GLOBAL CRISIS

Winner of the 2012 Heineken Prize for History, GEOFFREY PARKER is a renowned British historian who taught at the University of St Andrews, the University of Illinois, the University of British Columbia and Yale University before becoming Andreas Dorpalen Professor of European History and Associate of the Mershon Center at The Ohio State University. He is also a Fellow of the British Academy, the Netherlands Academy of Arts and Sciences, the Spanish-American Academy of Arts and Sciences (Cadiz), and the Royal Academy of History (Madrid). His many books include *The Grand Strategy of Philip II*, published by Yale in 1998 (winner of the Samuel Eliot Morison Prize), and *The Military Revolution* (1996; winner of the best book prize of the American Military Institute and the Society for the History of Technology), as well as seminal works on global military history and early modern Europe. *Global Crisis* was awarded a British Academy Medal in 2014.

GLOBAL CRISIS

WAR, CLIMATE CHANGE AND CATASTROPHE IN THE SEVENTEENTH CENTURY

GEOFFREY PARKER

YALE UNIVERSITY PRESS
NEW HAVEN AND LONDON

For information about this and other Yale University Press publications, please contact:
U.S. Office: sales.press@yale.edu   www.yalebooks.com
Europe Office: sales@yaleup.co.uk   www.yalebooks.co.uk

Set in Arno Pro by IDSUK (DataConnection) Ltd
Printed in the United States of America.

Library of Congress Cataloging-in-Publication Data

Parker, Geoffrey, 1943–
    Global crisis: war, climate change and catastrophe in the seventeenth century/
Geoffrey Parker.
        pages cm
    Includes bibliographical references.
    ISBN 978-0-300-15323-1 (cloth: alkaline paper)
1. History, Modern—17th century. 2. Military history—17th century.
3. Civil war—History—17th century. 4. Revolutions—History—17th century.
5. Climatic changes—Social aspects—History—17th century. 6. disasters—History—
17th century. I. Title.
    D247.P37 2012
    909'.6—dc23
                                                                                2012039448

A catalogue record for this book is available from the British Library.

ISBN 978-0-300-20863-4 (pbk)

10 9 8 7 6 5 4 3 2 1

This book is dedicated in admiration to all those
who fight multiple sclerosis

'It was so harsh a winter that no-one could remember another like it . . . only after Easter could the peasants go to their fields and begin to farm'

(Hans Heberle, *Zeytregister* [*Diary*], Ulm, Germany, 1627)

'The times here are so miserable that never in the memory of man has the like famine and mortality happened'

(East India Company officials, letter, Surat, India, 1631)

'Those who live in times to come will not believe that we who are alive now have suffered such toil, pain and misery'

(Fra Francesco Voersio of Cherasco,
Diario del contagio [*Plague Diary*], Italy, 1631)

'There have been so many deaths that the like of it has never been heard in human history'

(Hans Conrad Lang, *Tagebuch* [*Diary*], South Germany, 1634)

'Jiangnan has never experienced this kind of disaster'

(Lu Shiyi, *Zhixue lu* [*Diary*], South China, 1641)

'Among all the past occurrences of disaster and rebellion, there had never been anything worse than this'

(*County Gazetteer*, Yizhou, North China, 1641)

'The whole monarchy trembled and shook, since Portugal, Catalonia, the East Indies, the Azores and Brazil had rebelled'

(Viceroy don Juan de Palafox y Mendoza, Mexico, 1641)

'[These] days are days of shaking and this shaking is universal: the Palatinate, Bohemia, Germany, Catalonia, Portugal, Ireland, England'

(Jeremiah Whitaker, *Ejrenopojos* [*The peacemaker*], England, 1643)

'This seems to be one of the epochs in which every nation is turned upside down, leading some great minds to suspect that we are approaching the end of the world'

(*Nicandro* [*The victor*], pamphlet, Madrid, Spain, 1643)

''Tis tru we have had many such black days in England in former ages, but those parallel'd to the present are to the shadow of a mountain compar'd to the eclipse of the moon'

(James Howell, *Collected letters*, England, 1647)

'There was great hunger throughout the Christian world'
(Inscription, Old Sambor Cathedral, Ukraine, 1648)

'The pryces of victuall and cornes of all sortes wer heigher than ever heirtofore aneyone living could remember ... The lyke had never beine seine in this kingdome'
(Sir James Balfour, 'Some shorte memorialls and passages of this yeire', Scotland, 1649)

'If one ever had to believe in the Last Judgment, I think it is happening right now'
(Judge Renaud de Sévigné, letter, Paris, France, 1652)

'The elements, servants of an irate God, combine to snuff out the rest of human-kind: mountains spew out fire; the earth shakes; plague contaminates the air'
(Jean-Nicolas de Parival, *Abrégé de l'histoire de ce siècle de fer* [*Short history of this Iron Century*], Brussels, South Netherlands, 1653)

'A third of the world has died'
(Abbess Angélique Arnauld, letter, Port-Royale-des-Champs, France, 1654)

'I no sooner perceived myself in the world but I found myself in a storm, which hath lasted almost hitherto'
(John Locke, 'First Tract on Government', London, 1660)

'Because of the dearth sent to us by God, we wanted to sell our property to our relatives, but they refused, and left us to die from hunger'
(Gavril Niță, Moldavian peasant, 1660)

'Transylvania never knew such misery as this last year'.
(Mihail Teleki, Chancellor of Transylvania, *Journal*, 1661)

'So many prophets and prophetesses arose in all the cities of Anatolia that everyone believed wholeheartedly that the End of Days had come ... These were indeed miraculous occurrences and wonders, the like of which had never happened since the day the world was created'
(Leib ben Oyzer, *Beschraybung fun Shabsai Zvi* [*Description of Shabbatai Zvi*], on events in the Ottoman empire in 1665–6)

'The world was aflame from the time I was 15 [1638] to the time I was 18'
(Enomoto Yazaemon, *Oboegaki* [*Memoranda*], Saitama, Japan, 1670)

'Since [1641] I am not afraid of seeing dead people, because I saw so many of them at that time'
(Yao Tinglin, *Linian ji* [*Record of successive years*], Shanghai, China, c. 1670)

'Many people held their lives to be of no value, for the area was so wasted and barren, the common people so poor and had suffered so much, that essentially they knew none of the joys of being alive . . . Every day one would hear that someone had hanged himself from a beam and killed himself. Others, at intervals, cut their throats or threw themselves into the river'

(Huang Liuhong, *Fuhui quanshu* [*Complete book concerning happiness and benevolence*], about events in Shandong, China, c. 1670)

Contents

Illustrations

Preface to the Paperback Edition[1]

'THIS IS A BIG BOOK. HOLLOWED OUT IT WOULD SERVE AS A MAUSOLEUM FOR Ronnie Corbett, though hopefully not for some time': thus Hugh Macdonald began the first review of *Global Crisis* to appear in print, in *Herald Scotland* in March 2013.[2] Most subsequent reviewers also referred to the size of the book – a few of them even as they wondered why I had not added yet more pages to address other issues. 'We are not told', wrote sociologist Jack Goldstone,

> *Why* did the scientific revolution succeed in Europe, while similar efforts at more rigorous empirical investigation in other regions petered out? *Why* did north-western Europe's gains in income and productivity in the 18th century not simply get diluted by more rapid population increase, as happened in southern and central Europe? For that matter, *why* did China, which also experienced gains in long-distance trade and agricultural productivity in the late 17th and early 18th century, fail to build on these trends and make further gains?[3]

These are indeed fascinating and important questions, although as Goldstone conceded, it 'would take perhaps hundreds more pages to answer'. Most readers would surely endorse Samuel Johnson's verdict on John Milton's *Paradise Lost*: it 'is one of the books which the reader admires and lays down, and forgets to take up again. None ever wished it longer than it is.'[4]

So instead of addressing new questions or incorporating new research, in this paperback edition I have merely corrected some errors noted by my erudite colleagues – especially those that featured in two 'debates' and one 'review article' of the book.[5] Nevertheless, I should like to address here two substantive comments made by Jan de Vries and Kenneth Pomeranz.

In a thoughtful review article of *Global Crisis*, de Vries (an eminent economic historian whose work has inspired and enlightened me) stated:

> [A] nation that enjoyed population growth through the crisis era, as well as rising per capita output, enjoys no place of importance in Parker's account even though it appears prominently in the crisis literature. The Dutch Republic experienced what is now called its 'golden age' during the crisis . . . Although Parker knows this history well, he finds no place for it, and does not justify its omission.[6]

'Omission' seems an exaggeration, given that the index entry for 'Netherlands' directs interested readers to over twenty pages in *Global Crisis*, while the entry for 'Dutch Republic' lists over forty. Moreover, chapter eight discusses the three *coups d'état* that shook the Republic during the seventeenth century (1618, 1650/1 and 1672), as well as to the misery of 1648 to 1651, when (in the words of a contemporary) 'those towns that prospered most during the war declined during the peace – their industry lost, their merchants diminished, many of their houses up for sale', endless rain depressed everyone, and grain prices stood at their highest level in the Republic for a century (pp. 236–7). For many citizens of the Republic, 'what is now called its "golden age"' was apparent only in retrospect.[7]

In *Historically Speaking*, the noted Sinologist Kenneth Pomeranz (who not only inspired me through his work but also provided invaluable feedback while I was drafting *Global Crisis*) argued that 'Despite 16th-century warfare, Japan's population seems to have grown by between 30% and 50% during that period,' which 'calls into question Parker's claim that Japan entered the crisis era "underpopulated".'[8] The size of Japan's population in the sixteenth century is, admittedly, a highly contested field. Hayami Akira (the pioneer of Japanese historical demography) proposed a total population of only 12 million (± 2 million) in 1600, whereas Saitō Osamu and others have subsequently suggested much higher figures, ranging from 15 million to 17 million.[9] Nevertheless, even if we accept the higher estimate, almost all scholars agree that by 1700 the population of Tokugawa Japan had increased to some 30 million. Japan thus boasted an immense *capacity* for growth following unification around 1590, and even if the population 'only' doubled (as Saitō suggested) rather than almost tripled (as Hayami argued) such growth – which was unparalleled in the seventeenth-century world – was only possible because of an initial 'demographic cushion'. Japan really was different.[10]

Inevitably, new information about the Global Crisis has appeared since I completed my text, some in new sources and others in old material examined in different ways.[11] Thus chapter 19 discusses how alarming information about revolutions spread during the 1640s from one European capital to another, but it does not address a question posed by a colleague: did it also reach the Tokugawa regime in Edo? When I checked the records of the Dutch East India Company, I found a copy of a letter sent from Batavia on 28 June 1642 by Governor-General Antonio van Diemen to 'the royal council of Japan', providing a full account of the Portuguese revolution. Five years later, a Dutch delegation sent to Edo reported an animated discussion with the shogun's leading advisers about the progress of the Dutch Republic's war with Spain and Portugal (revealing that the Japanese government had already learned a good deal from other sources); while in August 1650, the Dutch provided the magistrates of Nagasaki with an account of the execution of Charles I, brought by a ship that had just docked at the Dutch factory at Dejima, in Nagasaki bay. The magistrates decided to send an express courier to Edo: it may have taken twenty months, but the horrifying news of the regicide eventually spread from one end of Eurasia to the other.[12]

In 2009, in his introduction to a special issue of *The Journal of Interdisciplinary History* on 'The Crisis of the seventeenth century: interdisciplinary perspectives', Theodore K. Rabb observed: 'Like it or not, the Crisis seems here to stay'; while three years later, in *The American Historical Review,* Julia Adeney Thomas reminded us that 'climate change – or climate collapse – and all of its related global transformations' is 'a world-altering force', one 'more devastating, and more definitive' than any other. She called for an 'environmental turn' in our field, one that foregrounds climate as a protagonist in human affairs.[13] As if in answer, over the winter of 2013/14 several new books that link climate and history appeared; hundreds of scholars attended the dozen or so panels at the annual meeting of the American Historical Association devoted to some aspect of the impact of climate on history; and *The Journal of Interdisciplinary History* published a special forum on 'The Little Ice Age: Climate and History Reconsidered', in which historian Sam White and climatologists Ulf Büntgen and Lena Hellmann documented the robustness and uniformity of evidence from around the world that a dramatic episode of global cooling occurred in the seventeenth century. The range of these scholarly endeavours demonstrates not only that the Global Crisis is 'here to stay,' but also that climate formed an integral part of the fatal synergy that produced it.[14]

Prologue
Did Someone Say 'Climate Change'?

CLIMATE CHANGE HAS FREQUENTLY CAUSED OR CONTRIBUTED TO WIDE-spread destruction and dislocation on Earth. After the various advances and retreats of glaciers, each one a major climate-related event, about 12,000 years ago, a final episode of global cooling wiped out most species of large mammals, such as the mammoths and saber-toothed cats. About 4,000 years ago, societies in south and west Asia collapsed amid general drought; while between AD 750 and 900 drought on both sides of the Pacific fatally weakened the Tang empire in China and the Maya culture in central America.[1] Then, in the mid-fourteenth century, a combination of violent climatic oscillations and major epidemics halved Europe's population and caused severe depopulation and disruption in much of Asia.[2] Finally, in the mid-seventeenth century, the earth experienced some of the coldest weather recorded in over a millennium. Perhaps one-third of the human population died.

Although climate change can and does produce human catastrophe, few historians include the weather in their analyses. Even in his pioneering 1967 study, *Times of feast, times of famine: a history of climate since the year 1000*, Emanuel Le Roy Ladurie averred that 'In the long term, the human consequences of climate seem to be slight, perhaps negligible'. By way of example, he stated that 'it would be quite absurd' to try and 'explain' the French rebellion between 1648 and 1653 known as the Fronde 'by the adverse meteorological conditions of the 1640s'. A few years later Jan de Vries, a distinguished economic historian, likewise argued that 'Short-term climatic crises stand in relation to economic history as bank robberies to the history of banking'.[3]

Historians are not alone in denying a link between climate and catastrophe. Richard Fortey, a noted palaeontologist, has observed that 'There is a kind of optimism built into our species that seems to prefer to live in the comfortable present rather than confront the possibility of destruction', with the result that 'Human beings are never prepared for natural disasters'.[4] Extreme climatic events therefore continue to take us by surprise, even if they cause massive damage. In 2003 a summer heatwave that lasted just two weeks led to the premature death of 70,000 people in Europe; while in 2005 Hurricane Katrina killed over 2,000 people and destroyed property worth over $81 billion in an area of the United States equivalent in size to Great Britain. In the course of 2011 over 106 million people around the world were adversely affected by floods; almost 60 million by drought; and almost

40 million by storms. Yet although we know that the climate caused these and many other catastrophes in the past, and although we also know that it will cause many more in the future, we still convince ourselves that they will not happen just yet (or, at least, not to us).[5]

Currently, most attempts to predict the consequences of climate change extrapolate from recent trends; but another methodology exists. Instead of hitting 'fast forward', we can 'rewind the tape of History' and study the genesis, impact and consequences of past catastrophes, using two distinct categories of proxy data: a 'natural archive' and a 'human archive'.

The 'natural archive' comprises four groups of sources:

- *Ice cores and glaciology*: the annual deposits on ice caps and glaciers around the world, captured in deep boreholes, provide evidence of changing levels of volcanic emissions, precipitation, air temperature and atmospheric composition.[6]
- *Palynology*: pollen and spores deposited in lakes, bogs and estuaries capture the natural vegetation at the time of deposit.[7]
- *Dendrochronology*: the size of growth rings laid down by certain trees during each growing season reflects local conditions in spring and summer. A thick ring indicates a year favourable to growth, whereas a narrow ring reflects a year of adversity.[8]
- *Speleothems*: the annual deposits formed from groundwater trickling into underground caverns, especially in the form of stalactites, can serve as a climate proxy.[9]

The 'human archive' on climate change comprises five groups of sources:

- *Narrative* information contained in oral traditions and written texts (chronicles and histories, letters and diaries, judicial and government records, ships' logs, newspapers and broadsheets).
- *Numerical* information extracted from documents (such as fluctuations in the date when harvesting certain crops began each year, in food prices, in sunspots observed, or in the number of men paid each spring to steer the detritus that swept down rivers along with snowmelt); and from narrative reports ('Rain fell for the first time in 42 days').
- *Pictorial* representations of natural phenomena (paintings or engravings that show the position of a glacier's tongue in a given year, or that depict ice floes in a harbour during a winter of unusual severity).[10]
- *Epigraphic* or *archaeological* information, such as inscriptions on structures that date flood levels, or excavations of settlements abandoned because of climate change.
- *Instrumental data.* Starting in the 1650s, in Europe, some observers regularly recorded weather data, including precipitation, wind direction and temperatures.[11]

The failure of most historians to exploit the data available in these two 'archives' for the seventeenth century is particularly regrettable, because an intense episode of global cooling coincided with an unparalleled spate of revolutions and state breakdowns around the world (including Ming China, the Polish–Lithuanian

Commonwealth and the Spanish Monarchy), while other states came close to revolution (notably, the Russian and Ottoman empires in 1648; and the Mughal empire, Sweden, Denmark and the Dutch Republic in the 1650s) (Fig. 1). In addition, Europe saw only three years of complete peace during the entire seventeenth century, while the Ottoman empire enjoyed only ten. The Chinese and Mughal empires fought wars almost continuously. Throughout the northern hemisphere, war became the norm for resolving both domestic and international problems.

Historians have christened this age of turmoil 'The General Crisis', and some have seen it as the gateway to the modern world. The term was popularized by Hugh Trevor-Roper in an influential essay, first published in 1959, which argued that

> The seventeenth century did not absorb its revolutions. It is not continuous. It is broken in the middle, irreparably broken, and at the end of it, after the revolutions, men can hardly recognize the beginning. Intellectually, politically, morally, we are in a new age, a new climate. It is as if a series of rainstorms has ended in one final thunderstorm which has cleared the air and changed, permanently, the temperature of Europe. From the end of the fifteenth century until the middle of the seventeenth century we have one climate, the climate of the Renaissance; then, in the middle of the seventeenth century, we have the years of change, the years of revolution; and thereafter, for another century and a half, we have another, very different climate, the climate of the Enlightenment.[12]

But of 'climate' in its literal sense Trevor-Roper said not a word, even though the upheavals he described occurred during a period marked by global cooling and extreme weather events.

The climatic evidence is both clear and consistent. Daily readings from an international network of observation stations reveal that winters between 1654 and 1667 were, on average, more than 1°C cooler than those of the later twentieth century.[13] Other records show that 1641 saw the third coldest summer recorded over the past six centuries in the northern hemisphere; the second coldest winter in a century experienced in New England; and the coldest winter *ever* recorded in Scandinavia. The summer of 1642 was the 28th coldest, and that of 1643 the 10th coldest, recorded in the northern hemisphere over the past six centuries; while the winter of 1649–50 seems to have been the coldest on record in both northern and eastern China. Abnormal climatic conditions lasted from the 1640s until the 1690s – the longest as well as the most severe episode of global cooling recorded in the entire Holocene Era – leading climatologists to dub this period 'The Little Ice Age'.[14]

This volume seeks to link the climatologists' Little Ice Age with the historians' General Crisis – and to do so without 'painting bull's eyes around bullet holes': without arguing that global cooling 'must' have somehow caused recession and revolution around the world simply because climate change is the only plausible common denominator. Le Roy Ladurie was absolutely correct to insist in 1967 that 'The historian of seventeenth-century climate' must 'be able to apply a quantitative method comparable in rigour if not in accuracy and variety to the methods used by

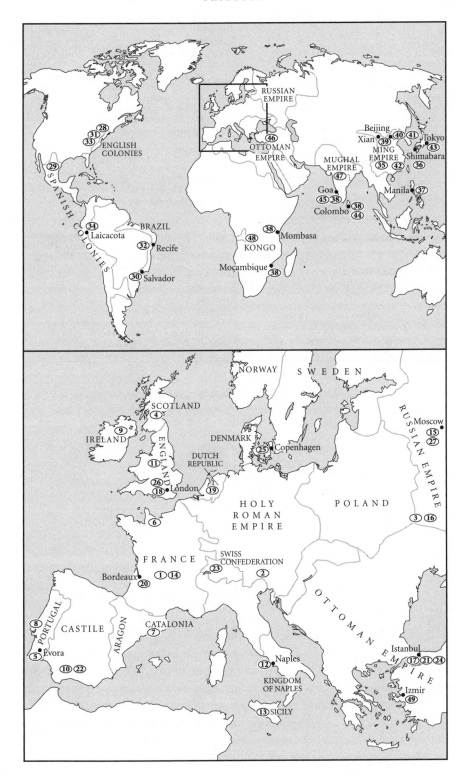

Major Revolts and Revolutions, 1635–66

EUROPE		AMERICAS	
1636	1. Croquants Revolt (Perigord)	1637	28. Pequot War
	2. Revolt in Lower Austria	1641	29. Mexico Revolt (to 1642)
1637	3. Cossack Revolt (to 1638)		**30. Portuguese Brazil rebels against Spain**
	4. Scottish Revolution (to 1651)	1642	31. English colonies in America take sides in Civil War
	5. Évora & S. Portugal Revolt (to 1638)	1645	**32. Portuguese colonists in Brazil rebel against**
1639	6. Nu-pieds Revolt (Normandy)		**Dutch (to 1654)**
1640	**7. Catalan Revolt (to 1659)**	1660	33. "Restoration" in English colonies
	8. Portugal rebels (to 1668)	1666	34. Revolt of Laicacota (Peru)
1641	**9. Irish rebellion (to 1653)**	ASIA AND AFRICA	
	10. Andalusia: Medina Sidonia conspiracy	1635	35. Popular Revolts spread from NW China to
1642	**11. English "Great Rebellion" (to 1660)**		Yangzi valley (to 1645)
1647	**12. Naples Revolt (to 1648)**	1637	36. Revolt at Shimabara (to 1638)
	13. Sicily Revolt (to 1648)	1639	37. Chinese (Sangleys) Revolt in Manila
1648	14. France: Fronde Revolt (to 1653)	1641	**38. Revolt of Portuguese in Mombasa,**
	15. Russia: Moscow and other cities rebel (to 1649)		**Mozambique, Goa and Ceylon against Spain**
	16. Ukraine Revolt against Poland (to 1668)	1643	**39. Li Zicheng declares Shun Era in Xi'an**
	17. Istanbul: Ottoman regicide	1644	**40. Li Zicheng takes Beijing and ends Ming rule**
1649	**18. London: British regicide**		**41. Qing capture Beijing and occupy Central Plain**
1650	**19. Dutch Regime change (to 1672)**	1645	**42. Qing invade South China; "Southern Ming"**
1651	20. Bordeaux: Ormée Revolt (to 1653)		**resistance (to 1662 in South China; to 1683 in**
	21. Istanbul riots		**Taiwan)**
1652	22. "Green Banner" Revolts in Andalusia	1651	43. Yui conspiracy in Tokyo
1653	23. Swiss Revolution	1652	44. Colombo rebels against Portugal
1656	24. Istanbul riots	1653	45. Goa rebels against Portugal
1660	**25. The "Danish Revolution"**	1657	46. Anatolia: Revolt of Abaza Hasan Pasha (to 1659)
	26. "Restoration" in England, Scotland, and Ireland	1658	**47. Mughal Civil War (to 1662)**
1662	27. Moscow rebellion	1665	**48. Overthrow of Kongo kingdom**
Events listed in **bold** are those that produced a regime change.			49. Shabbatai Zvi proclaimed Messiah at Izmir

1. The Global Crisis.
Although Europe and East Asia formed the heartland of the 'General Crisis', the Mughal and Ottoman empires, like the European colonies in America, also experienced episodes of severe political disruption in the mid-seventeenth century.

present-day meteorologists in the study of twentieth-century climate', and he regretted that this goal was then unattainable.[15] The sources now available, however, allow historians to integrate climate change with political, economic and social change with unprecedented precision. Accounts of climatic conditions in Africa, Asia, Europe and the Americas in the mid-seventeenth century abound, while millions of measurements of tree-rings, ice-cores, pollen deposits and stalactite formations are available.[16]

Nevertheless, the new data, however abundant and however striking, must not turn us into climatic determinists. As early as 1627, Joseph Mede, a polymath with a special interest in astronomy and eschatology who taught at Christ's College, Cambridge, pointed out a methodological pitfall: any increase in observations may simply reflect an increase in the number of observers. Thus when he heard almost simultaneously about an earthquake near Glastonbury and 'another prodigie from Boston [Lincolnshire] of fire from heaven', Mede observed sagely: 'Either we have more strange accidents than was wont, or we take more notice of them, or both.'' Subsequent research has corroborated Mede's surmise. For example, while modern astronomy has confirmed that the seventeenth century indeed witnessed an unusual frequency of comets, humans took 'more notice of them' – both because the proliferation of telescopes enabled more of them to be seen from earth, and because dramatic improvements in gathering and disseminating news meant that every sighting soon became known to more people.[17]

A second obstacle to the accurate assessment of climatic data by historians is the role of infrastructure and contingency. On the one hand, the deleterious consequences of colder or wetter weather may be mitigated if a community has either a well-stocked granary or access to food imported through a neighbouring port. On the other hand, war may create famine even in a year of bountiful harvest by destroying or disrupting the food supply on which a community depends. In the aphorism of Andrew Appleby: 'the crucial variable' was often 'not the weather but the ability to adapt to the weather'.[18] This volume therefore examines not only the impact of climate change and extreme climate events on human societies during the seventeenth century, but also the various adaptive strategies taken to survive the worst climate-induced catastrophe of the last millennium.

Introduction: The 'Little Ice Age' and the 'General Crisis'

IN 1638, FROM THE SAFETY OF HIS OXFORD COLLEGE, ROBERT BURTON informed readers of his best-selling book, *The anatomy of melancholy*, that 'every day' he heard news of

> War, plagues, fires, inundations, thefts, murders, massacres, meteors, comets, spectrums, prodigies, apparitions; of towns taken, cities besieged in France, Germany, Turky, Persia, Poland, etc; daily musters and preparations, and such like, which these tempestuous times affoord; battels fought, so many men slain, monomachies, shipwracks and sea-fights, peace, leagues, stratagems, and fresh alarums.

Four years later, the English Civil War started and a group of London merchants lamented that 'All trade and commerce in this kingdom is almost fallen to the ground through our own unhappy divisions at home, unto which the Lord in mercy put a good end. And as the badness of trade and scarcity of money are here, so is all Europe in little better condition, but in a turmoil, either foreign or domestic war.' In 1643 the preacher Jeremiah Whitaker warned his hearers that '[These] days are days of shaking, and this shaking is universal: the Palatinate, Bohemia, Germany, Catalonia, Portugal, Ireland, England.' Normally, Whitaker argued, God 'shakes all successively', but now it seemed that He planned to 'shake all nations collectively, jointly and universally'. Indeed, he speculated, so much simultaneous 'shaking' must herald the Day of Judgement:[1]

That same year, in Spain, a tract entitled *Nicandro* [*The victor*] made the same point.

> Sometimes Providence condemns the world with universal and evident calamities, whose causes we cannot know. This seems to be one of the epochs in which every nation is turned upside down, leading some great minds to suspect that we are approaching the end of the world. We have seen all the north in commotion and rebellion, its rivers running with blood, its populous provinces deserted; England, Ireland and Scotland aflame with Civil War.

'What area does not suffer,' the *Nicandro* concluded rhetorically, 'if not from war, then from earthquakes, plague and famine?'[2]

In Germany, a Swedish diplomat expressed alarm in 1648 at a new bout 'of revolts by the people against their rulers everywhere in the world, for example in France,

England, Germany, Poland, Muscovy, the Ottoman empire'. He was well informed: civil war had just begun in France, and continued to rage in England; the Thirty Years War (1618–48) had left much of Germany devastated and depopulated; the Cossacks of Ukraine had rebelled against their Polish overlords and massacred thousands of Jews; revolts rocked Moscow and other Russian cities; and an uprising in Istanbul led to the murder of the Ottoman sultan. The following year, a Scottish exile in France concluded that he and his contemporaries lived in an 'Iron Age' that would become 'famous for the great and strange revolutions that have happened in it'. In 1653, in Brussels, historian Jean-Nicolas de Parival used the same metaphor in the title of his book, *A short history of this Iron Century, containing the miseries and misfortunes of recent times*. 'I call this century the "Iron Century"', he informed his readers, because so many misfortunes 'have come together, whereas in previous centuries they came one by one'. He noted that rebellions and wars now 'resemble Hydra: the more you cut off their heads, the more they grow'. Parival also noted that 'The elements, servants of an irate God, combine to snuff out the rest of human-kind: mountains spew out fire, the earth shakes, plague contaminates the air', and 'the continuous rain causes rivers to flood'.[3]

Seventeenth-century China also suffered. First, a combination of droughts and disastrous harvests, rising tax demands and drastic cutbacks in government programmes unleashed a wave of banditry and chaos. Then, in 1644, one of the bandit leaders, Li Zicheng, declared himself ruler of China and seized Beijing from the demoralized defenders of the Ming emperor (who committed suicide). Almost immediately, China's northern neighbours, the Manchus or Qing, invaded and defeated Li, entered Beijing, and for the next 30 years ruthlessly extended their authority over the whole country. Several million people perished in the Ming-Qing transition.

Few areas of the world survived the mid-seventeenth century unscathed. North America and West Africa both experienced famines and savage wars. In India, drought followed by floods killed over a million people in Gujarat between 1627 and 1630; while a vicious civil war in the Mughal empire intensified the impact of another drought between 1658 and 1662. In Japan, following several poor harvests, in 1637–8 the largest rural rebellion in modern Japanese history broke out on the southern island of Kyushu. Five years later famine, followed by a winter of unusual severity, killed perhaps 500,000 people.

The fatal synergy that developed between natural and human factors created a demographic, social, economic and political catastrophe that lasted for two genera-tions, and convinced contemporaries that they faced unprecedented hardships. It also led many of them to record their misfortunes as a warning to others. 'Those who live in times to come will not believe that we who are alive now have suffered such toil, pain and misery,' wrote Fra Francesco Voersio, an Italian friar, in his *Plague Diary*. Nehemiah Wallington, a London craftsman, compiled several volumes of 'Historical notes and meditations' so that 'the generation to come may see what wofull and miserable times we lived in'. Likewise Peter Thiele, a German tax official, kept a diary so that 'our descendants can discover from this how we were harassed, and see what a terribly distressed time it was'; while the German Lutheran Pastor Johann Daniel Minck did the same because, 'without such records … those who come after us will never believe what miseries we have suffered'.[4] According to the Welsh historian James Howell in 1647, ' 'Tis tru we have had many such black days in England in former ages, but those parallel'd to the present are to the shadow of a mountain compar'd to the eclipse of the moon'; and he speculated that

> God Almighty has a quarrel lately with all Mankind, and given the reins to the ill Spirit to compass the whole earth; for within these twelve years there have the strangest Revolutions and horridest things happened, not only in Europe but all the world over, that have befallen mankind (I dare boldly say) since Adam fell, in so short a revolution of time … [Such] monstrous things have happened [that] it seems the whole world is off the hinges; and (which is the more wonderful) all these prodigious passages have fallen out in less than the compass of twelve years.[5]

In 1651, in his book *Leviathan*, Thomas Hobbes (then a refugee from the English Civil War living in France) provided perhaps the most celebrated description of the consequences of the fatal synergy between natural and human disasters faced by him and his contemporaries:

> There is no place for industry, because the fruit thereof is uncertain, and consequently no culture of the earth; no navigation, nor use of the commodities that may be imported by sea; no commodious building; no instruments of moving and removing such things as require much force; no knowledge of the face of the earth; no account of Time; no arts; no letters; no society. And, which is worst of all, continual fear and danger of violent death; and the life of man, solitary, poor, nasty, brutish and short.[6]

When did this fatal synergy commence? In his *History of the civil wars of these recent times* of 1652, the Italian historian Majolino Bisaccione traced the sequence of 'popular revolts in my lifetime' back to the rebellion of Bohemia in 1618, which had attracted the support of some German Protestants, led by Frederick of the Palatinate, and so began a civil war in Germany. Seven years later, the English antiquarian John Rushworth agreed. When he sought to explain, 'how we came to fall out among ourselves' in the English Civil War, he too started his account back in 1618 because his research convinced him that the conflict originated in 'the causes and grounds of the war in the Palatinate, and how far the same concerned England, and the oppressed Protestants in Germany'. Rushworth also noted the appearance of three comets of unusual brilliance in 1618, which (like almost all his contemporaries) he interpreted as a harbinger of evil. He therefore 'resolved that very instant should be the *Ne Plus Ultra* of my retrospect'.[7]

The available evidence amply vindicates the chronology proposed by Bisaccione and Rushworth. Although Europe had experienced many earlier economic, social and political crises, they remained largely isolated and relatively short-lived. By contrast, the Bohemian revolt began a prolonged conflict that lasted three decades and eventually involved all the major states of Europe: Denmark, the Dutch Republic, France, Poland, Russia, Sweden, the Swiss Confederation and, above all, the Stuart and Spanish Monarchies. The year 1618 also saw long-running crises commence in two other parts of the world. In the Ottoman empire, a palace faction deposed the sultan (the first such event in the history of the dynasty), unleashing a series of catastrophes that a generation later the scholar-bureaucrat Kâtib Çelebi would term *Haile-i Osmaniye*: 'The Ottoman Tragedy'. Meanwhile, in East Asia, Nurhaci, leader of a tribal confederation in Manchuria, declared war on the Chinese emperor and invaded Liaodong, a populous area of Chinese settlement north of the Great Wall. Some observers immediately realized the significance of this step. Years later, Wu Yingji, a gentleman-scholar, recalled 'a friend telling me, when the difficulties began in the eighth month of 1618 in Liaodong, that the state would have several decades of warfare; and my thinking that his words were absurd because the state was quite intact'. Nevertheless the 'friend' had been right: the Manchu invasion initiated almost seven 'decades of warfare'.[8]

These events took place against a background of extreme weather events. Many parts of sub-Saharan Africa suffered a serious drought between 1614 and 1619; Japan experienced its coldest spring of the seventeenth century in 1616; heavy snow fell in subtropical Fujian in 1618; the winter of 1620–1 was intensely cold in Europe and the Middle East; drought afflicted both the valley of Mexico and Virginia for five years out of six between 1616 and 1621. Finally, 1617 and 1618 marked the beginning of a prolonged aberration in the behaviour of the sun, signalled first by the reduction and then by the virtual disappearance of sunspots. For all these reasons, this book follows the lead of Bisaccione, Rushworth, Kâtib Çelebi and Wu Yingji's friend: 1618 is 'the *Ne Plus Ultra* of my retrospect'.

When did the fatal synergy end? Here the evidence is less consistent. In 1668 Thomas Hobbes began *Behemoth*, his account of the English Civil Wars, by observing that

> If in time, as in place, there were degrees of high and low, I verily believe that the highest of times would be that which passed between the years 1640 and 1660. For he that thence, as from the Devil's Mountain, should have looked upon the world and observed the actions of men, especially in England, might have had a prospect of all kinds of injustice and all kinds of folly that the world could afford.[9]

Yet exactly 20 years later another revolution occurred: William of Orange landed at the head of the largest army ever to invade first Britain and then Ireland, in both of which he created a new regime. On the European continent, most of the contentious issues unleashed by the revolt of Bohemia were resolved between 1648 and 1661, but France's invasion of the Palatinate in 1688 generated a new conflict. In the Ottoman empire, in the 1650s the Grand Vizier Köprüllük Mehmet managed to end the cycle of domestic rebellion and, during the following decade, his son and successor defeated all foreign enemies and the empire began to expand again; but the defeat of the Turkish army before Vienna in 1683 halted the Ottoman advance into Europe and led to the deposition of another sultan.

Nevertheless, the 1680s saw the end of several conflicts. The 'Eternal Peace of Moscow' in 1686 marked the permanent ascendancy of Russia over the Polish-Lithuanian Commonwealth; while in 1683, Manchu troops finally defeated the last of their opponents, allowing a government inspector to exult that the Qing emperor 'has crushed all the rebels and even the seas are calm. At present, the people have returned to their former lands. Their homes are protected and their livelihood is secure. They will respect and honour Your Majesty's benevolence for generations to come.'[10] China's seventeenth-century crisis had ended at last. Meanwhile, in Boston, Massachusetts, Increase Mather (preacher at the North Church in Boston and president of Harvard College) warned the world that the brilliant comets that appeared in 1680 and 1682 'are the presages of great calamities at hand'. Little did he know that these two comets would be the last 'fearful sights and signs in heaven' of the age.[11]

Nevertheless, although both political upheavals and comets became less frequent, the Little Ice Age continued. In the northern hemisphere, 9 of the 14 summers between 1666 and 1679 were either cool or exceptionally cool – harvests in western Europe ripened later in 1675 than in any other year between 1484 and 1879 – and climatologists regard the extreme climatic events and disastrous harvests during the 1690s, with average temperatures 1.5°C below those of today, as the 'climax of the Little Ice Age'. This time, global cooling did not produce a wave of revolutions. The fatal synergy had been broken. This book ends by examining why.[12]

Writing global history is not easy. In 2011 Alain Hugon prefaced his study of the revolt of Naples in 1647–8 by noting that, although 'contemporaries clearly stated that no barriers separated the various revolutions of the seventeenth century', nevertheless 'We historians of the twentieth and twenty-first centuries dare not study them in their totality, despite our awareness of this synchronicity, of the interdependence, and of the interactions that occurred'. Hugon reported that whenever he 'tried to make historical comparisons appropriate to the mid-seventeenth century, the problems that arise from the need to contextualize each historical event render the attempt vain'.[13]

It is easy to sympathize with this view. On the one hand, recent research has revealed both far more 'historical events' than previous scholars had imagined – Hugon himself uncovered evidence of over 100 revolts in the kingdom of Naples in 1647–8; over 20 towns and cities in Andalusia took part in the 'Green Banner Revolts' of 1648–52; almost half the communities of Portugal followed Évora into rebellion in 1637 – and far broader participation in many of the events already known (over a million Chinese joined the 'roving bandits' in the 1630s; perhaps a million people perished in France's Fronde revolt, 1648–53). On the other hand, although almost all regions of the northern hemisphere experienced both the Little Ice Age and the General Crisis in the mid-seventeenth century, each did so in different ways, for different reasons, and with different outcomes – not least because some structural causes (such as climate change) lie largely beyond human control, while others (such as wars and revolutions) involve so many people that they lie largely beyond the control of any individual. Nevertheless, modern historians must emulate the global vision of contemporaries of the Crisis and, as we 'contextualize each historical event', try to identify what united as well as what separated the victims.

A second problem in explaining the synchronicity, the interdependence and the interactions of the various revolutions is the role played by contingency. Minor events repeatedly produced consequences that were both unanticipated and disproportionate. As Dr Samuel Johnson observed:

> It seems to be almost the universal error of historians to suppose it politically, as it is physically true, that every effort has a proportionate cause. In the inanimate action of matter upon matter, the motion produced can be but equal to the force of the moving power; but the operations of life, whether private or publick, admit no such laws. The caprices of voluntary agents laugh at calculation. *It is not always that there is a strong reason for a great event.*[14]

Dr Johnson's warning requires historians to identify the precise moment in each revolution when 'the motion produced' was no longer 'equal to the force of the moving power', and 'the caprices of voluntary agents laugh at calculation'. Scholars used to describe this as 'the turning point', and recently John Lewis Gaddis adopted from physics the term 'phase transitions': the moment 'where water begins to boil or freeze, for example, or sand piles begin to slide, or fault lines begin to fracture'. I prefer another term, the 'tipping point', a metaphor popularized by Malcolm Gladwell, because it implies that such changes, however sudden and dramatic, may one day be reversed. Ice, after all, can easily turn back to water.[15]

This book studies the Global Crisis of the mid-seventeenth century through three different lenses. Part I presents evidence from both the human and natural archives to identify the channels by which the crisis impinged on humankind. Chapter 1 examines how global cooling affects the supply of food, above all of staple crops such as cereals and rice, around the world. Chapter 2 evaluates how the policies pursued by early modern states interacted with these climate changes, for example by waging wars that intensified economic hardship and by pursuing unpopular policies that destabilized societies already under economic stress, or (more rarely) by adopting initiatives that mitigated the consequences of global cooling. Chapter 3 examines four zones where a disproportionate number of key events of the mid-seventeenth century occurred: composite states; cities; marginal lands; and 'macroregions'. Composite states, normally created by dynastic unions, were vulnerable because the ruler's authority was often weaker in peripheral areas than elsewhere; yet in wartime, precisely because they were on the periphery, these areas experienced greater political and economic pressure and often rebelled first. Global cooling gravely affected the other three zones – cities, marginal lands and macroregions – because they relied disproportionately on the yield of crops vulnerable to climate change. In addition, cities regularly suffered both fiscal and military calamities because both governments and armies targeted places that boasted a large, compact population. For the same reasons, macroregions (densely populated areas that concentrated on producing goods for export rather than for local consumption) were also especially vulnerable to political and military changes – not just at home, but also in those areas on which they were economically dependent for imports or exports. Chapter 4 examines the demographic responses by the victims in different regions as the crisis increased an imbalance between supply and demand for resources – an imbalance that would eventually reduce the global population by perhaps one-third.

The chapters in Part II examine a dozen states in Eurasia that experienced the full intensity of both the Little Ice Age and the General Crisis in the mid-seventeenth century, proceeding geographically from east to west: China; Russia and Poland; the Ottoman empire; Germany and Scandinavia; the Dutch and Swiss Republics; the Iberian Peninsula; France; Great Britain and Ireland. Each chapter charts the interplay of human and natural forces right up to the 'tipping point' that ended the existing social, economic and political equilibrium; it then analyses the nature of the ensuing crisis; and, finally, it documents the emergence of a new equilibrium.

The choice of an east-to-west itinerary, starting with China, is arbitrary – it reflects neither chronological differences (in most cases the 'days of shaking' began in or around 1618 and ended in the 1680s) nor the intensity of the crisis (although in terms of physical and personal damage, China and Ireland seem to have suffered worst of all). By contrast, the decision to devote greater space to the experience of Britain and Ireland than to other states gripped by major trauma is deliberate. In the words of Christopher Hill, perhaps the most perceptive modern historian of the subject, 'The middle decades of the seventeenth century saw the greatest upheaval that has yet occurred in Britain'.[16] Moreover, the 'upheaval' lasted longer, and produced more dramatic changes, than anywhere else except China. However, the wealth of surviving British and Irish sources permits a more detailed understanding of the causes, course and consequences of the crisis than is possible for any other society. Chapter 11 therefore charts the path to state breakdown in England, Scotland and Ireland between 1603, when they became a single polity, and 1642, when the failure of his policies forced King Charles I to flee his capital. Chapter 12 examines the consequences of the prolonged wars and multiple regime changes in the three kingdoms between 1642 and 1660, including the first formulation of democratic principles now regarded as central to Western society; the attempts by the central government to overthrow them between 1660 and 1688; and their limited resurrection after the 'Glorious Revolution' of 1688–9.

Part III considers two categories of 'exception' to this pattern: those areas where at least part of the population apparently emerged from the seventeenth-century trauma relatively unscathed (some European colonies in America; South and Southeast Asia; Japan); and those regions where the impact of the Little Ice Age remains ambiguous (the Great Plains of North America; Sub-Saharan Africa; Australia). Within the first category, in Mughal India and some of its neighbours, abundant resources enabled the state to ride out the crisis (chapter 13); while in Spanish Italy, the government managed to overcome major rebellions by making major concessions (chapter 14). Elsewhere, notably in Europe's overseas outposts, the prosperity of a few (the European colonists) was achieved only at the expense of the many (the indigenous population: chapter 15). Only Tokugawa Japan seems to have avoided the full effects of the crisis as the result of human initiatives: although global cooling caused a major famine in the archipelago during the 1640s, a barrage of effective countermeasures first limited and then repaired the damage (chapter 16).

Despite the remarkable diversity of human experience in the states and societies afflicted by the General Crisis, some striking common denominators emerge, and Part IV considers three of them. First, popular responses to catastrophe exhibited a number of similar protocols and conventions, ranging from a surprising measure of restraint in violent protests around the world to striking similarities in what James C. Scott termed 'the weapons of the weak': 'foot-dragging, dissimulation, desertion, false compliance, pilfering, feigned ignorance, slander, arson, sabotage' (chapter 17).[17] Second, an investigation of the individuals and groups in different societies who exploited the mounting instability to produce a 'tipping point' also exposes similarities. In many areas aristocrats played a prominent role, as they had done in many earlier crises; but in the mid-seventeenth century, from China through the Muslim world to Europe, the most prominent 'troublemakers' included men (some clerical, others secular) who had made great sacrifices to acquire advanced education but then failed to find suitable employment (chapter 18). A third common denominator is the ease with which radical ideas developed and spread. Proliferation sometimes occurred because insurgents travelled directly from one area to spread information and seditious ideas. Thus in 1647 the transfer of news between Naples and Palermo synchronized the rebellions in the two capitals; while the following year, in Russia, many towns rebelled as soon as their citizens returned from Moscow and described the rioting there that had forced the tsar to make massive concessions. More often, ideas spread because the proliferation of printed works and of schools had created a literate proletariat of unprecedented size in much of Asia and Europe, capable of reading, discussing and implementing new ideas. Thus although the Catholics of Ireland hated and feared the Calvinists of Scotland, they were prepared to learn from them. A few days after the 1641 uprising, when a captured Protestant asked a leading Irish Catholic: '"What? Yow have made a Covenant amongst yow as the Scotts did?" "Yea", said hee, "The Scotts have taught us our A. B. C."' (chapter 19).[18]

Finally, Part V examines how the survivors coped with the crisis and its aftermath, and how their choices shaped a new equilibrium that emerged in various states and regions. Although the 1690s and 1700s saw further bouts of extreme weather, famine and (in Europe and China) almost continuous war, unlike the 1640s and 1650s, no revolutions and relatively few revolts occurred. So although the Little Ice Age continued, the General Crisis did not. Several changes help to explain this paradox. Throughout the northern hemisphere, massive depopulation encouraged elites to control migration: groups that had rigorously excluded newcomers now welcomed them; states that had allowed freedom of movement now sought to bind their subjects to the land (chapter 20). In most parts of the globe, the experience of state breakdown, and the 'continual fear and danger of violent death', cooled the ardour of many advocates of economic, political and religious change, leading to greater political stability, economic innovation and religious toleration. It also led many governments to switch resources from warfare to welfare, fostering economic regeneration (chapter 21). Finally, chapter 22 examines a variety of intellectual responses devised to cope more effectively with future crises, some (like compulsory universal schooling) imposed by the state, others emerging among subjects – including 'practical knowledge' in China and Japan, the 'new reason' in Mughal India and the 'Scientific Revolution' in Europe. For various reasons, these innovations put down deeper roots in the West than elsewhere and formed a crucial ingredient in the 'Great Divergence' between East Asia and Northwest Europe that later developed.

The Conclusion considers some implications of recognizing that, far from being an aberration, 'catastrophe' forms an integral part of human history, while the Epilogue suggests that the current debate on 'global warming' confuses two distinct issues: whether human activity is making the world warmer; and whether or not sudden climate change can occur. Although some may still legitimately question the first, the seventeenth-century evidence places the second beyond doubt. The critical issues are not *whether* climate change occurs, but *when*; and whether it makes better sense for states and societies to invest money now to prepare for natural disasters that are inevitable – hurricanes in the Gulf and Atlantic coasts of North America; storm surges in the lands around the North Sea; droughts in Africa; prolonged heatwaves – or instead wait to pay the far higher costs of inaction.

PART I

THE PLACENTA OF THE CRISIS

THE FRENCH PHILOSOPHER AND AUTHOR VOLTAIRE WAS THE FIRST to write about a Global Crisis in the seventeenth century. His *Essay on the customs and character of nations, and on the principal facts of history from Charlemagne to Louis XIII*, composed in the 1740s for his friend, the Marquise du Châtelet (who, although an eminent mathematician, found history boring), set the wars and rebellions a century earlier within a global framework. Thus, after describing the murder of an Ottoman sultan in 1648, Voltaire immediately noted:

> This unfortunate time for Ibrahim was unfortunate for all monarchs. The Holy Roman Empire was unsettled by the famous Thirty Years' War. Civil war devastated France and forced the mother of Louis XIV to flee with her children from her capital. In London, Charles I was condemned to death by his own subjects. Philip IV, king of Spain, having lost almost all his possessions in Asia, also lost Portugal.

Voltaire went on to consider the careers of Cromwell in England, Li Zicheng in China, Aurangzeb in India, and others who had seized power by force, concluding that the mid-seventeenth century had been 'a period of usurpations almost from one end of the world to the other'.[1]

Voltaire's *Essay* repeatedly stressed the global dimension of the crisis: 'In the flood of revolutions which we have seen from one end of the universe to the other, a fatal sequence of events seems to have dragged people into them, just as winds move the sand and the waves. The developments in Japan offer another example . . '. Eventually, fearing that the marquise might still find his 174 chapters and 800 pages of 'examples' boring, he delivered his analysis in a single sentence: 'Three things exercise a constant influence over the minds of men: climate, government and religion.' Taken together, Voltaire proclaimed, they offer 'the only way to explain the enigma of this world'. Two decades later, Voltaire re-read his *Essay* and added a number of *Remarks*, including a fourth 'thing' that, he now believed, could 'reconcile what was irreconcilable and explain what is inexplicable' in human history: changes in population size.[2]

Voltaire's global vision has attracted few imitators. Although many subsequent historians have provided accounts filled with facts on 'government and religion' in the seventeenth century, until very recently few noted population trends and virtually none considered the influence of the climate. Nevertheless, recent work by demographers and climatologists suggests that around 1618, when the human population of the northern hemisphere was larger than ever before, the average global temperature started to fall, producing extreme climate events, disastrous harvest failures and frequent disease epidemics. Human demographic systems can seldom adapt swiftly enough to such adverse events, yet instead of seeking ways to mitigate the natural disasters and save lives, most governments around the globe exacerbated the situation by continuing their existing policies, above all their wars. These various natural and human factors constituted a 'placenta' capable of nourishing a global catastrophe. Even though they did not constitute the catastrophe itself, an examination of the placenta explains why the catastrophe lasted for two generations, why it killed up to one-third of the human population, and why it transformed the world inhabited by the survivors.[3]

1

The Little Ice Age[1]

'A strange and wondrous succession of changes in the weather'

IN 1614 RENWARD CYSAT, BOTANIST, ARCHIVIST AND TOWN HISTORIAN OF Luzern, Switzerland, began a new section of his chronicle entitled 'The Seasons of the Year', because 'the past few years have seen such a strange and wondrous succession of changes in the weather'. He decided to

> Record the same as a service and a favour to future generations because, unfortu-nately, on account of our sins, for some time now the years have shown themselves to be more rigorous and severe in the recent past, and we have seen deterioration amongst living things, not only among mankind and the animal world but also in the earth's crops and produce.[2]

Cysat was correct: 'a strange and wondrous succession of changes in the weather' had begun around the globe – and it would continue for almost a century. In west Africa, records reveal a prolonged drought from 1614 until 1619 both for Angola and for the Sahel (the semi-arid belt of savannah south of the Sahara that stretches from the Atlantic Ocean to the Red Sea). In Europe, Catalonia suffered 'the year of the flood' in 1617: after over a month of continuous rain, a final four-day downpour washed away bridges, mills, drainage works, houses and even town walls. All Europe experienced an unusually cold winter in 1620–1: many rivers froze so hard that for three months they could bear the weight of loaded carts and, most spectacularly, the Bosporus froze over so that people could walk across the ice between Europe and Asia (apparently a unique climatic anomaly).[3]

Other parts of the northern hemisphere also experienced abnormal weather. Japan endured its coldest spring of the seventeenth century in 1616; while Chinese Gazetteers recorded heavy snowfall in 1618 in subtropical Fujian (almost as rare as the Bosporus freezing over). Four provinces reported a severe winter in 1620, as did four more in 1621. In the Americas, drought afflicted the valley of Mexico for five years out of six between 1616 and 1621, and reduced the crops in the Chesapeake basin so severely that the new Virginia colony almost failed. After six better harvests, the summer of 1627 was the wettest recorded in Europe during the past 500 years, while 1628 was a 'year without a summer', with temperatures so low that many crops never ripened. Between 1629 and 1632, much of Europe suffered excessive rains followed by drought. Conversely northern India suffered a 'perfect drought' in 1630–1 followed by catastrophic floods in 1632. All of these regions experienced dramatic falls in population.[4]

Some better weather followed in the 1630s, but then came three of the coldest summers ever recorded in the northern hemisphere. Drought and cold significantly stunted the growth of trees throughout the western United States between 1640 and 1644, while the Canadian Rockies experienced severe and prolonged drought from 1641 until 1653. Since virtually no rain fell in the valley of Mexico in 1640, 1641 and 1642, the clergy of Mexico City organized processions with the 'Virgen de los Remedios', an image believed to possess special efficacy in bringing rain, to beg God's intervention before everyone starved to death (the first time the image had ever been used in consecutive years). Early in 1642, John Winthrop, governor of the Massachusetts Bay colony, noted that

> The frost was so great and continual this winter that all the Bay was frozen over, so much and so long, as the like, by the Indians' relation, had not been so these forty years ... To the southward also the frost was as great and the snow as deep, and at Virginia itself the great [Chesapeake] bay was much of it frozen over, and all of their great rivers.

To the north, English settlers on the coast of Maine complained of the 'most intolerable piercing winter' and found it 'incredible to relate the extremity of the weather'.[5]

Abnormal droughts also prevailed on the other side of the Pacific. The Indonesian rice harvest failed in both 1641 and 1642; and between 1643 and 1671 Java experienced the longest drought recorded during the past four centuries. In Japan the first winter snow of 1641 fell on Edo (as Tokyo was then known) on 28 November, almost the earliest date on record (the average date is 5 January), and both that year and the next saw unusually late springs. According to a 1642 pamphlet published in the Philippines, because of the 'great drought' throughout the archipelago 'a great famine is feared'; and two years later, a resident of Manila recorded that once again 'there has been much famine among the Indians [Filipinos] because the rice harvest was a poor one on account of the drought'. In North China, numerous Gazetteers reported drought in 1640 and the following year the Grand Canal, which brought food to Beijing, dried up for lack of rain (another unparalleled event); while in the lower Yangzi valley chroniclers recorded abnormal rain and cold throughout the spring of 1642.[6]

The lands around the Mediterranean also experienced extreme weather at this time. In March 1640 a messenger approaching Istanbul, 'with snow up to the horses' knees', experienced 'such a frost that I caught two frozen birds on the way simply with my own hand'. Catalonia endured a drought in spring 1640 so intense that the authorities declared a special holiday to enable the entire population to make a pilgrimage to a local shrine to pray for water – one of only four such occasions in the past five centuries. In 1641 the Nile fell to the lowest level ever recorded while the narrow growth rings laid down by trees in Anatolia reveal a disastrous drought. In Istanbul, by contrast, a chronicler recorded that rain flooded areas near Hagia

Sophia so that 'the shops were under water and destroyed'; while in Macedonia, the autumn saw 'so much rain and snow that many workers died through the great cold'. Early in 1642 the Guadalquivir broke its banks and flooded Seville, and the years 1640–3 were the wettest on record throughout Andalusia.[7]

Further north, English men and women noted 'the extraordinary distemperature of the season in August 1640, when the land seemed to be threatened with the extraordinary violence of the winds and unaccustomed abundance of wet'; while in Ireland, frost and snow in October 1641 began what contemporaries considered 'a more bitter winter than was of some years before or since seen in Ireland'.[8] Hungary experienced uncommonly wet and cold weather between 1638 and 1641, while summer frosts repeatedly devastated crops in Bohemia. In the Alps, unusually narrow tree rings reflect poor growing seasons throughout the 1640s, while estate papers record the disappearance of fields, farmsteads and even whole villages as glaciers advanced up to 1.2 miles beyond their current positions (their furthest extent in historical times). In eastern France, each grape harvest between 1640 and 1643 began a full month later than usual and grain prices surged, indicating poor cereal harvests. In the Low Countries, all along the river Maas (or Meuse), floods caused by snowmelt early in 1643 created 'the greatest desolation that one could imagine: the houses all broken open and overturned, and people and animals dead in the hedgerows. Even the branches of the highest trees contained a number of cows, sheep and chicken.' In Iceland, the unusual cold and constant rain ruined the hay, and in 1640 farmers resorted to dried fish as fodder for their cattle. Perhaps most striking of all, a soldier serving in central Germany recorded in his diary in *August* 1640 that 'at this time there was such a great cold that we almost froze to death in our quarters and, on the road, three people did freeze to death: a cavalry-man, a woman and a boy'; while 1641 remains the coldest year *ever* recorded in Scandinavia.[9]

Data from the southern hemisphere reveal a similar climatic aberration. In Chile, drought in the 1630s led the chief inquisitor to apologize to his superiors that he could not send them any proceeds from fines and confiscations because 'for the past three years we have not collected a penny on account of the drought'; while glaciers, tree rings and carbon-14 deposits all show significantly cooler weather in Patagonia in the 1640s.[10] In Sub-Saharan Africa, a severe drought afflicted both Senegambia and the Upper Niger between 1640 and 1644; while Angolan records show a unique concentration of droughts, locust infestations and epidemics throughout the second quarter of the seventeenth century, with a major drought and famine in 1639–45.

The decade ended with another bout of extreme weather around the globe. In 1648, on the Isle of Wight in southern England, a local landowner lamented that 'from Mayday till the 15th of September, we had scarce three dry days together', and when a visitor asked him 'whether that weather was usual in our island? I told him that in this forty years I never knew the like before'. Meanwhile, in Scotland, 'The long great rains for many weeks did prognosticate famine', and produced 'so great a dearth of corn as Ireland has not seen in our memory, and so cruel a famine, which has already killed thousands of the poorer sort'.[11] The following winter, the river Thames froze over as far as London Bridge and the barge arrying the corpse of Charles I to its final resting place after his execution on 30 January 1649 avoided ice floes in the river only with difficulty. Other parts of northwest Europe also experienced unusual precipitation that year – 226 days of rain or snow according to a meticulous set of records from Fulda in Germany (compared with an upper limit of 180 days in the twentieth century) – followed by 'a winter that lasted six months'. In France, appalling weather delayed the grape harvest into October in 1648, 1649 and 1650, and drove bread prices to the highest levels in almost a century, while floods covered central Paris for much of spring 1649. In China, the winter of 1649–50 seems to have been the coldest on record.[12]

The 1650s brought no respite. In the Dutch Republic, so much snow fell early in 1651 that the state funeral of Stadholder William II had to be postponed because mourners could not reach The Hague, and then the combination of snowmelt and a storm tide caused the worst flooding for 80 years in coastal regions. Catastrophic floods caused by snowmelt also occurred along the Vistula and the Seine. Conversely, 1651 saw the longest recorded drought in Languedoc and Roussillon, the Mediterranean borderlands between France and Spain: 360 days, or almost an entire year. In the Balkans, in spring 1654 'it snowed abundantly, [and] the snow covered the ground until Easter. I have never before seen such snowstorms and frost, moisture and cold.' Even olive 'oil and wine got frozen in the jars'. England experienced an 'unusual drought, which has lain upon us for some years, and still continues and increases upon us, threatening famine and mortality'; while in 1658 John Evelyn judged that he and his compatriots had just lived through 'the severest winter that man alive had known in England: the crow's feet were frozen to their prey; islands of ice enclosed both fish and fowl frozen, and some persons in their boats'.[13]

The same 'landmark winter' of 1657–8 affected other parts of the northern hemisphere. Along America's Atlantic coast, Massachusetts Bay froze over while the Delaware river froze so hard that deer ran across it. In Europe, people rode their horses on the ice across the Danube at Vienna, across the Main at Frankfurt and across the Rhine at Strasbourg, while barge traffic along the rivers and canals of the Netherlands gave way to sledges. The canal between Haarlem and Leiden remained frozen for 63 days. A Swedish ambassador returning home from Edirne (modern Turkey-in-Europe) noted in February 1658 that the weather was so cold that even migrating birds turned back, 'causing everyone to wonder'; while the Baltic froze so hard that a horse and cart could pass easily from the mouth of the Vistula at Danzig to the Hell Peninsula, and the Swedish army with all its artillery marched 20 miles over the Danish Sound from Jutland to Copenhagen. Inevitably, the following spring brought disastrous flooding as the snow and ice melted: the Seine again inundated Paris and many other towns, while the dikes in the Netherlands broke in 22 different places. Lieuwe van Aitzema, the official historian of the Dutch Republic, devoted two pages of his chronicle to the extreme climatic events around Europe during 1658, 'a year in which the winter was as harsh and severe at the beginning as at the end'.[14]

The seventeenth century saw not only extreme climatic events but also unusual concentrations of them. Of 62 recorded floods of the river Seine in and around Paris, 18 occurred in the seventeenth century. In England (and probably elsewhere in northwest Europe), 'bad weather ruined the harvests of corn and hay for five years from the autumn of 1646 onwards', with five more bad harvests in a row between 1657 and 1661. Put another way, 10 harvest failures occurred within the space of 16 years. The Aegean and Black Sea regions experienced the worst drought of the last millennium in 1659, followed by a winter so harsh that the Danube at Girugiu (200 miles inland from the Black Sea) froze so hard in a single night that the Ottoman army marched across the ice into Romania, 'laying waste all the villages and leaving no blade of grass or soul alive anywhere'. An official noted in his journal that, thanks to war and the weather, 'Transylvania never knew such misery as this last year [1660]'.[15] Extreme weather conditions continued in Europe. Ice floes blocked the Vistula with unequalled frequency, and in March 1657 a ship entering the river Elbe encountered 'mountaines of ice coming downe the river' and, despite using 'long poles to keep off the ice' all night, 'at day light wee had a mountaine of ice gathered before us, much higher' than the vessel itself. In 1675 much of the northern hemisphere experienced a 'year without a summer'. Ice floes repeatedly clogged and even froze the Thames during the 1660s and 1670s, most spectacularly in 1683–4, when 'there was a whole streete called the broad streete framed quite over the Thames from the Temple to the Bear Garden, and booths built, and many thousands of people walking sometimes together at once'. For six weeks crowds enjoyed 'severall Bull baitings' and 'all manner of debauchery on the Thames'.[16]

Poland experienced frost on several summer days in 1664, 1666 and 1667, and 109 days with frost in the year 1666–7 (compared with an average of 63 days today). Further south, in Moldavia, in the summer of 1670,

Terrible floods, frequent showers and heavy rainfall day and night raged for three months on end, destroying all of the best wheat, barley, oats, millet and all types of crop. Because they lie in water and are attacked by too much moisture, they neither ripen nor can bear seeds. Nor can the grasses and herbaceous seeds in hay-fields grow, for frost and water; or, if they do, they cannot be harvested [because] the sun never warms or dries up the land.

In 1686 a military engineer on campaign in what is now Romania complained that 'for three years now, I haven't seen a single drop of rain'. Lakes and rivers dried up, and 'in the swampy soil, cracks were so deep that a standing man could not be seen … I doubt if there is another example of such a terrible and lasting drought'.[17] In Russia, tree-ring, pollen and peat-bed data show that the springs, autumns and winters between 1650 and 1680 were some of the coldest on record; and, in China, the winters between 1650 and 1680 formed the coldest spell recorded in the Yangzi and Yellow river valleys over the last two millennia. In Africa, finally, according to a Turkish traveller in the 1670s, 'no one in Egypt used to know about wearing furs. There was no winter. But now we have severe winters and we have started wearing fur because of the cold.' Meanwhile, in the Sahel, drought in the 1680s became so severe and so widespread that Lake Chad fell to its lowest recorded level.[18]

Two artefacts from these years still strikingly reflect the unusually cold climate that prevailed. First, the abnormal frost, snow and ice gave rise to the popular genre of 'winter landscapes' by Dutch painters: most art galleries possess at least one, and almost all date from the later seventeenth century. Second, the wooden backs of the peerless violins made by Antonio Stradivari of Cremona in northern Italy display remarkably narrow growth rings, reflecting the unique succession of cold summers in the mid-seventeenth century that stunted the growth of the trees with which he worked.

So much abnormal weather led some contemporaries to suspect that they lived in the middle of a major climate change. In June and July 1675 (the century's second 'year without a summer'), the Paris socialite Madame de Sévigné complained to her daughter, in Provence, that 'It is horribly cold: we have the fires lit, just like you, which is very remarkable'; and speculated that 'like you, we think the behaviour of the sun and of the seasons has changed'. A generation later the Kangxi emperor, who collected and studied weather reports from all over China, noted how 'the climate has changed'. For example, His Majesty noted, 'in Fujian, where it never used to snow, since the beginning of our dynasty [1636], it has'.[19]

The Search for Scapegoats

Early modern people had good reason to monitor and to fear climate change. In the eloquent assessment of historian Thomas C. Smith:

> Farming, with its allied tasks, was the principal occupation and nearly the sole source of income for most families, and its rhythms defined the annual cycle of work, rest and worship. Severe annual variations in the harvest reverberated through family life, determining whether the family ate well or meagrely, whether the old might live another winter, whether a daughter could marry.[20]

Men and women therefore searched anxiously for explanations.

Many attributed natural disasters to divine displeasure. In China, the heavy and prolonged snows in 1641–2 convinced the scholar Qi Biaojia that 'Heaven is extremely angry'; somewhat later, the Kangxi emperor claimed that 'If our administration is at fault on earth, Heaven will respond with calamities from above'; while a Chinese folk song from the period reproached the Lord of Heaven for the catastrophic conditions:

> Old skymaster, you're getting on,
> Your ears are deaf, your eyes are gone.
> Can't see people, can't hear words.
> Glory for those who kill and burn;
> For those who fast and read the scriptures,
> Starvation.

Similarly, a Jesuit living in the Philippines speculated that the simultaneous eruption of three volcanoes in 1641 meant that 'Divine Providence wishes to show us something, perhaps to warn us of some approaching catastrophe, which our sins so deserve, or the loss of some territory, because God is angry.'[21]

Such statements reflected the prevailing 'peccatogenic' outlook (from *peccatum*, the Latin word for 'sin'): attributing disasters, including military defeats as well as bad weather and famine, to human misconduct. A circular letter written in 1648 by a new president of the Council of Castile, the minister responsible for internal affairs, was typical: 'The principal cause of the calamities that afflict this kingdom are the public sins and injustices committed', and punishing the former and 'administering justice with due rectitude and speed are the most important ways to oblige Our Lord to provide the successes that this Monarchy needs so much.'[22] In Germany the Protestant magistrates of Nuremberg commanded citizens to avert divine displeasure by showing moderation in food, drink and fashion and by refraining from sensual pleasure (especially if it involved adultery, sodomy or dancing). For the same reason, their Catholic neighbour, Maximilian of Bavaria, issued a stream of orders that forbade dancing, gambling, drinking and extramarital sex; limited the duration and cost of wedding festivities; forbade women to wear skirts that revealed their knees; proscribed the joint bathing of men and women; and periodically prohibited carnival and *Fastnacht* celebrations. The same logic appears in an edict issued by the English Parliament in 1642:

> Whereas the distressed state of Ireland, steeped in her own blood, and the distracted state of England, threatened with a cloud of blood by a civil war, call for all possible means to appease and avert the wrath of God . . . [and whereas] public sports do not well agree with public calamities, nor public stage-plays with the seasons of humiliation . . . being spectacles of pleasure, too commonly expressing lascivious mirth and levity . . . all public stage plays shall cease.

Parliament would later ban Maypoles and prohibit the celebration of Christmas, and in 1648 it 'authorized and required' the magistrates of London 'to pull down and demolish' all theatres, to have all actors publicly whipped, and to fine all playgoers, because plays tended 'to the high provocation of God's wrath and displeasure, which lies heavy upon this Kingdom.'[23]

The search for scapegoats targeted individuals as well as activities. In Europe, the climatic and economic disasters of the mid-seventeenth century fed a 'witchcraze' in which thousands of people were tried and executed because their neighbours blamed them for causing their misfortunes. Most of the victims were women, many of them unable to support themselves unaided; many lived in marginal areas for crop cultivation – in Lorraine, the Rhine and Main valleys for vines; in Scotland and Scandinavia for cereals – where the impact of global cooling was felt first and worst. Thus in southern Germany, a hailstorm in May 1626 followed by Arctic temperatures led to the arrest, torture and execution of 900 men and women suspected of producing the calamity through witchcraft. Two decades later, the Scottish Parliament likewise blamed a winter of heavy snow and rain followed by a cereal harvest of 'small bulke' on 'the sin of witchcraft [which] daily increases in this land'; and, to avert more divine displeasure, it authorized more executions for sorcery than at any other time in the country's history. A 'witch panic' also gripped the Hurons of North America between 1635 and 1645, although most of the accused were men; while in China, too, 'To anyone oppressed by tyrannical kinsmen or grasping creditors', a witchcraft accusation 'offered relief. To anyone who feared prosecution, it offered a shield. To anyone who needed quick cash, it offered rewards. To the envious it offered redress; to the bully, power; and to the sadist, pleasure.'[24]

The popularity of stage plays, sodomy and sorcery as explanations for catastrophe in the seventeenth century paled in comparison with five 'natural' scapegoats: stars, eclipses, earthquakes, comets and sunspots. In Germany, a Swedish diplomat wondered in 1648 whether the spate of contemporaneous rebellions might 'be explained by some general configuration of the stars in the sky'; while, according to a chronicler in Spain, only 'the malign influence of the stars' could explain the coincidence that 'in a single year [1647–8] in Naples, Sicily, the Papal States, England and France', such 'atrocities and extraordinary events' had occurred. A few years later, the Italian historian Majolino Bisaccione likewise argued that only 'the influence of the stars' could have created so much 'wrath among the people against the governments' of his day.[25]

Others blamed eclipses. The author of a Spanish almanac felt complete confidence that a recent eclipse of the sun had produced 'great upsets in war, political upheavals and damage to ordinary people' between March 1640 and March 1642 (as well as future catastrophes meticulously charted down to the year 2400). A similar English compilation predicted that the two lunar eclipses and unusual planetary conjunction forecast for 1642 would bring 'many strange accidents', namely 'sharp tertian fevers, war, famine, pestilence, house-burnings, rapes, depopulations, manslaughters, secret seditions, banishments, imprisonments, violent and unexpected deaths, robberies, thefts and piratical invasions'. An otherwise hard-headed chronicler writing two years after the Naples revolution of 1647 blamed it all on a recent solar eclipse; while in Iran, another solar eclipse in 1654 led some 'Persian wise men' to assert that it meant 'that the King had died; others said that there would be a war and blood would be shed; still others said wholesale deaths would occur.'[26] In India, even the Mughal emperors took special precautions during eclipses, staying indoors and eating and drinking little; while in *Paradise Lost*, composed between 1658 and 1663, John Milton noted the popular panic whenever the sun

> ... from behind the Moon
> In dim Eclips disastrous twilight sheds
> On half the Nations; and with fear of change
> Perplexes Monarchs.[27]

Many seventeenth-century people also speculated that earthquakes and comets presaged catastrophe – perhaps because the frequency of both increased notably. Thus an account of the destruction wrought by an earthquake, volcano and tsunami in the Azores in 1638 concluded: 'Let the speculative ponder, and the philosopher search out the cause of so portentous an effect.' A few years later a Dutch pamphleteer assured his readers that the

> Earthquake not long since felt in the year 1640, was a token of great commotions, and mighty shakings of the kingdomes of the earth, for a little before and shortly thereupon was concluded the revolt of Cathalonia, the falling-off of Portugal, the stirres in Scotland, the rebellion of the Irish, [and] those civill (uncivill) warres, great alterations, [and] unexpected tumults in England.[28]

Likewise, when severe tremors shook the buildings of Istanbul in 1648, the Ottoman minister and intellectual Kâtib Çelebi solemnly noted that 'when an earthquake happens during daytime in June, blood is shed in the heart of the empire': he was therefore not surprised by the murder of Sultan Ibrahim two months later. Records from Romania mention over 40 earthquakes between 1600 and 1690; while according to the *Earthquake Catalogue*, a peak of activity occurred in the mid-seventeenth century, especially in the 'ring of fire' around the Pacific Ocean, where more than two-thirds of the world's major earthquakes normally occur. Contemporaries saw each eruption as a harbinger of disaster.[29]

The mid-seventeenth century witnessed not only a peak of seismic activity but also a rare 'fireball flux'. The English astronomer John Bainbridge was apparently the first to comment, in 1619, on the 'many new stars and comets, which have been more [numerous] this last century of the world than in many ages before'. He wrote just after the appearance of three comets in 1618, which excited widespread anxiety. Even before they appeared, Johannes Kepler, the foremost mathematician of his day, warned in his *Astrological Almanac* for 1618 that the conjunction of five planets in May would cause extreme climatic events; and if a comet appeared as well everyone should 'sharpen their pens', because it would presage a major political upheaval. Over the winter of 1618–19, a multitude of books and pamphlets in Europe reminded readers that comets 'signify wars' and brought in their wake 'discord, irritations, deaths, upheavals, robberies, rape, tyranny and the change of kingdoms', and they predicted dire consequences for humanity following the three 'blazing stars' of 1618.[30] Some observers were more precise: a Spanish friar argued that the comets would prove especially dangerous for the Habsburg dynasty 'because they have touched us to the quick with the deaths of the empress, the Archduke Maximilian, and most recently the emperor [Matthias] . . . May God preserve those members of the House of Austria who are left!'[31]

Astronomers in Ming China also interpreted the three comets of 1618 as a portent of major upheavals, while the chronicles of their northern neighbours in Manchuria contain 'an overwhelming number of reports of such heavenly signs'. In Russia, the same comets provoked discussion and doleful interpretations among 'wise men'; in India, a Mughal chronicler claimed that 'no household remained unaffected' by fear, and blamed the comets for both an epidemic of plague and the subsequent rebellion of the crown prince; while in Istanbul, writers blamed them not only for the extreme weather (especially the freezing of the Bosporus) but also for the deposition of one sultan in 1618, the murder of another in 1622, and the provincial revolts that followed.[32]

Belief in the baleful effects of the comets of 1618 proved remarkably enduring. In 1643 a Dutch pamphleteer claimed that the

> Star with a tail, seen in the year 1618, was a warning and type of a rod that should come over all Christendome, whereupon followed those bloody effects, those horrible warrs, lamentable wastings, barbarous destruction of countreys and cities, the ruine of so many costly buildings, of so many gentlemen, so many inhabitants, men and women, young and old, in Germanie.

In 1649 a London newspaper considered that the end of the Thirty Years War the previous year was 'foretold by the Blazing Star which, in the year the war began, appeared over Europe for thirty days and no more'. A generation later in Boston, Massachusetts, the Reverend Increase Mather devoted three pages of his *Kometographia, or a discourse concerning comets* to the 'prodigy' of 1618 which, he claimed, had 'caused' not only a major drought throughout Europe, an earthquake in Italy, a plague in Egypt and 'the Bohemian and Germanic war, in which rivers of blood were poured forth', but also 'a plague amongst the Indians here in New England which swept them away in such numbers, as that the living were not enough to bury the dead'.[33]

Some contemporaries blamed the catastrophes that afflicted them on a combination of these natural phenomena. A popular Chinese encyclopaedia argued that 'when Venus has dominated Heaven, wars have arisen on a great scale, and that when comets have dominated Heaven, there have been conflicts over the succession to the throne'; while the Spanish almanac of 1640 already quoted reminded readers that 'whenever eclipses, comets and earthquakes and other similar prodigies have occurred, great miseries have usually followed'. In 1638 Robert Burton's *Anatomy of Melancholy* provided the most comprehensive 'catastrophe catalogue' of all. He felt sure that

> The heavens threaten us with their comets, starres, planets, with their great conjunctions, eclipses, oppositions, quartiles, and such unfriendly aspects. The air with his meteors, thunder and lightning, intemperate heat and cold, mighty windes, tempests, unseasonable weather; from which proceed dearth, famine, plague, and all sorts of epidemicall diseases, consuming infinite myriads of men.[34]

Others doubted such precise links. One Italian historian expressly ridiculed the idea that 'certain celestial constellations have the power to move the spirits of the inhabitants of a country to sedition, tumults and revolutions' in many different places at once; while the comets of 1618 provoked animated debates between astronomers and astrologers over whether or not they were capable of causing 'catastrophes'. Such uncertainty prompted a handful of observers to suggest an alternative natural scapegoat for the extreme weather of the seventeenth century: fluctuations in the number of sunspots – those dark regions of intense magnetic activity on the solar surface surrounded by 'flares' that make the sun shine with greater intensity. Even though they incorrectly argued that *more* sunspots would produce cooler temperatures on earth (whereas the reverse is true), unlike comet and star-gazers, the early solar astronomers had stumbled on an important cause of climate change in the seventeenth century.[35]

The development of telescopes as astronomical instruments after 1609 enabled observers to track the number of sunspots with unprecedented accuracy. They noted a 'maximum' between 1612 and 1614, followed by a 'minimum' with virtually no spots in 1617 and 1618, and markedly weaker maxima in 1625–6 and 1637–9. And then, although astronomers around the world made observations on over 8,000 days between 1645 and 1715, they saw virtually no sunspots: the grand total of sunspots observed in those 70 years scarcely reached 100, fewer than currently appear in a single year. This striking evidence of absence suggests a reduction in solar energy received on earth.[36]

Four other sets of data confirm this hypothesis. First, trees (like other plants) absorb carbon-14 from the atmosphere, and the amount rises as solar energy received on earth declines; and many tree-rings laid down in the seventeenth century contain increased carbon-14 deposits, which suggests reduced global temperatures. Second, between October 1642 and October 1644, Johannes Hevelius of Danzig made daily drawings of the sun that recorded the precise location of all spots, and he later printed his findings in a series of 26 'composite disks' that showed not only the number but also the movement of the spots over a few days (Plate 1). Hevelius's 'disks' reveal that sunspots were already rare: he seldom saw more than one or two groups at a time. Third, the aurora borealis (the 'northern lights' caused when highly charged electrons from the magnetosphere interact with elements in the earth's atmosphere) became so rare that when the astronomer Edmond Halley saw an aurora in 1716 he wrote a learned paper describing the phenomenon – because it was the first he had seen in almost fifty years of observation.[37] Finally, neither Halley nor other astronomers between the 1640s and the 1700s mentioned the brilliant corona nowadays visible during a total solar eclipse: instead they reported only a pale ring of dull light, reddish and narrow, around the moon. All four phenomena confirm that the energy of the sun diminished between the 1640s and the 1710s, a condition normally associated with both reduced surface temperatures and extreme climatic events on earth.[38]

A further astronomical aberration also troubled seventeenth-century observers living in the northern hemisphere: the appearance of 'dust veils' in the sky that made the sun seem either paler or redder than usual. Thus a Seville shopkeeper lamented that during the first six months of 1649 'the sun did not shine once . . . and if it came out it was pale and yellow, or else much too red, which caused great fear'. Thousands of miles to the east, Korea's royal astronomers reported darkened skies during the daytime on 38 occasions during the seventeenth century. On some days they recorded that 'the skies all around are darkened and grey as if some kind of dust had fallen'.[39] Both the dust and the reddened skies stemmed from an unusual spate of major volcanic eruptions in the mid-seventeenth century. Each hurled sulphur dioxide into the stratosphere where it deflected some of the sun's radiation back into space and, thus, significantly reduced temperatures in all areas of the earth beneath the dust clouds.

Vivid descriptions have survived for two of these volcanic eruptions. In February 1640, in Chile, Mount Villarica 'began to erupt with such force that it expelled burning rocks ... So much burning ash fell into the river Alipen that the waters burned in such a way that it cooked all the fish there.'[40] Less than a year later, on the other side of the Pacific, a Spanish garrison in the southern Philippines saw one day at noon 'a great darkness approaching from the south which gradually extended over that entire hemisphere and blocked out the whole horizon. By 1 PM they were already in total night and at 2 PM they were in such profound darkness that they could not see their own hands before their eyes.' Ash fell on them for 12 hours until, early the following morning, 'they began to see the moon'. They had just witnessed a 'force six' eruption, an event so terrifying that the authorities in Manila mounted an inquiry in which 'various priests and other trustworthy people' testified that the eruption was heard at exactly the same time 'throughout the Philippines and the Moluccas, and as far as the Asian mainland, in the kingdoms of Cochin-China, Champa and Cambodia – a radius of 900 miles, a wondrous thing which seems to exceed the bounds of the natural world'.[41] The dust veils produced by the 12 known volcanic eruptions around the Pacific between 1638 and 1644 (apparently an all-time record) combined with the sunspot minimum both to cool the earth's atmosphere and to destabilize its climate (Fig. 2).

Blame it on El Niño?

The global cooling caused by reduced sunspot and increased volcanic activity seems to have triggered a dramatic change in the climatic phenomena known as El Niño. In normal years, the surface air pressure in the equatorial region of the Pacific is higher in the east than in the west, which means that easterly winds blowing from America to Australia and South East Asia prevail. In cooler years, however, surface air pressure in the equatorial region of the Pacific falls in the east and rises in the west, so the pattern reverses: westerly winds blowing from Asia to America prevail. El Niño episodes dramatically affect the world's climate. As the air above the equatorial Pacific warms each spring it creates massive rain clouds: in a normal year, these fall on Asia as the 'monsoon', which nurtures the harvest, but in an El Niño year the monsoon weakens and heavy rains fall instead on America, causing catastrophic floods. Today this reversal – also known as ENSO (El Niño-Southern Oscillation) – happens about once every five years, but in the mid-seventeenth century it happened twice as often: in 1638, 1639, 1641, 1642, 1646, 1648, 1650, 1651, 1652, 1659, 1660 and 1661. This same period saw some of the weakest East Asian monsoons of the past two millennia.[42]

Admittedly historians cannot 'blame El Niño' for everything. Some regional climates are El Niño sensitive; others, even though contiguous, are not. Thus, in southern Africa, the eastern Cape is susceptible to El Niño-related droughts whereas the western Cape is not; likewise, droughts in northeast Brazil appear to occur in El

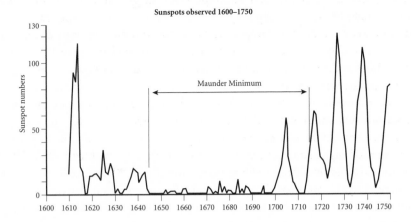

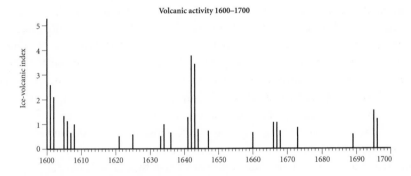

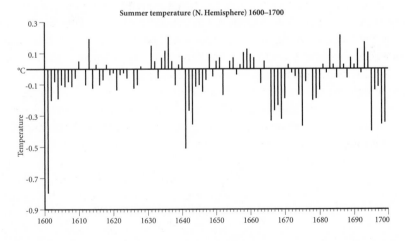

2. Sunspot cycles, volcanic anomalies, and summer temperature variations in the seventeenth century. The number of sunspots observed and recorded by European astronomers (*top*) shows the Maunder Minimum (1643–1715), in which fewer sunspots appeared in seventy years than appear in a single year now. Measurements of volcanic deposits in the polar icecap (the 'Ice-Volcanic Index') reveal a peak in the 1640s. Both phenomena show a striking correlation with lower summer temperatures in the northern hemisphere.

Niño years but those in western Mexico do not. The 'global footprint' of El Niño normally includes three regions besides the lands adjoining the Pacific: the Caribbean suffers floods; Ethiopia and northwest India experience droughts; and Europe suffers hard winters. In most of the 20 El Niño episodes recorded between 1618 and 1669, and in all 12 between 1638 and 1661, each of these regions experienced adverse weather.

The changed weather conditions in the Pacific Ocean during this period emerge starkly from two anomalies recorded in historical sources. On the one hand, the coastal province of Guangdong in southern China suffered more typhoon landfalls between 1660 and 1680 than at any other time in recorded history.[43] On the other hand, the voyages of galleons sailing from Acapulco in Mexico to Manila in the Philippines took longer than in any other period. In the first and last decades of the seventeenth century the crossing took an average of 80 days (a few took only 50 days), but between 1640 and 1670 the average duration rose to over 120 days (and three took over 160). Some ships never arrived: of the 11 galleons known to have sunk or run aground before reaching Manila during the seventeenth century, nine did so between 1639 and 1671. The return voyage from Manila to Acapulco also took much longer: the average duration rose from 160 to well over 200 days, and the longest voyages ever recorded (240 days, or eight months) took place in the 1660s. Nothing except a major shift in wind pattern could explain such a dramatic change. Diego de Villatoro, a crown official who had made the voyage twice, saw the connection clearly. In a memorial written in 1676 he noted sadly that 'now we consider a voyage from the Philippines to Acapulco that takes less than seven months to be good', and he perceptively ascribed the longer duration 'to a change in the monsoons'.[44]

Villatoro, of course, lacked the expertise either to blame this change on the increased frequency of El Niño activity or to associate El Niño with reduced solar activity, weaker Asian monsoons and increased volcanic activity. But we now know that in 'normal' years, when easterly winds prevail, the Pacific stands some 24 inches higher off the Asian than off the American coast, whereas in El Niño years, when westerly winds prevail, those levels reverse. The movement of such a huge volume of water places enormous pressure on the edges of the earth's tectonic plates around the Pacific periphery, where the most violent and most active volcanoes in the world are located, and this may trigger a spate of eruptions.[45] If this hypothesis is true, it creates a deadly cycle:

- Reduced solar energy received on earth lowers temperatures, which increases the risk of more, and more severe, El Niño events.
- El Niño events may trigger volcanic eruptions around the Pacific that throw sulphur dioxide into the stratosphere, which further reduces the solar energy received on earth.
- El Niño activity becomes twice as likely after a major volcanic eruption.

Whatever the exact connections between these natural phenomena (and not all scientists agree), the mid-seventeenth century certainly experienced both an unusual spate of earthquakes, fireball fluxes, volcanic eruptions and El Niño episodes, and a drastic reduction in sunspot activity, the weakest monsoons and some of the lowest global temperatures recorded in the past few centuries.

Climate and Crops

So what? To a sceptic, 'global cooling' that amounts to a fall of only one or two degrees Celsius in mean summer temperatures, and a modest glacier advance, may seem insignificant; but that is to think in linear terms. On the one hand, the mean global temperature has shown remarkable stability over the last six millennia: the difference at the equator between the 'Medieval Optimum' (the hottest temperatures recorded until the late twentieth century) and the Little Ice Age was probably less than 3°C. A change of even one degree is thus highly significant. On the other hand, in the northern hemisphere, home to the majority of humankind and site of most of the wars and revolutions of the seventeenth century, solar cooling reduces temperatures far more than at the equator, in part because increased snow cover and sea-ice reflect more of the sun's rays back into space. The extension of the polar icecaps and glaciers in the mid-seventeenth century would thus have reduced mean temperatures in northerly latitudes dramatically.

A recent 'model' of the probable global climate in the later seventeenth century shows significantly colder weather in Siberia, North Africa, North America and northwest India; colder and drier weather in central China and Mongolia; and cooler and less stable conditions in the Iberian Peninsula, France, the British Isles and Germany. As already noted, these same areas – the Russian and Ottoman empires in Eurasia; the Ming and Qing states in East Asia; and the dominions of Philip IV, Charles I, Louis XIV and Ferdinand II in Europe – reported not only cooler weather in the 1640s and 1650s but also a significant number of extreme weather events and serious political upheavals. The former should cause no surprise: an overall decline in mean temperatures is normally associated with a greater frequency of severe weather events – such as flash floods, freak storms, prolonged droughts and abnormal (as well as abnormally long) cold spells. All of these climatic anomalies can critically affect the crops that feed the people.

In the 'temperate zone', which stretches roughly from 30 to 50 degrees of latitude, crop yields suffer disproportionately from a cold spell during germination, a drought in the early growing season and a major storm just before harvest. To take a single example, a Gazetteer from Zhejiang in eastern China reported that 'When on the 13th day of the 5th moon in 1640 the fields were inundated, those who had planted out on the 12th or earlier had no disaster once the flood had subsided, but those who planted on or after the 13th' lost everything.[46] An unseasonable frost could prove equally disastrous. In areas of wet rice cultivation, a fall of 0.5°C in the average spring temperature prolongs the risk of the *last* frost by 10 days, while a similar fall in the average autumn temperature advances the risk of the *first* frost by the same amount. Either event suffices to kill the entire crop. Even without frosts, a fall of 2°C during the growing season – precisely the scale of global cooling in the 1640s – reduces rice harvest yields by between 30 and 50 per cent, and also lowers the altitude suitable for wet-rice cultivation by about 1,300 feet. Likewise, in cereal-growing regions, a fall of 2°C shortens the growing season by three weeks or more, diminishes crop yields by up to 15 per cent, and lowers the maximum altitude at which crops will ripen by about 300 feet. Drought, too, destroys harvests by depriving crops of the precipitation they required. As a Chinese manual of agriculture, published in 1637, warned: 'All rice plants die if water is lacking for ten [consecutive] days.'[47]

Extreme weather could also destroy crops indirectly. Excessive rain might allow rodents to multiply. In Moldavia in 1670 'myriads of mice' not only ate 'all they found in the vegetable gardens' but also, 'climbing up the trees, ate all the fruit, finishing them up; and to end the job' they 'finished the wheat in the field'.[48] Drought favoured locusts. In 1647 the Moldavian nobleman Miron Costin reported that 'about the time of the year when people pick up their sickles to harvest the wheat', he and some companions were on the road and 'suddenly noticed a cloud towards the south':

> We thought it was a rainstorm until we were suddenly hit by the locust swarm, coming at us like a flying army. The sun disappeared immediately, veiled by the blackness of these insects. Some of them flew high, at three or four metres, while others flew at our level, or even right above the ground ... They flew around us without fearing anything ... It took an hour for a swarm to pass, and then after an hour and a half there came another, and then another, and so on. It lasted from noon till dusk. No leaf, no blade of grass, no hay, no crop, nothing remained.[49]

In latitudes north of the 'temperate zone', where the growing season is shorter, the impact of climate change on crop cultivation increases. First, it radically reduces yields. In Manchuria, with a total of only 150 frost-free days in even 'good' years, a fall of 2°C in mean summer temperature reduces harvest yields by a stunning 80 per cent. In Finland, the growing season even in 'normal' years is the shortest compatible with an adequate harvest so that even a single summer night's frost can kill an entire crop. Seventeenth-century Finland saw 11 crop failures (compared with only one in the eighteenth century).[50] Second, global cooling increases the frequency of harvest failure in northerly latitudes.

- In the 'temperate zone', if early winters or summer droughts occur with a frequency of $P = 0.1$, the harvest will fail once every 10 years, and two consecutive harvests will fail once every 100 years. If, however, early winters or summer droughts occur with a frequency of $P = 0.2$, the harvest will fail once every 5 years (double the risk) while two consecutive harvests will fail every 25 years (quadruple the risk).
- In latitudes north of the 'temperate zone', each fall of 0.5°C in mean summer temperatures decreases the number of days on which crops ripen by 10 per cent, doubles the risk of a single harvest failure, and increases the risk of a double failure six-fold.
- For those farming 1,000 feet or more above sea level, a fall of 0.5°C in mean summer temperatures increases the chance of two consecutive failures 100-fold.

Climate and Calories

In densely populated parts of the early modern world, whether sub-boreal, temperate or tropical, most people relied on a single crop, high in bulk and in carbohydrates, known as a 'staple'. Cereals (wheat, rye, barley and oats) formed the principal staple in Europe, northern India and northern China. Rice occupied the same role in Monsoon Asia, maize in the Americas, and millet in upland India and Sub-Saharan Africa. The economic allure of staple crops is almost irresistible to farmers. An acre under cereals feeds between ten and twenty times as many people as an acre devoted to animal husbandry; furthermore, the same amount of money usually bought 10 pounds of bread but only 1 pound of meat. An acre planted with wet-rice yields up to 6 tons of food – three times as much as an acre of wheat or maize and sixty times as much as an acre devoted to animal husbandry. Not surprisingly, therefore, according to a Chinese textbook printed in 1637, '70 per cent of the people's staple food is rice', while in Europe, cereals likewise provided up to three-quarters of the total calorie intake of every family (not only in the form of bread but also as a 'filler' for soups and as the basic ingredient for beer and ale).[51]

Steven Kaplan has rightly insisted on the 'tyranny' of popular dependence on staple crops – cereals, rice, maize or millet, depending on the region – in the pre-industrial world. In Europe,

> Cereal-dependence conditioned every phase of social life. Grain was the pilot sector of the economy; beyond its determinant role in agriculture, directly and indirectly grain shaped the development of commerce and industry, regulated employment, and provided a major source of revenue for the state, the church, the nobility, and large segments of the Third Estate ... Because most of the people were poor, the quest for subsistence preoccupied them relentlessly. No issue was more urgent, more pervasively felt, and more difficult to resolve than the matter of grain provisioning. The dread of shortage and hunger haunted this society.[52]

'Shortage and hunger' could arise in three distinct ways. First, throughout the early modern world, food accounted for up to half the total expenditure of most families, and so any increase in staple prices caused hardship because most families had little spare cash and soon faced the risk that they could not feed themselves. Second, spending more on food left little or nothing with which to purchase other goods, leading to a fall in demand: this meant that many non-agricultural workers lost their jobs and reduced the wages received by the rest – that is, their income fell just as their expenditure rose. Third, since the impact of harvest failure on the price of cereals is non-linear, any shortfall in the harvest reduced the food supply geometrically and not arithmetically. Suppose that

- In a normal year a European farmer sowed 50 acres with grain and harvested 10 bushels an acre, a total of 500 bushels. Of this, he needed 175 bushels for animal fodder and seed corn and 75 bushels to feed himself and his family – a total of 250 bushels – leaving 250 for the market.

- If bad weather reduced his crop by 30 per cent, the harvest would produce only 350 bushels yet the farmer still needed 250 of them for his immediate use. The share available for the market therefore dropped to 100 bushels – a fall of 60 per cent.
- But if bad weather reduced crops by 50 per cent, the harvest would produce only 250 bushels, all of them needed by the farmer, leaving virtually nothing for the market.

This non-linear correlation explains why a 30 per cent reduction in the grain harvest often *doubled* the price of bread, whereas a 50 per cent reduction *quintupled* it. It also explains why, if the harvest failed for two or more consecutive years, starvation almost always followed.

Steven Kaplan concluded his study of famines in eighteenth-century France by suggesting that this cruel calculus 'produced a chronic sense of insecurity that caused contemporaries to view their world in terms that may strike us as grotesquely or lugubriously overdrawn'. However, a study by Alex de Waal of the Darfur famine of 1984–5 in East Africa rejected the notion of 'overdrawn' where harvest shortfalls are concerned because, even today, failures can 'cross a threshold of awfulness and become an order of magnitude worse'. Not only do large numbers of people die, so does their entire way of life.[53] De Waal identified three characteristics of these 'landmark famines':

- First, they force those affected to use up their assets, including investments, stores and goods. Although a family might choose to go hungry for a season in order to preserve its ability to function as a productive unit (for example by keeping back grain to feed its livestock or to use as seed corn instead of eating it all), it can rarely maintain that strategy for a second, let alone a third year. Two or three successive harvest failures therefore leave victims permanently destitute.
- Second, prolonged starvation also forces those affected to use up their social claims ('entitlements'). A hungry family may refrain from begging for assistance from other individuals and institutions for a short period, but once again it can rarely maintain that strategy for long. If a large number of families suddenly becomes destitute, it may cripple and even destroy the communities in which they live.
- Third, as communities cease to be viable, some families migrate. Initially, migration may form a reasonable 'coping strategy' in a famine because, although the migrants necessarily abandon both their assets and their 'entitlements' by leaving their local community, those who survive can return to their homes and their previous way of life when conditions improve. Prolonged dearth, however, will sever the links with the world they have left and thus, according to De Waal, lead to the 'mortality' of their entire way of life.

Calories and Death

Each day, every human needs to consume at least 1,500 calories to maintain her or his basic metabolic functions and to resist infection. Pregnant women and those who earn their living by physical labour require at least 2,500 calories. Few people in the early modern period were so lucky: during the Italian plague of 1630–1, hospital records show that each patient received a daily ration of half a kilo of bread, a quarter of a kilo of meat (probably in a stew), and half a litre of wine – a daily intake of scarcely 1,500 calories (and one seriously deficient in vitamins). Even in the 'normal' years of the seventeenth century, the average Frenchman consumed barely 500 calories more than his basic metabolic requirement, and the average Englishman barely 700 calories more.[54]

Two short-term 'safety mechanisms' help humans to adjust to malnutrition. We may cut back on energy demands (working more slowly, resting longer); and, as body weight declines, we can get by with fewer calories to sustain the basic metabolism (and the reduced physical activity). Nevertheless, in the long term, even a small reduction in our daily calorific intake can have dramatic consequences. A decrease of one-fifth, from 2,500 to 2,000 calories, *halves* our ability to work efficiently because the body's basic metabolism still requires 1,500 calories. In the case of a pregnant woman, a similar reduction imperils the health of both mother and child. Furthermore, a weight loss of 10 per cent reduces energy by about one-sixth, but a weight loss of 20 per cent reduces energy by about one-half, and if a woman or man loses 30 per cent of their normal body weight, blood pressure falls and the ability to absorb nutrients fails.

In this weakened condition, any additional stress on the body, such as disease, usually proves fatal – and, amid the social disruption normally associated with famine, infectious diseases often spread rapidly – while cold and damp further weaken those who are starving. According to a report on an Indian famine in the nineteenth century: 'The most common termination of life in those debilitated by famine was diarrhoea or dysentery, aggravated by damp and exposure ... Cold and damp had a most detrimental effect upon the starving poor, and those in a physically reduced condition from chronic insufficiency of food.'[55] Observers in the seventeenth century described the same fatal decline. According to Yang Dongming, a government official and philanthropist in central China:

> All beings are physically the same, alike in their intolerance of cold. Those people with old, tattered clothes ... go nearly naked in the dead of winter, their hair dishevelled and feet bare and their teeth chattering; crying out and terrified ... Being solitary, they have no place to go ... [and] falling snow covers their bodies. At this point, their organs freeze and their bodies stiffen like pieces of wood. At first they are still able to groan. Gradually they cough up phlegm. Then, their lives are extinguished.

Five thousand miles to the west, Sir Robert Sibbald, a Scottish physician and geographer, lamented that

> The bad seasons these several years past hath made so much scarcity and so great a dearth, that for want, some die by the way-side, some drop down on the streets, the poor sucking babes are starving for want of milk, which the empty breasts of their mothers cannot furnish them. Every one may see death in the face of the poor

that abound everywhere: the thinness of their visage, their ghostly looks, their feebleness, their agues and their fluxes threaten them with sudden death, if care be not taken of them. And it is not only common wandering beggars that are in this case, but many house-keepers who lived well by their labour and industrie are now by want forced to abandon their dwellings and they and their little ones must beg.[56]

Famines afflicted 'little ones' with especial severity. Starvation killed many infants because their mothers had no milk to feed them; but, famished children, especially when they are also cold and exposed to disease, suffer 'stunting'. Because simply staying alive and keeping warm absorbs so many calories, and a famine diet usually lacks adequate protein and vitamins, the long bones in the legs and arms of children cease to grow. Human remains from the Little Ice Age show unmistakable evidence of such 'stunting'. When archaeologists excavated the skeletons of 50 workers buried in the permafrost at Smeerenburg ('Blubber Town'), a whaling station maintained by the Dutch on Spitsbergen Island in the Arctic between 1615 and 1670 (when the intolerable cold forced them to withdraw), no fewer than 43 showed evidence of stunting and a corresponding reduction in height.[57] Even more striking, French soldiers born in the second half of the seventeenth century were on average about an inch shorter than those born after 1700; and those born in famine years were notably shorter than the rest. Thus 'stunting' reduced the average height of those born in 1675, the 'year without a summer', or during the years of cold and famine in the early 1690s, to only 63 inches: the lowest ever recorded. Once warmer weather and better harvests returned in the eighteenth century, the average height of Frenchmen increased by almost 1.5 inches – an unparalleled surge – and the 'bantam soldiers' never reappeared (Fig. 3).

'Stunting' does not only adversely affect the long bones of children: because malnutrition often impairs the development of major organs as well as long bones, it makes children more vulnerable to both contagious and chronic diseases, which can in turn further diminish stature. Children living in the countryside might experience a catch-up growth spurt, which partially compensates for stunting, but those living in overcrowded and insanitary towns often stayed short (which probably explains why recruits for the French Army from Paris were always shorter than the rest). John Komlos, the demographer whose research revealed the reduced height of Louis XIV's soldiers, was surely correct that the seventeenth-century crisis 'had an immense impact on the human organism itself'. His data provide perhaps the clearest – and saddest – evidence of the consequences of the Little Ice Age for the human population. The repeated famines not only killed: many of those who survived literally embodied Thomas Hobbes's assertion that 'the life of man' had indeed become 'solitary, poor, nasty, brutish and short'.[58]

An Overpopulated World?

Although Hobbes and his contemporaries apparently stood somewhat shorter than their grandparents, they were far more numerous. A run of warm summers in the

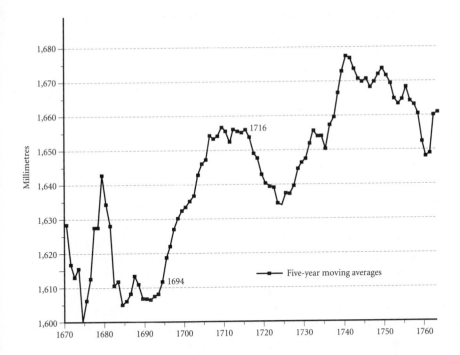

3. Estimated heights of French males born between 1650 and 1770.
John Komlos assembled 38,700 'observations' from the personal records of French males who
enlisted in the army between 1671 and 1786. Even though recruiting officers rejected the shortest
volunteers, the 'stunting' effect of global cooling is evident, especially for those born in 1675, 'the
year without a summer' (one of two experienced in the seventeenth century). The average height of
Louis XIV's soldiers was 1,617 mm, or 5 foot 3 inches.

sixteenth century had allowed the human population in most parts of Europe and
Asia to increase and in some areas to double – until by 1618 China boasted perhaps
150 million inhabitants, India 116 million and Europe 100 million. In some areas,
the number of inhabitants had increased so fast that local resources no longer
sufficed to feed them because of another cruel calculus: *population increases geometrically while agricultural output grows only arithmetically*. Just like 'compound interest', a
sustained demographic increase of 1 per cent per year over a century causes a population not merely to double, but to triple; while a 2 per cent increase over a century
produces a sevenfold growth. Since crop yields rarely increase at this pace, food
shortages can occur very rapidly.

Many people in the early seventeenth century realized that their part of the world
possessed more mouths than could be fed, and feared the consequences. China's
Lower Yangzi valley, known as Jiangnan, boasted a population of about 20 million
by 1618, equivalent to almost 1,200 persons per square mile (by way of comparison,
the overall population density of the modern Netherlands, the most densely settled
part of Europe today, is 1,000 persons per square mile). According to Alvaro
Semedo, a Portuguese Jesuit long resident in the region who wrote in the 1630s,
Jiangnan 'is so full of all sorts of people that not only the villages but even the cities

can now be seen one from another' and, in some areas, 'settlement is almost continuous'. Indeed, he mused,

> This kingdom is so overpopulated [*eccessivamente popolato*] that after living there
> for twenty-two years, I remain almost as amazed at the end as I was at the begin-
> ning by the multitude of people. Certainly the truth is above any exaggeration: not
> only in the cities, towns and public places ... but also on the roads there are
> normally as many people as would turn out in Europe [only] for some holiday or
> public festival.

Since 'the number of people is infinite,' Semedo concluded, 'there can be no capital
sufficient for so many, or money enough to fill so many purses'.[59]

Many of Semedo's contemporaries also considered Europe 'overpopulated'. John
Winthrop justified 'the plantation of New England' because England itself 'groweth
her inhabitants soe that man, the best of creatures, is held more base then the earth
they tredd on'; while Sir Ferdinando Gorges also claimed that England's 'peaceable
time affords no means of employment to the multitude of people that daily do
increase', and he sent colonists to settle the coast of North America primarily to
reduce population pressure at home. His rivals in the Virginia Company, fearing 'the
surcharge of necessitous people, the matter or fuel of dangerous insurrections', likewise sought to remove them from England to their new colony. These and other
measures enjoyed such success that by the 1630s thousands crossed the Atlantic
each year, promoting England's stability because the colonies 'serve for drains to
unload their populous state which else would overflow its own banks by continuance of peace and turn head upon itself, or make a body fit for any rebellion'.[60]

Scarcely had the ink dried on these words than the global population began to
contract sharply. In China, the victorious Qing believed that in the mid-seventeenth-
century crisis 'over half of the population perished. In Sichuan, people lamented that
they did not have a single offspring.' In the 1650s, after a decade of sectarian violence
and civil war in Ireland, according to one of the English victors 'a man might travel
twenty or thirty miles and not see a living creature' except for 'very aged men with
women and children' whose skin was 'black like an oven because of the terrible
famine'; and a generation later, another English eye-witness estimated that over
500,000 Irish men and women had died 'by the sword and famine and other hardships' in the troubles. Contemporaries elsewhere made similarly bleak assessments.
In southern Germany, one eye-witness of the Thirty Years War believed that 'there
have been so many deaths that the like of it has never been heard in human history';
while a Lutheran minister wrote despondently in 1639 that of his 1,046 communicants a decade earlier, barely one-third remained: 'Just in the last five years, 518 of
them have been killed by various misfortunes. I have to weep for them,' he continued
forlornly, 'because I remain here so impotent and alone. Out of my whole life
scarcely fifteen people remain alive with whom I can claim some trace of friendship.'
Perhaps most striking of all, in France, ravaged between 1648 and 1653 by war,
famine and disease, Abbess Angélique Arnauld of Port-Royal (just outside Paris)
estimated that 'a third of the world has died'.[61]

Subsequent research has corroborated each of these striking claims. In China, 'the cultivated area of land decreased by about one-third' during the Ming-Qing transition, while 'the demographic losses were nearly the same'. Sichuan suffered particularly badly, with perhaps a million killed. Ireland's population fell by at least one-fifth during the mid-seventeenth century. In Germany, 'about 40 per cent of the rural population fell victim to the war and epidemics [while] in the cities, the losses may be estimated at about 33 per cent' between 1618 and 1648. Many villages in the Île-de-France suffered their worst demographic crisis of the entire Ancien Régime in 1648–53.[62] Census data from Poland, Russia and the Ottoman empire suggest a population fall in the mid-seventeenth century of at least one-third, sometimes more. These staggering losses were not caused by the Little Ice Age alone, however: it required the misguided policies pursued by religious and political leaders to turn the crisis caused by sudden climate change into catastrophe.

The 'General Crisis'

'The century of the soldiers'

Most of those who lived through the seventeenth-century crisis identified war rather than climate as the principal cause of their misfortunes – and with good reason: more wars took place around the world than in any other era before the Second World War. The historical record reveals only one year entirely without war between the states of Europe in the first half of the century (1610) and only two in the second half (1670 and 1682) (Fig. 4). In 1641 the prevalence of conflicts led the Italian warrior and man of letters Fulvio Testi to claim that 'This is the century of the soldiers'; while according to the English philosopher Thomas Hobbes, 'man's natural state' was war. In Denmark, more than one-tenth of all texts printed between 1611 and 1669 concerned war, and publishing data from neighbouring countries would probably reveal a similar pattern. Beyond Europe, the Chinese and Mughal empires fought wars continuously for most of the seventeenth century, and the Ottoman empire enjoyed only ten years of peace.[1]

The 'Conflict Catalogue' compiled by Peter Brecke, a sociologist, shows that, on average, wars around the world lasted longer in the seventeenth century than at any time since 1400 (when his survey begins); while, looking only at Europe, Jack S. Levy, a political scientist, considered the sixteenth and seventeenth centuries 'the most warlike in terms of the proportion of years of war under way (95 per cent), the frequency of war (nearly one every three years), and the average yearly duration, extent, and magnitude of war'. The 'index of war intensity' proposed by Pitirim Sorokin, another sociologist, rose from 732 in the sixteenth century to 5,193 in the seventeenth – a rate of increase twice or three times greater than in any previous period.[2]

In addition to these interstate conflicts, the mid-seventeenth century also witnessed more civil wars than any previous or subsequent period. For six decades, supporters of the Ming and Qing dynasties fought for control of China. The rebellion of large parts of the Stuart and the Spanish Monarchies unleashed internal conflicts that lasted over two decades in the former and almost three in the latter. The states of Germany, with powerful foreign support, fought each other for 30 years. France endured a civil war that lasted five years; the Mughal empire suffered a succession war that lasted two years. Several other countries (including Sweden,

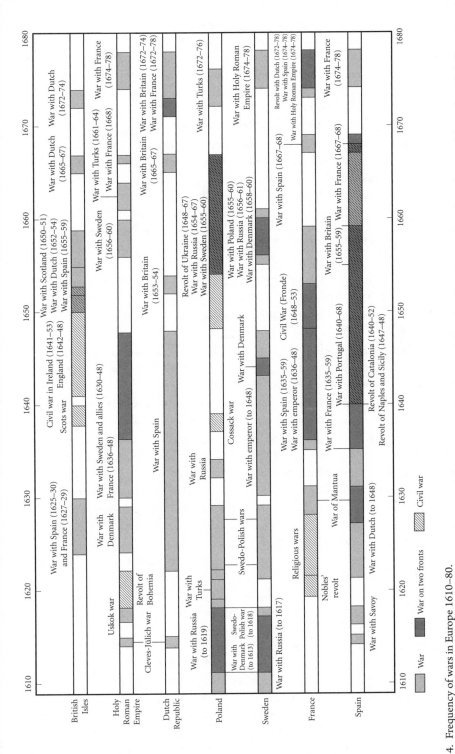

4. Frequency of wars in Europe 1610–80.

In the six decades between 1618 and 1678, Poland was at peace for only 27 years, the Dutch Republic for only 14, France for only 11, and Spain for only 3. Some states fought wars on several fronts at once. Virtually no European state avoided war during the 1640s.

Denmark, the Dutch Republic and the Swiss Confederation) experienced political upheavals that only just stopped short of civil war (see Fig. 1 above). War, rather than peace, had become the normal state of human society.

Although the business of the military in war has always been killing people and breaking things, many in the seventeenth century believed that the wars of their day were not only more frequent but also more harmful to both people and property. When, around 1700, Richard Gough researched the history of his village, Myddle (Shropshire, England), he found that 21 men (one-tenth of the community's adult males) had left to fight in the Civil War, of whom only seven returned. Of the other 14, six died in battle, one perished in a brawl over plunder, another was hanged for horse theft and the other six disappeared without trace. Some no doubt succumbed to war-related diseases (such as typhoid, revealingly known as 'camp fever') or suffered war-induced accidents (such as freezing to death on sentry duty); but whatever their fate, and wherever their unmarked grave, their families never saw them again – 'and if so many died from Myddle,' Gough speculated, 'we may reasonably guess that many thousands died in England in that war'.[3]

Gough was right – the catalogue of 645 'military incidents' fought in England and Wales between 1642 and 1660 compiled by historian Charles Carlton reveals that at least 80,000 men died in action – but they formed only part of the trail of destruction caused by war. As Patrick Gordon, a Scottish veteran, noted in the 1650s: 'One can scarse be a souldier without being an oppressor and comitting many crimes and enormityes', because those who failed to take what they needed by violent means 'were sure to be destroyed by vermine, or dy with hunger or cold'.[4] Hans Heberle, a German shoemaker, recorded in his *Journal* how the failure of civilians to appreciate this dynamic could destroy lives and livelihoods. In 1634 the Protestant army of Bernard of Saxe-Weimar approached Heberle's village but, since they too were Protestants, he and his neighbours 'did not regard him as our enemy' and so took no precautions. Nevertheless Bernard's troops 'plundered us completely of horses, cattle, bread, flour, salt, lard, cloth, linen, clothes and everything we possessed. They treated the inhabitants badly, shooting, stabbing and beating a number of people to death.' As they left, 'they set the village alight and burnt down five houses'. Heberle and his surviving neighbours had learned an important lesson: in the mid-seventeenth century, every soldier was an 'enemy'. Henceforth, 'we were hunted like wild beasts in the forest,' he wrote bitterly in his journal, and whenever troops approached, the villagers fled with whatever they could carry to Ulm, the nearest fortified city. Their sufferings did not end there, because Ulm lacked the resources to sustain the sudden influx of thousands of refugees. On at least one occasion water became so scarce that 'almost everybody drank their own urine, or the urine of their children . . . The thirst grew so intense that we did not care about being hungry.'[5]

To quote the lugubrious Thomas Hobbes again, 'warre consisteth not in battell onely, or the act of fighting, but in a tract of time, wherein the will to contend by battell is sufficiently known'. War, Hobbes argued, was like the climate: just 'as the nature of foule weather lyeth not in a showre or two of rain, but in an inclination thereto of many days together: so the nature of warre consisteth not in actuall fighting, but in the known disposition thereto during all the time there is no assurance to the contrary.' This led to widespread insecurity. When he returned to England from the continent in 1660, Charles II observed that the Civil War 'had filled the hearts of the people with a terrible apprehension of insecurity', and therefore worked hard on 'extinguishing this fear, which keeps the hearts of men awake'. Three years later, in Germany, a comedy by Andreas Gryphius made the same point with a joke, beginning one of his plays with the boast of 'Captain Daradiridatumtarides Farter of a Thousand Deaths' that

> The Great Shah of Persia trembles when I walk on the earth.
> The Turkish emperor has several times sent ambassadors to offer me his crown.
> The world-famous Mughal (emperor) knows his fortress is vulnerable to me . . .
> The princes of Europe ever more courteously become my friends –
> But more through fear than through true affection.

Looking back in 1683, ex-Queen Christina of Sweden wrote that 'In the present century, the whole world is at arms. We threaten each other, we fear each other. Nobody does what they want, or what they could do. No one knows who has lost or who has won, but we know well enough that the whole world lives in fear.'[6]

In China war became so common that a special word emerged to describe military atrocities: *binghuo*, 'soldier calamity'. According to the eminent sinologist Lynn Struve, 'no locale in China escaped some sort of "soldier calamity"' during the Ming-Qing transition.[7] As in Europe, the worst atrocities occurred when soldiers took a town by storm. A seventeenth-century Chinese play, *The Miraculous Reunion*, compared the treatment of a captured town or city with 'pounding fresh onion and garlic to pieces in a bowl'; while an eye-witness account noted that civilians who survived a successful storm 'had scorched pates, pulpy foreheads, and broken or otherwise injured arms and legs. They had sword gashes all over their bodies, the blood from which had clotted in patches, and their faces were streaked with trickles of blood like tears from burning red candles.'[8]

This description came from a chronicle kept by a scholar, Wang Xiuchu, of the six-day sack of Yangzhou, a large city north of the river Yangzi, by Qing forces in 1645. According to Wang, at one point 'through the compound wall I heard the voice of my youngest brother shrieking and the sound of a sabre hacking – three strikes and all was silent. After a short while I also heard my elder brother say pleadingly "I have silver at home in an underground vault. Let me get it and bring it to you." One strike, and again silence.' Somewhat later, a soldier caught another of Wang's brothers and 'cut him with his sabre to make him talk'; he died of his wounds a week later. His sister-in-law, nephew and niece also perished, and both Wang and his wife were badly beaten. Before the soldiers stormed Yangzhou 'there were eight of us,' Wang wrote, but 'now there are only three'. Another eye-witness claimed that 80,000 inhabitants perished in the sack; and because so much of the city lay in ruins, poets referred to it as the 'Weed-covered city'. Its fate in 1645 is still familiar to every Chinese schoolchild.[9] The European equivalent of the sack of Yangzhou was the sack of Magdeburg in 1631. Even in the nineteenth century,

Protestant preachers still used its fate as a warning in their sermons and for a time it gave a new verb to the German language: *Magdeburgisieren*, to 'make a Magdeburg' of somewhere.[10]

For women, war presented additional dangers: the high risk of being raped or abducted. Some suffered through a deliberate effort by the victors to dishonour a community, to prove it could not 'protect its women'; others became the victims of lust. At Yangzhou in 1645, Wang Xiuchu watched a group of soldiers argue over the fate of five women whom they had captured:

> Suddenly one of them hoisted one of the women and copulated with her under a tree. Then the two other younger ones were sullied while the two older ones wailed and begged to be spared. The three younger ones shamelessly thought nothing of it when about a dozen men took turns raping them before handing them over to the two soldiers who'd run up later.

Thousands of Chinese women committed suicide after they had been raped.[11] Rape also featured prominently during the sack of Magdeburg. Some monks watched horrified as six Catholic soldiers gang-raped a 12-year-old girl until she died in the courtyard of their convent; while Otto von Guericke, an eyewitness who survived to become a skilled inventor, reported that 'Things went very badly for many of those women, girls, daughters and maids who either had no men, parents or relatives who could pay a ransom on their behalf, or could not appeal to high officers for help or advice. Some were defiled and disgraced, and some were kept as concubines.'[12]

The diary of a Catholic soldier, Peter Hagendorf, shows what might happen next. He described how at the sack of a Bavarian town in 1634, 'Here I got a pretty girl as my booty as well as 12 thalers in cash, some clothes and a lot of linen.' A few weeks later, he participated in the sack of another town 'and here again I got a young girl out of it'. If the rest of the 'enlisted men' received similar 'booty', a very large number of 'women, girls, daughters and maids' from these two towns must have been abducted and, presumably, 'defiled and disgraced'.[13] Hagendorf's 'girls' were relatively lucky: he released each of them when the army moved on. Three years later, 20 Swedish soldiers rode into the small village of Linden, in central Germany, one afternoon, and violently demanded food and wine. Two of them, a 'fat soldier' from Finland and a 'white-haired young soldier', broke down the door of a farmer's cottage, where they raped his wife and then chased her, screaming, through the village. During the Irish rebellion of 1641, a Protestant prisoner claimed to have heard his Catholic captors

> Often in the night tyme with their pistolls come into the Chamber where the women servants were, and attempted their chastities, making them skrike and cry out; and, as the said woman affirmed, threatened to pistoll them if they wold not consent to their lustfull desires; and this deponent thincketh that those wicked rebells did assault them untill they had forced them to their lustful wills.

In Poland, finally, after the town of Graudiądz was 'taken by storme' in 1659, many inhabitants managed to swim across a river to safety but the 'others of all sexes and ages were taken to the leaguer (the besiegers' camp) and stripped of all, and the women abused'.[14]

The victims of such violent acts suffered psychological as well as physical damage. In Germany, soldiers raped Anna Hurter of Hawangen in 1633, and when she died in 1657 her parish priest noted in the burial register that 'for twenty-four years *she had not had one sane hour until suddenly she expired*'. In Ireland in 1641, during a brutal rape of a young woman, 'to prevent her crying out, one of (the) souldjers thrust a napkin into her mowth and held her fast by the haire of her head till the wicked act was performed'. Afterwards the victim could not move 'for three or four days', and even four years later 'thought shee should never bee well nor bee in her right mynd againe, the fact was soe fowle and grievous unto her'. Four years later, Wang Xiuchu noted that 'one of the younger women' he had watched being gang-raped at Yangzhou 'couldn't even get up to walk'.[15] Although in all ages and in all places war produces personal tragedies like these, the proliferation of conflict in the seventeenth century multiplied them. The profoundly disturbing alabaster sculpture by Leonhard Kern, which shows an officer abducting a naked girl, significantly called 'Scene from the Thirty Years War', no doubt commemorates a common occurrence (Plate 2).

'Feeding Mars'

Contemporaries also blamed war for the cost to them of maintaining the armies and navies of their rulers. The expenses associated with fighting wars, whether against neighbours or rebels, constantly increased – and not just because of their duration. Europe's Atlantic states built huge fleets of 'floating fortresses': sailing warships, each of them larger than a country house and carrying as many guns as a fort on land, that cost £33,000 each to build and £13,000 to keep at sea for a campaign. Europe's naval wars during the second half of the century saw battleships deployed in lines that stretched for 10 miles, with 3,000 heavy guns firing broadsides at each other, sometimes for several days – an enormous financial outlay. Naval arsenals and dockyards were the largest industrial plants in early modern Europe, whether they produced sailing ships or, as in the Mediterranean, galleys. Mediterranean warfare was labour-intensive. Each galley carried about 400 oarsmen and soldiers, so that (in the words of a French sailor) 'an infinite number of villages are far from having as large a number of inhabitants' as a single galley.[16]

Normally, land warfare cost even more than naval operations. Apart from raising and maintaining soldiers, most states also invested heavily in fortifications. The two largest states in the world, China and Russia, constructed continuous defences along their most vulnerable frontiers. The late Ming emperors extensively rebuilt the Great Wall of China in stone to take account of gunpowder technology, and although the Manchus breached it in both 1629 and 1642, it still reduced small-scale raiding. Meanwhile, the Russian empire constructed a 'Great Wall' consisting of fortified towns linked by earthen ramparts which, by 1658, ran for 800 miles along the steppe frontier from the Dnieper to the Volga (see Fig. 19). As in China, although the fortified line did not bring complete security, it compelled invaders from the south – whether Crimean Tatars or Cossack rebels – to follow certain paths where the tsar's troops could more easily intercept them.

Other European states eschewed 'lines' but invested in a network of 'artillery fortresses': each one a star-shaped complex with extremely thick walls protected by angled bastions, moats and outposts. When in a good state of repair, and defended by sufficient heavy guns and an adequate garrison, such positions could seldom be taken by assault, and so sieges played a crucial role in conflicts: the Russo–Polish wars of 1632–4 and 1654–5 hinged on control of the bastions around Smolensk, while the turning point in the Habsburg–Turkish wars came with the failed Ottoman blockade of Vienna in 1683. Further west, artillery fortresses proliferated in many contested areas: the north Italian plain; the borders of France; the lands around the Baltic; within the Iberian Peninsula as well as in Britain and Ireland after the civil wars began; and above all in the Netherlands, which contained by far the largest density of artillery fortresses anywhere in the world. When the Dutch Revolt against Spain began in 1572, 12 towns already possessed a complete set of the new defences, while 18 more had been partially updated; but when the Revolt ended in 1648, the same area boasted at least 50 artillery fortresses and a further 60 towns with partially modernized walls. Each one cost millions of pounds to construct.

Laying siege to these state-of-the-art fortifications formed the largest engineering enterprise of the age – trenches might stretch for 25 miles and operations could last for months – and their outcome dominated most campaigns. 'Battles do not now decide national quarrels, and expose countries to the pillage of conquerors, as formerly,' observed an Irish general who learned his craft during the wars of the mid-century, 'for we make war more like foxes, than lions; and you will have twenty sieges for one battle.' 'One scarcely talks any more about battles,' a German military instructor concurred: 'Indeed, the whole art of war now consists only of cunning attacks and good fortification.'[17] The Spanish and Dutch governments each maintained around 100,000 soldiers in the Netherlands from the moment war between them resumed in 1621 until they made peace in 1648 – and yet the two sides never fought a pitched battle. Instead, each year's campaign consisted of sieges.

Perhaps one million men served simultaneously in the various armies and navies of seventeenth-century Europe. Philip IV of Spain boasted that 'In the year of 1625 just past, we can count around 300,000 infantry drawing wages and more than 500,000 militiamen'. Louis XIII of France ordered the mobilization of over 150,000 men when he declared war on Spain in 1635, and he and his successor maintained at least 100,000 soldiers in arms until making peace 24 years later. Between 1672 and 1678, Louis XIV commanded about 250,000 troops.[18] In Germany, some 300,000 troops took part in each campaign between 1631 and 1634; and at least 200,000 men remained in arms when the Thirty Years' War ended in 1648. Over 100,000 soldiers fought the civil wars in England, Scotland and Ireland during the 1640s, and throughout the 1650s over 50,000 men served in the army and navy of the British Republic.

All these soldiers required training and equipment, as well as food and clothes. From the 1620s onwards, up to half of each army in western Europe carried muskets, and fought in parallel lines firing repeated 'broadsides' at their enemies. This tactic called for a level of proficiency and discipline from each individual soldier that only prolonged training could provide, leading to the creation of a 'standing army' of veterans who would form the backbone of the larger forces required in wartime. Some of the regiments raised by Emperor Ferdinand II to suppress the Bohemian revolt in 1618 remained in the imperial Habsburg army until the dynasty fell three centuries later; General George Monck's regiment of foot, formed in 1650 and now known as the Coldstream Guards, boasts the longest continuous service of any unit in the British Army (or indeed any army) today.

Many non-Western states adopted at least some of these expensive European innovations. Both the Ottoman and the Russian empires recruited infantry armed with muskets: the Janissaries (literally 'new troops') fought for the sultan in ranks with muskets; while Western instructors recruited by the tsars trained New Formation Regiments. Although the Mughal and Chinese emperors also made use of Western firearms and Western military experts, they normally fought wars that were labour-intensive (by mobilizing overwhelming numbers) rather than capital-intensive (by investing in new technology). Shah Jahan normally travelled with an army of 200,000 cavalry and 40,000 infantry, 50–60 heavy guns and numerous war elephants; the last Ming emperors, at least in theory, could call on 500,000 men and 100,000 cavalry horses; while to repress the Three Feudatories rebellion in the 1670s the Kangxi emperor mobilized over 150,000 'bannermen' (elite Manchu troops) seconded by 400,000 loyal Chinese troops. Even in times of peace, the Qing maintained 80,000 bannermen as a rapid reaction force, garrisoned in citadels specially created in China's major cities. All of them had to be paid.

The 'unit cost' of waging war rose inexorably. The Italian political theorist Giovanni Botero complained in 1605 that '[Nowadays] war is dragged out for as long as possible, and the object is not to smash but to tire, not to defeat but to wear down the enemy. This form of warfare is entirely dependent upon money.' 'The manner of making war at the present time,' echoed a Spanish commander in the 1630s, 'is reduced to a sort of traffic or commerce, in which he who has most money wins.' Six decades later, an English pamphleteer made exactly the same point:

> War is quite changed from what it was in the time of our forefathers; when in a hasty expedition, and a pitch'd field, the matter was decided by courage. But now the whole Art of War is in a manner reduced to money; and nowadays that prince who can best find money to feed, cloath and pay his army, not he that has the most valiant troops, is surest of success and conquest.[19]

All this had crushing financial consequences for civilians. In France, the tax burden on a family of four rose from the equivalent of 14 days' output a year to 34 days' output by 1675; the Ottoman empire spent 75 per cent of its total budget on war; while, in Muscovy, 'one-eighth of [all] productive resources went just to pay for the army'.[20]

Naturally, the diversion of so many resources to the pursuit of 'success and conquest' also involved indirect (or 'opportunity') costs. States that spent so much on war had little left for anything else – whether official salaries; goods and services; or welfare. Philip IV of Spain, who spent at least £30 million to finance his foreign wars between 1618 and 1648, claimed that he lacked the money to set up a national banking system; Charles I of Great Britain, whose wars between 1625 and 1630 cost £6 million, decided he could not afford to create public granaries for famine relief; and so on. Ming China offers perhaps the most graphic case of the 'opportunity costs' of prodigious military spending. After Manchu raiders broke through the Great Wall in 1629, the emperor's drastic reductions in non-defence spending included the closure of perhaps one-third of all courier and postal stations. Some of those who lost their livelihoods began to prey on those who used the routes they had once serviced: one of them was Li Zicheng, who became the leader of a bandit alliance and, briefly, emperor of all China.[21]

The Fiscal-Military State

Early modern governments resorted to a wide variety of expedients to fund their wars. The fiscal history of England, a relatively small country, was both striking and typical. Between 1605 and 1625, the government of James I (much criticized for its extravagance and corruption) raised and spent some £10 million, roughly 25 per cent of which went on military and naval spending; by contrast, between 1642, when the Civil War began, and 1660, when all soldiers and sailors then on foot laid down their arms, the London government raised and spent £34 million. The central government's defence spending thus rose twelve-fold – from an annual average of £117,000 in 1605–25 to an annual average of £1.5 million in 1642–60. Even so, debts of about £2 million remained unpaid in 1660, leaving subsequent generations of English taxpayers to amortize the cost of the Civil Wars.[22]

Such debts reflected the fact that, then as now, few governments can fund their wars from current revenues alone. In Europe, most states raised loans to bridge the gap between income and expenditure – but borrowing created a new set of problems, because bankers normally demanded a specific source of revenue as security for each loan, compelling governments to create new taxes. This vicious circle explains the apparently senseless fiscal decisions of so many rulers. Some stifled economic activity by taxing industrial production or exports just when conditions called for economic stimuli and 'tax breaks'; while others taxed items in general use, such as foodstuffs, which not only reduced the disposable income of most consumers but also provoked both widespread hardship and resistance. Many revolts began with rioting at the point of sale when a new tax unexpectedly increased the price of everyday items such as a loaf of bread or a basket of fruit. Other revolts materialized when rulers increased taxes on areas that they believed to be unusually prosperous. Thus when war broke out with Spain in 1635, the French government abruptly doubled the *taille* (the principal direct tax) payable by the area around the thriving port of Bordeaux from one million *livres* to two. In 1644, although poor harvests had caused grain prices to soar, the government increased the *taille* to three million *livres* and then in 1648, coinciding with the worst harvest of the century, to four million *livres*. Not surprisingly, Bordeaux supported the Fronde revolt that year and before long considered secession as an independent republic (see chapter 10).

Apart from imposing excise duties and increasing direct taxes, early modern governments at war frequently exploited and extended state monopolies (often known as 'regalian rights'), such as extracting minerals obtained from the sea or under the ground (including salt and coal, silver and copper), or maximizing the profits from minting coins. Currency manipulation became particularly common in the seventeenth century, with governments from Spain, through Russia, to China either adulterating silver coins with base metals, or issuing copper or paper money with little or no intrinsic value. Forcible devaluation could ruin whole societies. In 1634 in exile Pavel Stránský recalled the devaluation in Bohemia a decade earlier as the most traumatic experience of his life: 'Neither plague, nor war, nor hostile foreign incursions into our land, neither pillage nor fire however atrocious, could do so much harm to good people as frequent changes and reductions in the value of money'. Several major revolts broke out when governments manipulated the currency, notably in central Europe in 1621–3, in Spain in 1651, and in Russia in 1661–3.[23]

Nevertheless, as the Swedish historian Jan Glete reminds us, in early modern Europe 'Wars were not decided by the existence of resources but by how these resources were organized'. The key to improved organization, Glete argues, was 'the fiscal-military state': a polity dedicated to extracting, centralizing and redistributing resources to finance the use of violence.[24] Only its superior ability to organize available resources enabled Sweden, with scarcely a million inhabitants, to hold 20 million Germans to ransom during and after the Thirty Years War; and allowed the Dutch Republic, also with scarcely a million citizens, to defeat the Spanish Habsburgs, with over 30 million subjects. Yet even the Dutch Republic, the most successful fiscal-military state of the early modern world, experienced difficulties in funding its wars. The debt of the federal government rose from 5 million florins in 1618 to 16 million in 1670, and that of the richest province (Holland) from 5 million to 147 million. At the same time taxes, especially sales taxes, rose to dizzying levels both to pay for current wars and to service the debts created during previous wars: in the university town of Leiden, by the 1640s taxes accounted for 60 per cent of the price of beer and 25 per cent of the price of bread. When provinces fell into arrears with their quotas of the overall budget, the federal government imprisoned their citizens as hostages until the shortfall was made good.

Only such draconian measures enabled the Dutch government, at war for most of the seventeenth century, to maintain its credit intact while paying its army and navy regularly; other governments did not even try. Calculations in 1633 by the Swedish chancellor, Axel Oxenstierna, responsible for funding all Protestant troops fighting in Germany, show the magnitude of the problem. On paper, each of the 78,000 soldiers fielded by the allies earned an average of 125 thalers per year, or almost 10 million thalers for the entire army. Oxenstierna knew that this was far beyond his means. If, however, he provided each soldier with full wages for just one month, a small cash advance for the other 11, and one pound of bread every day, then the total annual cost fell to 5.5 million thalers, or 55 per cent of the original cost.[25] But what of the other 45 per cent? Oxenstierna, like other warlords of his day, expected two fiscal expedients to make up the shortfall. He expected his officers to use their own credit to supply their troops with essential items. It was no secret that his principal adversary, Albrecht von Wallenstein, had borrowed five million thalers (five times his personal fortune) between 1621 and 1628 to sustain his army until a victorious peace would bring reimbursement and rewards; and that most of the 1,500 or so colonels who raised regiments to fight in the Thirty Years War did much the same (albeit on a lesser scale). It was also no secret that Wallenstein had introduced a 'contributions system' that forced civilians living near his army to provide it with food and other necessities. His quartermasters worked out with the local magistrates of each community the precise quantities and the exact timetable for delivery, threatening that any shortfall or default would trigger the arrival of a detachment of soldiers who would burn everything to the ground. Oxenstierna expected his quartermasters to do the same.

Although it is hard to assess the precise financial impact of war on civilians, the records of the principality of Hohenlohe in southwest Germany show that in each year from 1628, when hostile soldiers first arrived, until the demobilization of 1650, its inhabitants paid at least double what they had done before the war, and that in some years they paid three, four or even five times as much. Yet even this did not suffice to 'feed Mars'. Just before his regiment was demobilized, one officer complained that he did not 'earn enough daily bread to support my wife and poor children'.[26]

Troops elsewhere seldom fared much better. In China, a Manchu Bannerman named Dzengšeo recorded in his campaign diary for 1680 that on some days he did not eat, but instead 'wept with sorrow under the blanket'; while on one desperate occasion he 'even sold a woman' whom he had received as booty at the capture of a town, to buy horses and food. Usually, however, like early modern soldiers elsewhere, when he was hungry Dzengšeo exploited the civilian population: when 'the food supplies for the whole army had been used up', he sent his servants to 'search for food in every single village' and to take what they found by force.[27]

Doing God's Work

Rulers in the mid-seventeenth century could not plead ignorance about the economic hardships that their wars inflicted on soldiers and civilians alike. In China, officials deluged their superiors with memoranda that pointed out (to quote one missive), 'The present dynasty commands the largest area of land in history. But land without people is worthless, and people without wealth are valueless; and in the present dynasty we find that the poverty afflicting the whole population is unprecedented in the history of China.' Likewise, in 1640, just before the outbreak of revolt in Catalonia and Portugal, a tract published in Madrid perceptively warned Philip IV of the dangers inherent in overtaxing his subjects:

The horror of civil unrest is more to be feared than the weapons of the enemy. The common people will prefer rebellion in order to avoid destitution. Hardship causes desperation; constant rigour incites hatred ... Subjects are more obedient when they are less taxed. A prince who in time of war avoids spending on himself will make the word 'tax' acceptable, and avoid being called 'ambitious'.

If the king read this, he paid no attention – just as, 12 years later, he ignored the protests of his spiritual advisor, Sor María de Ágreda, 'that, for the love of God, Your Majesty should introduce as few innovations as possible and avoid oppressing the poor, lest their misery leads them to revolt'. Instead Philip loftily assured Sor María that, although 'everything possible will be done for the relief of my poor vassals', nevertheless *the requirements of the army pull in the opposite direction*'. Spain's wars therefore continued.[28]

Why, exactly, did so many seventeenth-century rulers raise taxes to satisfy 'the requirements of the army' instead of taking steps to 'avoid oppressing the poor'? One reason lay in the lack of any restraint. In China, the emperor claimed to possess the 'Mandate of Heaven' for all his actions, and his subjects revered him as *Tianzi*, 'Son of Heaven', possessing supreme power in all things:

He judged whether a given offender should be punished severely or not at all. He judged the qualifications of candidates for high offices and for the civil service examination degrees. He validated or refused requests to do anything non-routine, such as whether to issue amnesties or disaster relief, or modify a ritual or bureaucratic procedure, or mount an attack against [foreign enemies] ... The outside world could not function without imperial decisions. No one else in the realm was empowered to make authoritative rulings.[29]

Every aspect of the emperor's official life proclaimed his unique status and untrammelled authority. At audiences he alone faced south and everyone else faced north; no one else could wear clothes designed like his; he alone used red ink (everyone else used black); the character for 'emperor' received a line of text to itself; no one else could use the character for each emperor's given name or the word he used for 'I' (*chen*).

Other Asian rulers also claimed to embody divine power on earth, which conferred the right to make war at will. Korean kings held that they both embodied the state and acted with divine sanction to bring the purposes of heaven and of human beings into harmony. In the words of a scholar and minister in 1660: 'The ruler regulates things in place of Heaven, and causes them to find their appointed places'.[30] Political rhetoric in South Asia also presented rulers as endowed with superhuman powers. Successful Buddhist monarchs claimed to be *chakhravarthi* ('world conquerors'), just as India's Mughal emperors projected themselves as *Sahibkiran* (the 'Shadow of God on Earth'). India's Hindu rulers claimed to be not only the incarnation of one of the gods but also sexual heroes: court poems and dance-dramas, the preferred media for political propaganda in southern India, portrayed the capital as a city of erotic delights and war as a sexual adventure. None of these political visions left room for restraint.[31]

Indonesian rulers likewise acknowledged no limits to their power. Thus in the 1640s the sultan of Mataram assembled 2,000 of his senior clerics shortly after his accession, accused them of disloyalty, and executed them all. A generation earlier, according to a foreign visitor, whenever Sultan Iskandar Muda of Acheh heard about an attractive 'woman, either in city or country, he sends for her to the court. Although she be married, she must come and if her husband seem unwilling or loath to part from her, then [the Sultan] presently commands her husband's prick to be cut off.' Iskandar Muda did not stop at 'pricks': he also (according to another foreign visitor) 'exterminated almost all the ancient nobility' in the course of his reign. Therefore by 1629 no one had the authority to restrain the sultan when he decided to lead the entire military and naval strength of his state to attack Portuguese Melaka, or to remind him of the need to fortify his own siege works – with the result that a Portuguese relief army destroyed almost all his army, his fleet and his guns.[32]

Most Muslim political writers extolled a powerful monarchy as both the only alternative to anarchy and the best way to advance the cause of Islam, often citing a paradigm known as the 'Circle of Justice':

> There can be no government without the military;
> There can be no military without wealth;
> The subjects produce the wealth;
> Justice preserves the subjects' loyalty to the sovereign;
> Justice requires harmony in the world;
> The world is a garden, its walls are the state;
> The *Sharî'a* [Islamic law] orders the state;
> There is no support for the *Sharî'a* except through government.[33]

A treatise of advice presented to Ottoman Sultan Murad IV in 1630 by a learned palace official, Mustafa Koçi Beg, ascribed the problems facing the empire to the failure of the sultan to use his divinely sanctioned arbitrary power to overcome anarchy and advance the cause of Islam. To implement this advice, Murad addressed a stream of requests to the Chief Mufti (*Şeyhulislam*) of Istanbul to certify (usually in the form of a written opinion, or *fatwā*) that a proposed action or edict conformed to the *Sharî'a*.[34] In 1638 Murad even took the *Şeyhulislam* with him on campaign, so that he could ensure that his military as well as his civilian decisions conformed to God's will. Occasionally the *Şeyhulislam* might defy a sultan – in 1648 one even issued a *fatwā* to legitimize the sultan's deposition (see chapter 7 below) – but normally the shoe was on the other foot: sultans deposed (and occasionally executed) a *Şeyhulislam* who challenged their authority.

The tsars of Russia likewise claimed divine status and encouraged writers and artists to portray them as the secular version of the transfigured Christ, as paragons of Old Testament kingship (especially David), and as the 'Image and likeness of God', while their subjects became the Chosen People, their country the Earthly Paradise, and their capital the New Jerusalem. The state apartments in the Kremlin sported paintings that interspersed the victories of Moses, Joshua and Gideon with the leading events of Russian history and portraits of the biblical 'tsars' with the princes of Russia. The main Moscow churches displayed icons in which an arch-angel and the heavenly host led the tsar and his troops on campaigns of conquest. When the tsar 'wishes to wage war or make peace with any state,' an experienced minister explained in the 1660s, 'or when he wishes to decide any other great or small affairs, it is in his power to do what he wishes'. As with the rhetoric of abso-lutism in Asia, the 'Paradise myth' fostered by the tsars left no room for discussion or dissent, let alone for loyal opposition.[35]

The equivalent of the 'Mandate of Heaven', the 'World Conqueror', the 'Shadow of God on Earth' and the 'Paradise Myth' for rulers in Latin Christendom was the 'Divine Right of Kings'. Many early modern European rulers claimed both that their power was *absolute* (a term derived from Roman law to describe the authority of one 'absolved' from obeying the laws he had made) and that their actions enjoyed divine approval. In 1609 James I of Great Britain boasted that 'The state of monarchy is the supremest thing upon earth, for kings are not only God's lieuten-ants upon earth and sit upon God's throne, but even by God himself they are called god.' Therefore, James continued, 'They exercise a manner or resemblance of divine power upon earth' because 'they make and unmake their subjects, they have power of raising and casting down, of life and of death, judges over all their subjects and in all causes and yet accountable to none but God only.' A generation later, the funeral oration for a German prince echoed the same sentiments. 'Just as the sun in the heavens above is made and fashioned by God, and is truly a wondrous work of the Almighty, so are kings, princes and lords placed and ordered by God in the secular estate. For that reason, they may themselves be called gods.' In France, a treatise written by a royal minister likewise argued that the king's commands must always prevail:

> One can ask the question, if a man's conscience tells him that what the king has ordered him to do is unjust, is he bound to obey? To this I respond that, if there are considerations for and against, he must follow the king's will, not his own ... One must pay attention to circumstance, because if [a measure] relates to a pressing necessity for the public good ... *Necessity knows no law.*

Later still, ex-queen Christina of Sweden wrote that 'Only monarchs must rule: everyone else must obey and execute their orders.' Specifically, she continued, a royal decision to wage war – even a war of aggression – obliged everyone to obey because sovereigns could discern the true interests of the state better than their subjects.[36]

Most European monarchs received an education crafted explicitly to reinforce these attitudes. They studied history (national, Classical and occasionally foreign) primarily 'to examine how each prince had acted well or badly' and to learn how to 'ascertain what our subjects are hiding from us'. Thus on hearing that France had signed the peace of Westphalia in 1648, Louis XIV's preceptor seized the chance to give his 10-year-old charge a crash course in German history, and especially on the history of the Rhineland (which Louis would later spend vast resources trying to annex); while during the Fronde revolt of 1648–53, Louis read chronicles that described how his predecessors had overcome rebellious nobles.[37] Princely instruction in language and geography was also utilitarian. Louis XIV, his son and his grandsons all studied Spanish history and literature, and learned to speak Spanish, in case they might one day succeed their ailing cousin, Carlos II. They likewise learned the principles of architecture and mathematics explicitly so that they would better understand how to attack and defend fortified towns; and Louis XIV commissioned a set of huge relief models of frontier fortresses so that his son could follow the progress of his wars until he was old enough to participate in person.[38]

Above all, seventeenth-century rulers believed that 'religion is the most important element in what must be taught to a young prince destined to wear the crown' – and this meant not only private but also public devotions. Throughout the Fronde, the official *Gazette de France* recorded not only the zeal and humility of the young Louis XIV during sermons but also his participation in pilgrimages; while between 1654 and 1663 it chronicled the 42 occasions on which he 'touched' (and, according to popular tradition, cured) subjects afflicted with scrofula – some 20,000 individuals in all – perhaps the most striking public demonstration of divinely delegated power in the early modern world.[39] French monarchs proudly styled themselves 'The Most Christian King', while their Spanish counterparts used the style 'The Catholic King' and English monarchs were Supreme Governors of the Established Church. Catholic and Protestant rulers alike appointed the prelates of their state (the former with papal concurrence) and expected their subjects to follow their theological opinions – or, in the formula that prevailed in the Holy Roman Empire, *Cuius regio, eius religio*: 'Rulers determine religion'.

The overlap of politics and religion influenced foreign as well as domestic policy. In the words of the governor of Louis XIV's heir, Christian princes must not only 'love and serve God' but also 'make others honour Him, avenge His injuries, and take up His causes'; and in 1672 the Dauphin, aged 11, composed a campaign history that justified his father's invasion of Holland because it advanced the Catholic faith.[40] Religion often served as a pretext for war in Europe in the first half of the seventeenth century. Thus when in 1619 the Bohemians offered their crown to the German Protestant leader, Frederick of the Palatinate, he accepted because, he claimed, it 'is a divine calling that I must not disobey. My only end is to serve God and his Church'. A similar confidence motivated Frederick's brother-in-law Charles I, who steadfastly refused to negotiate with his rebellious subjects because, as his wife Henrietta Maria put it in a confidential letter of 1642, on the eve of the English Civil War, 'This is no longer mere play. You must declare yourself; you have testified your gentleness enough, you must show your justice. Go on boldly: God will assist you'. The king complied. A few months later he informed a close colleague that 'no extremity or misfortune shall make me yield, for I will either be a glorious king or a patient martyr'. Even after his catastrophic military defeat at Naseby in 1645 Charles refused a suggestion that he should seek the best terms possible from his adversaries because

If I had any other quarrel but the defence of my religion, crown, and friends, you had full reason for your advice; for I confess that, speaking either as a mere soldier or statesman, I must say that there is no probability but of my ruin. Yet as a Christian, I must tell you that God will not suffer rebels and traitors to prosper, or this cause to be overthrown ... A composition with them at this time is nothing else but a submission, which, by the grace of God, I am resolved against, whatever it cost me; for I know my obligation to be, both in conscience and honour, neither to abandon God's cause, injure my successors, or forsake my friends.[41]

Charles continued to reject all compromise until, on 30 January 1649, he became a 'martyr'; yet even from the grave he continued to claim divine sanction for his actions. A posthumous volume of his prayers and meditations on recent events, *Eikon Basilike* ('The king's image'), circulated almost immediately, with a frontispiece that showed the king looking like Christ, putting aside his earthly crown and grasping a crown of thorns as he prayed (Plate 3).

Charles's uncle, Christian IV of Denmark, also stressed his special relationship with God. While championing the Protestant cause in Germany, he claimed to have seen a vision of Christ wearing a crown of thorns and, to make the most of this signal mark of divine favour, the painting commissioned to commemorate it made Jesus look strikingly like Christian himself. In similar vein, the Catholic emperor Ferdinand II claimed that, during the siege of Vienna by his rebellious subjects in 1619, as he knelt in prayer before a crucifix, Christ spoke from the Cross: 'Ferdinande, non te deseram' – 'Ferdinand, I will not desert you'. Shortly afterwards, a contemporary print depicted him as Christ on the Mount of Olives, surrounded by his sleeping noblemen. Many of Ferdinand's contemporaries also had themselves portrayed as characters from the Gospels (Anne of Austria and her son Louis XIV as Madonna and child; and, more remarkably, together with Louis XIII as the Magi); as Old Testament figures (Gustavus Adolphus as Judas Maccabeus; Philip IV as Solomon; Frederick Henry of Orange as David); or as saints (Louis XIII as his ancestor, St Louis; Anne of Austria and her sister-in-law Henrietta Maria of England as Saints Helena and Elizabeth).[42]

Most Christian rulers admitted only one restraint on their absolute power: like their Ottoman contemporaries, they consulted spiritual experts before taking controversial decisions. Thus in Russia, 'when discord and warfare break out with neighbouring powers, the tsar at that time consults with the patriarch, metropolitans, archbishops, bishops and with other hierarchs of the prominent monasteries'; while many Catholic rulers routinely asked their confessors to certify that they might 'in conscience' adopt a controversial policy. In addition, the kings of France and Portugal created a 'council of conscience' to advise them on more complex issues; while other Catholic monarchs periodically consulted theologians. Thus in the 1620s Philip IV asked a 'committee of theologians' to decide whether his sister should marry the Protestant Charles Stuart; whether he could send assistance to the French Protestants; whether he might intervene in the Mantuan succession; whether he should send troops into the Valtelline; whether he needed to honour concessions made to rebels; and so on.[43] Later in his reign, Philip even convened a 'summit' of men and women from his European dominions credited with prophetic powers, and asked them for advice on policy. Although he never repeated this experiment, for the next 25 years the king wrote a letter once every two weeks seeking advice and prayers from one of the spirit mediums at the 'summit', Sor María de Ágreda, who thus became the most influential woman in Spain.

Secular ministers, too, might try to convince their masters that even the most costly and destructive policies enjoyed divine favour. In a memorial of 1626 that listed the various successes of his ministry, Philip IV's chief adviser the count-duke of Olivares assured his master triumphantly: 'Sire, God has placed the armed forces of Your Majesty in this situation, with no other assistance or ally. I would be lying to Your Majesty, and a traitor to you, if I claimed that all this stemmed from human provision. No: God alone has done it, and only God *could* have done it.' A quarter of a century later, Philip himself attributed his ability 'to overcome not only my enemies but also storms at sea, epidemics on land and the domestic unrest of the towns of Andalusia' to the support of 'God's most mighty hand'.[44]

Pride and Prejudice

It is, of course, possible that early modern rulers used such rhetoric and imagery as propaganda without actually believing it. Queen Christina of Sweden asserted as much in 1649, when she debated with her council whether or not to support English royalists after Charles I's execution. Marshal Jakob de la Gardie argued that, since 'such a giddy spirit has arisen' in Europe, rulers of the same faith should support one other; but Christina (still officially a Lutheran) disagreed. 'People use religion as a pretext,' she replied, 'and it is used by us against Calvinists and Catholics alike.' 'The Pope, the Spaniards and the rest of the House of Austria have always sought to make use of religion,' de la Gardie reminded her. 'Like a raincoat when it's wet,' the queen quipped. In similar vein, three decades later (and now a Catholic), Christina noted that although princes should allow their confessors 'to speak freely to us, we must not blindly obey all that they tell us. We must be well aware that it is not always God who speaks to us through them.'[45]

Such overt cynicism was extremely rare in the seventeenth century. More typical was the providential vision of Philip IV of Spain, who in 1629 told a senior minister that 'I seek salvation, and want to placate God by obeying His laws and by making sure that others obey them, without exception' because then, 'even if misfortunes rain upon us, you need have no fear that they will harm us.' Therefore, the king explained, 'I desire the fear of God and executing his commands and doing Justice to be my guiding principle'. He still felt the same three decades later. Upon hearing in 1656 that Britain had joined France, Portugal and the Catalans in making war on him, Philip confided to Sor María de Ágreda that, although 'The risk is apparent and the distress is greater than any that this Monarchy has ever seen, particularly since we lack the means to withstand even one part of such a great storm', he intended to keep on fighting because 'I have firm faith that, unless our sins make us unworthy,

Our Lord will deliver us from this great storm without allowing these kingdoms, so loyal to the Catholic Church, to be brought down by heretics.'[46]

Naturally, a providential vision did not preclude secular motives for waging war. Many seventeenth-century rulers, like their medieval predecessors, saw waging war as a rite of passage to be performed at the outset of every reign. Thus, three months after his accession, when Charles I asked the English Parliament to vote funds for war with Spain, he said 'I pray you remember *that this being my first action*' as king 'what a great dishonor it were both to you and to me' if it 'should fail for [lack of] that assistance you are able to give me'. A few years later, when Philip IV heard that Louis XIII had just invaded Italy, he scribbled on a ministerial memorandum that 'My intention is to get my revenge on France for its recent behaviour', and to that end 'I shall be there in person. *Fame, after all, cannot be gained without taking personal part in some great enterprise.* This one will enhance my reputation, and I gather it should not be too difficult.'[47] All three kings – just like their contemporaries Gustavus Adolphus and Charles X of Sweden, Christian IV and Frederick III of Denmark, Emperor Ferdinand III and Tsar Alexei – not only commanded their armies in person but also claimed to relish military life. The same was true of their children. Louis XIV personally participated in over 20 sieges, starting in 1650 when he was 12, and ending in 1692, when he ceded the role to his heir, noting that 'If my son does not go on campaign every year, he will be totally despised and will lose all respect'. His cousin, the future James II, started the second Anglo-Dutch war in 1664 almost single-handed because, according to his secretary, 'Having been bred to arms' he sought 'an occasion to show his courage on sea as on land'. James eventually 'broke the measure of those ministers who should otherwise have preserved the peace at any price'.[48]

Several seventeenth-century rulers also advanced strategic arguments to justify starting (or prolonging) their wars. Thus in 1642 the French Court watched a 'heroic comedy' in five acts commissioned by Cardinal Richelieu in which 'Ibère' (Iberia: Spain) tries to win the love of 'Europe' but then, having failed, starts to place shackles on her until 'Francion' rushes in, exclaiming

Europe, it is better to perish than be enslaved.
Liberty must be bought with blood.

Francion warns Ibère to 'keep within your just boundaries'; and when Ibère pays no attention, Francion declares

In the end we must have war, and I am driven to it
Not by ambition but by necessity.[49]

'Necessity' served to justify many foreign wars. Thus, in 1624, despite much public rhetoric about Britain's dedication to upholding 'the Protestant cause' in Germany, a diplomat coldly informed his Palatine counterpart that 'England has no other interest in Germany apart from the Palatinate; *it does not matter to them whether all Germany is set in flames, provided they might have the Palatinate.*' The diplomat justified this with a 'domino theory': 'if we lose the Palatinate first, next we lose the Low Countries, then Ireland, and finally ourselves'.[50] Spanish ministers constructed a similar 'domino theory' to justify their numerous wars. For example, in 1629 they warned Philip IV that 'once the Netherlands are lost, America and other kingdoms of Your Majesty will also immediately be lost with no hope of recovering them'; a point repeated four years later by a Spanish official in Brussels: 'If we lose the Netherlands, we will not be able to defend America, Spain or Italy'. A few years later a veteran diplomat extended the argument yet further: 'We cannot defend the Netherlands if we lose Germany'.[51] Spanish troops therefore continued to fight on all fronts until 1648. Sweden's leaders likewise claimed that (initially) invading Germany and (later) occupying large parts of it were essential to Swedish security. 'Pomerania and the Baltic Coast are like an outwork of the Swedish crown; our security against the Emperor depends on them,' wrote Chancellor Axel Oxenstierna; Sweden was a fortress 'whose walls are its cliffs, whose ditch is the Baltic, and whose counterscarp is Pomerania,' echoed Ambassador Johan Adler Salvius.[52] Failure to retain any territorial gains would imperil national security – so Sweden, too, continued to fight until 1648.

These various factors threatened to eternalize many conflicts. Ending the Thirty Years War required sixty months of negotiations, with scarcely a break; talks to end the Eighty Years War between Spain and the Dutch took twenty months; those to end the Thirteen Years War between Russia and Poland required 31 sessions over the course of a year – and even then ended only in a truce. Such longevity also reflected other factors that tend to prolong all conflicts. First, it is always easier to start than to finish a war. The nobles of Russia made this point in 1652, when Tsar Alexei sought their approval to attack the Ottoman sultan: 'It is indeed easy to pull the sword from the scabbard, but not so easy to put it back when you want, since the outcome of war is uncertain.' Second, objectives changed. As the clergyman and cryptologist John Wallis observed when he looked back on the English Civil War, its ultimate objectives 'proved very different from what was said to be at first intended. As is usual in such cases; the power of the sword frequently passing from hand to hand, and those who begin a War, not being able to foresee where it wil end.' A generation later, another English clergyman noted that 'the ends that those who begin a war designe to themselves are seldome obtained, but oftentimes that which is contrary thereunto and dreaded by them is brought to pass'.[53]

Finally, in the seventeenth century as today, the more resources invested, and the more lives sacrificed, the more total victory seems the only acceptable outcome. As Arthur Hopton, Britain's ambassador in Madrid, observed in 1638 concerning Spain's struggle against France:

> The end of all these troubles (unless they outlast Time) must be peace, which nevertheless comes on so slowly as I cannot say appearances thereof are visible. That which I *can* discover is that on both sides they have reason to be weary of the war, and ... they would be glad of any good occasion to treat of a peace; *but they are so entangled on both sides, partly out of jealousy and partly out of avarice, being*

unwilling to forgo what they have gotten (and indeed have dearly enough paid for) as I find the way to begin a treaty to be very difficult.

At this point, the war was only three years old. Eight years later, when France's diplomatic delegation in Westphalia asked permission to conclude a settlement, Cardinal Mazarin made much the same point as Hopton. '*After all the many expenditures that the war has cost*', he insisted that his diplomats must 'find pretexts for delaying the signature of a peace treaty' in order to 'profit from the remainder of the campaigning season'.[54]

In addition, according to another British ambassador in Madrid, the Spaniards 'are not frendes to part with any thinge they have once gott'; and their rhetoric to postpone peace invoked reputation as often as religion.[55] A notorious example occurred in 1656 when secret talks with France took place. After three months of hard bargaining, the parties agreed that France would end all assistance to Portugal and in return would retain all its remaining conquests in Catalonia and the Netherlands; but Spain would not abandon the prince of Condé, Louis XIV's cousin, who had defied Mazarin and entered Spanish service (see page 285 below). Philip IV's chief minister, Don Luis de Haro, refused to countenance any peace that failed to restore Condé 'to the rank, dignities and positions' that he had previously held. 'We have considered first the question of honour,' Haro told a French envoy grandiloquently, 'and only in second place the conservation of the state, because without honour every state will eventually collapse.' The war continued for three more years.[56]

Finally, negotiating while hostilities continued made peace more elusive because, as Cardinal Mazarin put it in April 1647, each state's demands reflected 'how much the military situation has changed in our favour recently'. The count of Peñaranda, the chief Spanish negotiator at the Westphalian peace congress, agreed. In June of that year, he informed a colleague: 'You believe that the war will last many years, but you are entirely mistaken . . . My lord, the vassals of both kings (of France and Spain) find themselves so exhausted that asking them for more could lead either monarch to complete ruin . . . Whether we win or lose, we both must have peace.' News of the revolt of Naples deepened Peñaranda's pessimism yet further: 'The Naples rising has been widespread. For God's sake, Sir, we have to settle in some way' with France. Yet one month later, Peñaranda hailed news that the French siege of Lleida had failed as 'the most important and pleasing news I have ever had in my life because it shows that Our Lord in his mercy smiles upon us and wishes to remove the scourge from us'. He therefore urged the king to fight on. Philip duly obliged.[57]

Minorities and Tanistry

Succession struggles also increased the frequency of civil wars. Early modern states often experienced anarchy whenever a ruler died leaving no capable and universally recognized successor – and minorities proved unusually common in the seventeenth century. France experienced civil war soon after the accession of

Louis XIII at the age of nine in 1610, and again after his death in 1643 when he left an heir aged only five. Civil War also broke out in Russia when Tsar Alexei died in 1676 leaving three young sons. On the death of Charles IX (1611), Gustavus Adolphus (1632) and Charles X (1660) of Sweden, each of whom left a minor to succeed them, their nobles swiftly reduced the powers of the crown; while those of Denmark did the same in 1648 when Christian IV died before he could secure parliamentary acceptance for his heir (see chapter 8).

Instability was also endemic in elective Monarchies. Although the House of Habsburg retained the title of Holy Roman Emperor throughout the seventeenth century, the Electoral College only chose Ferdinand II in 1619 after a bitter contest that unleashed the Thirty Years War; and only voted for his grandson Leopold in 1658 after a year of intrigue and bargaining for concessions. Likewise, although Sigismund Vasa and his two sons occupied the Polish throne for almost a century, the death of each monarch gave rise to an interregnum while the federal Diet bargained for concessions before choosing a successor. The Dutch Republic suffered a constitutional crisis in 1650 when, on the death of William II of Orange, the States-General denied the title of Stadholder to his posthumous son; while in Japan the following year, the death of the autocratic Shogun Tokugawa Iemitsu, leaving only a child to succeed him, unleashed plots to overthrow the dynasty. China's Ming dynasty also experienced succession difficulties in the first half of the seventeenth century. The Wanli emperor (1573–1620) refused to recognize his eldest son as his heir, instead intriguing to gain recognition for the claims of another of his offspring; and although the eldest son eventually succeeded, he died shortly afterwards, leaving a young heir who suffered from what today would be called 'Attention Deficit Disorder'.

This instability paled in comparison with the succession disputes that character-ized some other Asian dynasties. The distinguished historian Joseph Fletcher observed that nomadic peoples such as the Mongols, as well as dynasties like the Qing, the Mughals and the Ottomans who claimed descent from Mongolian fore-bears, determined each transition of power through a practice he called 'bloody tanistry', after the Celtic practice in which each ruler had a recognized heir (the *Táinste*), who nonetheless had to prove himself by defeating, and often killing, all challengers before assuming the full powers of his predecessor. Tanistry created serious political instability, because everyone took part in succession disputes (there were no 'civilians' in nomad societies, only warriors) and so everyone had to guess which of the various potential successors would emerge victorious in the next generation and position themselves accordingly – knowing that those who had supported the victor would monopolize the spoils.

Perhaps tanistry made sense on the steppes of Central Asia – because the principal requirement of each clan leader was military talent, Fletcher observed, 'what better way for a nomadic nation to choose the best qualified scion of their royal clan than to see which son, brother, uncle, grandson, or nephew of the deceased ruler would win the grand khanship in an internal war?' – but the practice often brought more complex states to the brink of extinction.[58] On the death in 1626 of Nurhaci, 'great ancestor' of the Qing, his relatives fought among themselves for several years before a clear successor emerged: his eighth son, Hong Taiji. When he died in 1643, another bitter struggle broke out between his brothers and uncles until the survivors agreed to recognize the late emperor's ninth son, who became the Shunzhi emperor. In the end, half of the sons of Nurhaci who survived to adulthood were executed, forced to commit suicide or posthumously disgraced. When the Shunzhi emperor died in 1661, his only stipulation was that his successor should have already contracted and survived smallpox (the disease that killed him) and for this reason the throne passed to his third son, the Kangxi emperor, although he was only eight years old. For the next decade his ambitious relatives struggled to dominate the regency government.

In the seventeenth century, Ottoman sultans sought to avoid such chaos by confining their male relatives within the Istanbul palace in sealed apartments known as the *kafes* ('cage'). Even the crown prince rarely left the 'cage' to visit the world outside, but immediately after his accession he killed all his male relatives – both siblings and younger sons – in an attempt to avoid succession disputes. The system changed in 1617, when Sultan Ahmad died leaving only two young sons. The Ottoman elite allowed them and Ahmad's brother to live, but in 1622 palace factions murdered a sultan they deemed incompetent. When Ahmad's son Murad IV reached manhood, he executed three of his brothers so that, at his death in 1640, only one male member of the House of Osman survived: his youngest brother Ibrahim, who had never left 'the cage'. After eight years of erratic rule, he too was murdered, but the Ottoman elite once again allowed all his young sons to live because they were the only surviving male members of the dynasty (four of them would reign; the last of them would be deposed in 1687). These succession protocols may have been slightly less disruptive than the civil wars among male members of the Qing, but they destabilized the Ottoman state all the same.[59]

The Mughal emperors also faced repeated succession disputes. When Jahangir's heir rebelled the emperor impaled 300 of his supporters alive to form an avenue through which his son had to pass to beg forgiveness, yet a year later the heir conspired against his father again. This time Jahangir had the young man blinded and entrusted to his younger son, Shah Jahan, who himself rebelled in 1622–3. Once again the revolt failed, and once again Jahangir pardoned the miscreant so that Shah Jahan survived to succeed his father when he died a few years later – and promptly had all other male members of his family killed or blinded. This left Shah Jahan and his four sons as the only surviving male members of the dynasty. Each prince built up a powerful following until 1658 when, believing that their father was on the point of death, three of them rebelled and fought a civil war that lasted two years. Aurangzeb, the eventual victor, murdered all his rivals just as his father had done. Later he tried to partition his inheritance, hoping to avoid another succession war, but his ambitious sons refused to accept anything less than the whole empire – and fought each other after he died in 1707 until only one remained.

The Curse of the 'Composite State'

Although tanistry never took root in early modern Europe, over half the major seventeenth-century revolts occurred in 'Composite States' comprising a well-integrated core territory linked by loose and often contested bonds to other more autonomous regions, some of them far away. These composite states included Denmark (whose monarch also ruled Norway, Greenland, Iceland, Holstein and many Baltic islands) and Sweden (which included Finland, Estonia, Ingria and several Polish enclaves). Similarly, the Russian state included several areas annexed by treaties, many with distinct religious and ethnic groups, even before the annexation of Ukraine and Siberia in the seventeenth century; while the Ottoman empire likewise incorporated territories that contained disparate religious and ethnic groups (above all, Shi'ites, Christians of various creeds and Jews) as well as several provinces with separate legal codes and local traditions (notably the Crimea, the Balkan principalities and the North African states).[60] But the most volatile composite states were those created by earlier dynastic unions: the Stuart and Spanish Monarchies, and the lands of the Austrian Habsburgs.

These composite Monarchies were politically unstable for two reasons. First, they owed their origin to repeated endogamy among monarchs, which reduced the gene pool of the dynasty and therefore the viability of their offspring. This seems to have produced both more minorities and more disputed successions. For example, the intermarriage of several generations of his progenitors meant Philip IV of Spain boasted only 8 great-grandparents instead of the normal 16; and after he married his niece in 1649, he became the great-uncle as well as the father of his children, while their mother was also their cousin. This created the same genetic inheritance as the child of siblings, or of a parent and child. Only two of the couple's six children survived infancy, and although their son Carlos II lived to be 39, he was physically deformed, mentally challenged and sterile. His death unleashed a prolonged succession war between the various claimants that resulted in the dismemberment of the Spanish Monarchy.[61]

The second weakness of the composite Monarchies lay in the fact that many territories preserved their own institutions and collective identity, sometimes reinforced by a separate language or a distinct religion. An English pamphlet of 1641 noted the vulnerability of both the Stuart and Spanish Monarchies on this score: the former stood, it argued, on the brink of disintegration 'because there was not heretofore a perfect union twixt England and Scotland, incorporating both into one body and mind'; while in the latter the same 'reason has caused Portugal and Catalonia to revolt from the king of Spain'.[62] Diversity created instability because every political organism has a distinct 'boiling point' – or, as Francis Bacon put it in an essay entitled 'Of seditions and troubles': 'discontentments' are 'in the politique body like to humours in the natural, which are apt to gather a preternaturall heat, and to enflame'. When either natural disaster (such as famine) or human agency (such as war), 'enflame' the parts of a composite state, it becomes unstable and its 'discontentments' soon emerge. Not only was the political 'boiling point' unusually low in composite states, it was lowest on their peripheries, making them the least stable component.[63]

At first sight this may seem surprising: after all, global cooling, failed harvests and lethal epidemics affected the core as well as the periphery of each composite state. Indeed, cores often endured more intense government pressure – taxpayers in England and Castile paid far more than their neighbours in peripheral territories – and yet England was the last of Charles I's kingdoms to rebel against him, while (except for Andalusia) Castile did not rebel at all. The paradox has three explanations. First, the core of each state often escaped the worst consequences of war, and thus the full synergy between human and natural disasters. Thus the villages of Castile contributed soldiers and taxes to the wars, and also suffered from extreme weather, poor harvests and high food prices, but most of them remained safe from the devastation of war. Their inhabitants were rarely robbed or raped; troops seldom burnt their property or spread disease; and normally they even escaped billeting. By contrast, at a time of failed harvests and epidemics, the need to feed garrisons as well as the local population created a crisis in frontier regions like Catalonia long before enemy troops wrought further devastation. Second, several parts of Europe's composite states retained not only their own institutions and identity, but also their own economic, defensive and strategic agendas. The priorities of the local elite in Barcelona (as well as in Lima, Mexico, Manila, Naples, Palermo, Milan and Brussels) often differed from those of the imperial government in Madrid (just as the priorities of Edinburgh, Dublin, Jamestown and Boston often differed from those of the central government in London). Third and finally, diversity frequently led to 'sub-imperialism'. Peripheral parts of each composite state often possessed extensive privileges, permanently guaranteed by the sovereign, and whenever conditions became difficult, whether through war or weather, regional elites invoked their constitutional guarantees (often termed 'fundamental laws', 'charters' and 'constitutions'), while the central government sought to override them. Such confrontations could and did lead to rebellion. Thus in 1638, when his Scottish subjects refused to accept a new liturgy mandated by Charles I, the king told one of his ministers that 'I would rather die than yield to those impertinent and damnable demands' because 'it is all one, as to yield, to be no king in a very short time'. The following year, in Spain, the count-duke of Olivares, Philip IV's chief minister, reached the end of his patience with the insistence of the Catalan elite that he must respect their 'Constitutions'. He exclaimed: 'By now I am nearly at my wits' end; but I say, and I shall still be saying on my deathbed, that if the Constitutions do not allow this, then the Devil take the Constitutions'. In both cases, within a few months intransigence led to armed insurrection.[64]

Favourites

Olivares's insensitivity reflected his distinctive status: he was not only Philip IV's chief minister but also his 'Favourite' – a courtier who gained total control of his master's affairs. Favourites abounded across the early modern world and, like minorities and sub-imperialism, their existence made war and rebellion more common. Only the Ottoman empire made the position permanent, in the person of the Grand Vizier. Elsewhere, many Favourites gained a privileged position through the extreme youth of a new ruler: Philip IV and Tsar Alexei came to the throne aged 16; Louis XIV of France succeeded aged four (and only started to exercise his powers at 23). In each case, the monarch relied initially upon a much older man, often a member of his household as heir to the throne, to run the government for them (respectively Olivares, Boris Morozov and Jules Mazarin). Likewise, in China, the Tianqi emperor ascended the throne aged 14 and immediately surrendered his powers to one of the palace eunuchs who had helped to raise him: Wei Zhongxian. But youthful inexperience cannot explain why each ruler continued to rely on their Favourite after (often long after) they became adults, or why the institution (although not new) became so much more common during the first half of the seventeenth century than at any other time.[65]

The continued prominence of Favourites is all the more surprising in view of the hatred they provoked. The duke of Buckingham, who dominated policy and patronage under both King James I of Great Britain and his son Charles, was compared with Sejanus, the tyrannical adviser of the Roman Emperor Tiberius – a parallel deeply resented by Charles – and when the duke was murdered in 1628 songs, poems and pamphlets compared the murderer with the biblical David.[66] The fall and suicide of the eunuch Wei the previous year likewise caused rejoicing throughout China, as did the fall of most Grand Viziers in the Ottoman empire (an event that occurred every four months, on average, in the 1620s). Similar rejoicing would no doubt have greeted the success of any of the numerous assassination plots against Richelieu; or had Tsar Alexei bowed to popular demands and surrendered Morozov to the mob that screamed for his blood in the Kremlin in 1648. According to one of Charles I's more thoughtful English critics, 'The king's favour is tyrannie, when by that favour a man rules over them in fact, that can plead neither election nor succession to that power'; and, he concluded ruefully, if such men were truly deemed necessary, 'a king should have more than one Favourite, [because] emulation will make them walke the fairer wayes'. Charles paid no heed.[67]

The rise of the Favourites in part reflected the relentless increase in the administrative burdens that weighed upon monarchs. In the aphorism of Queen Christina of Sweden: 'If you knew how much princes have to do, you would be less keen to be one'. Copies and minutes of some 18,000 letters survive from the office of France's secretary for war between 1636 and 1642, an average of 2,500 a year; but by 1664 the total had risen above 7,000, and by 1689 above 10,000. In the Mughal empire, 'The state records and documents pertaining to the reign of Shah Jahan (1627–57) must have numbered in the millions'; while, in China, the Shunzhi emperor complained in the 1650s that 'The nation is vast and affairs of state are extremely complex. I have to endorse all memorials and make decisions by myself without a minute of rest.' His son, the Kangxi emperor, read and returned 50 memorials on normal days, but when on campaign the total rose above 400. He later recalled that the amount of paperwork generated by a rebellion in 1674 forced him to stay up until midnight.[68]

Favourites not only reduced the bureaucratic burden on their masters, they also simplified the process of decision-making by operating outside the traditional institutional channels. Each of them sought to monopolize both the people and the information reaching their master; and to this end they promoted their own relatives and clients, excluding all potential rivals. Cardinal Richelieu built up a network of *créatures*, literally people he had 'created': men 'who would be faithful to him and only to him without exception and without reservation'. The 'creatures' worked as a team: whether at court or in the provinces they exchanged information and did each other favours. They also took every opportunity to praise Richelieu to the king and made sure that their advice and proposals coincided with his, since they knew that their own political survival depended on the cardinal monopolizing Louis's confidence. Likewise, in Spain, as Philip III lay dying in 1621, his Favourite the duke of Uceda came face to face with Olivares, who enjoyed the complete confidence of the heir apparent. 'Now everything is mine,' Olivares gloated. 'Everything?' asked the doomed duke. 'Yes, without exception,' Olivares replied. He immediately set about replacing all Uceda's appointees with his own men.[69]

The reliance on Favourites promoted revolts and civil dissension for several reasons. First, rival courtiers excluded from power might lose patience and rebel, especially when the fall or death of a Favourite failed to change the status quo. Thus the duke of Híjar in 1648 began to plot against Philip IV not merely through resentment that Olivares had excluded his entire family from power because they had been allies of the duke of Uceda, but also because he had hoped to regain royal favour as soon as Olivares fell – whereas Philip now relied on the late Favourite's nephew, don Luis de Haro, who likewise excluded Híjar from court. Second, discontented subjects who hesitated to challenge the 'Divine Right of Kings' found it far easier to justify their disobedience by claiming that the ruler had been deceived by his wicked ministers; and the cry 'Long live the king; down with the evil ministers!', common in earlier rebellions, became a constant refrain in the mid-seventeenth century because the monopoly of power by a Favourite made it all the more plausible. Ming scholar-officials claimed that the orders issued by Wei Zhongxian lacked imperial sanction; opponents of Philip IV in Portugal and Catalonia claimed that they strove to free the king from the snare or satanic spell cast by Olivares; opponents of both Tsar Alexei and King Charles I demanded the sacrifice of unpopular ministers who, they claimed, had bewitched their master.

Absolutism and the 'willingness to wink'

Circumventing the checks and balances of traditional governments encouraged 'mission creep' on the part of the state. As Sheilagh Ogilvie has astutely observed, the new style of absolutism introduced by monarchs and their Favourites in the mid-seventeenth century 'affected more than taxation and warfare':

The administrative instruments developed for *these* purposes could also regulate activities previously inaccessible to government, and they could offer redistributive services to a wide range of favoured groups and institutions. Resistance to these *new* forms of redistribution, and competition to control them, were central elements in the 'crisis' of the mid-seventeenth century.

Whereas the traditional bureaucracy of most early modern states contained mechanisms (however rudimentary) by which subjects could legally protest (however deferentially), the 'alternative administrations' invented by Favourites – whether Buckingham, Richelieu, Olivares, Morozov or Wei – brooked no challenge. The imposition of government initiatives by proclamations, often resurrecting or extending a 'regalian right', enforced by royal judges with instructions to stifle any opposition in the courts, left those affected without legal redress. Everywhere, 'absolute' rulers displayed both inflexibility and ruthlessness in enforcing *all* government policies – not just those related to war.[70]

David Cressy has explained this phenomenon brilliantly in the context of Stuart England. Whereas the officials of James I 'were inclined to avert their gaze from local difficulties,' he has written, those of his son Charles 'went looking for trouble'. England, like most (if not all) early modern states, was rife with conflicts; but until the 1630s 'these conflicts were continually being resolved or mitigated by an overriding insistence on peace'. 'The famed "consensus" of Jacobean England consisted not in mutual agreement on issues but rather a determination to prevent divisive issues from disrupting the body politic. It was a social rather than an ideological consensus, and it worked by winking at the gap between theory and practice.' In the 1630s this 'willingness to wink' disappeared. Instead, Charles and his ministers (especially his bishops) developed a 'remarkable gift for seeing mild irregularity as intransigence, moderate nonconformity as sectarianism, and all disagreement as refractoriness or rebellion'. Eventually, 'in forgetting how to wink they tore the country apart'.[71] By way of example, Cressy cited the insistence that women wear veils when they came to church for the first time after giving birth; the demand that ministers make the sign of the cross at every baptism; and the requirement that communion tables in the centre of the church give way to altars at the east end. Earlier generations had regarded each of these as 'trifling matters' or 'things indifferent' and so, over time, each parish had developed its own ritual to which the congregation became strongly attached. Then, in the 1630s, the central government proscribed all three former practices (along with many others) and excommunicated those who would not conform, measures that affected literally thousands of churchgoers each year. Therefore, when the need to pay for war forced Charles in 1640 to return to the traditional institutional channels and summon Parliament, he faced an avalanche of grievances that paralysed the transaction of public business.

Some Asian rulers also seem to have gone 'looking for trouble' on matters previously regarded as peripheral. Sultan Murad IV forbade both smoking tobacco and drinking coffee throughout the Ottoman empire and had many offenders executed. A seventeenth-century ruler of Borneo forbade his subjects to

Dress like people from abroad, such as the Hollanders, the people from Keiling, the Biadju, the Makassarese, the Buginese. Let no one follow any of the Malay dressing customs. If foreign dressing-customs are followed this will unavoidably bring misery over the country where this is done ... [There will be] disease, much intrigue and food will become expensive because people dress like those in foreign countries.[72]

Most spectacular of all, in China, the Qing insisted that all their male subjects shave their forelocks, braid the rest of their hair in a pigtail, and adopt Manchu dress, on pain of death. Initially, the head-shaving edict made sense because it immediately distinguished friend from foe: the long hair of Ming loyalists could be shorn in a few minutes. Shaving the forelocks therefore seemed a perfect test of loyalty; but it also created constant provocation because compliance required constant repetition as each man's hair grew. Nevertheless the Qing refused to back down and instead decreed 'Keep your head, lose your hair; keep your hair, lose your head' (chapter 5 below).

Not one of these contentious issues – wearing a veil at the 'churching of women', smoking tobacco, dressing like Dutchmen, head-shaving and so on – threatened the integrity or security of the state; and not one of them arose from the problems created by the Little Ice Age. With goodwill, statesmanship, or just the 'willingness to wink', each of them could have been peacefully resolved; but the exalted rhetoric and claims of those leaders who believed in the Divine Right of Kings or the Mandate of Heaven prevented such an outcome. On the contrary, they produced crises out of trifles and exacerbated tensions created by more serious problems, thereby increasing the sum of human misery.

Untangling the connections between these distinctive and disruptive aspects of seventeenth-century government (Divine Right, Tanistry, Composite States, Favourites and Absolutism), and the increased frequency of war and rebellion, is nevertheless complicated by two factors: contingency and feedback loops. Thus, a well-informed English minister later believed that the Anglo-Dutch war that began in 1664 'arose by strange accidental things concurring from several parts and parties without any intent to help each other'.[73] Documenting feedback loops is more difficult, but the success of Favourites in removing checks and balances made it easier for monarchs to go to war; while war made Favourites more necessary, because monarchs needed to curtail checks and balances in order to extract more resources. A similar feedback loop existed between war and rebellion. On the one hand, inter-state war frequently caused intrastate rebellions by driving governments to extract resources from their subjects more aggressively. On the other hand, intrastate rebellions could turn into interstate wars when alienated subjects secured foreign intervention. It is therefore impossible to assert that one aspect was always the cause while the other was always the effect: the relationship between them varied according to time and place.

Nevertheless, one part of the feedback loop remained constant: war seemed uniquely capable of uniting opponents of a regime. The imperative to 'feed Mars' eventually led governments to impose burdens on every social group and all geographical regions, which often alienated everyone at the same time. To be sure, the heaviest burdens normally fell on the lower ranks of each state, but governments desperate to win a war also trampled on the rights of those with corporate rights such as cities, nobles and clergy in their efforts to extract resources, and upon certain regions that the Little Ice Age rendered particularly vulnerable.

'Hunger is the greatest enemy':
The Heart of the Crisis

IN ONE OF HIS CELEBRATED *ESSAYS*, PUBLISHED EARLY IN THE SEVENTEENTH century, the English politician and philosopher Francis Bacon warned rulers to ensure that their subjects, unless 'mowen downe by wars, *doe not exceed the stock of the kingdome that should maintain them*', because a prolonged imbalance between the production and consumption of food sooner or later produces famine, disruption and revolt.[1]

Subsequent writers agreed. In 1640 a historian 'embedded' with the army of Philip IV as it passed through the drought-parched fields of Catalonia noted ominously: 'Amid the distress to which human misery reduces us, *there is almost nothing men would not do*'. Seven years later, the minister responsible for law and order in Castile warned his master that 'The population [of Madrid] is very volatile and every day becomes more insolent ... because *hunger respects no one [la ambre a ninguno respecta]*. The people are so licentious that no day is safe' from the threat of violence. In case Philip missed the point, other ministers reminded him that '*Hunger is the greatest enemy*. Even the most frugal person cannot cope with it ... and in many states the shortage of bread has provoked unrest that ended in sedition'. In 1648, as several Italian towns faced the worst harvest of the century, officials reported 'murmurs among the people saying that "*it was always better to die by the sword than to die of hunger*"'; while in London 'the cryes and teares of the poore, who professe they are almost ready to famish' led some to fear that '*a sudden confusion would follow*'. Finally in Scotland, during the last famine of the century, an acute observer reminded his compatriots that 'Poverty and want emasculate the mindes of many, and make those who are of dull natures, stupid and indisciplinable', whereas 'those that are of a firy and active temperament, it maketh them unquiet, rapacious, frantick or desperate. Thus, *where there are many poor, the rich cannot be secure in the possession of what they have*'.[2]

Nevertheless, although the Little Ice Age afflicted almost the entire northern hemisphere, some areas suffered more than others. This should cause no surprise. Europe west of the Urals covers four million square miles, ranging from arctic to subtropical and containing hundreds of ethnic, cultural, economic and political divisions: naturally, developments did not take place uniformly in all regions. Even within Spain, different areas suffered at different times. Galicia in the northwest and Valencia in the southeast experienced population decline from about 1615 to the 1640s; but in the centre, although the decline around Toledo also began in 1615, it lasted until the 1670s, while around Segovia, where the decline also ended in the 1670s, it began only after 1625. Ming China, covering 1.5 million square miles, and also ranging from subarctic to tropical conditions, likewise experienced the Little Ice Age in many different ways. Thus low-lying Shandong in the northeast often experiences both droughts and floods, so that the province rarely generates a surplus – let alone a reserve on which to draw in bad years. Urgent petitions calling for food loans and tax relief therefore emanated from Shandong on an almost annual basis, in the seventeenth century as at other times. By contrast Sichuan province in the west enjoys a mild climate which in most years permits abundant crops of rice, wheat, cotton, sugar, silk and tea – thus reducing vulnerability to global cooling.

Amid the diversity, three broad economic 'zones' stand out as particularly exposed to climate change: marginal farming lands; cities; and macro-regions. Marginal lands were vulnerable because they produced enough to feed all their inhabitants only during years of optimal harvests. Cities, by contrast, were vulnerable because their prosperity made them strategic targets, which in turn led to the construction of a fortified perimeter that promoted overcrowding, poor hygiene and the spread of diseases inside the walls and, in wartime, exposed the inhabitants to the risk of extensive human and material damage. Finally 'macro-regions' – complex regional economies consisting of several adjacent towns and their overlapping hinterlands – were vulnerable because their prosperity rested on the ability to import the food on which their population depended and to export the specialized goods which they produced. Disruption of either activity, whether at home or abroad, caused almost immediate hardship.

Although the inhabitants of these three economic 'zones' formed a small minority of the global population, they featured disproportionately in the Global Crisis. On the one hand, they suffered earlier, longer and more intensely than others, because government policies exacerbated to a unique degree the disruption created by climatic adversity and overpopulation; on the other hand, they harboured a large number of articulate men and women eager to publicize their predicament at home and, whenever they could, abroad. These voices resonated longer and louder than those of others whose experiences may have been more typical.

Agriculture on the Margin

For most of the sixteenth century, warmer weather permitted the expansion of farming throughout the northern hemisphere and a good part of this process took place on lands already close to the limits of viable cultivation. The farmers who cultivated these lands initially reaped spectacular harvests, thanks to the nitrogen and phosphorus that had accumulated in the earth during the centuries when they lay fallow; but once this natural bounty expired, even in 'good' years they became trapped in a high-risk, high-input, low-yield operation that required constant attention to produce even a mediocre crop. In northerly latitudes, as noted in chapter 1, each fall of 0.5°C in the mean summer temperature decreases the number of days on which crops ripen by 10 per cent, doubles the risk of a single harvest failure, and increases the risk of a double failure sixfold. Moreover, for those farming 1,000 feet or more above sea level, a fall of 0.5°C in the mean summer temperature increases the chance of two consecutive failures a hundredfold.

This cruel calculus applies throughout the northern hemisphere. In Scotland, where the majority of all farmland is marginal, the benign climate of the sixteenth century encouraged the cultivation of fields at higher altitudes and on poorer soils than before, but the cold and wet summers of the 1640s, which drove down mean temperatures by up to 2°C, brought disaster. In the Lammermuir Hills near the English border, three-quarters of the farms were abandoned; while on the Mull of Kintyre, in the west, four-fifths of all townships were abandoned because 'Farmers were not able to plant nor crofters to dig. The corn when it came up did not ripen . . . People and cattle died, and Kintyre became almost a desert'[3] (Fig. 5). In southern Europe, Sicily saw the foundation of some 70 'new towns' in the sixteenth and early seventeenth centuries, specifically to produce grain for the fast-growing cities of the island. At first many farmers harvested up to ten grains for each grain of wheat sown, and more than ten for each grain of barley sown, but the extreme weather of the 1640s drove yield ratios down on some lands of the new towns to 1:2 – a reduction of 80 per cent, and the lowest recorded in the entire early modern period. Leonforte, one of

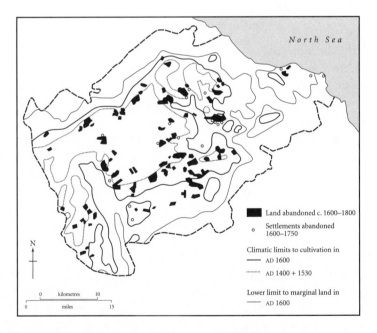

5. Farms in south-east Scotland abandoned in the seventeenth century.
Fourteen of the fifteen farmsteads that existed in the Lammermuir hills (south-east Scotland) in 1600 had disappeared by 1750, and three-quarters of the cultivated land reverted to permanent moorland. Global cooling, which increased the number of failed harvests, bears part of the blame, but the troops crossing between Scotland and England during the Civil War between 1639 and 1660 also contributed to the general insecurity of the region.

those new towns, grew from zero to over 2,000 inhabitants between 1610 and 1640, but the drought of 1648, which produced the poorest harvest ever recorded, brought catastrophe. The town's parish register recorded 426 burials but only 60 births.[4]

Clearing fields for cultivation led to a pernicious practice that could soon make even the most fertile land marginal: clear-cutting forests. A historian living in Shaanxi province in northwest China recalled that 'flourishing woods' used to cover its hills so that rainfall flowed down in gentle streams, and villagers cut 'canals and ditches which irrigated several thousand [acres] of land'. But as prosperity in the region grew,

> People vied with each other in building houses, and wood was cut from the southern mountains without a year's rest. Presently people took advantage of the barren mountain surface and converted it into farms. Small bushes and seedlings in every square foot of ground were uprooted. The result was that if the heavens send down torrential rain, there is nothing to obstruct the flow of water. In the morning it falls on the southern mountains; in the evening, when it reaches the plains, its angry waves swell in volume and break through the embankments, frequently changing the course of the river.[5]

New and old farms alike ceased to be viable.

The 'urban graveyard effect'

Although the decision to give up a farm – for whatever reason – is always heart-wrenching, the Little Ice Age forced many farmers on marginal lands to flee to the towns with their families in the hope of finding work or at least bread. Most of them met with bitter disappointment, in part because their flight helped to fuel unsustainable urban expansion.

The mid-seventeenth century was a 'metropolitan moment': never before had so many people lived in such close proximity. Beijing, the largest city in the world, had in excess of one million inhabitants, with almost as many in Nanjing. Six other Chinese cities numbered 500,000 citizens or more, while a score had 100,000 or more. Mughal India, the most urbanized area in the world after China, included three cities with 400,000 or more inhabitants and another nine with over 100,000. By 1650, 2.5 million Japanese, perhaps 10 per cent of the total population, lived in towns. By contrast, in the Americas, only Mexico and Potosí (the silver-mining centre of Peru) exceeded 100,000 inhabitants; while Africa's only metropolis was Cairo, with perhaps 400,000 residents. In Europe, the population of Istanbul, the capital of the Ottoman empire, may have approached 800,000, but no other city came close: only London, Naples and Paris exceeded 300,000. Ten other European cities numbered 100,000 inhabitants or more, while in Holland over 200,000 people lived in ten towns within a 50-mile radius of Amsterdam.

Every one of these metropolitan areas required prodigious quantities of housing, fuel, food and fresh water, as well as schemes to manage traffic, fight fires and keep public spaces clean. Failure to provide these essential services created the 'urban graveyard effect'. In the 1630s William Ince, a Dublin preacher, delivered a sermon that poured scorn on the desire of Abraham's brother Lot (in the Book of Genesis) to flee from Sodom to another city, where he hoped to find 'plentie, societie, and safetie', believing that in a 'Citie all these three concurre to make life securely happy', whereas, in fact, Ince reminded his audience, Lot found that urban living brought only 'povertie and solitarienesse'. And, indeed, as the French social historian Jean Jacquart observed, all early modern cities were 'a *mouroir*, a demographic black hole, accounting for disproportionately fewer marriages, fewer births and more deaths'. In London, which preserves particularly precise demographic records, burials in the seventeenth century were often twice as numerous as baptisms and both maternal and infant mortality were particularly high. Only massive immigration from other communities prevented major cities from shrinking in size, which meant that each capital exerted a pronounced 'dampening' effect on the population of the kingdom as a whole[6] (Fig. 6). As early as 1616, King James I predicted with alarm that 'all the country is gotten into London, so as, with time, England will only be London, and the whole country be left waste with everyone living miserably in our houses, and dwelling all in the city'.[7]

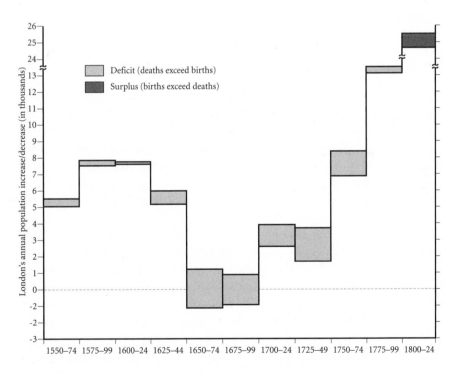

6. The 'dampening effect' of London on England's overall demographic growth.
Although other areas of England registered a surplus of some 120,000 births over deaths between 1650 and 1674, London accrued a deficit of 228,000 over the same period and only strong immigration allowed the capital to keep growing.

One of King James's subjects, Ben Jonson, published a satirical poem about the 'urban graveyard effect' created by the shortage of shelter, food and water, as seen through the eyes of a brave trio who travelled through the sewers of London, where

> Hung Stench, Diseases, and old Filth, their Mother,
> With Famine, Wants, and Sorrows many a Dozen,
> The least of which was to the Plague a Cozen.
> But they unfrighted pass, tho' many a Privy
> Spake to them louder than the Ox in *Livy*.

According to Jonson's contemporary James Howell, Paris was no better: it 'is alwayes dirty, and 'tis such a dirt, that by perpetual motion is beaten into such black onctious oyl, that wher it sticks no art can wash it off'. In addition, 'besides the stain this dirt leaves, it gives also so a strong scent, that it may be smelt many miles off, if the wind be in one's face as he comes from the fresh air of the countrey. This may be one cause why the plague is alwayes in som corner or other of this vast citie, which may be call'd, as once Scythia was, *Vagina populorum*'. Another contemporary, Xie Zhaozhe, made much the same complaints about Beijing:

> The houses in the capital are so closely crowded together that there is no spare space, and in the markets there is much excrement and filth. People from all directions live together in disorderly confusion, and there are many flies and gnats. Whenever it becomes hot it is almost intolerable. A little steady rain has only to fall and there is trouble from flooding. Therefore malarial fevers, diarrhoea and epidemics follow each other without stopping.[8]

Of course, city-dwellers at virtually all times and in virtually all places have made similar complaints; but in the mid-seventeenth century the problems they faced intensified. For example, by the 1630s population and building densities in the City of London both reached levels that 'have probably not been witnessed in Britain either before or since'. In some parishes, almost 400 persons squeezed into each acre, many of them living in six-storey houses, in one case with 'six rooms let to sixty-four persons' (an average of 11 per room). At least 30 per cent of London households lived at or below the poverty line.[9]

In many seventeenth-century cities, growing dependence on fossil fuels created new problems. Any disruption in supply soon produced general misery. Beijing welcomed the Manchu invaders in 1644 in part because they promised to restore the supply of coal from Shanxi on which householders and industrialists alike depended, disrupted for two years by civil war. Likewise, when that same year military operations interrupted the supply of Tyneside coal required by London's industries, an observer predicted 'there will be riots this winter'. However, fossil fuels damaged the health of city-dwellers through pollution. In 1656 the English poet Sir William Davenant published an 'entertainment' that complained that in London 'the plentiful exercise of your chimneys makes up that canopy of smoke which covers your city' and included a song that began:

London is smother'd with sulph'rous fires.
Still she wears a black hood and cloak
Of sea-coal smoak
As if she mourn'd for brewers and dyers.[10]

Since the sea-coal used by brewers, dyers and other manufacturers contained twice as much sulphur as that used today, its smoke darkened the air, dirtied clothes and curtains, stunted trees and flowers, blackened buildings and statues, and choked and killed the inhabitants. In an early condemnation of air pollution, published in 1661, John Evelyn compared the 'columns and clouds of smoke which are belched forth from the sooty throats' of London's chimneys with 'the picture of Troy sacked by the Greeks'. The capital's inhabitants, he claimed, 'breathe nothing but an impure and thick mist accompanied by a fulginous and filthy vapour'. Ladies used ground almonds to clean their complexion, while preachers in churches had to compete with the constant coughing and spitting of their congregations.[11] The situation was even worse in those Dutch towns where industrial plants burned peat for brewing, dyeing, soap factories and brick kilns, because (although far cheaper than coal) peat created toxic fumes.

The presence of industrial enterprises in the heart of cities greatly increased the risk of fire; so did the use of wood and other flammable material to build cheap and shoddy high-density housing for the influx of immigrants. In East Asia, the use of wood not only for residences and shops but also for temples, government offices and covered markets further increased the risk; so did the use of palm and bamboo for roofs and floors and the practice of cooking on an open brazier, using oil lamps for light, and setting off fireworks during celebrations. Even the occupants of stone and brick temples, tombs, fortresses and merchant warehouses remained nervous. 'Oh, this word *fire*!' wrote an English merchant in Java. 'Had it been spoken near me, either in English, Malay, Javanese or Chinese, although I had been sound asleep, yet I should have leaped out of my bed.' He recalled that while the merchants slept, 'our men many times have sounded a drum at our chamber doors and we never heard them; yet presently after, they have but whispered to themselves of *fire* and we all have run out of our chambers.'[12]

As Christopher Friedrichs has noted: 'Of all the elements, it was not earth, water or air that most persistently threatened the well-being of the early modern city. The most dangerous element was fire' – and, in the mid-seventeenth century, major fires became both more frequent and more destructive. A 'gazetteer' of accidental urban fires in England listed over one hundred between 1640 and 1689, at least ten of which consumed over a hundred buildings. London experienced so many fires in 1655 that many thought they presaged the Last Judgement; while six years later, when faced after the Sunday sermon for the fifteenth consecutive week with pleas for charity from those whose homes had burned down, Samuel Pepys became irritated and 'resolve[d] to give no more to them'.[13] He changed his mind in 1666, when the 'Great Fire' of London destroyed St Paul's Cathedral, the Guildhall, the Royal Exchange, 84 churches and 13,000 houses, leaving 80,000 people homeless and causing £8 million of damage. Although Londoners blamed the Lord Mayor, who had initially jested that 'a woman might piss it out' and failed to create fire breaks, the true culprit was the climate: after an unusually hot and dry spring, temperatures in the summer of 1666 rose 1.5°C above normal, and a precipitation shortfall of 6 inches turned London into a tinderbox. The same conditions prevailed in much of north-western Europe, giving rise to fires in a score of German cities. Only the spectacular destruction of so much of London has overshadowed the frequency of urban fires elsewhere in 1666.[14]

London was not the only capital city where unusual drought in the mid-seventeenth century produced a 'Great Fire'. In Moscow in 1648, after several months without rain, 'within a few hours more than half the city inside the White Wall, and about half the city outside the wall, went up in flames'; while a large part of the new Mughal capital Shahjahanabad (now Delhi) burnt down in 1662. Istanbul suffered more (and more devastating fires) in the seventeenth century than in any other period of its history: one in 1660, once again after a prolonged drought, burned down 28,000 houses and several public buildings[15] (Fig. 7). Major blazes also regularly devastated Edo, the largest city in Japan, notably the Meireki fire of 1657 – which, like those in Moscow in 1648, Istanbul in 1660 and London in 1666, broke out after an abnormal drought. Three separate

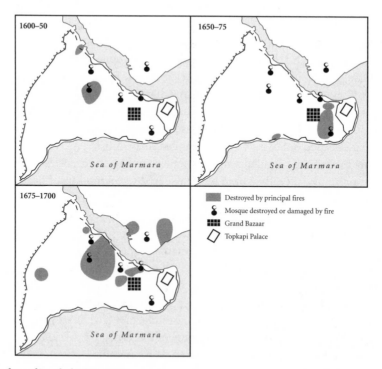

7. The fires of Istanbul 1600–1700.
Three maps show the areas of the Ottoman capital destroyed by fire in 1600–50, 1650–75 and 1675–1700. Note that the third quarter of the century experienced the worst damage, with major conflagrations in 1652, 1660, 1665 and 1673.

conflagrations combined to destroy three-quarters of Edo, including 50,000 homes of merchants and artisans, almost 1,000 noble mansions and over 350 temples and shrines. Even the shogun's magnificent new castle, the tallest building in Japan, 'which can be compared to one of the largest walled cities in Europe, has been completely destroyed by this horrendous fire'. Perhaps 160,000 people died. In the words of a Japanese contemporary account: 'When the fire drew upon them, burning up completely all that was near at hand, some people could no longer bear the heat and they formed themselves into a human shield to try to ward off the fire, but they were choked by the billowing smoke. Others were consumed by the fire, their limbs burned to ashes.' A Dutch eyewitness described how 'with horror and dread I saw this immense city ablaze, like Troy'; and how, the next day, 'passing through the streets', he saw 'innumerable burnt people, either completely or partly consumed, of which at least a third were small children, spread all over and lying dead on each other'. He also captured the desolation in a striking painting that showed empty city blocks, charred trees and scores of dead bodies in the streets[16] (Plate 4). No sooner had rebuilding commenced than another major fire 'destroyed an area about 1.5 miles in circumference', followed by a third in 1661 and a fourth in 1668 which 'devoured so many houses of nobles and civilians that it is estimated that two-thirds of the city of Edo has been destroyed'. According to one Dutch visitor, 'it seems that it has become customary for that all-consuming element (fire) to rage there around Japanese New Year'.[17]

It is possible to demonstrate the extraordinary intensity of the four Edo fires of the mid-seventeenth century. A 'core' of earth excavated in 1975 at a building site in Hitotsubashi, not far from the shogun's castle, revealed three prominent layers of ash. The most recent, representing the firestorm caused by the bombing of Tokyo in 1945, measured 4 inches; the second, caused by the fire that followed the Kanto earthquake of 1923, measured 6 inches; the third, representing the fires of the mid-seventeenth century, measured 8 inches. The fact that the burned debris from 1657–68 was twice as thick as that created by the most advanced pyrotechnics of the twentieth century is both striking and sobering.[18]

All these urban fires were apparently accidental; many more occurred because of wars. Thus during the 1640s, although 13 English towns experienced 'accidental' fires, soldiers deliberately caused at least 80 more, some of them large (over 80 houses destroyed in Birmingham and almost 250 in Gloucester, both in 1643). War also destroyed towns in other ways: constructing or extending fortifications, preparing for a siege, and fire from siege artillery brought down many buildings. At Exeter, the third largest city in England, between 1642 and 1646 the defenders deliberately razed all the suburbs, where one-third of the pre-war population had lived, while bombardment during two sieges left 'whole streets converted to ashes'. Although Exeter successfully resisted capture, it did not attain its pre-war extent for 60 years.[19]

The prevalence of war meant that every urban space needed walls – indeed, the Chinese character most commonly used for 'city' (cheng: 城) literally signifies 'city walls' because it is made up of the characters that signify 'earth' (土) plus 'complete'

(成) – but they did not always save the community within. Mainz, in western Germany, which surrendered without a struggle in 1631, over the next five years lost 25 per cent of its houses, 40 per cent of its population and 60 per cent of its wealth while it served as the headquarters of the Swedish expeditionary force. Although its massive walls allowed Pavia (Lombardy) to withstand an eight-week siege in 1655, success still ruined the city: lack of demand destroyed its industries; buying flour before and subsidizing bread prices during the siege bankrupted its treasury; and the besiegers' destruction of all municipal assets beyond the walls seriously impeded economic recovery. Nonetheless, Mainz and Pavia were lucky: cities taken by force during the mid-seventeenth century suffered far greater losses and might take over a generation to recover. The siege and sack of Mantua in 1629 reduced its population from 29,000 to 9,000; by 1647 it still had only 15,000 inhabitants and in 1676 only 20,000. The population of Warsaw, the capital of the Polish-Lithuanian Commonwealth, numbered perhaps 30,000 in the 1630s (and up to 100,000 whenever the Diet met there), but this fell below 6,000 after occupation by Transylvanian and Swedish forces in 1655-7. They also left over half its buildings ruined.[20] Perhaps the worst man-made urban catastrophe of the period occurred in 1642 when, after a siege that lasted a year, the Chinese rebel leader Li Zicheng decided to force the surrender of Kaifeng (capital of Henan province) by breaching the dikes on the nearby Yellow river. By a fateful coincidence, at exactly the same time the defenders broke another set of dikes hoping to flood Li's encampment and thus drive him off. According to a contemporary, water from both breaches poured through one of the city's gates, creating floods that 'suddenly rose twenty feet'. The following day Li sent men into the city on boats in search of ransoms and plunder, but they found not a living soul.[21]

Floods also contributed to the 'urban graveyard effect'. Because many cities grew up beside rivers and lakes, even without military intervention higher precipitation could cause immense flood damage. The worst inundation in the history of Mexico City occurred in 1629, when a combination of torrential rains and inadequate drainage caused the surrounding lakes to rise suddenly, submerging considerable parts of the city for five years. The catastrophe led some to consider relocating the capital, and although on this occasion the Spanish central government rejected the option, 30 years later repeated flooding led it to approve abandoning the regional capital of Santa Fé la Vieja, Argentina, and relocating it to higher ground. In Europe, the Seine burst its banks and flooded Paris 18 times in the seventeenth century, with particularly serious inundations in 1649, 1651 and 1658; towns in the low-lying province of Holland suffered even more frequently because storms in the North Sea periodically drove water over or through the dikes (as in 1651, flooding Amsterdam).[22]

A final cause of the 'urban graveyard effect' was the dependence of early modern cities on food produced far away. A Chinese magistrate near Shanghai foresaw with absolute clarity the danger inherent in this situation:

> Our county does not produce rice, but relies for its food upon other areas. When
> the summer wheat is reaching ripeness and the autumn crops are already rising,

the boats of the merchants that come loaded with rice form an unbroken line . . .
[But] if by chance there were to be an outbreak of hostilities . . . such that the city
gates did not open for ten days, and the hungry people raised their voices in
clamour, how could there fail to be riot and disorder?

His fears turned into reality in 1641–2 when, even without 'an outbreak of hostilities', global cooling destroyed the rice harvest throughout South China. Perhaps
500,000 people starved to death and public order collapsed.[23]

The 'Palace cities'

'Palace cities', those with a large population of otherwise unproductive government
officials to feed, were most vulnerable because they normally had to import a high
proportion of their food, and therefore sought supplies farther afield – and the
longer the supply chain, the more susceptible it was to disruption. Thus, every year,
huge convoys of barges carried 450,000 tonnes of rice (as well as vast quantities of
wheat, millet, beans and other foodstuffs) to Beijing along the Grand Canal, which
stretched almost 1,200 miles down to the fertile rice paddies of the Yangzi valley. In
1641 drought in Shandong caused the Grand Canal to dry up (for the only time in its
history); while, after 1642, fear of bandit attacks interfered with routine maintenance
(dredging, diking and repairing the locks) and disrupted the sailing of the convoys.
Since most of the imported rice nourished the 300,000 inhabitants of the Inner City,
the failure of the last Ming emperor to feed his own people no doubt contributed to
their decision to surrender his capital, scarcely firing a shot, in 1644.

The provisioning of seventeenth-century Istanbul, another 'palace city', strikingly
resembled that of Beijing. The Ottoman capital imported thousands of sheep
and lambs, over 500 cattle and 500 tonnes of bread daily, because the sultan (like
the Chinese emperor) needed to feed not only the imperial family, bureaucrats,
eunuchs, artisans, guards, merchants, and their households, but also students in the
colleges and medreses attached to the imperial mosques. Like Beijing, Istanbul also
boasted a proven supply network – Egypt, the Balkans and the lands around the
Aegean and Black Seas all regularly sent food to the city, some of it as tribute, just as
they had done since Roman times – but this network too was subject to disruption by
natural and human agency. Thus in 1620–1, the Bosporus froze over, while in 1641–3
unusually weak Nile floods caused an epic drought in Egypt: both climatically
induced events dramatically reduced the supply of food shipped to Istanbul. War
likewise disrupted the supply of food: between 1645 and 1658, when enemy fleets
repeatedly prevented ships from passing through the Dardanelles, food prices in the
Ottoman capital soared. On each occasion, whatever the cause, as in Beijing the
households of those normally fed by the state suffered first and most – which helps to
explain why palace personnel led the revolts that culminated in regicide in both 1622
and 1648.[24]

In Madrid, the capital of the Spanish Monarchy, magistrates imposed a daily
schedule according to which each nearby village had to deliver a specified amount

of wheat to the special granary maintained to feed the court. When supplies dwindled during the disastrous harvest of 1630, the magistrates extended the tribute system to include over 500 communities within a radius of 60 miles. Every house in each of these communities became responsible for providing a fixed share of the court's total requirement of 30 tonnes of wheat a day.[25] In 1647, when 'the torrential and persistent rain made traffic impossible on the roads to Madrid', a senior minister warned the king that 'The stocks of flour have almost run out and people cannot get into the countryside to find dry firewood to heat the ovens. Very few mills still have a wheel that works, because of the floods.' The city's granaries soon emptied and the minister worried that 'if the bread supply fails for a single day, instead of the 100 people who are protesting today, Your Majesty will find the entire population in front of the palace'.[26] To avert disaster, the government once again unilaterally extended the grain tribute system, rescinded all exemptions, dismissed all appeals from oppressed villages for relief, and sent agents 120 miles and more from the capital to requisition bread. Thanks to these rapid and radical responses, Philip IV never did 'find the entire population in front of the palace'.[27]

'Palace cities' were not alone in creating a sophisticated but vulnerable supply network. When other urban centres outgrew the capacity of their immediate hinterland to feed them, they too became dependent on distant market forces. Thus the burgeoning populations of the largest port cities around Europe's Atlantic and North Sea coasts (including London, Amsterdam, Antwerp, Lisbon and Seville) depended for their daily bread on importing large quantities of grain from the Polish-Lithuanian Commonwealth, which boasted fertile soil, cheap labour and easy access to water transport. By the early seventeenth century, between 150,000 and 200,000 tonnes of grain came down the Vistula annually for sale at Danzig, where an average of 1,500 ships loaded and shipped it to western Europe. Any interference in this commerce – for example when war broke out between Poland and Sweden in the 1620s, or when the Danish Sound froze over early in 1658 – caused the price of bread immediately to soar in the leading cities of Atlantic Europe, where the poorer members of their populations starved.

The Macro-Regions

No early modern settlement was entirely self-sufficient: all of them needed to import at least some items. Even the inhabitants of upland villages isolated for part of each year by winter snows or monsoon rains periodically trudged to the nearest market town to sell handicrafts or surplus agricultural produce and acquire such essentials as salt for food preservation and iron for tools. As population density increased in the sixteenth century, the number of market towns multiplied spectacularly. In China, the number of markets in Zhangzhou prefecture (Fujian) increased from 11 in 1491 to 38 in 1573, and to 65 in 1628. In Japan, market towns in most parts of the coastal plains stood by the 1630s between two and four miles apart; while by then, in England, men and women had to travel an average of only eight miles to the nearest market.

Markets achieved their greatest density around major cities – in the counties around London, markets were on average less than a mile apart – because they formed part of a zone of economic activity that contained the best arable land, the densest population, the hubs of communication and transport, and the largest capital accumulations. Economists call them 'macro-regions'. Ming China contained eight macro-regions, each one centred on a river system and separated from the others by natural barriers. The Indian subcontinent also included several macro-regions, including Gujarat and the Ganges valley; the Ottoman empire boasted Egypt, the lands around the Aegean, and the Black Sea region; in the Americas, Mexico City lay at the centre of a macro-region; so did the Kinai and Kantô plains in Japan. The macro-regions of Europe included the Genoa–Turin–Venice–Florence quadrilateral in Italy; the Home Counties in southeast England; the adjacent provinces of Holland, Zealand and Utrecht; and the Île-de-France. Many of the settlements within these macro-regions adopted a high-risk, high-reward economic strategy: they concentrated on producing cash crops which they sold to merchants and manufacturers, and imported the food they needed from farther afield.[28]

When times were good, the macro-regions created three golden economic opportunities for farmers – but at a high risk. First, thanks to rising external demand and stable transport costs, many individual agriculturists made the transition from generalist to specialist, investing in the tools, raw materials and labour required to produce a single crop, or a small range of crops, for the market. Thus in the duchy of Württemberg (southwest Germany), by 1622 many farmers and even entire communities had ceased to grow grain and converted all their land to producing the fine wines for which the area is still famous. This rendered almost everyone dependent on imported grain to bake their daily bread, and so when the harvest in most of Germany that year produced scarcely half the normal yield, much of Württemberg starved.[29] In many parts of eastern China, a lot of farmers likewise switched to producing cash crops for the market, such as sugar, tea, fish, silk and cotton. Initially, these shifts involved little disruption. On the one hand, rice requires intensive cultivation in March, May and July, whereas cotton requires most attention in April, June and between August and October; so the same labour force could produce both crops. On the other hand, fish ponds had long existed in the southern river deltas, with fruit trees planted on the surrounding embankments; the fish (mainly carp) fed on the organic matter that fell from the trees, and the muck scooped from the ponds fertilized the trees and the surrounding rice paddy. But as growing demand inflated the price of silk, farmers began to replace their fruit trees with the mulberries on which silkworms feed, and they also converted rice paddy into fish ponds with mulberries on the embankment. At first sight this formed a sustainable ecosystem, because almost all the necessary mineral and energy resources were recycled. It was not, however, a closed system: those who concentrated on producing fish and silk could no longer feed themselves and instead now depended totally on rice produced miles (sometimes hundreds of miles) away. The same dilemma faced Chinese farmers who abandoned cereals to plant cotton, at first in dry fields or on the ridges between their paddy, and then in their entire holding. Although smallholders could make a fortune from cotton in some years, the crop required twice as much fertilizer as rice and was more vulnerable to floods, droughts and high winds. Since no one stored the annual crop, its market value immediately reflected variations in the climate and the price of fertilizers, as well as in the demand for cotton itself – all of them factors over which farmers had no control. Sooner or later, therefore, either the 'miracle crop' would fail or the market would collapse. In both scenarios, its producers would starve.

The second golden opportunity for farmers that accompanied the growth of macro-regions in the sixteenth century was the chance to reclaim flooded land. In North Holland, the growth of Amsterdam and other adjacent cities encouraged entrepreneurs to reclaim 220,000 acres of lake, estuary and marsh between 1590 and 1640, creating 1,400 large new farms. In China, the sixteenth century saw the completion of over 1,000 new water-control projects, twice as many as the preceding century, while repairs brought many more abandoned projects back into service. In Japan, major land-reclamation projects between 1550 and 1640 more than doubled the area of rice paddy. Nevertheless, all these hydraulic projects were vulnerable. On the one hand, they needed constant maintenance: any inundation, however caused, requires immediate remedial action, because the longer the water is left, the harder it is to drain. On the other hand, hostile troops could easily destroy dikes and dams, and prevent repairs. Such action brought the risk of perpetuating a cycle of disorders, both because peasants who lost their land faced few alternatives to joining the aggressors, and because the floods created excellent redoubts where those aggressors could thrive (see chapter 5 for some Chinese examples).[30]

The third golden opportunity associated with macro-regions was that the warmer climate of the sixteenth century, which reduced the risk of frosts that killed early or late crops, allowed more intensive cultivation of crops to satisfy the increased demand for food from a growing population. The most spectacular increases occurred in southeast China, where the land tax varied according to acreage rather than output, encouraging farmers to plant two and even three crops per year. Many incredulous contemporaries in the 1620s described this system – some of them Chinese ('in Guangdong there are fields which get three harvests; the reason is the warm climate') and others European ('they obtain three consecutive harvests in one year, two of rice and one of wheat')[31] (Fig. 8). In both China and Japan, farmers experimented with different types of rice – quicker ripening (even if lower in yield); resistant to salt (for use near the sea); resistant to cold – until over 150 varieties were in use in Fujian alone, over two-thirds of them found in only one location.

Taken together, these improvements almost doubled rice yields in good years – but only in good years. Drought, cold and any other factor that prevented double-cropping impoverished farmers whose livelihood depended on selling the surplus crops. They also caused shortages or even starvation for their consumers, whether from lack of food or from inability to purchase it – often with long-lasting results. In India, the famine and floods of 1627–31 ended the production of indigo and cotton in Gujarat because, lacking both a market for their goods and food to eat, the weavers fled and never returned. Similarly at Luzhou, a once prosperous town in

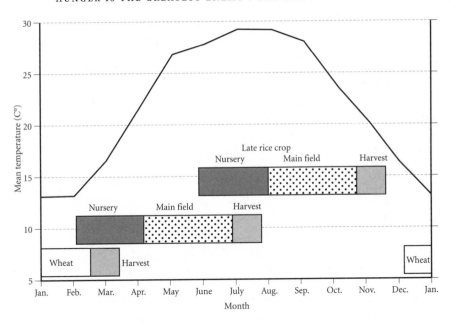

8. The double-cropping cycle in Liangnan, south-east China.
Rice price series reveal two distinct patterns: warm years (such as the 1620s) saw generally lower prices with two 'peaks', in April–May and again in July (just before each harvest reached the market); colder years (such as the 1640s) saw higher prices with only one peak, in June–July.

Shanxi province (northwest China) where until the disastrous harvest of 1640–2 'over 3,000 looms' wove imported raw silk, thereafter

> All the weavers had to take out loans and their debts piled up and ruined them, so by 1644 there were only two or three hundred looms left. Although the weavers worked hard for themselves and for official exactions, toiling day and night with their wives and children, they had to pay all their expenses out of their own pockets and accumulated only debts – how could they go on? Now in 1660 they are thinking of burning their looms and repudiating their debts and, in great sorrow, running away.

The collapse of weaving also, of course, affected those who produced the raw silk: sericulture vanished from the neighbouring province of Shaanxi, despite a tradition that went back 2,000 years. Those who ceased to grow foodstuffs, and instead concentrated on other commercial crops produced for export, such as sugar, tea, indigo, or the wide variety of artefacts made from bamboo (writing brushes, rain-hats, umbrellas and so on), all shared the same vulnerability: when the supply of staples failed, they lost both their market and their capacity to feed their family.[32]

Malevolence and the Macro-Regions

Besides the catastrophes caused by climate change, the macro-regions (just like cities) were also extremely vulnerable to human malevolence. To begin with, agricultural innovations and commercial crops normally required a substantial investment in fixed assets. Thus sugar production needed roller mills to crush the cane, pans to boil the juice, and trays to dry the crystals; silk manufacture required mulberry trees (each of which took six years to mature), vats for dyeing, and looms for weaving; making cotton fabrics required gins and looms.[33] Such fixed assets could be looted and burned by enemies, just like traditional crops and simple farm equipment – but the damage cost far more and took far longer to repair. Moreover, as with hydraulic projects, what marauders could destroy once they could destroy again.

A second way in which human agency could cause serious damage to macro-regions arose from the fact that, although they formed the largest coherent economic units of the seventeenth century, they did not form a single market (Fig. 9). Instead, in the felicitous image of economic historian Kishimoto Mio, they resembled

> Numerous shallow ponds connected one to another by channels. Because of their shallowness, the ponds were vulnerable to changes in external economic conditions. For example, too little inflow or too much outflow of money

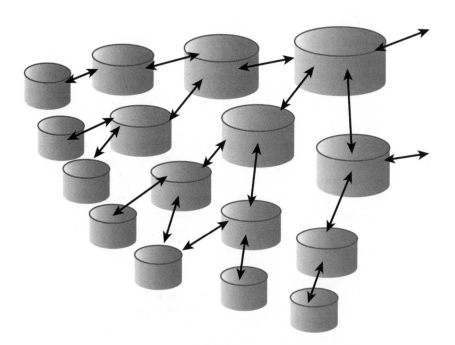

9. A simple model of early modern economic systems.
Japanese historian Kishimoto Mio has suggested that economic systems in the early modern world resembled an interconnected series of shallow pools, some deeper than others. Full integration of the 'pools' (Fig. 52 below) took place slowly.

or commodities could easily flood or dry up these ponds and paralyze local economies ... Even if we could calculate the 'total' size of an economy by aggregating the water stock of these ponds, it would not have real meaning in economic history until these ponds are organically integrated into a single economy. More meaningful, perhaps, is to study the flow of money and goods in and out of the 'shallow' local markets from the viewpoint of local inhabitants, listening to their complaints about the destructive effects of external market conditions.[34]

In the seventeenth century such complaints multiplied whenever wars and rebellions closed down markets and trade routes. Thus in 1621 two simultaneous wars – between the Dutch Republic and Spain, and between Sweden and Poland – involved blockades specifically intended to halt the export of Baltic grain: the former because Dutch ships carried most of it, the latter because its profits sustained the Polish war effort. Grain exports through the Danish Sound accordingly plunged from over 200,000 tonnes in 1618 to 60,000 in 1624 and 1625. Just as the blockaders intended, this fall both ruined Polish farmers and pushed food prices in the Dutch Republic to their highest level of the seventeenth century. Riots broke out in several towns and an alarmed Dutch politician wrote in his journal that 'the plague of God' lay on the land.[35]

A decade later, in East Asia, another blockade crippled those whose economic survival depended on selling Chinese silks in Japan. In the 1630s Shogun Tokugawa Iemitsu first ordered all Japanese residing abroad to come home and forbade all emigration; he then prohibited the construction of large ships in the archipelago; finally he forbade all trade with the Portuguese. Iemitsu had prepared carefully for the economic impact of these measures upon Japan. On the one hand, he issued new 'frugality and sumptuary laws' designed to reduce the consumption of imported products such as silk; on the other, he encouraged Dutch, Korean and Chinese merchants to increase their silk imports in order to maintain a steady supply.[36] But he miscalculated: although the Portuguese of Macao lost 'the most lucrative trade that His Majesty [Philip IV] has over here' (just as Iemitsu intended), the Dutch, who expected to gain, also lost because when they imported large quantities of silk, as requested by the shogun, they found that the new 'frugality and sumptuary laws' had decimated demand.[37] For the same reason the Chinese, too, could not sell their cargoes in Japan: the price of raw silk in the Yangzi valley therefore fell sharply and its producers starved. Finally, the native Japanese importers also suffered because they forfeited the capital – at least 800,000 *taels* of silver – previously sent to Macao to buy silks. Many went bankrupt, some fled and a few committed suicide in order to escape their creditors.[38] Everyone involved in the Sino-Japanese silk trade thus experienced serious losses, some of it terminal, because of a political decision over which they had no control and against which they had no defence.[39]

Those living in the macro-regions were also defenceless against other government initiatives. For example, since they normally used cash to settle commercial transactions, currency manipulation affected them far more than communities which continued to rely on barter. Currency in the early modern world came in two forms. One, used by merchants, monarchs and others who engaged in high-value transactions, consisted of silver and gold coins that had an intrinsic value like any other commodity. Therefore, by changing the amount of precious metal contained in each coin, governments could manipulate its exchange value against the coins of other states that contained precious metal. During the mid-seventeenth century, an unprecedented number of governments around the world tampered with the currency, both to *make* money when they re-minted existing coins at inflated values and to *save* money when they had to make payments (much as some governments today welcome currency devaluation because it reduces the real cost of their debts and increases the competitive edge of domestic products). The Spanish government took the lead, issuing cheap copper coinage (known as *vellón*) in 1618. Within eight years it had almost completely replaced silver in domestic transactions. Serious inflation took place, and the government first halted further issues of *vellón* and then halved the face value of all copper coins. Four more times between 1636 and 1658 the Spanish Mints called in all existing coins and re-stamped them at a higher value (two, three, or even four times their face value) – only to retreat after a few months in the face of public outcry and restore the earlier value.

Many Muslim rulers also resorted to currency debasement, causing similar economic dislocation. In the Ottoman empire, the weight and silver content of the standard silver coin, the *akçe*, dropped in a series of devaluations from 0.7 grams in the 1580s to 0.3 grams in 1640 and it all but disappeared as a medium of exchange. In Iran, an irate draper described in verse what he called the 'monetary revolution' of 1653–4, in which creditors feared payment in the shah's abundant but debased silver coins bearing a lion's head:

Money is in plenty, but beggars refuse it,
As if its lion were a man-eater . . .

The creditor flees the borrower,
Never did the world see such ways . . .

At the time of the monetary revolution
I was worried by both dearth and plenty.[40]

In China, the subjects of the last Ming emperors also worried as mounting defence spending led first to the issue of large quantities of copper fiat money and then, once copper supplies ran short, to coins adulterated with base metals. The exchange rate of silver to copper coins fell to 1:1700 in 1638 and to 1:3000 in 1643. At this point, the desperate Chongzhen emperor started to issue paper currency, but (understandably) no one believed the notes would ever be redeemed, and so that expedient also failed. Worse followed: the Qing refused to accept Ming copper currency as legal tender and so the exchange rate between silver and copper coins fell to 1:5000 in 1646, and to 1:6000 in 1647. Eventually, as in central Europe during the 1620s (page 35 above), copper coins became worthless: in the words of a contemporary, 'a hundred coins piled up hardly measured an inch in thickness and when they were thrown on the floor they broke into pieces'.[41]

Economic historians still debate the extent to which such drastic changes in liquidity affected the early modern world. Obviously, the importance of silver and gold currency to each geographical area and to each social group increased in proportion to its reliance on cash as opposed to barter; and, predictably, barter spread in many parts of the seventeenth-century world. Nevertheless, trade – and especially foreign trade – exerted a 'multiplier effect' on currency variations. To use another insight of Kishimoto Mio, unlike other commodities,

> Sooner or later money creates added income for others through spending. The silver that flowed annually into one regional market in turn created demand in other regional markets through chain-like successions of exchange. For example, producers of raw silk would sell their silk to outside merchants and obtain silver, with which they could buy foods from farmers in the neighbourhood. Those who obtained silver from the sale of food would buy cotton cloth or other miscellaneous commodities with that silver, and so on. If the inflow of silver was to stop for some reason, the silk producers would have no money to buy food, and food producers would also have no money to buy cotton cloth. The decrease of income spreads through a chain reaction.[42]

Kishimoto's 'model' explains why contemporaries paid special attention to the 'flow' of silver and other commodities, rather than to stock: what mattered was not the ability to amass goods, but the ability to sell them. In the 1650s, after three decades of war, disease and famine had drastically lowered demand in Jiangnan, a series of warm summers produced bumper rice harvests – but this spelled disaster for rice farmers. According to one of them, 'This year the price of rice was very low, at a level not seen for several decades. The humblest people in the poorest hamlets all ate fine rice and made cakes, while in my house we ate no midday meal on the last day of the year [traditionally a Chinese feast day].' During the following decade, the decision of the Qing government to forbid all maritime trade, cutting off Jiangnan from its traditional overseas export markets, again caused supply to exceed demand. According to a local source,

> Even the rich with much property rarely have any silver, so they are not able to buy grain, meal and cloth – all of which are cheap. Consequently the sellers of these commodities [have no business, lack money], and are also unable to consume goods . . . As a result, grain and hundreds of other unsold commodities pile up at the market centres in Suzhou. Good merchants lose their funds and the wealthy become penniless.

Or, more concisely, in a Chinese aphorism of the day, 'The rich become poor; the poor die.'[43]

'The haves and the have-nots'

In the second part of *Don Quixote*, published in Madrid in 1615, Miguel de Cervantes attributed to the phlegmatic squire Sancho Panza a now famous proverb:

'My grandmother used to say that there are only two families in the world: the haves and the have-nots.'[44] When Cervantes wrote, the village of Navalmoral de Toledo, in central Spain, had a population of around 250 families, of which 50 were 'have-nots' who owned no property. Instead they lived in shacks, sometimes without a single piece of furniture – the inventory of their property when they died recorded no chair, no table, no bed – and survived on what they earned from working for the 'haves'. In addition, 20 widows lived alone in the village without any apparent source of income; and 17 individuals, described as paupers, lacked even a permanent dwelling place of their own, sleeping in a barn or an attic in winter and under a hedgerow in summer (Fig. 10). In the early decades of the century, whenever a meagre harvest forced up the price of food but required fewer labourers, these 'have-nots' went hungry but they rarely starved because the 'haves' provided alms, while the church used the tithes (a 10 per cent share of the harvest) to provide charity. If dearth continued, however, not only did the number of have-nots increase but the yield of the tithe simultaneously decreased. Thus in 1618, a year of good harvest (and therefore of good tithes), the church of a Spanish village near Navalmoral distributed 12,000 maravedis (£5) in alms; but in the 1630s, as harvest yields fell, the

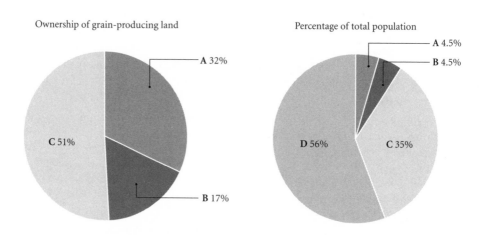

Group **A**: 11 families, 4.5% of the population, owned 32% of the land.
Group **B**: 11 families, 4.5% of the population, owned 17% of the land.
Group **C**: 86 families, 35% of the population, owned 51% of the land.
Group **D**: 135 families, 56% of the population, owned no land.

Navalmoral contained 243 familes (perhaps 1,100 people)
and 1,000 acres of grain-producing land.

10. The social structure of Navalmoral, Spain, in the early seventeenth century.
Of 243 families living in a remote upland village south of Toledo, 11 families owned one-third of the village's land, 22 families owned half of it, and 108 families owned all of it. The rest of the inhabitants were 'have-nots', many of them homeless.

sum declined to 2,000 *maravedis* annually; while in 1645, 1647 and 1649, the years that saw the worst harvests of the century, the parish priest wrote sadly in his account-book: 'No charity has been given, since there is nothing to give.'[45]

The lot of the have-nots was little better elsewhere. Even in England, the only European state that boasted an obligatory welfare system (the Poor Law), a failed harvest would double, triple or even quadruple the amount required from the rich to save the poor from starvation so that, in the words of social historian Steve Hindle, it is 'difficult to understand how the agricultural labourer and his family got through the year' in the mid-seventeenth century. Paid farm work was no longer 'a living in itself, but simply a vital cash supplement to a subsistence based on the cultivation of cottage gardens and the exploitation of common rights', occasionally augmented by poor relief; and this precarious situation 'rendered imperative the participation of all family members in the production endeavours of the household economy'. Unless prevented by disability or weakness, until the later seventeenth century most ordinary English men and women started to earn their living at age six or seven and 'literally worked themselves to death'.[46]

The situation of 'ordinary men and women' was, of course, even worse in war zones. In the Maas valley of the South Netherlands, the magistrates of St Truiden cancelled their annual fair in 1630 on account of 'these times of war, of shortage of grain, of contagious disease, and of misery'. Four years later the parish priest at neighbouring Emael wrote in his diary: 'This year, we have been tested in astonishing fashion by sickness, war, famine and fire. First a violent plague struck the village during the months of June and July, taking seventeen victims. Immediately afterwards, war unexpectedly came to us' when three Spanish regiments (that is, troops sent to defend them) 'lodged here. They behaved worse than barbarously: they destroyed everything; they cut trees, completely demolished many houses, and trampled whatever grain they could not steal, not even leaving enough to appease the hunger of the poor farmers. For that reason, we did not collect the tithe this year.' Although none of these individual disasters was unprecedented, they had rarely if ever coincided: throughout the Maasland, in 1634 tithe receipts (which mirrored agricultural production and, as in Spain, provided the principal form of relief for the poor) sank to the lowest level ever recorded between 1620 and 1750.[47]

In China, too, agricultural production fell to its lowest levels in the mid-seventeenth century and, once again, brought about the collapse of traditional forms of charity. Each county town maintained (at least in theory) a state-run 'Ever Normal' granary, with smaller additional repositories elsewhere to 'nourish the people'; but by the seventeenth century many lay empty, either through corruption or incompetence. In an attempt to avert disaster, groups of concerned citizens therefore created 'voluntary societies for sharing goodness'. Some distributed aid to impoverished widows, padded winter jackets to the poor, and coffins in which to bury unclaimed corpses; others set up soup kitchens and advanced money to small businesses in trouble; others still established orphanages, medical dispensaries and schools for the poor. Most voluntary societies, however, only provided assistance to a select few. Some conducted a 'background check' before issuing approved supplicants with a 'Ration Card'; others helped only those recommended by members (including their own relatives, in order to escape responsibility for maintaining them). Private charity therefore only scratched the surface of poverty. In 1641, on the eve of the great famine, the founder of a benevolent society in Zhejiang province claimed that although it now helped 'three to four hundred people' (compared with only a few dozen a decade before), he feared that 'the number of persons who are kept alive or given burials is still less than 10 to 20 per cent' of the total poor.[48]

Even this limited charity often ceased during the Ming-Qing transition. In Tancheng county (Shandong), the local elite informed a newly arrived magistrate in 1670 that the area 'has long been destitute and ravaged. For thirty years now fields have lain under flood water or weeds.' Famine, disease and bandits had depopulated the county in the 1630s; the Manchu army ravaged the county and sacked its capital in 1642; torrential rain caused the local rivers to flood, destroying the harvest, four times between 1649 and 1659. The county's assessment for forced labour therefore fell from just over 40,000 able-bodied males in the 1630s to under 33,000 in 1643 and to under 10,000 in 1646. By 1670, the new magistrate learned, 'many people held their lives to be of no value, for the area was so wasted and barren, the common people so poor and had suffered so much, that essentially they knew none of the joys of being alive'.[49]

The people of Shandong were not alone in believing that they had faced horrors of unprecedented severity. Others, especially those living on marginal lands, in towns, or in macro-regions, wrote similar laments. Enomoto Yazaemon, a Japanese salt merchant near Edo, thought that 'the world was in flames from the time I was 15 [1638] to the time I was 18'. In Europe, a German cloth merchant lamented that 'there have been so many deaths that the like of it has never been heard in human history'; while a chronicler in Burgundy saw 'everywhere the face of death' when war, plague and harvest failure struck simultaneously. 'We lived from grass taken from the gardens and the fields,' he wrote. 'Posterity would never believe it.' A German pastor expressed the same resignation: 'Our descendants will never believe what miseries we have suffered'; while one of his Catholic clerical colleagues asked rhetorically: 'Who could have described so many vile knaves, with all their evil tricks and wicked villainies? . . . I would not have had time or opportunity, nor could I have laid hands on enough pens, ink or paper.'[50] The incredulity and pessimism of these writers become explicable only when we look more closely at the scale of the demographic catastrophe which they had witnessed – a catastrophe that may have reduced the size of the global population by one-third.

'A third of the world has died': Surviving in the Seventeenth Century[1]

THE DRAMATIC REDUCTION IN FOOD SUPPLY IN THE MID-SEVENTEENTH century, whether through human or natural agency, forced many human communities to take urgent and extreme measures to reduce their food consumption. The easiest and most effective way to do this was to reduce the number of mouths to feed; and although this process took different forms in different parts of the globe, almost everywhere the population fell steadily from the 1620s until a new equilibrium emerged between supply and demand for basic resources – often not until the 1680s.

The exact scale of demographic contraction is hard to document. In 1654 the abbess of the convent of Port-Royal near Paris lamented that 'a third of the world has died', while, a generation later, the Chinese emperor asserted that during the transition from the Ming to the Qing dynasties 'over half of China's population perished'. Many surviving statistical data support such claims. Thus the parish registers from Île-de-France, where Port-Royal stood, show that 'almost one quarter of the population vanished in a single year'. In China, tentative reconstruction of population levels in Tangcheng county in Jiangnan between 1631 and 1645 shows that some areas suffered almost 60 per cent losses.[2] The number of taxable households in western Poland also fell by more than 50 per cent between the census of 1629 and that of 1661 while, further east, tax registers in what is now Belarus showed falls of between 40 and 95 per cent in urban populations between 1648 and 1667 (see chapter 6 below). In Germany, parts of Pomerania and Mecklenburg in the north, like parts of Hessen and the Palatinate in the centre, apparently lost two-thirds of their population between 1618 and 1648. Württemberg, in the southwest, boasted a population of 450,000 in 1618 but only 100,000 in 1639.

Even when detailed demographic records chart a decline, they do not always reveal the exact causes. Thus London's 'Bills of Mortality', which printed the weekly totals of burials in each parish of the capital together with the causes of death, included such esoteric afflictions as 'blasted', 'frighted' and 'headmouldshot' as well as different types of homicide ('murthered and shot'), recognizable diseases ('smallpox', 'French pox') and conditions ('childbed'), as well as suicide ('Hang'd and made away themselves': Plate 25). Taken together, the 'Bills' and other available data nevertheless reveal three distinct mechanisms that reduced the global population during the seventeenth century:

- More deaths through suicide, disease, or war;
- Fewer births, either through postponing or preventing marriage, or through infanticide and child abandonment;
- More migration.

I. Death: 'Never send to know for whom the bell tolls'[3]

Suicide

An unprecedented number of people in the mid-seventeenth century appear to have reacted to adversity by killing themselves. During a famine in Scotland in the 1630s, some clerics reviewed the grim alternatives that faced their parishioners: 'The picture of death is seen in the faces of many. Some devour the seaware [kelp and seaweed]; some eat dogs . . . Many are reduced to that extremity that they are forced to steal and thereafter are executed; *and some have desperately run into the sea and drowned themselves.*' At much the same time, a Catholic at the court of Charles I gloated over an epidemic of suicides among Protestant clergymen: 'a divine (and, they say, an excellent preacher)' had 'strangled himself with a garter, and the like did another minister lately in Manchester'; 'a third minister . . . fell upon his owne sword', while Dr Henry Butts, vice-chancellor of Cambridge University, 'on Easter daye in the morning hanged himself'. In 1637 the preface to a comprehensive English treatise on suicide (326 pages plus index) asserted that 'scarce an age since the beginning of the world has afforded more examples' of people who 'drowned themselves' or committed suicide in other ways. 'There are many more self-murderers than the world takes notice of,' it announced. 'Yea, the world is full of them.'[4]

In England, suicide was not only a felony, and so came before the courts, but also the subject of 'shaming' rituals such as dragging the corpse through the streets and (at least in some counties) burial in unconsecrated ground with a stake through the heart. So many mid-seventeenth-century records have disappeared that it is almost impossible to document fluctuations, but the surviving evidence suggests that twice as many English men as women took their own lives; that almost one-third of them were under 20 years old; and that about one-fifth were over 60. Although we can only guess at their motives, the court testimony of witnesses, as well as accounts by those who attempted to kill themselves but failed, suggest two broad categories. Some felt overwhelmed by a direct threat to their psychological or physical survival, such as bereavement, family strife and fear. Thus several mothers and a few fathers killed themselves after their children died; a 9-year-old boy tried to drown himself because he no longer wanted to live in poverty and misery; a young woman took her own life because she could not marry the man she loved; and a 12-year-old apprentice hanged himself when, after running away from a brutal master, his parents sent him back. A second group of unfortunates killed themselves because they had lost their social standing and could not live with the shame, such as women who became pregnant outside wedlock (especially as the result of incest or rape); and those who had suffered a public humiliation, such as a clerk who shot himself in prison after his arrest for debt.⁵ Meanwhile, in seventeenth-century Scotland more than three times as many men as women 'made away with themselves', and just over half were farmers while just over a quarter lived and worked in towns. Surviving data from Bavaria demonstrate the difficulty in achieving greater precision: of some 300 cases of suicide reported to the duchy's courts between 1611 and 1670, almost 90 per cent occurred before 1635 – a skewed distribution that presumably reflects the collapse of the judicial system during the Thirty Years War rather than an absence of suicides. But since surviving court records from other decades show that suicides often rose (or at least became more visible) during times of economic and political crisis, it seems highly likely that 'self-killing' increased during the mid-seventeenth century.⁶

Suicides in China certainly increased at this time, but not always for the same reasons. Although, as in Europe, motives included melancholy, economic misery and disappointment in love, as well as desperation during a period of turmoil, many also sought to humiliate, embarrass or harm someone else. This could be achieved relatively easily because Chinese law insisted that a dead body must remain untouched until the local magistrate came to make a full inquiry – one that often uncovered the provocations, the humiliating cruelties, the cheating and the insults that had forced the deceased to take their own life. To remove any possible doubt, many desperate people killed themselves at the exact site where the ill-treatment had taken place: the humiliated apprentice in his master's shop; the young childless bride outside the door of her abusive mother-in-law; the members of a starving family in the orchard of a local magistrate who had failed to 'nourish the people' – seen as the primary duty of government officials throughout imperial China (Plate 5).

Such 'revenge' suicides may have increased during the turbulent transition from Ming to Qing rule, as the shortage of resources exacerbated tensions and desperation within each family, but three other factors added significantly to the total of women who killed themselves. First, Confucian teaching encouraged virtuous women to commit suicide in two circumstances: those who had been raped or otherwise 'dishonoured' should kill themselves immediately to 'avoid the shame', while a virtuous widow should 'follow her husband' to the grave as soon as he died. The collapse of public order in the mid-seventeenth century dramatically increased the number of women affected by these precepts.

When Qing forces took Yangzhou by storm in 1645 (pages 29–30 above), many women in the city jumped into deep wells or hanged themselves while others burned themselves to death in their own home or slit their throats rather than fall into the hands of the soldiers and be raped, enslaved, or forced to watch the abuse and murder of their families.⁷ Some young women either slit their noses or cut off their ears, so that they could not be forced to remarry (Confucian rites required a 'whole body'); others, before killing themselves, composed a brief autobiography in prose followed by a few verses expressing anguish at their plight: a new genre of literature: *tibishi*, or 'poems inscribed on walls'. The 'suicide note' left by Wei Qinniang, 'a girl from Chicheng' (Zhejiang province), seems typical. Just three months after she got married, soldiers captured her and carried her away from her husband (whose fate she never discovered). Somehow she escaped and 'disfigured my face and covered myself with dirt to obliterate my tracks. During the day I begged by the side of the road and at night I laid low in the blue grass. I swallowed my sobs and wept in secret, fearing that others might find me.' At last she found shelter in an abandoned temple where 'I look at my shadow and pity myself: my pretty face has been ruined by dust and wind, and my clothes have all been muddied.' Eventually 'With no news from home, I recite a few quatrains and in tears write them on the wall. If some compassionate men of virtue would pass them on to my family, it would suffice to make my lonely parents understand.' She then killed herself. Her moving farewell, inscribed on the wall of her temple refuge, is all we know about her.[8] Other elite women killed themselves out of loyalty to the Ming. Just before her death, the foster-mother of the scholar-official Gu Yanwu told him: 'Although only a woman, I have received favour from the [Ming] dynasty; to perish with the dynasty is no more than my duty.' When news arrived that Qing troops were approaching her home, she stopped eating and died 15 days later.[9]

Many Chinese women killed themselves after war claimed the lives of their husbands. In 1621, for example, the wife of an official in a town in Liaodong heard that it had fallen to Manchu forces. Assuming that her husband had died heroically for the Ming cause, she 'led more than forty household relatives and retainers into suicide, jumping into a well with her own granddaughter in her arms'. Some husbands expected no less. Just before Yangzhou fell in 1645, Shi Kefa, the Ming commander, wrote two letters of farewell to his wife, both of them enquiring pointedly: '[Since] sooner or later I must die, I wonder whether my wife is willing to follow me?'[10] Even the junior scholar Wang Xiuchu expected his pregnant wife to commit suicide rather than survive alone, informing her: '"Enemy soldiers have entered the city. If things go awry, you should cut short your own life." "Yes," his wife replied: "Let me give you my few pieces of silver to keep." And then she sobbed, "Women like me in situations like this no longer think to live in the human world."' Both the soldier Shi and the scholar Wang thus (in the words of Lynn Struve) 'expected their wives to place the honour and well-being of their husbands and families above the preservation of their own lives. Times of acute disruption, such as the Ming-Qing conflict, demanded such sacrifices from hundreds of thousands of women.'[11]

'Times of acute disruption' also increased suicides among males. Many scholar officials of the Ming killed themselves in accordance with the Confucian adage: 'the commanders of the troops have to die when they are defeated; the administrators of the state have also to die when the state is in peril'. Many did just that, especially in the south. As the Manchu army approached Yangzhou one young scholar declared that 'matters having reached this point, I will read the sage's books and, retaining my honour, I will die': accordingly, with the Book of Changes open in his hand he jumped into a well and drowned. One colleague killed himself next to the image of Confucius, while others hanged themselves after writing appropriate poems. Others still drowned themselves in the Yangzi, the Grand Canal, or a local well, and a few hid and starved themselves to death.[12]

A few protested that such sacrifices were needless – in his *Credible record of 1644* the official Qian Xing argued (after shifting allegiance from Ming to Qing) that 'if everyone dies at the time of national calamity, the whole country will be ruined; the monarch will be killed; and the whole world will be handed over on a silver platter' – but suicide remained common. When in 1670 a new magistrate took up his post in Tancheng county, Shandong province, he noted that 'many people held their lives to be of no value, for the area was so wasted and barren' that 'every day one would hear that someone had hanged himself from a beam and killed himself. Others, at intervals, cut their throats or threw themselves into the river.' The practice remained common enough in 1688 to justify an imperial edict that forbade widows to 'treat life lightly' and kill themselves. Instead they must serve their parents-in-law and raise their children.[13]

Suicides rose notably during the mid-seventeenth crisis in two other societies: Russia and India. In the former, the practice mainly involved males. From the 1630s onwards, a group of Orthodox Christians became convinced that the end of the world was imminent and immured themselves in hermitages and convents. Some of them, later known as 'Old Believers', concluded that the tsar was the Antichrist whose mistaken religious innovations brought the apocalypse ever nearer; and from the 1660s they defied him. When the government sent troops against them, they killed themselves rather than submit. According to one study, 'the total number of suicides ran into tens of thousands'.[14]

In India, by contrast, suicide normally involved women. Hindus believe that a virtuous woman has the power to preserve and prolong her husband's life; and although this brought her great status while married, it brought blame if her husband died. Respectable Hindu widows were expected to expiate their 'guilt' by committing *suttee* (from *sati*, 'a virtuous woman'), either by casting themselves onto their husband's funeral pyre or by being buried alive beside it. Conveniently for their in-laws, suicide resolved another issue. Hindu custom gave a widow the right both to a share of her late husband's goods and to support from his surviving family – and suttee irrevocably ended both obligations. Widows who refused suttee immediately became marginalized: they could not remarry, and many became either slaves or prostitutes (indeed in Marathi, 'the word for widow and the word for prostitute were in some contexts interchangeable'). Although Muslim rulers (including the Mughals) tried to abolish suttee, many European visitors encountered it. Thus in 1630, in Gujarat, the Cornish world-traveller Peter Mundy watched in amazement as the beautiful widow of a Hindu trader climbed into a special structure atop the funeral pyre and took her husband's head on her lap before she herself set fire to the surrounding kindling.[15] Although no official total of suttee survives, a Dutch merchant residing in the Mughal capital in the 1620s claimed that 'in Agra this commonly occurs about *two or three times a week*'. It seems reasonable to suppose that the pressure on widows to commit suicide grew in response to both the higher mortality among males caused by war and the increased pressure on resources caused by famine.[16]

Sick to Death

Almost everywhere in the seventeenth-century world, the most lethal disease was smallpox. The smallpox virus spreads rapidly and directly between humans by inhalation, and before the introduction of preventive measures it killed around one-third of all those infected, and up to one-half of infected infants and pregnant women. In addition, according to an experienced French midwife, 'almost all women with child that are attacked' by smallpox 'miscarry, and are in great danger of their lives'. Smallpox survivors, after several weeks in agony, often emerged with disfiguring scars, with deformed or stunted limbs, or with impaired sight. Smallpox spared no one: among the ruling dynasties of western Europe, it carried off Philip IV's brother the Cardinal-Infante in 1641 and his son and heir Balthasar Carlos in 1646; Prince William II of Orange in 1650; two siblings of Charles II of England in 1660 and his niece Queen Mary II in 1694; and Louis XIV's heir in 1711. The only 'positive' aspect of the disease is that those who survive it acquire a lifelong immunity.[17]

Smallpox appears to have become both more deadly and more widespread in the seventeenth century. An English tract of 1665 about 'the tyranny of diseases' devoted a whole section to their apparent 'alteration from their old state and condition'; in particular, it claimed that smallpox was 'very gentle' until 'about forty years ago and less' and far more lethal thereafter.[18] Three considerations support this contention. First, given its highly infectious character, once smallpox entered a community it spread fast; therefore the proliferation of areas of dense settlement, such as cities and macro-regions, increased mass deaths from epidemics. Second, the transportation of African slaves to both western Europe and America introduced new and apparently more lethal strains of the disease from another continent. Third, communities rarely exposed to smallpox always suffer unusually high mortality at first contact and, as previously isolated areas entered the global economy in the seventeenth century, virtually all their inhabitants succumbed at the same time. In England, a single smallpox carrier in 1627 infected over 2,000 people on the Isle of Wight, normally shielded from outbreaks on the mainland, and most of those infected died. In East Asia, the Manchus, who had previously lived in small and relatively isolated communities on the steppe, likewise suffered heavily when they invaded China and encountered smallpox for the first time. In 1622, shortly after their first incursion into Chinese territory, the Manchu leaders established a 'Smallpox Investigation Agency' to identify and isolate suspect cases; and they later created 'Shelters for keeping smallpox at bay', to which those not infected by the disease could escape. To preserve the military effectiveness of their armies they only entrusted senior commands to smallpox survivors. Nevertheless in 1649 smallpox killed one of the emperor's uncles as he directed the conquest of south China, and 12 years later it killed the emperor himself.[19]

In the early modern world, only one other disease killed as many people as smallpox: bubonic plague. Although epidemics were less frequent, they too spared no one: men and women, children and seniors, saints and sinners, rich and poor all perished in agony – many within 24 hours and most within 48 hours of infection.

An epidemic could increase deaths in affected communities sixfold because, according to Geronimo Gatta, a doctor from Naples, whereas 'in the countryside it is possible to keep a suitable distance between the infected and the healthy', those living in towns had no escape. Gatta knew whereof he spoke: he had just survived a plague epidemic that in 1656 reduced the population of his native city from almost 300,000 to perhaps 150,000 in a matter of months. In the neighbouring town of Eboli, almost 1,000 families took Easter communion in 1656, but scarcely one-fifth knelt at their local altar unscathed one year later; the plague had totally eliminated over 80 families with one or two members, 27 families with three members, 15 families with four, and 14 more families with between five and seven.[20] The same epidemic that devastated Naples and Eboli had already ravaged large parts of the Iberian Peninsula, creating what the eminent historian Antonio Domínguez Ortiz called 'the worst demographic catastrophe to strike Spain in modern times'; and it went on to kill at least 39,000 people in Genoa. Many other port cities, including Seville and Naples, lost half their population. Some did not recover their pre-plague levels until the nineteenth century (Fig. 11).[21]

Many cities of northern Europe also suffered catastrophic losses from plague in the mid-seventeenth century. In 1654 an epidemic struck Moscow with particular ferocity. Although we lack totals for the entire city, within the walls of the Kremlin, 26 people at the Chudov monastery survived but 182 died, while in three convents of nuns 107 survived but 272 perished. In 1663–4 another epidemic afflicted Amsterdam (where it killed 50,000 people), and other Dutch cities, before crossing to London, where it killed well over 100,000 people in 1665 – perhaps 15,000 in the single week 12–19 September, 'the grimmest week for burials in London's long history' with 'between one and two thousand bodies' thrown into graves and anonymous 'plague pits' every night.[22]

Plague and smallpox, together with typhus, measles and fever, belong to a cluster of deadly diseases that correlate closely with harvest yields: that is, the number of victims in each epidemic to some extent reflected the food supply. It is therefore not surprising to find that both the frequency and the intensity of these diseases increased amid the famines caused by the Little Ice Age. England's demographic records, which have survived better than those of other European countries, show eight years of high mortality between 1544 and 1666 caused by plague, of which half occurred after 1625; while a survey of mortality crises in Italy between 1575 and 1886 shows more episodes between 1620 and 1660 than at any other time.[23]

Climatic adversity promoted sickness everywhere. In China, acute drought caused epidemics as well as famines: a study of County Gazetteers in Jiangnan revealed over 100 locations affected by disease in the famine year 1641. Meanwhile in Serrès, Macedonia, an Orthodox priest left a particularly vivid account of the same catastrophic combination. The trouble began with the constant rains of summer 1641, which turned into snow during the grape harvest, so that many labourers perished of cold in the fields. The weather turned unusually mild until more unseasonable snow fell in March and April 1642, and during this climatic anomaly the plague took hold in the region with unsurpassed severity: not only did

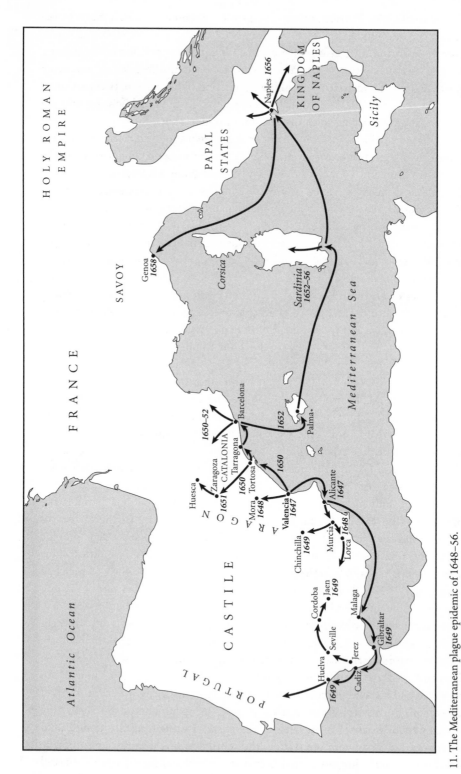

11. The Mediterranean plague epidemic of 1648–56.

After ravaging Andalucia, where it caused demographic losses that took two centuries to make good, the plague epidemic spread along Spain's eastern coast before crossing to Naples, and finally Genoa, where it killed half the city's population. Notably, Castile maintained an effective quarantine and escaped the epidemic.

it afflict virtually every family in town and country alike but 'of a hundred who fell ill, only one recovered'.[24]

Climate, corruption, hoarding and war could all intensify the effects of epidemics. According to the English merchants in Gujarat, India, all these factors increased mortality from the disease in 1631. The Mughal emperor's campaigns prevented 'the supplies of corne to these parts from those others of greatyr plenty; and the raynes hereabout having fallen superfluously; which, with bad government, is cause of the highest extreame of scarcity.' And 'to afflict the more,' the merchants added, 'not a family hath not been visited with agues, fevers and pestilentiall diseases'. In short, 'Never in the memory of man [has] the like famine and mortality happened.'[25] Italy also experienced an unprecedented demographic catastrophe at this time – indeed, according to a recent study, 'no other area of Europe came near to the overall losses suffered by the peninsula'. The crisis began in 1629 when torrential rains destroyed the harvest in northern and central Italy and so created serious overpopu-lation. Then large armies arrived from both Germany and France, where plague already raged, spreading the disease even as they consumed scarce resources and destroyed the fragile infrastructure. Cities and countryside were, it seems, equally affected, and of the six million people living in the north Italian plain in 1628, perhaps two million perished during the following two years.[26] The Alpine passes that served as military corridors suffered worst. In 1630 the plague travelled through the Aosta valley between France and Italy so swiftly that when news reached the regional capital, the secretary of the council (then in session) dropped his pen in mid-sentence – 'We further resolved to ...' – and fled. When he returned, of the valley's 90,000 inhabitants, no fewer than 70,000 had died.[27]

Like smallpox, plague afflicted the young and pregnant women with especial severity. Thus in Barcelona, during the plague epidemic of 1651 a disproportionate number of infants died, because their mothers either perished or lacked milk to feed them, so they were left at the Foundlings' Hospital 'with a ribbon or tag around their arms or leg or neck with the names of their parents written on it'. Miquel Parets, the Barcelona tanner who recorded these details in his diary, observed that 'hardly any' of these foundlings survived, 'because so many were sent there' that it proved impossible to find wet nurses for them all. Parets also noted sadly that children who had once lacked for nothing now became orphans, 'lost and wandering about the city begging ... and in this fashion many children fell sick and never grew up'; while 'of the poor women who were pregnant at this time ... perhaps two among every hundred survived. If they were in the last days of their term all they could do was to commend themselves to God, as most of them simply gave birth and died and many of their babies died with them.' Surviving parish records confirm this: far more women and children than men were buried in Barcelona in 1651 (Fig. 12).[28] Parets himself watched his wife and three of his children die within a month (a fourth child contracted plague but recovered) and his strong religious faith began to waiver. 'God knows why He does what He does,' he wrote in his diary after recording these devas-tating losses; but worse was to come. Although the plague abated, Catalonia was afflicted by one of the longest droughts ever recorded (360 days: almost the entire

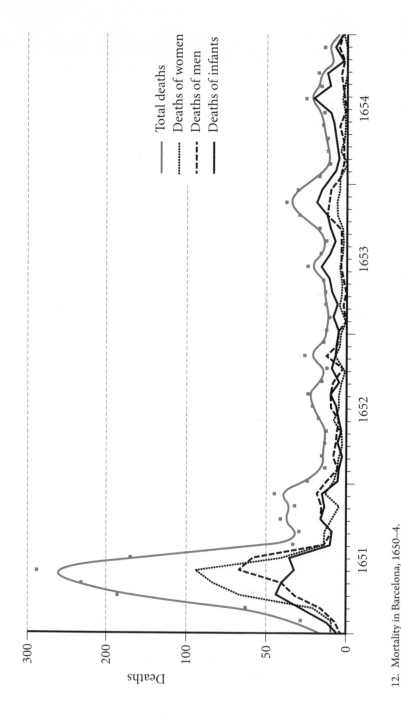

12. Mortality in Barcelona, 1650–4.

Drought had destroyed the Catalan harvest in 1650 and drastically reduced the seed corn available for 1651, when plague broke out. Then the troops of Phillip IV besieged the city, and by the time it surrendered, half the population of Barcelona had perished. The monthly burial totals in the parish of Santa Maria del Pi show that more women than men died in the summer of 1651, and unusually high infant mortality.

year); and, in addition, the troops of Philip IV now arrived to besiege the city, in revolt since 1640. Many of those who had survived the plague died during the blockade, and by the time Barcelona surrendered in October 1652 half its population had died.[29]

Climate change increased the lethality of other diseases, too. In the early eighteenth century, the Icelander Mathias Jochumssen sought to explain why the local population had declined over the previous century: although he acknowledged the importance of smallpox and plague epidemics brought by foreigners, he blamed primarily the 'unusually poor standard of living, and rotten food' caused by the adverse climate, which promoted deficiency diseases such as scurvy and reduced fecundity. A correlation of the variations in the weekly death totals recorded in London's 'Bills of Mortality' with the prevailing temperatures supports this interpretation. A fall of 1°C in winter temperatures coincided with a 2 per cent increase in mortality and with a 1 per cent fall in marital fertility. Medical research suggests some reasons: lower temperatures increase deaths through cardiovascular disease, while 'the elderly, the very young, [and] persons with impaired mobility' are 'disproportionately affected because of their limited physiological capacity to adapt'. In addition, the smoke from coal fires (a serious urban problem in the seventeenth century: see chapter 3 above) carries fine particles that exacerbate cardiac or respiratory diseases such as asthma or bronchitis. Finally, mortality from other common diseases such as mumps, diphtheria, influenza and malaria – all of which kill many people every year – no doubt rose whenever extremes of weather weakened bodily defences or social disruption compromised hygiene.[30]

The Killing Fields

Only wars can eliminate human populations faster than disease, and the greater frequency of armed conflict in the mid-seventeenth century sharply increased mortality. Thus burials in the English county of Berkshire during the seventeenth century show that although the plague epidemic of 1624–5 killed many, the armies who fought there in 1643 killed far more (Fig. 13). Battles, in particular, ended thousands of lives in a matter of hours if not minutes. Thus at Rocroi, France, in 1643 at least 6,000 Spanish veterans died in an evening as they tried to withstand a French artillery bombardment; while the following year at Marston Moor, England, the victorious Parliamentary-Scottish army cut down some 4,000 defeated Royalists in a little over an hour. Also in 1644 at Freiburg, Germany, according to the victorious commander, 'In the twenty-two years that I have been involved in the carnage of war, there has never been such a bloody encounter.' Perhaps 10,000 men perished.[31]

Naval combat also killed many men. During the 'Four Days Battle' between the Dutch and English fleets in June 1666, 'the most terrible, obstinate and bloodiest battle that ever was fought on the seas', the Royal Navy lost over 4,000 men killed, wounded or captured – more than a fifth of those engaged. Seafaring in the age of sail was a dangerous occupation at the best of times, and some officers 'reckoned

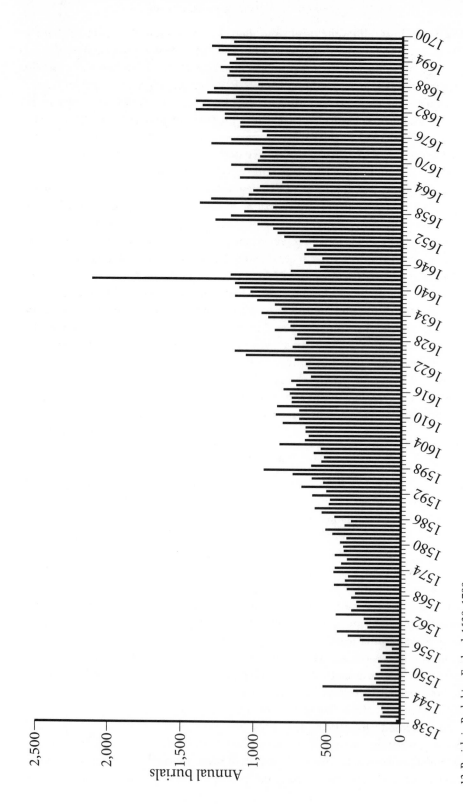

13. Burials in Berkshire, England, 1538–1700.
Plague ravaged almost every parish in Berkshire in 1624 and 1625, but twice as many burials occurred in 1643, when rival armies struggled for control. Almost all of those buried in local churchyards were civilians, not soldiers.

there were four deaths by illness or accident for every one killed in action'; but life for sailors ashore could also prove lethal, because neither the government nor the local population could adequately support the men aboard a fleet that stayed in port for long. Just before the 1667 fighting season began, the commissioner at an English naval base was 'Sorry to see men really perish for want of wherewithal to get nourishment. One [sailor] yesterday came to me crying to get something to relieve him. I ordered him 10 shillings. He went and got hot drink and something to help him, and so drank it, and died within two hours'.[32]

On sea as on land, battles were relatively rare in seventeenth-century Europe; but, one veteran estimated in 1677, 'you will have twenty sieges for one battle' (page 32 above) and sieges also claimed many lives. According to Lucy Hutchinson, an eyewitness of the siege of Nottingham Castle in 1644, 'no one can believe, but those that saw the day, what a strange ebb and flow of courage and cowardice there was in both parties' because, after the catharsis of passing through a killing ground, 'the brave turn cowards, fear unnerves the most mighty, makes the generous base, and great men do those things they blush to think on'. Countless atrocities illustrate her point. Thus the previous year, when the Royalists captured Preston in Lancashire, '"Kill dead! Kill dead!" was the word in the town, killing all before them without any respect . . . their horsemen pursuing the poor amazed people, killing, stripping, and spoiling all they could meet with, nothing regarding the doleful cries of the women and children.'[33]

Civilians everywhere suffered violence at the hands of soldiers. A verse play from the Maas valley in the 1630s stressed the unpredictability of the horrors that war could bring. A 'farmer' described how disaster struck just as he and his family sat down for a meal together:

> It was Wednesday, at dinner time,
> When Mansfeld's soldiers came.
> They had no warrant for lodgings or food,
> But at our hearth they began
> To steal and to plunder,
> Not saying a word, neither 'to the death' nor 'on guard',
> Competing to see who could take the most.

The narrator went on to relate how, while 'competing', the soldiers murdered his father because he tried to resist, then raped his sister, and finally set fire to the farm. Only the smoke allowed him to escape certain death.[34] Similar outrages fill the powerful prints entitled 'The misfortunes of the war' by engraver Jacques Callot from Lorraine, just south of Liège, which show the sack of villages, the torture and murder of their inhabitants, and the revenge of the peasants against isolated detachments of troops.

Two factors increased the likelihood of such atrocities in the mid-seventeenth century. First, the prevailing military conventions (sometimes called the 'Laws of War') held that rebels who took up arms to oppose their ruler 'ought not to be classed as enemies, the two being quite distinct, and so it is more correct to term the armed contention with rebel subjects *execution of legal process, or prosecution*, not war'. It followed that in 'a war waged by a prince with rebels . . . all measures allowed in war are available against them, such as killing them as enemies, enslaving them as prisoners, and, much more, confiscating their property as booty'.[35] The worst military massacres of the age often occurred during civil wars or during the repression of those regarded by the victors as rebels; and the mid-seventeenth century, we know, saw a spate of civil wars and rebellions.

The involvement of protagonists from different religions likewise raised the risk of mass killing. As Blaise Pascal observed in his *Pensées*: 'Men never do so much harm so happily as when they do it through religious conviction' – and the multiple conflicts of the mid-seventeenth century offer abundant examples. Thus in 1631 the Protestant city of Magdeburg in Germany refused to admit a Catholic garrison sent by its suzerain, Emperor Ferdinand II, made an alliance with his enemy and then derisively rejected Ferdinand's demand for surrender. When, after a long blockade, Magdeburg repudiated a final ultimatum, the besiegers launched a successful assault in which perhaps 20,000 men, women and children perished, while fire consumed all but the cathedral and 140 houses.[36]

Few European military leaders in the mid-seventeenth century seem to have felt remorse about such massacres carried out in God's name: on the contrary, they often claimed scriptural warrant, urging their soldiers to follow the Old Testament example of Joshua and the Israelites at Jericho and 'utterly destroy all that was in the city, both man and woman, young and old'.[37] Thus in 1645, at the fall of Basing House, the heavily fortified mansion of a Catholic peer, Protestant preachers whipped up a religious fervour among the besiegers so that when they at last forced an entry no quarter was given. The victors murdered in cold blood six priests found within, shot a former Drury Lane actor (with the sanctimonious comment 'Cursed be he that doth the Lord's Work negligently'), beat out the brains of a young woman who tried to stop a soldier from abusing her father, and stripped naked even those they spared (including the famous architect Inigo Jones, who escaped the slaughter clothed only in a blanket). A newspaper account reassured squeamish readers that such horrors were fully justified because the victims 'were most of them Papists. Therefore our swords did show them little compassion.'[38] Religious passion produced many other atrocities. The advance of a Cossack army through Ukraine in the Polish-Lithuanian Commonwealth in 1648 was accompanied by the massacre of at least 10,000 Jewish settlers; and six years later, as the Russian tsar prepared to invade the Commonwealth, he gave orders 'to burn alive Poles or Belorussians subsequently captured *who would not convert to Orthodoxy*' (see chapter 6). The following year, in Ireland, English troops commanded by Oliver Cromwell carried out a major massacre after they stormed the city of Drogheda. Cromwell later claimed 'I am persuaded that this is a righteous judgment of God upon these barbarous [viz Catholic] wretches, who have imbrued their hands in so much innocent [read: Protestant] blood'; and that accordingly, 'in the heat of the action' he had forbidden his troops 'to spare any that were in arms in the town'. At least 2,500 soldiers and at least 1,000 civilians (including all Catholic priests) perished.[39]

Nevertheless, death in face-to-face violence rarely formed the largest category of mortality in early modern wars. Thus in the century 1620–1719, although some 500,000 Swedish and Finnish troops died in the almost continuous wars waged by their monarchs, only 10 per cent fell in battle (including King Gustavus Adolphus) and only 5 per cent in sieges (including King Charles XII). Of the rest, 10 per cent perished in prison while the remaining 75 per cent succumbed to the normal hardships of war. The stunning scale and impact of premature deaths among these troops emerge from two sets of demographic data. First, between 1621 and 1639, the parish of Bygdeå in northern Sweden provided 230 young men to fight in the 'continental war', where 215 of them died and five more received injuries that left them crippled: only ten of them remained in service in 1639 – and, since the war still had nine more years to run, the odds of their survival were slim. Thus of the 28 conscripts from Bygdeå who mustered in July 1638, all of them under 18 and many of them under 15 years old, all but one had died within three months of reaching the continent. The second set of data comes from the duchy of Finland between 1638 and 1648. These records list every one of the 14,000 local infantrymen conscripted in the duchy to fight in Germany, and reveal that two-thirds of them never came home. Throughout the Swedish Monarchy, military service had virtually become a sentence of death for males.[40]

II. Only Women Bleed

The 'bitter living' of Women

The increased frequency of wars during the seventeenth century also brought serious demographic consequences for women. Some were direct, in that they sometimes became a primary target. Thus the (Protestant) government in Dublin in 1642 instructed their troops fighting the Catholic insurgents not to spare the women they encountered 'being manifestly very deep in the guilt of this rebellion, and, as we are informed, very forward to stir up their husbands, friends and kindred to side therein, and exciting them to cruelty against the English'.[41] Wars also had some indirect adverse impacts on women. Notably, the departure of husbands and sons to fight (and perhaps die) in the wars forced increasing numbers of women either to support families alone or to live as spinsters or widows. In Württemberg, an area of Germany devastated by war, the number of households headed by single women rose to almost one-third of the total – an unprecedented number. In some ravaged villages in Burgundy (France) widows were the *only* householders. In the Swedish parish of Bygdeå, the ratio of men to women in 1620 already stood at 1:1.5, but 20 years of compulsory military service more than doubled the ratio to 1:3.6, while the number of households headed by women multiplied sevenfold. Many of them were 'war widows': the archives of the Swedish central government contain thousands of petitions desperately requesting payment of the wage arrears, or reimbursement of the expenses, due to deceased soldier-husbands, because the petitioner and her children were starving.[42]

A German widow in 1654 spoke for all these indirect victims of war: she was, she lamented, 'a poor woman with only a small field or so to her name' who must therefore '*earn a bitter living*'. If she (or any other woman living alone) fell foul of the law, the males who ran the local courts would sentence her to hard labour; if she failed to behave in a subservient and docile way, her male neighbours would banish her; and, even if they allowed her to stay, they normally denied her the opportunity to learn or practise a trade (and thus compete with them).[43] A 'bitter living', indeed.

The lives of most urban women in the seventeenth century were scarcely sweeter. In many European cities two-thirds of those receiving welfare were women, most of them former servants. Their predominance is easily explained. In a world without domestic appliances or prepared food, as Olwen Hufton has noted, 'the first luxury that any family permitted itself was the services of a girl, a maid of all work, to take on the drudgery involved in carrying water – a major time and energy consumer – and coal or wood, going to market or performing laundry service'.[44] But as soon as a recession occurred, that 'first luxury' became the first casualty. Employers in 'hard times' had no scruples about getting rid of their maids; and even those who retained their jobs might have to forego wages and work in return for their keep. Either way, the chances of getting married and having children before the economy recovered remained slim. The fate of women who worked in industry was no better: unlike male apprentices, who enjoyed some job protection if their employer fell on hard times (or if women themselves fell ill or suffered injury), they would be thrown out of work without any 'social security' to sustain them.

A few Europeans fretted about the demographic consequences of economic recession. Thus in 1619, suspecting that the population in his region had recently declined, Sancho de Moncada, a priest from Toledo, Spain, examined local parish registers for proof (apparently the first person ever to use them in this way). He found that, in the wake of a severe episode of plague and famine in 1599, the registers recorded 'not one half of the marriages that there used to be', so that births in and around Toledo remained far lower than before. In Andalucía, half a century later, Francisco Martínez de Mata also consulted the parish registers and found, like Moncada, that both marriages and births had fallen catastrophically during the harvest failures of the 1640s. Subsequent research by demographers on parish registers has confirmed these findings – but also revealed another important consequence. In the words of E. A. Wrigley, throughout early modern Europe 'Marriage was the hinge on which the demographic system turned'; and when bread prices doubled, marriages normally fell by one-fifth and the age of brides at first marriage rose.[45]

Thanks to the expanding economy of the sixteenth century, European women married on average at age 20 and many gave birth to eight or nine children and some to ten or more. In the first half of the seventeenth century, however, brides were on average 27 or 28 when they married; few gave birth to more than three children; and an increasing number had no children at all. Equally important, more women remained celibate. In England, householders in the seventeenth century sometimes publicly objected at the reading of marriage banns, and after marriage refused to allow couples to live together, if they seemed too poor to raise a family (the prevailing Poor Law system made householders responsible for supporting the local poor). Of Englishwomen born around 1566 who might have married in the 1590s, only 4 per cent failed to do so; but of those born around 1586, who might have married in the 1610s, over 17 per cent failed to do so; and of those born around 1606, who might have married in the 1630s, over 25 per cent failed to do so.[46]

These developments reduced the total population in the seventeenth century more rapidly than they would do today because of remarkably high mortality among both mothers and children. In the words of a prominent (if somewhat patronizing) male midwife: 'Going with child is a rough sea, on which a big-bellied woman and her infant floats the space of nine months: and labour, which is the only port, is so full of dangerous rocks, that very often both the one and the other, after they have arrived and disembarked, have yet need of much help to defend them against divers inconveniences.' Or, as the terse French proverb put it: 'A pregnant woman has one foot in the grave' (*Une femme grosse a un pied dans la fosse*). Surviving records suggest that in Europe perhaps 40 women per 1,000 died as a result of childbirth (compared with 0.12 per 1,000 in much of western Europe today). The death of the mother became even more frequent if the child died in the womb (and since this becomes more frequent at times of scarcity and disease, it must surely have become more frequent during the 1640s). Moreover, as elsewhere in the early modern world, at least one-quarter of all children born in Europe died within their first year, and almost one-half died before reaching the age of reproduction. In the graphic phrase of the French demographic historian Pierre Goubert, in the seventeenth century 'It took two children to make an adult'.[47]

Mothers in the early modern world needed to give birth to at least four children simply to maintain a given population level – *at least* four, because not all of those who survived to adulthood would marry and be fertile. Even in periods of prosperity, a woman who married when she was 27 or 28 would find it hard to give birth to four children, since fecundity waned in her late thirties; and periods of adversity triggered important biological and behavioural responses that reduced fertility. On the one hand, malnutrition leads to more spontaneous abortions and fewer conceptions (sometimes because ovulation has ceased), decreased libido, a rise in the age of menarche, and a fall in the age of menopause. On the other hand, a serious food shortage often reduced coital frequency (either through abstinence or increased spousal separation). At the same time, the greater prevalence of disease associated with famine increased deaths, especially among pregnant women and new mothers. For all these reasons, the birth rate in many if not most European communities in the mid-seventeenth century fell below – often far below – the level required to maintain the overall population (Fig. 14).[48]

The rising age of brides when they first married, together with the increase in female celibacy, had one further deleterious effect: an increased risk of illegitimate pregnancies. Mid-seventeenth-century parish registers reveal that between one-fifth and three-fifths of all births took place only a few months (and sometimes only a few weeks) after the parents' marriage; while pregnancies also increased

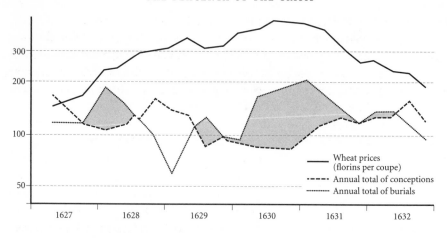

14. A subsistence crisis: Geneva 1627–32.
Burials increased and conceptions declined in step with the rise in the price of bread in Geneva, a
city of 15,000. Similar patterns occurred in communities throughout early modern Europe (and, if
similar serial date existed, probably elsewhere in the northern hemisphere).

among spinsters who never married. Urban court records throughout Europe are full
of testimony from or about young women who came to town looking for work and,
when they could not find it, were tricked or coerced into prostitution. One such
newcomer to London was reassured by her landlady 'that it is better to do so [become
a prostitute] than to steal and be hanged'. Although perhaps true in the short term,
this survival strategy seldom offered a permanent escape from poverty. Instead, it
increased the risk of sexually transmitted diseases, and also created a cruel dilemma
for single mothers if they became pregnant: either they aborted, abandoned or killed
their babies at birth, or else they faced the shame and hardship of having to survive
by begging – in which case they as well as their babies would probably die.[49]

In most of East Asia, the birth rate also fell in the mid-seventeenth century, and
although this decline also reflected a reduction in the reproductive capacity of
women, it reflected different social pressures. In China, several generations of a
family might live together in the same household – a proverb claimed that 'five
generations under one roof' was optimal. Although this happened rarely, a typical
Chinese household included one or more parents and one or more of their married
sons and their families, forming a single economic, religious, social and demographic
unit which could easily number 50 members from three generations. They produced
and consumed in common; they performed collectively the appropriate rites for the
well-being of family members both alive and dead; they shared the burden of caring
for aged and needy relatives; above all, they discussed and determined family size
together, because the purpose of marriage was production as well as reproduction.
'Demographic decisions' in many parts of China were 'never individual' but had to be
'negotiated with co-resident kin according to collective goals and constraints'.[50]

'Negotiation' was important because nearly all Chinese girls who reached puberty
in the seventeenth century married, often while teenagers. Moreover, if a wife failed

to produce a son, husbands with sufficient means might take one or more concubines: a peasant girl purchased for the purpose, a household servant, an entertainer, a prostitute – almost anyone except a woman from their own neighbourhood or 'name'. An active trade in concubines existed in the city of Yangzhou before the sack of 1645, where (according to one contemporary source) 'daughters are as numerous as clouds' and

> At age thirteen or fourteen,
> They are ready.
> Who cares if he is old,
> If he has gold?[51]

To ensure that early and widespread marriage, and the frequent resort to concubines, did not produce more children than each household could support, Chinese families employed one or more of four strategies. First, spouses started to reproduce late: the gap between marriage and becoming a mother for the first time averaged three years in China, compared with 18 months in western Europe. Second, wives stopped reproducing early: the mean age of Chinese women when they gave birth to their last child was 33 or 34, compared with 40 for their west European counterparts, and the average span between the first and last child was 11 years, against 14 in Europe. Third, Chinese mothers got rid of the children they (or their relatives) did not want. Many families either surrendered for adoption children they could not feed (especially boys, to families who lacked sons of their own) or sold them (especially girls, who became concubines or prostitutes). Some pregnancies were also either avoided or terminated. Early modern Chinese medical literature described many methods of contraception and abortion; Chinese physicians always placed the health of the mother before that of the foetus; and imperial law criminalized neither procuring nor performing an abortion. Finally, parents could and did murder their unwanted offspring – especially girls. Chinese families intensified their use of all four strategies for child limitation in the mid-seventeenth century – starting to reproduce later; ceasing to reproduce earlier; increasing birth intervals and giving up more children for adoption; and killing off more children at birth.

Infanticide and Abortion

In the words of Francesca Bray, an eminent historian of China: 'Infanticide is the most effective way of controlling family size in response to sudden crisis. It is also a foolproof way of exercising sex selection if all other means fail.' Overall, the ruling Qing dynasty (for whom remarkably precise data are available) killed perhaps 10 per cent of all their daughters, many of them at birth, but in the 1640s and 1650s poorer members of the dynasty 'killed almost twice as many of their daughters' as their richer relatives. Although no other family compiled figures of similar precision, it seems that in Manchuria, the Qing homeland, peasant families killed between one-fifth and one-quarter of their daughters at birth in 'normal' years, and more in years of dearth; while in Liaoning, just to the south, the sex ratio among the *last* children born to peasant families stood at 500 boys for every 100 girls. No biological circumstance can account for such gender imbalance: widespread female infanticide is the only possible explanation.[52] Female infanticide was also common in southern China. According to a county gazetteer from Fujian, 'When a baby is born, the midwife holds it in her hands for examination. If it is a girl she just throws her into a tub and asks the mother, "Keep it or not?" If the answer is "No", she calls for water and holds the baby upside down by the feet, dipping her head in the water.' A poem from Jiangnan, written in the form of an appeal from one woman to others in the region, ended bitterly:

> Even before you've heard me out, or sighed a few times in regret,
> In one town after another, *girls are no sooner born than dead.*

At times of economic adversity, poor families in China may have killed as many as half their children at birth.[53]

Infanticide was also widespread in Russia, where early modern households often consisted of three or four families (usually related) living together, and many women married at the age of 12 or 13. Children born out of wedlock and children born to the very poor seem to have been killed by their parents far more often than in the West – at least in part because both Church and State took a relatively lenient view of the matter. The medieval Russian version of St Basil's Rule forgave women who killed their children 'from simplicity or ignorance, *or because of scarcity of necessities*'; and although the comprehensive law code issued in 1649 decreed death for a mother who killed a child conceived in adultery, 'If a father or mother kills [their legitimate] son or daughter', the penalty was that 'they shall be imprisoned for a year', and after that 'they shall not be punished'.[54] The law said nothing about foundlings and orphans (a draft decree of 1683 establishing state orphanages remained a dead letter until 1712) – perhaps because Russia's harsh climate reduced their numbers anyway. The available records show that maximum sexual activity among the rural population took place just after the harvest, which produced a peak in births just before the next growing season. This in turn produced a peak in infant mortality because the short growing season made it essential for Russian women to work in the fields at seedtime and harvest, which meant that those who were still infants at that point might either receive solid foods too early or else get insanitary 'pacifiers' that killed them. As the Little Ice Age reduced the length of the growing season still further, the few surviving demographic records show an increase in infant mortality.[55]

Abortion and infanticide were also common in western Europe. In 1660, according to the Dean of the Faculty of Medicine in Paris, the local clergy 'have made a calculation that in the past year, six hundred women have confessed that they had killed and destroyed the fruit of their womb'.[56] Throughout the seventeenth century, infanticide constituted the commonest capital crime tried by the *Parlement* of Paris, the law court with the largest jurisdiction in early modern Europe. Its cases show that virtually all those accused were women, half of them spinsters and another quarter widows; and that their numbers rose in times of economic hardship. One quarter of the women tried for infanticide admitted that they had also attempted unsuccessfully to terminate their pregnancy.[57]

The increasing frequency of abortion and infanticide in the seventeenth century led many European states to pass harsh legislation against offenders. An English statute against infanticide in 1624 explicitly targeted unmarried mothers ('lewd women'), as even its title made clear: 'Act to Prevent the Murdering of *Bastard* Children'. Studies of prosecutions brought under the new law show that all the victims were illegitimate (mostly born to young women in domestic service) and that almost all died on their first day of life (most through strangulation, suffocation, exposure or drowning, though a few had been beaten to death or thrown into a fire). In Germany, the government of Württemberg in 1658 issued a law that enjoined the denunciation of all women suspected of killing their offspring: almost 130 cases came to trial over the next 40 years: the average age of the mothers was 25; almost all were single; and almost all were sentenced to death.[58]

Nevertheless, many infanticides in early modern Europe evidently went undetected, despite the diligence of neighbours (many of whom devoted considerable time to watching whether or not single women produced bloodstained laundry once a month). Perhaps the most striking evidence comes from the French city of Rennes, where workmen replacing old drains in 1721 found one that contained about 80 skeletons of infants – and yet no one had been charged with their deaths. The total of murdered infants, in Rennes and elsewhere in Europe, would surely have been higher had not two institutions offered legal opportunities for fertile women to avoid raising children in times of crisis: foundling hospitals and, in Catholic countries, nunneries.

'Get thee to a nunnery'[59]

In Italy, by 1650, perhaps 70,000 females lived in nunneries, most of them in towns. Nunneries housed 8 per cent of the total female population in Bologna, 9 per cent in Ferrara, 11 per cent in Florence and 12 per cent in Siena. By then France boasted at least as many nuns, while Spain had 20,000, with many more in Germany, the South Netherlands and Poland.[60] The cities of Russia and the Balkans also included a significant population of cloistered females, as did those of Catholic Europe's colonies – and in every region, the number of nuns increased markedly in the course of the seventeenth century. Why? Many nuns, like Isabel Flores de Oliva (later canonized as Santa Rosa of Lima), took the veil through a religious vocation; others did so because some disability placed them at a disadvantage in the outside world; others still sought temporary refuge in the cloisters from abusive husbands or while their husbands were away. A few, no doubt, felt attracted by the lavish lifestyle of certain convents, where servants and slaves made up half the population (and in some nunneries even outnumbered the nuns). But a considerable number of young women in the seventeenth century entered convents against their will. Elena Cassandra Tarrabotti (1604–52), daughter of a Venetian patriarch, was one of them.

Her father sent her to a nunnery at age 13 claiming that, because of the economic depression, he lacked the money for an appropriate dowry. There she wrote several books – with titles like *Innocence undone or the father's tyranny* and *The nun's hell* – lamenting her lot. 'Consider it a fact,' she thundered in one of them, 'that more than one-third of nuns, confined against their will, find their senses opposing their reason, and subject themselves unwillingly and out of fear to the outrageous misfortunes cruelly created for them' by their fathers. It would be a kindness, she continued provocatively, if parents strangled their daughters at birth rather than condemn them to a life behind bars against their will.[61]

Although Tarrabotti's works went straight onto the *Index of Prohibited Books*, the proportion of daughters of patrician families forced to take the veil increased as the seventeenth-century crisis deepened. In Venice, in 1642, 80 per cent of them became nuns, and in 1656, 90 per cent. Although patricians justified their 'sacrifice' of a daughter as an act of exemplary piety, they doubtless consoled themselves with the fact that marriage dowries averaged 1,500 scudi, whereas it cost only 400 to place a daughter in even a prestigious convent. Regardless of motive, incarcerating daughters in a cloister proved highly effective in reducing the number of elite women available to marry and reproduce: 40 Venetian patricians married annually in the 1580s, but under 30 in the 1650s.[62]

Many convents also accepted foundlings. Indeed, some institutions installed a special 'wheel of fortune' to make it easier for mothers to abandon their unwanted offspring: they could place their babies on the wheel outside anonymously and then rotate it inwards for collection within. At the Foundling Hospital of Milan, where desperate mothers left some 400 babies a year, use of the 'wheel of fortune' (*scaffetta*) followed the fluctuations in grain prices with sickening regularity: in a year of food scarcity four or five infants might be placed on the wheel in a single night (Fig. 15). Likewise, in Madrid, where almost 15 per cent of all children baptized in the mid-seventeenth century had been abandoned by their parents, the city's Foundling Hospital took in about 500 children a year; while the Foundling Hospital of Seville averaged almost 300 admissions a year – increasing notably during periods of economic adversity. In cities that lacked a Foundling Hospital, such as London, up to 1,000 infants a year were 'found on the streets, stalls and dunghills of the capital', their number likewise rising and falling in step with the price of bread.[63]

Parents who abandoned their babies on dunghills probably did not intend them to live, so their action might be seen as infanticide; others, however, not only left their child in a public place but also wrote a heart-wrenching note of explanation. By chance, about 150 notes have survived from the Madrid Foundling Hospital in the 1620s. All were small – some of them very small, written on a scrap of paper torn from a book or on the back of a document, and in one case on the back of a playing card – and stated whether the child had been baptized or not, and usually its name, date of birth and saint's day. A few provided a brief explanation (parents too poor; mother abandoned by her lover; mother died in childbirth; mother unable to produce milk; in one case 'a well-known lady who does not wish to be found out'). The saddest messages of all were those written in the first person (Plate 6):

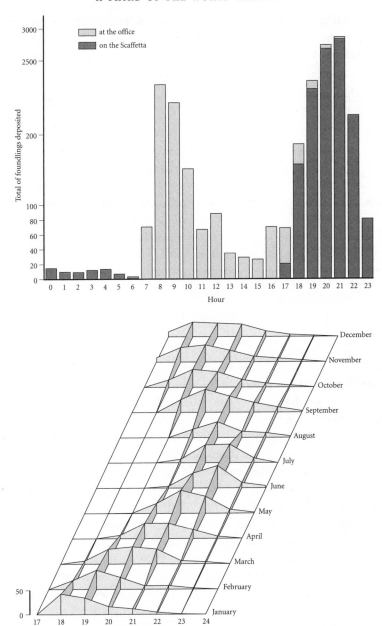

15. Children abandoned at the Foundling Hospital of Milan.

The upper graph shows the time at which parents delivered the children they could not feed to the Foundling Hosital of Milan. In daytime, foundlings were delivered to the staff, but the number rose after dark, with most infants left anonymously on the 'scaffetta' or 'wheel of fortune'. The lower register leaves no doubt about this: the hour that saw most infants abandoned changed according to the season of the year (between 5 and 6 p.m. in December and January; between 9 and 10 p.m. between June and August), presumably to spare the distraught parent the shame of being seen. Although these data come from the eighteenth century, the same patterns prevailed a century earlier.

My name is Ana. I have been baptized. My parents are honourable people who, because they are poor, entrust me to Our Lady and St Joseph. I beg you to entrust me to someone who will look after me.

A[64]

Almost certainly, Ana pleaded in vain. Most of those who entered a Foundling Hospital, whether in Madrid or elsewhere, died there – for the simple reason that almost half of all foundlings were abandoned within their first week, and at that vulnerable age, without the immediate intervention of a wet nurse, they would die. Moreover, since 'mortality tends to increase with admissions', life expectations fell as admissions rose: in the Hospital of the Innocents in Florence, one-third of the 700 foundlings abandoned in the famine year 1629 died on their first day; half died within a week; and almost two-thirds died within a month. Leaving a newborn baby on the 'wheel of fortune' may thus not technically have been infanticide, but the effect was much the same: it provided an additional method, brutal but effective, of rapidly reducing the number of mouths to feed in a crisis.[65]

III. Migration

Voluntary Migration

Well over one million West Europeans responded to economic adversity in the seventeenth century by migrating to find a better life abroad. So many Scots left the kingdom to make a living in Poland in the seventeenth century that the Poles invented the word *szot* (Scot: meaning 'tinker'); and, in all, between 1600 and 1650 perhaps 100,000 Scotsmen, or one-fifth of the kingdom's adult males, went to live abroad. In western Europe, only Portugal also suffered losses on this scale through migration: in the course of the seventeenth century perhaps 250,000 people set sail for its overseas colonies.[66] At the same time, further east, tens of thousands of Russian and Polish families – the majority of them unfree peasants – fled to join the Cossacks living on the rich 'black earth' lands in the south, and in the case of Russia (and in lesser numbers) also to Siberia (see chapter 6 below).

Thousands of Chinese families, too, elected to escape adversity by migrating overseas. Many, especially from the mountainous southeastern provinces, left for the Philippines and Southeast Asia, either as settlers or to 'service' the European colonies there. By 1700 some 20,000 Chinese lived in a special suburb of Manila known as the Parián (and its population would have been much larger but for the periodic massacres carried out by the Spaniards and their Filipino allies); and several thousand more lived in Batavia (now Jakarta), which became a 'Chinese colonial town under Dutch protection'.[67] The establishment of European colonies on Taiwan after 1624 created another opportunity for Chinese 'co-colonization'. Almost immediately, the governor of Fujian province allowed 'several tens of thousands' of those destitute through famine to migrate to the lands around the main Dutch settlement, providing each person with three *taels* of silver and every family with a cow. By 1683, when Qing forces annexed the island, some 120,000 Chinese lived on Taiwan alongside the indigenous population. In each of these locations – Manila, Batavia, Taiwan and so on – virtually no Chinese settlement had existed a century before.[68]

Thanks to the unparalleled prevalence of war in the seventeenth century, many more men than ever before left home to join an army. In India, perhaps one-tenth of the active male population of Hindustan formed part of a sophisticated military labour market because the Mughal emperors, like their Afghan predecessors and their British successors, raised Rajput troops on their northwest frontier and sent them to fight on the eastern and southern borders of their empire. Many of them married and settled there. A similar system of military expatriation characterized the Spanish empire. Every year, troops raised in the towns and villages of Castile left for the Netherlands where, in 1640, Philip IV's troops included over 17,000 Spaniards. Many of these expatriates, like the Rajputs of Mughal India, married and settled abroad, never planning to come home. As a Spanish patriarch told his younger brother when he left for the wars, 'I don't want you to enjoy the countryside in the Netherlands, but the war. The war must become your home.'[69] Every state found recruiting easier in years of economic adversity. In the words of the reluctant Spanish warrior who met Don Quixote on the way to join his regiment:

Necessity drove me to the wars;
If I had money truly I would never go.

Or, as a French general put it just after the 'Great Winter' of 1708–9: 'It might well be said that "it's an ill wind that blows nobody any good", for we could only find so many recruits because of the misery of the provinces ... The misfortune of the masses was the salvation of the kingdom.'[70]

Other forms of 'voluntary migration' during the mid-seventeenth century also mirrored economic conditions. For example, up to 6,000 people came to London every year, most of them either boys who became 'bound apprentice' to a merchant or artisan in return for instruction in his craft, or females and males who came to work as domestic servants until they had accumulated enough savings to become financially independent and marry – a goal that became more elusive whenever economic circumstances deteriorated. In the English capital, as elsewhere in western Europe, these migrants made up 10 per cent or more of the urban populations.

Other people migrated on an annual basis to work on the crops, because the cultivation of most staples requires many extra hands at certain predictable, intense, but short periods. In the case of rice, farmers needed to transplant seedlings and add fertilizer as rapidly as possible, and so throughout East and Southeast Asia itinerant labourers followed the rhythm of these activities. In cereal-producing areas, harvesting had to be accomplished rapidly and so required additional hands for a very brief period. In Catalonia, for example, every June 'by ancient custom, many reapers [the *segadors*] came down from all the mountainous regions and converged on Barcelona' to hire themselves out to farmers with land in the fertile plains of the principality.[71]

Itinerant labourers who lacked 'a house, a job or a fixed address' were extremely vulnerable to economic adversity – far more vulnerable than those who remained in their community, and so could claim at least some 'entitlements'. They were also far more dangerous. One eyewitness characterized the *segadors* as 'dissolute and bold men who for the rest of the year lived disordered lives' and 'normally caused disturbances and unrest wherever they went; but the absolute need for their services apparently made it impossible to stop them.' In June 1640, after a prolonged drought had caused great scarcity in the principality, some 2,500 restless reapers arrived in Barcelona and almost immediately 'caused disturbances and unrest' that led first to the murder of three royal judges and the viceroy, and eventually to the declaration of the 'Republic of Catalonia'.[72]

Except for those who became domestic servants, few migrants were female. In the seventeenth century only a handful of European women crossed the oceans alone, and even they sometimes disguised themselves as men (like the remarkable Basque transvestite 'lieutenant nun' Catalina de Erauso, who dictated memoirs describing her feats as a soldier of Philip IV in America). Rather more accompanied their husbands or parents as they sailed to overseas colonies – but males always outnumbered females.[73] Neither masquerading nor migration was an option for many Han Chinese women because from about the age of seven their mothers tightly bound their feet, just like their own. This produced, in its extreme form, 'the golden lotus': a foot measuring only three inches from the heel to the end of the large toe. A poem by Hu Shilan, a woman from a gentry family later forced to earn her living by teaching the daughters of more fortunate families, bitterly recalled the days when

> My little maid stood by me under canopy of flowers
> So that my tiny shoes wouldn't slip on mosses so green.
> Little did I know that in mid-life I would have to roam around
> Braving the scorched sun and furious storms.

In a crisis, a woman with bound feet would find it hard to 'roam around' – or, more important, to run away: a potentially fatal disadvantage during the Ming-Qing transition when China teemed with soldiers and bandits.[74]

Involuntary Migration

Besides those migrants who were 'pulled' from their homes through the prospect (whether apparent or real) of economic advancement elsewhere, the mid-seventeenth-century crisis 'pushed' hosts of others onto the roads through the threat of death or destitution if they remained. In Anatolia, the heart of the Ottoman empire, what contemporaries called the 'Great Flight' caused the tax-paying population of some communities to decline by three-quarters between the 1570s and the 1640s as landless unmarried men departed to find sustenance by serving in bandit armies, by seeking work in cities, or by studying in religious schools (*medreses*: see chapter 7 below). In central Europe, the Thirty Years War depopulated many communities. Martin Opitz, the most famous German poet of his day, asked rhetorically in his 1621 verse epic, 'Consolation in the Adversity of War':

Is there nowhere that war cannot come
So that we can live there without fear or flight? . . .
The trees stand no more;
The gardens are desolate.
The sickle and the plough are now a sharp blade.

In India, the famine and floods in Gujarat in 1628–31 likewise caused widespread flight, especially by craftsmen. According to an English observer, 'the greater part of [the] weavers, washers and dyers who (such as are escaped the direfull stroake of famine) are disperst into forraigne parts of greater plentie, leaving few or none of their faculty [skills]'.[75] In China, Chen Zilong, a scholar-official of the Ming as well as one of the finest poets of his generation, captured the agonizing fate of such refugees from disaster in 'The Little Cart':

The little cart jolting and banging through the yellow haze of dusk;
The man pushing behind: the woman pulling in front.
They have left the city and do not know where to go.
'Green, green, those elm-tree leaves: *they* will cure my hunger,
If only we could find some quiet place and sup upon them together.'
The wind has flattened the yellow mother-wort;
Above it, in the distance, they see the walls of a house.
'There, surely, must be people living who'll give you something to eat.'
They tap at the door, but no one comes; they look in, but the kitchen is empty.
They stand hesitating in the lonely road and their tears fall like rain.[76]

Those arbitrarily deprived of their freedom before being deported faced an even worse fate. Some were conscripted soldiers and sailors. Although, in Europe, only Sweden introduced a permanent 'draft', most states periodically resorted to 'impressment': the compulsory enlistment in armies and navies of men with no obvious means of support, of men who had beaten or abandoned their wives, and of men who had embarked on what the community considered a life of sin – adulterers and fornicators. In addition, since in wartime 'sin' seldom filled the ranks, governments periodically conscripted law-abiding citizens. In Castile, communities often met their quota for the draft through a lottery held among all eligible males, and the criteria for 'eligibility' widened notably as the seventeenth century advanced and the population declined. Thus in the university town of Salamanca, in 1630 all men over age 40 were exempt, but this limit had risen to age 70 by 1640. At the same time, traditional exemptions (for students and professors, for town officials and familiars of the Inquisition, for gentlemen and doctors, even for the disabled) were challenged, until the only categories recognized as exempt were clerics and gypsies (the latter regularly rounded up for compulsory galley service). The draft could soon depopulate entire communities. Thus in 1642 the Spanish town of Villarrobledo, with some 3,000 inhabitants, complained that impressment had removed some

400 men over the previous five years and asked for relief since it now lacked sufficient manpower to work the fields. (The government responded with a demand for
60 more men.) Sometimes recruits became so scarce that they were held in gaol
between enlistment and deployment to prevent escape. Thus a group of recruits
from Castile who had languished in gaol for eight months, awaiting transport to
fight in Italy, pleaded with the Council of War in Madrid 'for the love of God arrange
for us to get out of this prison so that we may serve His Majesty, even if it should be
in Hell itself'.[77]

Some states also deported large numbers of miscreants rather than executing them.
A number were captured in war and rebellion. The Mughals, for example, regularly
sold their prisoners in the slave markets of central Asia. Thus in the 1630s the
governor of Kalpi, in the foothills of the Himalayas, boasted that in repressing a
rebellion he had 'beheaded the leaders and enslaved their women, daughters and children, who were more than two lachs [200,000] in number', and sent them for sale.
While recognizing that chronicles tend to exaggerate numbers, historian Scott Levi
(who quoted this detail) estimated that 'over the years, Mughal military expansion in
India accounts for the enslavement and exportation of hundreds of thousands of individuals'. Other deportees were convicts. The Russian government deported many
criminals to defend the southern frontier against Tatar raids, rather than putting them
to death – including some convicted witches who received a sentence of permanent
exile and, ironically, spent the rest of their lives patrolling the frontiers of Orthodoxy
(in most parts of western Europe they would have been publicly executed). In
Scotland, exasperated by the constant lawlessness of one particular clan, in 1626 the
government deported all men named 'Macgregor' to continental Europe, 'sufficiently
guarded by some of their officers who will be answerable for their not escaping'.
Before leaving for the continent, every Macgregor had to swear 'that they shall never
return again within this kingdom under the pain of death'.[78]

Most British deportees were transported to America. England's Virginia Company
showed the way, rounding up in 1618 'a hundred young boys and girls that lay
starving in the streets' and sending them to Virginia. A few years later, the Company
similarly removed the 'super-increasing people from the city [of London] to Virginia'
so that it 'may ease the city of many that are ready to starve, and do starve daily in
our streets ... for want of food to put into their mouths'.[79] By the 1640s the
Company employed 'spirits' who 'did entice children and people away for Virginia'
aboard their waiting ships with the promise of food once they got on board, but,
according to Charles Baily (one of the thousands of victims), 'being once on board,
[I] could never get on shoar untill I came to America, where I was sold as a bond-
slave for seaven years'. Baily later believed that he and the other 'poor creatures had
better have been hanged, than to suffer the death and misery they did'. Some of these
'poor creatures' were defeated soldiers and rebels whom the victorious Republican
regime in London condemned to work as unfree labour in Barbados and other
American colonies. According to a recent study, 'tens of thousands of people from
Britain and Ireland ended up working as bond slaves in the Chesapeake and
Caribbean during the revolutionary period'.[80]

Some European governments deported not only convicts to work in their colonies in America and Asia during the seventeenth century, but also orphaned girls and prostitutes, hoping to redress the extreme gender imbalance that prevailed in most overseas colonies. It did not always work: a stunning 80 per cent of the married women in seventeenth-century Canada who died childless had come as 'Filles du Roy' ('daughters of the king', as the deportees were known).[81] Many male migrants also failed to reproduce. Some perished en route from the rigours of the journey, and others died soon after they reached their destination because they lacked immunity to the pathogens they encountered there. Thus between 1604 and 1634 some 25,000 European males died in the Royal Hospital in Goa, the capital of Portuguese India, most of them shortly after disembarking from their long sea voyage from Lisbon; and of over 5,000 Portuguese men who left Lisbon for India between 1629 and 1634, fewer than half arrived alive. Equally, despite the immigration of some 223,000 Europeans to England's Caribbean islands in the course of the seventeenth century, their total 'white' population in 1700 was scarcely 40,000.

The greatest forced migration of the seventeenth century also involved the greatest mortality: the deportation of Africans. Some, especially in east Africa, were captured and taken to Muslim states in the north. Throughout the seventeenth century slave caravans brought 5,000–6,000 African men and women to Ottoman Egypt each year, whence they were distributed throughout the empire – but, after the arrival of the Europeans in the west, far more Africans went involuntarily to the Americas.[82]

Estimating the overall size of the trade in slaves between Africa and the various European colonies in America is extremely difficult; nevertheless, around 1640 an official with extensive experience estimated that the slave population of Spanish America stood at about 325,000 and that just over 9,000 new slaves were required each year to maintain this level. In addition, a further 80,000 slaves probably laboured in Brazil, where the colony needed to import over 2,000 slaves annually just to replace 'losses'; while in 1656 alone 2,000 African slaves arrived in the English colony of Barbados. Taken together, these figures suggest that a total of at least 13,000 African slaves arrived each year in America in the mid-seventeenth century.[83] In addition, thousands more captured Africans died either en route to the Atlantic coast, or in the holding pens where they awaited shipment, or on the voyage. Adding these totals together, Europeans enslaved some two million Africans during the seventeenth century, half of them from west-central Africa and most of the rest from the states along the Gold Coast and the Bights of Benin and Biafra.

Negative Compound Interest

The various processes that reduced the human population in the mid-seventeenth century, and thus reduced short-term demand for resources (especially food), had five important long-term consequences that created a 'negative compound interest':

- **Depleting the next generation of mothers.** Pressure on widows to kill themselves decimates the current generation of mothers, already reduced by high mortality during and after childbirth (and, in Catholic countries, also by an increase in the number of nuns); but killing or abandoning girls at birth decimates the mothers of the *next* generation. *A female infanticide rate of 10 per cent will reduce population growth in the next generation by 10 per cent.* A Chinese poem bitterly noted this double assault on women:

  > Fujian custom leaves alive after birth only half the number of baby girls born;
  > Lucky survivors desire to be virtuous females.
  >
  > Daughters should die after their husband's death;
  > Poisoned wine is ready in cups and cords await on beams.
  >
  > A daughter clinging to life withstands great pressure,
  > Broken hearts are full of grievances;
  >
  > Death occurs at last amid clansmen's cheers,
  > Official distinction is bestowed to glorify the clan's name for a thousand years.[84]

- **Creating depleted cohorts.** Any short-term crisis that significantly reduces the size of an age cohort, whether through human or natural catastrophe, automatically reduces the ability of that cohort to reproduce itself. A rise of 50 per cent in the prevailing death rate means that those under 15 at the time of the crisis will lack the numbers to restore the previous population level. Moreover, by a tragic coincidence (and it seems to be no more than a coincidence, at least in Europe) each generation reduced by a major mortality crisis in the seventeenth century reached marriageable age just as another catastrophe struck. Thus the 'cohort' depleted by the plague of 1630–1 came of age just in time to face the famine of 1661–3, while their children reached the age of reproduction during the crisis of the 1690s. Similarly, the 'cohort' depleted by the crises of 1618–21 and 1647–53 came of age just in time to face the harvest failures of the mid-1670s, while their children reached the age of reproduction during the 'Great Winter' of 1708–9 and the resulting famine.[85] Each catastrophe thus reduced not only the size of the afflicted generation but also the size of the next one.

- **Death on the road.** In every age, it is hard to raise a family on the move. Parish registers all over Europe record the frequent death of 'strangers' – men, women and children who perished as they tried to get from one place to another, usually in search of work or food. Because each parish kept separate records, their entries rarely allow historians to recreate the losses of migrant families, but some qualitative sources come to the rescue. To take a single example, Peter Hagendorf, a soldier in the Thirty Years War between 1624 and 1648, kept a diary as he marched almost 15,000 miles around Europe with his regiment. He recorded meticulously the births, marriages and deaths of his family, later placing numbers beside the death of all four children by his first wife between 1627 and 1633, when she died, and of four more by his second wife between 1635 and 1648. Most of his eight children died as infants (one before baptism, and two more in their first week). In the course of the Thirty Years War Hagendorf thus sired ten legitimate children, but only two were still alive when it ended, one aged five and the other just an infant.[86] If Hagendorf's experience was representative, then active military service was a sentence of death not only for many soldiers, but also for their families; and since at least a million men fought in the European wars of the mid-seventeenth century, the overall demographic consequences were severe.

- **The hidden costs of migration.** Some of the villages of northern Portugal that supplied large numbers of men – both sailors and colonists – for the country's overseas enterprise boasted fewer than 60 men for every 100 women, and scarcely half the women in the community ever married. Similar gender imbalances characterized other villages where most of the men migrated to find work, producing two long-term demographic consequences. First, in cereal-producing areas with soils too heavy for women to till by themselves, the departure of too many men (whether to fight, as in Scandinavia, or to colonize, as in Iberia) could reduce food production so much that, although consumption fell (because the men no longer ate local food), the community might no longer be able to feed itself and so eventually atrophied. Second, at least in monogamous societies, male migration on this scale dramatically reduced the number of marriages and therefore the size of the next generation, once again creating a kind of 'negative compound interest'.[87]

- **'A young man's world'.** The sociologist Jack Goldstone drew attention to 'the extraordinary youthfulness of England's population in the 1630s', both absolutely and relatively.

Age as a percentage of England's total population

Year	Total Population	0–4	5–14	15–24	25–29	Total aged 15–29	Total aged 30+
1631	4,892,580	12.5	19.9	18.2	7.9	26.1	41.6
1641	5,091,725	11.8	20.5	17.3	8	25.3	42.4

As Goldstone noted, 'the cohort that reached ages 26–35 during the 1630s *was the largest youth cohort of the entire period 1500–1750*'; and a large number of them remained unmarried.[88] Such a demographic structure is inherently unstable, not only because those who are young and single are the ones more likely to voice their discontent, but also because (as Goldstone observed) 'the participation of people in demonstrations or opposition movements depends to some extent on how great they perceive the support of that opposition movement to be'. Therefore, since 'the more timorous among the discontented may only join an opposition that appears widespread and successful', the growth of the 26–35 age cohort to unprecedented size in the 1630s would also have increased the chances that people over age 35 would join the opposition. This, in turn, increased the volatility of the *whole* population.[89]

Chinese data, although not as precise as England's parish registers, record a parallel phenomenon. The prevalence of female infanticide inevitably increased the number of 'bare sticks' – the common Chinese term for unmarried men – in the next generation. A Fujian gazetteer claimed that during the 1650s almost half of all males remained single because they could not find women to marry; and, as in England, such an unusual demographic pattern would explain why so many people refused to see scarcity as a natural calamity to be stoically endured, but rather as the consequence of human agency to be vigorously protested.[90]

In his influential essay *Poverty and Famines*, inspired by his experience of the Bengal famine of 1943, Amartya Sen argued that 'Starvation is the characteristic of some people not *having* enough food to eat. It is not the characteristic of there *being* not enough food to eat. While the latter can be a cause of the former, it is but one of many *possible* causes.'[91] That is: famines arise more often from distribution problems caused by human agency than from supply problems caused by nature. Whether or not Sen is correct, such 'anthropocentric' views convinced many people (in the words of Stephen L. Kaplan) 'that they were the victims of a terrible conspiracy'. In the early modern world, Kaplan argued,

> Consumers found reasons to question the authenticity of the dearth. They uncovered signs that the harvest was not as bad as announced, that unusual and illegal acts were occurring in the grain trade, that the government was not performing as it was supposed to, and so on. As subsistence anxieties deepened . . . the conviction grew that the crisis was contrived, that there was a criminal conspiracy afoot against the people, that popular suffering was needless, and that the plotters somehow had to be resisted. The villains were virtually interchangeable from crisis to crisis. They included men of power (ministers . . . magistrates, and so forth), of great means (for example, financiers, tax farmers, bankers, military contractors), and members of the entourages of several of the key leaders (mistresses and relatives.)

Much the same anthropocentric assumptions surrounded major epidemics: that they were spread by evil and powerful men (and occasionally women).[92]

Such convictions led many people in the early modern period to insist that the authorities could and must do more to provide their subjects with sufficient food and security to ensure survival. The notion that the state's paramount duty was to 'Nourish the people' did not only hold sway in China. *Politics drawn from the very words of Holy Scripture*, a treatise written in 1679 for the heir to the French throne by his tutor, Jean-Bénigne Bossuet, stressed that 'The prince must provide for the needs of his people' (the title of one of the book's 'propositions'). Indeed, Bossuet chided:

> The obligation to take care of the people is the basis of all the rights that sovereigns have over their subjects. That is why, in times of great need, the people have a right to appeal to their prince. 'In an extreme famine, the people cried to Pharaoh for

food.' The famished people asked for bread from their king, as from a shepherd, or rather as from their father.[93]

That is why (Bossuet might have added) early modern rulers who followed Pharaoh's example, and ignored the 'appeal' of their people, soon faced more rebellions and revolutions. Indeed, the greatest population losses occurred in precisely the states that experienced not only most famines and wars, but also most rebellions and revolutions: China, Russia, the Polish-Lithuanian Commonwealth, the Ottoman empire, Germany and its neighbours, the Iberian Peninsula, France, Britain and Ireland.

PART II

ENDURING THE CRISIS

Peace does not become peace in a single day; a crisis does not become a crisis in a single day. Both become what they are through a gradual accumulation.

Jia Yi, *History of the Han*[1]

IN A SEMINAL ARTICLE, SIR JOHN ELLIOTT POINTED OUT THAT THE 'EPIDEMIC of revolutions' in the 1640s 'was not, after all, unprecedented', and he listed not only eight rebellions in western Europe between 1559 and 1569 but also contemporary statements deploring the ubiquity of those upheavals. Thus the Protestant Reformer John Knox warned the ruler of turbulent Scotland in 1561 that 'Your realm is in no other case at this day than all the other realms of Christendom are'; while John Calvin thought he discerned '*Europae concussio*: the shaking of Europe' – precisely the same metaphor used by Jeremiah Whittaker and others in the 1640s (page xxi above). And yet, Elliott added, 'I am not aware that any historian has grouped them together' and 'used them as evidence for a "general crisis of the sixteenth century"'.[2]

The 1590s, by contrast, have attracted more attention from historians, because the combination of global cooling, harvest failure, plague and war reduced agricultural and industrial production to the lowest levels recorded in three centuries. In addition, 'Probably never before in European history had so many popular rebellions coincided in time'. Once again, however, Elliott counselled caution. 'The signs of trouble,' he conceded, were 'all around: famine and epidemics, vagrancy and unemployment, riots and revolts. But these were hardly unusual phenomena in the life of early modern Europe'. The 1590s, Elliott suggested, saw not so much 'another full-blown "general crisis"', but rather 'an unusually interesting case of *fin de siècle* malaise'.[3]

In fact, Asia as well as Europe experienced the same 'malaise' in the 1590s: civil war in Anatolia almost brought the Ottoman empire to its knees, while Japanese invasions desolated Korea and destabilized both China and Japan itself. Moreover, the entire northern hemisphere experienced extreme climatic events that caused widespread famine and dislocation. In 1594 Yang Dongming, an official in China's Henan province, submitted perhaps the most vivid account of an early modern famine ever written, later printed under the title *Album of the Famished*, complete with 13 harrowing sketches of the effects of starvation on humans. He described and illustrated families fragmented by famine, children abandoned or sold for food, and entire families committing suicide (see Plate 5). Yang also recorded the extreme weather he had experienced.[4] Many of his European contemporaries did the same. In Germany, several Lutheran pastors composed hymns that reproached God for 'holding back the sunshine and sending heavy rain', while in England William Shakespeare's *A Midsummer Night's Dream*, first performed in 1595–6, lamented that

> ... the green corn
> Hath rotted ere his youth attain'd a beard;
> The fold stands empty in the drowned field ...
> And through this distemperature we see
> The seasons alter ...
> ... the spring, the summer,
> The chiding autumn, angry winter, change
> Their wonted liveries, and the mazed world,
> By their increase, now knows not which is which.

Ottoman chroniclers in Hungary and the Balkans also recorded unusually severe winters that froze the Danube solid and complained that 'The winter – the so-called "merciless soldier" – pressed with its full strength. Terrible storms and snowstorms occurred; all hands and feet were crippled'. The decade also saw both extreme droughts and floods that ruined the harvests. In Italy, when extreme weather destroyed the 1591 harvest, crowds in Rome mobbed the pope demanding food; the magistrates of Naples expelled 2,000 foreign students from the city, to reduce food consumption, and issued bread ration cards to citizens; while bread prices in Sicily reached their highest level for two centuries. In Scandinavia, people looked back on 1591 as 'the black year in which the grass did not turn green at all', while in 1596 and again in 1597 there was 'so dreadful a hunger that the greater part of the people had to [eat] bread made of bark'.[5]

These striking data from the 1590s remind us that the global cooling of the 1640s, like the 'epidemic of revolutions', 'was not, after all, unprecedented'; and so they support the scepticism of Niels Steensgaard, who wrote that the concept of a seventeenth-century 'General Crisis' has 'become a synonym for what historians in other centuries call "history"'.[6] This volume respectfully disagrees. It contends, by contrast, that the 1640s saw more rebellions and revolutions than any comparable period in world history. Admittedly, few of the new regimes endured (the Republican experiments in Catalonia, Naples and England collapsed in a matter of days, weeks and years, respectively); but some proved permanent (the Portuguese revolt) or lasted for centuries (the 'Great Enterprise' of the Qing in China; the demise of Spain as a Great Power; the Protestant ascendancy in Ireland).

The seventeenth century experienced extremes of weather seldom witnessed before and never (so far) since: the only known occasion on which the Bosporus froze over (1620–1); the only time that floods in Mecca destroyed part of the Kaaba (1630); the coldest winter ever recorded in Scandinavia (1641); and so on. This combination of natural and human disasters had profound human consequences. Infanticide and suicide in China rose to unequalled levels; far fewer European women married, and others did so only in their thirties; many Frenchmen, their growth stunted by famine and cold, were of shorter stature than any others on record. These diverse physical indicators all reflect conditions that were both unique and universal – but China, then as now the most populous state on the planet, apparently suffered worst and longest.

5

The 'Great Enterprise' in China, 1618–84[1]

Iᴺ 1645, ᴅᴇᴘʀᴇssᴇᴅ ʙʏ ᴛʜᴇ sᴜɪᴄɪᴅᴇ ᴏꜰ ᴛʜᴇ ʟᴀsᴛ Mɪɴɢ ᴇᴍᴘᴇʀᴏʀ ᴛᴏ ʀᴜʟᴇ from Beijing, a gentleman-scholar named Xia Yunyi decided to dictate his memoirs before he killed himself:

> In agony and wrath at the emperor's death, my reason to live has ended . . . So what more is there to say? I just fear that, regarding the rise and fall of the state, the advance and retreat of worthy and base men, the origins and ends of bandits, and the sources of arms and provisions, those who instruct later generations will miss the realities. Is what I remember worth putting into words? Well, if what I say here has the fortune to survive, later generations will be able to ponder that question.[2]

Later generations did indeed ponder Xia's *Account that will be fortunate to survive* long after he committed suicide, as well as more than 200 other accounts of the fall of the Ming dynasty, and virtually all laid the blame upon an unprecedented combination of domestic problems and foreign threats.

In 2010 the eminent sinologist Timothy Brook reached the same conclusion. 'The fall of the Ming dynasty is many histories,' he wrote:

> The history of the expansion of the Manchu empire on the northeast border, the history of the most massive rebellions to wash over China since the fourteenth century, the history of the disintegration of the Ming state, and the history of a major climate episode. Different in the stories they tell, they overlap and together constitute the same history.[3]

The immense size and complexity of the Ming state complicate the task of telling these overlapping 'stories'. By 1600 China included almost 200 million acres of cultivated land, spread over 20 degrees of latitude, with climates ranging from tropical to subarctic. It formed the most ecologically diverse state of its day. In addition, its two major river systems, the Yangzi and Yellow rivers, linked by the Grand Canal, underpinned the most diverse, unified, wealthy and populous economy of the early modern world. The Ming emperors ruled over far more subjects than anyone else (Fig. 16).[4] Nevertheless in spring 1644 the dynasty's northern capital, Beijing, fell twice: first to an army of rebels from the northwest, and a few weeks later to Manchu invaders from the northeast, who drove out the rebels. The victors then undertook campaigns of conquest that eventually created a

16. Ming China and its neighbours.
Most maps of East Asia use Mercator's projection, which increases the size of Ming China compared with the steppes where the Manchu dynasty achieved dominance in the early seventeenth century. In 1644, the Great Wall failed to protect Beijing (the Ming northern capital) from capture, first by a bandit army from the west and then by the Manchus from the north. Nanjing (the southern capital) fell the following year.

state twice as large as Ming China and endured for two centuries. No other political change in the mid-seventeenth century affected so many people, caused so much damage, or created such lasting consequences.

Manchus versus Ming

The late Ming regime suffered from three endemic weaknesses. First, although Chinese subjects revered their emperor as *Tianzi* ('Son of Heaven') and assigned him sole power to make authoritative rulings, he could only enforce them in cooperation with a bureaucracy of some 15,000 highly educated elite males. Although recruited through competitive examinations open to almost all, the bureaucrats came overwhelmingly from the land-owning class, and their personal wealth brought an independence that enabled them to criticize, disobey and even defy an emperor who failed to meet their expectations. Second, despite their economic independence, even the senior bureaucrats (the Grand Secretaries) had limited opportunities to convey their views in person because the late Ming emperors spent their entire lives isolated in the 'Forbidden City' in Beijing, a walled compound of some 200 acres surrounded by a wide moat where tens of thousands of eunuchs staffed the agencies that managed the imperial household (including its granaries and treasury as well as its ceremonies) and handled the emperor's correspondence. Third, since the prevailing Confucian ideology aimed to promote harmony and peace, Ming officials tended to favour the least disruptive and least expensive policies, to organize factions to preserve the status quo, and to denounce innovators as traitors.

These weaknesses became prominent in the early seventeenth century when the Wanli emperor (1573–1620), frustrated by the obstructionism and denunciations of his bureaucrats, left official posts unfilled and refused to sign orders. Instead, he used the imperial eunuchs who answered to the Director of the Ceremonial Department (in effect, the emperor's chief of staff and always a eunuch) to circumvent the civil service and carry out his orders. His successor, the Tianqi emperor (1620–7), went further: he made the eunuch Wei Zhongxian his chief minister and used the palace eunuchs, now 80,000 strong, as diplomats, trade and factory superintendents, tax inspectors and government supervisors, even generals and admirals. They thus formed an 'alternative administration' that reported directly to Wei.

Tianqi's half-brother the Chongzhen emperor (1627–44) initially relied less on eunuchs but proved both stubborn and suspicious in dealing with the bureaucracy. Of the 160 Grand Secretaries appointed during the entire Ming era (1368–1644) Chongzhen appointed no fewer than 50, almost all of whom he removed in response to a remonstrance or denunciation by a jealous colleague. Such inconstancy precluded the formulation and implementation of effective strategies to meet the numerous challenges that faced the empire: instead of discussing how to save it, ministers concentrated on finding someone to blame. The emperor, like his predecessors, therefore relied increasingly on eunuchs in both civil and military affairs.

As paralysis gripped the Ming government, a small nomadic group living beyond its northeast frontier created a new state. At first their leader Nurhaci (1559–1626) accepted Ming suzerainty, leading tribute missions to Beijing in person, learning to read Chinese, and studying Chinese history and military practice; but he also strove to unite into a single confederation the various tribes that inhabited the steppes of central Asia. By 1600 Nurhaci commanded at least 15,000 warriors organized into permanent companies (known as *niru*, from the Manchu word for 'arrow') containing some 300 fighting men, normally from the same village and sometimes from the same clan. Each *niru* formed part of a Banner (*gūsa*, the Manchu term for a 'large military division') commanded by a member of Nurhaci's family. Manchu warriors valued horsemanship and archery; they revered as their ancestors the Mongols who had conquered China four centuries before; and, like the Mongols, they shaved the hair on their foreheads and wore the rest in a queue behind. For some time, the new Manchu state prospered from trade (especially from exporting ginseng to China), from war booty (both property and persons), and from agriculture (mostly performed by their slaves).

The situation altered dramatically when climate change struck East Asia. In China, imperial officials reported in 1615 that they had received a deluge of petitions for disaster relief, and that 'Although the situation differs in each place, all tell of localities gripped by disaster, the people in flight, brigands roaming at will, and the corpses of the famished littering the roads.' The following year, a Shandong official submitted an *Illustrated handbook of the great starvation of the people of Shandong* (1616). The situation in Manchuria was even worse. When Nurhaci's advisers suggested that invading China might alleviate the famine, he retorted angrily: 'We do not even have enough food to feed ourselves. If we conquer them, how will we feed them?'[5] Nevertheless, perhaps to conserve his remaining resources, Nurhaci first declared himself independent of China and stopped sending tribute; then, in 1618, he followed his advisers' suggestion and invaded Liaodong, a province north of the Great Wall where subjects of the Ming cultivated wheat and millet during the short but intense growing season. This delivered into Manchu hands perhaps one million new subjects – but, almost immediately, global cooling produced the result that Nurhaci had predicted: a Manchu chronicle noted that the year 1620 was the first year of high rice prices, and added 'thereafter there were no years in which rice was not expensive.'[6]

The Ming failed to exploit the Manchus' problems because of an uprising in Shandong province by supporters of a Buddhist sect known as the White Lotus. In 1622 one of the White Lotus leaders declared himself the founder of a new imperial dynasty, and his followers promptly cut off the transport of rice up the Grand Canal, causing shortages in the capital. The Ming therefore withdrew troops from the northern frontier, which allowed them to crush the rebellion before it spread further, but also allowed Nurhaci to consolidate his control of Liaodong by abolishing the dues and services payable to landlords and confirming all peasants in possession of their land – provided they cut their hair and shaved their foreheads in the Manchu manner. According to a disgusted Ming commander, 'People are so happy that all of them, cutting their hair, have obeyed the Manchus.'[7]

The Erosion of Ming Power

Ming China had two capitals. Nanjing (literally 'Southern Capital'), in the lower Yangzi valley, never saw the emperor but possessed a full bureaucracy that mirrored the one in Beijing ('Northern Capital') located at the extremity of China's 'Central Plain'. The strategic vision of the two administrations differed considerably. With the Great Wall barely 30 miles away, ministers in the northern capital normally prioritized defence and the food supply: they not only needed to monitor developments among those who lived on the steppes but also, living in the largest city in the world, needed to ensure a constant supply of the essential goods on which the capital depended, especially the rice that arrived via the Grand Canal from the fertile paddies of the lower Yangzi valley, a region known as Jiangnan (literally 'south of the river'), and the coal brought by camel trains from the mines of Shanxi, hundreds of miles to the west. Ministers in the southern capital, by contrast, needed above all to maintain peace and productivity in the densely populated lands of Jiangnan, where many farms could no longer feed the families that worked them, either because they were too small or because they produced commercial crops rather than foodstuffs. Even abundant harvests left some people hungry, producing tension between landlords and tenants in the countryside and sometimes disturbances in the towns. Poor harvests almost immediately produced starvation, migration and disorder.

The ministers of the two imperial capitals, Beijing and Nanjing, nevertheless faced three similar problems: an inadequate fiscal system; a weak military; and ineffective imperial leadership. First and greatest among the fiscal problems was the fact that the Ming state never borrowed – a practice that greatly reduced flexibility in times of crisis, since expenditure could be funded only from current revenues, instead of being spread over several years (as in western Europe). This placed an enormous premium on the efficient collection of the land tax, the Ming government's main source of revenue; but by the 1630s, the distribution of this tax had become extremely uneven. Within each province, counties that had at some point earned imperial disfavour paid extra, whereas others contained tax-exempt lands and therefore paid less. Additionally, new inequities emerged in the wake of a major tax reform in the sixteenth century: mounting budget problems led the central government to combine two different obligations – labour services and land tax – into one, known as the 'Single Whip'. Ministers hoped to increase yields by using the detailed household registers of labour services (known as 'Yellow Books') to allocate tax obligations; but since the gentry enjoyed exemption from labour services, their names did not appear in the Yellow Books and so the Single Whip system exempted them from the land tax, too. Landholders therefore scrambled to register their households under gentry names, significantly increasing the tax burden on peasant farmers. Moreover, local officials determined the annual burden payable by each remaining taxable household, a process that opened the way to corruption and abuse, so that communities were said to dread the annual visit of the tax officials 'as much as if they were to be thrown into boiling water'.[8]

These fiscal discrepancies produced stunning cumulative inequalities. Thus Suzhou prefecture, with 1 per cent of China's cultivated land, paid 10 per cent of the total imperial revenue; Shanghai county paid three times as much as an entire prefecture in Fujian; while a single prefecture near Nanjing which had only three counties paid as much as the entire province of Guangdong which had 75 counties.[9] An imperial decree that made support of the emperor's relatives the first charge on each regional treasury greatly exacerbated these gross fiscal inequities: by the 1620s the cost of supporting 100,000 Ming clansmen – most of them with a wife, concubines, numerous progeny and a large household (all tax-exempt) – absorbed over one-third of the annual revenues in some provinces.

As long as China's agrarian economy continued to expand, as it did throughout the sixteenth century, these inequities remained tolerable; and even after the land tax increased from 4 million *taels* in 1618 to 20 million in 1639 (to fund the growing defence expenditure), the underlying tax rate in the richest and most fertile parts of China still lay at or below 20 per cent – a heavy but bearable burden. Moreover, 20 million *taels* should have sufficed to support an army of 500,000 men – more than enough to preserve the Ming state – but corruption and weak central control kept much of the yield from reaching the central treasury. By 1644 the government's budget projected receipts of less than 16 million *taels* but expenditure of more than 21 million, with no way to bridge the gap.[10]

The second common problem facing the ministers in Nanjing and Beijing was the poor quality of their troops. Ming culture disparaged martial virtues and achievements, which not only discouraged talented members of the elite from serving in the army but also demoralized the troops. Most soldiers did not know how to use their weapons properly, while most officers systematically overstated the size of their armies to the Ministry of Revenue to gain more resources (and understated it to the Ministry of War to avoid being sent into combat). Thus, according to a frustrated government inspector, if 100,000 names appeared on the army's lists, only 50,000 soldiers actually served; and, he concluded, 'of those 50,000 men, no more than half are of any use in combat. The Court thus pays for four soldiers but receives the services of only one.' Western observers agreed. A Spanish Jesuit who observed the drill of local garrison troops in Fujian in 1625 remarked that their firearms were 'badly made', their powder weak and their shot 'no larger than tiny pellets of lead'. Chinese drill, the Jesuit claimed, 'resembled games more than preparing to fight well'. A decade later, a Portuguese visitor who watched Ming troops drilling likewise noted that the soldiers simply 'waved their lances and swords as if they were in some stage play'.[11] Europeans also noted that officers frequently flogged their soldiers, making them 'drop their trousers and lie on the ground, as if they were schoolboys, to receive the blows'. Such treatment led many troops to desert and others to mutiny. Over 50 serious military revolts occurred between 1627 and 1644, reaching a crescendo as pay for the troops fell far in arrears.[12]

The third critical problem facing ministers in both Nanjing and Beijing was the existence of numerous 'academies' where intellectuals discussed current moral and social issues in the light of the teachings of Confucius. Although the goal of Confucianism remained the same for all – the need for each man to perfect himself so that he could serve heaven and human society as a sage ruler or minister – by the early seventeenth century two opposed paths to that goal existed. One required aspiring sages to search for moral principles in the outside world (specifically in the Confucian Classics, the words of past sages) and apply them; the other stressed self-examination, and believed that intuition based on each man's 'innate goodness' sufficed to ensure righteous actions. The *Donglin* ('Eastern Grove') Academy in Wuxi, a Jiangnan town, followed the first path: its associates downplayed intuition and introspection in favour of ending corruption and restoring moral rectitude throughout China by applying the ancient virtues enshrined in the Classics. They adopted the popular slogan *jingshi jimin*: 'Manage the world's affairs; provide for the people'. Although the Wanli emperor degraded or dismissed ministers who sympathized with Donglin goals, for a brief period after his death they prospered and even opened a branch of the academy in Beijing, with a library and a lecture hall where members debated the pressing issues of the day. They used their advantage to attack not only ministers who were corrupt but also those who tolerated corruption in the interests of social harmony. After Nurhaci's occupation of Liaodong, their criticisms focused on 'a man who sucks boils and licks haemorrhoids' whom they blamed for the humiliating defeat: the eunuch Wei Zhongxian, the emperor's childhood friend and now his principal minister.[13]

In 1624 a prominent member of the Donglin Academy submitted to the emperor a memorial that listed the 'crimes' committed by Wei against the interests of the state. Almost immediately a host of other officials, many of them also Donglin alumni, submitted similar memorials that called for Wei's dismissal. Their efforts backfired because Wei convinced the emperor that Donglin factionalism formed the true threat to government stability. Warrants went out for the arrest of 11 critics, all Donglin alumni, and imperial agents arrested and brought them to Beijing, where they were carried through the streets in cages like zoo animals, interrogated, tortured, publicly flogged, and then murdered. In addition, Wei abolished all private academies as well as compiling a 'blacklist' of military and civilian officials whom he considered sympathetic to the Donglin movement, replacing them with his own protégés (later known as *yandang*: 'associates of the eunuch').[14]

In 1627, however, the Tianqi emperor suddenly died and his 16-year-old half-brother succeeded as the Chongzhen emperor (a reign title that meant 'lofty and auspicious', but later black humour punned on the word *chongzheng*, meaning 'double levy', to create the 'Double Taxation Reign'). The new ruler declined to protect Wei, who hanged himself, and announced an 'era of renovation'. To achieve this he rescinded the order abolishing the private academies, exonerated most of the Donglin partisans still in prison, rehabilitated the reputations of those degraded, and issued his own 'blacklist' – this time of the *yandang*, most of whom lost their jobs and many of whom were punished. The Chongzhen emperor also urged his senior ministers to end their factional struggle. 'Consider this,' he told them at one meeting: 'We have alarms east and west, we have wars north and south, yet [my officials] have no anxiety for the dynasty. All they do is divide into camps, all they talk about is some clique, some Donglin – and of what benefit is that to national affairs?'[15]

The new emperor's pleas failed because, in the perceptive phrase of historian Ying Zhang, in his 'ambition to save the empire in crisis' he 'sought only instant successes and simple solutions'. Each administrative error and policy failure therefore provoked a spate of denunciations and memorials by rivals of the officials deemed responsible.[16] Not knowing whom he could trust to show 'anxiety for the dynasty' or seek 'benefit' for 'national affairs', the Chongzhen emperor changed the heads of the six major departments of state, on average, once every year: half of them he merely dismissed from office, and a quarter he also executed or disgraced.

Factional struggles among China's bureaucrats had two deleterious consequences. First, the repeated purges reduced the overall quality of senior bureaucrats. Of the 120 magistrates whose biographies appeared as exemplars for others in the official *Ming History*, composed a generation later, not a single one had served either the Tianqi or Chongzhen emperors. Second, although provincial postings were supposed to be distributed by lot, those who excelled in the civil service examinations went to the more prosperous counties, leaving several poor, remote and problematic areas virtually ungoverned. Thus in 1629 half of the prefectures and counties in the impoverished and turbulent Shaanxi province lacked a single magistrate.

In the words of the official *Ming History*, 'When a dynasty is about to perish, it first destroys its own people of quality. After that, there come floods, drought and banditry.'[17] From the first, the Chongzhen emperor and his dwindling cohort of 'people of quality' had to deal with 'floods, drought and banditry' in the northwest. The adjacent provinces of Shaanxi and Shanxi normally suffer from uncertain rainfall, a short growing season and poor communications; and, in the early seventeenth century, they lacked both adequate granaries and family lineages wealthy enough to sustain the poor. Neither province could support from their own resources the large garrisons required for their defence, leaving the troops there dependent for subsistence on wages and supplies sent from the capital. So long as these items arrived with reasonable regularity, all was well; but after 1618, when Beijing concentrated on repelling the Manchus, military units in the northwest received little or no pay. Many soldiers therefore deserted, taking their horses and weapons with them, forming fast-moving combinations known in the sources as 'roving bandits'. Little is known of the organization of these groups, and even their leaders usually appeared in the public record under nicknames: 'Lone Wolf', 'Dashing King' and (prophetically) 'Friend of the Red Army'.[18]

The brutal punishments for banditry stipulated by the Ming Law Code (death not only for each bandit but also for all male relatives 'up to second cousins' and for those who concealed or aided them) helped to keep the problem in check for a while; but a prolonged drought in Shaanxi province in 1628 changed the criminal calculus. Starving farmers now abandoned their land and joined the outlaws; existing hideouts therefore became too small to shelter the new recruits; and the increase in numbers enabled the bandit leaders to threaten more prosperous lands to the south. Then in 1629, with Manchuria also afflicted by drought, Manchu forces for the first time broke through the Great Wall and ravaged northern China.[19]

The Chongzhen emperor responded to these developments with two disastrous measures. First, he withdrew troops from Shaanxi to defend his capital against the Manchus, leaving the rest to fight the bandits without pay and supplies. Many of these abandoned troops, including a 23-year-old soldier named Zhang Xianzhong, joined the roving bandits. Second, to save money, the Chongzhen emperor closed roughly one-third of the courier stations that served foreign envoys, officials and messengers travelling to and from Beijing, and dismissed their employees. This not only reduced the central government's ability to receive news and convey orders in a timely fashion; it also caused great hardship in the northwest, where the courier network had traditionally provided many jobs in an area of high unemployment. Li Zicheng, aged 23, from a poor Shaanxi family, was one of the thousands of courier staff thrown out of work. Initially he transferred to the army but, when his unit received no pay, he led a mutiny and then (like countless others) joined the roving bandits.[20]

Climate change further exacerbated the situation. Some of the weakest monsoons recorded in the last two millennia produced droughts that destroyed the crops. A scholar-official lamented that 'Today, people are killed by bandit mobs; tomorrow, they may die at the hands of government troops. No one can tell how many fields have been left fallow by farmers fleeing disaster or in how many fields already-planted crops wither under the sun. No one can count how many families have been broken apart or number the dead lying piled in ditches.'[21] Not surprisingly, many of the starving survivors joined the roving bandits, who now began to ravage lands as far afield as the Yangzi in the south and Sichuan in the west.

The inequities created by the Ming fiscal system further aided the bandits and hurt agriculture. When a government official travelling through Jiangnan asked the remaining residents why almost 90 per cent of all farms lay abandoned, they replied that after a farmer fled,

> His land was left uncultivated but the land tax was still attached to it. His family was then summoned to pay the tax and if they failed to do so, the people of the [tax district] had to pay it for him . . . For a rich family, it was possible to pay what was owed, but the poor usually left the neighbourhood, abandoning all their property. This was why the villages were empty and the farms were left uncultivated.[22]

Even where no bandits threatened, extreme climatic episodes adversely affected agriculture: thus subtropical Lingnan (the 'lands south of the mountains': Guangxi and Guangdong provinces) saw heavy snowfall in 1633 and 1634, and abnormally cold weather in 1636. Crop yields plunged. Petitions flowed in to the central government from all over the empire, begging for action to end the bandit menace and to relieve the suffering caused by failed harvests, high taxes and bad weather; but the Chongzhen emperor did little because he was concentrating all his resources on resisting the Manchus.[23]

The 'Great Enterprise' Begins

While Ming China suffered from the problems created by the tax system, the bandits and the weather, the Manchus improved their military efficiency thanks to some opportune technology transfer. When he declared war on the Ming in 1618, Nurhaci's forces had consisted almost entirely of mounted archers whereas his Chinese opponents relied mainly on infantry using firearms. The Manchus' lack of artillery allowed the major towns of Liaodong to hold out – indeed, Nurhaci himself received a fatal wound as he besieged one of them. The Chongzhen emperor sought to build on this advantage by importing Western artillery, and soon about 50 bronze cannon defended the Great Wall. It was too late. During the 1629 raid into China, Hong Taiji (who, after a savage succession struggle, followed his father Nurhaci as Manchu leader) acquired not only Western guns but also conscripted a Chinese gun crew 'familiar with the new techniques for casting Portuguese artillery'. He also offered huge enlistment incentives to any engineer, and anyone proficient in the art of making and using cannon, who agreed to serve him. When the Manchus resumed the war in Liaodong in 1631, they possessed 40 Western-style artillery pieces and the crews to work them, and they built palisades and forts to cut off the heavily fortified regional capital. It surrendered within a few weeks. Hong Taiji also incorporated both his Chinese volunteers and conscripts alike into the Banner system (see page 118 above). By 1642 each of the eight Banners of his army had parallel Manchu, Mongol and Han Chinese components.[24]

All this formed part of the Manchus' ambitious programme to challenge the Ming for mastery of China, known as 'The Great Enterprise' (*Da ye*). In 1627 Hong Taiji issued a list of 'seven grievances' not only against the Ming but also against Korea: both documents presented the Manchu state as an independent political entity that dealt with its neighbours as a sovereign power. He also established a chancery and six administrative Boards, modelled on the Chinese system; devised a new script to communicate his orders in Manchu; and commanded scholars to search historical works for accounts of previous conquests of China by northerners, and of Chinese who switched allegiance to the conquerors at an early stage, as well as examples of bad Chinese rulers whose overthrow had been justified. Hong Taiji also moved to a new capital (present-day Shenyang), named both Shengjing ('Flourishing Capital' in Chinese) and Mukden (from the Manchu word 'to arise'), where his court combined Manchu, Mongol and Chinese imperial protocol. In 1636 he proclaimed himself the founder of a new multi-ethnic state called *Da Qing* ('Great Qing'). He also received from Tibetan lamas consecration with the powers of Mahakala, the warlike deity who protected Buddhist Law, and he claimed that the 'mind of Heaven' now guided his actions.[25]

Equally innovative, Hong Taiji decreed how his subjects should look and dress. An edict of 1636 required that 'All Han [Chinese] people – be they official or commoner, male or female – [in] their clothes and adornment will have to conform to Manchu styles ... Males are not allowed to fashion wide collars and sleeves; females are not allowed to comb up their hair or bind their feet'. Above all, males must shave the front part of their head and wear the rest in a long pigtail or queue like the Manchus. Two years later, a further decree specified that 'all those who imitate' Ming customs 'in clothes, headgear, hair-bundling and foot-binding are to be severely punished'. Hong Taiji's legislation thus reconfigured both attire (clothes) and the body itself (hair and feet) to proclaim political allegiance and cultural identity; and it construed failure to conform as treason.[26]

The Little Ice Age Strikes

Just as Nurhaci's decision to invade China in 1618 reflected climatic imperatives – global cooling affected Manchuria more severely than more temperate areas – so the cool and wet weather that ruined several harvests in the 1630s made it imperative for the Manchus to seize as much food as possible from their neighbours. Hong Taiji therefore launched another raid deep into China and also invaded Korea, the most important tributary state of the Ming; but, as in 1618, expansion brought only short-lived relief. Even the expanded lands under Qing rule no longer sufficed to feed those who lived there, and in 1638 some of Hong Taiji's advisers recommended that he seek a peace treaty with the Ming.[27]

Extreme weather conditions also afflicted China. The laconic entries in the section on 'famines' in the *Veritable Records of the Ming*, compiled from provincial reports to the Chongzhen emperor, are eloquent:

> In the ninth year [of the reign: 1636] severe famine affected Nanyang [Henan province] during which mothers killed and cooked their daughters [for food]. That year there was also a famine in Jiangxi province. In the tenth year [1637], there was a severe famine in Zhejiang province during which fathers and children, siblings and husbands resorted to cannibalism. In the twelfth year [1639], there was a famine in the Northern and Southern Metropolitan regions and in Shandong, Shanxi, Shaanxi and Jiangxi provinces. In Henan there was a severe famine during which people resorted to cannibalism . . . In the thirteenth year [1640], there were famine conditions in the Northern Metropolitan Region, Shandong, Henan, Shaanxi, Shanxi, Zhejiang, and the lower Yangzi delta.[28]

Recent climatic reconstructions reveal that in 1640 – a year of extreme El Niño and volcanic activity (see chapter 1 above) – north China experienced the worst drought recorded during the last five centuries. According to a magistrate in Henan province, 'there have been eleven months without rain. In the past year people have suffered from floods, locusts and drought. The drought was so bad that people could not plant the wheat, and what little was planted was eaten by locusts . . . The people all have yellow jaws and swollen cheeks; their eyes are like pig's gall.' He commissioned 16 sketches of famine conditions, regretting that the pictures could not transmit 'the screams from hunger and the howls from the cold' that he had witnessed.[29] The year 1641, which also saw extreme El Niño and volcanic activity, proved even worse. Jiangnan experienced severe frost and heavy snow, followed by the second driest year recorded during the sixteenth and seventeenth centuries. A telegraphic entry in the Shanghai county gazetteer is eloquent:

Massive drought.

Locusts.

The price of millet soared.

The corpses of the starved lay in the streets.

In July the Grand Canal dried up in Shandong province, cutting off the supply of rice to the imperial capital, and smallpox halved the population of some villages. The gazetteer of Yizhou county (Shandong) noted sadly: 'Among all the past occurrences of disaster and rebellion, there had never been anything worse than this'(Fig. 17; Plate 7).[30] Even subtropical Lingnan reported snow and ice four or five inches deep on the fish ponds in 1642, so that all the fish died; while the colder weather made it impossible to gather two annual rice harvests as before, dramatically reducing the yield of the south's staple crop both for local consumers and for export. At one point a tiger – the first one seen in the area for over a century – stalked its prey right outside the walls of Canton, no doubt driven from its normal haunts by the famine.[31]

Confucian doctrine saw flood and droughts as 'heaven-sent disasters' (*tianzai*) and an increased incidence of natural disasters as a cosmic portent that a 'Change in the Mandate [of Heaven]' was imminent. The failure of so many harvests in the Chongzhen reign therefore led his ministers to propose drastic remedies. *A complete treatise on agricultural administration*, composed in the 1620s and published in 1637, devoted one-third of its text to famine control, explaining not only how to build and manage granaries but also how to cultivate crops capable of withstanding adverse weather, and which wild plants one could safely eat. By then, however, lack of funds and central direction had left many (if not most) of the public granaries empty and the run of poor harvests made it impossible to replenish them.[32]

Lacking assistance from the central government, individual county magistrates searched for other ways to 'nourish the people' during the worst crisis to afflict East Asia in early modern times. Since the central government devoted all available resources to resisting the Qing, many pinned their hopes on charity to feed the hungry – but this also produced too little, too late. Thus when the magistrate of Shanghai county, faced by famine and disease in 1641–2, persuaded some gentry and merchants to 'contribute rice to cook gruel' for communal kitchens, starving people came 'in unbroken streams, leading their elders and bearing their children on their backs. In extreme cases, they fell down dead on the roads before reaching the gruel kitchens; or else, having eaten their fill, they died by the wayside just as they were returning ... Outside the city, from winter till the following summer, on the roads the corpses lay on top of one another.' The spring brought no relief. The same source described 'the joy that lit up the faces of those able to obtain a few pecks of husks by borrowing; the rush of the starving people to clear the countryside of green vegetation indiscriminately as it appeared in spring 1642; unbroken lines of beggars; sale of child slaves and women; abandonment of little children; active infanticide; cannibalism'.[33] Others reported that 'the human price of a peck of rice – barely enough to feed one person for a week – was two children'. Lu Shiyi, a young

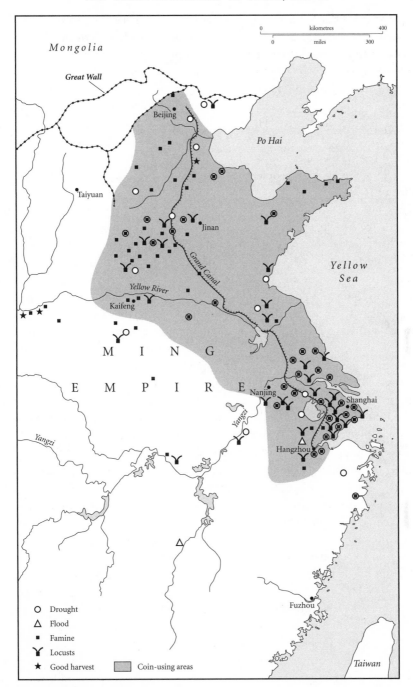

17. Disasters and diseases cripple Ming China, 1641.
Over 100 County Gazetteers from the provinces of Henan, Hubei, Shandong and Jiangsu recorded a major natural disaster – drought, flood, famine, locusts – in the year 1641. At the same time, a sudden dearth of silver coins dislocated the economic hub of Ming China.

scholar so poor that he had to beg, recorded in his diary the 'red dust skies', the drought and locusts, the bandit and pirate attacks of 1641, and concluded 'Jiangnan has never had this kind of disaster'. But then came 1642, when 'an especially severe food shortage, coupled with freezing weather, caused an unknown number of people to die of starvation; in villages and alleyways, no sign of life could be found,' he wrote, adding: 'I have heard of many cases in which women let themselves be violated in order to survive.' He himself watched a woman eating her own child outside the office of the sub-prefect. Many years later, Yao Tinglin, a minor official who had been a teenager in Shanghai at the time, wrote that ever since then 'I am not afraid of seeing dead people: that is because I saw so many of them' during the famine of 1641–2.[34]

Thus, just as the Manchu and bandit threats reached a crescendo in north China, the Little Ice Age struck the south. The fertile soil and benign climate of Jiangnan, which had allowed enterprising farmers to harvest double and even triple rice crops, had produced by the 1620s an overall population density of 1,200 per square mile – one of the highest on the planet. In 1637 the Jesuit missionary Alvaro Semedo, who had lived for two decades in Jiangnan, correctly concluded that the region was 'overpopulated': since the number of 'people is infinite, they cannot create a capital or stock sufficient for so many, or money to fill so many purses'. He therefore deduced, also correctly, 'hence it comes to pass that the partition [of resources] among them is such that a few get a lot, not many get enough, and almost everyone gets [too] little.'[35] Many Ming officials shared Semedo's view. One noted that the 'population has grown so much that it is entirely without parallel in history' and worried about the consequences. Another estimated that the population of Jiangnan had quintupled over the previous 250 years so that the province's arable land could no longer support it. Such prodigious population growth, coupled with the habit of dividing farms among all sons, had by the 1630s reduced some holdings to half an acre (two *mou*) – insufficient to provide enough rice to sustain even a small family – but many farmers still managed to survive by raising cash crops such as cotton (which could grow on higher land than wet-rice) or tea (which thrived on hillsides), or by switching from rice cultivation to raising silkworms.[36]

This shift created a new source of vulnerability, however. Farmers who raised cash crops needed to produce and sell enough both to buy a year's food and to pay their taxes – but, unfortunately for them, climatic adversity coincided with a drastic reduction in the silver coins in circulation. In 1639, no doubt because the changing Pacific wind system made navigation more hazardous (see chapter 1 above), two galleons laden with silver from Mexico foundered with the loss of their entire cargoes. The Chinese merchants therefore could not sell their silk in the Philippines in exchange for Mexican silver as usual. In normal times, increased trade with Japan might have filled this shortfall because the archipelago (like Mexico) both produced silver and craved silk; but in the late 1630s, fearful of foreign influence, the Japanese government restricted all overseas trade, and so little silver left the country. Overall, China's silver imports fell from almost 600 metric tons in 1636–40 to under 250 metric tons in 1641–5, disrupting the trade and production of those who normally used silver, just as the central government increased its tax demands (payable in silver) to unprecedented levels. The farmers of southeast China could scarcely have picked a worse time to rely on cash crops.[37]

Under the cumulative pressure of so many catastrophes in so many areas, the social fabric of Ming China began to unravel. Many towns became battlegrounds where 'fighters guilds' would, for a fee, 'bully, beat, maim or even kill as directed'; and gangs with names like 'The 36 Heavenly Scourges' and 'The 72 Earthly Plagues' terrorized the streets. In Suzhou, 'the most populous, and most prosperous, non-capital city on the face of the earth', a run of drought-induced harvest failures, rent strikes and food riots had by 1642 brought the city to its knees. According to the autobiography kept by the retired magistrate Ye Shaoyuan, 'Most of the residences in the city are empty and they are falling into ruins. Fertile farms and beautiful estates are for sale but there is no one to buy them.' He added, 'It is natural that after a period of prosperity a period of depression should follow; but I never dreamed that I should have to witness these misfortunes in the days of my [own] life.'[38] Ye also reported that 'everywhere in hamlets and villages, people came shouting at the door, breaking down gates to enter' and loot. Many men and women committed suicide to escape agonizing choices or dishonourable fates; others migrated in desperation, like the couple who pushed their 'little cart' hoping in vain to find food, shelter and jobs elsewhere (see chapter 4 above); while others sold themselves into slavery. Rural rebellions multiplied as bondservants rebelled against their masters, while peasants attacked their landlords, defaulted on their rent, abandoned their homes – and, in many cases, joined the outlaws.[39]

Many contemporary writers commented on the link between the rise of the 'roving bandits' and the weather. Manuals on statecraft stressed that 'hunger and cold make a bandit' and that 'in famine years, if there is no government relief, and tax collection is not relaxed ... those who did not die of famine will rise to become bandits'; while books of advice for merchants warned that 'there are bandits along the small rivers in bad years' and 'bandits roam among the lakes, especially in famine years'. Officials of the central government concurred. According to Ming ministers, 'Famine breeds banditry' and 'There will be more banditry when we have successive years of famine'; while a Qing official later observed that 'When people are suffering, they can either risk death by flouting the law and becoming bandits, or face starvation if they do not; so the weak starve and the strong become bandits.'[40] Instead of taking strong measures, however, many Ming ministers exacerbated the problem by selling pardons to captured bandits in order to raise revenue. When in 1642 officials in Shandong captured and then ransomed a bandit leader, a local aristocrat (whose men had participated in the capture) pointed out reproachfully: 'If you release plundering and homicidal rebels like this, without question there will be more people who, seeing this, will imitate it.' Yet the officials had little choice, as even the Qing had to admit, because the bandit gangs were different:

Rural rebels never go beyond flocking like crows and scattering like beasts, but these types set up encampments and build forts. Local rebels never go beyond blocking the roads and stealing goods, but these types attack cities and seize land. Local rebels never go beyond cutting spears and making staves, but these types train soldiers to use firearms, and come completely equipped.[41]

The Alienated Intellectuals of Ming China

In the mid-eighteenth century Qin Huitian, a senior government official, summarized the problem in two lapidary sentences: 'The demise of the Ming was due to banditry. The rise of banditry was due to famine.'[42] Qin's explanation nevertheless omitted one other critical factor in the 'demise of the Ming': the role of an alienated academic proletariat whose influence far exceeded their numbers. Throughout China, tens of thousands of male children learned to read, write and memorize a set of classical works on ethics and history, and then took a formal examination in the county town under the personal supervision of the district magistrate, who also graded their papers. Those who passed this examination became eligible to take a more advanced test in the prefectural capital, once again under strict supervision, and all who passed achieved the rank of *shengyuan* ('licenciate'). Gaining *shengyuan* status brought numerous rewards: a modest stipend; exemption from labour services, physical punishments and certain taxes; the right to wear a special 'scholar's uniform' and to take precedence in all public places over other men, however senior, who lacked the degree. In a famine, they also received government relief before others. All *shengyuan* were expected to prepare for a further round of rigorous examinations, held triennially, which required them to write essays on assigned topics from the classics set by, and supervised by, a team of senior officials who left Beijing in a carefully calibrated sequence so that students sat the same examination on the same day over the entire state. Those who passed became *juren* ('elevated candidate'). They could then proceed to take a final set of exams held once every three years in the huge examination halls of Nanjing and Beijing, followed (for the successful) by an additional test administered by the emperor himself. Those who passed gained the coveted status of *jinshi* ('advanced scholar'): a passport to the highest offices in the state.[43]

This sophisticated system provided a strong administrative backbone for imperial China, and in many ways it served the state well. First, since it was open to most males able to memorize the classical curriculum and write literary Chinese, the central government mobilized its human resources for public service to an extent unequalled in the early modern world. Second, the existence of a 'common curriculum' in a single language and script provided remarkable cultural and linguistic uniformity across the state, despite its immense size and diverse population. Finally, the civil service never completely succumbed to either corruption or absolutism because, however incompetent, capricious or lazy the emperor at the apex of the system, every three years a new cohort of articulate and classically literate men in their prime began their measured progress up China's 'ladder of success'. Anyone who hoped to become a senior minister had to climb it.[44]

Nevertheless, the size of each successful triennial cohort remained very small: seldom more than 500 *juren* candidates and 300 *jinshi*. With such long odds, few candidates passed on their first attempt and some graduated only after many failures, long past their prime. Indeed, the combination of relatively easy access to *shengyuan* status with very strict quotas on higher degrees meant that 99 per cent of the men who competed in each triennial *juren* competition failed, as did 90 per cent of those who took each *jinshi* examination.[45] Accordingly, the number of *shengyuan* holders without government jobs soared from perhaps 30,000 in the early fifteenth century to over 500,000 in the early seventeenth – one in every 60 adult males – and below them lurked those who had devoted years of study at the county schools but still failed to pass any of their examinations.[46]

What happened to this academic proletariat? Although those who achieved their *shengyuan* degree were allowed to retain for life the economic and social privileges it brought, the impact of failing subsequent examinations on candidates who had devoted so much of their lives to study (and on the families that had sacrificed so much to support them) could be devastating. A few committed suicide; many suffered a nervous collapse; most went home and either worked while they continued to study (perhaps as secretary to an overworked magistrate or as tutor to the talented son of a rich family), or else vented their frustrations on the local population (a reaction so common that the 'failed candidate' became a stock character in Chinese novels). Some abandoned the examination mill and turned to business or medicine; while others still 'ploughed with their ink stands' (in the contemporary phrase), producing biographies, plays, novels, essays, epitaphs and (ironically) manuals on how to pass the civil service examinations.[47]

All these men (and many of their wives and daughters) could read, and thus become familiar with the unprecedented number of printed works available both in urban shops and from rural pedlers. Reading convinced some of these thwarted scholars that they could cope with China's problems better than their successful competitors now in the bureaucracy – a belief confirmed through the numerous 'scholarly societies' (*wen she*), where educated men debated not only literature, philosophy and history but also practical ways of restoring effective government. In 1629 a scholar from Tiacang, close to both Suzhou and Wuxi, called for these societies to join in an amalgamated federation, which would bring together gentlemen-scholars interested in 'revitalizing and restoring the ancient learning and thus be of some use at a later time. The name of our society, therefore, shall be the Restoration Society (*Fu she*).' The following year, when the society already boasted over 3,000 members, 30 of them took and passed the provincial examination in Nanjing, gaining one-fifth of the total *juren* granted, and the following year twice as many became *jinshi*.[48] Each successful alumnus of the Society worked to advance his colleagues within the bureaucracy through patronage and recommendations while others published collections of 'model essays' couched in a new pragmatic style both to popularize their ideas and also to put pressure on the examiners – for if the authors of such meritorious essays should fail, it would suggest bias and corruption.[49]

Nevertheless, bias and corruption increased. After 1620, the central government, desperate for money, allowed certain localities to sell *shengyuan* degrees; and in 1643, the last full year of Ming rule in Beijing, money even determined the outcome of the metropolitan examination, with the first and second places going to those who paid the highest price. Rising numbers of examination candidates tried to beat the system by resorting to religion or fortune-tellers; by trying to bribe or intimidate the examiners or the guards; or by cheating – by writing on their clothes or their bodies in special 'invisible ink' one of the thousands of successful essays from earlier examinations available in print. Naturally, such practices discouraged honest candidates; so did the Chongzhen emperor's habit of punishing any minister who failed to produce instant success. Many talented civil servants therefore either declined promotion or resigned rather than risk disgrace (and possible death) because, as a contemporary proverb put it, 'at any time, the jug could strike against the tiles'. Eventually, scores of disenchanted scholars threw in their lot with the 'roving bandits' led by Li Zicheng, the former official of the courier service.[50]

The Rise of 'the Dashing Prince'

The demoralization of the Ming's educated subjects, and above all of their officials, helped to facilitate the triumph of their enemies. In 1642 Li Zicheng, now known to his followers as 'the Dashing Prince', captured Kaifeng, once the capital of all China, while later that year a large Qing army broke through the Great Wall for the third time, pillaging northern China for several weeks before returning home with enormous booty (including copious quantities of food to sustain their own hungry subjects). In their wake, one town in Shandong reported that 30 per cent of its population had died of starvation, with another 40 per cent so poor that they could only survive by joining the bandits.[51]

This desperate situation produced desperate remedies. The emperor even authorized a secret approach to the Manchu leaders to see whether they might negotiate – until a clerk inadvertently published one of the clandestine documents in the government's official gazette. This slip provoked an avalanche of memorials from the bureaucracy condemning such pacifism, leading the emperor to abandon the talks.[52] Meanwhile, some Ming officials agreed to administer their regions in Li's name, and a few accepted an appointment at his 'court', encouraging the Dashing Prince to believe that (like other men from humble backgrounds in Chinese history) he could found his own imperial dynasty.[53] To win popular support, Li's followers fashioned populist slogans – 'Equalize land!', 'Three years remission of taxes!', 'Equal buying, equal selling!' – and propagated catchy ballads:

Kill the swine, prepare the wine,
Open the gates, prepare a welcome line.
When the Dashing Prince comes,
We won't pay a dime.[54]

In 1643, with the aid of disaffected officials, Li Zicheng set up a formal government in Xi'an (once the imperial capital), including a chancery and the traditional six ministries, and then declared himself the founder of a new state, *Da Shun* (meaning 'Great Compliance' [with the Mandate of Heaven]) with a corresponding 'Shun era' calendar. He also minted his own coins, elevated his leading supporters to noble status, and held civil service examinations to produce his own cadres of administrators. At this stage Li may have thought only in terms of a power-sharing arrangement – either with the Ming or with the Manchus – but early in 1644, perhaps encouraged by the lack of effective Ming resistance to the recent Manchu raid, he led his followers in one of the most extraordinary military feats in Chinese history: a 'long march' from Xi'an to Beijing.[55]

Li demanded exemplary behaviour from his troops – 'kill no one, accept no money, rape no one, loot nothing, trade fairly' he ordered – and this tactic encouraged most local commanders and officials in his path to surrender either immediately or after only token resistance. Li 'pardoned' most of them and confirmed them in office. The Dashing Prince and his lieutenants also imitated the heroes of the popular novel *Water Margin* (some took the names of characters from the book), while the literati in his entourage continued to produce catchy ditties:

You'll feed your mates,
You'll dress your mates,
You'll open wide your city gates.
When the Dashing Prince arrives there'll be no more rates.[56]

In addition, they drafted proclamations that exuded confidence and reassurance: 'Our army is made up of good peasants who have worked the fields for ten generations; we formed this humane and righteous army to rescue the population from destruction.' As soon as he arrived in an area, Li established tribunals that allowed tenants to press claims against their landlords and granted titles to abandoned domain land. To widespread popular acclaim he also arrested, humiliated and executed all Ming clansmen who fell into his hands, while his followers tore down the arches and temples erected by forced labour as memorials to illustrious local dignitaries.[57]

The Chongzhen emperor and his remaining advisers continued to debate extreme remedies: demanding forced loans from all ministers and eunuchs (which raised only 200,000 *taels*); issuing paper money to pay the troops; evacuating the crown prince to Nanjing; making a deal with either Li or the Manchus; recalling the only remaining reliable army, commanded by General Wu Sangui, from the Great Wall to defend the capital. Only the last measure took effect – and even then Wu was still far away when on 23 April 1644, a mere eight weeks after they had left Xi'an, Li and his army stood before the capital of the Ming empire.

Although defended by walls that stretched for over 20 miles, with 13 huge fortified gates and the largest urban population in the world, Beijing presented a soft target: the garrison had not been paid for five months and food reserves had run low. Some disaffected defenders opened one of the outer gates to Li but, since the

Imperial City remained intact, the emperor summoned his ministers and prepared to make a last-ditch stand there. When no one came, he disguised himself as a eunuch and tried to escape, but his own palace guards fired on him and he turned back. So finally, after a reign of 17 years, he went into the palace garden, where he wrote an epitaph on his white robe that combined (in characteristic fashion) self-criticism with blame of his advisers:

> My inadequate virtues and weak flesh have invited punishment from Heaven. Now the treacherous rebels are invading the capital. My officials have caused all this! I must die, but I am ashamed to face my ancestors. Therefore I take off my crown and cover my face with my hair.

He then hanged himself to avoid being captured, humiliated and executed by his subjects.[58]

Li now controlled most of northern China, including its capital, but he faced three urgent problems. First Zhang Xianzhong, the ex-soldier turned bandit leader (page 123 above), had conquered Sichuan where he proclaimed himself the 'Great King of the West'. Although Zhang did not threaten the capital, his brutal administration devastated one of the wealthier provinces of China and undermined both the resources and the reputation of the central government. Second, although Li's troops had kept good order on their march to Beijing, they now expected their reward. To avoid looting, the Dashing Prince needed to arrange for taxes to flow into the capital once more – but his earlier depredations complicated this task. A traveller from the south who reached Beijing at this time marvelled that in the 'villages we passed through' on the way 'there were only broken-down walls and ruined chimneys leaning against one another. For several hundred miles there was no sign of human habitation.'[59] Finally, Li urgently needed to pay and win over the army of Wu Sangui – all that stood between the capital and the Manchu forces beyond the Great Wall.

At first, not knowing whether the crown prince might still be alive somewhere in the city, and anxious to win over Wu and his loyalist troops, the Dashing Prince behaved with great prudence. For example, he sat beside the imperial throne (not on it) to receive the obeisance of the civil and military personnel in the capital. Once again his moderation succeeded: of the 2,000 or more Ming officials in Beijing when it surrendered, fewer than 40 elected to follow the example of their late master by committing suicide – amazing testimony to how the Chongzhen emperor had alienated his ministers. Li now ordered former civil servants in the capital to make 'substantial contributions' to his new treasury, preferably voluntarily but if necessary under duress. The Shun treasury received some 70 million *taels* in this way (compared with only 200,000 offered to the Ming emperor a few days before), which allowed the Dashing Prince both to pay his troops and to 'forgive' the tax arrears of all areas that recognized his authority.

Most senior officials initially seem to have regarded their ordeal as a just punishment for failing to serve their late master better (and to commit suicide on learning of his death); but before long Li lost control over his followers, who started to plunder the houses where they lodged, to abuse their hosts, to attack their neighbours and to abduct or rape teahouse servants, female entertainers, and finally elite women in their homes. When the new master led his troops out of the city on 18 May, only three weeks after their triumphant entry, Beijing rejoiced.

The Tipping Point: China's 'Battle of Hastings'

The Dashing Prince left his new capital to deal with Wu Sangui, the Ming general whose troops manned the Shanhai pass, where the ridge of mountains that carries the Great Wall reaches the sea north of Beijing. Wu had refused to recognize the 'Shun state' and, when a detachment of Li's army attacked him, he defeated it, provoking the Dashing Prince to murder Wu's father and other relatives whom he had captured. Almost immediately, Wu appealed to the Qing for help against Li.

Why did Wu take this fateful decision? Apart from resentment at the death of his relatives, several other considerations played a part. First, commanding scarcely 40,000 soldiers, no doubt Wu feared that the victorious Shun army, numbering perhaps 100,000 men, would overwhelm him if he fought alone (as indeed they almost did). Second, several of his surviving relatives had surrendered to the Manchus in Liaodong and an alliance with the Qing would secure their continued good treatment. Third, several Chinese regimes in the past had survived by appealing to a northern neighbour for assistance in time of peril. Fourth, the Manchus had previously shown no interest in permanent conquest: their earlier invasions of China had targeted booty not land. Finally, the Qing ruler Hong Taiji died late in 1643, leaving two quarrelsome brothers as regents for his 6-year-old son, and Wu may have assumed that this family squabble would fatally undermine Manchu strength and cohesion.

All these considerations were valid, but Wu overlooked the crucial impact of climate change. Long before they received his appeal for help, the Manchus had concluded that the recent famines would force them to invade China or perish: the tree-ring series for East Asia shows 1643-4 as the coldest years in the entire millennium between 800 and 1800, and the winter monsoons brought little rain (Fig. 18). The Manchu leaders therefore assembled a Grand Army of 60,000 or more warriors close to the Great Wall, while their Han Chinese advisers prepared announcements to persuade their compatriots to support the new invasion: 'The righteous army comes to avenge your ruler-father for you. It is not an enemy of the people. The only ones to be killed now are the [Shun] bandits. Officials who surrender can resume their former posts. People who surrender can resume their former occupations. We will by no means harm you.'[60]

The Grand Army stood poised to break through the Great Wall into Shanxi when Wu's desperate appeal revealed the widespread hostility to the Shun regime. This, according to Wu, offered a unique 'opportunity to rip down what is withered and rotten. Certainly there will never be a second chance!'[61] The Manchu leaders therefore abandoned their plan to invade Shanxi and instead led their troops to the Shanhai pass where Wu, threatened by Li's approaching army, let them through.

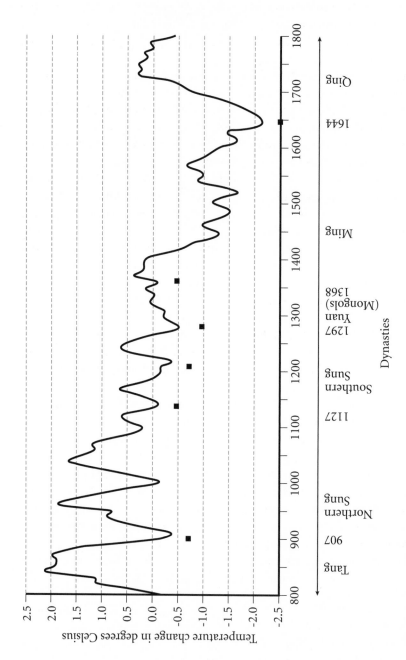

18. East Asian temperatures, 800–1800.

Although temperatures, as measured by tree-ring width, began to fall in the fourteenth century, with a partial recovery in the sixteenth, the lowest temperatures – more than 2°C cooler – occured in the mid-seventeenth century with the nadir in 1644, the year the Manchus drove the Ming from north China.

The Qing Regent Dorgon ('badger' in Manchu), in command of the Grand Army, skilfully exploited his advantage. His troops took no part in the battle between Wu and Li, which sinologist Mark Elliott has called 'China's battle of Hastings', until the last moment, when they charged the Shun flanks. As a result, Wu's forces bore the brunt of the battle and sustained heavy casualties, leaving them too weak to confront the Manchus. Dorgon therefore called upon Wu to become a Qing vassal. If he did this, Dorgon promised, 'your ruler will be avenged and you and your family will be protected' (an unsubtle reference to the presence of Wu's relatives in the Qing camp). In addition 'your posterity will enjoy wealth and nobility as eternal as the mountains and rivers'.[62] Powerless to resist, Wu and his surviving soldiers shaved their heads in the Manchu manner as a dramatic gesture of submission.

Meanwhile, Li and his defeated troops fell back on Beijing, which they re-entered on 31 May 1644. The Dashing Prince now had nothing to lose by proclaiming himself emperor, and the hasty enthronement of the first (and last) Shun emperor took place. The following day, realizing that the approach of Wu and the Manchus made his position untenable, Li set fire to the Forbidden City and ordered his men to retreat. The wits of Beijing jested:

Zicheng hacked his way to power –
But he's not the Son of Heaven.
He mounted the throne on horseback –
But not for very long![63]

The population of the capital prepared to greet Wu Sangui, perhaps accompanied by the missing Ming crown prince; but instead, on 5 June 1644, Dorgon mounted the ceremonial platform they had prepared and told the onlookers: ' "I am the prince regent. The crown prince will arrive in a little while. Will you allow me to be the ruler?" The crowd, astonished and uncomprehending, was only able to lamely answer "yes." ' Since the few remaining palace guards offered no resistance, a detachment of Manchu troops took possession of the smouldering Forbidden City, the hub of the entire Chinese state.[64]

Many people in Beijing only realized that a new dynasty had seized power when they read a proclamation issued by Dorgon later that day. It first declared that the 'Great Qing Dynasty' had long sought harmonious relations with the Ming 'hoping for perpetual peace', and in the past had invaded only when their letters were ignored. Meanwhile the bandits had taken control, but now the Qing had exacted 'revenge upon the enemy of your ruler-father':

We burned our bridges behind us, and we have pledged not to return until every bandit is destroyed. In the counties, districts and locales that we pass through, all those who are able to shave their heads and surrender, opening their gates to welcome us, will be given rank and reward, retaining their wealth and nobility for generations. But if there are those who resist us and act disobediently, then when our Grand Army arrives, the stones themselves will be set ablaze and everyone will be massacred.

Dorgon took immediate steps designed to win support for the new regime. He announced that the Manchu troops were about to 'unstring their bows' (viz. stand down); he abolished several unpopular taxes; and he reduced the land tax by one-third in all areas that submitted to the Qing. Above all, he visited the body of the late Chongzhen emperor to pay his respects and ordered three days of public mourning, inviting all former Ming officials to do the same. This proved an extremely shrewd move, because any official who *now* committed suicide could be seen as expressing loyalty to the Shun regime, and Dorgon capitalized on their dilemma by promising to reinstate and remunerate all former Ming bureaucrats prepared to resume their former office, and an instant one-grade promotion to those who also shaved their heads in Manchu fashion and adopted Manchu dress.[65] Almost the entire bureaucracy of the capital complied. A prominent official who two months earlier had switched his allegiance to the Shun spoke for many when he declared: 'I am a minister of the Ming but the Ming have perished and there is nothing to belong to. Whoever has the ability to take revenge upon the enemies of the Ming, those murdering bandits, is therefore my ruler.' On 29 October 1644 China's new ruler, the 7-year-old Shunzhi emperor for whom Dorgon served as regent, entered Beijing. The following day he performed the customary sacrifice to the Supreme Ruler of the Universe at the Temple of Heaven, south of the Forbidden City, and thereby established his claim to be the sole intermediary between Heaven and Earth. A few days later, an official noted in his diary with relief: 'My alarmed spirit has begun to settle. Within the last ten days officials high and low' had begun to work once again in the Imperial City, so that 'it is just like old times'. He spoke too soon: it would take a generation before all China again enjoyed peace – and, even then, 'old times' would never return.[66]

China Partitioned

Since China had two capitals, the Dashing Prince's capture of Beijing automatically made Nanjing the Ming capital. It possessed many assets. Lying in the lower Yangzi valley, the richest region of the empire, amid copious supplies of food and a bustling trade, it was the cultural centre of China. It was also the second largest city in the world (after Beijing) and boasted powerful defences. Admittedly, the southern capital tended to attract officials with little enthusiasm for war, ill-suited to resist skilful and determined invaders; nevertheless, some weeks before the fall of Beijing, officials in the southern capital made plans for the Ming crown prince to escape and join them and began to mobilize naval and military forces.

Although Chinese history offered a promising precedent – four centuries earlier, the Song dynasty had survived in the south for 150 years after Mongol invaders overran northern China – the situation in 1644 was very different: crop failures in 1633, 1634, 1635, 1638 and 1640, followed by the worst drought in five centuries (1641–4) had depopulated parts of Jiangnan and left the survivors weak, poor and demoralized. In addition, the sudden scarcity of silver after 1640 (see pages 128–9 above) crippled both trade and tax collection. Amid such weakness, news of the

Chongzhen emperor's suicide, and the disappearance of the crown prince, immediately created chaos: many people considered an interregnum to be a period without laws and acted accordingly.

According to an eyewitness living near Shanghai, 'seeing that there was no emperor, the bondsmen made a body of many thousands, and asked their lords for papers of [manumission] because [with the fall of] the Chinese government they were already free. And taking up arms they first turned on the lords in the countryside, killing, robbing and doing a thousand other insults without anyone taking up arms against them.' They also warned magistrates in nearby towns that, unless they received 'the papers of their freedom immediately', they would 'kill all without mercy'. According to another contemporary, thousands of bondservants took up arms 'under rebel leaders. They ripped up pairs of trousers to serve as flags. They sharpened their hoes into swords and took to themselves the title of "Levelling Kings", declaring that they were levelling the distinction between masters and serfs, titled and mean, rich and poor.' They also 'opened the granaries and distributed the contents'.[67] The leader of one uprising claimed: 'Now we are endowed by heaven with a special opportunity, for our masters are all weak and feeble and are not able to take up arms. We can take advantage of their crisis. Even if they want to suppress us, they do not have time.' His followers agreed: 'The emperor has changed, so the masters should be made into servants to serve us; master and servant should address each other as brothers.' In the words of the gazetteer of a county near Shanghai, 'an uprising like this has not been seen for a thousand years'.[68]

The collapse of central authority also encouraged other, lesser forms of resistance. Peasants presumably deployed their traditional repertory of 'foot-dragging, dissimulation, desertion, false compliance, pilfering, feigned ignorance, slander, arson, sabotage' (page 512 below), and withheld rents and services whenever possible. Even when defiance stopped short of murder, it spread disorder that proved particularly deleterious in areas where successful agriculture depended on hydraulic projects: inland, the destruction or neglect of dikes created marshes and lakes that offered a sanctuary to bandits (many of them, no doubt, peasants deprived of their livelihoods by the floods); in coastal areas, it supplied recruits to pirate enterprises. The towns of the Yangzi and Pearl river estuaries in particular fell prey to attacks by ferocious river pirates.[69]

Unlike their colleagues in Beijing, many Ming officials in the south responded to the news of the Chongzheng emperor's death by committing suicide. Gazetteers record some southern gentry families in which a dozen or more members either set themselves on fire or, one after another, jumped into a well; while students, inspired by an ardent colleague or teacher, either drowned or hanged themselves. Yet not all Ming loyalists gave up. In Nanjing, ministers discussed which member of the imperial family should become the 'caretaker' of the realm until the crown prince reappeared. The prince of Fu, a first cousin of the late emperor, who had supported the hated eunuch Wei's persecution of Donglin, attracted the allegiance of surviving *yandang* officials, but was unacceptable to the self-proclaimed 'righteous ministers';

so although he became first 'caretaker', and then emperor, bureaucratic factionalism continued to plague the Ming state.

Nevertheless, for a moment it seemed that the new ruler in Nanjing might stabilize the situation. He immediately promoted all officials by one grade, scheduled civil service exams, and granted all provinces between the Yangzi and the Yellow rivers tax relief until they recovered from the crisis of the preceding years. He also divided these provinces into four military zones and charged Shi Kefa, one of the few Ming generals to have campaigned successfully against the roving bandits, with coordinating defensive operations. Shi made Yangzhou, on the Grand Canal just north of the Yangzi, both the linchpin of a new defensive system and a springboard for a future offensive to reunite China under its former dynasty.

In Beijing, Dorgon considered his options. When his Chinese advisers urged him to conquer all China, he at first ridiculed the notion – 'Unify it?', he is alleged to have asked: 'We can do no more than gain an inch and hold on to an inch, gain a foot and hold on to a foot' – but he soon discovered that his huge new capital could not survive without rice from Jiangnan, controlled by the Southern Ming, and without coal from Shanxi, controlled by Li Zicheng.[70] Dorgon decided to deal with the second problem first.

Since Li still commanded some 350,000 soldiers whereas the Manchu Grand Army probably now numbered fewer than 100,000 warriors, only half of them Manchus, the regent made several further concessions to win the support of his new Chinese subjects. He barred eunuchs from handling revenues from imperial estates and from participating in court audiences; he also reduced their numbers to about 3,000. He accepted the services of magistrates and ministers who had served both Ming and Shun (although they were later known by the unflattering label *Er chen*, 'ministers who served both dynasties'), and welcomed back many reforming ministers, often associates of the Donglin and other Academies, who had lost their posts under the Tianqi and Chongzhen emperors. These officials began to rationalize the legal system (issuing a standard set of penalties, updating the civil code, promulgating new criminal regulations) and improve revenue collection ('forgiving' tax arrears in areas that submitted to the Qing and confiscating the vast estates held by Ming clansmen). To Frederic Wakeman, an outstanding historian of 'the Great Enterprise',

> What is most surprising is how little was actually required in the end to bring the bureaucratic administration up to a reasonable level of efficiency. Adjustments, not replacements; overhaul, not wholesale substitution, were the characteristics of this reform effort. Moreover, the reforms ... were mainly the work of men who had seen service under the Ming, and were now given the opportunities denied them earlier to carry out the kinds of adjustment that would make the system with which they were already familiar work best.[71]

The Qing also courted some important constituencies which the Ming had alienated – above all, by extolling martial virtues and rewarding military merit, they won over many generals and troops whom the Ming had treated with contempt.

Moreover, the ability of the new dynasty to tackle the bandit menace that had made life miserable for so many Chinese won both admiration and support from property owners. Shandong offers a testament to the success of Dorgon's policy of reconciliation. After the great Manchu raid of 1642–3, provincial officials estimated that seven households out of ten depended on some form of criminal activity for their survival. A few weeks after entering Beijing, Dorgon 'forgave' all Shandong's tax arrears, and the following year he significantly reduced its quota and sent some of his elite troops to restore order. Just five years after being traumatized by Qing marauders, Shandong provided the new dynasty with the largest provincial quota of 'twice-serving ministers'; and its largest landowners, the dukes of Kong (direct descendants of Confucius), became the dynasty's staunch allies.[72]

By contrast, two of Dorgon's other initiatives proved highly divisive and unpopular. First, the regent decided to create 'Tatar towns' in a number of strategic cities. In Beijing, Dorgon decreed that only Manchus could live in the Inner City, around the palace, and he forcibly relocated perhaps 300,000 Chinese residents to the Outer City beyond. The Qing took similar steps throughout their territory, eventually creating 34 'Tatar towns' – basically citadels – reserved for Manchu soldiers and their families, while all others had to live outside.[73] This measure naturally infuriated those compelled to abandon their ancestral homes.

A second innovation proved even more divisive and unpopular because it affected all males, whether living in town or countryside. Long before 1644, the Qing decreed that their supporters must make themselves look like Manchus; but realizing that it would take time to acquire new clothes (or adapt old ones), Dorgon at this stage insisted only that all males must shave the front of their heads and wear the rest in a queue at the back. He failed to anticipate how much resentment even this would cause. Han Chinese culture had for millennia viewed correct attire and appearance as an essential distinction between civilization and barbarism; and bundling his hair into a topknot (*shufu*) formed part of the etiquette that marked the passage of a Han male to adulthood. Dorgon's tonsure decree thus challenged a fundamental aspect of traditional Chinese culture – and not once but repeatedly, since to keep the front part of the head bald required regular shaving (Plate 8).[74]

Revolts against head-shaving broke out almost immediately in some areas near the capital and, after three weeks, Dorgon prudently backed down. 'Formerly,' he explained,

> Because there was no way of distinguishing people who had surrendered, I ordered them to cut their hair in order to separate the yielding from the rebellious. Now I hear that this is directly contrary to the people's wishes, which contradicts my own [desire] to settle the people's minds with civil persuasion. Let each of the ministers and commoners from now on arrange their hair in the old [style], completely according to their convenience.[75]

This compromise convinced most 'ministers and commoners' in northern China to accept the Qing, while Wu Sangui and a part of the Manchu Grand Army set off in pursuit of Li, who had retreated to Xi'an, his 'western capital'. He could not hold it:

instead, in February 1645, the Dashing Prince took to the hills with a handful of followers, where some months later he met a violent end. Wu, having won control of all his strategic objectives in the northwest (including the vital Shanxi coalfields), now invaded Sichuan to destroy Zhang Xianzhong's 'Great Western State'.

In Beijing, Dorgon bought time by plying the Southern Ming with reassuring messages that hinted at a negotiated partition of China. 'As for those who have not forgotten the Ming [dynasty] and have supported and enthroned a worthy prince, putting forward their fullest effort with unified hearts to protect the lower Yangzi [against the bandits]', he wrote soothingly to them, 'that is as things should be. We will not stop you. But you should contact us for peaceful, amicable discussions and not rebuff our dynasty.'[76] The Nanjing regime countered with an embassy that thanked the Qing for expelling the bandits from the capital and promised that if they withdrew beyond the Great Wall, they could keep all land beyond it and receive a handsome annual tribute. This was totally unrealistic: the Manchus had come too far, and needed the resources of the Central Plain too much, simply to go home. Nevertheless Dorgon entertained the embassy from Nanjing with false hopes until, in March 1645, he felt it safe to recall some of his Banner troops from the west. His brother, Prince Dodo, now led a devastating attack on the Southern Ming.

'Keep your head, lose your hair; keep your hair, lose your head'

Appalling weather continued to afflict Jiangnan: the winter of 1644–5 saw the weakest monsoon in more than a millennium, prolonging the drought. As the Grand Army advanced southwards from Beijing most cities opened their gates and offered tribute to the conquerors. By May 1645 only Yangzhou held out north of the Yangzi river, and its makeshift defences proved no match for the heavy artillery brought by the Qing. When the city fell, Dodo allowed his troops to sack it for a week, and only unseasonable rain prevented the fires lit by the looters from consuming the entire city. Nevertheless, the destruction of life and property was so great that poets began to refer to Yangzhou as *Wucheng*: 'the weed-covered city'.[77]

Dodo's strategic use of terror bore immediate fruit: Nanjing and most other cities of Jiangnan surrendered to avoid the fate of Yangzhou. Nevertheless a few Ming loyalists elsewhere in the south organized resistance, forcing the Manchus once again to seek some way to distinguish friend from foe – albeit more sensitively than before. Instead of insisting that all Chinese males must shave their heads, a new tonsure decree of June 1645 announced that 'In all of the places occupied by the Grand Army we will shave the military and not shave the civilians; we will shave the soldiers and not shave the people'; but a group of Chinese scholars in the capital unwisely protested against even this compromise, claiming that their traditional 'System of Rites and Music' required Han Chinese to preserve intact all they had inherited from their parents, so that shaving forelocks was a kind of tonsorial castration.[78] This proved too much for Dorgon, who angrily retorted:

Does *our* dynasty not have a System of Rites and Music? If officials say that people should not respect our Rites and Music, but rather follow those of the Ming, what can be their true intentions? There may be some sense in the idea that one's hair and skin are from one's parents and, thus, ought not to be harmed, but I will not stand for this incessant 'Rites and Music' rubbish. I have hitherto loved and pitied the [Han] officials, allowing them to follow their own preference [in matters of dress and tonsure]. Now, however, because of this divisive talk, I can but issue a decree to all officials and commoners, ordering that they all shave their foreheads.

Dorgon further insisted that the tonsure decree must be implemented within ten days of its receipt in each locality: disobedience would be 'equivalent to a rebel's defying the Mandate [of Heaven]', and any official who sought 'to retain the Ming institutions and not follow those of this dynasty' would face immediate execution.[79]

This angry overreaction, a marked departure from Dorgon's previous moderation, perhaps reflected a new confidence born of his appointment as sole regent and the successes of Qing armies on all fronts; but, whatever its cause, it proved a catastrophic error. As a Jesuit eyewitness tartly observed, the Chinese elite now 'grieved and fought more valiantly for their hair and habit than they had done for their kingdom and emperor'.[80] An incident near Nanjing illustrated this point. After the surrender of the southern capital, the new Qing authorities urgently sought information on the resources of the region, dispatching commissioners to secure the tax and population registers of each county. Since the Qing lacked their own reliable cadres, many of these commissioners were former Ming officials: Fang Heng, a young *jinshi* official sent to the town of Jiangyin, was one of them. He arrived still wearing Ming insignia on his robes and was on the point of securing the registers when four Manchu soldiers turned up with the tonsure decree and orders for its immediate implementation. Fang therefore prepared a simple Chinese version of Dorgon's proclamation – *'Keep your head, lose your hair; keep your hair, lose your head'* – which provoked armed peasants to converge on Jiangyin, where they killed all four Manchu soldiers and Fang – but not before he had sent a secret appeal for reinforcements. Qing troops arrived with 24 siege guns, which breached the town walls and enabled a successful assault. Dorgon had ordered his troops to 'fill the city with corpses before you sheathe your swords', and his troops duly obliged. Tens of thousands of Ming loyalists at Jiangyin 'kept their hair and lost their heads'.[81]

Similar events took place elsewhere in the lower Yangzi valley, as places changed hands (sometimes several times). Yao Tinglin, scion of a gentry family from Shanghai, later recalled how in 1645,

Whenever the Qing army approached every household in the towns and villages would paste pieces of yellow paper on the door with the characters *Da Qing shunmin* ('obedient subjects of the Great Qing') written on, but would tear them down as soon as the loyalist rebellion seemed to get the upper hand, only to paste them again when the Qing troops were supposed to come back.

This explains why Dorgon enforced the tonsure decree so ruthlessly as a touchstone of loyalty: one could opportunistically paste up and tear down pieces of paper, but no man could fake his tonsure. By the end of 1645 the Qing had prevailed throughout Jiangnan. In Shanghai, Yao Tinglin recognized that 'nothing would be the same as before: it was to be a new dynasty, people looking differently, new social hierarchies, new rituals, and so forth – in short, "another world, with no restoring of the old order".'[82]

'China in Tigers' Jaws'

The Qing conquest of Jiangnan marked an important stage in the success of the Great Enterprise because it secured Beijing's food supply. Rice, millet, wheat and beans once again came up the Grand Canal, to be stored in the capital's enormous granaries. Although most of these supplies went directly to the Manchu families of the Inner City, other residents benefited because the government used the granaries to keep prices low and to run soup kitchens for the poor.[83] The Qing also preserved the traditional examination system for the civil service. They held the first triennial metropolitan examination in 1646, just three years after the last Ming exercise, a supplementary one in 1647, and then a regular cycle from 1649. They also tightened up the lax examination standards that had prevailed under the late Ming, for example by executing candidates found to have cheated.

As one Qing minister wearily noted, however, 'Seizing the empire is easy; ruling it is difficult.'[84] The absence of any effective geographical barrier separating Beijing from the lower Yangzi had greatly facilitated the Qing's progress thus far, but extending control into areas of the south and west loyal to the Southern Ming presented greater challenges. First, the Little Ice Age continued to cause hardship and disruption. The winter of 1649–50 seems to have been the coldest on record in both north and east China, while the capital experienced such a serious drought in 1657 and again in 1660 that the emperor personally conducted prayers for rain. In the south, 17 counties in Guangdong province reported frost or snow in the 1650s – the highest number in two centuries. Guangdong also suffered more typhoon landfalls between 1660 and 1680 than at any other time in recorded history.[85] Second, troops raised in the steppe had seldom encountered smallpox and so possessed little immunity when they entered China: the sudden death from the disease of so many Manchu troops and commanders began to undermine campaign plans. The Qing adopted several panic measures: they banished from the army any soldier who contracted the disease, and they ordered that only princes who had survived smallpox should command their armies. These measures failed: inevitably, not all cases of smallpox were detected before they spread to other soldiers; and, in pursuit of honour and booty, some princes disregarded the risk of infection and insisted on campaigning and promptly died.[86]

Losses from smallpox, and the need to garrison initial conquests with reliable soldiers, reduced the number of Banner troops available for the conquest of the south, forcing the Qing to rely on former Ming units of questionable loyalty. In

1645, for example, a small Qing force captured the great port of Guangzhou (Canton) by a ruse and entrusted it to a general who had defected from the Ming; but he soon declared for the Southern Ming. Forces loyal to Beijing only returned five years later and blockaded Canton for eight months, until a defector opened one of the gates, allowing the besiegers to rush in. Over the next two weeks, they 'never spared man, woman or child; but all whosoever were cruelly put to the sword; nor was there heard any other speech, but "Kill, kill these barbarous rebels"'. Well-informed sources placed the number of slain at 80,000, and even a century later a mound of congealed ashes marked the spot where their corpses had burned on a huge funeral pyre.[87] The Qing now entrusted the unruly southeastern provinces of Guangxi, Guangdong and Fujian to three Chinese generals from Liaodong who had joined them at the outset.

Despite abundant proof that head-shaving united their opponents, the Qing persevered with the policy after Dorgon died in 1650. Thus when the principal Ming naval commander, Zheng Chenggong ('Coxinga'), seemed willing to defect, at first the Qing offered him a ducal title and lands, promised that he could keep all his troops under arms, and conceded that all shipping off the coast of Fujian 'shall be subject to your management, inspection, and collection of taxes'. Then, just when Coxinga seemed about to accept these terms, the envoys sent by Beijing to handle the final negotiations bluntly stated: 'If you do not shave your head, then you cannot receive the [emperor's] proclamation. If your head is not shaven, then we need not even meet.'[88] Outraged, Coxinga used his warships – some of them armed with Western-style artillery – to dominate all trade in the South China Sea until by 1659 he had gathered sufficient funds and support to mount a campaign up the Yangzi. Thirty-two counties and seven prefectural capitals declared their allegiance before a Qing counter-attack forced Coxinga first to retreat to the coast and eventually to abandon the Chinese mainland, making the island of Taiwan his new base.[89] Lacking a fleet capable of pursuing him there, the Qing now imposed another draconian and deeply unpopular measure on their Chinese subjects: in the hope of starving out Taiwan, they ordered all who lived within 20 miles of the mainland's southeast coast to abandon their homes and move inland. They then forbade all seaborne trade, destroyed all buildings, and issued orders to kill any human found in the 'no go' area.

The trade embargo produced what the Chinese called *shu huang*: 'dearth in the midst of plenty'. Famines, war and disorder had already decimated domestic consumption in southeast China: now the government removed all export markets so that, once better weather increased rice yields, supply rapidly outstripped demand. The price of a bushel of rice fell one hundred-fold and, according to a local source, 'with such low grain prices, peasant-farmers could not pay taxes or support their families, thus much land was abandoned'.[90] The entries in a county gazetteer in Jiangnan epitomized the agonizingly slow process of restoring domestic order. Three times – in 1649, 1654 and 1664 – it optimistically recorded that 'now that the bandits have been pacified, the dikes were at last rebuilt'; but only on the third occasion did lasting repairs to the irrigation system, the vital precondition for wet-rice cultivation, actually get underway.[91]

One cannot blame the Qing alone for this prolonged devastation. As Lynn Struve noted in her path-breaking study of the Southern Ming: 'The long struggle between the Ming and Qing was not so much a direct clash between two states as a competition to see which side would prevail over, or be defeated by, a third state, so to speak: that of socio-political anarchy':

> In the whole eighteen-year span of the Southern Ming, there were not more than a handful of instances in which the Qing had to fight to wrest control of a community from Ming officials and military forces that had been in place there prior to the dynastic crisis. The problem for the Ming had been to maintain control, and for the Qing it was to re-establish control, over a patchwork quilt of districts, prefectures, and circuits the size of a subcontinent. Generally speaking, the Ming lost in this competition more rapidly than the Qing won.[92]

First the Southern Ming court fled south to Fujian, then westward to Yunnan and finally into Burma where in 1661 Wu Sangui hunted down the last claimant and executed him. After this regicide, the jubilant Qing granted Wu extensive powers in Yunnan, where he settled with his victorious troops and created a prosperous fief.[93] That same year, Coxinga and his followers departed for Taiwan, and with that all organized resistance to the Qing on the Chinese mainland temporarily ceased.

Nevertheless, for several reasons Qing power remained fragile. First, the death of the Shunzhi emperor in 1661 left a vacuum in which the regents for the young Kiangxi emperor competed for power, destabilizing the entire state. Second, fiscal shortfalls caused by the cost of the various Manchu conquests led the central government to decree that all tax arrears must be paid immediately and to threaten that all officials would be denied promotion, or even demoted or dismissed, unless they delivered outstanding tax quotas in full. In Jiangnan, a combination of unusually high tax evasion and lingering loyalty to the Ming led the Qing to institute a crackdown, imprisoning or executing 'tax resisters' and barring them from holding office. Although these savage measures worked in the short-term – tax evasion by the gentry dropped dramatically – they created a reservoir of discontent: in the words of a Jiangnan gentleman-scholar, the 'laws were like a frost withering the autumn grass'.[94] Finally, global cooling continued to afflict most if not all regions of China: 9 of the 14 summers between 1666 and 1679 were either cool or exceptionally cool, and a recent study of Chinese glaciers suggests a late seventeenth-century climate on average more than 1°C colder in the west and more than 2°C colder in the northwest than today.[95]

The factional struggles, fiscal shortages and bad weather undermined Qing power, but a further challenge arose in 1675 when Wu Sangui submitted a formal petition to the Kangxi emperor requesting, on grounds of old age, that he be allowed to resign his fief of Yunnan, and that his son should succeed him. The emperor, now aged 19, granted only the first request and took steps to establish central control over the region. Alarmed, two other Chinese generals appointed to rule southeastern provinces as fiefs decided to test Qing resolve by submitting identical petitions.

Most of the imperial council favoured rejecting these petitions, especially the one from Wu Sangui, fearing that acceptance would lead him to rebel; and they urged the Kangxi emperor to temporize, but he opted for confrontation and terminated Wu's authority. As the councillors had predicted, Wu promptly rebelled and (despite having executed the last ruler of the former dynasty) he adopted the slogan 'Fight the Qing and restore the Ming' and proclaimed that all men could once again dress and wear their hair in the traditional Chinese fashion.

The two other feudatories joined Wu in rebellion, hence the name 'The Revolt of the Three Feudatories', and so did many other disgruntled Chinese (including some of the Jiangnan gentry imprisoned for tax evasion a decade before as well as troops from Taiwan commanded by Coxinga's son). Yet Kangxi still underestimated the scale of the challenge he faced, sending a mere 10,000 troops to confront the rebels, who therefore gained control of almost all China south of the Yangzi, as well as of Sichuan and Shaanxi provinces. Wu demanded that the Manchus withdraw beyond the Great Wall, while the Dalai Lama (then as now a major Buddhist leader) offered to broker a deal that would partition China between Wu and the Qing. Even though Wu died in 1678, partly because of the difficult terrain and partly because the rebels practised a scorched-earth policy as they retreated, it took three years and the deployment of over half a million troops to regain all the rebel territories.[96]

Once Qing forces had crushed the Three Feudatories, they turned to Taiwan, where in 1683 they forced Coxinga's successor and the last Ming loyalists to surrender. The emperor now authorized the return of local inhabitants to the coastal areas of southeast China from which they had been banned for a generation, and allowed the resumption of maritime trade. After almost 70 years of disruption, destruction and disaster, the Qing had completed their 'Great Enterprise'.

The Cost of 'Changing the Mandate'

The victorious Kangxi emperor now visited the tombs of his ancestors at Mukden to 'perform the rites of reporting success', and then toured much of Manchuria and Shanxi. In 1684 he set off to visit Jiangnan: the first emperor to do so in almost three centuries. His aim, according to his 'official diary', was to 'investigate the unknown sufferings of the people'; but he did not investigate too closely. On his 2,000-mile tour, the emperor avoided places punished for their loyalty to the Ming, such as Yangzhou; he slept in the segregated and safe 'Tatar Towns'; and he returned to Beijing after two months.[97]

The imperial party also bypassed the provinces that had suffered the worst devastation, such as Hunan, where a government survey revealed a shortfall in taxpayers of up to 90 per cent. Nor did it visit Lingnan, where the prohibition on coastal trade had caused a population loss of one-fifth and the abandonment of up to one-half of all cultivated land; or Sichuan, where the savagery of Zhang Xianzhong's 'Great Western Kingdom' and the brutal conquest meant that 'well over a million people must have been killed and the local gentry was virtually exterminated'.[98] Nevertheless, the emperor must have seen abundant evidence of depopulation and devastation along his route. The total of cultivated land in the empire had fallen from 191 million acres in 1602 to 67 million in 1645, with a partial recovery to only 100 million in 1685, the year after his tour. Even a generation after the conquest, when pious family members in Anhui province sought to update their collective genealogies, they found that 'entire households had been massacred or had died of disease, "so that the lineage was barely saved from extinction"', while 'some of their survivors were unable to name their ancestors and degree of kinship to one another'. Meanwhile, in Jiangxi province, 'wherever you look, you see signs of abandonment,' a visitor noted in 1662, 'and you realize that before the upheavals there must have been a dense and thriving population here'.[99]

Human losses were qualitative as well as quantitative: thousands of members of the elite met a premature death by suicide, by imperial decree, or at the hands of soldiers or bandits. In 1647 the closet Ming loyalist Gu Yanwu lamented the 'uncles, and brothers and cousins who have died in the last two years, those in-laws and friends who have died, those who were older than I and have died, those who were younger than I and have died, and the number is uncountable'. Many more would perish over the next quarter century. In 1702 historians commissioned by Kangxi to compile the official *Ming History* included the biographies of almost 600 men who killed themselves out of loyalty to the Ming dynasty and of almost 400 women who either 'followed their husbands into death' or died after being dishonoured.[100] Since they only included those who had definitely taken their own lives out of principle, and omitted the rest, the true total must have been far higher: many other members of the elite, both male and female, died because they simply got in the way of soldiers, rebels or bandits, and left no surviving documentary trace. It therefore seems appropriate to speak of a 'lost generation': in no other part of the seventeenth-century world did such a high proportion of the elite meet a violent end, with the exception of Germany – and Germany was a fraction of the size of China.

The compilers of the *Ming History* omitted many other victims of the transition – such as the millions of Han Chinese who became slaves, either because Bannermen took them as booty or because they sold themselves and their families into servitude to escape debts, taxes or starvation. Qing Beijing had a lively slave market; and the dynasty enforced draconian fugitive slave laws. The Dutch diplomatic envoy Johannes Nieuhof provided a graphic example of the consequences. As he and his colleagues travelled by boat upriver from Canton towards Nanjing,

> We saw into what a miserable condition the Chinese were reduced by the last war of the Tartars, who put them upon this slavish labour of towing and rowing their boats, using them worse than beasts at their pleasure, without any exception of persons, either young or old. Often the track'd ways on the riverside are so narrow, uneven and steep, that if they should slip, they would infallibly break their necks, as many times it happens. Now and then they walk up to the middle in water, and if any of them grow faint and weary, there is one that follows, having charge of the boat, who never leaves beating of them, till they go on or die.[101]

The *Ming History* likewise omitted the suffering of Chinese women during the transition because of new legislation introduced by the Qing. Thus female slaves (both married and unmarried) were considered the sexual property of their masters: although a female slave could in theory resist rape by her master, if she struck or injured him in doing so she would be punished according to the severe laws against resisting one's 'owner'. The Qing Law Code, promulgated in 1646, also required a woman who sought redress for being raped to prove that she had struggled against her assailant *throughout* the entire ordeal; her body must show bruises and cuts; her clothing must be torn; and witnesses must have heard her *repeatedly* cry for help.[102]

Many Han Chinese women committed suicide rather than live in such a world, some of them leaving suicide notes in verse that explained how fate had ruined their lives (see chapter 4 above). Others wrote heart-rending prose letters and verse laments concerning their lot. Thus Huang Yuanjie, abducted by soldiers who probably raped her before selling her to a brothel, escaped and later became a celebrated poet and painter. In 1646 she marked the Qingming Festival (the day when families gathered around the family graves to remember their dead) by writing a poem that recalled not only her misfortunes but also her husband, lost in the anarchy of the previous year:

Leaning against a pillar, I am besieged by worries about the nation;
Others, as always, go to the pleasure houses.
My thoughts persist like unending drizzle;
Tears fall like fluttering petals without end.
Since we parted, a new year has already arrived . . .
Thinking of my family I stare off into the white clouds.
My small heart overwhelmed by grief.[103]

There can have been scarcely a woman in Jiangnan, and in many other parts of China, who did not feel 'overwhelmed with grief' for a relative or friend who perished during the Ming-Qing transition.

Even the Chinese men and women who survived the transition often lived in fear. Ding Yaokang, a gentleman scholar from Shandong, wrote a personal memoir evocatively entitled *A Brief Account of My Escape from Disaster*. It described how he and his family had to abandon their ancestral lands twice – once in 1642, to avoid the great Manchu raid, and again in 1644 when Li Zicheng retreated from Beijing. They survived only because they could afford to charter a boat to take them (and other gentry families) to safety on an island off the coast. On both occasions he noted the death of many who remained, because troops stole and destroyed everything they could, and any crops still in the field could not be harvested for lack of labour. In the adjacent province of Henan, Li Tingsheng was studying for his *shengyuan* degree when the bandits came in 1642. He too fled, spending the next two years on the move while he evaded both rebel forces and government armies, disguised as a food vendor and impersonating a carter until it was safe enough to resume his life as a scholar and to write *A Record of Hardship*, which made clear that only the support of other gentry families had allowed him to survive.[104]

Although the Kangxi emperor would have met few such 'losers' on his southern tour in 1684, he mingled with members of the largest group of 'winners' of the mid-seventeenth-century crisis anywhere in the world: the Banner troops and their families. When Nurhaci declared war on the Ming in 1618, he commanded only a few thousand followers, with the grudging support of some of his Mongol neighbours, and he worried about how to feed them. Twenty-five years later, his son Hong Taiji commanded a powerful confederation of steppe people and ruled over perhaps a million Chinese settlers; but he too worried about how to feed them. In 1684, by contrast, tens of thousands of Manchus and their Mongol allies lived comfortably in the vast empire they had conquered. Each received a salary in silver, a grain subsidy, a housing allowance, arms and ammunition, pensions, wedding and funeral expenses, loans and land. Most of them also owned slaves.

Eventually, many of the Qing's Chinese subjects joined these 'winners'. First in northern China and then in the south, the new dynasty restored law and order and secured the frontiers, enabling the surviving population to prosper and multiply even before the return of a benign climate in the early eighteenth century improved farming conditions. The Qing also solved other problems that had beset their predecessors. The high losses among civil servants, whether through death or resignation, opened up thousands of positions in the bureaucracy and allowed the promotion of many 'alienated intellectuals' whose constant criticisms had weakened the former dynasty. Similarly, in many rural areas, mortality and migration made available much rich farmland, and allowed surviving farmers to join several small plots together and enjoy greater prosperity. The central government also revitalized the infrastructure of their realm, above all the roads and granaries, and pioneered the technique of variolation, which dramatically reduced deaths from smallpox (see chapter 21 below). Finally, as Joanna Waley-Cohen has stressed, the 'Great Enterprise' strengthened 'the empire by uniting its diverse people through the creation of a common basis, one that was founded on loyal pride in imperial achievement and in which all could participate'. When Yao Tinglin completed his 'Record of successive years' in Jiangnan in the 1680s, he commented on how the administration of justice was now much faster and more efficient; he listed commodities unknown in Ming times now offered for sale; and he considered the Qing fiscal system a 'revolution' (gaige), with lighter taxes and far fewer demands for labour services. Yao had no doubt that 'at the end of the seventeenth century the people of Shanghai were living in a more prosperous and more peaceful world than has ever existed'.[105]

Perhaps, however, Yao's comparison was unfair to the Ming. The Chongzhen emperor had faced problems that possibly no ruler could have overcome: an inefficient and inequitable tax burden; contempt for martial values at a time when the state needed to defeat both domestic and foreign enemies; factionalism that paralyzed the bureaucracy; corruption that eventually 'penetrated' even the examination system; above all, the Little Ice Age. As Timothy Brook wrote, 'No emperor of the Yuan or Ming faced climatic conditions as abnormal and severe as Chongzhen' – adding, 'the greatest puzzle might well be to figure out how the Ming remained standing for as long as it did'.[106]

The invaders, for their part, twice placed their Great Enterprise at risk, and thereby prolonged the suffering of their subjects – once in 1645 with Dorgon's tonsure decree and again in 1673 with Kangxi's decision to remove the Three Feudatories – but Qing military prowess eventually prevailed and the new dynasty went on to conquer extensive territories in Inner Asia, doubling the area controlled from Beijing to more than four million square miles (larger than all of Europe west of the Urals and far larger than China today). Westward expansion might have continued further, but for the fact that the Qing encountered the outposts of an even larger state marching east: Romanov Russia.

'The great shaking': Russia and the Polish-Lithuanian Commonwealth, 1618–86[1]

The Humiliation of Russia

In September 1618 troops commanded by the Polish Crown Prince Władysław Vasa stormed Moscow. Although the assault failed, Tsar Michael Romanov agreed to the truce of Deulino, by which he relinquished all Russian lands conquered over the previous decade by the Polish-Lithuanian Commonwealth, which now became the largest state in Europe, twice the size of France. The tsar had little choice: 20 years of famines, rebellions, civil wars and invasions by both Sweden and Poland had reduced Russia's population by perhaps one-quarter. In some areas more than half the villages and even entire towns had been abandoned. The intervening period soon became known in Russian history as *smuta*: 'The Great Trouble'.[2] A generation later, in 1648, angry Muscovites broke into the Kremlin, sacked the apartments of the tsar's leading ministers, and murdered two of them, triggering rebellions elsewhere in the empire. Astonishingly, Michael's son Alexei Romanov (r. 1645–76) not only survived this crisis but went on to vanquish the Polish-Lithuanian Commonwealth, regain all the lands surrendered at Deulino, and extend the bounds of Russia until it covered six million square miles, making it the largest state in the world.

The extent of the tsar's dominions so impressed the Danish traveller Adam Olearius as he traversed Russia from north to south and back that he used longitude and latitude as well as 'German miles' to estimate the distances he covered: 450 miles from the Baltic to Moscow, and 900 miles more from there to the Caspian Sea. Olearius never crossed the Urals into Siberia, where in the course of the seventeenth century Russian settlers founded and fortified a chain of forts all the way to the Pacific and the Amur basin, on the Chinese frontier. Tobolsk, the administrative centre of Siberia, lay 1,500 miles from Moscow; Okhotsk, founded on the Pacific in 1649, and Irkutsk, founded on Lake Baikal in 1652, lay over 3,000 miles from Moscow. Messages to and from the tsar might take two years to arrive. Russia's rulers therefore faced an important dilemma: whether to leave local affairs in local hands, and risk political disintegration, or to maintain central control, and sacrifice both efficiency and potentially constructive local initiatives.[3]

Admittedly, environmental features reduced the dilemma somewhat. Above all, although the major rivers of Siberia – Ob, Yenisey and Lena – run north–south, their tributaries form an almost continuous east–west waterway from the Urals to

Lake Baikal. Likewise the broad rivers that run from Muscovy south towards the Black and Caspian Seas – Dnieper, Donets, Don and Volga – allow communications by boat in the summer and on the ice in winter. These natural 'corridors' permitted not only mass migration, the transmission of orders, tribute and trade, but also dramatic military raids: Cossack adventurers captured Sinop in Anatolia in 1614 and Azov near the Crimea in 1641.

The principal strategic challenges to the Russian state nevertheless lay elsewhere. Smolensk, forward bastion of the Polish-Lithuanian Commonwealth, stood just over 200 miles west of Moscow, while Narva, a Baltic outpost of the Swedish state, stood scarcely 400 miles to the northwest. Each of the three neighbours adhered to a different branch of Christianity: Russia was solidly Orthodox, Poland-Lithuania was predominantly Catholic, and Sweden was overwhelmingly Lutheran.

Russia's two western neighbours, both ruled by branches of the House of Vasa, also covered vast areas. The Swedish state stretched from the southern shore of the Baltic to the North Cape, a distance of over 600 miles, while the Polish-Lithuanian Commonwealth (*Rzeczpopolita*) stretched from the Baltic almost to the Black Sea, also a distance of over 600 miles. Yet although the dimensions of all three states dwarfed the size of their west European neighbours in the mid-seventeenth century, their populations remained far inferior. Russia and the *Rzeczpopolita* scarcely boasted 11 million inhabitants each, while the Swedish crown included only about 2 million; by way of comparison, both France and the Holy Roman Empire contained about 20 million inhabitants. These figures disguise striking differences in population density. Whereas parts of western Europe boasted 22 inhabitants per square mile, Poland averaged 8, Lithuania 6, and Muscovy not even 1. Moreover, according to the first reasonably complete Russian census, in 1678, almost 70 per cent of the tsar's subjects lived in the lands north of Moscow while only 1 per cent inhabited the vast expanse of Siberia. The rest lived in the steppe south of Moscow, especially on a zone of *chernozem* ('black earth', so called because of its colour) some 200 miles wide that ran from the Black Sea into Siberia: 270 million acres of soil so fertile that, according to a western traveller, the 'grass grew so tall that it reached the horses' stomachs' and, wherever farmers chose to sow grain, 'everyone is confident of a rich annual harvest'.[4]

Throughout the seventeenth century three groups vied for control of the 'black earth'. Initially, Muslim Tatar raiders based on the Crimea and owing nominal obedience to the Ottoman sultan predominated, but gradually Russian farmers spread southwards, first along the banks of the Don and then along the Dnieper, where they faced subjects of the Polish-Lithuanian Commonwealth settling in Ukraine.[5] Paradoxically, the colonization of their southern frontier destabilized both states. In Russia, the cost of defending the borderlands required heavy taxes, while the southward flight of so many peasant families to the new lands led northern landlords to demand draconian measures from the crown to prevent the haemorrhage of their servile labour force. In the Polish-Lithuanian Commonwealth, the southwards migration not only of serfs but also of Jews, trying to escape the restrictions imposed on them by various towns, increased the burdens on those who remained.

The fact that the Russian, Polish and Swedish Monarchies were all 'composite states' also caused instability. The tsar ruled over numerous distinct ethno-linguistic groups, including Muslims along the middle and lower Volga and nomads in Siberia, some of which preserved considerable political autonomy and even some of their own institutions after incorporation.[6] Likewise, although the kingdom of Sweden boasted remarkable religious and administrative uniformity, its overseas territories – Finland, Estonia and (later) parts of Germany – retained great political autonomy, boasting their own separate Estates, languages and legal systems. Finally, each component of the Polish-Lithuanian Commonwealth retained its own legal systems, treasury, army and local representative assemblies (*Sejmiki*). In addition, the Commonwealth boasted great ethnic diversity: large communities of Tatars, Scots and Armenians lived among the Poles, Germans, Lithuanians and Ruthenians; while Westerners predominated in many Baltic cities such as Danzig and Riga.

The Constitution of the Commonwealth deepened this diversity. At the death of each monarch, representatives from every region assembled in a federal Diet (the *Sejm*) to negotiate concessions from the various claimants before electing one of them king. Thereafter, representatives from the *Sejmiki* met together for six weeks at least once every two years, with emergency sessions when necessary, and at the end of each Diet, a plenary session debated all the legislation recommended for enactment. At this stage, the veto of just one representative on just one issue required the king to dissolve the Diet without passing any legislation (not even measures already agreed upon). Although both foreign contemporaries and most subsequent historians castigated the *Liberum Veto* as a weakness that doomed the Commonwealth to decline, they exaggerate: no one used it until 1652 – and even in that year a new Diet convened four months later and passed all pending legislation. In fact, the *Liberum Veto* safeguarded regional rights (which is why attempts to replace unanimity with some form of majority rule always failed); and the *Sejm* offered the earliest example in world history of a federal parliament that bound together a multi-national and multi-ethnic state.

The Commonwealth's principal weakness lay in its religious pluralism. Catholicism predominated in Poland, but in both Lithuania and Ukraine it competed with a powerful Orthodox Church and, after 1596, with a distinct 'Uniate Church', created specifically to reconcile an important group of Orthodox Christians with Rome. In addition, the Commonwealth was home to numerous other religious groups. Each landlord had the right to determine the faith of his subjects, and major cities had the right to grant toleration to whomever they pleased. Thus the city of Lwów (Lviv) contained 30 Catholic churches (and 15 monasteries), 15 Orthodox churches (and 3 monasteries), 3 Armenian churches (one of them a cathedral) and 3 synagogues. Nevertheless the Roman Catholic hierarchy, strongly supported by the crown, used a wide range of economic, social and political inducements to win converts. Their success can be measured by the fact that although the federal Diet in 1570 included 59 non-Catholic lay senators, that of 1630 included only 6; while over the same period the number of Protestant communities in Poland fell from over 500 to scarcely 250. In addition, especially in the 1630s, large numbers of Orthodox clerics and laity deserted either to the Catholic or the Uniate Church.

Despite such political and religious diversity, for the first half of the seventeenth century the Commonwealth held its own against its neighbours, largely thanks to its rapid adaptation of new military technology. 'Antiquity has its virtues', a Lithuanian nobleman who had served in the army of the Dutch Republic reminded his sovereign loftily in 1622, but 'every century teaches soldiers some new trick. Every campaign has its own discoveries; each school of war seeks its own remedies.' He therefore recommended that the army of the Polish Commonwealth should increase its gunpowder weapons just as the Dutch had done.[7] King Sigismund III (r. 1587–1632) paid heed and created special musketeer infantry formations, standardized artillery calibres, and added field guns modelled on Western prototypes. Although progress remained slow – mainly because the Polish nobles resisted any measure that might enhance the power of the monarchy (such as hiring foreign mercenaries, arming serfs, and fortifying royal cities) – the military effectiveness of the Commonwealth's troops remained high.

The humiliating 'Time of Troubles' convinced Tsar Michael Romanov (r. 1613–45) that he must imitate the military methods of the Commonwealth. He therefore welcomed foreign military advisers to train and command 'New Formation Regiments' equipped with Western weapons; and when, on the death of Sigismund III in 1632, the *Sejm* bargained with Crown Prince Władysław before electing him, the tsar launched an invasion to recapture the lands sacrificed at Deulino. The Russian army, including the 'New Formation Regiments', swiftly captured 20 towns before they laid siege to Smolensk. Yet Smolensk held out until Władysław, now elected king of Poland, arrived with a relief army and besieged the besiegers. In February 1634 the Russian commanders surrendered, prostrating themselves at the feet of Władysław while his horse trampled on their standards. A few weeks later Michael reluctantly concluded the 'Eternal Peace of Polianovka', by which he not only confirmed all Poland's territorial gains at Deulino but also promised to dissolve his New Formation Regiments and to pay a huge war indemnity. The cost of this new defeat created tensions and problems that would shake the Romanov state to its foundations.

The 'imaginary little world' of the Muscovites

Understanding the Russian crisis of the mid-seventeenth century is complicated by the paucity of sources. Only Sweden maintained a permanent diplomatic representative in Moscow, and on some events his dispatches form the only surviving source; but normally foreigners in Russia filled their letters with laments about the conditions in which they had to serve – above all, poor communications. In winter, there never seemed to be enough sledges for transport; in summer, the rivers often lacked sufficient water to carry boats; and the spring thaw and autumn rains made all roads impassable for about a month (called *rasputitsa*, 'quagmire season', in Russian). The foreigners also lamented the complexity and malevolence of the Russian bureaucracy and, above all, the fact that the Russians refused to talk to them because they were either too fearful or too absorbed in what one of them dismissed as 'upholding their imaginary little world'.[8]

Few *Russian* sources remain from which to reconstruct that 'imaginary little world'. The archives of almost all the central departments of state have suffered grievous losses: some were burned (fire twice consumed the entire archive of the 'Kazan chancellery' which administered the lands along the Volga annexed in the 1550s) while others were lost when the Soviet government consolidated all 'ancient documents' in a single archive. Only the records of the Siberian chancellery have survived relatively intact for the early modern period.[9] Luckily for historians, the 'natural archive' of the period supplements deficiencies in the 'human archive'. Climatic reconstructions reveal notably cooler and drier conditions in the 1640s, with severe drought in 1639 and 1640 in Ukraine; poor harvests in the south in 1642; drought and a plague of locusts in 1645 and 1646; and early frosts and poor harvests in the south in 1647 and 1648.[10] When the government carried out a land survey in 1645–6, the commissioners found that many communities paid significantly less than the amount assessed in the previous survey two decades earlier because they had shrunk in both size and wealth. One of the few detailed studies of this census data (for Karelia, the area between Lake Ladoga and the White Sea) reveals that between 1628 and 1646 the overall number of households declined by one quarter, and gentry households by almost one half, while the proportion of landless peasants doubled.[11]

Tsar Michael nevertheless increased the tax burden on this dwindling population. The unsuccessful war with Poland in 1632–4 created massive debts (an indemnity payable to the Poles plus the wages earned by the defeated Russian troops); while to remedy the weaknesses exposed by that conflict the tsar purchased costly foreign munitions and recruited more Western officers to train more New Formation Regiments. A far larger item of defence spending arose on the southern frontier where, between 1636 and 1654, the central government ordered the construction of almost 50 fortified new towns linked by wooden and earthen ramparts that ran for 800 miles from the Dnieper to the Volga. The western half of Russia's 'Great Wall' became known as the Belgorod Line, after the town at its centre, and the eastern half as the Simbirsk Line, after the town on the Volga where it terminated. Although the principal function of the new towns was defence, in the 1660s their inhabitants petitioned with mounting frequency 'against rapidly increasing tax burdens, suggesting that the incorporation of these regions into the main stream of Muscovite life had been swift and sure'(Fig. 19).[12]

These 'lines' represented perhaps the greatest military engineering feat of the seventeenth century – but the cost proved crippling. Apart from the capital outlay required for construction, each of the new towns and fortresses required a permanent garrison. In addition, each summer, the government mobilized an army of 'servitors' (*deti boiarskie*: gentry who held lands in return for military service) and sent them south to guard against Tatar invasion. Beyond the fortifications, the central government also supported thousands of Cossacks (perhaps from *kazac*, the Turkic word for 'free man'), fiercely Orthodox warriors who patrolled the steppe to disrupt any attack by the Muslim Tatars or their Ottoman overlords.[13]

19. The Russian empire and the Polish-Lithuanian Commonwealth.

Imperial Russia had to defend itself against two enemies: the Polish-Lithuanian Commonwealth in the west, and the Crimean Tatars in the south. Against the latter, the Romanov tsars constructed the fortified Belgorod and Simbirsk 'lines' that made use of natural features such as forests and rivers. In 1670, the 'lines' also halted a Cossack invasion. The Polish-Lithuanian Commonwealth had no such defences, and in 1648 a Cossack invasion fatally weakened the state, opening the way to invasions by both its Russian and Swedish neighbours. The Commonwealth briefly ceased to exist.

The tsars nevertheless sought to avoid outright provocation of their southern neighbours. Thus when a band of Cossacks seized the town of Azov at the mouth of the river Don from vassals of the Ottoman sultan, and offered in 1641 to place the town under Moscow's suzerainty, the tsar convened the Zemskii Sobor (the 'Assembly of the Land') and asked for their advice on two questions: whether to accept the Cossacks' offer, which would inevitably provoke open war with the Ottomans; and, in case of acceptance, how to finance that war. Although almost everyone in the assembly favoured retaining Azov, they did not want to pay for a new war. The provincial gentry, for instance, refused to provide the necessary funds without a detailed land survey to equalize tax demands between large and small estates. They also demanded a thorough reform of the central government: 'We are ruined by Moscow red tape (*volokita*) and injustice more than by Turks and Tatars,' they protested. Likewise, Moscow merchants refused to pay more unless the tsar revoked the special trading privileges granted to their foreign competitors, which placed them at a disadvantage. Perhaps shaken by the demand for so many reforms and concessions, the tsar ordered the Cossacks to return Azov to Ottoman control forthwith.[14]

Despite the tsar's military restraint (so rare in the mid-seventeenth century), Russia continued to expand southwards. To begin with, whereas the growing season in Karelia begins in April and ends in September, around Belgorod it begins a month earlier and ends a month later. This important discrepancy enhanced the attraction of the *chernozem* farmland now protected by the Belgorod and Simbirsk Lines. Admittedly, cutting down forests to create fields gave rise to hotter summers, colder winters, and a greater risk of extreme events such as droughts in the region; but *chernozem* continued to produce bountiful crops in all except years of exceptional climatic adversity (such as 1647 and 1648). Furthermore, in the 1630s the tsar exempted the pioneers from paying taxes for a decade or more. Not surprisingly, this combination of advantages attracted a substantial migration of peasants from the north. Some joined the Cossacks beyond the Belgorod and Simbirsk Lines, seeking Tatar booty, while others fell victim to Tatar raiders and begged to be ransomed; but most settled and prospered on the hundreds of thousands of acres of virgin farmland now available behind the Lines.

This mass migration created a crisis for the 'servitors' of the northern regions, on whom the tsars relied to defend the empire. To finance their military service, most servitors depended on the labour and services exacted from the unfree inhabitants of their estates. Now, the servitors claimed, no sooner had they departed on campaign than either their serfs fled southwards or else neighbouring noblemen kidnapped them as extra hands to work their own estates: they could therefore no longer fulfil their military obligations for lack of peasants. Contemporary evidence bears them out. Servitors claimed that they each required at least 20 peasant households to maintain themselves as a soldier of the tsar, but by the 1630s, at least in the Moscow region, they owned on average only 6 peasant households.[15] Not surprisingly, the servitors repeatedly petitioned the central government to compel fugitive serfs to return, and to abolish the time limit for their recovery; but the central government demurred. Although in 1636 the tsar decreed that all former serfs in the south must return, he limited the measure to those who had fled *before* 1613 and he exempted those who had fled to Siberia. Likewise, although the tsar later raised the time limit for legal recovery to ten years, this fell far short of the total control over serfs which the servitors regarded as essential if they were to discharge their military duties to the sovereign.

The tsar and his 'slaves'

The rapid territorial growth of imperial Russia led to an equally rapid expansion of the central bureaucracy. Tsar Michael created 44 new departments of state in Moscow (known as *prikazy*: chancelleries), and his son Alexei created 30 more. Both the volume of business handled by each *prikaz* and the staff employed to handle it grew exponentially. For example, the Military Chancellery employed 45 men in the 1620s but over 100 in the 1660s, and issued orders that ranged from major troop movements down to how many cubic feet of earth should be moved to create ramparts, and how many timber beams of a specified dimension should be used to construct the main gate, of a frontier town.

The willingness of the tsar's subjects to tolerate such intrusion in their daily lives no doubt reflected the chaos and destruction of the Time of Troubles which 'profoundly shocked most Russians psychologically, emotionally and spiritually'. According to Chester Dunning, 'Some regarded the Troubles as God's punishment for the sins of the Russian people or their rulers and concluded that, if God allowed the country to survive, there would be need for significant moral and spiritual reform.' Most Russians henceforth 'rejected innovation in favour of restoring as much as possible of the pre-crisis old order'.[16] The Romanovs capitalized on these sentiments by stressing their role as patrons of 'Holy Russia' (a term first used in 1619): they regularly undertook ostentatious pilgrimages to religious sites, and they occupied pride of place in the annual processions organized every Epiphany and Palm Sunday by the Orthodox Church through what is now Red Square. A chrono-graph of Russian history written in the second half of the seventeenth century 'began with the creation of the world based on the Old Testament and then traced a lineage of emperors from Alexander the Great through the Romans and Byzantines' until it arrived at those sacred defenders of the faith, the Russian tsars, culminating in Michael Romanov.[17]

Even as imperial Russia became more hierarchical, one exception remained. In the admirable formula of Valerie Kivelson: 'All interactions with the state, whether legal disputes in court or communications between provincial and central offices, were framed as humble petitions addressed directly to the tsar.' 'Humble' seems an understatement: the phrase for 'petition' in Russian, *bit' chelom*, literally means 'to beat one's brow [to the ground]'; and all petitioners addressing the tsar called them-selves 'Your slave' and 'Your miserable orphans'. Even nobles used demeaning diminutives of their names ('I, little Ivashko, Your slave, beg you ...').[18] Since petitions to the tsar formed the only legal channel by which subjects might request redress of their grievances, and as government intervention in daily life (and, consequently, opportunities for abuse) steadily increased, both grievances and petitions multiplied. To cope with them, Michael Romanov created a special 'Petitions Chancellery' and one of its officials always travelled with him in order to direct each petition to the appropriate department of state.

On Michael's death in 1645 his 16-year-old son and successor Alexei faced so many petitions, many of them from groups of servitors protesting about the shortage of serf labour, that the Swedish envoy in Moscow believed they presaged a general uprising; but the new regime averted disaster by reducing the military service obligation of the gentry by one day, and promising to undertake a new census of all Russia as a preliminary step towards abolishing all restrictions on reclaiming fugitive serfs.[19] Inspectors from the central government duly visited each administrative region to ascertain the number of taxable households (and whether they paid less or more now than before); the amount of land under cultivation (as well as land abandoned); and the economic activities of each village (including estimates of crop yields). They also compiled lists of all serfs who had fled their original estates during the previous ten years. But no edict abolishing the time limit for recovering fugitive serfs materialized – not least because Alexei's chief adviser (and brother-in-law) Boris Morozov led the way in welcoming runaway serfs to his own extensive estates and in concealing them from the government's inspectors.

Morozov acted much like royal 'Favourites' in western Europe. First he drove from office those who had advised the previous tsar and then, in order to fund military expenditure (primarily hiring foreign army officers, and building the Belgorod and Simbirsk Lines), he made some highly unpopular fiscal decisions. He instructed another of the tsar's brothers-in-law, treasury minister Peter Trakhaniotov, to freeze the wages earned by the *streltsy* – the corps of musketeers recruited from the gentry, on whom the government relied to preserve law and order in the capital – creating a group of discontented subjects who were both organized and armed. Moreover, Morozov approved a proposal from Nazarii Chistyi, a prosperous Moscow merchant, to introduce indirect imposts modelled on Dutch prototypes. In 1646 imperial decrees imposed a 'stamp tax' on the paper required for all official transactions and created state monopolies for the sale of tobacco and salt. The salt monopoly, in particular, provoked widespread resentment because it increased prices fortyfold. Faced with such brutal inflation, consumers purchased far less salt (causing sales and tax revenues to fall dramatically) and made protests. Late in 1647 the tsar brought some 10,000 musketeers into the capital to preserve order, but when popular unrest continued he reluctantly revoked the salt monopoly.[20]

Other anomalies in the Russian tax system also caused unrest. Morozov entrusted control over the commerce of the entire capital to another of his relatives, Levontii Pleschcheev, who not only increased the bureaucratic 'red tape' but also extorted bribes of unprecedented size in return for rendering justice. Moreover, in an attempt to make good the shortfall caused by the revocation of the salt monopoly, the treasury began the ruthless collection of tax arrears from the previous two years. A recent study estimates that these measures together 'tripled the tax burden for

1648.[21] Morozov had thus managed to alienate almost simultaneously the town elites, the servitors and the ordinary taxpayers of Muscovy.

In April 1648, Morozov ordered the servitors to mobilize and march south to parry an anticipated Tatar raid – but when no incursion occurred, he disbanded them without pay. The Moscow contingent was still in the capital, alienated and angry, when the following month some of the tsar's subjects decided to present their grievances to him in the accustomed manner: through a formal petition. The local servitors no doubt shared the outrage of the crowd as they watched the imperial entourage intercept the petition so that the tsar would not see it. Instead, he and his family left the city on a pilgrimage to a nearby monastery.[22]

'The whole world is shaking'

According to Adam Olearius, Moscow was always a dangerous city. The Russians, he asserted, were drunken, sex-crazed sodomites whose lust spared neither horse, man nor boy. Violent street crime posed a constant threat, he continued, because of the large number of underpaid household slaves who could not afford to live on their allowance and so survived by robbery. Patrick Gordon, who served in the tsar's army for almost four decades, agreed. The Russians, he wrote, were 'morose, avaricious, niggard, deceitful, false; insolent and tirrannous, where they have command; and, being under command, submissive and even slavish, sloven and base, and yet overweening and valuing themselves above all other nations'.[23] The failure of Tsar Alexei to receive his subjects' petition stirred up these passions and, while he was absent on his pilgrimage, crowds gathered in and around the churches of the capital to vent their grievances. They decided to try again to make him listen when he returned, and on 11 June 1648 a large group of citizens emerged from the city to greet their ruler, bearing not only the customary bread and salt but also copies of a petition denouncing the corruption of Levontii Pleschcheev. Once again, the imperial entourage intercepted the documents and Alexei's guards used their whips to drive the crowd back. At one point they opened fire.

A few of the enraged protestors now followed the tsar into the Kremlin with their formal 'Supplication', but Morozov had them imprisoned. Half an hour later, as the tsaritsa returned from the monastery in her carriage, the crowd tried to present their grievances to her, but once again the guards drove them back. At this, 'the entire crowd, totally exasperated, threw stones and used cudgels against the guards'.[24] Both parties had transgressed important boundaries: the tsar had unexpectedly and inexplicably rejected a petition, the only legitimate avenue for subjects to bring their problems to his attention; while a group of subjects had forced their way uninvited into the Kremlin, a sacred space for both Church and State.

A far worse 'transgression' occurred the next day during a religious festival, when the royal family left the Kremlin to worship. Crowds surrounded the tsar as he returned from church, begging that he accept their 'Supplication'. Although the document used the customary self-abasing style of petitions to the tsar ('Your slaves and poor subjects'), it also contained some notable innovations. First, it claimed to speak in the name of the 'common people of Russia' (not just of Moscow or a particular group), and it lamented the intolerable 'bribes, presents and gifts' demanded by bureaucrats in return for any official act (the tsar could easily identify the offenders, the document claimed, because they 'build themselves houses that are not appropriate to their stations'). The supplicants complained that they had already presented petitions, but 'great ones' had intercepted them, so that

> It has been brought to this: that they [the great ones] have stirred up Your Imperial Majesty against the people and the people against Your Imperial Majesty. So it now appears that such injustice has driven the whole population of the entire Moscow region and its adjoining provinces to revolt. As a result great confusion is brewing in your Imperial capital and in many other regions and towns.

They boldly reminded the tsar of 'the history to be found in your imperial palace [the Kremlin] of the Greek king in Constantinople, Justinian', who averted divine punishment by issuing laws that ended the oppression of the poor:

> Now Your Imperial Majesty can do the same, if you wish to avoid the punishment of God that now threatens your kingdom. Let the unjust judges be rooted out; get rid of the incompetent; punish all bribery and injustice, the obstruction of justice, and all unfairness. Delay and prevent the many innocent tears that fall. Protect the lowly and the weak from violence and injustice.

Just in case Alexei missed the point, the Supplication reminded him that his father Michael had been 'designated and chosen by God and the whole people' to rule 'when the land of Muscovy was nearly completely exhausted by evil people'; and yet currently 'all one hears from the common folk is [talk of] uprising and revolt because of the injustices inflicted on them by the powerful'.[25]

This time the 'great ones' in the imperial entourage tore this petition 'into tiny pieces and flung the pieces in the petitioners' faces' while their servants thrashed the supplicants. Again the crowd pursued the tsar towards the Kremlin – but this time, when Morozov ordered the musketeers to close the gates to the complex, they refused. Several thousand demonstrators gathered in front of the tsar's apartment and demanded immediate redress of their grievances, which now included the execution of the hated Levontii Pleschcheev.[26] When Morozov appeared on the palace balcony to reason with the crowd, they shouted back 'Yes, and we must have you too!' Morozov's servants urged the musketeers in the Kremlin square to fire on the crowd; but the troops, no doubt remembering Morozov's refusal to pay their arrears, 'replied that they had sworn [allegiance] to His Imperial Majesty and to no other, and that they would not fight for the nobles against the common people'. A delegation of musketeers told the tsar to his face that 'They would not make enemies of the people for the sake of the traitor and tyrant Pleschcheev', while those in the square assured the demonstrators that they 'would not oppose the crowd but would much rather give them a helping hand'.[27]

Together, troops and rioters broke into Morozov's luxurious apartments in the Kremlin, smashing his fine furniture with axes and crushing his jewels to dust; but 'they suffered not the least thing to be carried away, crying aloud *To naasi kroof*, that is to say, "This is our blood"'.[28] Although the tsar pleaded for moderation, the crowd murdered three of his household officials and forced their way into the residence of Nazarii Chistyi, architect of the hated salt monopoly, and immediately killed him with their axes and clubs, exclaiming 'Traitor, this is for the salt!' Then they 'hauled him down the stairs by the heels, dragging him like a dog' around the interior of the Kremlin, and 'having stripped him, they flung him stark naked upon the dunghill'. Next the rioters attacked the residences of Pleschcheev, Trakhaniotov and other ministers of Alexei who had given offence. Although when 'the night approached the plundering ceased a little, with the day break they began to plunder again'.[29]

On 12 June 1648 the crowd torched some 70 residences of nobles and merchants, apparently following some plan, and almost 40 more the following day; then they 'ran' (the word used by all the sources) back inside the Kremlin and demanded that the tsar surrender Pleschcheev, Trakhaniotov and Morozov.[30] Alexei immediately surrendered Pleschcheev, and even provided two executioners, 'but as soon as he arrived in the market place the common people [*gemene mannen*] put him to death there, and eventually a monk threw his body onto a fire'. The tsar now asked for two days to consider the fate of his other ministers, and the demonstrators (perhaps surprisingly) dispersed. No sooner had they done so than fires broke out in five distinct places across Moscow. Thanks to the prolonged drought, the fire spread rapidly and, according to the terrified Swedish ambassador, 'within a few hours more than half the city within the White Wall, and about half of the city outside the wall, went up in flames'. Some calculated that 50,000 homes and 2,000 people perished in the conflagration.[31]

The musketeers captured some of the arsonists who, 'being racked, have confessed that they were hired to do it with money by Morozov' – but some went further and claimed 'that the tsar himself instigated these [fires] in order to distract the common people and those who had houses [in the city] from the uproar, since they would be called back to save their own [possessions] from the fire'. If so, the ruse did not 'distract the common people' for long: on 15 June they surged back to the Kremlin and demanded the immediate surrender of Trakhaniotov and Morozov.[32]

In the words of an irate citizen: 'the whole world is shaking ... There is great shaking and the people are troubled'. The fate of Romanov rule now hung in the balance. Some people in the crowd declared 'His Imperial Majesty to be a traitor as long as he refused to banish Morozov from his court and capital. They also resolved that, if His Imperial Majesty did not comply with their wishes, they would use force to make him do so.' A few even asserted that 'the tsar is young and stupid' and, while attributing his obstinacy to wicked advisers, added 'They manage everything and the Sovereign keeps silent. *The devil stole his mind*' – an accusation of Satanism that challenged the tsar's claim to be the champion of Orthodoxy, and thus his right to rule.[33]

Realizing the seriousness of his situation Alexei now delivered Trakhaniotov, too, to the crowd. He also promised, kissing a golden crucifix held by the patriarch, that Morozov would become a monk and retire to some distant monastery, and would never again hold government office. Because of the evident religious solemnity, the crowd believed him and once again dispersed, while the tsar distributed a substantial cash payment to all musketeers to regain their loyalty. According to the Swedish resident, he also ordered his Western 'officers, to train 20,000 soldiers near the Swedish border'.[34]

Long before these loyal troops were ready, Morozov managed to precipitate another confrontation. Perhaps imagining that the crisis had passed, he recommended that Alexei should not pay the servitors still in Moscow their promised bonus, and on 20 June a new petition, this time in the name of the gentry, merchants and 'people of all ranks', again insisted that Morozov must go. It also demanded that the tsar summon the Zemskii Sobor. In desperation, Alexei recalled the ministers of his father whom Morozov had displaced in 1645, and sent the hated chief minister into 'perpetual exile' under heavy guard. Over the next eight weeks more than 70 petitions flowed in from discontented groups and the tsar approved all of them: to appease native merchants, he abolished the trading privileges of the English; to content ordinary Muscovites, he promised money to rebuild structures damaged by the fire; to pacify the servitors, he paid their promised bonus and also returned all fugitive serfs found on Morozov's estates.[35] Above all, Alexei reluctantly agreed to convene the Zemskii Sobor.

These sweeping concessions did not arise only in response to the troubles in Moscow. A combination of drought and locusts ruined the harvests of 1647 and 1648 throughout Russia, even on *chernozem* lands, creating not only widespread food shortages but also heightened anxiety. Moreover, as the Supplication of 12 June had predicted, revolts also broke out in 'many other regions and towns' of the empire.[36] Tomsk, 2,500 miles from Moscow in the middle of Siberia, led the way. Its multi-ethnic community (some 700 Russian and about 300 Tatar and other non-Russian households) suffered from poor harvests throughout the 1640s, with yields about one-third below the norm; yet the governor raised taxes while withholding wages from the musketeers and other troops. In April 1648 the town magistrates seized the governor and placed him under house arrest, while the servitors, merchants, peasants, urban taxpayers and Tatars all petitioned the tsar to remove him. Instead the tsar ordered the governor's reinstatement, which provoked a second wave of rioting. This time the insurgents created an alternative regime with its own 'rebel chancery' (*Voroskii prikaz*), its own candidate for governor and its own assembly (*krug*) which issued manifestos, sent circulars to incite other communities to join them, and petitioned Moscow to recognize their actions. Peace only returned in June 1649 when the tsar recalled the former governor in disgrace.[37]

Urban uprisings broke out elsewhere as soon as news arrived of the riots in Moscow. The new town of Kozlov on the Belgorod Line had already sent three petitions to the tsar denouncing the tyrannical practices of its governor, which resulted in a commission of inquiry in 1647; but the governor bribed or intimidated many protestors so that the inspectors found little substance to the accusations and left him in post. The disastrous harvest of that year produced new tensions, however: even servitors with extensive estates had to sell their weapons and clothing in order to buy grain, while the governor's exactions, corruption and abuse of justice continued. Early in 1648 a wave of murders, assaults, arson and thefts suddenly convulsed the town, and a large delegation took another petition to Moscow, arriving just in time to witness the collapse of the tsar's authority. As soon as they returned to Kozlov with the news, the town rose in rebellion. The governor just managed to escape, but the rioters beat to death several of his supporters and 'threw them into the depths of the river. And they plundered many houses and shops.' Rioting also broke out in neighbouring forts and Cossack villages, where mobs beat or killed neighbours who had wavered in their support for the earlier campaign against the governor, plundering their shops and houses. Nevertheless, although some documents mention a community (*mir*), council (*sovet*) or assembly (*krug*) of insurgents, the rebels failed to unite the town behind them by the time a new governor with a detachment of musketeers arrived from Moscow. Eventually almost one hundred men were tried and punished – among them the petitioners who had brought news of the Moscow riots and thereby (the judges asserted) provoked the troubles.[38]

Frustration at corruption and at Moscow's 'red tape' combined with dearth had also created an atmosphere conducive to revolt elsewhere. Thus by the time Kursk rebelled in July 1648, it had suffered from a prolonged food shortage (caused by bad harvests coupled with Tatar raids), and now it faced increased tax demands. The town had sent numerous petitions to the tsar pleading for relief but none succeeded; and so upon hearing of the events in Moscow, peasants, townsmen, Cossacks and servitors combined to overthrow the governor held responsible for the town's misfortunes. There and elsewhere, only the arrival of musketeers from Moscow restored order.[39]

The Great Compromise of 1649

Although the 'great shaking' affected large areas of Russia, the fate of the Romanov state was decided in Moscow. According to one of the tsar's advisers, it was 'the rebellion of the common people' of his capital, supported by the local gentry and the musketeers, which led Alexei to summon representatives of his subjects – 'not willingly, but out of fear'.[40] First, an elite group of clerics, nobles, servitors, merchants and representatives of the main towns assembled in the Kremlin in July 1648 and requested that the tsar should 'order to be written up on all sorts of judicial matters a law code and statute book (*Ulozhennaia kniga*), so that henceforth all matters would be done and decided according to that statute book'. They also wanted the tsar to convene the Zemskii Sobor to ratify the new laws.[41] The tsar duly established a five-man commission to draft a new law code, and they had completed their task by October, when some 600 representatives arrived in Moscow to attend a Zemskii Sobor.

For a moment it seemed that the assembly (and therefore the new law code) was doomed because, having bought the musketeers' compliance with another substantial gift, Alexei summoned Morozov back to Moscow where he resumed his post as chief minister. Many leading Muscovites, fearing that this blatant breach of the tsar's solemn promise would produce another wave of popular violence, fled the capital, while some wealthy merchants moved into the residence of the Swedish envoy, defended by his staff and some of the tsar's musketeers.[42] Perhaps this reaction unnerved Morozov, or perhaps he came to realize that a comprehensive law code might benefit the central government, for he allowed the assembly to continue its deliberations. Many of the provisions of the new law code (*Sobornie Ulozhenie*), which contained almost 1,000 articles, closed off the avenues that had led to the troubles. Article 1 ('Blasphemers and Church troublemakers') ensured the sanctity of churches and church services (precluding any further attempt to intercept the tsar on religious holidays), while Article 3 ('The sovereign's palace court') did the same for the sovereign's palace (making any forced entry to the Kremlin treason). Article 10 ('The judicial process') decreed that, in future, subjects must submit their petitions through the local governor to the appropriate chancellery, not to the tsar: anyone who tried to circumvent this procedure would be imprisoned and flogged. Article 19 ('Townsmen') required all citizens to register in the town where they resided on publication of the law, and forbade them and their descendants ever to leave it.

In return for these measures, the tsar made numerous concessions, including many demanded in past petitions. The *Ulozhenie* granted the registered inhabitants of each town a monopoly over all local trade and crafts activities; abolished the tax exemptions enjoyed by most privileged orders; and allowed the pursuit and recapture of all former citizens who fled in order to escape paying taxes. Above all, Article 11 ('Judicial process for peasants') settled the matter of fugitive serfs. Henceforth no peasant could legally leave the estates of his lord; no time limit existed for reclaiming fugitive serfs; and all those who had previously fled could now be reclaimed. The peasants also lost their right of full ownership of personal property: the law deemed all their goods to be possessions of their lord. Moreover, these measures applied to the serf's family: 'a peasant who married a fugitive, or the child of a fugitive, was transferred with his spouse when the latter was reclaimed by the fugitive's rightful lord'. Almost immediately government commissioners began to track down and return fugitive serfs, finding that in some regions up to one-fifth of the population consisted of runaways. Although in some areas (notably the southern frontier and Siberia) fugitives could still live in relative safety, the *Ulozhenie* deprived perhaps half the rural population of their freedom of movement. Noblemen could now buy and sell serfs (and their families), move them around, trade them and even (by the end of the century) wager them in card games. A nobleman's power over every servile family living on his estates was limited only by murder: 'premeditated murder of a peasant' by a lord, any lord, 'was punishable by death'.[43]

The government had resisted restricting peasant migration for as long as possible because of its importance for the expansion of Siberia and the southern frontier; but Alexei's dependence on his servitors both to preserve domestic law and order and to fight foreign enemies eventually led him to give way. The trauma of the 'great shaking' of 1648 must have made the sacrifice of the serfs seem a cheap price to pay for the return of political stability – especially since the Zemskii Sobor showed no interest in demanding more concessions (at a time when Alexei could hardly have refused to make them).[44] The compromise of 1649 brought gains to both sides. On the one hand, landholders gained total control over their serfs for the next two centuries; on the other, the restoration of domestic harmony allowed the tsar to rearm. By the end of the year, the Swedish ambassador reported that foreign officers had begun to drill Russian soldiers in Moscow 'almost daily, because they must become capable of training the others who are to be enlisted'. This would soon allow Alexei to annexe large parts of the Polish-Lithuanian Commonwealth.[45]

The Ukrainian Revolt

The 'Eternal Peace of Polianovka' bound only the two principal signatories, and so technically it lapsed with the death of Michael Romanov in 1645; but Władysław IV made clear his desire to renew the peace, and he immediately sent an embassy to Moscow to negotiate not only this but also a common strategy for an attack on the troublesome vassals of the Ottoman sultan: the Crimean Tatars. Anticipating Moscow's agreement, Władysław set out to persuade the Cossacks living along the Don and Dnieper rivers in Ukraine to spearhead the venture.

Until 1569 Ukraine formed part of the Grand Duchy of Lithuania, which boasted weak government control and a strong Orthodox Church; but in that year Lithuania joined Poland in a closer union, and the region passed under Polish control. This transfer produced three destabilizing consequences. First, the crown strove to impose Polish officials, laws, troops and the Catholic faith on the newly incorporated lands. Second, the underpopulated Ukraine attracted many immigrants from many areas: Poland, Lithuania, Russia; the Balkans and even further afield. Some settled on the Black Earth farmlands (just as fertile as those in Russia: page 153 above), while others went to the towns – both to new settlements founded by the nobles and to established cities like Kiev, the capital, which by the 1620s numbered between 10,000 and 15,000 inhabitants – where they formed a reservoir of malcontents. The third destabilizing consequence arose because the crown granted huge estates in Ukraine to a few great nobles, on the grounds that they required extensive resources in order to coordinate frontier defence. By 1640 about one-tenth of the landholders controlled two-thirds of the population. The rapid growth of some noble estates almost defies belief: for example, the Wiśniowiecki family possessed some 600 settlements in Ukraine in 1630, over 7,000 in 1640, and no fewer than 38,000 (with 230,000 'subjects') in 1645. To maximize the yield of their vast new estates, these nobles appointed aggressive estate managers, and tasked them both with collecting tolls, taxes and rents more efficiently and with exporting as much as possible of the crops raised on the rich soil. Many of the estate managers came from the expanding Jewish population of Ukraine, which rose from perhaps 3,000 in 15 localities in 1569 to at least 45,000 in almost 100 communities by 1648.[46]

The relative ease of river access (for both settlers and exporters) meant that these developments occurred primarily along the Dnieper and its tributaries, challenging the independence of the Cossacks there who lived from a combination of fishing, hunting, farming and raids to secure Tatar booty (both human and material). Nevertheless, since the crown still needed the Cossack 'Host' (as its warriors were known) to defend its southern border, it maintained a 'register' of veterans who received an annual stipend. The Cossacks elected their own officers and a commander, the *Hetman*, who in wartime led them on campaign; but in most years, the 'Cossack register' included scarcely one-tenth of the available warriors. Only they were entitled to a stipend, leaving a disgruntled and heavily armed population living along the Dnieper 'below the rapids' (*Zaporizhia*), for whom raiding offered the only chance of preserving the lifestyle they had adopted.

In 1630 the Cossacks rebelled, appealing to 'both clergy and laymen of the Greek [Orthodox] religion' because their faith 'was being taken away, and asking them to stand up for the faith'.[47] Alarmed by the unity between Cossacks and clergy, the government increased the number of registered Cossacks from 6,000 to 8,000. Nevertheless, the influx of Polish settlers to the Dnieper valley continued, as did the demands of the new noble landowners. In 1635 the federal Diet provocatively reduced the number of registered Cossacks to 7,000 and called for a fort to be built at Kodak on the lower Dnieper, garrisoned by units of the regular army. These measures provoked a new revolt by the Cossacks, who sacked Kodak and murdered its garrison. Although payment of wage arrears to the registered men allowed the capture and execution of the leading rebels, according to Adam Kysil (a Ukrainian nobleman appointed by King Władysław as a commissioner to pacify the revolt) the Cossack problem remained 'a boil perennially on the verge of bursting'; and, indeed, almost immediately, another rebellion broke out.[48] Once again, the Cossacks claimed that they sought to defend the Orthodox faith as well as the civilian community, and to that end (according to a chronicler) they 'treated the Poles with contempt, killed the Germans like flies, burned towns, and slaughtered the Jews like chickens. Some burned monks in Roman Catholic churches.'[49]

Such brutality alienated many supporters, allowing Polish troops to force the Cossack rebels to surrender. They reluctantly swore an oath, drawn up by the secretary of the Zaporozhian warriors, Bohdan Khmelnytsky, that they would henceforth obey the crown in all matters. They also agreed to a reduction in the number of registered Cossacks to 6,000 again, and they promised not to attack the Tatars (or the Ottomans) without express royal permission. Above all, they promised to take orders from a Cossack commissioner appointed by the crown (instead of from their elected *Hetman*), and agreed that the commissioner would appoint the colonels and captains formerly elected by their men. Naturally, Władysław appointed Polish magnates as commissioners; equally naturally, the commissioners appointed their Polish supporters to serve as colonels and captains. The newcomers soon began to exact much the same taxes and services from the Cossacks as from their peasants, and they punished non-compliance with confiscation of property and even outlawry.

Adam Kysil, who negotiated the treaty that ended the revolt, urged Władysław not to press his advantage too hard. He observed that although war, execution and flight had significantly reduced the number of unregistered Cossacks, the new social order backed by Warsaw rested upon a very narrow base: a few troops, a few managers (mostly Jewish), and a few nobles. The central government, Kysil warned, must realize that 'it is just as important to take control of the free villages [along the Dnieper] and their peasants, so that they do not have time to run wild, as it is to keep the Cossacks themselves in order, for the peasants cannot stand firm without the Cossack name and advice, nor can the Cossacks do so without the peasants' strength'.[50] Władysław did not listen. Instead, he continued to grant huge estates in Ukraine to leading Polish nobles, who continued to increase the burdens on the peasantry. He also stationed Polish troops in the leading cities where, in the absence of punctual pay, they extracted food, lodging and other goods at gunpoint.

Rabbi Nathan Hannover, who lived in Ukraine, described the cumulative impact of these changes in his *Abyss of Despair*, an account of the massacre of the Ukrainian Jews in 1648–9. Władysław, he observed, had

> Raised the status of the Catholic dukes and princes above those of the [Ukrainians], so that most of the latter abandoned their Greek Orthodox faith and embraced Catholicism [or joined the Uniate Church]. And the masses that followed the Greek Orthodox church became gradually impoverished. They were looked upon as low and inferior beings and became the slaves and the handmaids of the Polish people and of the Jews ... Their lives were made bitter by hard labour in mortar and bricks, and in all manner of heavy taxes, and some [lords] even resorted to cruelty and torture with the intent of persuading them to accept Catholicism.[51]

Although anti-Semitic exaggeration has distorted the record (for example, claiming that Jews had acquired the lease of churches and only allowed Christian services to take place in them in return for hefty payments), Jewish estate managers often did gain extensive powers over the rural population. For example, in many areas Jewish entrepreneurs acquired the exclusive right to distil and sell vodka: this meant that they operated the only taverns in the region, where they could charge whatever prices they liked, and they called in the army to destroy illegal stills. Unsurprisingly, these measures enraged the local population and alienated them from their Jewish neighbours.[52]

Rabbi Hannover did not mention one more factor that helped to precipitate the rebellion that would cost half of Ukraine's Jews their lives and property: adverse weather. The failure of the 1637 revolt triggered a mass migration of Cossacks to the lower Dnieper which, even at the best of times, suffered from almost unbearable humidity and heat in summers and intense cold in winters. As elsewhere in the northern hemisphere, these were not 'the best of times'. The diary of Marcin Goliński of Kraków recorded the deteriorating situation, with high bread prices in 1638; an exceptionally cold summer in 1641 (during which the sparse grain harvest ripened late and the wine was sour); spring frosts in 1642 and 1643 that blighted all crops; and heavy snow and frosts in the early months of 1646 that gave way to daily rains so torrential that the roads became impassable. Further south, a French resident concurred. After noting that, even in normal years, the Ukrainian winter 'has as much power and force to destroy anything as fire has to consume', he wrote that plagues of locusts in 1645 and 1646, followed by the cruel winter of 1646, had destroyed the harvests and made it impossible for the Cossack communities along the lower Dnieper to feed themselves.[53]

Amidst this climate-induced adversity, Władysław's plan to launch a massive Cossack raid against the Tatars possessed considerable appeal: war would double the number of registered (and therefore paid) Cossacks to 12,000, offering them a providential escape from overpopulation and hunger. But the federal Diet refused to approve the necessary funds for the venture, while the Cossack commissioner and his subordinates behaved outrageously towards individual Cossacks, including Bohdan Khmelnytsky. While he was away in Warsaw in 1646 to receive the king's instructions for the projected Ottoman campaign, a Polish officer seized some of Khmelnytsky's property and publicly flogged one of his sons so brutally that he subsequently died. Another officer allegedly abducted Bohdan's betrothed and married her; while the following year, Polish troops ravaged his estates. Khmelnytsky therefore fled to the unregistered Cossacks of the lower Dnieper, but he found little solace there: autumn and winter 1647 saw torrential rains that destroyed crops and caused widespread floods; spring 1648 was exceptionally hot and dry, and locusts destroyed the harvest. An inscription carved into the cathedral wall of Old Sambor, not far from Lviv, said it all: 'There was great hunger throughout the Christian world.'[54]

Khmelnytsky chose this moment to declare that he possessed Władysław's personal blessing for another Cossack revolt. He asserted that the king had listened sympathetically when he described the abusive system under which the Cossacks now lived and had stated that, although he lacked the power to restrain his nobles, 'since you cannot proceed otherwise, avenge your grievances with the sword'. Khmelnytsky also claimed to possess letters signed by the king authorizing the Cossacks to mobilize against their oppressors.[55]

Although the royal letters were almost certainly forged (nobody ever claimed to have seen the originals), many believed Khmelnytsky's claim that he held some sort of commission from the king – thanks in part to his charismatic character, which impressed virtually everyone he met. Born into a minor noble family in Ukraine around 1595 and educated at a Jesuit college, he acquired extensive military experience and boasted personal contacts not only in Istanbul (where he had spent two years as a captive) but also in Warsaw (where as Secretary of the Host he met not only the king but also his leading ministers). Although at first Khmelnytsky commanded barely 250 followers, within a few weeks several thousand Cossacks – including registered men whose pay had fallen into arrears – rallied to his cause and elected him their *Hetman*. He also requested and received assistance from the sultan's vassal, the Tatar Khan of the Crimea, whose subjects were also starving (according to a chronicle, 'last year [1647] there was no harvest, and now the cattle, sheep and cows are dying').[56]

In May 1648, Khmelnytsky led his Cossack followers and their Tatar allies towards Kiev where they ambushed a Polish army: the hated Cossack commissioner and almost all the Commonwealth's regular troops either died or surrendered. Almost immediately afterwards, King Władysław died, creating an interregnum. Adam Kysil saw at once the seriousness of the situation. 'We are no longer dealing', Kysil warned his colleagues in Warsaw, with the Ukrainians of earlier days who 'only mounted their horses armed with bows and boar-spears, but with a brutal and impassioned army whose proportions we must reckon thus: that for every one of us there will arise a thousand [of them] with firearms'.[57] Whereupon, all over the region, peasants rose up against their lords while the Orthodox clergy called for vengeance against the Catholics; the outnumbered Polish nobles withdrew, hastily followed by their retainers and their estate managers. According to a noble refugee, 'Every peasant has either killed his lord or driven him out with just the shirt on his back, his life, and his children.' Most abandoned the weapons in their armouries and arsenals, which the Cossacks promptly appropriated.[58]

Although Kysil persuaded Khmelnytsky to halt his army and send back his Tatar allies, a Cossack leader nicknamed 'Crook-Nose' continued to march northwards, encouraging the native population to turn on their remaining oppressors The 'Victory March' composed during the uprising describes what happened next:

Hey, Crook-Nose leads a small army,
Seven hundred Cossacks together,
He chops the soldiers' heads off their shoulders
And drowns the rest in the water.

There on the Vistula, there hang the Polacks,
There like a black cloud they're hanging.
Now Polish glory's shattered and sorry,
While the bold Cossack goes dancing.[59]

But the Cossacks did not just chop off the heads of soldiers, 'hang the Polacks' and then go dancing: they also turned on the Jews. Rabbi Hannover left a chilling description of the massacres that started in June 1648 at the town of Nemyriv, where the local population helped the Cossacks to enter the citadel in which their Jewish neighbours had taken refuge. As the raiders cut down the men, many women jumped off the walls and drowned themselves rather than be raped and then murdered. In all, Hannover estimated that 6,000 died in two days at Nemyriv. July saw similar tragic events further north: 2,000 Poles and 12,000 Jews killed at Polonne when the Ukrainians persuaded the servants within the town to open the gates ('Why fight us to protect the nobles?'), with more at Zasław (the rabbi's home town) and Ostrog (where the Ukrainians also looted and wrecked the Catholic monasteries).[60]

It is hard to establish the exact scale of the killings. Early Jewish estimates range from 80,000 to 670,000, but more recent calculations suggest 10,000 killed in the violence itself, at least 8,000 more fugitives to Jewish communities elsewhere (from Amsterdam to Egypt), and perhaps 3,000 sold to the Tatars as slaves. An unknown number survived only because they converted to Orthodoxy. In all it seems likely that the Jewish population in Ukraine fell by half in the summer of 1648. In the opinion of a Jewish chronicler in Kraków, writing later in the century, 'from the time of the Destruction of the Temple there has not been such a cruel slaughter in the community of the Lord'.[61]

Three unrelated developments now affected the outcome of the revolt in Ukraine. First, although Khmelnytsky had written a letter to the tsar requesting that he take the entire Cossack Host under his protection, the letter arrived just as Moscow erupted in rebellion: Alexei could not help. Second, the murder of the Ottoman Sultan Ibrahim ruled out aid from the Crimean Tatars, because the khan expected a summons to restore order in Istanbul (chapter 7 below). Finally, while the Polish nobility debated the election of a new king, they appointed three joint commanders for the regular army – and even then created a supervising committee of senators to keep them in check. This divided command made it easy for Khmelnytsky to rout the Poles again in September 1648 and lead his men towards Warsaw (see Fig. 19).

In Kraków, Marcin Goliński saw the perils of the situation clearly. Normally (he wrote in his diary), whenever the Cossacks rebelled the Poles struck first; but the defeat of the Commonwealth's field army left Poland with no defence except prayer. The Danzig correspondent of a London newspaper agreed: 'The kingdom of Poland is in a most miserable perplexed condition, being troubled within and from without. The peasants of that kingdom massacre all their landlords for [the] great slavery they kept them in, under which they groaned so long. And the Cossacks are 200,000 strong in arms.' The reporter blamed the crown's refusal to permit the Orthodox Cossacks 'the exercise of their religion, that restraint having caused more bloodshed than all the other'.[62] Eventually the Sejm elected Władysław's brother John Casimir as their king and also authorized a truce with the Cossacks. Khmelnytsky was agreeable (he had supported the candidacy of John Casimir), and he led his men back to Kiev, the ancient capital, where the landmark winter of 1648–9 changed the entire nature of the revolt.

Since the great nobles had all fled, and the lesser ones who stayed lacked any corporate identity, almost by default the Cossack Host became the focus and mouthpiece for the entire community. The policies articulated by this body reflected the fact that the Catholics and most other religious minorities had also fled, leaving the militant Orthodox clergy of Kiev in almost sole control of the pulpits. They hailed Khmelnytsky (despite his Catholic upbringing) as 'Moses, saviour, redeemer, and liberator of the Ruthenian nation from the slavery of the [Poles], he who was given by God, hence called Bohdan [which literally means God-given]'. Whenever Khmelnytsky attended church he received pride of place, and the Metropolitan compared him to Constantine the Great, the founder of Orthodox piety, and hailed him as 'prince of Rus'' – the descendant of the ancient rulers of Kiev.[63]

This concerted clerical campaign to turn Khmelnytsky into a national hero affected his style of leadership. He put it best in a speech early in 1649 to Adam Kysil and the other negotiators sent by John Casimir. 'True enough, I am a wretched little man, but God has granted that I am the sole ruler and autocrat of Rus,' he began. 'The time was ripe to negotiate with me when I was being sought and hounded . . .

on the Dnieper', or 'when I was on the march to Kiev'; but now 'I shall fight to free the whole Ruthenian nation from Polish bondage. At first I fought for my own damages and injustice – now I shall fight for our Orthodox faith.'[64] Khmelnytsky and his supporters therefore submitted an ultimatum to the crown that included many ecclesiastical demands: apart from a general amnesty and doubling the number of registered Cossacks entitled to a state salary to 12,000, they required the admission of Orthodox prelates to the federal Diet, the restitution of all former Orthodox churches taken over by the Catholics, and the expulsion of all Jesuits and Jews.[65]

Kysil and his colleagues realized that the Cossacks had decided to renew the war. As they returned home with the ultimatum they noted that, on the one hand, no crops had been sown whereas, on the other, 'the masses are arming themselves, savouring freedom from labour and dues, and they do not want to have lords ever again'. They feared that 'even if Khmelnytsky himself wanted peace, the peasant masses and the Ruthenian priests do not want to allow it – but [rather want] him to finish the war against the Poles, so that the Ruthenian faith may spread, and so they may not have any lords over them'. The next two decades would see (in the words of an early chronicle) 'the greatest, bloodiest and, since the beginning of the Polish nation, unprecedented war'.[66]

The Cossack declaration of war is easily explained. Thanks to the landmark winter of 1648–9 and the likelihood of another plague of locusts, a further harvest failure loomed; and so, without crops and without wages from the central government, war alone offered the Cossacks the prospect of sustenance for the coming year. On the other hand, if the nobles and Catholic clergy who had fled should ever return, they would no doubt exact a terrible revenge upon the former rebels – amnesty or no amnesty. Khmelnytsky therefore wrote a series of letters begging assistance from Tsar Alexei, from the Don Cossacks, and from the Tatars. Although the tsar, still facing urban rebellions, again refused to aid the Cossacks openly, he allowed them to import bread and other foodstuffs duty free, which saved many from starvation; and he invited prominent churchmen from Kiev to come to Moscow and work towards a union of all Orthodox churches (naturally under Muscovite aegis). By contrast, Khmelnytsky had more success with his overture to the Tatar khan, who arrived with a huge following in August 1649. Together they ambushed another Polish army, this time led by King John Casimir in person, near Zboriv on the Strypa river. The resulting 'Zboriv Agreement' granted almost everything in Khmelnytsky's ultimatum: a general amnesty, the expulsion of all Jesuits and Jews, and complete toleration. In addition, the new king promised that no Cossack would be tried by non-Cossacks; no royal troops would be stationed in Ukraine; some Orthodox bishops could sit in the Diet; no Jewish settlement would be allowed in the region; and the number of registered Cossacks entitled to government pay would rise to 40,000 – a huge increase that in effect made Khmelnytsky (now confirmed as *Hetman*) the head of a new autonomous unit within the composite Polish-Lithuanian Commonwealth.[67]

The Zboriv agreement solved nothing. The Tatars forced Khmelnytsky to allow them to enslave numerous Christian families as the price of their withdrawal to the

Crimea, which caused general outrage; while the Diet refused to ratify the king's concession that Orthodox bishops could join its deliberations, and instead voted money to raise a new army which in 1651 defeated the Cossacks and their Tatar allies and occupied Kiev. Khmelnytsky reluctantly signed a treaty that conceded some territory to the Commonwealth and reduced the number of Cossacks on the 'register'. At the same time, however, the *Hetman* renewed his plea for Tsar Alexei to send military assistance.

The Tipping Point: The Commonwealth dismembered

This time the tsar was more sympathetic. According to Peter Loofeldt, a Swedish diplomat in Russia, no sooner had Morozov returned to Alexei's side than he welcomed the chance 'to seek war with Poland over the disputed borders' as a means of diverting the 'increased hatred and resistance' directed towards him. But, Loofeldt continued, when Alexei asked the Zemskii Sobor to discuss assisting the Cossacks, 'The secular lords protested strongly against war, saying that "it is indeed easy to pull the sword from the scabbard, but not so easy to put it back when you want, and that the outcome of war was uncertain".[68] Only an unrelated religious development undermined this consensus and allowed Morozov to get his way.

In 1652 Alexei appointed the zealous monk Nikon as Patriarch of Moscow and encouraged him to undertake a comprehensive campaign of church reform. Nikon aimed to improve the behaviour of the laity: there must be no smoking or swearing; no working on Sundays; no 'pagan' practices (such as celebrating the winter solstice and staging carnivals during Lent); and limited liquor sales (one store in each town and one bottle per customer at a time, with no liquor sales at all on Sundays, holidays, or during Lent). Nikon also tried to raise clerical standards (censuring drunken priests, demanding that the holy offices be chanted audibly) and to demonstrate that the Russian Church was the one true descendant of the Church of the Apostles. To this end he introduced liturgical practices from Greek Orthodox communities; he collected and ritually defaced all icons painted in the Western style; and he sponsored Old Testament imagery suggesting that Moscow had become the New Jerusalem – a conceit most clearly expressed in the vast monastic complex that he constructed just west of Moscow, which included features named for the River Jordan, Golgotha, Nazareth and, at its centre, a cathedral closely modelled on the church of the Holy Sepulchre. On his first visit, Tsar Alexei named the complex 'New Jerusalem' (the name by which it is still known).

Morozov soon persuaded Nikon to see the war to save the Orthodox Cossacks as part of his reform programme. The Patriarch duly 'declared the undertaking to be a holy enterprise and the tsar as the protector and saviour of all the persecuted brethren of the old Greek religion, comparing him with the Kings David, Josiah, and Constantine the Great, who wanted to defend' their faith. 'This made quite an impression upon ordinary people,' wrote Peter Loofeldt, 'making them much more willing to become involved in attacking Poland again. So now preparations for the war began in earnest.'[69]

Events in the Commonwealth encouraged Russian belligerence. The first ever use of a *Liberum Veto* in the *Sejm* of 1652, which brought about the dissolution of the Diet before it had voted the taxes necessary for a new campaign, encouraged several cities in Lithuania to defy the central government and attempt to ally with Khmelnytsky; but then the following year, although resistance continued in Lithuania, the *Sejm* voted funds to invade Ukraine. These developments led the tsar to send two diplomatic delegations westward: one went to Warsaw to demand the return of Smolensk and other territories ceded at Polianovka which, as Alexei had anticipated, the *Sejm* rejected; the other went to Ukraine with an offer of Russian protection, provided that Khmelnytsky ended his alliance with the Tatars. Again as Alexei had anticipated, the *Hetman* accepted. The tsar now invited the Zemskii Sobor's advice, and in October 1653 the assembly voted unanimously to declare war on the Commonwealth and to place Ukraine under Russian protection.

Because of the long distance and the dangerous conditions, the tsar's envoys only reached Khmelnytsky at his camp in Pereiaslav in January 1654 – but, as it happened, their timing could scarcely have been better. Military success by Commonwealth forces the previous year had convinced Khmelnytsky that he could not succeed alone, and as soon as the Russians arrived he summoned all his lieutenants and declared that 'We now see that we can no longer live without a ruler'. He therefore asked his followers to choose between four candidates: the sultan, the Crimean khan, the Polish king and the tsar. Unanimously they chose their co-religionist Alexei and the tsar's officials spent the next few days administering oaths of loyalty. They also invested Khmelnytsky as *Hetman* in the tsar's name; promised that Russian troops would arrive to strengthen defences against the Poles; and agreed that the number of registered Cossacks should be 60,000. In addition, they confirmed all the concessions made by John Casimir at Zboriv. Cossack envoys accompanied the tsar's officials back to Moscow, where in March they formally accepted the terms of what became known as the 'Union of Pereiaslav'.[70]

The continuing unrest in Lithuania had convinced Morozov and Alexei that they should launch a pre-emptive invasion of the Grand Duchy, and in May 1654 the tsar led an enormous army, numbering perhaps 100,000 troops and including all the New Formation Regiments equipped with the latest Western weapons, towards Smolensk. While Khmelnytsky tied down the main Polish army, John Casimir's Orthodox subjects welcomed their co-religionists: several towns in Lithuania changed hands with scarcely a struggle. In July the Russians reached Smolensk and re-entered the siegeworks abandoned 20 years earlier. After three months, the city surrendered to the tsar.

According to Peter Loofeldt, 'the Russians almost remained stationary' after the recapture of Smolensk 'and could have been induced to [make] peace'. But another exercise of a *Liberum Veto* dissolved the *Sejm* before it had voted any taxes and, since 'the Poles could offer little opposition', Alexei decided to 'continue the war with great earnestness'. The tsar once again led his forces in person and, according to Loofeldt,

Took one fortified place after another and did not want to give them up again, especially because for the most part the general population in these places belonged to the Orthodox religion and firmly regarded the tsar as their protector. Also since the Russians had set foot so deep into the country, they could not abandon it easily or with honour. For these reasons, the tsar allowed the war to proceed, sending in greater reinforcements.[71]

In July 1655, Alexei captured Vilnius, the capital of Lithuania, and proclaimed himself its Grand Duke.

The tsar's rapid and complete success alarmed Sweden. Realizing that if he remained neutral, Russia would occupy the entire Commonwealth, King Charles X Gustav (r. 1654–60) and his council debated whether they should help the Poles resist another Russian onslaught, or attack and secure some territory for themselves before the Commonwealth collapsed.[72] They decided on the latter and in July 1655, just as Alexei entered Vilnius, Charles invaded Poland. He entered Warsaw in September and Kraków in October. John Casimir fled the country, while most of his magnates accepted Swedish authority. It was the most complete and rapid state breakdown seen in Europe during the entire early modern period.

'Potop' and 'ruina'

Sweden's spectacular military success rested on slender foundations. Charles X commanded only 36,000 troops – far too few to hold down the vast tracts of the Commonwealth that now lay at his feet. Moreover, the king lacked a clear plan for exploiting his sudden triumph. He failed to convene the Sejm, as he had promised; he failed to restrain his Lutheran troops from assaulting and even murdering Catholic clerics, or from looting Catholic church property; he failed to uphold the privileges of the Polish nobles (for example, their exemption from billeting); and he failed to arrange adequate supplies for his troops, so that they levied contributions from the towns and countryside they occupied. Before long, such ineptitude and brutality alienated large segments of the Polish population and local resistance began.

Tsar Alexei had no intention of sharing any of his gains with Sweden, and in May 1656 he declared war on King Charles and laid siege to the heavily fortified Swedish outpost of Riga; but although he ruled the largest state in the world, Alexei could not mobilize sufficient resources to prevail in two wars at the same time. In order to concentrate on his new war with Sweden, the tsar concluded an armistice with the exiled John Casimir, who swiftly regained Warsaw.

The Russian volte-face infuriated Khmelnytsky, who still regarded the Commonwealth as the Cossacks' greatest enemy. He therefore refused to follow the orders received from Moscow and break with Sweden: instead he tried to build an anti-Polish coalition (going so far as to propose an alliance to Oliver Cromwell), but many Cossacks defied Khmelnytsky and continued to obey the tsar. The Hetman's death in 1657 did not end this division: most Cossacks on the west bank of the Dnieper continued to favour Poland, whereas those on the east bank mostly favoured Russia. These developments plunged the entire region into a period of bloody anarchy that Ukrainian historians eloquently call *Ruina*, and Polish writers, with equal eloquence, call *Potop*: 'the deluge'.[73]

Three factors prolonged the conflict. First, geography confined hostilities to largely predictable locations. In particular, the impenetrable forests forced both troops and supplies to use the rivers, where they could be more easily intercepted, while huge marshlands provided refuge to defeated units and allowed them to regroup for attacks on enemy lines of communication, reducing the chances of a knock-out blow. Second, the Russian army pursued a policy of deliberate brutality that eventually proved counter-productive. In 1654 Alexei instructed his generals 'to present the inhabitants of Belorussian towns with written surrender requests, but if they spurned them, to burn alive Poles or Belorussians subsequently captured who would not convert to Orthodoxy'.[74] The following year, when troops under the tsar's personal command took Vilnius, the capital of Lithuania, they started fires that raged for 17 days and killed perhaps 8,000 people. Throughout the annexed areas, Russian troops persecuted Catholics, Jews and especially members of the Uniate Church (page 154 above). Third, natural disasters intensified the devastation caused by the war. Plague epidemics struck Poland twice in the 1650s and the Little Ice Age produced more long, cold winters and disastrous harvests – including the landmark winter of 1657–8 when the Baltic froze hard enough to allow the Swedish army to march from Jutland to Copenhagen (see chapter 8 below). In central Poland, the thaw began only in early April and (according to a courtier) 'no one can remember such a long winter'.[75]

Eventually, the protagonists became too exhausted to continue fighting: Alexei concluded an armistice with Sweden at the end of 1658, and a peace three years later that sacrificed all his gains. It is hard to disagree with the lapidary verdict of Brian Davies: 'Nothing had been gained from the war with Sweden'.[76] The Commonwealth, too, concluded peace with Sweden in 1660 but for another six years continued its campaigns against the tsar and his Ukrainian allies.

During 'The Deluge', the Polish-Lithuanian Commonwealth encountered all of the 'Four Horsemen of the Apocalypse' – pestilence, war, famine and death – with catastrophic consequences. In 'Great Poland', the western flank of the Commonwealth, fought over and occupied by the Swedes, the number of taxable households fell from 612,554 in the census of 1629 to 305,585 in the census of 1661. Warsaw, occupied by hostile troops between 1655 and 1657, saw its population decline from around 30,000 to barely 6,000. Almost two-thirds of its buildings lay in ruins. Further east, urban tax registers in present-day Belarus (the area invaded by the Russian army) showed catastrophic falls between 1648 and 1667: Pinsk declined from almost 1,000 households to under 300; Mogilev from over 2,300 to under 600; Vitebsk from almost 1,000 to just 56. Thousands perished in sieges; tens of thousands became the victims of persecution like the Jews of Ukraine, slaughtered by Cossacks who saw them as oppressors, or those of Mogilev, slaughtered by Russian troops who feared they might side with an advancing Polish army. In all, the population of the Commonwealth fell by at least one-third.[77]

The population of Russia also plummeted during the 1650s and 1660s through a lethal combination of climatic change, war and plague. Tree-ring, pollen and peat-bed data show that the springs, autumns and winters between 1650 and 1680 were the coldest recorded in Russia during the past 500 years. Repeatedly, crops either failed or produced little food.[78] Probably, as in other parts of Europe, many men who could not find enough to eat at home joined the army, where most of them perished. In 1678, a decade after peace returned to Russia, a detailed census of one community in Karelia, in the far north, revealed that 1,000 of its young men perished in the war – almost 400 of them killed in action – leaving half the households with only young sons.[79] Since Alexei's campaigns involved up to 100,000 troops, communities elsewhere presumably suffered similarly high casualties.

An epidemic of bubonic plague in 1654–7 also caused widespread depopulation. An official survey found that the epidemic had killed four-fifths of the monks and three-quarters of the nuns living in convents within the Kremlin, as well as half the officials in the Foreign Ministry and nine-tenths of those in the Revenue Ministry. A Polish visitor to Russia in 1656 described the 'terrible and considerable devastation' in graphic terms:

> There is a lawless desert in the towns and villages and especially in the capital itself. The Muscovite wages war on the Commonwealth, and the Lord wages war on him in the form of a terrible plague. Food is expensive, especially bread; with the men away at war, the fields are not sown; and famine is to be expected in Moscow. The people are strongly opposed to going to war; they have to be driven to it by force, leaving few people in Moscow.[80]

Alexei's wars also created a fiscal disaster. A recent study by Richard Hellie, an eminent historian of imperial Russia, concluded that 'the real cost of the Muscovite military establishment in the mid-1650s must have been at least three million rubles a year', over one million of which went on the New Formation Regiments. In all, Hellie suggested, 'above one-eighth of Muscovy's productive resources went just to pay for the army'.[81] Building the Belgorod and Simbirsk Lines absorbed perhaps as much again.

The tsar therefore introduced desperate expedients to balance his budget, including currency debasement. The Imperial Mint began to issue copper coins as well as silver, but in 1662, desperate for funds to defeat Poland, the tsar decreed that taxes could only be paid in silver. The exchange rate between the two currencies now shot up from parity to 1:15, and producers refused to accept copper coins for their goods, including grain, creating a famine in Moscow. As in 1648, thousands of citizens and soldiers in the city now gathered to petition the tsar to hand over the ministers whom they blamed for their plight, while rioters looted and burned some of the offenders' houses. This time, however, the tsar used his foreign troops to restore order, executing some 400 protestors out of hand and imprisoning hundreds more (some of them boys as young as 12). After being branded on the cheek for future identification, the tsar sent some 2,000 rioters and their families into permanent exile in Siberia and the lower Volga. Yet they did not suffer in vain: the following year, the tsar recalled all copper money and prices quickly fell to their earlier levels.[82]

John Casimir threw away the golden opportunity presented by these disorders by over-reaching himself (just as Alexei had done by attacking Sweden). He demanded that the *Sejm* elect his successor during the own lifetime, but supporters of the electoral principle repeatedly used the *Liberum Veto*, forcing the king to dissolve the Diets four times in 1665 and 1666. This starved the government of resources for the war against Russia, provoked an aristocratic rebellion that created new devastation, and encouraged the Cossack leaders to seek Ottoman support once more. With Russia and the Commonwealth both paralyzed, the representatives of John Casimir signed a truce at Andrusovo (a village near Smolensk) in February 1667 that not only ceded Alexei's conquests (Smolensk and the lands along the upper Dnieper) but also agreed to partition Ukraine, transferring to the tsar Kiev and all lands east of the Dnieper.

Foreign diplomats quickly saw the significance of these concessions. 'You see in what a state Poland finds itself,' wrote the French ambassador, 'without help, without compassion from its friends because of its bad conduct; and thus must throw itself into the arms of the Muscovites or perish'. His English colleague agreed: 'Ukraine was, in a manner, lost to Poland and with it the safety of Poland'.[83] An Ottoman invasion in 1672 proved this: no longer able to resist, the Commonwealth swiftly made humiliating concessions (see chapter 7 below). But 'the Muscovites', too, still faced many problems.

Russia's Religious Schism

Before Tsar Alexei left Moscow on campaign in 1654 he conferred the title 'Great Sovereign' on Nikon, which allowed the Patriarch to sign decrees in the tsar's name during his absence. Nikon now oversaw the printing of three separate editions of a new liturgy that incorporated numerous innovations, and at a Church Council in 1656 he enjoined the exclusive use of the new ritual and denounced as heretics all who objected. Although the changes were small, they could not be ignored. Above all, demanding that priests and congregations henceforth make the sign of the cross with three fingers instead of two, as Nikon required, affected the most common visible symbol in Orthodox worship.

The Old Believers (as Nikon's critics came to be known) argued that the true Christian faith was timeless and not subject to change: to add or subtract anything was to destroy the truth. They also argued that the Russian Church alone had (in the words of Avraamii, a 'holy fool': one of the earliest and most articulate Old Believers) preserved the 'true Orthodox faith, handed down by the holy Apostles, confirmed at the seven ecumenical councils and sealed with the blood of the holy martyrs'. Heresy, he added, 'comes in by a single letter of the alphabet'.[84] It followed that, if Russia alone had preserved the true faith, every divergent belief or practice must be heretical. Unlike Nikon, the Old Believers despised the numerous Greek Orthodox prelates who visited Moscow to raise money for their beleaguered churches (and found that a declaration in favour of Nikon's liturgy helped their cause), because they all lived under Ottoman rule – a clear sign of divine disfavour. They also dismissed the new liturgies produced by the Moscow printers because they were based on texts printed in Venice, at the heart of Latin Christendom.

In Russia, as elsewhere in Europe, lay people tended to see strict observance of traditional church practices as their pathway to salvation – especially after the Great Plague of 1654–7, which intensified devotion to the local icons and liturgical practices that had 'saved' a family or a community. Many people later recalled that 'the plague had led them to change their way of life': all over Russia, ordinary people began to participate in commemorative religious processions, to worship at votive chapels dedicated to plague victims, to construct special churches in a single day, and to discover new relics – all to exalt their devotion to 'Mother Russia'. They also fasted, self-flagellated and prayed more than ever before.[85]

Imposing religious uniformity throughout the largest state in the world presented unique challenges. It was easy for discontented clergy, whether Old Believers or not, to turn popular insecurities into intransigence – and imperial Russia had no shortage of discontented clergy. Many lived in the small religious communities and hermitages that abounded in remote areas; others were itinerant priests, monks and nuns who wandered the country, many of them defrocked for resisting authority. In addition, every parish had its own service book (usually manuscript), and it took time for the new printed texts to reach outlying areas; moreover, since individual copies were expensive, many parishes remained without one. Nevertheless, two more church councils in 1666–7, presided over by Alexei in person and attended by all Russian and many foreign bishops, repeated the injunction to use only the new liturgy and anathematized as 'heretics and recalcitrants' all who refused to conform (anathemas that remained in force until the 1970s). Most critics of the reform now recanted, but a handful remained obdurate. Some, like the 'Holy Fool' Avraamii, died at the stake in Moscow as a heretic; others went into exile in the far north (where the tsar's servants put many to death as well); but, as long as they lived, these and other Old Believers tirelessly gathered and copied ancient church texts and wrote martyrologies of the fallen.

Stenka Razin

Moscow's religious intransigence also contributed to the major uprising in 1670 by the Cossacks of the Don and Volga valleys, who lived on hunting, fishing and raiding. Over the previous quarter-century, thanks to peasant migration from the north, the number of Don Cossacks had tripled to perhaps 25,000, which severely increased pressure on the scarce resources of the region. The situation remained tolerable in the Cossack settlements along the lower Don and its tributaries, where an elite of long-established families, known as the 'householders', monopolized the best hunting, fishing and grazing, pocketed the subsidies from Moscow, and held all political power; but conditions deteriorated for the immigrants, significantly known as 'the naked ones' (*golytba* or *golutvennye*). They lacked land, property and subsidies, surviving only if the 'householders' gave them work. In the words of a government report, 'runaway peasants have come from neigh-bouring areas with their wives and children, and as a result there is now great hunger on the Don'.[86]

The truce of Andrusovo between Russia and Poland in 1667 hurt the Cossacks. Not only did it deprive them of a fruitful source of booty, but it also reduced pressure on the tsar, no longer dependent on their services, to send grain and munitions punctually. Later that year, one of the disgruntled householders, Stepan ('Stenka') Razin therefore decided to lead an expeditionary force of 'naked ones' on a raid around the Caspian Sea. Like Bohdan Khmelnytsky in the Polish Commonwealth, Razin was familiar with the corridors of power long before he became a rebel: he had visited Moscow and also headed an embassy from the tsar to neighbouring steppe rulers. Now, despite the tsar's express prohibition, Razin and his men sailed safely down the Volga to the Caspian, where they took advantage of a series of natural disasters that weakened Iran (see chapter 13 below) to institute a reign of terror in 1668 and 1669.

Razin's remarkable success in securing wealth during a famine year won over many more 'naked ones', and in spring 1670 he decided to lead his forces back to the Volga and advance on Moscow. His declared aim was to move 'against the Sovereign's enemies and betrayers, and to remove from the Muscovite state the traitor boyars' as well as the tsar's councillors, provincial governors and town magistrates, 'and to give freedom to the common people'.[87] In the event Razin's followers, who now numbered 7,000, determined otherwise: having advanced up the Volga as far as Tsaritsyn, which they captured, they voted to move south again and seize control of all Russian settlements down to the Caspian. This they accomplished thanks to two strokes of fortune. First, the Crimean Tatars, who normally attacked Russian outposts along the lower Volga each summer, campaigned elsewhere, relieving Razin of a potential enemy. Second, Tsar Alexei had deported many of those involved in the Moscow revolt of 1662 (page 178 above) to the lower Volga and these exiles, eager for revenge, betrayed their towns and joined the rebels.

Nevertheless, Razin's position remained vulnerable because the economy of the entire lower Volga depended on goods, and especially grain, sent by the tsar. Razin therefore persuaded his followers that they must campaign against Moscow in order to secure the supplies without which they would starve. As he moved north in summer 1670, Razin won the support of others alienated by Moscow's oppressive policies – fugitive serfs, political exiles, unpaid soldiers, Muslims dispossessed by Christians – as well as of oppressed peasants anxious to take revenge on their brutal masters and of townsfolk impoverished because the tsar imposed a trade embargo on all areas in revolt. Many women joined the movement and disseminated propa-ganda; a few, including Razin's mother, commanded rebel detachments. Many clerics alienated by Nikon's reforms provided spiritual support and drafted 'sedi-tious letters' (as the government termed them) inviting those along Razin's line of march to help him 'eliminate the traitors and the bloodsuckers of the peasant communes', and proclaiming that he was on his way to Moscow 'to establish the

Cossack way there, so that all men will be equal'. The clerics cleverly tailored each message to its audience – for example, writing to Muslim communities in their own language and claiming 'this is our watchword: *For God and the Prophet'*. Razin even claimed that he had received letters of support from Nikon and that he represented the crown prince. By September 1670, the revolt that had originated with a subsistence crisis on the lower Don affected a swathe of territory along the Volga that stretched for 800 miles. Even subjects of the tsar in Siberia and Karelia received copies of Razin's 'seditious letters'.[88]

The revolt failed because of the 'Great Wall' created expressly to protect the capital against attacks from the south. The tsar sent reinforcements, bonus pay and extra ammunition to garrisons along the fortified ramparts, which foiled the attempts of Razin and some 20,000 men to secure Simbirsk, at the eastern end of the Lines. After a month, a counter-attack drove Razin back with heavy losses. He himself suffered serious head and leg wounds, impairing his aura of invincibility, and he retreated to the fortified base on the Don from which he had started. Meanwhile his brother, with another army, failed to take Voronezh, a key fortress on the Belgorod Line, and also fell back. When the tsar sent his New Formation Regiments southwards, the Cossack 'householder' elite decided that it would be prudent to arrest Razin, which they did in April 1671, and to send him to Moscow where Tsar Alexei had him tortured and executed.[89]

In January 1672 victory celebrations in Moscow demonstrated Alexei's power. The shah of Iran, whose subjects had suffered from Razin's raiders, sent his congratulations; so did Charles II of Great Britain, who recalled with gratitude the tsar's refusal to recognize the Republican regime that had executed his father. For a while, some of Razin's followers found shelter in the Old Believer Solovetsky monastery, apparently impregnable on an island in the White Sea; but in January 1676, a defector revealed a breach in the monastery walls to the imperial besiegers, who broke in during a snowstorm. Many of the dissidents they killed, and many more killed themselves. Only 14 of the 200 defenders escaped to spread the story of the Old Believers' heroic resistance.[90]

Nevertheless, when Alexei died in his bed a few days later, leaving three minor sons to succeed him, the troubles resumed. Abroad, war broke out with the Turks in 1677 and lasted for four years; at home, opposition resumed in the smaller monasteries, which still resented the efforts of the bishops to put Nikon's liturgy into effect. In May 1682 a dispute over which of Alexei's sons should succeed led a group of musketeers, resentful of the growing prominence and higher pay of the New Formation Regiments, to storm the Kremlin. They received support from Old Believers in the capital and, the following month, submitted a petition calling on the Regent Sofia, Alexei's daughter, to restore the traditional liturgy. Sofia agreed to a 'debate' on the validity of the Nikonian reforms, but when an Old Believer spokesman suggested that not only the Patriarch but also her father had been a heretic, Sofia stormed out of the meeting and fled the capital, leaving it under the control of the mutineers until she could raise an army capable of defeating them. She had her revenge two years later when, having regained Moscow without firing a shot, Sofia issued draconian legislation against the Old Believers: all who failed to attend their local parish church must be questioned; all suspected of heresy must be tortured; all who refused to recant must be burned at the stake; and anyone who sheltered an Old Believer must be severely punished. Henceforth, Old Believers flourished only on the periphery of the state, where some staged mass suicides when threatened by government forces – and won new converts by their devotion. Although religious dissent never again threatened the integrity of the Romanov state, and although 'the total number of suicides ran into tens of thousands', by 1900 one Russian in six was an Old Believer, and the faith today numbers millions of adherents.[91]

The New Order

In the words of Frank Sysyn, 'modern national relations' in eastern Europe 'begin with the Khmelnytsky revolt' of 1648. Even a flurry of provincial rebellions a generation later failed to change the new political configuration in which, in the words of Brian Davies, 'the circle of serious contenders for hegemony had been narrowed to the Ottoman Empire and Muscovy'.[92] The vast Polish-Lithuanian Commonwealth never recovered from the mid-century crisis: its population had declined by at least one-third; one year after signing the 1667 truce of Andrusovo, John Casimir abdicated and emigrated; and the 1686 'Eternal Peace of Moscow' perpetuated the transfer of all territory ceded to Russia.

War and rebellion also ruined Ukraine. The measure of self-rule secured by Khmelnytsky between 1648 and 1654 did not survive, although for the next seven decades the tsar's guarantee that 60,000 Cossacks (and their families) would receive a regular salary from state revenues allowed the Cossack Host to evolve into both the civil administration and the social elite of the region. Moreover, the flight of Polish landowners ended Catholic patronage of builders and artists, allowing a renaissance in Ruthenian art, architecture and literature which profoundly influenced Russia. Throughout the Romanov state, Orthodox seminaries followed the model of Kiev; most bishops came from Ukraine; and Russian art and music embraced Ukrainian forms. Nevertheless, the *ruina* fully deserved its name. The death or flight of half its Jewish population in the massacres of 1648 created, in the phrase of Rabbi Nathan Hannover, an 'abyss of despair' for the survivors; while the continuation of war and extreme weather decimated the rest of the Ukrainian population. Even in 1700 the former Cossack state contained scarcely a million inhabitants – one-third of its former size – and those survivors remained dependent on support from the tsar. Although they retained some internal autonomy for a while longer, they could never again boast that 'the tsar rules in Moscow but the Cossacks rule on the Don'.[93]

Conversely, taken together, the 'Time of Troubles', the 'great shaking' of 1648–9 and the Thirteen Years War strengthened the Romanov regime. Even the *Ulozhenie* of 1649, which stemmed directly from the 'great shaking', reinforced the power of the tsars. Admittedly, the code gave most landholders what they wanted – total control over their serfs – but it also established the obligations of servitors and musketeers to the tsar, and the punishments for those who fell short; it extended the fiscal responsibilities of townspeople; and it established the religious protocols of the Church and the acceptable behaviour of priests. The code also offered equality before the law to Russians and non-Russians alike – one no longer needed to convert to Orthodoxy, or even to speak Russian, in order to plead in a Russian court – and it standardized court protocol, forensic procedures and fees. A single document thus laid out the entire Russian social and legal system with the tsar at the apex, and it proved a 'best-seller': two editions of 1,200 copies by the Government Printing Shop each sold out almost immediately, and regional administrators as well as many individuals soon possessed their own copy.[94]

Tsar Alexei's wars also brought significant material gains, adding perhaps 120,000 square miles (about the same size as modern Italy or Nevada) and over a million new subjects to the Romanov state. They also discredited the military pretensions of the servitors so that, ironically, just as they received the economic benefits they had long sought, they became militarily obsolete. Instead of cavalry drawn from reluctant landowners, the tsars relied increasingly on highly trained New Formation Regiments under highly paid Western officers of unquestioned loyalty – even if some of them, like General Patrick Gordon, constantly considered 'how I might ridd my self of this country so farr short of my exspectation and disagreeing with my humour . . . strangers being looked upon by the best sort as scarcely Christians, and by the plebeyans as meer pagans'.[95]

Gordon was not alone in perceiving limits to Russia's 'Westernization'. A few years later an English envoy belittled the Russians for their 'rustick and barbarous humor, which is so natural to them' and hoped they would 'learn by degrees to live with more civility'. Indeed, he mused, if they 'were under a gentler government, and had a free trade with every body, no doubt but this Nation would in short time be taken with our civility and decent way of living'.[96] Even without such 'civility', however, the Romanovs had not only wrested important concessions from the Polish-Lithuanian Commonwealth at Andrusovo and again at the 'Eternal Peace of Moscow', but also forced both the Ottoman sultan in 1681 and the Chinese emperor in 1689 to recognize the tsar as their equal. The General Crisis, combined with the Little Ice Age, thus enabled Russia to emerge as a Great Power, a position it has never lost.

The 'Ottoman tragedy', 1618–83[1]

'The greatest [empire] that is, or perhaps that ever was'

In the early seventeenth century the Ottoman empire overawed European visitors. A Venetian consul marvelled that it had acquired 'like a lightning bolt' so much territory that it 'included 8,000 miles of the circuit of the world' and 'a great part' of three continents, namely Asia, Africa and Europe; while an English traveller considered it 'the greatest [empire] that is, or perhaps that ever was'. Such awe was justified: the sultan ruled over 20 million subjects and 1 million square miles. Although Istanbul lay more than 700 miles from Vienna, and 1,000 miles from Baghdad, thanks to the empire's efficient logistical infrastructure, imperial couriers carried orders from the capital to officials in Hungary and Mesopotamia in 14 days or less, while an army leaving the Bosporus in spring could normally reach either the Tisza or the Tigris in 10 weeks.[2]

Nevertheless, in the mid-seventeenth century the empire saw two regicides, three depositions and significant loss of territory in both Europe and Asia, and by 1700 it had become 'the sick man of Europe'. Until recently, the nature of this process remained obscure because, in the words of a recent article, 'The seventeenth century has been the black hole of Ottoman history'; but the careful study of the available human and natural 'archives' reveals that the lands around the eastern Mediterranean suffered more from both the Little Ice Age and the General Crisis than almost any other part of the northern hemisphere.[3]

Effective Ottoman government depended on a complex balance of forces. Every sultan claimed absolute and indivisible jurisdiction in all matters not explicitly covered by existing Islamic Law (the *sharīʿa*), and issued decrees known as *kanūn* on fiscal, penal and administrative matters that every subject must obey. Although some sultans occasionally acted as supreme judge and heard cases in person, they ceded executive authority to a single minister, the Grand Vizier, while their council normally heard and decided the thousands of petitions that flowed in from subjects every year.[4] In the seventeenth century most sultans lived in the imperial palace, and seldom strayed far from its grounds. This arrangement conferred immense power on those who controlled access to the imperial apartments, and particularly to the palace harem where the sultan's concubines lived under the supervision of several hundred eunuchs. Since no seventeenth-century sultan married, each concubine who bore a son intrigued ceaselessly to ensure that her offspring succeeded and, later, to influence his policies. The sultan's mother was the most powerful woman – and often the most powerful person – in the empire.

The Ottomans divided their subjects into two categories: the *reaya* (literally 'subjects', those who paid taxes) and the '*askerī* (literally 'of the military', those who served the state). Among the latter, a select group of soldiers and government officials known as the *kullar*, the 'sultan's slaves', exercised great power. Until the 1630s, the sultans recruited their *kullar* by conscripting boys from Christian communities under their control in the Balkans and Anatolia: a practice known as *devşirme* ('gathering' in Turkish). Once the boys reached Istanbul, they began rigorous training to turn them into obedient, skilled and 'Ottomanized' converts to Islam, and afterwards they either joined the Janissaries (literally 'new troops', infantry equipped with firearms) or became palace officials (though they too received a military training – appropriately enough in a state that regarded war as its principal activity).[5] The *devşirme* system enhanced the power of the Ottoman dynasty in three distinct ways. First, only the *kullar* could legally own and use firearms (both muskets and artillery). Second, since each regional centre boasted a similar provincial cadre – governor, provincial council, treasurers, garrison commandant and presiding judge – the imperial government could rotate its 'slaves' easily from one post to another because, wherever they went, the *kullar* encountered familiar administrative systems, procedures and expectations. Finally, the young converts who prayed, ate, slept and trained together developed a remarkable cohesion and loyalty; and, since they could never leave the sultan's service, risking loss of life and property if they refused or disobeyed an order, they normally formed a principal pillar of the state. Nevertheless the system possessed one obvious weakness: without constant supervision, the *kullar* might usurp their master's power and dictate policy.

Muslims by birth dominated only two professions in the Ottoman empire: the heavy cavalry and the clergy. In the sixteenth century ethnic Turks formed the cavalry (*sipahis*: from the Persian word meaning 'army'), maintaining themselves and their followers with a fief (*tîmâr*) granted by the sultan. By 1600, however, few fiefs produced enough to support a *sipahi* and his retainers, and the number of cavalry troopers had fallen to around 8,000. The central treasury therefore began to pay salaries to the sipahis who formed part of the permanent garrison of Istanbul and various provincial capitals (just like the Janissaries), and their numbers rose to 20,000 by 1650. This increase placed an intolerable strain on the central treasury, which sometimes could afford to pay either the Janissaries or the sipahis, but not both, leading to rivalry and sometimes pitched battles between them.[6]

The clergy, or '*ulema* (the plural of the Arabic word for 'knowledgeable person', '*ālim*), were all Sunni Muslims. They not only provided public worship and religious education but also administered pious foundations and served as judges. At their head stood the *Şeyhulislam* (Chief Mufti), appointed by the sultan and paid a state salary like the rest of the '*ulema*, who received a stream of requests from the central government to certify (usually in the form of a written opinion, or *fatwā*) that a proposed action or edict conformed to the *sharî'a*.[7] On occasion, the Chief Mufti withheld such certification, producing a political crisis that might result in his deposition or, in extreme circumstances, his murder. One Chief Mufti survived for just half a day. The sultans also founded religious schools (*medreses*: literally 'places of study') and paid preceptors to provide basic education in Arabic grammar and syntax, in logic and in rhetoric, as a prelude to instruction in theology and law. The size of the *'ulema* tripled between 1550 and 1622, reflecting a rapid expansion in the number both of *medreses* and mosques (Istanbul had none of either when the Ottomans captured the city in 1453, but by 1600 it boasted almost 100 *medreses* and over 1,200 mosques). This enabled each *medrese* student to find a position as either preceptor, preacher or judge on graduation, and to receive a state salary.

In the seventeenth century, however, further expansion ceased and jobs dwindled. Graduates might wait years for the chance to pass the examination to obtain a licence, without which they could neither teach nor preach; and even those who gained their licence often remained at the bottom of the hierarchy because a select group of elite families (known as the *mevali*) virtually monopolized the elite positions and passed them on to relatives. Thus four-fifths of the 81 Chief Muftis and senior judges appointed between 1550 and 1650 were related, and almost half came from just 11 families.[8] This concentration of power in the hands of the *mevali* naturally created widespread frustration among other members of the *'ulema* who found their careers blocked, and some began to claim that the path to salvation required a return to the original practices and beliefs of Islam.

Frustration also mounted among some Muslims who did not belong to the *'ulema* but nevertheless claimed supernatural powers. Some, not unlike Christian friars, wandered from one community to another, surviving on alms from the faithful; others, not unlike Christian hermits, lived in solitary ascetic devotion in one place; while others still practised as healers – like 'Slimey' Hüseyn in the Istanbul hippodrome, who claimed that his snot healed those on whom it landed. Many more men and women, known as *sufis*, believed that the path to God lay through experience rather than scholarship and therefore performed their devotions publicly, sometimes accompanied by music and dance. The majority belonged to one of Islam's religious Orders, each one headed by a *sheikh*, and either lived in or supported one of the Order's 'lodges' (not unlike Christian monasteries). Several Orders enjoyed close connections with members of the Ottoman elite: thus the Bektashi Order enjoyed a venerable association with the Janissaries, while the Mevlevi and Halveti Orders counted many followers in the imperial palace.[9]

Although the Ottoman empire lacked a tradition of clerical collective action, extreme climatic events in the mid-seventeenth century, as well as the multiplicity of political and economic problems that faced the empire, provided charismatic preachers of all persuasions with convincing evidence of divine discontent and the need for rapid and radical change. Many began to take their message directly to the faithful in passionate sermons delivered in mosques during Friday services, attended (at least in theory) by all males throughout the empire. On several occasions, their preaching imperilled the Ottoman state itself.

Climate and Depopulation

Climate change did not affect all parts of the Ottoman state with equal force. The coastal plains that surrounded the Mediterranean, which formed the heart of the empire, coped best with the Little Ice Age, because farmers from Greece to Morocco normally enjoyed sufficient sun and rain to produce cereals, vegetables, tobacco and even cotton without irrigation. Here, serious food shortages would occur only when January temperatures fell below 5°C or annual precipitation below 300 millimetres. By contrast, farmers on the hills and plateaux overlooking the sea who produced cereals and a few vegetables by dry farming still needed to irrigate their fruit crops. In this zone, even small climatic changes could produce major problems. The situation was worse further inland, where farmers could produce crops only if they invested in extensive irrigation systems (Fig. 20). Here, even a short drought or unseasonable frost could ruin the entire harvest. In several regions of Anatolia, the number of rural taxpayers fell by three-quarters between 1576 and 1642, and almost half of all villages disappeared, while throughout Anatolia heavy spring precipitation in both 1640 and 1641 and droughts later in the decade destroyed many harvests and no doubt caused even more depopulation.[10]

Balkan farmers also suffered intensely during the Little Ice Age. Surviving tax registers show that the population of Talanda (central Greece) fell from 1,166 households in 1570 to 794 in 1641, while that of Zlatitsa (Bulgaria), fell from 1,637 households in 1580 to 896 in 1642 – a loss of almost 50 per cent in both cases. Around Manastir (now Bitola in Macedonia), in 1641 one-quarter of all taxpaying households were abandoned; while to the east, in Serrès, farmers found an abundance of grapes when they began to harvest them in September 1641, but then came 'so much rain and snow that many workers died through the great cold' (Fig. 21).[11] It was much the same in other parts of the empire. In Crete, rains in 1645 more intense than anything recorded in the twentieth century destroyed crops and buildings; while in Palestine, repeated droughts ruined many settlements, including the Jewish religious centre of Safed, where visitors can still see the ruins along dried-up riverbeds of 25 textile mills abandoned in the seventeenth century. Egypt, too, experienced drought when the Nile reached its lowest level of the century in 1641–3, and again in 1650, because El Niño episodes produced low summer rainfall in the Ethiopian highlands and the Sudd swamps of Sudan, which began the river's annual water cycle. Since, in the aphorism of Alan Mikhail, 'Egypt is a desert with a river running through it', a poor Nile flood drastically reduced the crop yields of the entire province – which in turn reduced the food available to supply Istanbul, the sultan's armies and the holy cities of Arabia. To quote Mikhail again, Egypt was 'the caloric engine of the Empire. Its surplus energy supplies fueled the political authority and function of the Ottoman state – powering the brain of the palace and the capital, the religious heart of the Hijaz, and the Empire's military muscle.'[12] Loss of income forced charitable institutions throughout the empire to close their doors (and their soup kitchens), adding to the misery of the local poor.

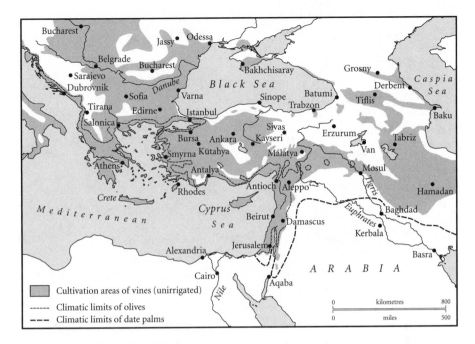

20. The climatic zones of the Ottoman empire.
The staple crops of the eastern Mediterranean – olives, vines and date palms – can survive even where little rain falls in summer; but a shift in rainfall patterns, as occurred in the mid-seventeenth century, can cause long-term damage. The more frequent droughts and colder weather also destroyed grain and citrus fruit.

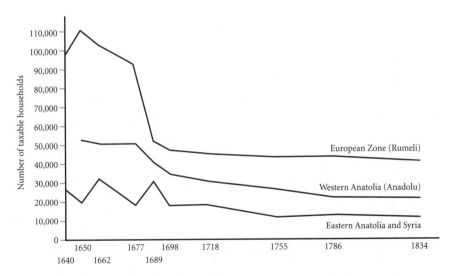

21. Tax yields in the Balkans, Anatolia and Syria, 1640–1834.
The dramatic fall in taxable households after 1640 helps to explain the decline of Ottoman power. The simultaneous decline in the Balkans, Anatolia, and Syria is striking – and it proved fatal to the tax receipts of the Ottoman state.

As usual, overpopulated areas, where supply barely satisfied demand even in good years, felt the effects of the Little Ice Age most acutely. In parts of Anatolia, for example, a benign climate in the sixteenth century allowed rural population density to reach levels that would 'never be reached again, even by the turn of the twentieth century'. The price of land rose steeply and the size of some peasant holdings shrank until, in some settlements, landless unmarried men made up three-quarters of the total adult male population. No community like this can long survive, and from the 1590s onwards single men left their villages in increasing numbers for three destinations: the cities (where some sought employment and others entered the *medreses*), the army, and the outlaw bands known as *Celalis*. Oktay Özel suggests that 'there were at least as many uprooted peasants-turned-Celalis in the Anatolian countryside as those who remained in the villages and were listed in the survey registers of the 1640s'.[13]

Although Ottoman law forbade peasants to leave without the permission of their lord, until the 1630s emigrants only had to pay modest compensation if they did so. Thereafter, as in Russia (see chapter 6 above), landowners serving in the imperial cavalry complained that they could no longer sustain themselves while fighting for the sultan, impelling the central government to demand the forcible return of fugitives: a decree of 1636 allowed pursuit for up to 40 years after the initial flight. Soon afterwards, however, another edict reduced the period to ten years, and a third decree in 1641 restored the principle of merely paying 'compensation'. Nothing seemed able to halt the exodus, because human agency intensified the impact of the harsher climate: pirates in coastal areas and brigands inland preyed upon those who continued to till the land. Although those who lived in poorer villages (less attractive to booty-seekers) and in communities protected by forests or mountains (less accessible to outsiders) fared rather better, the central problem of the Ottoman economy now became a chronic shortage of labour.

'The Ottoman tragedy'

Against this backdrop of rural crisis, a series of political upheavals called by one contemporary historian 'the Ottoman tragedy' rocked the empire between 1617 and 1623.[14] The 'tragedy' began with an unprecedented dynastic crisis. All male members of the Ottoman dynasty normally lived in sealed apartments in the imperial palace, appropriately known as 'the cage' (*kafes*), until one of them became sultan and executed all the others. In 1595 Sultan Mehmet III had followed tradition and executed all 19 of his brothers, some of them infants, as well as pregnant slaves in the harem, and he later executed the crown prince on suspicion of treason, so that at his death in 1603 only two male members of the Ottoman dynasty survived: his sons Ahmed (aged 13, who became the new sultan) and Mustafa (aged 4). Prudence dictated that Mustafa should be allow to live (even if, some speculated, he was 'nurtured like an innocent little sheep who must soon go to the butchers') and he was still alive when Ahmed died in 1617.[15] His survival created unprecedented confusion: should the next sultan be Mustafa, now aged 18, or Ahmed's oldest son

Osman, aged 14? Initially, supporters of the former prevailed but he behaved so erratically that, after three months, a household faction imprisoned him – the first sultan to be deposed by a palace coup – and engineered the proclamation of Osman in his stead.

Osman also ruled erratically. His preceptors had instilled in him a determination to follow the Prophet Mohammed's injunction to 'enjoin right and forbid wrong', and the new sultan soon forbade the cultivation and use of tobacco (on the grounds that it wasted money, induced laziness and, above all, imitated a habit introduced by infidels). He also punished the senior religious leaders who had supported Mustafa's succession, especially the elite *mevali* families, by abolishing their salaries during periods of unemployment and in retirement, as well as their right to appoint a successor (usually one of their relatives). Osman thus made the most powerful Muslim clerics his bitter enemies – an especially unwise move, given the severity of the winter of 1620–1.[16] For 40 days the Bosporus froze over (an unprecedented event) and ice floes prevented grain from reaching Istanbul: the vast city, totally dependent on imported food for its survival, began to starve. Osman exacerbated the shortages by mobilizing troops and supplies for a campaign against Poland, which had attacked one of his vassals in the Balkans. They left the capital in May 1621 but severe cold and torrential rains (this was an El Niño year), combined with unexpectedly tenacious Polish resistance, forced the sultan to conclude a humiliating truce. When he and his demoralized troops returned to Istanbul in January 1622, they found it in the grip of 'famine and high prices'. According to an Ottoman eyewitness, 'Among the people such hardship and misery appeared that it was thought the Day of Judgement had arrived or that it meant death for the entire people'; according to an English contemporary, 'Everyone complained, and though it was remedilesse by the pollicy of man', the sultan himself 'did not escape scandall and calumniation'.[17]

The poor performance of Osman's troops in Poland convinced him of the need to replace the elite Janissaries and *sipahis*, who formed the core of both the field army and the garrison of Istanbul, with troops from Anatolia, Syria and Egypt. At first the sultan stated that he would undertake a pilgrimage to Mecca, but then he ordered the principal institutions of government, and the imperial treasury, to cross the Bosporus to Asia. Once again the sultan's timing proved unfortunate. Unprecedented Nile flooding had ruined the harvest in Egypt in 1621, and then came drought, reducing the food supply even further. According to a chronicler, the sultan's troops protested that they 'could not go into a desert without water, and without doubt their animals will perish too'; according to another, they asked rhetorically 'After the Polish campaign, what fool among the soldiers would go now?'[18] On 18 May 1622, the appointed day for the sultan's departure, the Janissaries of the city garrison demanded that Osman remain in the capital and hand over to them those who had advised him to move. They returned the following day, this time accompanied by the Chief Mufti and other *mevali*, and when the Grand Vizier came out to negotiate, they murdered him and burnt down his residence (and those of some other advisers). Osman and the rest of his counsellors procrastinated until some alienated officials opened the gates of the Topkapı Palace complex and the mutineers swarmed in. One group found Mustafa (who had languished in the 'cage' in the four years since Osman's accession) and took him to the Janissaries' mosque, where they proclaimed him sultan again, while another found Osman and dragged him through the crowded streets of the capital in a cart, subjecting him to public insults, and cast him in prison where he was first mutilated and then strangled – the first regicide in Ottoman history.

The Ottoman chronicler Ibrahim Peçevi, an eyewitness to these events, marvelled that 'the streets were full of people' and 'the world full of rebellion and disorder'; while Sir Thomas Roe, the British ambassador in Istanbul, recorded his amazement that, although thousands of men served in the palace expressly to protect the sultan, not one of them had done so. 'Thus one of the greatest monarchs in the world is first affronted by mutinied troops, his own slaves, almost unarmed, and few in number, no man taking up the sword to defend him; and they who began this madness, not meaning to hurt him, by the increase of their own fury, which has no bounds, depose him ... and at last expose his life'. Moreover, as Roe accurately predicted, given Mustafa's nature (which Roe considered 'fitter for a cell, than a sceptre'), 'they have set up another [sultan] that in all likelihood they must change for disability'. Roe also predicted that the troops in Asia would 'attempt some revenge for that [sultan] who was their martyr; or that some great pashas, far removed from court, will apprehend this occasion not to obey a usurper, set up by treason'. He was right.[19]

Several provincial governors in Anatolia, including those whom Osman expected to provide the troops for his new army, refused to recognize the coup and turned on the Janissaries and sipahis in local garrisons. The capital too remained in uproar as food prices rose to the highest levels recorded in the entire seventeenth century. In desperation, the government paid new bribes to retain the loyalty of the Janissaries and, when this created an unacceptable budget deficit, reduced the silver content of the currency to its lowest level of the century. The next few months saw five Grand Viziers come and go (some of them murdered). As the Venetian ambassador observed, 'It is impossible to portray the confusion and disorders that occurred in the ten months that Mustafa reigned, while the soldiers who committed the crime went around unrestrained, full of anger and pride, absolute masters of affairs.' Meanwhile shops and markets stayed closed, food ran short and plague spread. Finally, in January 1623, the coalition of mutineers and *mevali* who had engineered Mustafa's restoration deposed him again: the Chief Mufti declared that a madman could not be sultan, and proclaimed Osman's oldest surviving brother, the 11-year-old Murad, as his successor – the fourth sultan in six years.[20]

Several groups now vied for control of imperial resources and power: Murad IV's Greek mother, Kösem Sultan; the senior palace officials, especially the eunuchs; the Janissaries and sipahis of the Istanbul garrison; and the *mevali*. Thanks to their intrigues, the average tenure of a Grand Vizier in the 1620s fell to four months. Meanwhile, in the provinces, rebellions and roaming bandit gangs in Anatolia deprived the central treasury of revenues, while the unpaid garrison of Baghdad mutinied and betrayed the city and most of southern Iraq to Iranian troops.

Murad IV's 'Personal Rule'

The nadir of Murad's rule occurred in 1630, another El Niño year, when over 10 feet of rainfall flooded Mecca, a city that normally sees virtually no rain, destroying two walls of the Kaaba (those that stand today were rebuilt by the sultan during the following decade). Extreme weather also disrupted operations by the Ottoman army fighting in Mesopotamia: in January 1630, according to one chronicler, 'the Tigris and Euphrates all overflowed and floods covered the whole Baghdad plateau', while another compared the torrential rains to 'the times of Noah'. The following August, by contrast, he noted that the waters of the Tigris sank so low that no ships could use it, leaving the army 'desperately in need of munitions and provisions'.[21] In 1630, 1631 and 1632 the Nile fell far below the level needed to irrigate the fields of the delta, causing a major famine accompanied by lethal epidemics. In Istanbul, drinking water ran short in summer 1630.[22] Reports of poor harvests abound; so do reports of rural insurrection. The Ottoman government's 'Registers of Important Affairs' (*Mühimme Defteri*) in 1630 and 1631 recorded an unusual number of petitions arising from provincial unrest, while the sultan's council issued over 150 orders in response to complaints about brigands and peasant revolts, almost 70 arising from abuse by provincial officials, and over 50 more about local elites who colluded with brigands.[23]

In 1632 the chaos in Istanbul reached such a pitch that the leading protestors demanded an emergency meeting with the sultan in person to secure the redress of their grievances. Murad complied, and reluctantly delivered to the mob his Grand Vizier, Chief Mufti, and several others. All immediately met a violent death. For several weeks, the insurgents held the city to ransom, threatening to burn down the house of anyone who refused to pay them, until the exasperation of the citizens of the capital at last allowed the sultan to eliminate many of those involved in the disorders (including the new Grand Vizier and Chief Mufti), to purge corrupt judges, and to crack down on bribery. Perhaps 20,000 perished in the disorders – but Murad, now aged 20, at last held the initiative and began eight years of 'Personal Rule'. Every year, he ordered the execution of hundreds of officials and subjects for failing to maintain local roads, for indiscipline on campaign, for selling adulterated bread and for a host of other infractions. In addition, suspecting that his critics hatched plots in coffee-houses and taverns, Murad ordered all of them to close, and he forbade all consumption of coffee, alcohol and tobacco. The sultan took up enforcement of the last prohibition in person: according to the English ambassador in Istanbul, 'so great is his hatred that in person he doth walk up and down (day and night disguised)' in search of secret smokers, ordering the summary execution of all offenders.[24]

These initiatives paralleled the reform programme of the empire's most prominent Muslim preacher, Kadizade Mehmet (1582–1635), the son of an Anatolian judge (and thus a member of the 'ulema), who after spending time in both a *medrese* and a Sufi lodge came to Istanbul in 1622, the year of the regicide. At first he joined another Sufi lodge, but soon concluded that the chaos he saw around him stemmed from a failure to adhere strictly to the dictates of the shari'a. Finding no support among either the 'ulema or his Sufi brothers, Kadizade Mehmet decided to take his message directly to the faithful through sermons. Although Istanbul by then boasted over 1,200 mosques, not all enjoyed equal prestige: chief among them stood the seven 'imperial mosques', each of them a structure so enormous that those who delivered sermons there could address tens of thousands at a time. Even Katib Çelebi, a scholar and official unsympathetic to the movement, admitted that Kadizade Mehmet 'was a good and effective speaker whose sermons never failed to move his hearers'. When he composed his autobiography 30 years later, Katib still recalled passing by a mosque in which Kadizade was preaching and feeling 'it was as if he had taken hold of the reins of his hearer's mind'.[25] In 1631, impressed by these oratorical gifts, Murad licensed Kadizade Mehmet to preach at Hagia Sophia, the most prestigious mosque of all.

From the start of his ministry, Kadizade blamed the chaos that afflicted the capital and the empire on religious innovation. He repeatedly quoted the hadith (Prophetic tradition), 'Every innovation is heresy; every heresy is error; every error leads to hell', and argued that God would continue to punish the entire empire until everyone returned to the beliefs and practices of the Prophet Mohammed. He focused on those 'innovations' associated with Sufis. He condemned their habit of singing, playing, chanting and dancing while reciting the name of God (on the grounds that the Qur'an expressly forbade 'entertainments' or 'plays'), as well as their prayers to the righteous dead for intercession with God. He demanded the abolition of all new social habits: the consumption of tobacco, alcohol or coffee; shaking hands or bowing before superiors; allowing women to prophesy; and wearing or using anything except traditional Muslim garments and artefacts. When a bystander sarcastically asked one of Kadizade's followers: 'Will you also get rid of underwear?' (a garment apparently unknown to the Prophet), the preacher shot back: 'Yes – and spoons too!'[26]

Apart from the huge congregations enchanted by his oratory – some slept overnight in the mosque to be sure of hearing his sermons – Kadizade won many disciples among unemployed medrese graduates. According to Paul Rycaut, an English resident in the Ottoman empire, the Kadizadelis (as Kadizade's followers came to be called) included 'tradesmen, whose sedentary life affords opportunity and nutriment to a melancholy and distempered fancy', as well as apprentices and slaves (many of them former Christians). He added that the Kadizadelis 'addict themselves to the study of their Civil Law, in which they use constant exercises in arguing, opposing and answering, whereby to leave no point undiscovered or not discussed'. 'They are,' Rycaut continued with relish, 'great admirers of themselves and scorners of others that conform not to their tenets, scarce affording them a salutation or common communication'; 'they admonish and correct the disorderly'; and those who spurned their teaching 'they excommunicate'.[27]

The Sufi leaders, many of whom danced and drank coffee to keep going as they ceaselessly chanted the divine name, reacted to Kadizade's criticisms swiftly and in kind. Those who served as preachers used their sermons to mobilize support among both *medrese* graduates and their congregations for their innovations, creating (in the words of an unsympathetic Muslim observer),

> A trap of imposture and a snare for disreputable fools. This is the reason why the brutish common people flock to them, and [why] votive offerings and pious gifts pour into their lodges. Since their gyrations play an important part in this, they will not abandon their spinning [round]. There is no rhyme or reason to any of it; they falsely extol their sheikhs to the skies and put on an act for the sake of a dinner.[28]

The tide turned in 1633 when, following a prolonged drought, a great fire destroyed at least 20,000 shops and houses, the barracks of the Janissaries and the state archives in Istanbul. Kadizade blamed the disaster on religious 'innovations' and warned of more catastrophes to come unless they ceased. After one particularly vivid sermon, his hearers sacked the taverns of the capital. Since Murad did nothing to stop the disorders, the Kadizadelis advanced one step further: citing the Qur'anic injunction to 'enjoin right and forbid wrong', they called on the faithful not only to amend their own lives but to seek out and punish sinners. Individual Sufi sheikhs were denounced and beaten, their lodges vandalized, and their adherents given the choice of either reaffirming their faith or being put to death.

Since Murad saw coffee shops and taverns as potential centres of sedition, he used the Kadizadelis' ire as an excuse to shut them down, killing those who gathered to consume coffee, alcohol and tobacco because in doing so he believed he was also killing his political critics. The sultan's support for the 'Puritans of Islam' thus helped to discipline his subjects; but it also kept the preachers on edge because they never knew when some small miscalculation or oversight might lead their cruel and capricious sultan to take their lives too. (In 1634 Murad had another Chief Mufti executed for refusing to approve one of his actions.) No doubt Istanbul breathed a collective sigh of relief when Murad left with an army to recover Mesopotamia from the Iranians.

In 1638, after a long siege, the sultan recaptured Baghdad. Perhaps mindful of the huge costs (both human and material) of the war, he promptly accepted Iran's offer to make peace, ending over a hundred years of conflict and bringing most of Iraq under Ottoman control for the next three centuries. Then in 1640 Murad died after a short illness – during which he characteristically threatened to kill his physicians if he did not recover, and tried to have his sole surviving brother Ibrahim strangled (he had already killed all three of their siblings). The new ruler was 25: the first sultan in a generation to reach the throne as an adult and also, as the sole surviving male member of the entire Ottoman dynasty, the first to rule unchallenged by rivals. Nevertheless, Ibrahim had spent his entire life confined in a 'cage' in the Topkapi Palace, reading the Qur'an, practising calligraphy and living in constant fear of sharing the violent fate of his other brothers. Just like Murad, therefore, he came to the throne lacking political experience.

The 'mad sultan'

For the first four years of Ibrahim's reign, Kara Mustafa Pasha, Murad's last Grand Vizier, managed public affairs competently. Abroad, he promoted peaceful relations with both Iran and the Austrian Habsburgs; and, although in 1641 he failed to recapture Azov from the Cossack adventurers who had seized it, he secured it the next year by negotiation (see chapter 6 above). At home, Kara Mustafa stabilized the coinage (albeit after another sharp devaluation), initiated a new land survey in an attempt to create a more equitable tax base, reduced the garrison in the capital and banned the Kadizadelis from delivering inflammatory sermons. Although a provincial governor defied him and led an army to within sight of Istanbul, the capital remained loyal and the rebellion crumbled. This loyalty seems surprising because the summer months of 1640, 1641 and 1642 all saw torrential rains, as well as plague, throughout the empire, while a drought in Egypt (page 188 above) reduced the supplies of several staples normally consumed by the palace; but Kara Mustafa's ability to find alternative sources to feed the capital assured his survival. By 1643 the Ottoman treasury registered a small surplus.[29]

Kara Mustafa also worked hard to train the inexperienced sultan, and the Topkapi Palace archive contains some rescripts written in the sultan's own hand urging his ministers to attend promptly to business.[30] But the Grand Vizier failed in one crucial respect: he could not cure Ibrahim's numerous medical complaints. On the one hand, the sultan suffered from perpetual headaches and repeated attacks of physical exhaustion; on the other, he worried that he, the last surviving male of the dynasty, might be impotent. In 1642, since the doctors provided by Kara Mustafa failed to provide remedies, Ibrahim turned to charlatans recommended by his mother, Kösem Sultan. One of these, Cinci [meaning 'sorcerer'] Hoca, seems to have cured at least Ibrahim's impotence, because in the next six years he sired several children, including four future sultans; but Cinci Hoca used the imperial favour thus earned to build a faction against Kara Mustafa, and early in 1644 engineered his downfall. The next 12 years would see the rise and fall of 23 Treasurers, 18 Grand Viziers, 12 Chief Muftis and countless provincial governors. Since each official tried to get rich and to enrich as many of his followers as quickly as possible, the 60,000 government officeholders of 1640 had grown to 100,000 by 1648.[31]

The number of troops paid by the Ottoman treasury also increased, from 60,000 to 85,000, due to the outbreak of war with the Venetian Republic. The two states had remained at peace since the 1570s, although each allowed its allies to prey on the trading vessels of the 'other side' and to carry out coastal raids. Late in 1644 some galleys of the Knights of Malta seized a convoy carrying pilgrims from Istanbul to Mecca. Some died in the struggle, including the former Chief Eunuch of Ibrahim's harem, and the victorious galleys steered to the Venetian island of Crete, where the authorities allowed them put ashore some of their spoil and captives and to take on supplies.

This breach of neutrality infuriated Ibrahim, and he ordered immediate retaliation. In a striking demonstration of imperial power, by April 1645 some 50,000 men had embarked on a fleet of 70 galleys, 20 sailing warships and 300 transports. The Venetians, who refused to believe that the Ottomans could mount a serious military or naval threat, assumed that the problem could be resolved through judicious bribery: 'It will not be difficult to put forward our case, using money as our vehicle,' they informed their resident in Istanbul.[32] They seemed unaware both of the unpopularity of their rule with many sections of the Cretan population and of the dilapidated state of Crete's defences – especially after a catastrophic storm in January 1645 that severely damaged the fortifications of Khaniá, not far from Herakleion, the administrative capital. The Ottoman expeditionary force exploited these advantages to the full: in June its Janissaries stormed ashore near Khaniá and took it. Before long they controlled most of Crete – but the Venetians counter-attacked by blockading the Dardanelles, which cut off not only relief for the Ottoman garrisons on Crete but also the supply of grain to Istanbul.

The war would last until 1669, costing the lives of some 130,000 Ottoman troops and absorbing around three-quarters of the imperial budget. It also coincided with more episodes of extreme weather. Torrential rains in 1646 and drought in 1647 destroyed the harvest surpluses on which Istanbul depended, creating another food shortage. The Ottoman capital normally consumed some 500 tonnes of bread each day, of which about half went to feed the palace employees, the capital's garrison and the students in the *medreses*, so that the sultan's immediate entourage were among the first to feel (and resent) any shortfall. Perhaps this explains why Ibrahim (like China's Chongzhen emperor: see chapter 5 above) reacted so savagely when his ministers failed to produce instant success. For example, in a tantrum following news of another military defeat, Ibrahim had his Grand Vizier strangled in the middle of the street. When his mother, Kösem Sultan, predicted (correctly) that 'the same thing will happen to you as happened to your brother Osman', namely that 'the soldiers and the people will cut you to pieces', Ibrahim banished her.[33]

Late in 1647 a new Grand Vizier persuaded his master to retreat to his private quarters in the Topkapi Palace, where he could be shielded from adverse news; but, in seclusion, Ibrahim's behaviour became ever more eccentric. He developed an extravagant taste for luxury items, especially furs, and became irrationally impatient for the goods he craved: on occasion he made the shops of the capital open at midnight while his men requisitioned items for him and his concubines. Foreigners in Istanbul noticed widespread 'murmuring' among the capital's residents that 'the sultan ought to spend on the Arsenal what he spends on women and gypsies for dancing and skits [*mattacine*]'. 'The extravagant prodigality of Sultan Ibrahim', an English merchant in the capital wrote self-righteously, 'was such as the wealth of his whole empire could rather only feed than satisfy: all costs and curiosities being too little to reward his pleasing bedfellows.'[34]

Funding the war as well as the sultan's exotic tastes proved a challenge. Since the continued predations of pirates and bandits kept many rural areas depopulated, in the 1630s Ottoman fiscal experts moved away from dependence on taxes on agricultural production, long the mainstay of the treasury, in favour of personal taxes – above all the *avariz* ('extraordinary levies' paid in either cash or kind, such as chickens for the imperial kitchens or repairs on road and bridges) and the *cizye* (a poll tax on non-Muslims). Each year, the treasury held a public auction at which it sold the right to collect these personal taxes to the highest bidder, receiving payment in cash and in advance. Since even this did not suffice to fund Ibrahim's war with Venice, his ministers adopted desperate fiscal expedients: levying new excise duties on goods; demanding that even the *'ulema* contribute; selling still more public offices, including judgeships; and withholding pay from the Janissaries and *sipahis* of the Istanbul garrison. Venice exploited Ottoman weakness to recapture fortresses both on Crete and in the Balkans while its agents incited revolts in the Ottoman province of Albania. Above all, its fleet continued to blockade the Dardanelles, cutting off the capital from some of its principal food suppliers. As usual, this deprivation immediately affected those who received their food directly from the sultan: the officials and garrison of the palace.

Meanwhile, locusts destroyed crops in Moldavia, another area on which Istanbul depended for its food. An eyewitness described vividly how 'a locust swarm came at us like a flying army. The sun disappeared immediately, veiled by the blackness of these insects' and afterwards 'No leaf, no blade of grass, no hay, no crop, nothing remained.' The same disaster destroyed the next two harvests, and an English traveller found the soil of Moldavia 'covered with Locusts; such as were of a veneniferous Colour; some alive but most dead; having allready destroy'd almost all the Grass in these parts; all of which are most certein and fatall Signes of a Pestilentious Aire; sadly experienced at Constantinople in the times of theyr Prodigious Plagues there'.[35]

Such was the tense situation when in June 1648 a major earthquake rocked Istanbul. According to Katib Çelebi, 'an earthquake like this has not been seen in our times. According to some experienced and enlightened ones, when an earthquake happens during daytime in June, blood is shed in the heart of the empire.' Four minarets at the Hagia Sophia collapsed and the mosque built by Ibrahim's father Ahmed sustained severe damage during Friday prayers, killing several thousand worshippers. The earthquake also demolished the city's main aqueduct so that drinking water ran short just as the summer heat began: the price charged by water vendors soared and many died of thirst. Once again, the Kadizadeli preachers blamed these natural disasters on failure to follow the teachings of the Prophet, and a Venetian observer in the city reported that 'the wise made diverse predictions of unrest in the city in the near future, and of imminent ruin and discomfort'. 'The wise' were right.[36]

A Second Regicide

The sequence of events that led to Ibrahim's assassination began with the arrival in Istanbul on 6 August 1648 of a senior Janissary officer from Crete, bearing urgent requests for reinforcements and supplies. While awaiting an audience with the sultan, the officer informed his colleagues of the failure of the central government to supply the troops on campaign. Hearing of this, and fearing that he would be blamed, Grand Vizier Ahmed Pasha attempted to have the officer killed, but he escaped and complained about the chaos in Crete to the Chief Mufti, who consulted with other members of the clerical elite and the leading judges of the city. The following day a group of conspirators met in a mosque to discuss appropriate action.

After consulting Ibrahim's mother, Kösem Sultan, the Chief Mufti went to the palace to demand the appointment of a new Grand Vizier. Ibrahim started to shout abuse and attacked bystanders with his stick; the conspirators retaliated by strangling Ahmed Pasha, and throwing his body into the street where the crowd swiftly dismembered it (hence his later nickname *Hezarpare*: 'Thousand pieces'). Early on 8 August the conspirators sent a letter to Ibrahim demanding that he get rid of some concubines and all of his furs, that he pay the arrears of his troops, and that he restore all the goods unjustly confiscated from his subjects. Ibrahim read their letter and promptly tore it up. The angry troops now asked the Chief Mufti 'what did someone who refused to accept the justice of God deserve; and he replied, having read the books of the Law, that the subjects of such a prince were dispensed of their duty to be faithful to him'. He therefore issued a *fatwā* ordering Ibrahim's deposition on the grounds that he was incapable of ruling the empire and protecting the Muslim faith.[37]

Guards now persuaded Ibrahim that, for his own protection, he should retire to an inner apartment – and promptly locked the door behind him. Shortly afterwards a large number of Janissaries, accompanied by the Chief Mufti, forced their way into the palace. Finding Ibrahim already confined, they sought out his oldest son Prince Mehmet, aged seven, and 'in the name of the '*ulema* and the soldiers', hailed him as the new sultan. The next day, the Janissaries opened the treasury of the late Ahmed Pasha and found a huge fortune in cash, which they appropriated as their traditional 'accession bonus' (equivalent to a full year's salary); but at this point Ibrahim escaped from confinement (probably freed by one of his concubines) and, with a sword in his hand, searched the palace intending to kill Mehmet. Eventually guards overpowered him and locked him in the 'cage' where he had lived before his accession, and there the leading conspirators (including the Chief Mufti) confronted him and denounced his failures: 'You have ruined the world by neglecting the affairs of *shari'a* and the religion of the people. You spent your time with entertainment and slothfulness while bribery became widespread and wrongdoers fell upon the world. You wasted and squandered the state treasury.' Balthasar de Monconys, a French visitor in the capital, claimed that 'such a peaceful revolt has never been seen: the whole process took only 40 hours, and affected only the sultan, his chief vizir and one judge'.[38]

Nevertheless, Ibrahim continued to scream and rage in his sealed room, gaining the sympathy of some members of his household, while outside the palace the sipahis, who had not received an 'accession bonus' like the Janissaries, resolved to restore him. To avoid such a development, on 18 August 1648 the Chief Mufti issued another *fatwā* that legitimized the second regicide in Ottoman history and personally ensured that his decree was put into immediate effect. In the words of Monconys:

This unfortunate monarch, who 12 days before exercised absolute command over large parts of three continents, was strangled by a hangman in the capital city of his empire, and in the palace where his son was acknowledged as king and where his mother issued the principal orders of state.[39]

Up to this point, the capital had remained calm but now rioting broke out, led by *medreses* students and junior palace officials. Both groups, their career aspirations blocked by the lack of money to pay salaries, gathered in the Hippodrome to make their protest; but the Janissaries surrounded and butchered them. Such savagery, coupled with the continuation of high food prices as a result of the Venetian blockade, provoked widespread rioting. Robert Bargrave, an English resident in the city, complained of the 'daily hazards of being stabbed by the drunken sottish Turks, who supposing all to be Venetians that wore our western [dress] (as if the world were divided between Venetians and Turks)', and 'having lost in the war perhaps some near relations, were always apt to mischief us'.[40]

Kösem Sultan – Mehmet's grandmother as well as Ibrahim's mother – and her supporters retained power until the summer of 1651, when continuing food shortages, heavy taxation, currency devaluation and military defeats provoked a new round of rioting in Istanbul. The city's tradesmen, who claimed that they had received a dozen demands for new taxes that year alone, shut their shops and demanded that the Chief Mufti go to the palace, as in 1648, to demand reforms. The frightened sultan, only nine years old, agreed to abolish all taxes imposed since the reign of Suleiman the Lawgiver a century before. To restore order, Kösem Sultan turned once more to the Janissaries for support, but she faced a more formidable adversary within the palace: Turhan, Mehmet's mother, supported by a faction among the eunuchs. In a desperate bid to retain power, Kösem decided to kill the young sultan and replace him with one of his brothers – one with a more docile mother – but Turhan's supporters acted first and had her strangled and dragged naked from the harem.

The brutal murder of Kösem, after more than three decades at the centre of power, outraged her allies among the Janissaries, who swore vengeance; but Turhan and her associates thwarted them by unfurling the Standard of the Prophet, one of the most sacred objects of Islam, and sending out town criers to urge all Muslim men and women to rally to the Standard. Thousands flocked to the palace from all over the capital, fully armed, and for three weeks the fate of the empire hung in the balance until the recalcitrant Janissary leaders perished. Their confiscated wealth served to win the allegiance of the rest.

Nevertheless the new regime failed to solve the two most pressing problems that faced the empire: balancing the budget and defeating the Venetians. In 1653 Sultan Mehmet, now 14, invited his leading advisers to suggest solutions. 'My expenditure is not as great as that of my father, and the revenues are the same,' he pointed out. 'What then is the reason that the income of the state no longer suffices to cover the expenditure, and why is it that money cannot be raised for the fleet and other important matters?' After some discussion, Mehmet invited each of his ministers to submit written recommendations. One of them, Katib Çelebi, calculated that in 1648, the year of the regicide, the central treasury had received 362,000,000 akçes but spent 550,000,000. Two years later, income had soared to 532,000,000 akçes, but expenditure had risen, to 677,000,000. By 1653, according to Katib Çelebi, 'expenditure exceeds revenue by 160,000,000 akçes' and the government had already committed the yield of several taxes payable in future years. The main problem, he argued, was the catastrophic fall in receipts from the principal tax on property, while the war with Venice continued to drain the emperor's available resources (Fig. 22). Katib Çelebi suggested that only reducing the size of the standing army would cut spending significantly, and that only restoring the rule of law to the countryside, so that peasants would return to their land and resume farming and taxpaying, would increase revenues sufficiently. If the state failed to act, he predicted, 'it is certain that the curse of disobedience to the law, and the burden of injustice and violence, will ruin the empire.'[41]

Katib Çelebi had no illusions about the fate of his proposal: 'Since I knew that my conclusions would be difficult to apply,' he wrote in another of his works, 'I took no further trouble about it.' He merely hoped that 'a sultan of some future time will become aware of it' and act before it was too late. Instead, however, in 1653 Mehmet and his council rejected a Venetian peace offer (because the Republic refused to abandon Crete), and two years later they ended another military revolt in Anatolia by incorporating the mutineers and their leaders into the standing army, thus raising its size from 71,000 to 130,000 soldiers – and adding 262,000,000 akçes to the expenditure of the central treasury.[42]

As Katib Çelebi observed in another of his numerous writings, 'It is a fact that when disputation and disagreement on any topic have once arisen among a people it is not possible, even after they have reached agreement, for that disputation or disagreement to be entirely eradicated.'[43] As long as the Venetian forces maintained their blockade of Istanbul, and held out on Crete, the palace factions in Istanbul continued their fruitless 'disputation and disagreement' on how to reverse the empire's decline. A stream of ministers came to power, each with a new policy initiative, only to lose their heads when they failed to produce instant success: in 1655 and 1656, seven Grand Viziers came and went, some within a matter of weeks. One lasted a single day. In March 1656 another attempt to balance the budget through a savage currency devaluation provoked another mutiny, when the city garrison found that no shopkeepers would accept payment in the virtually worthless new coins. The Janissaries once again marched on the palace and demanded 30 of the sultan's 'wicked advisers'. Mehmet reluctantly complied, and they were murdered and hanged upside down from a great plane tree in the main public square of the capital – the fourth regime change in eight years.

With no effective government to oppose them, the Venetians routed the Ottoman fleet yet again and this time occupied the Aegean islands of Tenedos and Lemnos, which virtually cut Istanbul off from the Mediterranean. Many inhabitants, fearing that the Venetians would launch a direct attack, sold their property and left the capital. With provincial governors refusing to send money to the central administration, and

22. The Ottoman empire at war, 1630–1700.
The sultans were almost constantly at war during the seventeenth century. Until the 1680s, they mostly managed to fight on only one front at a time, but for the last fifteen years of the century the Ottoman empire faced attacks from all its European enemies – as well as domestic rebellions and mutinies.

the capital on the brink of starvation, the future of the Ottoman state seemed bleak indeed. Popular discontent reached such a level that, once again, the sultan's fate hung in the balance: 'Public talk ran very hard against him,' noted a foreign visitor, 'so that upon the least unlucky turn and new disgrace in their public affairs, he stood in great hazard of a revolution.'[44]

The Return of Stability

The Kadizadeli preachers, as usual, blamed all disasters on religious innovation. They had lost some influence while Kösem Sultan dominated government policy because she favoured Sufis, but after her murder in 1651 the Kadizadelis secured new legislation against smoking and drinking and approval for the destruction of certain Sufi lodges. Now, in 1656 they laid plans to demolish all dervish lodges throughout the capital, and all minarets except one on each mosque 'to ensure that Istanbul would reflect the Prophet's Medina'.[45]

The onslaught never took place, because on 15 September 1656 Mehmet IV appointed Köprülü Mehmet Pasha as Grand Vizier. A *devşirme* boy from Albania, now aged almost 80, Köprülü had previously held only minor government offices, but he possessed a deep understanding of the inner workings of the Ottoman state. Before accepting office as Grand Vizier, he conducted intense negotiations with 'the palace', gaining the support of Turhan Sultan, Mehmet's mother, and of the Chief Mufti and the *'ulema* for a pre-emptive strike against the Kadizadelis. When a few days later they refused to call off their planned attack on the Sufi lodges, Köprülü had their leaders arrested and exiled. Following this success, he executed several unpopular individuals, most notably the Greek Orthodox Patriarch, whom he accused of treason, and many of the Janissaries who had surrendered Tenedos to the Venetians. When part of the capital's garrison rebelled against these arbitrary acts, Köprülü played off the sipahis against the Janissaries, thus cementing his authority. He then asked the Chief Mufti to certify that all the actions he had taken thus far had been legal. The official obliged but expressed surprise at the request. 'In this day and age,' Köprülü Mehmet replied, 'when everyone constantly changes his mind and switches allegiance, I wanted to secure your support on paper.'[46]

Köprülü also mobilized religious support for an offensive against Venice. He ordered all the palace pages named Mehmet (after the Prophet) to recite the opening verse of the Qur'an every day until the end of the campaign; and he commanded 101 men to recite the entire Qur'an 1,001 times in the principal mosques of the capital.[47] Confident that these measures would produce a miracle, Köprülü led the Ottoman fleet in person to fight the Venetians. He was not disappointed: the Venetian garrisons surrendered Lemnos and Tenedos, thus at last breaking the blockade of the capital and restoring the vital supply of food from Egypt. Next, Köprülü led an army into the Balkans, apparently intending to attack Venetian possessions on the Adriatic coast, but a revolt in Anatolia called him back. The rebel leader, Abaza Hasan, governor of Aleppo (the third city of the empire), had won widespread support from other regional governors in Anatolia and Syria, and preachers began to hail him as the 'renewer' and the 'messiah' who would restore the Islamic community to purity. He and his supporters demanded that the sultan depose his Grand Vizier.

This presented Mehmet IV with a major challenge. Although he realized that refusal to sacrifice Köprülü would probably unleash a civil war, the sultan secured a *fatwā* from the Chief Mufti condemning the rebels: 'Since they committed an act of oppression against the sultan, their blood can be shed lawfully: those who cause Muslim armies to abandon their fight with infidels by perpetrating sedition are worse than infidels.' After endorsement by the *'ulema* of Istanbul, multiple copies of the *fatwā* went out, together with a call for all adult males to fight against the rebels. The Little Ice Age also helped to rescue Köprülü: the landmark winter of 1657–8 followed by a failed harvest in Anatolia made it impossible for the rebels to maintain their army, and gradually support for the insurrection dissipated. Early in 1659 Abaza Hasan and his lieutenants surrendered against a promise of clemency – only to be executed.[48] Köprülü Mehmet now sent his trusted lieutenant, Ismail Pasha, to round up renegades, to end unjustified tax exemptions and to confiscate all illegally held firearms. His success is reflected in two celebrated contemporary anecdotes. The first concerns a town in Anatolia that boasted 2,000 descendants of the Prophet Mohammed, each one therefore entitled to tax exemption: Ismail's investigation sustained the claims of only 20 individuals and he ordered the other 1,980 to pay not only current taxes but also full tax arrears for the preceding decade. The second anecdote relates that, after the sweep to confiscate guns (said to have secured 80,000 weapons), a peasant noticed a partridge chirping defiantly in the woods: 'Well, you may chirp,' he said wistfully, 'your patron, Ismail Pasha, got all our guns.'[49]

The Little Ice Age also produced the greatest setback of Köprülü Mehmet's five-year tenure as Grand Vizier. In 1659–60 the lands around the Aegean and Black Seas experienced the worst drought in a millennium: no snow fell over the winter and no rain fell during the spring. In Romania, according to a peasant sale contract, 'because of the dearth sent to us by God, we wanted to sell our property to our relatives, but they refused, and left us to die from hunger'; while, according to a chronicler, hunger forced others to sell their children. In Transylvania, a senior official noted in his journal that meagre harvests caused widespread starvation, so that 'Transylvania never knew such misery as this last year'.[50] The combination of drought and extreme heat turned the wooden buildings of Istanbul into a tinderbox, and in July 1660 a fire of unparalleled ferocity destroyed two-thirds of the capital, causing the minarets on the mosques to burn like candles. The chief casualty was the area where most of the capital's Jewish and Christian populations lived: 7 synagogues and at least 25 churches burned to the ground.

Such was Köprülü Mehmet's hold on power that he survived these disasters, too, and the following year he died in his bed and passed on his office of Grand Vizier to his 26-year-old son Köprülü Fazil Ahmed: a peaceful transition with few parallels in seventeenth-century Ottoman history (and the first time a son had ever succeeded his father to the office). Almost immediately the new Grand Vizier, who had previously been a preceptor in a *medrese*, invited a charismatic Kadizadeli preacher named Vani Mehmet Efendi to join him in Istanbul. Following the example of Kadizade Mehmet a generation before, Vani attributed the Great Fire to abandoning the religious practices of the first Muslims. Once again, the sultan paid heed and forbade the consumption of tobacco, coffee and alcohol; condemned musical performances, public singing, dancing and chanting; prohibited any unsupervised meetings between unmarried people of the opposite sex; and insisted on the strict enforcement of the *shari'a*. He also destroyed popular Sufi tombs, and exiled or executed Sufi leaders.[51] Vani and other preachers also claimed that the disproportionate destruction of property belonging to Jews in the Great Fire of Istanbul was a sign of divine displeasure and called for legislation to prevent them from returning to the area. Köprülü Fazil Ahmed duly confiscated all the lands where synagogues had stood before the fire and put them up for auction: since he forbade non-Muslims to make a bid, the area became instantly Islamized. To symbolize the change, and to proclaim her own growing authority, the sultan's mother Turhan sponsored the completion of the huge 'new mosque' (Yeni Cami) in the area. When it opened in 1665, Vani Mehmet Efendi became its first preacher and his sermons there continued both to assert the supremacy of Muslim traditions and to criticize the Jews.[52]

The Messianic Moment of Shabbatai Zvi

These changes profoundly unsettled and alarmed the Jewish population throughout the Ottoman empire. Some were already on edge because the Jewish calendar had just begun a new century (5400: 1640 in the Christian calendar) and each new century normally occasioned a resurgence of Jewish Messianism. In addition, the years before 5400/1640 had witnessed a weakening of the authority of both rabbis and traditional texts (Torah and Talmud) among some Jewish groups, in favour of new sources of authority. One of these was Kabbalah (literally 'something received'), a strain of Judaism that exalted mysticism and revelation as well as tradition and Torah, and revered prophets and healers as well as rabbis. A distinctive brand of Kabbalah, developed in the town of Safed in Palestine, spread throughout the Jewish world, first by word of mouth, then by manuscript and eventually by printed works, finding especially fertile soil in Italy and Poland. It was a tragic irony that some prominent Jewish writers argued that 'in the year 408 of the fifth millennium [AD 1648] they that lie in the dust will arise'. Naphtali ben Jacob Bacharach published *Emeq ha-Melekh* (*Valley of the King*, 1648), predicting that the redemption of the Jews and the end of the world fast approached, while two years later Manasseh ben Israel brought out *Esperança de Israel* (*Hope of Israel*), soon translated into other languages, with much the same message.[53]

Four disasters kept tensions high within the global Jewish community. First, in 1645, Portuguese settlers in the parts of Brazil conquered by the Dutch rebelled (see chapter 14 below). Whereas the Dutch colonial regime had actively encouraged Jewish settlement, the Portuguese now destroyed Jewish property and killed (or delivered to the Inquisition) all the Jewish settlers they could find. Second, that same year, the outbreak of war between Venice and the Ottoman empire ended a lucrative commerce that had sustained Jewish communities living in both states. Third, in 1647 Philip IV declared a state bankruptcy in Castile and confiscated the capital of all loans made to his government over the previous two decades, most of them by Jewish bankers from Portugal. All were ruined. Fourth and finally, in Ukraine the Cossacks massacred thousands of Jews (see chapter 6 above).[54]

Harrowing reports of all these catastrophes reached Izmir (Smyrna), a prosperous port-city whose Sephardic community included a religious student called Shabbatai Zvi. One day in 1648, while walking in solitary meditation outside the city, he 'heard the voice of God speaking to him: "Thou art the saviour of Israel, the Messiah, the son of David, the anointed of the God of Jacob, and thou art destined to redeem Israel, to gather it from the four corners of the earth to Jerusalem."' From that moment on, Shabbatai later told his disciples, 'he was clothed with the Holy Spirit' and felt empowered to behave in extravagant ways. He went on to demolish a synagogue door with an axe on Shabbat, to arrange a wedding ceremony in which he married the Torah, and to pronounce repeatedly the forbidden Tetragrammaton. Such ostentatious flouting of Jewish laws led the rabbis of Izmir first to condemn him as a fool and then in 1651 to send him into exile.[55] Shabbatai now travelled widely in Europe, Asia and Africa, living in various cities of the Ottoman empire until his outrageous behaviour caused his expulsion. Then in May 1665, in Hebron, a young kabbalist called Nathan of Gaza transformed the situation by proclaiming that Shabbatai was the true Messiah.

Much had happened since Shabbatai had first made the same claim two decades earlier. He himself had married a refugee from the Ukrainian massacres and so he became personally aware of the catastrophe; a group of Portuguese Jewish exiles in Izmir published a new edition of Manasseh ben Israel's *Hope of Israel*; and the destruction and displacement of the Jewish community in Istanbul after the Great Fire of 1660 raised anxieties among their co-religionists throughout the Ottoman empire.[56] Meanwhile, many Christians calculated from a passage in the Book of Revelation that the world would end in 1666 and predicted that, immediately beforehand, a charismatic leader would unite all the Jews of the world, wrest Palestine from Muslim control, and then become a Christian.

By 1665, therefore, many Jews and Christians were predisposed to accept Nathan of Gaza's claim – circulated by sermons, letters and a remarkable series of forged documents – that the long-awaited Messiah had come. Acclamation began in Safed, the former centre of Kabbalistic study now ruined by prolonged drought, where ten prophets and ten prophetesses began to proclaim Shabbatai's Messianic status. Thanks to letters exchanged between Jewish scholars and study groups, the news spread rapidly; and before long male and female prophets had proclaimed Shabbatai as the Messiah in Aleppo, Izmir, Edirne, Thessalonica and, above all, Istanbul, where

There were women and men, youths and maidens, even young children, all of whom prophesied in Hebrew or the language of the *Zohar* ... They would fall to the ground like one afflicted with epilepsy, foaming at the mouth and twitching, and would speak Kabbalistic secrets in Hebrew on many matters. The sense of all of them, each in his unique language, was this: Shabbatai Zvi is our lord, king and Messiah.

The writer continued that, 'because so many prophets and prophetesses arose in all the cities of Anatolia, everyone believed wholeheartedly that the End of Days had come' – adding apologetically for the benefit of later readers: 'These were indeed miraculous occurrences and wonders, the like of which had never happened since the day the world was created.'[57] Followers of the new Messiah had visions in which they claimed to see pillars of fire above his head, while Nathan of Gaza's pamphlets pictured Shabbatai as the Messiah sitting on the throne of kings as angels placed the imperial 'Crown of Zvi' on his head.[58]

By 1666, Shabbatai had won widespread support. In Africa, rabbis in Morocco, Tunisia and Libya became staunch adherents, and some of their followers set out for Jerusalem. Reports in newspapers and pamphlets kindled enthusiastic support for the movement in the Jewish communities of Europe, especially in Italy and the Dutch Republic (with followers of Manasseh ben Israel in the forefront), while in London, Samuel Pepys reported that the Jewish community 'offer[s] to give any man £10 to be paid £100, if a certain person now at Smyrna be within these two years owned by all the princes of the east, and particularly the Grand Signor [the Sultan], as the king of the world ... and that this man is the true Messiah.'[59] In Moscow, Tsar Alexei himself listened intently while his ministers read Russian translations from perhaps two dozen pamphlets and newspaper stories received from the west, based not only on letters written by Jews but also on correspondence from European merchants and missionaries living in the Ottoman empire, anxious to know whether the Day of Judgement was nigh.[60]

Meanwhile, in the Near East, devout Egyptians who had known Shabbatai while he lived in Cairo elevated belief in his mission to the same level as belief in the Torah. The Jewish community in Yemen, perhaps in response to news of the Messiah, marched into the palace of the local governor to demand that he abdicate in Shabbatai's favour. Before he left Izmir for Istanbul in February 1666, the new Messiah not only performed 'miracles' (at least according to the gushing reports distributed by Nathan of Gaza and others) but also appointed several of his leading believers to govern specific regions as kings under the overall supervision of his two brothers, one for the Islamic world and the other for Christendom – dramatic reminders that Shabbatai's claims possessed a political as well as a religious dimension.[61]

According to a Western eyewitness in Istanbul, now the entire Jewish community's 'conversation turned on the war [in Crete] and the imminent establishment of the kingdom of Israel, on the fall of the Crescent and of all the royal crowns in Christendom'; and when Shabbatai arrived, many underwent 'transports of joy such as one can never understand unless one has seen it'. Not surprisingly the Grand Vizier imprisoned Shabbatai almost immediately. Nevertheless, the mass hysteria continued and Jews in the capital continued to fast and pray instead of working and paying taxes.[62]

Clearly, the Ottoman authorities could not allow this situation to continue. In September 1666 the sultan's council presented Shabbatai with a stark alternative: they would execute him (and, according to some sources, all his followers) unless he either proved immediately by some miracle that he *was* the Messiah, or else converted to Islam. Shabbatai chose the latter course. He apostatized and lived as a Muslim pensioner of the sultan until he died a decade later – but some followers kept the faith: until the nineteenth century in eastern Europe the 'Frankists', although outwardly Catholic, continued to regard Shabbatai as the Messiah, as did the 'Dönme' (meaning 'converts' in Turkish) in parts of Greece and Turkey. For most disciples, however, apostasy ended Shabbatai's appeal and abruptly terminated 'the most important messianic movement in Judaism since the destruction of the Second Temple'.[63]

The Tipping Point

Köpülü Fazil Ahmed's 15-year tenure as Grand Vizier, one of the longest on record, saw not only the return of stability to Istanbul but also notable territorial gains. First he led an invasion of Hungary and captured a number of fortresses before securing an advantageous truce with the Austrian Habsburgs; then he joined the soldiers in the trenches in Crete until in 1669 they forced the last Venetian garrisons to surrender. The whole island now became an integral part of the Ottoman empire, and remained so until 1898. Fazil Ahmed followed up these victories with three campaigns against Poland, one of them led by the sultan in person, forcing the Commonwealth to cede parts of Ukraine and increasing the boundaries of the empire to their largest extent. He even managed to balance the state budget. In 1675, to celebrate all these successes, Mehmet IV and his Grand Vizier held 'a scrupulously orchestrated exhibition of dynastic splendour and munificence' that lasted 15 days.[64]

Few observers of the sultan's 'exhibition' can have guessed that 12 years later mutinous troops would force him to abdicate. The process began that same year, 1675, one of the two 'years without a summer' in the seventeenth century, which initiated a period of intensely cold winters and unusually dry springs. A major erup-tion of Mount Etna in 1682 seems to have reduced crop yields all over the eastern Mediterranean and produced a particularly cold winter and wet spring.[65] Fazil Ahmed did not have to face these challenges, since he died in 1676, succeeded as Grand Vizier by his brother-in-law Merzifonlu Kara Mustafa ('Black Mustafa from Merzifon'), who almost immediately campaigned in Ukraine, in an attempt to exploit his predecessor's gains. Having done so, he made an advantageous settle-ment in 1681 – the first formal treaty between the sultan and the tsar. The Grand Vizier also commissioned a meticulous survey of the new Ukrainian lands (although the devastation of war was reflected in the fact that of 868 settlements surveyed, only 277 were still inhabited). Then, two years later, the Ottomans rejected the Austrian Habsburgs' offer to renew the truce between the two empires, despite the refusal of the Chief Mufti to authorize a declaration of war. Instead, encouraged by

Vani Mehmet Efendi, still the most influential preacher in the empire, Merzifonlu Kara Mustafa prepared a campaign to capture Vienna, the Habsburg capital.[66]

The campaign went badly from the start. Unusually severe winter snows and spring rains delayed the advance of the imperial army, which reached Vienna only on 14 July 1683. Its garrison therefore managed to hold out until Polish troops, resentful at their losses to the Ottomans, spearheaded a charge that not only relieved the city but killed large numbers of the besiegers. Mehmet IV had Merzifonlu Kara Mustafa executed and exiled Vani, but it was too late: Ottoman forces in Hungary fell back, while the Venetians exacted their revenge for the loss of Crete by gaining several Ottoman outposts along the Adriatic coast. Then, the severe winter of 1686–7 caused the Golden Horn to freeze over, and afterwards Istanbul went without rain for seven months. The central treasury spent over 900 million akçes, but received scarcely 700 million, and the deficit left the army in Hungary short of provisions – even as it endured a summer of exceptional rain – and in September 1687 it mutinied, defied orders to winter in Belgrade and instead marched on Istanbul. There they forced Mehmet IV to abdicate: the fifth forcible removal of a sultan in 60 years. In 1699, just after the Golden Horn froze over for the third time in a century, the Ottomans signed the peace of Carlowitz, which ceded most of Hungary to the Habsburgs and parts of Greece to the Venetians. It marked the first major territorial retreat of the empire in almost three centuries.[67]

One must not exaggerate the scale of these defeats. After all, the pivotal year 1683 saw the Ottoman army at the gates of Vienna, the Habsburg capital, whereas no Christian army threatened Istanbul until the twentieth century. Moreover, the Ottomans remained in control of all their other European possessions, including Crete. Nevertheless the speed with which the gains and the stability of the Köprülü era evaporated requires explanation. First Vienna lay at the outer limit of the effective *Aktionsradius* of the Ottoman state: even if the weather had allowed the sultan's troops to arrive earlier in the year and capture the Habsburg capital in 1683, it seems unlikely that they could have held it against a spirited Christian counter-attack. Second, although the Köprülüs helped the Ottoman state to recover from the bankruptcy of the mid-1650s, they failed to accumulate a substantial reserve in the central treasury. Admittedly the bribes paid by ministers in return for appointment, and the confiscation of their fortunes when they fell, provided substantial windfalls; but this could never replace the reduced inflow of taxes from the depopulated heartland of the empire. Other provinces also bore the scars of the mid-seventeenth century crisis. In Egypt, which suffered from plague and drought in the 1640s, a serious power struggle broke out between two factions, one supported by units of the garrison raised in the Balkans and Anatolia, the other upheld by troops raised in the Arab provinces of the empire. The rival factions would divide Egyptian society for over a century.[68]

Moreover, the Little Ice Age seems to have struck the lands around the eastern Mediterranean with particular force. Most areas suffered drought and plague in the 1640s, the 1650s and again in the 1670s, while the winter of 1684 was the wettest recorded in the eastern Mediterranean during the past five centuries, and the winters of the later 1680s were at least 3°C cooler than today. In 1687 a chronicler in Istanbul reported that 'This winter was severe to a degree that had not been seen in a very long time. For fifty days the roads were closed and people could not go outside. In cities and villages, the snow buried many houses'. In the city's gardens, 'lemon, orange, pomegranate, fig, and flowering trees withered', while near the Golden Horn, the snow 'came up higher than one's face'. The following year, floods destroyed crops around Edirne, ruining the estates that normally supplied the imperial capital with food.[69]

Nevertheless, the combination of climatic adversity with human ineptitude in the Ottoman empire had been far worse in the 1640s and 1650s – and yet no territory was lost to the Christian powers until 1683 (on the contrary, Mehmet conquered Crete). The relatively late 'tipping point' seems to have reflected above all a change in the military balance between the Ottomans and their enemies. In the earlier seventeenth century the principal Western states deployed most of their resources elsewhere: the Habsburgs fought in Germany (1618–48); Spain fought the Dutch Republic and France (1621–59); Poland fought the Cossacks, Sweden and Russia (1621–9, 1632–4, 1648–67). This European in-fighting allowed the Ottomans not only to make gains in the west, but also to defeat Iran. The end of the domestic wars of Christendom meant that Merzifonlu Kara Mustafa's 1683 offensive against the West triggered a far more effective response.

Moreover, European wars gave rise to three important technological advances which the Ottomans replicated only with difficulty, if at all. First, at sea the West deployed sailing warships capable of firing a broadside that could usually destroy any oar-driven galley with impunity; and the Ottomans proved incapable of constructing galleons to match them. Second, on land, the Europeans constructed fortresses of enormous sophistication, and at the same time developed siege techniques capable of taking all but the strongest Ottoman fortress: very few of the fortified places captured after 1683 in Hungary and the Adriatic ever returned to Ottoman control. Finally, the Europeans deployed massed musketry salvoes and artillery barrages to far greater effect in battle, which now became more common. Only three battles took place in Hungary between 1520 and 1665, of which the Ottomans lost only one, compared with 15 battles between 1683 and 1699, of which the Ottomans lost 11. The empire, as before, proved an adept imitator, and its Janissary corps successfully adapted the volley fire technique of its Western enemies, but it seemed incapable of innovating. The 'decline' of the Ottoman empire was thus relative rather than absolute: it eventually recovered from the mid-seventeenth-century crisis – but its European rivals recovered more quickly and more completely.

8

The 'lamentations of Germany' and its Neighbours, 1618–88[1]

The Long Shadow of the Thirty Years War

In 1962 the regional government of Hessen sent out a questionnaire that asked respondents to place in rank order the 'seven greatest catastrophes' ever suffered by Germany. Most respondents mentioned the Black Death, defeat in the Second World War and the Third Reich, but the Thirty Years War topped the list. It is easy to understand why: the loss and displacement of people were proportionately greater than in the Second World War, the material and cultural devastation caused were almost as great; and both the catastrophe and its aftermath lasted far longer. Germany not only experienced these misfortunes, however, it also exported them to its neighbours. Britain, Denmark, the Dutch Republic, France, Poland, Sweden, the Swiss Confederation, and several states of northern Italy all became involved in the Thirty Years War, and in each case that involvement created an economic and political crisis and, almost, state breakdown. Helmut G. Koenigsberger was correct to suggest that the conflict that began in Bohemia in 1618 and ended in 1648 amounted to a 'European Civil War'.[2]

Within the borders of the 'Holy Roman Empire of the German Nation' (which included almost all of modern Germany and Austria, as well as Slovenia, the Czech Republic, and parts of western Poland and eastern France) lived some 20 million people.[3] Although its population was thus much the same as that of France, whereas just one sovereign ruled France, public authority in the empire was divided between some 1,300 territorial rulers. At the apex stood the seven Electors (*Kurfürsten*) who met periodically to choose each new emperor: the archbishops of Mainz, Cologne and Trier (all of them ruling small states in the Rhineland); the Electors of Saxony and Brandenburg and the king of Bohemia, all ruling large territories further east; and the Elector Palatine, who governed territories both on the lower Rhine and on the border of Bohemia. Collectively, the seven Electors governed almost one-fifth of the empire's population, and at meetings of the imperial Diet (*Reichstag*) they formed the most prestigious of its three 'colleges'. Spiritual princes who ruled 50 fiefs, together with lay colleagues who ruled another 33 fiefs, formed the Diet's second College; while approximately 50 'Imperial Free Cities', most of them in the south and west of Germany, formed the third College. About one thousand lesser rulers, both lay and secular, most of them also in the south and west, governed the rest of Germany – but lacked direct representation in the Diet.

The political geography of the empire therefore possessed striking disparities. Whereas just four states, all Protestant (Brandenburg, Saxony, Pomerania and Mecklenburg), dominated the sparsely populated north and northeast of Germany, the more populous south and west contained a multitude of smaller political entities, some Protestant but most Catholic. Swabia, for example, covering some 16,000 square miles just north of Switzerland, was fragmented between 68 secular lords, 40 spiritual lords and 32 city-states. Among these, Württemberg (Swabia's largest state) contained 400,000 subjects; but some of its neighbours consisted of a single village. Moreover, since the imperial Constitution allowed rulers to determine the religion of their subjects, Württemberg was staunchly Lutheran, whereas most of its neighbours were equally staunchly Catholic.

Throughout the empire, rulers great and small strove to reinforce their independence. On the one hand, they created schools and universities to train (some might say 'indoctrinate') clergy and teachers who would faithfully follow the state religion. On the other hand, they also created tariff barriers designed to protect local production as well as to raise revenues: thus a ship carrying merchandise along the river Elbe between Hamburg and Prague (just over 300 miles) had to pay tolls at 30 border checkpoints; and a barge travelling along the Rhine between Mainz and Cologne (just over 100 miles) had to pay tolls 11 times. In addition, some German rulers spent heavily on defence (both fortifying their towns and raising militia units); several joined a confessional alliance (the Protestant Union from 1608, the Catholic League from 1609); and all sought financial independence. Maximilian, ruler of Bavaria from 1598 to 1648, made no secret of his ambitions. 'I believe that we princes only gain respect, both from spiritual and secular powers, according to "reason of state",' he wrote at the beginning of his reign; adding 'and I believe that only those who have a lot of land or a lot of money get that respect'.[4] Over the next two decades he doubled his tax revenues and used the proceeds to build state-of-the-art fortifications, to fund the Catholic League and to create a war chest of four million thalers.

Despite these impressive achievements, Maximilian was not an independent prince: like all other German rulers he owed obedience to the Holy Roman Emperor, an elective office held since the mid-fifteenth century by one of the Habsburg Archdukes of Austria. The Habsburgs also held the elective crowns of Hungary and Bohemia; but in all these territories, unlike Germany, the representative assemblies ('Estates') had forced their rulers to grant religious toleration to their vassals. Indeed, in 1609 the Estates of Bohemia extorted from the King-Emperor Rudolf II the 'Letter of Majesty', an edict that guaranteed full religious toleration throughout the kingdom, and then created a standing committee, known as 'the Defensors', to ensure that the concessions went into effect. Rudolf and his successor Matthias fought back by replacing Protestant officials with Catholics, often either foreigners or recently ennobled townsmen with a legal education: both groups became dedicated supporters of the crown and, in return, the crown showered rewards and offices on them. Matters came to a head in the winter of 1617–18 when

Matthias, supported by his 'heir designate' Archduke Ferdinand, ordered his regents in Prague to prohibit the use of Catholic endowments to pay Protestant ministers, to deny civic office to all non-Catholics and, most inflammatory of all, to forbid Protestant worship in all towns built on church lands. The Defensors determined that these measures contravened the Letter of Majesty and summoned the Bohemian Estates to assemble in Prague in May 1618. Meanwhile Protestants excluded from power produced polemics that criticized the 'pettiness, deceit and envy' of the Catholic-dominated court.[5]

The Prague Spring

Unusually cold and wet conditions ruined the harvests in 1617 and 1618 throughout central Europe, so that economic tension was already high by the time the Bohemian Estates convened. Polyxena Lobković, the perceptive wife of the Chancellor of Bohemia (and a staunch Catholic), predicted that 'Things were now swiftly coming to the pass where either the Papists would settle their score with the Protestants or the Protestants with the Papists.'[6] She was soon proved right. When the regency council declared the meeting of the Estates illegal, in May 1618 the Estates invaded the chamber where they met and threw two councillors, together with their secretary, out of a high window in an event that became known as the Defenestration of Prague. They then created a provisional government – not one member had held office under the crown – and began to raise an army in preparation for the inevitable Habsburg backlash.

Religious tensions also ran high in Germany, fuelled by Protestant celebrations in 1617 of the first centenary of Martin Luther's successful defiance of the papacy. Hans Heberle, a shoemaker living near Ulm, a city with both Catholic and Protestant inhabitants, later noted in his diary that 'This Jubilee became one of the causes of the war' because it set German Protestants and Catholics at each other's throats. Indeed, Lutheran broadsheets, pamphlets and sermons called for an immediate crusade against Rome, centre of idolatry, sodomy and other 'vices', while Catholics responded with angry calls for a counter-jubilee, dedicated to the abolition of 'heresies'. A spate of inflammatory pamphlets and broadsheets flowed from the presses (Fig. 23).[7]

The Bohemian Estates made haste to exploit these tensions, appealing for military and financial assistance to the German Protestant Union; but although the Union raised an army of 11,000 men 'to protect liberty and law' and 'to maintain our religion like true patriots', it refused to deploy them outside Germany.[8] Then in March 1619 Matthias died, creating a double succession crisis, one as king of Bohemia and the other as Holy Roman Emperor, because both were elective offices. On 25 August 1619, although they had previously recognized Ferdinand as 'king-designate', the Estates of Bohemia elected as their new ruler Elector Frederick of the Palatinate, the Director of the German Protestant Union as well as son-in-law of James I of England and nephew of Maurice of Nassau, the dominant figure in the Dutch Republic.

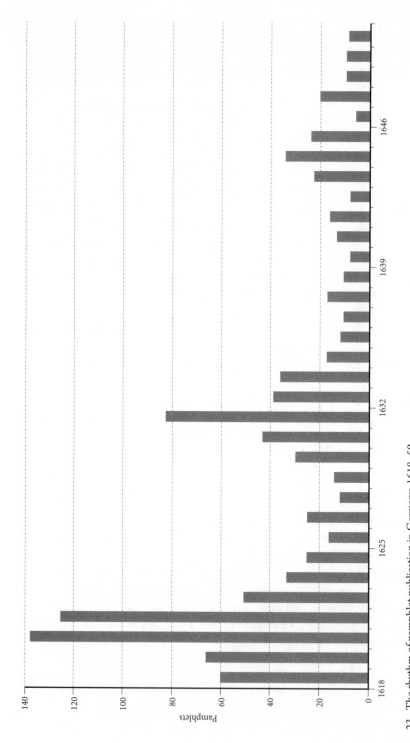

23. The rhythm of pamphlet publication in Germany, 1618–50.
The Gustav Freitag Collection of pamphlets, in Frankfurt, contains over 1,000 items printed between 1610 and 1650, with major peaks in 1618–22 (40 per cent of the total) and 1629–33 (20 per cent). The first peak, predominantly Catholic, centred on the Bohemian Revolt and the intervention of Frederick of the Palatinate; the second, almost entirely Protestant, reflected the hopes aroused by Sweden's intervention in the war.

Had this momentous event occurred only slightly earlier, it would have affected the choice of the next Holy Roman Emperor, because the king of Bohemia was one of the seven Electors. Instead, as soon as all the Electors (or their representatives) had arrived in Frankfurt-on-Main, according to custom the city was sealed so that no one could legally enter or leave. Therefore on 28 August 1619, when Ferdinand was elected unanimously as Holy Roman Emperor, neither he nor his colleagues knew that, 300 miles away in Prague, he had just been deposed as king of Bohemia.

The danger created by this double election was immediately apparent. 'Let everyone prepare at once for a war lasting twenty, thirty or forty years,' an observer in Frankfurt wrote presciently, because 'the Spaniards and the House of Austria will hazard everything to recover Bohemia . . . rather than allow their dynasty to lose control of it so disgracefully'. A few days later, a British diplomat likewise warned that 'this business of Bohemia is like to put all Christendom in confusion'. If the Bohemian cause was 'neglected and by consequence suppressed', he predicted, the German Protestants 'are like to bear the burden of a victorious army'.[9]

Frederick of the Palatinate, aged 23, now held the fate of Europe in his hands: would he accept the crown offered by the Bohemian Estates or not? Several of his advisers argued that allowing the Bohemian cause to founder would open the way for a concerted Habsburg attack on Protestants throughout Europe. Other advisers saw the matter in providential terms, arguing that since the Bohemians' cause was just, God would clear away all obstacles. This argument seems to have convinced Frederick: the opportunity 'is a divine calling that I must not disobey. My only end is to serve God and his Church,' he confided to his wife and in November 1619, eighteen months after the Defenestration, he travelled to Prague for his coronation.[10] Meanwhile, his supporters laid siege to Vienna, Ferdinand's capital.

This marked the zenith of Frederick's fortunes. The following month, disputes among his commanders caused them to abandon the siege of Vienna – an event that Ferdinand and his supporters interpreted as an unmistakable sign of divine favour for their cause – while Duke Maximilian of Bavaria promised to help Ferdinand defeat his rebellious subjects. In return, Ferdinand promised to reimburse all of Maximilian's military expenses and to grant him any of Frederick's possessions that he could capture (including, in the event of total victory, Frederick's Electoral title). The Catholic League authorized Maximilian to raise 25,000 men, and the following summer the new army (whose many notable volunteers included René Descartes) invaded Bohemia.

Frederick's troops fell back until in November 1620 they made a desperate stand at the White Mountain (Bílá Hora), just outside Prague. The engagement lasted only two hours and 'the loss of soldiers was not much unequal' but, as an English diplomat on the spot noted:

> The loss of cannon, the baggage, reputation, is the Imperials' victory who, as it
> seems, hold Bohemia now by conquest . . . And if a new establishment by petition
> shall be obtained, it will be only the Law of the Conqueror, who does already

finely call those of the [Protestant] Religion to account for what they have, and put it into safe keeping, so that they taste already their condition to come.[11]

Frederick, whom Catholic polemicists cruelly dubbed 'The Winter King', because his reign had lasted barely one year, promptly fled from Prague, while Catholic troops invaded and occupied his German territories.

Ferdinand immediately pressed home his advantage. He created a judicial commission to try his opponents. He approved the execution of almost 30 ring-leaders, and condemned almost 600 more to lose their landed estates – which he promptly sold in order to pay off his troops. It was, in the words of Peter Wilson, 'the largest transfer of property in Europe before the seizures during the Communist takeover after 1945'.[12] This imposition of 'the Law of the Conqueror' on the king-dom's elite, though brutal, affected relatively few; but another initiative affected almost everyone. Although his forces had won their victory relatively swiftly, the cost of the campaign far exceeded Ferdinand's available funds. He therefore allowed a consortium of his creditors to mint debased currency, and used it to pay his debts. The rulers of many neighbouring states followed this example and set up mints expressly to produce cheaper coins, causing runaway inflation known as the *Kipper-und Wipperzeit* (the 'see-saw' era) in much of central Europe. Meanwhile, some of Frederick's supporters fought on, preventing Ferdinand from demobilizing his troops. In Württemberg, a chronicler wrote of 1622: 'This year cannot sufficiently be described, how wretchedly and damagingly it went' – not only because of 'murder, robbing and burning, with the quartering of the soldiery whom the people were forced to serve with all their means, with the imposition of war costs' but also because 'One no longer traded with money, but with bartered exchange'. The wages of some urban workers fell by half between 1619 and 1621, and by half again by 1623, provoking riots in several central European towns. One pamphleteer claimed that 'The last days which Christ prophesied have come'. By the time Ferdinand decreed a return to the old coin values in 1624, many families had lost 90 per cent of their savings. Even a decade later, the Bohemian exile Pavel Stránský recalled the *Kipper- und Wipperzeit* as the most traumatic of his life.[13]

The effects of devaluation were felt far beyond Germany, because it reduced the cost of manufactures there so drastically that no one bought imported goods. Thus the number of English woollen cloths exported to the continent from London fell from over 100,000 in 1618 to 75,000 in 1622, and even those brought no profit because 'the monies [have] become so variable, that when a merchant has sold his cloth, and hopes to have gained something thereby, by the time that the term for payment is expired, he receives less in value than the cloths cost', because of the devaluation. At the same time, cheap foreign imports flooded the English market, reducing domestic demand for home manufactures. According to a contemporary economist, the recession caused the English to become 'improvident and careless ... besotting ourselves with pipe and pot, in a beastly manner, sucking [tobacco] smoke and drinking healths until death stares many in the face'.[14]

Germany's other trading partners also suffered from the decision of Ferdinand and his neighbours to devalue. In Italy, the reduced demand and the currency shifts in central Europe ruined many merchants (and, therefore, those whom they employed). Spanish Lombardy, whose economy depended heavily on German demand, experienced a dramatic setback: between 1618 and 1622 unemployment in the capital rose to 50 per cent; the trade of Cremona (a centre of cloth production) fell by 90 per cent; and the quantity of coinage issued by the Milan mint fell by 97 per cent. In Spanish Naples, where the poor harvests of 1619, 1620 and 1621 coincided with orders from Madrid to send money to assist Ferdinand, the viceroy allowed the city's public banks to issue paper money to cover the outflow of specie. They preserved their solvency only because the viceroy allowed them to refuse to pay any credit note worth more than ten ducats. Urban and rural property values fell by about half and the economy of the kingdom languished. In the biblical phrase used by a Neapolitan economist of the day, 'seven lean years began in 1623'.[15]

The Crisis of the Dutch Republic

Meanwhile, civil war almost broke out in the Dutch Republic. The conclusion of a Twelve Years Truce with Spain, in 1609, unleashed deep domestic tensions previously held in check by the common war effort. Neither history nor tradition linked the seven 'United Provinces' that composed the Republic. Friesland and Gelderland had spent much of the fifteenth century fighting Holland and Zealand, with Groningen, Overijssel and Utrecht as both prize and battleground. All preserved their local laws and liberties intact, and they even spoke different languages: Dutch in the western provinces, Fries in Friesland, and either Oosters or German in the eastern provinces. The religious complexity of the Republic was even greater. 'After having consulted the local people', one foreign observer estimated that 'one might divide the population of these provinces into three parts, each more or less equal': one-third were Calvinists, another third Catholics, and the rest either Anabaptists, Lutherans, Jews, members of some other 'sect', or atheists. The pattern of distribution was not uniform. Thus the Anabaptists constituted more than half the population of some areas of Friesland, and perhaps one-tenth of the whole province; while almost one-tenth of the 20,000 inhabitants of Rotterdam were Catholics, with the rest belonging to one of ten other religions, or to none.[16]

The House of Orange-Nassau provided a degree of cohesion. Count Maurice of Nassau (prince of Orange after 1618) served as captain-general of the confederate army and governor (*Stadholder*) of five provinces, while his cousin governed the other two. Certain institutions also served the entire Union – the Council of State (for military matters), the Admiralty boards and the Audit Office – but executive power rested with the individual assemblies (the *Staten* or States) of the seven United Provinces, each of which sent delegates to the States-General. This central body remained surprisingly small, seldom more than 12 deputies (and often only four or five), because most decisions (including those on war, peace and new taxes) required ratification by the seven provincial assemblies. Naturally, unanimity often proved difficult (sometimes impossible) to achieve; but until 1618 the views of Holland, which provided almost two-thirds of the Union's tax revenues, generally prevailed.

Securing the consent of each provincial assembly required much time and patience, because even there the delegates could settle little without reference to their 'principals': the magistrates of each major town and the local nobility. The States of Holland (for example) could only discuss an agenda of issues that had circulated beforehand among the magistrates of 18 towns and the representative of the province's nobles. This requirement gave great influence to their chief legal officer, Johan van Oldenbarnevelt, who prepared the agenda for each meeting and led the discussions. Although the States of some other provinces proved more tractable, their decisions still involved large numbers of the local elite. In all, perhaps 2,000 magistrates (known as 'regents') in 57 towns, plus scores of noblemen, participated directly in the Republic's decision-making process. It was not 'democratic' by modern standards, but in virtually no other major state in the early modern world did so many people help to shape national policy.

With so many protagonists in decision-making, friction frequently developed – particularly over contentious issues such as finance, religion and foreign policy. Holland, for example, normally favoured peace with Spain because war was expensive and Holland paid more in taxes than all the other provinces combined. Its southern neighbour Zealand, by contrast, normally opposed peace with Spain because the province prospered from piracy at Spain's expense and from the revenues generated by tolls and passports to trade with the enemy. The Calvinist clergy, too, vociferously favoured war with the Catholic 'arch-enemy', using not only the pulpits but also their contacts with individual regents (often their brothers, nephews and fathers) to sabotage peace initiatives. Finally, most of those who had fled Catholic persecution in Flanders and Brabant likewise opposed any settlement with those who had driven them into exile.

The discussions of 1607–9 over whether or not to make peace with Spain polarized these diverse groups. On one side stood the regents of Holland and Utrecht, led by Oldenbarnevelt, who wanted peace abroad and a measure of religious toleration at home. They faced a coalition that comprised Zealand and other areas that profited from the war; most Calvinist ministers; and most southern immigrants, supported by Maurice of Nassau (who stood to lose much of his influence and patronage once the Republic demobilized its armed forces). These divisions deepened once the Truce began because of a controversy between two Calvinist theologians at Leiden University. Francis Gomarus, a refugee from Flanders, preached that everybody's spiritual destiny had been determined from the beginning of time; while Jacob Arminius, a Hollander, argued that an individual's life choices affected their chance of salvation. A vicious pamphlet war on these issues of salvation gathered momentum, with almost 200 published in 1617 and over 300 in 1618. Alarmed by attacks on Arminians, the States of Holland passed a resolution authorizing each town to raise special militia units (known as *waardgelders*) to preserve law and order whenever necessary, and ordered them to obey the orders issued by the town that raised them. Maurice, who sided openly with the Gomarists, declared these measures an 'affront to the true Reformed religion and to our person' (since as captain-general all troops in the Republic owed obedience to him) and he toured the inland provinces to remove Arminians from office.

Oldenbarnevelt and his supporters retaliated by raising more militia units, whereupon Maurice used regular troops to disarm and disband them, and to arrest Oldenbarnevelt. He also purged the town councils, replacing experienced magistrates with novices who lacked the ability to monitor the Stadholder's policies effectively. Maurice also removed all Arminians from schools and universities, while a National Synod of the Calvinist Church convened at Dordrecht (Dort) condemned the Arminians as heretics and 'perturbers of the peace' in both Church and State, and deprived some 200 of their ministers of their livings. In 1619 Maurice persuaded the States-General to sentence Oldenbarnevelt to death, and he used his unchecked authority to welcome his nephew Frederick of the Palatinate and to encourage and fund the latter's efforts to recover his lands. Maurice also welcomed the renewal of war with Spain in 1621, when the Twelve Years, Truce expired.

Frederick's renewed defiance prompted Emperor Ferdinand II to honour his promise (page 215 above) to transfer the Electoral title to Maximilian. This provoked a spate of hostile pamphlets within Germany, because it was unconstitutional: the Golden Bull of 1356, universally regarded as the fundamental and immutable law of the Holy Roman Empire, ordained that the Electorate should remain in the Palatine house in perpetuity. Even the Spanish Council of State, which normally supported Ferdinand to the hilt, disapproved, realizing that it would 'mean the renewal of war permanently in Germany'.[17] The Spanish ministers were right: now, at last, Frederick found the international support that his cause had previously lacked, and he forged alliances with France, England, Savoy, Sweden and Denmark, as well as the Dutch Republic. All promised to fight until Frederick had recovered his forfeited lands and titles, and Christian IV of Denmark prepared to lead 20,000 soldiers into the empire to achieve this goal.

Enter Denmark

King Christian commanded prodigious resources. His dominions stretched from the North Cape to Holstein in Germany and from Greenland to Oland in the Baltic, and included both sides of the Danish Sound. Since every ship entering or leaving the Baltic needed to pass beneath the guns of his castle at Elsinore, the Danish king derived a huge income from the Sound Tolls; and by 1625 his total assets amounted to almost 1.5 million thalers. Despite a propensity for binge drinking, Christian was a devout Lutheran who firmly believed in the existence of a Catholic conspiracy that aimed to extirpate Protestantism throughout the empire; and events after White Mountain confirmed his fears. The victorious Catholic forces began a relentless campaign of 'Catholicization', expelling Protestant ministers, prohibiting public Protestant worship, and reclaiming secularized church lands. Thoroughly alarmed, Christian proclaimed himself 'Defender of German Liberties' and, despite the objections of his councillors and his lack of military experience, in spring 1626 he led his army across the Weser towards the Palatinate.[18]

This development in turn alarmed Count Tilly, commander of the army of the Catholic League, who realized that he could 'not gain superiority alone'. He warned his master, Maximilian of Bavaria, that 'The Danes hold great advantages: they will act first and overwhelm us'.[19] Maximilian therefore asked Ferdinand for reinforcements and the emperor obliged by ordering Albrecht von Wallenstein, a military entrepreneur who had grown rich from buying up confiscated lands acquired in his native Bohemia, to raise and maintain an army of 24,000 men. With considerable skill, Wallenstein halted the advance towards Bohemia of a Protestant army financed by Christian's allies, and sent reinforcements to Tilly just before he confronted the Danish army at the battle of Lutter-am-Barenberg. Although Christian wrote in his diary only that he 'Fought with the enemy and lost the battle', he had in fact sacrificed half his army and all his field artillery.[20]

Christian and most of his nobles managed to escape to the Baltic islands, but for the next two years Catholic troops occupied Jutland as well as northern Germany and forced the inhabitants to finance them through 'contributions': payments in cash and commodities made directly to local troops. The effectiveness of this system is reflected in a letter written by Wallenstein to the imperial treasurer, boasting that although his army cost at least 12 million thalers annually to maintain, he would only need from Vienna 'a couple of million thalers every year to keep this long war going'.[21] Paradoxically, despite the apparent savings, Wallenstein's system required a steady increase in the size of his army to collect the 'contributions'. He therefore raised more troops, which in turn necessitated more contributions, until by 1628 he commanded (and had to support) no fewer than 130,000 men.

Meanwhile, cold winters, late springs and wet summers reduced the supplies available to support civilians and soldiers alike. In south Germany, in May 1626, hailstones the size of walnuts combined with a heavy frost killed many crops; while the following year, according to the diary kept by Hans Heberle, 'a great snow fell' just after New Year and covered the ground until Easter Day. 'It was so harsh a winter that no-one could remember another like it', and 'only after Easter could the peasants go to their fields and begin to farm'. The autumn also saw heavy precipitation, and in 1628 some Alpine villages experienced snowfalls, sometimes heavy, every month: it proved to be the first 'year without a summer' to afflict Europe during the seventeenth century. In many areas, neither grain nor grapes ever ripened.[22] Many sought scapegoats for this extreme weather: an unparalleled spate of witchcraft trials occurred, some involving the execution of hundreds of suspects at a time, while others blamed the Jews. A popular print from 1629 (Plate 9) showed a Jew who has secured a monopoly of the wine harvest, with a series of political and extreme weather events in the background (one of the few contemporary images that explicitly linked climate and catastrophe), and noted the general 'unrest' of the time.[23]

The most serious case of this 'unrest' occurred in Upper Austria, which had rashly joined the Bohemians in revolt but rapidly fell to the army of the Catholic League.

After White Mountain, the emperor granted Upper Austria to his ally Maximilian as a pledge against the repayment of his war expenses, and allowed him to use the duchy's taxes both to pay interest on this debt and to sustain the army of occupation. Taxes in the region rose fourteen-fold, all payable in silver at a time when the *Kipper- und Wipperzeit* had destroyed the savings of most taxpayers. The cowed population might have tolerated these burdens had the government not also ordered the expulsion of all Protestant pastors and schoolteachers, and allowed Catholic creditors to foreclose on Protestants in order to force the sale of their property. When it decreed that by Easter 1626 all residents of the duchy must attend Catholic worship or leave, open opposition broke out, led by a prosperous Protestant farmer, Stephen Fadinger. The rebels routed the governor and his troops and chased them back to Linz (the duchy's capital), which they besieged. They also sent an envoy to beg for Danish aid, but the defeat at Lutter prevented this; then a bullet killed Fadinger in the trenches around Linz, and a general assault on its defences failed. Eventually 12,000 imperial troops restored order and executed scores of rebels (the nobles by decapitation, the commoners losing their right hands before being disembowelled). The government again ordered Protestants either to convert or leave, but the Little Ice Age delayed the process: the appalling weather made it virtually impossible for anyone to liquidate their assets before they left, and so the deadline for departure was reluctantly extended.[24]

Meanwhile, all over Germany, resentment of Wallenstein and his army continued to grow. Thomas Robisheaux's exhaustive study of the Lutheran county of Hohenlohe in southwest Germany shows how the demands of the imperial troops not only quadrupled taxes but also forced the civilian authorities to become far more aggressive in collecting them. By 1628 the county had, 'for all practical purposes, lost its autonomy and become an extension of Wallenstein's tax state'.[25] Catholic rulers suffered almost as much, and a group of them protested directly to Ferdinand that Wallenstein had authorized 'exorbitant rates of pay to regimental and company staff officers' and created a contributions system that ruined 'poor widows and orphans'. All 'territorial rulers,' they concluded bitterly, 'are at the mercy of colonels and captains who are war profiteers and criminals, breaking the laws of the Empire'. They called on the emperor to reduce the size of Wallenstein's army, to end all recruiting, to replace the army's 'contributions' with taxes raised and administered by civilians, and to appoint a special commissioner to audit the general's accounts.

Although Ferdinand rejected these demands, he attempted to placate his Catholic allies with religious promises. He informed them that, after nine years of war, he wished to reconfigure the religious state of the empire, and in particular to repossess church lands secularized by Protestant rulers. These steps, he claimed, would be 'the great gain and fruit of the war', and he promised his fellow Catholics that 'just as up to now we have never thought to let pass any chance to secure the restitution of church lands, neither do we intend, now or in the future, to have to bear the responsibility before posterity of having neglected or failed to exploit even the least opportunity'.[26]

'The root of all evils'

As long as Christian of Denmark remained in arms, the emperor deemed the 'opportunity' too risky; but in 1628, with peace negotiations underway, he prepared a document known as the Edict of Restitution that required Protestant rulers to return to the Church all lands secularized since the peace of Augsburg of 1555, which had brought Germany's religious wars to an end. He had 500 copies of the Edict secretly printed and distributed, with instructions for simultaneous publication on 28 March 1629. Two months later, Christian made peace and Tilly and Wallenstein immediately deployed their troops to enforce the Edict, making no distinction between previously loyal and rebellious Protestant states. Within 18 months, the secularized lands of 6 bishoprics and 100 convents were back in clerical hands, with 400 more convents scheduled for restitution. Naturally such a drastic measure caused uproar throughout the empire. On the title page of one copy of the Edict – one printed in a *Catholic* stronghold – a contemporary hand added the words *Radix omnium malorum*: 'The root of all evils'.[27]

International affairs now distracted the emperor from further enforcement of the Edict. First, the Dutch captured a treasure fleet sailing to Spain from America, compromising the Spanish Habsburgs' ability to fund their troops in both northern Italy, where they sought to crush the defiant duke of Mantua, and in the Netherlands, where they faced the largest Dutch army ever assembled. Ferdinand therefore instructed Wallenstein to send one expeditionary force to the Netherlands and another to Mantua, plus a third to help the king of Poland withstand an invasion by King Gustavus Adolphus of Sweden. Then a French army crossed the Alps into northern Italy, compelling Ferdinand to divert Wallenstein's expeditionary force from the Netherlands to Italy; and although Wallenstein's reinforcements helped the Poles to inflict a stinging defeat on Gustavus, French diplomats brokered a truce in the Baltic that freed the battle-hardened Swedish army to invade Germany.

These developments compelled Wallenstein to recruit yet more troops, until by spring 1630 he commanded 151,000 men, spread out over all Germany and northern Italy. The increased demands of his army's commissioners for contributions further outraged his Catholic allies, who now insisted that Ferdinand dismiss his expensive general. The emperor reluctantly agreed to meet the other Electors at Regensburg to resolve this and other contentious issues.

Since his election as emperor in 1619, Ferdinand had deposed rulers and transferred their lands, created the huge imperial army under Wallenstein and issued the Edict of Restitution – all without convening an imperial Diet. Representatives of German rulers and foreign powers alike therefore converged on Regensburg in the summer of 1630, anxious to make their views known to the Electors; to restore the *status quo ante*; and, especially, to get rid of Wallenstein. Since the cost of his army far exceeded the available resources, the imperial commander himself made no effort to stay on. 'There is no other way,' he thundered to one of his lieutenants. 'If they want to wage a war in which affairs are arranged and managed in such a way that quartering gives the Empire pleasure and not displeasure, let them appoint Our

Lord God himself to be their general – not me!'[28] In August 1630 Ferdinand duly replaced his general – not with God, but with Count Tilly, commander of the army of the Catholic League, who reduced the imperial forces by two-thirds. Wallenstein retired stoically to his estates in Bohemia; his banker committed suicide.

The Electors capitalized on their success in eliminating Wallenstein by extracting a promise from the emperor that, in future, 'no new war will be declared other than by the advice of the Electors', but they failed to persuade him to modify the Edict of Restitution. Many German Catholics, even Maximilian of Bavaria, considered some relaxation advisable in view of increasing foreign support for the Protestant cause; but Ferdinand's confessor, William Lamormaini S. J., answered that the emperor did not care whether he lost 'not only Austria but all his kingdoms and provinces and whatever he has in this world, provided he save his soul, which he cannot do without the implementation of his Edict'.[29] Ferdinand thus made two fatal errors. By sacrificing Wallenstein, he lost the one man who might have defeated all his enemies; and by retaining the Edict intact he convinced the north German Lutherans that they would soon experience its terms themselves.

Enter Sweden

Gustavus Adolphus arrived on German soil at the head of a powerful army just as the Electoral meeting commenced. He immediately issued a manifesto in five languages that rehearsed his personal grievances (particularly Ferdinand's dispatch of 'armies into Poland against His Majesty and the kingdom of Sweden') and his fear that the Habsburgs aimed to dominate the Baltic. Only at the end did the manifesto mention, briefly, the maintenance of German liberties as a motive for invasion. It said nothing about saving 'the Protestant cause'.[30] At first, Gustavus attracted little support: his sole German ally when he landed was the small port-city of Stralsund, and only the dispossessed and those under direct threat of imperial occupation (such as the city of Magdeburg) declared for him. In addition, just before Gustavus landed, Habsburg troops captured and sacked the city of Mantua. The outlook for the Swedish expeditionary force looked bleak.

Under intense pressure from the Catholics at his court, Louis XIII of France had sent negotiators to Regensburg with orders to resolve all outstanding disputes with the emperor (albeit without detailed instructions on how to do so). News of the fall of Mantua unnerved his negotiators, who signed a treaty with Ferdinand that not only stipulated the joint evacuation of French and imperial forces from northern Italy, but also committed Louis to refrain in future from offering support to anyone who opposed the emperor. In a remarkable volte-face, in October 1630 Louis repudiated the treaty signed in his name. It was, he raged at his envoys, 'Not only contrary to your powers, to the orders in the Instructions you took with you, and to those I have sent you at various times since, but it even contains several items that I never even thought about, and that are so prejudicial that I could not hear them read out to me except with extreme displeasure.'[31] In addition to repudiating the treaty of Regensburg, Louis concluded an alliance with Sweden that promised Gustavus one million *livres* annually for five years to finance a war for 'the safeguarding of the Baltic and Oceanic Seas, the liberty of commerce, and the restoration of the suppressed states of the Holy Roman Empire'. The French subsidy enabled Gustavus to raise more troops and occupy the duchies of Mecklenburg and Pomerania, turning the eastern Baltic into a Swedish lake.

Meanwhile, Count Tilly and his troops were tied down in blockading the Protestant city of Magdeburg, Sweden's only ally in central Germany, until in May 1631 they stormed and brutally sacked it (see chapter 4 above). The following month Habsburg and French negotiators, assisted by a young diplomat in papal service named Giulio Mazzarini, signed a treaty that brought peace to northern Italy, freeing all imperial troops there to fight in Germany. Once again it seemed as if Ferdinand would be able to expel the Swedes single-handed, but Tilly rashly decided to confront Gustavus before the reinforcements arrived from Italy. To this end, he invaded Lutheran Saxony, which had previously remained loyal to Ferdinand, causing its outraged ruler to join forces with the Swedes. Tilly caught up with them at Breitenfeld, near Leipzig, where on 17 September 1631 the superior discipline and firepower of Gustavus's troops put an end to the Catholic tide of victory: having lost 20,000 men, his field artillery and his treasury, Tilly rapidly retreated.

Rather like Lutter five years before, the battle of Breitenfeld transformed the military balance – and thus guaranteed that the war would go on. Meeting with no effective resistance, Gustavus sent one army to Bohemia, allowing the return of the exiles who had fled in 1620, while he plundered his way through Germany's Catholic heartland to the Rhine. Meanwhile, his principal Swedish minister, Axel Oxenstierna, created a 'government-general' to administer all the occupied territories and organized 'contributions' to maintain the 120,000 victorious soldiers deployed across northern Germany.

Ferdinand now saw no choice but to recall Wallenstein because, as one of his councillors put it: 'Now we shout "Help, Help", but nobody is listening'.[32] But before the general could recruit a new imperial army, Tilly and the battered troops of the Catholic League rashly attacked the nearest Swedish positions. Gustavus promptly defeated Tilly (who died of battle wounds soon after) and, accompanied by a jubilant Frederick of the Palatinate, systematically plundered Bavaria while Maximilian pleaded with Wallenstein for help. Instead, the new imperial army retreated to the Alte Veste, a huge fortified camp near Nuremberg that Gustavus vainly besieged for two months before withdrawing northwards; but on 16 November 1632 he launched a surprise attack, and at the battle of Lützen, near Leipzig, Wallenstein lost so many soldiers that he decided to retreat. He did not learn until some days later that the Swedes, too, had suffered heavy casualties – among them King Gustavus himself.

For the next 16 years rival armies moved to and fro across the empire, seeking to gain a decisive strategic advantage – and leaving death, devastation and insecurity in their wake. Initially Axel Oxenstierna, who after Gustavus's death became both head of the Swedish regency council and director of the Protestant war effort, tried to negotiate a favourable settlement with Wallenstein; but in February 1634 Ferdinand had his general murdered (on the grounds that he was supposed to wage war, not make peace), and the following September, at Nördlingen, Habsburg forces won a crushing victory over the Swedes and their German allies. Oxenstierna now withdrew his forces to the Baltic and sought to renew the peace talks ended by Wallenstein's death but, deeming the emperor's terms unacceptable, he decided to fight on. Ferdinand, by contrast, concluded the peace of Prague with some of Sweden's allies in May 1635, and a few months later declared war on France. Oxenstierna renewed Sweden's alliance with France, promising (among other things) that neither side would make peace without the other. The alliance – and therefore the war – would last for 13 more years.

The Tipping Point: The Rape of Germany

The battle of Breitenfeld in 1631 saved the Protestant cause, but in doing so it transformed both the scope and the impact of the war. Previously, most Germans had seen hostilities as both exceptional and temporary: in the words of a Protestant miller's daughter near Nuremberg, until the summer of 1632 'we had indeed heard of the war, but we had not thought that it would reach us [here]'. The situation changed abruptly when imperial troops sacked both her town and her mill during the siege of the Alte Veste, leaving 'not a grain of wheat, not a speck of flour'. Likewise, a Lutheran pastor near Ulm scarcely mentioned military operations in his chronicle until 1628, when 'a new and frightening catastrophe threatened us' in the shape of Wallenstein's army of occupation. For the next three years he still interspersed comments about billeting and contributions with reports of the harvest, weather and freak accidents, but that too changed after Breitenfeld, when the victorious Swedish army advanced into central Germany. Henceforth war dominated the pastor's narrative – which also became far more detailed. On the other side of the religious divide, a monk near the Swiss border who had filled his diary with details on the weather and the wine harvest suddenly changed his focus and tone when the Swedish army approached, and 'the trouble really started around here'. Looking back a decade later, the author regretted that he had not applied himself 'more assiduously to noting everything' as it happened; but 'I did not suppose that this protracted and disastrous Swedish situation would drag on for so long'.[33]

Many rural areas saw a complete collapse of public order as the secular and religious elite fled whenever 'their' side suffered a defeat. A region of strategic importance, like the county of Hohenlohe in the southwest, might change hands so often that 'at times one cannot say with certainty who actually controlled the territory'.[34] Not far away, in the villages ruled by the Benedictine abbey of Ottobeuren, parish priests recorded some of the 'evil tricks and wicked villainies' committed by troops in Swedish service. In Unteregg they beat little children with sticks and dragged them around on ropes like dogs; and they bored through a miller's leg and roasted his wife in her own oven. In Niederrieden they disembowelled and tortured to death the parish priest. In Westerheim 'Jerg Lutzenberger was stripped by the soldiers in the woods [and] in an inhuman and worse than barbarous manner was tortured in his secret parts and shockingly tormented'. Three days later, two soldiers 'stabbed him in the hands and one in the back; he died shortly thereafter.' Many entries in the local burial registers record parishioners who 'died of hunger', sometimes after eating mice and 'such things as heretofore [even] the pigs didn't eat', and in a few cases after eating human flesh. The duchy of Württemberg suffered a 'coal-black, bitter hunger, in which many therefore starved'. People lived on 'grass, thistle and greenery of that kind' because 'hunger is a good cook'. Others begged for scraps and 'those who were ashamed to do that died of hunger'.[35] Philip Vincent, a peripatetic English pastor who had visited Massachusetts and Guyana as well as Germany, also saw Breitenfeld as a turning point in his graphic book of 1638 entitled *The lamentations of Germany. Wherein, as in a glass, we may behold her miserable condition and read the woefull effects of sin.* 'Before the king of Sweden's coming,' he asserted, the war 'had consumed no less than 100,000. If that be true, what has it done since? How many millions have miserably perished?' Vincent saw no silver lining because there was now 'No tilling of the land, no breeding of cattle; for if they should, the next year the soldiers devour it.' Instead 'there is now no other abode but some camp, no other plough to follow, no other employment but the war'.[36]

Abnormal weather also increased the 'lamentations of Germany'. A Catholic soldier in central Germany reported in *August* 1640 that 'at this time there was such a great cold that we almost froze to death in our quarters', while in January 1641 the river Danube froze so hard at Regensburg that the Swedish army and its artillery could cross over and bombard the city. In Hessen-Kassel, a chronicler recorded in 1639 that 'The corn froze this year', while a pastor noted sadly that 'the little that we could sow in the winter anno 40 [1640], and also the summer crop [of 1641] was all eaten by mice, so we did not harvest much. One went to the fields to cut, and the grain was stripped away so bare that one could not tell what kind of – or even if – grain had been planted there … Anno 1642, all the misery continued just as bad as in the previous year, so that the despair pressed all the harder'. Yield ratios for grain crops fell from 1:6 to 1:1 in these years. In Bavaria, an abbot living in the Alpine foothills filled his diary in these years with reports of the misery caused by the 'coldest winter', the 'raging storms', the 'wintery spring' and the 'stormy summer'; and, in 1642, by 'a flood that was worse than any in human memory', by 'hailstones weighing up to a pound', and by a hoarfrost that covered the fields in mid-June and ruined the harvest. He also noted the 'multiplication' of wild boars and wolves, 'making the roads and paths of all places unsafe'.[37] Many civilians fled their homes in panic at least once. Pastor Lorenz Ludolf and his parishioners abandoned their village in Hessen for 18 weeks in 1646 and for much of both 1647 and 1648, hiding in neighbouring woods because their region had become a war zone. Farmer Caspar Preis, also in Hessen, felt 'so afraid and panicky that even a rustling leaf drove us out'. Shoemaker Hans Heberle complained that he and his family 'were hunted like wild beasts in the forest', and they fled from their village no fewer than 30 times during the war in search of safety.[38]

Peace Breaks Out in Germany

Remarkably, only one of the printed eyewitness accounts blamed the rulers of Germany for their misfortunes. Peter Thiele, a tax official in Brandenburg, pulled no punches: 'This whole war has been a veritable robbers' and thieves' campaign. The generals and colonels have lined their purses while princes and lords have been led about by the nose. But whenever there has been talk of wanting to make peace they have always looked to their reputations. That's what the land and people have been devastated for.'[39] Yet although Thiele condemned one obsession of the rulers of his day, 'reputation', he remained silent about another: religion.

Many Protestants, like Frederick of the Palatinate, firmly believed that they fought in response to a direct call from God (page 215 above); most Catholics consulted their confessors, and sometimes special committees of theologians, before making painful decisions concerning war and peace. Thus in 1634–5, the imperial confessor Lamormaini opposed any accommodation with the Protestant rulers who sought to negotiate with Ferdinand in the wake of Nördlingen. Unconvinced, the emperor convened a committee of 24 theologians and asked them whether he could make religious concessions to achieve peace without falling into mortal sin, or whether (as Lamormaini claimed) he must reject all compromise in the expectation that divine intervention would produce a Catholic triumph. Some of the theologians supported the confessor because 'God, who up to this point has rescued our most pious emperor from so many dangers, in this extremity will also show us the way either to continue the war or to obtain a better peace'; but most approved limited religious concessions to Protestants as 'the lesser of two evils'. Ferdinand therefore signed the Peace of Prague with Saxony and some other Lutheran princes.[40] When in 1640 the Diet of Regensburg debated whether Protestants might retain secularized church lands, even the hard-headed Maximilian of Bavaria ordered his advisers to consult theologians about their 'scruples' against making peace with Protestants; while in 1646 Emperor Ferdinand III consulted the 'court theologians' on the same issue. In each case, the theologians favoured modest concessions, provided they improved the chances of peace.[41]

The agreements reached at Prague and Regensburg settled most of the German disputes, and they formed part of the final peace settlement; so why did the war drag on until 1648? Part of the problem lay in the fact that, although most of the German protagonists sought the redress of a specific *past* injustice, first Sweden and then France had invaded Germany primarily to prevent a potential *future* injustice – namely the threat that a Habsburg victory might pose to their national security. This goal meant that the 'two crowns' (as contemporaries called France and Sweden) could not be bought off with the transfer of one or even several tracts of land (although both did indeed make territorial demands): instead they refused to sign an agreement until they had created structures to guarantee its implementation.

European history offered no precedent or guidance for achieving such aims and so, despite prayers, pamphlets, broadsheets, medals and plays calling urgently on the 'two crowns' to make peace, they continued to make war. In April 1643 the Swedes sent an open letter to all Protestant rulers pointing out that 'the emperor [had] usurped everything by right of sovereignty. This is the highroad to absolute rule and the servitude of the territories. The "two crowns" are seeking, as far as they are able, to obstruct this, because their security rests on the liberty of the German territories.'[42] Sweden (and, to a lesser extent, France) therefore sought to create a balance of power between the emperor and the states of the empire, and between Catholics and Protestants. They insisted that only the imperial Diet, not the emperor, could legally declare war, and that all territorial rulers with seats in the Diet should have the right both to arm themselves and to make alliances. The 'two crowns' hoped that these measures would make any future war in Germany virtually impossible because, in the words of a Swedish diplomat, 'The first rule of politics is that the security of all depends on maintaining the equilibrium between each individual state. When one begins to become more powerful and formidable, the others throw themselves onto the scale [Waagschale] by means of alliances and federations in order to offset it and maintain a balance.'[43] The 'two crowns' hoped to impose their vision on the diplomats representing almost 200 European rulers (150 of them German), who late in 1643 began to arrive in Westphalia: those of the Protestant states gathered at Osnabrück, while those representing Catholic states assembled 30 miles away at the city of Münster.

Negotiations ceased for a few months, while Sweden launched a surprise attack on Denmark (page 231 below), but in December 1644 the four major protagonists (France and Sweden on the one side, Spain and the emperor on the other) exchanged documents that set out their peace terms. However, they refused to suspend hostilities while they negotiated. France 'and its allies had no intention of reducing the fires of war by a ceasefire,' Cardinal Mazarin explained, 'but rather sought to extinguish them totally by a good peace'. This meant that the demands of each side waxed and waned with the changing fortunes of war – as Mazarin well knew: 'We have always said that we would increase our demands to reflect how events improved in our affairs,' he reminded his diplomats at the peace conference, and so his variable bargaining position reflected 'how much the situation has changed in our favour recently'. He continued unconvincingly, 'It is not we who have changed, but circumstances'.[44]

The 1645 campaign gave France and its allies a decisive advantage. A Swedish army invaded Bohemia, routed a Habsburg army under the personal command of Emperor Ferdinand III (r. 1637–57), and then spent the summer ravaging the Habsburg lands; while one French army destroyed the field army of the Catholic League in Germany, and another captured ten towns in the Spanish Netherlands. In October 1645, Ferdinand faced the inevitable and drew up in his own hand a secret instruction for his chief negotiator at Westphalia that authorized a layered sequence of humiliating concessions on all the major issues. In religious matters, Ferdinand hoped to turn the clock back to 1630, the high watermark for the Catholic cause following the Edict of Restitution; but, if that proved impossible, he would settle for 1627; and 'in extremo casu' (when writing his final concessions, the emperor invariably switched from German to Latin) he would accept 1618, the optimal date for the Protestant cause. In political matters, Ferdinand would allow the Palatine and Bavarian branches of the Wittelsbach family to hold a seat in the Electoral College *alternately*, but 'ad extremum' he would create an *additional* (eighth) Electorate so that each branch would enjoy permanent representation. Furthermore, Sweden could keep eastern Pomerania plus, 'if it cannot be avoided', the archbishopric of Bremen and parts of Mecklenburg *for the lifetime of the present ruler* – and 'in ultimo necessitatis gradu' *in perpetuity*. Finally, 'in extremo casu', France could annexe the Habsburg lands in Alsace and, 'in desperatissimo casu', Breisach too.[45]

Since further defeats placed Ferdinand 'in desperatissimo casu', he eventually made all these concessions, and in September 1646 his negotiators signed a 'preliminary treaty' with France that granted even Breisach – but the terms would only come into effect when Sweden also made peace. Only now did the Congress turn serious attention to thorny religious issues, such as a 'normative date' for the religious settlement.[46] Like Ferdinand, the German Catholics (supported by France) wanted to turn the clock back to 1630, while the Protestants (supported by Sweden) pressed for 1618: in the end the peace congress annulled the Edict of Restitution and settled on a 'normative date' of 1624. Those who had fled their homes to avoid religious persecution since then received the right to return (thus granting, for the first time in European history, legal protection to religious refugees). The Congress also determined that, in future, any religious change required an 'amicable composition' between Catholics and Protestants, instead of a simple majority vote – a remarkable compromise in such a devout age.

Yet even after settling the crucial religious issues, the war dragged on for six more months while the French tried to extract a promise from the emperor that he would never again assist the Spanish Habsburgs, and the representatives of the Swedish army tried to extract 30 million thalers to pay its wage arrears. Perhaps unexpectedly, the second issue proved easier to resolve. On the one hand, after three decades of taxation, recession, depopulation and material destruction, it was obvious that the surviving inhabitants of Germany lacked the resources to raise such a sum; and in any case, as France's chief minister observed dryly, 'there are not enough coins minted in the whole of Germany to satisfy the claim' of the Swedish veterans.[47] On the other hand, the Little Ice Age indirectly facilitated a compromise, because appalling weather continued to afflict Germany. The summer of 1647 was exceptionally cold: according to a Spanish diplomat in Münster, July was 'like November' and in August 'the weather is so cold that it could be the end of October'. The winter that followed proved unusually long and hard – in March 1648, a Bavarian nun recorded that 'there came such a great cold spell that everyone might have frozen' – followed by an exceptionally wet summer.[48] The bedraggled Swedish troops eventually settled for 5 million thalers (1.8 million immediately in cash, 1.2 million in assignations and the remaining 2 million payable within two years), and with everything resolved, on 24 October, the 'plenipotentiaries' of the major states signed multiple copies of the complex 'peace instruments' that had taken so long to finalize. The news reached the Swedish troops besieging Prague on the 31st and the fighting there ceased immediately. The Thirty Years War was over.[49]

After so many years of fighting, news of the settlement at first seemed scarcely credible. A German poet in Nuremberg captured the surprise of many:

Something you never believed in
Has come to pass. What?
Will the camel pass through the Needle's Eye
Now that peace has returned to Germany?

Hans Heberle went to Ulm one last time to take part in the 'thanksgiving and joyous' festivities which, he claimed, 'were celebrated as vigorously and thoroughly as one ever did Holy Christmas'.[50] Over 40,000 copies of the peace agreement rolled off the printing presses and some of its provisions went into immediate effect: Protestants returned to the cities and territories from which they had been banned (provided Protestant worship had existed there in 1624), while church lands reclaimed under the Edict of Restitution changed hands again. Specific amnesties also took immediate effect. The son of Frederick of the Palatinate assumed a seat in the Electoral College, now expanded to eight, and those who had lost lands and property for supporting France or Sweden (although not those condemned for rebellion) received them back. Those who had sought refuge in Switzerland and elsewhere now returned.

Disengaging and disbanding the 200,000 troops under arms proved more difficult, not least because the soldiers continued to draw pay until the day of their demobilization: the Swedish army alone earned almost a million thalers a month, on top of the arrears agreed at Westphalia. Bad weather throughout northern Europe continued to complicate the task – widespread flooding ensued in spring 1649 when the snow eventually melted after 'a winter that lasted six months'; the following year, parts of central Germany experienced rain or snow on a record 226 days (compared with a twentieth-century maximum of 180 days of precipitation) – but eventually the war-weary German governments collected enough money to allow the foreign troops to begin a phased withdrawal, on prearranged days, from the areas they occupied. Swiss troops returned to Switzerland; French forces to France; and in October 1650 the Swedish high command embarked at Wismar (a Baltic port not far from Stralsund, where Gustavus Adolphus had landed just over 20 years before) and sailed home. They found their fatherland on the brink of revolution.

Denmark and Sweden on the Edge

The extreme weather that afflicted most of Germany throughout the 1640s also ruined harvests in Scandinavia, causing bread prices to climb far beyond the reach of families already weakened by two decades of war. A remarkable combination of adverse social, dynastic and constitutional circumstances then almost brought both the Swedish and Danish monarchies to their knees between 1648 and 1651. Denmark suffered more. Although Christian IV did not intervene directly in Germany after his defeat in 1629 (page 222 above), he could not resist the temptation to exploit the continental involvement of his rival Sweden and (as Axel Oxenstierna once joked) 'repeatedly chucked us under the chin to see if our teeth are firm in our heads'.[51] Then in 1643 the Swedish army in Germany invaded Jutland while another occupied all Danish territories east of the Sound, and the Swedish navy routed the Danes. These hammer blows forced Christian to accept a humiliating peace that ceded several Danish territories and, more significantly, virtual exemption from the Sound Tolls to Sweden. Although the king retained considerable personal prestige as a sort of national patriarch – few Danes could recall any other monarch, since he had reigned for 60 years – he now had to defer to the nobles on the Council of the Realm. Moreover, when he died in February 1648, Christian left a constitutional crisis because the Estates had not yet recognized a successor. Even though his oldest surviving son, Crown Prince Frederick, was the only viable candidate, the Council of the Realm (which according to tradition acted as the executive during an interregnum) delayed his election until he agreed to a coronation charter that forbade the monarch to involve the kingdom in foreign wars.

The new king faced a difficult task. To begin with, the recent Swedish occupation had caused widespread damage to farms and a sharp drop in agricultural production; now disastrous harvests almost doubled the price of bread, and most areas also suffered from plague. These natural disasters came on top of sharp economic setbacks. The end of the war in Germany led both to a sudden drop in foreign demand for Danish agricultural produce and to the return of many demobilized soldiers in need of domestic employment. Then the Council imposed heavy taxes to liquidate the debts of previous wars – taxes from which its members, by virtue of their noble status, were exempt. This combination drove many smaller landowners into debt as they raised capital to repair the damage of the war years and pay their taxes at a time when their profits plunged, creating a dangerous divide between the great nobles who ran the government and everyone else.

The climate also contributed to a remarkably similar crisis in the Swedish Monarchy. A prolonged period of cold weather had reduced crop yields and trade, and the harvest of 1650 'was the worst Sweden had known for fifty years, or was to know for near fifty more', and in March the Stockholm bakers fought each other at the city gates to secure some of the scarce flour.[52] As in Denmark, the harvest failure coincided with unprecedented fiscal pressure to liquidate the debts created by Sweden's 'continental war'. Although no foreign troops had crossed the frontiers of the kingdom and caused damage, the constant demand for taxes and recruits created widespread hardship. The remarkable territorial gains secured at Westphalia did not impress Gabriel Oxenstierna (brother of Axel and a member of the Swedish Council of the Realm): 'The common man wishes himself dead,' he opined. 'We may indeed say that we have conquered our lands from others, and to that end ruined our own', because although 'the branches expand, the tree withers at the roots'.[53]

Queen Christina, Gustavus Adolphus's daughter who came of age in 1644, did nothing to solve these problems. Not only did she spend vast sums on herself (court expenses soared from 3 per cent of the state budget in 1644 to 20 per cent in 1653), she also alienated so many crown lands that her revenues fell by one-third. Once her officers and soldiers returned from Germany, demanding their wage arrears and rewards for their services, 'donations were given faster than the land registers could record them [and] sometimes were given twice over'. Christina also doubled the number of noble families in Sweden within a decade, creating a new title almost every month. As in Denmark, such prodigality caused bitter divisions among the queen's subjects. So did the continuing political dominance of Axel Oxenstierna and his aristocratic allies, who by 1648 held 20 of the 25 seats on the Council, a concentration of power that provoked a spate of angry pamphlets.[54]

The opposition drew strength from the fact that Christina lacked an heir. After she made clear in 1649 that she did not intend to marry, she worked towards securing the succession for her cousin Charles Gustav (commander-in-chief of Sweden's troops in Germany), for which she required the approval of the Diet (*Riksdag*). The queen therefore summoned delegates to assemble in Stockholm in July 1650, despite the probability that they would seize the opportunity to air their numerous grievances.

The Swedish Diet, which included not only noble, clerical and urban chambers but also a peasant estate, began their 1650 session with a concerted attack by the representatives of the towns on the increased number and excessive privileges of the nobles. 'Do they want to introduce into Sweden the same servitude for men born free that prevails in Poland?' they asked indignantly. The clerical estate also criticized noble abuses. 'Is it just,' they demanded, 'that a small number of people should be the only ones to benefit from the return of peace, to the exclusion of the other groups who have contributed so powerfully, by sacrificing their lives and goods, and nonetheless must now live in servitude without enjoying the allure of liberty?' Both groups complained that the queen preferred to appoint nobles to all the best positions in Church and State, depriving them of valuable career opportunities – a development that caused especial frustration because, as in so many early modern states, Sweden now boasted more university graduates than ever before.[55]

The grievances of the peasants were both more vehement and more extensive. They complained not only of excessive demands from their lords (some claimed that their farms had to provide 500 and 600 days' service annually; others that they had to travel 100 miles to reach the place where they had to perform their services), but also about the alienation of crown lands, which delivered peasants to noble control. This not only decimated crown revenues, because the noble lands paid less tax (or no tax at all) to the state, but also reduced the size of the Estate of the Peasants in the Diet, because only peasants on crown lands could take part.[56] These issues proved a rallying cry for all three non-noble Estates because, in the words of Archbishop Lennaeus of Uppsala,

> When the nobility have all the peasants subject to themselves, then the Estate of Peasants will no longer have a voice at the Diet; and when the Estate of Peasants goes under, [the Estates of] Burghers and Clergy may easily go under too . . . ; and since the Estate of Nobles has all the land in the kingdom under its control, where is the crown's power? For he who owns the land is the ruler of the land.[57]

The three Estates therefore held joint meetings, forged common resolutions, claimed that the will of the majority of the four Estates should prevail, and refused to discuss the crown's proposals before it had redressed their grievances. Led by the burgomaster and town secretary of Stockholm (both lawyers), and the Historiographer Royal, they cloaked their demands in appeals to the 'Fundamental Laws' of the kingdom, and published them in a joint Supplication drawn up in October 1650. The document included demands 'that all without distinction shall enjoy equality before the law' and 'that all private prisons and torture . . . may be abolished'. No crown lands should be alienated in future, and those already alienated should be recovered if the Estates demanded it. The Supplication even condemned Sweden's foreign policy: 'What have we gained beyond the seas, if we lose our liberty at home?'[58]

Hundreds of printed copies of the Supplication circulated, serving as a rallying call to all opponents of the central government. One week later a delegation from the lower Estates of the Diet met Oxenstierna and the Council of the Realm, but the delegates' complaints about high taxes by the state and extensive abuses and exactions by their lords made little impression. On the former, Oxenstierna pointed out that 'wars were not what they are now': although in the past, the crown had financed its armed forces from domain revenues, 'The German War was a very different affair from any that preceded it: it needed more men, more ammunition, higher pay; and how far would the old revenues have gone in such circumstances?' When a peasant delegate complained that the lords 'take from us all that we have', another councillor blurted out 'You may complain of your burdens all you like; but I tell you that you have never had it better than now . . . Clergy, burghers and peasants, they are all in clover these days' – but then, recalling the appalling weather and failed harvests, he conceded 'though just at the moment, perhaps, they may be suffering some hardship as a result of the unexpected scarcity which prevails this year'. At this, Archbishop Lennaeus chimed in: 'What [the peasants] say is true, all the same; we know it, because whereas in former times there was a handsome income from tithes, they have now dropped very much. And I am afraid that there are more of those who treat the peasants badly than of those who help them. There are certainly grievances.'[59]

Yet the opposition failed to achieve any of its goals, mainly due to its lack of coordination. Sweden possessed no plausible alternative leader except Prince Charles Gustav, Christina's heir presumptive, and he had nothing to gain from overthrowing his cousin. The major nobles likewise had nothing to gain from overthrowing Christina, and in any case they had plenty of examples around them of where rebellion led. The Swedish council regularly received and discussed the latest news about the uprisings in other states – especially in England. According to one councillor, just as the troubles 'there in England originated with impatient priests, so it is also occurring here. It sets the worst possible example and does much harm.'[60]

Queen Christina skilfully exploited her critics' divisions. She won the nobles' goodwill by promising not to revoke the grants of crown land she had made to them. She divided the other Estates by offering limited concessions to each of them: the clergy received some of the privileges they asked for (such as a guarantee that the crown would favour only orthodox Lutheran theology); the leading townsmen were promised open access to some crown offices (albeit mostly in remote areas); and the peasants won some limitations on the labour services they could be required to perform for their lords. In October 1650 the deputies recognized Charles Gustav as heir presumptive and dispersed.

Although a political victory, the Diet proved a fiscal failure: only the general recovery of alienated crown land (a process known in Sweden as a *Reduktion*) could have solved the financial crisis facing the Swedish Monarchy. Therefore, despite imposing new indirect taxes, the queen could not pay the wages of her soldiers, sailors and household servants, and she lacked any resources for relief when the harvest of 1652 failed all over Scandinavia. Shouts of 'Death to the nobles' and 'Devil take the bailiffs' soon rang out and, in one area, the peasants elected a 'king', with councillors, and drew up a list of nobles whom they intended to murder; but when Christina sent troops to repress the insurgency, the peasant king ended up broken on a wheel while his councillors (one of them a priest) were hanged.[61]

An ambassador who travelled through the areas affected by the uprising remarked on the overall poverty of the population, the neglect of the roads and the dead animals in the fields; and one might wonder why these dire conditions failed to provoke broader unrest. The central government believed that the answer lay in its military system. 'The only means to keep the peasant under discipline is conscription,' according to one councillor: that is, the constant forced migration of Swedish and Finnish young men to fight on the continent removed both potential leaders and marginal (and therefore dangerous) elements.[62] The detailed records of the parish of Bygdeå (which, with only 1,800 inhabitants scattered over 1,200 square miles, was already thinly populated) give some idea of the impact. The parish had 500 adult males in 1620 but 20 years later only 365, whereas the number of adult females rose from 600 to 655. Moreover, all but 14 of the 230 men who left for Germany during those two decades died there.[63]

Although the detailed records of Bygdeå end in 1639, data from other parts of the Swedish Monarchy reveal the heavy cost of conscription elsewhere. Of the 25,000 Swedish and Finnish soldiers sent to Germany in 1630 and 1631, more than half died within two years; and of over 1,000 conscripts in one regiment within that same period, one-third died of disease, one-sixth died of wounds, and one-eighth deserted. As young men began to realize that military service was virtually a sentence of death, recruiting efforts faltered. Thus, over the course of the Thirty Years War, Finland supplied some 25,000 young men to fight on the continent – equivalent to perhaps one-quarter of its total adult males – but although six conscription drives in Viborg province during the 1630s produced some 4,000 men, eight drives in the 1640s produced fewer than 3,500, and eight more in the 1650s produced fewer than 2,500. Those who managed to avoid the draft included deserters (some 'hid in the forest' before the first muster, others fled during the march to the coast), the injured (some of them clearly with a self-inflicted wound), and the sick – including the unusual if not unique claim of Jakob Göransson who, when conscripted in 1630, asserted that 'every month he has a period like a woman and during that time he lies as if he were dead'.[64] Yet whether they served, deserted or menstruated, no conscript could take part in peasant insurgency. The war that ruined so much of Germany probably provided a safety valve for both Finland and Sweden and thus paved the way for the abdication of Christina and the peaceful succession in 1654 of her cousin as King Charles X Gustav.

The Second Crisis of the Dutch Republic

As soon as peace was concluded with Spain in 1648, some inhabitants of the Dutch Republic looked back on the war years with nostalgia. 'War, which has made all other lands and countries poor, made you rich,' wrote one pamphleteer in 1650: 'Your country used to overflow with silver and gold; the peace [with Spain] makes you poor.'[65] At first sight, such claims seem ridiculous. By the 1640s, almost 90 per cent of the total expenditure of the Dutch Republic went on defence, creating a huge tax burden, above all in the form of indirect taxes: in the city of Leiden, excise duties accounted for 60 per cent of the price of beer and 25 per cent of the price of bread. Still, revenues fell far short of the Republic's military and naval spending: between 1618 and 1649, the debt of the States of Holland soared from under 5 million to almost 150 million. At the same time, the war had harmed the Republic's economy in other important respects. Villages near the frontiers paid 'protection money' to enemy garrisons or else risked being ravaged; merchants who shipped goods abroad risked having them confiscated; privateers in Spanish service not only caused serious direct losses – in 1642 alone, they captured 138 Dutch ships – but also forced up freight and insurance rates.

Many in the Republic, led by the States of Holland (which, thanks to its critical role in financing the war, had regained some of the power lost in 1618: page 219 above), therefore favoured a settlement with Philip IV. In 1635 France had declared war on Spain and, in concert with the Dutch, launched an immediate assault on Philip's possessions in the Netherlands. Although French forces made little progress before 1640, thereafter they made some major gains. Each victory caused alarm in the Republic. 'France, enlarged by possession of the Spanish Netherlands, will be a dangerous neighbour for our country,' declared the States of Holland; it would be 'Hannibal at the gates' echoed a pamphleteer.[66] Popular opinion shifted towards concluding peace before Spanish power collapsed totally. Nevertheless, hammering out a settlement acceptable both to the Stadholder, now Maurice's brother Frederick Henry, and to all seven provinces, proved difficult. Zealand held out (mainly because its privateers prospered from the war) but after prolonged haggling, in January 1646 the delegates of the other six provinces left for Münster in Westphalia, headquarters of the Spanish delegation at the peace congress.

From the first Philip IV's negotiators assured the Dutch that their master was now ready to concede full sovereignty to the Republic. They also slyly leaked a French proposal to marry the young Louis XIV to a Spanish princess, with the Netherlands as her dowry. This duplicity, as well as the spectre of the French just across the border, accelerated Dutch willingness to talk. Philip was by then prepared 'to give in on every point that might lead to the conclusion of a settlement' – indeed, according to an unsympathetic observer, he was so desperate for peace that 'if necessary he would crucify Christ again in order to achieve it'.[67] Spain therefore proposed a new truce, to last 12 or 20 years; the Dutch countered with a list of 71 conditions, almost all of which Philip IV accepted. The States of Holland therefore recommended that the States-General upgrade the talks from a truce to a full peace. Again, Zealand dissented and again it was overruled: in November 1646, by six votes to one, the Dutch agreed to work for peace, and two months later the two parties signed a provisional agreement that ended both the fighting and the economic sanctions.

Almost immediately, a run of bad harvests in the Republic drove up food prices and created popular pressure for the tax reductions that only peace could bring. At the same time, the ceasefire on both land and sea caused a surge in Dutch trade and this too fuelled pressure within the Republic for a permanent settlement that would perpetuate such prosperity. Naturally the French tried desperately to derail the peace initiative, creating (in the phrase of a dispirited Spanish diplomat) 'an artificial labyrinth, constructed in such a way that those who allow themselves to be led into it can never find the exit'.[68] Ironically for a cardinal of the Catholic Church, Mazarin concentrated his efforts on wooing the Dutch Calvinist clergy, some 1,200 in number, almost all of them implacably opposed to a peace with Spain. The death of Frederick Henry in March 1647 provided a new ally because his son and successor as Stadholder, William II, also strongly opposed the peace; nevertheless, the States-General approved the final agreement and, after another round of fruitless bargaining to secure Zealand's consent, in May 1648 at Münster the delegates of Spain and of six Dutch provinces solemnly swore to uphold a permanent peace. The longest revolt in European history was over.

Supporters of the settlement predicted glittering prosperity, universal harmony and even a new Golden Age as soon as the war ended; some improvements duly occurred – freight and insurance rates declined even further; trade with Spain, Spanish Italy and Spanish America soared – but the benefits accrued mostly to the merchants of Holland. The rest of the Republic's citizens may have been – and certainly felt – worse off in 1648–50 than before. To begin with, they suffered the same appalling weather as other parts of the world: in some areas it rained every day between April and November 1648, so that the hay and grain rotted in the fields – a local bard wrote a poem entitled 'The rainy weather of the year 1648' – and then came six months of frost and snow during which the canals froze over, stopping all barge traffic. Many complained of 'the winter that lasted six months'. The summer of 1649 was also unusually wet, and the summer of 1650 unusually cold. Between 1648 and 1651, grain prices in the Republic stood at their highest level for a century.[69]

Paradoxically, peace with Spain intensified the impact of poor harvests in frontier regions. As soon as the fighting ceased, the central government reduced the garrisons in the fortified towns in the east and south, and since the Dutch state normally paid its troops in full and on time, the dramatic reduction in military consumers put many local suppliers (especially tailors, saddle-makers, boot-makers and innkeepers) out of business.[70] Zealand also suffered because the province had invested heavily in creating a colony in northwest Brazil, and its leaders acquiesced to peace with Spain only in return for promises of aid from their neighbours against the Brazilian settlers still loyal to Portugal. An expeditionary force duly set out, but the Portuguese settlers routed it (see chapter 15 below).

This major setback led Zealand to view with favour proposals to renew the war on Spain made by three other influential protagonists: France, the House of Orange, and the Calvinist clergy. Desperate for a second front that would divert the Spanish Army of Flanders, Mazarin tried to persuade William II (Stadholder of five of the provinces after Frederick Henry's death in 1647) and his cousin William Frederick (Stadholder of the other two provinces) to engineer a rupture. Since the Stadholders' authority arose in large part from their command over the troops of the Republic, the reduction in army size (from 60,000 in 1643 to 35,000 in 1648 and to 29,000 in 1650) drastically diminished their power. Demands by the States of Holland for yet more military economies angered William. The States also angered the Calvinist clergy, the third group opposed to the peace, because they refused to pass laws that promoted Protestantism and restricted Catholic worship in the lands newly acquired from Spain. To gain support for his own agenda, like his uncle Maurice a generation before, William II posed as a champion of Calvinism.

The year 1650 saw another torrent of polemical Dutch pamphlets, many of them written by Calvinist pastors who blamed the peace for all subsequent misfortunes. 'War caused all industry and trade to grow and prosper; peace makes them wither and decline,' one asserted. Moreover, 'War became a bond of union and unity; peace brings quarrels and disunity.' Ever since the fighting stopped, the anonymous author continued relentlessly, the price of food had risen to unprecedented heights. 'Do we not see those towns that prospered most during the war decline during the peace – their industry lost, their merchants diminished, many of their houses up for sale?' He also claimed (as did some clerics in their sermons) that even the weather revealed God's disapproval of peace with Spain: had it not rained almost incessantly ever since?[71] Such crude propaganda found its mark: in March 1650 the Spanish ambassador in The Hague warned his government that 'the common people certainly do not like the peace, blaming it for all the shortages they suffer, especially that of grain, without remembering the sterility of past years'.[72]

The ambassador was unaware that William II had already decided to exploit the general discontent to his own advantage. In October 1649 he confided to his cousin William Frederick that, unless the States of Holland ceased to insist on further reductions in the armed forces, he intended to eliminate its leaders, above all the magistrates of Amsterdam. He sponsored pamphlets that criticized their policies: the lack of help for Brazil, the refusal to ban Catholic priests in the new conquests, and the failure to provide cheap bread. Unbowed, in May 1650 the States of Holland ordered several more units on their payroll to disband; the next day, the prince instructed the units' commanders to disregard these orders and complained to the States-General – where Holland had but one vote among seven – about the province's usurpation of his power. As in 1618, the States-General authorized the prince to visit each town in Holland and remove every magistrate who had opposed him. Amsterdam offered to negotiate an agreement over troop reductions, but when the prince refused, it composed a statement that reminded everyone that the Stadholder was the servant of the state and not its master. William, it argued, must accept Holland's order for troop reductions so that everyone could 'enjoy the fruits of the present peace, which the further retention of an unnecessary and unregulated militia would make impossible'.[73]

Outraged by such defiance, on 30 July 1650 the prince arrested and imprisoned his leading critics in the States of Holland, believing that his cousin William Frederick and 12,000 soldiers had just forced their way into Amsterdam – but contingency had disrupted his plan. The previous night, a large part of the troops destined for the operation lost their way in a thunderstorm and arrived at the rendezvous thoroughly soaked. While they dried out, a postal courier bound for Amsterdam rode by and (since the troops had no orders to detain passers-by) managed to warn the city. Thanks to this extraordinary chance, by the time William Frederick and his men finally arrived, the magistrates had armed the citizens, closed all the gates and flooded the moat around the city.

When William of Orange heard the news he retired to his room, stamped his feet and threw his hat on the floor; but after his tantrum subsided, he decided to see whether a personal appearance might intimidate Amsterdam. He joined his troops outside the walls, and after a few days the city meekly agreed to surrender its outspoken magistrates and acknowledged the Stadholder's sole right to issue orders to the army, to determine troop levels, and to decide foreign policy. William, with his domestic base secure, now issued an ultimatum to Philip IV: unless Spain immediately opened peace talks with France, the Dutch Republic would attack.

Once again, contingency disrupted his plan. The victorious prince took to his bed, stricken by smallpox, and on 6 November 1650 he died of it. Since he lacked an acknowledged heir, his new-found powers – and his threat of a new war with Spain – died with him. The States of Holland immediately freed their imprisoned colleagues and invited representatives from all the provinces to join them in a special session of the States-General, armed with full authority to fill the unprecedented constitutional vacuum.

Even before the 'Great Assembly' met in January 1651, the States of Holland took several revolutionary steps. Above all, they resolved not to appoint a Stadholder for the province and instead made clear that all troops within the province took their orders from them. In the absence of a Stadholder, the States also permitted the patrician elite of each town to choose their own magistrates and name their representatives to the States. The 'Great Assembly' both confirmed these initiatives and introduced some more. It appointed a Holland nobleman 'Field Marshal' of the Republic's army, and reduced the autonomy of the military: henceforth courts martial would try only military offences (such as desertion and disobedience), leaving soldiers accused of all other crimes to be tried by civil courts. In religious affairs, the States granted freedom of worship to Catholics and Jews; and, although they agreed to tolerate non-Calvinist churches only where they already existed, this effectively guaranteed toleration for all who desired it. Finally, the assembly's sensible decision to ignore pleas to prosecute those who had promoted William II's agenda restored the domestic harmony imperilled by the controversies of the previous four years.

This constitutional revolution received widespread praise – the philosopher Baruch Spinoza termed it 'the System of True Liberty' – and it brought unprecedented prosperity to most parts of the Republic for a generation. Nevertheless, it suffered from two linked weaknesses: the very prosperity of the Dutch provoked envy and attacks by its neighbours; and, without a Stadholder to coordinate military and naval operations, the Republic had difficulty in winning its wars. Thus when Britain attacked in 1652, the Dutch navy lost almost every battle; while the following year, although Dutch success in closing off both the Baltic and the Mediterranean to English shipping led to peace in 1654, that same year, the last Dutch outposts in Brazil surrendered to Portugal. The Republic did rather better when Britain attacked again in 1664, but the spectacular raid that destroyed or captured several English warships at anchor in the River Medway scarcely compensated for the loss of New Netherland, the last Dutch outpost in North America. Then, in 1672, Britain attacked a third time, this time in alliance with France.

Dutch forces crumbled before the invasion of Louis XIV at the head of 130,000 troops and one month later, the States-General reversed its position on civil-military relations and reluctantly appointed William III, posthumous son of the late prince of Orange and now aged 22, commander of its army and navy. It was almost too late: having captured every Dutch town in his path with scarcely a struggle, in June 1672 Louis entered Utrecht in triumph. As urban riots rocked Holland, the remaining delegates in the States-General voted to surrender on ignominious terms. Luckily for them, Louis rejected their offer and demanded more, allowing Prince William to restore order, and to focus the energy of everyone on resisting the French – but his efforts might have failed without a sudden change in the weather. Extreme drought in the spring of 1672 had facilitated the French invasion by reducing the level of the Rhine and other rivers so that the French cavalry could wade across and create a bridgehead, allowing the king's engineers to build bridges for the infantry. The drought also prevented the Dutch from using their ultimate defensive strategy: opening the dikes to create a water barrier between Holland and the French. Until mid-July, the water rose painfully slowly. Then torrential rain fell, rendering all routes into Holland impassable, and at the end of the month Louis left Utrecht and returned home. Under the firm hand of William III, Dutch naval and military organization steadily improved until first England (1674) and then France (1678) made peace.[74]

Louis XIV did not accept failure gracefully, especially since the peace of 1678 included important economic concessions that favoured Dutch merchants trading with France. In the course of 1687, Louis rescinded almost all these concessions, drastically increasing tariffs on some Dutch imports and totally banning others; and, since France was the largest market for many Dutch goods, the effects on the Republic were both immediate and serious. In summer 1688 the French ambassador in The Hague warned his master that 'the trade of Holland is reduced by more than a quarter, and the population is severely affected and extremely angry with France'. Moreover, he added, many of the Republic's leaders favoured a reciprocal ban on French imports, even if this brought with it the risk of war.[75] Prince William and his advisers began to discuss what to do in the worst-case scenario: a repeat of the joint attack by France and Britain in 1672; but developments in each neighbouring state brought salvation.

In 1685 the Elector Palatine, grandson of Frederick, died without male heirs, but recognized his closest male relative as his successor. This did not satisfy Louis XIV, who claimed a share of the Palatinate on behalf of his brother, married to the late Elector's sister, and in September 1688 French forces crossed the Rhine to enforce his demands, capturing or devastating the whole Palatinate. Although the invasion was thus a tactical triumph, it proved a strategic disaster, because it not only turned virtually all German rulers into France's enemies but also distracted Louis from noting the invitation sent by some of James II's English subjects to William, begging him to invade before the end of the year. Louis warned the Dutch leaders that should they attack His Britannic Majesty, France would immediately attack them, but the invasion of Germany meant that he lacked the resources to make good his threat. Instead, William III managed to assemble a fleet of almost 500 vessels and an army of over 40,000 troops for the invasion – and still leave enough ships and soldiers behind to defend the Republic. They had gained control of all England by Christmas, and, although Louis declared war, the new ruler of Great Britain and the Dutch Republic forged alliances with Spain, the Holy Roman Emperor and other German rulers explicitly to deprive France of all its gains since the Peace of the Pyrenees. Although the Republic remained at war with France for most of the next 25 years, it survived as an independent state for over a century.

The 'Swiss Revolution'

The Dutch Republic was not the only state that prospered during – and partly because of – the Thirty Years War: another beneficiary was the Swiss confederation. In 1648, although the Peace of Westphalia stopped short of granting the 13 Swiss cantons (and some associated territories) sovereign status, it recognized their 'exemption' from the laws and institutions of the Holy Roman Empire – in effect making them independent. This did not, however, make them unified: each canton maintained a unique relationship with the others. The million or so inhabitants of the confederation spoke four different languages (German, French, Italian and Romansch, with many dialects of each) and professed different creeds (some were Catholics; most belonged to one of the Protestant creeds; a few had lords of one faith and subjects of another). Political and economic divisions also existed. On the one hand, in most cantons a single town dominated the countryside, controlling production and collecting taxes for its own benefit. On the other, despite the harsh environment (70 per cent of Switzerland is mountain), the economic boom and milder climate of the sixteenth century encouraged both the cultivation of new lands and specialization in the production of hardy cash crops such as hemp and flax for export.

When the hero of Hans von Grimmelshausen's novel *Simplicissimus* managed to escape the Thirty Years War and cross into Switzerland, he described a country that

> Seemed so strange to me in comparison with other German lands that I might have been in Brazil or China. I saw the people there buying and selling in peace; the stables full of cattle; the farmhouses full of chicken, geese and ducks; the roads safe for travellers; the inns full of people making merry. There was absolutely no fear of the enemy, no worries about being plundered, and no dread of losing goods, and life or limb . . . So I considered this country to be an earthly paradise.[76]

Grimmelshausen exaggerated. Climatic deterioration raised food prices in many Swiss cantons to their highest level for two centuries in 1636–41; and between 1642 and 1650, agricultural prices fell on average to at least half their former value. But as long as the Thirty Years War lasted, men who could no longer make a living from farming found highly paid employment as mercenaries abroad, and the wages and booty which they acquired boosted the Swiss home economy.[77] The war in Germany affected Switzerland in two other ways. First, it benefited several towns because it caused a massive influx of refugees who brought with them both wealth and economic skills: by 1638, the 7,500 refugees in the city of Basel almost outnumbered the native residents. Second, in 1633 and again in 1638 German armies violated Swiss neutrality, leading several cities to embark on an expensive defence programme, building or improving their fortifications and increasing the number of their defenders.

Until 1648, the prosperity created by the Thirty Years War made such military spending bearable; but while the Peace of Westphalia brought security, it ended prosperity. German demand for Swiss produce, including soldiers, plunged; and the refugees from Germany returned home, causing a collapse in both urban house prices and overall tax revenues. Coincidentally France, which had paid the cantons a 'retainer' both to hold troops as a strategic reserve and to prevent them from serving another power, defaulted on its payments because of its own fiscal problems (see chapter 10). Finally, Switzerland experienced the same disastrous weather and ruined harvests as other parts of western Europe.

As in the Dutch Republic, many people in Switzerland now began to look back on the Thirty Years War as a Golden Age. 'During the war years,' the peasants of Canton Basel complained to their rulers in 1651, '[we] were able to sell a great variety of harvested crops at a high price and in considerable quantities above and beyond what was required for the maintenance of our households.' Fearing that 'the worst that can possibly happen to us approaches', they begged their magistrates to abolish all excise duties and to reduce interest rates.[78] The peasants of Basel did not exaggerate: between 1644 and 1654 prices in northern Switzerland fell by about 75 per cent, while those who had borrowed money during the prosperous years now found it hard to pay interest, let alone repay capital. The appearance in 1652 in the skies above Switzerland of a bright comet whose tail seemed like a 'flaming sword' led the local pastors, as they had done in 1618, to claim that it was a warning from God of disasters to come. And disaster duly came: in a desperate attempt to cope with the sudden economic crisis, the northern cantons (the ones hardest hit by the fall in German demand) debased their currencies by 50 per cent. The 'Swiss revolution' began two weeks later.[79]

In January 1653, 40 local officials in the isolated Entlebuch valley south of Luzern met in secret to discuss the economic crisis caused by the increase in taxes and the devaluation. They voted to send a delegation led by Hans Emmenegger, the senior magistrate (and one of the richest inhabitants), to request emergency relief from the cantonal authorities in Luzern. The delegates met with a total refusal: any concession to the peasants, such as reduction of debt interest or rural taxes, would adversely affect the wealthy citizens among whom they lived (and of course the magistrates themselves). Instead, the canton authorities mustered their militia companies.

This was a rash move. Luzern boasted some 4,000 citizens, of whom scarcely a quarter could bear arms – far fewer than the peasants of Entlebuch. Moreover, several neighbouring areas had recently experienced collective violence, including Canton Bern (1641) and Canton Zürich (1644–5); and, just across the border, the archbishopric of Salzburg (1645–7), Upper Austria (1648) and Styria (1650) – but in each case the government soon regained control and imposed draconian penalties on those who had 'raised the banners' (*Fähnlilups*: the traditional call to collective resistance in the Alpine regions). These successes led the magistrates of Luzern to underestimate the threat in Entlebuch.[80]

They were not alone in their complacency. In his letters of December 1652, the French ambassador to the confederation stressed the 'profound tranquillity which these cantons have enjoyed for so long'; and even when reporting 'the devaluation of the copper currency', he added that, although in other parts of Europe 'this could produce some unrest, people here act very slowly in everything'.[81] The ambassador overlooked some important local circumstances: the people of Entlebuch felt unusual confidence that, despite the failure of popular revolts elsewhere, their own resistance would prosper. First, the valley possessed not only a papal privilege to place the 'weapons of Christ' on its coat of arms and seal, as a constant reminder that God would protect them, but also a fragment of the True Cross, universally taken as another sign of special protection. Second, like everyone else in Switzerland, the inhabitants of Entlebuch knew by heart the story of William Tell, who had successfully defied the region's brutal governor in the past – a powerful reassurance that resistance in a just cause could succeed. The rebels entitled their political anthem 'The new song of William Tell, made in the Entlebuch in 1653'.[82] Finally, the valley possessed a considerable measure of political and religious autonomy, a cadre of experienced and respected leaders and a well-developed communications network that facilitated rapid mobilization.

On 26 February 1653 a gathering of peasants from all over the region approved a manifesto drafted by Hans Emmenegger that blamed their desperate situation on a synergy of human and natural factors:

The common farmer can scarcely hold on to his house and home, let alone pay his mortgage, debts and interest on them, or support his wife and children ... Drought or the loss of horses or cattle has forced people to leave their houses and homes, to give up their property and to move to a distant place to make their living.

Later that day, the assembled peasants swore to oppose the policies imposed on them by the authorities in Luzern. In particular they demanded the restoration of currency at its former value and permission to pay interest on their debts in kind instead of in cash.[83] Peasant communities in Cantons Bern, Basel and Solothurn as well as Luzern soon took up the call, and over two thousand men from the four cantons attended an assembly that drew up a 'letter of union' (*Bundesbrief*) demanding a return to the 'eternal, God-given and inviolable laws' of Switzerland and the abolition of all innovations (a shrewd ploy, since a *Bundesbrief* of 1291 between three cantons formed the founding document of the entire Confederation). The assembly also declared that henceforth no one would pay interest on their debts or tithes (another shrewd move that improved the insurgents' liquidity while simultaneously harming that of the towns). Finally, the assembly amalgamated all militia units, creating a force of 24,000 men, and elected a council of war to direct its efforts. While some units attacked isolated castles belonging to their lords, the main peasant army laid siege to Luzern.

Magistrates all over Switzerland now began to panic. Whereas in January 1653 their official correspondence (both with the federal authorities and with each other) had mentioned 'unrest', the following month they wrote of 'revolt' and in April of a 'general uprising', a 'general conspiracy' and a 'revolution' that aimed at 'the extermination of our confederate state'.[84] In May the authorities in Canton Bern made concessions that secured a separate peace with their rebellious subjects, and groups of insurgents elsewhere also made the best terms they could until only Entlebuch remained in revolt. This allowed the magistrates of Luzern to defeat their rebellious subjects and hunt down the survivors. The process proved protracted, given the mountainous terrain, but by the end of the year all resistance had collapsed and scores of peasant leaders had been tortured and executed.[85]

Nevertheless, the rebels won some lasting gains. Before 1653, Swiss city magistrates and the federal government had reduced (and, where possible, abolished) the participation of the peasants in the political process; they had sought to restrict local industry by imposing guild control over rural workers; and they had used the courts to overrule local traditions and customs with newly passed laws that, naturally, favoured citizens over peasants (for example, by protecting creditors rather than debtors). The 'Swiss Revolution' arrested this development. At the federal level, even victory over the rebels failed to produce absolutism: the cantons did not even create a single political structure until 1803. Political and economic power therefore remained with the cantonal authorities, and the towns in which they resided. These now created a more 'paternalist' state in which taxes on peasant farmers remained low, rural industry enjoyed exemption from guild rules and local communities retained their customs, traditions and autonomy. All this created a favourable environment for the development of proto-industrialization and a democratic state. Although Hans Emmenegger never became a local hero like his contemporary Masaniello, he and his associates won far more permanent concessions.

The Danes 'forge their own chains'

After the humiliating concessions extracted in return for his coronation in 1648, Frederick III of Denmark worked hard to reach a better relationship with his subjects, and in spring 1657 he persuaded both the Council of the Realm and the Diet to authorize a declaration of war against Sweden, since Charles X appeared to be mired in a simultaneous war against Poland and Russia (see chapter 6 above). The war almost cost Frederick his kingdom. Charles left Poland at once to deal with his new enemy, marched across Germany and occupied much of Jutland. The Swedes had planned an amphibious attack on Copenhagen, but the onset of one of the coldest winters of the Little Ice Age in mid-December suggested another possibility. According to an English diplomat at the scene,

> the extraordinary violent frost was by this time increased to such a degree, that the Little Belt which divides Jutland from the isle of Funen was so intensely frozen, as suggested to the Swedish king an enterprise (full of hazard, but not disagreeable to a fearless mind edged with ambition) of marching over the ice into Funen with horse, foot and cannon.

The astonished Danish defenders 'made large cuts in the ice' but they soon 'congealed again' because of the extreme cold. The Swedes therefore stormed ashore and swept all before them because 'Funen [and] the other Danish isles are all open and unfortified, and have no defensible places'. For the first time in European history, meteorologists now decided military strategy: they persuaded Charles to disregard the misgivings of his senior officers and follow the itinerary where they indicated that the ice had frozen hard enough to allow some 8,000 Swedish veterans with their artillery to cross from Funen to Zeeland, and to advance upon Copenhagen.[86]

Although the Danish capital lacked the strength to resist a siege, Charles (ignorant of its weakness) granted an immediate ceasefire in return for Frederick's promise to cede almost half his kingdom to Sweden and to send military and financial assistance to Charles's campaign in Poland. It is easy to see why the boastful legend on the campaign medal minted by Charles claimed *Natura hoc debuit uni* ('Nature owed this to me'); but pride came before a fall. Realizing in 1659 that Frederick had no intention of sending him the promised assistance, Charles determined to reduced Denmark 'to the position of a province of Sweden': its nobility would be exiled, its recalcitrant bishops replaced with docile Swedes and its university 'moved to Göteborg' (on the Swedish side of the Sound). But before he could attempt these ambitious goals, the redoubtable Charles X suddenly died, leaving a 4-year-old son under a regency council. A few months later the two governments concluded a treaty that obliged the Swedes to restore a few of the lands they had captured, but advanced their frontier permanently to the Sound. Never again would Denmark be able to control shipping entering and leaving the Baltic.

Frederick III nevertheless faced other serious problems. The adverse weather (of which the frozen Baltic was merely the most memorable extreme event) had drastically reduced harvests and this shortfall, coinciding with a plague epidemic and enemy occupation, left many areas devastated and depopulated. The total population of Jutland and the home islands fell by about a fifth between 1643 and 1660; some parishes claimed that three-quarters of their farms lay abandoned; and almost half the Danish clergy died between 1659 and 1662. In addition, the war had created huge debts. To address these issues, Frederick III ordered the representatives of the nobles, the towns and the clergy to assemble in Copenhagen in September 1660.

All members of the Danish Diet agreed that the kingdom's fiscal crisis could be solved only by reducing spending and raising taxes – but here consensus ended. The representatives of the burghers and clergy insisted on creating new excise taxes to be paid by everyone without exception, but the nobles insisted on exemption. After four weeks of haggling, on 14 October 1660 a group of outraged clerics and citizens proposed extensive reforms to the prevailing political system, including the abolition of the elective character of the Monarchy in favour of the hereditary principle – a move that would involve a revocation of Frederick's 1648 coronation charter and thus of the privileged position enjoyed by the nobility. It seems likely that the authors of this revolutionary proposal meant it merely as a tactical manoeuvre to scare the nobles into agreeing to pay their share of the new taxes, but the king and his courtiers swiftly exploited their unexpected opportunity. One week later, Frederick doubled the guards on the capital's ramparts and closed its gates, ordering all ships to stand off so that no one in the city could leave.

The nobility promptly crumbled, and on 23 October 1660 delegates of all three Estates gathered in the royal palace and offered Frederick full hereditary rights. The king graciously accepted, ending over a century of aristocratic dominance, and appointed a constitutional commission to propose the necessary changes to perpetuate his new status. After a couple of days, however, the commissioners obsequiously declared that Frederick himself should formulate a new constitution. The Diet agreed, asking only that the king should not dismember the kingdom or change its faith, and that he should respect the ancient privileges (without specifying which). On 28 October, Frederick received the unconditional homage of his people: the Danish Diet would not meet again for two centuries.

The king and his advisers now remodelled the central government (ironically imitating the system of the hated Swedes) with administrative 'colleges', a supreme court to replace the judicial functions previously exercised by the Council of the Realm, and an army raised through conscription. Frederick also sold almost half the crown lands to pay off his war debts and introduced new taxes, direct as well as indirect, which the nobles had to pay along with everyone else. In 1665 the new 'absolute and hereditary monarchy' received its definitive form in the Royal Law (*Kongelov*), a constitution that remained in force until 1849 (making it the longest-lasting constitution in modern European history). The king received 'supreme power and authority to make laws and ordinances according to his own good will, to expound, to alter, to add and take from, indeed simply to abrogate laws previously made by himself or by his forefathers and also to exempt what and whom he pleases from the general authority of the law'. Other clauses gave the crown 'the supreme power and authority to appoint and dismiss all officials, high and low'; 'supreme power over the clergy, from the highest to the lowest'; and sole 'control over the armed forces and the raising of arms, the right to wage war, to conclude and dissolve alliances with whom and when he sees fit, and to impose duties and other levies'.[87]

Frederick III had thus achieved in Denmark by popular consent what many of his fellow monarchs failed to win by force. Thirty years later Robert Molesworth, sometime British ambassador in Copenhagen, still found it hard to believe that 'in four days' time' an entire kingdom had 'changed from an estate little differing from aristocracy to as absolute a monarchy as any is at present in the world'. In Molesworth's cruel jibe, 'To the [Danish] people remained *the glory of having forged their own chains*, and the advantages of obeying without reserve: a happiness which I suppose no Englishman will ever envy them.' They were now 'all as absolute slaves as the negroes are in Barbados; but with this difference, that their fare is not so good'.[88]

The Second Serfdom

Molesworth might have penned similar insults about Denmark's eastern neighbours, Mecklenburg, Pomerania and Brandenburg, where relative depopulation caused by a generation of war forced each state to enact legislation intended both to increase the labour services required from its peasants and to terminate their freedom of movement: as in Russia, fugitive serf laws empowered landowners to pursue, recover and punish all who escaped.

The 'Second Serfdom' in eastern Europe

State	Year in which the courts deprived peasants of freedom of movement
Ducal Prussia	1633
Mecklenburg and Pomerania	1645
Brandenburg	1653

Although exceptions existed – some lords freed serfs after long service or as a reward for bravery in warfare, while others did so because they believed compulsory servitude to be wrong – serfdom soon became as basic to the economy of eastern Europe as slavery had been to that of the Roman empire. In Brandenburg, all the children of serfs could be required to work as household servants of their lord; in Danish Holstein, peasants produced not only grain, wool, butter, cheese and horses for their lord, but even took his ships to sea and caught herring and other fish for him to sell to merchants; and so on. Historians have termed this process the 'second serfdom'.

Even in areas of central Europe far from the Baltic, the demographic and economic collapse caused by the Thirty Years War reduced peasant power. In the past, feudal courts across Germany had heard cases brought by peasant communities and, in many if not most cases, redressed their grievances: they reduced taxes, restricted labour services, pardoned opposition and even (in extreme cases) permitted a change in ruler. This sympathetic attitude steadily evaporated after 1618. The history of the duchy of Friedland in Bohemia, once ruled by Wallenstein, is instructive. Its manorial court records, which have survived in large numbers, show that although in the 1620s peasant communities brought hundreds of complaints before the duke's judges, the number steadily dwindled. Villagers lost the freedom to migrate, to marry, or to divide their inheritances without their lord's explicit consent; they also found that the ducal courts no longer heard their protests about abuse from local oligarchs but instead referred them back to the community. In the words of a judgment in 1676, in 'conflicts which are of *no importance*, the village headman and jury shall bring about a settlement out there [in the village], and the parties shall be satisfied, in order that so many people [in court] do not need to attend to a few unimportant persons.'[89] These changes delivered weaker villagers, especially women and outsiders, into the hands of their stronger neighbours who dominated the courts, while it maintained intact the lord's complete economic, fiscal and legal control over all his subjects. By the eighteenth century, the second serfdom had turned each noble estate (in the words of the Prussian reformer Baron Stein) into 'the den of a predator which lays waste everything around it and surrounds itself with the silence of the grave.'[90]

'The all-destructive fury of the Thirty Years War': A Myth?[91]

The survivors of the Thirty Years War who recorded their experience had no intention of surrounding themselves with 'the silence of the grave'. On the contrary, Maria Anna Junius, a nun in Bamberg, kept a chronicle specifically 'so that when pious sisters come after us who know nothing of these distressed and difficult times, they can see what we poor sisters suffered and endured, with the grace and help of God, during these long years of war'. Near Berlin, the tax official Peter Thiele concluded his account: 'Our descendants can discover from this how we were harassed, and see what a terribly distressed time it was. May they take this to heart and guard themselves against sin, begging God for mercy so that they may be spared such dread.' In Hessen, farmer Casper Preis lamented that 'to tell of all the misery and misfortune [of the war years] is not within my power, not even what I know and have seen myself'; and in any case, he added, even 'if I did report everything which I have seen and so painfully experienced, no-one living in a better age would believe it' because 'the times were awful beyond measure'. Pastor Johann Daniel Minck, also living in Hessen, wrote in his journal that 'without such records . . . those who come after us will never believe what miseries we have suffered'; while his neighbour Pastor Lorenz Ludolf predicted that 'Whoever has not himself seen and lived through such circumstances cannot believe what I note here.'[92]

Such eyewitness accounts are extremely vivid – but how typical were they? To begin with, of the tens of millions of Germans who lived through the war, the accounts of fewer than 250 eyewitnesses have survived; moreover, of these we know that 226 authors were male and only 9 female. Protestant pastors made up the largest single category with 58 accounts, but only 11 of the accounts come from farmers – a gross distortion, since at least three-quarters of the German population worked on the land whereas pastors constituted less than 1 per cent. Even the geographical distribution was atypical, because the authors of two-thirds of the surviving accounts (including all the women) lived within a quadrilateral bounded by Münster, Magdeburg, Basel and Munich.[93] Other discrepancies arose because most eyewitnesses covered only part of the period: many began to record events only after the war affected them; others stopped before the war ended; and several left gaps in their narratives – usually because it became too dangerous to write. Finally, the motive for keeping a journal varied. None of the authors seems to have envisaged publication: the majority wrote a private record to remind families or their descendants of the horrors that they had experienced, and a few wrote just 'for myself'.[94]

Despite these disparities, and although none of these authors knew what the others had written, they described many of the same experiences. Thus three-quarters of the civilians stated that they had been plundered by troops – some of them repeatedly. Johann Georg Renner, a rural pastor near Nuremberg, noted that soldiers passed through his village 61 times in 1634 alone, causing serious damage. On one occasion, a spiteful parishioner told passing troops that their pastor was a wealthy man who 'ate off silver dishes' and had a large balance on deposit in the city. The soldiers kept him and his son confined until he paid a handsome ransom.[95] Over half of the writers reported having to flee their homes at least once; almost half reported the murder by soldiers of individuals whom they had known personally; and about one-fifth described being assaulted themselves. The most striking omission is rape: only three of the printed accounts written by civilians mentioned violence committed against women they knew (such as 'Hannes Trosten's wife was raped by two cavalrymen near the castle wood on her way back from holy almsgiving'). No doubt, authors who wrote to inform their descendants of what they had seen and endured felt either too traumatized or too ashamed to include the personal tragedies and humiliations that had befallen them and their loved ones.[96]

Human history is, of course, full of people who claimed that they had experienced misfortunes unparalleled in other ages; yet subsequent research has corroborated the extreme claims of those who lived through the Thirty Years War. Careful analysis of all the 800 or so German parish registers that survive for the period 1632–7 found that only five did *not* record a significant mortality crisis. The Swedish demographic historian Jan Lindegren has used the records of the Swedish army to calculate that two million soldiers, most of them Germans, perished as a direct result of the war, as did two million German civilians.[97] Moreover deaths, whether through violence, starvation or disease, formed only one of three variables that affected all early modern populations. In addition, during the Thirty Years War:

- Births fell because brides postponed their marriage and conceived fewer children, either through abstinence or infertility.
- Migration soared as civilians left their homes either to find security or sustenance elsewhere, or to join an army.

The exact combination of these variables affected not only the magnitude of the demographic decline in each community but also the rate of its recovery. Losses through adult mortality were, paradoxically, the easiest to replace because death might leave a vacant farm or firm that would provide economic opportunities that allowed the next generation to multiply. Migrants were more difficult to replace, because either they took their fortune with them or else they had none to take: only a community with assets would attract migrants from elsewhere to replace those who had left. A shortfall in births – especially female births – proved the hardest to replace in demographic terms because, apart from creating a 'missing generation' (children who would have been born but for the trauma of war), a generation that numbered fewer mothers would itself produce fewer children, so that the 'deficit' perpetuated itself.[98]

All this explains why most areas did not recover their pre-war populations until the eighteenth century. Some historians have suggested that Germany's population fell by between six and eight million, or between 20 to 45 per cent, during the Thirty Years War – far more, in relative terms, than the population loss during either of the world wars of the twentieth century – and did not recover its pre-war level for 50 years or even more.

Given the political fragmentation of early modern Germany, all these 'national' aggregations are tentative, and trying to identify regional demographic variations is even more hazardous. Nevertheless, a careful study of local records led John Theibault to suggest that most of the losses occurred in a relatively small area: '*More than a quarter of the population of the empire may have lived in areas that had no losses or lost less than 10 per cent of their population, while only about a tenth lived in areas that lost more than half their population.*'[99] Figure 24 shows the location of the principal states in these two categories. It appears that, in the southern half of Germany, only the Rhine Palatinate (a battleground almost from the moment when Frederick accepted the Bohemian crown) and Württemberg (savagely contested between Catholics and Protestants from 1631 until the war's end) lost one-half – and perhaps more than one half – of their pre-war population. Of those alive in 1655, nearly half

German demographic evolution, 1600–1750 (in millions)[100]

	Germany (1871 frontiers)			Holy Roman Empire		
Year	Abel	Bosl/Weis	Sagarra	Kellenbenz	Dipper	Mitterauer
1600	16	16	18	18–20	18–20	21
1650	10	10	10–11	11–13	11–13	16
1700	–	–	–	–	15–17	21
1750	18	18	18	18–20	18–20	23

24. The depopulation of Germany during the Thirty Years War, 1618–48.
The political fragmentation of Germany means that the demographic impact of the Thirty Years War can only be reconstructed from regional data. These reveal a few areas, notably in the north-west (and in Austria and Switzerland in the south), that lost one-tenth or less of their pre-war population; while the Bohemian lands, where the war began, lost up to one-third. By contrast, some Protestant areas in the north-east and south-west lost over half of their people, while parts of the Catholic South lost between one-third and one-half.

were under the age of 15. The number of communicants in the lands of the monastery of Ottobeuren, for example, fell from almost 6,000 in 1626, the last year of peace in the region, to scarcely 1,000 around 1640; even in 1659 it stood at 2,566, still under half of the pre-war total.[101] By contrast, Bavaria, Franconia and Hessen seem to have lost between one-third and one-half; while some other areas lost less. In the northern half of Germany, only Mecklenburg and Pomerania (both of them fought over and then occupied by Sweden) lost one-half or more than one-half of their population; while Saxony and Brandenburg (also a battle ground almost continuously between 1631 and 1648) lost between one-third and one-half. Many strategically important regions suffered staggering material as well as demographic losses: two-thirds of the buildings in the once prosperous and densely populated countryside around Magdeburg and Halberstadt were destroyed between 1625 and 1647; the debts of the city of Nuremberg rose from under 2 million gulden in 1618 to over 7 million by 1648; and so on. For all these communities, the Thirty Years War might indeed be described as a 'catastrophe' – a phrase used by German writers of the day in its original Greek sense of 'terminal'.[102]

The war destroyed culture as well as people. The booksellers of Germany, the birthplace of the printing industry, brought out 1,780 titles in 1613 but only 350 in 1635; and the international book fair at Frankfurt collapsed. Many of the thriving urban music societies of Germany closed their doors – the *Musikkranzlein* at Worms and Nuremberg, the *Convivia Musica* at Görlitz, the musical 'colleges' at Frankfurt and Mühlhausen – and princes, too, reduced their musical patronage. Even popular music declined: of over 600 songs from the period 1618–49 that make some reference, direct or indirect, to the Thirty Years War, scarcely 100 appeared after 1634. As early as 1623, one composer recalled how the Devil had given Saul a spear to kill the harpist David and asserted that 'Saul's spear is ... in the hands of court finance ministers who lock their doors when they hear musicians approach.' Heinrich Schütz, court musician of Electoral Saxony and the finest composer of his day, began to produce short choral pieces of religious music for only 'one, two, three or four voices with two violins, 'cello and organ' because 'the times neither demand nor allow music on a big scale'.[103] Soon afterwards, Schütz left Germany.

Many other intellectuals fled to avoid the war. The largest single group came from the lands ruled by Ferdinand II. The polymath Jan Amos Comenius, who supported the Bohemian revolt, left his native Moravia after White Mountain and sought refuge in Poland where he started work on an 'encyclopaedia of universal knowledge', which he believed could solve the world's problems. Later he moved to Holland, to England, and finally to Sweden, with the intention of founding a special college where colleagues could work on his project. The poet Martin Opitz, from Silesia, also fled to Poland after White Mountain and ended his days there as a refugee. The astronomer and mathematician Johan Kepler had to flee twice: first from Graz in 1600, when Archduke Ferdinand expelled all Protestants in Styria, and then from Linz in 1626 when the brutal suppression of the Upper Austrian peasants' revolt (page 221 above) made him fear for his life. In 1675 the artist and art historian Joachim von Sandrart filled his *German Academy of Architecture, Sculpture and Painting,* with bitter laments about the cultural consequences of the war:

> Time and again, Queen Germania saw her palaces and churches, decorated with splendid paintings, go up in flames, and her eyes were so darkened with smoke and weeping that she no longer had the desire or the strength to pay heed to art ... Those that made art their profession fell into poverty and contempt: and so they put away their pallets and took up the spear or the beggar's staff instead of the paint-brush, while the gentle born were ashamed to apprentice their children to such despicable people.

He provided numerous biographies of artists whom 'bloodthirsty Mars' had forced to flee, or else (like Sandrart himself) compelled to 'give up laborious copperplate engraving and take up painting in its stead' (because it was portable in an emergency). Others lost 'all their work' through some act of theft or spite. Thomas Robisheaux has argued that the enormous impact of the war came not just 'from the harsh and inhuman conduct of the soldiery, but from the way all social, political, and religious order vanished and so contributed to the wild disorder and confusion at every level of society'.[104]

'The outstanding example in European history of meaningless conflict'?

In the conclusion to her classic study of the Thirty Years War, first published in 1938, Dame Veronica Wedgwood stated sadly: 'The war solved no problem. Its effects, both immediate and indirect, were either negative or disastrous. It is the outstanding example in European history of meaningless conflict.'[105] The evidence presented in this chapter lends some support to her verdict: not only Germany but also northern Italy, the Dutch Republic, Sweden, Switzerland and Denmark all suffered effects that were 'either negative or disastrous'. Nevertheless, the Peace of Westphalia brought eventual benefits not only to Germany but also to at least some of its neighbours. First, pressure from France and Sweden eventually created a political 'balance' within the Holy Roman Empire by enhancing the power of the Diet (which after 1648 alone possessed the power to declare war) and of territorial rulers (who could now both take up arms and make alliances), while reducing the powers of the Habsburgs. Second, the new principle of 'Amicable Composition' reduced the risk of another religious war: for almost a century, no German state declared war on another – and none would ever wage war again for religion. Moreover, once the states of central Europe ceased to be ravaged by religious and civil wars, foreign powers lacked a plausible excuse to intervene in their disputes – a development that promoted international stability. Finally, the Congress also provided a new model of conflict resolution. In future, international conferences modelled on Westphalia terminated the major wars between European states – the Pyrenees (1659), Breda (1667), Nijmegen (1678), Rijswijk (1697) and Utrecht (1713) – paving the way for the Concert of Europe that would successfully maintain peace among the Great Powers after 1815.

Germany was therefore fully justified in organizing joyous ceremonies to commemorate the Peace of Westphalia. The city of Augsburg organized two celebrations: a general day of rejoicing followed by a peace festival for children, at which the Lutheran clergy distributed copperplate 'peace etchings' to remind young people of the horrors they had escaped. After 1748, the first centenary of Westphalia, schoolchildren received a booklet, to be recited rather like a catechism, with 91 questions and answers about the war; and almost 200 textbooks used in German schools depicted the war as a national disaster.[106] Small wonder, then, that in 1962 the people of Hessen still regarded a conflict fought more than three centuries before as the greatest catastrophe ever suffered by Germany; or that, even today, Augsburg gratefully commemorates the peace that brought that conflict to an end.

The Agony of the Iberian Peninsula, 1618–89[1]

'The target at which the whole world wants to shoot its arrows'

A T HIS ACCESSION IN 1621, AGED 16, PHILIP IV GOVERNED AN EMPIRE ON which (as his spin doctors put it) 'the sun never set', comprising the Iberian Peninsula; Lombardy, Naples and Sicily; the southern Netherlands; and the colonies of Spain and Portugal in the Americas, the Philippines, Asia and Africa. Nevertheless, this global extent brought weakness as well as strength. A letter written in 1600 to Don Balthasar de Zúñiga, a senior diplomat, underlined the strategic dilemma:

> We are gradually becoming the target at which the whole world wants to shoot its arrows; and we know that no empire, however great, has been able to sustain many wars in different areas for long. [We] think only of defending ourselves, and never manage to contrive a great offensive blow against one of our enemies, so that when that is over we can turn to the others . . .

This assessment proved prophetic. Over the next two decades, the Dutch Republic forced Spain to recognize its de facto independence and seized some Iberian outposts in Asia and Africa, while several states in Italy successfully broke free of Spanish influence. In 1619 Zúñiga, now Spain's chief minister, lamented that 'when matters reach a certain stage, every decision taken will be for the worst, not through lack of good advice, but because the situation is so desperate that it is not capable of remedy'.[2]

Zúñiga died in 1622, and his position as chief minister fell to his nephew, already the king's *Privado* or Favourite: Don Gaspar de Guzmán, count of Olivares and later duke of San Lúcar (hence his clumsy title 'the count-duke') – a man who, at least initially, rejected such pessimism. 'I do not consider it useful to indulge in a constant, despairing recital of the state of affairs,' he chided a critic in 1625. 'I know it, and lament it, without letting it weaken my determination or diminish my concern; for the extent of my obligation is such as to make me resolve to die clinging to my oar till not a splinter is left.'[3]

Time would prove Zúñiga right – in the seventeenth century, even an empire on which the sun never set could not 'sustain many wars in different areas for long' – but the extraordinary energy of his nephew initially concealed many underlying weaknesses. Olivares normally rose at five, confessed and took communion, and then roused the king from his slumbers to discuss the day's programme. He spent the rest of the day 'receiving and dispatching letters, giving more audiences, holding meetings . . . until eleven o'clock at night'. The hectic routine killed four of Olivares' secretaries, and the count-duke himself suffered from a chronic lack of sleep. This may explain the breathless quality of his state papers (which constantly referred to the matter under discussion as 'without exception the most important thing that has happened in Your Majesty's Monarchy') and the attraction of doing the unexpected, or doing things in unexpected ways, in part because they saved time. One ambassador considered Olivares 'by nature very inclined to novelties, without taking account of where they might lead him'.[4]

At Christmas 1624, Olivares presented his master with a comprehensive programme of 'novelties'; but almost immediately, Britain declared war and attacked Cadiz, while the duke of Savoy laid siege to Genoa, Spain's most important ally in the Mediterranean. Olivares deferred his novelties while in 1625 he not only organized the relief of Genoa and repulsed the attack on Cadiz, but also recovered from the Dutch both Bahía in Brazil and Breda in the Netherlands. 'God is Spanish and favours our nation these days,' Olivares crowed to a colleague; but the need to react simultaneously to attacks in so many different areas convinced him of the importance of an integrated imperial defence strategy. A few days after hearing of the relief of Cadiz, he unveiled the 'Union of Arms'.[5]

The scheme aimed to create a 'rapid reaction force' of 140,000 men, drawn from the Monarchy's various component parts: if any part came under enemy attack, a portion of the force would immediately come to its rescue. Olivares expected that the Union would not only share the costs of imperial defence, but also 'familiarize [the word used in government circles] the natives of the different kingdoms with each other so they forget the isolation in which they have hitherto lived'; and in January 1626, he set out from Madrid with the king to 'sell' the Union of Arms to the *Corts* (representative assemblies) of Aragon, Catalonia and Valencia. Afterwards, they intended to move to Lisbon, to prepare an invasion of Ireland in retaliation for Charles I's attack on Cadiz.[6]

The Union of Arms had little chance of success, because Olivares used unreliable data to fix the obligations of each part of the Monarchy. Thus he calculated that Catalonia's population numbered one million, so that it should therefore provide 16,000 paid soldiers for the defence of the Monarchy; but subsequent research suggests that Philip had only 500,000 Catalan subjects.[7] Moreover, by unilaterally imposing the demands of the central government on regional authorities accustomed to autonomy, the Union provided a common focus for previously separate grievances. In Aragon, where the king and his minister called for a permanent standing army of 3,333 soldiers, with a further 10,000 as a strategic reserve, tenacious opposition forced them to accept just 2,000 for 15 years. The Valencian Corts granted only one quarter of the crown's request. The Catalan Corts refused to vote anything.

Undeterred, in July 1626 Philip signed orders that put the Union of Arms into effect in Portugal, Italy and the Netherlands. He also ordered the Council of the

Indies to apply it to America and the Philippines. Everywhere, the scheme provoked opposition. The governors of Portugal, charged with providing 16,000 men, claimed that the Union could not be introduced legally without a meeting of the Cortes. In Mexico, the magistrates of the leading towns demanded a special assembly of delegates to discuss the proposal, while the viceroy of Peru attempted the same tactic as the kingdom of Aragon. He reminded the king that 'what matters to his royal service is not just the imposition of taxes but that his subjects should accept and pay them with obedience and enthusiasm. And to achieve this it would be good that some should hope for, and others feel certain of, a reward.' When the central government rejected this strategy out of hand, the viceroy simply declined to put the Union into effect.[8]

The Castilian treasury therefore continued to bear the brunt of defending the Monarchy, forcing the king to issue a 'decree of bankruptcy' in February 1627 that froze the capital of existing loans, most of them from Genoese bankers, and suspended all interest payments. Olivares had already secured an undertaking from Portuguese bankers, almost all of them 'New Christians' (as people of Jewish descent were termed) to lend over a million ducats and, just as the government hoped, the emergence of these rivals led the Genoese bankers to accept low-interest bonds in repayment of their old debts, and also to provide new loans. On the very day the government finalized these generous arrangements, news arrived at court that the duke of Mantua in northern Italy had died, leaving a disputed succession. Philip and Olivares regarded the coincidence as providential and decided that, notwithstanding the numerous wars already afoot, they could afford to intervene in order to prevent a French candidate from gaining Mantua. They would soon regret their choice.

The Portuguese New Christians expected repayment of their loans from the silver bullion scheduled to arrive in Spain from America, but in September 1628 a Dutch fleet ambushed the entire treasure fleet and captured its cargo intact. Even a year after the disaster, Philip admitted that 'whenever I speak about it my blood boils in my veins, not for the loss of money, because I pay no attention to that, but for the reputation that we Spaniards lost.'[9] The king's bankers, however, did not share his insouciance: without the anticipated silver they defaulted on their loans, so that Philip's armies abroad received no funds for several months. In the Netherlands, Spain's unpaid troops failed to prevent the Dutch capture of the heavily fortified city of 's Hertogenbosch and almost 200 surrounding villages. In Madrid, some councillors feared catastrophe because 'once the Netherlands are lost, America and other kingdoms of Your Majesty will also immediately be lost with no hope of recovering them'. In Italy, Spain's unpaid troops could not prevent Louis XIII with a large army from crossing the Alps to Italy to support the French claimant to Mantua. Olivares predicted (with uncanny accuracy) that France had just started a war that would last for 30 years.[10]

So many setbacks might have disposed some rulers towards peace, but Philip gushingly reassured his councillors that 'none of these losses that I have suffered and continue to suffer have afflicted or discouraged me, because God Our Lord has given me a heart that has room for many troubles and misfortunes without becoming overcome or fatigued'. All his wars must therefore continue. One month later, he announced his intention to travel first to Italy and then to the Netherlands to take personal command of his armies. Realizing that his great adventure would involve enormous costs, he invited each of his ministers to suggest ways of funding it.[11]

Characteristically, the king appointed a 'committee of theologians' to evaluate the proposals received. The theologians immediately rejected every suggestion that called for reduced spending (that the king should stay in Spain; that he should make peace in Italy in order to have more money to fight in the Netherlands; that he should make 'the best peace treaties possible, postponing until a better occasion the royal intentions of Your Majesty in the hope that God will return to fight for His cause'). Instead they approved three proposals for new taxes: stamp duty on all official documents (*papel sellado*); a national salt monopoly (*estanco de la sal*); and retaining part of the first year's salary of every newly appointed office-holder, secular and ecclesiastical (*media anata*). They also made the radical suggestion that the new taxes should be imposed universally throughout the empire, and not just in Castile.[12]

Olivares welcomed the theologians' report, praising in particular the 'universal measures, that will affect all kingdoms', because they would 'give Your Majesty the means and resources to lay down the law to the whole world from your watch-tower and thus to control personally, by your orders, the fleets, armies, wars and peace treaties, that Your Majesty considers justified'. He therefore ordered ministers to draw up plans to introduce each new tax, payable by everyone, even the clergy, throughout Castile and Portugal.[13] Although some ministers warned about the dangers inherent in such innovations – 'This is a matter, Sire, on which we must embark with great caution because every novelty brings with it great hardships' – the king pressed ahead with the *media anata* at once, signing letters that imposed it first on Portugal and Spain and later on Italy and America, with the solemn promise that it would be used exclusively 'for the wars against heretics and infidels'.[14]

Open Opposition Begins

The new taxes pleased Olivares in part because they were the king's ancient 'regalian rights', which could be imposed and changed at will; but since the precedents for most of them lay deep in the past (many had not been levied for decades if not centuries), government apologists ransacked historical works for justifications. Opponents of the taxes therefore searched for counter-precedents that restricted or precluded each royal initiative. In Naples, several scholarly books condemned government by a viceroy as an unjustified novelty and extolled the city's 'republican' past when a 'doge' had maintained parity between the nobles and the 'people'. They called upon the king of Spain to restore the 'ancient constitution'. In Catalonia, lawyers published historical accounts of the 'fundamental laws' or 'constitutions' of the principality that no ruler could violate; clerics published tracts defending the duty to preach in Catalan (not Castilian, as the central government insisted); and trade officials wrote discourses in favour of protecting economic goods produced in

Catalonia against imports (especially from Castile). All three groups of writers fostered a sense of 'us' versus 'them', and a distrust of everything that emanated from Madrid.

Olivares's opponents had no difficulty in recruiting university-trained historians and lawyers, because early modern Spain and Italy, like other European countries, possessed a surfeit of them. By 1620 some 20,000 students attended university in Castile, representing more than one-fifth of their age cohort. The majority studied law and what today would be called 'liberal arts'. Only a small proportion of these students entered government service: rather more devoted their learning to researching and writing critiques of government policy.

The government's critics gained strength when extreme weather caused a series of catastrophes throughout the Spanish Monarchy. In 1626–7 the worst floods ever recorded inundated Seville; in 1629 disastrous floods left much of Mexico City under water for the next five years (see page 64); Spanish Lombardy suffered from a drought-induced famine and plague, which killed about one-quarter of the population in 1628–31 (see chapter 14 below); in 1630–1, according to a contemporary chronicler, Lisbon 'lacked everything, especially grain' because of drought.[15] Castile also suffered from the climatic downturn. The magistrates of Madrid sent officials as far as Andalusia and Old Castile to requisition additional grain – a measure without parallel in the seventeenth century – and in 1630–1 the capital's granaries distributed 1.5 million bushels of wheat: twice as much as in any other year. The rural population was less fortunate. To take a single example: at the village of Hoyuelos, near Segovia, the tithe yield (a fixed percentage of the harvest) fell from 19 *fanegas* of wheat in 1629 to 2 in 1630 and to only 1 in 1631. Shortfalls like this decimated the population: some towns and villages lost half of their inhabitants and the king's ministers warned that, owing to 'the shortage of grain, Your Majesty's vassals find themselves in great need and incapable of serving you as they would wish'.[16]

Olivares ignored these warnings of catastrophe and instead began a massive recruiting drive throughout Castile to create armies capable of winning his foreign wars. The minister in charge of this operation protested that 'I see this kingdom exhausted, and especially Old Castile, where most communities have failed to grow even a little barley with which to make bread, and so they are losing their population. If recruiters arrive, it will complete their destruction.' In any case, he continued relentlessly, they would find few recruits,

> Because with the constant levies of troops for America, the Netherlands, Italy, the garrisons and the fleet, and with those who die and are drowned, the kingdom is very short of men. So it would be good to decide which of these two inconveniences would be less damaging: raising fewer men or doing universal damage to Castile?[17]

Olivares ignored this warning, too, expecting the salt monopoly to fund everything; but, as with the Union of Arms scheme, the lack of accurate demographic data doomed the venture.

This time, ministers tried to estimate the total size of Castile's population, and thus to project the total consumption of salt, on the basis of the number of religious indulgences distributed in recent years; but this failed to take account of the death and migration of so many 'consumers', which sharply reduced the demand for salt. Once he realized the scale of the shortfall, Olivares demanded that every household declare under oath their anticipated salt consumption for the coming year, which would cost 69 reales per *fanega* – a figure that included no less than 58 reales of tax. Consumers could acquire more salt at the price of 176 reales, but they could not take less. Local officials registered before a notary each householder's estimate of his or her expected consumption; and every four months they recorded the amount of salt purchased by each family, to ensure that they had bought their quota – and thus paid their huge new tax burden in full (see Plate 10).

Such heavy reliance on 'regalian rights' provoked widespread opposition. Some Castilian taxpayers resisted the salt monopoly passively, either declaring that they would consume no salt or giving improbably low estimates; others organized protests.[18] In Seville, the cathedral chapter claimed that the salt monopoly infringed their traditional exemption from lay taxation, and the papal nuncio authorized them to suspend all church services if the king's ministers tried to force their compliance. The yield of the salt tax therefore continued to fall. The decline proved particularly serious because, apart from the need to sustain wars in Italy and the Netherlands, in 1630 a Dutch expeditionary force landed in Brazil, where they brought the province's sugar-rich coastal plain under their control (see chapter 15 below). Meanwhile, storms sank some treasure ships returning from America, with the loss of over six million ducats. 'Given the present state of the royal treasury and our foreign commitments,' Olivares glumly informed a colleague, 'we can assume that this Monarchy is about to collapse suddenly and that His Majesty's crown is at stake.'[19]

Philip now convened the Cortes of Castile, and called on the delegates to 'give the last drop of blood in your veins, if necessary, to uphold, defend and preserve Christianity'. He provided them with details on each recent campaign, and its cost, and warned them that Spain now faced 'the greatest, the most urgent and desperate situation that has arisen or could arise'. The assembly responded that the extreme weather, failed harvests and high mortality precluded raising any new taxes – unless the king agreed to abolish the salt monopoly. Reluctantly, he did so.[20]

Olivares and his master therefore decided to make another personal attempt to persuade Catalonia to participate in the Union of Arms. To the count-duke, the principality seemed 'of all provinces in the Monarchy the one least burdened with taxes, and ... the most extensive, abundant and populous'.[21] Nothing could have been further from the truth. Even in good times, Catalonia seethed with social tensions and lawlessness. The town-dwellers clashed constantly with those who lived in the countryside over agrarian policies (the former wanted cheap grain while the latter welcomed high prices); ancient rivalries divided the rural nobility, some of whom used bandit gangs to conduct feuds with their neighbours; in the background lurked the *segadors* (reapers) who depended on finding enough employment during the harvest every summer to sustain them through the rest of the year. Many of the feuds across the principality were interconnected, and their protagonists assumed the names of two rival families: the *Nyerros* (followers of the lords of Nyer, although in Catalan 'nyerro' also meant 'pig') and the *Cadells* (after the family of that name, which in Catalan also meant 'dog'). Since each faction numbered almost 200 principals, and since a census of firearms in the principality revealed some 70,000 weapons – one for almost every household – confrontations between the Nyerros and Cadells usually left a considerable trail of dead and wounded. These feuds even penetrated the principality's government: according to the viceroy, 'all the ministers, from the big ones to the small, have within them the original sin of being *cadells* or *nyerros*, so that members of one faction cannot be entrusted with anything that conflicts with its interests'.[22]

Catalonia, like the rest of the Iberian Peninsula, had also suffered a series of natural disasters. During the winter of 1627–8, in the words of a diarist, 'the earth and sky seemed made of brass', and the clergy of Barcelona led no fewer than 34 processions to pray for rain. Their prayers were answered with storms that washed away another harvest. Then in 1630 a new drought caused food prices to rise sharply while trade and industry slumped. Barcelona introduced bread rationing and, although the authorities foiled a plan by the *segadors* to storm the customs house, starving citizens attacked the city's granaries, pulled half-baked loaves from the ovens, and devoured them.[23] Coming on top of such hardships, the demand in 1632 for new taxes to fund the Union of Arms rallied virtually all Catalans around their 'Constitutions' and so, as in 1626, even the presence of the king and his chief minister failed to persuade the Corts to vote any new taxes. They departed empty-handed once again.

Open unrest had already broken out among the Basque population of the northern lordship of Vizcaya. Although technically part of the kingdom of Castile, and so subject to the new salt tax, Vizcaya (like Catalonia) boasted powerful privileges (*fueros*) and a local representative assembly (the *Junta General*). In 1631, during a meeting of the Junta, 'some women from the coastal areas' denounced the local officials who tried to impose the salt tax as 'traitors' whom 'it would be better to kill'. Local officials prudently suspended both the session and the salt tax. One year later, when the magistrates of Bilbao announced their intention to collect the new salt duty, the city streets filled with rioters and once more women took the lead, 'Saying publicly to the town elite: "Now our sons and husbands will be magistrates and officials, and not the traitors who have sold our republic . . . And since we are all equal in Vizcaya, our estates should all be the same: it is not right that they should be rich and us poor, that they should eat chicken and we eat sardines."' The crowd sacked the houses of the tax collectors. News of these events appalled the king: 'I saw these papers and this consulta with sadness,' he scribbled on the dossier forwarded by his council, 'to see in Spain something unheard of for centuries'.[24] Nevertheless he trod warily, dispatching mediators rather than troops; and when mediation failed, he merely imposed an economic boycott on Vizcaya until 1634, when he abolished the salt monopoly and issued a general pardon.

THE AGONY OF THE IBERIAN PENINSULA, 1618–89

The Spanish Netherlands also hovered on the edge of rebellion. Its nobles resented the loss of their political influence after 1623, when the king resolved that a small committee (made up mostly of Spaniards) should discuss and decide policy, instead of the Council of State (on which the nobles sat). For a time, Habsburg military success in Germany and the Low Countries, combined with a measure of prosperity, muted criticism; but the Dutch capture of the treasure fleet in 1628 and of 's Hertogenbosch the following year caused widespread disillusion. A group of South Netherlands nobles now solicited military intervention from the king of France and the prince of Orange in support of an uprising; but when the Dutch invaded in June 1632, virtually nobody stirred. The conspirators therefore turned to France again and begged the duke of Aarschot, the senior nobleman in the South Netherlands, to take the lead; but he refused and opposition collapsed.

The defiance of Catalonia, Vizcaya and the South Netherlands nobles, coupled with the success of Gustavus Adolphus and his Protestant allies in Germany, deeply depressed Olivares. 'You get to the mountaintop,' he wrote despondently in autumn 1632, 'and then everything falls, everything goes wrong. We never see a comforting letter; not a dispatch arrives that does not tell us that everything is lost because we had failed to provide the money.' Realizing that the problems arose in part from trying to fight on all fronts all the time, Spain tried to maintain the peace in at least some areas. For example, Philip instructed the viceroy of India that he must 'always maintain peace with the Mughal' emperor 'since he is our very close neighbour and his power [encircles] our territories. If he is offended, he may break off with us to the great damage of' Portuguese India, 'which is not in a condition to resist so great an enemy'.[25] Olivares saw no need for such restraint in European affairs: instead, eager to 'die doing something' (as he put it), he convinced his master that sending a large army overland from Italy to the Netherlands under the personal command of Philip's brother, the Cardinal-Infante Fernando, would at a stroke drive the Protestants out of southern Germany and induce the Dutch to make peace. At first the gamble worked amazingly well. In the summer of 1634 the Cardinal-Infante crossed the Alps and joined the imperial army in Germany, where together they routed the Swedes at the battle of Nördlingen: 12,000 Protestants perished and 4,000 more, including the Swedish commander, fell prisoner. The triumphant Spaniards then marched on to Brussels while the imperialists reoccupied almost all of southern Germany. Olivares could be forgiven for hailing Nördlingen as 'the greatest victory of our times'.[26]

The count-duke, nevertheless, remained in thrall to a 'domino theory' – that failing to defend any imperial interest would imperil the rest. He therefore argued that 'The greatest dangers' facing the Spanish crown were

Those that threaten Lombardy, the Netherlands and Germany, because a defeat in any of these three is fatal for this monarchy; so much so that if the defeat in those parts is a great one, the rest of the monarchy will collapse, because Germany will be followed by Italy and the Netherlands, and the Netherlands will be followed by America; and Lombardy will be followed by Naples and Sicily, without the possibility of being able to defend either.

The only alternative, he argued, was a pre-emptive strike on France. He planned 11 coordinated assaults from Spain, Italy, Germany, the Low Countries, the Atlantic and the Mediterranean, and convinced himself that 'there is no possibility that the blow can misfire'.[27]

Of course the blow did 'misfire': no state could make large-scale preparations on so many fronts and escape detection, and so Louis XIII decided to make his own pre-emptive strike. He secured a Dutch commitment to invade the Netherlands; he persuaded Sweden not to make a separate peace with the Habsburgs in Germany; and in May 1635 he sent a herald to declare war on Philip IV. At first Olivares rejoiced, since he could now present his long-prepared 'blow' as a response to unprovoked French aggression. Fatefully, he selected Catalonia as the principal theatre of operations, envisaging that the king would go there in person and invade France with 40,000 men.

In the event, another disastrous harvest in Catalonia left both the army and the civilian population starving, while a French invasion of the Low Countries tied down the Spanish troops tasked with advancing on Paris. So although Olivares had mobilized (and paid for) two fleets and 150,000 soldiers, they achieved nothing. Nothing daunted, he prepared another knock-out 'blow' for 1636 – and this time he came close to achieving his goal. An imperial army invaded eastern France, while troops from the Netherlands captured Corbie and came within sight of Paris. Refugees from the French capital streamed southwards until pressure from the Swedish army in Germany compelled the Habsburg forces to retire.

The capture of Corbie convinced Olivares that France could not withstand one more assault, and to fund it he again resorted to manipulating regalian rights: he recalled all copper coins and re-stamped them at three times their face value, and he introduced *papel sellado* (stamp duty: another recommendation of the Committee of Theologians in 1629) (Plate 11). Once again, the Little Ice Age thwarted his efforts. According to Don Francisco de Quevedo, at this stage the government's most eloquent apologist, 'We need to light candles at midday. No one has sown crops, nor can they, and there is no bread, Most people eat barley and rye. Every day we bring in people who have died in the streets from hunger and poverty. Misery is everywhere and terminal.' Dearth afflicted Andalusia, and flash floods destroyed half the houses in Valladolid, a former capital. Olivares saw no alternative to reducing the cost of the cheapest stamped paper required for simple transactions from 10 *maravedíes* to 4, 'because poor people were not transacting any business because of the tax'.[28]

So in 1637, Olivares turned once more to Catalonia for help, ordering 6,000 men to mobilize for the defence of their fatherland, citing a 'constitution' known as *Princeps Namque*; but the Catalan authorities pointed out that this measure could be invoked only when the sovereign resided in the principality. Since Philip remained in Madrid, they declared the proclamation void. When a royal army eventually invaded France, it contained troops from various parts of the Monarchy but not a single Catalan – and few Portuguese, because a serious rebellion had just broken out there.

The Portuguese Emergency

At the heart of the unrest lay a dispute over who should pay for the defence of Portugal's overseas empire. Already in 1624, when the Lisbon authorities begged the king to send funds to recover Bahía in Brazil from the Dutch, ministers in Madrid complained that 'the Portuguese are by their nature grumblers and spongers'. Some also considered that 'Wanting to wage an offensive war in the 15,000 miles of coast of Africa and Asia, where the Portuguese garrisons are split up' was impossibly unrealistic.[29] Although on this occasion Olivares relented, organizing a massive and successful Luso-Spanish relief expedition, the Dutch capture of Pernambuco five years later led to a new dispute: Portugal begged for central funds while Madrid insisted that the Portuguese pay more to defend their empire.

Union with Spain had never been popular with some Portuguese, but until 1620 many members of the elite studied at Spanish universities, served in the Spanish Army and administration, took Castilian spouses, and wrote in Castilian. Thereafter, however, the loss of overseas trade and territory to the British and the Dutch caused widespread resentment. As Stuart Schwartz has written, 'More than any other single issue, the colonial situation created a sense and perception of crisis in Portugal'.[30] Olivares himself contributed mightily to this 'perception of crisis', by terminating the profitable overland trade between Portuguese Brazil and Spanish Peru, and by encouraging the Inquisition to investigate Portuguese merchants in search of any Jewish practices (over half of the Portuguese merchant class was of Jewish descent, and many of them languished in prison while the inquisitors carried out their lengthy enquiries). These developments reduced the taxes and profits of colonial trade, which provided two-thirds of the total revenues of the Portuguese crown as well as the livelihood of most of the kingdom's merchant elite.

As in Castile, Olivares initially decided to increase revenues by manipulating regalian rights, above all by imposing the *media anata* and a salt monopoly, and asked the Portuguese Cortes to approve them. When they refused he forced the Vicereine, the king's cousin Margaret, duchess of Mantua, to introduce other fiscal 'novelties' to pay for imperial defence. On his orders she withheld one-quarter of all payments due in pensions and bond interest; extracted forced donations from the towns; required nobles to raise troops for the crown; increased excise duties by 25 per cent; and imposed a tax on meat and wine known as the *real d'água*, previously levied by towns (not the crown) as an emergency measure. She also prepared to impose a tax on capital and rents, and ordered officials throughout Portugal to register the possessions of every household, however poor. In August 1637 a crowd gathered outside the house of the mayor of Évora, the third largest city in the kingdom, and instructed him to stop the compilation of the new registers. When he refused, boys began to throw stones and, after a while, the crowd stormed his house and made a bonfire of his furniture. They then ransacked the houses of those compiling the registers and those who had collected other new taxes (such as the *real d'água*), burning their papers and possessions. Posters appeared in the streets signed by 'Manuelinho', formally the town's simpleton but now hailed as 'secretary of the young people, ministers of divine justice', that threatened the 'tyrant Pharaoh' (King Philip) and his agents with death because they had imposed new taxes without popular consent. Within a few weeks, some 60 places in southern Portugal had also rebelled. Some would defy Madrid for six months (Fig. 25).[31]

Despite the fact that wheat at Évora hit its highest price of the decade in 1637, Olivares insisted that the opposition was 'not about food but about the *fueros*', claiming that the Portuguese 'pay less [in taxes] than anyone else in Europe'. He added: 'they are not asked for, nor do we want from them, revenues beyond those that pay for their own needs'. The count-duke feared that if Philip gave the rebels of Évora what they wanted, 'not only the rest of Portugal but also all His Majesty's realms in Europe, in America and in India would want the same – and with very good reason, because they would risk nothing in doing so since they would know that one miserable town, just by rebelling, had obliged its king to agree to terms favourable to them'. Nevertheless, recognizing the need to settle the matter before either the French or the Dutch intervened, Olivares declared himself ready to offer a pardon based on 'the most generous models; and to that end we are studying what we did in Vizcaya'.[32] The king, too, could not decide how to proceed. He gave orders to prepare 10,000 troops to invade if necessary, adding that 'I will go there, even on foot and in the depths of winter, because nothing on this earth will stop me from taking care of my vassals and saving them from perdition'. However, he recognized that 'although these rebels are prodigal sons, they are still "sons"', he suspended collection of the *real d'água*. This combination of stick and carrot worked well: by the end of 1637 all the towns in revolt had submitted and the king issued a generous pardon – which was indeed modelled on that for Vizcaya – that condemned only 5 rebels to death and another 70 to the galleys.[33]

Olivares at Bay

The pacification of Portugal temporarily salvaged Olivares's reputation, as did the repulse of a French attack on the port of Fuentarrabía in 1638; but elsewhere Spain's enemies triumphed. In Germany, French forces captured Breisach on the east bank of the Rhine, cutting the 'Spanish Road' used by troops and treasure travelling from Lombardy to the Netherlands. In west Africa, the Dutch took São Jorge da Minha, the oldest Portuguese colony in the Tropics; in India, they blockaded Goa, the capital of Portuguese India; in Brazil, they attacked the viceregal capital, Salvador, with a large fleet, and the citizens only just managed to repel them. Therefore, in 1639 Olivares sought to regain the initiative with two characteristically dangerous and expensive gambles. First, he appointed the relatively inexperienced count of La Torre as 'Governor and Captain-General on sea and land of the State of Brazil', entrusted him with 'the largest fleet that ever entered the hemisphere' (46 ships and 5,000 men), and instructed him to bring the Dutch to battle.[34] Second, he decided to launch another invasion of France from Catalonia with the express intention of forcing the Catalans to become 'directly involved, as up to now they seem not to have been involved, with the common welfare of the Monarchy'. He therefore sent

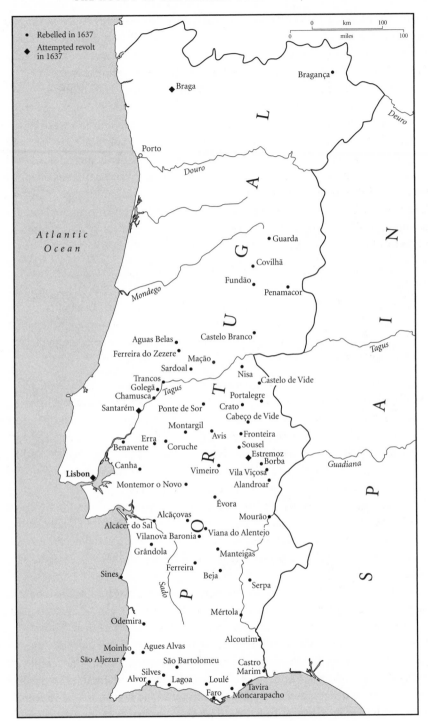

25. The revolt of Portugal, 1637.
An epidemic of revolts against Spanish rule affected almost all the southern half of the kingdom, in some areas lasting six months.

troops raised in Castile, in Italy and in the South Netherlands to the principality, expecting the Catalans to feed, lodge and pay them. When this move provoked complaints he smugly reassured the count of Santa Coloma, his viceroy in Barcelona, 'Better that the Catalans should complain, than that we all should weep.'[35]

Olivares overlooked not only the strength of Catalonia's institutions but also its geographical unsuitability for major military operations. In the north, the frontier with France ran through high mountains and arid plateaux. In the west, a barren wasteland separated Catalonia from Aragon, while in the south the vast Ebro delta prevented easy communication with Valencia: all of them geographical barriers that made it hard to launch a Habsburg invasion of France. Even within the principality, the steep hills and deep river gorges made interior communications a labyrinth. Finally, the unpredictable climate limited agricultural yields in many upland areas, leaving little surplus to feed an army even in good years. As a senior minister of Philip IV observed ruefully some years later:

> War in Catalonia is the most expensive and most difficult to sustain, because the countryside cannot provide support as other areas do, and it lacks the long-distance trade that facilitates the use of bills of exchange and letters of credit, so that there is no way to maintain armies except with ready money; and where that is lacking, since the need to eat brooks no delay, it gives rise among the soldiers to robbery, plunder, violence, rape, much licence and no discipline.[36]

Contingency created a new political obstacle to Olivares's decision to turn Catalonia into the principal theatre of operations in 1638. Once every three years, a small boy stood beside a silver urn containing 524 slips of paper, each one bearing the name of an eligible member of the Corts, and drew out slips until he had the names of two clerics, two nobles and two burgesses. These six men immediately began a three-year term as the *Diputació*, or Standing Committee of the Corts, whose main task was to ensure that their ruler respected and obeyed the 'Constitutions' of the principality. In 1638 the small boy drew from the silver urn a slip of paper bearing the name of Pau (or Paul) Claris, a canon of Urgell Cathedral and a trained lawyer, who became the senior clerical *Diputat*, followed by another bearing the name of Claris's cousin Francesc de Tamarit, who became the senior noble *Diputat*.[37]

Unfortunately for Madrid, both the new Diputats possessed a passionate and uncompromising devotion to their native land and its 'Constitutions', seeing the Catalans as God's chosen people and condemning every political innovation as tyranny. Since Olivares's decision to bring the war to Catalonia was bound to produce innovations, the stage was set for political confrontation. For example, after the French captured the frontier fortress of Salces in 1639 the judges in Barcelona received orders to ignore their oath to observe the Constitutions whenever they conflicted with the needs of the army. '[If] the Constitutions do not allow this,' Olivares informed Viceroy Santa Coloma, 'then the Devil take the Constitutions'. Neither the viceroy nor the judges dared to remind the all-powerful Favourite that this attitude would surely drive the new Diputats to protest; instead, in the words of a perceptive observer, they preferred to 'write, consult, doubt and obey'. In less than a year, almost all of them would pay for this complicity with their lives.[38]

The Revolt of the Catalans

Early in 1640, thanks to relentless pressure by the judges and naked blackmail by Santa Coloma (who promised a patent of nobility to all landholders who spent 30 days with the army), the Catalans recaptured Salces – but the victory impressed neither the royal commanders in Catalonia, preoccupied by the need to lodge and feed their victorious troops, nor Olivares, who now issued orders to raise 6,000 new troops in the principality for service in Italy. Anticipating trouble, Santa Coloma forbade any lawyer to take up complaints lodged by peasants against soldiers; and when the Diputats protested at this further innovation, Olivares ordered a magistrate, Miquel Joan Monrodón, to arrest Tamarit (the senior noble of the *Diputació*) and commanded the church authorities to prosecute Claris (the senior cleric). An eyewitness underscored the dangers inherent in such arbitrary policies, 'because in truth the greatest grief of the downtrodden is removing their ability to ask for redress', and (he continued ominously) 'Amid the distress to which human misery reduces us, there is almost nothing men would not do'. One of Olivares's own agents in Catalonia drew the same conclusion. The principality, he remarked, 'is very different from other provinces'.

> It contains a villainous populace, which can easily be excited to violence, and the more it is pressed, the harder it resists. For this reason, actions which would be sufficient to make the inhabitants of any other province submit to orders of any kind from above, only succeed in exasperating the inhabitants of this province, and in making them insist more stubbornly on the proper observance of their laws.[39]

Extreme weather early in 1640 made the Catalans even more 'villainous'. Following a meagre harvest the previous year, no rain fell on the fields of the hinterland in spring 1640, producing a drought so intense that the authorities declared a special holiday to allow the entire population to make a pilgrimage to a local shrine to pray for water – one of only four such occasions recorded in the past five centuries. Since still no rain fell, unless the villagers could exclude the troops, they faced starvation; but when Santa Coloma de Farners, a hamlet about 60 miles northeast of Barcelona, refused orders to quarter an approaching regiment of Castilians, the viceroy sent the same magistrate who had arrested Tamarit to intimidate them. Even loyalists felt that the viceroy had made a serious error in choosing Monrodón – a man 'irritable by nature, hasty, arrogant, proud' – to perform a task that required 'guile rather than force'. They were soon proved right. On 30 April 1640, Monrodón ordered the arrest of any civilian found carrying a firearm; the villagers responded by chasing Monrodón and his officials into the local inn, which they then set on fire, chanting 'Now you'll pay for putting Tamarit in prison.' Monrodón and most of those inside died in the flames.[40]

The villagers of Santa Coloma de Farners now rang the church bells to summon aid, and hundreds of armed men soon stood ready to protect the community. Their resistance forced a regiment travelling behind the Castilians to make a sudden detour and they took their revenge on the next village on their route, Ruidarenes, where they burnt down several houses and the church. Meanwhile, outraged by the murder of Monrodón, the viceroy ordered his troops to march back to Santa Coloma de Farners and burn it to the ground. This they accomplished on 14 May, leaving the church and most homes in ashes. For good measure, they also destroyed the rest of Ruidarenes.

That same day, the local bishop excommunicated the troops for sacrilege, and shouts of 'Long live the king and death to the traitors' soon rang out as the inhabitants of some 50 villages attacked any soldiers still billeted in their area and plundered the property of royal officials and loyal inhabitants (Fig. 26). A little rain now fell, saving the harvest, but everyone feared what might happen when the *segadors* entered Barcelona for their annual hiring fair on 7 June 1640, Corpus Christi Day. Santa Coloma received several warnings about his safety, including one from a holy woman who predicted that 'he would die on Corpus Christi'. Nevertheless on 6 June, on orders from Madrid, the viceroy sent the squadron of galleys that normally defended Barcelona, manned by most of the city's garrison, to fight the French. The preconditions for disaster were now all in place.[41]

That night hundreds of *segadors*, some armed with muskets and others carrying firewood, entered the city under cover of darkness, and on the morning of the Corpus holiday circulated among the crowds amid occasional shouts of 'Long live Catalonia' and 'Death to the Castilians'. Then one group sighted a servant of the late Miquel Joan Monrodón, who fled into his house with the *segadors* in hot pursuit. When a shot from within killed one of them, his comrades used their firewood to burn down the door, broke into the house and sacked it. Others now sought out the hated judges, who fled from one convent to another seeking sanctuary while the crowd burned their possessions and papers, smashed the windows and walls of their homes and even chopped down the trees in their gardens. The rioters spared only religious images (although they burned the frames), and when some priests tried to intervene, they angrily replied that the judges 'had watched the Castilians burn churches and sacraments', and although 'they could have stopped it, they had done nothing; it was thus reasonable that they should pay for it'.[42]

When the crowd – by now some 3,000 strong – came under fire from the house of a government minister, they chased its occupants to the royal shipyards, where the viceroy had taken refuge. With no galleys and a depleted garrison, the *segadors* soon forced an entry, seized the weapons stored in the royal arsenal, and fanned out to search for those who had fired on them. The viceroy tried to escape along the beach, but two of the pursuers intercepted him and stabbed him to death.

'While these events were taking place in the shipyard,' wrote an eyewitness, 'the *segadors* went about Barcelona with such fury, cries and loud noises that it seemed as though the world was coming to an end or as though the city had become the very stage of the Last Judgment'. The city militia, drawn from Barcelona's middle class

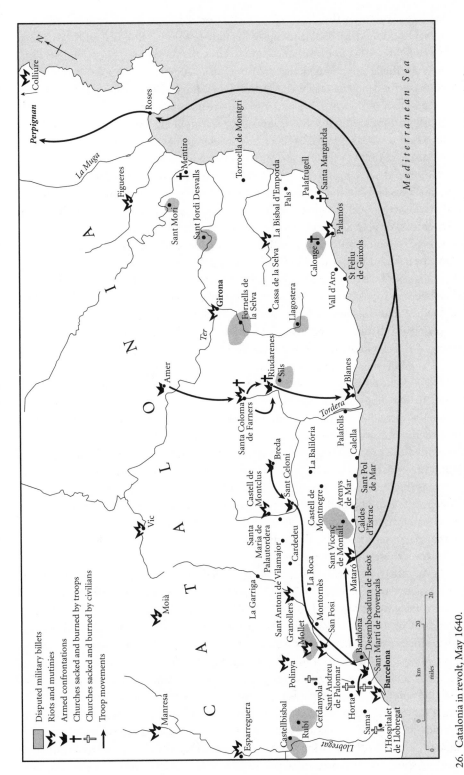

26. Catalonia in revolt, May 1640.

Even before the 'Corpus de Sang' in Barcelona on 7 June 1640, a large part of Catalonia was in arms, with both royal troops and outraged peasants involved in confrontations that in some cases culminated in the burning down of churches.

Map labels:

Mediterranean Sea

Perpignan
Collioure
Roses
Figueres
La Muga
Mentiro
Sant Mori
Sant Jordi Desvalls
Torroella de Montgri
La Bisbal d'Emporda
Pals
Palafrugell
Santa Margarida
Palamós
St Feliu de Guixols
Calonge
Vall d'Aro
Girona
Fornells de la Selva
Cassa de la Selva
Llagostera
Ter
Amer
Riudarenes
Sils
Blanes
Santa Coloma de Farners
Tordera
Palafolls
Calella
Breda
La Baliloria
Sant Celoni
Sant Pol de Mar
Castell de Montclus
Castell de Montnegre
Arenys de Mar
Vic
Santa Maria de Palautordera
Cardedeu
Caldes d'Estrac
Sant Vicenç de Montalt
Moià
La Garriga
La Roca
Montornès
Mataró
Sant Antoni de Vilamajor
Granollers
San Fost
Desembocadura de Besòs
Mollet
Badalona
Sant Martí de Provençals
Manresa
Sant Andreu de Palomar
Barcelona
Esparreguera
Polinyà
Cerdanyola
Horta
Castellbisbal
Rubí
Sama
L'Hospitalet de Llobregat
Llobregat

C A T A L O N I A

Legend:

- Disputed military billets
- Riots and mutinies
- Armed confrontations
- Churches sacked and burned by troops
- Churches sacked and burned by civilians
- Troop movements

km 0 20
miles 0 20

which also resented the ceaseless demands of the central government, did not intervene – indeed, according to one of the judges, some militiamen said ' "We don't have to fight against our brothers" and mixed with [the rioters] like friends'.[43] One terrified official complained that 'No one was secure in his house' because the rioters 'seemed possessed by the Devil'. They dragged Castilians who had taken sanctuary out of the churches and into the streets, where they murdered them. An English visitor dared not leave his house for fear of being 'taken for a Castellano: it is not safe to speak Spanish, such is the inveterate hatred against them'.[44] Similar violence occurred in other communities of Catalonia.

News of the *Corpus de Sang* ('Bloody Corpus', as it became known) stunned Philip. 'This is something the like of which has never been seen in any province or kingdom of the world,' he wrote. 'If Our Lord does not come to our aid with a rapid settlement, or else with a general peace, Spain will be in a worse state than it has been in for many centuries.' The British ambassador in Madrid agreed: 'It will be now a very hard matter to compose' the revolt, he opined, 'without discomposing the king's authority', adding archly, 'which might have been prevented if the business had been undertaken in time'. Nevertheless, at least one critic at court believed that Olivares could still have pacified Catalonia simply 'by leaving it alone; by not always harrying its inhabitants' and 'by using temperate words and temperate actions'.[45] But the count-duke knew that if he bowed to Catalan pressure and suspended recent taxes and billeting demands, other parts of the Monarchy would demand the same.

He also knew that the Catalan cause was far from united. Many nobles remained loyal to the king; and although a few bishops joined the rebels, most did not. Likewise, although most monks and friars defied Madrid, most nuns did not. Above all, each community and each social group possessed its own agenda and many exploited the general disorder to settle old scores. In the countryside, the landless rural underclass attacked those who exploited their labour; in the cities ordinary citizens threatened the oligarchs who regulated their lives and monopolized office. Meanwhile bandits robbed and murdered anyone who crossed their path, and the feud between *nyerros* and *cadells* revived. The *Diputats* lamented 'how the principality tears itself apart with domestic passions', and worried about 'the grave consequences if these civil wars persist'.[46]

In August 1640 Olivares issued a declaration that accused the Catalans of treason and instructed the marquis of Los Vélez, from an eminent Catalan family, to mobilize an army to restore royal control. He also announced that the king would hold a Catalan Corts and restore 'in the principality the free exercise of justice, which has been violated and made impossible by certain wicked and seditious persons'. Almost immediately, the southern town of Tortosa staged a counter-revolution, seizing the leading rebels and hanging 15 of them. Loyalists in the principality now possessed a rallying point that made possible the growth of two 'parties' in Catalonia. The rebels cited the brutality and sacrilege of the king's troops in the past, and the chaos that would doubtless attend their return, while the loyalists stressed the danger of anarchy posed by the uprising – but their cause suffered a setback with the publication of some of Olivares's intemperate letters to the late viceroy, expressing his contempt for the 'Constitutions' and suggesting that Madrid really did intend to destroy Catalan autonomy.[47]

In September the *Diputació* summoned some 250 clerics, nobles and burgesses to Barcelona, where they drew up a formal refutation of Olivares's charge of treason, asked for support from Valencia, Aragon and Mallorca, and took steps to mobilize resistance. Meanwhile Claris secretly requested French protection for a possible 'Catalan Republic'. His envoys met with a cool reception because (in the words of France's chief minister, Cardinal Richelieu) 'most disorders of this type are normally a brush fire'; but eventually Richelieu instructed a relative, Bernard de Duplessis-Besançon, to travel to Barcelona and promise the Catalans that France would supply gunpowder, muskets and artillery as well as 6,000 French infantry and 2,000 cavalry in return for three guarantees: that the munitions would never be used against France; that the Catalans would never make a separate peace with Philip; and that they would hand over three ports and some hostages. Even after an agent of the *Diputació* signed a draft treaty conceding all these points, Richelieu remained sceptical: the Catalans 'have no leader of much stature, and no religious disagreement' with Castile, he noted, and so he doubted that their resistance would last long.[48]

The cardinal's caution was understandable – albeit ill-founded. Although at this stage few Catalans contemplated reneging on their oath to obey Philip IV, they were unwilling to fight for him. Olivares's policies had alienated every major social group in Catalonia. The nobles resented the appointment of non-Catalans to lucrative military commands and the repeated demands for military service without pay or reward; the clergy resented the appointment of non-Catalans to plum posts and the imposition of heavy taxes; while the town oligarchs resented the ceaseless pressure from Madrid to provide loans which they knew would never be repaid and to implement policies, such as billeting, which earned them the hatred of their citizens. The *Diputació* now administered an oath of loyalty to the new regime – over 300 citizens took the oath on the first day; over 1,000 had done so within a week – and began to raise both troops and money. They also summoned a special committee of theologians to debate the legality of their policies (and published its favourable findings); and commissioned and distributed pamphlets depicting themselves as lawful subjects enforcing a contractual relationship with their ruler, and as the 'avenging hand of God' against the royal troops who had profaned His churches. One tract, the *Universal Description of Catalonia* by Francesc Martí i Viladamor, a lawyer, not only listed each occasion on which Olivares had breached the 'Constitutions' but also suggested for the first time that the principality might secede from the Spanish Monarchy.[49]

Claris and his colleagues sent copies of these publications to Madrid, Naples, Valencia, Zaragoza and other outposts of the Monarchy, as well as to Paris and Rome, where they soon won support for the rebellion. As soon as news of the 'revolution in Catalonia' arrived in the Dutch Republic, the States-General set up a special committee to organize support, recognizing their 'common interest' with all other rebels against Philip IV – but only France actually sent assistance, and by the end of 1640 it numbered only 3,000 foot and 800 horse.[50] Likewise, in Barcelona, a public bond issue raised 1.2 million ducats with purchasers from among all sections of the population – but, even with taxes on the clergy and increased excise duties, that sum sufficed to pay only 8,000 soldiers. Even the strategic advantages conferred by geography seemed unlikely to protect the principality against the royal army of 23,000 infantry, 3,100 cavalry and 24 artillery pieces that the marquis of Los Vélez reviewed on 7 December 1640, just six months after the Corpus de Sang.

At first the campaign went very well for the king. Cambrils, the first major stronghold in the path of his army, resisted for only three days before it surrendered 'at discretion'. Although Los Vélez pardoned the French defenders, he argued that 'neither oath nor word oblige the king when dealing with his vassals', and therefore hanged several Catalan officers while his troops massacred about 500 other defenders in cold blood. This example of strategic terror encouraged several other towns to surrender.[51] The royal army lived on the ample supplies found in these captured towns, especially Tarragona (captured on 23 December), supplemented by food and munitions received by sea. The revolt of the Catalans seemed doomed – until news arrived of a revolution in Lisbon.

The Revolt of Portugal

The Portuguese rebellion – the only one in mid-seventeenth century Europe to achieve permanent success – originated in 1634, when three Portuguese gentlemen (fidalgos) visited the Royal Armoury in Madrid and viewed with disgust the collection of trophies secured when Spanish forces invaded their country to enforce the union of crowns in 1580. There and then they took an oath to restore Portugal's independence, but by 1637 only five fidalgos had joined the plot: they therefore failed to exploit the revolt in Évora, and many other places, that year (pages 263–4 above). Duke John of Bragança, Portugal's premier aristocrat, also stood aloof. He possessed enviable fiscal, ecclesiastical and military resources and, unique among Europe's aristocracy, he could create nobles himself. He maintained a permanent representative in Rome as well as Madrid and closely monitored political developments, but his principal political aim was 'conservation': to maintain and consolidate what he already owned. He scrupulously avoided any entanglement that could put his inheritance at risk. He lent full-hearted support to the central government against the rebellion of Évora; and when, in 1638, Cardinal Richelieu offered to send French troops if he rebelled (and threatened to support a rival claimant to the Portuguese throne if he did not), the duke did nothing.[52]

Nevertheless in 1639 Arthur Hopton, the British ambassador in Madrid, predicted that the 'unquietness' of Portugal 'is not yet settled, the minds of the people being as ill-disposed as ever'. He believed that only the improvidence of the nobles, whom royal favour shielded from bankruptcy, stood in the way of another rebellion.[53] Olivares shared this analysis and, in the wake of the Évora riots, summoned 80 members of the Portuguese elite (though not Bragança) to Madrid – ostensibly to advise him on how to improve relations between the two kingdoms but in effect to keep them under surveillance. He did not seem to realize that removing them from the kingdom weakened, rather than strengthened, government control.

Meanwhile two of Olivares's henchmen – Miguel de Vasconcelos, the principal minister in Lisbon, and his brother-in-law Diogo Soares, secretary for Portuguese affairs in Madrid – established a stranglehold on the administration of Portugal. They controlled all patronage, packed the administration with their relatives and clients, and sold offices and titles of nobility to the highest bidder. In addition, despite virulent anti-Semitic feeling in the kingdom, they protected the 'New Christian' bankers on whose loans Philip's armies and navies depended. Despite widespread hostility (and an assassination attempt), Vasconcelos and Soares managed to marginalize all their rivals, but they remained dangerously isolated. As Vasconcelos warned his brother-in-law in September 1640, 'anything might provoke a great conflagration':

> Truly, I do not know how to isolate the seditious without provoking a storm, because even exiling them would create a scandal. Should we get His Majesty to summon them? It has already been done and they did not obey. To announce that His Majesty will grant those who go [to Catalonia] the land of those who refuse to go would only increase the frustration ... I tell you the truth, dear colleague: I don't know what to do.[54]

Vasconcelos's misgivings were well founded. Few Portuguese now saw any benefit in the union with Castile; nor did vassals living overseas. When a new viceroy of India arrived at Goa early in 1640 he found the entire population 'disheartened'. The 'constant presence of the Dutch naval squadrons over the past four years' and the 'lack of relief from Portugal' had paralyzed trade and led to the loss of many outposts in Sri Lanka. Worse, the Dutch had laid siege to Melaka, the key to all seaborne trade between south and east Asia, and the viceroy lacked the resources to save it. Moreover, in Japan, the shogun had just expelled the Portuguese and forbade them to trade further. Although Philip was not responsible for this setback, he refused all requests for Portuguese Macao to trade directly with Spanish Manila – a measure that would have provided some relief to the exposed outpost.[55] The Portuguese settlers in Brazil were even more 'disheartened'. In June 1640 the leading citizens of its capital, Salvador, wrote an urgent letter begging Philip, their 'father, king and lord', to send help because their colony was about to collapse. Because they lived 'in a faraway place, persecuted for so many years with the losses of war, with the robberies and cruelties of our enemies', the colonists felt 'in immediate and eminent danger'. The need to fortify their borders deprived them of the labour of their slaves on the plantations; while the native population helped the Dutch, showing them routes to the interior, killing planters and burning sugar mills. Worst of all, the 'people from Guinea [their African slaves] seem on the brink of rebellion'. When the colonists heard about 'the events in Catalonia' most of them despaired, because their needs would now inevitably move further down the list of imperial priorities, causing further 'delays in sending us relief'.[56]

Despite these deep-seated problems, Philip IV only lost Portugal because of another miscalculation by Olivares. In November 1640, having relocated most of the Castilian troops in Portugal to Catalonia, the count-duke commanded the duke of Bragança to raise a regiment of his vassals and lead it to the Catalan front in person. The duke, fearful that he would never be allowed to return, pleaded that the responsibilities of his estate precluded his departure; but Olivares 'replied that this was unacceptable'. Ambassador Hopton saw the danger clearly: if another rebellion materialized in Portugal, he considered it 'almost certaine that the duke of Braganza shall ingage himselfe herein'. And indeed, on 1 December 1640, it was Bragança's agent in Lisbon who gave the order for the discontented *fidalgos* (still only 40 in number) and their followers to storm the viceregal palace.[57]

Even with the duke's support, the conspirators ran grave risks. The Portuguese capital was the largest city in the Iberian Peninsula, with perhaps 170,000 inhabitants, and it normally boasted a powerful Spanish garrison – but here too, Olivares's earlier policies worked against him. He had withdrawn to the Catalan front all but two of the companies guarding the viceregal palace, and they proved unable to stay the intruders who hunted down Miguel de Vasconcelos and murdered him. Shortly afterwards, one of the *fidalgos* appeared on the palace balcony and shouted 'Long live King John IV' – meaning Bragança – and the crowd immediately took up the cry. To avoid further bloodshed, Vicereine Margaret of Mantua ordered the outnumbered Castilian troops to surrender; and a few days later Bragança arrived in the capital to receive oaths of fealty from his new subjects.

The Tipping Point

Olivares flatly refused to believe the first rumours of the coup in Lisbon. 'We have heard so far of no motive that could have caused it, nor has there been any grievance, tax or other [likely] cause that could have occasioned such an event,' he told the king. 'It is possible that a popular tumult might have produced a good deal of what we have heard, but to proclaim a king the same day is not credible.' When irrefutable confirmation arrived, the count-duke's spirits sagged. 'In many centuries there cannot have been a more unlucky year than the present one,' he lamented – but, once again, he exaggerated. The year 1641 would prove even worse.[58]

For a few weeks more, Olivares pinned his hopes on a quick victory in Catalonia, where Los Vélez and the royal army continued to advance, meting out exemplary punishment to the towns taken by force. Yet these 'examples' failed to intimidate the people of Barcelona. When news of the massacre at Cambrils arrived, crowds hunted down and killed any remaining Castilians they could find; and when they heard of the fall of Tarragona, they murdered three of the surviving royal judges (and some others suspected of collaboration with 'the enemy'), disfigured them with repeated blows and shots, and then hanged them from the gallows in the city square. Shaken by the rising disorder, Claris persuaded the Junta de Braços to proclaim the Catalan Republic on 16 January 1641; but when, five days later, Los Vélez's troops captured and sacked nearby Martorell, the Junta de Braços gave up their brief bid for independence and recognized Louis XIII as their new ruler. In return, the king agreed that all officers of justice, all clerics and all military governors would henceforth be Catalan; that the Constitutions would prevail; that several unpopular taxes would cease; and that the Inquisition would continue its work with full powers (a special concern of the Catalan leaders). He even graciously agreed that the Catalans could choose another lord if he did not treat them well.

Duplessis-Besançon, Richelieu's representative, now took charge of military affairs within Barcelona, while the city's clergy (reinforced by those who had retreated from the surrounding villages rather than surrender) organized round-the-clock services and frequent processions to beg the city's patron saints for protection against 'the regiments of the count-duke'. According to one royalist, 'the efforts of the most committed friars in their writings and pulpits' upheld the cause as much as 'the *segadors* in the streets'.[59] They needed all their persuasive powers when on 24 January 1641 a herald from Los Vélez arrived and threatened that unless the city surrendered at once, it too would be sacked.

Duplessis-Besançon later remarked in his memoirs, 'In war, the least circumstance, difficult to assess [at the time], often produces major effects', and indeed, on the very day that Los Vélez issued his summons, a ship arrived in Barcelona bearing two envoys from John IV of Portugal with an offer of alliance. This gave the Catalans new 'vigour and strength', and thousands of men and women flocked to join the city's defenders.[60] Just as Los Vélez's troops tried to capture the hill of Monjuich, from which they could bombard the city, Duplessis-Besançon rushed in 2,000 reinforcements. They turned the tide. The royal assault failed and many royal soldiers (especially the Portuguese) deserted as they retreated. Los Vélez soon lacked sufficient men to mount a formal siege. In addition, the marquis had relied on finding supplies in Barcelona: without them, he had to fall back, pursued by French troops.

Olivares nevertheless drew consolation from the sudden death of Pau Claris, probably poisoned by royal agents, and began to contemplate diverting resources from the Catalan to the Portuguese front.[61] As he pointed out to Philip, 'unless action is taken immediately against Portugal, there will be no chance of recovering that kingdom for many years, since each day's delay will make the enterprise more difficult'; but, once again, circumstances beyond his control thwarted him. The count-duke had planned to use the silver aboard the 1640 treasure ships from the Americas as security for loans to fund the 1641 campaign, but none arrived: although the viceroy of Mexico had amassed over 750,000 ducats to send to Spain, he decided to hold the entire shipment back 'because of so many rumours of enemies'. With no silver to offer, Spain found few bankers willing to lend.[62]

As Olivares had feared, Spanish inaction allowed John IV to consolidate his control over Portugal. The Cortes 'acclaimed' him as their new king and, after he abolished the hated regalian rights newly imposed by Madrid, they voted new taxes (including a property tax – the very imposition that had provoked the revolt of Évora three years before). They also presented a list of 'grievances' for redress, including improved administration of justice, punishment of corrupt public officials, and better government control over the bankers who collected the taxes assigned to repay their loans. Other grievances revealed deep social divisions. The nobles and representatives of the towns in the Cortes begged the king to limit the number of clerics (Portugal boasted 30,000 seculars and 25,000 regulars); to limit the jurisdiction of the ecclesiastical courts; and to levy more taxes on the Church. The towns called for the closure of all universities and colleges for five years (save only for Coimbra), because they produced more clerics and lawyers than the kingdom needed; while the towns and the clergy wanted strong measures against the New Christians (none should be admitted to university or allowed to become doctors, lawyers, priests or public officials). The Cortes thus focused on individual groups and sought to return to 'normal times' because 'it is not wise to innovate': they showed little awareness of national issues or collective interests.[63]

Olivares tried to exploit these social divisions by supporting a conspiracy hatched by a group of Portuguese prelates, nobles and New Christian bankers to assassinate John IV and restore Madrid's control. They failed, however, and the new king executed most of the noble conspirators. He also suspended the prelates and appropriated the revenues of their sees, and allowed the Inquisition to persecute the New Christian merchants. He also sponsored sermons and printed propaganda against Castile, while his agents concluded treaties with France, Sweden, Britain – and, most important of all, the Dutch Republic, which in August 1641 sent a fleet to defend Lisbon. Bragança would not become a 'Winter King' like Frederick of the Palatinate (see chapter 8 above).

The Fall of Olivares

Olivares enjoyed no respite. Instead, news arrived of sedition in another previously loyal part of the Monarchy, the kingdom of Aragon, and suspicion fell principally on the viceroy: the duke of Nochera, a Neapolitan. In 1639 Nochera had warned about the discontent in Aragon caused by recruiting, taxation and the loss of trade with France; the following year he sent a defeatist letter urging the king to conciliate the Catalans 'or they will be like Hydra, where instead of one you find seven'; now he offered his services as intermediary between the two sides. Olivares interpreted this as treason and ordered the duke's arrest. He died in prison.[64]

Some nobles in Castile also became restless. Although many of them privately disapproved of the expensive yet unsuccessful policies pursued by Olivares, they made no headway because they lacked a constitutional forum for expressing their grievances (the aristocracy no longer attended the Cortes). According to one of them, 'We grandees are to blame for what has happened to us, because each of us gloated over the harm done to the others. If we had joined together as we should have done, this would not happen.'[65] Nevertheless, two 'grandees' took matters into their own hands. Early in 1641, Olivares ordered the duke of Medina Sidonia, together with his relative and neighbour the marquis of Ayamonte, to initiate secret talks to see whether John IV (married to the duke's sister) might be reconciled with Madrid. Instead, the two nobles sought Portuguese support to 'turn Andalusia into a republic' with Medina at its head. King John offered to send a flotilla from Lisbon to Cádiz, where it would burn the Spanish warships in the harbour and seize the treasure fleet expected from America. Evidence of the plot reached Madrid only a few days before the Portuguese ships arrived off Cádiz, and Olivares reacted both punctually and forcefully. When Medina Sidonia ignored a direct summons to come to court, an envoy arrived with a vial of poison and orders either to bring the duke to Madrid or 'to send him to meet his Maker'. Realizing that the game was up, Medina complied and threw himself (literally) at the king's feet, unchivalrously blaming everything on Ayamonte.[66]

These events – the first aristocratic plots in Castile for 150 years – took place amid another spate of climatic disasters. In spring 1641 a prolonged drought threatened the harvests of Castile; and in August 1642 a tornado struck the city of Burgos with such force that it destroyed the nave of the cathedral, 'lifting beams, boxes and other pieces of wood as if they were feathers'. This natural disaster seemed so remarkable that the king sent hundreds of letters to his subjects in Spain and America soliciting contributions for the cathedral's repair. The years 1640–3 saw the highest precipitation ever recorded in Andalucía, and in January 1642 the Guadalquivir burst its banks, flooding Seville.[67]

The government added to the misery through desperate measures to find money for the wars with Catalonia and Portugal – especially through another devaluation of the currency of Castile, calling in all copper coins and re-stamping them at triple their value. The king also tried to ascertain the number of his Castilian vassals in preparation for levying yet another tax and, since he still lacked census data, he collected data on the number of 'bulls of the crusade' distributed by the Church each year (in theory one to each family). He found that the number of households had declined from 4.3 million in the 1630s to 3.8 million in 1643. As Arthur Hopton, the British ambassador in Madrid, reported to his government:

> Concerning the state of this kingdom, I could never have imagined to have seen it as it is now, for the people begin to fail, and those that remain, by a continuance of bad success, and by their heavy burdens, are quite out of heart . . . The greatest mischief of all is that the king of Spain knows little of all this, and the count-duke is so wilful as he will break rather than bend.[68]

King Philip was not quite as ignorant of the public affairs of his Monarchy as Hopton supposed, however. He fully comprehended the first *consulta* announcing the Portuguese rebellion, because his rescript is stained with his tears (Plate 12); and in spring 1642 he finally emulated his brother-in-law Louis XIII and joined his troops in Aragon. It did little good: he failed to recapture Lleida (Lérida, the last barrier to a march on Madrid), while the French forced the surrender of Perpignan, the second city of Catalonia – which, as the British ambassador in Paris observed, was 'the most important and considerable action the French have accomplished since the beginning of this last war', because it allowed them to advance to the Ebro.[69]

Philip returned to Madrid disconsolately, to find that almost all his nobles had boycotted his court: on Christmas Day, only one man sat in the pews reserved for the grandees – the son of the murdered count of Santa Coloma. Criticisms of the count-duke now became more public, with special venom reserved for the Buen Retiro palace, which Olivares had built for his master on the outskirts of Madrid using tax revenues. Many saw the palace as a symbol of his misguided policies: even its name – 'Retreat' – served as a stick with which to beat the minister as his armies retreated on all fronts. A French cartoon of 1642, 'The plundered Spaniard', memorably portrayed the situation: it showed four 'bandits' (one French, one Portuguese, one Dutch and one Catalan) robbing a Spanish traveller of his clothes, with the loss of Breda, Salces, Catalonia, Portugal, Thionville and Perpignan in the background – all disasters that occurred in the last five years of Olivares's ministry.

So many defeats and humiliations fatally undermined Olivares's position. On 16 January 1643 his secretary noted: 'My master is utterly worn out and broken, but even with the water over his head, he keeps swimming,' adding '[t]he storm is great, but God is above all, and one single event can change everything for the better'.[70] Perhaps he imagined that news of the death of Olivares's nemesis, Cardinal Richelieu, which had just become known in Madrid, would 'change everything'; but if so, he erred. The following day Philip gave his Favourite and chief minister of almost 22 years permission to retire.

The fall of Olivares led to a long-overdue reappraisal of the Monarchy's strategic priorities. As early as July 1641 one minister had warned the Favourite that 'Seeking to arrange the affairs of Spain must come before the conservation of other provinces, because if the war lasts long there, we shall lose them all, whereas once Catalonia and Portugal are regained, everything can be maintained and we can recover what has been lost [elsewhere].'[71] As usual, the count-duke paid no attention, but two weeks after his fall, the king and his Council of State together reviewed imperial priorities and concluded that less money should go to Germany, Italy and the Netherlands until all enemy forces had been expelled from Spanish soil, and that the war in Catalonia must take precedence over recovering Portugal. Philip therefore ordered his commanders in all theatres except Catalonia to assume a defensive posture. He also opened peace talks with both France and the Dutch, and instructed don Francisco de Melo, governor-general of the Spanish Netherlands, to forward conciliatory personal letters to his sister Anne, now the regent of France, with orders to 'deploy every seemly and feasible means to secure a treaty'.[72]

Melo was a career diplomat who had gained his exalted office by default: he was the senior Spanish minister in Brussels in 1641 when smallpox claimed Philip's brother the Cardinal-Infante – but he reassured the king that his relative lack of military experience did not matter, because nowadays 'a mere doctor of philosophy' could lead an army to victory. The following year he vindicated this arrogant view by using a portion of his troops to hold the Dutch at bay while he led the rest to victory over a French army in battle and captured five French towns.[73] Melo's success seems to have weakened the peace initiative. When the Council of State met early in 1643 in the presence of the king to discuss whether or not to open peace talks with France, the count of Oñate (another career diplomat) argued:

When the situation and developments are favourable, it is desirable for Your Majesty to bring relief to your vassals through peace, and when they are unfavourable, it seems essential; but it must always be done while maintaining the ruler's reputation and dignity as much as possible, especially a ruler to whom God has given as many kingdoms and possessions as Your Majesty; because otherwise, when we make peace, it will be neither sure nor respected.

Of course Oñate professed that he did not oppose negotiations in the long run; he only opposed them at this juncture: 'We should leave a little time for Time,' he quipped.[74] Melo agreed and invaded France again, laying siege to the heavily fortified town of Rocroi. This time a relief force arrived promptly, drove off his weak cavalry, and then attacked the Spanish infantry until they either died or surrendered. 'To tell the truth,' Melo admitted sheepishly after the fiasco, 'we used to regard war here as a pastime; but the profession [of arms] is serious and it gains and loses empires.'[75]

Although the battle of Rocroi did not destroy 'the empire on which the sun never set', it certainly transformed its strategic vision. The king, now 38 years old, sought consolation in spiritualism, summoning men and women renowned for their prophetic powers from all his dominions to give advice on what he should do next, culminating in a 'summit' of prophets in October 1643; and for the next 22 years Philip wrote a holograph letter once every two weeks to one of the spirit mediums, Sor María de Ágreda, begging her to erect a barrier of prayer against his enemies that might take the place of the human resources he lacked.[76] Philip's ministers also hoped that God 'would give Your Majesty's armed forces the results that reflect the justice of your cause' – but in view of 'the variety of events and accidents that normally occur in wars', they recommended that Spain should concentrate its resources on fighting the Dutch and the Catalans, requiring Italy to fund the other wars of the Monarchy, as well as paying for its own defence.[77]

Even so, the cost to Spain of continuing Philip's wars exceeded what his subjects could bear. Don Juan Chumacero, the minister responsible for law and order in Castile, had already warned the king that his vassals 'cannot withstand the burden of their taxes, so that everything may collapse at the same time'. In particular, he feared that the towns will 'shake off their yoke at the same time, through frustration' at the endless demands of the tax collectors, especially when 'the crops are generally poor' because 'storms have destroyed a large part of them, and what has been harvested is of poor quality'.[78] Don Luis de Haro, Olivares's successor as chief minister, felt equally pessimistic when early in 1646 he went to Cádiz to get the Atlantic fleet to sea. 'Everything comes down to difficulties and more difficulties' because of the extreme weather, he complained. 'Three months of snow and rain, and the harshest weather ever seen by Man' had created 'difficulties or rather impossibilities', and he began to contemplate suicide: 'Sire, I do not know how to deal with this, unless it is to drown myself.'[79]

These and other extreme climatic events ruined the harvest in 1646, and the following winter saw continual rain. According to a Madrid newspaper, 'In Spain, and even they say in all Europe, the era of Noah's flood came again with a vengeance, because the rains that fell were so heavy and so continuous, and the rivers rose so excessively, that commerce and communication ceased between the cities, towns and villages. Many lives were at risk; many buildings collapsed.'[80] The inhabitants of the capital suffered in spite of an elaborate supply network created to feed them with grain from the vicinity, so that when the harvest failed again in 1647 (an El Niño year), Chumacero despaired:

> God has chosen to wear out these realms with every calamity – war, famine and plague – each one of which normally suffices to raise great anguish and a sense of panic ... The population is very volatile and every day becomes more insolent, which leads to fears of some violence ... Hunger respects no one, and so it is necessary to do all we can to help, and to avoid any decision which the people might regard as a burden.

He concluded wearily: 'There is no shortage of people who blame Your Majesty, saying that he does nothing, and that the council is at fault – as if we had any control over the weather!' Other ministers reinforced Chumacero's point: 'Hunger is the greatest enemy,' they warned the king 'and in many states the shortage of bread has provoked unrest that ended in sedition.'[81] They knew whereof they spoke: adverse weather had just triggered riots in Andalusia.

The 'Green Banner' Revolts

In January 1647, following a disastrous harvest, a group of 'over 70' men armed with swords and clubs marched through the streets of Ardales, a mountain town inland from Málaga, shouting 'Long live the king and down with the bad government!' The marquis of Estepa, a local nobleman, mused that 'the poverty of some inhabitants, and the hardship that causes when they pay taxes imposed on them', and the greed of the tax collectors, 'may perhaps have caused them to lose patience'; but he fully realized the extreme danger posed by domestic rebellion at a time when 'we see our king so beset by enemies, with a real risk that the kingdom in which we live may be lost'. After two months of talks, Estepa therefore put together an army of retainers and, even though the rebels were heavily armed, they crumbled. Three of their leaders were hanged and 15 others fled. Estepa's firm action seems to have averted unrest elsewhere for a while.[82]

In May 1647, just when the new grain harvest seemed safe, all over Andalusia 'the weather turned very cold, even worse than the coldest January day'. Freak frosts killed the ears of grain and produced the worst harvest of the century. It also left little seed corn for the next year: according to a chronicler, 'the peasants did not sow one third of what they should have sowed'. In March 1648 the senior magistrate of Granada, the third largest city in the kingdom, reported that he had never seen so many children begging in the street and noted that the Foundlings Hospital was full and could scarcely feed those already there. A loaf of bread, he noted, cost triple its usual price. There now followed 'the most important urban uprising in Castile since the revolt of the Comuneros' over a century before. A group of men armed with swords and clubs marched on the city hall shouting (again) 'Long live the king and down with the bad government!' Rumours circulated that 'the people want to elect a king and declare a state of rebellion', but instead they elected a respected gentleman, as the new chief magistrate: the pious (and aptly named) Don Luis de Paz ('Peace'). The new leader did his best to bring to market all the grain stored in the city and thus assure bread at a reasonable price until the next harvest; but for several weeks Granada defied the central government.[83] In Madrid, the king's ministers proclaimed that disorder should always be punished without mercy – but opined that the extreme circumstances of 1648 made moderation advisable. The troubles had arisen from 'need and hunger', and many vassals lived 'on the edge of desperation'; therefore, the ministers reasoned, 'because of the unfavourable disposition of the weather, we need to give way and dissimulate in order to avoid greater setbacks'. The king agreed: later that month he paraphrased these views in one of his breast-beating letters to Sor María de Ágreda. He favoured clemency, he told her, 'because it is not possible to squeeze my vassals more, as much because of what they would suffer as because of the risk we would run of suffering more misfortunes'.[84]

Philip showed no such restraint towards the duke of Híjar, a discontented courtier who aspired to be king of Aragon. The Híjar conspiracy stemmed from the succession crisis left by the death from smallpox of Crown Prince Balthasar Carlos in 1646. The prince's mother had died two years before, leaving Philip IV with only one legitimate descendant: his daughter María Teresa, aged eight. As Don Luis de Haro pointed out to his master: 'Without a royal male to succeed, the Monarchy is in critical danger of passing under the control of foreign rulers. It is a circumstance that places the whole future of Spain at risk.' Haro studiously avoided mentioning that this 'circumstance' also placed his own future at risk, since the identity of the princess's husband would determine whether or not he remained at the helm.[85] A change of ministers already appealed to some courtiers – especially to those who had hoped for some reward upon the fall of Olivares but found their ambitions thwarted by the rise of Haro, the count-duke's nephew. One of those disappointed was the duke of Híjar, with extensive estates in Aragon. During the king's 'spiritual summit' (page 279 above), one of the prophets apparently told Híjar that he would rule Aragon after Philip IV died, leading the duke to prepare genealogies to justify his claim to the throne and to seek out 'astrologers and mathematicians, so that they would tell him what would happen'. He also spent time – too much time – discussing with others at court possible strategies to overthrow Haro. A servant betrayed these indiscretions, and Philip immediately ordered the arrest of Híjar and others. Under torture, they revealed two separate (and incompatible) plots. Both started with the abduction of Princess María Teresa, who would be taken either to Paris to marry Louis XIV (with Catalonia and Navarre as her dowry) or to Lisbon to wed John IV's heir (with Galicia as her dowry); and both ended with the grateful princess making Híjar king of Aragon. Philip IV himself considered that '[what] they plotted (or wanted to plot) against my crown was so ridiculous that they seem fools rather than traitors' – but in December 1648 he sentenced the duke to life imprisonment and executed the rest. He would face no more aristocratic rebellions.[86]

The king settled for good two other issues that same year – the count of Peñaranda, Spain's chief negotiator at the Congress of Westphalia in 1648, signed treaties that ended the long-running wars in both the Netherlands and Germany (see chapter 8 above) – but he stopped short of concluding a general peace. Although Peñaranda observed pointedly, 'I leave it to the superior intelligence and prudence of Your Majesty to consider if this is the right moment' to settle with France or 'to remain at war while all Europe makes peace', the outbreak of the Fronde revolt led Philip to miss his chance (see chapter 10 below); but the continuation of extreme weather prevented him from exploiting to the full his rival's weakness.[87] In October 1648 the town council of Cádiz lamented that 'the grape harvest of this year is ruined' and the following month that 'for several days the butchers have had no meat'. The following spring, torrential rains and gales battered Seville so severely in Holy Week that participants could not leave their homes to take part in processions: 'The darkness, wind and rain on Maundy Thursday' were the worst ever known in the city, one chronicler recorded; 'it was as cold as January,' wrote another. One-third of the city lay under water, making it impossible to bring in sufficient food and flour to feed the population. To complete the misery, a devastating plague epidemic carried off half the city's inhabitants before spreading eastwards, ravaging one coastal city after another. Although a strict quarantine spared the rest of Castile from the epidemic, even in Madrid in the mid-century births plunged, deaths soared, and infant mortality reached levels never equalled in early modern times (Fig. 27).[88]

Deputies in the Cortes lamented 'the calamities that surround us: kingdoms lost, vassals impoverished, wars, plague in Andalucía, locusts which destroy the fields of

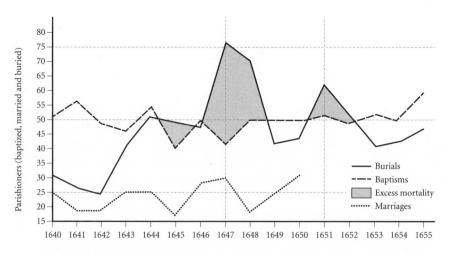

27. The subsistence crisis in Madrid, 1647–8.
The registers of the parish of Santa María de la Almudena, a poor parish in the heart of Madrid, shows that burials peaked while baptisms and marriages plunged in 1647–8, just as the granaries of the capital ran out of flour.

Castile, and other signs of the wrath of God'; while a royal minister expressed concern that the 'complaints of the Monarchy are so numerous that I fear they may suck us under', but then added more positively that 'if we can capture Barcelona, stoke the fire in France, and save the Low Countries, then it will all have been worth it and all can be saved'.[89] This seemed absurdly optimistic. In November 1651 the government debased Castile's copper currency in the hope of making a profit of 12 million ducats, but according to a chronicler in Seville, 'even without the effects of the devaluation, the scarcity of all foodstuffs would have sufficed to cause dearth'; as usual, tampering with the coinage disrupted all market transactions. By April 1652, a loaf of bread cost more than a working man could earn in a week. A new wave of insurgency started in Córdoba the following month, when several hundred men from a poor parish took to the streets armed with 'arquebuses and other weapons' and, 'encouraged by the women', shouted 'Long live the king and death to the evil government!' They found huge quantities of grain hidden in the houses of the rich and, to avoid further disorders, the clerical and lay leaders of the city set up an interim government charged with supplying cheap bread. Desperate to avoid any confrontation that might compromise his ability to fund his wars, the king ordered the immediate dispatch of 6,000 bushels of grain from Madrid to Córdoba; and, as in the case of Granada in 1648, he accepted that the rioters had not 'intended to forget their obedience to me' but had rather acted through 'the anguish caused by hunger, their lack of foresight in not laying by the wheat required for their sustenance, and the exploitation of many people who sold wheat at excessive prices'. Philip therefore pardoned them all.[90]

Such leniency created a dangerous precedent: everyone could see that collective violence had 'worked' in Córdoba, because the city turned into an oasis of plenty. Starving people from all over Andalucía therefore arrived to consume the grain graciously provided by the king, while a wave of insurgency, known as the 'Green Banner' revolts, eventually affected some 20 Andalucían towns and probably involved more people than the revolt of the Catalans (Fig. 28). Seville was the first city to follow the example of Córdoba. In May 1652 rioters attacked the houses of those suspected of hoarding grain while others entered the city's arsenal and distributed armour, weapons and even artillery. Others still broke into the prisons and freed the inmates. The magistrates made haste to restore all copper coins to their former value, abolished recent royal taxes (including excise duties on food and the hated *papel sellado*) and proclaimed – falsely – that the king had issued a general pardon. These measures pacified the situation until, a month later, a large force of city merchants and gentlemen suddenly attacked the headquarters of the rebels. Lacking the expertise to use their artillery, they surrendered. The cycle of Green Banner revolts ended as suddenly as it had begun.[91]

The Spanish Phoenix?

Against all the odds, the year 1652 turned out well for Philip IV. His troops recaptured Dunkirk, the principal port of the South Netherlands; Casale, reputedly the

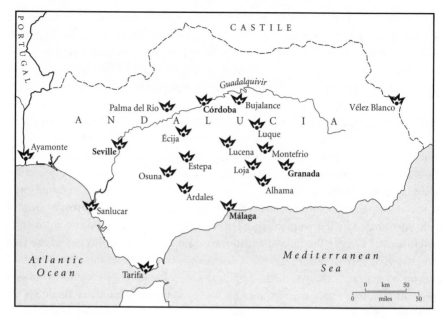

28. The 'Green Banner' revolts in Andalusia, 1647–52.
The extent of these urban revolts has been seriously underestimated by historians: they probably involved more people and places than the revolt of Catalonia. All the towns and cities named on the map experienced rebellions in these years.

most formidable fortress in Italy; and Barcelona, whose surrender led almost all of Catalonia to submit. Although French forces, assisted by a few Catalans, retained the northern areas, after 12 years of savage and continuous war Madrid again controlled most of the principality. Philip IV's ability 'to overcome not only my enemies but also storms at sea, epidemics on land and the domestic unrest of the towns of Andalusia' astonished Pietro Bassadonna, the Venetian ambassador in Spain. Back in 1647, he recalled, rebellion had reigned in Naples, Sicily and Andalusia; Híjar planned to create an independent Aragon; a devastating plague epidemic raged; while 'the king's revenues were alienated; his credit was exhausted; his allies were either declared enemies or neutral or undecided'. In short, the Spanish Monarchy had then resembled 'the great Colossus [of Rhodes] which had been for so many years the wonder of the world until brought down by an earthquake in just a few minutes.' Despite several 'earthquakes', Bassadonna noted, the Spanish Colossus remained almost intact. Nevertheless, he continued, in large part this reflected 'the present commotions of the kingdom of France, which has chosen to turn its victorious arms against its own breast, and exchanged a glorious war for a dreadful slaughter of the French themselves'.[92] He predicted that the 'earthquakes' would resume as soon as the French stopped slaughtering each other.

Bassadonna failed to foresee another setback for Spain: the British Republic declared war in 1655 (see chapter 12 below). This development profoundly depressed Philip IV. He assured Sor María de Ágreda that the situation was worse 'than any that this Monarchy has ever seen, particularly since we lack the means to withstand even one part of such a great storm'; but, as usual, he refused to contemplate a negotiated settlement. Even when Cardinal Mazarin sent a secret envoy to Madrid in 1656, and the parties agreed that France would end all assistance to Portugal and in return retain all its conquests in Catalonia and the Netherlands, the talks foundered on the status of the prince of Condé, Louis XIV's cousin and the victor of Rocroi, who had defected to Spanish service. The king refused to abandon his ally. The war therefore continued, and Spain lost more ground. Meanwhile Castile experienced exceptional precipitation throughout the 1650s, reducing the yield of one harvest after another.[93]

The unending sequence of disasters alarmed Philip's advisers, who warned him in January 1659 that peace with France, whatever the price, 'is absolutely essential for the conservation of the Monarchy of Your Majesty' – adding that 'experience has shown that the more we delay it, the more we lose, and the more difficult recovering it becomes'. The king declared his willingness both to sacrifice Condé (on the grounds that 'when one places in the balance the conservation of the Monarchy, the importance of this necessity cannot be compared with that of the prince of Condé') and to marry his daughter María Teresa to Louis XIV (although in making this concession he compared himself with Abraham sacrificing Isaac). Later that year, the peace of the Pyrenees ended 25 years of continuous war.[94]

Now, Philip could at last concentrate on the reconquest of Portugal, but almost two decades of independence had allowed the Bragança regime to consolidate its position both at home and abroad. Above all, Portugal controlled Angola and Brazil, generating both trade and tax revenues, while French and British troops arrived to defend the frontiers. Nevertheless in 1663, after signing a fourth and final decree of bankruptcy, Philip launched a powerful invasion of Portugal which captured Évora. Its fall provoked rioting and an attempted coup in Lisbon; but an Anglo-Portuguese army mounted a successful counter-attack. The councillors of Philip IV summed up the futility of the situation perfectly. 'A truce with Portugal is the only way to ensure that we will not lose everything and to repair the desperate state in which we find ourselves,' they lamented – only to continue lamely that 'considering that the army is already on campaign, and that it would not be right to sacrifice all the treasure it has cost, or to despair of some happy outcome, it seems we should wait and see what happens'.[95] Only the king's death in 1665 opened the path to peace.

Of the vast Lusitanian empire that Philip IV had inherited, the heralds could proclaim his sickly 4-year-old son 'Carlos I of Portugal' in only two tiny outposts: Ceuta and Tangier. After two more inconclusive campaigns, the regents for the young king accepted English mediation, and in 1668 they signed a peace that recognized Portugal as an independent kingdom and 'restored everything to the state it had enjoyed before the union with Spain'. They returned all the property confiscated from Spaniards who had sided with Bragança, and even the duke of Medina Sidonia received the lands confiscated from his father after his conspiracy to create an independent Andalusia in 1641. It was the most humiliating treaty ever signed by the Spanish Habsburgs – and it still did not bring peace.

In 1667 Louis XIV declared war on Spain, on the grounds that the terms of the peace of the Pyrenees had not been fulfilled, and his troops seized Lille and other towns in the Spanish Netherlands, which became a permanent part of France when the parties made peace. Further aggression by Louis secured more territorial gains, in part because harvest failures in 1665–8 and 1677–83, plus another plague epidemic in 1676–85 and yet more harvest failures in 1685–8, prevented Spain's demographic and economic recovery. In 1687 the abuses that normally arose from billeting troops during a time of dearth provoked another major rebellion in Catalonia, and thousands of peasants marched on Barcelona. Just as in 1640, some ministers in Madrid advocated firm repression, but others had learned their lesson, recognizing that 'force is a very dangerous remedy when the civilians are more powerful than the army'. They therefore hesitated to do anything rash lest 'all Catalonia should be lost in a few hours, *as we saw in the days of the count of Santa Coloma*'. Nevertheless, France again intervened, conquering much of Catalonia (including Barcelona) and also invading the Spanish Netherlands (destroying most of Brussels in a ferocious bombardment). It is hard to dissent from the verdict of the Venetian ambassador in 1695: 'The whole of the present reign has been an uninterrupted series of calamities'.[96]

Counting the Cost

What had Philip IV gained by fighting so many wars? In material terms, nothing: he acquired no new territory and instead lost the vast Portuguese empire, Jamaica, important parts of the Netherlands, and northern Catalonia. Yet this negative outcome entailed immense Spanish sacrifices, both political and material. Repeatedly, strategic overstretch forced the crown to postpone measures aimed at recovery and retrenchment, and to make substantial concessions to its rebels. When Barcelona surrendered in 1652, for example, Philip confirmed its privileges almost exactly as they had been in 1640, issued a general pardon that exempted only one person, and swore to respect the 'Constitutions'.[97]

Olivares's attempts to innovate in Catalonia thus neither diminished the principality's independence nor increased its contribution to imperial ventures – but they caused great personal and material losses. Troops had destroyed countless villages like Santa Coloma de Farners and Ruidarenes, and butchered the defenders of numerous towns like Cambrils and Tarragona: between 1640 and 1659 thousands of ordinary Catalans died violently and thousands more fled into exile. The loss was qualitative as well as quantitative: at least 200 gentlemen lost their lives during the revolt – executed, killed in action or disappeared – and over 500 more went into exile. By the time Barcelona surrendered in 1652, its population halved by famine and plague, it had run up a debt of over 20 million ducats; the diocese of Tortosa, which changed hands in 1640 and again in 1648, saw its revenues drop from over 30,000 ducats annually in the 1630s to virtually nothing.[98]

Everywhere, Philip IV had far fewer subjects at his death than at his accession. In Naples, the revolt of 1647–8 cost the lives of at least 6,000 people; repeated harvest failures expedited the death of tens of thousands more; and over 150,000 people in the capital city alone died during the plague of 1656 (see chapter 4 above). A census of 1650 in Aragon showed that settlements near the Catalan and French frontiers had fallen at least one-third below the levels recorded at the end of the Middle Ages; while the Castilian population living near the Portuguese border also fell dramatically because the king's troops exacted so much money, food and other local resources. The burden on smaller communities often proved insupportable and their inhabitants fled because they could not feed both themselves and the troops billeted on them. Baptisms in Extremadura fell by more than a quarter (Fig. 29). As Henry Kamen has observed: 'No other single event in Castilian history of the early modern period, excepting only epidemics, did more to destroy the country' than the 28-year war with Portugal.[99]

Nevertheless, most of Castile lay far from any theatre of operations and so avoided direct devastation by troops; also, thanks to ruthless enforcement of a cordon sanitaire, it avoided the plague for much of the seventeenth century. The steady demographic decline apparent in Figure 29 therefore reflects other causes. It is possible to identify three potential culprits. First came extreme weather, starting with the drought of 1630–1, which ended the viability of many settlements on marginal land. Numerous subsequent floods, droughts and other climatic anomalies also periodically caused sterility, dearth and famine. Second, every year saw the emigration of thousands of people from Castile. Some went involuntarily, as conscripts to fight for the king overseas or as prisoners captured by north African pirates. Many more took ship for America because, in the words of the French ambassador in 1681, 'they cannot live in Spain'. Inevitably, this reduced the number of subjects left at home.[100]

The third culprit for the depopulation of Castile was taxation. According to a recent calculation, the crown's taxes absorbed approximately '8 per cent of national income in the 1580s and 12 per cent in the 1660s' – an increase of 50 per cent – and, on top of this rising burden, taxpayers also had to satisfy the competing demands of the Church, of landlords (for the rural population) and of the towns (for the rest).[101] As in any fiscal system, this burden was not shared equally. Some Castilians enjoyed tax exemption: those able to produce certain goods for themselves (olive oil, wine and so on) escaped paying excise duties on what they consumed, while certain social groups achieved collective exemption. Thus when in 1648 the magistrates of Cádiz discussed how to allocate the 'millones' tax, they noted that many citizens 'were tax exempt on a variety of counts: some because they were gentlemen or clerics', others 'because they served in the cavalry, as gunners, as ministers of the Cruzada, and as Familiars of the Inquisition'. Hence, they continued, the burden would fall on the relatively few citizens involved in the city's trade, and on the poor, causing them disproportionate hardship.[102] The system of making each community pay a fixed quota for each tax, whatever the number of taxpayers, hit smaller communities particularly hard in times of falling population, because almost

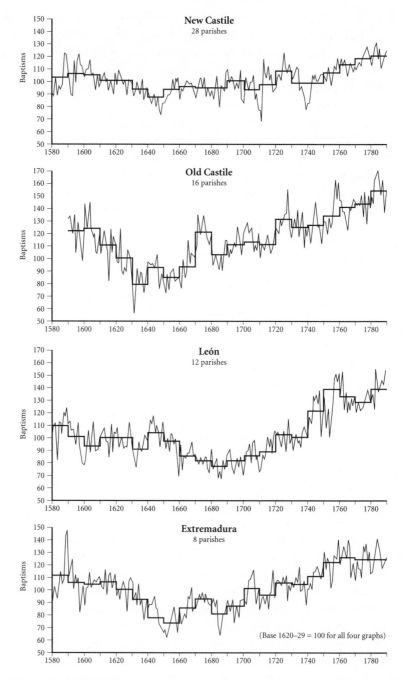

29. Baptisms in Castile, 1580–1790.
Baptismal registers from 115 Spanish parishes all showed a fall during the seventeenth century, but
with different rhythms. Old Castile suffered its sharpest fall during the drought of 1630–1, New
Castile and Extremadura during the plague years of 1649–50, and León during the famine of 1662.
Extremadura also suffered losses because of the war with Portugal between 1640 and 1668.
Other regions adversely affected by Philip IV's wars – Aragon, the Basque provinces, Navarre and
Valencia – are not represented.

inevitably a point came when the remaining taxpayers could no longer afford the collective assessment and so abandoned the settlements. Fiscal pressure also caused indirect harm. As the council of finance warned the king in 1634, 'people need food more than they need clothes and shoes', so raising taxes reduced demand for manufactured goods and caused lay-offs and migration.[103]

As Alberto Marcos Martín forcefully stated:

> In the last analysis, we should assess a fiscal system (any fiscal system, past or present) not by what it raises but by what it collects (and by what methods and processes it chooses to accomplish this task), and by what it does, what it creates, and how it spends what it has amassed in taxes and contributions.

By this yardstick, the record of the Spanish Habsburgs is abysmal. First, they borrowed enormous sums from foreign bankers, creating a 'sovereign debt' far beyond Spain's capacity to service: over 112 million ducats by 1623, over 131 million by 1638, almost 182 million by 1667, and almost 223 million by 1687.[104] Second, public-sector borrowing drained capital and raw materials from Spain, undercut local manufactures, and encouraged a 'rentier' mentality among those sectors of the population with the potential to be entrepreneurs. Third, the need to raise and create taxes to repay lenders led to onerous fiscal expedients with high social and economic costs. Finally, most tax revenues were remitted abroad, to fund armies and navies fighting to achieve international goals that mattered to the dynasty but not to most Spaniards. Between 1618 and 1648, the government exported at least 150 million ducats – a sum almost exactly equal to the increase in Castile's public debt.

In the case of China, Timothy Brook pointed out that no previous emperor had 'faced climatic conditions as abnormal and severe as Chongzhen', and one could make much the same excuse for Philip IV. During his reign, Spain suffered extreme weather without parallel in other periods, particularly in 1630–2 and 1640–3; but more than any other seventeenth-century ruler, Philip intensified the impact of climate change by disastrous policy choices. In the words of Arthur Hopton, one of the shrewdest ambassadors in Madrid, in 1634: 'It is no wonder that many of their designs fail in the execution, for though this great vessel [the Spanish Monarchy] contains much water, yet it has so many leaks it is always dry' – in other words, in trying to do too much, the crown achieved nothing.[105]

The Spanish Habsburgs seem to have sincerely believed their mantra that foreign wars, however expensive and inconclusive, offered the best way to defend Spain itself: 'With as many kingdoms and lordships as have been linked to this crown it is impossible to be without war in some area, either to defend what we have acquired or to divert our enemies,' as Philip once observed.[106] Nevertheless, although the king spent every day of his 44-year reign at war – against the Dutch (1621–48), against the French (1635–59), against Britain (1625–30 and 1654–9) and in the Iberian Peninsula (1640–68), as well as in Germany and in Italy – he could surely have avoided (or more swiftly ended) some conflicts, and thereby reduced the fiscal pressure that crushed his subjects and provoked so many of them to rebel. In the

Netherlands, he could certainly have renewed the Twelve Years' Truce with the Dutch Republic when it expired in 1621; and he might have exploited the capture of Breda and the simultaneous imperial victories in Germany in 1625 to negotiate an advantageous settlement. The king himself later admitted that he should have stayed out of the war of Mantua in 1628: 'I have heard it said that the wars in Italy over Casale in Monferrat could have been avoided,' he wrote ruefully, and 'if I have made a mistake in some way and given Our Lord cause for displeasure, it was in this'.[107] Above all, Spain fumbled every opportunity to make a peace with France. In 1637, after just two years of war, Richelieu sent a secret agent to open informal peace talks, but Olivares insisted on a public overture: 'Let those who broke the peace, sue for peace,' he pompously chided the French envoy. Two years later, the count-duke warned his master that 'we need to think about bending in order to avoid breaking' and sent a special envoy of his own to Paris to start talks – but his willingness to negotiate ended as soon as the *Nu-pieds* rebellion in Normandy seemed to weaken his rival.[108]

Shortly after his fall in 1643, Olivares realized the foolishness of a faith-based foreign policy, confessing to a former colleague 'This is the world, and so it has always been, even though we thought we could perform miracles and turn the world into something it can never be' – but for 22 years he had acted on the assumption that 'God is Spanish and favours our nation'. In 1650 an English statesman in Madrid still marvelled at the capacity of Spain's leaders for self-deception. They were, he wrote, 'a wretched, miserable, proud, senseless people and as far from the wise men I expected as can be imagined; and if some miracle do not preserve them, this crown must be speedily destroyed'. A generation later, one of those ministers made the same point: 'I fear deeply for Italy; I am very worried about Catalonia; and I never forget about America, where the French already have too many colonies. We cannot govern by miracles for ever.'[109] The miracles ceased when Carlos II died childless in 1700, and a savage succession war resulted in the partition of the Spanish Monarchy, with the larger part falling to a grandson of Louis XIV, whose descendants rule Spain to this day.

France in Crisis, 1618–88[1]

La Grande Nation?

'BOTH GEOGRAPHICALLY AND SOCIALLY,' WROTE LLOYD MOOTE IN 1971, THE Fronde revolt in France (1648–53) 'was the most widespread of all the rebellions in mid-seventeenth-century Europe'.[2] Its extent should not cause surprise, because France was the largest state in western Europe, covering almost 200,000 square miles. More striking is the extensive social support for the revolt: almost all the leading nobles defied the crown at some point, including the king's uncle, Gaston of Orléans, as did judges and civil servants, cardinals and curates, lawyers and doctors, industrial workers and field hands. About one million French men and women died, either directly or indirectly, because of the Fronde.

Like its neighbours, Spain and Britain, France was a 'composite monarchy', the product of territorial unification during earlier centuries. Seven provinces on the periphery (Brittany, Burgundy, Dauphiné, Guyenne, Languedoc, Normandy and Provence) retained considerable autonomy, guaranteed by their own fiscal institutions, sovereign law courts and representative assemblies (the *États*: these seven provinces were therefore known as *Pays d'États*, 'provinces with Estates'). The central government in Paris directly controlled the remaining two-thirds of the country (known as the *Pays d'élections* after the tax officials, the *élus*, who apportioned tax quotas). Traditionally, legislation and taxes for the kingdom had been voted by another representative assembly, the *États-Généraux* (States-General), but after 1600 it met only twice. As a result, Louis XIII (r. 1610–43), like two of his brothers-in-law, Philip IV and Charles I, augmented his revenues whenever possible by manipulating existing taxes and by enforcing regalian rights, and he relied on his senior judges (those sitting in the ten *Parlements*, or sovereign law courts, of the kingdom) to enforce them (Fig. 30).

Louis XIII ruled the most populous state in Europe, with perhaps 20 million inhabitants (against 7 million in the Iberian Peninsula and perhaps the same in Britain and Ireland), and French farmers produced an abundance of staples as well as some new crops, more resistant to climatic adversity, such as maize, buckwheat, beans, tomatoes and potatoes. The duke of Sully, the chief fiscal officer of Louis's father, Henry IV, placed the finances of the French state on a sound basis. He stabilized the public debt by repudiating foreign obligations and unilaterally reducing the interest payable on

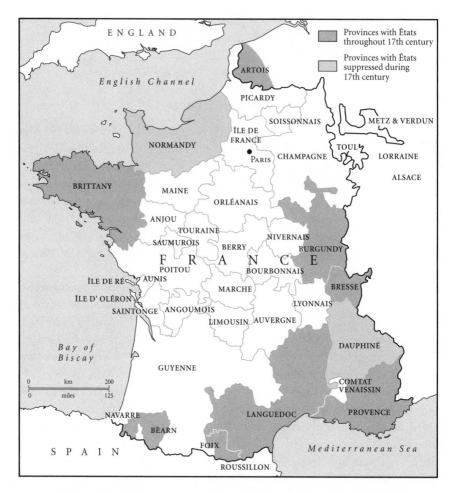

30. Seventeenth-century France.

The kingdom comprised both *Pays d'élections*, governed directly from Paris, and *Pays d'États*, most of them on the periphery, where the central government ruled through provincial institutions. The crown suppressed the Estates of Dauphiné in 1628, and those of Normandy in 1666, and gradually increased its authority over the rest.

remaining loans; and he raised revenue by introducing new indirect taxes, including the *Paulette*: a nine-year agreement (renewable) that allowed holders of government office the right to pass on their posts to anyone they chose in return for annual payments to the treasury. The *Paulette* soon became indispensable to the government because it yielded 10 per cent of total revenues, but it gave rise to a serious disadvantage. Members of the bureaucracy, who numbered over 50,000 men, including the judges, henceforth enjoyed almost complete job security and could sell or bequeath public offices as they pleased. The crown could no longer control them.

Seventeenth-century France was also weakened by the coexistence of two religious communities that had spent the later sixteenth century fighting each other. In 1598 Henry IV issued the Edict of Nantes, which granted full civil rights to France's Protestants (often known as Huguenots), who made up about 10 per cent of the kingdom's population, and guaranteed their right to think, speak, write and worship as they wished within their own homes. They could also worship publicly in specified areas where they were numerous, and convene at regular intervals in assemblies to discuss both religious and political issues. But the Edict also legalized Catholic worship and assemblies everywhere, and the French Catholic Church rapidly gained in strength. The total number of convents in France doubled between 1600 and 1660, and diocesan seminaries to train the secular clergy rose from 8 to perhaps 70.

The murder of Henry IV in 1610 and the accession of his 9-year-old son Louis XIII produced several changes. First the Queen Regent, Marie de Medici, dismissed Sully and used the resources he had accumulated to pay pensions and bribes to her noble supporters; then, when several nobles supported by the Huguenots nevertheless challenged her authority, Marie promised to include more nobles in her council and granted the Huguenots permission to turn their principal port, La Rochelle, into an artillery fortress capable of resisting a long siege. In 1617, resentful at his mother's maladroit handling of public affairs, Louis seized power and banished Marie and her chief adviser, Bishop Armand-Jean du Plessis de Richelieu, from his court; but Louis rashly allowed his mother to retain all her revenues, lands and offices. These allowed her to defy her son when, in 1619, she escaped from confinement; but the following year, Richelieu mediated a settlement that allowed Marie to resume her place on the royal council. At last, the French crown was free to address three pressing problems: the power of the Huguenots; the insubordination of the nobles; and the growing strength of the Habsburgs, whose territories in Spain, Italy, Germany and the Netherlands encircled and threatened France.

Louis determined to eliminate the Huguenots before embarking on costly foreign ventures. He claimed that the Edict of Nantes did not apply to Navarre (a kingdom that he ruled separately from France) and when in 1621 the Huguenot National Assembly protested, he invaded. This unleashed a religious war that, combined with a succession of cold winters and summers between 1618 and 1623 which caused widespread dearth, ruled out an assertive French foreign policy; and in frustration in 1624 Louis recalled Richelieu, now a cardinal. His ministry would last 18 years.[3]

Initially, Richelieu too prioritized domestic over foreign policy, largely because his patron, Marie, supported the *dévots*, a group of courtiers whose chief political goal was the destruction of Huguenot independence. After some vacillation, he and the king in person laid siege to La Rochelle, despite its impressive fortifications, and did nothing while Spain mobilized troops in northern Italy to prevent a French claimant from acquiring the duchy of Mantua (see chapter 9 above). Luckily for Richelieu, Spain still had not prevailed when La Rochelle surrendered in October 1628. He and Louis immediately led a powerful army across the Alps.

France Goes to War

France's efforts to dominate northern Italy failed in part because extreme climatic events produced another economic crisis. A sequence of unusually wet winters and summers between 1625 and 1631 (including the 'year without a summer': 1628) either reduced or destroyed the crops, culminating in a famine that coincided with a plague epidemic. Lyon, France's second city, lost half its population, and hundreds of thousands died in the countryside.[4] The catastrophe also reduced the demand for industrial goods and paralyzed trade, making it far harder to mobilize the necessary human and material resources to win the war. Developments within Italy also worked against effective French intervention. Exercising his rights as feudal overlord of Mantua, Emperor Ferdinand II diverted 12,000 soldiers from Germany to fight in northern Italy alongside 25,000 Spanish troops, far outnumbering France's forces.

Richelieu also undermined his own foreign policy by provoking a new domestic crisis. Convinced that the provincial Estates were shirking their fiscal responsibilities, the cardinal sent special commissioners into Burgundy, Dauphiné, Languedoc and Provence with orders to raise taxes. In addition, he threatened to suspend the *Paulette* when its nine-year term ended unless the senior judges provided full support to these commissioners. This was a dangerous gambit. The central government depended absolutely on the services of its 25,000 *officiers* (civil servants) and especially on its judges. Despite the similar name, the *Parlements* of France (law courts filled by judges who had either purchased or inherited their positions) differed significantly in composition from the Parliaments of England, Scotland and Ireland (with nobles and bishops in one chamber and elected representatives from towns and counties in another); and yet the institutions also possessed some important similarities. First, both assemblies conducted their business in public view. Just as the English Parliament met in the same building as the central law courts, and their debates could normally be heard by anyone who chose to listen at the door (see chapter 11 below), so could the cases before the French judges: only two doorkeepers stood outside the court. Second, although smaller than the English Parliament, the *Parlement* of Paris was still a considerable body (indeed, larger than most representative assemblies). Normally some 200 judges, sitting in ten different 'chambers', heard cases referred to them by inferior courts that covered almost half the kingdom; but they could also meet in plenary sessions, presided over by the senior judge (the *premier président*: the only judge directly appointed by the crown), in which every member possessed the right to speak and to vote. The *premier président* controlled debating and voting protocols, and (just like the Speaker of the English House of Commons) when necessary liaised with the monarch; moreover (again like the Speaker) unless the *premier président* presided, all debate ceased. Finally, much as the English House of Commons claimed that no tax could be legally collected without its approval, so in France no tax legislation could be enforced until the local *Parlement* registered it – and both before and after registration the judges had the power to 'interpret' (i.e. modify) government edicts in the light of legal appeals concerning exemptions and exceptions.

The king in person could override the obstruction of any *Parlement* by making a personal appearance in court to enforce the registration of any law or edict he had issued, in a process known as a *lit* or 'bed' of justice; but such action demeaned the power of the monarchy and could cause embarrassing confrontations. At a *lit de justice* in 1629 at the *Parlement* of Paris, Louis XIII forced his judges to register some contentious tax edicts, but they reminded him that 'Great in the law though he is, the king will not wish to overturn the basic laws of the kingdom ... *Our* power is great too.' As harvest failure and plague caused widespread hardship, others emulated the defiance of the Paris judges. One regional *Parlement* commandeered royal funds held by tax collectors to pay their own wages; another ordered the grain collected for the army to be sold to starving civilians; two more encouraged popular riots against royal policies and refused to punish those who took part.

Alarmed by this domestic unrest and infuriated by France's wars against Catholics abroad, the *dévots* determined to get rid of Richelieu. They argued that unless France withdrew from all foreign commitments and allowed time for retrenchment and reform, the monarchy would collapse. According to one of their papers of advice:

> France is full of sedition, but the courts punish no one. The king has appointed special judges for these cases, but the *Parlements* prevent the execution of the sentences so that, in consequence, they legitimize the rebellions. I do not know what we should hope or fear in all this, given the frequency of revolts, of which we learn of a new one almost daily.

Richelieu did not dispute either these facts or the urgent need for reform, but he presented his master with a stark choice: 'If the king resolves upon war, it is necessary to abandon all thought of peace, retrenchment and good order within this kingdom. If, on the other hand, he wants peace, then he should abandon all thought of Italy for the future.'[5]

While Louis pondered these options, the *dévots* made their move. On 10 November 1630, Marie publicly deprived Richelieu of all offices in her household and banished him from her presence. The next day, he returned to tender his formal resignation, as protocol demanded, to find Marie locked in conversation with her son. She immediately launched into a tirade about the cardinal's wickedness, telling Louis that he must choose which of them he wished to retain as his advisor. Richelieu left disconsolate, and his enemies flocked to congratulate Marie on her victory (and to make bids for the offices that the cardinal and his numerous relatives and clients would soon vacate.) Louis, however, spent the rest of the day sitting on his bed petulantly pulling the buttons off his waistcoat while he pondered the agonizing decision required by his mother. Eventually he summoned Richelieu and, together, they planned how to govern without Marie.

The 'Day of Dupes' (as contemporaries called it) accelerated France's slide into a 30 years war with Spain. Marie fled abroad, never to return, while Richelieu executed, imprisoned or banished those who had rashly revealed their opposition to him. Nothing now restrained his resolve to check Habsburg expansion, whatever the domestic cost, and he promised large subsidies to support both Sweden and the Dutch Republic. This support required tax increases, however, which produced more protests; in 1631, another famine year, six more urban revolts rocked France; and 1632 was little better. The governor of the province of Guyenne spoke for many worried ministers when he warned Paris that 'the misery is so general, in all areas and among all classes, that unless there is an immediate reduction [in taxes] it is inevitable that the people will be driven to some dangerous course of action.'[6] Louis made some concessions – he reluctantly restored the provincial estates in Burgundy, Languedoc and Provence; and he renewed the *Paulette* for nine years – but in 1634, realizing that Philip IV planned to attack, the king explained to Richelieu his reasons for waging a 'vigorous open war against Spain in order to secure a beneficial general peace'. It would forestall a Spanish–Dutch peace; it would limit imperial gains in Germany; it would reawaken anti-Spanish sentiment in Italy. Louis even claimed that, given the size of the subsidies he already paid to the Swedes and the Dutch, it would cost only one million *livres* more each year to declare outright war. For all these reasons, the king concluded, 'I believe it is better for us to attack them now than to wait for them to attack us'. In May 1635 a French herald delivered a declaration of war on Spain.[7]

Louis mobilized 150,000 men (at least on paper) for the new campaign – but, unwisely, he deployed them on numerous fronts: against Spain, in the Spanish Netherlands, in Italy and in Switzerland. He also built up a navy in both the Atlantic and the Mediterranean. None of these forces achieved anything of note: indeed, the invasion of the South Netherlands ended in humiliation when, following an unsuccessful siege of the university town of Louvain, the French had to withdraw northwards and beg the Dutch to rescue them. One of the defenders of Louvain, Cornelius Jansen (a professor of theology), wrote a vitriolic book during the siege that used both Scripture and history to discredit France's alliances with heretics: *Mars Gallicus* sold thousands of copies in several editions and several languages.[8]

War and Insurgency

Contrary to Louis XIII's prediction, outright war increased state expenditure by a great deal more than a million *livres*. Apart from an immediate rise in taxes, the government had to feed and lodge its troops at a time when the war depressed trade and industry in many areas, causing widespread economic hardship. Fourteen urban revolts occurred in 1635, the year war broke out, and although a reasonable harvest helped to preserve order in the countryside, a wet winter followed by an unusually hot and stormy spring produced widespread opposition to the recruiters and tax collectors in 1636. Many prepared formal complaints to the crown. Shaken by an invasion from the Spanish Netherlands that captured Corbie and threatened Paris (see chapter 9 above), the king graciously agreed to overlook the seditious nature of these assemblies and 'forgave' tax arrears; but the continued military pressure soon led him to make new demands for both men and money. In 1637 these provoked one of the largest popular uprisings in French history: the Croquants of Périgord, in south-western France.[9]

The trouble began when Louis ordered royal judges to sequester grain for the troops assembling to attack Spain, revoked the 'forgiveness' of past taxes and increased the *taille* by about one-third. The speed of the hostile reaction stunned everyone. According to a chronicler, 'most uprisings of this kind tended to pass through various stages: one could see the plan take shape before the trouble broke out. But from the first, this one reached such excesses that, just like a great fire that has been covered for a long time, suddenly flames burst out that were virtually impossible to extinguish.'[10] In May 1637 men from a group of forest villages formed an army that included many local veterans who lived among them, led by the lord of La Mothe La Forêt, a retired professional soldier, who called on each parish to produce 20 recruits and 5 *lives* a day for their support. When the veterans had drilled and trained the rest, La Mothe led some 8,000 men to Bergerac, a largely Protestant town, which welcomed him. Several more members of the elite – including 14 lawyers, 12 'gentlemen' and 4 priests – rallied to the Croquant cause and started to compose sophisticated manifestos. Many have survived, filled with complaints about the 'insupportable, illegitimate and excessive [taxes] unknown to our forefathers' levied since the war with Spain began, and exacted by financiers who 'consume the poor labourers down to the bone', coupled with laments about the loss of trade and industry caused by the war. They petitioned the king (who, they claimed, had been deceived by his evil counsellors) to restore justice and liberty by reducing their tax burden to its pre-war level.[11]

The government only managed to restore order in Périgord by recalling troops from the Spanish front. Afterwards, in an attempt to discourage others from rebellion, judges arrived with instructions to seek out 'those with something to lose' and to administer 'exemplary punishments' that would 'horrify the rest of the rebels'. A dozen of the leaders, including several gentlemen, were degraded and publicly executed; but many others (including La Mothe) faded into the backwoods from which they had come – in many cases becoming bandit leaders. Louis was so shaken by the extent of the unrest that in December 1637 he made a formal 'vow' placing France under the protection of the Virgin Mary – an act of public humiliation celebrated in popular processions throughout the kingdom, and in a powerful painting by Richelieu's protégé, Philippe de Champaigne.[12]

Open revolts like that of the Croquants formed only the 'public transcript' (to use the language of James Scott) of French popular resistance. Many other communities, especially in remote areas, defied the government in ways that have left few archival traces: people delayed tax payments as long as possible and fled whenever recruiters approached. Elsewhere, the mere threat of violence led local authorities to make concessions that averted open revolts. Thus at Caen in Normandy in 1631, when harvest failure drove up the price of bread by 50 per cent, the crowds in the marketplace 'terrorized the merchants and took their grain at the price they wanted' – all the sources emphasize that they stole nothing – 'and made themselves masters of the grain market, distributing the goods at a fair price to those who wanted them'. At this point the local militia intervened to maintain the new 'fair price', which prevented further trouble. Likewise, six years later (the year of the Croquants), faced with demands from the central government for more revenue, the magistrates of Caen imposed a tax on each serge cloth manufactured in the city. This inevitably forced up prices and drove down demand, leading manufacturers to lay off workers. One morning the new unemployed gathered outside the town hall and, in orderly fashion, placed their grievances before the magistrates: as soon as the magistrates promised to revoke the new tax, the crowd dispersed.[13]

Although such tactical retreats preserved public order in the localities, they left the central government short of taxes – taxes whose yield it had already alienated to the *partisans* (bankers who had loaned money under a contract, or *parti*, which assigned repayment, with interest, from a specified source of income). So Richelieu began to appoint special commissioners known as *intendants* to enforce payment of the taxes assigned to the *partisans*, and to seize the possessions and even the persons of delinquent taxpayers. Whenever local judges showed sympathy with the taxpayers, Richelieu evoked the case from the *Parlements* to the king's council for judgment. He also forbade any appeal to the courts in tax disputes that involved less than 100 *livres* – equivalent to three years' wages for many workers.[14]

Much of France's war expenditure came from the yield of a single direct tax on land, the *taille*. As usual in the early modern world, the burden did not fall evenly. First, certain areas (such as enclaves ruled by foreign princes) and certain social groups (including university professors, judges and tax collectors as well as nobles and clergy) did not pay *taille* at all. As the government's fiscal needs rose, it naturally tried to reduce these exemptions, but although this strategy produced a short-term advantage in the form of increased tax yields, it brought a long-term danger because those newly subjected to fiscal pressure often favoured and sometimes fomented tax strikes and tax revolts by others. In addition, some provinces paid far more *taille* than others, and within provinces some areas enjoyed special exemptions – which meant that the rest had to pay more. Each round of tax increases accentuated these disparities: thus the tax burden on Lower Normandy quintupled between 1630 and 1636, and had doubled again by 1638. The following year, the chief treasury minister warned Richelieu that the region 'pays almost a quarter of the taxes of the entire kingdom'.[15] Small wonder that Lower Normandy saw the greatest of the seventeenth-century tax revolts: the *Nu-Pieds* (the 'Bare Feet') (Fig. 31).

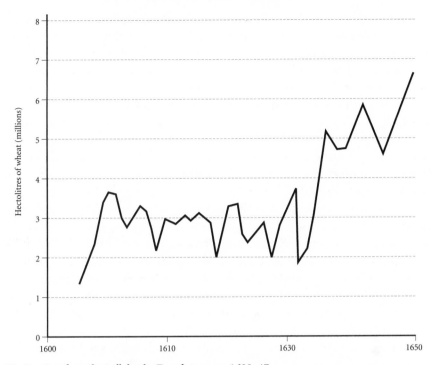

31. Receipts from the *taille* by the French treasury, 1600–47.
The dramatic fiscal impact of France's war against the Habsburgs emerges clearly when expressed in terms of its equivalent in wheat. The spikes in 1643 and 1647 soon translated into popular revolts.

The economic stagnation caused by the war also reduced tax yields. Many who could not afford to pay simply abandoned their homes and farms and fled – but since the government apportioned most direct taxes by community, not by individuals, the flight of any taxpayer automatically increased the burden on those who remained. Tax arrears therefore mounted: whereas the government received four-fifths of its impositions in 1629, it received less than one-half a decade later. The central government therefore supplemented the *taille* with indirect taxes, labour services, billeting obligations (both for soldiers and for prisoners of war) – so many new burdens that 'their number wearies the memory', according to a group of irate taxpayers in 1638.[16] Richelieu subjected civil servants to particularly harsh burdens. He arbitrarily reduced their salaries and delayed paying the residue; he demanded 'loans' from them that he had little or no intention of repaying; and he both doubled the number of positions in established institutions (which halved the months of the year when the officers could draw a salary) and founded new institutions that reduced the jurisdiction of existing ones (which reduced the income of each official from fees). This constant fiscal pressure encouraged the judges of the *Parlement* of Normandy to defy the cardinal in 1639: the judges refused to register a new crop of tax edicts, the prosecutors went on strike in protest against a royal edict that doubled their number, and the courts took no action when the *Nu-Pieds* revolt broke out.[17]

The *Nu-Pieds* revolt took its name from 'the poor miserable salt-workers', some 10,000 of whom walked barefoot on the sand as they carried wood to heat the saltpans on the beaches of Lower Normandy, and then salt from the pans to the nearest town. In July 1639 they murdered an official who, they believed, brought orders to extend to Normandy a salt monopoly (known as the *gabelle*) that existed in other French provinces, requiring each householder to agree in advance to purchase a set quantity of salt at inflated prices. In various violent demonstrations over the summer, angry crowds in Lower Normandy murdered about one hundred people – most of them tax collectors – and maimed or threatened many others; they also burnt down tax offices and the houses of those suspected of enriching themselves from taxes. Sometimes the perpetrators numbered a few score, at other times a few hundred, and eventually they coalesced to form 'The Army of Suffering' with perhaps five thousand members. As with the Croquants two years earlier, a minor nobleman, the lord of Ponthébert, took charge (calling himself 'General Nu Pieds') and appointed some veterans as 'Brigadiers' to command and drill his followers. With a cleric to serve as his secretary, the 'General' also composed and circulated manifestoes that denounced the new salt tax and called for a return to the 'Charter' of 1315 that formed the basis of Normandy's incorporation into the kingdom of France.[18]

Richelieu initially blamed the revolt on his financial advisers – 'I fail to understand why you do not devote more thought to the consequences of the decisions you take in the council of finance,' he scolded them: 'It is easy to prevent even the worst misfortunes, whereas after they occur no remedy can be found' – and, since the alienated civil servants (including local judges) refused to act against the rebels, he agreed to suspend some of the unpopular new taxes. Nevertheless, as Hugo Grotius (then Sweden's ambassador in Paris) correctly predicted, 'winter, when the soldiers return to their garrisons, will cool these hot tempers'; and in November 1639, Richelieu sent an army into Normandy, where it defeated the 'Army of Suffering' in a pitched battle that lasted several hours (as with the Croquants, the Nu-Pieds included many army veterans).[19] The troops then executed the captured leaders and imprisoned the rest before they dispersed into garrisons. Meanwhile Chancellor Pierre Séguier, head of the kingdom's judicial system, toured the duchy and imposed 'exemplary punishments' in order 'to rule out any recurrence of similar disorders in the future'.[20]

Nevertheless domestic discontent continued. Late in 1639, Louis's finance minister complained presciently that 'People want to pay nothing more, neither old nor new taxes. We are scraping the bottom of the barrel, no longer having the ability to choose between good and bad policies. I fear our foreign wars will degenerate into a civil war.' This risk increased after catastrophic weather in 1640 and 1641 ruined the crops, drove up bread prices and caused many to abandon their farms. Richelieu now predicted that 'If the council of finance continues to allow the tax-farmers and bankers full liberty to treat His Majesty's subjects according to their insatiable appetites, France will surely fall victim to a disorder similar to that which has befallen Spain. . . By wishing to have too much, we shall create a situation in which we shall have nothing at all.'[21] But the cardinal saw no way out. 'Given the small experience that I have in financial matters,' he complained petulantly in February 1642, 'it is impossible for me to judge whether to accept or reject' a new fiscal expedient. Admittedly, he drew up an ambitious plan for reform that would both reduce expenditure dramatically and shift the tax burden from direct to indirect levies – but acknowledged that it would only take effect 'après la paix [after the peace]'. It therefore remained a dead letter.[22]

Meanwhile, France's war effort produced few results. For a moment, in 1640, the revolts of Catalonia and Portugal against Philip IV held out the promise of a speedy victory (see chapter 9 above). France's envoy in Barcelona later recalled that

> Our affairs, which were not going very well in the Low Countries, and still worse in Piedmont, suddenly began to prosper on all sides (even in Germany) because our enemy's forces, being retained in their own country and recalled from else-where to defend the sanctuary [Castile] became weak and slow in all the other theatres of war. [This] gave us the means to gain the upper hand.

Meanwhile a Francophile observer likewise gloated that 'These internal ailments are the true means to abase the pride of Spain, or to force it to make a reasonable peace.'[23]

These hopes were quickly dashed because France suffered its own 'internal ailments'. In 1641 the count of Soissons, a disaffected cousin of the king exiled for his part in an earlier plot, issued a manifesto that promised 'to restore everything to its former place: re-establishing the laws that have been overthrown; renewing the immunities, rights and privileges of the provinces, towns and personages that have been violated; ... ensuring respect for churchmen and nobles'. The conspirators mobilized an army, but Soissons foolishly lifted the visor of his helmet with a loaded pistol and pulled the trigger as he did so. Even the cardinal's agents believed that 'If monsieur the count had not been killed, he would have been welcomed by half of Paris. Indeed such is the general feeling of all France that the whole country would have rallied to his side.' The following year a plot by Louis's catamite and favourite courtier, the marquis of Cinq-Mars (known as 'Monsieur le Grand': 'Mr. Big'), to get rid of Richelieu as a prelude to making peace with Spain and retrenching at home, came within an ace of success. But then Louis's troops forced the surrender of Perpignan and advanced to the Ebro. Richelieu's gamble therefore seemed to have paid off – but he died in December 1642. Louis XIII accepted Richelieu's suggestion that Giulio Mazzarino, now known as Cardinal Jules Mazarin, should become his chief minister; but, four months later, Louis himself died and his widow, Anne of Austria, Philip IV's sister, immediately named Mazarin president of the council of regency for her 4-old son, Louis XIV.

Anne's decision astonished almost everyone, and alienated both those who had aspired to the position and all xenophobes. Many believed that the cardinal also became Anne's lover – a suggestion supported by the passionate letters they exchanged when they were apart – but the physical relations of the couple (what-ever they might be) were irrelevant, because the cardinal obviously enjoyed Anne's complete confidence, so that only armed rebellion could dislodge him. In any case, the victory of the future prince of Condé over the Spaniards at Rocroi five days after Louis XIII's death gave the new regime a spectacular boost. So despite another disastrous harvest in 1643 – which caused the price of bread to reach its highest level in half-a-century, and frosts that destroyed the vines so that in May 1644 rioters in Paris surrounded Chancellor Séguier shouting 'Have mercy!' – Mazarin decided to keep on fighting.[24]

The tense domestic situation alarmed France's negotiators at the peace congress in Westphalia (see chapter 8 above). In April 1645 one of them reminded Mazarin that although recent successes placed within his grasp 'a glorious peace that would greatly extend the boundaries of the French empire', it would be rash to expect 'the same for some future date, because public affairs, which are so subject to revolutions, could be transformed either by the recovery of our enemies' fortunes, or by the decline of our own, or by the birth of some domestic division that would destroy in an instant all our advantages and our hopes'.[25] It was prescient advice, but Mazarin ignored it: instead he made refusal to pay taxes a capital offence and sent out more of the hated *intendants* to supervise the collection of as much revenue as possible.

For a while, Mazarin's gamble worked. With better harvests, popular revolts abated and tax revenues increased, permitting new conquests at the Habsburgs' expense in Flanders, Germany, Italy and Catalonia. Still, some of the cardinal's colleagues feared for the future and, as soon as the 1646 campaign ended, advocated the immediate conclusion of a settlement

> That is solidly grounded, rather than hold out for a better one that can only be gained by prolonging the war, in which events are always doubtful. Victories are not won by the manifest justice of the cause or by the size of the armies: instead God, whose secrets cannot be known, gives victory to those He wishes to raise up; and, to humiliate others, brings setbacks that are beyond human understanding.

Mazarin expressed some sympathy for this view, even extolling *'the art of quitting when one is ahead, because then one keeps what one has won'*, but he failed to follow his own admirable advice.[26]

Matters came to a head in 1647. The crown not only spent all its revenues for the year in advance, but also anticipated those for 1648, 1649 and part of 1650. The funds required to keep the army fighting could now come only by creating more new taxes and mortgaging their future yields to some banker in return for immediate advance payments in cash; but each edict creating a new tax required the approval of the judges of the various *Parlements*, who might either refuse to 'register' the edict (and thus prevent its collection) or 'interpret' it (that is, reduce its application, and therefore its yield, in some way). To avoid this outcome, Mazarin silenced outspoken judges (and other critics) by issuing *lettres de cachet* (which placed the recipient under house arrest) and took the young king to a *lit de justice* at the recalcitrant *Parlement* of Paris, which obliged its judges to register controversial new tax edicts. Some judges protested that such conduct was 'tyranny' and thereby emboldened some of those affected by the new taxes to withhold payment; but Mazarin paid no attention, and instead in November 1647 sent another set of edicts creating new taxes for registration. Three of them would prove especially contentious: an excise duty on foodstuffs coming into Paris; a tax on lands alienated from the royal domain; and the creation of several new public offices for sale to the highest bidder. The cardinal made clear that the *Paulette* would not be renewed until all these measures had been registered.

Mazarin had chosen a dangerous moment for confrontation on three counts. First, as a Parisian diarist observed, these new taxes came at a time when the government had imprisoned 'people of all social backgrounds, not after due process before a court of law, but simply on a warrant from the royal council and a list [of names] signed by the minister of finance'. In the year 1646 alone, some 25,000 people went to jail for failing to pay their taxes. Second, the failed harvest of 1647 left both the capital and the court short of food. As Mazarin complained to a colleague: 'If some astrologer had predicted that, at the end of this year, the king and queen would have no bread to eat, he would have been dismissed as mad and outrageous; and yet he would have told the truth.' Finally, the cardinal failed to heed his predecessor's warning about treating Paris with great care: 'One must never awake this great beast,' Richelieu had written. 'It should be left asleep.'[27]

Paris was the largest city in Christendom in the mid-seventeenth century, with 20,000 houses and over 400,000 inhabitants, but it had enjoyed exemption from most taxes. The new edicts threatened to change this, by levying excise duty on incoming foodstuffs and taxing alienated domain lands (many of them near the capital). Early in January 1648, hundreds of Parisians gathered outside the Palace of Justice, while the *Parlement* debated the new edicts, chanting 'Naples, Naples' – a pointed reminder of the rebellion in another capital city provoked by imposing an unpopular tax (see chapter 14 below). Someone in the crowd struck one of the judges as he emerged, and when guards attempt to make an arrest, the women in the crowd counter-attacked and forced them to flee. Two days later, when the regent went to hear Mass in Notre Dame, several hundred women 'shouted at her and demanded justice'.[28] That night Anne and Mazarin deployed troops around the capital – but, in response, the city's militia companies assembled and ostentatiously 'tested' their firearms as a sign that they would fight if attacked. Instead, therefore, on 15 January 1648 Anne and Mazarin brought the young king to another *lit de justice* at the *Parlement* of Paris to force through some of the other tax edicts previously sent for registration.

The Revolt of the Judges

During the discussion of the unpopular tax edicts, Pierre Broussel, a 73-year-old judge in the *Grand Conseil* (and also one of the city's militia captains) made a bold statement in defence of the *Parlement*'s right to reject 'royal actions contrary to the well being of the state and God's commandments, as these edicts are, not only because they contain clauses prejudicial to the well being of the state but because they were presented in contravention of the customs and protocol of the assembly, which must always enjoy its powers freely'. Just like opponents of government innovations elsewhere, Broussel and his colleagues sought to ground the discussion of individual grievances on general principles, citing in support Scripture, history and institutional custom. The King's Advocate, Omer Talon, did the same. At the *lit de justice*, he reminded the 9-year-old king: 'Sire, you are our sovereign lord. Your Majesty's power comes from above and, after God, you are responsible for your actions to no one except your own conscience. But your glory requires that we should be free men and not slaves.' Warming to his theme Talon reminded Louis that

> For the past ten years, the fields have been ruined and the country folk reduced to sleeping on straw because they have sold their furniture to pay their taxes – which even then they cannot do in full. To maintain the luxury of Paris, millions of innocent souls are obliged to live on black bread and oats. All that your subjects have left, Sire, is their souls – and if they could, they would also have put those up for sale long ago.

Talon then reviewed the hardships created for both townsmen and civil servants by the new taxes that the *Parlement* had just been forced to register and then, turning to Anne, admonished her:

> Tonight, in the solitude of your oratory, think of the sorrow, bitterness and consternation of all the servants of the state who today see their goods confiscated, even though they have committed no crime. And add to that thought, Madam, the desperation of the countryside, where the hope of peace, the honour of battles won, and the glory of provinces conquered cannot feed those who lack bread.[29]

The speeches of Broussel and Talon immediately appeared in print, and encouraged several groups directly affected by recent taxes to petition *Parlement* to 'interpret' (that is, to modify) the edicts that they had just been forced to register. The most surprising petitioners were the *maîtres de requêtes*: lawyers who worked for the royal council. Since on appointment each *maître* gained noble status, which exempted him and his family from paying most taxes, aspiring lawyers were willing to pay 150,000 *livres*, plus the annual *Paulette*, in order to guarantee such a lucrative position. The *maîtres* therefore objected vehemently to the tax edict forcibly registered on 15 January 1648 that created 12 new similar positions – because it would inevitably reduce the number of lucrative cases that each would handle and hence the resale value of existing offices. The following month, the *maîtres* went on strike and asked the *Parlement* to 'interpret' the edict. The judges not only agreed to investigate their grievance: they also authorized an examination of the other edicts just registered.

The government now made a serious error. Instead of restricting discussion to a specific (albeit contentious) issue, Anne invoked issues of principle. She ordered the judges to consider whether or not *any* edict registered during a *lit de justice* could be modified. She thus overlooked the danger inherent (in the words of one perceptive protagonist, Cardinal de Retz) in 'lifting the veil that must always cover what one might say and what one might believe concerning the rights of the People and the rights of kings, which always keep the best harmony when silent'.[30]

Meanwhile the opposition of the Paris judges stimulated defiance from colleagues elsewhere. The *Parlement* of Brittany arrested and imprisoned the officials sent from Paris bringing similar tax edicts for registration, while the *Parlement* of Toulouse sentenced to hard labour any excise collector who began to collect the new duties. The order to double the number of judges in the *Parlement* of Provence excited such passionate opposition that the first man to purchase one of the new offices was stabbed to death, and posters went up warning other prospective purchasers to expect the same. Everywhere tax payments ceased.

It seems surprising that Mazarin did not foresee the consequences of his policies but, like most other seventeenth-century European statesmen, he rejected the modern political consensus that governments should always place domestic imperatives above foreign issues. Instead (not without reason) he felt supremely confident that the revolt of Sicily and Naples would lead Philip IV to use force to regain control, which would benefit France in three ways: first, the troops sent to Naples would come from Catalonia, allowing French forces there to make progress; second, a Spanish attack on Naples would 'kindle rather than put out the fire'; and, third, that 'fire' would prevent Spain from defending its positions in northern Italy.[31] Mazarin therefore rejected the advantageous peace terms offered by the beleaguered king of Spain: to cede all France's gains in the Low Countries permanently, and those in Lombardy and Catalonia for 30 years, in return for peace. Had Mazarin accepted these terms – far better than France would ever receive again – he could have immediately diverted the troops in the Netherlands to Germany, and thus extracted far better terms at the Peace of Westphalia. Instead, in the hope of gaining yet more, he poured all available resources into campaigns in Catalonia and Lombardy.

The decision to continue the war with another Catholic monarch alienated not only the *dévots*, but also another religious group who became known as the 'Jansenists'. In 1640 a huge Latin treatise entitled *Augustinus* had appeared from the pen of Cornelius Jansen (author of the best-selling *Mars Gallicus*, above). It argued at great length that humans had fallen so far from their original innocence and perfection that only the most rigorous and sincere devotion could merit salvation: conventional piety would not suffice. Resenting the numerous editions and translations of Jansen's earlier anti-French polemic, Richelieu secured papal condemnation of the *Augustinus* and had it banned. Nevertheless, shortly after the cardinal's death Antoine Arnauld, a Paris priest, published *Frequent Communion*, an eloquent tract in French that popularized the main ideas of Jansen's virtually unreadable Latin folio tomes. In particular, it condemned the practice of taking frequent communion, advocated by the Jesuit Order (among others), as a way of 'appeasing' God: instead, Arnauld argued, the laity should take the sacrament only when they had purged all impiety from their hearts and minds. Following Richelieu's example, Mazarin sent a copy of *Frequent Communion* to Rome and requested a papal condemnation. He also planned to send its author there for trial on charges of heresy – but whereas Jansen was a subject of Philip IV, Arnauld was the son of a French judge and scion of a prominent Parisian family. The judges of the *Parlement* of Paris argued not only that France had plenty of theologians competent to determine the orthodoxy of Arnauld and his work, but that sending a French subject to Rome would open the door to papal intervention in the affairs of the French Church. In the words of Orest Ranum, Anne's decision gave Arnauld and 'the Jansenist cause more support in Parisian society than he or his predecessors had ever hoped for. For the first time, radical members of the Parlement argued that the Queen Mother was a foreigner subverting French laws.'[32]

The opposition of the judges and Jansenists, together with another cool wet spring that spoiled the crops, led Anne and Mazarin to change their minds about peace: in May 1648 they indicated to Madrid a willingness to open talks on the basis of the generous terms offered by Spain five months before. By then, however, Philip had made peace with the Dutch and repressed the revolts of both Naples and Sicily: he therefore determined to increase the military pressure on France. 'All we need now,' mused a Spanish diplomat, 'is some moderate victory in the Netherlands in order to start some commotion in France that will open up a highway to an honourable peace.'[33] A few weeks later, a far greater 'commotion' than even the most optimistic Spaniard could have imagined paralyzed the French capital.

The Tipping Point: The Barricades of Paris

In April 1648 Mazarin attempted to drive a wedge between his domestic opponents. He offered the judges of the *Parlement* of Paris (and only them) the opportunity to renew the *Paulette* on the normal terms. Other officials could renew only if they agreed to forego their salaries for four years; while the *maîtres de requêtes*, still on strike, lost their right to renew altogether. This blatant attempt to divide and rule backfired disastrously. The judges of the *Parlement* voted to issue an *arrêt d'union* expressing support for all their colleagues and invited the other three 'sovereign courts' that met in Paris – the *Cour des Aides* and the *Chambre des Comptes*, which handled tax appeals and audits, and the *Grand Conseil*, which heard ecclesiastical disputes – to send delegates to meet with them in a special room in the Palace of Justice known as the Chambre Saint-Louis.

This defiance encouraged other discontented groups of civil servants to defy the regent, starting with the officials who administered direct taxes in the provinces: the *Trésoriers de France*. The *trésoriers* enjoyed many social and economic privileges, including automatic elevation to noble status after three generations of service as well as exemption from billeting, compulsory service in the militia and certain taxes. They therefore attracted men from good families (for example, Blaise Pascal and Antoine Arnauld came from *trésorier* families). The *trésoriers* also maintained their own trade union (*syndicat*), which held annual general meetings and supported a permanent secretary, a standing committee and permanent deputies in Paris as well as producing a newsletter. Despite this impressive organization, Mazarin revoked some of the tax exemptions of *trésoriers* and ended their freedom from billeting troops. The standing committee of the *trésoriers* retaliated by instructing its members to use any revenues they collected to pay their own salary arrears first, and to seek out and publicize any evidence of malversation of funds by any official appointed by Mazarin to raise new taxes. By mid-May 1648 the entire fiscal machinery of the French state had ceased to function.[34]

Realizing the dangers that now faced them, Anne and Mazarin put pressure on the judges by withdrawing the offer to renew the *Paulette*, prohibiting any further meetings in the Chambre Saint-Louis, and imprisoning some *trésoriers* in the Bastille – but these provocations fuelled further defiance. Starting on 30 June 1648, 14 judges from the *Parlement* and six from each of the three other central courts met daily in the Chambre Saint-Louis to discuss the various grievances of the kingdom. In a desperate attempt to produce a compromise that would allow the tax collectors to resume their work, Anne dismissed an unpopular finance minister and released the imprisoned *trésoriers*; but once again, concessions increased the self-confidence of the opposition. The judges now demanded that no civil servant be imprisoned without showing due cause; an end to the creation of new judicial offices; timely payment of salaries to judges; 'forgiveness' of all tax arrears; annulment of all loan contracts; and, above all, the abolition of the *intendants*.

In the *Parlement* of Paris, the frequent meetings produced greater confidence among the judges. They interrupted speeches of which they disapproved by hissing and stamping their feet; they held 'divisions' on important issues (thus the proposal to abolish the *intendants* passed by 106 votes to 66); and on occasion they forcibly held the *premier président* in his seat so that he could not halt the debate and passage of controversial measures.[35] When she learned that the Spanish Army of Flanders was massing along the northern frontier, Anne capitulated. She agreed to renew the *Paulette* for nine years for all officials; to reduce the *taille* by one-eighth for the current year; to 'forgive' all tax arrears from before 1647; to free all those imprisoned for non-payment of taxes; and to revoke all commissions to the hated *intendants*.

Mazarin felt confident that these measures would end the crisis. In July 1648 he boasted to one of his colleagues that 'Not only has all opposition ceased, but His Majesty has drawn inestimable advantage from [the situation], which clearly demonstrates that God dearly loves this government, leading it to its greatest good fortune by ways that seemed to lead exactly the other way.' In particular, he enthused that, 'for fear of something worse', a consortium of *partisans* had 'promised to provide a fixed sum to prolong the war as long as the obstinacy of the Spaniards makes it necessary. We had spent all [the revenues] of this and the next two years; now we have found a way of spending them a second time.'[36]

Then, to the cardinal's horror, the *Parlement* of Paris voted to investigate the accounts of some *partisans* for evidence of fraud and excessive profits. All lending to the government immediately ceased, and Mazarin reluctantly instructed his negotiators at Münster to end the war in Germany immediately on the best terms available. 'It is almost a miracle,' he observed, 'that amid so many self-made obstacles we can keep our affairs going, and even make them prosper; but prudence dictates that we should not place all our trust in this miracle continuing any longer.' The cardinal lamented that the opposition of the law courts and the spreading tax-strike had brought the government to the edge of bankruptcy. 'Shedding tears of blood', he regretted that it had all happened at a time when, in Germany, 'our affairs have never been in a more prosperous state', but concluded: 'The end of this long discourse is to convince you of our need to make peace at the earliest opportunity.'[37]

Ironically, just one week after Mazarin signed this letter, the prince of Condé routed the invasion by the Spanish Army of Flanders at the battle of Lens – but the cardinal immediately threw away his advantage. Calculating that a *Te Deum* for the victory celebrated in Notre Dame Cathedral would provide the ideal opportunity to arrest the leading judges, including Pierre Broussel, the regent personally invited all of them to attend. A tiny miscalculation thwarted the plan. Normally, bodyguards surround the persons they are meant to protect and so when, at the end of the service on 26 August 1648, some judges noted the queen's guards lingering in the church after she had left, they raised the alarm. Since it was a market day, the areas around Notre Dame were all packed and some of Mazarin's targets escaped – including Broussel, who lived close to Notre Dame, but a detachment of guards arrived in hot pursuit and abducted him from his home.[38]

The arrest of Broussel, who was a militia captain as well as a judge, outraged his neighbours and dense crowds began to rampage through the streets shouting 'Long live the king! Free the prisoner!' and smashing doors and windows. To prevent looting, the militia companies mobilized and brought out the heavy chains that most Paris streets still maintained for emergency use, hanging them across the street and erecting barricades behind them to repulse any attack. As dawn broke on 27 August, Paris boasted over 1,200 barricades. According to one eyewitness, 'Everyone, without exception, took up arms. One saw children five and six years old with daggers in their hands, and mothers arming them themselves.' The militiamen declared that they would not lay down their arms until the regent freed Broussel; more alarmingly for the crown, at the royal palace the guards made clear that they would not fire on their compatriots.

Although Broussel's release and triumphant return home the following day calmed tempers and brought down the barricades, a 'Great Fear' continued to grip the French capital as householders worried that their property might be damaged if either the 'populace' or the troops attacked. The judges, led by Broussel, took advantage of the uncertainty to continue their scrutiny of recent tax edicts, rejecting some outright and asking Anne to modify others. They also did nothing to prevent a torrent of literary attacks on her chief minister: the *Mazarinades*.[39]

The cardinal had made many enemies. Several prominent courtiers had hoped to succeed Richelieu, and envied the man who beat them; many clerics resented his practice of naming political allies to vacant ecclesiastical positions and his persistence in making war on fellow Catholics; while the judges loathed his fiscal innovations, which deprived them of authority and income. In the wake of the botched arrest of Broussel, a wave of pamphlets condemned the cardinal's policies, protested his foreign birth and mimicked his Italian accent. Coachmen intimidated recalcitrant horses with the threat, 'Mazarin will get you'. Above all, gangs of young

Parisians took to the streets with slings, known as *frondes*, which they used to smash the windows of the opulent Palais Mazarin. That 'weapon of the weak', reminiscent of David's overthrow of Goliath, gave its name to the revolt that would last for five years: the Fronde.[40]

The judges of the *Parlement* now systematically challenged the legality of each recent tax, encouraged by periodic demonstrations outside the court by irate taxpayers, until in October the regent abolished some taxes and reduced the *taille* for 1648 and 1649 to one-fifth of the previous level. Mazarin calculated that her concessions 'deprived the king, in one way of another, of over half his revenues' and once again instructed his negotiators in Westphalia to extricate France from the German war immediately on the best terms possible. 'It would perhaps have been more advantageous for the conclusion of a universal peace had the war in the Empire continued a little longer, rather than hastening the settlement of outstanding matters as we did,' he protested, because the emperor would now escape 'the total ruin which, considering the lamentable situation to which his fortunes had been reduced, was imminent and almost ineluctable'. He was wasting his breath: recognizing their precarious situation, the French diplomats at Münster had already signed the final instruments of peace.[41]

The Fronde

Madame de Motteville, a perceptive member of the regent's household who had been in the royal palace on the 'Day of the Barricades', now lamented that 'the people, in the hope of saving themselves from dues and taxes, dreamed only of tumults and changes' and feared that the anti-royalist revolts in progress in England and Spain as well as in France formed part of an 'evil constellation that menaced the well being of kings'.[42] Anne of Austria evidently shared this pessimistic view, because she now issued a proclamation that accused the judges of plotting with Spain to seize her sons, hinting that they aimed to establish a Republic, and commanded all four sovereign courts to leave the city immediately for four separate destinations. She also ordered the prince Condé and his victorious army to blockade the capital.

Once again, the regent's maladroit actions united her opponents. Since she had lumped all the judges together as traitors, even those who had remained loyal until this point now subscribed to a declaration that Mazarin was 'an enemy of the king and the state'. In January 1649 the royal family fled from their capital. The blockade forced the judges to make common cause with other opposition groups in Paris. The city magistrates loaned one million *livres*, while militiamen garrisoned the Bastille, the Arsenal and the city walls. The judges also sequestered all royal assets they could find in the capital and set up a wartime administration with committees to handle military, financial, 'diplomatic' and other business. The Paris clergy (many of them Jansenists), led by Paul de Gondi, archbishop-designate and later Cardinal de Retz, also lent their support with advice, sermons and pamphlets. So did many nobles, who flocked to Paris to join the judges, bringing their troops with them.

Initially, at least, most of the noble recruits to the Fronde acted out of principle. Richelieu had imprisoned them, sequestered their property and demolished their castles not only for plotting but also for lesser offences such as duelling. Now they sought to dismantle the machinery of prerogative rule that had both humiliated them and impoverished their vassals. They also favoured opening peace talks with Spain, believing that continuing the war would ruin France.[43] Although the nobles lacked an established forum for discussing grievances – they could only meet legally in the States-General (none had been called since 1614) or in the provincial Estates (and by 1649 only those on the periphery of the kingdom still met regularly) – at first this scarcely mattered because it proved so easy to circulate their views in pamphlets. Paris boasted over 350 print shops, many of which had prospered from producing the multiple copies of government edicts required for distribution throughout the kingdom: when the flight of the royal family ended this lucrative source of business, printers compensated by publishing cheap political pamphlets (*libelles*, to use the more expressive French term of the day). Contemporaries commented on 'the frightening quantity of pamphlets', and one writer joked that 'Half Paris prints or sells pamphlets and the other half buys them.' He may have been right: the total number of publications between 1649 and 1653 far exceeded those produced during the rest of the century (Fig. 32).[44]

The pace of publication varied in response to political and military events: whereas fewer than one hundred items appeared in 1648, while the court still resided in the capital, over a thousand *Mazarinades* appeared in the first three months of 1649 after it left, with sometimes a dozen or more published in a single day (Fig. 33). The *Mazarinades* covered a wide range of topics and approaches. Some provided erudite discussions of political obligation, arguing that previous writers had 'attributed more power to princes than is expedient for them to have, even for their own security'; that kings 'owe us their protection just as we owe them our obedience'; and that the *Parlement* of Paris had replaced the defunct States-General as the lineal descendant of the Assemblies of the ancient Franks so that 'no taxes can be levied on the king's subjects ... without the consent of the *Parlement*, which represents the general assent of the people'.[45] Others turned the great issues of the day into obscenities, such as the eight-page verse pamphlet about Anne's sex life that opened with the stanza:

> People, doubt it no longer: It's true that he's fucked her
> And through her hole Jules [Mazarin] pelts us with shit.

According to the *Mazarinades*, the cardinal's involvement in government ensured that everything in France ended up (in the words of one of them) 'like either a brothel or a cemetery'.[46]

The quantity of political pamphlets is remarkable given that the winter of 1648–9 lasted almost six months, with intense cold followed by a rapid thaw and torrential rains that caused the Seine to burst its banks, inundating the city hall and surrounding houses. Floods south of Paris, which normally provided most of the capital's bread, combined with Condé's blockade, caused the price of a loaf of bread to leap from

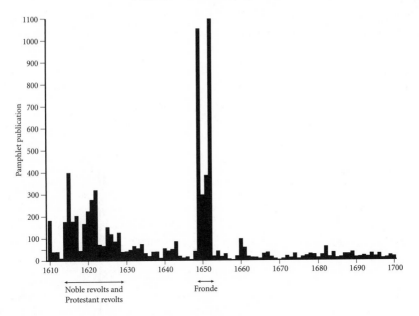

32. Pamphlet publication in seventeenth-century France.
The Bibliothèque Nationale de France, in Paris, boasts a remarkable collection of pamphlets, whose contours reflect the political stability of the kingdom. The assassination of Henry IV in 1610 led to the publication of over 100 items, and the subsequent rebellions of Protestants and nobles sometimes produced over 400 items in a year; but these totals were dwarfed by the *Mazarinades* (tracts attacking the chief minister Cardinal Mazarin), which exceeded 1,000 in 1649 and again in 1652.

9 to 18 *sols* in February 1649. Since an unskilled labourer at this time earned 12 *sols* a day (on days when he could find work), this increase spelled starvation.[47]

Those who lived outside Paris had to contend not only with snow, floods and famine but also with Condé's troops. As the regent's entourage travelled by coach near the capital in February 1649 they passed 'through several villages where we noted a frightening desolation. They had been abandoned by their inhabitants. The houses were burnt and torn down, the churches pillaged.'[48] Those who could took refuge in the nearest convent, like Port-Royal-des-Champs southwest of the capital, where Abbess Angélique Arnauld (sister of Antoine) did her best to provide protection, building barricades and putting horses in the chapterhouse, cows in the cellar, chicken and turkeys in the courtyard, and grain in the chapel. Nevertheless, as she lamented to a nun living in Paris, although

> Nothing has happened to us yet, thank God, we have reason to fear that if this weather continues we will die of hunger just like you, because if they [the soldiers] take everything from us, as they do with others, we have no idea where to find food, since nothing remains in the countryside... The famine is at least as great here as in Paris, and in addition we are burdened with soldiers.

She also lamented that Port-Royal was 'surrounded by the cruellest troops in the world, who have ravaged all the countryside around with all sorts of cruelty,

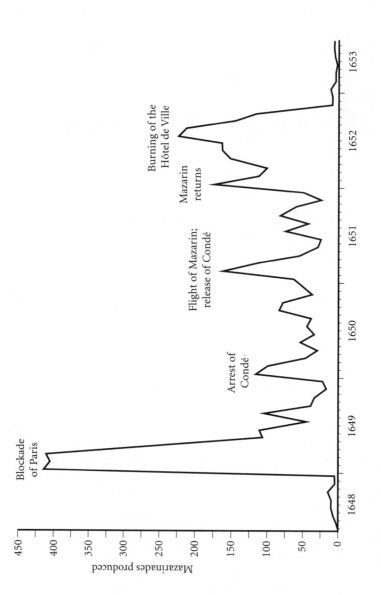

33. Monthly production of *Mazarinades*, May 1649–July 1653.
Pamphlets attacking the Cardinal rose dramatically in January 1649 after the Court left the capital and lost its ability to censor printers. Although the total production of *Mazarinades* during the siege of Paris early in 1649 dwarfs the titles triggered by subsequent events – such as the arrest of the prince of Condé in January 1650 and his release one year later – the monthly total still exceeded the annual total of previous years (see Fig. 32). Production fell equally dramatically when Mazarin returned to the capital – from 1,093 titles in 1652 to 18 in 1653.

sacrilege and malice'.[49] Within the capital, starving crowds surrounded the Palace of Justice and shouted 'Give us bread or give us peace.' They welcomed an agent of Philip IV who arrived to invite the *Parlement* to mediate a peace between France and Spain. The Fronde seemed about to succeed – but, later that day, news arrived that in London a 'High Court of Justice' had tried, condemned and beheaded Charles I.

News of the regicide spread rapidly, thanks to the *Gazette de France*, published by Théophraste Renaudot (the king's doctor) every Saturday, sometimes supplemented midweek by 'extraordinary issues'. Copies sold for two *sols*, and those who could not afford a copy of their own could still read one at a newsstand or listen to others reading aloud. Each issue of the *Gazette* balanced domestic stories that stressed the stability and felicity of France and its royal family (the ballets and religious devotions attended by the king; the victories of his armies) with stories from abroad that revealed chaos or catastrophe (atrocities in Germany; prodigies and portents that foretold misfortunes for others). News of the regicide in London, coming so soon after news of the murder of Sultan Ibrahim in Istanbul, produced a wave of incredulity, indignation and revulsion throughout France. It was 'the most remarkable thing to happen in many centuries,' claimed one commentator. 'Let people just consider what has happened in neighbouring kingdoms,' screamed a pamphlet. 'Ask Renaudot what happened in Constantinople a few months ago, because the case of England is too odious. Is it possible that people remain in ignorance of these events? Is it possible that they do not see where it all leads?'[50]

The Paris judges saw 'where it all leads' clearly enough. To distance themselves from the 'parricide' in England, they offered their condolences and a pension to Queen Henrietta Maria, and opened peace talks with the regent. Eventually, in return for Anne's promise to confirm all her previous concessions and to grant an amnesty to her opponents, in March 1649 the *Parlement* of Paris annulled its edicts against Mazarin.

This defection shattered the Fronde. Many nobles, whose paramount goal had been to remove the cardinal from power, continued their defiance; while crowds of Parisians gathered outside the Palace of Justice shouting 'No peace! No Mazarin' and, more alarmingly 'Republic!' At this point, Philip IV again offered to open peace talks with France, but (in view of the weakness caused by the Fronde) he now demanded not only the withdrawal of all French troops from Catalonia and Lorraine but also an end of all aid to Portugal. Mazarin angrily rejected these 'exorbitant demands' and early in 1650, in exasperation, the prince of Condé joined the Fronde.

'Monsieur le prince' (as everyone called him) enjoyed many advantages. He was the king's close relative, third in line to the French throne; he enjoyed enormous prestige as the victor of Rocroi and Lens; he possessed both wealth and eloquence (in Latin as well as French). He also maintained a printing press in his Paris headquarters and a team of writers who produced a stream of propaganda. Nothing suggests that Condé wanted to displace his royal cousin on the throne, or to dismember France by carving out a state of his own: he probably aimed to replace Anne as regent, and seemed close to achieving this goal when, in January 1650, Mazarin acknowledged that he was Condé's 'very humble servant' who would further the prince's interests in all matters. The prince's triumph lasted just two days: Anne's guards suddenly arrested and imprisoned him, together with his two principal supporters.[51]

Most of the judges regarded these arrests as another example of arbitrary power and immediately declared their support for the prince, while Condé's supporters and relatives in Normandy, Burgundy and Guyenne promptly defied the central government. Their revolt unleashed a conflict that lasted for three years because the central government lacked the money to prevail. 'If you were here,' Mazarin confessed to a colleague abroad in spring 1650,

> You would know that every day the royal household is on the verge of bankruptcy, that the queen of England [Henrietta Maria] has dismissed her household and entered a convent because we cannot provide a monthly pittance, and that the treasury ministers have not yet found a penny for . . . our troops in Flanders.

The following summer, wet and windy, brought no relief; and (according to a contemporary history) 1651 began with 'a deluge that seemed to presage the misfortunes that later afflicted the poor kingdom' of France. 'War had led to excesses; taxes had ruined the population; famine had sent many to their graves; and despair had led to uprisings.'[52] Virtually all French troops at home were either mutinous, because they lacked pay and food, or commanded by nobles in open defiance of the crown. Even areas that saw no fighting suffered from natural disasters. In Provence, the combination of plague and the highest grain prices of the century provoked almost 70 popular revolts; while in Picardy, local clergy visiting their parishioners found families too weak even to answer their door because they had not eaten for several days.[53]

In February 1651, Anne bowed to the demands of both nobles and judges and released Condé and his colleagues; while Mazarin, fearing that the former prisoners would seek their revenge, fled ignominiously to Germany. He left Paris in chaos. On the one hand, torrential rains caused the Seine to burst its banks again, flooding many Parisians' houses; on the other, the hundreds of aristocrats who had gathered to demand release of the three princes now created a forum, the 'Assembly of Nobles', wherein they could express their numerous grievances against the central government: non-payment of interest on bonds; lack of employment (and therefore salaries); repeated violation of their traditional immunity from taxation, recruiting and billeting. Unusually, the Assembly admitted no distinction of rank, so that its pronouncements (all printed and widely circulated) went out in the names of princes, peers, barons and ordinary gentlemen alike. Everyone took turns to preside at the daily meetings. The Assembly insisted that Anne convene the States-General, and in order to get the nobles to go home, she eventually promised to convene one on 8 September 1651.[54]

It seems astonishing that the nobles took Anne's promise seriously, because three days before the scheduled meeting, Louis XIV would turn 13: when, according to French law, he would come of age and the regency would end. Although several groups optimistically drew up lists of grievances (*Cahiers de doléances*) the government did not even bother to issue writs to summon the deputies: the States-General would not meet again until 1789. Realizing that he had been duped, Condé fled Paris and signed a formal alliance with Philip IV. Soon afterwards, Anne and Louis also left the capital to join Mazarin, who had re-entered France at the head of a powerful contingent of German troops.

The court's departure from Paris provoked another flood of *Mazarinades*: no fewer than 1,600 appeared in the course of 1652 – sometimes 10 published on the same day (see Fig. 33). As before, the pamphlets targeted Mazarin; so did a series of striking broadsheets affixed in public places. One of these took the form of a 'wanted poster', which sentenced the cardinal to death for the damage he had done to France: each copy came with a rope that passed through two holes around the cardinal's neck, so he could be hanged in effigy.[55] Jansenists also now entered the fray, led by Robert Arnauld, brother of Antoine and Angélique, with a pamphlet entitled *The Naked Truth*, which offered a penetrating analysis of the origins of the Fronde that laid equal blame on Mazarin and Condé – and for good measure compared them with Cromwell, the 'usurper and tyrant of England' and 'the Mohammed of this century'.[56]

This second peak in the production of *Mazarinades* coincided with a new siege that produced starvation in the capital. Condé returned briefly in April 1652, hoping to create a new central government, but when his supporters seized the Hôtel de Ville and murdered his leading opponents, popular opinion turned against him. At one point scores of women gathered outside Condé's headquarters vociferously demanding peace. The prince got into a shouting match with the 'peace women' and unwisely accused them of accepting money from Mazarin: 'We are not for hire,' they shouted back, 'unlike your murderers at the Hôtel de Ville.'[57] Condé fled from Paris again, and this time made for Bordeaux, where a coalition of craftsmen, lawyers and merchants had set up a city government, known as the *Ormée*, which sought inspiration and assistance from England. With the help of some English advisers, the city's leaders drew up a republican constitution as shouts of 'No kings! No princes!' echoed through the streets.[58]

Meanwhile, Mazarin prepared a counter-attack. He persuaded a group of financiers to provide him with enough loans to win over some of the judges by paying their debts and granting them pensions, while Anne conferred lands and titles on potential supporters: 17 noble families became 'peers of the realm (*duc et pair*)', a relatively new and extremely rare honour. In October 1652, Louis XIV re-entered his capital and immediately held a *lit de justice* that annulled all legislation enacted by the *Parlement* over the previous four years. He also forbade the judges in future from meddling in 'affairs of state and the management of finance'; prohibited any proceedings 'against those whom the king has appointed to govern' (such as Mazarin); abolished the 'Chamber of Justice' established in 1648 to investigate profiteering among the crown's bankers; and exiled his most obdurate critics.[59]

Nevertheless, Louis still faced many domestic enemies. Guyenne remained in full revolt, supported by Spanish and British troops, while Condé and several regiments commanded by his clients and noble allies fought in the Spanish Netherlands alongside the troops of Philip IV. Above all, the Paris clergy openly opposed Mazarin after December 1652, when he arrested Pierre de Gondi, Cardinal de Retz and the designated successor ('coadjutor') of the archbishop of Paris. Although by no means Mazarin's only clerical critic – even Vincent de Paul, later sanctified for his pious life and works, demanded that the cardinal should abandon ministerial office – Retz took the lead in fomenting anti-government intrigue in the capital, first in the hope of replacing Mazarin as chief minister and then, as that prospect waned, with a view to turning France into a republic on the English model.[60] From prison, Retz begged his noble relatives and clerical colleagues to organize an uprising that would secure his release, and a 'clerical Fronde' began among the parish clergy of Paris, almost all Jansenists who already resented the government's persecution of those who revered the *Augustinus*. In May 1653, Mazarin persuaded the pope to issue a bull that categorically condemned Jansenism, naming five propositions allegedly contained in Jansen's writings as heretical; but this tactic only served to intensify the opposition of the Paris priests – some 50 in number – who now assembled regularly to discuss the affairs of the archdiocese.[61]

The 'clerical Fronde' drew strength from Mazarin's inability to crush his other opponents. Although royal troops forced the surrender of Bordeaux, ending the *Ormée*, Condé took command of Spain's armies in the Netherlands and in 1654 seemed poised to march on Paris. At the same time Retz escaped from prison, intending to rally his supporters once more. Hundreds of people converged on Notre Dame, where the cathedral chapter – in defiance of the government – sang a *Te Deum* to celebrate their hero's escape, but chance now saved Mazarin: while escaping, Retz fell and dislocated his shoulder and could not ride. Instead he had to rest and, during his recuperation, the Paris clergy attacked the Jesuits (many of them outspoken apologists for the government). These unseemly clerical disagreements unleashed the wickedly funny series of *Provincial Letters* by Blaise Pascal, which purported to explain the various controversies while discrediting virtually all the protagonists.

Then came the landmark winter of 1657–8, followed by snowmelt augmented by torrential rains: many rivers burst their banks, including the Seine which flooded Paris for the third time in a decade. Since farmers could not sow their crops, the following harvest was very poor, forcing even Mazarin to recognize that, since he lacked the resources to mount another campaign, it was time to practise 'the art of quitting when one is ahead'. In spring 1659 he accepted Philip IV's peace overtures and gained for France northern Catalonia and some areas in the South Netherlands (see chapter 9).[62]

The Audit of War

The quarter century of war, climatic adversity and political crisis between 1635 and 1659 reduced France to a shadow of its former self. The year 1652 saw the worst demographic crisis of the entire *ancien régime*. Grain prices in the capital rose so high that even charlatans failed to make a living – 'I have not pulled a tooth or sold any of my magic powders for three months', the most famous of them complained – while in the surrounding countryside, the combination of hostilities and harvest failure made the rural population 'believe everything and fear everything'. At Port-Royal-des-Champs, Angélique Arnauld observed that 'we see nothing but poor people who come and tell us that they have not eaten today, and some say they have not eaten for two or three days'.[63] As soldiers destroyed crops, burnt houses and stole possessions, it seemed to Abbess Arnauld that 'the war has ruined everything. Almost everyone is dead and the rest recruited and gone to the war, so we will have trouble tilling the fields for lack of labourers.' The surviving parish registers confirm her bleak assessment. In one parish, the 'great cruelties and great ravages' of the troops, combined with poor weather, 'forced the inhabitants to flee to safety, and 250 people died' – a fourteen-fold increase in normal mortality – and, throughout the Île-de-France, burials soared while conceptions plummeted, leading demographers to conclude that 'almost a quarter of the population vanished in the single year' (Fig. 34).[64]

The exhaustive research of Pierre Goubert on the Beauvaisis, a region of rich farmland north of Paris, likewise revealed a 'crisis – economic, social, demographic, physiological and moral – of an intensity and duration hitherto unknown'. Goubert noted that 'For five consecutive years, from 1647 to 1651, agriculture was the victim of bad weather; the most disastrous harvests being those of 1649 and 1651'; and, he added, 'The result was a steep rise and heavy extension of poverty and mortality, and

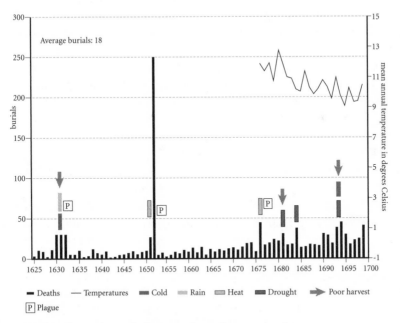

34. War, climate and mortality in Ile-de-France during the seventeenth century.
The records of Créteil, a village seven miles south-east of Paris, reveal a close link between climate and mortality throughout the seventeenth century: burials rose with the cold and rain of 1631 and 1693–4, and the heat wave of 1676. The worst demographic crisis of the village – indeed, of all Bourbon France – occurred in 1652 during the Fronde revolt, when a combination of floods, a catastrophic harvest, and military operations increased burials fourteen-fold.

a sharp fall in births.' The population of the Beauvaisis fell in these years by about one-fifth and did not regain its pre-Fronde level until the mid-eighteenth century. The demographic crisis also produced a major change in landholding. On the one hand, 'crushed by debt, the small peasants had to give up a large part of their land to their creditors'; on the other, the burgesses of Beauvais bought up 'hundreds of hectares of land' from impoverished peasants and nobles, while those able to produce more grain than they required sold it at a huge profit, which they used to buy up vacant freeholds and acquire leases on the numerous ecclesiastical estates of the region. 'In short, the terrible years of 1647 to 1653, which decimated the Beauvaisis, left a profound mark on peasant society and decisively widened social differences.'[65]

Depopulation and devastation on this scale demoralized even the most resilient. 'If one ever had to believe in the Last Judgment,' wrote one Parisian in 1652, 'I believe it is right now'; while the following year another claimed that 'two-thirds of the inhabitants of the villages around Paris are dead of illness, want and misery'. Abbess Arnauld feared that the general desolation 'must signify the end of the world'; while in 1655 the king's uncle Gaston of Orléans declared that 'the Monarchy was finished: the kingdom could not survive in its present state. In all the Monarchies that had collapsed, decline began with movements similar to the ones he discerned [now]; and he launched into a long list of comparisons to prove his statement from past examples.'[66] Some historians have gone even further than the duke, suggesting that the plight of the French Monarchy during the Fronde was greater than in 1789, and that the territorial integrity of the kingdom might not have survived a *Frondeur* victory.[67] Moreover, another disastrously wet winter and spring in 1661 caused another famine: the price of bread in the capital tripled, exceeding even the level during Condé's siege a decade before, while in many parts of the kingdom marriages fell by half, and conceptions by three-quarters. In all, Louis XIV may have lost another 500,000 subjects.[68]

The Sun King

Nevertheless, the French Monarchy survived the Fronde and Louis XIV became the most powerful ruler in western Europe. In part, this outcome arose from contingency. Abroad, France benefited from miscalculations by its enemies. Above all, the intransigence of Philip IV between 1648 and 1655, when he held the upper hand, saved Mazarin from having to trade land for peace, while Spain's eventual decision to concede virtually all its territorial losses appeared to vindicate the policies that the cardinal had pursued so recklessly. At home, Mazarin's most dangerous rivals either overplayed their hand (like Condé) or else lost the initiative at a critical moment (like Retz after he fell off his horse). Moreover, the various opponents of the crown lacked a single agenda: the judges, princes, nobles, clerics, urban patricians and popular leaders all stood for something different and often devoted more energy to destroying their erstwhile allies than to wresting concessions from the crown. Sometimes even individual groups splintered: in 1652 two of the leading *Frondeur* princes fought a duel that killed one of them (and both of his noble seconds). The movement also lacked a unifying ideology: Protestantism had become a spent force, while Jansenism still looked to Rome rather than to Paris for inspiration. Finally, the nobility was deeply divided between the hereditary ('sword') aristocracy and the newer 'robe' nobility, made up of judges and other royal officials who had purchased their exalted status. Had the States-General met in 1651, the 'robe nobility' would probably have sat with the urban delegates in the Third Estate (as they had done in 1614) rather than with the 'sword nobility' in the Second Estate (as they would do in 1789).

Such fundamental divisions, together with the hardship caused by the Little Ice Age and by the civil war, eventually enabled the crown to present itself as the only alternative to anarchy. As Louis XIV wrote in the 1670s in his *Mémoires*, as soon as he began to rule: 'I began to cast my eyes over all the various parts of the state; and not the eyes of a bystander but the eyes of the master.'[69] Mazarin had already shown the way, because peace with Spain enabled the cardinal to eliminate several groups of his domestic opponents. Almost immediately he terminated the assemblies of both the Paris clergy and the *Trésoriers de France* (whose defiance had started the Fronde), and then he dissolved an association of devout Catholics known as 'The Company of the Holy Sacrament'. According to the Company's official historian, when Anne of Austria asked Mazarin why he wanted to persecute 'such good servants of the king', the cardinal responded that although they had not yet done any harm, thanks to their impressive organization they could present a threat in the future. The legislation that ended the Company's legal existence outlawed meetings of *all* religious 'confraternities, congregations and communities' in Paris or in the provinces, on the grounds that 'under the veil of piety and devotion' they might foment 'cabals' and 'intrigues'.[70]

After Mazarin's death in 1661, Louis XIV continued to eliminate individuals and corporations who offered alternative foci of loyalty, starting with the late cardinal's wealthy and corrupt Finance Minister, Nicholas Fouquet, who had fortified the island of Belle-Île off the Breton coast, where he maintained a large arsenal and a private squadron of warships. Equally provocative, to the 'eyes of the master', Fouquet had spent 14 million *livres* on creating the most extensive and expensive private residence ever built in early modern France, at Vaux-le-Vicomte near Paris, where he maintained a glittering artistic following, including the playwrights Molière and Racine and the poet La Fontaine. A few months after Mazarin's death, Louis XIV arrested and imprisoned Fouquet, charged him with treason, and set up a commission of inquiry to investigate all who had grown rich from lending money to the crown in wartime. The commission eventually convicted almost 250 individuals of defrauding the treasury and collected fines that totalled 125 million *livres* – almost twice France's annual budget.[71]

The commission of inquiry was one of several royal initiatives that corresponded to demands by the Frondeurs. Others included Louis's decision to create fewer new offices, to end the punitive taxation of office-holders and to renew the *Paulette* automatically. In addition, Fouquet's successor as Finance Minister, Jean-Baptiste Colbert, paid both loan interest and official salaries punctually and in full; redeemed many costly long-term bonds; and, above all, reduced reliance on direct taxes like the *taille* (whereas indirect imposts had produced less than 25 per cent of the royal budget in the 1640s, they brought in 50 per cent by the 1670s). Although Colbert's fiscal reforms only raised the crown's notional revenue from 83 million *livres* in 1661 to 95 million in 1667, they more than doubled the amount that actually reached the central treasury from 31 million to 63 million *livres*.[72]

Louis also excluded from the central government three groups which, he believed, had grown too powerful during the regency: his relatives (even Anne of Austria lost her seat on the council and he never consulted his brother on matters of state); his nobles (in the course of his long reign, he appointed only two to the rank of minister of state); and his prelates (there would be no more Richelieus or Mazarins). Instead, Louis entrusted major tasks to men of relatively humble origins (like Colbert, whose father was a bankrupt provincial draper) with whom he worked diligently, either separately or in council, while reserving all the key decisions for himself. In the provinces, Louis not only restored the *intendants* abolished during the Fronde but appointed them on a permanent basis with wide-ranging functions (reflected in their full titles 'Intendants of justice, police and finance': the ancestors of the modern Prefects). In the *Pays d'État*, a series of edicts removed the power of the *Parlements* to challenge royal edicts before registering them, and Louis held no *lit de justice* after 1675. The local Estates likewise lost their right to present grievances before voting taxes. John Locke (at the time operating as an English spy in France) witnessed a session of the once-powerful Estates of Languedoc in 1676, and observed that the assembly had 'all the solemnity and outward appearance of a Parliament: the king proposes and they debate and resolve about it' – but, he continued, 'they never do, and some say dare not, refuse whatever the king demands'.[73] The language of politics in France had shifted from negotiation and compromise to obedience and subordination.

Louis tackled with similar vigour another inherited domestic challenge: the Huguenots. He issued a stream of edicts that restricted the religious and personal liberty of France's 250,000 Protestants; he quartered troops on the households of those who refused to convert; and in 1685 he revoked the Edict of Nantes (page 293 above). The king now ordered the destruction of all Protestant churches, proscribed all Protestant worship, public and private, closed all Protestant schools, and ordered all Protestant ministers either to convert or to leave the kingdom within two weeks. At least 200,000 Protestants followed their pastors into foreign exile, while the rest remained and, at least outwardly, conformed.

Louis also used force to impose his will on the cities of France, assailing their physical as well as their political strength. He ordered the demolition of almost all fortifications in the interior – including those of Paris, replacing its walls with the tree-lined Grands Boulevards that dominate the right bank of the city to this day. According to a treatise on the administration of the capital, France now enjoyed such security that its capital no longer needed walls to defend it.[74] This was no idle boast. Louis's military architects created a ring of artillery fortresses around the periphery of France, christened *Le pré carré* (the duelling field), designed to prevent any enemy from penetrating to the heart of the kingdom. The king also steadily increased the size of France's standing army. In the 1650s, through desertion and demoralization, the effective strength of France's armies probably did not exceed 150,000 men, and after the Peace of the Pyrenees the total fell to around 55,000. During the 1670s, by contrast, France's armies exceeded 180,000 men in peacetime, rising above 250,000 in wartime – the largest and most expensive defence establishment in Europe. Soldiers became more numerous in France than clerics, and military buildings (barracks as well as fortresses) dwarfed even the largest cathedrals and monasteries.

'Louis le Grand' (as his sycophants dubbed him) also constructed a vast palace complex at Versailles just outside Paris (using the same team of architects, painters and garden designers who had created Vaux-le-Vicomte for Fouquet), where he took decisions, patronized the arts and, with some secretarial assistance, prepared his *Reflections on the Craft of Kingship*, in which he justified his claim to exercise absolute power not solely because monarchs were God's lieutenants on earth (although Louis firmly believed that to be true), but because they combined unique benefits of nature and nurture. Inheritance, he argued, gave rulers a superior natural intelligence; but to succeed (like him) they must still work hard at 'the craft of kingship (*le métier du roi*)'. Thanks to his own dedication, Louis observed smugly, he now dominated both France and its neighbours.[75]

Louis showed the same inflexibility in both foreign and domestic policy. Like Richelieu and Mazarin before him, he viewed Christendom as a hierarchy in which some states naturally played a greater role than others: he therefore believed that an enduring 'balance of power' in Europe required France to be pre-eminent, and seemed genuinely astonished that other states would see his kingdom as a dangerous threat to be contained rather than as the vital guarantor of stability. Yet fears of French dominance were already current even when Louis ascended the throne. In 1644 a Swedish envoy at Westphalia remarked to his imperial counterpart that he 'was not unaware of the fact that [the French] aimed at superiority and at becoming the arbiters of the affairs of the Christian world', and he indicated that Sweden would oppose it; while one of his French colleagues observed that 'In my humble opinion it would be more advantageous to gain less, with the true and cordial affection of the Germans, than to retain more while forfeiting their friendship.' Two years later another French diplomat warned his government that 'If Breisach, Pinerolo and Perpignan are not sufficient to secure our frontiers, I have no doubt that the same thing will happen to us as to the Spaniards for wanting to extend their power so far.'[76] Louis paid no attention. Every one of the peace conferences of his reign – the Pyrenees in 1659, Breda in 1668, Nijmegen in 1678, Rijswijk in 1697 and Utrecht in 1713 – convened to end a war that France had begun.

Plus ça change?

Louis's ignorance reflected his education. Even before he became the royal preceptor, François de La Mothe le Vayer had written: 'One cannot deny that the art of governing people and subjugating enemies, which is the true vocation of princes, consists primarily of action rather than thought'; and that 'One of the great maxims of politics is that a king must wage war in person, because someone who is only king in his palace runs the risk of finding his master on the battlefield.' By the age of 13, when his practical military education began, Louis had already translated the whole of Caesar's *Commentaries* from Latin into French; and he spent the next five years learning how to fight with pike and musket, how to attack and defend fortresses, and how to command. The one exception was arithmetic, which La Mothe le Vayer considered a matter for merchants and 'something inappropriate for a king' – thus depriving Louis of a vital tool for assessing the costs of his policy decisions.[77]

Just like Richelieu and Mazarin, however, Louis XIV fought his wars at a time when climatic adversity reduced the available resources. Tree-ring data from western France show a long period of cooler and drier weather in the later seventeenth century, with several years of extreme adversity. The year 1672, when the Dutch war began, saw the worst harvest in a decade (thanks to drought followed by torrential rain), and those of the two succeeding years were scarcely better. Then came 1675, a 'year without a summer', almost certainly reflecting the powerful eruption of two volcanoes in Southeast Asia. In July, in Paris, Madame de Sévigné complained to her daughter that 'we have the fires lit, just like you.' Her daughter lived in Provence, where a diarist lamented that 'the seasons were so disorderly that all the crops were incredibly late' and predicted that they would not be harvested until late October, 'something never before seen here'. He was right: the grape harvest of 1675 ripened later throughout France than in any other year since records began in 1484. In Languedoc, John Locke noted that 'the rents of land in France [had] fallen above one-half, in these [last] few years by reason of the poverty of the people and want of money', while 'merchants and handicrafts men pay above half their gain' in taxes.[78]

Admittedly, Louis took some steps to ameliorate the adverse effects of climate change. During the famine of 1661 he bought grain in Aquitaine, Brittany and the Baltic and brought it to the capital – something neither Richelieu nor Mazarin had attempted – and this became standard operating procedure for the French central government in times of dearth for the rest of the *ancien régime* and beyond. Elsewhere, however, the king showed little concern and so each period of climatic adversity produced not only famine but also a spike in popular rebellions. At least 300 revolts broke out in 1661–2, a few of them suppressed only after troops arrived; and 1675 saw popular protests in western France from Bordeaux to Nantes. Those in Lower Brittany reached the scale of earlier uprisings. Louis had introduced several new indirect taxes to fund the Dutch war – notably a duty on all products made of tin, a state monopoly on tobacco and a stamp duty on all legal documents – and obliged the *Parlement* to register them. As before, raising taxes in a time of climatic adversity produced cries of 'Long live the king – without excise taxes'. Several Breton cities saw assaults on the offices that issued stamped paper, while peasants stormed and sacked the mansions and castles of their lords. By September 1675 the movement had a leader, the lawyer Sébastien Le Balp, a collective name

(*Les bonnets rouges:* 'The red bonnets') and several printed lists of grievances; but it collapsed when a nobleman managed to murder Le Balp, and regular troops entered the duchy to carry out systematic reprisals. Louis signed a general amnesty in February 1676 that excluded more than 150 people (including 1 gentleman, 1 notary and 14 priests) in order to concentrate on the next campaign.

The 'year without a summer' thus produced consequences that resembled those that followed climatic disasters in the first half of the seventeenth century; but there were also three differences. First, the revolts of 1675 neither produced sequels nor did they attract aristocratic involvement. Louis XIV would face no more Frondes. Second, they left a permanent visual legacy. The king ordered his troops to 'decapitate' the church steeples in Brittany whose bells had summoned insurgents, and some of the truncated towers still stand as a stark reminder of the revolt and its consequences. Finally, as already noted, the record cards (*fiches*) compiled for each of the thousands of men who enlisted in the French army reveal an average height of only 5 ft 3 inch) for those born between 1666 and 1694; and of those, the shortest of all, standing at 63 inches, were born in 1675. Moreover, among that disadvantaged group, those born in the west of France, the areas that had rebelled, were the shortest cohort of Frenchmen *ever* recorded.[79] This vindicates the claims made by some of Louis's subjects, from Madame de Sévigné to Sébastien Le Balp, that the conditions they faced were 'without parallel in past centuries'. Even the Sun King was no match for the Little Ice Age.

The Stuart Monarchy: The Path to Civil War, 1603–42[1]

T HE HISTORY OF SEVENTEENTH-CENTURY ENGLAND HAS ALWAYS ATTRACTED controversy. In 1659 John Rushworth published the first volume of a work entitled *Historical Collections or private passages of state*, dedicated to Lord Protector Richard Cromwell (son of Oliver Cromwell), which charted the origins of the English Civil War from a Republican point of view. Since the 1620s, Rushworth had held a variety of appointments that enabled him to witness events and amass printed and manuscript material (Plate 13). In 1682 James Nalson, a cleric, published a royalist alternative to Rushworth, entitled *An impartial collection of the great affairs of state*, dedicated, 'To the king's most excellent majesty'. Although both authors ended with the execution of Charles I on 30 January 1649, Rushworth started with the revolt of Bohemia in 1618 and the reaction of Charles and his father James I, which (as Nalson pointed out) implicitly saddled the Monarchy with 'the guilt of all the calamities and miseries of the late rebellion'. Nalson, by contrast, started with 'the Scotch rebellion' against King Charles in 1637, a chronological choice that focused blame on the king's opponents, and he accused his predecessor of including only documents that 'justify the actions of the late rebels'. Rushworth wisely ignored these barbs: 'Dr Nalson,' he wrote to a friend, 'finds fault with me; but I leave it to Posterity to judge.'[2]

'Posterity' can now draw on far more sources than either Rushworth or Nalson. Many of the leading protagonists recorded their innermost thoughts and justified their actions in writing, which historians can link with other written records as well as with sources on the prevailing climate. These data, richer and more varied than those available for any other country in the seventeenth century, make it possible not only to reconstruct just how Charles I and his subjects in Britain and Ireland 'came to fall out among ourselves' (as Rushworth put it), but also to study exactly how human and natural causes interacted to produce that outcome. And then we can 'judge'.

'Great Britain': A Problematic Inheritance

The Civil Wars would have been impossible without the creation of a new 'composite state' in 1603, when James VI of Scotland inherited England, Wales, Ireland and the Channel Isles from his childless cousin, Elizabeth Tudor. It was an unequal union from the first. Ireland's population in 1603 was perhaps 1.5 million, and Scotland's population was well under a million, whereas England's exceeded four million. The disparity was even greater a century later, when the totals had risen to 2.5, 1 and 6 million respectively. London, with 250,000 inhabitants in 1603 (and perhaps twice as many in 1640) had no equal in the Stuart Monarchy. The contrast overwhelmed King James, who admitted sheepishly to Parliament that 'my three first yeeres [in England] were to me as a Christmas' so that it might have appeared 'that the king had been drunke with his new kingdome'.[3]

England and Scotland had spent much of the previous four centuries at war, leaving a reservoir of mutual hatred and suspicion, and the economic, social and political differences of the two kingdoms were exceeded only by their incompatible religious establishments and doctrines, each enforced through a panoply of laws and courts. Although both states were officially Protestant, in Scotland bishops appointed by the king contended with regional assemblies (known as presbyteries) of parish ministers who followed the theology of John Calvin; whereas in England the monarch, who was also the Head of the Church, appointed all bishops and upheld a Protestant theology hostile to both Catholics and Calvinists (normally known as Presbyterians). England's Catholics inspired disproportionate popular hatred and fear, because although they numbered under 5 per cent of the total population, they included many prominent adherents (including the spouses of both James and his son Charles and many of their courtiers) as well as some extremists (such as the group led by Guy Fawkes who in 1605 attempted to blow up the royal family and both Houses of Parliament in the Gunpowder Plot).

Ireland, too, proved a troubled inheritance. In 1603, after a bitter nine-year struggle, English forces managed to suppress a major Catholic rebellion, supported by Spain, and soon afterwards James confiscated the lands of many former rebels and granted them to settlers from Britain. By 1640 some 70,000 English and Welsh, and perhaps 30,000 Scots, had settled in Ulster (the northern province of the island), mostly in new towns and in 'plantations' (lands confiscated from the native Irish and granted to groups of British immigrants). These newcomers joined either the Protestant Church of Ireland (closely modelled on the Church of England, with bishops appointed by the crown) or one of a growing number of Presbyterian communities; but everywhere they remained heavily outnumbered by Catholics obedient to the bishops and abbots appointed by Rome.

Geography, too, posed a serious challenge to effective government of the new composite state. Even England possessed some 'dark corners of the land' (such as Westmoreland and the Cambridgeshire Fens) where few heeded the religious and political measures decreed by London, while much of Wales proved even less tractable. In Ireland rivers and bogs separated the staunchly Catholic hinterland from the Protestant enclaves along the coast and in Ulster. In addition, commands and resources sent from London could take weeks to cross the Irish Sea, which storms or the prevailing westerly winds often rendered impassable. Although James boasted to the English Parliament 'This I must say for Scotland, and I may truly vaunt it: here I sit and governe it with my pen; I write and it is done', and although royal messages regularly travelled between London and Edinburgh in four days, in the Highlands and Islands clan chiefs normally ignored the crown and pursued the vicious feuds and rivalries that had lasted for centuries.[4]

To overcome such diversity, and to guard 'against all civill and intestine rebellion', James strove to foster a common loyalty among his subjects. He assumed the title 'king of Great Britain' and stated that 'his wish above all things was at his death to leave one worship to God, one kingdom entirely governed, [and] one uniformity in laws' throughout his realms. In Ireland, his agents completed the work of their predecessors in imposing English law and administrative practices until by 1612, according to an official addicted to metaphors, 'the clock of civil government [in Ireland] is now well set, and all the wheels thereof do move in order; the strings of this Irish harp, which the civil magistrate doth finger, are all in tune'. That 'tune' became steadily more Protestant. The Catholics lost their majority in the Irish Parliament, thanks to the grant of Irish peerages to British Protestants and of parliamentary seats to the new towns of Ulster; and when some Catholic leaders protested, James excoriated them as 'half-subjects of mine, for you give your soul to the pope and to me only the body – and even it, your bodily strength, you divide it between me and the king of Spain'. His efforts to advance both the religious and political influence of Ireland's Protestant minority therefore continued.[5]

James also strove to 'Anglicize' his native Scotland. In secular affairs he worked through the Privy Council, a body of nobles and officials sitting in Edinburgh whose proclamations had the force of law. After 1612, a standing committee of the Scottish Parliament, known as the 'Lords of the Articles', prepared legislation for ratification by the full assembly and enabled James to control the parliamentary agenda. Sometimes arguments arose over the imposition of taxes – which tripled between 1606 and 1621 – but every increase eventually received approval. The only area of policy where James encountered spirited resistance was religion. When he returned to Scotland in person in 1617 and tried to impose English liturgical practices on the General Assembly of the Church, his efforts provoked the first public discussion in Stuart Britain of the limits of royal authority. When the Presbyterian minister David Calderwood explained his refusal to obey the king's direct commands on worship, James shot back:

> *King.* I will tell thee, man, what is obedience. The centurion, when he said to his servants, to this man, Goe, and he goeth, to that man, Come, and he cometh: that is obedience.
> *Calderwood.* To suffer, Sir, is also obedience, howbeit not of that same kind . . .
> *King.* Consider, I am here. I am a king. I may demand of you when and what I will.

Although James silenced Calderwood for a time by ordering him to be deported to Virginia, he lost the argument because any ruler who finds it necessary to justify his authority to his subjects automatically undermines it.[6]

Shortly after this exchange, foreign events began to undermine the king's authority further. Elector Frederick of the Palatinate, husband of James's daughter Elizabeth, accepted the crown of Bohemia and provoked a counter-attack by both Austrian and

Spanish Habsburg forces, who confiscated his hereditary lands (see chapter 8 above). James decided to assist his son-in-law in two ways: first, by sending him money and (later and very grudgingly) troops; and second, by seeking to marry his son and heir Charles to a Spanish princess, with the restoration of the Palatinate to Frederick as (in effect) her dowry. When marriage negotiations languished, in 1623 Prince Charles travelled to Madrid together with the duke of Buckingham, his father's Favourite, to advance his suit in person. Meanwhile, to facilitate the 'Spanish Match', James relaxed anti-Catholic penal laws in England – a move guaranteed to alarm and alienate his Protestant subjects at any time, but especially during an economic depression.

The El Niño autumn of 1621 brought torrential rains that ruined the harvest throughout Britain. In Scotland, 'there was never seene in this countrie in so short a time suche inequalitie of prices of victuall; never greatter fear of famine nor scarsitie of seede to sow the ground'. Before long, 'everie man was carefull to ease himself of suche persones as he might spaire' – that is, to dismiss employees and servants. 'Pitifull was the lamentation not onlie of vaging [wandering] beggars, but also of honest persons.' Northern England also saw many 'wandering beggars'. In 1623 the vicar of Greystoke in Cumbria buried 'a poor fellow destitute of succour' in January; 'a poor hunger-starving beggar child' and 'a poor hunger-starved beggar boy' in March; and 'a poor man destitute of means to live' in May. Marriages in Greystoke and elsewhere in England plunged to their lowest point between 1580 and 1640 (because no one could afford to set up a new home) while conceptions fell by half (either through abstention or amenorrhoea). Even in areas that normally exported grain, the magistrates feared that 'this time of so extraordinary a want both of corn and of work' would 'breed in those of their condition a dangerous desperation'.[7]

Amid such tensions, and with English tracts, poems and sermons railing against the 'Spanish Match', some foreign ambassadors predicted rebellion should Prince Charles bring back a Spanish bride. Instead, the marriage negotiations failed and the prince's return as a bachelor precipitated ecstatic rejoicing. Charles and Buckingham became national heroes and they exploited their popularity by persuading James to declare war against Spain, primarily to put pressure on Philip IV to restore Frederick of the Palatinate's confiscated estates. To pay for the war, James summoned Parliament, where Charles and Buckingham persuaded the House of Commons first to impeach a minister who opposed the war and then to vote £300,000 in new taxes to fight it.

Although this assembly earned the epithet 'Felix Parliamentum, the happy Parliament', it created two serious problems for Charles. First, resort to impeachment (common in the fifteenth century but little used since then) set a dangerous precedent that could be used against any royal official who displeased Parliament. Second, as James himself had observed many years before, 'a wise king will not make warre against another, without he first make provision of money' – but in 1624, although the war with Spain was predicted to cost £1 million a year, the English treasury had no such 'provision'. This shortage made the crown a hostage to Parliament as long as hostilities lasted, and Charles reconvened Parliament as soon as he succeeded his father in March 1625, and requested more funds to prosecute the war. The acrimonious debates that marked this and the three subsequent sessions destroyed both the king's popularity and the national unity created by the failure of the Spanish Match. In the words of Richard Cust, the king's most perceptive biographer, 'Charles's honeymoon with the English people was over'. How did it end so fast?[8]

'The crisis of Parliaments'

One major reason for popular disenchantment in the later 1620s lay beyond Charles's control. No sooner had he secured a declaration of war on Spain than another run of poor harvests drove up food prices and drastically reduced the demand for manufactured goods. The magistrates in Buckinghamshire in 1625 complained that poverty 'enforces many to steal or starve', while those of Lincolnshire thought the 'country was never in that want it now is' and reported that thousands had 'sold all they have, even to their bed-straw, and cannot get work to earn any money. Dog's flesh is a dainty dish, and found upon search in many houses.' Meanwhile plague broke out in London, killing some 40,000 people and halting trade. In Essex, normally a prosperous county, 'Scarce any man has half an ordinary crop of corn, clothiers have no vent [sale] of their wares, graziers and marketmen have no sale on account of the infection in London.' The adverse weather continued: on the Isle of Wight, normally a grain-exporting region, a landowner noted in 1627 that 'the coldness of the summer and the great fall of rain in August and September' ruined the harvest; while 'the winter of 1629 was one of the wettest that ever I knew. It rained almost every other day', killing most of the cattle and destroying the winter wheat. At the same time, a smallpox epidemic of particular virulence killed and disfigured many people as well as disrupting travel and trade. Charles could hardly have chosen a worse time to wage war.[9]

The king exacerbated the situation with two policy decisions. First, in the hope of creating an anti-Habsburg alliance to support his Palatine policy, he proposed marriage to Henrietta Maria of France – but her brother Louis XIII demanded a measure of toleration for English Catholics before he would consent. Accordingly, Charles suspended the penal laws again, provoking the predictable anti-Catholic agitation. Second, he and Buckingham (still the royal Favourite and chief minister) decided to spend the funds voted by Parliament for the new war on two ambitious ventures: an army to raise the Spanish siege of the Dutch city of Breda and a fleet to capture the Spanish port city of Cádiz. By the time Charles met his second Parliament in 1626, both operations had failed (see chapter 9 above) and these setbacks, combined with famine, plague and the failure to persecute Catholics, produced widespread exasperation.

The English Parliament was a volatile body. With almost 150 peers in the House of Lords and almost 600 members in the House of Commons, it formed the largest representative assembly in the entire early modern world; and, since every freeman with property worth £2 could vote, a general election of 'Members of Parliament'

(MPs, as those who sat in the Commons were known) could involve up to 500,000 people. Moreover, since both Houses normally held their debates in the Palace of Westminster, which also housed the central law courts, Parliament functioned under the gaze of thousands of spectators: lawyers, petitioners and supplicants; servants, families and advisers; those who wished to see and be seen; those who sought to influence the outcome (Fig. 35). Finally, London itself – where almost one-third of all families lived at or below the poverty line, and perhaps 6,000 young men and women arrived each year in search of employment – constituted an enormous reservoir of potential unrest. Securing approval for the crown's proposals, and avoiding any attempt to exploit the crown's fiscal needs to extract concessions, therefore required careful 'management' not only of general elections and of the two Houses, but also of the capital in time of Parliament. No seventeenth-century government succeeded in these vital tasks, creating a fundamental and recurring instability at the heart of the state.[10]

Charles summoned and then dissolved Parliament three times between 1626 and 1629. In each instance, the House of Commons began by blaming the crown for pursuing disastrous policies and demanded redress for its grievances before it would vote money to fund the king's wars; Charles took offence at its demands, tried to bully it into submission by arresting recalcitrant members; and when those efforts failed, he dissolved it. Since the war with Spain continued, in the absence of

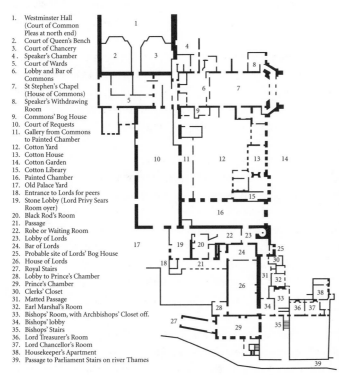

1. Westminster Hall (Court of Common Pleas at north end)
2. Court of Queen's Bench
3. Court of Chancery
4. Speaker's Chamber
5. Court of Wards
6. Lobby and Bar of Commons
7. St Stephen's Chapel (House of Commons)
8. Speaker's Withdrawing Room
9. Commons' Bog House
10. Court of Requests
11. Gallery from Commons to Painted Chamber
12. Cotton Yard
13. Cotton House
14. Cotton Garden
15. Cotton Library
16. Painted Chamber
17. Old Palace Yard
18. Entrance to Lords for peers
19. Stone Lobby (Lord Privy Sears Room oyer)
20. Black Rod's Room
21. Passage
22. Robe or Waiting Room
23. Lobby of Lords
24. Bar of Lords
25. Probable site of Lords' Bog House
26. House of Lords
27. Royal Stairs
28. Lobby to Prince's Chamber
29. Prince's Chamber
30. Clerks' Closet
31. Matted Passage
32. Earl Marshal's Room
33. Bishops' Room, with Archbishops' Closet off.
34. Bishops' lobby
35. Bishops' Stairs
36. Lord Treasurer's Room
37. Lord Chancellor's Room
38. Housekeeper's Apartment
39. Passage to Parliament Stairs on river Thames

35. Plan of the Palace of Westminster, England. Parliament and the Law Courts shared the same complex of buildings at Westminster. The House of Commons met in St Stephen's Chapel (7), but members could enter and exit in various ways, including by 'Parliament Stairs' to the river Thames (39), used by the 'Five Members' when Charles I came to the Commons to arrest them in January 1642.

parliamentary funding the government raised money by demanding loans from leading subjects (and imprisoning those who refused) and by enforcing regalian rights (such as billeting soldiers in private households). But Charles's decision in 1627 to declare war on France as well forced him to summon another Parliament. Much was at stake when it met the following year. As one MP put it, 'This is the crisis of Parliaments. By this we shall know if Parliaments will live or die', adding perceptively that 'our lives, our fortunes, our religion, depend on the resolution of this assembly', because 'if the king draws one way, and the people another, we must all sink'.[11] Some MPs nevertheless refused to vote further taxes until Charles had redressed what they saw as the abuses of previous years, invoking principles and precedents drawn from a careful study of history and the Classics. 'Every man knows,' stated one MP about billeting, that 'our houses are our castles, and to have such "guests" put upon us, our wives, and children, is a violation of the laws'. 'The subject of our discourse is to vindicate the fundamental liberties of the kingdom,' claimed another. After several weeks of wide-ranging debate, MPs incorporated their various grievances into a single document, known as 'The Petition of Right', which not only required the crown to cease billeting soldiers and sailors in private homes and to stop subjecting civilians to martial law, but also forbade the imposition of taxes without parliamentary consent and the imprisonment of any subject without showing due cause – two prerogatives that Charles regarded as an integral part of monarchical power. They also begged Charles to 'take a further view of the present state of your realme' and to dismiss his Favourite, the duke of Buckingham, whom they blamed for 'the miserable disasters and ill successe that hath accompanied all your late designes and actions'. The king once again responded with an immediate dissolution of Parliament.[12]

By the time Charles made peace with both France and Spain in 1630, his debts totalled four times his annual revenues. In addition, both economic malaise and bad weather continued. The year 1629 saw 'so wonderful and great a flood as had not been seen of forty years'; 1630 saw widespread harvest failure; the summer of 1632 was 'the coldest that any then living ever knew'; spring 1633 was 'wet, cold and windy' and the following autumn 'a marvellous ill seed-time'; summer 1634 brought drought; and the following winter saw such 'very intense cold' that the entire Thames froze over. Then came two summer droughts, that of 1636 so 'excessive' that 'everyone declares that there is no memory of such a misfortune in England, whose usually damp climate is so changed that the trees and the land are despoiled of their verdure, as if it were a most severe winter'.[13]

Nevertheless, Charles managed to govern without Parliament for 11 years – in part because England's foreign trade underwent a rapid expansion: since war ravaged Europe while Britain enjoyed peace, many merchants shipped their wares through English ports, despite high customs duties. By 1639 the king had both paid off his debts and raised his annual revenues to £900,000, almost twice as much as a decade before. Customs duties accounted for only half the crown's increased income, however. Much of the rest came from the ruthless enforcement of 'regalian rights', such as fines for encroaching on royal forests, fees from those eligible to become knights, and (most lucrative of all) 'Ship Money', a levy to pay for the Royal Navy. Legal doubts surrounded every one of these extra-parliamentary income streams. The customs duties consisted principally of an ancient tax known as 'tonnage and poundage', which the 1625 Parliament had granted to Charles for only one year; thereafter his officers collected it without parliamentary approval. 'Forest fines' increased largely because crown lawyers arbitrarily extended the boundaries of the royal forests to their former, medieval limits; while Ship Money, which had no precedent except in maritime counties, was now collected everywhere. When a few courageous subjects challenged the legality of each of these levies, Charles brought a test case to the law courts – and each time his judges ruled in his favour. The king's courts, formerly the arbiters of his subjects' lives, had become partisan protagonists. When in 1637 the judges upheld the legality of Ship Money, some landholders in Kent argued that their king was now 'more absolute than eyther France or the great duke of Tuscany'.[14]

Charles also strove to become 'more absolute' in religious matters. Although he neglected the penal laws against Catholics, he persecuted Presbyterians. Throughout the 1630s his bishops enforced conformity to the doctrine and liturgy of the Church of England by summoning resisters – and there were thousands of them – to the church courts and, when convicted, handing down harsh punishments. Those who remained unbowed came before the king's courts, especially the Courts of High Commission and Star Chamber, where they received even harsher punishments. The most spectacular example occurred in 1637, shortly after the Ship Money decision, when Star Chamber condemned three prominent critics of episcopacy: William Prynne, Henry Burton and John Bastwick. All three were gentlemen who had attended university and also received professional training (Prynne as a lawyer, Burton as a preacher, Bastwick as a physician). At the instigation of William Laud, archbishop of Canterbury and the king's principal adviser on ecclesiastical affairs, the judges of Star Chamber (which included Laud) charged each man with seditious libel and condemned them to pay the enormous fine of £5,000 (equivalent to perhaps £1 million today); to life imprisonment without access to their family or to pen, ink or paper; and, despite their elite status, to have their ears sliced off by the common hangman in a degrading public ceremony. Such savagery, coupled with flagrant contempt for social status, caused widespread outrage. Many regarded the three men as martyrs.[15]

Although these legal victories by the king caused some to grumble, many of his subjects would probably have agreed with the claim of Edward Hyde, a prominent royalist and author of the influential *History of the rebellion and civil wars in England*, that in the 1630s England 'enjoyed the greatest calm and the fullest measure of felicity that any people in any age for so long time together have been blessed with', rather than with the verdict of Nehemiah Wallington, a London craftsman, who compiled a record of the 1630s expressly so 'that the generation to come may see what wofull and miserable times we lived in'. In any case, those who thought like Wallington had limited outlets for their views so long as Parliament remained out of session – and, as one observer put it, 'none could expect a Parliament, but on some necessity not now imaginable'.[16]

The success of Charles's 'Personal Rule' required him to avoid creating such a 'necessity' because, as Anzolo Correr, the Venetian ambassador in England, observed, Charles had 'changed the principles by which his royal predecessors have governed' by 'ceasing to rule by Parliament as his predecessors used to do'. He continued:

> It remains to be seen if he will continue and if he can achieve through royal authority what former kings did by the authority of the realm. It is a difficult matter, and all the more dangerous now because, it seems, the kingdom is agitated about two great matters, religion and the reduction of the liberty of the people, both of which the king has thoroughly stirred up [*perturbate*]. This will produce a major confrontation if not a great upheaval [*gran turbolenza*].

The ambassador invoked 'the example of Henry III, who suffered prolonged disasters and upheavals in what was called "the Barons' Wars"', four centuries before, because, Correr opined, 'the people are so discontented that if they had leaders – which they have not – it would be impossible to placate them'. Correr's analysis, although admirable for England, completely omitted Scotland and Ireland. He even failed to mention the riots that three months earlier had shaken Edinburgh, starting a chain of events that would lead Charles into war, produce a formidable cadre of English 'leaders' and create 'prolonged disasters and upheavals' far more damaging than 'the Barons' Wars' against Henry III.[17]

The Scottish Revolution

Charles had offended the Scots ever since his accession in 1625, when as part of his mobilization plans for the war with Spain he resolved to create among his kingdoms 'a strict union and obligation each to [the] other for their mutual defence': a 'Union of Arms' modelled on Spain's ill-fated scheme (see chapter 9 above). To obtain funds for the Scottish contingent of the Union army, the new king announced a 'Revocation', a device traditionally used by Scottish monarchs at their accession to reclaim lands usurped from their immediate predecessor; yet despite numerous precedents, the manner in which Charles presented his initiative provoked widespread opposition. Although the king eventually made some grudging concessions, the final version (put into effect in 1629) still required those who had obtained church and crown lands to surrender them to him, before receiving them back under less favourable terms. Just like the Edict of Restitution promulgated in Germany that same year (see page 222 above), the Act of Revocation subsequently appeared even to loyalists as the 'root of all evils'. Looking back in the 1640s, the historian Sir James Balfour saw in the Revocation 'the groundstone of all the mischief that followed after, both to this king's government and family', and believed that it 'laid open a way to rebellion'.[18]

The resentment generated by the Revocation had scarcely abated before Charles took steps to create a single 'form of public worship', so that just as his Monarchy 'has but one Lord and one faith, so it has but one heart and one mouth ... in the churches that are under the protection of one sovereign prince'. Above all, the king wished to end the 'diversity, nay deformity' of worship he observed when he returned to Scotland in 1633 because 'no set or public form of prayer was used, but preachers or readers or ignorant schoolmasters prayed in the church' extemporaneously. He charged the energetic but inflexible Archbishop William Laud with devising a remedy.[19]

Archie the Fool, the Scottish jester who entertained Charles I and his courtiers with droll remarks, immediately saw the danger. On hearing of the plan to impose a new liturgy on his homeland by royal proclamation, Archie turned to Archbishop Laud and asked: 'Who's the Fool now?' Laud responded by banishing the jester from court and instead prepared a 'Code of Canons' for Scotland that prohibited extempore prayer and other ancient liturgical customs. Charles published them by virtue of 'our prerogative royal, and supreme authority in causes ecclesiastical' – apparently forgetting that the Church of Scotland recognized no such 'supreme authority'. The king also ordered every church to buy and use a Prayer Book and, when reminded that no Scottish Prayer Book existed, he instructed Laud to prepare one that contained set prayers and responses based on (albeit not identical to) English practice. Then, using 'Our royall authority, as king of Scotland', Charles enjoined the exclusive use of the new Prayer Book, with effect from Sunday, 23 July 1637. Ministers who failed to acquire a copy, and to use it on that date, would be declared rebels and outlaws.[20]

The king had chosen a dangerous moment to innovate because Scotland suffered from more extreme weather than England. In June 1637 the Privy Council in Edinburgh issued emergency legislation to deal with a plague epidemic, an acute shortage of coins, and a universal 'scarcity of victuals' because of the poor harvest. According to the earl of Lothian, one of Scotland's worried landowners:

> The earth has been iron in this land . . . and the heavens brass this summer, till now in the harvest there have been such inundations and floods and winds, as no man living remembers the like. This has shaken and rotted and carried away the little corn [that] came up, [so] that certainly they that are not blind may see a judgment come on this land. Besides there is no kind of coin in it, [so] that men that are in debt can not get their own to give their creditors, and the few that have money keep it for themselves for the[ir] great advantage in this penury and necessity.

Small wonder, then, that imposing the new Prayer Book, derisively known as 'Laud's liturgy', unleashed a revolution – especially since its opponents were already well prepared.[21]

In April 1637 a group of ministers led by Alexander Henderson (a man of obscure origins whose abilities as a preacher and organizer would soon catapult him to international prominence) met secretly in Edinburgh with some 'matrons of the kirk' (the wives of prominent Presbyterians) and warned them that the king aimed to abolish Scotland's traditional forms of worship, in which spontaneous prayer formed a central part, and thus imperil their chances of salvation. A strange accident provided irrefutable confirmation of Henderson's claim: once the government's printer had corrected the proof sheets of 'Laud's Liturgy', he discarded them – but, since good paper was valuable, the sheets were promptly recycled by 'the shops of Edinburgh to cover spice and tobacco' and so became public knowledge, convincing everyone that 'the life of the Gospel' would be 'stolen away by enforcing on the kirk a dead service book'. The 'matrons of the kirk' therefore authorized their maid-servants to stage a riot whenever it was first used.[22]

The maidservants obliged. No sooner had the dean of Edinburgh begun to read the new set prayers at the morning service on Sunday, 23 July in St Giles Cathedral, in the presence of the king's judges and the city magistrates, than the young women sitting on their folding stools at the front 'with clapping of their hands, cursings and outcries, raised such a barbarous hubbub in that sacred place that not any one could either hear or be heard'. The young women then 'threw the stools they sate on at the preacher' and then 'did rive [rip] all the service bouk[s] a peisses'. The dean, judges and magistrates ran for their lives, and when they tried to use the new Prayer Book in the afternoon, the crowd threw stones at them (Plate 14).[23]

Charles responded by commanding the Scottish Privy Council to punish all 'authors or actors', and to enforce use of the new Prayer Book forthwith. The Council duly summoned the leading members of the Edinburgh clergy – but instead of decreeing punishments, they determined that 'the service books cannot be orderly used in the kirks', and therefore authorized the ministers to continue to preach in the traditional form. They also freed those imprisoned for involvement in the riots.[24] Henderson and his colleagues used their reprieve to draw up a 'supplica-tion' against religious innovations, to be presented to the king in the name of the godly nobles, burgesses and ministers. Charles regarded this collective act as sedi-tion and ordered the committee to disperse; but instead Henderson, ably assisted by Archibald Johnston of Wariston, a determined and devout Edinburgh lawyer, drafted a formal protest that they called 'The National Covenant' to solidify popular support. Although the Covenant claimed to safeguard 'the true worship of God, the majesty of our king, the peace of the kingdom, for the common happiness of ourselves, and the posterity', its content was profoundly subversive since it condemned all innovations in ecclesiastical and secular government made since the Union of 1603. Moreover, it obliged every Scottish householder to take a solemn and public oath that they would 'to the uttermost of our powers, with our means and lives' defend 'the foresaid true religion, liberties and laws of the kingdom *against all sorts of persons whatsoever*' – a formula that could be used to justify rebellion.[25]

On the third Sunday in March 1638, a day named by Henderson and his colleagues as 'a solemn fast day appointed for subscription', in each Scottish parish the congregation rose to its feet and, with right hands raised, repeated in unison the oath to uphold the Covenant 'against all sorts of persons whatsoever'. They then signed their names, after which (Wariston reported) 'such a yell' came from the throats of the assembled crowd 'as the like was never seen or heard of'.[26] Wariston was right: Scotland – perhaps the world – had never seen such an exercise in popular democracy. After more sermonizing, a messenger set forth for London bearing both the Covenant and a list of eight demands (composed by Wariston) 'containing the least of our necessary desires to settle this church and kingdom in peace' to present to the king. Wariston then 'prayed the Lord *to preserve us from that great sin of retiring one single inch in this cause of God* out of diffidence and worldly fears'. For Wariston, at least, there would be no surrender and no compromise.[27]

The marquis of Hamilton, who arrived in Scotland as Charles's personal representative in June 1638, immediately recognized the danger posed by such intractability. 'The conquering totally of this kingdom [Scotland] will be a difficult work,' he warned the king, even if 'you were certain of what assistance England can give you'; but, the marquis continued presciently,

> It fears me that [the English] will not be so forward in this as they ought, nay that there are so many malicious spirits amongst them that no sooner will your back be turned but they will be ready to do as we have done here, which I will never call by another name than rebellion. England [lacks] not its own discontents.

Charles took no notice. Since he believed that 'not only now my crown but my reputation for ever lies at stake' in Scotland, he informed Hamilton that nothing 'can reduce that people to their obedience, but only force'. Therefore, he added imperiously, 'I would rather die than yield to those impertinent and damnable demands' because 'it is all one, as to yield, to be no king in a very short time'. Returning to the theme in another letter, he repeated: 'So long as this covenant is in force, I have no more power in Scotland than as a Duke of Venice, which I will rather die than suffer.' He therefore reiterated his determination to use overwhelming force 'to suppress rebellion' there.[28]

It was, once again, a dangerous moment to make such ambitious plans. On the one hand, whereas Scotland had seen 'such inundations and floods and winds as no man living remembers the like' in 1637, the following year proved to be the driest year that some parts of Scotland had experienced in a century. On the other hand, a new Venetian ambassador saw clearly that Charles's Personal Rule was doomed. He perceived 'a disposition to revolution in England also, to force the king to obey the laws' according to 'the example of the Scots'; while 'the people of Ireland also are discontented and ill-treated by the Viceroy there [Thomas Wentworth] without regard for their privileges or anything else. As their outcry makes no impression on His Majesty they complain bitterly.' In short, the ambassador concluded, '*the king has no friends in England, less in Ireland and none in Scotland, and if he does not change the nature of his rule one foresees some irremediable disaster*'.[29]

For the time being, Charles cynically authorized Hamilton to make concessions to the Covenanters: 'Flatter them with what hopes you please,' he wrote, '*your chief end being now to win time . . . untill I be ready to suppress them*'. In October 1638, since it was too late for military intervention, Charles even gave his consent for the General Assembly of the Scottish Church to convene for the first time in 20 years, and hundreds of ministers and pious laymen (many of them heavily armed) attended its opening session. 'It is more than probable that these people have somewhat else in their thoughts than religion,' warned Hamilton (who presided over the Assembly in the king's name): rather, religion 'must serve for a cloak to rebellion', and to 'bring them again to a dutiful obedience'. He, too, now saw no alternative to a full-scale invasion.[30]

Wariston could think of only two avenues by which Scotland might escape this fate: the outbreak of troubles in England itself ('either by a mutiny of the Protestant people' or 'by the king of France's invasion'); or else 'the Lord's removal of Charles' – the first known reference to the king's death as a solution to the problems of the Stuart Monarchy (a full decade before it happened). Realizing that these convenient scenarios were improbable, and knowing that insistence on 'the absolute rooting out of bishops' would mean 'taking up arms' to oppose an English invasion, Wariston and his colleagues began to study the theories of political resistance advanced by continental writers.[31] Thus enlightened, they spread their views through pamphlets and preaching; they cultivated links with known opponents of Charles's policies in England (in the hope of provoking a 'mutiny' that might divert Charles from attacking Scotland); and they persuaded the Swedish government both to allow Scottish soldiers in their service to return home and to provide arms and munitions. Chancellor Axel Oxenstierna, who equated Scotland's cause with Sweden's war of independence over a century before, eventually sent almost 30 heavy guns, 4,000 muskets and 4,000 suits of armour, and released over 300 Scottish officers in Swedish service, including General Alexander Leslie, a veteran with 30 years' experience of continental warfare.

The Tipping Point

In 1639 these reinforcements gave the Scots a critical advantage in opposing the king, who had decided to lead 20,000 men to the Scottish border in person, while Hamilton with the Royal Navy both blockaded the east coast of Scotland and landed troops to assist opponents of the Covenant in the northeast, and an Irish army invaded the southwest. It was a promising strategy (four years later an invasion of Scotland from Ireland would prove devastatingly effective), but three flaws ruined it. First, the joint commanders of the Irish army (the earls of Strafford and Antrim) refused to cooperate with each other. Their sole achievement was to alienate the leading landowner in southwest Scotland, Archibald Campbell, earl of Argyll, who now threw in his lot with the Covenanters. Second, the royalists in the northeast surrendered before English reinforcements arrived. Third, extreme weather delayed the mobilization of Charles's English army. Spring 1639 saw a 'most grievous tempest of wind, thunder, lightning and rain' followed by a ten-week drought, followed by 'the greatest wind that ever I heard blow', and finally 'aboundance of raine [which] made foule travelling' and 'two of the coaldest dayes' that 'ever I felt'. 'I feare,' a royalist commander fretted, that if the cold 'continues, it will kill our men'.[32]

When the royal recruits mustered at York, their numbers 'came farr short of the king's expectacion' and many men lacked weapons. According to an officer who watched the king's troops advance through Newcastle, 'I dare saye ther was never soe raw, soe unskillfull, and soe unwilling an army brought to fight ... They are as like to kill theyr fellowes as the enimye'. A solar eclipse three weeks later, which many in the army 'construed' as 'an ominous presage of bad successe to the king's affaires', did nothing to improve morale – especially since, according to John Aston, a member of the royal entourage, 'the greatest enemy' was 'hunger, which had soe assaulted the campe' that 'there was a mutinie in the army for want of bread'.[33] Nevertheless, at the end of May 1639, King Charles reached the river Tweed, the border between the two kingdoms, at the head of 20,000 soldiers, where they pitched their tents and fortified their camp facing the army of the Covenant, entrenched just across the river.

Charles I's 1639 campaign fully vindicated the warning of Louis XIV's preceptor: 'One of the great maxims of politics is that a king must wage war in person, because someone who is only king in his palace runs the risk of finding his master on the battlefield.' The naivety of the king, and of the commanders whose advice he sought, allowed Alexander Leslie, drawing on his lifetime of military sacrifice, to trick them. According to John Aston, 'the great bruite [rumour] of the ennemye's strength, and their able commanders, did beget a distrust in most, and a murmure in others'. They did not discover until later that General Leslie had drawn up his troops expressly 'to beguile men's view' and prevent the English from realizing either that they faced scarcely 12,000 men, many of them poorly armed, or that the Royal Navy's blockade had deprived the Scots of 'any natural means or ordinary way either of our convening or subsisting together, remaining or retiring or going on, for want of victuals, money or horses'. So instead of leading his far larger army in an attack, on 18 June 1639 Charles signed a ceasefire and opened negotiations with his rebellious Scottish subjects.[34]

Just as he had insisted on leading his army in person, despite his lack of military experience, Charles now insisted on conducting the negotiations in person, despite his lack of diplomatic experience. The Scots immediately demanded that their sovereign ratify the acts of the last General Assembly of the Church (which meant abolishing all bishops), summon a new Parliament and return for trial and punishment the 'incendiaries' (as they termed the king's supporters who had fled to England). Charles withdrew to consult his leading advisers and, since the talks took place under canvas, the Scots overheard Hamilton warn his king that 'if he consented to yearly General Assemblies he might quit his three crowns for they would trample over them all'. They breathed a sigh of relief when Charles rejected Hamilton's prescient advice and instead consented to the Pacification of Berwick, which not only granted all the Covenanters' demands but also required him to demobilize his army and lift the naval blockade. He had just made, in John Adamson's words, 'the greatest single mistake of his life'.[35]

The Pacification of Berwick weakened Charles I in four important ways. First, by failing to exploit his military superiority, he forfeited his best (if not his only) chance of victory over his Scottish rebels. Second, the king's retreat from his earlier stated position ('I would rather die than yield to these impertinent and damnable demands') discredited not only him but also his leading advisers. As Hamilton pointed out: because 'those particulars which I have so often sworn and said Your Majesty would never condescend to, will now be granted', the Covenanters 'will give no credit to what I shall say there after, but will still hope and believe, that all their desires will be given way to.'[36] He was soon proved correct. The Scottish Parliament that met in autumn 1639 acted from the first on the assumption that the king would sooner or later concede everything they demanded. Third, and equally damaging, the pamphlets generated in England by the Scottish crisis initiated debate on issues that had been taboo: liturgy and church government, the limits of authority and obedience, even the possible justifications for resistance. Fourth and finally, Charles was now bankrupt: the campaign itself, which had cost about £1 million, drained the English treasury of its reserves; while the king's craven concessions emboldened many to withhold payment of Ship Money and other regalian rights (and encouraged royal officials to leave offenders alone, fearing another change of the royal mind). Tax revenues therefore declined sharply. To solve the problems that his policies had created, Charles turned to the only minister who could apparently 'achieve through royal authority what former kings did by the authority of the realm': Thomas Wentworth, Lord Deputy of Ireland.

'Thorough' in Ireland

In Ireland, Charles had sought to fund his 'Union of Arms' scheme (page 332 above) by offering the Catholics there concessions, known as the 'Graces', in exchange for new taxes to pay for the island's defence. Among other things, he promised to relax the requirement that all holders of public office must recognize the king as Supreme Governor of the Church of Ireland (something no Catholic could do), and also to guarantee the titles of all families that had held their lands for 60 years (which would virtually end the further creation of 'plantations'). As soon as he had made peace with France and Spain in 1630, however, Charles reneged on these promises and instead ordered a strict application of the anti-Catholic laws, commanded the dissolution of all Catholic convents and required all magistrates either to take the Oath of Supremacy (recognizing Charles as Supreme Governor of this Church) or be dismissed. The king entrusted enforcement of these measures to a group of militant Protestant landholders, who carried out their work with efficiency and enthusiasm – until Charles reversed course yet again in 1632, when he named Thomas Wentworth, an Englishman with extensive administrative experience but no Irish connections, to serve as Lord Deputy.

From the first, Wentworth exploited the fragmentation and divisions of Irish society. Thus he hinted to Catholics that the 'Graces' might be confirmed in return for approving some tax increases, and duly relaxed some anti-Catholic measures – but he also tampered with charters and franchises so that Catholic membership of the Irish House of Commons fell dramatically: although 112 Catholics sat in the 1634 assembly, only 74 did so in 1640. Wentworth also systematically reviewed all property titles, increasing royal rents and services wherever possible and dispossessing those with titles deemed to be defective, targeting newcomers (both Scots and English Protestants) as well as natives (including families who had come over to Ireland generations before, known as the 'Old English'). As Aidan Clarke has observed, although 'the confiscation of property was not a new experience for the Irish, it was for the Old English'. Even the new settlers from Britain 'were threatened as much as anyone by the systematic violation of common law rights upon which landholders relied to protect their property'.[37] Thanks to these measures, and to increased customs revenues, the Irish budget went into surplus for the first time in decades.

Wentworth realized that his innovations, which he boastfully termed 'Thorough', would alienate most segments of Irish society, but he relied on their deep-seated mutual hatred to prevent cooperation. He therefore left Dublin for London full of confidence. In December 1639 he – supported by Laud and Hamilton – met Charles and persuaded him to summon the Westminster Parliament and demand funds for a new invasion of Scotland – although all four recognized that it might be necessary to resort to 'extraordinary ways, if the Parliament should prove peevish, and refuse' to vote taxes.[38] The quartet also decided to launch another attack on Scotland in 1640, repeating the strategy of the previous year: Charles would invade with a major army from England while the Royal Navy once again blockaded Scotland's east coast and another army from Ireland attacked in the southwest. Wentworth, now raised to the peerage as earl of Strafford, returned to Dublin and persuaded the Irish Parliament to authorize taxes sufficient to raise an army of 8,000 foot and 1,000 horse for the invasion of Scotland. Mobilization began at once and as the new troops converged on Ulster, the area nearest to Scotland, the new earl returned to London just in time to take his seat as a peer in the first English Parliament to meet in 11 years.

England on Edge

The 500,000 Englishmen entitled to vote in parliamentary elections seized the unexpected chance to protest against the controversial policies of the previous decade, rejecting candidates who had allocated Ship Money, collected regalian rights, or enforced Laud's liturgical innovations. Instead, their representatives took with them to Westminster long lists of grievances which they debated at length, ignoring the government's pleas for new taxes. Charles tolerated this irritating behaviour until he learned that on the morning of 5 May 1640 the Commons planned to debate a motion urging 'reconciliation with . . . his subjects in Scotland'. Since such a motion would destroy the entire moral foundation of his Scottish policy, the king dissolved the assembly, soon to be known as the 'Short Parliament'.[39] Angry crowds soon roamed the streets, and a group of about 500 surrounded Lambeth Palace, Laud's official residence as archbishop of Canterbury, because they blamed him for the king's decision to dissolve the assembly. It was the first major episode of mob violence in the Stuart capital; it would not be the last.

Laud was not in Lambeth Palace because, as soon as Charles returned from dissolving Parliament, he summoned his archbishop to attend a 'committee of war' to discuss whether, despite the lack of parliamentary funds, 'the Scotts are to bee reduced or noe?' The rough minutes taken at the meeting by Secretary of State

Henry Vane reveal that some councillors favoured a compromise – 'If noe more mony than what proposed, howe then to make an offensive war?' one asked – but Strafford dismissed this concern because a 'defensive warr' would involve 'losse of honor and reputacon'. He then argued that since 'the quiett of England will hold out longe', the king should 'goe on with a vigorous warr, as you first designed'. He also stressed that 'You have an army in Ireland, which you may imploy here to reduce this kingdome' (the ambiguity of 'here' and 'this kingdome' would come back to haunt him). 'Scotland shall not hold out five monthes. One sumer well imployed will doe it,' Strafford predicted. The earl also repeated the arguments he had advanced the previous December: now that the king was 'loose and absolved from all rules of government, beinge reduced to extreame necessitie,' Strafford declared, 'everythinge is to be done as power might admitt' – that is: since Parliament had refused its support, the king should fund his army via regalian rights and forced loans from the leading London merchants.[40]

As soon as he left the meeting, the army's designated general, the earl of Northumberland, assured his lieutenant in Newcastle, the largest city in the north-east, that 'We are going upon a conquest with such a power that nothing in that kingdom [Scotland] will be able to resist us' – although, he added, because Parliament had not voted funds, the rendezvous of England's troops scheduled for 20 May had unfortunately been pushed back to 10 June. This delay did not worry Strafford, because he expected Spain to fund the war. The previous December he had met Philip IV's envoys in London to request a loan of £100,000; now he asked them for £300,000. Philip expressed support, but the uprising in Barcelona, which began one month later (see chapter 9 above), deprived him of funds to help Charles regain Scotland. As John Adamson observed, 'The revolt of the Catalans is no less important than the revolt of the Covenanters in explaining why civil war in England became a serious probability after the summer of 1640.'[41]

The collapse of the Spanish deal left Charles dangerously exposed. He had ordered 35,000 English troops to mobilize for service against Scotland and could not abandon his war plans now without 'losse of honor and reputacon'. Postponing the date of the rendezvous twice more (first until 1 July and then 'till the middle of August') multiplied the risks because, as Northumberland noted, mid-August was 'a season not so proper for the drawing an army into the field in these northerne countries'. 'The season' soon became even less 'proper' than the earl had anticipated. An outbreak of plague prevented the levies from Devon and Cornwall from reaching York while, thanks to the El Niño episode of that year, much of England experienced 'an abundance of rains and cold winds: the spring is wonderfully late'. In August 'the land seemed to be threatened with the extraordinary violence of the winds and unaccustomed abundance of wet'. Even Strafford, appointed to lead the king's army after Northumberland resigned, arrived late: by 24 August 1640 he had only reached Huntingdon, where he found 'the waters mightily risen and the ways as foul as Christmas'.[42]

Meanwhile, in Dublin, news of the failure of the Short Parliament combined with Strafford's absence encouraged the Irish Parliament to suspend collection of the taxes already voted. This delayed the raising of the troops designed to invade Scotland, so that although the infantry regiments had assembled in Ulster by June, the cavalry (which required more money to equip) had not. In addition, neither the weapons for the recruits nor the transport ships to carry them across to Scotland arrived. Most of the 'New Army' therefore remained in Ulster, consuming local supplies already much reduced by a run of bad harvests.

The Scottish Parliament took advantage of these setbacks to reassemble in Edinburgh and, in the words of Sir James Balfour, passed a legislative programme 'memorable to be recommended to posterity as exhibiting the real greatest change at one blow that ever happened to this church and state these 600 years by past' – for in effect it 'overturned not only the ancient state government, but fettered monarchy with chains'. Parliament passed a Triennial Act, requiring an assembly to convene at least once every three years, with or without a royal summons, and an Act excluding all bishops from the assembly. It also created an elaborate structure of standing committees to govern Scotland while Parliament was not in session.[43] The Covenanting leaders also received a letter signed by seven English peers, promising that 'upon the first assurance of your entry into the kingdom', to 'unite themselves into a considerable body, and to draw up a Remonstrance to be presented to the king'. It would contain the grievances of both Scotland and England, to which they would 'require' (not 'request') redress.[44] The seven dissident (and traitorous) peers included the earls of Bedford and Warwick (both of whom Charles had previously imprisoned for criticizing his policies), and the earl of Essex (whom Charles had blamed for the failure of the 1639 campaign). All three had used their influence to secure the election of malleable MPs to the Short Parliament – including John Pym, a protégé and former employee of both Bedford and Warwick, who became the dominant voice in the House of Commons – and they bitterly resented its dissolution.

The treasonable promise of collusion by the seven peers persuaded the new Scottish government to make a pre-emptive strike. They sent one army into the north under Argyll, with orders to destroy the property of all potential royalists who might open a second front, and they authorized General Leslie – who had spent the previous year training and arming his soldiers – to invade England. On 20 August 1640 he led 18,000 men across the Tweed. Scotland and England were at war again.

Charles left London that same day for York, where he 'spake with the lords, colonels and gentlemen', urging them to march against the Scots. Instead of mobilizing, however, on 28 August they sent Charles a 'humble petition' protesting that the last campaign had cost the county over £100,000, so that 'for the future, the burden is so heavy that we neither can, nor are able, to bear it'. They were equally blunt about the king's demand that they billet soldiers until the campaign began: 'billeting of unruly soldiers, whose speeches and actions tend to the burning of our villages and houses' was forbidden by the 'ancient laws of this kingdom, confirmed by Your Majesty in the Petition of Right'. That same day, Leslie led the Scottish army across the Tyne, routed the small English force facing him at the battle of Newburn and captured Newcastle, before sweeping south to capture Durham as well.[45]

Although many historians have overlooked the scale and significance of these military defeats, contemporaries did not. The king, who was leading his army from York towards Durham in person, panicked and beat a hasty retreat when he heard about Newburn; while Secretary Vane feared that England now faced the 'greatest [danger] that had threatened this state since the [Norman] Conquest'. Indeed, the occupation of northeast England not only guaranteed Scotland against the imposition of the 'perfect union' envisaged by Charles and Laud; it also opened the way for the Scots to impose on England a 'perfect union' of their own by cutting off the supply of Tyneside coal on which London depended.[46]

Many in England openly rejoiced at their king's defeat. When news of Newburn arrived in London, the church bells rang out in celebration and the Privy Council, which had already placed artillery around Whitehall Palace to guard against a popular insurrection, fled the capital and prepared Portsmouth, on the south coast, as 'a retreat' for the royal family 'in case of extremity'. Archbishop Laud expressed the defeatist temper of the Council best: the king, he said, must understand that '*We are at the wall, and that we are in the dark*', and that the only way to organize effective resistance to the Scots was by summoning a council of peers 'or the calling of a Parliament'.[47]

Laud's fears were well founded. Although London saw no insurrection at this stage, the dissident English peers honoured their promise to their Scottish colleagues and sent to the king a 'Petition' that bore 12 noble signatures and made two categories of demands. First, they asserted that 'By occasion of this war, your revenue is much wasted, your subjects burdened with ... military charges ... and your whole kingdom become full of fear and discontents'. To solve these problems, the peers proposed a simple and immediate solution: peace with the Scots. Second, and at greater length, they complained of 'the sundry innovations in matters of religion'; 'the great increase of Popery, and employing of Popish recusants'; the rumours 'of bringing in Irish and foreign [i.e. Catholic] forces'; 'the urging of Ship Money' and imposition of sundry taxes on 'the commodities and manufactures of the kingdom'; and 'the long intermission of Parliaments'. To address these issues, the 12 Petitioner Peers demanded that Charles

> Summon a Parliament within some short and convenient time, whereby the causes of these and other great grievances which your people lie under may be taken away, and the authors and counsellors of them may be there brought to such legal trial and condign punishment as the nature of the several offences shall require.[48]

No one could overlook the significance of the increase in noble signatories to 12, for it recalled 'the example of Henry III' cited by the Venetian ambassador three years before (page 332 above): in 1258 the king had reluctantly agreed under duress that 12 peers could summon a parliament in their own name if he refused to do so. Would the Petitioner Peers now invoke that same right?

Charles decided not to put the matter to the test. On 5 September 1640, after discussing the Petition with his advisers, and upon learning that the Scots 'plant garrisons and take up their winter-quarters throughout Northumberland and the bishopric' of Durham, while his own 'army cannot be in a posture fit to fight these six weeks', Charles summoned a 'Great Council' consisting of all the English peers (a body that had not met since Tudor times) to meet him.[49]

Foul weather continued to impede the transaction of public affairs – 'we have had so great rains these two days, and the waters are so out,' Vane complained, 'that there is scarce means to pass anywhere upon the roads' – but in late September just over 70 peers joined their king at York. Those who had signed the Petition arrived ostentatiously in a single cavalcade with their carriages, servants and retainers – a clear sign of unity that seems to have sapped the king's morale. 'In the first place,' he announced in his opening speech to the Great Council, 'I must let you know that I desire nothing more than to bee rightly understood of my people, and to that end *I have of myself resolved to call a Parliament.*' It would assemble in Westminster on 3 November 1640.[50] The king next asked for advice on what to do about the Scots and expressed the hope that his nobles would fund a campaign to avenge Newburn. They refused, and instead insisted not only on the appointment of a committee of 16 peers with full powers to conclude an armistice with the Scots, but also on the inclusion within that number of 11 of the Petitioner Peers, including Bedford, Essex and Warwick – men who could hardly deny the invaders' demands, given that the Scots possessed their treasonable letter of July.

The king had thus surrendered a significant part of his prerogative – the power to make war and peace – and the Peace Commissioners used their new-found authority to conclude the treaty of Ripon, which made three crucial concessions to the Scots. First, it left them in control of the Tyneside collieries, on which London depended both for its manufactures and for heating – a measure that gave them critical leverage over their English allies because, until Parliament authorized the taxes necessary to buy them off, and thus allow the colliers to start supplying London again, the capital would both starve and freeze. Second, it stipulated that negotiations for a final settlement would take place at Westminster, which offered the Petitioner Peers and their allies in Parliament and in Scotland a unique opportunity to reshape the entire political structure of Charles I's monarchy. Third, it guaranteed that the Scots would receive the enormous sum of £850 a day to maintain their soldiers in England until a permanent settlement could be arranged – a requirement that not only compelled Charles to feed and pay his own army in Yorkshire, despite the fact that 'these great rains that have fallen have made an ill harvest, and corn is likely to prove very dear', but also prevented him from dissolving the new Parliament until it had voted sufficient funds to disband both of the armies in England and also Strafford's army in Ulster.[51]

In his opening speech to Parliament on 3 November 1640, Charles could not refrain from blaming his audience for his predicament. Had the previous assembly believed him, he chided, 'I sincerely think that things had not fallen out as now we see', and he called for the immediate vote of funds for a new campaign to expel the invaders. His belligerent stance did not lack supporters: a number of MPs felt either bound to obey the king, right or wrong, or insulted by the Scots' success ('if the

Scots should be too refractory, [let us] bring them by force of true English courage to reason'; 'We should get them out by fair means or foul').[52] The number of MPs sympathetic to the king's argument soon became apparent. Both the Petition and the treaty of Ripon had called for the 'legal trial and condign punishment' of those responsible for the unpopular policies of the previous decade, Strafford chief among them. His opponents hoped to decide his fate in a small committee, but by a vote of 165 to 152 the king's supporters ensured that the whole House, which was more sympathetic, would make the decision.

This emboldened Charles to summon Strafford (still commander of the royal armies in both England and Ireland and still the strongest advocate of resuming the war against the Scots) back to London, where he immediately started to strengthen the Tower's defences. As if that were not enough to alarm the king's critics in Parliament, rumours spread that Strafford and the king were preparing charges of treason against those whom they now knew had maintained seditious contact with the Scots. On 11 November the fearful MPs therefore decided to act first, accusing the earl himself of high treason. He was promptly taken into custody. This halted not only plans for a third campaign against the Scots, but also the transaction of most other public business, while Parliament collected the 'particular accusations and articles' of treason ready for Strafford's impeachment.

The trial took place in March 1641 in Westminster Hall, the 'largest secular covered space in England', so that as many members of the public as possible could look on and listen. Although Parliament sold entrance tickets, the demand for seats far exceeded supply and vast crowds hovered around the doors to catch a glimpse and hear a few words – it was, as John Adamson wittily observed, 'perhaps the first exercise in broadcasting the proceedings of Parliament' (Plate 15).[53] The earl expertly rebutted all the charges, but his enemies could not afford to let him go because, in the words of a popular pamphlet of the day: just as 'the madde Bull wounded and let loose doth more mischief, so if the earle shall get out of the net he will be more savage then before'. The Commons therefore prepared a Bill of Attainder (a procedure that denied the accused a hearing), pinning their hopes on the hasty notes taken by Sir Henry Vane at the meeting of the Committee of War on 5 May 1640. These, it may be recalled, recorded Strafford's advice to the king that since he was now 'loose and absolved from all rules of government ... everythinge is to be done as power might admitt'; and, even more damaging, that 'You have an army in Ireland, which you may imploy *here* to reduce *this kingdome*'. Strafford's enemies argued that 'here' and 'this kingdome' referred to England, so that the earl had not only counselled arbitrary rule but also urged the king to use foreign (Irish) troops to crush his domestic critics.[54] Furious at this turn of events, the king decided both to dissolve Parliament and to summon some officers serving with his army in Yorkshire to rescue Strafford from the Tower; but news of his plans leaked, and thousands of Londoners rushed to Westminster to form a human shield while the Commons finalized the articles of Attainder. The Bill passed by 204 votes to 59, revealing how far Charles's actions had shifted opinion against the earl. The House of Lords prepared to try him.

Once again, contingency intervened. Since not even the king could pardon a person found guilty by the process of Attainder, Charles pinned his hopes of saving Strafford on persuading moderates in the House of Lords, such as the earl of Bedford, to bring in a verdict of banishment or imprisonment but not death. On 23 April, believing his efforts had succeeded, the king wrote an affectionate letter (signed 'Your constant faithful frend') informing Strafford that 'upon the word of a king, you shall not suffer in lyfe, honnor, or fortune' – but no sooner had he given this solemn promise than Bedford, the most influential moderate, went down with smallpox, and so lost his ability to influence the peers' discussions.[55]

On 1 May 1641 the king therefore paid another visit to Parliament to repeat what he had told Bedford. Explaining that he did not believe Strafford to be guilty of high treason, he expressed the hope that the two Houses would vote for the lesser charge of misdemeanours. His audience remained unmoved. As the earl of Essex (whose own father had been executed for treason) put it, if the earl lived, Charles would restore him to his former offices 'as soon as the Parliament should be ended', and then the 'madde bulle wounded' would seek his revenge. By contrast, said Essex, shaking his head as he uttered his most memorable phrase: 'Stone-dead hath no fellow'.[56]

Perhaps realizing that his speech to Parliament had missed its mark, Charles now set in motion another plot to seize control of the Tower and free his faithful minister. Yet again news leaked out, and by nightfall on 2 May 1641 a crowd of about 1,000 had gathered near the Tower to make sure that the plotters stayed outside while Strafford stayed inside. The following day, some 15,000 people assembled at Westminster, both to protect Parliament and to protest the king's attempted coup. 'Surely,' the craftsman Nehemiah Wallington wrote in his diary, 'I never did see so many together in all my life. And when they did see any Lords coming they all cried out with one voice "Justice! Justice!"' One of the lords claimed that someone in the crowd warned him that 'if they had not justice tomorrow, they would either take [i.e. lynch] the king or my Lord Strafford' – the first recorded public suggestion of regicide as a solution to England's political problems.[57] Meanwhile, in the House of Lords, Lord Stamford proposed that the peers 'Give God thanks for our great deliverance, which is greater than that from the Gunpowder-treason'. The comparison quickly spread. The Dutch ambassadors in London averred that the recently discovered 'conspiracy was much more widespread and horrible than the Gunpowder Plot', while John Pym convinced the House of Commons that they faced another 'popish conspiracy' that aimed 'to subvert and overthrow this kingdome'. Pym also exploited the general panic to rush through a document entitled 'The Protestation', with authorization to print enough copies for every parish in the kingdom.[58]

Like the Scottish National Covenant (which probably served as its model), the Protestation required a universal public pledge to defend the Established Church against its enemies, and to seek punishment for all who had endeavoured 'to subvert the fundamental laws of England and Ireland, and to introduce the exercise of an arbitrary and tyrannical government'. Again as in Scotland, the clergy read the document aloud to their congregations from the pulpit before subscribing their names; and then they called upon 'all masters of families, their sons and men-servants' to 'subscribe his name, with his own hand or mark' in a special register. Tens of thousands, including apprentices and servants, duly swore the oath and affixed their signatures or marks, and then flocked 'in troops to the Parliament house with the Protestation on the top of their swords', while the city militia swaggered through the streets with the 'Protestation fastened to their pikes or hats'. Over 3,000 of the Protestation returns survive today, bearing the names of over 37,000 individuals. 'Never before,' writes David Cressy, 'had so many subjects been invited to act as citizens, regardless of rank.'[59]

On Friday, 7 May the House of Lords approved Strafford's Bill of Attainder and a delegation from both Houses set out to present it to Charles, along with another bill that forbade the dissolution of Parliament without its own consent. A crowd estimated at 12,000 escorted the delegation to Whitehall Palace, which they then blockaded for 36 hours, shouting slogans, until Charles – having consulted both his bishops and his ministers to try and find a way to keep 'the word of a king' to his minister, and having wept at the council table when he could not – finally signed both documents. As William Sanderson, an eyewitness, wrote in his *Compleat history of the life and raigne of King Charles from his cradle to his grave*, 'at one time, the same instant, the same pen and ink, the king lost his prerogative and Strafford's life also'. A crowd perhaps 200,000 strong immediately gathered around the scaffold on Tower Hill to gloat over the earl's execution, and afterwards those who had come from afar to see the spectacle 'rode in triumph back, waving their hatts, and with all expressions of joy, thro' every town they went, crying "His head is off, his head if off!" ... and breaking the windowes of those persons who would not solemnize this festival with a bonfire'.[60]

The 'Long Parliament' had already earned its epithet – it had sat continuously for longer than any previous assembly – and, having gained the upper hand, it now made the most of its advantage. The day after Charles signed Strafford's death warrant, Parliament approved a draft peace treaty with the Scots; and the day after the earl's execution, it voted the funds required to demobilize the English and Scottish armies in the north. Nevertheless, until those funds arrived, in the anguished words of Secretary Vane, 'We are here still in the labyrinth and cannot get out.' Soon after it assembled in November 1640, the Long Parliament printed and distributed a pamphlet urging 'persons in every county of the kingdom' to exploit 'the present opportunity, by giving true information' to document cases of royal misrule during the previous decade. Almost all of England's 40 counties obliged, presenting petitions that bore over half a million signatures. Some were printed in multiple copies; others were presented by thousands of petitioners – 3,000 arrived from Buckinghamshire on horseback 'riding three and three', 10,000 from Kent, and so on – forcing the House of Commons to appoint marshals to 'regulate and prevent such disorders as are committed by the disorderly multitudes that press in'.[61] England had seen nothing like this exercise in direct democracy, and Parliament used the information to prepare for the king's signature a stream of legislation designed to destroy both the agents and the apparatus that had enabled him to govern England for 11 years without their participation. By September 1641, when the two Houses finally went into recess, they had brought impeachment proceedings against no fewer than 53 of the king's senior appointees, including Archbishop Laud, 12 bishops and almost half the judges, many of whom languished in the Tower pending trial; and approved bills that declared Ship Money illegal, restricted forest laws, abolished knighthood fines, Star Chamber and High Commission, and outlawed Tonnage and Poundage. Between 7 and 10 August, Charles grudgingly gave his assent to all these measures and also approved a peace treaty that ended the 'late troubles' with his Scottish subjects, one of whose clauses forbade the king to make 'war with foreigners without consent of both Parliaments'. He was now, in effect, a king in name only.[62]

On 11 August, Charles left London, first to oversee the demobilization of the Scots and English armies and then to ensure the acceptance of the peace treaty by his northern kingdom. At first, all went well: the Scottish Parliament demobilized its troops and ratified the treaty. When this news arrived in London, Parliament held a public thanksgiving 'for the peace concluded between England and Scotland' during which the preacher Stephen Marshall gave a sermon that compared the situation in 'the three Nations of England, Scotland and Ireland' with that in Germany, which 'remains a field of blood, when their Cities and Towns are desolate, their wives ravished, their children kill'd, when many of them eat their dead carcasses, and die for want of food'. Although it had sometimes looked as if England might become 'a wonder to all the world in our desolations', instead 'God hath made us a wonder to the world in our preservation.'[63]

It was indeed a remarkable achievement, and if the king's opponents had been able to stop there, they might have retained the upper hand. Instead, the composite nature of the Stuart Monarchy – which had previously been such an asset for them – turned into an asset for the king. The Scots insisted on immediate compliance with their demand for 'one confession of faith, one form of catechism ... and one form of church government in all the churches of His Majesty's dominions' – modelled, of course, on Scotland's Presbyterian system. It could not be done. Ireland's Catholic majority was invincibly opposed, and few of Charles's English opponents were Presbyterians. Moreover, unlike the Scots, England lacked a single rallying point: instead of the National Covenant, there were two rival documents, the Protestation and the Book of Common Prayer. Choosing between them would divide communities and even families throughout the kingdom. However, Charles decided to build up a royalist faction in both Scotland and Ireland capable of defeating his opponents. The result was what Conrad Russell called a 'billiard-ball effect'.[64]

The 'Incident': Scotland on Edge

Charles spent the summer of 1641 in Edinburgh, where he did his best to win over the Covenanters by attending Presbyterian church services, and by showering rewards on their leaders (Leslie became earl of Leven, Argyll became a marquis, Wariston became a knight). These gestures did not prevent his opponents from demanding yet more concessions, notably the right of veto over all major appointments (councillors, judges, great officers of state). Charles reluctantly granted this on 16 September – but in so doing, he created at last a royalist faction, composed of men whom the Covenanters would surely veto, and who therefore faced permanent exclusion from office. Over the next four weeks William Murray, Groom of the Bedchamber and Charles's intimate companion since boyhood, put together a plot to eliminate those whom he perceived as the king's leading Scottish enemies. One evening, in the king's bedchamber – a highly unusual location for a meeting – Colonel John Cochrane, a royal sympathizer in the Covenanting army, proposed to Charles a plot to lure Hamilton and Argyle into the royal apartments in Holyrood Palace, at a time when 'the king were out of the way'. There he would arrest them both and take them under guard to Edinburgh Castle. Should their followers attempt to rescue them, then (in the words of one of the conspirators) 'I would have the traittors' throats cut'.[65]

The plot was thwarted because two of the soldiers charged with the arrests (and if necessary murder) revealed the plan to their potential victims, who fled Edinburgh on 12 October, leaving Charles to explain the 'Incident' to the Scots Parliament. Although the king denied all knowledge, three pieces of evidence incriminate him. First, during their interrogation by the Scots Parliament, Murray and the other plotters expressly stated that they had acted with his knowledge and consent. Second, it is hard to explain either the bedtime meeting with Cochrane or the plan to stage the coup in his private apartments, unless Charles was complicit. Finally, the king gave himself away when on 5 October he annotated a letter from Sir Edward Nicholas, his Secretary of State in London. Next to Nicholas's news that the English parliamentary leaders were in high spirits because they believed events in Scotland favoured them, the king (in Edinburgh) wrote in the margin 'I belive before all be done that they will not have such great cause of joy'; and that 'when ye shall see littell Will: Murray', Nicholas would know 'how all will end heer' – 'littell Will: Murray' being none other than the architect of the plot to arrest Hamilton and Argyll, as well as the confidential courier to whom the king often entrusted his secret letters.[66] Nicholas immediately realized the significance of this message: the same day that he received the king's cryptic comments he observed to a colleague: 'I wish that those who have been the cause of these miserable distraccons in his Majestie's dominions may feele the weight of punishment they deserve,' adding 'I doubt not that they will doe [so] in due time.'[67]

Whatever the truth about Charles's role in the 'Incident', it had immediate and immense consequences for his cause. Not only did its miscarriage prevent him from imposing 'the weight of punishment' on his critics, both in England and Scotland, but it also led many to question his integrity. A member of the royal household in Edinburgh feared that 'all will end in an agreement to our master's disadvantage, and what will be required by the [Scottish] Parliament at first must be yelded to at laste, and soe putt everie thing into a wors condition then wee fownde it'. Almost immediately, the assembly exercised its new power of veto over the king's nominees to executive and judicial office, thus realizing Charles's fears that he would have 'no more power in Scotland than as a Duke of Venice' (page 335 above).[68] In England, news of the Incident also 'putt everie thing into a wors condition'. The interrogations of 'littell Will: Murray' and the conspirators (duly forwarded to Westminster), coming just months after the Army Plot to rescue Strafford, suggested that Charles would stop at nothing to eliminate his enemies. However, the 'accons and successes' of Charles's opponents in the Edinburgh Parliament encouraged their colleagues at Westminster to 'take a patterne for their proceeding' and frame demands 'according to the Scottish precedent' as soon as the king returned to England. But first, events put Ireland into a far 'wors condition'.[69]

The Irish Revolution

The Irish political elite found the developments in Charles I's other kingdoms deeply troubling. One protagonist in the Irish rebellion later recalled hearing 'that the Scotts hadd peticioned the Parliament howse of England that there should not bee a Papist left alive either in all England, Ireland or Scotland', so that the only effective response was 'to ryse vpp in armes and take all the stronghouldes and forts into their handes'.[70] Ireland's Catholic leaders were therefore receptive to hints from Charles that if they organized military and financial support for him against his enemies in Britain, he would confirm the 'Graces' (page 338 above). Working principally through the earl of Antrim (who had married the duke of Buckingham's widow and, through her, enjoyed a close relationship with the monarch), the king apparently approved a plan 'that the castle of Dublin should be surprised and seized' and an army of 20,000 men mobilized to be 'employed against the [Irish] Parliament' and then 'against the Parliament of England if occasion should be for so doing'. In other words, Charles envisaged starting a civil war first in Ireland and then in England.[71]

Antrim did his best, but again the climate intervened. Adverse weather ruined the harvest in Ireland in 1641, as it had done in 1639 and 1640, causing widespread food shortages and reducing exports (almost all farm produce) by about one-third. The province of Ulster suffered worst because the presence of the troops raised by Strafford for the invasion of Scotland soon consumed all available resources. According to a resident of Belfast, the combination of hungry troops and scarce food meant that the poor 'are so much impoverished that they can no longer subsist'. Throughout the province, land rents fell by half, creating great tensions between natives and newcomers. Those who had 'lived by [their] husbandry', now 'haveing noe mantainance', saw rebellion as their only option.[72] In this highly charged atmosphere, in August 1641 the king gave his consent for the Irish Parliament to debate the 'Graces'; but when the news arrived in Dublin, the 'Lords Justices' (a commission of Protestants entrusted by Charles with governing Ireland after Strafford's fall) immediately dissolved the assembly.

This surprise move, which blocked the road to constitutional reform for the foreseeable future, outraged the Catholic members of the Irish Parliament. Seeing that the Scots' armed insurrection had secured concessions, first from the king and then from the English Parliament, they concluded that only military strength could now overthrow 'the tyrannicall governement that was over them', and decided that they would 'imitat Scotland, who gott a privilege by that course'.[73] Over the next few weeks, one group of conspirators under Connor, Lord Maguire, made plans to take Dublin Castle, while another led by Sir Phelim O'Neill, a prominent landowner and a justice of the peace, would seize all the fortresses in Ulster garrisoned by Protestants. Everyone agreed to act simultaneously on 23 October, a market day in Dublin, which would make the arrival of the conspirators in the capital the night before less conspicuous. Maguire intended to equip his followers with the weapons stored in Dublin Castle and then force the English government to grant religious and political freedom.

On the night of 22 October Maguire's plot miscarried. Owen Connolly, one of the few Protestant conspirators, slipped away to tell the Lords Justices all he knew. The latter 'gave at first very little credit to so improbable and broken a [story], delivered by an unknown, mean man, well advanced in his drink' and so sent him away; but Connolly later made a second attempt to warn the authorities. This time, 'being in better temper' (that is, being less 'advanced in his drink') 'he found more belief for his then less distracted story'. The plotters, he warned, intended 'that in all the seaports and other townes in the kingdome, all the Protestants should bee killed this night'. The government immediately arrested Maguire and the other plotters in the capital, and sent urgent messages to warn Protestants elsewhere.[74]

They arrived too late. On the night of 22 October, just as the drunken Owen Connolly betrayed the plot in Dublin, Sir Phelim O'Neill and his allies used a variety of ruses to capture the major fortresses in Ulster, and Catholics elsewhere rejoiced. In County Meath, 'the very first night after this rebellion was knowne, generally all papists houses' round about 'were sett upon a merry pin, danceing, singing, and drinkeing, as if hell had bin broken open among them'; while in County Monaghan an insurgent boasted that 'this was but the beginning' because 'by the next night Dublin would bee too hott for any of the English doggs to liue in'. Insurgents in many other counties immediately declared their opposition to British rule, and well over one hundred members of the Irish Parliament eventually joined the rebellion.[75]

Like the Scots Covenanters, whose example had both inspired and alarmed them, the initial aims of the Irish confederates were conservative: they did not seek the return of forfeited lands, only an end to further plantations; they did not demand independence from England, only an end to London's power to alter the status quo; they did not strive to overthrow Protestantism, only to end the persecution of Catholics. In the absence of leadership from Maguire, however, groups of Catholics exploited the temporary collapse of public authority to settle scores with local Protestants.

Although several confrontations were intensely personal – some attackers stabbed, hanged, burned or drowned neighbours whom they had known for years (see chapter 17 below) – most Catholics did not intend to kill their victims, but rather to expel and humiliate them by stripping them as they gloated 'Now are you wild Irish as well as we' (Plate 16). But the Little Ice Age often rendered these activities lethal. Contemporaries considered 1641–2 'a more bitter winter than was of some years before or since seen in Ireland', with severe snow and frost afflicting the whole island – a part of the world that rarely sees any snow. The cold weather started in October, just before the rebellion began, and it either killed or almost killed thousands of half-naked Protestants as they tried to flee.[76] In County Tyrone, in the north, Reverend John Kerdiff was 'stript of al my clothes and left stark naked', and was then compelled by the local Catholics, 'without any thing to cover my lower parts' to 'travell about two miles in the frost and snow'. In the Midland, Dorcas Iremonger 'and her 2 chyldren were by the rebells stript of all their clothes' who then 'exposed her to great and unwonted cold': she 'and 220 poore English more were inforced to lye a whole night almost stark naked on the snow upon a rock soe as two of her children dyed since of the cold'. In the southwest, Gilbert Johnstone, an innkeeper from Tipperary, was one of 'fortie more yong and ould in one company with him being all stripped' by the local Catholics, and 'in one flock starke naked driven to one of the gates of the said Cittie' where he was stabbed and 'left for dead amonge the rest of the corpses'. He 'layed from foure of the clocke in the forenoone till foure in the afternoone dureing which time (being frostie weather) this deponents body (after he came to himself) was soe frozen and fast to the ground with his owne blood and the bloode of those that were killed closeby with him that the deponent had much to doe to loose himselfe from the ground'.[77]

The surviving accounts of those affected by the uprising record more deaths from 'snow and frost' and 'extreme cold' than directly from violence, indicating that the Little Ice Age at least doubled – and may have tripled – the number of Protestants who met an unnatural death in autumn 1641.[78] The most harrowing and heart-wrenching (and for English readers, the most inflammatory) accounts involved the suffering of women and children. A Protestant sailor recorded how, shortly after the uprising began, he and 'his wife and five smalle children' were 'stript of all their clothes' by their Catholic neighbours. That night, 'flying away for safftie naked in the frost, one poore daughter of his, seeing him and her mother greeve for their generall misery, in way of comforting said she was not cold, nor would crye', but immediately afterwards 'she died by that cold and want. And the first night this deponent and his wife, creepeing for shelter into a poor [shack], were glad to ly upon their children, to keep in them heate and save them alive.'[79]

A second factor that increased the death toll was more predictable: sectarian passion. On the one hand, some of the Catholic clergy, especially in Ulster, presented the rising as a Crusade, a chance to regain Ireland for the True Faith, and encouraged Catholic gangs to round up Protestant settlers (Scots as well as English) and either stab them to death, burn them alive in their houses, or drive them into icy water where they perished. As soon as they could, the Protestants responded in kind, ordering the troops 'sent into the enemies [Catholic] quarters to spare neither man, woman nor child'.[80]

How many died in the violence? Few paused to count the corpses at the time, and some who did found the task overwhelming. When Anthony Stephens, a farm hand from Roscommon who became a soldier, gave his impressions five years later, he

admitted that 'as to murthers and cruelties comitted by the rebellious Irish upon
and against the persons and estates of the Brittish in those parts, they were soe
many in number, and soe fowle and wicked in nature that this deponent is not able
to expresse them'. His most vivid memory was seeing about 140 people at Coleraine
buried 'in one deepe holle or pitt, and layd soe thick and closse together as he
may well compare it *to the makeing or packing up of herrings*' – a peculiarly vivid and
disturbing image. In all, Stephens was 'perswaded there died noe fewer within three
months after the begining of the Rebellion within the said towne of Colraine then
seven or eight thowsand of the Brittish nation'.[81]

Although this account outraged the many British Protestants who read it,
Stephens's claim was impossible – Coleraine, a small town, could not have sheltered
so many people – but it is hard to be more precise. After a diligent study of the
surviving records, one historian recently estimated that 4,000 Protestants in Ireland
were massacred, while a further 8,000 succumbed to hunger and cold; but another,
after equally diligent study, has argued that no more than 'ten thousand men,
women and children, *Catholic and Protestant*' perished 'through direct violence,
exposure and privation'. What mattered at the time, however, were the estimates that
circulated (like that of Anthony Stephens), all of which (like his) put the total of
victims far higher. The figure that received the widest currency in Britain at the time
(and for many decades afterwards) was provided by the Reverend Robert Maxwell,
Archdeacon of Down, that the Catholics had massacred 154,000 English and
Scottish settlers in Ulster alone. This absurdly exaggerated figure (there were not
154,000 Protestants, dead or alive, in the whole of Ireland), coupled with the horrifying individual examples, explains why the survivors and their families, friends and
co-religionists found such a sympathetic audience when they called for immediate
revenge against the Irish rebels.[82]

A King without a Capital

News of the Irish rebellion quickly spread around Charles's composite monarchy.
The king himself, still in Edinburgh, remained curiously – to some, suspiciously –
unmoved. Upon hearing news of the massacre, he went out to play a round of golf;
and he later scribbled on a message from one of his ministers, 'I hope this ill newes
of Ireland may hinder some of theas follies in England'. In Ireland, many openly
claimed his support. O'Neill and other Ulster rebels brandished 'a parchment or
paper with a great seal affixed which he affirmed to be a warrant from the King's
Majestie for what he did', and it convinced even many Protestants that Charles
supported the Catholics and may even have sanctioned their rebellion.[83]

The English Parliament, which received the first news just after returning from its
summer recess, saw the massacres as clear justification for their fears of a general
Catholic uprising against them and lost no time in organizing countermeasures. It
resolved to 'make use of the friendship and assistance of Scotland' in restoring
Protestant control in Ireland, and solicited loans from leading Londoners to raise
and arm troops for an immediate counter-attack. But who would control these

soldiers? John Pym, now so prominent in parliamentary business that he was known as 'King Pym', feared that Charles might use any troops raised for Ireland against his English opponents, and so compiled a Remonstrance with 204 individual points, asserting that without redress of outstanding grievances 'we cannot give His Majesty such supplies for support of his own estate, *nor such assistance to the Protestant party beyond the sea [in Ireland], as is desired*'. The 204 points included not only the demands for religious uniformity made by the Scots but also many constitutional novelties based on Charles's concessions to the Scots, such as the requirement he appoint only officials approved by Parliament.[84]

Like the Petition of Right in 1628 (page 330 above), the Remonstrance of 1641 situated individual acts of 'misgovernment' by Charles since his accession within the overall framework of a Catholic conspiracy to subvert the 'fundamental laws' and religion of England and Ireland. Not all MPs accepted this – 'I did not dream that we should remonstrate downward, tell stories to the people, and talk of the king as of a third person', as one MP put it – and after 14 hours of bitter debate, it passed the Commons by only 159 votes to 148. Nevertheless, Pym made sure that copies were available for purchase the following day, 24 November 1641. On the 25th Charles entered London, escorted by over 1,000 soldiers from the recently disbanded northern army.[85]

For the next six weeks 'popular tumults' rocked the capital. Gangs of unemployed young men roamed the streets of London shouting 'Down with the bishops, hang up the popish lords'. The king responded provocatively: he ordered the Lord Mayor to 'kill and slay such of them as shall persist in their tumultuous and seditious ways and disorders'; he commanded his courtiers to start wearing swords; and he built a barracks just outside Whitehall Palace to accommodate the soldiers he had brought with him from Yorkshire. Clashes between anti-royalist gangs and Charles's guards steadily increased until, following the worst frosts in living memory, early in January 1642 some 200 Londoners armed with staves and swords marched through the cold to Whitehall shouting anti-Catholic slogans. One threw a 'clot of ice' at the soldiers guarding the palace gates, who promptly gave chase and injured several civilians.[86]

On 3 January 1642 the Commons asked the London magistrates to call out the city militia (its 'Trained Bands') to protect them, but Charles forbade this move. Instead he presented to the House of Lords articles of impeachment against one peer and five MPs, ordered his agents to seal and search the residences of the 'five members', and sent a messenger to the House of Commons to demand their immediate arrest. The king's printer published and distributed the articles of impeachment against them. Parliament responded by ordering the unsealing of the residences; refusing to deliver the five; and calling for the printer of the 'scandalous publication' to be punished.

This triple slap in the royal face, combined with unseasonable floods that prevented about 200 MPs from returning to the capital after the Christmas recess, encouraged Charles to undertake a *coup d'état*. According to one source, it was his wife Henrietta Maria who triggered this disastrous course of action: 'Go, you coward,' she allegedly yelled at him, 'and pull those rogues out by the ears, or never see my face more'. Unfortunately for her plan, one of the queen's confidantes, Lucy, countess of Carlisle, overheard this exchange and sent 'timely notice' of Charles's plans to the House of Commons. The heavy rains had turned the streets of London into a quagmire, so that on the afternoon of 4 January Lady Carlisle's messenger got from Whitehall to Westminster faster than Charles and his 500 soldiers. Even so, as one of the five members later recalled, 'the king came immediately in, and was in the House, before we got to the water' (the Thames), where they found a boat to take them to safety in the City of London.[87] As his soldiers ostentatiously brandished their weapons at the door to the Commons chamber, Charles entered and 'commanded the Speaker to come out of his chair, and sat down in it himself, asking divers times whether these traitors were there'. When no one replied, he carefully scrutinized the faces in the chamber before uttering his most famous words, 'All my birds are flown'; after which he rose and returned empty-handed to Whitehall.[88] The next day, 5 January, having learned that his 'birds' had alighted in the City, Charles led his swordsmen on another hunt but, again, he failed to find them and returned empty-handed.

Charles's flagrant breach of parliamentary privilege caused the Commons to cease their deliberations, and as he returned through the streets to Whitehall, the king found that the shopkeepers had pulled down their shutters and stood menacingly at their doors bearing arms. Worse, 'the rude multitude followed him, crying again "Privileges of Parliament! Privileges of Parliament!"' and clutching the Protestation. Charles experienced 'the worst day in London', according to one eyewitness, 'that ever he had'.[89]

Charles's attempted coup confirmed all previous suspicions that he was prepared to use violence against his English subjects. On the night of 5 January 1642 rumours flew 'that there were horse and foot coming against the city. So that the gates were shut and the [port]cullices let down and the chains put across the corners of our streets, and every man ready in his arms'. In open defiance of the king, the London magistrates now called out the Trained Bands which escorted the 'five members' denounced by the king as traitors back to Westminster in triumph. Since the armed men in London loyal to Parliament now heavily outnumbered the 'cavaliers' (as Charles's swordsmen were known), had he remained in his capital (according to one contemporary) 'the king had been like to have been torn in pieces by the citizens'. So on 10 January he fled with his family to Windsor Castle. Henrietta Maria fully realized the significance of this move: her husband, she told an ambassador, 'was now worse than a duke of Venice'.[90]

Charles I: A Problematic King

In a celebrated passage of his history of the First World War, Sir Winston Churchill tried to reduce his own responsibility for the failure of an initiative by presenting the outcome as the result of a 'sinister fatality': a series of contingencies. 'The terrible "Ifs" accumulate,' he wrote, and he presented eight decisions that, 'if only' the protagonists had chosen differently, could have produced a positive outcome. Much the same argument has been made for the English Civil War: that it resulted from '"*a sequence*" *of largely contingent events*, which at a number of points might have ended in a peaceable victory for the king'.[91] Like Churchill, we can easily list these 'largely contingent events' to create a 'sinister fatality'. A 'peaceable victory for the king' might indeed have occurred *if only* the assault on Cádiz in 1625 had achieved even the partial success of the English attacks on the same city in 1587 and 1596; *if only* Charles had dismissed Buckingham and allowed other political leaders access to power and patronage; *if only* he had married a Protestant instead of a Catholic princess; *if only* he had left the liturgy of the Scots alone (or *if only* the government printer had not recycled the Prayer Book proofs, allowing its opponents time to mobilize); *if only* Charles had remained resolute at Berwick in 1639 (or *if only* the Scots had lacked an experienced commander like Leslie); *if only* Sir Phelim O'Neill had not acted a day early, so that some warning of the Catholic conspiracy could have reached the Protestant garrisons in Ulster . . .

Although each link in this 'sinister fatality' may seem superficially plausible, they all rest upon three major 'rewrites' of history: a different inheritance; a different monarch; and different opponents. The newly created 'kingdom of Great Britain' was a composite state, and therefore had a lower political 'boiling point' than other polities, meaning that upheaval tended to arise sooner at times of stress (see chapter 3 above). Composite states required particularly sensitive handling when a ruler embarked on war, especially at a time of adverse climate – as Charles I did between 1625 and 1630 and again in 1639 and 1640. One can reasonably object that no sovereign could have foreseen the unusually adverse weather that would complicate military operations, but Charles could hardly plead ignorance of the fact that *any* war would force him to raise new taxes, and that this would inevitably cause both a clash with the House of Commons and popular resentment; yet on each occasion he decided to press ahead.[92]

Charles likewise seemed oblivious to the disruptive consequences of changing traditional forms of worship at a time of economic crisis and spiritual uncertainty. As Conrad Russell perceptively remarked: 'Measures designed to bring about unity in religion' in more than one of the Stuart kingdoms, 'no matter in the name of which religion they were undertaken, could unite a faction across the Border, *but only at the price of the internal division and disruption of [the] countries to which it was applied*'.[93] Tens of thousands of Charles's subjects became involved in the political process mainly if not solely because they believed the king's policies imperilled their salvation. First in Scotland and then in England, ordinary citizens subscribed their name to public documents – the National Covenant and the Protestation, respectively – that they hoped would preserve their ancient faith, even though doing so set them on a collision course with their sovereign.

Once again, Charles could hardly plead ignorance. As the late Kevin Sharpe noted, Charles worked hard at being king and exhibited an 'obsession with ordering'. He regularly presided at Privy Council meetings (even convening special Sunday morning meetings to monitor the collection of Ship Money); he read and annotated incoming correspondence and scrutinized the credentials of candidates for state offices; and in matters of religion he commanded while his bishops executed. His personal intervention in the crafting and promulgation of both the Canons and the Prayer Book for Scotland did not stand alone. Charles also demanded from Laud an 'annual account' of his ecclesiastical province, which he read and returned with a barrage of schoolmasterly comments ('This must be remedied one way or other; concerning which I expect a particular account of you'); demands for further information ('I desire to know the certainty of this'); and promises to back up his archbishop's decisions with the full force of the Law ('Informe mee of the particulars, and I shall command the judges to make them abjure').[94]

The 'Obsessive personality' (or, as Freud termed it, the 'Anal personality') is not rare among rulers, and in Charles's case it might have stemmed from his unhappy childhood, overshadowed until age 12 by his charismatic brother Henry, whose posthumous fame set a standard that Charles could never match – not least because of his diminutive stature and a life-long stammer. It is less easy to explain two other characteristics that complicated relations between the king and his subjects: inconstancy and irresolution. James I had once assured the English Parliament that 'I will not say anything which I will not promise, nor promise anything which I will not sweare; what I sweare I will signe, and what I signe, I shall with God's grace ever performe.'[95] Charles was different: although he frequently and ostentatiously gave his 'word as a king', he often later reneged. Thus his policy towards the Scots in 1638–9 oscillated between implacable obstinacy ('I would rather die than yield to those impertinent and damnable demands') and abject capitulation at the Pacification of Berwick, with the result that his subjects gave 'no credit' to anything he said. Likewise, in 1641, two weeks after promising Strafford 'upon the word of a king, you shall not suffer in lyfe, honnor, or fortune', he signed the earl's death warrant; while the following year, after many vehement denials, he signed into law a bill depriving bishops of their right to vote in the House of Lords. Such retreats, in the words of Lord Clarendon, 'exceedingly weakened the king's party' strategically as well as tactically, because many of his supporters 'never after retained any confidence that he would deny what was importunately asked'. Henrietta Maria saw inconstancy as her husband's greatest weakness and deluged him with rebukes about it. 'Remember your own maxims, that it is better to follow out a bad resolution than to change it so often,' she chided. 'To begin, and then to stop, is your ruin – experience shows it you.' Or 'You are beginning again your old game of yielding everything'; and '[I hope] that you will not have passed the militia bill. If you have, I must think about retiring for the present into a convent, for you are no longer capable of protecting anyone, not even yourself.'[96]

Nevertheless, opposing Charles in the expectation that he would eventually give way was a high-risk strategy, eloquently expressed by the earl of Manchester, a parliamentary general whom Charles had earlier sought to arrest along with the 'five members'. 'It concerns us to be wary,' he warned his colleagues, 'for in fighting we venture all to nothing. If we beat the king ninety-nine times he would be king still, and his posterity, and we subjects still; but if he beats us but once we should be hanged, and our posterity be undone.'[97] Charles had often displayed both intolerance and vindictiveness. Admittedly, as Kevin Sharpe noted, he executed not a single subject for treason or crimes of state (a striking contrast with both his fellow monarchs and the Republican regime that followed), but he had imprisoned and banished those who criticized him, ranging from Archie the Fool to the earl of Bedford. Moreover, in 1628 he urged his judges to torture John Felton (who had assassinated his Favourite Buckingham) and 12 years later he wrote out *in his own hand* the warrant authorizing the torture of a man suspected of leading the attack on Lambeth Palace after the dissolution of the Short Parliament. In 1639 and again in 1640 he led an army to 'suppress' his Scottish subjects, and in 1641 he almost certainly approved a plan to murder Hamilton and Argyle (the 'Incident'). He would surely have executed Manchester and the 'Five Members' as traitors had Parliament passed their bills of attainder (they were, after all, guilty as charged).[98]

For many of his opponents, Charles's actions not only smacked of political arbitrariness: they also raised fears of a Popish Plot. Every English parish church was supposed to have on public display a copy of John Foxe's *Book of Martyrs*, filled with graphic examples of how in the past Catholics had tortured and killed English Protestants. A few political leaders in 1640 had witnessed Spain's attempt to invade England in 1588 (indeed, one of the 12 'Petitioner Peers' had fought against the Armada), some could remember the 'Gunpowder treason', and almost all recalled the 'Spanish Match'. Fear of 'popery' therefore formed a permanent part of opposition rhetoric in Stuart England. Its resurgence in 1641-2, in the wake of the traumatic news from Ireland served up almost daily in lurid pamphlets, was thus likewise not 'contingent' but entirely predictable.[99]

These circumstances explain the insistence of Charles's enemies in the case of Strafford that 'stone-dead hath no fellow' – even though forcing the king to commit judicial murder significantly increased the risk of civil war. As Charles later wrote, 'The failing to one friend has indeed gone very near me; wherefore I am resolved that no consideration shall ever make me do the like' again. He refused to trust or keep faith with those responsible; and henceforth he made promises that he had no intention of keeping, because 'I have set up my rest upon the justice of my cause, being resolved that no extremity or misfortune shall make me yield, for I will either be a glorious king or a patient martyr.' In doing so, he plunged all his kingdoms into the most turbulent and destructive decades they would ever experience.[100]

Politics, it is often said, is 'the art of the possible' – but what exactly was 'possible' in early Stuart Britain? Johnston of Wariston explicitly ruled out 'retiring one single inch in this cause' and he was not alone. In June 1638 Hamilton summed up Charles's Scottish dilemma with remarkable perspicacity: 'How far your Majestie in you greatt wisdome will think itt [fit] to *wink at ther madnes*, I dare not nor presume to advise,' but 'I dare assure you, till sume part of their madness hes left them, that *they will sooner loose ther lives than leive the Covenantt, or part frome ther demands*'.[101] Once Charles had decided to impose a Prayer Book, come what may, nothing short of full independence for the Scottish Church would have satisfied Wariston and his associates. Likewise in Ireland, after the sudden dissolution of the Dublin Parliament in the summer of 1641, only implementation of the 'Graces' would have satisfied Maguire and his fellow conspirators.

Perhaps Wariston was right: a peaceful resolution of the tension that developed in the Stuart Monarchy in the 1630s could only have been achieved through 'the Lord's removal of Charles' – *if only* he had died before January 1642, either from disease (he contracted smallpox in 1632, but in a mild form) or some accident such as a fatal fall from his horse (which would kill his grandson, William III).[102] Given the temperament of the protagonists, once the Little Ice Age, combined with the 'two great matters, religion and the reduction of the liberty of the people', led subjects like Wariston, Maguire and Essex into opposing a monarch like Charles I, civil war became the most likely if not the inevitable outcome.

Britain and Ireland from Civil War to Revolution, 1642–89

I N 'THE CRUEL AND UNNATURAL WARS FOUGHT IN RECENT YEARS'

Much innocent blood of the free people of this nation hath been spilt, many families have been undone, the publick treasure wasted and exhausted, trade obstructed and miserably decayed, vast expence and damage to the nation incurred, and many parts of this land spoiled, some of them even to desolation.

Although this bleak assessment resembled those made about Germany during and after the Thirty Years War, it formed part of the indictment read out on 20 January 1649 by John Cook, 'Solicitor-general for the Commonwealth' of England at the first 'war crimes' trial of a sitting Head of State ever held: that of King Charles I. His execution ten days later brought about Britain's only experience thus far of Republican government, its first written Constitution, the first effective political union between all parts of the Atlantic Archipelago, and the foundation of the first British empire. It was, as Christopher Hill observed, 'the greatest upheaval that has yet occurred in Britain'.[1]

Moreover, in the words of Martyn Bennett, war 'invaded the fields, the yards and the kitchens of the people. It took the linen off their beds and the mirrors off their walls'. It also killed about 250,000 men and women in England, Scotland and Wales, or 7 per cent of the total population (compared with some 700,000 people, fewer than 2 per cent of the total population, in the First World War and just over 300,000, not quite 1 per cent of the total population, in the Second World War). Between 1640 and 1660, several hundred thousand men and women were maimed or rendered homeless; and tens of thousands more were taken prisoner and enslaved by the conquerors in either England or America. In addition, a series of failed harvests and a plague epidemic produced in Scotland a famine of which 'the lyke had never beine seine in this kingdome heretofor, since it was a natione'; and 'so great a dearth of corn as Ireland has not seen in our memory, and so cruel a famine, which has already killed thousands of the poorer sort'. In 1652 an English soldier in Ireland reported that 'You may ride twenty miles and scarce discern anything, or fix your eye upon any object, but dead men hanging on trees and gibbots'; while three years later one of his colleagues echoed that 'a man might travel twenty or thirty miles and not see a living creature' except for 'very aged men with women and children' whose skin was 'black like an oven because of the terrible famine'. In the words of an Irish poet:

This was the war that finished Ireland,
And beggared thousands.
Plague and famine ran together.

In all, Ireland's population may have fallen in the 1640s and 1650s by one-fifth.[2]

The conflict also caused unprecedented material devastation. In England and Wales, at least 150 towns and 50 villages suffered severe damage; and over 11,000 houses, 200 country houses, 30 churches and half a dozen castles were destroyed (and many more seriously damaged). The total cost of property losses exceeded £2 million.[3] Moreover, to pay and deploy its armies, the central government in London extracted over £30 million in taxes and fines from the population, while the soldiers extracted many millions more directly. It is impossible to calculate a global cost for the war, but the experience of Cheshire between 1642 and 1646 offers an eloquent example: its inhabitants paid at least £100,000 in taxes and a further £120,000 in goods and services requisitioned directly by the soldiers. When sequestration, plunder and wanton destruction are included, the First Civil War cost Cheshire at least £400,000, or £100,000 a year. By contrast, the county's annual Ship Money assessment, which had featured so prominently in provoking the constitutional crisis of 1640, had been just £2,750. Moreover, like every other county, the citizens of Cheshire continued to pay huge sums to support the government and its troops for another 14 years.[4]

Such precise calculations of material damage remain unavailable for Charles I's other dominions, but documents from the 1650s reveal serious depopulation in some areas of Scotland and Ireland (such as abandoned farms in the Borders and the lands of Clan Campbell in the former, and parts of Ulster in the latter), due to deliberate damage inflicted by soldiers. In addition, the rioting in Edinburgh in 1637 began a train of events that resulted in the demise of Scotland as an independent nation for almost a decade; while the Irish troubles that began in 1641 opened social and cultural wounds that remain unhealed to this day.

After considering these and other data, Ian Gentles observed that by any standard, Britain and Ireland paid an extremely high price 'for overthrowing an arbitrary king, crushing the menace of popery, and conducting an 18-year experiment in republican government'; while J. H. Plumb noted that 'By 1688 conspiracy and rebellion, treason and plot, were a part of the history and experience of at least three generations of Englishmen'. Plumb attributed this chronic instability to three defects: inadequate monarchs, badly advised; a Parliament at Westminster which the court could neither control nor ignore; and the 'implacable hostility' of London towards its Stuart sovereigns – a hostility graphically reflected in the decision of King Charles to abandon his capital in January 1642.[5]

The Uncivil Wars

A 'Great Fear' swept England in the winter of 1641–2, comparable in intensity to the 'Great Fear' that gripped France in 1789; but instead of reflecting the fear of famine, it arose from the perceived 'danger from the papists and other ill-affected persons' who stood 'ready to act the parts of those savage blood-suckers in Ireland if they be not speedily prevented'.[6] The mention of Ireland was significant, because news of the massacres that followed the uprising on 23 October 1641 – and rumours that the king himself had sanctioned the revolt – seemed to authenticate the long-standing fear of a similar atrocity in England. One-quarter of all pamphlets published in London in December 1641 carried news of Ireland, and this figure rose steadily to one-third in April 1642. None had more impact than the *Remonstrance of diverse remarkable passages concerning the church and kingdom of Ireland* drawn up by Dr Henry Jones, one of those who had taken down the sworn depositions of survivors of the uprising (see chapter 11 above). Having showed Parliament copies of the depositions of over 600 victims, he included lurid extracts from 78 of them in his *Remonstrance*.[7]

It is almost impossible to exaggerate the impact of this information. When, in 1659, the Puritan preacher Richard Baxter recalled by 'what reasons I was moved to engage myself in the Parliament's warre', he stressed above all 'the odious Irish rebellion', with 'so many thousands barbarously murdered, no less (by a credible testimony) than a hundred and fifty thousand murdered in the one province of Ulster'. 'If you say "What was all this to England"?' Baxter continued, 'I answer: We knew how great a progress the same party had made in England', and therefore feared 'to have been butchered by thousands, or fall into such hands as Ireland did. . . . Of all my acquaintances, I remember few that went into the Parliament Army but such as by their fears upon the Irish Massacre did seem and be moved to it, thinking that there was no other way to safety' in England. The Irish events of October 1641, and the fear that Charles would allow the same to occur in England, was 'the main matter that so satisfied so many of the intelligent part to side with the Parliament when the Civil War began'.[8] Baxter's recollection is amply confirmed by the decision in February 1642 of the House of Commons, shamed and shaken by the depositions, to offer 2.5 million acres of land, to be confiscated from the Irish rebels, as security to those who would 'adventure' funds to raise troops to restore Protestant control, and to authorize an emergency tax of £400,000, to be assessed and collected by Parliament, not by the king.

Ireland was not, of course, the only pressing issue that required urgent attention from Charles and Parliament. Petitions poured in demanding action to end the recession. One from Essex, allegedly signed by 30,000 people, highlighted the crisis in the textile and farming sectors, where 'many thousands are like to grow to sudden want' – but it, too, came linked to sectarian demands: 'Nor can we expect any redress thereof unless the bishops and popish lords be removed out of the House of Peers'. Outside Parliament, mobs of angry men and women 'tumultuously demanded the exclusion of the bishops and of the Catholic lords also, and that the goods of both shall be distributed for the relief of their present needs, otherwise they threaten orally and in writing that necessity will compel them to take more violent measures'.[9] The Lords succumbed, agreeing to exclude the bishops, and then also approved the Impressment Bill, which allowed Parliament to use duress to raise soldiers for the defence of Ireland. Charles grudgingly assented to both bills in March 1642, and then he left for northern England.

The parliamentary leaders continued to usurp the crown's executive functions – appointing men whom they trusted to take charge of the Tower of London, the arsenals of Hull and Portsmouth, and the Royal Navy – which so demoralized the king that when he arrived at York in April 1642 with only 39 gentlemen and 17 guards, even to one of his loyal supporters he 'appeared almost abandoned by all his subjects'.[10] Two months later a parliamentary committee charged with finding 'how to prevent a Civil War' presented him with 'The Nineteen Propositions', a document that sought to curtail yet more of the crown's executive powers: privy councillors, ministers, judges, fortress commanders and even the tutors for the king's children could henceforth take office only after parliamentary approval; there must be no more Catholic queens; Parliament must approve in advance the marriage of any member of the royal family; above all, the king must accept Parliament's right to raise soldiers when it chose.

Charles, now at York, warned that if his opponents persisted in demanding such radical concessions, then 'at last the common people' would discover 'that all this was done by them, but not for them'; and then it would only be a matter of time before they 'set up for themselves; call parity and independence "liberty"'. It would inevitably end with 'a Jack Cade or a Wat Tyler' (the leaders of popular revolts in 1450 and 1381 respectively). If he accepted the Nineteen Propositions, the king continued, 'we shall have nothing left for us but to look on' while Parliament 'destroy all rights and properties, all distinctions of families and merit' until *this splendid and excellently distinguished form of government end in a dark, equal chaos of confusion'.* He therefore rejected the document.[11]

The Nineteen Propositions thus allowed the king to present himself as the champion of English tradition. He could now credibly claim that he stood for law and order against the 'dark, equal chaos of confusion', and his rhetoric soon gained widespread support. In July a pamphlet (originally delivered as a sermon) warned that in war 'there is no distinction betweene the magistrate and the people, but Cade, and Straw and Tyler will beard the king, and give all judgements out of their lawlesse lips'; while a few weeks later a royalist peer wished that 'my children had never been borne, to live under the dominion of soe many Cades and Ketts, as threaten by their multitudes and insurrections to drowne all memory of monarchy, nobility, gentry in this land'.[12] The king also reminded his subjects that 'I am constant for the doctrine and discipline of the church of England as it was established by Queen Elizabeth and my father, and resolved (by the grace of God) to live and die in the maintenance of it.' His firm stand 'caused much rejoicing, the people crying out "God bless His Majesty, we shall have our old religion settled again!"'; while several counties presented petitions to Parliament in support of episcopacy and the traditional liturgy. Moreover, since the king had brought a printing press with him, he now made full use of it both to issue orders and to stress that only the king could enact the measures 'whereby the good and quiet people of our kingdom' – what today would be called 'the silent majority' – 'may be secured and the wicked and licentious may be suppressed'.[13]

King Charles's political instincts proved sound. The collapse of censorship had allowed radical religious groups to spring up, above all in London, which alarmed many ordinary English men and women. Moreover, Parliament proved powerless to end the widespread economic dislocation. The cloth merchants of Suffolk complained that they had sold virtually no wares for 18 months, while in Essex textile production fell by more than half, reaching the lowest level of the century. 'The cries of the poor for work and their curses and threats' spread fear that the unemployed 'are now like to be reduced to extreme want and misery as they will be enforced to take some violent course for the relief of themselves and to spoil the richer and abler sort'. In August 1642 large gangs of unemployed workers in Essex and Suffolk began to attack and sack the houses of both local Catholics and prominent Protestant royalists.[14]

Both developments worked to the king's advantage. Those who dreaded either a collapse of public order or a religious free-for-all now made their way to York, where they joined high-profile courtiers terrified that they might share the fate of Strafford, Romans Catholics alarmed by Parliament's blood-curdling rhetoric and those who considered that, right or wrong, 'majesty is sacred'. By July 1642 the House of Commons, which had once contained almost 600 Members, rarely saw even one-third of them turn up to vote, while the House of Lords numbered only 30 peers (one-quarter of the total). Many of the rest had rallied to the king.

The migration of 'royalists' (as they would soon be called) allowed those who remained at Westminster to take more radical steps. 'King Pym' and his dwindling group of supporters lashed out at anyone who spoke against them: scores of 'scandalous ministers' and discontented laymen joined half the bench of bishops and half the judges in prison. They also created a 'Committee of Safety', which levied forced loans on pain of confiscation (something expressly prohibited by the Petition of Right (page 330 above)); and, conscious that a successful English challenge to Charles still required Scottish involvement, they pushed through a religious programme expressly aimed at winning the support of the Covenanters – thereby further alienating those Englishmen who stood by the Book of Common Prayer.

Meanwhile Parliament's opposition to freedom of conscience in Ireland, along with rumours that it planned to send troops to 'destroy and extirpate all that is there Irish and Catholic', alienated many in Ireland; while the permission granted by the Lords Justices to its military officers to 'execute to death or otherwise by martial law any pillager, or any rebel or traitor', and their resolution to target Catholic women, 'being manifestly very deep in the guilt of this rebellion', suggested what might happen when the reinforcements arrived.[15] Therefore in June 1642, just as the king read and rejected the Nineteen Propositions, Ireland's Catholic leaders drafted an Oath of Association for their own defence. They also created a formal 'confederation' with its own General Assembly and Supreme Council headquartered in Kilkenny, which for the next seven years governed Catholic Ireland and pursued an active foreign policy, sending diplomatic representatives abroad and receiving accredited envoys from continental Catholic powers. The Confederation also raised and maintained its own army and navy to repel an English invasion.

They need not have worried. In August 1642, Parliament resolved to use the funds levied for Ireland to raise instead an army of 10,000 volunteers for its own defence, and named the earl of Essex its Lord General. Charles responded with a proclamation 'for the suppressing of the present rebellion under the command of Robert earl of Essex', and issued commissions authorizing his supporters to raise troops – an unequivocal declaration of war. Once he had gathered some 14,000 volunteers, the king embarked on his third campaign in three years and advanced on London, while Essex led his volunteers to stop them. On 23 October 1642, the first anniversary of the Irish rebellion, the two armies fought a pitched battle at Edgehill – the first on English soil for well over a century. Both sides suffered serious losses and disengaged, but instead of making a dash for London, Charles marched to Oxford, which he fortified and made his 'temporary capital'. His choice gave Parliament time to organize the defence of London, and by the time the king's army reached the western outskirts it was outnumbered and had to withdraw to winter quarters.

By the end of 1642, Charles's supporters held Wales, the west of England and most of the Midlands and the north, while Parliament controlled the southeast, a few enclaves (many of them ports) elsewhere, and the navy. To win the war, Charles needed only to take London whereas his opponents could declare victory only after they had forced the king to surrender and secured control of the whole country. Scotland's leaders, exploiting the leverage provided by this unequal equation, offered to send Parliament military assistance on condition that every Englishman over the age of 18 swore to accept the Covenant and that the English Parliament took an oath to impose Presbyterianism in both Ireland and England. This programme enjoyed limited appeal in England and virtually none in Ireland; but the parliamentary leaders had little choice. In the despairing words of one observer in December 1643, 'Our country makes as much haste as it can towards the miserable state of Germany, contrary parties having been all this winter in many counties still acting hostilities against one another, to the undoing of the inhabitants.'[16] The Westminster Parliament therefore accepted the divisive demands of the Scottish Covenanters, and in January 1644 the latter's well-trained troops entered England and joined Parliament's field army. The allies now far outnumbered the royalists when they met in July on Marston Moor, near York, in the biggest battle ever fought on English soil. In just two hours, the royalists lost 5,500 soldiers and control of northern England.

Nevertheless, Marston Moor did not end the war. First, Charles persuaded the Irish Catholic Confederates to send an expeditionary force to Scotland, compelling the Covenanters to recall most of their forces from England to defend their homeland. Next, the king lured Essex with the main parliamentary army deep into Cornwall, where in September 1644 he forced their surrender. Finally, the following month, Charles almost defeated the earl of Manchester, commanding the rest of Parliament's field army. These signal failures outraged many Members of Parliament including Oliver Cromwell, one of the architects of victory at Marston Moor. 'The members of both Houses have got great places and commands,' Cromwell warned the Commons in December 1644, and they will 'not permit the war to speedily end, lest their own power should determine with it'. He therefore proposed (in effect) the dismissal of both Essex and Manchester and the creation of a new 'national army'.[17]

Although Cromwell and his associates got their way in the Commons, the Lords refused to humiliate their colleagues. This paralysis encouraged the moderates on both sides to propose negotiations aimed at resolving differences on three contentious issues: religion, control of the armed forces, and Ireland. Although Charles agreed to the talks, he had already made up his mind on the first two issues. As he wrote in a secret letter to his wife (a strong opponent of negotiating with rebels), even before the talks began: 'The settling of religion and the militia are the first to be treated on: and bee confident that I will neither quit episcopacy nor that sword which God hath given into my hands.'[18] The failure of the peace talks led the House of Lords to agree (albeit by only one vote) to appoint Sir Thomas Fairfax as Lord General of a 'New Model Army', to number 22,000 men, with Cromwell as his second-in-command, and in June 1645 they brought the king to battle at Naseby. Although this engagement, like Marston Moor, was soon over, the victory of the New Model troops proved decisive, for they captured most of the royalists' infantry, artillery and baggage. They also captured Charles's coach, in which they found his personal archive.

The King 'uncloath'd'

'The king's letters taken at the late fight at Naseby' proved (in the words of a London newspaper) 'of as much concernment as all the wealthe and souldiours that we tooke'. After John Wallis, a young mathematician, had deciphered them, the House of Commons arranged a public reading of a selection of the secret correspondence between Charles and his wife and trusted ministers, notably the marquis of Ormond in Ireland. The audience greeted them with a combination of hissing ('exhibilations') and 'a shout, as loud as that which the people gave Herod' (a telling image). Parliament then commissioned a pamphlet, *The king's cabinet opened*, that included some of the letters together with a devastating commentary. Not only did the pamphlet sell well: it 'sparked more controversy, measured in terms of other publications it prompted, than almost every other work of those prolific Civil War years'.[19] Almost all of London's dozen or so newspapers reported it and one serialized it. A host of royalist pamphlets argued that the letters were forged (though obviously they were not); that they had been incorrectly decoded (hard to sustain); or that they should not be read because they had been written as private documents (too late to enforce). Two years later, a royalist writer admitted that publishing the letters had 'uncloath'd the king', and (as Derek Hirst has argued) helped 'bring Charles to his trial, and to the executioner's block'.[20]

How could a pamphlet with fewer than 50 pages achieve so much? Some recent changes had created an unprecedented public interest in political developments both at home and abroad. First, thanks to the proliferation of schools in England and Wales, by 1640 a significant part of the population could read about the political and religious affairs of the kingdom directly. Second, due to the collapse of royal censorship, there was an unprecedented number of publications for them to read, many of them about politics: over 2,000 printed works appeared in England in 1641, more than in any previous year, and the number doubled in 1642 – an annual total unequalled for almost a century. By spring 1642 a London craftsman found 'so many of these little pamphlets of weekly news about my house I thought they were so many thieves that had stole away my money before I was aware of them.'[21] Third, although only one newspaper appeared in England in 1639, over 60 came out in 1642 (Figs 36 and 37). Each issue carried foreign and domestic news, including accounts of sermons and speeches taken down in shorthand by paid 'reporters' (another innovation), so that those who thirsted for political news could now 'feel how the pulse of the king and kingdom beats' on a regular basis. Thanks to these three innovations, England in the 1640s boasted the most animated 'public sphere' in the early modern world, 'where claims and counter-claims could be asserted and negotiated, and where the range of princely and imperial power could be questioned and contested.'[22]

Few pamphlets or newspaper articles packed the punch of *The king's cabinet opened*, however. As the preface promised, the 'curtain is drawn, and the king writing to Ormond and the queen, what they must not disclose, is presented upon a stage'. Charles's secret letters complained about the stultifying dullness of his entourage in Oxford, ridiculed the peers and MPs who had rallied to him in Oxford as 'our mungrell parliament here', and made fun of the ambition of his ministers. In addition, the correspondence revealed that the king transacted 'nothing great or small' without his wife's 'privity and consent', even though (in the sanctimonious language of the editors) 'she be of the weaker sexe, borne an alien, bred up in a contrary religion'. There was more to this charge than meets the modern eye: most people in the seventeenth century saw uxoriousness as a weakness. In the words of the best-selling manual *A godlie forme of householde government* (1612): 'It is impossible for a man to understand how to govern the commonwealth, that doth not know how to rule his own house.' The deference that pervaded Charles's letters to his 'dear heart', Henrietta Maria, would thus have led most readers to doubt his fitness to rule.[23] Even more compromising were the king's attempts to solicit foreign military assistance; his promises to repeal the penal laws against English Catholics in England 'as soon as God shall inable me to do it'; and, worst of all, his promise to grant full toleration to the Irish Catholics provided '*they engage themselves in my assistance against my rebels of England and Scotland*'. The last pages of the pamphlet contained a devastating selection of Charles's public statements that his private letters flatly contradicted. In the words of the editors: 'The king will declare nothing in favour of his Parliament so long as he can finde a party to maintaine him in this opposition; nor performe anything which he hath declared, so long as he can finde a sufficient party to excuse him from it.' *The king's cabinet* thus robbed the king not only of his 'cloathes' but also of his credibility.[24]

After Naseby, Charles gradually lost his other assets. In England, the remaining royalist garrisons surrendered, while in Scotland the Covenanters crushed an army of Irish invaders at the battle of Philiphaugh: only the soldiers of the 'Confederation of Kilkenny' continued to fight for the king. Although the Irish Catholics boasted a robust administrative structure (with a single-chamber General Assembly, and a

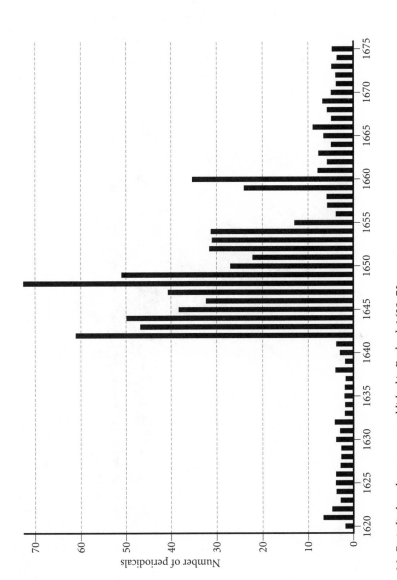

36. Periodicals and newspapers published in England, 1620–75.

In the 1640s, newspapers not only proliferated but acquired permanence: sequential issues with continuous pagination throughout the year; advertisements and special features; full coverage of domestic and foreign news. Issue 202 of *The moderate intelligencer*, for the week ending 1 February 1649, carried a report of the execution of Charles I and also an obituary in regard this is the last time mention will be made of him as a king'; while the next five issues provided readers with 'An epitome of the late thirty years' war in Germany' which had just ended.

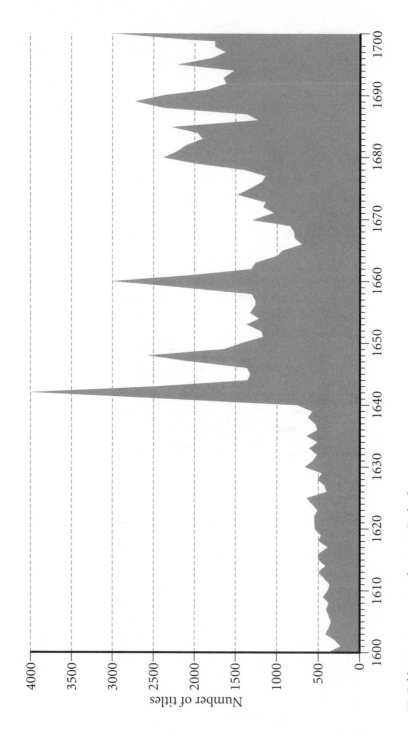

37. Publications in seventeenth-century England.

As in France a few years later, the abolition of government censorship triggered an unprecedented surge in printed works (as reflected in the titles of all known published works). The negotiations between Parliament, the Army and the king in 1647–8, and the debate in 1659–60 over the best form of government for the British state, likewise produced surges of printed works; but the totals of 1641–2 would not be equalled for almost a century.

Supreme Council, both operating under Ireland's first written Constitution, the 'Model for Government'), and enjoyed foreign support, the conflicting aims of the papacy, France and Spain (all of which maintained diplomatic envoys and sent money and munitions) fostered Confederate divisions. Above all, the first papal nuncio ever sent to Ireland, Giovanni Battista Rinuccini, became president of the Confederate Council and insisted on the restoration of all former properties of the Catholic Church as a precondition to any settlement with England – something that neither Charles nor the Westminster Parliament would ever grant. Competition between the various factions paralyzed the Confederation of Kilkenny and prevented it from sending the king any relief. Therefore, as Fairfax's army prepared to besiege Oxford, in May 1646 Charles rode out of his 'temporary capital' and surrendered to a detachment of Scottish troops.

The New Model Army Takes Charge

Charles I's surrender to the Scots created a power vacuum in England and Wales. Without the guiding hand of John Pym, who had died in 1643, the Westminster Parliament became bitterly divided between a Presbyterian majority committed to imposing the Solemn League and Covenant throughout the three kingdoms and a minority, known as 'Independents', who opposed it. The former found much support in London and the Home Counties, which perhaps concealed from them the fact that the rest of the country detested Presbyterianism – as did many officers and men in the New Model Army.

Early in 1647, after the surrender of the last royalist outposts in England, the Presbyterian caucus at Westminster voted to transfer about half the New Model Army to Ireland and disband the rest. They sent commissioners to the Army's head-quarters to put these measures into effect, offering to pay six weeks' wage arrears immediately to those who agreed to serve overseas – but nothing to the others. This was outrageous: Parliament's soldiers had fought with great valour and outstanding success, and it owed them at least £1 million in unpaid wages. Fairfax and his senior officers therefore refused to discuss any demobilization plan with the commissioners sent by Parliament until they had clarified questions on full payment of arrears, indemnity for past actions and other matters. Pamphlets on these issues circulated among the rank and file, including one stating that no soldier should agree to go to Ireland until all had received their pay arrears in full.

Irritated by the unexpected (though foreseeable) resistance to their plans, the Presbyterian MPs declared the authors of these pamphlets to be 'enemies of the state and disturbers of the public peace'. This accusation outraged the entire army, and at the urging of Henry Ireton, deputy commander of the cavalry (and Cromwell's son-in-law), several regiments elected representatives, popularly known as Agitators. In an unprecedented exercise in military democracy these men from the rank and file met their officers and together resolved that they 'would sooner die than disband without the utmost farthing of their arrears'.[25] Amazingly, the Presbyterians failed to perceive the imminent danger and peremptorily ordered Fairfax to disperse his troops as a prelude to disbanding them. In response, and with the full support of his senior officers, Fairfax defied Parliament by summoning all units to a 'general rendezvous' near the town of Newmarket on 4 June 1647.

Once again, contingency intervened. Parliament had recently paid the Scots £400,000 in return for the withdrawal of their troops from England and the surrender of the king, whom the Presbyterian leaders planned to bring to London; but while they debated the terms of the new constitutional settlement they intended to impose on Charles, he remained under guard at his palace of Holdenby, in the Midlands. On 3 June 1647 George Joyce, a former tailor and now a 'Cornet' (the most junior commissioned rank in the cavalry) arrived at Holdenby with a flying column of 500 troopers and took charge of the king's person. When Charles asked to see Joyce's commission, the cornet simply pointed to the soldiers arrayed behind him; and together they rode to Newmarket, where the king had a hunting lodge – and where Fairfax had summoned the New Model Army to assemble the following day. At first the Lord General was furious, refusing even to speak to Joyce, but he soon realized that control of the king's person provided the New Model Army with a priceless asset in their negotiations with Parliament, which now offered the troops full payment of arrears and an act of indemnity for wartime actions.

No doubt Parliament hoped that the improved terms would destroy the army's unity, and indeed many officers and men accepted these terms and promptly left for Ireland; but the exodus included most of their Presbyterian allies, and 'Independent' officers now took their place. The regiments assembled at Newmarket approved a radical pamphlet entitled *The Solemn Engagement of the Army*, prepared by Ireton in association with the Agitators, which pledged that they would remain under arms until Parliament had not only redressed their material grievances but also enacted legal protection from oppression both for the troops and for *'other freeborn people of England, to whom the consequence of our case does equally extend'*.[26] The troops also approved the creation of a General Council consisting of two officers and two Agitators from each regiment, as well as Fairfax and his senior officers.

The General Council promptly resolved to march on London, accompanied by the king. They took with them a printing press, which produced multiple copies of a radical *Declaration* (again mostly drafted by Ireton) boldly stating that 'We shall, before disbanding, proceed in our own *and the kingdom's behalf* to propound and plead for some provision for *our and the kingdom's* satisfaction and future security' by virtue of the fact that 'We were not a mere mercenary army, hired to serve any arbitrary power of a state, but called forth and conjured by the several Declarations of Parliament to the defence of our own *and the people's just rights and liberties.'* The document drew explicit parallels with the Scots, the Dutch, the Portuguese 'and others' who had secured their goals through armed resistance to arbitrary power, and demanded that Parliament do five things:

- Provide full accounts of the money levied and spent during the war;
- Issue a 'General Act of Oblivion' in order to remove 'the seeds of future wars or feuds';

- Grant freedom of worship for all law-abiding subjects;
- Conduct a drastic electoral redistribution that would 'render the Parliament a more equal representation of the whole' kingdom;
- After that, Parliament must dissolve itself so that the king could summon a new assembly according to the new franchise.[27]

For the first time in England, a powerful group of citizens demanded both freedom of conscience and electoral reform – issues that would dominate political debate in England, and indeed in the entire West, for the next two centuries. It is easy to forget that they were first articulated and discussed by the West's first national army.

The 'Young Statesmen'

In July 1647 the Army's General Council discussed a yet more radical document, entitled *The Heads of the Proposals*, which both detailed the Army's terms for reaching a settlement with the king and proposed a new English Constitution, with a Parliament elected every two years according to a franchise apportioned according to taxation; the abolition of regalian rights and imprisonment for debt; and the right for the accused in criminal trials not to incriminate themselves. One cavalry trooper attending the General Council expressed a sense of awe at debating these weighty issues, 'having relation to the settling of a kingdom', because 'We are, most of us, but young statesmen'. After ten days of animated debate, the senior officers shared the *Proposals* with King Charles. Having read them, he enquired what the Army proposed to do if Parliament rejected their suggestions. After an awkward silence, Colonel Thomas Rainborough blurted out: 'If they will not agree, we will make them'.[28]

The king had put his finger on a crucial weakness: London now boasted powerful new walls and could easily withstand a siege. Nevertheless, the capital was restless and the recent harvest had proved poor. Ralph Josselin, an Essex clergyman, complained in his diary about the 'very hard times: I never knew the like want of money in my life'; while in London a crowd enraged by high meat prices burned down the excise office in Smithfield cattle market and destroyed all its records. Somewhat later, a diligent farmer on the Isle of Wight wrote that, although his homeland had been 'the paradise of England, now, Anno 1647, it is just like the other parts of the kingdom: a melancholy, dejected, sad place'.[29] With rapidly rising food prices, a plague outbreak and the ceaseless tax burden to support the army that refused to disband, hardship and discontent increased while in the capital trade and industry atrophied.

These tensions created new divisions in Parliament between the 'Independents' who wanted to appease the Army and the Presbyterians who did not. As the latter lost ground they organized a mass demonstration outside the Palace of Westminster that got out of hand. On 26 July 1647 a mob of apprentices and ex-soldiers burst into both Houses of Parliament yelling 'Traytors, put them out, hang their guts about their necks' and 'if they will not grant your desires, cutt their throates'. The

Speakers of both Houses, followed by over 60 MPs and peers, now fled to the Army and appealed for its protection.[30] A week later, sympathetic units of the capital's garrison opened one of the gates, which allowed Fairfax and his soldiers to enter London without firing a shot. They wore laurel leaves as they escorted the fugitive parliamentarians back to Westminster in triumph, and installed the king (under guard) at Hampton Court Palace, before withdrawing to Putney, strategically located on the Thames between Parliament and the king. There the Army's General Council resumed its discussions on how best to arrange the affairs of the kingdom.

The composition of the Army had changed since it left Newmarket. Above all, many London radicals known as 'Levellers' enlisted to fill vacant places in the regiments – and also to influence the Army's political agenda. Many secured election as 'Agitators'. Unlike most of the radical groups that flourished in the 1640s, the Levellers had no religious programme but instead demanded wide-ranging social and political reforms, including the right of each male citizen to participate in selecting his rulers. In October 1647 the General Council listened to a reading of *An Agreement of the People for a firm and present peace upon grounds of common right*, a concise and eloquent pamphlet approved by the Agitators. After repeating the demand that Parliament must dissolve itself, the *Agreement* argued that sovereignty should pass to a single-chamber assembly, chosen every two years by an electorate 'proportioned according to the number of the inhabitants', whose primary function was to secure certain 'native rights' for all Englishmen: freedom from religious compulsion and from conscription; a universal indemnity 'for anything said or done in reference to the late public differences'; laws that applied to all citizens equally; and a written Constitution. Finally, the document called on the army to impose its revolutionary programme by force if necessary.[31]

Some 50 officers and men, including some of the new Leveller Agitators, now took part in one of the most famous debates in the history of democracy. After lengthy common prayers, the participants began to debate the *Agreement*. Colonel Thomas Rainborough, a recent convert to the Leveller cause, made the case for universal manhood suffrage with particular eloquence, using words that still inspire readers today:

> Really I think that the poorest he that is in England has a life to live, [just] as the greatest he; and therefore truly, sir, I think it's clear that every man that is to live under a government ought first by his own counsel to put himself under that government. And I do think that the poorest man in England is not at all bound in a strict sense to that government that he has not had a voice to put himself under.

When Ireton continued to insist that only those who owned property should vote, Trooper Edward Sexby (formerly a grocer's apprentice but, after four years of valiant service, now one of the Army's leading activists) proudly spoke for the rank and file: 'We have engaged in this kingdom, and ventured our lives, and it was all for this: to recover out birthrights and privileges as Englishmen.' He continued: 'There are many thousands of us soldiers that have ventured our lives [in the war]; we have had little property in the kingdom as to our estates, yet we have had a birthright. But it seems now [that] except a man has a fixed estate in this kingdom, he has no right in this kingdom – I wonder we were so much deceived!'[32]

Hot exchanges on the franchise (and its limits) continued until the weary steno-graphers laid down their pens. We therefore do not know for certain the outcome of the debate at Putney, but the majority apparently agreed 'that all soldiers and others, if they be not servants or beggars, ought to have voices in electing those that shall represent them in Parliament'. The Levellers thus carried the day, and immediately sought to capitalize on their success. Although the senior officers imposed a news blackout, the Agitators circulated printed copies of the *Agreement* and invited soldiers to sign it in anticipation of another march on London, this time to dissolve the Long Parliament by force. Other pamphlets at the time advocated mutiny. 'You have men amongst you as fit to govern as others to be removed', *A call to all the soldiers of the Army* insisted, 'AND WITH A WORD YOU CAN CREATE NEW OFFICERS. Necessity has no law.' The pamphlet also described King Charles as 'a man of blood' – a biblical term with the clear connotation that he should be put to death.[33] Two regiments stationed at Ware, not far from London, promptly expelled their officers, placed copies of the *Agreement* in their hatbands, and chanted 'England's freedom! Soldiers' rights!'

Fairfax reacted forcefully. Showing great personal courage, he and a group of senior officers rode among the mutineers at Ware, beating them with their swords until the papers disappeared. Afterwards he convened a court martial that condemned several of them to death (although, in the end, only one was executed) and drew up a *Remonstrance* in which he pledged to 'live and die with the army'; to secure its full pay arrears and an amnesty; and to replace the Long Parliament with a new representative assembly whose 'freedom and equality of elections' would 'render the House of Commons (as near as may be) an equal representative of the people that are to elect'.[34]

In one sense, the failure of the mutiny at Ware doomed the Leveller cause. Fairfax's *Remonstrance* was less 'democratic' than the *Agreement*, yet it went far beyond any of the Army's earlier constitutional pronouncements – and its programme was attainable, whereas that of the Levellers was not. No royalist could accept a settlement that excluded the king, while no Presbyterian would accept a scheme that granted an equal voice in parliamentary elections to saints and sinners alike. Anarchy would have resulted had the Levellers got their way in 1647 and persuaded the Army to dissolve the Long Parliament by force; and the only person who stood to profit from anarchy was Charles Stuart.

'We suffer dearth: if warrs renue twixt the twoe kingdomes, both shall rue': The Second Civil War[35]

The king had followed the Putney Debates closely. Expressions like 'man of blood' led him to fear assassination, and in November 1647 he fled from Hampton Court. He was soon recaptured and, this time, the Army leaders (who saw his flight as breaking his parole) locked him up in prison. Cromwell and some other senior officers seem to have decided at this point that no understanding could be reached with Charles, and instead envisaged depriving him of his office. The royal prisoner, fully aware of this development, therefore entertained the 'propositions' clandestinely proffered by commissioners from the Scots, his erstwhile captors, who had concluded that their English allies were not capable of obtaining a settlement that would guarantee all the concessions they had gained. In December 1647 the king signed a secret 'Engagement' to establish Presbyterianism in England for a trial period of three years and to allow a committee of theologians nominated by both sides to determine a permanent religious settlement. In return, the Scots promised to send an army 'into England for preservation and establishment of religion, for defence of His Majesty's person and authority, and restoring him to his government'.[36] The Scots had thus declared war on the Westminster Parliament and its Army.

For a time, economic hardship worked in favour of the king and the 'Engagers'. Throughout England, 'bad weather ruined the harvests of corn and hay for five years from the autumn of 1646 onwards, and every succeeding year until the harvest of 1651 exacerbated the problems left by the previous one'. In Essex, Parson Ralph Josselin noted in May 1648 'when rye was earing and eared, such terrible frosts [came] that the ear was frozen and died and cometh unto nothing'; while in June he reported 'corn laid [flat], pulled down with weeds: we never had the like in my memory'. In the Isle of Wight, when King Charles asked a landowner 'whether that [wet] weather was usual in our island', he replied 'that in this forty years I never knew the like before' and predicted that 'wheat and barley will bear such a price as was never known in England'.[37] In London, according to James Howell, 'a famine doth insensibly creep upon us, and the Mint is starved for want of bullion. Trade, which was ever the sinew of this island, doth visibly decay and the insurance of ships is risen from two to ten in the hundred'. Howell continued, *''Tis true we have had many such black days in England in former ages, but those paralleled to the present are as the shadow of a mountain compared to the eclipse of the moon'.* The Leveller John Wildman agreed. In January 1648 he warned the House of Commons that 'trading was decayed and the price of food so excessive that it would rend any pittiful heart to heare and see the cryes and teares of the poore, who protest they are almost readie to famish'. According to Wildman, the clothiers 'professed that trading was so dead, that some of them, who set at work formerly 100 did not now set at work above a dozen' and that 'The poor did gather together in troops of 10, 20 [and] 30 in the roades and seized upon corne as it was carrying to market, and devided it among themselves before the owners' faces, telling them they could not starve'. He predicted that 'a sudden confusion would follow, if a speedie settlement were not procured'.[38]

Such dire predictions led the leaders of both Parliament and the Army to make major concessions. The former promised immunity to serving soldiers and financial relief to their wounded comrades, as well as to the widows and orphans of the slain; the latter agreed to demobilize some 20,000 veterans, some from garrisons and regional forces and the rest from among the radicals who had joined the New Model Army during the occupation of London. Parliament failed, however, to address the grievances of the navy, which allowed royalist agents to provoke a mutiny among the unpaid crews of many warships; and, without naval protection, London's seaborne trade virtually came to a halt.

Now, with the navy mutinous and the New Model Army reduced in size, the second Civil War began. Charles's supporters seized and fortified Pembroke Castle, to serve as a bridgehead for Catholic troops expected from Ireland; rebellions spread in Kent and Essex; and royalists in the north seized both Carlisle and Berwick in preparation for the invasion of the 'Engager' army from Scotland. Cardinal Mazarin, in Paris, complained with some justification that 'the affairs of that country [Great Britain] are in perpetual motion, [creating] an impenetrable uncertainty of what will happen next'.[39]

Gradually, Cromwell recovered south Wales and routed the Scottish invasion, while Fairfax and his men pacified the southeast; and afterwards the victors converged on London, angry and embittered. Fairfax and his troops had spent 11 weeks in the trenches around Colchester, the weather being 'very wet, the season very sad'; while Cromwell's men in the northwest, having struggled all day along roads turned by the constant rain into quagmires, slept at night 'in the field close by the enemy, being very dirty and weary, having marched twelve miles'. Cromwell complained that his cavalry ended the campaign 'so exceedingly battered as I never saw them in all my life' while 'these ways and the weather have shattered [the infantry] all to pieces'.[40] Such privation helps to explain the Army's implacable treatment of its adversaries during and after the 1648 campaign. Whereas in the first Civil War, with few exceptions, both sides had treated at least their English enemies with respect, the victors now severely punished those who fell into their hands. When Colchester surrendered, Fairfax court-martialled and shot two of its commanders and sentenced many other defenders to penal servitude in the West Indies. In Wales, Cromwell shot two royalist commanders as soon as they surrendered and sold over 200 more to merchants for transportation to Barbados.

But what penalty should await the monarch who had done most to cause the late war? Since English Law offered no precedents for bringing a wayward sovereign to justice, the Army's leaders took the matter into their own hands: on 20 November 1648 they demanded that Parliament execute 'capital punishment upon the principal author and some prime instruments of our late wars' (namely Charles and his leading supporters), and the following morning troops surrounded the Palace of Westminster and either excluded or arrested all Members of Parliament thought likely to vote against a trial. Since many other members prudently stayed away, the House of Commons was reduced to a 'Rump' (as it became derogatorily known) of scarcely 150 members (down from almost 600 before the war); and the Rump obligingly created a 'High Court of Justice' consisting of 135 judges, including both MPs and officers.

Proceedings began on 20 January 1649, when the king was brought into court under guard. John Cook, 'solicitor-general for the Commonwealth', read out the charges against him. 'Out of a wicked design to erect and uphold in himself an unlimited and tyrannical power to rule according to his will', Charles had tried 'to overthrow the rights and liberties of the people'; and to that end had 'traitorously and maliciously levyed war against the present Parliament and the people therein represented'. Some 50 eyewitnesses gave depositions concerning 12 specific acts of violence (what today would be called 'War Crimes') between 1642 and 1645 in which the king had taken part. The king refused to recognize the jurisdiction of the court, showed no contrition, and even smiled as he listened to some of the evidence against him, until on 27 January 1649 his disrespectful demeanour, together with the evidence marshalled by Cook, persuaded 59 members of the High Court of Justice to 'adjudge that he, the said Charles Stuart, as a tyrant, traitor, murderer, and publick enemy, shall be put to death, by the severing of his head from his body'. Only on the scaffold on 30 January (a day of exceptional cold, with icebergs floating down the Thames) did Charles assert his innocence. Moments later, the masked executioner – whom some believed to be Cornet George Joyce – cut off his head.[41]

Creating the British Republic

The 'Rump' now became the supreme executive as well as the supreme legislative authority in England, but at first it did not know what to do with its unlimited power. It took three weeks for them to remove the name 'king' from all legal documents and to vest the monarch's executive functions in a Council of State; six weeks formally to abolish the House of Lords; and almost four months to declare 'the people of England and of all the dominions and territories thereunto belonging' to be a 'Commonwealth'.[42] Meanwhile, a volume entitled *Eikon Basilike* ('The king's image'), in which the late king 'set down the private reflections of my conscience, and my most impartial thoughts, touching the chief passages . . . in my late troubles', had by year's end appeared in 35 English and 25 foreign editions (see Plate 3).[43]

As *Eikon Basilike* rallied royalist opinion, the heavy taxes required to maintain the army and navy reduced support for the Rump. Three permanent taxes established by Parliament in 1643 proved particularly burdensome: a reorganized customs tax (whose yield was applied directly to the navy); the 'assessment' (a tax on wealth and income, ironically allocated among towns and shires on the same basis as the hated Ship Money, to pay the army); and excise duties (initially levied only on alcohol and certain goods considered non-essentials, but later also on staples, which both paid the army and paid off debts). Their collection proved particularly difficult in 1649, because of the extreme weather and failed harvest. Even in London, normally the best-supplied region of England, the price of flour reached a level unequalled for another half century, and the soldiers of the New Model Army received a wage supplement so that they could buy enough food to live. Civilians enjoyed no such assistance, and London's extant Bills of Mortality show an excess of burials over baptisms. In Essex, Ralph Josselin recorded in his diary the persistent 'great dearth and want of all things' in almost every month of 1649, and claimed that 'the times were very sad in England, so that men dared not travel and, indeed, rich men were afraid to lie in their houses, robbers were so many and bold'.[44] The magistrates and clergy of Lancashire clearly perceived 'the hand of God':

In this county hath the plague of pestilence been ranging these three years and upward, occasioned manifestly by the wars. There is a very great scarcity and dearth of all provisions, especially of all sorts of grain ... which is full six-fold the price that of late it hath been. All trade (by which they have been much supported) is utterly decayed. It would melt any good heart to see the numerous swarms of begging poore, and the many families that pine away at home, not having faces to beg; ... to see paleness, nay death appear in the cheeks of the poor; and often to hear of some found dead in their houses or high-wayes for want of bread.[45]

Amid such dearth, domestic critics of the new regime multiplied. In April 1649 some Levellers accused the Rump of 'tyranny' and their imprisonment provoked a demonstration outside Parliament by several hundred women, and the presentation of a protest signed by some 10,000 people. New radical groups also appeared: the 'Fifth Monarchists', who wanted to set up a regime ruled by 'saints' to prepare for the imminent Second Coming; the 'Diggers', who proclaimed that all property should be held in common; the 'Ranters', who believed that they had discovered a divinity within themselves that freed them from conventional morality; and the 'Quakers', who admitted no distinction in social rank between men and women, or between rich and poor. None of them supported the new Republic.

Critics of the Rump also multiplied outside England. Immediately after the regicide, the Scots Parliament provocatively proclaimed their allegiance to 'Charles the Second, *king of Great Britain and Ireland*' and, even more provocatively, declared that before he could exercise his royal powers, he must promise to uphold 'the security of religioun, the union betwix the kingdoms, and good and peace of [all] his kingdoms *according to the Solemn League and Covenant*'.[46] This was, in effect, a new declaration of war on England. In Ireland, the Catholic Confederates also recognized Charles II as their legitimate king, and agreed to maintain 18,000 soldiers to fight for his cause: by July 1649 only Dublin and Londonderry lay beyond their control. In addition, royalists controlled the Scilly and Channel Islands while, across the Atlantic, Virginia not only proclaimed its allegiance to Charles II but also outlawed those who denied that he was the rightful king of England. The governors of Bermuda, Antigua, Newfoundland and Maryland soon followed suit and, even in New England, only Rhode Island formally recognized the Commonwealth: settlers elsewhere regarded the regicide as 'a very solemn and strange act' and awaited evidence that the new regime enjoyed divine approval before committing themselves.[47] In Europe, virtually no government recognized the Commonwealth; the tsar of Russia expelled all English merchants; and royalist exiles murdered the diplomats sent abroad by the young Republic to Spain and Holland, and almost killed a third in Russia.[48]

Faced by such hostility, the Rump debated the terms of an oath of allegiance known as the 'Engagement' to be taken by the new Council of State. A proposal to include language approving Parliament's trial of Charles I was defeated by 36 votes to 19 (an indication both of the small size of the Rump and of doubts concerning the regicide). In the end, the councillors simply swore to serve the current government, 'without king or house of peers', to the best of their abilities. The Rump soon imposed a similar oath on all members of Parliament, state employees and members of the armed forces, as well as on clerics, teachers and students at universities and schools. Finally, in January 1650 all males aged 18 and over had to swear that 'I do declare and promise that I will be true and faithful to the Commonwealth of England as it is now established, without a king or House of Lords.' Nevertheless, one member of the Rump (although not a regicide) lamented that 'all the world was and would be their enemies' and that 'the whole kingdom would rise and cut their throats on the first good occasion'; another committed suicide on the first anniversary of the king's execution; and a third died a month later of depression.[49]

Ireland presented the most immediate problem for the Commonwealth, and in August 1649 Cromwell sailed for Dublin with 12,000 veterans from the New Model Army, together with a train of 56 siege guns and a war chest of £100,000. The brutal sack first of Drogheda and then Wexford persuaded most of the remaining rebel strongholds to surrender, and within a year London controlled Ireland more effectively than ever before. The poet Andrew Marvell euphorically hailed the regicide as the foundation stone of a new and glorious Roman empire. According to his 'Horatian Ode upon Cromwell's return from Ireland',

So when they did design
The Capitol's first line,
A bleeding head where they begun
Did fright the architects to run;
And yet, in that, the State
Foresaw its happy fate.
Now the Irish are ashamed
To see themselves in one year tamed ...

And Marvell predicted that his hero would soon do the same in Scotland:

The *Pict* no shelter now shall find
Within his party-coloured mind;
But from this valour sad
Shrink underneath the Plaid.[50]

The 'Picts', like the Irish, had left the Rump little choice. No sooner had Cromwell returned in triumph to London in June 1650 than news arrived that Charles II planned to return to Scotland, swear to impose the Covenant on all his hereditary dominions, and invade England. The Rump therefore decided to launch a pre-emptive strike and once again sent Cromwell and veterans from the New Model Army against them. The Scottish Covenanters suffered from several disadvantages. Since 1636, Scotland had experienced the worst sustained drought in a millennium (page 335 above) culminating, according to historian Sir James Balfour, in heavy snow followed by a cereal harvest of 'small bulke' in summer 1649, so that the prices of foodstuffs 'of all sortes were heigher than ever heirtofoe aney[one] living could remember'. Indeed, he averred, 'the lyke had never beine seine in this kingdome heretofor, since it was a natione'. Balfour also noted a panic reaction common to many countries during the Little Ice Age: claiming that 'the sin of witchcraft daily increases in this land', and fearing divine punishment if it continued, the Scots Parliament issued some 500 witchcraft commissions in 1649–50, resulting in more executions for sorcery than at any other time in Scottish history.[51]

The Covenanter leadership also attempted to avert the Lord's wrath by purging their army of all 'malignant, profane, scandalous persons' – but this fatally weakened their strength when in July 1650 Cromwell did what Charles should have done a decade before: crossed the Tweed with a large army, an artillery train, a large fleet to cover his right flank and a war chest of over £1 million. At the battle of Dunbar on 3 September some 3,000 Scottish soldiers died and 10,000 more fell prisoner. Cromwell hailed his victory as a 'high act of the Lord's Providence to us'.

For many, both at home and abroad, the victory at Dunbar confirmed the Republic's legitimacy. In London, the Rump confidently struck commemorative medals, which it issued to all soldiers who had taken part (the first 'campaign medals' since Roman times). In Boston, Massachusetts, the Reverend John Cotton hailed the victory as the long-awaited sign that God approved of the new republican regime, celebrated a special day of thanksgiving and wrote a personal letter of congratulation to Cromwell. In Paris, Thomas Hobbes put the finishing touches to the first masterpiece of political philosophy in the English language: *Leviathan, or the matter, form, and power of a commonwealth, ecclesiastical and civil.* Despite its lasting fame, the book was 'occasioned by the disorders of the present time'. Seeking to show 'the mutuall Relation between Protection and Obedience', Hobbes argued that 'If a monarch subdued by war render himself subject to the victor, his subjects are delivered from their former obligation, and become obliged to the victor' – namely the Rump.[52]

Naturally, Charles II (to whom Hobbes thoughtlessly presented a special copy of his book) disagreed. Refusing to accept that God would uphold a regicidal regime against an anointed king, he assembled a 'national army' in Scotland that included Highland clansmen and royalists as well as Covenanters, and in summer 1651 they swept southwards, covering 330 miles in three weeks until they reached Worcester, where they hoped to receive reinforcements from the surviving English royalists. Instead, on 3 September 1651, the anniversary of Dunbar, Cromwell attacked and once more prevailed: another 3,000 Scots fell on the field and 10,000 more became prisoners. Relatively few escaped, like Charles II, to fight another day. To Cromwell, this 'most remarkable, seasonable and signal victory' was 'for aught I know, a crowning mercy' to the young Republic. The Rump organized a victory parade in London, which included some 4,000 Scots prisoners who promptly went into penal servitude – some to drain the Fens and mine Tyneside coal, the rest to labour in the American colonies – and declared that 3 September should forever be celebrated as a day of thanksgiving. It was just getting started.[53]

Creating the First British Empire

No sooner had Cromwell triumphed at Dunbar than he urged the Rump to seek wider horizons: 'you shall shine forth to other nations, who shall emulate the glory of such a pattern, and through the power of God turn into the like'. Specifically, Cromwell proposed *exporting* England's Revolution and the Rump, by now a relatively homogeneous assembly that met almost every weekday to exercise both the executive and legislative functions of government, accepted this new charge with enthusiasm.[54]

Its first target was North America. Although most of London's merchant elite had supported the king during the Civil Wars, most of those who traded with the American colonies supported his opponents: they repeatedly loaned money to Parliament and eight of them sat in judgement on Charles I. In return for their material and moral support, the 'colonial merchants' demanded protection for their trade against royalist privateers, and the Rump obliged by building sleek frigates, suitable for long voyages escorting convoys, to replace unwieldy battleships suitable only for fleet actions in the Channel; by creating a Council of Trade (on which many 'colonial merchants' sat) to promote overseas commerce; and by prohibiting foreign vessels from trading with England's American colonies without prior licence. In 1651, again at the insistence of the 'colonial merchants', the Rump passed the Navigation Act, which stipulated that all goods imported into the territories of the Republic should be carried either on English vessels or ships from the country of origin.

The following year, a fleet left England to enforce the Commonwealth's new policies in the Caribbean, and captured 27 Dutch ships trading with the prosperous royalist outpost of Barbados. The Dutch regarded this as a declaration of war, but after 18 months of bitter naval conflict, made peace and promised to respect the Navigation Act. The Republic's warships also secured Barbados and forced the royalist governor of Virginia to surrender (albeit only after securing a compromise that acknowledged the authority of the Commonwealth without renouncing the king). The Rump now deported its defeated opponents from both Britain and Ireland, and increased the forced migration of African slaves, to England's New World colonies, whose population may have quadrupled during the 1650s.[55]

The Commonwealth also brought Scotland to heel. Immediately after the 'crowning mercy' at Worcester in September 1651, Cromwell called on the Rump to incorporate Scotland and England into a single polity, and a month later a parliamentary *Declaration* called for a political union predicated on religious toleration; a pardon for virtually everyone not still in arms; the abolition of all existing legal jurisdictions in favour of the English system of justices of the peace; and the destruction of all insignia of royalty. Parliamentary commissioners met representatives from each Scottish shire and town who reluctantly accepted the 'incorporation' of the two kingdoms and agreed on Scottish representation in a new Union Parliament (thus succeeding where James VI and I had failed: see chapter 11 above). Meanwhile, English troops established garrisons in the Highlands and Islands where no central government – from Edinburgh let alone from London

– had ever ruled. As David Scott ironically observed, 'What had begun back in 1637 as a rebellion to prevent Scotland's reduction to the status of an English province had ended in precisely that fate.'[56]

These measures were mild compared with the Rump's treatment of Ireland. Once again the 'colonial merchants' took the lead. They had 'adventured' large sums of money to uphold the Protestant cause in Ireland; now they demanded the confiscated lands that Parliament had offered as collateral security. In August 1652 the Rump passed a comprehensive 'Act for the settling of Ireland', which required all Irish to accept the authority of the Commonwealth; condemned all priests and all participants in the 1641 Uprising to lose their lives and property; deprived all landowners (Protestant or Catholic) who had 'born [sic] arms against the Parliament of England or their forces' of two-thirds of their estates; and confiscated between one-fifth and one-third of the lands of any Irish Catholic who could not demonstrate 'constant good affection to the interest of the Commonwealth of England' between 1641 and 1650.[57] The Act thus declared all Irish landowners guilty unless they could prove themselves innocent – and now the 'depositions' taken down after 1641 by Henry Jones and his colleagues, which named all those who had terrorized and robbed the Protestant settlers, came into their own. Organized by county, and ominously entitled 'Books of Discrimination', the evidence served to deprive hundreds of Catholics of their lives and over 44,000 more of their property. Whereas in the 1640s Catholics owned about 60 per cent and Protestants 40 per cent of the island's cultivable land, after the 1650s the Protestants owned 80 per cent and the Catholics only 20 per cent. The redistribution of Irish land represented one of the most dramatic and permanent consequences of the seventeenth-century crisis (Fig. 38).

The Rump had thus achieved a great deal in a short time. It had created a Republic; it had defeated the Dutch; it had crafted new administrative and economic structures for its colonies in America; and it had imposed effective English rule on both Scotland and Ireland. In short, it had created the first British empire. Nevertheless, the 'Commonwealth' lasted fewer than five years, because the Rump failed to take one final step dear to the New Model Army, whose troops had largely created that empire: it refused to arrange elections for a new Parliament according to a franchise based on personal assets, not just property, with additional representatives for Scotland and Ireland.

The Road to Restoration

In April 1653 Cromwell lost patience. At his direction, in the middle of one of the Rump's debates on constitutional reform, a detachment of musketeers marched in, removed the Speaker by force from his seat, cleared the chamber, and finally locked up the premises. A wit pinned a notice to the door of the Commons' chamber: 'This House is to be let, now unfurnished'; while Dorothy Osborne, a royalist who had lost two brothers in the Civil War, wrote wickedly: 'Well, tis a pleasant world, this: if Mr. Pim were alive again, I wonder what hee would think of these proceedings and

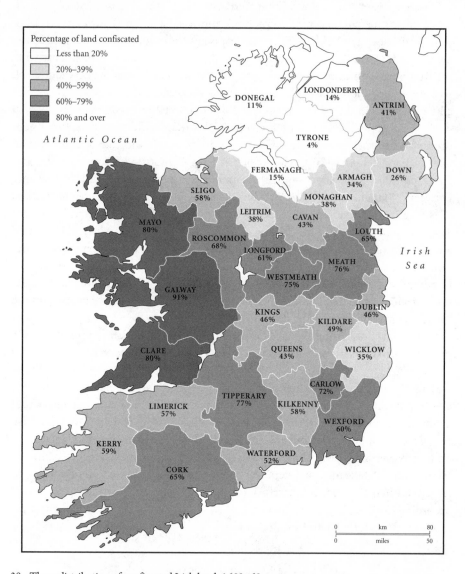

Percentage of land confiscated

Less than 20%

20%–39%

40%–59%

60%–79%

80% and over

Atlantic Ocean

DONEGAL
11%

LONDONDERRY
14%

ANTRIM
41%

TYRONE
4%

FERMANAGH
15%

ARMAGH
34%

DOWN
26%

SLIGO
58%

MONAGHAN
38%

LEITRIM
38%

CAVAN
43%

Irish
Sea

MAYO
80%

ROSCOMMON
68%

LONGFORD
61%

LOUTH
65%

MEATH
76%

GALWAY
91%

WESTMEATH
75%

KINGS
46%

DUBLIN
46%

KILDARE
49%

CLARE
80%

QUEENS
43%

WICKLOW
35%

CARLOW
72%

TIPPERARY
77%

KILKENNY
58%

LIMERICK
57%

WEXFORD
60%

KERRY
59%

WATERFORD
52%

CORK
65%

38. The redistribution of confiscated Irish land, 1653–60.

The overall pattern of redistribution, which reduced the proportion of lands owned by Catholics from almost half to less than one-quarter, conceals even more dramatic regional shifts. A detailed reconstruction for three Ulster counties showed that only 5 of 58 Gaelic Catholic landowners in 1641 retained their lands 20 years later. Most of the rest had been forcibly resettled in the far west.

whither this would apeare as great a breach of the Privilidge of Parliament as the demanding of the five members' in 1642.[58] It was an astute comparison, for by invading the Palace of Westminster, Cromwell, like Charles I a decade before, had made a permanent constitutional settlement more elusive.

Cromwell at first replaced the Rump with a new Council of State (numbering, with suitable biblical symbolism, 12 besides the Lord General), as a caretaker executive, and he invited 140 representatives, nominated by godly communities in Scotland and Ireland, as well as in England and Wales, to assemble in London and frame a new Constitution for the state. After four months of fruitless discussion by the Nominated Parliament, however, Cromwell again sent his troops to clear the chamber, and instead considered a written Constitution drawn up by General John Lambert, called the *Instrument of Government*, which entrusted the 'supreme legislative authority' in 'England, Scotland and Ireland, and the Dominions' to a Lord Protector, advised by a council. Every three years the Protector was required to convene a Parliament comprising 30 members from Scotland, 30 from Ireland, and 400 representatives from England, Wales and the Channel Islands, elected from new constituencies created according to their respective tax obligations. Every Englishman with assets worth £200 or more could vote in the elections (unless they had fought against Parliament). Cromwell, who now became 'Lord Protector of England, Scotland and Ireland' for life, summoned the first Parliament elected by the new franchise to assemble on the next 'national holiday', 3 September 1654. The 'Instrument' thus created a new political framework that balanced monarchy (Protector), aristocracy (Council) and democracy (Parliament); but it did much more. Above all, for the first time in Western history, it guaranteed freedom of public worship to almost all Christians; and for the only time in its history, Britain had a written Constitution. It did not last long.[59]

An attempt to carve out a British empire in Latin America fatally undermined the Protectorate. Cromwell seems to have fallen under the sway of visionaries like John Cotton of Massachusetts (who begged him to 'take from the Spaniards in America' the island of Hispaniola), and Thomas Gage (a Dominican missionary for 12 years in Spanish America before he converted to Protestantism and published *The English-American*, which advocated an English empire in Guatemala and Mexico, failing which in the Caribbean). Both men argued that England's existing American colonies would supply sufficient settlers; and the same 'colonial merchants' who had invested in the subjugation of Ireland, Barbados and Virginia now offered to fund a 'Western Design' aimed at 'promoting the glory of God, and enlarging the bounds of Christ's kingdom' by creating a British empire in the Caribbean.[60]

Cromwell overcame the doubts of his Council of State (who, according to the *Instrument of Government*, had to give their consent before Britain could make war) by emphasizing the religious aspect of the venture. 'God has not brought us hither where we are but to consider the work that we may do in the world as well as at home,' he told them, 'and to stay from attempting until you have superfluity is to put it off for ever, our expenses being such as will in probability never admit it. Now Providence seemed to lead us hither.' He duly enjoined the commander of the expeditionary force 'to set up the banners in the name of Christ, for undoubtedly it is His cause', and to remember that 'we fight the Lord's battles'.[61] Late in 1654, 38 warships carrying 9,000 soldiers and sailors left England for the Caribbean, but they captured only Jamaica. Although the island later became a powerful base for future operations, most of those who landed (including Thomas Gage, who had sailed as a chaplain) died there. Soon afterwards, with sickness in the fleet as well, its commander abandoned all ashore and sailed for home.

According to one of the disappointed 'colonial merchants', the failure of the Western Design involved 'the disgracefullest defeat' that 'ever this kingdom suffered in any age or time'. Cromwell reacted by suppressing all but a handful of newspapers (for fear of the political consequences of widespread press criticism); by dividing England into 12 military districts, each under a major general (through fear that the fiasco might encourage royalists to rebel); and to decree a day of public fast and humiliation throughout England and Wales (because 'the Lord has been pleased in a wonderful manner to humble and rebuke us, in that expedition to the West Indies'). Fearful that he had somehow provoked God's wrath, Cromwell also summoned another Parliament to advise him. The assembly produced *The humble petition and advice*, a Constitution to replace the Instrument (and the major generals), with Cromwell as hereditary monarch, a second chamber (known as 'The Other House'), and a reformed Council of State (renamed the Privy Council). After much soul-searching, Cromwell rejected the crown but accepted the rest of the constitutional amendments, and in June 1657 he was reinstalled as hereditary Lord Protector.[62]

Nevertheless, 'the Lord' continued to 'humble and rebuke' the regime. In London, burials exceeded baptisms in 1652, 1654, 1656 and 1658; and the winter of 1657–8 seemed 'the severest' that any 'man alive had known in England: the crow's feet were frozen to their prey; islands of ice enclosed both fish and fowl frozen, and some persons in their boats'. In the depths of this landmark winter Cromwell convened a Parliament with two chambers, but after a month of wrangling once again he dissolved it – the third time he had so acted.[63] He had made plans to summon another when he died on the National Holiday and the anniversary of his two greatest victories: 3 September 1658. Under the terms of the *Humble petition and advice*, Cromwell's eldest son Richard automatically became Lord Protector, despite the fact that he lacked any military or executive experience (he had served on the council for only nine months). As his father had intended, he immediately convened a new Parliament.

The *Humble petition* allowed the Protector and his council to choose the franchise for the new assembly, and they decided to revert to the traditional franchise in England, allowing all free men with more than £2 of property (as opposed to £200) to vote in the traditional constituencies – a fatal error, because broadening the electorate created a less manageable assembly. Moreover, Parliament convened during 'tedious winter weather, formerly frost, now rain, snow, cold: [a] hard time for the poor, who pine exceedingly, nipped with want and penury'. It soon became clear that many opposed the new regime (the motion to recognize Richard Cromwell as Lord Protector passed by only 191 votes to 168) and, soon after the session started, Sir Arthur Haselrig (one of the 'five members' whom Charles I had tried to arrest and now a vigorous opponent of the Protectorate) launched into a bitter denunciation: 'In five years we have had greater mal-administration than in five hundred years before. . . The people care not what Government they live under, so as they may plough and go to market.'[64] But although Haselrig and other opponents of the Protectorate proved adept at pulling down what they did not like, they could not agree on what should take its place.

The fundamental obstacle to creating a stable Republic lay in Oliver Cromwell's practice of employing men from a wide spectrum of political opinions, from former royalists to ardent Presbyterians, in order to create a broadly based polity – because it created a regime cemented only by loyalty to the Protector. Once Oliver's death removed that bond, the regime was doomed. In April 1659 the General Council of the Army demanded that Richard Cromwell dissolve Parliament, since in three months it had achieved so little; but, having done so, he resigned as Lord Protector. After two weeks of anarchy, the army leaders reconvened the Rump, which resumed its discussions on how to create a permanent form of republican government. It, too, made little progress, and frustrated army units led by General John Lambert (who had drafted the *Instrument of Government*) therefore surrounded Westminster and dissolved the assembly yet again. A 'Committee of Safety' served as a provisional government while Lambert and his colleagues decided what to do next.

By December 1659, a vacuum of power existed. In England the central law courts, which had continued to function despite all previous changes of regime, ceased to operate; taxpayers united to oppose the levy of any imposition that lacked parliamentary sanction; and local garrisons, left without financial support, began to collect their wages directly from the local community. Three groups, apparently operating independently, now intervened. In England, the Republic's navy sailed up the Thames, blockaded London, and demanded the restoration of the Rump; in Scotland, General George Monck, commander of the English garrisons, assembled an army with the same intention – marching on London to restore the Rump; while in Ireland, army officers loyal to the Rump seized Dublin Castle (just as the conspirators of 1641 had hoped to do) and gradually gained control of the other garrison towns of Ireland. On 26 December 1659 the 'Committee of Safety' accepted the inevitable and restored the Rump, which (although now barely 50 strong) resumed its executive and legislative functions; but its survival depended on solving two pressing problems. First, it needed to pay the Republic's armed forces not only their wages but also their mounting arrears. Cromwell's conquests had created standing armies in Ireland, Scotland, Jamaica and Dunkirk (captured from Spain in 1658), as well as throughout England; and paying for the army and navy now absorbed over three-quarters of the Republic's expenditure, while its debts totalled at least £2 million – equivalent to a whole year's revenue.

The Rump's second pressing problem was George Monck. He had condemned the seizure of power by his army colleagues in London, and purged the English garrisons in Scotland of officers whom he considered unreliable. Now, on 2 January

1660, he led 7,000 of his troops across the border into England. Although his forces were far inferior in strength to the various regiments opposing him, repeated purges since the death of Oliver Cromwell and the lack of wages shattered their morale. 'Honest George Monck' therefore reached York, where he received the Rump's commission to bring his army south to protect them. Once he reached London on 3 February, Monck held the political fate of the entire Anglo-Atlantic world in his hands. Over the next two weeks, he tried to persuade the Rump to readmit the other surviving members of the Long Parliament, excluded because they had opposed the trial of Charles I (page 375 above), and when they refused he approached the excluded members directly and secured a promise from each one that, if readmitted, they would immediately authorize writs for new parliamentary elections and then dissolve themselves. Once the excluded members had agreed to his terms, on 21 February 1660 Monck's musketeers escorted them back to the Commons Chamber and stood guard until they kept their promise. Monck, for his part, agreed to accept whatever constitutional arrangement the new assembly should approve; and he, too, kept his promise.

The first general election held since 1640 was contested by an unprecedented number of candidates and produced, perhaps surprisingly, an assembly dominated by royalists. It convened on 25 April 1660 and immediately authorized all peers currently in England to come to Westminster and form a House of Lords in the traditional manner. Some members of Parliament, including Monck (who sat in the Commons as well as holding the rank of commander-in-chief of all army units in Britain), may have hoped to impose conditions on Charles in return for his restoration, but the king-in-exile pre-empted this by his 'Declaration of Breda' (named after the Dutch city where he had taken up residence), because it made four key concessions. Charles promised a free and general pardon to all who pledged loyalty to him, except those whom Parliament should exclude; the resolution by Parliament of all disputed titles to property; religious toleration for all who lived in peace, unless Parliament decided otherwise; and a promise to honour whatever measures Parliament took to pay the arrears of Monck's soldiers. Despite its apparent magnanimity, the Declaration cleverly made Parliament responsible for all the difficult and unpopular outstanding decisions: whom to punish, whom to tolerate, whom to reward, whom to tax.[65] On 1 May, after hearing the Declaration read out, the peers at Westminster formally resolved 'that according to the ancient and fundamental laws of this kingdom, the government is, and ought to be, by King, Lords and Commons'. A week later, both chambers declared that Charles II had been England's lawful king since the death of his father, and invited him to return. Monck was the first person to embrace the king when he landed at Dover on 25 May. According to a contemporary, 'There is nothing now to be seen or heard but joys and jubilees throughout the British Empire, for the royal physician is come to heal the three bleeding nations and to give them again the life of free-born subjects.' To this end, Charles immediately issued writs for a new Parliament to assemble in each of the three 'bleeding nations' according to the traditional franchise.[66]

The 'Happy Restoration'

Some of the king's new subjects required more healing than others. Tens of thousands of men and women bore the physical and mental scars of what they had seen or had done to them – females as well as males. In 1640 a woman in Gloucestershire was 'ravished' by 'eight several soldiers' on their way to join the king's army; the colours of a royalist infantry company displayed a naked soldier with an unsheathed sword and an erect penis, together with the motto 'Ready to use both', and presumably many men did so; some depositions made after the Irish rebellion of 1641 described gang-rape in chilling detail (seven 'rebells hadd ravished and had carnall knowledge of an English Protestant woman, one presently after another, soe as they gaue her not tyme to rise till the last act performed'). And so on.[67] Tens of thousands of women also suffered the anguish of separation and some consulted astrologers such as William Lilly for reassurance. As Sir Keith Thomas has observed, 'It is hard to think of a source which gives a more vivid indication of the human suffering caused by the Civil War' than Lilly's neatly kept ledgers of advice given to distraught women desperate to know whether the absent soldiers they loved were alive or dead.[68] Many saw their worst fears come true. So many men died in the wars that the number of English women who remained spinsters all their lives increased to almost one-quarter; while many others grieved as widows. Margaret Eure considered the loss of her husband – one of 23,000 English soldiers killed in combat in 1643 alone – 'the greatest misfortune that could ever happen to me in this world', because it meant 'the death of the gallantest man that I ever knew in my life'. On hearing of her husband's death in a skirmish that same year, Lady Alice Moore described herself as 'a wretched woman, desolate and distressed', adding 'I am not capable of receiving comfort myself in this dreadful extremity.'[69]

In the immediate aftermath of the Restoration, however, Charles II and his 'Cavalier Parliament' paid little attention to such personal issues and instead concentrated on turning the clock back to 1641. The insignia of the Republic were the first to go: its coat of arms and flags were removed from all public places; its coins were recalled and melted down; its warships were renamed; its monuments were smashed. The anniversary of the regicide, 30 January, replaced 3 September as a national holiday – and on the first one, in 1661, the corpses of Cromwell and other republican leaders were disinterred and strung up on the common gallows at Tyburn. By then, the courts had tried and punished perhaps 100 of their colleagues, restored the confiscated estates of some 800 English royalist landowners (summarily depriving those who had 'usurped' them during the Interregnum), and allowed a further 3,000 royalist families to buy back their sequestered property.

Charles II thus honoured the first two promises contained in the Declaration of Breda – a general pardon and a resolution of property disputes – but he failed to persuade Parliament to approve the religious toleration he favoured. Instead, the assembly enacted measures 'for preventing Dangers which may happen from Popish Recusants' and penalized all who refused to 'conform to the liturgy of the Church of England as it is now by law established'. Above all a 'Test Act' required all preachers, town magistrates and teachers at schools and universities, and later all peers and Members of Parliament, to take a 'test' on oath to demonstrate their orthodoxy. Those who refused – including perhaps 2,000 clerics who refused to accept the Book of Common Prayer – immediately lost their jobs. The Cavalier Parliament also renewed the Established Church's monopoly of legal worship: henceforth, fines awaited all who failed to attend their parish church each Sunday, all who attended a non-conformist meeting of five or more, and all officials who failed to enforce the law. Persistent non-conformists went to prison – including John Bunyan, who composed *The Pilgrim's Progress* (the most popular work of prose fiction in English written in the seventeenth century) during his 12 years in jail, and George Fox, the leading Quaker, who composed a best-selling autobiography during his long periods of incarceration. Neither work circulated in print for many years because another early measure of the Cavalier Parliament, the Licensing Act, prohibited the printing of any work in England without government permission. The publication of newspapers temporarily ceased and the spate of pamphlets became a trickle.[70]

The Cavalier Parliament also restored to Charles II most of the powers exercised by his father. Although both the prerogative courts (whether secular, like Star Chamber, or ecclesiastical, like High Commission) and the regalian rights (like Ship Money) that had caused such controversy in the 1630s disappeared, the king gained sole control of the kingdom's armed forces (the dispute that had precipitated the Civil War); and, once Parliament obligingly revoked the Triennial Act in 1664, he could convene and dismiss assemblies as he pleased. Three years later, he also recovered the right to appoint and remove judges at will.[71] Above all, Charles inherited the three principal taxes that had formed the mainstay of the republican regime – customs, excise and the assessment – and, as the English economy burgeoned, the yield of the first two revenue streams steadily increased, making the crown once again largely independent of Parliament in peacetime. Between 1679 and 1684 only 7 per cent of the crown's income came from parliamentary taxes – a quinquennium in which no Parliament sat – and between 1684 and 1688 the figure fell below 1 per cent.[72] A return to 'Personal Rule' by the monarch seemed a distinct possibility.

The Restoration in Scotland and Ireland took a different form – not least because Charles had been proclaimed king of both Scotland and Ireland in 1649, so the concessions contained in the 'Declaration of Breda' applied only to England. A small cadre in London therefore guided the Parliaments of both kingdoms through a Restoration process modelled on the measures passed by the Cavalier Parliament at Westminster. In Scotland, Charles restored the separate Parliament and judicial courts abolished by Cromwell; voided all legislation passed by his father's opponents; and (like his father) handpicked his Privy Councillors, who both implemented the policies decreed in London and named 'the Articles' (the committee that shepherded through Parliament all legislation desired by the king). A few leading Covenanters (including Argyll and Johnstone of Wariston) went to the scaffold for their role in bringing down the monarchy. In religious matters, Charles did not tamper with the traditional liturgy (the immediate cause of the revolution in 1637) but required all ministers to accept the authority of bishops (and deprived of their livings the 300 who refused). He also gained the right to maintain a considerable standing army, ready to stifle any opposition.

In Ireland, Charles also restored the Parliament and legal system abolished by Cromwell – but otherwise did very little because, as his chief adviser, Edward Hyde (later Lord Clarendon), slyly realized while in exile: 'Cromwell is no doubt very busy ... [re-settling] that kingdom without opposition. And truly, *if we can get it again, we shall find difficulties removed which a virtuous prince and more quiet times could never have compassed.*'[73] Although after the Restoration a 'Court of Claims' heard petitions from those who had lost their lands, it reinstated few royalists. By contrast, almost 8,000 veterans of Cromwell's army and many civilian supporters of the Republic received confirmation of their titles to lands confiscated from the rebels; and every year, on 23 October, Protestant clerics delivered sermons to remind their congregations that, despite the massacres carried out on that day in 1641, the rebellion had failed and its perpetrators had received due punishment.

The king changed even less in Anglo-America. Although, as in Britain and Ireland, orders went out to restore the 'Established Church', Charles instructed his officials in America 'not to suffer any man to be molested or disquieted in the exercise of his religion' and he showed little enthusiasm for hunting down even the regicides fled who had there (John Dixwell, William Goffe and Edward Whalley all eventually died of natural causes in Connecticut).[74] He also continued the Republic's policy of populating the colonies with both African slaves and British criminals, political opponents and paupers; he reissued the Rump's Navigation Acts that protected the colonists from foreign competition. He retained and developed Jamaica, the Republic's sole Caribbean conquest from Spain.

Nevertheless, the Restored Monarchy at first seemed precarious. In England the years 1661–2 saw a marked rise in deaths and fall in marriages and conceptions due to a poor harvest; 1665 witnessed a plague epidemic that killed perhaps a quarter of London's population; in 1666 a great fire destroyed most of the capital's historic centre; and in 1667 the Dutch, on whom Charles had rashly declared war, launched a surprise attack up the Thames, coming almost within sight of London, and then destroying several ships of the Royal Navy at anchor and taking its flagship home as a trophy. Samuel Pepys, who both as a Londoner and as Secretary of the Navy was well placed to judge the situation, reported that 'never were people so dejected as they are in the City all over at this day; and do talk most loudly, even treason; as, that we are bought and sold – that we are betrayed by the papists and others about the king'. On 13 June 1667, fearing that the Dutch might attack London itself, Pepys sent his family, most of his money and his precious diaries 'into the country' for safety (noting that 'hundreds' of other Londoners now 'remove their families and rich goods' from the City).[75]

The next decade was less restless, but in 1679 and 1680 part of England's political elite tried repeatedly to persuade Parliament to pass an act excluding from the succession Charles's brother and heir James, an open and devout Catholic whom some suspected of wanting to turn Britain into an absolute monarchy like 'France, where the subjects are at the disposal of the king for life and limb, and to invade other nations' property for the luxury of the Court; and little men of low fortunes are the ministers of state.' Yet despite three general elections in two years (a record still unmatched in British history), Charles managed to avoid signing an Exclusion Bill into law. He also managed to rule without Parliament for the rest of his reign.[76]

Thus Edward Sexby's proud boast in the Putney Debates of 1647 – 'We have engaged in this kingdom, and ventured our lives, and it was all for this: to recover our birthrights and privileges as Englishmen' (page 372 above) – had miscarried. Only the reckless behaviour of James, who became king when Charles died in February 1685, provided a second chance.

The Glorious Revolution

At first, the new monarch seemed secure on his throne. A few months after his accession, Charles's illegitimate Protestant son the duke of Monmouth invaded, but he attracted little support and James's troops swiftly defeated him (see chapter 17 below). Encouraged by this display of loyalty, James decided to reduce the size of the electorate to the English House of Commons (a process started by his late brother), and so to create a more manageable assembly. He pressured the nobles and gentry in each county to agree in advance on two 'knights of the shire' to represent them, and thus avoid a contested election. He then systematically revoked the charters of parliamentary boroughs then and reissued them in a form that allowed the crown to appoint – and remove – the officials who chose its members of Parliament. Any corporation that resisted incurred heavy legal costs (and, in the end, usually lost). At least 35 boroughs were 'regulated' (to use the king's terminology) between March and September 1688.

James had an ulterior motive in modifying the franchise in this way: he was determined to repeal the 'Test Acts' that restricted all government posts in England to members of the Church of England. He therefore engaged in a practice known as 'closeting', in which he personally interviewed members of England's political elite to secure an undertaking that, when he next summoned Parliament, they would favour the election of men committed to repeal the Test Acts. He dismissed anyone who refused and replaced them with someone more compliant – often either Catholics or 'Dissenters' (Protestants who did not belong to the Church of England). Lords Lieutenants, justices of the peace and other prominent men throughout England lost offices that they and their families had held for generations: 'Not since the Norman Conquest,' wrote Sir John Plumb, 'had the crown developed so sustained an attack on the established political power of the aristocracy and major gentry.'[77]

Because the 'attack' involved several thousand individuals, it took longer than James had anticipated and in April 1688 he decided to act. Instead of summoning a Parliament, he used his prerogative powers to issue a 'Declaration of Indulgence'. In it, the king declared that 'all manner of penal laws in matters ecclesiastical' were now suspended and that all his subjects might 'meet and serve God after their own way or manner'. Catholics, Quakers, Jews and all other religious groups would now enjoy the same freedoms as Anglicans. Moreover – and here lay the fatal flaw – James required all members of the Anglican clergy to read out his Declaration from their pulpits on two successive Sundays.[78]

Just before the first day appointed for the public reading, seven bishops (including the archbishop of Canterbury) presented a petition to the king stating that they could not comply because no English king had the unilateral power to suspend a parliamentary statute (namely the Test Acts). Only Parliament could do that. James responded by charging the seven bishops with 'seditious libel'. Given the subject matter, the ensuing trial of the bishops almost inevitably led to a discussion of the limits of royal power and, like his grandfather James I when confronted by a cleric who protested on ground of conscience (page 326 above), James II would discover the folly of submitting such matters to public debate. 'I do not remember in any case in all our law,' one judge observed on the last day of the trial, in which the king had overridden a law enacted in Parliament. Moreover, '*I can see no difference, nor know of one in law, between the king's power to dispense with laws ecclesiastical and his power to dispense with any other laws whatsoever. If this be once allowed of, there will need no Parliament; all the legislature will be in the King.*'[79] After deliberating all night, on 10 July 1688 the jury declared the bishops 'Not Guilty' and they emerged to a tumultuous welcome.

That same day, a group of seven peers sent a letter inviting James's son-in-law, Prince William of Orange, to invade England in 'such a strength' that it 'were able to defend themselves' against James's army and navy if attacked. Like their predecessors who in 1640 had promised widespread support for a Scottish invasion (see page 341 above), the peers assured William that 'there are nineteen parts of twenty of the people throughout the kingdom who are desirous of a change' of regime, and urged him 'to venture upon the attempt' before the end of the year.[80] Unlike the petition by the seven bishops, the invitation of the seven peers was manifestly treason: they had called on a foreign power to invade and overthrow their anointed king.

In logistical terms, expecting that a powerful amphibious expedition requested in mid-July could arrive before the end of the campaigning season was totally unrealistic; and any amphibious expedition in winter involved a high risk of disruption or damage from storms. Moreover, even if the prince managed to evade the Royal Navy and land his forces, James had some 40,000 troops with which to oppose them; and, even should William secure a bridgehead, as a shrewd English observer noted, 'it's well known he cannot stay long here without a manifest exposing of his own countrey to the French'.[81] Nevertheless, by a combination of good logistics and good luck, on 5 November (15 November by the Gregorian calendar), 500 Dutch ships arrived off the Devon coast and the prince, his 23,000 veteran troops, 5,000 horses and artillery train began to disembark.

Contrary to the assurances of the seven peers, scarcely one nobleman in ten provided William with active support as he marched on London, but he also encountered remarkably little opposition. Eventually deserters, including even James's second daughter Anne and her husband, joined the prince and undermined James's ability and will to resist; and, just before Christmas, a detachment of Dutch troops discreetly 'escorted' James from his London palace, creating an Interregnum for the second time in a generation in England (whose Parliament determined that James had abdicated) and Scotland (where he was declared deposed).

The political situation in the winter of 1688–9 was similar to that in the winter of 1641–2: the anointed king had fled, and although his opponents mostly agreed that they did not want him back, they remained divided on what they wanted to place in his stead. But whereas 'King Pym' had only the London Trained Bands to rely on, Prince William placed all the key points in London and the Home Counties under the control of his veteran troops – most of them Dutch, assisted by some of the Danish, German, English and Scots units that normally served in the Dutch Army. They remained there for more than a year while he persuaded those who had invited him over, and their allies, to make him their sovereign – a step none of them had intended. William refused to talk with those who 'would have a duke of Venice' (just like Charles I before him); while to those who wanted to make his wife Mary (James's eldest daughter) their sole sovereign, he replied that he 'would not like to be his wife's gentleman usher'. Therefore in February 1689 William and Mary accepted an invitation from a 'Convention' of peers and commoners to become joint sovereigns in England. In return – indeed, in the same document – they promised to redress specified grievances (such as recognition that 'suspending the laws, or the execution of laws, by regal authority, without consent of Parliament, is illegal') and also to guarantee certain 'liberties'.[82]

Shortly afterwards, the new monarchs approved several critical measures. The Mutiny Act left them in charge of the kingdom's armed forces – but only for six months, which in effect meant that they would need to convene Parliament frequently in order to renew it. The Toleration Act, although it did not mention Catholics (nor indeed the word 'toleration'), abolished the mechanisms that had allowed the bishops and the law courts to enforce conformity. Above all, instead of allowing the crown to levy customs and excise, Parliament retained control of all state taxation and from this allotted William a 'Civil List' to defray the expenses of the crown's household, officials, judges and diplomats. Parliament had now regained almost all the powers it had won in 1641 – and this time it would keep them.

After the Revolution

Many participants in the 'events of 1688' nevertheless felt betrayed by the 'Revolution Settlement'. In England, John Locke and some of his radical colleagues did not want to stop merely after 'mending some faults peice meale, or anything lesse than the great frame of government'. They therefore saw the Convention as 'an occasion, not of amending the government, but of melting itt downe and make all new'.[83] Their expectations were just as dangerous (and unrealistic) as those of the Levellers a generation before, and they found little support because they were equally unacceptable to the political elite. The wisdom of the 'minimalist' revolution in England appears most clearly in comparison with the settlements implemented elsewhere. In Scotland, the insistence of the Presbyterian majority on excluding from power all who did not share their views strengthened the Jacobites (as the supporters of James II and his descendants were known), and although a Jacobite uprising in 1689 failed, the victors lacked the strength to resist another forced union with England in 1707. No Scottish Parliament would meet again until the late twentieth century. In Ireland, the Jacobites (with French aid) triumphed until William invaded in person, at the head of his foreign troops, and in July 1690 the battle of the Boyne consolidated the 'Protestant Supremacy' established by Cromwell, reducing Catholic influence and prosperity even further.

Some observers made an explicit comparison between the two leaders. One verse in a poem entitled *The weasel uncased*, sung to the tune of 'For he's a jolly good fellow', claimed:

So let O. P. or P. O. be king,
Or anyone else, it is the same thing

'O. P.' stood for 'Oliver Protector', and 'P. O.' for the 'Prince of Orange'. Other English works in the 1690s, both in prose and verse, compared and condemned both men as tyrants and usurpers. The return of extremely cold weather and a succession of disastrous harvests added to the misery of what became known as 'King William's Ill Years'. In London, John Evelyn reported in May 1698 that such unseasonably cold weather 'had not ben known by any, almost, alive' with 'all tree fruits ruined and threatning the rest with famine'. Scotland suffered far more: in upland regions, cold and wet summers caused the harvest to fail *every year* between 1688 and 1698, a year when the Scottish government lamented the onset of '*a perfeit famine, which is more sensible than ever was known in this Nation*'. The population of the northern kingdom fell by one-tenth in the course of the decade, with losses of up to one-third in upland communities. Even in the 1780s, a survey of Scottish parishes recorded several areas abandoned at 'the end of the last century, when that part of the country was almost depopulated by seven years of famine: and now they lie neglected, along with many thousand acres, in like situation, in different parts'.[84]

The political legacy of the seventeenth-century revolutions also endured. In a debate on the repeal of the American Stamp Act in 1766, an English Member of Parliament asked 'Shall we stay until some *Oliver* rises amongst them?'; and in 1775, an *Essay upon government adopted by the Americans, wherein the lawfulness of revolutions are demonstrated*, published in Philadelphia, juxtaposed a section on 'the late civil war condemned', which dwelled upon 'the barbarous murder of King Charles I' by 'a few particular persons', with one on 'The Revolution justified'. If a monarch should refuse his subjects protection, it argued, 'they may refuse him their obedience', the anonymous author conceded (following Thomas Hobbes), 'but this does not give them any power over his person':

[If] such principles and such practices upon such pretences were to be allowed, they would make the right of princes and the peace of society the most precarious thing that can be; and lays [rulers] open to the insults of every *Massinello*, who has but impudence enough to charge the government with popery or tyranny . . . and cunning enough to time it with some popular discontent.[85]

The *Essay* therefore expressed the hope that America might experience a bloodless revolt by 'the whole society', like the Glorious Revolution of 1688, and thus avoid the violence of the 1640s.

Not all colonists saw the past in this way. Although most New England patriots recalled with pride their ancestors' struggle against Charles I's tyranny, many in the Upper South nourished with equal pride their ancestors' victory over the Puritan regicides. Thomas Ingersoll has argued that these conflicting memories of the 1640s constituted one of the principal impediments to a Declaration of Independence; and that taking this decisive step became possible only after a collective amnesia developed about the English Civil War. 'Pamphlets written by the leading rebel politicians in the last year of the crisis before July 4, 1776,' Ingersoll notes, unlike those written earlier, 'do not mention the revolution of 1649'.[86]

English politicians also continued to wrestle with the ideological debris left by 'Oliver' and the regicides. When in 1791 Edmund Burke reflected on the likely outcome of the recent revolution in France, he noted how England's troubles in the 1640s had begun with modest constitutional demands but ended in civil war, concluding that violence formed an inseparable element of rebellion. 'These politics of revolution,' he claimed, 'temper and harden the breast, in order to prepare it for the desperate strokes which are sometimes used in extreme occasions.' 'Plots, massacres, assassinations, seem to some people a trivial price for obtaining a revolution,' he continued caustically, and on the very next page launched into a diatribe on the regicide. Burke viewed the Glorious Revolution in a very different light. 'What we did' then, he wrote in another publication of 1791, 'was in truth and substance, and in a constitutional light, a revolution not made but prevented', because (he continued) the events of 1688–9 resolved most of the contentious issues that had led to civil war in all three kingdoms, and also in New England, where James had worked to suppress representative assemblies throughout in favour of an authoritarian viceroyalty.[87]

To Thomas Babington Macaulay, writing in 1848 as 'all around us the world is convulsed by the agonies of great nations', and 'governments which lately seemed likely to stand during ages have been on a sudden shaken and overthrown', it might 'seem almost an abuse of terms to call a proceeding, conducted with so much deliberation, with so much sobriety, and with such minute attention to prescriptive etiquette, by the terrible name of Revolution. And yet,' he continued, the events of 1688–9 in England, 'of all revolutions the least violent, has been of all revolutions the most beneficent'. It brought to an end all three sources of chronic instability discerned by J. H. Plumb – inadequate monarchs, badly advised; a Parliament at Westminster that the court could not control; and the implacable hostility of

London towards its sovereigns – and instead ushered in a state dedicated to the vigorous promotion of economic development, broad religious tolerance and free competition among political interests, characteristics that still define liberal democracies today. The Glorious Revolution therefore remained, as Macaulay proudly proclaimed, 'our *last* revolution'. It provided for England, albeit at a very high cost, a complete and (so far) permanent escape from both the General Crisis and the Little Ice Age.[88]

PART III

SURVIVING THE CRISIS

IN 1623 AN ITALIAN PREACHER, SECONDO LANCELLOTTI, BECAME IRRITATED BY those who complained about the unprecedented harshness of the world and set out to refute them. His best-selling book *Nowadays, or how the world is not worse or more calamitous than it used to be*, identified 49 'fallacies' held by contemporaries whom Lancellotti called *hoggidiani* – 'whiners' – and then listed examples in each of the 49 categories to prove them wrong. Thus 'princes nowadays are *not* more avaricious or indifferent towards their subjects than they used to be', while 'human life nowadays is *not* shorter, so that men do *not* live for less time now than they have done for thousands of years'. Lancellotti devoted his last chapters to natural phenomena. He reviewed recent accounts of famines, fires and plague epidemics as well as natural disasters (such as earthquakes, floods and cold weather) 'nowadays', and argued that such catastrophes in the past had been far worse and far more frequent. According to Lancellotti, life had never been so good – but proving his case took over 700 pages.[1]

Although *Nowadays* sold so well that Lancellotti wrote a sequel (claiming to show that science and literature too were 'not worse than before'), his vision was deeply flawed.[2] To claim that seventeenth-century princes were no more 'avaricious or indifferent towards their subjects' than their predecessors (in itself hardly a ringing endorsement) obscured the fact that, in many cases, their misguided policies caused far more damage than those of their predecessors; while the data in this book reveal that 'human life' was indeed 'shorter' than in the past, and that famines, fires and epidemics as well natural phenomena (not only earthquakes, floods and cold weather but also fireball fluxes, volcanic eruptions and El Niño episodes) all increased markedly. Not surprisingly, as the seventeenth century advanced, the ranks of 'whiners' swelled and their assessments became ever more pessimistic. 'The worst news keeps coming in from everywhere,' the Spanish intellectual Francisco de Quevedo lamented to a friend in 1645. 'I cannot be sure whether things are breaking up or have finally broken up. God knows!' A few years later, in Paris, Thomas Hobbes complained about the 'continual fear and danger of violent death' in which he and his contemporaries lived, while Renaud de Sévigné, a rebellious lawyer, believed that 'If one ever had to believe in the Last Judgment, I think it is happening right now'. In a nearby convent, Abbess Angélique Arnauld thought that the death of 'one-third of the world' and the prodigious material destruction 'must signify the end of the world'. Meanwhile the Spanish Jesuit, Baltasar Gracián, published *El Criticón* (The Critic), a vast allegorical novel that divided human life into four 'seasons', and divided each season into chapters that Gracián entitled 'crisis'. Each of the 38 'crises' presented a bitter and desolate survey of the human condition.[3]

Nevertheless, Lancellotti had a point. On the one hand, some of the pessimists lived longer than their 'whining' might have predicted: although Gracián was only 58 when he died, Quevedo and Sévigné both died aged 65; Arnauld died aged 70; and Hobbes died aged 91. Moreover, all five died in their beds of natural causes. On the other hand, although unparalleled hardships befell many of those who lived in composite states, in urban areas, in marginal lands and in macro-regions during the mid-seventeenth century, the inhabitants of some other regions largely escaped. Put differently, even if 'one-third of the world died', the other two-thirds survived. Thus, although Mughal India, Safavid Iran and Tokugawa Japan all experienced extreme weather events and some rebellions in the seventeenth century, they avoided the fatal synergy between human and natural factors that elsewhere turned crisis into catastrophe. Moreover, parts of Sub-Saharan Africa, Australia and the Americas appear to have remained largely unscathed by both the Little Ice Age and the General Crisis (although this conclusion may reflect absence of evidence rather than evidence of absence). Finally, although government oppression at a time of climatic catastrophe provoked major rebellions in two of the Italian states ruled by Spain – Sicily and Naples – strategic concessions restored control in a matter of months; while Spanish Lombardy remained loyal. The experience of these regions thus supported the vision of Secondo Lancellotti: life was *not* 'worse' or 'more calamitous than it used to be'.

Four of the areas where Lancellotti's optimism seems valid – areas where the 'footprint' of the seventeenth-century crisis appears lighter – nevertheless shared an important negative common denominator: Japan, Australia, Sub-Saharan Africa and the Americas all entered the seventeenth century with a relatively low population density. The reasons for this circumstance varied – a century of civil war in Japan; the perennially harsh climate of Australia; the elimination by Europeans of indigenous peoples in both Africa and the Americas – but the result was the same: the Little Ice Age struck societies in which the demand for food did not already exceed supply. This seems to have mitigated disaster and, in the case of Japan, it also promoted recovery.

The Mughals and their Neighbours[1]

'The most potent monarchs on earth'

IN APRIL 1639, AT THE EXACT SECOND DETERMINED BY THE IMPERIAL astrologers, a lark was sacrificed on a bluff overlooking the Jumna river near the ancient city of Delhi, and workers immediately placed the bodies of several freshly beheaded criminals around the cornerstone of the new capital of the Mughal empire, to be called Shahjahanabad: the *abad* or city of Shah Jahan. Nine years later, Shah Jahan made his ceremonial entry and took up residence with some 10,000 followers in his palace citadel, surrounded by the huge red sandstone wall that gave the complex the name it still bears: the Red Fort. The emperor also supervised the construction of a *medrese*, a hospital, the largest mosque in the entire Muslim world, and a massive stone wall with 14 gates (most of them still standing) to defend the city's population of 400,000. Shah Jahan, who ruled from 1627 to 1658, created the only capital city in the world built entirely during the mid-seventeenth century.[2]

John Ovington, an English visitor, ascribed this and the Mughals' other costly achievements to the fact that 'the vast tract of land' under their rule 'reaches near 2,000 miles in length, some say more', and that it provided them with 'more than double the incomes of any [of] the most potent monarchs on earth'.[3] It did indeed. The Mughals ruled an area half the size of Europe and a population of perhaps 100 million (the same as the whole of Europe and second only to Ming China). Most of their subjects lived in a 'fertile crescent that extended from the mouth of the Indus River, northeast to the rich, well-watered, densely populated lands of the Punjab, and then down the even richer Ganges Valley to the Bay of Bengal'. Farmers there cultivated 19 spring and 27 autumn crops, sometimes securing two harvests each year. Although primarily an agrarian state, the empire included three cities with 400,000 or more inhabitants and nine others with over 100,000 people and, in both the cities and the countryside, craftsmen manufactured a vast range of high-quality goods for export.[4]

Although the emperors ruled substantial areas in this heartland directly, from the 1570s onwards they granted the rest to prominent supporters (known as *mansab-dars*, literally 'men who hold rank') in return for serving in the imperial army with a specified number of troops. Shah Jahan maintained over 400 *mansabdars*, but not all received the same amount of land: by far the largest share went to his four sons, who between them ruled almost 10 per cent of the empire. Each grant of territory was known as a *jagir*, literally 'holding place' because the emperors regularly rotated their *mansabdars* from one *jagir* to another. As Stephen Dale has pointed out, 'This system required accurate land-revenue estimates, which in turn necessitated land surveys in order to make assignments that generated sufficient funds to support the number of troops commanded by each officer. These features necessarily generated an enormous financial bureaucracy.'[5] Controlling such a vast and diverse empire turned the Mughal emperors into workaholics. Whether in their capital, on progress or on campaign, every day they publicly bestowed titles and promotions, received petitions, heard claimants, and dispensed justice: a chronicler claimed that in the 1660s the emperor 'appears two or three times every day in his court of audience . . . to dispense justice to complainants.'[6]

The Mughals constantly presented their decisions as divinely sanctioned. Shah Jahan's father Jahangir (r. 1605–27) enrolled and initiated religious 'disciples' and sought advice from eminent Muslim holy men, while his son Aurangzeb (r. 1658–1707) could recite the entire Qur'an from memory, spent 'whole nights in the mosque which is in his palace', and enjoined his judges to uphold the *shari'a* (Muslim law derived from the Qur'an and other ancient religious texts).[7] The Taj Mahal, built by Shah Jahan between 1631 and 1653, emphasizes the central role of Islam in his government: lengthy inscriptions from the Qur'an explain how each part of the structure and the surrounding gardens replicate Paradise, with the dome representing the throne of God. Lest anyone miss the point, Shah Jahan ordered that his own tomb be placed immediately below that dome, together with an epitaph that described him as *Rizwan*, the gatekeeper of Paradise.

Nevertheless, no Mughal emperor placed his trust in God alone. Even the names they chose breathed absolute power: *Jahangir* means 'conqueror of the world'; *Shah Jahan* means 'king of the world'; Aurangzeb took the regnal name *Alamgir* ('world conqueror') at his accession. John Ovington noted that each emperor constantly employed 'a numerous army to awe his infinite multitude of people, and keep them in absolute subjection'; and that he did so in person. According to Aurangzeb, 'An emperor should never allow himself to be fond of ease and inclined to retirement,' and he warned his successors that they should 'always be moving about as much as possible':

> It is bad for both emperors and water to remain at the same place;
> The water grows putrid and the king's power slips out of his control.
> In touring lie the honour, ease and splendour of kings:
> The desire of comfort and happiness makes them untrustworthy.[8]

True to his own advice Aurangzeb, like his predecessors, spent over one-third of his reign on the move – although, also like them, he seldom strayed further than 800 miles from Delhi (Fig. 39). Three factors explain this precise radius. First, the Mughal emperors moved slowly (never more than 10 miles a day and often less) because it took time to receive in person (and thus overawe) the major vassals along their route. Second, the court normally returned to the capital before the monsoon, which halted travel throughout Hindustan between July and October. Finally,

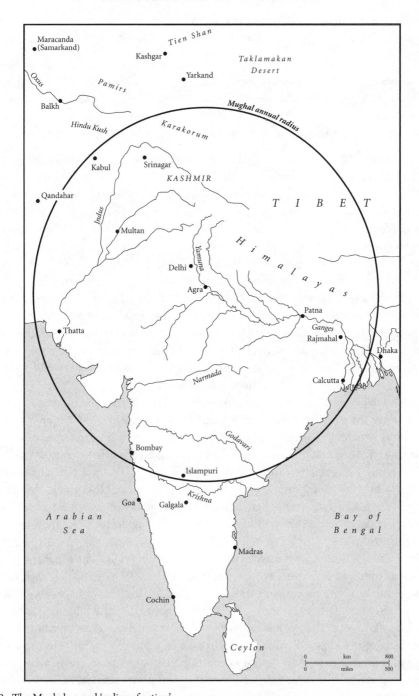

39. The Mughal annual 'radius of action'.
Although the Mughal emperors went on progress every year, they almost always returned to their capital ahead of the annual monsoon. Since this limited the time for travel to nine months, and since the Court travelled at an average speed of about five miles a day, the emperor's effective 'radius of action' was around 800 miles. Significantly, this included Kabul (which the Mughals managed to retain) but not Qandahar or Balkh (where repeated campaigns failed).

moving too far or too long from any given area might encourage rebellion. As Ovington noted:

> The frequent revolts in India render those parts very miserable, and reduce the inhabitants to a very distressed state. For hoping to retrieve their liberty, and regain the kingdoms they have lost, they often declare for a rajah (which is a native Indian prince), and stand by him till the Mogul overpowers their forces, defeats their rebellion, stints their progress, and reduces them to a tame obedience again.

This state of affairs, he added, 'makes fear and distress, poverty and famine the universal air and genius of those unquiet abodes'.[9]

Ovington exaggerated: only the 'rajahs' on the periphery of the Mughal state possessed the means to defy the emperor, drawing strength from regional cultures distinct from the Persian idiom adopted by the central government. Moreover, the Mughals often chose to end these rebellions by negotiation and compromise rather than by force, not least because India boasted a vast military labour market that favoured the 'seller': the emperor was merely the largest, never the only, ruler recruiting troops each year. According to the calculations of Mughal ministers, some four *million* men in northern India possessed military equipment and training, and the emperor needed to raise enough of them not only to execute his own designs, but also to prevent any of his rivals from creating an army capable of mounting a challenge. Shah Jahan therefore maintained an army of 200,000 cavalry and 40,000 infantry, supported by elephants, horses, camels and oxen.[10]

Since such unparalleled concentrations of humans and animals could not live off the country, the emperor not only took with him on campaign enough money to pay his troops punctually and in cash, but also prepared large strategic reserves of specie along the line of march, and arranged for bankers travelling with the army to transfer revenues from outlying territories to the 'sublime camp'. This practice allowed his troops to buy their food from merchants who set up bazaars every time the camp halted. The Mughal military system had no peer in the early modern world, and for almost the entire seventeenth century it allowed the emperors to rule their territories effectively.

Nevertheless, like other dynasties with Central Asian origins, the Mughal regime suffered from one serious weakness: the system of 'tanistry', by which each ruler emerged only after a process of ruthless competition, sometimes between siblings but also between father and sons (see chapter 2 above). When rumours spread in 1622 that Emperor Jahangir had fallen ill, his eldest son Shah Jahan demanded sole command of the imperial armies and, when he failed to receive it, he led an army from Gujarat in the west to Bengal in the east in an attempt to create a coalition strong enough to depose his father. He failed, and only the surrender of his own sons as hostages secured a reconciliation. A succession struggle ensued when Jahangir died in 1627, with court factions supporting the claims of various rival princes, and after Shah Jahan prevailed he executed his rivals. Thirty years later, rumours that Shah Jahan was mortally ill would trigger a civil war between his sons; and the same would happen in 1707, after the death of the victor, Aurangzeb.

'A perfect drought': The Great Indian Famine of 1630–2

No sooner had Shah Jahan consolidated his authority and murdered his male relatives than a natural catastrophe struck his empire. The well-being of India and its
neighbours has depended for at least six millennia on the annual monsoon, which
brings 90 per cent of the subcontinent's annual rainfall. But whereas a catastrophic
monsoon failure normally occurs only once per century, the seventeenth century
saw four: in 1613–15, in 1630–2, in 1658–60 and again in 1685–7. Each failure
produced widespread famine, especially in Gujarat whose population relied heavily
on imported food. The worst catastrophe occurred in 1630 (a year that saw both
strong volcanic activity and a major El Niño episode, which often coincide with a
weak monsoon) when virtually no rain fell, and 1631 (another year of high volcanic
activity). The emperor's official chronicle recorded that

> Throughout the Deccan and Gujarat a perfect drought prevailed. Consequently
> the inhabitants of those regions suffered severely from the dearness of grain and
> the want of the common necessaries of life. The cravings of famine compelled
> parents to devour their offspring, and high and low were clamouring for their
> bread and dying from sheer exhaustion... he mortality was so dreadful that in all
> the cities, towns and villages of those kingdoms, the streets and marketplaces were
> so thronged by the immense number of corpses that a [traveller] could scarcely
> make his way through them.[11]

One of the 'travellers' was the Cornish merchant Peter Mundy, who recorded
distressing details of the famine in his *Journal*. He witnessed parents

> driven to that extremity for want of food that they sold their children for 12, 6 and
> [even fewer] pence a piece; yea, and to give them away to any that would take
> them... No less lamentable was it to see the poor people scraping on the dunghills
> for food, yea the very excrement of beasts, as horses, oxen, etc, belonging to travel-
> lers, for grain that perchance might come undigested from them, and that with
> great greediness ...

Like the Mughal chronicler, Mundy noted that 'All the highways were so full of dead
bodies that we could hardly pass from them without treading on or going over
some.' Other Europeans commented on the 'Universal dearth over all this continent, of whose like no former age has record, the country being wholly dismantled
by drought', and noted that the 'weavers, washers, dyers' abandoned 'their habitations in multitudes', only to perish 'in the fields for want of food to sustain them.'
Then, in 1632, 'At last it pleased God to send rain, but in so great abundance that it
drowned and carried away all the corn and other grain.' The region suffered 'such
inundations as have not been known or heard of in those parts', unleashing water-
borne epidemics, above all malaria and dengue fever, with the result that 'Not a
family' escaped 'agues, fevers and pestilential diseases ... so that the times here are
so miserable that never in the memory of man [has] any the like famine and
mortality happened' (Plate 17).[12]

Although no census and (as yet) no 'natural archive' exists to quantify the scale of the disaster, Peter Mundy believed that 'The famine itself swept away more than a million of the common or poorer sort; after which the mortality succeeding did as much more amongst rich and poor.' Foreigners did not escape: of the 21 Englishmen living in the East India Company's factory at Surat in 1630, 17 died in the following three years – a mortality rate of over 80 per cent. In Goa, 500 miles to the south, the viceroy of Portuguese India estimated that famine and plague had killed four million Mughal subjects, and (he claimed) although a hardened soldier he could hardly bring himself to recount the suffering he had seen.[13]

As usual during such climatically induced catastrophes, the purchasing power of most families fell as food prices rose, and since buying staples now absorbed almost all their income, the demand for services and manufactured goods fell. At the same time, high prices for staples encouraged farmers to plant more grain and fewer 'industrial crops'. Both manufacture and trade therefore atrophied, producing unemployment among artisans and transportation workers. In Gujarat, trade and industry came to a standstill. Even in 1634 the English merchants at Surat found no textiles for sale on account of

> The great price which all sorts of grain has yielded for some years past, which has undoubtedly disposed the country people to those courses which have been most profitable for them, and so [they] discontinued the planting of cotton, which could not have been vented [sold] in the proportion of former times, because the artificers and mechanics of all sorts were so miserably dead or fled.[14]

In the event, neither the production of cotton nor indigo in the region *ever* recovered their previous levels. The famine thus proved the 'universal calamity of this country', because what 'was in a manner the garden of the world is now turned into a wilderness, having few or no men left to manure their ground, nor to labour in any profession; so that places here that have yielded 15 bails [bales of] cloth made there in a day hardly yield now 3 [bales] in a month'. Ahmadabad, the capital of Gujarat, 'that likewise yielded 3,000 bails of indigo yearly or more, now hardly yields 300'. Peter Mundy predicted that with 'the country in a manner desolate, scarce one left of ten . . . in my opinion it will hardly recover its former estate in fifteen, nay in twenty years'.[15]

Welfare State versus Warfare State

Mundy's forecast proved too pessimistic only because Shah Jahan used some of the vast resources at his disposal to respond to the disaster with a series of measures eschewed by most other rulers of the time. First he established soup kitchens and almshouses 'for the benefit of the poor and destitute. Every day sufficient soup and bread was prepared to satisfy the wants of the hungry.' At this time the emperor resided in the capital of one of the Hindu states of the Deccan he had recently conquered, and he ordered that, as long as he remained there, '5,000 rupees should be distributed among the deserving poor every Monday, that day being distinguished above all others as the day of the emperor's accession to the throne. Thus, on twenty Mondays, one *lach* [100,000] of rupees was given away in charity.' Moreover, since 'Ahmadabad had suffered more severely than any other place', Shah Jahan 'ordered the officials to distribute 50,000 rupees among the famine-stricken people'; while, since 'want and dearness of grain had caused great distress in many other countries', he 'forgave' taxes worth seven million rupees, 'amounting to one-eleventh part of the whole revenue' in order to 'restore the country to its former flourishing condition and the people to affluence and contentment'. The emperor ordered his major vassals to take similar steps.[16]

Once the monsoons resumed their normal rhythm, Shah Jahan sponsored a number of initiatives to promote economic recovery: he donated ploughs to the poor as he visited each region, 'so that the forests might be cleared and land cultivated' in order 'to populate the country'; and he and his principal courtiers founded hundreds of market towns. The emperor also took steps to increase exports. He sponsored the cultivation of cotton, sugar cane, silk, tobacco and indigo in Bengal to attract European merchants; and, since the newcomers paid for what they bought with silver bullion, their purchases stimulated rapid growth in the regional economy and also produced vast customs revenues for the emperor. Shah Jahan ordered the construction of great ships in Gujarat, which allowed him to participate in the lucrative carrying trade between Mughal India and the Persian Gulf and Red Sea. Thanks to this combination of 'tax breaks' and 'stimulus spending', within a decade Gujarat (as well as other regions) once again reported a revenue surplus. In the opinion of Indian economic historian Tapan Raychaudhuri, although 'it would perhaps be an exaggeration to say that the Mughal age saw the emergence of an integrated national market', nevertheless 'the commercial ties which bound together different parts of the empire had no precedent'.[17]

Expenditure on famine relief still left Shah Jahan with plenty of money to spend on other things: ten million rupees on his 'Peacock Throne', encrusted with jewels; seven million on the Taj Mahal (a sumptuous mausoleum for his late wife); seven million more on Shahjahanabad; and almost a million on creating the Shalimar gardens at Lahore. He also waged war almost constantly. The illustrated chronicle by Abdul Hamid Lahori, based on documents in the state archives, devoted well over half its pages and images to campaigns by the emperor's forces against the Hindu states of the Deccan and against the Portuguese in Bengal. In the northwest, Shah Jahan also campaigned against the Sikhs, led by Guru Hargobind, the sixth 'master' of the faith, whose predecessor had been captured and executed by Jahangir. This action radicalized the Sikhs, who had previously eschewed violence, and Guru Hargobind encouraged martial training and built up armed forces that repulsed four Mughal assaults. Nevertheless, even after all this expenditure during his first two decades on the throne, Shah Jahan had accumulated a reserve of 95 million rupees.

Three reasons explain this unique fiscal outcome. First, the productivity of both rural and urban workers, coupled with the fertility of many areas under Mughal rule, yielded high tax revenues. Second, Shah Jahan's wars often turned a profit – both in booty and in the massive number of Hindu captives sold into slavery in Central Asia. Finally, the emperor limited his expenditure on foreign-policy goals. Although the Mughals campaigned in the Deccan, they never seem to have contemplated an attack on the Tamil lands further south or on Sri Lanka; and although they expanded into Bengal and founded Jahangirnaga (now Dhaka), a Mughal city that by 1640 numbered over 200,000 inhabitants, they made no serious plans to advance into Burma. As Sanjay Subrahmanyam has observed: 'We may see the Mughal empire as an unfinished project, in a territorial sense, but also as one that had a proper sense of its limits.'[18] The sole area of imprudence was Afghanistan.

Afghanistan: The Perpetual Battleground

The Mughals prided themselves on their direct descent from both Chinggis Khan and Timur (Tamerlane), and their official chronicles frequently noted plans to recapture Central Asia, their ancestral home; but only Shah Jahan attempted to achieve this goal. According to his historians, 'the mighty soul of the world-subduing monarch had been bent upon' conquering the lands 'which were properly his hereditary domains' ever since 'the time of the last emperor Jahangir's death' in 1627. Twelve years later, Mughal troops seized Qandahar in southern Afghanistan from its Safavid defenders, and the emperor and a massive entourage crossed the Khyber Pass for the first time. They spent the summer at Kabul while they prepared to conquer the lands beyond, 'which were once included in the kingdom of his imperial ancestors', but the Uzbeks, who had occupied the Mughal 'homeland' ever since expelling Shah Jahan's ancestors more than a century before, mounted such an effective defence that the emperor's 'mighty soul' decided to return to India.[19] Then a succession dispute arose between two Uzbek rulers, one of whom appealed for Mughal assistance. In spring 1646 Shah Jahan therefore returned to Kabul, whence a Mughal army at last crossed the Hindu Kush and occupied the fertile alluvial plain around the great trading city of Balkh. When news of this success reached the emperor, still at Kabul, he hosted a party that lasted eight days and wrote a boastful letter to the shah of Iran predicting that his troops would soon also take Timur's former capital, Samarkand.

Admittedly, Shah Jahan had much to boast about. His armies had overcome remarkable logistical obstacles in crossing the Khyber Pass (3,000 feet above sea level) to Kabul, more than 800 miles from the Mughal capital, and in advancing a further 200 miles over the Salang Pass (almost 12,000 feet above sea level) to Balkh. His expeditionary force was probably the largest ever to enter the region before the Soviet invasion of 1979. Nevertheless, even at the best of times, Afghanistan lacked both the crop surpluses and the credit networks required to feed a large slow-moving army like that of Shah Jahan – and the Little Ice Age was far from the best of times. Unusually heavy snowfalls in the 1640s reduced both the campaign season and the quantity of supplies that could be brought over the passes from India, while a shorter growing season throughout the Himalayan region reduced local crop yields. Both factors made the Mughal troops dependent on what they could forage from the countryside, but the 'scorched-earth' policy pursued by the Uzbeks made foraging impossible. So although the gold, jewels, silk and brocade of the imperial army, as well as their weapons, horses and war elephants, initially impressed the population of Balkh, the winter of 1646–7 brought such intense cold that the Mughal garrisons 'burned themselves in the fires they lit for warmth, and no one left their house for fear of being frozen'.[20]

Rather than give up, in spring 1647 the emperor returned to Kabul for the third time while his son Aurangzeb led another army across the Hindu Kush. The prince used his war elephants as well as his new troops to defeat Uzbek counter-attacks (incidentally winning immense renown when he calmly dismounted in the middle of a battle to perform his ritual prayers), but three months later he had to admit defeat and abandon Balkh. The Central Asian 'wolves' now closed in and captured large numbers of Indian 'slave sheep' as they retreated. Many of them did eventually see Samarkand, but as slaves: prisoners from the Mughal army were so numerous that the price of Indians in the slave markets of Central Asia fell by two-thirds. It took Aurangzeb and the survivors a month to regain Kabul, arriving just in time to accompany the emperor back across the Khyber Pass.[21]

The Mughals' spectacular failure encouraged Shah Abbas II of Iran to demand the return of Qandahar and, when no satisfactory answer came, in 1649 his forces recaptured the city. Shah Jahan promptly returned to Kabul, but even his official chronicler noted that at the siege of Qandahar the Mughals had brought 'with them neither a siege train of battering guns, nor skilled artillerymen'. Therefore, when 'grain and fodder were beginning to get scarce' after 14 weeks, the emperor recognized that 'the reduction of the fortress without the aid of heavy guns was impracticable' and withdrew his troops. In 1651 he tried again, this time bringing a few siege guns, but two 'cracked from constant firing' and became 'quite unserviceable', while although the other five 'continued to be discharged, yet as they were not served by scientific artillerymen, their fire was not so effective as could be wished'. Once again, the besiegers ignominiously withdrew. In 1652 Shah Jahan made one more attempt to take Qandahar; but after 'five months, the winter began to set in, all the lead, powder and cannon-balls were expended, and neither was there any forage left in the meadows, nor provisions with the army', and so the survivors and their emperor retreated. They never returned.[22]

Shah Jahan's efforts had advanced the Mughal frontier scarcely 30 miles beyond Kabul, yet it resulted in 'the killing of thirty to forty thousand' soldiers and the expenditure of over 35 million rupees.[23] The war also caused extensive damage to Afghanistan – Qandahar became an almost permanent battleground – but the fragmentary nature of the surviving sources makes it extremely difficult to assess the exact impact. The records of the shrine at Mazar-e Sharif ('Tomb of the holy one'), close to Balkh, shed a rare beam of light. The shrine had prospered in the earlier seventeenth century as local Afghan rulers granted lands and founded *medreses*, until its activities involved over 3,000 people either as producers or consumers; but when Mughal troops entered the valley, the local merchants and many farmers fled, so that in their first year the army of occupation collected only half of the previous year's revenues, and in their second year only half of that. Grain prices skyrocketed, and firewood (essential for survival at that altitude) could not be found. The Uzbeks invaded after the Mughals withdrew, and only in 1668 did the administrator of the shrine dare to leave Mazar-e Sharif to secure a charter from the nearest ruler that restored the lands and revenues lost 'because of the turmoil in the world'.[24]

The Crisis of Mughal India

Shah Jahan's eldest son, and his favourite, Dara Shikoh, resided with him at court and boasted *jagirs* (fiefs) almost equal to those of his three brothers combined. In contrast, the three younger sons resided in distant provinces as the emperor's representatives, and from time to time he entrusted them with command of major campaigns. Shah Jahan intended this arrangement to avoid any rebellion similar to the one that he and his brothers had mounted against their father, Jahangir, but he reckoned without the ambition, ability and charisma of his third son, Aurangzeb. In 1636, aged 18, the prince began to govern the newly conquered regions of the Deccan for his father. Over the next eight years Aurangzeb took a personal interest in all aspects of the administration and built up a retinue of loyal followers whom he rewarded with lands acquired in frontier warfare. He constructed a new city, which he named Aurangabad, and both there and in his conquests he made lavish grants to individual mosques and *medreses*; forged ties with religious zealots; and encouraged conversion to Islam by new subjects.

This military prowess in the Deccan led Shah Jahan to entrust the reconquest of Central Asia to Aurangzeb and, although his efforts failed, the prince gained valuable experience of command. He also became convinced that his brother Dara Shikoh had held back supplies and reinforcements for his campaigns, and so in 1652 Aurangzeb met his two other siblings to 'make plans for the preservation of their life and honour and the management of their affairs' in case the emperor suddenly died.[25] Aurangzeb then returned to the Deccan where, in preparation for the inevitable succession struggle, he developed links with religious leaders and ethnic groups whom Shah Jahan had failed to integrate into the imperial fabric. He also built up a cadre of talented and devoted military officers, and with their assistance he led successful campaigns against the empire's southern neighbours that secured substantial treasure and tribute. Aurangzeb thus possessed immense political, military and financial resources when, late in 1657, rumours spread that the emperor 'was unable to attend to business' through illness and that Dara Shikoh had taken 'the opportunity of seizing the reins of power'.[26] The princes governing Gujarat and Bengal at once seized the local treasuries, issued their own coinage and had Friday prayers read in their name.

The ailing emperor responded by charging Dara Shikoh with restoring order; but the prince foolishly divided his forces and sent armies simultaneously against both usurpers. Aurangzeb now joined his rebellious sibling in Gujarat, but skilfully ensured that his brother's troops took heavier casualties in the decisive battle.

Therefore when Dara Shikoh retreated, Aurangzeb's troops secured Agra and, with it, the imperial treasury, the principal arsenal and the person of Shah Jahan. The emperor now offered to partition the empire among his sons, but Aurangzeb, confident that he could triumph alone, declared himself emperor and undertook campaigns against each of his brothers in turn, executing them and any of their sons who defied him. He kept his father in prison until he died.

Unfortunately for the new emperor's subjects, as a Mughal chronicler observed, 'The disturbances and the movement of large armies for two years [1658–60] in different parts of the empire, particularly in the northern and eastern territories', coincided with another 'failure of the monsoons'. In Delhi, grain prices rose precipitously, and in an attempt to reverse the process Aurangzeb abolished 'more than eighty taxes' as 'a relief measure to lessen the hardships caused by the rising prices of grain'.[27] Nevertheless in 1659 southeast India saw 'so great a famine' that, according to resident English merchants, 'the people [are] dying daily for want of food', while in Gujarat 'the famine and plague' became 'so great' that (as in 1630–2) they 'swept away the most part of the people, and those that are left are few'. The monsoon failed again in 1660, and the same English merchants lamented the 'great dearth' in the southeast 'now these eighteen months'; while their colleagues in Gujarat believed that 'never famine raged worse in any place, the living being hardly able to bury the dead'.[28]

Meanwhile, according to a Mughal chronicler, 'the scarcity of rains' caused famine in the Ganges plain:

> The scarcity of foodstuffs grew every day and the poverty of the destitute people increased to such an extent that most of the *parganahs* [administrative units] became desolate. Large crowds of people from distant parts of the country and from the vicinity of the capital took the road to the city.

Aurangzeb set up ten 'free feeding houses' in his capital, with more in surrounding communities, 'besides the permanent public distributing centres of cooked and uncooked food', and he obliged the leading noblemen to do the same. He also reissued his edict abolishing taxes until 'at last a change for the better appeared in the condition of the people'.[29] It did not last. In 1662 a major fire destroyed large parts of Shahjahanabad, while the price of grain in Gujarat approached famine levels because the 'very little rain this last year' was 'not sufficient to produce corn except in some particular places, and [even] there not more than half and quarter crops'. The English merchants feared that the extreme drought would 'utterly dispeople all these parts' because 'there are more than 500 families of weavers that are already fled, and the rest will certainly follow, if the famine should increase'.[30] Although the 1664 monsoon was normal, 'the past year's dearth' produced widespread disease in Gujarat, where 'all these towns and villages hereabouts are full of sickness, scarce a house free'. Meanwhile, famine, drought and disease also caused a sharp increase in the price of staples in Bengal; and, in the south, Kerala experienced three years of drought.[31]

A French physician residing in Delhi noted in 1668 that 'of the vast tracts of country constituting the empire of Hindustan, many are little more than sand, or barren mountains, badly cultivated, and thinly peopled; and even a considerable portion of the good land remains untilled from want of labourers'; while a new revenue survey compiled for Aurangzeb's treasury showed that receipts from the ten core provinces of the empire had fallen 20 per cent below pre-war levels. The civil war also allowed Shivaji, a Maratha nobleman, to build up a powerful Hindu state that would defy and even defeat the Mughals (Shivaji sacked Surat, their principal port, in 1664 and again in 1670).[32]

Although Shireen Moosvi, an economic historian, has suggested that the crisis of 1658–70 formed the watershed between Mughal expansion and decline, the empire continued to expand for four decades more.[33] In the 1670s Aurangzeb captured, tried and executed the charismatic Sikh leader Tegh Bahadur, and thus halted a movement that had won both Hindu and Muslim converts; and in the 1680s he defeated a Rajput revolt led by one of his own sons, conquered the Deccan kingdoms of Bijapur and Golconda, and captured and executed the leader of the Maratha confederacy. After these spectacular successes, Aurangzeb seems to have forgotten his own advice that 'It is bad for both emperors and water to remain at the same place' (page 400 above), because he spent 27 years campaigning against the Marathas in the Deccan, despite monsoon failures in 1686 and 1687 (both years of intense El Niño activity and weak monsoons), which intensified the deleterious effects of his campaigns. According to the English merchants in the city, 35,000 people died in Madras while parents gave away their children and adults sold themselves into slavery in order to avoid starvation.[34] Nevertheless, when the emperor died in 1707, despite spending millions on war, his treasury contained 240 million rupees – far more than the total left by previous rulers and almost certainly more than the resources of any other ruler in the world. Throughout the seventeenth century, the yield of taxes, tribute and plunder always exceeded the needs of the Mughal state. Nevertheless, Aurangzeb's Rajput, Sikh and Maratha neighbours all stood poised to exploit the inevitable succession war that erupted immediately after his death. Even the wealthiest state in the world could not overcome the weaknesses caused by 'bloody tanistry'.

Southeast Asia: Turning Plenty into Poverty

Several rulers in the Indonesian archipelago in the early seventeenth century also boasted vast wealth – and for much the same reasons as the Mughal emperors: the tax yield from unusually fertile land and profitable commerce, combined with few wars. Nevertheless, also like Mughal India, their lands suffered from the unusual frequency of both El Niño and volcanic events in the mid-seventeenth century. Although most of the archipelago normally receives 4 inches or more of rainfall *every month* (there is no 'dry season'), tree-rings from central Java between 1643 and 1671 reveal the longest period of low rainfall ever recorded. Not a single year during this period received the normal amount of rain, and 1664 was the driest year recorded in the last five centuries. Surviving written sources from Java, the most densely populated island, show famines in six years and poor rice harvests in ten more between 1633 and 1665, while those from the outer islands of the archipelago show famines in two years and poor rice harvests in ten more, with universal shortfalls in four years: 1633, 1657, 1660 and 1664 (Fig. 40).[35]

Three natural advantages mitigated these effects of the Little Ice Age. First, since the archipelago straddles the equator, changes in solar energy had less impact: a fall in mean temperatures there is far less serious than in more northerly latitudes. Even during the great drought, abundant arable land remained available. According to Francisco de Alcina, an envious European visitor in the 1660s, 'many and very extensive lands remain, lacking anyone to cultivate them. Although it is true that each village or populated area has its own boundaries ... anyone who comes to settle among them, even though he was never seen or heard of, is given an option to select voluntarily all and as much land as he might wish, without asking him for a cent for it.' Second, the tropical climate and fertile soil of the archipelago allowed a wide variety of edible crops to flourish, some of them resistant to adverse weather. William Marsden, who visited Sumatra, noted that if their staple crop failed, people turned 'to those wild roots, herbs, and leaves of trees, which the woods abundantly afford in every season'. Therefore, Marsden continued, 'failures of crops or grain are never attended with those dreadful consequences which more improved countries and more provident nations experience'.[36] Third, the densely populated coastal areas managed to avoid some consequences of the drought by importing rice from unaffected areas. Above all, the ships of the Dutch East India Company normally brought rice from India to relieve famines, because crop failures in the archipelago and in the subcontinent rarely coincided.[37] For all these reasons, although 20 million people inhabited the Indonesian islands in the mid-seventeenth century, few of them starved. The situation changed when, despite such natural abundance, human agency managed to create a crisis.

The eagerness of several groups of merchants – Portuguese, Dutch, English, Muslim, Chinese and Japanese – to acquire individual spices (nutmeg on the Banda Islands, clove on Amboina, and so on) inexorably led to monoculture: each island concentrated on cultivating cash crops and abandoned all others. Until the 1630s, local growers prospered and, thanks to export taxes, so did their rulers; but this state of affairs changed rapidly as political and military events closed off one market after another. First, in 1638, the Japanese government prohibited all foreign trade both by its own subjects and by the Portuguese (see chapter 3 above); then in 1641 the Dutch East India Company captured Melaka from Portugal and thus gained a stranglehold over all ships passing through the Straits; finally after 1644 Chinese maritime trade contracted during the Ming-Qing transition. These three developments conferred enormous commercial advantages on the Dutch. On the one hand, they exploited their control of the sea lanes to exclude competitors, especially the Muslim traders and intermediaries who had grown rich from the long-distance commerce in high-value spices, and to increase the price of the food they imported to Indonesia. According to one estimate, rice prices quintupled once the Dutch wrested control of the import trade from their indigenous competitors. On the other hand, the Dutch could always blockade the ports of producers

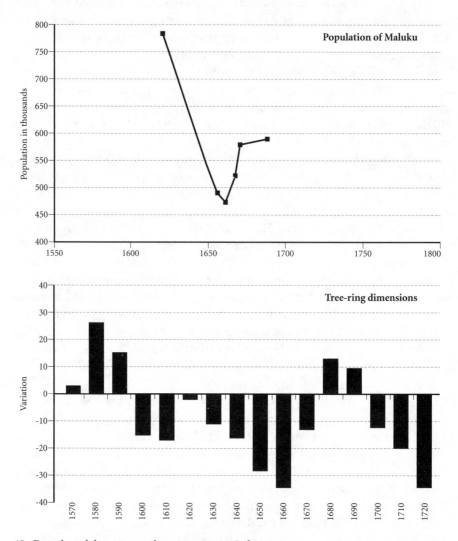

40. Drought and the seventeenth-century crisis in Indonesia.
The dramatic fall in the population of Maluku, a group of spice-producing islands in the Indonesian archipelago, exactly paralleled the longest and most severe drought in the region's recorded history.

dependent on imported foodstuffs, creating an artificial famine that compelled the victims to sell spices cheap. In the 1650s, for example, pepper prices fell by half.[38]

The falling price of spices and the rising cost of food staples had profound consequences for the peoples of the archipelago. Some destroyed their pepper vines and reintroduced rice cultivation because, in the words of a verse epic composed in Acheh, the largest Muslim state of the archipelago:

> Marketing does not yield much profit, even if you grow pepper, my friends.
> If there is no rice in the country, nothing else will be of use ...
> If there is nothing to eat, your children will starve and you will have to sell all you possess...
> What can you feed on if there is no food?
> If there is no rice in the country, the entire country starves.

Other rulers in Monsoon Asia stopped producing spices for reasons of security. One Muslim prince forbade his subjects to plant pepper 'so that they did not thereby get involved in war, whether with the [Dutch] or with other potentates'.[39] Achieving this outcome was easier said than done, because the Dutch usually attacked in alliance with a rival 'potentate'. Thus, in southern Sulawesi, the sultans of the prosperous port-city of Makassar overran the neighbouring state of Bone and then defied Dutch pressure to grant then monopoly trading privileges, instead welcoming all traders. They prudently invested some of the resulting revenues in constructing a large fortress (Sombaopu) around the royal palace which, on the seaward side, boasted walls 14 feet thick with four bastions equipped with heavy guns donated by Danish, English and Portuguese traders, all of whom maintained factories in the city. After the fall of Melaka in 1641, between 2,000 and 3,000 Portuguese transferred their activities to Makassar, and the sultanate enjoyed unprecedented prosperity until Arung Palakka, the exiled prince of Bone, sought Dutch help. In 1667, at Palakka's request, Dutch warships bombarded the new fortifications of Makassar until they had secured important trading concessions. Two years later, claiming that the sultan had breached the agreement, the allies returned and took the city by siege. Arung Palakka now became the new sultan of Makassar, while the Dutch created a citadel from which they controlled all seaborne commerce in southern Sulawesi. A verse epic written just after the allied victory expresses local sentiment:

> Listen, sirs, to my advice:
> Never make friends with the Dutch.
> Possessed of a sort of devilish cunning,
> No country can call itself safe when they're around.[40]

The war between Makassar and the Dutch came at a high cost for all protagonists: it left much of Makassar in ruins and, although the Dutch eventually gained from the elimination of a competitor, several decades passed before profits from trade equalled the cost of the two naval expeditions.

The First World War: The Dutch versus the Portuguese

The Dutch also ran up heavy losses fighting the Portuguese in what the distinguished historian Charles Boxer christened 'the first world war', because it took place on all four continents as well as on the seas around them.[41] Throughout the 1630s Dutch warships blockaded Goa, the capital of Portuguese India, and its profitable outposts in Monsoon Asia: Sri Lanka (Ceylon), Melaka and Macao, all of which depended on the ability to export high-value cargoes. In 1640 an English merchant in India observed that the Portuguese were 'in a most miserable predicament: Melaka and Ceylon besieged and (the Dutch say) as good as seized; their galleons fired; their soldiers decayed; themselves disheartened'. Unless 'sudden and ample succour from Europe reinforce them,' he predicted, the Portuguese would plunge to their 'utter ruin, while the insolent Dutch domineer in all places, styling themselves already kings of the Indian seas'.[42] Shortly afterwards a new viceroy arrived in Goa with reinforcements from Lisbon; but when, a year later, news arrived of Portugal's revolt against Spanish rule, he – like virtually all the Portuguese in Asia – declared for the new regime headed by King John IV (see chapter 9 above).

The new monarch could not defend all his overseas possessions against the Dutch, however. Even as he wrote to advise the viceroy in Goa of his accession, he warned that 'as greatly as I might want to help India', he could send no funds because 'at present it is necessary to spend much money to secure our frontiers against Spain'. The viceroy responded emphatically that, in that case, 'it is necessary to make a peace or truce with the Dutch in these parts at once – at once! – because they are so powerful and the forces of Your Majesty are so weak'. Without an immediate peace, the viceroy continued relentlessly, 'Your Majesty should arrange with the same urgency to send relief each and every year. Right now we need at least eight or ten powerful galleons, absolutely full of soldiers, sailors, artillery and money.'[43] But the new government in Lisbon had other priorities: not only the defence of the homeland but also the recovery of Brazil from Dutch control – indeed, King John and his council discussed the affairs of Brazil four times more frequently than those of India, having decided that 'Asia, by reason of its distance and its size, is more difficult and costly and less useful to conserve', and that therefore 'we should give up in Asia as much as we need to, in order to leave us free [to act] in Brazil'.[44] So, 'each and every year', King John sent a letter to his viceroy in Goa apologizing for not sending galleons 'absolutely full of soldiers, sailors, artillery and money' because of the paramount need to defend both Portugal and Brazil.

The king's subjects in Asia deeply resented their new sovereign's neglect, and some of them staged armed protests. The first outbreak occurred in the port-city of Macao, near Canton in China, with a population of perhaps 30,000. Although its inhabitants, like Portuguese settlers elsewhere, enthusiastically welcomed the 'Restoration' of independence, the news arrived at the city just after the loss of Melaka and Japan's decision to end all trade with the Portuguese. These two events ruined most of the city's merchants. In 1643–4 a group of Spaniards, supported by some of the local clergy, almost managed to retake the city for Philip IV; then in

1646 the unpaid garrison mutinied and a group of irate citizens murdered the governor. In accordance with his 'Brazil-first' policy, King John instructed his officials in Asia to 'dissimulate in order to avoid causing another disturbance': they must not try to identify (let alone punish) the murderers.[45] Six years later, frustrated by the absence of state support against the Dutch, a group of Portuguese colonists in Sri Lanka also rebelled. Yelling 'Long live the faith of Christ! Death to bad government!', they entered Colombo, the largest Portuguese fortress in Sri Lanka, where they imprisoned the royal governor and replaced him with their leader. In 1653 Goa also rebelled. Deprived by the Dutch of both seaborne trade and lucrative plantations in Sri Lanka, the capital of Portuguese Asia – formerly a thriving city of some 75,000 Europeans, Indians and Africans but now, thanks to the Dutch blockade, reduced to 'only one-third of the inhabitants it used to have' and with 'many parts depopulated, and the majority of its houses in ruins'. A group of frustrated Portuguese colonists deposed the viceroy and installed a successor by 'acclamation' (a significant term, since it had been used in Lisbon at the ceremony recognizing John IV as the new ruler). They 'gave as justification that Portugal had done the same, and so had the people of England – while, near at hand', they added, 'Ceylon had done it'.[46]

Although royal agents would eventually suppress all three insurrections, the Portuguese empire in Asia never recovered from the mid-seventeenth century crisis. At his accession in 1640, John IV controlled 26 outposts stretching from Sofala in Africa to Macao in China, but only 16 remained when his son made peace with the Dutch in 1663. As Manuel Godinho, a Jesuit long resident in Portuguese India, eloquently put it, the empire that had 'formerly dominated the whole of the east, and comprised eight thousand leagues of sovereignty' had now atrophied so that 'If it has not expired altogether, it is because it has not found a tomb worthy of its former greatness. If it was a tree, it is now a branch; if it was a building, it is now a ruin; if it was a man, it is now a limb; it was a giant, it is now a pigmy; if it was great, it is now nothing.' Portugal controlled only the outposts 'that our enemies have left us, either as a memorial of how much we formerly possessed in Asia, or else as a bitter reminder of the little which we now have there'.[47]

Godinho's eloquent epitaph nevertheless failed to explain why Portugal had lost most of its empire in Asia *to the Dutch Republic* – an even smaller state. Many Portuguese blamed the problems posed by distance: as one viceroy plaintively reminded the king, 'Sire, India is a long way off, and its voice can only be heard very late and very faint' in Lisbon.[48] There was, of course, some truth in this – the return journey between Lisbon and Goa involved sailing 24,000 miles and spending 300 days at sea – but Amsterdam lay even further than Lisbon from Goa (as well as from Colombo and Melaka, both of which the Dutch captured). Even if the Little Ice Age affected the wind patterns in the Atlantic and Indian Oceans so that journeys took even longer, as happened in the Pacific (page 16 above), they would have affected Dutch no less than Portuguese vessels.

The outcome of the 'first world war' reflected human rather than natural differences. The Portuguese ambassador in the Dutch Republic summed them up bitterly in 1649: 'In our country,' he complained, '*it takes two months to do what others do in two hours*. Above all, the Portuguese repeatedly failed to get the annual fleet bound for Goa ready to depart before the end of March, despite the fact that (in the words of an irate viceroy in 1650) 'any ship which left Lisbon after the first day of April could only reach Goa in the same year by a miracle'. Significantly, the irate viceroy wrote these words from southwest Africa after his fleet, having set sail on 21 April, ran aground and was wrecked.[49] John IV's ministers agreed: just the previous year they lamented that 'It is painful to see the enemies of your royal crown so favoured in their conquests and voyages, for out of nine ships not one is lost, and of those of Your Majesty which go and come there is such miserable news'. And indeed the surviving records show that the Dutch lost *only one out of every twenty* ships sailing to Asia during the mid-seventeenth century, whereas the Portuguese lost *one out of every three*.[50] This striking disparity arose only partly from the superior ability of the Dutch to get their outbound fleets to sea in good time: it also reflected the superiority of the entire Dutch command and control system over that of the Portuguese.

Above all the Portuguese crown, which directly controlled all Asian initiatives, entrusted almost all positions of responsibility in their empire to noblemen who not only lacked practical experience themselves, but also refused to listen to their social but competent inferiors. Hence Portuguese troops repeatedly ran into ambushes because the *fidalgo* in charge rejected advice from the professional soldiers under his command, while many Portuguese ships foundered because the noblemen in command disregarded the views of the mariners aboard. Moreover, many Portuguese colonial administrators were egregiously corrupt and incompetent. As one crown official reminded a critic preparing to leave Goa for Lisbon: 'You can go and say whatever you like in Portugal, for when the punishment comes thence, either Portuguese India will no longer exist or else we will no longer be around. . . This place is a long way off from Portugal.'[51]

Dutch Asia, by contrast, was controlled directly by the 17 'directors' of the United East India Company, whose primary concern was to make money. They therefore entrusted executive power to men of proven talent, irrespective of their background. The three most successful 'Governors-General of India' during the mid-seventeenth century were all improbable choices: Antonio van Diemen (1636–45) had fled to Batavia as a bankrupt using a false name; Johan Maetsuycker (1653–78) was a Catholic trained at the university of Louvain in the Spanish Netherlands; and Rijkloff van Goens (1678–81) was born in Germany. These men combined an ambitious vision with a steely determination to reject any advice or even commands from their superiors with which they disagreed. Van Diemen proved particularly successful, using the 85 warships at his command to coordinate attacks on Goa, Sri Lanka and Melaka while sending Abel Tasman on a voyage that placed Tasmania (originally named Van Diemen's Land), New Zealand and Fiji on European maps for the first time. When in 1641 van Diemen received a reproach from the company's directors in Holland for taking too many risks, he reminded them of his recent successes (notably the capture of Melaka) before continuing defiantly 'We have said, and by this letter confirm, *that the affairs of Asia must be entrusted to us*; and therefore we cannot wait for orders if we are to serve the Company. Your Honours

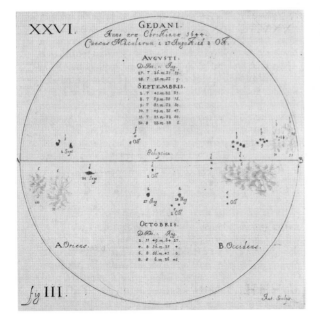

1 Sunspot observations by Johannes Hevelius in Danzig, 1644. (See page 13.)
Hevelius, a brewer, and his wife noted all the sunspots they observed, and later created composite disks that recorded their movement (in this case between 27 August and 8 October 1644), a task facilitated by the relative absence of spots between the 1640s and the 1710s. With the insouciance characteristic of the age, Hevelius published these solar observations as an appendix to his book about the moon.

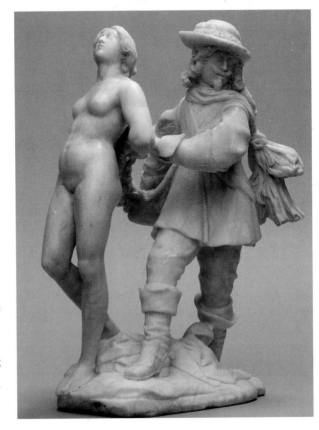

2 Leonhard Kern, 'Scene from the Thirty Years War'. (See page 31.)
This shocking alabaster sculpture, carved in the 1640s, shows a Swedish officer abducting a young naked woman, presumably to rape her. In preparation, he has tied her hands and presses his blade into her back.

3 King Charles I exchanges his worldly crown for a crown of thorns. (See page 41.)
While in prison, Charles 'set down the private reflections of my conscience, and my most impartial thoughts, touching the chief passages . . . in my late troubles', in a book called *Eikon Basilike* ('The king's image'). Printed copies circulated on the day of his execution, 30 January 1649, and 35 English and 25 foreign editions had appeared by year's end.

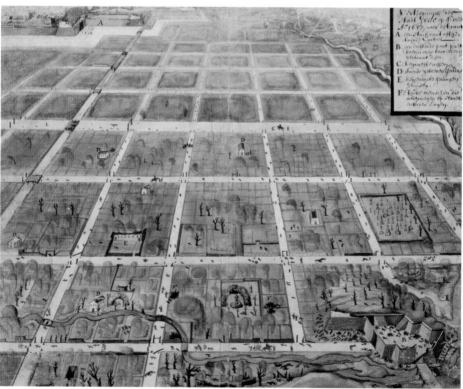

4 'Drawing of the city of Edo on 4 March 1657 after the fire'. (See page 63.)
Zacharias Wagenaer, a Dutch merchant who had trained as a draughtsman, graphically depicted the desolation caused by the Meireki fire. Dead bodies lie in the street (F), and the castle of the shogun, once the largest edifice in Japan, lies in ruins (A). Only a few merchant 'Godowns' made of stone remain intact (D).

5 Famine kills: Henan, China. (See page 79.)
In his *Album of the famished* (1688), Yang Dongming, a government inspector, showed how hunger produced suicide. Here, five members of a starving family of seven have hanged themselves from a tree in the garden of the local magistrate whom they blamed for failing to feed them. They leave two young children to fend for themselves.

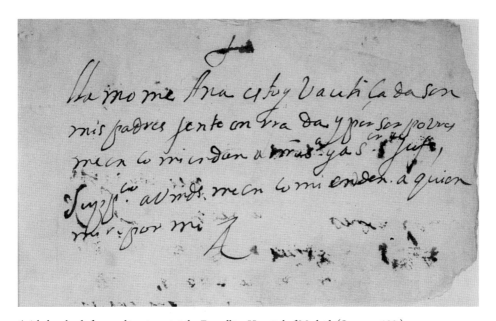

6 A baby pleads for good treatment at the Foundling Hospital of Madrid. (See page 100.)
'My name is Ana' begins the label written by distraught parents when they abandoned their daughter in 1628. It ends: 'I beg you to entrust me to someone who will look after me. A.'

7 Weather in China, 1640 and 1641. (See page 126.)
Chinese historians of climate have reconstructed the prevailing weather in each of the last 500 years by plotting data from local Gazetteers on a scale from 1 (very wet) to 5 (very dry). Both 1640 and 1641 emerge as years of extreme drought in northern China and Manchuria, with abnormal precipitation in parts of the south.

8 A Chinese male undergoes 'tonsorial castration'. (See page 141.)
The Qing edict that all their male subjects must shave their foreheads and wear the rest of their hair in a pigtail provoked widespread opposition not only because it provided unequivocal proof of allegiance to the new dynasty, but also because it required constant repetition. Han Chinese had to re-affirm submission to their conquerors on a regular basis.

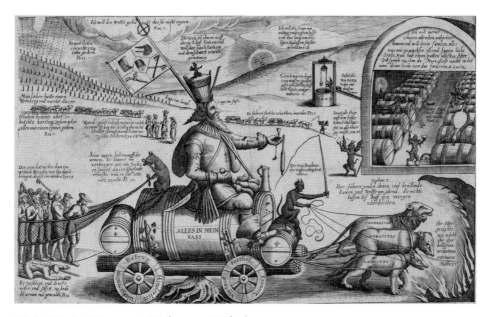

9 'The Wine Jew', Germany, 1629. (See page 220.)
A popular print shows the devil guiding a Jewish wine-merchant to Hell. The upper register records the climatic disasters of the previous 'year without a summer', linked to a Biblical warning. On the left, vineyards are destroyed by torrential rain ('He serves you a storm for a punishment': Psalm 11) and drought ('I will command the clouds not to rain': Isaiah 5:6). In the centre, clouds obscure the sun ('I will make the sun go down at noon and darken the land': Amos 8:9).

10 The 'salt register' for Calle Fuencarral, Madrid, 1631. (See page 259.)
To enforce its new salt monopoly, the Spanish government pre-printed forms where each head of household had to state his or her name, the size of the household, and how much salt it would buy in the coming year. They then either signed it or (like all these householders) authorized the notary to sign 'because they do not know how'.

11 Spanish stamp duty (*Papel Sellado*). (See page 262.) Another fiscal innovation introduced by the Spanish government in the 1630s was 'stamp duty' payable for official transactions. The recipient of this grant, personally signed by the king (*Yo el Rey*), had to pay 272 *maravedis* to the treasury of 'Philip III, the Great' for the paper on which it was written.

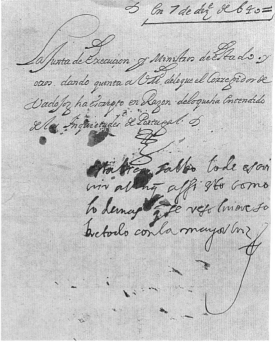

12 Philip IV weeps, 7 December 1640. (See page 277.) A consulta from his 'Executive committee' concerning rumours of 'unrest in Portugal' noted the absence of any news from the duke of Bragança, suggesting that the duke had defected. The tear stains and poor script suggest that Philip lost his self-control as he wrote his response and added his initial (the large 'J' at the end).

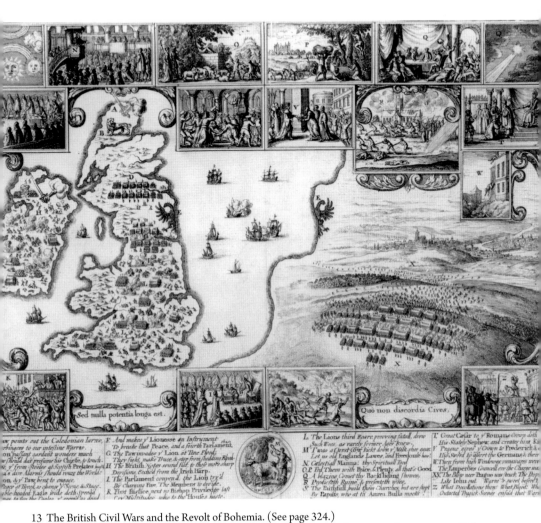

13 The British Civil Wars and the Revolt of Bohemia. (See page 324.)
The Czech engraver Wenceslas Hollar, a fugitive in England, summarized in images the argument of John Rushworth's *Historical Collections* concerning the origins of the Civil Wars. Like Rushworth, Hollar began with the 'blazing comet' and defenestration of Prague in 1618 (Q and W, upper right), leading to the battle of White Mountain (the large right-hand image: X); while in Britain the Edinburgh riots (C, top centre), the pacification of Berwick, the battle of Newburn, the Irish Rebellion (D, G and H, on the large left-hand image), and Charles's attempt to arrest the Five Members (I, bottom centre), combined to produce war.

14 Rioting against the first use of 'Laud's Liturgy' in Edinburgh, 1637. (See page 334.)
Although this crude woodcut implied that only men participated, women took the lead in the rioting that broke out in St Giles Cathedral during the morning service on 23 July 1637.

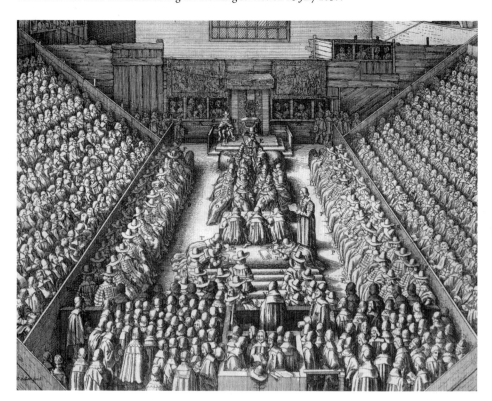

15 The earl of Strafford's impeachment in Westminster Hall, 1641. (See page 344.)
Wenceslas Hollar's engraving shows England's 70 peers (wearing their hats and robes) surrounded by grandstands where almost 600 members of the House of Commons sit bare-headed. Behind Strafford (standing front centre) over 1,000 members of the public who had purchased tickets listened and watched as the trial unfolded.

16 'Now are ye wilde Irisch as well as wee.' (See page 350.)
One of several graphic illustrations that accompanied later propaganda accounts of how Catholics murdered their Protestant neighbours in the uprising that began on 23 October 1641. Note the reference to 'the frost & snowe' – then, as now, a rarity in Ireland.

17 Selling children for food: Henan Province, China. (See page 403.)
Another haunting image from Yang Dongming's *Album of the Famished*, shows one of the desperate acts described by observers of the 'perfect famine' in Gujarat in 1630–2 as well as in China: in the left-hand panel, a starving mother sells her child for a pot of rice, while on the right other mothers line up to do the same.

18 'The revolt of Masaniello' in Naples, 1647, by Micco Spadaro. (See page 438.) In one of the earliest European pictorial records of 'current events,' the young painter Domenico ('Micco' for short) Gargiulo (also known as 'Spadaro' because his family made swords) depicted what happened in the Piazza del Mercato during the first few days of the Naples revolt. On the left, Masaniello speaks to the crowd, as he did on 7 July 1647, while various groups of his followers (including armed bare-footed boys) mill around him. In the centre, the 'Epitaph' displays the naked torso of Don Giuseppe Carafa and the severed heads of others who tried to assassinate Masaniello. In the lower centre, Masaniello rides to meet the viceroy in the silver costume he wore on 11 July. The tower of Santa Maria del Carmine, headquarters of the rebels (upper right), and high-rise apartments dominate the square.

19 The Massacre of the Pequots at Mystic Fort, Connecticut, in 1637. (See page 450.)
The English colonists burst into the palisaded Pequot encampment at Mystic and set fire to 'The Indians
houses'. They then form a circle and use their muskets to shoot down those who try to escape, while a wider
circle of their Native American allies wait to kill with their arrows any Pequots who get past the English.
Recent archaeological excavations suggest that some 400 Pequots died in the massacre.

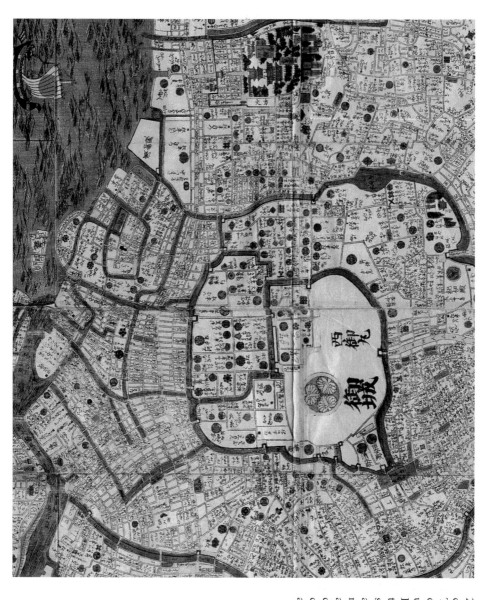

20 Knowledge is power: mapping Edo, capital of Tokugawa Japan. (See page 502.) The central panel of one of the many maps of Edo created from the exhaustive surveys undertaken by the Tokugawa authorities. Edo castle lies at the centre, marked with the trefoil Tokugawa crest in red and gold, surrounded by moats, canals, and rivers, as well as streets, alleys and bridges – all meticulously identified. Temples, shrines, and warehouses are clearly shown; each daimyō complex is identified by names, crests and regalia; commoner residences are left blank.

21 'The Execution of Don Giuseppe Carafa' in Naples, 1647, by Micco Spadaro. (See page 522.)
A striking 'capriccio' shows Masaniello, in his fisherman's overalls and red bonnet, addressing his supporters on 10 July 1647 as they execute and mutilate the noblemen who had just tried to assassinate him. Other members of the crowd wave red flags.

22 'Smoking kills' (See page 602.)
Death, decay and debility dominate the frontispiece to a verse satire by Jakob Balde, S. J., *Dry drunkenness*, published in Latin in 1657 with a German translation the following year. The vomiting smoker in the centre reminds viewers of some side-effects of the habit; while the skeleton on the right, with smoke pouring out of its eye sockets, leaves readers in no doubt where tobacco use leads. Modern anti-smoking images pale in comparison.

Ich ward gleich wie ein phoenix durchsfaier geboren
Ich flog durch die Lüffte? ward doch nicht verloren
Ich wandert im wasser ich streiffte zu Land,
In solchem Umschwermen machts ich mir bekant
was offt mich betrübet und selten ergetzet.
waß war das? Ich habs in dieß Buch hier gesetzt
Damit sich der Leser gleich wie ich ut thu,
entferne der Torheit, und Lebe in Ruh.

23 Frontispiece to Grimmelshausen, *Abenteurlicher Simplicissimus.* (See page 612.) A phoenix, wearing only a sword and bandolier and trampling below its feet several theatrical masks, points to images of war in a book. In an age of limited literacy, images were carefully chosen and this engraving epitomized the message of *The adventures of a German simpleton*: the Thirty Years War is over; Germany has risen from its ashes.

24 The Grand Canal at Tianjin, China, 1656. (See page 622.)
The ingenious pen of Johannes Nieuhof, secretary of a Dutch embassy to the Qing emperor in 1656, captured the bustling scene as his barge reached the end of the Grand Canal at Tianjin, the 'staple' where 'whatsoever vessels are bound for Peking from any other part of China must touch'.

25 The General Bill of Mortality for London, 1665. (See page 630.)
Burials during the year of the Great Plague are organized both by location (upper register: one column for the total, another for plague deaths) and by cause (lower register). The different 'diseases and casualties' include 'Abortive and stillborne' (617) and suicides ('Hang'd & made away themselves' 7). Overall, burials in 1665 numbered 97,306, an increase over the preceding year of 79,009.

26 A fire engine in action during a major freeze, Amsterdam, 1684. (See page 636.) Jan van der Heyden, artist, inventor and fire-master, wrote a book – part description, part sales catalogue – about the powerful new fire engines he designed, capable of pumping water from rivers and canals even when they had iced over. He devoted three pages to how they extinguished a fire in a house on a canal in January 1684 (although he kept secret exactly how the engines worked and how he manufactured the hoses).

27 René Descartes gloats in his study. (See page 649.)
The scholar plants his foot disparagingly on one book labelled 'Aristotle' as he annotates another – surely not the *Discourses* of Galileo, which Descartes purchased on its publication in 1638 only to complain: 'I just spent two hours leafing through it, but I found little there with which to fill the margins'.

28 'A scheme At one View representing to the Eye the Observations of the Weather for a Month', England, 1663. (See page 661.)
Robert Hooke, 'Curator of experiments' for the newly founded Royal Society of Great Britain, proposed to its Fellows a method for collecting data for 'A history of the weather', mobilizing observers in various stations throughout England. Although the 'scheme' came to nothing, the Society's first historian, Thomas Sprat, considered it worthy of commemoration.

A SCHEME

At one View reprefenting to the Eye the Obfervations of the Weather for a Month.

Dayes of the Month and place of the Sun. Remarkable houfe.	Age and fign of the Moon at Noon.	The Quarters of the Wind and its ftrength.	The Degrees of Heat and Cold.	The Degrees of Dryneſs and Moyfture.	The Degrees of Preffure.	The Faces or vifible appearances of the Sky.	The Notableſt Effects.	General Deductions to be made after the fide is fitted with Obfervations: As,
4 8 14 II 12.46 12	27 12 ♉ 9. 46. 4 8 Perigeû.	W. 2. 3. 3½	9 12 16	2 ½ ½	5 8	29 ⅛	Clear blew, but yellowiſh in the N. E. Clowded to-ward the S. Checker'd blew.	A great dew. Thunder, far to The South. A very great Tide.	From the laſt quar: of theMoon to the changethe weather was ve-ry temperate but cold for the fea-fon; the Wind piety conſtant betwen N. and
15 II 13.40	8 4 ♉ 24. 51. N. 10	N.W. 3 2 1	9 8 7	2 3 ½ 2	8½ 2 2	29 9 1029	A clear Sky all day, but little chec-ker'd at 4. P.M. at Sun-fet red and hazy.	Not by much as yeſterday. Thunder in-the North.	W. A little before the laſt great Wind, and till the Wind roſe at its higheſt, the Quickſilver con-tinued defcend-
16 II 14.37	10 N.Moon. S. at 7. 25' A.M. II 10. 8.	1	10	1	28 ½	Overcaſt and very lowr-ing.	No dew upon the ground, but very much upon Marble ftones,	ing till it came very low ; after which it began to reafcend,
	&c.	&c.	&c.	&c.	&c.	&c.	&c.	&c.

know why: namely that time will not allow it.'[52] The Portuguese empire in Asia may have 'expired altogether' during the Little Ice Age, as Manuel Godinho claimed, but it did so through human rather than natural causes.

The Enigma of Iran

The surviving evidence suggests that Safavid Iran, too, should have 'expired altogether' during the mid-seventeenth century. Confederations of pastoral nomads, constantly at each other's throats, had long dominated Iran's history. They had provided all of Iran's ruling dynasties, including the Safavids, and also the shah's elite troops: the Qizilbash ('red heads', named after their red turbans). The first Safavid shah, Ismail, the charismatic head of a Sufi brotherhood, had claimed around AD 1500 to be the Messiah and called upon all who shared his Shi'ite faith to support him. His project succeeded only in Iran, leaving his country surrounded by the Sunnite Ottomans, Mughals and Uzbeks; while Iran itself included sizeable Sunni Muslim and Armenian Christian minorities as well as Jews and Hindus. Moreover, by 1600 the shahs ruled scarcely 10 million subjects (compared with 100 million Mughal and perhaps 22 million Ottoman subjects), leaving their state extremely vulnerable whenever their mighty neighbours decided to declare war.

At the core of the Safavid state lay the Iranian plateau, a vast but arid interior basin in which almost all large settlements are located around the edge, whereas the centre is sparsely populated. The French jeweller Jean Chardin, who lived in Iran for much of the 1660s and 1670s, observed that 'There is not in all the world that country which hath more mountains and fewer rivers. There is not so much as one single river that can carry a boat into the heart of the kingdom, nor serve to transport goods from one province to another.' He noted that 'The country of Persia is dry, barren, mountainous and but thinly inhabited', and continued:

> The twelfth part is not inhabited, nor cultivated; and after you have pass'd any great towns about two leagues, you will never meet a mansion-house, nor people in twenty leagues more. The western side above all the rest, is the most defective, and wants to be peopl'd and cultivated the most of any, and nothing is to be met with there almost, but large and spacious deserts. This barrenness proceeds from no other cause, than the scarcity of water; there is want of it in most parts of the whole kingdom, where they are forc'd to preserve the rain-water, or to seek for it very deep in the entrails of the earth.

Chardin went on to note that many farmers had created in these 'entrails' elaborate 'subterranean canals' to bring mountain streams to their fields, but added shrewdly 'there are not people enough everywhere to look after it, and draw up a sufficient quantity. Hence the want of people does not proceed from the barrenness of the soil, but the barrenness of the soil from the want of people.'[53]

Chardin attributed the survival of the Safavid state, despite such natural disadvantages, to the innovations of Shah 'Abbas (r. 1588–1629). In politics, 'Abbas introduced two Ottoman practices. First, he abandoned tanistry: to avoid the risk of sons challenging and deposing their fathers (as he himself had done), he killed or blinded his own sons and created a *harem* where his grandchildren would live until one of them succeeded. This brutal practice, repeated at each accession, put an end to succession struggles (although, as in the Ottoman empire, it also produced inexperienced rulers). Second, 'Abbas counterbalanced the power of the Qizilbash by recruiting slave soldiers (*ghulam*) whom he armed with muskets and artillery. To pay his 'new troops' 'Abbas confiscated lands from tribal rulers and entrusted their administration to *ghulam*. 'Abbas also undertook economic reforms: he improved roads and created a corps of highway police to protect their users; he constructed bridges and caravanserais; he fostered the cultivation of cotton, rice and silk (forcibly converting the two main silk-producing provinces into crown land). Above all, he brought Armenian merchants to his new capital, Isfahan, where they oversaw the production and sale of silk thread, which soon became both Iran's most lucrative export and the shah's principal source of revenue. Ironically, Shah 'Abbas used the silver produced by selling silk to the Ottoman empire to fund a war that wrested Iraq and most of the Caucasus from Ottoman control. He also captured both the Persian Gulf ports of Gombroon (which he renamed Bandar 'Abbas after himself) and Hormuz from the Portuguese, thus opening further markets for Iranian silk. In all, 'Abbas virtually doubled the size of the territories under Safavid control, and Isfahan grew to a metropolis of perhaps 500,000 inhabitants.

As soon as 'Abbas died in 1629, his oldest grandson, Safi, murdered or blinded all his male relatives in the hope of avoiding civil war. He nonetheless faced a serious uprising against high taxes in the silk-producing region of Gilan led by a discontented Qizilbash who claimed to be the 'Messiah'; the new shah prevailed only after executing the 'Messiah' and 2,000 of his followers. Three years later, after thwarting an attempt to poison him, Safi massacred all the surviving female descendants of 'Abbas and also all clerics at his court save one, who served as the shah's 'minister of religion, education and justice'.[54] The 3,000 eunuchs and 1,000 *ghulam* of the palace ran the rest of the government. This new regime failed to conserve 'Abbas's gains, however. In the north, Cossack raiders terrorized the Caspian; while in the east, Uzbek chieftains launched repeated raids; and, in the west, the Ottomans recaptured Iraq, leading Safi in 1639 to agree to the peace of Zuhab, which returned all of Mesopotamia to Ottoman control (see chapter 7 above).

Although the Safavids would never again rule Iraq, their brief period of dominance there had long-lasting consequences. The Iranians had exalted their new Shi'a subjects and oppressed the Sunni majority, and so when Safi relinquished the region, he abandoned not only the Shi'ite holy cities of Najaf and Kerbala but also a large Shi'a population. They would suffer political exclusion and oppression until the collapse of Ottoman control in 1916, and again under Saddam Hussein in the later twentieth century. As in Ireland (see chapter 12 above) the roots of an insurgency that has lasted into our own times thus originated in the sectarian struggles of the mid-seventeenth century.

Iran itself enjoyed a 'peace dividend' after the peace of Zuhab, which reopened the Silk Road to the Mediterranean. The shah and his Armenian merchants prospered, and when Safi died three years later, his 10-year-old son 'Abbas II (r. 1642–66) succeeded peacefully. In 1649, at the request of the Afghans, he captured Qandahar from the Mughals and retained it despite three desperate sieges (page 407 above), celebrating his success in a series of historical wall paintings that can still be admired in the gardens of the Chihil Sutun ('forty columns') palace in Isfahan – one of several splendid architectural complexes built by 'Abbas II to adorn his capital. Stephen Dale has suggested that Chihil Sutun may represent the shah's 'own perception of his reign as a kind of Safavid golden age', but soon after its completion a run of extreme climatic events caused widespread suffering.[55]

Iran regularly experiences droughts, high winds, violent hailstorms and earthquakes; but the second half of the seventeenth century saw far more of these natural disasters than normal. For six months in 1663 the northwest of the country received neither rain nor snow, so that 'wells dried up and crops withered', and in 1665–6 a poor harvest led to several bankruptcies among the merchant community. The combination of plague and famine persuaded 'Abbas's successor in 1666 to abdicate and re-enthrone himself under a new name the following year, but plague still raged and locusts destroyed the harvests for another three years. In addition, repeated devaluations of the currency created economic instability; the Cossacks of Stenka Razin raided lands around the Caspian (see chapter 6 above); and torrential rains ('the worst in living memory') destroyed 2,000 houses in the wine-producing area of Shiraz. When Jean Chardin returned to Iran in 1676, he believed that the wealth of the country had diminished by 50 per cent since his first visit a decade earlier.[56]

Two factors helped the Safavid state to survive both economic instability and political ineptitude. First, its rulers rebuffed the numerous invitations from Russia, Venice and other states to join their hostilities against the Ottomans. Rather like the Mughal empire, we may see the Safavid state as 'an unfinished project, in a territorial sense, but also as one that had a proper sense of its limits'.[57] Second, and no less important, although we lack any precise demographic records similar to the parish registers of Europe, many visitors to Iran during the Little Ice Age commented on its 'depopulation'. Jean Chardin advanced three explanations:

> First, the unhappy inclination which the Persians have, to commit that abominable sin against Nature, with both sexes. Secondly, the immoderate luxury of the country. The women begin there to have children betimes, and continue fruitful but a little while; and as soon as they get on the wrong side of thirty, they are look'd upon as old and superannuated. . . There are also a great many women who make themselves abort and take remedies against growing pregnant. The third reason is, that within this last century, a great many Persians, and even entire families, have gone and settl'd in [India.][58]

Now although Chardin was fluent in Persian, and had lived many years in Iran, he was not qualified to pontificate on the frequency of sodomy (impossible to measure) or the exact number of emigrants (whilst the Mughal rulers of India did indeed welcome thousands of Persians, thousands of Indians migrated to Iran). He was on firmer ground in suggesting that birth control was common, however. Although the

Qur'an was silent on reproductive matters, several 'Hadith' (commands attributed to the Prophet Mohammed) enjoined birth control, while Islamic Law allowed abortions within the first three months of pregnancy (albeit officially only to preserve the life of the mother and not as a way to control population size). By the seventeenth century, those who read medical treatises in Arabic could find descriptions of almost 200 techniques of contraception and abortion, and pharmacies stocked many of the medications mentioned therein. Some of these treatises explicitly argued that contraception (including early abortions) was 'permitted when times are bad' or 'to attempt to escape having too many dependants, or to escape having any dependants at all'. Iran therefore avoided the 'overpopulation' that plagued states elsewhere.[59]

Nevertheless, the Safavid state remained fragile – a fact reflected in the remarkable freedom of speech it allowed its subjects. In the 1640s a French traveller marvelled that the government 'allowed them to talk and argue about religious matters', and it 'freely admitted when it had lost a battle or a town (whereas the Ottomans always asserted that some treason was to blame)'. A generation later, Jean Chardin noted with surprise that in urban coffee houses 'political criticism was voiced in full liberty, free of government scrutiny, for the court was not concerned with what people said' – but as usual in the seventeenth century, toleration reflected weakness, not strength.[60] The Safavid regime endured mainly because it lacked external challengers, and when this changed early in the eighteenth century, the shahs proved powerless to prevent both the Ottomans and the Russians from making territorial gains, while their Afghan neighbours first rebelled, then invaded and finally murdered the last male members of the dynasty – before defeating the Mughals and conquering Hindustan in 1739.

Since both the Safavid and Mughal states collapsed into anarchy soon after 1700, some might infer that they had merely deferred catastrophe rather than averting it; but this is unfair. Like other parts of south and Southeast Asia, their territories suffered natural disasters (notably droughts) in the mid-seventeenth century, yet they escaped political catastrophe. Instead, for another two generations, and for most of their subjects, life in much of South Asia was indeed 'not worse or more calamitous than it used to be'.

Red Flag over Italy[1]

M ANY CONTEMPORARIES EXPECTED THE REVOLT OF THE CATALANS IN JUNE 1640 to produce the collapse of the Spanish Monarchy. In Paris, Swedish ambassador Hugo Grotius gloated that 'in time this flame could spread to Aragon, Valencia and Portugal'; while in London, James Howell predicted that 'the sparkles of this fire will fly further, either to Portugal, or to Sicily and Italy; all which countries, I observed, the Spaniard holds, as one would do a wolf, by the ear'.[2] And, indeed, Portugal rebelled in December 1640 and Aragon came close the following year (see chapter 9 above); while rioting against conscription and tax increases paralyzed much of the kingdom of Valencia after a drought produced the worst harvest of the century in 1645. Two years later a broadsheet bore the menacing slogan:

If it's good government you want
Naples, Messina and Palermo
Have shown you the way.[3]

By then 'the sparkles' of rebellion had flown not only to Naples, Messina and Palermo but also to Milan – but in each case they failed to start a conflagration. Whereas the revolt of the Catalans lasted 19 years, and Portugal achieved independence after 28 years of war, in Spanish Italy the government prevented the 'fire' from taking hold in Lombardy, and extinguished it in Naples and Sicily within a year. Why?

Sicily in Revolt

Spain began to impose heavier taxes on its Italian subjects in 1619, when Philip III demanded three million ducats from his Italian vassals to pay for the troops he sent to assist Emperor Ferdinand II defeat his enemies in Germany (see chapter 8 above). Despite their unequal size and wealth, the split was equal – one million each from Lombardy, Naples and Sicily – but Sicily presented a particularly tempting fiscal target. First, the island's fertile soil normally produced yields of 7–10 grains of wheat and 9–11 grains of barley for each grain sown, the highest recorded in seventeenth-century Europe. Second, three-quarters of Sicily's population lived in towns, 70 of them founded on the uplands of the interior specifically to produce grain for export (see chapter 3 above). Thanks to the benign climate of the sixteenth and early seventeenth centuries, most of them thrived, and the population of the island doubled from 600,000 in 1500 to 1,200,000 in 1623, including 130,000 in Palermo and perhaps 120,000 in Messina, the two principal cities.

Nevertheless, there were two Sicilies. The west and centre of the island, including Palermo, the administrative capital, produced and exported primarily grain; while the east, including Messina, the commercial capital, produced and exported primarily silk. Despite their prosperity, both parts of the island were economically vulnerable. Messina and its hinterland produced virtually no grain, and so the population depended on being able to import bread and export textiles. When war broke out between Venice and the Ottoman empire in 1645 (see chapter 7 above), silk exports from Messina fell by one-quarter, throwing thousands out of work. Crisis could strike western Sicily with equal severity and suddenness, because drought rendered the marginal lands around the new towns of the central uplands barren. During the 1640s, yield ratios on some estates fell to 1:3 – the lowest recorded on the island during the entire early modern period – which drastically reduced the grain available to feed Palermo.[4] The two Sicilies also differed politically. The king appointed most local government officials in the west, whereas the eastern cities enjoyed a considerable degree of autonomy. Luis Ribot García has suggested that Messina, in particular, ruled by a Senate composed of six magistrates elected annually, 'had gained a greater degree of self government than any other city in Sicily – perhaps in the Hispanic world – making it in effect a sort of republic under Spanish protection'. The king appointed directly only the *straticò*, the official who commanded his garrison and enforced his laws.[5]

The decision by Philip IV and his Spanish ministers in 1643 to make Italy contribute more for his foreign wars (see chapter 9 above) almost doubled the tax burden on his Sicilian subjects over the next four years. The government of the island, headed by a viceroy, met these demands with many of the same fiscal strategies adopted elsewhere during the mid-seventeenth-century crisis: it exploited 'regalian rights' (such as the 'media anata' and stamp duty); it bullied the island's Parliament into voting new taxes, and then farmed their collection out to bankers in return for cash advances; and it imposed excise duties on almost all commodities in common use. When these measures fell short of the king's demands, the viceroys also alienated crown lands and rights (although this reduced revenue), sold public offices (although this undermined the loyalty and integrity of the civil service) and issued bonds (although the interest payable greatly increased expenditure). The fiscal pressure forced the major towns to take similar measures: they sold lands, imposed new taxes and borrowed money at interest (by the 1640s, the public debt of Palermo stood at over four million ducats). This meant that both central and local governments lacked resources when a series of natural disasters struck the island.

Starting in September 1645, rain fell almost continuously on Sicily for a year, destroying first the winter crops and then drastically reducing the yield of the summer harvest. In addition, floods destroyed houses and washed away bridges, gales destroyed the olive trees and an eruption of Mount Etna 'did notable damage'. Nevertheless, the king commanded his viceroy to send 300,000 bushels of grain to Spain the following spring and rejected all the viceroy's pleas that the island's own food shortages made this impossible. Philip also issued express orders that the city magistrates must not subsidize grain prices (as they had been doing) to cushion the impact of rising food prices on the poor. In August 1646, with wheat prices higher than ever previously recorded, the Senate of Messina ordered all bakers to reduce the size of a standard loaf by 10 per cent – the only alternative to raising its price. Three weeks later, as wheat prices continued to rise, they did the same again.[6]

A crowd of 'boys and women' now took to the streets of Messina, brandishing the small loaves on the end of pikes and shouting 'Long live the king and down with the evil government!' The rioters killed one of the magistrates, burned down the houses of two others and stoned the homes of several nobles; but the viceroy, the same marquis of Los Vélez who had performed so dismally in the campaign against the Catalans in 1640–1 (see chapter 9 above), reacted swiftly. He ordered the soldiers aboard the galleys that happened to be in Messina harbour to march through the streets to restore order; he sent grain from the government's 'strategic reserve' to the city; then he travelled to Messina in person and supervised the arrest and execution of the leading rioters.

Although these measures pacified Messina, they did nothing to address the crisis caused by harvest failure in the rest of Sicily. On the contrary, in autumn 1646, 'having ploughed and sowed the land, the peasants desired rain, but a great drought occurred, not only then but for almost the whole succeeding winter, and into the spring of 1647', which seemed to 'threaten a universal catastrophe'. The drought coincided with (or caused) a serious epidemic in Palermo that killed hundreds each week as bread prices reached their highest level in three centuries. When the king ordered the city's magistrates to cease subsidizing the price of bread, at a cost of 300 ducats a day, they refused because (recalling the events in Messina) they feared a riot if they obeyed.[7]

Meanwhile the local clergy organized processions to pray for rain and beg forgiveness for the sins that, they claimed, had brought God's punishment on the land. 'Day after day and hour after hour' the men, women and children of Palermo took to the streets 'showing their penitence in a variety of ways, with crowns of thorns on their heads, iron chains around their necks and feet, flagellating themselves, continuously weeping'. Then a miracle occurred: it rained for two days and the crops began to grow again. Just as popular anxiety subsided, 'a Sirocco wind blew day and night, so fierce that it dried the breath in your throat and killed off both grain and fruit crops' – but on 19 May 1647 a second miracle occurred: a ship docked in Palermo harbour carrying several tons of grain.[8] Unfortunately, the ship also brought new letters from the king, threatening that unless the city magistrates ended the bread subsidy they would have to pay for it personally. The bakers therefore received orders to reduce the size of the standard loaf by 15 per cent 'in order to align the price with the cost'.[9]

The prospect of mass starvation, the outpouring of religious zeal and then two apparent miracles of deliverance created emotional overload in Palermo. Some women went to the cathedral carrying the small loaves which they laid on the altar, shouting 'Look what we get, Lord, after so much penitence.' On 20 May about 200 people, many of them women and boys (as in Messina the previous year), gathered outside the city hall and shouted 'Long live the king and down with the evil government', 'Big loaves, no excise' and, more simply, 'Bread, bread'. Their cries attracted a much larger crowd and some began to throw stones at the windows and set fire to the doors. They also broke into the principal prison and freed over 1,000 inmates.[10]

The convicts transformed the situation. The following day one of them, Antonino la Pelosa, incited the crowd to storm the treasury and burn the tax documents within. In a desperate attempt to restore order, Viceroy Los Vélez issued a proclamation abolishing excise duty (*gabella*) on five basic foodstuffs and fixed the prices at which each should be sold; and he restored the bread subsidy so that the bakers could produce larger loaves for the same price. More surprisingly, he also deposed the city magistrates who had decreed the reduction; granted 'the people' the right to elect two magistrates themselves; and formally pardoned not only all rioters but also those freed from prison. The violence subsided until the city magistrates, perhaps still fearful that the king would hold them responsible for any food subsidy, insisted that all items *except bread* should be sold at cost price. La Pelosa and his supporters denounced this move as a breach of faith and burned down the houses of officials and merchants involved in tax collection.

The escalating violence produced panic. The archbishop instructed all clergy in the city to keep loaded guns by them at all times, while Los Vélez authorized the city guildsmen to bear arms. Together with the nobles and their bands of retainers, the guildsmen restored order to the streets and captured La Pelosa, who confessed under torture that he had intended to distribute among his followers the money taken from the city treasury, expecting to be hailed as king, and that he had brought into the city 'some Greeks' (farmers of Greek descent) who planned to murder all the nobles (and any others he deemed to be his enemies) on the feast of Corpus Christi, the seventh anniversary of the Catalan uprising. The following day the viceroy had him and other leading 'incendiaries' executed, after which he wrote a letter to the king boasting that he had just toured the streets in his carriage in perfect safety.[11]

Los Vélez boasted too soon. Famished citizens in other Sicilian towns drew the obvious lesson from the ease with which Palermo had won concessions, and crowds led by 'women and youngsters carrying sticks and stones in their hands' took to the streets shouting 'Long live the king of Spain, down with the excise.' Almost everywhere the magistrates complied, and, if they refused, the crowds broke open the prisons and started burning the houses of the rich until they received the concessions they demanded. In Catania, a port 60 miles south of Messina, rioters led by a local nobleman set free all prisoners, burnt all trial papers and forced the city authorities to abolish excise duties, to issue a pardon and to allow the guilds to elect two magistrates who would serve for life. In Caltabellotta, a small upland town, a public meeting demanded not only the abolition of the excise but also a new census to serve as the base for allocating future taxes, because the existing one listed '8,000 souls, the greater part of them very prosperous; but at present there are scarcely 3,500 impoverished and miserable souls'.[12]

Palermo, too, faced a financial crisis because, without the excise duties, it lacked money to pay its creditors. On 1 July 1647 the viceroy met the newly elected magistrates and the guild leaders, and they agreed to impose taxes that targeted the rich: duty would henceforth be paid on every window, door and balcony of the city's houses; on every pound of tobacco; and on every horse-drawn carriage. They also decreed that there would be no exemptions for either nobles or clerics. This represented the first 'progressive' fiscal system of early modern Europe, and it might have produced a lasting settlement had not news arrived of a revolution in Naples.[13]

'I find nothing more difficult than walking around Naples'

The kingdoms of Sicily and Naples were adjacent, enjoyed numerous cultural and commercial ties, obeyed a common master and closely monitored events on the other side of straits of Messina. Reports of the Palermo revolt, and its remarkable outcome, spread swiftly to Naples where, before long, posters criticizing the Spanish government appeared. There was much to criticize. The kingdom of Naples was more than twice as large as England, with a smaller population (about three million), but its capital (with perhaps 350,000 inhabitants) was the largest city in the Spanish Monarchy and one of the largest in Europe. In 1634 Giulio Cesare Capaccio published a guide to Naples, complaining that the streets 'are bursting with people on foot, on horseback, in carriages, with a buzzing everywhere as if it were a beehive. I find nothing more difficult than walking around Naples and going where I want, whatever the time of day.' Capaccio also noted the prodigious quantities of food consumed by this huge population, most of it bought and sold every day in the city's principal marketplace, the Piazza del Mercato.[14]

Many observers noted the striking contrast between the ostentation of the city's patrician elite (a French visitor considered that 'there was not a race in the world more presumptuous and more boastful' than the nobles of Naples) and the destitution of the rest of the population, many of whom eked out a living in 'high-rise' apartment buildings in the city centre, in shacks around the periphery, or in the streets. The Neapolitans called them *lazzari* (Lazaruses) because their ability to arise from their beds and walk seemed miraculous – but Capaccio considered them 'the dregs of the state, prone to rebellions, to revolutions [*rivoluzioni*], to break laws, customs, obedience to superiors'. They were, he believed, 'capable of reducing everything to disorder with every tiny movement'.[15]

To minimize the risk of 'revolutions', the viceroys exploited the rivalry between different social groups. The nobles in Naples belonged to one of six groups of families (known as *Seggi* or 'seats'), and a representative from each served on the city council, together with a candidate chosen by the viceroy from a list submitted by the non-noble householders (misleadingly known as the *Eletto del popolo*, 'the man elected by the people') who served for a six-month term, which the viceroy could terminate or prolong at will. Despite his title, the holder reflected the views of the government. In 1620 a major political crisis ensued when the lawyer Giulio Genoino, then serving as *Eletto del popolo*, proposed a programme of constitutional

reform that included equal representation in the city's government of nobles and
popolo. One of his manifestos justified the new division on the basis of their respective numbers – '300,000 against 1,000' – but although the viceroy endorsed the
plan, Madrid vetoed it and condemned both the viceroy and Genoino to prison.[16]

Genoino and other members of the city's intellectual elite had consulted legal and
historical sources, which convinced them that the Spanish government had tampered
with the 'Ancient Constitution'. They found, for example, that 'Naples was born a
free Republic, divided into Senate and People'; that it had paid no taxes until the
time of the Normans; and that it had 'elected a doge pleasing to the [Byzantine]
emperor or to another friendly prince who offered protection'. The historian
Camillo Tutini published an erudite but controversial book which argued that, since
Roman times, *popolo* and nobles had shared power in Naples equally, with the
implied argument that they should do so again.[17] By contrast, the Neapolitan
reformers kept silent about another innovation: the capital's exemption from all
taxes imposed on the rest of the viceroyalty. Representatives from the rest of the
kingdom met every two or three years in a Parliament dominated by the nobility
and voted taxes that, for the most part, fell on their vassals. It could scarcely be
otherwise, because by 1640 only ten towns besides Naples remained under direct
royal control: the crown had sold the rest, along with most of its domain lands, to
the nobles. As in other countries, it had also sold titles of nobility – the 161 peers of
1613 rose to 271 in 1631 and to 341 in 1640 – and to raise cash it also sold to the
nobles (both new and old) public offices, regalian rights and, above all, jurisdiction
over their vassals (including the right of final appeal). Once they had acquired these
comprehensive legal rights, the nobles used armies of retainers to compel their
tenants to sell produce to them far below the market price, to exact numerous
(and sometimes new) feudal services and to suppress any opposition by force.
A book published by a retired judge in 1634 listed hundreds of recent cases of
feudal abuse, all of them unpunished. Such excesses generated anger and protests
throughout the kingdom.[18]

The mounting fiscal burden imposed by Madrid exacerbated these dangerous
tensions. Each year between 1637 and 1644 over one million ducats left the
kingdom to pay for Philip IV's wars – one viceroy protested that Naples contributed
more than the Americas to imperial defence – but with the revolts of Catalonia and
Portugal to suppress, and war with France on multiple fronts, the government's
requirements for 1641 reached an unprecedented nine million ducats and 14,500
troops. Demands on this scale forced the viceroys to triple tax revenues by using
much the same combination of old and new taxes as other regional governments of
the Spanish Monarchy. They also resorted to loans from local bankers, which
dramatically increased public sector borrowing, until by 1647 the total public debt
lay between 120 and 150 million ducats – not far short of the kingdom's gross
domestic product. The viceroys also 'squeezed' the eight public banks of Naples
to surrender their cash deposits, which they then exported, issuing paper currency
in lieu of the absent specie (probably the first true paper money in Europe). By 1647
all eight banks were effectively bankrupt, while private financiers demanded

ever-higher interest on each loan transferred to Spain and Lombardy: 8 per cent in the 1630s but 40 per cent in 1641, 55 per cent in 1642, and 70 per cent in 1643.

These fiscal developments affected the entire population of the kingdom. Tens of thousands of Neapolitans subscribed to the loans – either directly or through bankers – attracted by the high interest secured on the yield of future taxes. They faced ruin when those taxes failed to materialize. However, as in Castile, depopulation reduced tax revenues. A census of the kingdom (excluding the capital) in 1595 revealed some 550,000 households; half a century later, another census recorded scarcely 500,000. The viceroy's financial advisers blamed the decline on migration to avoid the inexorable increase in fiscal pressure: 'from Calabria they move to Messina; from the Abruzzi to the Papal States; and, saddest of all, from the area around Otranto to the Ottoman empire'. Migration also created such a shortage of recruits for the army that the government sometimes placed conscripts in manacles as they marched to their port of embarkation 'in order to prevent their escaping'.[19]

In the face of the unremitting fiscal pressure from Madrid, the viceroys of Naples searched for new sources of revenue. In 1642 the Parliament of the kingdom agreed to raise an unprecedented 11 million ducats, financed largely by a hearth tax to be paid by every household in the kingdom with exemption only for those in the capital – but only on condition that it would not be asked to vote new taxes for a decade. This agreement meant that only the magistrates of the city of Naples could raise new taxes, and they duly imposed duties on certain 'luxury' imports such as tobacco and fruit until, according to a city chronicler, 'there was no item of food that did not carry as much tax as its actual cost'. He underestimated: by 1647 taxes on some items tripled their sale price.[20]

Although the fruit excise (*gabella della frutta*) targeted the rich, because most of the fruit purchased went to well-to-do households, its imposition had caused riots in the past and it now symbolized unjust and oppressive taxes. Nevertheless, when the *Seggi* offered to advance a million ducats against the yield of a new fruit excise the viceroy accepted. Before long, 'placards went up throughout Naples, inciting the people to "make a revolution" like that of Palermo'; and unknown persons blew up the excise office, located in the Piazza del Mercato, surrounded by the shacks and 'high-rise' projects that housed the poor.[21] In June 1647, as he passed through the piazza on his way to hear Mass at the church of Santa Maria del Carmine, which housed an image of the Virgin widely reputed to perform miracles, the viceroy received numerous protests against the fruit tax. Don Rodrigo Ponce de León, duke of Arcos, had been viceroy of Naples since 1646, and before that viceroy of Valencia for three years: he should have known better than to promise to suspend a levy whose yield had already been promised to creditors, because it required him to find an alternative source of revenue. Arcos proposed a tax on those who owned carriages, but when the *Seggi* (who owned most of the carriages) objected vociferously, he reimposed the fruit excise.

At this point, a French fleet appeared off Naples, and the viceroy immediately sent part of the city's galley squadron, manned by troops from the garrison, to drive them away. Coincidentally, an urgent command arrived from the king to defend Genoa from a French assault, and so Arcos dispatched another detachment of the garrison aboard the rest of the galleys, leaving Naples virtually undefended. The viceroy's decisions, at a time when he was well 'aware of the ill-will of the Neapolitans on account of the new tax on fruit, and knew equally well that for the same reason – excessive taxes – the people of Palermo and of almost every other place in Sicily had rebelled', mystified some loyal Neapolitans. It seemed to them that Arcos had committed political suicide. And so it proved.[22]

Red Flag over Naples

Since popular violence often occurred on Sundays and holidays, when everyone was either in the streets or in the taverns, Archbishop Ascanio Filomarino of Naples prudently cancelled the customary St John's Day celebrations on 24 June. He also planned to cancel the festival honouring the Virgin Mary on 16 July, because it involved a ritual battle in the Piazza del Mercato between two teams of young men from the area, dressed as 'Moors' and 'Christians' and armed with sticks. One defended a mock castle of wood and painted canvas erected in the square, while the other attacked it. They 'rehearsed' in the piazza on Sunday mornings.

On the morning of Sunday, 7 July, a dispute broke out between the stallholders of the Piazza del Mercato and the local producers over who should pay the fruit excise. Eventually, one of the fruit vendors 'flew into such a rage that, throwing two great baskets [of figs] upon the ground, he cried out "God gives plenty and the ill government creates a dearth. I don't care about the fruit. Help yourselves."' When the *Eletto del popolo* arrived to try and restore order (and secure payment of the tax), 'the women and girls' in the marketplace 'began to shout "Long live the king and death to the evil government"'. Suddenly a man dressed in white overalls and wearing a red bonnet leaped onto a fruit stall and shouted 'No excise! No excise!' and threw first fruit and then stones at the *Eletto*.[23]

The demagogue was a 27-year-old fishmonger named Tommaso Aniello, commonly known as Masaniello, born and raised in one of the lanes adjoining the Piazza del Mercato, and leader of the 'Moorish' team during the festival. He had already drilled his *ragazzi* ('boys'), dressed in red and black, to a high level of cohesion, and 'in the twinkling of an eye, thousands and thousands of common people' came into the square, and under Masaniello's lead they seized some weapons stored in the tower of the Carmine church and 'unfurled the red flag on the tower of the church as a sign of war'. When some refugees from Sicily in the crowd 'called them cowards because they were satisfied with only one thing and incited them to demand everything, as had happened in Palermo', Masaniello directed the crowd into the streets leading to the viceroy's palace.[24] Meanwhile, other rioters forced open the prisons, setting free the inmates.

Archbishop Filomarino, who loathed 'this Masaniello', expressed his amazement that a simple fishmonger could 'acquire such authority, command, respect and obedience that he has made this whole city tremble at his orders, which are carried out by his followers punctually and rigorously. In short, he has become a king in this city, and the most glorious and triumphant king that the world has seen.' Masaniello's supporters also proclaimed that 'he is a man sent by God' and compared him to Moses.[25] Masaniello's genius lay in his ability to inspire not only his *ragazzi* and the *lazzari*, who had little to lose, but also the artisans and shopkeepers who normally sided with the forces of law and order. By midday on 7 July 1647 the insurgents numbered 30,000, and when they reached the viceroy's palace, they demanded the immediate abolition of all excise duties. Fearful of the fiscal consequences of such a sweeping concession (estimated at five million ducats in lost revenue), Arcos replied that he would abolish only some of them. This angered the crowd, which surged forward, and the viceroy's guards (who had orders not to fire) fell back. Arcos was lucky to escape the fate of Viceroy Santa Coloma in Barcelona, seven years before.

Masaniello had chosen his moment well. After the galley squadron departed with most of the garrison, Arcos had only 1,200 soldiers left to preserve order in one of Europe's largest cities. When the viceroy started to create defences around the Castel Nuovo, the crowd sealed off the area while reinforcements arrived from the country armed with 'ploughshares, pitchforks and shovels', and 'women were seen in great numbers, armed with fire shovels and iron tongs, with spits and spikes, and their children with sticks and canes'.[26] The following day, two important figures emerged at Masaniello's side: Giulio Genoino and his nephew Francesco Arpaja, both of them veterans of the attempt to change the city's Constitution in 1620. Together, the triumvirs compiled a list of houses to be sacked and burned each night – a list that contained the residences of Genoino's personal enemies as well as of those connected with the oppressive fiscal system.[27] Archbishop Filomarino, acting as mediator, persuaded Arcos to abolish all excise duties and to issue a general pardon, in order to restore at least a temporary peace, but once again the viceroy misstepped: his pardon unwisely characterized the rioters as 'rebels'. Such disrespect provoked a new wave of violence, and the houses of several more ministers and tax collectors went up in flames.[28]

On 9 July 1647 Genoino and his associates drew up a list of 22 *Capitoli* ('Articles') that insisted not only on a comprehensive pardon but also on a host of specific concessions which, they claimed, had been granted to the city in previous charters – including an end to all excise duties on food, the equalization of the tax burden between the capital and the provinces, and the selection of the *Eletto del popolo* by the popular assembly. (Arcos ruefully observed that the *Capitoli* incorporated the reforms Genoino and his supporters had proposed almost 30 years before.) As the list was read out in the crowded Carmine church, a member of the audience shouted out an objection: the Spanish government had reneged on promises made to its opponents in the Netherlands, Catalonia and Portugal, so what could be done to secure compliance this time? Arcos agreed that, until the king confirmed the *Capitoli*, the insurgents could continue to bear arms – a dangerous concession given that Masaniello's well-drilled militia now numbered 10,000.[29]

Meanwhile, some local priests assured the insurgents that 'because they were oppressed by excessive taxes, and were attacked and provoked by the Spaniards', their struggle was just; while others formed a regular militia company, and others still preached sermons that compared Arcos with Nebuchadnezzar, Goliath and Pharaoh, and the insurgent leaders with Daniel, David and Moses. All this, according to one source, 'animated the people so that they went freely to fight, and believed they would be martyrs and go to Paradise'.[30] Masaniello skilfully used militia to prevent the royal galleys from re-entering the harbour when they returned from chasing off the French. He also placed an embargo on the export of grain from the city, and abolished all excises within it, which 'reduced the price of almost all foodstuffs to the levels not seen since the reign on Charles V'.[31] Filomarino persuaded Arcos to give in and accept all the rebels' demands.

The revolt of Naples might have ended at this point had a group of heavily armed horsemen not ridden into the Piazza del Mercato and tried to assassinate Masaniello. They missed their mark, and when the crowd overpowered and tortured them, the ringleaders revealed that they had the viceroy's approval for their attempt, that they had planted barrels of gunpowder around the square (which they intended to detonate in order to kill as many rioters as possible), and that they had poisoned the city's water supply (in order to kill the rest). The plot radicalized the rebels, some of whom now called for an independent republic. In desperation Arcos appointed Genoino as head of the treasury, while his nephew Arpaja became *Eletto del popolo*, and he promised them that the rest of the kingdom should pay a new hearth tax to replace the city's excise duties; that a new census should be undertaken to establish a more equitable tax base; and that the people might continue to bear arms until the king confirmed his concessions. In return, the viceroy made only one demand: the elimination of Masaniello.

At this point, many insurgents were prepared to sacrifice their leader. Genoino and the lawyers despised him; those whose property had been burnt wanted revenge; many felt alienated by his increasingly erratic personal behaviour. On 16 July four conspirators (each of whom later received a handsome reward from Arcos) murdered Masaniello, and the crowd then mutilated his body. Many believed that this event would end 'the great revolution of the people', after just ten days; but, once again, unforeseen and unrelated developments transformed the situation.[32]

One of the viceroy's guards celebrated Masaniello's murder by riding through the streets shouting that the nobles would soon make the people eat dirt again, while rumours spread that the viceroy would reduce the size of loaves of bread. Several bakers anticipated this order, whereupon angry consumers seized their pikes and, spearing the small loaves, marched on the viceregal palace in protest. They also recovered Masaniello's mutilated body and a procession of 40,000 men and women followed his coffin through the streets, 'saying the rosary and the litany, to which they added "St Masaniello, pray for us"'. Archbishop Filomarino himself conducted the exequies.[33] News also arrived that other places in the kingdom had followed the example of the capital, starting with Salerno, where on 10 July a crowd of peasants and citizens demanded the abolition of all excise duties, as had happened in Naples. When the excise collectors refused, the crowd torched their houses and elected a *Capopopolo* (also a fisherman). By the end of the month, in over 100 towns (in the words of a French observer) 'the people took a cruel revenge for the ill treatment they had received from their lords', hundreds of whom fled abroad. By the end of the year (according to the Tuscan envoy) 'There was not a village left that has not experienced revolution, with arson, murders and robbery'.[34] Only church lands seem to have escaped popular violence (Fig. 41). As Genoino and his colleagues consolidated their control over the capital, they reached out to the local lawyers and other 'intellectuals' who, as in Naples, had taken the lead in uprisings elsewhere in the kingdom. And then news arrived of a fresh uprising in Palermo.

Red Flag over Sicily

It took only four days for tidings of Masaniello's revolt to reach Palermo, where it immediately upset the delicate balance of forces created by Viceroy Los Vélez in the wake of the May riots. As elsewhere in the northern hemisphere, appalling weather presaged another thin harvest, causing food prices and tensions to mount. Giuseppe d'Alesi, an artisan who had witnessed 'the revolution in Naples', returned to Palermo bearing a copy of the 22 *Capitoli* conceded by Arcos and at once began to plot with some colleagues how to secure similar concessions. Having laid their plans, the conspirators decided to follow Masaniello's example and wait until the next religious festival – 15 August 1647, Assumption Day – when they rode through the streets shouting 'Death to the evil government, out with the Spaniards'. The viceroy and his outnumbered Spanish guards fled.[35]

His supporters now hailed Alesi as chief (*Capopopolo*) of the city, and they burned over 40 buildings belonging to nobles and merchants before meeting the viceroy to negotiate an agreement acceptable to all parties. The resulting 49 *Capitoli* included concessions to the common people (abolition of excise duties throughout the kingdom), to the guilds (who would henceforth appoint three of Palermo's six city magistrates as well as many subordinate officers), and to the lawyers (who secured a promise that the legal system would be reformed and the laws returned to the 'days of King Peter of Aragon'). Above all, Los Vélez swore that henceforth only native Sicilians would hold secular and ecclesiastical posts and pensions.[36]

The viceroy nevertheless fomented opposition to Alesi, and on 22 August a combination of disaffected guildsmen and vengeful nobles murdered the *Capopopolo* and 12 of his close supporters. Then, just like Arcos in Naples, Los Vélez misstepped: when he arrested some guild leaders, thousands of armed citizens waving red flags took to the streets until the viceroy published the 49 *Capitoli*. The guilds regained control of both the fortifications and the government of the city, but their power depended upon continuing to provide cheap food. Since the sparse harvest caused grain prices to rise further, this could only be done by subsidizing the bakers, at a cost of over 1,200 ducats a day. By the end of October the city faced a deficit of almost 150,000 ducats.

The new masters of Palermo hoped to make common cause with rebels else-where on the island, but given the fierce particularism of the Sicilian towns, and the refusal of Messina to join the cause, this remained a chimera. Los Vélez now issued

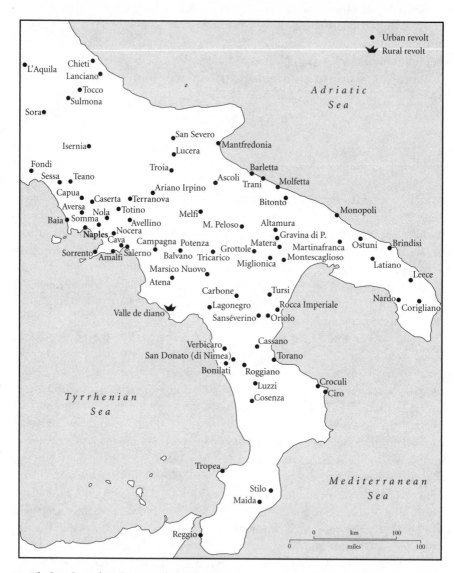

41. The kingdom of Naples in revolt, 1647–8.
Although insurgency began in a few rural regions before the revolt of the capital on 7 July 1647, Salerno was the first town to follow its example (three days later). By the end of the year, over 100 communities had rebelled. Almost all continued their defiance until after the capital surrendered on 6 April 1648.

a proclamation ordering all who had fled the capital to return within three weeks or face the confiscation of all their goods, and the return of the fugitives – mostly royalists – eventually gave him numerical superiority over the insurgents. He therefore ordered the surrender of all weapons taken from the city arsenals and forbade anyone henceforth to carry arms without a permit. 'Immediately, and it was a strange thing to see, boys and priests began to hand them over.' Los Vélez's victory thus seemed complete. Then the stunning news arrived that a powerful fleet commanded by Don Juan of Austria, Philip IV's illegitimate son, had tried to take Naples by storm – and failed.[37]

The Empire Strikes Back

News of the disorders in Palermo reached Madrid on 16 June 1647. As his ministers immediately reminded the king, the conflict with France had turned the entire Mediterranean into a war zone, which meant that orders could take weeks and even months to arrive. This delay made it 'impossible to provide remedies from here in time, because of our distance from the place where they are needed, so that before the dispatches carrying orders can arrive there, the danger may have ceased or increased'. Concessions therefore could not be avoided. News of the revolt of Naples at first failed to change the council's prudent stance, 'because the state of affairs over there changes from one moment to the next, and what seems appropriate today might not be so tomorrow'; nevertheless, Philip IV now took several steps to free up resources.[38] In January 1647 he had declared himself ready 'to give in on every point that might lead to the conclusion of a settlement' in the Netherlands and signed a ceasefire with the Dutch Republic (see chapter 8 above). In September he heeded a warning from the archbishop of Valencia that 'things are so impossible that it would be most unwise to think of adding new taxes, because at present they are both odious and dangerous', and granted the concessions demanded by the kingdom's elite. 'In these stormy times,' he informed Sor María de Ágreda, 'it is better to utilize deceit and tolerance rather than force' where rebels were concerned – but he deceived his confidante, because he had just ordered his navy to set sail for Naples.[39]

Poor planning and bad luck had often thwarted the plans of Philip IV, but this time promised to be different. Don Juan had already set sail from Cádiz with Spain's main battle fleet to blockade Barcelona, when news of the French siege of Genoa arrived. The king therefore ordered his son (like the galleys of Naples) to save the city, but Don Juan had only reached Minorca when news of the revolt of Naples arrived. Philip therefore ordered him to sail there instead, in the hope of ending the troubles speedily.

The vast city had become a soft target. After the murder of Masaniello, several 'special interest groups' disrupted public order: on a single day, 300 students, 500 silk workers and even the musicians and chaplains of the viceroy's palace took to the streets in protest against their situation. The fickle crowds blamed Genoino for this chaos, and he fled to Arcos seeking protection – but the viceroy promptly arrested him and sent him to Sardinia with secret instructions that he should be murdered on arrival.[40] In the last week of August, Francesco Arpaja, still *Eletto del popolo*, persuaded the viceroy to accept a new constitutional programme known as the 58 *Capitoli*. This document confirmed the division of power in the city between nobles and the people; it exiled and deprived of civil rights those whose houses had been torched during the riots; and it reserved all offices in the kingdom for natives, and ordered all 'foreign' clerics to depart. More radical still, Arpaja persuaded the viceroy to depose the royal judges and replace them with 12 new ones, all of them local lawyers who had proven their ability to defy the Spanish authorities. Not without reason, the local chroniclers called these developments 'a new revolution'.[41]

Such was the situation when, on 1 October 1647, Don Juan of Austria arrived off Naples with his battle fleet and 9,000 troops. Instead of using his advantage to 'negotiate from strength', Don Juan unwisely accepted Arcos's advice to attack, and for more than a day the guns of the fleet and the citadels bombarded the city, in preparation for a massed assault. However, artillery fire directed by Gennaro Annese, an armourer who lived in the Piazza del Mercato, forced the Spanish fleet to withdraw from the harbour while the city militia (honed by three months of drill) repulsed the Spanish troops with heavy losses. Don Juan agreed to a truce, but refused to ratify the 58 *Capitoli*, and so on 17 October 1647 Annese, assisted by the lawyer Vincenzo d'Andrea, issued a 'Proclamation' that repudiated Philip IV's sovereignty over Naples. Five days later Annese became 'Generalissimo of the People' of Naples and 'the people raised a black and red banner on the tower of the Carmine church, signifying that they would fight to the death'. Annese 'read out in a loud voice' a letter from the French ambassador in Rome offering on behalf of Cardinal Mazarin to send a fleet and money to support the 'Most Serene Republic of Naples', which would 'henceforth live under the protection of the king of France'.[42] Spanish power in Italy – and therefore perhaps the future of Spain as a great power – now hung in the balance.

Naples expected much of Mazarin, a native of the kingdom, but he remained cautious, knowing better than anyone that Francophiles formed a minority there and that a French invasion might alienate the majority. He therefore rejected the offer to place Naples under French protection. Instead, the cardinal concentrated on the 'big picture' – how best to exploit recent developments to secure an advantageous peace on all fronts – and he believed that the mere prospect of losing Naples and Sicily would suffice to secure more concessions without having to lift a finger (and, more important, without spending a *sou*). He therefore deployed all remaining resources on a campaign to wrest Milan from Spanish control.[43]

The Enigma of Lombardy

In the early seventeenth century, the duchy of Lombardy boasted a population of about 1.2 million, a density of almost 200 people per square mile – the highest in Europe outside the Low Countries. An English traveller found it 'plentifully furnished with all things' and 'so pleasant an object to mine eyes, being replenished with such unspeakable variety of all things, both for profit and pleasure', that it seemed 'the paradise of the world. For it is the fairest plain, extended about some two hundred miles in length, that ever I saw, or ever shall.' War and devaluation in Germany, Lombardy's principal trading partner, temporarily wrecked this paradise; but the duchy slowly recovered until in 1628–9 torrential rains ruined two harvests, raising bread prices to the highest level of the century just as troops from both Germany and Spain arrived to fight the war of Mantua. They brought with them bubonic plague.[44]

Perhaps one-third of the duchy's population died between 1628 and 1631, and its economy collapsed. In the cities, house rents plunged by up to three-quarters and the textile industry atrophied; in the countryside, up to one-third of all farmland lay uncultivated for lack of labour and demand. Once more, Lombardy recovered swiftly. An Italian who resided in the duchy's capital later wrote that from 1630 to 1634 'I saw a sudden transformation: from being an almost depopulated city, it again became recognisable as Milan.' Admittedly the city's woollen textile industry never recovered, but other economic activities took its place – above all the manufacture of silk, glass and armaments. As late as 1646, an English visitor to the capital found it had enough 'trade to support it in a flourishing condition' so that it was 'thronged with artisans of all sorts'; while another noted that the city was 'full of . . . rare artists, especially for the works of crystal'.[45]

Few visitors mentioned that Philip IV maintained a standing army of 10,000 men in Lombardy, with sometimes as many again marching through on their way to uphold Spain's interests in northern Europe, while in wartime the duchy might be defended by 40,000 combatants. Each soldier required food, lodging and pay, and many used force to extract them from the local population, creating widespread hardship and resentment. In May 1640 the city of Milan sent a special envoy, Carlo Visconti, to protest to the king and his ministers about the 'excesses' of the soldiers, about the city's annual deficit of over 200,000 ducats and public debt of almost five million, and about 'the introduction of so many new taxes and the notable increase in old ones'. Visconti arrived at court just after the Corpus de Sang, and stressed to the king how 'the events in Catalonia' stemmed from precisely the same 'excesses of the soldiers' experienced by Lombardy. Visconti claimed that, as he described the abuses, the count-duke of Olivares 'exclaimed "Jesus, Jesus" many times'.[46] Some ministers warned the king that 'although the loyalty of your vassals [in Lombardy] is so great, in such turbulent times we should not reduce them to total despair' and 'that right now we should treat vassals with much kindness', but instead Olivares demanded more contributions towards the war effort in Spain. 'It is easier to recover all the places' lost in Italy, he argued, 'after we have regained what we have lost in Spain, than to keep them if we lose what we have here'.[47]

The fall of Olivares and the crushing French victory at Rocroi in 1643 (see chapter 9 above) led the central government to resolve that, 'With the scarce resources that exist to make war on all fronts, it seems that we must try to reduce our commitments as much as possible'. Henceforth, Italy would have to pay for its own defence, leading a royal official in Milan to warn the king in July 1647 that 'we have only survived until now by selling our assets, by imposing extraordinary taxes, and by suffering miseries that would not be believed'. At just this moment, the rebellions in Naples and Sicily reduced the flow of funds to Milan even further, so that, 'having used all the techniques that human ingenuity can devise', and having spent in advance all revenues for the next three years, the soldiers and civilians faced starvation.[48]

Cardinal Mazarin confidently expected this desperate situation to provoke a rebellion and sent troops across the Alps ready to exploit it. His expectations came close to realization in August 1647 when, inspired by the revolt of Naples the previous month, manifestos went up in the streets of Milan 'saying, in so many words, "Long live the king of Spain, but let the loaves of bread be big and let the excise duties be abolished"', and threatening that the houses of government ministers would be burnt down.[49] Two months later Giuseppe Piantanida, a Milan confectioner, was arrested in possession of numerous printed manifestos calling on his fellow citizens to support a forthcoming French invasion that would 'end the insupportable oppression that the entire people [of Lombardy] suffer under the evil government and tyranny of the ministers of Spain'. Afterwards, Piantanida promised, all would 'again enjoy the same inviolable privileges conceded to them by the most august Emperor Charles V' a century before.[50] Under torture, Piantanida implicated not only some Milanese nobles but also the neighbouring duke of Modena; and, shortly afterwards, the duke invaded at the head of a French army – but the extreme weather thwarted them: torrential rains, which made all roads impassable, stopped the campaign in its tracks. 'The heavens,' Mazarin wryly observed, 'sent the Spaniards reinforcements in the form of rain.'[51] A year later another group of conspirators, hoping to exploit Spain's preoccupation with the revolts of Catalonia, Portugal, Naples and Sicily, divided the city of Milan into four quarters, each one with its own 'squadron' of insurgents who would converge on the city centre yelling 'Long live liberty' and 'Death to the tyrants'. Meanwhile French forces besieged Cremona, the second city of the duchy, until the Fronde suddenly deprived Mazarin of the resources to support them (see chapter 10 above). Once again, the revolt fizzled out.

France's inability to send effective assistance to the conspirators cannot by itself explain why chronic fiscal pressure combined with war and disastrous harvests failed to shake the loyalty of Lombardy. Many contemporaries remarked on this paradox. A Francophile Venetian observer expressed his exasperation at the 'incorruptible loyalty' of the Milanese at a time when 'the Spanish Monarchy was preoccupied with the rebellions in Catalonia and Portugal, the uprising of Naples, [and] the attacks on the [Spanish] Netherlands by powerful French and Dutch armies'. It was particularly remarkable, he continued, that no member of the elite had faltered in his loyalty; rather 'many of them have fought worthily in this war, raising infantry and cavalry at their own expense, and devoting their own wealth' to uphold the Spanish cause 'in the most pressing needs of state'.[52]

Why? Some might ascribe such passivity solely to the troops stationed in the duchy, many of them in citadels that dominated the leading towns; but, although a few thousand ill-paid troops certainly acted as a deterrent, they could not hold down a hostile population of more than a million indefinitely. Rather, the potential of

France to exploit any revolt in a matter of weeks encouraged Philip IV and his minis-ters in both Milan and Madrid to avoid confrontations and to foster a 'convivenza' (convergence of interests) with his Lombard vassals. On the one hand, the king abated or abridged several fiscal privileges previously enjoyed by the elite, and tried to ensure that all social groups paid a reasonable share of the 'many new taxes' about which Carlo Visconti complained. In particular, Spain did its best to equalize the burden of both taxation and billeting between town and countryside, and between the various social groups. Although these efforts did not always produce the desired results, they mitigated at least some grievances and created a favourable general impression. On the other hand, the government left the balance of power within Lombard society largely intact, while offering numerous economic, political and career opportunities to ensure that the elite (whether nobles, clerics, university professors or local government officials) became 'stakeholders' in the survival of Spanish rule. Thus, the government offered attractive rates of interest on its loans, and never declared bankruptcy, encouraging the elite to buy government bonds – which committed them to Spanish success, because a French victory would mean the loss of both principal and interest. Likewise the government increased the number of troops raised locally by the elite to defend the duchy (the proportion of the total rose to one-third in the 1650s) – again committing the elite to Spanish success, because if the troops mutinied, or if their officers defected, those who had raised them would forfeit everything that the king of Spain owed them. Finally, the clergy deposited 1.5 million ducats in the duchy's public bank, which paid higher returns than agriculture, trade or industry – creating another important group of stakeholders, because the bank made substantial loans to the government, and therefore a successful rebellion against Spain would jeopardize all investments in it, including those of the clergy.[53]

Finally, two economic factors softened the impact of both war and climate change in seventeenth-century Lombardy. First, as every foreign visitor noted, the duchy was extraordinarily prosperous: the high-value manufactured goods of the towns gener-ated profits for the elite and jobs for the rest, while its fertile fields produced an abun-dance of crops and livestock. Although the burden of billeting remained heavy, Lombardy could thus absorb its impact far better than (say) Catalonia. Second, the catastrophe of 1628–31 had drastically reduced demographic pressures. Precisely because famine, plague and war in those years reduced the duchy's population by perhaps one-third, many of the survivors accumulated substantial assets, so that during the 1640s, when the extreme climatic events stunted the growth of even the hardy trees that Antonio Stradivarius would later use to make his unique violins (see chapter 1 above), consumption did not dangerously exceed production. The earlier trauma helped Lombardy to survive the Little Ice Age without political insurrection.[54]

The Republic of Naples

Gennaro Annese did not lie when he announced 'in a loud voice' in the Carmine church that the new Republic of Naples enjoyed French support. Although Cardinal

Mazarin did not 'believe that the [Republican] project could succeed' and was reluctant to accord it official recognition, Duke Henry of Guise, a descendant of the French rulers of Naples and Sicily, who happened to be in Rome when the troubles began, claimed to have a letter of commitment signed by Louis XIV, and he travelled to Naples to provide assistance.[55] The new regime displayed remarkable self-confidence, issuing over 250 printed edicts during the winter of 1647 that commanded or forbade a wide variety of acts in the name of 'The Most Faithful Republic'. It also sponsored publications about other successful revolts against Spain (for example, by the Dutch and the Catalans); commissioned an 'official history' of its achievements by Giuseppe Donzelli, a celebrated physician and chemist of the city who had kept a diary of events; and sponsored a series of paintings of the main events of the revolution from a talented young artist, Micco Spadaro (Plates 18 and 21).[56] On the political level, the new regime discussed convening a 'States-General' (on the Dutch model) for the 12 provinces of the kingdom and urged all Neapolitans to defy the Spaniards 'in defence of the liberty of this kingdom, which involves at the same time working for the longed-for liberty of Italy'.[57]

Nevertheless, shortage of bread remained the principal problem facing the young Republic. Not only were the grain harvests of 1647 and 1648 extremely poor, but the nobles and their troops blockaded the city and virtually cut off all supplies. Annese, as 'Generalissimo of the most faithful people of this most serene republic of Naples', therefore decreed in December 1647 that bakers must reduce the size of the standard loaf from 40 to 24 ounces and supply the militia with loaves before anyone else, 'so that we can continue the present war'.[58] Both measures naturally provoked widespread hostility within the city; and when French warships at last arrived off Naples, the duke of Guise exploited the discontent to proclaim himself *Duce* (leader) of a new 'Royal Republic of Naples'. He also unfurled a 'new banner of the Republic on the tower of the Carmine church', published a new Constitution and started issuing coinage in his own image.[59]

News of these events completely unhinged the ministers of Philip IV. 'What I hear from Naples is incredible,' one of them wrote, 'because losing one of the finest kingdoms in Christendom is no small thing'. He asked a colleague rhetorically: 'When extreme necessity forces a monarch, for the sake of his conscience and repu-tation, to adopt extreme remedies, how long must we wait for those remedies to be taken?' This time, the king took notice. In October 1647 he signed a new Decree of Bankruptcy, confiscating the capital of his creditors and regaining the sources of revenue assigned to them; and four months later he reluctantly offered to conclude a permanent peace with the Dutch that acknowledged their full independence and allowed them to keep all their conquests in both Asia and America.[60]

Philip also offered the French humiliatingly favourable terms, but Mazarin unwisely rejected them, confident that he could do better by sabotaging the Hispano-Dutch peace talks and exploiting the revolts of Naples and Sicily. He miscalculated on both counts: the Dutch accepted Philip's terms and, shortly after-wards, the 'Royal Republic of Naples' began to fall apart. The fleet sent by Mazarin to 'protect Naples' failed to defeat its Spanish adversaries and withdrew; and although the *Duce* continued to issue grandiloquent proclamations to his new subjects – for example, ordering the public banks to reopen, 'giving our word as a prince' that all deposits would be repaid – Annese and many others no longer obeyed his orders.[61]

The Tipping Point

According to Vincenzo d'Andrea, the lawyer who had advised Masaniello and Genoino and now served as Annese's principal counsellor, Neapolitans now faced five choices: they could declare for Spain, for France, for Guise, for the nobles, or for the former republican leaders. Such confusion could not continue indefinitely. In March 1648 letters arrived in the city reporting 'a revolution of the people of Paris' in which the crowds chanted 'Long live Naples, we don't want any more taxes or wars'.[62] Far from feeling flattered, the Neapolitans realized that France could not now help them. D'Andrea, seeing no alternative course of action, opened secret talks with Don Juan, whom Philip had appointed viceroy in place of the hated Arcos, and with the count of Oñate (who had closely monitored the situation from Rome, as Spanish ambassador, and now served as Don Juan's principal political adviser). Both men agreed to confirm most points in the 58 *Capitoli*, including a general pardon; to abolish stamp duty, the *media anata* and all excise duties on foodstuffs; to appoint only native Neapolitans to most offices; to confirm those appointed by the Republic; and to grant equality of votes between the nobles and the 'people' in the city's government. In addition, they promised compensation for the damage caused by the bombardment the previous October and agreed that citizens could retain their weapons until the king solemnly ratified all his concessions. On 6 April 1648 Annese and his followers opened the gates of Naples and Don Juan and his Spanish troops marched in.

Many leading republicans had already fled, and (despite the general pardon) Annese and a number of others found guilty of active collaboration with the French went to the scaffold. In June 1648 the *Capopopoli* of all cities received orders to come to Naples at once 'on pain of being deemed rebels and confiscation of all their goods'. All were imprisoned and some executed. Nevertheless, Philip IV deemed it prudent to confirm all the concessions granted by his son and Oñate; he even put the duke of Arcos on trial. Most remarkable of all, some of the rebel leaders continued in power: Vincenzo d'Andrea became a trusted adviser to Oñate, who even persuaded the king to confirm in office the judges appointed by the 'Most Serene Republic'.[63]

Three reasons explain such concessions. First, the revolt had severely weakened Naples: arson and bombardment had destroyed much property (one contemporary estimated the damage at six million ducats, roughly equivalent to a year's revenues from the entire kingdom), while between ten and fifteen thousand people had either died or fled abroad. Naples could no longer pay for imperial defence. Second, adverse weather ruined the harvest of 1648 throughout southern Italy: the price of grain in Naples itself quadrupled, increasing the risk of more popular violence.

Third, rioting continued in Palermo, prolonging the risk of copycat movements on the mainland.

News of the failed bombardment of Naples arrived in Sicily on 18 October 1647 and, although Viceroy Los Vélez imposed a news blackout, 'all day, from dawn until dusk, people awaited nothing except news from Naples'. The guilds, fearful of similar aggression, demanded the restoration of the privileges granted by Charles V, while torrential rain, so 'abundant and cruel that it broke the machinery of the mills', reawakened fears of famine.[64] Dispirited by these continuing setbacks, Los Vélez sickened and died; but the death of this unpopular and unsuccessful minister actually benefited Spain, because Cardinal Teodoro Trivulzio, the primate of Sicily who boasted extensive diplomatic and military experience, happened to be in Naples. Don Juan immediately appointed him acting viceroy of Sicily. Trivulzio arrived in Palermo just two weeks after the death of his predecessor, and deftly exploited the divisions among the insurgents to assert his authority. Paradoxically, the continuation of extreme weather conditions helped him: gales blew down walls and trees; torrential rains caused floods on a scale unequalled in living memory. The new farming towns established on marginal lands earlier in the century harvested virtually nothing and so sent no grain to the cities that had become dependent on them. Finally, an unusually cold winter filled both the hospitals and the church shelters for the homeless. It was easy for Trivulzio to represent these misfortunes as evidence of divine disapproval of rebellion. News of the fall of the Neapolitan Republic strengthened the cardinal's hand further and he immediately arrested several former associates of Alesi, even though they had previously been pardoned. The demoralized guilds then evacuated the fortifications, and Trivulzio demanded that everyone give up their weapons. As in the kingdom of Naples, the *Capopopoli* of other cities also relinquished power, and collection of the new excise taxes began again on 1 September 1648, just before Don Juan arrived in Palermo with his galleys and troops.

As in Naples, the prince prudently made major concessions. Collection of the restored taxes became the responsibility of a specially elected body, the 'Deputies for the new excises', with wide-ranging powers; imposts fell mainly upon luxury goods (tobacco, bottled wine and carriages) and less on everyday items (flour, barley, meat and olive oil); above all, there were now no exceptions. When collection of the 'new excises' commenced, Cardinal Trivulzio made a point of paying first, and he formally waived his right to exemption both for himself and all other clerics. The king henceforth took care to appoint only Sicilians to lucrative church livings: when one fell vacant in July 1648, Philip wrote: 'Although I could appoint a foreigner to this abbacy without prejudice to Sicily, to please the kingdom I want it to be a native'.[65] It was a far cry from the imperious commands of earlier years.

A Final 'epidemic of uprisings'

Despite all these concessions, in 1672 'the most important domestic conflict faced by the Spanish Monarchy in the second half of the seventeenth century' broke out in Messina.[66] The city had received major rewards from the crown in return for its loyalty during the uprising in 1647–8; above all, Don Juan granted Messina a monopoly of all silk exports from the island, exempted it from several taxes and promised that every viceroy would spend as long in the eastern city as he did in Palermo, bringing with him all the institutions of the central government. Needless to say, Palermo bitterly opposed this concession (the presence of the central government brought profit as well as prestige), and few viceroys complied. The Senate of Messina therefore sent a stream of petitions and envoys to Madrid to demand compliance, and when in 1669 the viceroy – obdurately remaining in Palermo – attempted to collect a new tax from Messina, widespread rioting resulted.

In Madrid, the ministers of the infant King Carlos II resolved that 'the affairs of Messina have reached such a state that no other remedy will be effective other than using force' – even though some voiced concern that this might drive the Senate 'to despair so that they commit the ultimate crime: to surrender to the enemies of this crown the port that is the key of the two kingdoms of Naples and Sicily'. The appearance of a French fleet off the island allowed the viceroy to increase the garrisons of Spanish troops stationed in the fortresses in and around the city, and in 1671 he appointed as *straticò* Don Luis del Hoyo, an official 'versed in all the political arts, having served in the "school" of the count of Oñate during the time of the revolution of Naples'.[67] These measures coincided with a spell of excessive heat and drought that destroyed the harvest throughout the island. Grain prices reached almost the same level as in 1647–8, forcing the viceroy to introduce rationing and the governments of most cities to subsidize the price of grain. Nevertheless, the famine caused heavy mortality and drove the major cities into debt while filling the city streets with beggars and the country roads with bandits. Several urban riots broke out against magistrates who had failed to make adequate provision for the consequences of famine.

The existence of factions in most towns exacerbated the tensions, especially in Messina, where the Senate accused the *straticò* of exploiting the dearth to undermine the city's independence. Hoyo took his revenge in March 1672 when rioting broke out, and he encouraged the crowds to assault the Senate building and open all the city's gaols, releasing some 500 prisoners into the streets. After an uneasy two-week truce, under cover of the religious festivities on Ash Wednesday, the senators and their supporters organized another riot – but the *straticò* turned the crowds against them, and the mob burnt down the houses of the leading magistrates (in many of which they claimed to have found hidden reserves of grain). The victorious faction, known as *merli*, outlawed the Senate's supporters, known as *malvizzi* (the factions took their names from two varieties of Sicilian sparrow), so that when the viceroy arrived in May 1672, 'the city was virtually deserted, the nobles and principal citizens having fled'.[68]

Hoyo and the viceroy now set out to destroy Messina's autonomy, revoking many of its privileges and imposing new taxes – but then orders arrived from Madrid to send all available resources to fight in a new war against France. Like the duke of Arcos in Naples a generation before, the viceroy complied – even withdrawing the galleys that normally patrolled the Straits of Messina. On 7 July 1674, the anniversary of Masaniello's rebellion, the *malvizzi* staged another riot. This time they succeeded, and although they professed loyalty to the king, and displayed his image prominently on the facade of the Senate building, they arrested and executed over 50 *merli*, exposing their mutilated bodies to public contempt.

The viceroy of neighbouring Naples urged Madrid to overlook this provocative behaviour, and to show 'mildness, kindness and dissimulation' to the rebels because 'the same influences and grievances' existed elsewhere; and, he continued, '*as we saw in the years 1646 and 1647*, having begun in Palermo, the epidemic of uprisings immediately attacked Naples'. His words went unheeded, and instead government forces blockaded Messina, hoping to force its submission. The *malvizzi* responded by 'committing the ultimate crime' identified five years before: they invited Louis XIV to take their city under his protection.[69]

At first Louis declined the honour, thinking (like Richelieu and Mazarin before him) that any revolt that lacked aristocratic backing would soon fail; but in September 1674 he changed his mind, announcing that 'it is in my interest not to allow a fire that has spontaneously broken out to be extinguished'. Sending support to Messina, he reasoned, would compel Spain 'not only to apply to the uprising all the resources it can extract from its Italian possessions, but even to divert some of its military and naval forces fighting in Catalonia'.[70] A few weeks later, a French fleet arrived in Messina with troops and food, and for the next three years Sicily became a minor theatre of operations in Louis XIV's 'Dutch War' (see chapters 8 and 10 above). Nevertheless, Louis had little interest in 'liberating' Sicily from Spanish rule. As soon as financial pressure compelled him 'to deploy my forces only in the places where they are absolutely necessary', he abandoned his supporters on the island to their fate. French warships evacuated the last of their troops, and several hundred *malvizzi*, in March 1678.[71]

The Spanish authorities now exacted their revenge: every town in rebellion suffered 'civil death' by losing all its privileges. Messina also lost its tax exemptions and its leading institutions, including the Senate, the Mint, the University and even the office of *straticò* (which originated in Byzantine times). In addition, the victors shipped the city's historical archive and its principal art collections to Spain; razed the palace in which its Senate had met (replacing it with a statue that showed Carlos II killing the hydra of rebellion); and erected a vast citadel to preclude any further unrest. On top of all this, another drought struck Sicily – grain prices in 1679 again reached famine levels – which compounded the misery caused by the new taxes and the abandonment of many farms as a result of the war. Messina's population in the 1681 census stood at 62,279, barely half its pre-war total.

'We need to think about bending in order to avoid breaking'

A generation before, when faced with domestic rebellions, the count-duke of Olivares had advised his master that 'we need to think about bending in order to avoid breaking'; and seldom had the need for concessions been greater than during the rebellion of Messina because, as Luis Ribot observed, it 'put to the test the entire Spanish system in the kingdom of Sicily, laying bare both its weaknesses and its strengths'.[72] On the one hand, the *malvizzi* received support both from neighbouring communities in eastern Sicily and from sympathizers across the straits: several barons of Calabria, eager not only to make an exorbitant profit but also to make trouble for their suzerain, sent both supplies and reinforcements to Messina. On the other hand, the rebels and their French allies made little progress by force of arms: no community welcomed them spontaneously and no anti-Spanish uprising occurred elsewhere on the island. Given that bitterly opposed factions like the *merli* and *malvizzi* existed in every town, and given the four-year duration of the conflict, the absence of a general uprising is notable: those who hated Spanish rule had ample opportunity to act, yet few did so. By contrast, pro-Spanish riots took place in some areas under French control while several areas under government control staged demonstrations of loyalty.[73]

In part, this outcome reflects the ancient hostility between the leading cities of Sicily. Messina had rebelled alone in 1646 and it had stood aloof when Palermo and other cities rebelled the following year. It also reflected a tradition of hostility towards the French, originating in the massacre known as the 'Sicilian Vespers' in 1282, which ended their rule over the island. Nevertheless, Spain did not prevail solely by default: despite the xenophobic propaganda of the *Risorgimento*, in the seventeenth century Spanish rule was accepted by most of its vassals in other areas. In the Netherlands, for example, many citizens of Lille lamented their transfer from Spanish to French rule after Louis XIV captured the town in 1667. They regarded the ensuing settlement as 'a peace without joy, because it left us under the king of France', and for several decades afterwards they celebrated the births and marriages of the Spanish royal family, drank the health of Carlos II and protested at any criticism of him.[74] Had Spain lost its Italian territories, there is every reason to suppose that similar loyalty to the Habsburgs would have persisted.

Furthermore, as in Lombardy, so in Sicily, Madrid created a *convivenza* that turned important groups of its vassals into 'stakeholders' in the regime. In the wake of the rebellion of 1647–8, the government curtailed the political powers of the nobles, abolished tax exemptions for the privileged and entrusted collection of the new taxes (which fell upon luxury goods rather than everyday items) to a new *elected* body ('the Deputies for the new excises'). In addition, henceforth the treasury paid interest on its bonds at 4 per cent for Palermitans, 3.5 per cent for other Sicilians, and 3 per cent for foreigners, and it created a 'sinking fund' to amortize the debt in an orderly fashion. The new system proved so successful that it remained in force, with only minor alterations, until the revolution of 1860.[75]

Philip IV and his ministers went to considerable trouble to create the same *convivenza* in Naples after Masaniello's revolt. A single example demonstrates the lengths to which they were prepared to go: the count of Oñate, the new viceroy, decided to confirm in office the judges appointed by the revolutionary regime, instead of reinstating those previously appointed by the crown. 'This decision has caused great astonishment,' the king protested, reminding his viceroy that 'the nomination of these judges on 21 August 1647 was at the insistence of the populace during the seditions and tumults: that is what obliged and compelled that decision. Now that these disturbances have ceased, it does not seem appropriate to confirm it.' Furthermore, 'when we saw that the appointments failed to include Spaniards, as has always been the case, it caused even greater astonishment', and so, he thundered, 'it seems that neither the appointments then nor the decision now can be legal'. And yet, after rehearsing all these arguments, the king crumbled. 'Considering the zeal with which you serve me, and the need to authorize all your actions,' he concluded meekly,

> You should govern according to the state of affairs in that city and kingdom, paying chief attention to its peace and relief, which is what matters most and is the goal to which everything we do has to aim. So we remit everything to your prudence, and what I have told you here is for your information only.[76]

The judges appointed by the revolutionaries retained their offices. Such flexibility, and the desire to preserve *convivenza* at all costs, helps to explain why, even though catastrophes caused by both human and natural agents continued, the revolt of Messina remained the only serious challenge that the Spanish Habsburgs faced in Italy after 1648. Unfurling the 'red flag as a sign of war' offered too few attractions.

The 'dark continents': The Americas, Africa and Australia[1]

ALTHOUGH THE HUMAN AND NATURAL 'ARCHIVES' FROM THE MID-SEVENTEENTH century are abundant, they relate overwhelmingly to only two continents: Europe and Asia. We lack a human archive for much of the Americas and most of Africa, because few indigenous populations left written or pictorial records that can be precisely dated; and although the natural archive (above all tree rings), supplemented by archaeological remains, indicates that global cooling afflicted both these continents, its impact on their human population remains obscure. Thus while many Europeans in North America realized that the indigenous population was declining rapidly – in New Mexico, 'where three Pecos had lived in 1622, only two lived in 1641 and only one in 1694'; in New England 'by the 1640s the number of Iroquois (and of their Indian neighbours) had probably already been halved' – none suggested the probable causes.[2] In Australia, although only archaeology and the natural archive provide reliable testimony, little of it is currently available, and (as elsewhere) much of it lacks chronological precision. So despite the immense size of these continents (16 million square miles for North and South America, almost 12 million for Africa, and 3 million for Australia), historians can reconstruct the experience of their inhabitants in the seventeenth century only for those areas where literate residents or travellers from other regions – most of them Europeans – compiled written records that have survived.

The Americas

In both North and South America, substantial records exist only for the European colonies that stretched from the tundra of Newfoundland at 49 degrees north, through the rain forests of Brazil, to the tundra of Chile at 39 degrees south: the French settlements along the St Lawrence river and the southern Great Lakes; the English colonies of New England, the Chesapeake and the Caribbean; the Spanish viceroyalties of New Spain and Peru; and coastal Brazil. Despite the distance that separated these colonies, and their environmental differences, their histories in the seventeenth century shared five striking similarities:

- From Newfoundland to Patagonia, the Americas experienced notably colder winters and cooler summers in the 1640s and 1660s; while 1675, a 'year without a summer', remains the second coldest recorded in North America during the last six centuries.[3]

- Areas normally affected by episodes of El Niño suffered more, because the frequency of these episodes doubled in the mid-seventeenth century: more rain and floods along the Pacific coast and throughout the Caribbean; more droughts in the Pacific Northwest; more cold winters in the Atlantic Northeast. Moreover, both seismic and volcanic activity along America's Pacific shores increased.[4]
- Almost all surviving harvest records show dearth in the 1640s and 1650s.
- In the words of John McNeill, 'From Canada to Chile, the Americas in the seventeenth century served as a playing field for the ambitions of several European statesmen and countless independent warrior-entrepreneurs.'[5] Several regions experienced wars of unusual ferocity: the Pequot War and King Philip's War in New England; the 'Beaver Wars' in New France; and the Dutch–Portuguese struggle in Brazil. As in Europe and China, wars waged at a time of climatic adversity caused extensive damage to both property and people.
- Finally, all the indigenous peoples who came into contact with Europeans, whether directly or indirectly, suffered losses – sometimes catastrophic losses. In New England and New France (but only there), this decline was partially offset by a dramatic growth in the number of settlers, both through strong immigration and because many appear to have lived longer than any other group of humans in the entire early modern world.

'Our people must at least be doubled every twenty years': The Anglo-Atlantic at Peace

According to Benjamin Franklin in 1751, New England's white settlers had never been 'afraid to marry' because:

> They see that more land is to be had at rates equally easy, all circumstances considered. Hence marriages in America are more general, and more generally early, than in Europe. And if it is reckoned there, that there is but one marriage per annum among one hundred persons, perhaps we may here reckon two; and if in Europe they have but four births to a marriage (many of their marriages being late), we may here reckon eight, of which if one half grow up, and our marriages are made (reckoning one with another) at twenty years of age, our people must at least be doubled every twenty years.[6]

Although Franklin lacked any statistical basis for his estimate, as usual he was right. As early as 1634, John Winthrop had commented on the unusually low mortality among the settlers around Massachusetts Bay, and a few years later English pamphleteers likewise extolled the general good health of the colonists, contrasting it with the situation back home. 'In public assemblies it is strange to hear a man sneeze or cough as ordinarily they do in Old England,' one wrote; while another claimed that 'No man living there [in New England] was ever knowne to be troubled with a cold [or] a cough.' Most comprehensive of all, a group of 'New-England men' who had briefly returned to their native land thanked God for 'Blessing us generally with health and strength ... more than ever in our native land; many that were tender and sickly here [in England] are stronger and heartier there.' And they all knew why: 'God has so prospered the climate to us that our bodies are hailer, and children there born stronger, whereby our numbers [are] exceedingly increased'.[7]

The church records of seventeenth-century New England confirm this claim: over 90 per cent of all colonists married; most women married young (aged 23 or younger at first marriage); and half of all settlers seem to have survived to age 70. 'Completed marriages' (ones where both parents survived to bring up their children) produced, on average, six children – most of whom, unlike those born in Europe, survived to childbearing age. Thanks to this remarkable fecundity, and to continued immigration, the settler population of New England increased from about 14,000 in 1640 to over 90,000 in 1700 – a sixfold increase in two generations.

The experience of British colonists elsewhere in North America was very different. Almost from its foundation in 1607, Virginia experienced (in the words of its first governor) 'a worlde of miseries', because drought caused its early settlers 'to feele the sharpe pricke of hunger', forcing some to eat 'doggs, catts, ratts and myce' as well as 'bootes, shoes or any other leather'. In desperation, 'many of our men this starveinge tyme did runn away unto the salvages' – but the 'salvages' could offer little help because the years 1607–12 saw the most prolonged drought registered in the Tidewater region near Jamestown in eight centuries, and it affected natives as well as newcomers.[8] Demographic growth therefore remained slow: although at least 6,000 English men, women and children had come to Virginia from England since 1607, by 1624 the colony still numbered only 1,200.

Several other circumstances contributed to this slow growth. First, although in 1618 the Virginia Company decided to recruit and send out far more colonists than before, it failed to send sufficient provisions to feed them – and the newcomers arrived just as a new drought reduced the local crops. Many soon died, and in 1621 the Company complained petulantly that 'some have beene pleased to write' that their colonial venture was no more than 'a more regulated kind of killinge of men'. The following year was far worse, because another severe drought forced natives and newcomers to compete for the scarce food, culminating in a massacre that cost the lives of almost 350 English men, women and children. Then, according to a prominent settler, there followed 'a generall sicknes, insomuch as wee have lost I believe few lesse than 500, and not manie of the rest that have not knockt at the doores of death'. Nevertheless, he continued,

> With our small and weake forces wee have chased the Indians from their aboade, burnt their houses, taken their corne and slayne not a few. The great king now sues for peace and offers a restitucion for his prisoners; for whose sakes wee seeme to bee inclineable thereunto, and will trie if wee can make them as secure as wee were, *that wee may [later] follow their example in destroying them.*

The strategy succeeded: by 1670 a combination of wars and diseases had reduced the indigenous population of the Tidewater from perhaps 20,000 to fewer than

2,000. When Benjamin Franklin and others extolled the fruitfulness of '*our* people', they meant only people of European descent like them.[9]

Even though the English settlers in Virginia successfully 'chased the Indians from their aboade', they still suffered from the hostile climate. In 1637 a New England pamphleteer gloated that 'many men' had come to Massachusetts 'sick out of Virginea', but had 'instantly recovered with the helpe of the purity of that aire'; and that the Bay Colony 'in seaven yeares time could show more children livinge that have beene borne there, then in 27 yeares could be shewen in Virginea'. Then in winter 1641–2 the entire Chesapeake Bay froze over, while in winter 1657–8 the Delaware river was 'frozen so hard that a deer could run over it . . . an extraordinary case, which the oldest Indians had never known'.[10] Even in 1650 only 15,000 colonists lived in Virginia. Not until the 1680s, when their number had reached 60,000 settlers, did the white population become self-sustaining.

That milestone took even longer to reach in England's Caribbean colonies, thanks largely to tropical diseases – especially two mosquito-borne viruses, malaria and yellow fever, which thrived in the wetter conditions created in the region by increased El Niño activity. Of the 7,000 Englishmen who invaded Jamaica in 1655 as part of Cromwell's 'Western Design', more than 5,000 perished during the first ten months; and although some 223,000 Europeans came to Barbados, Jamaica and the Leeward Islands in the course of the seventeenth century, their combined white population rose from 34,000 in the 1650s to only 40,000 in the 1690s.[11]

Mortality in the seventeenth century among the indigenous inhabitants in Anglo-America was also high. In 1621, in one of the first sermons preached at Plymouth plantation, Reverend Robert Cushman noted how the '[Indians] were very much wasted of late, by reason of a great mortality that fell amongst them three years since, which together with their own civil dissentions and bloody wars, hath so wasted them, as I think the twentieth person is scarce left alive'. Archaeologists have found around Massachusetts Bay several Native American mass graves from the early seventeenth century that lack the customary grave goods, suggesting unusually rapid mortality, probably due to smallpox; while Thomas Morton, who arrived in 1622, found piles of 'bones and skulls upon the severall places of their habitations'. The copious evidence of sudden death 'made such a spectacle' that 'it seemed to mee a new-found Golgotha'.[12]

Morton's chilling image reflects the crucial difference between European and Native American aetiology. Although the native peoples of the Americas suffered from a variety of illnesses before they came into contact with Europeans, to many early colonists they seemed robust, healthy and 'unusually free from any apparent physical defects and deformities'.[13] In part, this reflected the absence of diseases that produced 'stunting' and disfigurations, such as smallpox and measles; but, unfortunately, this created a virgin population with no immunity whatsoever when the Europeans arrived. Widespread vulnerability, combined with the probability that several 'Old World' diseases (notably smallpox and yellow fever) became more virulent in the seventeenth century (see chapter 4 above), explains not only why Thomas Morton encountered a 'new-found Golgotha' in Massachusetts, but also why the same uncommonly high mortality among the indigenous population of New England persisted. In Massachusetts, John Winthrop commented on this phenomenon in 1634, musing that 'If God were not pleased with our inheriting these parts, why did he drive out the natives before us? And *why does He still make room for us, by diminishing them as we increase?*'[14]

Nevertheless, some early settlers of New England still felt overwhelmed by what Roger Williams of Providence colony called in 1637 the 'ocean of troubles and trialls wherin we saile'. Perhaps he had in mind the hurricane that two years earlier 'threw down all the corn to the ground, which never rose more', followed by a harsh winter that forced many settlers who had recently established farms in Connecticut to return starving to the Bay Colony – where they also encountered a 'great scarcitye of corne' thanks to a combination of drought and the arrival of more settlers than the plantation could support.[15] But most of all, Williams referred to the Pequot War.

'It was Captain Hunger that threatened them most': The Anglo-Atlantic at War

Smallpox at first spared the Pequot Nation, whose members occupied some 2,000 square miles of southern New England. Most of them followed a semi-sedentary lifestyle in groups of 10–20 households, although perhaps 70 households lived in a fortified settlement at Mystic (modern Connecticut). Thanks to their numbers and their strategic location, by 1630 the Pequots controlled almost all the trade of the English colonies with the Dutch to the north and east and with other Indian nations to the west – but this increased their exposure to European diseases, and their numbers fell from some 13,000 in 1620 to only 3,000 by 1635. This loss destabilized the entire area and in 1634 John Winthrop noted that the Pequots 'were now in war with the Narragansett whom till this year they had kept under, and likewise with the Dutch', so that 'by these occasions they could not trade safely anywhere'.[16] The number of colonists, by contrast, continually increased and groups in search of viable farmland returned to the Connecticut valley. Since the indigenous inhabitants heavily outnumbered them there, the Governor of Massachusetts engaged Lion Gardiner, an engineer with extensive military experience in Europe, to build a new fort at Saybrook. Gardiner advised caution, because

> War is like a three-footed stool: want one foot, and down comes all. And these three feet are men, victuals and munition. Therefore, seeing in peace you are like to be famished, what will or can be done in war? Therefore I think, said I, *it will be best only to fight against Captain Hunger, and let fortification alone for a while.*[17]

Governor Henry Vane, 24 years old and only six weeks in office, did not listen. Instead, early in 1637 he sent a force of colonists, reinforced by Narragansetts and other Native Americans opposed to the Pequots, to launch a surprise attack on Mystic. It succeeded far beyond Vane's expectations. His troops penetrated the palisade and set fire to the wigwams within, which 'burnte their bowstrings, and made them unservisable', allowing the colonists and their native allies to shoot down without risk those who tried to flee. Between four and seven hundred Pequots perished in less than an hour. Only seven escaped (Plate 19). The scale of the slaughter and the 'fear-full sight' of human beings 'thus frying in the fyer and the streams of blood quenching the same' shocked the 'young soldiers that never had been in war'. Some asked 'Why should you be so furious?' But the colonial veterans reassured them that 'Sometimes the Scripture declareth women and children must perish with their parents. . . . We had sufficient light from the Word of God for our proceedings.'[18]

As Neal Salisbury has observed, 'For many settlers, the Pequot slaughter was the ideological as well as military turning point in the war and in their conquest of New England.' Following the massacre at Mystic, the colonists 'in a short time, pursued through the wildernesse, slew and took prisoners about 1,400' Pequots, 'even all they could find, to the great terrour and amazement of all the Indians to this day', until in September 1638 representatives of the victorious English and their allies gathered at the Dutch trading post in Hartford to divide up both the vanquished and their assets. The treaty of Hartford forbade the surviving Pequots to use their name and native language, or 'to live in the country that was formerly theirs but is now the English's by conquest'. It also incorporated the first 'fugitive slave law' in North American history: any former Pequot who escaped must be returned to his or her original captor. By 1643, according to the proud boast of a group of Harvard gradu-ates, 'the name of the Pequots (as of Amaleck) is blotted out from under heaven, there being not one that is or (at least) dare call himself a Pequot'.[19] The gender ratio among the Pequots after 1640 sank to one male for every 20 females, and the tribe continued to decline until it numbered just 66 people by the beginning of the twen-tieth century. By contrast, by 1643 the English population of the Connecticut valley and Long Island already exceeded 5,000, with 2,500 settlers in New Haven alone.

The maize seized from the Pequots during the war helped the colonists in New England to survive another 'very hard winter' when 'the snow lay from November 4th to March 23rd, half a yard deep' and a drought in 1639; but then in 1641–2 came the second coldest winter in a century, when Massachusetts Bay 'was frozen over, so much and so long, as the like, by the Indians' relation, had not been so these forty years'. After this, drought and cold significantly stunted the harvests throughout New England – just as the English Civil War broke out (see chapter 11). Although in 1640 John Winthrop rejoiced when he heard of the Scots' invasion of England and the summoning of the Long Parliament, he regretted that 'some among us began to think of returning back to England' and others of 'removal to the south parts [Virginia], supposing they should find better means of subsistence there, and for this end put off their estates here at very low rates'. Between May and October 1640 the price of grain in Massachusetts fell by almost one-half, and of cattle by three-quarters, which caused,

> A sudden and very great abatement of the prices of all our own commodities . . . whereby it came to pass that men could not pay their debts, for no money or beaver were to be had, and he who last year or but three months before was worth £1,000, could not now if he should sell his whole estate raise £200, whereby God taught us the vanity of all outward things.

Winthrop's 'vanity' received another blow in June 1641, when his joy at the execution of Strafford and the arrest of Archbishop Laud ('our great enemy') was tempered by the fact that 'this caused all men to stay in England in expectation of a new world, so as few coming to us, all foreign commodities grew scarce, and our own of no price'.[20]

The situation of the New England colonies remained perilous throughout the decade. The Massachusetts preacher Increase Mather later claimed that 'more persons have removed out of New England than have gone thither'. He might have added that those who 'removed' to support the parliamentary cause included many of the colony's elite: 14 of Harvard College's first 24 graduates (one of them George Downing, who rose to be Oliver Cromwell's spymaster); Hugh Peter, who became Cromwell's favourite preacher; and at least seven colonels in the parliamentary army (including Stephen Winthrop, son of John). Two more New Englanders (including Henry Vane, victor over the Pequots) won seats in the Long Parliament, one sat in the Westminster Assembly of Divines and one signed the king's death warrant.[21] Many of those who remained in New England also became parliamentary warriors – albeit 'in ambush', seeking to kill royalists with their prayers and sending sermons, poems, letters and treatises of encouragement back to England. Thus early in 1643 Anne Bradstreet of Cambridge, Massachusetts, Anglo-America's first published poet, composed a verse 'Dialogue between Old England and New concerning their present troubles' in which the loyal colonial 'daughter' urged her 'mother' to show no mercy towards royalists:

> Go on brave Essex, shew whose son thou art,
> Not false to king, nor country in thy heart;
> But those that hurt his people and his crown
> By force expel, destroy and tread them down:
> Let gaols be fill'd with th'remnant of that pack
> And sturdy Tyburn loaded till it crack.[22]

Although New England supported Parliament, Virginia (and several other colonies) remained loyal to King Charles, who denounced Parliament's efforts to spread 'this horrible rebellion even unto those remoter parts'. Barbados, by far the most prosperous English settlement in the New World, saw neutrality as the best way to survive, and its freeholders swore 'not to receive any alteration of government, until God shall be so merciful unto us as to unite the king and Parliament', and vigorously pursued a policy of free trade.[23] Initially the regicide changed little – only Rhode Island immediately recognized the English Commonwealth as the legitimate government – but in 1652 the young Republic dispatched one fleet to enforce its authority in the Caribbean and another to subdue Virginia. It also created a Council of Trade to promote overseas commerce and passed a Navigation Act that restricted all trade in the Anglo-Atlantic to English merchantmen. In addition it sent to America thousands of its defeated British and Irish opponents who toiled alongside tens of thousands of slaves imported from Africa; while because (in the words of a group of boastful colonists in 1643) New England enjoyed 'peace and freedome from enemies, when almost all the world is on a fire', the migration of freeborn English men and women also rose. In all, the population of the Anglo-American colonies quadrupled from around 50,000 to 200,000 during the 1650s.[24]

The British revolution strengthened Anglo-America in other ways. The collapse in local prices and the interruption of transatlantic trade after 1640 forced the colonists to fall back on their own resources. Instead of importing what they needed from Europe, they mined and worked local iron and lead, invested more in fishing and logging and manufactured their own textiles and ships. By 1660 almost 100 ships – many of them built in New England – docked annually in Boston, exchanging goods from Europe, the southern colonies and the West Indies. Distinctive new economic, demographic, social and constitutional structures emerged in Anglo-America, from Newfoundland to Trinidad during the mid-seventeenth century; and the Restored Monarchy in London left what the Republic had wrought alone until 'a concatenation of disasters' in 1676 led to some significant changes.[25]

In spring 1676 the Governor of Barbados noted that although his island had suffered some 'misfortunes, by the negroes' [revolt] first, and then by the hurricane', its inhabitants still 'retain one advantage':

> They sleep not so unquietly as the rest of their neighbours in America, from whence they receive nothing but ill news of daily devastations by the Indians who increase in strength and success which spread like a contagion over all the continent from New England, where they have burnt some towns and destroyed many people, to Maryland where they have done the same, likewise at Virginia.[26]

The 'daily devastations' in New England originated in the Pequot War, which had opened the Connecticut valley to European settlement. The newcomers' increasing demand for land and food alarmed even their most loyal Indian allies and in 1642 Miantonomo, one of the Narragansett leaders who had helped to exterminate the Pequots, called upon his neighbours to unite before it was too late. Just as 'we [are] all Indians as the English are, and say "brother" to one another, so must we be one as they are, or we shall be all gone shortly,' he told the Montauks of Long Island.

> You know our fathers had plenty of deer and skins, our plains were full of deer, as also our woods, and turkeys, and our coves and rivers were full of fish and fowl. But these Englishmen have gotten our land, they with scythes cut down the grass, and with axes felled the trees. Their cows and horses eat the grass, and their hogs spoil our clam banks, and we shall all be starved.

Miantonomo announced that he and 'all the sachems from east to west' had resolved 'at one appointed day' to 'fall on and kill [English] men, women and children – but no cows, for they will serve to eat till our deer be increased again'.[27]

Miantonomo's appeal backfired. A Montauk favourable to the English betrayed the plot, while the following year a rival Mohegan sachem captured and murdered its author; moreover, fear of a pan-Indian alliance encouraged the various groups of colonists to band together. The preamble to the 'Articles of Confederation of the United Colonies of New England' (1643) noted not only the 'sundry insolence and outrages' committed by 'the natives' but also 'those sad distractions in England, which they have heard of, and by which they know we are hindered' from receiving protection. The new alliance promised general cooperation (including the return of fugitive criminals and indentured servants) and mutual military assistance in case of attack.[28]

Within a generation, the New England colonists had created precisely the crisis predicted by Miantonomo. As Sir William Berkeley, Governor of Virginia, observed in 1676: 'All English planters on the main[land] covet more land than they are safely able to hold'. This craving, he asserted, 'was the cause of the New England troubles, the Indians complaining that strangers had left them no land to support and preserve their wives and children from famine'.[29] His analysis contained much truth, in that the cultivable land available to the 'Indians' did fall below subsistence level – but it did so for a variety of reasons. First, the rapid growth of the European population (both through immigration and through the natural increase praised by Benjamin Franklin) automatically drove up the number of mouths to feed and the number of fields required to produce the food. Second, the settlers cultivated not only subsistence crops but also cash crops like tobacco, and this diversification, too, reduced the amount of arable land. Third, the settlers' livestock also required space – a lot of space: their cattle trampled down crops as they grazed while their hogs rooted up clams and corn stores, and while the natives begged the newcomers to fence in their pastures, the newcomers retorted that the natives should fence in their crops. Finally, the 'natural archive' of what is now the eastern United States suggests a cooler climate in the mid-seventeenth century that reduced the total yield of crops, and so increased anxiety in both communities about their long-term prospects for survival. On top of all these changes the virtual extinction of the fur-bearing animals of New England, especially beavers, through excessive hunting, meant that the natives had fewer trade goods to offer the settlers. This shortfall in turn meant that, whenever the colonists' courts fined Native Americans for some transgression, land was often the only asset they had left with which to pay. This dynamic precipitated King Philip's War, which almost ended the existence of New England.

In 1671 the Court of Massachusetts Bay imposed on the sachem of the Wampanoags, known to posterity as Philip (his English name) or Metacom (his Algonquian name), a fine of £100 – a large sum that he could pay only by surrendering some of his land to the colonists. According to a well-informed settler, Philip planned to take immediate revenge by an attack on the settlers of Massachusetts, 'and would have done so had not God's immediate hand prevented him at that time, twice at least by great rains', which ruined the harvest on which his people depended. So Philip began to follow Miantonomo's example and forged alliances with his neighbours, as well as acquiring guns and constructing forts. In June 1675, during the 'year without a summer' when unusually cool weather threatened the crops of natives and newcomers alike, 'King Philip' (as the English now called him) launched a coordinated attack that eventually involved some 8,000 Native Americans.[30]

Philip commanded far more fighting men than the colonists, and they excelled in 'the skulking way of war' that consisted of raids and ambushes. Nevertheless, two critical weaknesses undermined his cause: not only the tensions inherent in any alliance, but also the lack among the New England tribes of any tradition of following a single leader – indeed, several of the traditional enemies of the Wampanoags fought for the United Colonies. So although (to quote Governor Berkeley again) Philip 'made the New England men desert about a hundred miles of ground they had divers years seated and built towns on', he and his allies suffered some serious defeats.[31] Above all, the unusually cold winter of 1675–6 froze the 'Great Swamp' that normally protected an important Narragansett fort, allowing a colonial army to march across the ice to the fort and slay all within it. Then early in 1676 the Mohawks, a member of the Iroquois Confederation, assaulted Philip's winter encampment, forcing him and his followers to disperse. For a while, another poor growing season combined with hostilities to produce dearth in New England, but the colonists received supplies by sea, and from each other, whereas Philip's supporters starved.[32] In addition, the colonists belatedly adopted 'the skulking way of war' and conducted joint operations with their Native American allies, until in August 1676 they cornered Philip and killed him. Although the war continued for another 18 months, Indian power east of the Connecticut river was broken forever.

Nevertheless, victory came at a high price. Perhaps 3,000 Native Americans died through combat, disease and hunger; 2,000 more fled; and another 1,000 were sent in servitude to Bermuda; whereas of the 90 settler towns in New England before the war, Philip's forces attacked 52, pillaged 25 and razed 17. Some of the smaller outposts perished for ever, and 'the work of a generation would be required to restore the frontier districts laid waste by the conflict'. It was, in proportion to population, 'the costliest in lives of any American war. Out of a total population of some thirty thousand, one in every sixteen men of military age was killed or died as a result of war; and many men, women, and children were killed, carried into captivity, or died of starvation or exposure as a result of the Indian raids.' The war also 'all but wrecked the colonial economy', disrupting the trade in furs and commerce with the West Indies, and it 'eliminated so much of the capital invested in colonization by the two founding generations that per-capita income did not achieve 1675 levels again until 1775'. In addition, Plymouth colony alone spent over £100,000 in the war, and Connecticut £30,000 more. Since human and material losses on this scale threatened New England's 'continued prosperity, perhaps even its survival', in April 1676 its leaders appealed to London for assistance.[33]

Shortly afterwards, another appeal arrived from Virginia. In July 1676 some of the Chesapeake planters demanded that Governor Berkeley sanction attacks on their Indian neighbours. When he refused, malcontents led by the well-connected and newly arrived Nathaniel Bacon issued a 'Declaration' in the name of 'the Commons of Virginia' that commanded 'in his Majesty's name' the arrest of the governor and his supporters 'as traitors to the King'. They also garnered support in Maryland. Both sides offered freedom to any servants and slaves of their opponents who agreed to take up arms (an unprecedented step); and in September, Bacon and his supporters subjected Jamestown, the colonial capital, to an artillery bombardment. They then entered and 'sett fire to towne, church and state house' so that by 'dawn,

21 September 1676, property worth £45,000 sterling was destroyed. Not a habitable house was left.'[34]

In the event, the unhealthy environment of the Tidewater nipped rebellion in the bud – dysentery carried off Bacon and many of the other rebellious planters newly arrived from England – but several commentators linked the events in Virginia and New England in 1676 with those in Ireland in 1641 ('The tyranny of the natives *exceeds that of the rebellion in Ireland*, if possible'; they have '*imbrued their hands in the blood of so many of His Majesty's good subjects*'). The government in London there-fore dispatched a fleet of 14 warships with 1,300 regular troops, and orders first to pacify Virginia and then to proceed to Boston and restore order there.[35]

James, duke of York and Albany, the future James II, played a leading role in formulating the new policy. He was already 'proprietor' of the North American territories acquired in 1674 from the Dutch (hence their name 'New York', as well as the names of the two principal towns); and his governor, Sir Edmund Andros, played a leading role in defeating King Philip by mobilizing the Iroquois against him. In 1677 Andros sealed a lasting agreement, known as the Covenant Chain, with the entire Iroquois Confederation, which brought peace to the Anglo-Indian frontier from Maine to the Carolinas – but at a price: colonial expansion westward ceased for almost a century.[36] Charles II and James now took other steps to restrain the colonies. As in England (see chapter 12 above), throughout the 1680s they revoked charters and other royal concessions, while in 1686 James (now king) created the Dominion of New England, with Andros as his first governor general.

Early in 1689 Sir Edmund was in Boston, consolidating his authority, when news arrived of the Glorious Revolution in England. A group of Massachusetts colonists immediately seized and imprisoned the governor general (and some of his appointed council); then, followed by other New England colonies, they restored the form of government laid down in their confiscated charters. The colonial elite in Massachusetts (as well as in Maryland and New York, which also supported the rebellion against James) later proclaimed William and Mary their sovereigns, but their capacity for independent action worried the new rulers: although they dismantled the Dominion created by James, the new rulers also issued new colonial charters that gave the crown far more authority.

The memory of the great Anglo-Indian wars of the mid-seventeenth century – and their outcome – lived on beyond the Appalachians. In 1811, in a vain attempt to unite the Indian Nations of the Midwest, the Shawnee leader Tecumseh asked rhetorically 'Where today are the Pequot? Where are the Narragansett, the Mohican, the Pocanet, and other powerful tribes of our people? They have vanished before the avarice and oppression of the white man, as snow before the summer sun ... Will we let ourselves be destroyed in our turn?'[37] It seems curious that Tecumseh omitted from his appeal some other 'powerful tribes of our people' destroyed in the mid-seventeenth century, including the Lenape (or 'Delaware Indians') of New York and New Jersey, and his own forefathers, the Algonquian speakers who lived around Lake Huron. Tecumseh's ancestors were not directly the victims of 'the avarice and oppression of the white man', but of the Iroquois.

New France and the 'Beaver Wars'

The history of the lands along the St Lawrence and around the Great Lakes in the seventeenth century resembled that of neighbouring New England in several respects. Above all, the European population increased very rapidly. Almost 70 per cent of all women who arrived in the colony from France married before they turned 20; while one-half of the married settler families produced four or more children and one-quarter produced ten or more. After 1650, some parishes in Québec registered three or four births for every death. The French metropolitan government rewarded this remarkable fecundity handsomely. After 1669 each French Canadian female who married before the age of 16 received 20 *livres* (as did each male who married before 20), and each father received an annual pension of 300 *livres* if he supported 10 children, and 400 *livres* if he supported 12. Thanks to all these factors, the number of French settlers increased from 800 in 1660 to 15,000 by 1699, the year in which Marshal Vauban (Louis XIV's leading statistical adviser) predicted that the colony's population would double every generation.[38]

As in New England, even this spectacular increase failed to offset the decline of the Native American population. In part, the decrease was deliberate, because the Iroquois were matrilineal and practised 'inheritance through the female line; female-headed households; pre- and extra-marital sexual relations for women; female-controlled fertility; permissive child-rearing; trial marriages; mother-dictated marriages; divorce on demand; maternal custody of the children in case of divorce; [and] polyandry'. Finally, Iroquois women also sometimes used herbs for abortion (and perhaps also for contraception, since they rarely seem to have had two pregnancies in less than two years). All these practices mitigated the intensity of the mid-seventeenth century crisis by easing the demand for limited or falling food supplies.[39] But the Iroquois women could not withstand new European diseases.

According to Adriaen van der Donck, a Dutchman who spent the 1640s in the Hudson valley and then wrote a detailed 'Description' of the region, the Native Americans 'affirm that, before the arrival of the Christians, and before the small pox broke out among them, they were ten times as numerous as they now are; and that their population had been melted down by this disease, whereof nine-tenths of them have died'.[40] 'The Christians' began to arrive in 1609, when Henry Hudson sailed a Dutch ship up the river that today bears his name, reaching the site of the future Albany, while a French party led by Samuel de Champlain advanced from Québec (which he had founded the previous year) up the St Lawrence as far as Crown Point. Both Hudson and Champlain hoped to find a 'northwest passage' to China and profit from its riches; and although they failed, they did profit from the abundant North American beaver, whose thick pelts made warm, rain-proof hats. In Albany alone, according to van der Donck, '80,000 beavers are annually killed', and he went on to note that 'There are some persons who imagine that the animals of the country will be destroyed in time, but this is unnecessary anxiety. It has already continued many years, and the numbers brought in do not diminish'. But van der Donck, who never went east of the Appalachians, was misinformed. The beaver became 'prey to one of the longest sustained hunts for a single species in world history' and the resulting 'fur rush' drastically reduced not only the number of beavers but also, in due course, the number of native hunters.[41]

Many Native Americans along the St Lawrence died in the wars of the seventeenth century. At Crown Point in July 1609 Champlain and several hundred Huron and Algonquin allies, who farmed and hunted in the woodlands north of Lake Ontario, encountered a war party of Mohawks, members of the Iroquois Confederation, which controlled the woodlands south of the lake. The French used their firearms to kill all three Mohawk chiefs at the outset, as well as several warriors as they fled, leaving the field to the Franco-Huron allies. This victory marked a turning point in the relations between Europeans and Native Americans in the region: 'the beginning of the long, slow destruction of a culture and a way of life from which neither side has yet recovered'. The defeated Mohawks sought an alliance with other groups of Europeans – but whereas the Hurons exchanged beaver pelts primarily for metal artefacts, above all tools, the Mohawks and other Iroquois groups exchanged them primarily for brandy and firearms. Before long, the Iroquois not only possessed many 'fowling pieces, muskets, pistols etc.' but were also 'far more active in that employment' – firing guns accurately – 'than many of the English, by reason of their swiftness of foot and nimbleness of body'.[42]

For a time the Hurons continued to prosper, since the metal tools supplied by the French enabled them to increase their maize crops, and their numbers rose to perhaps 25,000; but the Europeans they encountered exposed Huron traders to measles and smallpox in a form to which they apparently possessed no resistance. After a particularly savage epidemic in 1639–40 the Hurons numbered scarcely 12,000 and they now lacked the strength to resist the attacks by Mohawks and other Iroquois groups. Worse, the acquisition of European firearms and ammunition, and the drunken rages induced by consuming European brandy, gave Iroquois warfare a new ferocity. The 'design' of the Iroquois, wrote the Jesuit missionary Isaac Jogues in 1643, 'is to take, if they can, all the Hurons; and, having put to death the most considerable ones and a good part of the others, to make of them both but one people and only one land'.[43] Jogues failed to perceive that the Iroquois also fought in order to replace their own losses from disease by integrating prisoners captured from other Indian nations, a form of conflict known as 'mourning-war' in which the women (especially the widows) of the tribe separated the captives suitable for breeding, whom they saved, before torturing and then killing the rest.

The Hurons did their best to defend themselves. In 1645 they concluded a peace with the Iroquois; and, lest it should fail, they persuaded the Jesuits and French settlers living among them to provide firearms and teach them how to fortify their villages more effectively. But still the Iroquois burned Huron maize and stole their furs until, during the famine year 1649, they launched an all-out assault. The Hurons had made plans for an orderly withdrawal in case of need, and they now burned their villages and retreated to an island in Lake Huron, accompanied by about 50 French missionaries, artisans and soldiers; but since drought killed the maize planted by the refugees, many of them (especially children) starved to death.

An excavation in 1987 of a fort and the adjacent Huron village revealed a grave filled with the tiny skeletons of malnourished children – victims of the Europeans' obsession with firearms and fur hats.[44]

Their orderly migration plan enabled enough Hurons to survive the 'Beaver Wars' and the ensuing famine winter, and thus to preserve their collective identity after they abandoned their homeland; but, as with all migrations, groups who were intimately familiar with the resources, ecology and natural balance of their ancestral lands found it far harder to survive as malnourished refugees in an unfamiliar environment. For example, the Hurons took with them to their new homes, in what is now northern Illinois and Wisconsin, a lifestyle dependent on the staple crops that had sustained them further east. In the words of Nicholas Perrot, a Frenchman who lived among them for two decades: 'The kinds of food which the savages like best, and which they make the most efforts to obtain are the Indian corn [maize], the kidney bean, and the squash. If they are without these, they think they are fasting, no matter what abundance of meat and fish they have in their stores, the Indian corn being to them what bread is to Frenchmen.'[45] Unfortunately for the refugees, maize requires a 160-day growing season but, even in periods of benign climate, northern Illinois rarely provides more than 140. In years of late or early frost, or if too much rain or drought, the harvest failed. Tree-ring data from Illinois indicate that, as elsewhere in the northern hemisphere, adverse weather occurred more frequently during the mid-seventeenth century, and so no doubt many Hurons starved.

None of these misfortunes affected Europe's demand for beaver hats, and so in 1665 Nicholas Perrot established a base at Sault Sainte Marie, where Lake Huron joins Lake Superior, and began to exchange furs for guns, alcohol and tools with the Ottawas and other Indian nations around the Great Lakes. From there, together with Louis Joliet, he advanced to what is now Green Bay, and again established a trading post. In 1673 Joliet travelled down the Mississippi to its confluence with the Arkansas river; and a decade later the Chevalier de la Salle canoed all the way down to the Gulf of Mexico. On his odyssey, La Salle met a group of Huron exiles who gave vivid testimony concerning the insupportable hardship of life back home. When asked whether they would like to return north with the French they absolutely refused, because 'being in the most fertile, healthy, and peaceful country in the world, they would be devoid of sense to leave it and expose themselves to be tomahawked by the Illinois or burnt by the Iroquois on their way to another land where the winter was insufferably cold, the summer without game, and ever in war'.[46]

Perhaps these refugees exaggerated. In his magisterial study, *The Unending Frontier: An Environmental History of the Early Modern World*, John Richards assessed 'the effects of the fur trade on those Indian groups caught up in it. Every year,' he wrote, 'Europeans enlisted tens of thousands of Indians to serve as hunters, processors, carriers, and traders of huge numbers of furs and skins for export from North America.' He discerned 'three intertwined questions':

- Did the involvement of Native Americans in the fur trade cause weakness, dependence and cultural disintegration among them?

- More specifically, did the glut of European manufactured goods cause the Native Americans to abandon their cultural beliefs, institutions and behaviour?
- Finally, did insatiable European demand also cause the Native Americans to abandon sustainable hunting practices and embark on a policy of indiscriminate slaughter of fur-bearing animals that adversely changed the environment?[47]

Richards cautiously rejected each of these claims, at least for the seventeenth century. Although European diseases decimated most Indian groups in North America, the acquisition of metal tools, woollen textiles and accurate firearms 'enabled them to dispose of surplus goods in exchange for the means to live better and more comfortably'. With the partial exception of alcohol, they were 'cautious consumers who restrained their wants in both variety and quantity'. And although by the 1660s beavers had been hunted to near extinction in coastal New England and along the lower St Lawrence, Richards noted that the hunters who harvested more than 150,000 pelts every year in the 1690s seemed to have experienced few problems in satisfying European demand.[48]

The experience of other indigenous populations in North America during the seventeenth century, however, remains a mystery. Where European visitors to the central Mississippi valley in the mid-sixteenth century had encountered impressive hierarchical chiefdoms, French explorers in the 1670s did not mention them. Instead they reported widespread desolation. Patricia Galloway, a leading historian of the Choctaw of the Mississippi valley, has speculated that, since the area had limited lands capable of feeding large settlements from maize cultivation, 'a point came when some of the river valleys could no longer support their population, or when populations right at the edge of need experienced a run of bad years or even climatic change, and the people had to disperse or starve'.[49] Perhaps the mid-seventeenth century, when tree-ring series from the region show serious drought, formed such a 'point'? Likewise, dendrochronological data from the Great Plains suggest that a major drought occurred there in the mid-seventeenth century, which may correspond with what some Native American oral histories describe as 'the dog-less period' – that is, a time when all livestock, even dogs, perished – but greater precision seems impossible without a more extensive 'human archive'. Indeed, the entire period 1550–1650 has been dubbed the 'black hole' of Native American history beyond the Appalachians.[50]

Nevertheless, it is worth recalling that, despite the setbacks in the northeast, in 1700 Native Americans still far outnumbered both Europeans and Africans throughout the northern subcontinent; and that, thanks to their growing proficiency with both firearms and horses, they controlled most of its territory. The number of native inhabitants of the Mississippi and Arkansas river valleys may have been fewer than before, but they still occupied what Kathleen DuVal has called 'the Native Ground' of North America, from which they excluded all European settlers, negotiating with them (if at all) from a position of great strength. To the east of this region, lay a 'Middle Ground' where Native American peoples formed new relationships both with each other and with the Europeans. Their value as allies enabled them for another century both to impose their diplomatic protocols (such as the 'Covenant Chain') on their European neighbours and to avoid dependence on a single European group. Given the ravages of lethal diseases and savage wars, such resilience was a remarkable achievement.[51]

'This land of Brazil'

Although European colonists in the Americas sometimes went to war against each other in the seventeenth century as part of broader conflicts – the English against the Dutch in the 1660s, and against the French in the 1670s and 1690s – they seldom fought for long or deliberately destroyed much European property. The viceroyalty of Brazil formed a significant exception. By 1630, the Portuguese 'captaincies' of Bahía in the centre, with its capital at Salvador, and of Pernambuco in the north, with its capital at Olinda, each boasted around 12,000 settlers, many of them living on sugar plantations where *engenhos* (mills) made sugar from cane to sell in Europe; while perhaps 60,000 people inhabited the entire viceroyalty, roughly half of them Portuguese and the rest African slaves and Native Americans. Then two catastrophes occurred. First, sailors aboard two fleets that arrived from Lisbon introduced yellow fever, picked up from African slaves, which swiftly decimated the unprotected indigenous population of the colony. Second, a Dutch expeditionary force captured Pernambuco and, having destroyed Olinda, gradually expanded its control southwards down the coastal plain, until in 1640 Salvador itself came under siege. A young Jesuit in the city now delivered perhaps the most remarkable sermon of the seventeenth century in the form of a tirade against God modelled on those delivered by Moses and Job in the Old Testament. 'Consider, Lord, from whom You are taking this land of Brazil and to whom You are giving it,' António Vieira began sternly: 'You are taking it from those same Portuguese whom You chose from among all the nations of the world to be conquerors for Your faith.'

> How will it look, Supreme Lord and Governor of the Universe, if the sacred 'five shields' of Portugal and the insignia and wounds of Christ are replaced by the emblems of the heretics from Holland, rebels to their king and to God? If You had decided to give these lands to the Dutch pirates, why did You not give them when they were wild and uncultivated, instead of now?[52]

Perhaps the tirade (like those of Moses and Job) found its mark, because a few days later a relief force arrived and raised the siege, while in 1641 Salvador celebrated the apparently miraculous news of the 'restoration' of Portuguese independence (see chapter 9 above). But any hope that shifting their allegiance from Philip IV to John IV would bring peace and prosperity soon evaporated. In 1641–2 smallpox 'raged so violently among the Indians that entire aldeias [villages] were almost totally extinguished. The survivors retreated into the forests since they no longer dared to remain in their homes.'[53]

By contrast, Dutch Brazil prospered until, by 1644, some 15,000 settlers inhabited the fertile coastal plain that stretched from the Amazon delta to the São

Francisco river. Almost half the newcomers lived in the handsome new capital Mauritsstad (now the heart of Recife), built with bricks and tiles shipped out from Holland and boasting a fine palace for the governor, numerous churches and the first Jewish synagogue in the New World. Meanwhile, an expeditionary force captured Luanda, the capital of Portuguese Angola and the principal source of slaves required to produce sugar, thus apparently securing the economic future of the new colony. Everything changed in 1645 when the Portuguese settlers mounted a counter-attack that drove the Dutch back into a few coastal fortresses. For the next nine years, civil war between the Dutch and Portuguese colonists and their Native American allies caused widespread devastation. The Dutch seized hundreds of Portuguese ships carrying sugar to Europe, while in 1648 their warships entered the Bay of All Saints, the heart of the Portuguese colony, and torched the *engenhos* around its shores. The Portuguese retaliated in kind, burning so many *engenhos* in Pernambuco that the province lost for ever its position as the colony's leading exporter of sugar. Human casualties were also high. 'The Heavenly Court had decreed,' wrote the rabbi of Mauritsstad, 'that the marauding bands should spread out and invade forest and field. Some of them looked for plunder, others hunted human beings, for the enemy came with the intention to destroy everything.'[54]

The rabbi had good cause to know: the Portuguese treated captured Jews with especial cruelty, either killing them in cold blood or surrendering them to the Inquisition for trial and eventual execution. In all, at least 20,000 Dutch settlers perished in Brazil, and at the fall of Mauritsstad in 1654 the survivors – perhaps 6,000 in number, including at least 600 Jews – lost almost all their assets. Some of the Gentiles sailed on the next fleet to Batavia, intending to make their fortunes in Dutch Indonesia, while many of the Jews migrated to England, hoping that the belligerent Republic might provide them with another chance to settle legally in America.[55] Meanwhile Portuguese Brazil prospered, especially after the discovery of massive gold deposits in the interior in the 1690s, expanding until it covered (as it does today) almost half of South America.

'Panic in the Indies'

In the rest of Latin America, news of the revolt of Portugal ignited what Stuart Schwartz has called a 'panic in the Indies'. According to Don Juan de Palafox y Mendoza, bishop of Puebla and inspector general of the viceroyalty of New Spain in July 1641, 'the whole monarchy trembled and shook, since Portugal, Catalonia, the East Indies, the Azores and Brazil had rebelled'. Rumours spread that rebels had murdered the Spanish garrison in Salvador and that the settlers had made common cause with the Dutch to bring down Spanish power. Both stories proved false, but when an agent from Lisbon arrived in Cartagena and attempted to seize the treasure galleons (which assembled in the port every year), according to Palafox 'apprehension and hysteria' gripped the capital, whose 6,000 Portuguese residents were (he claimed) armed to the teeth and likely to enjoy the support of their numerous African slaves in any rebellion.[56]

The adverse climate, probably related to the unusually frequent El Niño events, made the situation even more volatile. The valley of Mexico normally receives copious rain from May to August, with little precipitation in the other months; but an intricate irrigation system, the creation of artificial floating horticultural beds (*chinampas*) in the lakes, and the maintenance of year-round granaries made it possible to sustain a relatively high population density. In 1639, however, the entire valley suffered the first of five years of drought, during which the price of maize quintupled, leaving the granaries without food and the citizens without water.[57] Blame for these disasters gradually shifted to the viceroy, the marquis of Escalona – who, although a member of one of the oldest aristocratic families in Castile, was not only married to the duke of Bragança's sister (which might tempt him to transfer New Spain to Portuguese hands) but also had Jewish ancestors (which, some thought, led him to protect the local New Christians).

In June 1641 Palafox wrote a secret letter suggesting to the king that Escalona would be better employed elsewhere, preferably in Europe. Philip IV took no chances: he signed three distinct secret orders, authorizing Palafox to use whichever one he judged appropriate: one invited Escalona to return to Spain where the king wanted his advice; a second censured the duke's conduct and ordered him to transfer his authority to Palafox; the third authorized the bishop to have Escalona killed. In each scenario, Palafox would become both archbishop of Mexico and interim viceroy. In June 1642, as soon as he received the package containing these remarkable letters, Palafox entered Mexico City to take up his new ecclesiastical position. Four days later, in a dawn raid, his agents arrested Escalona and confined him in a convent outside the town under guard until he could be shipped back to Spain.

Amid the resulting chaos emerged the remarkable figure of William Lamport, better known as Don Guillén Lombardo de Guzmán, an Irish protégé of the count-duke of Olivares (whose surname he took). Having arrived from Spain with the same fleet as Palafox, Don Guillén worked hard in 1641 to win support from the Creoles (the American-born descendants of Spaniards) for Palafox's plan to over-throw Escalona, but the following year he claimed to be the natural son of Philip III and shared with his Creole allies a plot to liberate Mexico 'from Spanish captivity' and declare himself 'king of New Spain'. By the time a neighbour denounced him to the Inquisition in October 1642, Don Guillén had prepared a declaration of Mexican independence that included the abolition of slavery and forced labour; the establishment of free trade with China and Europe and the manufacture of goods without regulation from Spain; and the creation of a representative assembly in which 'Indians and freedmen are to have the same voice and vote as Spaniards'. He had arranged for a militia of 500 Indians and African slaves to take over the viceregal palace, and waited only for one of the visions induced by the hallucinogens he ingested to reveal the most auspicious moment to launch his revolution. Rumours spread far and wide 'that don Guillén was plotting to make himself king' until the Inquisition suddenly seized him and his papers.[58]

Other parts of Spanish America also saw plots, both real and imagined. In Panama, the entrepot for all goods travelling between Peru and the rest of the

Hispanic world, just as news arrived that a Dutch expeditionary force had sailed round Cape Horn and fortified a base at Valdivia in Chile, a fire broke out that gutted 100 homes and much of the cathedral, followed by another blaze three days later. Once again the Spanish authorities blamed Portuguese nationals and rounded them up – only to find that they numbered just 17. Further south, when the viceroy of Peru, the marquis of Mancera, first received news of the Lisbon revolt, he did not believe it; only on receiving confirmation from Buenos Aires, together with a plea for help, did Mancera send troops across the Andes to secure the settlement.[59] Conscious that he was '500 leagues from the Caribbean and 800 leagues from Buenos Aires', Mancera also fretted that the Portuguese residents of Lima might persuade the African slaves to revolt, because 'the first religious instruction that these slaves receive is from the Portuguese, and they maintain love toward them'; so Mancera rounded up and disarmed some 500 Portuguese residents in the capital, forcibly moving the younger males inland.[60]

Spanish America was thus safe again from political danger, but not from natural disasters. Earthquakes destroyed churches, houses and fortifications in Santiago de Chile (1647), Concepción de Chile (1657), and in Lima and Callao, Peru (1687). Tree-ring series reflect the unusual frequency of both El Niño events and volcanic activity in the mid-seventeenth century which, then as now, caused extreme weather throughout Spanish America. In Argentina, serious floods of the Paraná river in 1643, 1651 and 1657–8 inundated one-third of the regional capital, Santa Fé, and persuaded the magistrates to abandon the city, despite its splendid public buildings, and relocate to higher ground. Meanwhile, the viceroyalty of New Spain continued to suffer repeated droughts. In 1642 the northern town of Monterrey experienced 'such a shortage' that the inhabitants 'sold rotten maize that could no longer be eaten – something neither heard nor seen [before] in New Spain, even in time of greater famine'; and between 1641 and 1668 local officials authorized eight public processions of Our Lady of Guadalupe, an image reputed to possess a miraculous ability to produce rain, and sponsored books to reassure readers of the statue's powers (one in Spanish and the other in Nahuatl).[61]

The prolonged droughts also depopulated the northern frontier of New Spain. In 1638 the Jesuit Provincial of New Spain, who had served in the missions of Sinaloa and Sonora in New Mexico, wrote that 'of the 300,000 Indians who had been baptized by the Jesuits, only one-third were still alive'. Shortly after that, prolonged drought forced the Christian communities on the Salinas plains to use their own urine both to irrigate their crops and to make bricks for the lavish mission churches, while Apache bands (no doubt also suffering from the extreme drought) launched repeated attacks. By 1678, every mission had been abandoned.[62] Meanwhile, in the valley of Rio Grande, between 1629 and 1641 a particularly lethal smallpox epidemic and repeated raids by Apaches killed two-thirds of the population and destroyed half of the Christian pueblos. According to Daniel T. Reff, 'The Pueblo population, in effect, declined by over 80 per cent between 1608 and 1680, much as populations did in north-western Mexico'.[63]

In the Caribbean, the torrential rains associated with the increased frequency of El Niño created optimal breeding and feeding conditions for the vector of both malaria and yellow fever: the mosquito. The first yellow fever pandemic in the New World began in 1647, a year that saw a 'strong' El Niño. In Barbados, attracted both by the sugar and by population densities above 200 per square mile, mosquitos spread the disease, killing one in every seven Europeans on the island as well as decimating other Caribbean islands and then Yucatán. The Mayan chronicle *Chilam Balam de Chumayel* reported that in 1648 'there was bloody vomit and we began to die' – a clear reference to yellow fever, to which (unlike many Africans) neither Europeans nor Native Americans possessed inherited immunity. The rains were followed by 'such a hard and extraordinary drought that it rendered the land sterile and produced such intense heat' that wildfires raged throughout Yucatán, destroying all crops left by the drought. The local chronicler Diego López Cogolludo claimed that 'Almost half the Indians perished with the mortality caused by the plague, famine and smallpox which since the year 1648 until the present one of 1656, in which I am writing this down, have so exhausted this land.'[64]

Two demographic strategies intensified the deleterious impact of these natural disasters on the human population of the Americas. First, according to Maria Sybilla Merian, a botanist who toured the Caribbean in the later seventeenth century, both African and Native American women frequently aborted their offspring to spare them a life of servitude and humiliation. Merian provided a detailed description of the 'peacock flower' (*Poinciana pulcherrima*), one of over a dozen abortifacients that she and other European observers found in use in the colonial West Indies, asserting that 'The black slaves from Guinea and Angola have demanded to be well treated, threatening to refuse to have children. In fact, they sometimes take their own lives because they are treated so badly.' Perhaps realizing that some readers would find this difficult to believe, Merian added 'They told me this themselves.'[65] Second, many women had no children because they entered convents. As in Europe, the number of nuns (which included many cloistered against their will in times of economic hardship) reached astonishing proportions: in Lima, popularly known as the City of Kings, the number of women in convents rose from 16 per cent of the total female population in 1614 to 21 per cent in 1700. By then, there were three Spanish and *mestiza* females for every Spanish and *mestizo* male living in Lima, as well as three *mulatta* and black females for every *mulatto* and black male. As Nancy van Deusen wittily observed, 'the City of Kings had become a city of women.'[66]

Revolt and Resistance in Spanish America

Seventeenth-century Latin America differed from Europe in one important respect: it experienced relatively few revolts. The most serious exception broke out in New Mexico, where (as already noted) prolonged drought produced famines that reduced the population and induced many Pueblo Indians to return to their traditional faith in the hope of bringing rain. Punitive measures by the authorities, both secular and religious, produced a major revolt in August 1680 that drove the Spaniards out of Santa Fé, the regional capital, for a decade – but the continuing drought eventually weakened the victorious (but disunited) Pueblos, and by the end of the century the Spaniards had regained control of the region. In the valley of Mexico, despite the prolonged drought of the 1640s and 1650s, and the activities of Don Guillermo Lombardo de Guzmán, no rebellion occurred; and Spanish South America likewise experienced few serious revolts. In 1656 Pedro Bohorques Girón, a Spaniard of Morisco descent who grew up in Cádiz and then migrated to America, appeared in the remote city of San Miguel de Tucumán (now in northwest Argentina) and proclaimed that he was the grandson of the last Inca ruler and therefore true king of the region. This was not the first insurrection by the settlers of Peru during the seventeenth century (others occurred in 1613, 1623 and 1644), but Bohorques boasted dangerous military skills (including the ability to found light artillery) and won considerable support from the indigenous population. After two years of defiance, Spanish forces defeated and captured him and sent him to Lima for trial on charges of rebellion. He was still there, pending the outcome of an appeal to Spain, when another insurrection broke out in Upper Peru.[67]

The fleets that brought most European settlers to the Americas left from Seville and, not surprisingly, many of the newcomers (like Bohorques) came from Andalusia. Nevertheless, a substantial number came to America from elsewhere, and some preserved their regional identity – none more so than men and women from Spain's Basque provinces, many of whom communicated in their native language. Although the Basques always remained a minority, the rest of the Spanish community envied their expertise and success in mining. The most serious rivalry occurred in Laicacota, a silver-mining region in the Altiplano region of the Andes. Two Andalusian prospectors discovered silver there in 1657 and founded a town that soon became the fourth largest in the region, with perhaps 1,500 inhabitants, many of them Basques. Almost immediately, the region experienced a series of natural disasters: both the maize and coca harvests failed between 1659 and 1662, while epidemic diseases struck in 1660–1. Rioting broke out that pitted not only Basques but also native mineworkers (both Indian and *mestizo*) against the Andalusian mine owners. Although government forces restored order, in 1665 the Basque insurgents, supported by sympathetic magistrates, seized control of Laicacota and its rich mines. The following year, however, the Andalusian mine owners, aided by a militia of Indians and *mestizos*, counter-attacked, chased out the magistrates, and sacked the town to shouts of 'death to the Basques'.[68]

No sooner did news of this open defiance of royal authority, and of the alliance between Spaniards and Indians, arrive in Lima than the viceroy died. In Arequipa, the town council discussed cancelling religious processions, for fear that discontented elements might exploit the crowded streets to begin a riot (as had happened in both Barcelona and Naples: see chapters 9 and 14 above). Rumours circulated that some Indians in Lima intended to flood the city while other groups throughout the viceroyalty would rise up at Epiphany 1667 to kill all the Spaniards and restore Inca rule; but the authorities acted promptly and executed potential ringleaders. Basque fugitives from Laicacota in the capital convinced the new viceroy, the count of Lemos, that 'the kingdom had come within an ace of a great disaster' and persuaded him to lead a punitive expedition into the Altiplano – the first viceroy to visit the area for a century. Lemos executed over sixty insurgents (including Pedro Bohorques for good measure), imprisoned many more and razed the rebel strongholds.[69] When the government in Madrid undertook a formal inquiry into the troubles at Laicacota, however, having collected and considered 25,000 pages of testimony, it concluded that Lemos had overreacted. There had been no risk of a 'great disaster', only manipulation of power by factions: claims that Lima 'tottered on the verge of insurrection' had no more substance than those of Pedro Bohorques to be an Inca, of Don Guillermo Lombardo de Guzmán to be Philip III's illegitimate son, or of Palafox and Mancera that Portuguese residents were poised to seize Spain's colonial capitals.

Why did Spanish America largely escape the political upheavals that afflicted so much of the planet in the mid-seventeenth century – especially since both climatic adversity and epidemic diseases caused widespread mortality and economic dislocation? Admittedly, in some areas, such as the isthmus of Panama, the pool of available Native American labour fell so drastically that by the 1630s many towns lacked sufficient food and the colonists' country estates lacked enough hands to bring in cash crops (above all cacao and indigo). The economy of the entire area entered a half-century of depression.[70] Elsewhere, however, the European settlers found other ways of compensating for labour shortages: they imported more African slaves; and they also increased the labour required from the Native Americans who worked in their mining, farming and textile production – creating appalling conditions that probably led to overall population decline.

Many towns also failed to thrive. An acute shortage of potential brides not only inhibited population growth but also led to some of the highest illegitimacy rates recorded in the Western world. Thus in the largest parish of Lima, over half of all registered births in the seventeenth century were illegitimate and about half of *those* were born to slaves – indeed, 80 per cent of all registered births to slave mothers were illegitimate: yet another tragic consequence of the abusive power relations that prevailed. As in Europe, a grim future awaited most bastards. The devoted staff of the Foundling Hospital of Lima 'walked day and night through the streets, corrals, stables, [and by] rivers and waterways to see if desperate people had given birth there', and carried those they found either to the hospital, where most of them died, or to a convent, where the survivors eventually became the celibate servants of the nuns.[71]

Taken together, these various limits on human reproduction may have averted the 'overpopulation' found elsewhere and thus shielded Spanish America from the 'General Crisis'; but the diversification of the colonial economy also brought relief. The records of the 'House of Trade' in Seville, which show a sharp fall in official commerce between Europe and Spanish America from 1623 to 1650, have led many historians to suppose that all long-distance trade in the Hispanic world stagnated; but, although disastrous for the Spanish government, the decline brought tangible benefits to America (Fig. 42). Transatlantic trade tied up capital for at least a year – several years in the case of Peruvian merchants, because of the greater distances involved – while Philip IV frequently confiscated goods aboard the fleets as soon as they arrived in Seville in order to fund his wars. To avoid such disasters, American

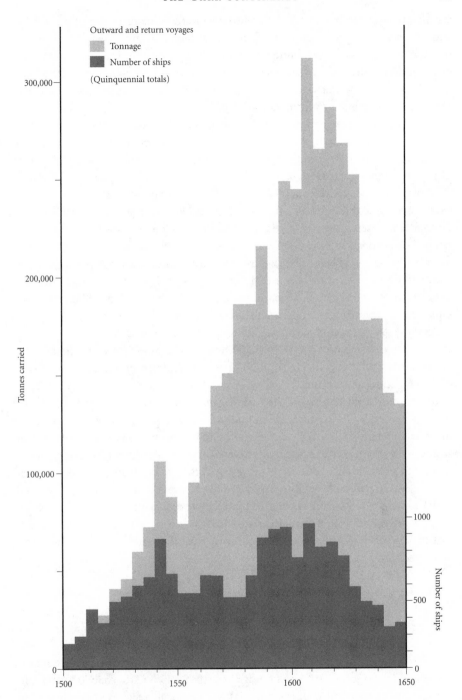

42. Trade between Seville and America, 1500–1650.
The records of the House of Trade (*Case de la Contratación*) in Seville charted the rhythm of official trade between Europe and Spanish America. Following a century of sustained and rapid growth, after 1620 both the number of ships crossing the Atlantic and the volume of their cargoes declined. By 1650, the quantity of goods carried was less than half the level in 1600.

merchants began to buy and sell clandestinely both in Spain (especially in Cádiz) and in the Caribbean, escaping both the surveillance of the House of Trade and the risk of confiscation, and often avoiding all taxes and duties. As the Peruvian historian Margarita Suárez has observed: 'Rather than a general crisis' of the Latin American economy, 'the seventeenth century produced a crisis in Spain's ability to extract economic benefits from its colonies'.[72]

This shift generated great domestic profits in Spanish America, encouraging many regions to develop specialty crops for export to other colonies: thus by the mid-seventeenth century Peruvian sugar, conserves, wines and vinegars were shipped to Chile, Panama and even Mexico, where they displaced Spanish competition. Moreover, most of these goods came from relatively modest units of production that proved hard for the government to monitor and tax – even had local officials proved vigilant. But they did not: instead, reports of administrative corruption, inefficiency and extortion reached such a pitch that in 1663 the crown appointed special inspectors to investigate the treasury officials of Peru. They uncovered over a million pesos in unpaid back-taxes; and although the viceroy had some of the corrupt officials executed, revenues remitted to Spain continued to fall. Whereas in the 1630s an average of 1.5 million pesos left Lima every year for Seville, in the 1680s the average fell below 150,000 pesos.[73]

All these developments meant that more wealth remained in America, as reflected in the output of coins by the leading Mints of the viceroyalty, which doubled between the 1620s and the 1680s, and in the magnificent public buildings (especially churches) constructed in the second half of the seventeenth century in virtually every colonial town of the period. Put another way: although the Little Ice Age affected Philip IV's American colonies, the king lacked the power to exacerbate the impact of natural disasters via his costly and inappropriate policies. If, in spite of all these favourable circumstances, rebellions still occurred, then the king's representatives acted swiftly – often executing suspects (like Lombardo and Bohorques) without waiting for authorization from Madrid – because, as the century advanced, they had more to lose from rebellions than the crown. In effect, the government in Madrid and the elites in its American dominions developed a *convivencia* similar to that of Spanish Italy (see chapter 14 above) that benefited both parties and thus preserved stability.

Africa

South Africa

Sub-Saharan Africa forms the largest area of the globe for which evidence is either ambiguous or absent concerning the impact of climatic change in the mid-seventeenth century on economic, social and political structures. We know that both extreme climatic events and important structural changes occurred there, but it is extremely difficult to link them.

The Cape of Good Hope, where in 1652 Dutch settlers established a small fort to guard the stores to refit and replenish the ships sailing between Southeast Asia and the Netherlands, offers a good example of the limitations of the available evidence. As soon as the Dutch began to establish farms beyond the walls of their fort, the Khoekhoen (whom the Dutch pejoratively called 'Hottentots') complained to Governor Jan van Riebeeck that the newcomers 'were living upon their land, and they perceived that we were rapidly building more and more as if we intended never to leave'. They then 'declared boldly that this was not our land but theirs'.[74] Since mere words appeared to make no impression, the Khoekhoen tried to halt the colonists' expansion by force, but after about a year of indecisive fighting they resumed negotiations. In 1660 their leaders once again 'strongly insisted' that the Dutch 'had been appropriating more and more of their land, which had been theirs all these centuries, and on which they had been accustomed to letting their cattle graze etc. They asked *if they would be allowed to do such a thing supposing they went to Holland*' – a telling point indeed – 'and they added: "It would be of little consequence if you people stayed here at the fort, but you come right into the interior and select the best land for yourselves, without even asking whether we mind or whether it will cause us any inconvenience"'. To this, van Riebeeck retorted:

> There was not enough grass for their cattle as well as ours; to which they replied: 'Have we then not reason to prevent you from getting cattle, since, if you have a large number, you will take up all our grazing grounds with them? As for your claim that the land is not big enough for us both, who should rather in justice give way, the rightful owner or the foreign intruder?' They thus remained adamant in their claim of old-established natural ownership.

Since the Khoekhoen were evidently getting the better of the argument, 'eventually' (van Riebeeck recorded dryly in his *Journal*) 'they had to be told that they had now lost the land as the result of the war and had no alternative but to admit that it was no longer theirs. . . Their land had thus fallen to us in a defensive war won by the sword, as it were, and we intended to keep it'. When the Khoekhoen leaders 'complained bitterly' that the colonists 'had done them much mischief' by stealing from them and 'by beating and striking them', van Riebeeck admitted (at least in his *Journal*) that 'there is some truth in this' but warned them that they should lodge formal complaints and not 'take their revenge by means of robberies and thefts' because then 'peace could never be maintained between us, and then by right of conquest we should take still more of their land from them'.[75] Later the Khoekhoen gave ground and agreed that they would graze their herds only on lands unoccupied by Dutch farmers; and before long, the influx of colonists and the ravages of European diseases (above all smallpox) among the native population tipped the balance permanently in favour of the newcomers. A century later, Cape Colony was the largest Dutch outpost overseas.

These developments at the Cape of Good Hope thus had effects that were both important and long-lasting – but can they be linked to the Little Ice Age? It would be reasonable to suppose that the adverse climate of the 1640s and 1650s affected the crops of southern Africa as it did elsewhere, thus reducing the available grazing and food resources of the region just as a new group of consumers (the Dutch) arrived, and that this scarcely contributed to the confrontation between them and the native inhabitants – but without a 'natural archive' for the period to reveal the prevailing climate, no such connection can be drawn. In addition, generalization would be doubly hazardous because in three important respects the Cape was not typical of Africa. First, the Dutch newcomers found the sole concentration of temperate land in an almost entirely tropical continent. Second, they encountered only herders and gatherers who (unlike other indigenous peoples in the region) lacked iron, and above all iron weapons, and who could therefore be either expelled or enslaved with relative ease. Finally, the Cape boasts a safe anchorage (except in winter) and relatively easy access to the interior, whereas most of sub-Saharan Africa lacks both the profusion of natural harbours and navigable rivers leading far inland that mark other continents. Instead, less than 100 miles inland, most African rivers descend precipitately from the central plateaux to the sea over powerful waterfalls virtually impenetrable to ships.

East Africa

Ethiopia and some adjacent regions normally suffer drought during episodes of El Niño – and the increased frequency of episodes in the mid-seventeenth century is reflected in the flood waters of the Nile in Egypt, which in 1641–3, in 1650 and again in 1694–5 fell to some of the lowest levels ever recorded.[76] This suggests that severe drought periodically afflicted the Ethiopian highlands, where the Nile rises, in the seventeenth century; yet the surviving records of the area, and of other regions of East Africa, mention no political unrest, social upheavals, or economic depression. Of course, this may merely reflect absence of evidence. Attempts to reconstruct the experience of the Iteso (or Teso) people, whose hereditary lands lie between the great lakes of East Africa, have so far failed because (according to James B. Webster, a modern researcher) the Iteso are 'a people whose ethnic identity and community depend on the art of forgetting'. He continued sourly: 'The field researcher has listened to a coherent and detailed account of an historical episode with exciting analytical possibilities. The elders have stopped speaking. There is a pause pregnant with expectation':

> Researcher: 'When did that happen?'
> Elders: 'Noi!'
> Interpreter: 'Long ago'.
> Researcher: 'How long ago?'
> Elders: 'Noi! Noi!'
> Interpreter: 'Long, long ago'.

'During research into Iteso history "Noi! Noi!" becomes the most often heard and, to the researcher, most depressing expression in the language.' It is the one 'he learns first and forgets last'.[77] Nevertheless the silence of seventeenth-century sources from East Africa may constitute evidence of absence rather than absence of evidence, because two factors probably rendered the region 'underpopulated' when the Little

Ice Age struck. First, in modern Uganda (the Iteso homeland), a protracted rainfall deficit in the late sixteenth and seventeenth centuries culminated in a total crop failure and famine between 1617 and 1622, which apparently caused mass migration and (presumably) heavy mortality. This may have created a more sustainable balance between food supply and demand a generation later, despite climatic adversity. Second, throughout the seventeenth century, two slave caravans assembled in Sudan, one in the city of Sennar on the Nile and the other in Darfur, which brought at least 5,000 men and women every year to Cairo, to be sold as slaves to toil in various parts of the Ottoman empire. This forced migration may also have relieved the demographic pressure at times of climatic adversity.[78]

West Africa

In West Africa, for which somewhat better records survive, water dominates both the ecology and the economy: climatic change is therefore registered primarily in changes in the rainfall regime. *Sahara* means 'wilderness' or 'desert' in Arabic, and even on its southern margins in most years only 4 inches of rain falls. This meagre precipitation in the Sahel, the semi-arid tropical savannah belt south of the Sahara that stretches from the Atlantic Ocean to the Red Sea, is sufficient to sustain only small nomadic groups that herd camels, sheep and goats on seasonal grasses and other hardy vegetation. Just south of the Sahel, the land receives between 4 to 16 inches of rain per year, which make it possible to breed and raise cattle, sheep and goats – provided the herders move south in winter (the dry season) and north in summer (the rainy season) to find water for themselves and their herds. Further south still, annual precipitation of between 16 and 24 inches allows the cultivation of millet, the hardiest of cereal crops; and where annual rainfall exceeds 24 inches and produces the rolling tropical grassland known as savannas, farmers can grow sorghum and other rain-dependent crops. The majority of West Africa's people lived in these 'savannas', which stretch from latitude 15° North to latitude 30° South.

It is important to note both the vulnerability and the incompatibility of these three farming strategies. Small variations in rainfall can produce major consequences. If the rains fail in an area that normally receives 16 inches of precipitation, all agriculture ceases and its cultivators must either migrate or become pastoralists – and those who opt for the latter course will soon encounter nomads forced by the same desiccation to migrate south in search of grazing for their herds and flocks. Farmers and herders who previously traded grain and textiles for milk, meat and animals, therefore begin to compete directly for land that has become marginal, and to this end both sides may deploy either force or the threat of force. It is also important to note that all these rainfall levels are averages. Thus at Podor, in northern Senegal, between 1887 and 1927 the annual rainfall averaged 12.5 inches, but this included one year with over 20 inches and another with only 5; while at Ziguinchor in southern Senegal over the same period the annual rainfall averaged 60 inches, which included one year with over 80 inches and another with scarcely 28. These variations were crucial for the survival of crops, herds and humans. Significantly, Ziguinchor's worst year was better than Podor's best, and enough rain fell to sustain cereal crops in every year; moreover, Ziguinchor enjoyed not only five times the mean rainfall but also a growing season twice as long as Podor (five months as against barely two). Farmers in Podor therefore faced permanent insecurity – and yet the distance between the two location s is only 300 miles: less than the distance that separates Boston from Baltimore, or London from Newcastle (Fig. 43).[79]

Vulnerability and insecurity in the Sahel also arise from oscillations in the Intertropical Convergence Zone (ITCZ): the point where the rain-bearing winds from the South Atlantic meet the dry trade winds that prevail further north. In the sixteenth and early seventeenth centuries the ITCZ lay further north than today, allowing an expansion of cultivable land in the Sahel. After 1630, however, it moved southwards, probably because of the cooler temperatures in northerly latitudes associated with the Little Ice Age, and this movement produced a southward advance of the deserts, prolonged droughts and political instability. The surviving records from Senegambia, the region between the Senegal and Gambia rivers, mention 'famine' 15 times during the seventeenth century, with especially intense events in 1639–41, 1666–8, 1674–6 and 1681. Visiting Gorée (an island just off modern Dakar) during the last of these great famines, the French trader Jean Barbot reported that 'several thousand persons have lost their lives and a greater number their liberty' and that the survivors 'looked like perfect skeletons, especially the poor slaves'. Barbot also stated (presumably on the basis of local information) that 'there were even worse famines in 1641 and 1642' – years of unusual cold in north-erly latitudes.[80] In the interior, Timbuktu and the region around the Niger Bend also suffered their greatest 'famine of the seventeenth century' at this time, with '1639 and 1643 virtually without rain, and low rainfall in the intervening years'; and they experienced famine again in 1669–70, after two years of drought. Meanwhile lands further east evidently experienced an epic drought in the 1680s (also a time of unusual cold in the northern hemisphere) because Lake Chad fell to the lowest level ever recorded (Figs 44 and 45).[81]

These landmark famines of West Africa did not all arise solely through drought: two forms of political disruption exacerbated the situation. First, an essential skill for successful West African rulers was 'rainmaking'. Naturally a prolonged drought called this ability into question and might lead to a challenge from someone, such as a religious leader (in Muslim areas often a sufi Sheikh: *marabout* in many West African languages) who claimed supernatural powers. Second, a ruler of pastoral communities whose rainmaking skills failed during a drought might still retain his authority through a successful war, using surprise and mobility to expel or subjugate neighbouring populations, and thus provide his followers with access to adequate water and grazing grounds. The latter no doubt explains the migration of nomads from what would soon be called 'the Empty Quarter' of the Sahel to prey upon the farmers immediately to the south, which in turn led those displaced to attack their own southern neighbours in a tragic domino effect. The 'war of the Marabouts' exemplifies the former.

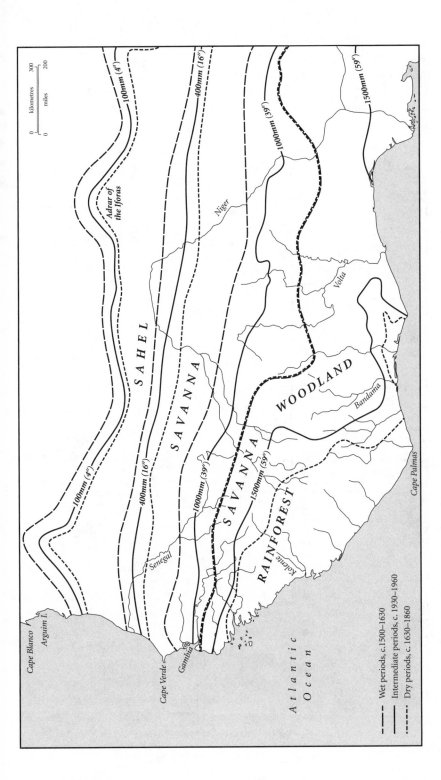

43. The southward advance of the Sahara from 1630.

Rainfall patterns in West Africa range from an annual average of 4 inches in the 'Sahel' on the fringe of the Sahara desert to almost 60 inches in the rain forests along the coast, with several critical thresholds that determine what types of agricultural endeavour are viable. After about 1630, each of these thresholds moved southwards, forcing farmers to migrate.

Within the map:

Cape Blanco
Arguim I.
Cape Verde
Gambia
Senegal
Adrar of the Ijoras
Niger
Volta
Bandama
Kolente
Cape Palmas

SAHEL
SAVANNA
WOODLAND
SAVANNA
RAINFOREST

Atlantic Ocean

100mm (4″)
400mm (16″)
1000mm (39″)
1500mm (59″)

kilometres 0 — 300
miles 0 — 200

- - - Wet periods, c.1500–1630
— — Intermediate periods, c. 1930–1960
- · - Dry periods, c. 1630–1860

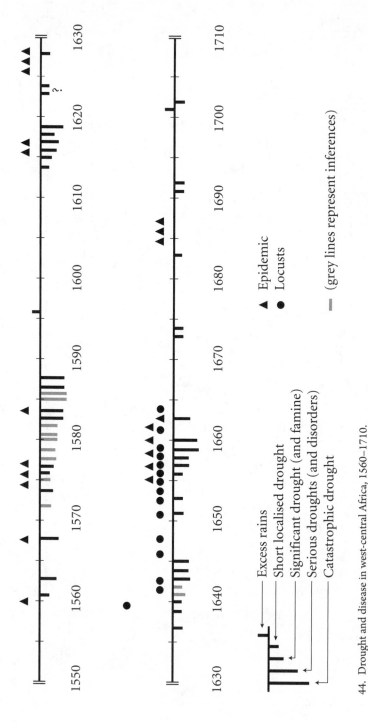

Legend:

Excess rains

Short localised drought

Significant drought (and famine)

Serious droughts (and disorders)

Catastrophic drought

▲ Epidemic
● Locusts

━ (grey lines represent inferences)

44. Drought and disease in west-central Africa, 1560–1710.
Although the surviving records show that several droughts afflicted the areas occupied today by Congo and Angola, the mid-seventeenth century saw an unparalleled combination of natural catastrophes, with drought, locusts, and epidemics.

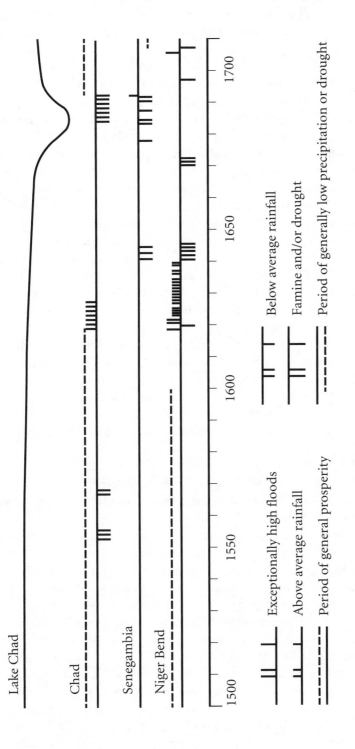

45. Famine and drought in Chad, Senegambia, and the Niger Bend, 1500–1710.
After a period of general prosperity in the sixteenth century, the states of Sahara Africa experienced frequent famines and draughts in the 1640s and, even more severely, in the 1680s – when Lake Chad fell to the lowest level ever recorded.

Louis Moheau de Chambonneau, a French trader in Senegal, attributed the famine of 1674–6 largely to a civil war caused by a charismatic Muslim sheikh, aged about 30, who 'claimed that he was sent by God' and who attracted many adherents in the various Wolof kingdoms along the Senegal river by 'preaching penitence entirely naked, disdaining clothes, with his head entirely shaved. He spoke only of the law of God and of welfare and freedom.'[82] While Chambonneau called the sheikh *Toubenan* (from the Arab and Wolof word *tuub*, meaning 'Convert to Islam'), and Arabic sources called him Nasir al-Din (and claimed he came from Mauritania), everyone agreed that 'the war of the Marabouts' targeted those whom the sheikh deemed insufficiently Islamized. Chambonneau reported that in 1674 the new French base at St Louis, at the mouth of the Senegal river, already suffered a 'scarcity of foodstuffs because of these wars', but the situation soon became far worse when one of the Wolof rulers counter-attacked, and 'for the entire year 1676 he did nothing but kill, take captives, pillage and burn the countryside' belonging to Muslim zealots, 'destroying the millet harvest and cutting it down while still green, forcing the local population to eat boiled grass'. When Chambonneau sailed up the river to trade, 'whole families offered themselves to me as prisoners, provided they were fed, having reached the extremity of killing each other in order to steal some food'.[83]

Worse followed. Nasir al-Din's version of Islam enjoined, among other things, a shift from agriculture to herding, and he therefore required his disciples to cease sowing crops. This shift left them totally unprepared when severe drought returned in the 1680s. Desperate for food, Toubenan's converts killed their animals to stay alive, but having done so, they either fled or starved. The number of slaves known to have been transported by sea from the states of Senegambia reflect these changes, almost doubling from over 8,000 in the 1670s, the decade of the 'war of the Marabouts', to over 14,000 in the 1680s. Even a century later, visitors found no farmers at all in the region.[84]

Similar instability, caused by a combination of human and natural agency, prevailed further south. After visiting the Bights of Benin and Biafra in 1678–9 and 1681–2, Jean Barbot asserted that the local states were 'ruined by the continual wars which have caused continual famines'. According to historian John Thornton, 'probably more than half of the people of Atlantic Africa lived in polities that measured around 50 kilometres [30 miles] across and had only a few thousand inhabitants, comparable in size to an American county or perhaps to a parish' in western Europe. Unlike Americans and Europeans, however, African states did not engage in their 'continual wars' for land, but for people: African legal systems did not regard land as private property, so that 'ownership of slaves in Africa was virtually equivalent to owning land in western Europe or China'.[85] Until the mid-seventeenth century, when the ITCZ migrated southwards and the climate of West Africa deteriorated, most of these conflicts for slaves remained small scale and involved elite warriors who fought with javelins and clubs; but thereafter, rulers began to create much larger armies of slaves and mercenaries, armed first with bows and then with muskets, who fought over far larger areas and took far more captives. This change, seen by some subsequent historians as a 'military revolution', triggered an arms race in which rulers eager to acquire firearms for their defence traded them for slaves, feeding the dramatic expansion in the transatlantic slave trade as European demand for slaves to work their American sugar plantations escalated.

Forced Migration: The African Slave Trade

African slavery, which existed long before the Europeans arrived, took two forms. First, rulers used enslavement to remove troublemakers from society: those found guilty of (for example) adultery, witchcraft or theft might be fined more than they could pay and, if their kin-group would not help them, the offenders were sold as slaves (the sale price paid their fine). Second, men and women captured during wars or raids also became slaves. 'The distinction between these two processes was crucial,' Robert Harms reminds us. 'Slaves in the former category [criminals], were unlikely to run away because they had no place to go' and so often remained in the area; whereas a captured slave 'had quickly to be taken from the point of capture so that he [or she] could not return home'. The demand of both European and Arab traders for cheap labour increased both forms of slavery, but especially the second. According to an eighteenth-century missionary who interviewed slaves in the Caribbean about their background, 'most of them were captured in open warfare'. The same was no doubt also true earlier.[86]

The fate of the two million or more men, women and children forcibly deported from Africa to the Americas during the seventeenth century has recently become better known thanks to the remarkable database constructed from almost 35,000 documented slave voyages (roughly 80 per cent of the total) by David Eltis and his colleagues. Almost one-half of the slaves came from West Central Africa (the 500 miles of coast on either side of the Congo estuary); almost one-quarter came from the Bights of Benin and Biafra (the coastal areas on either side of the Niger Delta); and almost one-tenth from Senegambia. Until 1641, ships from Spain and Portugal accounted for 97 per cent of the slave trade organized in Europe, but the separation of the two crowns and the ensuing war between them (see chapter 9 above) opened the way for French, Dutch and British ships to deport slaves to work on their rapidly expanding sugar plantations in the Caribbean. Of 160,000 slaves who disembarked in the Americas during the 1680s, over 141,000 went to the Caribbean (Fig. 46).[87]

The Little Ice Age played its part in increasing the slave trade, not only via the political, social and economic disruption caused by the southward shift of the ITCZ in the hinterland of Senegambia and the Bights of Benin and Biafra (see above), but also via an increase in droughts, epidemics and wars in West Central Africa. Of an estimated 12,569 slaves deported to the Americas in 1639, all but 285 came from West Central Africa. That year saw the beginnings of a severe drought in the region that lasted until 1645, while the simultaneous Luso-Dutch struggle to control Angola profoundly affected the neighbouring native states, especially Kongo, one of the few large states of Atlantic Africa.[88] The kings of Kongo, with perhaps 500,000 subjects, had long maintained an ambiguous relationship with the Portuguese, converting to Catholicism but otherwise striving to remain independent, while the

	Senegambia	Sierra Leone	Windward Coast	Gold Coast	Bight of Benin	Bight of Biafra	West Central Africa	South-east Africa	All regions combined
1601–10	16,251	0	0	0	583	507	74,532	51	91,923
1611–20	18,700	0	0	211	4,880	1,154	124,795	62	149,807
1621–30	8,185	0	0	0	4,854	3,884	165,502	821	183,246
1631–40	7,650	0	0	0	3,546	1,855	105,679	0	118,730
1641–50	28,563	521	0	4,250	5,307	28,749	56,014	0	123,404
1601–50	79,353	521	0	4,461	19,170	36,149	526,522	934	667,110
1651–60	30,836	989	707	1,790	15,681	27,102	79,325	0	156,429
1661–70	21,126	151	0	22,233	30,918	40,300	110,210	4,399	229,337
1671–80	11,821	0	0	32,083	40,843	47,434	78,819	11,776	222,775
1681–90	23,493	1,539	0	19,218	117,956	21,996	65,570	10,931	260,703
1691–1700	23,797	2,268	0	33,630	163,246	40,777	74,694	2,770	341,182
1651–1700	111,073	4,947	707	108,954	368,644	177,609	408,618	29,876	1,210,426
1601–1700	190,426	5,468	707	113,415	387,814	213,758	935,140	30,810	1,877,536

46. Slaves captured and shipped from Africa, 1600–1700.
The Europeans exported twice as many slaves in the second half of the seventeenth century as in the first. Of this total, one-third of them came from West Central Africa, one tenth from Senegambia and Sierra Leone, and over-half from the Gold Coast and the Bights of Benin and Biafra. The table does *not* include the overland deportation of slaves living in Sub-Saharan Africa to the Ottoman empire.

Portuguese constantly sought to impose economic and political as well as spiritual control. The Dutch capture of Angola in 1641 changed this situation. According to Bento Teixeira de Saldanha, a Portuguese resident, the Dutch let the indigenous inhabitants 'live in their own lands, allowing them to produce in their own way everything they needed to live, without permitting a single white man to disturb them in their homes – as the Portuguese have always done, and still do, molesting them and robbing them'.[89]

Teixeira wrote just after an expeditionary force from Portuguese Brazil regained Angola in 1648 and immediately recommended 'molesting' the native population, and just as a new episode of drought, locusts and disease disrupted life in the interior and led to a succession dispute in Kongo. After a few years of restless coexistence, in 1665 a Portuguese force from Luanda invaded and routed the main army of Kongo at Ambuila (Mbwila), killing the king and ending the existence of his realm as a coherent kingdom. Henceforth, regional chiefs maintained themselves by fighting wars to secure slaves, whom they sold to European traders in return for guns and ammunition.[90] The decennial total of slaves exported from West Central Africa leaped from almost 60,000 in the 1650s to almost 100,000 in the 1660s and to over 120,000 in the 1670s. Right up to abolition of the slave trade, the region continued to export more slaves than any other part of the continent.

Did this high level of forced migration perhaps mitigate the impact of the Little Ice Age on those humans who remained in sub-Saharan Africa? After all, migration from a community normally reduces its food requirements, and certain areas near to the principal ports of deportation experienced significant out-migration – especially when we include not only the deportees who reached America, but also those who succumbed to disease as their captors took them from drier inland areas to the coast, where they lacked immunity to new disease environments, and those who perished in the overcrowded and unsanitary coastal holding pens or on the voyage. Malnutrition, ill treatment and despair all took their toll: many of the logs kept by the slaving ships record the cause of death of their precious cargo, and they included 'stubbornness' and 'lethargy' as well as 'dysentery', 'scurvy' and 'a violent blow to the head'. Not for nothing did the Portuguese call the ships that carried slaves from Africa to America *tumbeiros*: 'coffins'.

If we include all forced migrations from East, Southeast and West Africa, seventeenth-century European and Arab traders between them apparently deported some 30,000 slaves annually from a continent with perhaps 100 million inhabitants – which at first sight makes the overall impact seem marginal (except, of course, for the victims). But the slaves did not come from all parts of the continent: on the contrary, most of them seem to have lived within 150 miles of coast – and, within that restricted area, often in specific regions. Although we currently lack data on the exact origin of seventeenth-century slaves, those from the eighteenth century show 'a remarkable degree of geographic concentration'. For example, the 'profile of slaves' that embarked on vessels leaving the Bight of Biafra reveals that 'most captives originated in the small Cameroon Highlands area'. In addition, over half the slaves deported to the Caribbean from the Bight of Biafra in the seventeenth century were female and one-tenth were children; while almost one-fifth of those deported from West Central Africa were children and over one-third were female. Deporting women and children intensified the impact of emigration by removing (in effect) the next generation.[91]

Yet even with all these exacerbating factors, it seems unlikely that even the areas of Africa most involved in the slave trade lost more than 10 per cent of their population through forced migration – whereas a drought, and drought-induced epidemic, could wipe out three times as many people. So, to return to the earlier question – did forced migration mitigate the disruptive impact of the Little Ice Age on those humans who remained in sub-Saharan Africa? The answer may well be affirmative. If we add famine and disease mortality to the high level of forced migration in coastal regions, the synergy of human and natural agency in sub-Saharan Africa may have removed one-third of the total population, as it did in much of Asia and Europe, and these disasters may have assisted those who remained to survive even prolonged climatic adversity.

Australia

Australia, the driest inhabited continent, covers 5 per cent of the planet's land mass and yet it has (and has probably always had) one of the lowest population densities in the world. The reason for this disparity lies in a combination of climate and isolation. Only the southeastern and southwestern corners of Australia boast both a temperate climate and fertile soils; but since they lie furthest away from the other continents, until the late eighteenth century they remained almost entirely isolated from the rest of the world, both demographically and economically. Deserts and semi-arid lands, known as 'the outback', cover more than two-thirds of Australia, and the annual rainfall in some locations there can vary from under 4 inches to over 36 inches. As in sub-Saharan Africa, the critical variable is not the *average* annual rainfall but its *seasonable reliability*. Even in the temperate zone, drought and the threat of drought are constant concerns.

Two factors preclude precision about the experience of Australia's population in the seventeenth century: the paucity of the 'natural archive', especially the rarity of tree species that produce distinct annual growth rings; and the complete absence of a 'human archive'. Although several groups of Europeans visited after 1606, none of them described climatic conditions; while although the indigenous inhabitants probably referred to catastrophes in their rich oral traditions, attempts to date these events have so far failed. Nevertheless, some generalizations can be offered. Australia, in the words of the pioneering historian of climate Richard Grove, has 'above all other places a claim on the epithet, "the el Niño continent".[92] This means that the same droughts that afflict China, Southeast Asia, Indonesia and India in El Niño years also afflict Australia – and therefore that the doubled frequency of El Niño events in the mid-seventeenth century would have struck Australia with unusual force. In particular, the continent presumably experienced the same major drought registered in nearby Indonesia between 1643 and 1671, with particularly intense episodes between 1659 and 1664 (see chapter 13 above.) Reconstructed tree-ring sequences from the island of Tasmania in the south appear to confirm this surmise, showing a succession of poor growing seasons in the mid- and late seventeenth century, a period that saw the 'most prolonged cool period in the past 700 years'.[93]

How much would these climatic events have affected the population of Australia in the seventeenth century? To survive the extreme climate even in 'normal' times, native Australians needed adaptive strategies in much the same way as many of the unique flora and fauna of the continent. Many Australian plants survive because they have developed deeper roots and an enhanced resistance to fire, while some Banksia species produce cones that release seeds only after experiencing both a bushfire *and* the subsequent onset of rains – precisely the environment most favour- able to germination and seedling survival. Likewise the red kangaroo has evolved uniquely efficient mechanisms to cope with the unpredictable extremes of rainfall: it eats vegetation high in moisture, and so can go for long periods without drinking; it hops, which enables higher speeds of travel with no increase in energy expended; and its reproductive cycle, known as *embryonic diapause*, supports three babies at different stages of development at the same time, which allows a rapid increase in population as soon as a drought ends.[94]

The annual life cycle of the aboriginal population of Australia's Western Desert in the mid-twentieth century suggests that its human population also adopted unique strategies in order to survive in some of the harshest environments on earth. The annual cycle began with the 'wet season' between December and February, when huge thunderstorms unleash torrential rains, which provide abundant water but do not immediately produce food. Family groups therefore moved around, foraging in areas neglected since the last wet season until seeds, root crops and fruit began to appear in March; then they settled down, living for two months or so by waterholes on the plains and harvesting crops (albeit often amid periodic drizzle and temperatures that fall to 6°C at night). This 'cold time' ended in August as temperatures rose rapidly and the landscape gradually dried out. Men now set fire to vegetation on the plains, both to trap game and to improve the yield of seeds and tubers the following year, while women prepared and stored the vegetables that would sustain the group through the rest of the year. Eventually in the 'hot time' or 'hungry time', as temperatures rose to 50°C, the waterholes on the plains dried up, forcing people to retreat to rock holes for the rest of the year. There they reduced their daily activities and tried to make their food and water last as long as possible, but since drought and heat stress limited foraging to areas near the rocks, the average calorific daily intake might fall as low as 800 per person – roughly half of what is necessary to sustain even someone of small stature. Sometimes the weak drank blood drained from the stronger members of the group in order to get through the last few weeks until the torrential rains returned and allowed them to leave their rock holes and spread out on the plains once more.

Although the environment of the Western Desert is harsh, its human inhabitants found and used 120 plants to satisfy their needs. Of these, 70 yield edible parts and over 40 produce seeds, which the women of the group would laboriously husk, winnow, grind and turn into a paste to be either baked in the campfire or eaten raw. Tubers and bulbs were far easier to turn into food – they were simply pulled up and roasted – while large game (such as kangaroo), once caught, would be gutted and grilled, and small game (birds, lizards and snakes) would be baked.

Since both the seasons and the availability of each resource followed the same pattern each year, the aboriginal populations of the Western Desert survived through their intimate environmental expertise, combined with knowledge of when each source of nutrition would become available as the seasons changed, and the use of fire to trap game and stimulate future crops. The one unpredictable variable was the precise duration of the 'hungry time', which determined whether or not there would be sufficient water and food to sustain the group from one annual cycle to the next, and thus who would die (either from thirst or starvation) and who would be born (because famine amenorrhoea would prevent conception).

Scott Cane, whose research on aboriginal subsistence strategies in the Western Desert is summarized above, noted one other feature of life in the 'hungry time': 'If the rains fail to come, tensions run high and fights are common'. All Aboriginal groups carried weapons – some of them offensive: spears, often used with spear-throwers which produced a velocity of 100 miles per hour and accuracy up to 164 feet; boomerangs; and clubs, sometimes with sharp shells attached to the head. Clearly these weapons were used against people, as well as game, because warfare features in many Aboriginal oral traditions, while when the British arrived in Sydney in 1788, they 'found Aborigines with wounds that could only have [been] caused by fighting with other Aborigines'.[95] It seems probable that wars between rival groups – like fights between group members – became more common in years when the 'hungry time' dragged on and reduced essential resources. It therefore also seems probable that a fatal synergy between natural and human factors prevailed in Australia, and that its population shrank in the seventeenth century until the reduced resources available sufficed to satisfy its minimum demands.

Scott Cane believed that his study of the Aborigines of the Western Desert presented 'the last reliable data on hunter-gatherer subsistence economies from arid environments anywhere in the world' because the way of life he described ended in the 1950s when the hunter-gatherers 'moved from the [Western] Desert onto cattle stations, missions and government settlements, scattered around the desert fringe'.[96] Nevertheless, a modern aboriginal bark painting shows a keen awareness of the destructive power of the weather. It depicts Namarrkon, the 'Lightning Spirit', holding in his hands conduits of power that run from his large testes, while his knees contain stone axes: both serve to remind viewers of how bolts of lightning destroy trees and start wildfires – and thus of the need to complete all activities, both farming and social, before the season of powerful storms begins.[97]

In the seventeenth century, hundreds of thousands – if not millions – of 'hunter-gatherers' populated the various 'arid environments' of the planet. In large parts of Africa and the Americas, in Central Asia and in the far north of Europe, human populations must have evolved coping strategies similar to those of the aboriginal population of Australia, allowing them to survive; and, as in Australia, those strategies no doubt proved only partially adequate whenever the annual 'hungry time' grew longer. Although the absence of a 'human archive' for these various groups precludes certainty, it is possible that in arid environments, too, 'one-third of the world died' in the seventeenth century. If so, it means that the only large area to register rapid and sustained population growth in this period, apart from New France and New England, was Japan.

Getting it Right: Early Tokugawa Japan[1]

The Pax Tokugawa

Eᴀʀʟʏ ɪɴ ᴛʜᴇ sᴇᴠᴇɴᴛᴇᴇɴᴛʜ ᴄᴇɴᴛᴜʀʏ, ᴛʜᴇ ꜰᴏʀᴇᴍᴏsᴛ Jᴀᴘᴀɴᴇsᴇ ᴄʜʀᴏɴɪᴄʟᴇʀ of his day rejoiced that 'In this age, there are none even among peasants and rustics, no matter how humble, who have not handled gold and silver aplenty. Our empire enjoys peace and prosperity; on the roads not one beggar or outcast is to be seen.' A few years later one of his colleagues went even further: 'What a marvellous age! Even peasants like me enjoy tranquillity and happiness... They dwell in the land of bliss. If this is not a [Buddhist Paradise], then how is it that I and other men could meet with such great fortune?' Admittedly, a few of their contemporaries elsewhere also expressed confidence in the immediate future: an English ambassador who gloated in 1618 that everywhere 'the gates of Janus' had shut, which 'promised Halcyonian days' to 'the greatest part of Christendom'; the Italian preacher Secondo Lancellotti (scourge of 'whiners') five years later. But whereas Europe suffered wars, revolution and economic collapse for the rest of the seventeenth century, Japan experienced the *Pax Tokugawa*: rapid demographic, agricultural and urban growth – and no wars.[2]

Tokugawa Japan: The First Century

Year	Population size (in millions)	Urban population (in millions)	Arable land (in million acres)	Harvest yield (in million bushels)
1600	12	0.75	5	100
1650	17	2.5	6	115
1700	27	4	7	150

The figures in the above table are striking not just because of the dramatic population growth – some parts of the archipelago experienced a fourfold increase during a century when most of the world experienced a sharp demographic decline – but because of the simultaneous increases in total land cultivated, harvest yields and urban population. Over 7,000 new villages sprang up during the seventeenth century, many of them on lands brought under the plough for the first time thanks to complex hydraulic engineering projects (153 in 1601–50 and 227 in 1651–1700), while average rice production per village rose from around 2,000 bushels in 1645 to over 2,300 bushels in 1700. These averages concealed some spectacular achievements: thus almost 400 new villages were founded in Musashi province (the area around Tokyo) between the late sixteenth and the late seventeenth centuries, and their rice production soared from 3.3 million to over 5.5 million bushels.[3]

Early Tokugawa Japan also experienced 'urbanization without precedent in history': between 1600 and 1650 the number of people living in towns and cities tripled, and between 1651 and 1700 it almost doubled again. Most of this urban population lived in 'castle towns', over one hundred in number. Kanazawa, for example, with some 5,000 inhabitants in 1583 when it became the headquarters of the largest domain in western Japan, numbered 70,000 by 1618 and perhaps 100,000 by 1667. Edo (as Tokyo was then known) grew from little more than a fishing village in 1590, when it became the headquarters of the Tokugawa domain, to a metropolis of perhaps one million a century later.[4]

These unique achievements did not stem from a benign environment: on the contrary, the Japanese archipelago has always been extremely vulnerable to climate change. To begin with, its northern areas are subject both to the Chishima Current, which brings arctic water southwards, and the 'Yamase effect', which produces cool air for considerable periods of the summer. Both climatic events can cause crop failures. Furthermore, most of Japan consists of mountains thrown up by the collision of the earth's tectonic plates, which has three adverse consequences. First, the archipelago – like many other parts of the Pacific rim – has an unusual number of active volcanoes, and their eruptions could and did trigger the 'Yamase effect'. Second, the majority of the Japanese population lived (and still lives) on the coastal plains of three islands – Honshu, Shikoku and Kyushu – and the abrupt gradients that rise from these coastal plains make it harder to bring new land under cultivation. Finally, the pressure to house and heat the rapidly growing population led to 'clear-cutting' the tree cover (that is, removing *all* grades of wood rather than only certain trees) on those steep slopes, which caused serious soil erosion and magnified the risk of frost, flood and drought.

According to Conrad Totman, the eminent environmental historian of Japan, the combination of aggressive cultivation of recently deforested land and the prevalence of 'clear cutting' on steeply sloping ground 'crowded the biological boundaries of crop viability' and made the transition from relative abundance to ecological overload in marginal lands exceptionally abrupt, and 'increased the portion of total food production chronically at risk of failure'.[5] The archipelago therefore could not escape the effects of the Little Ice Age. During the landmark winter of 1641–2, the first winter snow fell on Edo six weeks earlier than usual; and according to the memoirs of Enomoto Yazaemon, a merchant living near Edo, 'on New Year's Day, pots and pans full of water froze and seemed likely to burst; and one foot of frost covered the fields. Thereafter I observed seven snowfalls until the spring.' The prolonged cold weather created 'the Kan'ei famine' (named after the Japanese era in which it occurred). The price of rice rose from 20 silver *monme* in 1633 to 60 in 1637–8, and to 80 in 1642.[6] Even in Osaka, the 'kitchen of Japan' where in normal years merchants, lords and officials maintained huge stockpiles of food, rice became so scarce in July 1642 that 'the common man cannot maintain himself, his wife and his children, so that many people died of hunger'. Crowds congregated before 'the house of the city governor and lamented . . . begging His Excellency to provide them with some means by which they could stay alive'. To pacify the protestors, 'the afore-said governor distributed rice from various storehouses, and from the granary in Osaka castle, to the destitute at a low price. This ended the disturbances.'[7]

Another revolt, at Shimabara in the southern island of Kyushu, arose from the imposition of oppressive taxes at a time of climatic adversity. According to a Dutch merchant living nearby, when the lord of Shimabara demanded 'taxes and demands for so much rice that they could not be met', his agents tied up those unable to pay and dressed them in 'clothes made of straw', which they then set on fire. They also humiliated 'their wives by stringing them up with their legs entirely bare'. Outraged by such atrocities, weary of being asked 'to pay far more in taxes than they are able to do', and unable to 'subsist on roots and vegetables', the villagers resolved 'to die one single death instead of the many slow deaths to which they were subject': so in December 1637 they rebelled. Their defiance encouraged the peasants of neighbouring Amakusa Island, also long abused by their superiors, to kill their magistrate and the soldiers sent to restore order, after which they crossed to the mainland to join the revolt. European missionaries in the region had converted many Japanese to Christianity, including Amakusa Shirō, a 16-year-old boy who claimed to be the reincarnation of Christ; and many converts joined the rebellion. Some 200 discontented samurai (warriors) likewise joined the rebels and offered invaluable military advice. Some 25,000 insurgents, marching 'under banners bearing the sign of the cross', now burned down the town of Shimabara, the headquarters of the domain, and collected food and weapons before retiring to the neighbouring castle of Hara, on a promontory surrounded by the sea. For three months, Amakusa Shirō 'preached and celebrated Mass twice a week', confidently proclaiming that 'judgment day is at hand for all Japan' and that 'all Japan will be Christian', until the army of over 100,000 men sent by the central government took Hara Castle by storm and slaughtered everyone within – including Amakusa Shirō.[8]

The rebellions at Osaka and Shimabara proved a turning point in Japanese history. The first four decades of the seventeenth century had seen some 40 major rural revolts (*hōki*) and 200 lesser uprisings (*hyakushō ikki*), as well as almost 80 feuds fought out between the major landholders; but during the next 80 years both revolts and feuds virtually ceased.[9] The food riots in Osaka also had no sequel: most Japanese towns remained peaceful for a century or more. Most remarkable of all, the Shimabara campaign proved to be the last major military action in the archipelago for two centuries. Seventeenth-century Japan thus presents a curious contrast with the rest of the world: although initially its experience did not differ markedly from that of other countries, since it suffered from both the Little Ice Age and the General Crisis, in the 1640s it broke free. How?

The Industrious Revolution

The eminent Japanese historian Hayami Akira has identified two paths of escape from the tyranny of subsistence agriculture. The first path, typical of western Europe, is capital-intensive and labour-saving: investing money in agriculture to make production more efficient, thereby creating a pool of cheap labour to fulfil factory demands, and so facilitate an Industrial Revolution. The second path is the exact reverse: a labour-intensive and capital-saving strategy that Hayami christened 'the Industrious Revolution' in which peasants escaped from subsistence farming by investing more time and energy, rather than more money, in agricultural endeavour. Although improved farm tools and techniques played their part in Japan's Industrious Revolution, output improved primarily because farming families rationalized production and worked both harder and longer. 'Self-exploitation', Hayami argued, is the principal explanation for why the amount of cultivated land doubled, population tripled and output quadrupled in Tokugawa Japan between 1600 and 1868.[10]

Japanese families also adopted four additional prudential strategies to ensure that demand for basic resources would not outrun supply. First, many people worked away from home for prolonged periods: in some villages, up to one-third of all adolescents left to work either in a neighbouring community or in a town. Hayami's research revealed that 'the lower the social stratum, the more people work away from home, and the higher their age upon return to the village to marry'; and that, on average, the daughters of poor Japanese families married five years later than their wealthier sisters. This delay significantly reduced the number of children they could bear.[11] Second, those women who stayed home worked long hours in the field, which no doubt both reduced fertility and increased infant mortality (see chapter 4 above). Third, in the absence of animal milk (for few Japanese farmers raised livestock), mothers breast-fed their children intensively, often exclusively, until the age of three or four, a practice that normally suppresses ovulation.

Fourth and finally, as in China, when families faced economic hardship in spite of these prudential strategies, they regularly resorted to abortion and infanticide – procedures significantly termed, in Japanese, *mabiki*: 'thinning out' (as with seedlings). Qualitative data suggest that both practices were common. In 1646 the central government banned the public advertisement of 'menstrual medicines' within the capital, and in 1667 made it illegal to carry out abortions there. Nevertheless, 1692 saw the publication of *A guide to ladies good fortune*, dealing with all aspects of pregnancy, including abortion. Although most methods were herbal, the book also described how to insert sticks into the uterus and how to vibrate the womb.[12] As for infanticide, in the words of the English merchant Richard Cocks, one of the most astute Japan-watchers of the seventeenth century: 'The most horriblest thing of all is, that parents may kill their own children so soon as they are born if they have not the wherewithal to nourish them'. Even children's names reflected the determination of Japanese parents to limit family size: some were called *Tome* (meaning 'Stop') and *Sue* ('The Last'), while visitors to some temples can still find special plaques placed by distraught mothers in the Tokugawa era to 'apologize' to their aborted foetus.[13]

Besides these 'negative strategies' for survival in time of hardship, Japanese villages also implemented certain positive policies that promoted collective survival. Above all, the average community was divided into many holdings of different sizes: one or two large ones, rather more middle-sized ones and a majority of small or very small ones. Although this distribution pattern was true of villages throughout the early modern world, in Japan many farmers included in their households both serv- ants and sub-tenants, while most villagers with no land at all were also attached to one of the landholding households. Documents often referred to the household head as *oyakata* ('one who takes the role of parent') and to the servants and sub- tenants as *kokata* (or 'child': in Japanese, the term 'orphan' does not mean 'without parents' but 'without family'). Thus each village was not a collection of autonomous farming units, but rather a cluster of mutually dependent households. Ideally, the *oyakata* furnished the capital goods needed periodically by the smaller households, while the *kokata* provided the labour required at certain crucial periods by the larger farms (above all transplanting rice seedlings which, despite the large amounts of water needed to flood each paddy in turn, had to be effected in each field within a matter of hours). Communities also cooperated to perform certain collective func- tions that exceeded the resources of individual households, such as building or re-thatching a dwelling, repairing communal dikes, or dredging the irrigation chan- nels. Above all, during food shortages, the *oyakata* were expected to feed their *kokata* (whether servants or sub-tenants) and not abandon them.[14]

All these strategies helped to mitigate the impact of the Little Ice Age on early Tokugawa Japan, but two other factors played a greater role. First, although Japan had enjoyed the same benign climate in the sixteenth century as the rest of the northern hemisphere, a century of civil war (known as the 'Warring States Era': *sengoku jidai*) ensured that most of the archipelago was underpopulated rather than overpopulated. According to a European who lived in Japan during the 1580s, which saw the last decade of the civil war,

> Much of the land was not tilled, and when the cultivated parts were sown they were destroyed and plundered by neighbours and opposing factions. Men killed each other everywhere. Thus the entire kingdom and the nobles were left in the greatest poverty and wretchedness as regards their dignity and everything else, and the only law was military power. Men chastised and killed one another as they saw fit.[15]

In the 1590s Japan deployed vast resources in a vain attempt to conquer the Korean Peninsula; and even after that venture failed, huge armies manoeuvred and fought for control of the archipelago until 1615. Second, the 'Warring States Era' left a favourable political legacy: the ceaseless power struggle eventually eliminated alter- native foci of power until only one remained – the Tokugawa dynasty and their allies. In 1614 Richard Cocks termed Tokugawa rule 'The greatest and powerfullest tyranny that ever was heard of in the world', and over the next two centuries the dynasty used its power to coordinate responses that neutralized some of the worst effects of the Little Ice Age and created conditions favourable to rapid economic and demographic growth.[16]

'The greatest and powerfullest tyranny that ever was heard of in the world'

Although Japan has always been an empire, by the sixteenth century the emperor exercised no executive authority. Instead political and military power in the archipelago were divided between *daimyō* (literally 'great names') until, in the last three decades of the century, Japan was reunified by three powerful warlords: Oda Nobunaga (d. 1582), Toyotomi Hideyoshi (d. 1598) and Tokugawa Ieyasu (d. 1616). After a series of brilliant military operations that eliminated all his rivals, Hideyoshi (who had risen from peasant foot-soldier to general, and so possessed a unique understanding of the dynamics of Japanese society) imposed a series of measures that promoted social and economic stability. He commanded farmers throughout Japan to surrender all their 'swords, bows, spears, muskets, or any other form of weapon': henceforth, farmers could not legally own any weapons and must instead 'engage completely in cultivation'. Next, Hideyoshi decreed that samurai could no longer be farmers and farmers could no longer be samurai: henceforth magistrates must 'not harbour anyone who neither performs military service nor engages in [the cultivation of] fields'.[17] Although a few samurai gave up their weapons and remained in their community as farmers, most of them relocated with their households to the headquarters of the local daimyō where they became salaried retainers, largely living in the new towns that grew up around their lord's headquarters. As Hideyoshi intended, these measures both separated the samurai from their traditional rural power base and demilitarized the countryside.

To ensure that no one could commit abuses 'in the collection of annual taxes and thus foment uprisings', Hideyoshi also commissioned a vast cadastral survey. Inspectors toured the archipelago to measure all land parcels, to identify their purpose (rice paddy, dry field, residential lot) and their quality (from 'superior' to 'very inferior'), and to estimate their potential productive yield according to a standard measurement: the *koku* (approximately 5 bushels in the case of rice, the commonest but not the only commodity assessed). Land was therefore measured in the number of *koku* it could produce: the *kokudaka*. Hideyoshi permitted no exceptions or exemptions to the survey: his officials must 'pursue a lord to his castle and put him to the sword along with all of his vassals' and 'kill all the recalcitrant peasants in a whole district' if they refused to cooperate.[18] Although a few areas had still not been surveyed by 1598, the year of his death, Hideyoshi had created a far more complete inventory of the productive capacity of his country than any other ruler of the early modern world.

Hideyoshi's death without an adult heir in 1598 reopened the civil wars, but two years later Tokugawa Ieyasu defeated a coalition of his opponents and in 1603 secured from the emperor the title 'Shogun' (in full, *Sei-i taishōgun*: 'Great generalissimo who overcomes the barbarians'). Ieyasu and his immediate family now controlled the major towns and about one-quarter of Japan's arable land, while some 200 daimyō – most of them either his other relatives or long-term allies – held the rest of Japan as fiefs.

Ieyasu levied no direct taxes on the daimyō: instead he requested 'donations' for specific purposes (such as building materials and labour to expand and fortify his headquarters at Edo) and 'invited' each of his allies to spend prolonged periods with him in Edo, where he could keep them under surveillance. He also continued Hideyoshi's practice of accumulating information that enhanced his power. Thus his cartographers used the cadastral surveys to produce a uniform 'national map' of unprecedented detail, size and scope. Measuring 12 by 14 feet, it showed all the provinces and towns, as well as all the sea routes and harbours, the roads and post stations, and the travelling distances by land and sea between the principal centres. The map presented Japan as a seamless unity – it omitted all regional, administrative or social differences – and, since the shoguns allowed copies and prints to be made, the map soon became a logo of the newly unified state. No other government of the day produced (let alone mass-produced) anything like it.[19]

Ieyasu also invested in a comprehensive communications infrastructure centred on the network of trunk roads known as the five highways (gōkaidō), each with checkpoints where travellers had to show their papers. Whereas the Chongzhen emperor dismantled China's courier system (see chapter 5 above), the new shogun provided post-stations at regular intervals, each one equipped with fresh horses, porters, supplies and lodgings, and linked by relays of professional runners who travelled in pairs (one carrying documents or small parcels and the other with a lantern so that they could travel by night and day).[20] The system worked so efficiently that the Tokugawa government could predict precisely how long messages would take to reach their destination. For example 'on the afternoon of December 21 [1637] an urgent letter relating news of the insurrection in Shimabara arrived at Osaka Castle by messenger boat'. The senior Tokugawa officials there, conscious that 'in the meantime, the insurrection may have progressed, and that before it could grow bigger it must be quelled', discussed all their options and then,

> As the night turned into day, a warning letter was sent off to the Edo government. The lord of Bichû [the senior official] noted that the distance between Edo and Osaka was 325 miles, and the roundtrip by relay couriers would take 10 days. Then, discussion [in Edo] would take at least one day [making the return time] 11 days. When a response was finally received, it would take at least 10 days for it to make the 878 mile trip by sea [back], and if the favourable westerly winds were not as they are now, it would take 14 to 15 days to arrive.[21]

In the event, thanks to the government's remarkable communications system, two generals and thousands of elite troops dispatched from Edo reached Shimabara by 17 February – less than six weeks after the shogun received the 'warning letter' and less than two months after the outbreak of the revolt. No European government possessed the ability to react so effectively to an emergency on the periphery of the state.

As soon as he had destroyed the remaining strongholds of his opponents in 1614–15, Tokugawa Ieyasu issued a plethora of regulations to be obeyed by daimyō and their followers, by the imperial court and even by the emperor himself (who, although lacking effective power, still enjoyed immense prestige). They ranged from the petty (court nobles must micturate only in urinals) to the drastic – above all, henceforth each daimyō could retain only one castle and must destroy all the rest. Ieyasu died the following year, but his son Hidetada (who ruled until 1623) and grandson Iemitsu (r. 1623–51) inherited his title of shogun and further consolidated and expanded the power of the central administration.[22]

The shoguns periodically dispatched inspectors to assess each fief's defensive disposition, legal system, economic means and general morale. An unfavourable report could mean confiscation. Perceived incompetence (for instance provoking peasant rebellion through heavy-handed policies or allowing vendettas among vassals) could also result in forfeiture of a fief. Thus, after his troops had brutally suppressed the rebellion by the vassals of Shimabara and Amakusa, Shogun Iemitsu deposed both of the daimyō whose unreasonable demands had caused the revolt, forcing one to commit suicide and keeping the other in prison. He then annexed Shimabara to the Tokugawa domain and issued an edict that ordered everyone to 'return to living peaceably as in previous times', forbade 'riotous behaviour', outlawed Christianity and prohibited 'giving shelter or assistance' to fugitive peasants or samurai. However, the same edict also addressed the vassals' grievances: it forbade 'the buying and selling of persons', abolished all outstanding tax debts and labour services, and offered the farms of condemned rebels to anyone who wanted to take them.[23] In all, between 1615 and 1651 the Tokugawa confiscated the fiefs of 95 daimyō who thus lost all means of support – as did their retainers, who lost their stipends and became rōnin (masterless samurai). Over the same period the shoguns also transferred 250 other fiefs from one daimyō to another. According to Harold Bolitho: 'Never in the history of Japan had so much violence been done to local autonomy.'[24]

Iemitsu also extended his control over daimyō in other ways. He forbade them to build big ships, levy tolls, or settle disputes among themselves; he required them to maintain roads, bridges and post-stations in their domains; he commanded them to extirpate Christianity and to decide all legal cases 'according to the laws of Edo'. Above all, he transformed their visits to Edo into a closely managed 'alternate attendance' system (sankin kōtai: the first word meant 'reporting for audience', the second 'to rotate').[25] Henceforth each daimyō had to reside in the capital for 12 months out of every 24, and leave his principal consort and his heir there permanently (in effect as hostages). Iemitsu appointed different months of the year for specific groups of daimyō to 'report for audience', both to prevent possible plotting among them and to avoid depleting sensitive areas of all local leaders at the same time. In addition, his guards at all checkpoints on the roads leading to and from Edo searched for weapons coming in, women going out (since a lord who removed his wife might be plotting treason), and 'anybody else suspicious' who could not produce written permission to travel. When a prominent daimyō arrived slightly late for his scheduled *sankin kōtai* in 1636, Iemitsu sentenced him to three years of house arrest.

Trying to avoid humiliation and punishment at the hands of the shogun encouraged the daimyō to compete among themselves in constructing and maintaining more (and more luxurious) mansions in Edo for themselves, their family and their retainers. Moreover, since 'alternate attendance' was, in theory, military service, each daimyō had to travel to Edo fully armed, with an entourage of samurai appropriate to his rank (in the case of less important lords, virtually all retainers might have to accompany their lord, and the greater ones might travel in a procession of several thousand people) and the various expenses created by 'reporting for audience' absorbed half the total revenues of some domains. By 1700 the capital contained over 600 daimyō compounds, housing at least 250,000 people.[26]

Iemitsu also issued uniform codes to regulate the behaviour of other groups of subjects. In 1643 he promulgated 'Regulations for villagers' on Tokugawa lands, which codified appropriate behaviour in annoyingly comprehensive detail, with special regard for the type of clothes and ornaments permitted for each social group. Thus only village headmen could wear silk, have gates at their compound or covered ceilings in their homes; no peasant could use red or purple dyes when making textiles; and so on. 'Fashion was to be regulated by decree because it had to express degree', in the felicitous phrase of Robert Singer, an art historian. 'Consumption, especially public consumption, should not express personal wealth but should demonstrate one's subordinate or superior place in the polity, and one's acceptance of it.'[27] Similarly, since all major commercial and industrial centres remained under the shogun's direct rule, Iemitsu issued edicts to regulate the production and distribution as well as the consumption of goods, and to urge urban craftsmen, artisans, artists and architects to increase their productivity through hard work. This comprehensive legislation formed the foundation of 'the industrious revolution'.

Iemitsu also took drastic steps to limit Japan's overseas trade. Whereas his predecessors had encouraged Japanese merchants to build large vessels that traded with numerous ports in Southeast Asia, and promoted overseas trading colonies in Cambodia, Taiwan and Indonesia, in the 1630s Iemitsu banned all foreign trade, and residence abroad, by any Japanese. The only exceptions were a compound near Pusan in Korea and another at Okinawa in the Ryukyu Islands, where Japanese merchants handled trade with the Asian mainland. For a while, Iemitsu tolerated the presence of Portuguese merchants – although in 1636 he confined them to Dejima, an artificial island in Nagasaki bay connected to the mainland by a single bridge and dependent on the Japanese authorities for everything, even drinking water.[28] Three years later, since he blamed their missionaries for the Catholic overtones of the Shimabara rebellion, the shogun expelled all the Portuguese in Japan; and when, in 1640, an embassy with over 50 members returned to plead for the restoration of free trade, he killed them all and posted a notice at the site warning that

> A similar penalty will be suffered by all those who henceforward come to these
> shores from Portugal, whether they be ambassadors or whether they be sailors,

whether they come by error or whether they be driven hither by storm. Even more, if the king of Portugal or [Buddha] or even the God of the Christians were to come, they would all pay the very same penalty.

Iemitsu seems to have expected the Portuguese to seek revenge, and so ordered daimyō with fiefs near Nagasaki to stay at home with all their retainers instead of visiting Edo, but he need not have worried. Distracted by the rebellion against Philip IV (see chapter 9 above), the Portuguese dared not raise their hands against him. In 1641 Iemitsu relocated all Dutch merchants to the vacant island of Dejima, and for almost two centuries they remained the only Europeans allowed to visit and trade with the archipelago legally.[29]

The savage treatment of the Portuguese formed part of a coordinated campaign to control the religious beliefs of Iemitsu's subjects. In 1638 the shogun required everyone living on Tokugawa domain lands to present proof to the local magistrate that they belonged to a Buddhist temple. In 1665 his successor extended the same requirement to daimyō lands; and from 1671 the proof had to be presented annually. The magistrates compelled anyone suspected of deviance to trample on images of the Virgin Mary to 'prove' their indifference to Christianity; those who refused, and any missionaries captured, were tortured and executed.[30] Tokugawa apologists sought to 'sacralize' the new dynasty, propagating the cult of the founder Ieyasu as *shinkun* or 'divine ruler' and sponsoring shrines in his honour. Over 40 'Tōshōgū shrines' existed by 1624 (most of them erected by Ieyasu's son Hidetada) and many more followed (some built by Iemitsu, and the rest by nobles anxious to please him). The most important of these still stands at Nikkō, 80 miles north of Edo, where in 1634–6 Iemitsu constructed a stunning architectural complex covering over a square mile and filled with over 500 paintings and more than 5,000 sculptures.[31] The shogun also sponsored tracts that mixed texts drawn from Buddhist, Confucian and Shinto sources to explain how the dynasty had acquired the Mandate of Heaven, and how Japan's warrior code (*Bushidō*) formed the ideal instrument to preserve it. Most of those who wrote such tracts were either warriors or the sons of warriors, and they stressed absolute obedience to authority as the supreme virtue for subjects, exalted military norms in peace as well as in war, and compared the primary task of civil leaders with that of generals: directing and coordinating the movement of great masses of people. According to Suzuki Shōsan, a samurai who became a monk, in a tract of 1652: 'To receive life as a peasant is to be an official entrusted by Heaven with the nourishment of the world'. Suzuki also suggested (like Thomas Hobbes in England: see chapter 12 above) that subjects owed obedience to any ruler who provided them with peace and justice.[32]

Coping with the Kan'ei Famine

Tokugawa Japan thus enjoyed several structural advantages over other states in confronting the Little Ice Age. At the local level, the *oyakata/kokata* system provided a safety net for many of the most vulnerable people; while the *kokudaka* system created granaries that could be opened in case of famine. The separation of daimyō and samurai from their hereditary lands, together with the 'sword hunts', made resistance more difficult to organize; while the stream of edicts regulating behaviour both accustomed the central government to take the initiative in social and economic matters and predisposed its subjects to obey. Nevertheless, climatic adversity placed Japan under severe stress. During the terrible winter of 1641–2 (according to the memoirs of Enomoto Yazaemon) 'the corpses of those who had starved to death filled the streets'; Edo 'was full of beggars clad only in straw'; and 'from 50,000 to 100,000 people starved to death in Japan'. One upland village informed the shogun in 1642 that the famine had eliminated one-third of its population: 147 householders had starved to death, 92 had been forced to sell all their land and 38 more had fled.[33]

To cope with the Kan'ei famine, Iemitsu convened a series of emergency meetings with officials from the regions around the capital to discuss appropriate measures. At the most basic level, he set up food kitchens and shelters for the starving, and instructed all daimyō and city magistrates to do the same. He also authorized magistrates to release rice held in the government's granaries both to the starving and to farmers who lacked seed grain, and he ordered daimyō residing in Edo as part of the *sankin kōtai* system to return to their domain and organize famine relief. Most striking of all, he forbade daimyō to impose labour services on their peasants without government permission, and he drastically reduced the state's tax demands. The outstanding records of one village showed that it paid to the central government 23 per cent of its total production in 1636, but 21 per cent in 1640, 11 per cent in 1641 and only 6 per cent in 1642.[34]

Despite all these prudent measures, food prices continued to rise and Iemitsu therefore ordered farmers to plant only staple crops (for example, no tobacco and other cash crops could be planted as long as the famine lasted); and prohibited the use of rice to make *sake*. His officials erected notices all over the country urging farmers to be frugal, to continue tending their fields, and to bring their crops to market. In July 1642, when he received accusations that certain granary officials and rice merchants were withholding rice reserves in the hope of getting a better price, Ietmitsu had eight of them executed, required four others to commit suicide and exiled many more after confiscating their property. The hoarding ceased. The shogun also issued a stream of other economic legislation: the peasants of each village would be held collectively responsible for paying its tax quota, so better-off farmers must help the rest; any abandoned smallholding could be confiscated to the common good; roads and bridges had to be maintained to expedite the transport of foodstuffs to famine areas; 'because of the poor harvests, people are suffering extreme poverty so daimyō should be careful to avoid measures that would make their situation even worse'. When the lord of Aizu nevertheless provoked a peasant uprising, Iemitsu immediately confiscated his fief.[35] Iemitsu's comprehensive response to the famine also included legislation that limited the ability of vassals to organize collective protests against abusive lords, and made petitioning higher authorities a capital offence. Henceforth discontented vassals of an abusive daimyō had recourse to only one 'safety valve': they might migrate collectively to a neigh-bouring domain, a procedure known as *chōsan ikki*, 'organized flight'.[36]

Iemitsu's raft of proactive measures seems to have worked. Although Japan, like other areas in the northern hemisphere, continued to suffer periodic climate adver-sity, after the 1640s the surviving records no longer mention people dying in the streets. Moreover, the number of revolts by vassals against their daimyō dropped from 17 between 1631 and 1640 to 9 between 1641 and 1650; while scarcely 50 *chōsan ikki* episodes occurred between 1640 and 1680. Yet the shogun did not rest on his laurels. To prevent any recurrence of disorders and subsistence crises, he undertook more cadastral surveys and issued a stream of further edicts in 1648–9, later known as the Kei'an Laws. Some decrees aimed at reducing conspicuous consumption. Thus townsmen must not build three-storey houses, use gold in their homes (either in the structure or in household articles), ride in palanquins or wear wool capes, and their servants must not wear silk. Even the fabric used to make men's underwear was regulated (no silk!).[37] Daimyō, for their part, must not commission elaborate woodcarvings, metal ornaments, lacquered mouldings or lattice work for their dwellings; they should serve only modest meals, accompanied by a small (prescribed) amount of sake. In short, the shogun ordered: 'Do not have a liking for articles which you do not need, that is, articles other than military equip-ment. Do not indulge in personal extravagance. In all things, be frugal.' Iemitsu left no doubt concerning the rationale for all this: at a time of general crisis, he stated, it was imperative to conserve resources. 'Unless you are generally frugal, you will not be able to govern the country. If the superiors indulge increasingly in luxury, the land tax and corvées of their subordinates will increase and they will be in distress.'[38] Iemitsu also sponsored public works that increased food production (especially canals, land reclamation and irrigation schemes: the annual rate of construction doubled after the 1640s) and set up a system of emergency loans that were immedi-ately available to daimyō in the wake of a natural disaster (whether fire, flood, earth-quake or volcanic eruption) and repayable in easy stages.[39]

The Kei'an Laws of 1648–9 also micromanaged everyday behaviour. The shogun instructed villagers to arise early each morning to cut grass and pull weeds, to cultivate fields all day, and to spend their evenings making ropes and sacks. They should eat only barley and millet, except on a few specified holidays, leaving the rice they produced to pay their taxes; they must drink neither sake nor tea; they should plant trees around their house to supply firewood; and their toilets should have ample storage for human waste to provide fertilizer for their crops. Other articles dealt with the care of livestock, filial piety, health care and the need for all men to marry and procreate (the laws designated bachelors as 'bad villagers' and authorized farmers to divorce wives whom they deemed lazy). Others still repeated earlier legislation to limit peasant spending: farmers could not wear silk (even if they produced and wove the thread) or wear clothes dyed in patterns; only headmen could wear cotton rain capes and use umbrellas (everyone else must use straw capes and hats); and the ban on the consumption of tobacco, tea and sake became permanent.[40]

These energetic reactions demonstrate what a clearheaded early modern ruler *could* attempt and achieve in the face of a major catastrophe. Moreover, the shogun's example spread to daimyō fiefs. Thus, after the peasant rebellion at Aizu in 1642 (page 494 above), Iemitsu transferred the fief to his own half-brother, Hoshina Masayuki, who immediately imitated the shogun's policies. First, Hoshina initiated a new survey of the rice-producing capacity of each village, eliminating land made barren by floods or landslides. Second, he granted tax relief to villages whenever their crops failed, and he reduced the overall tax rate 'in order to help those whose need is greatest and to prevent peasants who might otherwise default from being forced to become indentured servants'. Third, Hoshina established funding agencies that made loans (some of them interest-free) to villagers in distress or to outsiders wishing to settle in the fief. Finally, he sponsored land-reclamation schemes that added substantially to the areas under cultivation. Thanks to these measures, between 1643 and 1700 the population of Aizu – a fief with some 200 villages – rose by 24 per cent, and although the tax yield rose by 12 per cent, the average tax per capita fell by 11 per cent.[41]

Other Japanese lords followed Iemitsu's example whenever their estates faced a crisis. Thus in August 1654 Ikeda Mitsumasa, lord of Bizen province (central Honshu), confided to his diary that 'this year's drought and flood are the greatest disasters to befall my tenure as daimyō', and he therefore decided that 'we must avail ourselves of the wisdom of the entire domain. Consequently a suggestion box will be set up. All, from the elders to men of those of lowest status, should write recommendations anonymously and place them in the box.' Ikeda also instructed his tenants to harvest the local rice early and purchased additional supplies in Osaka; he postponed tax payments and 'forgave' arrears; and he heard petitions from the poor and exempted those deemed incapable of paying.[42] Although the survival of his diary may make Ikeda seem particularly solicitous, he was far from unique in seeking to preserve and protect his vassals: other daimyō emulated Tokugawa 'policies even when they were not, strictly speaking, required to do so' and always took care to articulate policies that fell 'within the broad outlines established' by the central government. Thus the lord of Okayama (central Honshu) reminded his officials in 1657 that the shogun

> Desires nothing but that there be no one in the entire country who is starving or cold, and that the entire country prosper. However, since he cannot accomplish this alone, he has entrusted whole provinces to [major vassals like me] ... Likewise, I cannot compass all the affairs of the domain alone, and so I have entrusted [parts of it] to all of you in fief, and have commanded you to govern them in accordance with my original intentions. And yet you act as if [these fiefs] were your own private property, so that things have now come to the point that you exploit the lower orders, and you do not even realize that there are people starving... If we rule carelessly, and govern so that there are people starving and cold, or so that parts of the province are depopulated, then we shall not escape confiscation of the domain by His Majesty.[43]

It would be hard to find a better summary of Tokugawa domestic policies during the Little Ice Age.

Pursuit of a risk-averse foreign policy formed the last critical element in Iemitsu's efforts to preserve Japan from crisis. Not only did he strictly limit all contact with foreigners, confining to islands in Nagasaki Bay first the Portuguese, then the Dutch, and finally also the Chinese, he also forbade all except occasional Korean and Ryukyuan embassies to enter the country. More important, the shogun scrupulously avoided foreign intervention. Admittedly, when the Manchus invaded Korea, in 1627–8 and again in 1637, Iemitsu offered to send troops to help repel the invaders (recalling the devastating Japanese invasions in the 1590s, the Koreans naturally declined). Then in 1646, the shogun's officials at Nagasaki turned away Chinese junks manned by crews 'whose heads were shaved like Tartars' – that is, who had followed the orders of the Qing and shaved their foreheads – 'with orders to return only if they looked like Chinese.'[44] Even more provocatively, Iemitsu offered asylum to some Ming loyalists. But he went no further: in 1646 and again in 1650 the shogun rejected requests for military assistance from Ming loyalists who opposed the Qing 'usurpers' (see chapter 5 above). Likewise, in 1637 and in 1643 he declined Dutch invitations to launch a joint attack on Spanish Manila – although on the latter occasion he had a Spanish renegade draw him a map of Manila, and then checked it for accuracy with a Dutch merchant visiting Edo. He also personally interrogated some Dutch captives about how they had captured a Spanish fort on Taiwan, and how they fought at sea, before releasing them.[45]

The importance of avoiding foreign entanglements cannot be overestimated. Whereas Europe knew only four years of *peace* during the seventeenth century, and China knew none, Tokugawa Japan knew only four years of *war* (and none at all after 1638). By avoiding war, the sink that drained the revenues of most other early modern states, the shoguns managed to keep tax rates relatively low and yet still accumulate resources with which to respond effectively in case of a natural disaster.

The Tipping Point: Onwards and Upwards

In 1651 Iemitsu died after a long illness, leaving a 10-year-old son to succeed him, guided by a council of regency – but, because they had been the shogun's catamites, two of the senior regents immediately 'followed their lord in death' by committing suicide. This created a vacuum of power for which some of those whom the Tokugawa had oppressed had long prepared.[46]

Iemitsu's success in avoiding war both at home and abroad had deprived the samurai of their *raison d'être*, and many of them either taught or studied at schools and academies. In the words of Mary Elizabeth Berry: 'For peacetime soldiers, stripped of battleground activity and notoriously underemployed by the shogunal and daimyō bureaucracies, learning became both a rationale for privilege and an opportunity for work – as doctors, political advisors, tutors, teachers, and authors.'[47] Not all samurai managed to adjust to being 'peacetime soldiers', however. Above all, each time the shogun confiscated a fief he created tens of thousands of *rōnin*, 'masterless samurai', each of whom harboured bitter resentment towards the Tokugawa; and the ability of just 200 *rōnin* to turn the Shimabara rebellion into a major challenge to the regime graphically revealed their disruptive potential. Reports of Iemitsu's prolonged final illness gave time for several groups of disgruntled samurai to lay plans to seize power as soon as he died.

Yui Shōsetsu, who taught at a military academy in the capital, led one group of samurai conspirators that aimed to capture and blow up the Edo arsenal (whose deputy commander they had suborned), set fires in 20 places around the capital, seize the great castle built by Iemitsu as his headquarters and kill the remaining regents during the ensuing chaos. They might have succeeded but for the fact that, at the moment of Iemitsu's death, one of the leading conspirators was ill and Yui decided to wait until he recovered. During the interval another leader developed a fever, and in his delirium betrayed details of the plot. The government therefore managed to nip the conspiracy in the bud, crucifying or beheading over 30 rebels. Tokugawa power remained intact for the next two centuries.[48]

There was much more to Tokugawa success in surmounting the crisis of 1651 than contingency and a few executions, however. Elsewhere, the succession of a child ruler (for example, in France after the death of Henry IV or Louis XIII, or in the Dutch Republic after the death of William II), like the death or incapacity of an old one (such as Christian IV of Denmark or the Mughal Shah Jahan), often caused either regime change or civil war, and no sooner had news of the death of Iemitsu and his principal ministers arrived in Nagasaki than the Japanese interpreters attached to the Dutch embassy predicted disaster. The 'alternate attendance' system filled Edo with daimyō, some of whom had opposed the Tokugawa during the civil wars, accompanied by thousands of devoted samurai; and the interpreters noted 'the alterations and feelings this great change had created among the community. Because the prince [Iemitsu's son] is still a minor and the government of this empire will be entrusted to the councillors in the meantime, they fear that jealousy and thirst for power among the nobles will ignite disorder and revolts.'[49] Why, then, did these violent outcomes not occur?

On the negative side, the arbitrary policies pursued by the first three Tokugawa shoguns had destroyed or weakened their opponents so effectively that by 1651 no viable alternative focus for loyalty remained. The emperor, the major temples and most of the daimyō had all incurred heavy debts (often through providing the 'donations' required by the shoguns for their building projects, and in maintaining lavish mansions in Edo dictated by the 'alternative attendance' system). They therefore lacked the resources to exploit the temporary vacuum of power caused by Iemitsu's death. In addition, the 'one castle per fief' policy left the daimyō at a severe disadvantage in challenging the central government, which held dozens of strongholds, strategically located throughout the country – including the great castle in Edo that, according to a Dutch envoy, 'can be compared to one of the largest walled cities in Europe' and contained enough weapons to equip 100,000 soldiers.[50]

In addition, the military effectiveness of Japanese warriors of 1651 was not what it once had been. On the one hand, many of the samurai who defended their lord in

Edo had only a tenuous link with his fief – indeed some men, born in Edo, had never met their colleagues in the fief. On the other, whether or not they lived in Edo, none were 'combat ready'. The siege of Shimabara in 1637–8 marked the only military operation most of them could remember, and even then only samurai from a few fiefs had seen action; the rest lacked any combat experience. Moreover, since the Tokugawa stored huge quantities of weapons in its arsenals, and closely monitored (and reduced) the production of guns, any armed confrontation between Tokugawa and daimyō forces risked becoming a bloodbath. Tokugawa Ieyasu had made pacification his foremost policy goal; by 1651 his grandson had virtually achieved it.

Furthermore, despite its arbitrary aspects, Tokugawa rule had brought tangible benefits to almost all social groups. The daimyō gained because the shoguns protected lesser lords against their larger neighbours: for 250 years, no daimyō attacked the lands of another (a major contrast with the sixteenth century), and those with a grievance could always seek redress in Edo. The towns prospered because the samurai and other retainers who now thronged the castletowns increased demand for both food and artefacts. Merchants appreciated the creation of beacons, lighthouses and rescue facilities, which made seaborne trade safer, while improved roads and bridges facilitated land commerce. All these developments increased the demand for manufactured goods: a manual published in 1637 tabulated over 1,800 'notable products' for sale in Japan.[51]

Finally, Tokugawa rule also brought both peace and prosperity to the peasantry. Politically, the shoguns promoted mechanisms for defusing 'contentious events': they permitted 'organized flight', and although rebellion inexorably brought repression, the protestors normally achieved at least some of their goals (albeit often posthumously).[52] Economically, the state's fiscal demands declined. As Hayami Akira observed: 'Taxes in Tokugawa Japan were based on the principle of establishing a fixed level of production, and levying taxes on that' – that is, most communities continued to pay their taxes on the basis of the surveys carried out under Hideyoshi in the 1590s, which excluded the yield of new or improved arable lands. Thus a tax rate of 50 per cent on a village with a registered production of 1,000 *koku* of rice in the 1590s required the payment of 500 *koku* in tax, even if by 1651 the village actually produced 2,000, 3,000 or more *koku*. This would be the same as taxing US farmers today according to the yield of their fields in (say) 1945. In addition, neither the shogun nor the daimyō taxed income from the non-agricultural activities of their peasants – cotton fabric, silk thread, paper, soy sauce, and so on – while the Tokugawa levied no income tax, no inheritance tax, and no regular taxes on commerce.[53]

These measures not only favoured the 'industrious revolution' but also promoted economic growth. Whereas past generations of peasants had worked only for sustenance and to pay their taxes, increased market demand and the prospect of retaining their profits encouraged peasants to increase their production. Since low tax rates by the state also benefited landlords, they too promoted the 'industrious revolution': some imported new strains of rice and improved existing ones, allowing farmers to select the seed best suited to local conditions, while others distributed iron-tipped farming tools among their peasants and promoted technological improvements in civil engineering (above all irrigation and water supply). Finally, peasants gained from the requirement that samurai migrate from their villages to the lord's castle, because whereas resident samurai could determine the assets and income of each peasant household by personal inspection, surveyors sent by absentee samurai could more easily be deceived.[54]

Despite all these benefits, the Tokugawa regime might yet have crumbled in 1651 had the regents failed to address the principal grievances that had motivated the conspirators. Henceforth, they drastically reduced demands for daimyō 'donations' to Tokugawa building projects. For example, although several regents wanted to rebuild Iemitsu's proud tower at Edo Castle after the Meireki fire of 1657, Hoshina Masayuki (the late shogun's half-brother and now the senior regent) 'argued that the Tokugawa peace was so stable that the shogun's castle no longer needed a tower'. Instead he devoted all available resources to rebuilding the city. A Dutch delegation to the city a few months later noted with astonishment the passage of 'fifty of the shogun's horses, each packed with three chests or 3,000 taels of silver'; and were more astonished still when their landlord informed them that the treasure came from the Tokugawa reserves held in Osaka Castle, and that 'from now till the end of their year, which is another 10½ months, this will be done every day. . . The money will be distributed by the shogun for the rebuilding of houses in Edo.'[55] In addition, after 1651 the shoguns seldom interfered in how the daimyō ran their domains, allowing them to issue their own coinage (and, later, paper money) as well as their own legal codes; while the daimyō respected the shogun's exclusive right to mediate their disputes, to determine all matters of national concern (such as religion, defence and overseas trade) and to regulate public display. They accepted the obligation of 'alternate attendance' at Edo, arriving and departing on schedule and maintaining lavish mansions in the capital where many of them had been born and raised.

The only major problem that the Tokugawa failed to solve after 1651 was samurai unemployment. They did their best. They virtually ceased to confiscate fiefs, thus eliminating the principal cause of the masterless samurai whose resentment had threatened the regime. They then provided salaried positions for as many samurai as they could – for example, employing 1,200 of them as an elite fire brigade in Edo after the Meireki fire, and paying others to employ their pens in creating an ideology of unconditional obedience. Herman Ooms has noted the extraordinary durability of the tracts written by Suzuki Shōsan and other samurai (page 493 above). In the 1930s, 'when an even sharper delineation of nationhood was needed, one that could mobilize the Japanese to the highest degree', the state deployed the absolutist writings of the seventeenth-century Tokugawa apologists. 'Social and political values in present-day Japan maintain the structure they received in the seventeenth century.'[56]

Japan in Print

Just as the Tokugawa knew what they liked, so they knew what they did not like. In 1630 Iemitsu issued an edict banning 32 books in Chinese (most of them translations of European works), and also set up a censor's office in the Confucian Academy in Nagasaki to examine and report on all foreign books arriving in the city, the principal entrepot for trade between Japan and the outside world. On the basis of the censors' reports, the city magistrates burned and banned any condemned work, and obliterated or removed from other works any page that contained any reference to Christianity. In addition, the shogun commanded booksellers throughout Japan to bring in for scrutiny any Japanese work that mentioned foreign religions, and the surviving evidence suggests that they complied: printing blocks were destroyed and publishers punished (although manuscript copies of a few banned works circulated). Those found with Christian literature faced draconian penalties. Thus in 1643, three years after the massacre of the delegation from Macao (page 492 above), a boat carrying four European priests and six Japanese converts came ashore on the island of Kyushu, where the local population immediately captured them and turned them over to the magistrates. Iemitsu ordered them to be brought to Edo and imprisoned at the house of one of his catamites, and he made 11 visits to supervise the torture that secured the apostasy of two and the death of the rest.[57]

The Tokugawa censors showed less vigilance in non-religious matters. On paper, the government proscribed unauthorized items about the dynasty itself, its advisers and its policies, or about Hideyoshi and his family; any work that criticized the elite, or contained pornography, anything about 'strange events that have happened recently' (including love suicides, adultery, vendettas and major fires as well as foreign news), or (in the words of an Edo ordinance of 1673) 'anything that might offend others, or that deals with new and curious matters'. An ordinance of 1686 not only forbade the publication of 'such outrageous materials as reckless songs and rumours about recent events' but also ordered the arrest of 'those who sell these items on street corners'. Nevertheless, practice rarely matched theory. Most of the shogun's edicts concerning printed materials responded to an individual transgression, and tended to be exhortatory rather than prescriptive. Occasionally the government placed the author and publisher of a condemned work under house arrest, but even then some printed copies normally remained available and manuscript copies abounded. From the 1680s (if not before) street vendors sold broadsheets containing news of current non-political events thanks to a subterfuge: although their activity breached the ban on mentioning current events in publications, they wore masks and so the government tolerated them. Authors also circumvented the censors by producing fictionalized accounts: thus Japan's best-known playwright, Chikamatsu Monzaemon, even managed to publish and perform a play about the 1637–8 Shimabara uprising by ostensibly setting it in the twelfth century. Except where Christianity was concerned, Tokugawa censorship was far from the thought control exercised by the Qing, the Romanovs, the Papacy and other European rulers.[58]

The Tokugawa fully realized the power of print and promoted works of which they approved. Starting in 1643, just after the *sankin kōtai* system became mandatory, Edo printers began to publish personnel rosters giving the name, rank, age, crest, income and address of each daimyō; their families and their retainers, their schedule of attendance on the shogun; the distance travelled from each fief; the gifts presented; and so on. Starting in 1659, other printed rosters listed the main office-holders of the Tokugawa, both in the capital and in the provinces, together with their duties, address, stipend, deputies, tenure in office and previous appointments. Tens of thousands of copies flowed from the presses every year, each one duly updated (Plate 20).[59]

Although Tokugawa literary culture at first served primarily samurai readers in the cities, and especially in the 'three metropoles' (santō: Edo, Kyoto and Osaka), the spate of legislation issued by the central government, copied by most daimyō, and the insistence on receiving petitions and reports in writing, meant that every one of the archipelago's 70,000 villages required at least some literate males to read out and copy each text into a special register before passing it on to the next village according to a fixed schedule (the headman of the last village on the schedule certified that the original had completed its required circulation). The same was true of the trade guilds and city wards: both required men with skills in literacy.[60]

According to Eiko Ikegami's study of the culture of Tokugawa Japan, whereas around 1600 'most Japanese with good reading ability – including the ability to read Chinese characters – were either upper-class townspeople or farmers who did not have to perform manual labour', literacy soon expanded dramatically. A story of the day nicely illustrates the cumulative impact. The father of a family that runs a rice-cleaning shop is telling his children (as fathers everywhere tend to do) how incredibly lucky they are:

> When your dad was young, kids weren't given a tutor for writing and reading unless the family was really well-off. In any town ward there were at most only three to five people who could write. Your dad, of course, didn't have a tutor. I can't even form the character 'i' [the first character in the Japanese syllabary] correctly. Somehow, though, I managed to learn to read from experience. Nowadays the world has changed, and even a daughter of a humble household like ours can have lessons in writing and reading.[61]

The lucky and literate daughters of such diligent but deprived fathers could choose from a wide range of reading material. Before 1590, Japanese printers, most of them attached to Buddhist monasteries, had brought out fewer than 500 titles (almost all of them Buddhist religious texts in Chinese); but thereafter a rapidly increasing number of commercial publishers produced books: 12 firms by 1615, over 120 by 1650, and almost 800 by 1700 (Fig. 47). Although many of these firms engaged in other activities besides printing, their collective output was impressive. By 1625, another 500 titles had appeared, doubling the total of Japanese works ever printed, and in 1666 the first List of Japanese and Chinese books in print included over 2,500 titles. The pace continued to quicken, with almost 4,000 titles in the 1670 list, almost 6,000 in the 1685 list, and over 7,000 in the 1692 list.[62] This rapid expansion reduced but did not eliminate the preponderance of religious texts, which even in 1693 made up almost half of the total titles – but the other half displayed an amazing intellectual range. Books of haikai no renga ('playful linked verse') poetry grew

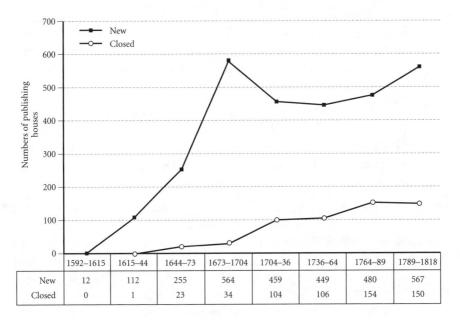

	1592–1615	1615–44	1644–73	1673–1704	1704–36	1736–64	1764–89	1789–1818
New	12	112	255	564	459	449	480	567
Closed	0	1	23	34	104	106	154	150

47. The growth of publishing houses in Japan, 1591–1818.
Starting in the late sixteenth century, Japanese printing burgeoned until more publishing houses existed in 1700 than at any time in over two centuries. The majority of the publishers at that time worked in Kyoto, followed by Osaka and Edo.

fastest: from 133 titles in 1670 to 676 in 1692. Although now associated principally with Bashō Matsuo (1644–94), Bashō was only one exponent among many masters of *haikai*, and he could only undertake the famous journeys during which he composed his verses because other *haikai* enthusiasts all over Japan welcomed and entertained him. These practitioners also paid to enter poetry competitions, some of which offered substantial prize money. In the year of Bashō's death, a Kyoto booklet announced the results of one recent competition that had attracted over 10,000 entries from 15 provinces.[63]

Although some entrants no doubt learned to compose poetry from Bashō or another master, others would have consulted one of the numerous printed reference books that taught the rules of composition. By the 1690s, Japanese readers could find reference works describing almost every aesthetic pursuit and hobby: how to arrange flowers, perform the tea ceremony, play *shamisen*, and write letters. They could also consult travel guides, or illustrated works containing the different patterns of the kimonos and other garments worn by the Kabuki actors and courtesans of the big cities. Fifty-five titles in the 1685 *List of Japanese and Chinese books in print* described the 'amorous arts', as did 119 titles in the 1692 *List*. Despite the shoguns' ban on pornography, some of these works contained striking woodblock illustrations (often hand coloured) representing sexual acts – both heterosexual and homosexual – with the protagonists' genitals prominently displayed.[64]

The prolific writer (and former samurai) Asai Ryōi popularized these and other delights in a book entitled *Tales of the floating world*, published in 1661. He wrote in the name of those who

> Live only for the moment, turning our full attention to the pleasures of the moon, the snow, the cherry blossoms and the maple leaves; singing songs, drinking wine, diverting ourselves in just floating, floating; caring not a whit for the pauperism staring us in the face, refusing to be disheartened, like a gourd floating along with the river current: this is what we call the *floating world*.[65]

The 'floating' took place in two principal locations, both of them new in the seventeenth century. The first was the theatre district in each major city, where actors (and until 1627 actresses) staged *kabuki* (literally 'not straight') plays, an art form that emerged from a combination of classical Noh drama with Shinto dances and popular pantomime. The second was the 'pleasure-quarter' (*akusho*; literally 'bad place'), licensed by the magistrates of almost every major town. Edo's pleasure-quarter, Yoshiwara, was by far the largest, in part because the *sankin kōtai* system brought a huge number of single adult males to the capital. By the 1680s, several tourist guides to Edo provided a convenient list of the names, ranks and residences (plus, in some cases, the fees, physical appearances and specialties) of over 1,000 courtesans.[66]

Asai published his *Tales of the floating world* only four years after the Meireki fire destroyed three-quarters of Edo, and so he did not exaggerate when he described his protagonists as 'living only for the moment' and 'caring not a whit for the pauperism staring us in the face'. Some of the survivors lived literally among ashes and ruins. When another fire threatened the lodgings of a Dutch delegation to Edo in 1661, they noted that 'our poor landlord, three times in four years, namely in 1657, '58 and '60, had been afflicted' and had lost 'his home and many goods'. Shortly afterwards, their successors noted that 'it is dangerous to have a long stay in this fearsome seat of fires'; while on their arrival in the shogun's capital in 1668, another group of merchants found that 'yet another fire had consumed four more streets than the great [Meireki] fire'.[67]

Getting it Right?

Tokugawa Japan thus did not differ significantly from the rest of the world in exposure either to the Little Ice Age or to other natural disasters (such as urban conflagrations): both regularly devastated the archipelago. The main distinctions lay elsewhere. First, where other regions became overpopulated, thanks largely to the expansion of agriculture into marginal areas, Japan began the seventeenth century underpopulated, due mostly to the 'Warring States Era'. Second, Tokugawa rulers made policy choices that mitigated rather than exacerbated the effects of adverse climate. The risk-averse foreign policies of the shoguns meant not only that their subjects never suffered the devastation caused by armies on the rampage, but also that no major social group had to pay higher taxes and few had to make forced loans that stood little chance of being repaid. Moreover, from 1615 onwards, the Pax Tokugawa turned the warrior elite into urban consumers living on stipends, and thus dependent upon a commercial economy that delivered cheap labour, goods and services. It was therefore in their interest to promote initiatives (such as land-reclamation schemes and improved crop strains) that maintained or increased that supply of cheap labour, goods and services.

Nevertheless, 'getting it right' in Tokugawa Japan did not stem from the consistent and rational application of sound economic policies by the ruling elite – although Ieyasu's investment in roads and bridges, and Iemitsu's response to the Kan'ei famine, were both remarkably adroit measures. On the contrary, many beneficial outcomes of Tokugawa rule stemmed from inertia (failing to tax most forms of commerce and production), from complicity (allowing villages to under-report increased productivity and improved crop yields) and from an atavistic intellectual outlook (enjoining frugality and other traditional virtues) – because, in a time of economic crisis, sometimes 'less is more'. In particular, minimizing taxes on the population at large, which allowed demand for goods and services to grow, served as a powerful stimulus to the Industrious Revolution; and avoiding wars both at home and abroad also avoided the deleterious fiscal policies that stunted growth in so many other states.

The Pax Tokugawa nevertheless came at a cost. In political terms, the shoguns deprived their subjects of many freedoms: no Japanese could engage in foreign trade, travel abroad, embrace a religion prohibited by the regime, or handle certain forms of literature. Vassals lost their right to organize collective protests against abusive lords or petition the shogun for redress. In economic terms, although the Industrious Revolution significantly increased output, it required not only relentless and ruthless 'self-exploitation' by producers but also (in the case of farmers) massive deforestation and the tillage of low-quality soils on sites that required constant maintenance. In the lapidary verdict of Conrad Totman, in the course of the seventeenth century farmers 'became trapped in an inflexible, high-risk, high-input, low-yield operation that could be sustained only by the most attentive husbandry'; while the widespread deforestation to build and heat the new towns meant that

> Nearby crop land faced a greatly increased risk of frost, flood and drought. Even without abnormalities or fluctuations of climate, the sharp reduction in forest cover was bound to multiply incidents of crop failure. In addition, during that same century more and more upland and northerly areas were opened to tillage, and these new lands crowded the biological boundaries of crop viability (for reasons of both climatic marginality and soil character) and exacerbated the danger of crop failure.[68]

Likewise, in military terms, avoiding war led to the neglect of military innovation, so that when in 1853 navies arrived from states that had invested heavily in military technology, the Tokugawa regime was powerless to resist them: Japan had to accept humiliating trading agreements, and rebellions brought down the shogunate.

By then, the Tokugawa system had brought peace to all Japan for more than two centuries – an unparalleled achievement for such a large population – and protected the archipelagos from the famines that afflicted much of the northern hemisphere in the 1690s, the 'climax of the Little Ice Age', when average temperatures fell 1.5°C below those of the later twentieth century. The first major food crisis after the Kan'ei famine of 1641–2 did not occur until 1732 – a respite of almost a century: another unparalleled achievement. For most subjects of the Tokugawa, after 1642 the Global Crisis was something that happened to other people.

PART IV

CONFRONTING THE CRISIS

MANY SEVENTEENTH-CENTURY WRITERS ATTRIBUTED THE VIOLENT disorders they saw around them to the innate defects of human nature. According to Thomas Hobbes in 1641, 'man's natural state, before they came together into society, was war; and not simply war, but the war of every man against every man'. In 1643, with civil war raging in England, a London pamphleteer considered that 'we see such an eager division in all families, and it is so universal, that no county, scarce any city or corporation, is so unanimous but they have division enough to undo themselves. And it is evident enough, that this rent will increase until we shall be quite torn in pieces.' That same year, one of Philip IV's Spanish chaplains asserted that 'God wanted the wide world, and the small world which is Man, to be governed by opposition, and everything on earth to be a continual war' – a point that Blaise Pascal put more concisely a decade later: 'All men by their nature hate one another.'[1]

These writers, like many of their contemporaries, saw life as a 'zero-sum game' in which assets could only be redistributed, not created – or, in the aphorism of Francis Bacon: *whatsoever is some where gotten is some where lost*. In every rural community, this zero-sum mentality led to intense, unstable and endless competition, encapsulated in the Arab proverb: 'Me against my brother; my brother and me against my cousin; my brother, my cousin and me against our neighbours'. A recent study of early modern France has noted that 'amity and enmity shaped all social relationships among individuals and groups'; while a historian of rural India also found that 'inequality and conflict' (and not 'simple homogeneous harmony') characterized village life: 'Diversity within a peasantry and conflict among various villagers define rural settings.' Another scholar who found the same 'inequality and conflict' among Japanese villagers noted that rivalry was normally 'covert rather than open, but [it was] fierce and unrelenting nevertheless. Farming was the arena of conflict, and the tools of victory were skill, ingenuity, hard work and perseverance.'[2]

The same 'zero-sum game' created similar rivalries in towns – where, as in the country, the only way to maintain one's position in the community was constantly to protect all assets against encroachment; but because towns were more complex organisms, and because the contrasts between rich and poor were greater, families tended to form associations to protect their assets: guilds for economic concerns, confraternities for religious and social issues, and factions for politics. In the seventeenth century, factions formed 'part of the landscape in towns of any size', each one of them capable of generating 'programmes and slogans and organized public demonstrations' that, just like other forms of conflict, normally became more common and more intense whenever resources ran short because, as the Scottish philanthropist and politician Sir Robert Sibbald put it, whereas 'poverty and want emasculate the mindes of many . . . those that are of a firy and active temperament, it maketh them unquiet, rapacious, frantick or desperate'.[3]

Most of the 'organized public demonstrations' by those of a 'firy and active temperament' in the seventeenth century fell into certain distinct categories. Lü Kun, a gifted bureaucrat of late Ming China, identified the most important of them. 'From of old,' he informed his emperor, 'there have been four kinds of people who like to rebel':

> First are those who have no means of support, no food or clothing, whose families are in difficulties, and who consider rebelling in hopes of delaying their demise. Second are people who do not know how to behave, who have high spirits and violent natures, who violate the laws to make life easier for themselves, who are fond of jade and silk and sons and daughters but cannot get them legitimately, and who think that if there is a rebellion they can steal what they want. Third are the people of heterodox beliefs . . . whose teachers preach and attract crowds, and who will respond to and join up with anyone who calls them. Fourth there are the people without self-control, who turn petty rifts into major fights, who think only of being strong, who hope only for a change, and who take no pleasure in the existing peace in the world.[4]

The categories identified by Lü Kun applied not only to China but also to other areas in the seventeenth century. Chapter 17 examines the motives and protocols of those who rebelled because they 'have no means of support, no food or clothing, whose families are in difficulties' due to economic adversity (especially dearth, unemployment, high taxation and state oppression), as well as the fellow travellers with 'high spirits and violent natures' who 'think that if there is a rebellion they can steal what they want'. Chapter 18 considers protests by 'people of heterodox beliefs' (that is, critics of the government) 'who hope only for a change' – above all the nobles, clerics and intellectuals who created ideologies to underpin political as well as economic grievances, and advanced alternative solutions for the problems of the day. Chapter 19 focuses on how these and other groups of rebels managed to 'preach and attract crowds', using all available media to 'spread the word' about their grievances and their strategies of redress, in the hope that attracting wider domestic and foreign support would not only gain greater concessions but also avoid repression by the authorities. In the mid-seventeenth century, the combined actions of these 'unquiet, rapacious, frantick or desperate' people would bring almost half the states of the northern hemisphere to their knees.

'Those who have no means of support': The Parameters of Popular Resistance[1]

Public and Hidden Transcripts

COLLECTIVE RESISTANCE WAS PERHAPS THE MOST COMMON HUMAN reaction to the seventeenth-century crisis. As a disgruntled English landowner observed, 'The meaner sort of people [are] always apt to rebel and mutiny on the least occasion' – and, indeed, the total number of food riots in England rose from 12 between 1600 and 1620 to 36 between 1621 and 1631, with 14 more in 1647–9. In Germany and Switzerland, more than half of the total of major peasant revolts recorded in the seventeenth century took place between 1626 and 1650; while in France, popular revolts peaked in the middle decades of the century.[2]

The Frequency of French Popular Revolts, 1590–1715

Date	Aquitaine (southwest France)		Provence (southeast France)	
	Number	Annual average	Number	Annual average
1590–1634	47	1	108	2.4
1635–1660	282	11.3	156	6.3
1661–1715	130	2.7	110	2

Records from other states reveal a similar crescendo of revolts in the mid-seventeenth century. In Russia, a wave of urban rebellions in 1648–9 shook the central government to its foundations; while at least 40 rural uprisings took place in Japan between 1590 and 1642 – a total unmatched for two centuries. In China, finally, the number of major armed uprisings rose from under 10 in the 1610s to over 70 in the 1620s and over 80 in the 1630s, affecting 160 counties. According to contemporary historian Zheng Lian, rebel leaders 'rose like spines on a hedgehog' and 'all of them attracted the masses to make themselves strong; they constructed forts and fought for territory. Whole prefectures and counties followed them and served as their ears and eyes, and local officials did not dare to cross them.'[3] In all, over a million people took part in this wave of revolts against the late Ming (Fig. 48).

Popular revolts also seemed a constant menace elsewhere. In India, Emperor Jahangir (r. 1605–27) complained that 'notwithstanding the frequent and sanguinary executions which have been dealt among the people of Hindustan, the number of the turbulent and disaffected never seems to diminish. . . Ever and anon, in one

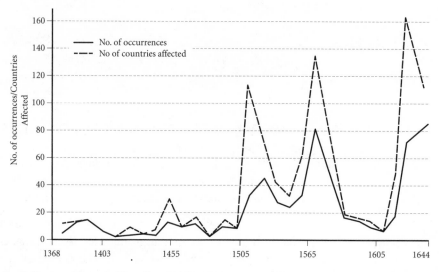

48. Collective violence in Ming China, 1368–1644.
James Tong found 630 cases of collective violence (rebellion and banditry) recorded in the surviving
Gazetteers of Ming China. Of these, four-fifths occurred in the second half of the dynastic era,
affecting almost all of the 1,000 counties included in his survey and reaching a crescendo between
1620 and 1644.

quarter or another, will some accursed miscreant spring up to unfurl the standard of
rebellion; so that in Hindustan never has there existed a period of complete repose.'
A generation later, in central Italy, two officials complained that 'when the people
(*plebbe*) rise up in unison they are a beast without restraint and without reason.
Governed only by their present needs', they become 'so rash and insolent that they
neither obey nor fear those who govern them.'[4]

Nevertheless, official documents and memoirs record only a fraction of the
occasions when the 'standard of rebellion' was unfurled: most revolts have left
scarcely a trace in the surviving archives. Thus, in Spain, a major disorder occurred
in Zaragoza in 1643 when a contingent of foreign soldiers, quartered in the area for
its defence, began to rob those who brought food to market, provoking a group of
students to drive them off with stones. When the troops opened fire, a general
uprising broke out. Perhaps 140 soldiers died before a thunderstorm sent everyone
scurrying for shelter – yet only two surviving manuscripts record these events.[5]
Likewise, only one document mentions an uprising at San Lúcar de Barrameda
in 1641, 'caused by the presence of soldiers, which has caused many deaths', or
a riot the following year by the students at the university of Santiago de Compostela
against attempts to draft them into military service. Virtually no documents
recorded the sort of violent protest on which Pedro Calderón de la Barca based his
most famous play, *The Mayor of Zalamea*, first published in 1651: the riot caused
by the rape of a village girl by a soldier on his way to the front – yet, since

Habsburg Spain was almost constantly at war, such tragic incidents must have abounded.[6]

Those who defied the authorities with words rather than deeds left even fewer archival traces. According to the English social historian John Walter, 'grumbling was the easiest and probably the first weapon of the weak' in the seventeenth century, and it took place mainly in 'unregulated spaces' such as alehouses or coffee houses. He speculated that 'dearth years doubtless saw increased grumbling' – and so must years of armed conflict, religious innovation and political tension.[7] In England, the Bishops' Wars of 1639 and 1640, and the ensuing conflict between king and Parliament, led to verbal protests of unprecedented frequency and vehemence. In Kent, a young man publicly called a member of a distinguished local family a 'rogue and rascal and bidding him kiss his arse, with other saucy and unseemly terms'; in Essex, a group of poachers 'laughed at the warrant' issued by the greatest nobleman in the region summoning them to court, asserting that 'there was no law settled at this time'; while in Sussex, a churchwarden asked rhetorically 'What care we for His Majesty's laws and statutes?' Some grumblers accompanied their opprobrious words with insulting gestures. In 1640, as the dignitaries of the city of Norwich attended Sunday service in the cathedral, a Bible fell from the upper gallery and hit the mayor on the head, breaking his glasses; 'at another time, one from the said gallery did spit upon Alderman Barrett's head'; and on a third occasion 'somebody most beastly did conspurcate [defile] and shit upon' one of the magistrates below.[8]

Yet even if historians could compile a comprehensive list of all recorded 'contentious events', scatological and opprobrious words, insulting gestures and grumbles – it would still fall far short of a complete inventory of popular resistance during the seventeenth century. On the one hand, magistrates or other members of the elite strove to avert protests before they got out of hand and so entered the 'public transcript'. In Europe, pressure from those with influence in the locality forced parties to end their disputes with a public gesture, such as a handshake or (in southern Europe) a kiss, as a sign of reconciliation, and a promise to pay a fine should either party break the peace in future. A similar process occurred in China. Thus, near Shanghai,

> Whenever there was a dispute, Mr. Wang [a wealthy merchant] could always resolve it immediately, even if it was quite serious . . . . [For example] when Mr. Chu set up dikes, a dispute occurred which involved thousands of people. The official tried to straighten out the merits of the case, but still it could not be resolved. Therefore the official asked Mr. Wang to take a hand in the matter. He successfully managed the dispute merely by sending out a long letter.[9]

On the other hand, many protesters took great care to ensure that their resistance left no trace in the public record. 'To the historian,' wrote Marc Bloch in 1931, 'agrarian revolt seems as inseparable from the seigneurial regime as, for example, strikes are inseparable from large-scale capitalism.' Nevertheless, he continued, 'The great insurrections were too disorganized to achieve any lasting result and almost always ended in failure and sometimes massacre. *The patient, silent struggles stubbornly carried on by rural communities accomplished far more.'* Half a century later, anthropologist James C. Scott reprised and developed Bloch's thesis by suggesting that the poor normally adopted a 'risk-averse' strategy when dealing with their neighbours, with the elite, and with the state, waging 'defensive campaigns of attrition' that included 'foot-dragging, dissimulation, desertion, false compliance, pilfering, feigned ignorance, slander, arson, sabotage'. These everyday acts of disobedience, Scott noted, 'require little or no co-ordination or planning; they make use of implicit understandings and informal networks'. They therefore did not 'make headlines' but instead left what he termed a 'hidden transcript' preserved, if at all, in narrative accounts and oral traditions.[10]

Even when material conditions were at their worst, and mass revolts occurred with unparalleled frequency, the 'patient, silent struggles' and 'defensive campaigns of attrition' far outnumbered them, because the risk-averse strategies discerned by Bloch and Scott reflected the central concern of the poor in all periods: survival. To make sure they had enough food to survive, the poor applied a simple calculation: *How much do I have left?* Only when the calculation dictated a shift from clandestine to open resistance and even revolt, did collective protest move from the hidden to the public transcript; and such shifts occurred with particular frequency during the seventeenth century.

Articulating Grievances

Three scenarios provoked serious popular revolts with the greatest frequency: a failed harvest; the arrival of troops requiring food and lodging; and the imposition of either a new tax or increases in an existing tax. Each scenario had its own tempo. Normally, because of the prevailing peccatogenic outlook (see chapter 1 above), most disasters in the early modern world initially led those afflicted to seek someone to blame. Often this process began with introspection: a community tried to expiate its own collective sins through acts of penitence such as processions, rogations, pilgrimages and self-flagellation. If this did not work, attention shifted to local individuals or groups whose conduct might have offended God. Some blamed their neighbours, denouncing them as witches, Jews and so on, and tried to eliminate them through the legalized violence of the courts. Others suspected their superiors of selfishly creating an artificial shortage, and took the law into their own hands. Irate crowds might threaten the grain merchants and bakers who failed to provide sufficient food at an affordable price, or the carters and bargees who transported grain, and force them to distribute their precious stock either free or at an artificially low price.[11]

If these strategies still failed to feed all the hungry, the crowds blamed the local authorities. Sometimes they demanded that the magistrates mandate lower prices in the market, purchase supplies elsewhere, or conduct an inventory of all grain reserves; at other times they attacked the town granary, the mansions of anyone suspected of hoarding grain, and the abbeys and church barns that stored the yield of the tithes. Finally, communities could try to prevent outsiders from exporting food from the area, whether merchants hoping to maximize profits or agents buying up grain on behalf of a city or an army – although this often escalated the level of collective violence. Normally, intimidating the local people who handled grain required only threats and the confiscation of their goods, whilst influencing local authorities might also involve throwing stones and tearing down walls; but preventing the export of grain often meant hamstringing draft animals, and sometimes also beating or even killing the perceived perpetrators.[12]

Billeting was the second major precipitant of popular revolt. Throughout Europe, soldiers quartered in a community demanded free light and heat, clean bed linen and three meals a day from their hosts. In Spain, according to a contemporary source, 'The soldier consumes in just one week what the farmer expected would feed himself and all his children for a month'; while in France, Cardinal Mazarin reminded his agents 'that three days' billeting, with the accustomed licentiousness of the soldiers, is harder for a man to bear than a whole year's *taille* and other taxes'. Such equations help to explain how the pressure of billeting troops played such a large role in generating popular revolts in Catalonia in 1640 and in Ulster the following year.[13]

Although three days of billeting may have done far more harm than the government's fiscal demands for a year, as Mazarin claimed, taxes also produced an abundance of revolts – especially in wartime. In seventeenth-century Aquitaine, for example, more than half of all known uprisings against tax collectors took place in the war years between 1635 and 1659. Tax revolts arose not only from the amount demanded by the state but also from the way in which it distributed the burden. Normally, states apportioned direct taxes among entire communities, not among the individuals who lived in them, and so a fall in the number of taxpayers in a given community inevitably increased the burden on those who remained. Thus, in 1647, the small Sicilian town of Caltabellotta complained that 'according to the past enumeration of inhabitants, it appears that this town and its lands contained about 8,000 souls', but 'at present there are scarcely 3,500 impoverished and miserable souls. So this town ... finds itself burdened with large arrears of dues and royal taxes, and the situation gets worse every day'. In Lombardy, another Italian farmer sighed that 'what land I own I would gladly give away if I only could find someone willing to pay' the back taxes he owed. It was the same in France, where a government inspector reported that 'The parishes that have paid least, and which are most in arrears with their land tax, are as poor (or more so) as those that have paid most'.[14]

The difficulty (and unpopularity) of increasing existing taxes explains why many early modern governments resorted to two alternative fiscal strategies in wartime: taxing *items* previously exempt, and taxing *categories of subjects* previously exempt. The decisions to impose a salt monopoly in Vizcaya in 1631 and in Normandy in 1639, a new tax on property in Portugal in 1637 and in Paris in 1648, and a new excise duty on fruit in Naples in 1647, all triggered major revolts. In Japan, the arrival of inspectors in a village to conduct a land survey – measuring individual holdings of irrigated and dry land and sampling the harvest for quality – was the commonest single cause of rural rebellion, because everyone knew that surveys normally heralded a tax rise. Likewise, in the Ottoman empire, Osman II's decision to end the privileged tax status of the clerical elite, and his threat to do the same to his palace guards, triggered his deposition and murder in 1622; while the demands made by his brother Ibrahim on the clergy of Istanbul led them to support a second regicide in 1648. In both Portugal and Castile, the attempt to make the clergy pay stamp duty provoked determined resistance. In France, the central government's constant erosion of tax exemptions enjoyed by the aristocracy and the civil service eventually turned both social groups into rebels. Finally, the resort of Charles I and his ministers to 'regalian rights' (such as the 'Revocation' in Scotland, 'Thorough' in Ireland, and 'Ship Money' in England – all of them meas-ures introduced by royal prerogative) imposed heavy burdens on social groups previously exempt. Thus in the county of Essex, where scarcely 3,000 households normally paid the taxes voted by Parliament, over 14,000 households faced Ship Money assessments – indeed, the king's commissioners wrote '£0-0s-0d' beside a few names, showing that they had visited and assessed even the poorest residents in the realm. Small wonder that so many of Charles's subjects protested.

Provoking opposition was doubly dangerous for governments in times of hardship, because people who took up arms for one protest might well later use them for another. In 1699 a Qing magistrate eloquently described this process of 'mission creep': 'Incidents that begin as expedients to get food for empty stomachs often end up as organized rebellion', because a threat to one or more of life's neces-sities – not just food but also jobs, welfare and traditional rights – could provoke an entire community first to unite and then to rebel. A generation earlier, an agent of the French government made exactly the same point at slightly greater length:

> If one allows the export of grain [from an area where it is already scarce], all the people will run to attack the [grain] merchants. Once they are exhilarated by having got something for nothing, they will undoubtedly form bands and, from there, will close the roads to all who want to transport the king's money, putting at risk the receipt of the tax revenues of His Majesty; *for the people, once armed and in rebellion, will use its weapons against everyone who asks them for money.*

An example of this process occurred at the village of Abjat in Périgord in 1640. The Croquant revolt had only just been suppressed (see chapter 10) and now, in a year of dearth, a cavalry company marching to join the royal army on the Spanish frontier arrived and demanded free quarters. The inhabitants refused them entry, shouting: 'We must kill all these thieves and not allow them lodgings.' When the troopers tried to find quarters in neighbouring hamlets instead, a gang of several hundred peasants ambushed them and killed their captain, whose body they then mutilated and dragged around the town. Afterwards, the royal courts indicted not only 109 named individuals – including the local priest, 12 village office-holders, 4 royal officials, 4 merchants and 14 craftsmen, but also 'all other inhabit-ants and householders of the town and parish of Abjat' – because almost everyone became involved, including local gentlemen who sheltered the peasants' cattle, and the nearest town, which sheltered the ringleaders. Thanks to this united front, the inhabitants who manned the barricades around Abjat successfully defied the government for five years.[15]

Deterrents to Collective Violence

Given the existence of so many grievances, and their correlation with adversity, it is surprising that revolts did not occur even more often; and in his study of peasant societies, James Scott gave detailed consideration to this paradox. He discerned four factors that normally deter villagers, however desperate, from open resistance. First, the need to earn a daily wage formed a powerful restraint on rebellion: a family that did not work – whether because on strike, in rebellion, or unemployed – might not eat. Second, the vertical links of kinship, friendship, faction, patronage and ritual in each community created ties between the dominant and the dominated that discouraged violent action. Third, and paradoxically, any economic development within the community that increased social divisions also militated against collective action. Thus a shift towards producing crops (especially industrial crops) for export normally created groups of prosperous cultivators who, as long as strong demand for their goods lasted, remained largely insulated from the frustrations and sufferings of those still tied to subsistence farming; and this significantly reduced the likelihood of unified resistance. Fourth and finally, in most farming communities of the early modern world, the poor often depended for their survival on deference and subordination. Better-off neighbours were more likely to provide relief in time of need to those who showed constant respect and obedience, whereas neglect or surliness might lead to denial of charity and even expulsion from the community. However much the poor may have resented their subordination and humiliation, their circumstances compelled them to conform: they might try to negotiate the terms of subordination, but they rarely dared to challenge it.[16]

For all these reasons, despite desperate economic circumstances and apparently intolerable provocations, the poor normally ensured that their protests did not break any laws. They took care not to steal (often ostentatiously burning the property of their targets, and beating anyone seen absconding with goods belonging to their victims) and they rarely carried prohibited weapons. In England, at least, those who destroyed property did so two by two, because the law stated that a 'riot' (severely punished) began only when three or more people became involved; while in both England and China, resentful subjects might await the interval between the death of one monarch and the proclamation of the next to seek revenge for a perceived wrong – because even some judges had doubts whether laws remained in force during an interregnum.[17]

'Chicks up front'

Except for a few privileged groups, those who tried to form associations larger than the family to achieve social and economic goals ran grave risks, and therefore in the West – in the seventeenth as in the twentieth century – women took a prominent role in many collective protests. According to a study of bread riots in western France, 'the most constant element was the presence of women' – indeed, throughout France, women outnumbered men in more than half of all known rural food riots and in more than three-quarters of all known urban food riots; while 'some crowds consisted entirely of women'.[18] In part, this disparity reflected the realities of daily life – in the villages the men spent the day working in distant fields, leaving only women at home, while in the towns women spent much of their time in the streets, either shopping or selling – but it also reflected long traditions. Jean Nicolas, who discovered this imbalance, noted that the women who took the lead in early modern food riots

> Had inherited patterns of ritualized behaviour that transcended time. From one end of France to the other, and across the centuries, the tempo of their actions seemed universal: first they shouted, then they overturned any structure easily tipped over, emptied the baskets full of grain, rushed into the shops, and blocked the way . . . To turn disorder into a riot required only stones to hurl, ashes to throw into the eyes of merchants, knives to slit the sacks.[19]

Women likewise took the lead in popular disorders elsewhere in seventeenth-century Europe. In the Dutch Republic, when the magistrates of Haarlem invited bids for collecting a new excise duty in 1628, a group of women attacked the first man to make a bid, shouting: 'Let's sound the drum and send our husbands home; then we'll get the bastard and beat him up because we cannot be punished for fighting.' In England, when in 1645 a group of women mounted a protest against the collection of excise duties in Derby they 'went up and down beating drums and making proclamations . . . that such of the town as were not willing to pay excise should join with them and they should beat the [excise] commissioners out of town'. When the commissioners tried to discuss the matter with the town council, one of the women banged her drum outside the council chamber so loudly that it drowned out the debate; and when a soldier tried to collect excise, a crowd tethered him to the bull ring in the marketplace whilst 'the women did beat the drums as before'. Collection only began after the authorities agreed that the proceeds would be used locally and not sent to London.[20] Dutch rioters often chanted the slogan 'Women can do no wrong!', and English magistrates agreed. 'If a number of women (or children under the age of discretion) do flocke together for their own cause, this is none assembly punishable,' wrote the author of a standard handbook for magistrates in 1619; while that same year the Court of Star Chamber, asserted (in a case that involved breaking down the fences around enclosed fields) that women were 'not subject to the lawes of the realme as men are, but might . . . offend without drede or punishment of lawe'.[21]

In part, this double standard reflected the realization that a woman and her family might cross the threshold between survival and starvation in a matter of days if not hours. In 1930 Richard Tawney, a social historian of early modern England, visited China (then in the grip of famine) and reported that, in some areas, 'the position of the rural population is that of a man standing permanently up to the neck in water, so that even a ripple is sufficient to drown him'. An English pamphlet published during food riots in Essex in 1629 described the plight of the local weavers in remarkably similar terms: most 'cannot live unless they bee paied every night, many hundreds of them havinge no bedds to lye in, nor foode; but from hand to mouth mainteyne themselves, their wives and children'. In France, insurgents half a century later exclaimed when faced by famine that 'you only die once' and so they 'would prefer to be hanged than to die of hunger', and that 'they were dying of hunger, and would rather hang to finish their lives sooner'. In Paris 'you could hear women in the market-place cry out that they would rather slit their children's throats than watch them die of hunger'. In such circumstances, 'survival' could easily lead to resistance and even revolt.[22]

European women lost their immunity only when resistance got out of hand. During the famine year of 1629, Ann Carter, a butcher's wife from the town of Malden in Essex, led a large crowd of women to prevent the export of grain from the region and, motivated by 'the crie of the country and her own want', they forced the would-be exporters to pour their grain into their bonnets and aprons. Her conduct on this occasion reflected the accepted protocols of early modern protest, but over the next two months Ann toured the area to mobilize support, took the title 'Captain' and proclaimed 'Come my brave lads of Malden, I will be your leader for we will not starve.' This time, a crowd of several hundred unemployed cloth-workers broke into a grain store and removed the contents. A week later the government arrested Ann, put her on trial for sedition, and after the (all male) jury convicted her, hanged her the next day. In the Netherlands in 1652, 45-year-old Grietje Hendrickx was likewise arrested, tried and sentenced for collecting stones in her apron, carrying them to the rioters and 'inciting bystanders to join in'. The following year, the authorities issued a warrant to arrest two women who had led a riot:

> Griet Piet Scheer, aged 36, blond hair, thin face with blue eyes, fairly tall, slim figure, soberly dressed. She dresses at times in black and at others she wears a blue overall with red sleeves; she acted as captain. Alit Turfvolster, bearer of the flag, is as tall but somewhat stouter than the above-mentioned Griet; she sniffs somewhat through her nose, is brown of complexion with black hair and untidy clothes; she wears a bodice with a linen apron, and her age is 30.

Court records show that few of the women charged with leading street protests were under 25 years, and fewer still were over 60: most were (like all the above mentioned insurgents) between 30 and 45.[23] Lungs as well as age counted, and here too women enjoyed an advantage because many of them worked as street-vendors who spent their days singing and shouting out their wares as they passed through the streets. One observer in 1643, the year with more grain riots than any other in seventeenth-century France, noted that unrest in Bordeaux ended when the authorities distributed bread to 'the women who shouted most'.[24]

Women might also lead other forms of collective protest. The riots against drainage schemes that threatened common rights in eastern England in the 1630s involved mostly 'women, boys, servants and poor people whose names cannot be learned', who broke open the new dykes, chased off the workmen and smashed their wheelbarrows; while a shouting and stool-throwing group of women in Edinburgh in 1637 started the Scottish Revolution. During the Corpus de Sang in Barcelona three years later, an observer noted the role of 'a cruel woman – and most of them were cruel on this occasion – who told the rioters that she had seen a Castilian' enter a local church. The men then went in and 'beat him to death'.[25] Protestant survivors from seven Irish counties commented on the prominent role played by women in 'hurting' British settlers during the rebellion of 1641. According to a woman from Newry in County Down, her female Catholic neighbours were 'more scornfull and cruell then the men, swearing and vowing they would kill them becawse they were of English kynd', while a women in County Armagh 'was soe cruell against the English and Scottish that she was very angrie with the souldjers becawse they did not putt them all to death'. Three other deponents in County Armagh (all women) described how a 'bloudy virago', had used a pitchfork to 'force and thrust' over a dozen of her Protestant neighbours into 'a thatcht howse', which she then 'sett on fyre' so that all 'were miserably and barbarously burned to death'.[26] Another female survivor testified that 'the Irish women would follow after the Irish rebel soldiers and put them forward to cruelty with these and such wordes, "Spare neither man, woman nor child"'. A male deponent recorded that another 'bloudy virago' had, 'out of divellish and base spite and malice to the English and Scottish', been 'the principall cawser and instigator of the drowning of fifty Protestants – men, women and children – all at one time'. Meanwhile at Kilkenny, the Confederate capital, the heads of several British soldiers defeated in battle were brought out and 'sett upon the Markett crosse, where the Rebells – but especially the women there' – gathered round and 'stabbd, cutt and slasht those heades'. One of them drew her dagger and 'slasht at the face of the [late] William Alfrey and hitt him on the nose'.[27]

Although accounts of revolts outside Europe sometimes mention the participation of women, they always appeared in subordinate roles. Thus in India during the 1650s, when villagers resisted Mughal efforts to collect taxes, 'the women stood behind their husbands with spears and arrows. When the husband had shot off the matchlock his wife handed him the lance, while she reloaded the matchlock.'[28] In China, although women appear in some exploits recorded in *Water Margin*, the popular Ming novel about outlaws, they do so only as helpers to their bandit husbands. Doubtless some women participated in the popular rebellions of the late Ming period – although Chinese officials normally named only the leaders (all male) and dismissed their followers as 'thugs' or 'wastrels' – but two considerations make it improbable that Chinese women could have taken the lead in revolts like Ann Carter, Griet Piet Scheer or Alit Turfvolster: first, neither Chinese law nor custom had a concept similar to 'women can do no wrong'; second, the practice of first binding the feet and then secluding 'respectable women' from puberty to menopause would have severely limited their ability to lead street protests.[29]

Clerics and Fools

In Europe, the clergy formed a second group who served as proxies during popular protests. Some became quite outspoken. A mid-seventeenth century French catechism, for example, condemned as guilty of homicide those 'who failed to calm and disperse popular sedition when they have the power to do so, such as magistrates'. A French priest had no doubt that his flock's opposition to billeting would prosper, because 'since the soldiers lacked just aims, and thought only of pillaging the city and other base designs, God would withdraw his blessings and grant that the first to be assigned and ordered [to seek billets] would perish'.[30] In Naples in 1647, some priests assured the insurgents that their struggle 'was just, because they were oppressed by excessive taxes and attacked and provoked by the Spaniards'; and many Spaniards questioned the allegiance of Archbishop Filamarino, who remained in Naples throughout the revolution and on several occasions appeared in public ceremonies alongside the rebel leaders.[31]

Clerics from other faiths intervened as proxies in popular revolts elsewhere. Throughout the Ottoman empire, local sheikhs (the heads of a Sufi or dervish lodge: see chapter 7 above) handled negotiations between the central government and a community either oppressed by taxes or by local officials, often securing redress of grievances before violence began. For example, in Cairo, protesting merchants and artisans would habitually march from the principal souk, Khan al-Khalil (also known as the 'Turkish bazaar'), to the al-Azhar mosque to request the intervention of a sheikh with known ties to the governing elite.[32] In China, Buddhist monks sometimes became spokesmen for the oppressed. Thus in 1640, in a Jiangnan town, a monk organized a 'strike for grain' (*da mi*) in which crowds of over a hundred peasants visited the houses of the rich asking for food: they spared houses that provided sustenance and burned those that refused. In general, however, Buddhist (and Daoist) clerics lacked the local authority wielded by their Christian and Sufi counterparts, partly because most of them lived in temples largely isolated from the rest of the population, and also because the dominance of Confucian ethics undermined any claim to moral leadership made by others.[33]

A third proxy occasionally able to speak truth to power was the 'fool', whom ancient tradition allowed to voice unwelcome criticisms to rulers. Most Islamic rulers grudgingly tolerated the criticisms and claims voiced by a *Majdhūd* ('holy fool') – indeed the Ottoman authorities may have initially overlooked the Messianic claims of Shabbatai Zvi because they considered him a 'holy fool'.[34] Holy fools were also common in Orthodox Christianity: they wore no clothes, draped themselves in chains and wore an iron hat, living in extreme poverty and begging for food. Although they normally spoke nonsense, they sometimes slipped sharp criticisms into their silliness, thus managing to confront even the tsar with unpalatable truths. In the 1660s the Old Believer Avraamii got away with his vociferous opposition to the liturgical reforms supported by Tsar Alexei by posing as a 'holy fool', which allowed him to speak (though not to write) with impunity. Likewise in Portugal in 1637, those who rioted against attempts to impose a new tax at Évora made a simpleton their leader: 'Manuelinho, secretary of the young people, ministers of divine justice' signed the manifestos posted in the streets against the 'tyrant Pharaoh'. That same year, when Archibald Armstrong, Charles I's Scottish Fool, heard of the rioting in his native land provoked by imposing a new Prayer Book on English lines, he asked the architect of the proposal, Archbishop Laud, 'Who's the Fool now?' in an attempt to change government policy. Although Laud had Archie banished from the court and confiscated his Fool's coat, the jester still had the last laugh. A courtier who encountered Archie without his fool's coat, and asked where it was, received the reply: 'Oh, my lord of Canterbury [Laud] has taken it from me, because he or some of the Scots bishops may have use for it themselves!'[35]

The Etiquette of Collective Violence

With or without proxies, most early modern rebels issued 'warnings' before they resorted to violence. Posters would appear in the streets warning an individual whom the community identified as an oppressor to change his (or, less often, her) ways; women would gather and kneel together in the open and noisily weep and wail in front of the house of an abusive landlord. If such 'shaming' tactics failed to produce concessions, satirical songs might be composed and sung at night outside the offender's house. Artefacts might be used to convey a message: a cart left in the doorway, implying that another would soon carry away a coffin; a bonfire lit, suggesting that the owner's house would be next; or someone hanged in effigy from a gallows – the ultimate sign of disapproval short of violence. If all of these coded warnings, too, failed to produce the desired changes, the aggrieved graduated to destroying property, starting with distant assets such as vines, fruit trees, mills and storehouses, moving on to stoning windows or smashing down the front door. After that, the terrified victims usually fled.[36]

Those who ignored these warnings ran the risk of serious harm – although even then, violence against property and people was normally applied with precision. In England in 1642 a group called the 'Colchester plunderers' ransacked a score of country mansions in Essex so thoroughly that later visitors found merely 'bare walls' or ruins 'desolate without inhabitant' – but the plunderers only targeted the property of those whom parliamentary and Puritan propaganda denounced as 'Papists and malignants' (that is, royalists). That same year, crowds surrounded the Palace of Westminster vociferously calling for the exclusion of bishops – but, as a French diplomat observed, 'If this were any other nation, I believe the city [of London] would be in flames, and blood flowing within 24 hours'.[37] And, indeed, rioters in some parts of continental Europe often showed little restraint. In Barcelona, after the murder of the viceroy in June 1640, a royal judge watched in horror from his hiding place in a church steeple as rioters murdered every Castilian they could find, filled with 'an incredible rage, without sparing the church where they killed someone hiding beneath the altar, without seeing or knowing who it was until the blood running out from under the frontal revealed that some unfortunate was hiding there'. Angry Catalans surged through the streets of Barcelona again the

following December, seeking out and murdering all those suspected of collaboration with 'the enemy' (viz. their former sovereign, Philip IV): this time they
disfigured their victims with repeated blows before hanging them from gallows in
the city square.[38]

The following year, the Irish rebellion also saw acts of extreme violence towards
individuals. Thus a Catholic in County Down exclaimed, as he ran his neighbour
'twice or thrice throrowe the body' with his rapier: 'That will make an end of him,
that he shall never write a *mittimus* [arrest warrant] to send mee to Down jaoyle
[jail] againe.' In County Antrim, another Catholic cut his Protestant neighbour
into 'many pieces' and then 'lay downe his bloody sword and put his fingers' in his
victim's 'mouth, and nipped his flesh to see if he were dead or not; and, beinge
dead, he sayes that "I am glade that I haue gotten thee, for I had rather haue had
thee then all the rest in the towne".'[39] For southern France, William Beik has
postulated the existence of a 'culture of retribution': once an angry crowd had
decided that someone ' "had it coming to him", there was no such thing as excessive
force'. In the province of Aquitaine, for example, at least 30 of the 50 known
tax rebellions in the course of the seventeenth century involved the humiliation,
execution and (often) mutilation of a tax collector by the rioters.[40]

The anthropologist David Riches has noted that violence serves not only as a
convenient and economical instrument to transform society, but also as an 'excellent
communicative vehicle' with which to make symbolic statements. In many parts of
Europe, crowd violence therefore often followed an etiquette that mirrored legal
protocols. Rioters paraded their victim, often a tax collector, around the town with
his hands bound and dressed only in a shirt, forcing him to make 'honourable
amends' at each crossroads and square – just as happened to those convicted by the
king's judges. Sometimes the crowd then set the victim free, so he could warn others
of the fate that awaited all tax collectors, but others they executed and quartered –
again following the same measured ritual, often performed in the same places, as in
state trials.[41]

Nevertheless, even the most enraged European crowds rarely killed promiscu-
ously. In Portugal, the conspirators who took over Lisbon on 1 December 1640
murdered Miguel de Vasconcelos, the hated agent of the central government, and
hurled him from a palace window into the square below where 'a workman cut off a
finger to get the ring that he wore'. Then, with women and adolescents playing a
prominent part, the crowd stripped his corpse, 'tore out his teeth, pulled out his
moustache and beard and stabbed him repeatedly. They then cut off both his ears,
which later the crowd displayed and offered for auction.' But Vasconcelos died
alone: no other servant of Philip IV perished in the 'Restoration'. The rioting in
Istanbul that ended the life of Sultan Ibrahim that same year involved the death of
relatively few other than the ruler himself and his Grand Vizier. Admittedly, like
Miguel de Vasconcelos, the vizier met a spectacularly barbarous end – 'strangled and
minced into mammock-pieces [shreds], one pulling out an eye, another cutting off
an ear, a third a finger' – but he perished alone. In Moscow in 1648, although rioters
burned scores of noble and merchant residences, they first compiled a list of houses

belonging to their perceived oppressors and then systematically worked their way through. In the revolution of Naples in 1647–8, several noblemen were butchered and their mutilated, naked bodies exposed on a special monument erected outside the rebel headquarters, but these men had attempted to slay Masaniello and kill his followers. More typical was the rebels' protocol in burning houses, in accordance with a written list of 60 targets, most of them belonging to those involved in either imposing or collecting taxes (Plate 21).[42]

In China, too, popular protests often displayed restraint. Many began with ritual wailing at local Confucian temples, and public lamentations by aggrieved subjects who carried placards through the streets that stated their petitions and grievances. In southern China, distressed villages also formed a covenant (known as a *gang*, or net) in which all participants recorded their names in a register, made sacrifices to their ancestors, swore that none of them would pay rent and visited the houses of the rich to beg for food. If such methods failed, crowds started to burn houses; but, as in Europe, they not only worked from a list of residences belonging to tax collectors but also notified the residents of adjacent houses in advance so that they could take steps to prevent the fire from spreading. In addition, they strictly forbade theft and often beat looters to death.[43]

Popular protests arising from non-material grievances also often possessed a distinctive etiquette and involved public displays. Thus in England in 1641, opponents of the ecclesiastical innovations of the preceding decade made sure that everyone could see their contempt for items like the surplice worn by ministers and the Book of Common Prayer. Surplices were not simply discarded, but ostentatiously shredded (often by women using knives and scissors) and put to a variety of profane uses: a bandage, a handkerchief, a shirt and (most eloquently) a sanitary towel; while in London, four horsemen rode through the streets 'in great pomp and triumph' wearing a surplice and 'with the Book of Common Prayer in their hand, singing in derision thereof, and tearing it leaf by leaf, and putting every leaf to their posterior'. Ironically, that same year Irish Catholics publicly and gleefully desecrated the religious objects venerated by the Protestants. They smashed and set fire to pulpits and other items of church furniture, and burnt or defaced liturgical texts; but they reserved special treatment for the Bible. One man watched as his captors took his Bible and, 'laying the open side in a puddle of water, lept and stamped on it, saying "A plague on't. This booke has bred all this quarrel"'; a Protestant minister saw a friar take 'the poor men's Bibles that he found in a boat, and cut them in pieces and cast them into the fire with these words, that he would "deal in like manner with all Protestant and Puritan Bibles"'; while an outraged settler reported that a Catholic, 'Opening the sacred bible, pist upon the same, saying "If I could doe worse with it I would"'.[44]

Place and Time

Popular resistance seems to have occurred most frequently in two completely different zones: in regions where a reservoir of discontent developed most rapidly (cities and 'macroregions': see chapter 3 above), and in communities previously insulated in some way from the attentions of the government. Among the latter, in times of hardship, areas protected by natural barriers such as marshes, forests or heaths often became 'oases of insurrection'. In the Riez marshes along Brittany's eastern border a group of villages maintained a permanent tax-strike between 1636 and 1660. Each community occupied an 'island' amid the marshes, normally accessible only by water and, since only the inhabitants knew the channels through the bogs, every government attempt to send in troops to collect taxes failed. Moreover, the success of the marsh-dwellers encouraged defiance in neighbouring communities, which rebelled six times between 1633 and 1658 rather than pay their taxes, secure in the knowledge that, if necessary, they could flee to Riez.[45] Turenne, the largest fief in Aquitaine, with around 100,000 inhabitants in almost 100 parishes, formed another oasis of insurrection by virtue of its legal status: its lord claimed to be an independent prince who owed the French king only homage. The men of Turenne paid an annual tax to their lord, and supplied him with troops when required, but not only did they vigorously resist any intervention by the crown (such as allowing royal troops to march across their territory) but they helped their neighbours to resist too. Throughout the seventeenth century, 'in all the revolts of Aquitaine, [Turenne] served as an assembly point and a provocative example'.[46]

Similar oases of insurrection existed elsewhere. Within Europe, the Austrian estates of the Schaunberg family, which could claim exemption from outside jurisdiction, lay at the heart of peasant revolts in 1620, 1626, 1632–3 and 1648, just as they had done in those of previous centuries. Likewise, men from St Keverne's, a remote Cornish-speaking parish in England's deep southwest, led a major revolt in 1648, just as they had done in 1497, 1537 and 1548. Certain areas also seem to have sustained an intellectual tradition of resistance: Kingston, commanding a strategic bridge across the Thames, sheltered the most outspoken critics of Queen Elizabeth and openly rejoiced over the murder of Charles I's 'Favourite', Buckingham, in 1628, just as they would later shelter both the Diggers (a group that cultivated common land and advocated sharing all things) and the Quakers.[47]

Frontier societies boasted even larger oases of insurrection. The southern borderlands of Russia and the Polish-Lithuanian Commonwealth, where forest turned into steppe, offered a constant refuge to the oppressed and discontented, who periodically staged rebellions against the states to the north (most memorably in Ukraine after 1648 when Bohdan Khmelnytsky led a Cossack rebellion against its Polish overlords, and in 1670 when Stenka Razin defied Moscow: see chapter 6 above). In the Americas, 'Maroons' – black slaves who escaped from European settlements – created fortified camps in several parts of Brazil, central America and the Caribbean islands where jungle, canyons or swamps offered a measure of protection. From these refuges, often under the command of those who had been rulers before their abduction from Africa, they made common cause with Native Americans and welcomed any fugitive European servants and outlaws. Together they posed a constant threat to the colonies (especially by burning down plantations of sugar cane – a conveniently combustible crop).[48] In China, finally, in the 1620s and 1630s rebels like Li Zicheng found refuge in the deep forests between Shanxi and Henan provinces, just as Mao Zedong would do three centuries later; while in the 1640s the marshes around Liangshan mountain in Shandong province sheltered large bandit groups, just like those in *Water Margin*, the popular novel of the day set in the twelfth century.[49] As in Europe, the mere proximity of an oasis of insurrection could encourage resistance. In Russia and the Polish Commonwealth, the abundance of fertile 'free' lands on the southern frontier made the threat of flight a powerful bargaining tool for peasants who wanted a better deal from their lords. As a group of Bengalis pointed out to their rulers, flight was always an option when one had 'A thousand countries to go to'.[50]

The calendar also influenced popular resistance. Revolts often began in spring, as grain from the previous harvest ran out, on market days and (in Catholic Europe) on religious holidays: Normandy erupted into violence on a festival in honour of the Virgin Mary in 1639; Barcelona on Corpus Christi, 1640; Palermo on Assumption Day, 1647. The explanation is simple: because the Church prohibited work on holidays, people thronged the street and the taverns, talking and drinking, so that an insurrection could quickly gather momentum. In June 1647 the viceroy of Sicily ordered that the Festival of the Holy Sacrament be celebrated by the clergy alone, without the participation of confraternities, guilds and other lay associations, lest 'because of the great multitude of people, a brawl might occur and turn into a more serious disturbance'. The following month, the same fear led the archbishop of Naples to cancel a festival in honour of the Virgin.[51] Market days also offered opportunities to rioters. Thus, in 1641 the leading Irish conspirators planned to take Dublin Castle on a market day because large numbers of people would (like them) be entering the city the night before and so they would attract less suspicion. Finally, revolutionary anniversaries could provoke repetition: Fermo in 1648 and Messina in 1674 both rebelled on the anniversary of Masaniello's revolt, 7 July; while in 1647 Antonino la Pelosa planned an uprising in Palermo on the same day as the Corpus de Sang in Barcelona, seven years before.[52]

The calendar also influenced popular resistance in Muslim countries. In the Ottoman empire, the garrison of Istanbul became restless at the end of the month of Ramadan, when tradition demanded that they receive a bonus pay: if the treasury could not meet this obligation, or met it only in part, the troops might mutiny.[53] Moreover, throughout the Muslim world religious holidays that involved public processions, like Muharram, could easily give rise to riots – particularly in areas like Mesopotamia that boasted both Sunni and Shi'ite populations, where supporters of one creed might disrupt the devotions of the other (a practice that continues to this day).

Weapons, Cadres and Emblems

A final common denominator of popular revolts was the transformative role of groups already used to acting in unison, especially if they were familiar with weapons. In a society that lacked an effective police force, owning a weapon, especially a firearm, offered a measure of security against perceived threats: bandits, 'insolent' beggars, personal enemies and, in the countryside, natural predators (above all, wolves). In some frontier zones of Europe and in Anglo-America, possession of firearms was seen as essential to survival. In France, the government itself supplied arms to the coastguards of Normandy and Brittany, and the Peace of the Pyrenees in 1659 guaranteed the right of every inhabitant of Roussillon to bear arms; while two decades later a French *Intendant* near the Spanish frontier regretted that 'It would be difficult to prevent the Basques from bearing arms, because they have been able to do so for so long'.[54] In India, seventeenth-century government records and visitors' accounts alike noted the abundance of 'labourers with their guns, swords and bucklers lying by them while they ploughed the ground', and the Mughals designated some areas *mawas* (rebellious lands) or *zor-talab* ('requiring coercion') because the villagers there were armed and refused to part with their wealth, whether to the government or to bandits, 'without at least one fight'. 'In order to defend themselves, these villagers hide in the thorny scrub or retire behind the slight walls surrounding their villages,' wrote Niccolò Manucci in the 1650s, and fought with bows, lances and firearms 'until they were no longer able to continue'.[55] In the 1640s the English 'Clubmen' often managed to protect their communities from billeting and plundering by the main armies during the Civil War, even when only 'armed with clubs, swords, bills, pitchforks and other several weapons'; while in Virginia in 1676, the year of Bacon's rebellion, Governor Berkeley lamented that his opponents were 'poor, indebted, discontented and armed'.[56]

Weapons became far more effective when in the hands of those familiar with their use, such as army veterans and outlaws. Whenever rioters forced open the gates of the local gaols they released into the crowd hundreds of men with experience of defying government, as well as links with other discontented groups still at large. Although some of the freed inmates immediately fled the country in search of safety, others seized the opportunity to inflict destruction on their oppressors. When rioters opened the prisons of Palermo in 1647, Antonino la Pelosa, a miller, set about organizing neighbouring farmers to murder all the nobles of Palermo; while Giuseppe d'Alesi, who had fled to Naples on his release from gaol, returned to his native city once he heard of the viceroy's general pardon and organized a more radical rebellion. Meanwhile, in Naples, Giulio Genoino and Francesco Arpaja emerged after a quarter-century in various royal prisons to direct the revolution against their former gaolers.

The participation of veterans also had a transformative effect on revolts, because they possessed not only familiarity with weapons but also discipline under fire and the ability to coordinate manoeuvres. In France, one contemporary claimed that the 8,000 armed peasant insurgents ('Croquants') who mobilized in Périgord in 1637 were 'mostly veterans from the most warlike provinces of the kingdom', serving under captains with extensive military experience, 'the best that one could find'. The Croquants certainly behaved like regular troops: not only posting sentries and issuing formal summons for towns in their path to surrender on pain of being 'ruined, razed and burnt to ashes', but also destroying the farms, killing the cattle and burning the crops of all who refused to join them.[57] The presence of a cadre of 40 or 50 'coquins' (rascals) and of many former soldiers and perhaps some officers among the Norman rebels in 1639 enabled the lord of Ponthébert ('General Nu Pieds') and his 'Army of Suffering' to withstand repeated assaults by regular troops in pitched battle.[58] Likewise, in Naples, Masaniello's regular drilling of his *ragazzi* – the 'boys' whom he had trained for a mock battle in the Piazza del Mercato – explains both the cohesion of his followers and his 'skill in digging trenches and keeping watch with sentries' (something that all commentators noted with surprise); while the city militia – originally created to fend off a possible Turkish attack, regularly trained and led by experienced army officers – managed to defeat every assault by forces loyal to the crown. Familiarity with artillery could also provide a critical advantage. In 1647 the ability of Gennaro Annese, an armourer by trade, to direct an effective bombardment of the Spanish fleet, saved Naples; whereas the inability of the Seville rebels to do the same five years later, even though they had captured several big guns, doomed them to defeat. In Peru, Pedro Borhorques alarmed the government in part because of his vaunted ability to cast as well as fire light artillery. Finally, neither the Scots in 1639–40 nor the Irish in 1641–2 could have prevailed without the return of large numbers of veterans of continental armies with their equipment and expertise.[59]

In Asia, too, many revolts gained at least initial success thanks to the participation of veterans. At Shimabara (Japan) in 1638, 200 former samurai taught the rest of the rebels how to use firearms to defend Hara Castle against over 100,000 government troops. In China, deserters from the regular army strengthened the 'roving bandits' in the 1620s and 1630s: Zhang Xianzhong, the 'Great King of the West' in Sichuan, was one of them. After 1640, the influx of deserters from the Ming Army probably explains Li Zicheng's sudden ability to capture fortified towns. By 1644, Li's troops had reached such a high level of military effectiveness that they came close to defeating the elite Ming troops of Wu Sangui at the Shanhai pass, and only the intervention of fresh Manchu forces turned the tide.[60]

Besides weapons and discipline, emblems and insignia could enhance the effectiveness of resistance to government. In America, the magistrates of Mexico City gradually replaced the Habsburg coat of arms with the ancient Aztec symbol of an eagle poised on a cactus devouring a serpent until 1642, when the viceroy, suspicious of any hint of insurgency in the wake of the revolt of Portugal and Brazil, forbade it. Governor John Endicott of Massachusetts had more success when in 1634 he decided to create a new flag for the colony by cutting the red cross out of the royal ensign, on the grounds that it was a symbol of popery: the colony retained its insignia almost until the end of the century. Meanwhile, in Japan, the Catholic rebels at Shimabara in 1638 placed 'many small flags with red crosses' around their parapets; and the following year the Chinese insurgents in the Philippines also waved distinctive banners in defiance at the Spaniards, while rebellious groups on the Chinese mainland flew red banners (although this may merely have reflected the fact that in China red was the colour of felicity).[61]

In several parts of Europe, red also became the colour of revolution. In 1647, in Naples, the rebels 'unfurled the red flag (*lo stendado rosso*)' at their headquarters 'as a sign of war', and soon insurgents throughout the city displayed red flags. The following month in Palermo, insurgents also waved red flags as a sign of defiance; while six years later, the Swiss insurgents followed the red 'Entlebuch banner'. In 1647 Masaniello wore a red bonnet while the soldiers of the New Model Army in England tied a red ribbon around their left arms to show 'that we will defend the equity of our [cause] with our blood'. In France, the Ormée rebels of Bordeaux (1651–3) wore a 'chapeau rouge', while the 'red bonnets' of the Breton rebels in 1675 gave their name to the province's rebellion against Louis XIV.[62]

Likenesses of many revolutionary leaders also circulated, to inspire their followers. Images of both Sabbatai Zvi and Nathan of Gaza not only appeared in books but were also paraded around the streets of Poland in 1666; while most leaders of the English Revolution – John Pym, Sir Thomas Fairfax and, above all, Oliver Cromwell – were frequently portrayed by both supporters and detractors in paintings, engravings, sculptures, medals and even artefacts. None, however, rivalled the posthumous fame of Masaniello of Naples. Although his 'reign' lasted only nine days, the humble fisherman achieved an iconic status that anticipated that of Che Guevara in the twentieth century: artists captured his likeness in paintings, medals and wax statuettes (some for export); intellectuals composed epigrams extolling his achievements; plays about him were later published in England, Germany and the Dutch Republic. The Dutch philosopher Benedict Spinoza hung in his rooms a picture of himself dressed to resemble Masaniello. Before long, tour guides for foreign travellers to Naples included his haunts in their itineraries.[63]

Finally, in societies where many protagonists were illiterate, slogans and songs also played an important role in maintaining the coherence of rebellions. Chronicles of the Naples revolution of 1647–8 record some 30 popular slogans, ranging from alarms when the crowd feared a Spanish counter-attack (*'Arme, arme! Serra, serra!'*: 'To arms, close ranks!') to more aggressive chants (*'Ammaza, ammaza'*: 'Kill, kill'). Some of them rhymed:

> May the people of Naples always advance;
> Long live God and the king of France!

By far the commonest slogans, in Naples as elsewhere in western Europe, were either economic or political: 'Long live the king and down with the evil government!' and 'Long the king and down with taxes!'[64] Some crowds also made social demands in rhyme. In England, a popular song first heard in 1640 had the refrain 'Heigh then up go we' attached to verses that attacked the social hierarchy, good manners, 'wanton women', subordination and the universities. Many contemporaries later remembered this as the 'revolutionary catchphrase that preceded the Civil War', but many more followed. *Rump: or an exact collection of the choycest poems and songs relating to the late times. By the most eminent wits, from anno 1639 to anno 1661*, published in 1662, contained 210 'scandalous, libellous songs' that had entertained and animated English men and women during the previous decades of turbulence.[65]

Other European revolutionary songs included the 54-verse 'Fadinger Song' (Upper Austria, 1626); an anthem in honour of Martin Laimbauer (Lower Austria,

1636); the Cossacks' 'Victory march' (Ukraine, 1648); and the 'New Song of William Tell in the Entlebuch' (Swiss Confederation, 1653). In Ireland, Gaelic bards composed and sang poems of freedom, and many accounts of the 1641 rebellion record pipers entertaining rioters.[66] Some rousing rebel songs composed in the seventeenth century enjoyed a long life. The melody of one of the many songs that commemorated Stenka Razin's revolt of 1670 entered the Western 'hit parade' three centuries later as 'The carnival is over'. Two seventeenth-century revolutionary songs are still sung by crowds today. The *Song of the Segadors*, with verses protesting against the troops and the policies imposed by the count-duke of Olivares and calling for an armed defence of Catalan liberty, first heard in the summer of 1640, has become the 'hymn of Catalonia' (albeit with some modernization of both words and tune).[67] In the Dutch Republic, a volume entitled *Netherlands Anthem of Commemoration*, first published in 1626, included patriotic songs and dances honouring major successes against 'Spanish tyranny'. One of the most powerful songs – *Merck toch hoe sterck* ('See now the strength'), written to celebrate Bergen-op-Zoom's successful resistance to a Spanish siege in 1622 – is still sung today at tense moments during Dutch football matches.[68]

Concession or Repression?

Sophisticated popular revolts placed governments everywhere in a quandary. On the one hand, many saw rebellions as dominoes and feared that failure to respond swiftly and harshly would embolden others. In the words of a bishop in Spanish Peru in 1635 seeking to justify strong measures against a critic of royal taxation, from 'small sparks are great fires easily set alight, and it is more prudent to remedy the damage in its beginning than to attempt to quench it when difficult or impossible'. The count-duke of Olivares heartily agreed. Two years later he feared that granting concessions to the rebels of Évora

> would lead not only the rest of Portugal but also all His Majesty's realms in Europe, in America and in India to do the same, and with very good reason, because they would risk nothing in doing so since they would know that one miserable town, just by rebelling, had obliged its king to come to terms – and to come to terms favourable to them.

Shortly afterwards, in Scotland, faced with demands for major constitutional concessions, the marquis of Hamilton (Charles I's cousin and senior adviser on Scottish affairs) issued a similar warning that unless the king refused 'he might quit his three crowns for they [his opponents] would trample over them all'.[69]

On the other hand, although Olivares and Hamilton were correct, ignoring the pleas of desperate or intransigent subjects could also provoke disaster. In the 1620s Francis Bacon asserted that 'rebellions of the belly are the worst', and two decades later the English parliamentary leader John Pym worried about the 'tumults and insurrections of the meaner sort of people' that would arise if they could not buy bread, because 'nothing is more sharp and pressing than necessity and want: what they cannot buy they will take'.[70] In 1648, facing the worst harvest in living memory, a petition to Parliament from the porters of London warned that unless they received relief, their economic straits would 'force your petitioners to extremities, not fit to be named, and to make good that saying, that *necessity has no law*'. A pamphlet entitled *The mournful cries of many thousand poor tradesmen* likewise reminded Parliament that 'necessity dissolves all laws and government and hunger will break through stone walls'. That same year, in Italy, the rioters of Fermo opined that 'it is better to die by the sword than to die of hunger'; while in France a lawyer at Bordeaux reported philosophically to the central government after a major food riot: 'There is nothing so natural as to fight to save one's life. Since bread is the most common source of food, men work all the harder to possess it. The poor fear that they will never have enough of it, because they are not always sure of having it; and this fear translates, in their minds, shortage into famine.'[71]

Mindful of these dangers, many governments granted short-term concessions to protestors. Caprice or scruples on the part of a ruler could also sometimes bring relief. In China, each emperor normally forgave unpaid taxes to celebrate his accession or the birth of an heir. In 1641 Philip IV even established a 'committee on conscience' to examine whether any of the taxes he had imposed might have been unjust and therefore offended God, because 'I do not want to benefit from any tax that has the slightest suspicion of injustice'.[72] Many governments also established permanent machinery to consider individual appeals for tax relief. In China, magistrates regularly petitioned the central government for forgiveness or reduction of taxes, or at least for a delay in collection, because their district had suffered from some natural disaster. Not all did so in vain. In Tancheng county, in Shandong province, for instance, the magistrate petitioned the Board of Revenue for tax relief in the wake of a devastating earthquake in 1668: officials from the Board made a personal inspection and, 18 months later, local taxpayers received a 30 per cent reduction, either as 'forgiveness' or, if they had already paid, as a rebate. The Board also reduced the county's compulsory labour services for the upkeep of roads and bridges. In the Ottoman empire, the sultan's council spent one day of each week hearing appeals from individuals, villages or groups of villages for a reduction in their tax assessment. Some cited a recent drought, flood or bandit attack, or general depopulation, to argue that the community could no longer meet its obligations; others argued that they were wrongly included in a tax register (often because they were already on another); a few protested against extortion. Although the subsequent inquiry sometimes discovered taxpayers falsely trying to reduce or escape their obligations, normally the government agreed that an error existed in the registers, and therefore reduced or 'forgave' the taxes specified in the thousands of petitions they considered.[73] In Castile, the law code decreed that royal commands contrary to conscience or the Catholic faith need not be obeyed, and many taxpayers therefore appealed to local judges against overassessment, or pleaded misfortune or changed circumstances to justify non-payment. The judges often reacted sympathetically and, if they did not (as in the Ottoman empire), the taxpayers might send a petition directly to the crown protesting against their burdens. The king's financial advisers duly considered them – often favourably.[74]

Admittedly, the same legal code that tolerated disobedience on grounds of conscience in Castile also treated resistance to authority as a capital offence, but the judges often hesitated to impose draconian penalties for fear of provoking a back-lash. Thus although the supreme court of Castile tried 336 people involved in nine separate anti-seigneurial riots between 1620 and 1685, it sentenced only 10 to death and fewer than 100 to forced labour. Obviously, Castile experienced far more than nine anti-seigneurial riots in this period, so what happened to the rest?[75] The saga of a riot at Aldeanueva de Ebro (a village in Spain's Rioja region) and its aftermath offers an instructive example of how sustained procrastination could minimize repression. In 1663 news arrived that the king had sold Aldeanueva, until then part of the royal domain, to a nobleman. Its inhabitants rioted, shouting the universal slogan in such situations – 'Long live the king and death to the bad government!' – along with grievance-specific shouts of 'Let's kill whoever wants to sell us like dogs!' and, more remarkably, 'Fuenteovejuna! Fuenteovejuna!' The last slogan referred to a play of that name written 50 years before by Spain's most famous dramatist, Lope de Vega, about the medieval peasant community of Fuenteovejuna that had rioted against abuse by its lord but afterwards refused to identify the ringleaders. Likewise at Aldeanueva, when agents of the new lord tried to round up some of the philo-thespian rebels none of them would name the ringleaders. A judge therefore declared 67 villagers guilty, but the community appealed the decision right up to the Supreme Court of Castile which, 20 years after the events, ruled that the evidence against those convicted was insufficient and ordered a re-trial – by which time most of the participants were dead. Only two of the rioters ever seem to have received any punishment.[76]

In a few cases, violent resistance could produce permanent concessions. Thus in 1641, in southwest France near to the war-zone with Spain, rioters burnt the offices of the king's tax collectors to the ground and ran his officials out of town to shouts of 'Thieves and taxmen: we'll kill you and exterminate all your kind so that no memory [of you] will remain.' The town magistrates, fearing reprisals, sent agents to Paris to explain the hardship from which their town suffered and, on this occasion, the king acknowledged the justice of his subjects' complaints and the unreasonable behaviour of the tax collectors: a letter arrived from the agents that began 'Gentlemen: give thanks to God! No more taxes!'[77] Royal concessions like this received massive publicity – printed posters proclaiming the news went up everywhere – giving the impression that popular resistance 'worked'; but govern-ments seldom crumbled like this.

Revolt and resistance always involved high risks because governments normally treated those who opposed them as traitors.[78] When the Chinese community in the Philippines rebelled in 1639, for example, the Spanish governor had all Chinese held in captivity shot in cold blood, murdered all Chinese servants in Christian households, and set fire to Manila's Chinese suburb, incinerating all within it. The insurgents would have fared no better in their native land, since both the Ming and Qing Law Codes laid down draconian penalties for all rebels and their families, and most Chinese uprisings therefore ended in mass executions.[79] Rebels against the

Romanovs in Russia met a similar fate. After the Moscow rising of 1662 against currency debasement and high food prices, the tsar

> Dealt horribly with those involved in the uprising: over 400 persons, not counting those who drowned, have been executed, some beheaded, and [some] hanged. Others have had their feet and hands cut off and their tongues cut out of their throats. They have put 700 [persons] in chains, and these will be sent as soon as possible to Siberia with their wives and children, each one [of the men] with a brand mark burned into his left cheek ... Each of the young boys who were found among the rebels – 12 or 14 years old – has had an ear cut off as a warning to others.[80]

Likewise in India, according to Emperor Jahangir, although 'there is scarcely a province in the empire in which, either in battle or by the sword of the executioner, five and six hundred thousand human beings have not, at various periods fallen victims to this fatal disposition to discontent and turbulence'.[81]

Many governments in western Europe also made sure defeated rebels received 'exemplary punishment' – a phrase that appears repeatedly in official documents, such as those discussing the proper measures to take in the aftermath of the *Nu-Pieds* of Normandy in 1639. In the event, Louis XIII sent his senior judge, Chancellor Pierre Séguier, to punish the guilty, and he tried over 300 prisoners, sentencing almost 30 to death and 15 more to perpetual exile (with many more sentences passed in absentia on those who had fled). Séguier also levied huge fines on all towns involved, ordered reparations for those whose property had been destroyed, and demanded immediate payment of all tax-arrears (enforced by the troops he brought with him). In 1648, in the wake of the food riots at Fermo in Italy, the town's overlord (the Pope) sent 1,500 troops, who immediately began to hunt down the rioters. Aided by denunciations, printed descriptions of the ringleaders and a papal dispensation to enter churches to arrest those who had sought sanctuary, they eventually captured and tried 30 men. Of these, they executed six and sent ten more as prisoners to row the papal galleys (often equivalent to a sentence of death). They then proceeded to raze the rioters' houses and those of the other accused who had fled; to confiscate their moveable goods; and to ban 17 of the ineffective magistrates (almost one-third of the town's elite) and their descendants from ever holding public office again.[82]

In England, finally, the victors in the Second Civil War executed Charles I and scores of his followers (especially those from Scotland and Ireland), and sentenced thousands more to perpetual servitude (draining the Fens, mining Tyneside coal, and labouring in the American colonies); and in 1685, the Catholic James II exacted a terrible price from the rebels who supported the attempt of his nephew, the Protestant duke of Monmouth, to seize the throne. According to Monmouth's own account, he landed in Devon, in the southwest of England, with scarcely 80 men but four weeks later, when he confronted the royal army he commanded perhaps 7,500. Few escaped. 'The fight actually continued half an hour,' the duke observed, with few losses on either side, but 'great slaughter was made in the pursuit'. Of the

1,300 men captured, the government butchered some immediately, executed almost 300 more (including the duke) after a rapid trial, and sentenced 850 to penal servitude in the American colonies.[83]

Even governments that promised pardon and concessions to rebels who surrendered might renege as soon as they had the upper hand. The most notorious example occurred in Naples. When Gennaro Annese and the other rebel leaders agreed to surrender, Don Juan of Austria promised the city's inhabitants a 'general pardon for all crimes, whether committed through ignorance or malice, even if they involved treason, together with immunity from all excise duties', and the restoration of the privileges granted by Charles V. But Philip IV later asked a committee of theologians 'if we were obliged to uphold the pardons granted to the Neapolitans and respect the oaths sworn to respect the privileges. Their response was negative.' The count of Oñate, who took over from Don Juan as viceroy, announced that his predecessor 'had acted according to the status he then held, but now it was up to him to proceed according to what he found', and almost immediately created a network of agents and spies to denounce enemies of Spain, and special courts to try them. Over the next three years, several hundred former rebels – called *Masanielos* in the Spanish sources – were executed, starting with Annese and several *Capopopoli* of other towns in the kingdom, and several thousand more were proscribed (they survived only because they fled abroad). Oñate also reneged on many other concessions agreed at the surrender, destroying the marble tablets on the 'Epitaph' (*Tavolato*), which contained a 'permanent' copy of the *Capitoli* secured by Masaniello. Then he tore down the structure itself, replacing it with the 'Oñate fountain' that now stands in front of the State Archives.[84]

Whether governments opted for concession or repression to restore order, most regarded rebellions as inconsequential unless or until members of the elite became involved. Thus on hearing of a popular uprising in Évora, Portugal's second city, in 1637, the count-duke of Olivares wrote dismissively: 'Normally we would take very little notice because we see popular tumults every day without any ill-effects' – yet half the kingdom was soon in revolt. Cardinal Richelieu was equally dismissive when he first heard of the Catalan revolt three years later, doing nothing because 'most disorders of this nature are normally just a brush fire (*un feu de paille*)' – yet the rebellion continued for almost two decades.[85] More rashly, in 1648, Cardinal Mazarin dismissed the 'Day of the Barricades' in Paris with exactly the same metaphor: 'The mild disorders that occurred in this city,' he reassured a colleague, were 'just a brush fire which we extinguished as easily as it began' – yet the French capital had just experienced the worst disorders it had seen in 60 years, or would see again until the French Revolution.

What Olivares, Richelieu and Mazarin failed to realize was that significant segments of the social elite seethed with resentment, that they sought any plausible excuse to 'turn petty rifts into major fights', and that they 'think that if there is a rebellion they can steal what they want'. An official in the Papal States, forced to flee from rioters in 1648, had a better grasp of the nature of popular revolts: 'One must never underestimate the facility with which the common people [*la Plebe*] allow themselves to be persuaded by anyone who expresses concern for their fate,' he warned the Pope. In particular 'impassioned gentlemen are highly effective in making the people believe the impossible, especially when clothed in zeal for the public good'.[86] Amid all the disasters of the mid-seventeenth century, 'impassioned gentlemen' became 'highly effective in making the people believe the impossible'. They were not alone.

'People who hope only for a change': Aristocrats, Intellectuals, Clerics and the 'dirty people of no name'[1]

I N 1644 NICHOLAS FOUQUET, LATER LOUIS XIV'S CHIEF FISCAL OFFICER but then his representative in Valence on the river Rhône, pondered the current unrest among the city's inhabitants. He concluded that, although the *origins* of the disorders he faced 'do indeed lie in the misery of the common people, their *progress* proceeds from the division that exists among the most powerful people, the ones who should oppose them'. A few years later, the marquis of Argyll, a leading protagonist in the Scottish revolution, made the same point in a different way: 'Popular furies,' he wrote, 'would have no end, if not awed by their superiors'.[2] In the early modern world, three groups of 'powerful people' possessed the power to turn 'popular furies' into something that threatened state breakdown – the nobility; literate lay men and women; and the clergy – and every major revolt in the mid-seventeenth century involved at least one of them. Sometimes, however, 'powerless people' from humble backgrounds also played important (albeit ephemeral) roles, especially in urban revolts; and they, like their social betters, sometimes developed sophisticated theories and arguments to justify their opposition.

The Crisis of the Aristocracy

Although bitter rivals, Richelieu and Olivares totally agreed on one maxim of state. In 1624 the cardinal (from an aristocratic family) warned Louis XIII that 'keeping the nobles under the king's authority is the sole pivot around which the State turns'; while that same year the count-duke lectured Philip IV on the necessity of keeping the nobles 'always reined in without letting any one of them grow too powerful'. Kings must 'under no circumstances allow noblemen, great or small, to make themselves popular'.[3] Over the next two decades both ministers followed their own advice ruthlessly. French aristocrats who openly challenged the government's policies, both domestic (for example, by defying Richelieu's ban on duelling) and foreign (by plotting peace with Spain), went either to the scaffold, to prison, or into exile. Philip IV, for his part, condemned to death the South Netherlands nobles who conspired against him in 1632; imprisoned the duke of Medina Sidonia and executed the marquis of Ayamonte, two of Spain's most powerful aristocrats, after their attempt to create an independent Andalusia came to light in 1641; and ordered the duke of Híjar to be tortured to reveal details of his alleged conspiracy. When Olivares first heard rumours of rioting in Lisbon in December 1640, he professed little concern 'because the nobles have not declared themselves and, in Portugal, unless the nobles are involved there is no reason to be afraid of the people'. His sole concern was that 'it is some days since the duke of Bragança wrote' – and, he added presciently, 'since he is so close to these disturbances, and since it would be so easy for him to write', his silence 'may cause some suspicion'. Just one week had elapsed since Bragança's acclamation as King John IV of Portugal.[4]

Nobles presented a greater political danger in Europe than elsewhere in the seventeenth-century world, and the continent contained three distinct 'aristocratic zones'. At one extreme stood areas where noble families made up a substantial proportion of the total population: Castile with 10 per cent, the Polish Commonwealth with 7 per cent, and Hungary with 5 per cent. By contrast, France, the British Isles, the Dutch Republic and the Scandinavian kingdoms belonged to a second zone, in which nobles were relatively scarce: 1 per cent or less of the total population.[5] The rest of the continent fell somewhere in between these extremes, but almost everywhere the nobility expanded. Between 1644 and 1654, Queen Christina doubled the size of the Swedish aristocracy; between 1600 and 1640, Kings Philip III and IV almost tripled the number of titled nobles in the kingdom of Naples and almost doubled it in Castile; and James I and Charles I almost quadrupled the Irish peerage and more than doubled that of England.

Many of the new peers received their title for the traditional reason – to reward outstanding service to the state – but many more became aristocrats either in return for money or services supplied to a monarch unable to reward their services in any other way, or as part of a strategy to empower one group (such as the relatives of the 'Favourite') at the expense of others. The new nobles therefore included many bankers, many generals, many lawyers and many people with the same surname (Guzmán in Spain; Oxenstierna in Sweden; and so on). New or old, however, most peers envisaged a threefold political role for themselves. First, they believed they should help the king to govern; second, they tried to bring to the king's attention the needs and interests of their family and followers; third, to preserve the 'liberties' won by the blood of their ancestors in the service of the crown to be their birthright, they felt (in the happy phrase of French historian Arlette Jouanna) a 'duty to rebel'.[6]

Domineering ministers and Favourites like Richelieu, Olivares and Oxenstierna irritated and eventually alienated their fellow aristocrats in two distinct ways. First, the ministers' insistence that 'necessity knows no law' resulted in the repeated violation of aristocratic immunities by recruiters in search of troops, by tax collectors in search of funds, and by commissioners demanding that nobles document their tax-exempt status. Second, Favourites strove to restrict the king's attention solely to the views and interests of their own followers. Previously the economic health of each noble house had depended upon royal benevolence – the grant of a lucrative state office, or an edict that unilaterally reduced interest rates on their debts and offered protection against their creditors – but now it depended upon the benevolence of the Favourite. At a time of economic adversity and heavy taxation, many peers faced economic catastrophe if the Favourite persuaded the king to with-hold his financial favours.[7]

Nevertheless, slighted nobles could still fight back. The Edinburgh maidservants whose 'barbarous hubbub' during a church service in 1637 began the Scottish revolution came from the households of disaffected noblemen who had issued careful instructions on when and how their servants should act. The involvement of the nobles explains not only the maids' temerity but also the government's decision not to apprehend or punish any of them. In England, formal opposition to Charles I began in 1640 with a petition signed by seven (later over twenty) peers demanding that the king should both 'remove and prevent' certain grievances and bring the 'authors and councillors of them' to 'legal trial and condign punishment'. Their actions forced the unwilling king first to convene a 'Great Council of Peers', attended by over seventy noblemen, and then to summon Parliament in which the House of Lords played a prominent role in securing further concessions. One-third of the English peerage would eventually fight in the Civil War.

Nobles found it harder – though not impossible – to rebel when they lacked a constitutional forum. In Castile, where the aristocracy had abandoned its right to attend the Cortes, rebellions by individuals (Medina Sidonia and Ayamonte in 1641, Hijar in 1648) came to nothing; but collective action occurred after the surrender of Perpignan (Catalonia's second city) to the French in 1642. The grandees of Castile boycotted the court and made clear that they would continue to do so until His Majesty dismissed Olivares. As the aristocratic 'strike' entered its third week, Philip crumbled. Although aristocratic solidarity on such a scale did not recur during the Habsburg period, collective protests by the landed elite persisted at the regional level. Thus four rebellions against the lords of Nájera and Navarrete in 1652 and 1653 involved 33 knights in Castile's Military Orders, and all four rebellions won major concessions (albeit only for the local communities).[8]

France's nobles, too, lacked a common forum in which to air their grievances. Although several provinces boasted a representative assembly that could meet legally in the absence of the king, affording the nobles of the regions a collective voice, the States-General, where representatives of the whole kingdom gathered, could convene only when summoned by the crown – and the crown issued no summons after 1614. As in Castile, the French nobility attempted to force their views on the monarch by collective action only once during the seventeenth century. In 1651, after the arrest of the prince of Condé and two aristocratic allies, some 800 nobles from all over France converged on Paris, where for six weeks they demanded the release of their leaders and the redress of their grievances – including a new assembly of the States-General. The government eventually promised to comply and persuaded the nobles to return to their provinces and draw up *Cahiers de doléances* (the Petitions of Grievance presented at the start of each assembly), but it was a bluff: no States-General met until 1789.

In the absence of a constitutional forum, discontented nobles found other ways to express their grievances. Some stated them in print: almost one-half of the authors of pamphlets published in France between 1610 and 1642 were aristocrats; while during the Fronde, several nobles maintained a stable of writers to propagate their views (Condé also installed a printing press in his Paris mansion).[9] Other nobles led local rebellions. Antoine Dupuy, lord of La Mothe La Forêt, recently retired from an active army career, agreed to lead the 'Croquant' rebellion of Périgord in southwest France in 1637; two years later, in Normandy, the lord of Ponthébert became 'General Nu-Pieds' and commanded an 'Army of Suffering'. Neither secured lasting concessions, but sometimes grandees achieved greater success. Thus in 1641 the duke of Bouillon ordered that if any royal troops tried 'to lodge in any parish' of his territories 'without an express order from the king, the said parishes should ring the church bells to alert the neighbouring parishes, which are obliged to assist them immediately' in driving the troops away.[10] Only one French noble, Louis de Bourbon, prince of Condé, took the 'duty to rebel' to the extremes seen in earlier centuries: he created a national following, sought to become chief minister, and when his attempt failed he entered the service of his country's arch-enemy (Philip IV) to further his cause.

Three considerations explain why Condé's extreme action remained virtually unique in seventeenth-century Europe. First, most attempts to create a 'national following' foundered on an intense local hatred of the capital and the court. As an account of the Croquants' revolt noted, 'the very name "Parisian" excites such hatred and horror in everyone that just to say it is to risk being killed'. Local rebels, in France and elsewhere, normally 'resolved not to welcome any prince or lord fleeing the Court'.[11] Second, rebellion was so expensive that most dissident nobles lacked the means to sustain their defiance for long: few could resist when the crown offered a settlement that restored their financial solvency. Thus in 1651 Mazarin purchased the allegiance of the duke of Bouillon by recognizing his French possessions as sovereign lordships and granting him extensive royal domains. Third, most of Europe's great noble houses simply had too much to lose by outright defiance of the government. Thus, long before he became king of Portugal, Duke John of Bragança boasted more power than any other Portuguese nobleman, if not more than any other aristocrat in western Europe. His vast revenues maintained not only a household of 400 people, modelled on the royal court; he exercised extensive ecclesiastical patronage; and, unique in all Europe, he could create nobles himself. Duke John therefore stayed out of court politics, because he had nothing more to gain, and instead concentrated on conserving the assets, privileges and pre-eminences which he had inherited. He only abandoned this prudent stance in 1640 because Olivares insisted that he raise and personally lead troops to fight in Catalonia, a venture from which he feared (probably correctly) that he might never be allowed to return – and so he threw in his lot with a group of conspirators who declared him king. His dynasty would rule Portugal and Brazil for almost three centuries.[12]

Many other magnates besides Bragança placed the preservation of their inheritance at the top of their political agenda, even if it compromised their allegiance.

Thus the determination of Randall MacDonnell, marquis of Antrim, to protect intact his extensive lands and interests in Ireland, England and Scotland throughout the upheavals of the mid-seventeenth century led him to remain loyal to Charles I until 1645 (no mean feat, in view of the king's frequent changes of policy) and then, once the king could no longer protect him, to make deals with others. He became, in turn, President of the Irish Catholic Confederation, privateer and warlord, a Cromwellian collaborator and, finally, a supporter of the Restoration. Some contemporaries condemned him for 'pulling down the side he is on', while others accused him of 'making poison out of everything' and thus infecting 'the greater part of the kingdom'. Yet, as Antrim's biographer Jane Ohlmeyer has remarked, 'concepts such as "treachery" and "patriotism" meant little in the early modern Gaelic world where a man's first loyalty was to his family and kinsmen, then to his religion, and only finally to his sovereign and country'. 'Antrims' emerged in western Europe whenever the changing fortunes of war led aristocrats to make similar compromises in order to preserve their heritage intact.[13]

In some states, the nobility had already acquired such extensive economic and political powers that they needed to make no such compromises to get their own way – and therefore felt no 'duty to revolt'. In Sweden, and also in Denmark until 1660, the aristocracy possessed not only vast landed estates but also controlled the royal council, without whose approval the ruler could do little; while the nobles of the Polish-Lithuanian Commonwealth acquired such a stranglehold on the federal Parliament (*Sejm*) that a single veto could paralyze all business and force dissolution. In Russia, the nobles used their prominent place in the 'Assembly of the Land' (Zemskii Sobor) to agitate for legislation that granted them absolute authority over their serfs and shamelessly exploited the wave of popular disturbances that swept the empire in 1648–9 to secure the tsar's compliance (see chapter 6).

No group of hereditary nobles outside Europe played an important role in the political upheavals of the mid-seventeenth century. Indeed, some states lacked any hereditary nobles. Thus, although the Mughal emperors granted fiefs (*jagirs*) to their leading followers, the grants never became hereditary; and while the Ottoman sultans also granted fiefs (*timars*) to their cavalrymen, they never became an 'aristocracy' in the European sense. Ming China boasted great landholding families, but most belonged to the ruling dynasty (which paid them lavish allowances). The Ming clansmen remained staunchly loyal because they realized that, without imperial protection, they would lose everything – as indeed occurred in the 1640s, when rebel armies publicly humiliated and executed all the princes they encountered, and then confiscated their goods. Finally, the Tokugawa shoguns deployed a wide range of policies to control the 200 daimyō of Japan: they ordered them to demolish all but one castle in each fief; they demanded huge 'donations' to their own construction projects; and they required all daimyō to spend half their time in attendance at Edo, and to leave their wives and children there permanently as a guarantee of loyalty. In addition, until 1651, the shoguns dismissed and occasionally executed daimyō who displeased them, arbitrarily rotated others from one fief to another, and took over direct administration during minorities. Although in 1651, after the death of Shogun Iemitsu, some discontented samurai conspired to overthrow the Tokugawa system, they received no daimyō support (see chapter 16).

Education and Revolution[14]

In many parts of the mid-seventeenth century world, a second category of 'powerful people' (to use the terminology of Nicholas Fouquet) fostered political resistance: literate lay men and women. Ironically, the very systems created by the state to generate highly educated officials also generated highly educated critics and opponents. In China, according to scholar Wang Daokun, most families found the rewards offered by success in the educational system irresistible:

> It is not until a man is repeatedly frustrated in his scholarly pursuits that he gives up his studies and takes up trade. After he has accumulated substantial savings he encourages his descendants, in planning for their future, to give up trade and take up studies. Trade and studies thus alternate with each other, with the likely result that the family succeeds either in acquiring an annual income of ten thousand bushels of grain or in achieving the honour of having a retinue of a thousand horse-carriages.[15]

Wang, the descendant of tradesmen who became a successful bureaucrat, knew well that although trade might bring profit, 'scholarly pursuits' brought prestige – and he must also have known how many men were 'repeatedly frustrated in [their] scholarly pursuits'. The arithmetic was simple: 99 per cent of the 50,000 shengyuan ('licenciates') who competed in each triennial provincial juren examination failed it, as did 90 per cent of the 15,000 men involved in each triennial metropolitan jinshi examination (see chapter 5 above). Although the overall population of China may have doubled under the Ming, if one includes all the men who prepared and sat for their examinations but failed, its student population by the 1620s probably reached five million, a twentyfold increase, and some counties boasted over 1,000 frustrated scholars. As the problems that faced the state multiplied, some started to criticize and even oppose the government.

One of the boldest disturbances led by scholars occurred in 1626 in the prosperous Jiangnan city of Suzhou, when the emperor's chief eunuch, Wei Zhongzian, ordered the arrest of one of his critics, Zhou Shunchang, a retired official who had displayed outstanding honesty and (according to one source) 'hated evil as a personal enemy'. Around 500 licentiates donned their formal attire and gathered in the courtyard of the local magistrate, begging him not to execute the warrant because it had been issued by Wei rather than by the emperor. Although the magistrate hesitated, the guards started to shackle Zhou anyway, and according to an eyewitness this provoked 'an uprising such as a thousand antiquities never experienced. . . The affair got completely out of control, so that law and order could not be enforced.' The scholars beat one guardsman to death and chased away the rest. The riots lasted for three days. Wei later had five of the insurgent Suzhou scholars executed, degraded five more and sentenced several others to hard labour.[16]

Although these draconian measures temporarily halted collective academic insurrections, some individual intellectuals continued to criticize the policies pursued by the Ming government, while others denounced those who carried them out. Tang Xianzu (1550–1616), who passed all his examinations and began a promising career as an official, resigned at age 47 and devoted himself to writing the celebrated play *The Peony Pavilion* and several tracts that portrayed his former colleagues in the bureaucracy as corrupt and incompetent pedants. Feng Menglong (1574–1646), who repeatedly failed his examinations, collected and published novels, poetry, jokes and short stories that likewise portrayed scholars and officials as corrupt buffoons. Ai Nanying (1583–1646) achieved fame when his successful *juren* examination in 1624 was deemed to contain material critical of Wei Zhongzian, who decreed that Ai would have to wait nine years before attempting his *jinshi*. Ai responded by writing critical essays, letters and poems that proved so popular that 'Suzhou and Hangzhou booksellers paid him to come and write something – anything – they could publish'. Three editions of his collected works had appeared by the end of the century.

Zhang Tao, a county magistrate who had passed all his examinations, provided perhaps the most damaging critique, in an essay published in a Gazetteer in 1609, comparing Ming China with the four seasons of the year. According to Zhang's scenario, 'winter' corresponded with the early years of the dynasty, when 'every family was self-sufficient, with a house to live in, land to cultivate, hills from which to cut firewood, gardens in which to grow vegetables. Taxes were collected without harassment and bandits did not appear.' Then came 'spring' – roughly the later fifteenth and earlier sixteenth centuries – when 'Those who went out as merchants became numerous and the ownership of land was no longer esteemed. Men matched wits using their assets, and fortunes rose and fell unpredictably.' This caused the moral order to weaken, as 'deception sprouted and litigation arose; purity was sullied and excess overflowed'. The process accelerated in the later sixteenth century, the 'summer' of the dynasty, as 'the rich became richer and the poor, poorer. Those who rose took over, and those who fell were forced to flee. . . Corrupt magistrates sowed disorder. . . Purity was completely swept away and excess inundated the world.' Now, in the seventeenth century, Zhang perceived 'autumn' all around him: 'One man in a hundred is rich, while nine out of ten are impoverished. The poor cannot stand up to the rich who, though few in number, are able to control the majority. . . Avarice is without limit, flesh injures bone, everything is for personal pleasure.'[17]

As public order and economic conditions deteriorated, alienated intellectuals gained confidence when they joined one of the 2,000 or so 'Academies' founded under the late Ming, of which the most famous was the Donglin Academy in Wuxi, where officials and candidates for the civil service exams met other intellectuals to discuss current social issues. After the Academy's suppression, many Donglin alumni joined the *Fu she* ('Restoration Society', founded in 1629) or another 'scholarly society', where they debated not only literature, philosophy and history but also practical ways of ending government corruption and dealing with threats to the traditional order, both foreign and domestic. Although the leading lights of the Academies and later the Societies managed to introduce their ideas into the curriculum of the civil service examinations, they failed either to halt the corruption or to influence the policies of the central government (see chapter 5), and some therefore defected either to Li Zicheng or to the Qing (and, in some cases, to both). Others formed their own bandit gangs. Thus in 1643 an agent of the dukes of Kong in Shandong who captured a gang of 24 bandits was astonished to find that most of them were graduates of the county academy. The scholars bribed a local official to release them and they returned with 1,000 retainers to the residence of the ducal agent, which they burned down, killing many of his relatives before stealing 'grain, donkeys, horses, oxen, sheep, all my accumulated savings, along with over eight thousand' ounces of silver belonging to the dukes of Kong, the most powerful family in the province.[18] Thanks to such successes, the graduate gang prospered until the Qing restored order in the province.

The full potential for disruption of the literate elite of Ming China only emerged after the Qing 'tonsure decree' of 1645 (see chapter 5 above). Tens of thousands of scholars in southern China, whatever degree they held, now mounted a desperate resistance to the foreign dynasty, in which many perished rather than shave their heads and dress like Manchus. Admittedly, they still failed to force the state to change its policies, but their learning and their shared values served as a 'force multiplier' and rendered their political opposition far more formidable.

In Europe, as in China, the methods adopted by the state to produce highly educated officials also produced highly educated critics and opponents. By the 1620s, European men could study at almost 200 institutions of higher education, some of which were surprisingly large (Fig. 49). The student population of Naples University numbered about 5,000, and that of Salamanca University around 7,000. Almost 1,200 students graduated from Oxford and Cambridge Universities each year during the reign of Charles I, while several hundred more studied law at the Inns of Court. In the 1650s, according to the Scottish visitor James Fraser, 'the number of the Inns of Court students and Gentlemen are at present computed to a 1,000 or 1,200', while Cambridge 'could boast of 3,200 students and above', and Oxford ('much decayed of late') had somewhat fewer.[19]

In most European states, the student body included many aristocrats. In Bavaria, almost one-fifth of those who matriculated at Ingolstadt University between 1600 and 1648 were nobles; and by 1620, one-half of the Protestant nobles of Lower Austria had acquired higher education. In England, according to James Fraser, 'all Gentlemen and a considerable number of ye higher Nobility' were 'versed and accomplished here in rhetherick, logick, arithmetick, mathematicks, the French to argue, and Latin'. The majority studied law – albeit, according to Fraser, they only 'learn[ed] so much of it as may be necessary to preferre their estates and to make themselves accomplished and polished in such qualeties as are necessary for Gentlemen'.[20]

In Spain, too, many students came from noble families and studied law. Don Gaspar de Guzmán, the future count-duke of Olivares, arrived at Salamanca

49. Universities founded in Europe, 1600–60.
Although the expansion of institutions of higher education in Europe slowed after 1600, the
following decades also saw numerous foundations, particularly in areas where Catholics and
Protestants struggled for control. Some institutions did not last long: the university college founded
at Durham in 1658 closed its doors the following year.

University aged 14 to study canon law. He attended both morning and afternoon
lectures, studied his lecture notes at night, and also memorized six new legal
precepts and their glosses daily. In his third year, his fellow students elected Don
Gaspar their rector, and he seemed set to enter the Church after graduation, but his
older brother died and his father summoned him to court. Had Don Gaspar persevered with his clerical career, he might have pursued advanced studies at one of
Castile's *Colegios Mayores* (graduate colleges), which prepared men not only to be
bishops and abbots but also to fill senior administrative and judicial positions in
Castile and its American colonies. As Richard Kagan remarked in his classic study
of the universities of Habsburg Spain, 'no other occupation or career offered such
possibilities for economic and social advancement'.[21] Even Wang Daokun might
have felt a twinge of envy.

By the 1630s, perhaps one young Englishman in forty, and perhaps one young
Castilian in twenty, attended university – proportions that would remain unequalled
until the later twentieth century. In addition, perhaps one-third of all adult males in
England acquired direct experience of law enforcement at some level, whether as
magistrates, constables or jurors – a remarkably high participation ratio. As in Ming
China, their learning and their shared values served as a 'force multiplier' that

rendered their political opposition far more formidable; also as in Ming China, no European government managed to employ all the alumni of its institutions of higher education. By the 1630s, perhaps 300 graduates left Oxford and Cambridge each year for a church living and another 200 went on to practise medicine or law – but this left some 700 others with no secure employment. The situation in Spain and other countries was similar: although many graduates entered the Church and a few became university professors, many more left university without a job.

This 'overproduction' of graduates terrified governments because, in the lapidary phrase of England's senior judge, a graduate of both Oxford and the Inns of Court, 'learning without a living doth but breed traitors' and, he opined, 'we have more need of better livings for learned men, than of more learned men for these livings'. In Spain, the acerbic writer Francisco de Quevedo (a graduate of the Complutense University) also argued that universities undermined rather than strengthened states: monarchies 'have always been acquired by generals and always corrupted by graduates,' he wrote. 'Armies, not universities, win and defend' states; 'battles bring kingdoms and crowns while education gives you degrees and pompoms'. In Sweden, the chancellor of Uppsala University complained that 'there are more men of letters and learned fellows, especially in political matters, than means or jobs available to provide for them, and they grow desperate and impatient'. Emperor Ferdinand II, a graduate of Ingolstadt University, blamed the revolt of Bohemia and Austria against him on the universities, where his noble subjects had, he claimed, 'in their youth imbibed the spirit of rebellion and opposition to lawful authority'.[22]

They made a good point: alienated intellectuals took a prominent part in fostering many European rebellions. In Bohemia, the rebel government included a dozen university graduates; in France, the Fronde began with a group of frustrated lawyers (the *Maîtres de requêtes*) and reached its first crescendo with the imprisonment of an outspoken judge (Pierre Broussel). In Sweden, two university-trained lawyers (the burgomaster and town secretary of Stockholm) and the Historiographer Royal led the opposition to Queen Christina in 1651. Many of Philip IV's leading opponents were also university-trained lawyers (Giulio Genoino, Francesco Arpaja and Vincenzo d'Andrea in Naples; Joan Pere Fontanella, his son Josep and Francesc Martí i Viladamor in Catalonia), supported by university-trained historians (Francesco Baronius in Sicily, Francesco de Petri in Naples and Joan Luis Montcada in Catalonia).[23]

Most striking of all, almost every one of Charles I's leading opponents – in both the New World and the Old – had attended an institution of higher education. Of the first 24 graduates from Harvard College, no fewer than 14 travelled to England to support Parliament. The architects of the Scottish revolution included Robert Baillie, who taught at Glasgow University; his pupil Archibald Johnston of Wariston; and Alexander Henderson, who studied (and briefly taught) at St Andrews University. In Ireland, Sir Phelim O'Neill (leader of the Ulster rebellion), had studied at the Inns of Court in London, as had about one-fifth of Ireland's Confederate General Assembly; while Lord Maguire (mastermind of the 1641 plot) had attended Magdalen College Oxford. Finally, at least four-fifths of the English House of Commons elected in 1640 had also studied at either a university or the Inns of Court, or both. In *Behemoth*, a retrospective in dialogue form concerning the causes of the Civil War written in 1668, Thomas Hobbes claimed that Oxford (his *alma mater*) and Cambridge 'have been to this nation as the wooden horse was to the Trojans' because 'out of the universities came all those preachers that taught' resistance. Moreover 'our rebels were publicly taught rebellion in the pulpits'. Hobbes did not limit his remarks to England. Later on in the dialogue, a crusty survivor of the English Civil War states that 'The core of rebellion, as you have seen by this, and read of other rebellions, are the universities', prompting his young inter-locutor to reply: 'For aught I see, all the states of Christendom will be subject to these fits of rebellion, as long as the world lasts' – and, indeed, every one of the major rebellions of western Europe in the mid-seventeenth century involved a large numbers of graduates.[24]

The Contentious Clergy of Latin Christendom

The clergy formed the third group of 'powerful people' with the capacity to transform popular revolts into revolutions, especially in Latin Christendom. At first sight their role may seem surprising because, as the marquis of Argyll wrote in 1661: 'True religion is rather a settler than a stickler in politics and rather confirms men in obedience to the government established than invites them to the erecting of a new' – and, indeed, both the Bible (especially the New Testament) and many religious writers stressed the need to obey. Yet Argyll assuredly knew better. He had seen Scotland's Calvinist clergy use their authority first to denounce the government by law established, then to erect a new one, and finally to compel their king to subscribe to their faith as a condition for allowing him into the kingdom. The Scottish historian (and slave to metaphor) Sir James Balfour did not exaggerate when he denounced the clergy of Scotland as 'the chiefest bellows that has blown this terrible fire' of civil war, because 'the best instruments, misapplied, doe greatest mischieffe and prove most dangerous to aney stait'. And, he continued bitterly, if the clergy chose to

> Misapplay ther talent and abandon themselves to the spirit of faction, they become the bitterest enimies, the most corroding cankers, and worst vipers in aney commonwealthe, and most pernicious to the prince; in regard that they, having the sway over the conscience, which is the rudder that steers the actions, wordes and thoughts of the rationall creature, they transport and snatche it away whither they will, making the beast with maney heads conceive according to the colour of thesse rods they use to cast befor them.[25]

Protestant clerics also acted as 'the chiefest bellows' of sedition elsewhere. In England, according to a preacher in the 1640s, whereas 'the Clergy had at first the golden ball of government amongst themselves', now 'the interest of the people of Christ's kingdom is not only an interest of compliancy, and obedience, and submis-sion, but of consultation, of debating, counselling, prophesying, voting &c; and let us stand fast in that liberty wherewith Christ hath made us free'. One of his colleagues was more specific: 'Ministers might by degrees prepare the people' to participate directly in politics, so that 'by the Sundayes sermon, or a lecture, they could learne, not onely what was done the weeke before, but also what was to be done in Parliament the weeke following' and thus prepare their parishioners 'for comming in tumults to the House [of Commons] for justice'.[26] A generation earlier, in the Dutch Republic, Pastor Adriaan Smout of Amsterdam used his sermons to denounce both the city magistrates and the States-General for sending warships 'to assist the child of destruction, the child of Satan . . . the king of France, Louis XIII'. Smout's oratory eventually secured the recall of the Dutch ships – shortly before the Amsterdam magistrates expelled Smout from their city in an attempt to silence him.[27]

Smout's fate was far from unique. A few years before, the Dutch Reformed Church had expelled some 200 ministers because they supported 'Arminian' views of which their colleagues disapproved. In Scotland, all the bishops and more than 200 ministers lost their posts after 1638, as did over 300 more after 1660, because they opposed the form of church government (Episcopalian and Presbyterian by turns) decreed by the state. For the same reason, in England, all bishops and almost 3,000 ministers (one-third of the total parish clergy) lost their pulpits in the 1640s, and a further 2,000 ministers lost theirs in the 1660s. These deprived ministers joined others who, though highly qualified, had failed to secure a permanent position: both groups posed a latent threat to public order.[28]

Catholic clerics, too, frequently fomented discontent. A Spanish propagandist claimed that 'once the Portuguese people had rebelled, they remained resolute thanks to the persuasion of many clerics who justified their uprising, both with signed opinions and dangerous manifestos . . . as well as with scandalous sermons'. He was right: in 1637, the Jesuits of Évora (where they ran the university) openly supported the rebellion against Spain and toured adjacent areas spreading sedition; while in the 1640s, almost 80 Portuguese preachers are known to have delivered sermons that supported the 'Restoration'. Some called on John IV to rebuild the kingdom of Portugal as Solomon had restored the Temple in Jerusalem, or to lead the Portuguese out of bondage as Moses had led the Hebrews out of Egypt, while others warned their hearers that death would be preferable to 'returning under the vile yoke' of Spain, and that death in the Bragança cause would be equivalent to martyrdom. In France the list of persons whom Louis XIV excluded in 1676 from his General Pardon after the 'red bonnet' rebellion in Brittany included 14 priests.[29]

In Catalonia, too, the clergy played a crucial role in legitimizing the revolt against Spain. In 1640 both bishops and Inquisitors excommunicated the king's soldiers who set fire to churches in two villages that defied them; during the ensuing siege of Barcelona, clerics preached sermons, staged processions and heard confessions around the clock to rally resistance; and, as in Portugal, others assured their congregations that to fight Philip IV and 'die for the Fatherland is to gain eternal life'.[30] Seven years later, in Naples, dissident clerics (especially friars) 'animated the people so that they went freely to fight, and believed they would be martyrs and go to Paradise', while a group of priests took up arms and formed a regular militia company (they and many other clerics found it prudent to flee when the revolt collapsed). At least three bishops of the kingdom were later charged with fomenting the trouble; and at the provincial town of Nardò, the government executed four cathedral canons for inciting the rebels.[31] Even Cardinal-Archbishop Ascanio Filomarino became directly involved in the revolution. In November 1647 he presided at the ceremony in his cathedral at which the duke of Guise became 'Dux' of Naples: he listened to the formal reading of the treaty between France and the Republic; he took Guise's oath to serve as perpetual 'Protector' of the Republic; and he blessed his ceremonial sword and baton. Then, after celebrating a *Te Deum* with the new Dux, the two rode through the crowds shouting 'Long live the king of France'. Although a few months later Filomarino also rode beside Don Juan of Austria when the Spaniards regained possession of the city, at least one chronicler asserted that the archbishop 'was really a supporter of the popular movement and had little love for Spain'.[32]

The Catholic clergy of Ireland proved the most bellicose of all. Although they apparently played little part in planning the 1641 uprising, many priests immediately lent their support. Some urged the rebel troops on in battle: 'Dear sons of St Patrick, strike hard the enemies of the holy faith,' said one; while another, during Mass, 'exhorted them all present to fall to this course of rebellion', and called for extreme measures, 'assureing them that though the English did discharge musketts, and that some of them should be kill'd yet they should not feare, for such as soe died should be saints; and they should rush on with a multitude and kill all the Protestants'. In Ulster, 'the preestes amongst the rebells' allegedly claimed 'that it was noe sinn to kill all the Protestants, whoe are damned' already; in Connacht, the prior of a monastery assured his clerical colleagues that 'it was as lawfull for them to kill' Protestants 'as to kill a sheepe or a dogg'; while in Munster a Dominican friar when asked about the Catholics' plan for his Protestant neighbours, replied '"Why, to kill them," quoth he, "for they will never be ridd of them in this kingdome till they take that course"', adding ominously 'for we have an example in France in the like, for untill the greate massacre there they could never be free of the heretickes' – a clear reference to the Massacre of St Bartholomew in 1572, which claimed the lives of 12,000 Protestants.[33] Equally radical, in 1645 Conor O'Mahony, an Irish Jesuit teaching at the university of Évora, published a tract that congratulated his compatriots on the slaughter of 150,000 of the Protestant newcomers, urged them to make haste to kill the rest, and then replace King Charles with a native Irish monarch.[34]

The involvement of clerics in European revolts mattered because they constituted such a large proportion of the continent's 'public intellectuals': those who helped to shape popular opinion through the spoken and the written word, through the pulpit and sermon as well as the pamphlet and book. In Spain, for example, although clerics made up scarcely 5 per cent of the population, over half of the intellectual elite in the seventeenth century had taken Holy Orders. In addition, a catalogue of all Spanish works published between 1500 and 1699 included 5,385 religious texts, almost all of them written by clerics, compared with 5,450 items in all other categories combined (many of them also written by clerics).[35] Elsewhere in Catholic Europe, clerics wrote two-fifths of all books published in the kingdom of Naples in the course of the seventeenth century, while over half the authors of tracts that supported the revolution of 1640 in Portugal, and one-fifth of all known authors of pamphlets published between 1610 and 1643 in France, were clerics.[36]

Catholic and Protestant clerics alike used the spoken as well as the written word to foment and encourage resistance. The English preacher Stephen Marshall reminded those who heard his sermon entitled *Meroz cursed* that 'the Lord allows no neuters' and rebuked those who 'are sorry for Germany, when they think on it, and that is but seldom', but did nothing to uphold the Protestant cause there; and he predicted that those who failed to embrace 'the cause of God' in England would be cursed just like Meroz in the Book of Judges, 'because they came not to the help of the Lord ... against the mighty'. In the year before the English Civil War began, Marshall delivered his sermon to some 60 different congregations, including the House of Commons, who had it printed.[37] Some seventeenth-century sermons, Catholic as well as Protestant, lasted several hours, during which skilful clerics managed to excite their devout auditors to near hysteria. One Irish Jesuit in the 1640s 'was interrupted so often by the sobs and cries of the faithful that he had to give up preaching, as his voice could not be heard'; while one of his French colleagues regularly reduced his audiences to tears, and the press of the congregation trying to touch his garments or kiss his hand sometimes knocked him over.[38]

The clergy of Latin Christendom enjoyed such influence largely thanks to their education and their elite background. Thus in Ireland, by 1641 every Catholic bishop, the provincials of every Order of Regulars, and hundreds of rank-and-file clergy had received a strict seminary education on the European continent. This training created not only a capacity for unified action, but also a level of learning, discipline and demeanour that empowered the clergy of Ireland both to mould and to channel popular behaviour. Although the senior Catholic clergy in France probably did not attain the same level of learning or discipline, of the 90 bishops nominated between 1640 and 1660, over three-quarters came from noble families, and some of them from the most powerful dynasties in the kingdom (Cardinal de Retz was the brother of a duke). Finally, almost half the 79 Portuguese clerics known to have preached in support of the 'Restoration' of 1640 came from noble families.[39]

Although normally of less exalted birth than their Catholic counterparts, almost all Protestant ministers boasted impressive academic credentials. An analysis of some 400 Scottish clerics in the 1640s – all of them involved in the revolt against Charles I – revealed that only one-quarter were the sons of landowners (and only 20 came from noble families), but every one of them held a university degree. Alexander Henderson epitomized Scotland's 'clerical troublemakers'. He taught at St Andrews University immediately after graduation, and then became pastor of a small neighbouring parish until he came to Edinburgh, where he displayed formidable oratorical and organizational skills in opposing 'Laud's Liturgy'. In 1638 he drafted the National Covenant and presided over the General Assembly that abolished episcopacy; and later he delivered sermons and published pamphlets to justify armed resistance to Charles I, negotiated directly with the king and masterminded the negotiations to oblige England and Ireland to adopt the Solemn League and Covenant (see chapter 11 above). He had become, in the unkind phrase of one of the deposed bishops, 'the Scottish Pope', and such was his fame that Sir Anthony van Dyck, the king's painter, did a full-length portrait of him.[40]

Two clerical contemporaries of Henderson, both Catholic priests, also led European revolts. In Catalonia, Pau Claris (from a family of Barcelona lawyers) studied law at the university of Lleida before becoming a canon of Urgell Cathedral. He achieved prominence in 1638, the same year as Henderson, when he emerged from the triennial lottery as the senior member of the Standing Committee of the Estates (*Diputació*: see chapter 9 above). From this position, he orchestrated first defiance and then armed resistance to Philip IV, until in 1641 he declared Catalonia to be an independent republic, with himself as its head. In Ireland, the constitution of the Confederation of Kilkenny in 1642 gave every Irish bishop the right to sit in the General Assembly (17 bishops did so), while the Supreme Council (the executive branch of government) always contained at least five bishops. Three years later, the papacy sent Giovanni Battista Rinuccini as nuncio to provide the Confederation with leadership and guidance. Rinuccini, from a Florentine patrician family, had gained a doctorate in civil and canon law before his appointment as archbishop of Fermo, a town in the Papal States where he resided for 20 years, writing and publishing books as well as administering his diocese, until his departure for Ireland. In 1646 he became president of the Supreme Council and thus chief executive of the Confederation.[41]

Contentious Clerics Elsewhere

Clerical opposition also threatened the stability of other states in the mid-seventeenth century, most notably the Ottoman empire, where a group of elite families (the *mevali*: see chapter 7 above) gained the right to pass on their offices and revenues to other family members. This privilege had a limited impact as long as Ottoman expansion continued to create new posts for the graduates of the *medreses* that trained the state's preachers, teachers and judges; but once expansion ceased, some graduates waited years for a licence either to teach or to preach, since vacancies remained few, and a disaffected clerical proletariat soon developed.

Even clerics lucky enough to get jobs could still make trouble. In the 1630s the charismatic preacher Kadizade Mehmet won widespread support, first in Istanbul and then throughout the Ottoman empire, through his call for a return to the beliefs and practices of Islam in the time of the Prophet Mohammed. Kadizade focused on 'innovations' associated with the Sufis, members of devout religious orders, excoriating both the way they practised Islam (such as singing, chanting and dancing while reciting the name of God) as well as their social innovations (such as the Sufis' consumption of stimulants like tobacco and coffee to maintain their stamina as they sang, chanted and danced). When some Sufi leaders fought back, the Kadizadeli (as they became known) denounced and beat up individual Sufi sheikhs, vandalized their lodges, and threatened to kill their adherents unless they changed their ways.

Paul Rycaut, an English resident in the Ottoman empire during the 1650s, regarded the proliferation of extreme Muslim groups like the Kadizadeli as 'dangerous, and apt to make a considerable rupture in [the] long continued union [of the Ottoman state] *when time changes and revolutions of state shall animate some turbulent spirits to gather soldiers and followers under these doctrines and other specious pretences*'.[42] Nevertheless Sultan Murad IV attended Kadizade's sermons in person during the 1630s and embraced several elements of his programme (for example, banning the consumption and possession of tobacco or coffee and dismembering or impaling smokers and coffee-drinkers). The Kadizadeli lost ground for a decade after Murad's death in 1640 because his mother, Kösem, used her considerable political authority to protect the Sufis; but after her murder in 1651, the government issued new legislation against smoking and drinking, and approved the destruction of certain Sufi lodges. The Kadizadeli vision enjoyed official support until the deposition of Mehmet IV in 1687, which ended a half-century during which their violent quarrel with the Sufis had not only 'spread extremist notions and so provoked the people and sown dissension among the community of Mohammed' but also severely weakened the empire.[43]

Clerics also played an important role in inspiring resistance in three other states. In Russia, a small group of literate clergymen and monks, protected by a few prominent lay patrons, articulated the cultural system of 'Old Believers' in the 1650s and 1660s, creating a movement that challenged the right of the Romanov dynasty to rule (see chapter 6 above). In Ukraine, when Bohdan Khmelnytsky led the Cossacks in revolt against their Polish overlords in 1648, the Orthodox clergy offered enthusiastic support from their pulpits. Khmelnytsky reciprocated by including many ecclesiastical grievances in the Cossacks' demands to the crown: the admission of Orthodox prelates to the federal Diet, the appointment of Orthodox local officials, the restitution of all former Orthodox churches taken over by the Catholics, and so on (see chapter 7 above). Finally, in India, the charismatic Guru Hargobind, the sixth Sikh Master, radicalized his followers and in the 1630s led them in battle against the forces of the Mughal emperor (see chapter 13 above).

'Dirty people of no name'

The political upheavals of the mid-seventeenth century empowered many others besides discontented members of the traditional elite. In East Asia, Nurhaci, the 'Great Ancestor' of the Qing dynasty, later accorded divine status, began his meteoric career as chief of a minor Manchurian clan that (by his own admission) initially possessed only 13 suits of armour between them. The Ming loyalist leader Coxinga was the illegitimate son of a Japanese samurai's daughter and a Chinese pirate. Li Zicheng, who overthrew the Ming and proclaimed himself the first emperor of the new Shun dynasty, had worked as a minor official at a provincial postal station. In Russia, both Bohdan Khmelnytsky and Stenka Razin, who led the greatest Cossack rebellions of the early modern period, came from poor families; while Patriarch Nikon, who for a time enjoyed powers equal to those of the tsar of Russia, was the son of peasant.

In Europe, too, many rebel leaders came from obscure backgrounds – a fact that profoundly irritated Edward Hyde, earl of Clarendon. In his penetrating *History of the rebellion and civil wars in England* and in other writings, Clarendon frequently condemned the king's opponents as 'men of no name and contemned interest', 'inferior people who were notorious for faction and schism', and even 'dirty people of no name'. There was some truth in such snobbery. Even John Pym, who led the king's opponents in the House of Commons, remained so obscure in the early months of the Long Parliament that one colleague referred to him (with delicious inappropriateness) as 'Mr. Pope'; while an official record listed Oliver Cromwell, the later Lord Protector, as 'Mr. Cornewell'. Another MP protested about 'the illuminated fancies of this all-knowing age', in which

> Old women without spectacles can discover popish plots; young men and apprentices assume to regulate the rebellion in Ireland; seamen and mariners reform the house of peers; poor men, porters, and labourers spy out a malignant party and discipline them; the country clouted-shoe [clog, meaning 'bumpkin'] renew the decayed trade of the city; the cobbler patch up religion.[44]

The Civil War and Interregnum would catapult many more Englishmen from humble backgrounds to prominence. Edward Sexby, once apprenticed to a grocer, in 1647 argued the 'rights of man' with assurance and eloquence at the Putney Debates and later drew up *The principles, foundation and government of a Republic* for the city of Bordeaux; while the most charismatic religious leaders of the period included George Fox, a former shepherd and apprentice shoemaker; John Bunyan, a tinker; and James Nayler, a yeoman. The grandfather of Oliver Cromwell had been a brewer.[45] Many leading Italian revolutionaries in 1647 came from obscure urban backgrounds: Giuseppe d'Alesi (Palermo) was a craftsman who had languished in prison until freed by rioters; Giuseppe Piantanida (Milan) was a confectioner; and Masaniello (Naples) was an illiterate fishmonger.

Political upheaval and war also empowered some European women of humble birth. In England, they not only led riots, like their continental sisters (see chapter 17 above), but also took an active role in the political process. In several parishes of southern England in 1642, when asked to express public support for Parliament by signing the Protestation 'as well women and youth of both sexes gave their full consent, though they put not hereunto their hands because they could not write'.[46] In addition, 'several young Puritan virgins gave expression to their evangelical and millennial zeal through inspired speeches delivered in a trance-like state induced by prolonged fasting and physical weakness', a condition that has been labelled 'holy anorexia'. At least one of them secured a hearing from the nation's rulers: in 1648–9, the Army Council granted two audiences to allow Elizabeth Poole (despite expulsion from her church for immorality and heresy) to explain her vision of what was best for the kingdom – and when they refused to heed her prophecies, she published them in pamphlets. Mary Cary, who described herself as 'minister or servant of the Gospel', also published several hundred pages of prophecy between 1647 and 1653, setting out God's plan for England and the world, based on twelve years' study of Scripture which started when she was 15. 'In a different world', it has been observed, 'such women might have become ministers'.[47]

Some Catholic women also achieved prominence during political upheaval. In Spain, in 1640 the beleaguered viceroy of Catalonia turned for advice to a holy woman who 'enjoyed a reputation for virtue on account of her unusual life, since she was said to have eaten nothing for six days, and gone forty without defecating, which increased the esteem in which she was held and authenticated the warning that she gave the viceroy: that he would die on Corpus Christi' (as he did). Between 1643 and 1665, Philip IV of Spain wrote letters to Sor María de Ágreda, a nun who claimed prophetic powers, at least twice a month setting out the problems he faced and soliciting her advice as well as her prayers (see chapter 9 above). This made her the most powerful woman in the Spanish Monarchy.[48]

Whatever their social background, many of those empowered by the chaos of the mid-seventeenth century were surprisingly young. Nathan of Gaza was 22 when he proclaimed Shabbatai to be the Messiah; and Elizabeth Poole was 26 when she shared her visions with the English Army's council of officers. Masaniello was 27 when he became ruler of Naples, as was Johnston of Wariston when he drafted the National Covenant, and Mary Cary when she published her first pamphlet. The prince of Condé was 28 when he tried to displace Mazarin as chief minister to Louis XIV. When the English Civil War ended in 1648, the Agitators of the New Model Army and most leaders of radical religious groups like the Quakers were still under 30. Dorgon and Wu Sangui were both 32 in 1644 when they made the agreement at the Shanhai Pass that settled the fate of China for almost three centuries. The duke of Guise was one year older when he seized control of Naples. Sir Thomas Fairfax was 33 when he took command of the New Model Army in 1645, and 38 when he resigned it. Coxinga was 35 when he led his great army of Ming loyalists up the Yangzi and almost took Nanjing in 1659. Neither Shabbatai Zvi nor James Nayler had turned 40 when their followers hailed them as the Messiah. Lesser protagonists were also young, although the shortage of sources makes verification more difficult. In Naples, the 'boys' who obeyed Masaniello were in their teens or twenties, just like the apprentices at the forefront of most London riots in the 1640s, and the 'young people' who took the lead in almost one-tenth of the popular revolts in France. Christopher Hill's comment about Revolutionary England could be applied to the entire northern hemisphere in the 1640s and 1650s: it 'was a young man's world while it lasted' – but how long it lasted depended in large measure upon the ability of the 'people who hope only for a change' to mobilize others through arguments that justified their resistance.[49]

Justifying Disobedience I: Back to the Past

The commonest justification for disobedience in the seventeenth century was the deployment of religious, legal and historical texts that evoked a real or imagined 'Golden Age'. Thus in the Ottoman empire, while insurgents demanded that the sultan abolish all taxes imposed since the reign of Suleiman the Lawgiver, the Kadizadeli clerics cited the Qur'an and the Hadiths of the Prophet Mohammed to demand the abolition of *all* novelties, and the Sufi Sheikh Niyāzī-i Mīṣri cited ancient history, such as the deeds of Alexander the Great and his 'sheikh' Aristotle.[50] In China, too, rioters often demanded a return to a 'Golden Age'. Thus in the 1640s, dissidents invoked the memory of a rebel hero from Fujian two centuries before, popularly known as the 'Pare-equal king' who had 'pared down master and serf, noble and menial, poor and rich, to make them equal'. In many areas 'The tenants put on their masters' clothing, entered by the main gate, seized and divided their houses, handed out the storage grain, tied the masters to posts and whipped them', claiming that everyone was born equal and boasting that 'From now on, it's going to be turned upside down.'[51]

Egalitarian ideas abounded in the popular culture of Ming China – both oral (local opera performances, stories, poems and songs) and written (above all the historical novels, *Romance of the Three Kingdoms* and *Water Margin*, both proscribed by the government). The *Romance*, which featured the evil power of eunuchs and their role in the downfall of the Han dynasty in the third century BC (an obvious parallel to the hated eunuchs of the Ming), became 'a veritable textbook on how regional militarists might bring the [ruling] dynasty to an end'.[52] *Water Margin*, set in the mountains of Shandong in the early twelfth century, portrayed a Chinese 'Sherwood Forest' peopled not only by heroic and selfless outlaws but also by itinerant monks, beggars, tricksters and experts in the martial arts. All of them opposed the corrupt and brutal government officials. During the late Ming period at least 30 editions of *Romance* appeared, half of them in the form of abridged texts written in simplified characters with pictures that took up the top third of each folio, while paintings and even printed playing cards popularized images of the protagonists. In the 1620s a prominent rebel adopted the name of a general from the *Romance*, and many of Li Zicheng's lieutenants adopted the names of the heroes of *Water Margin*. Nurhaci later claimed that he had learned about Chinese politics and military strategy from reading the *Romance*, and his grandson ordered the book to be translated into Manchu and required all his followers to read it.[53]

The Manchus also ransacked Chinese history for precedents to justify attacking the Ming, and studied chronicles that described the rise and fall of earlier dynasties. In a letter written in 1621 to his Chinese neighbours, Nurhaci provided a list of unworthy rulers (going back to the eleventh century BC) who 'immersed themselves in liquor, women, and wealth and no longer troubled themselves about the country', and asserted that 'The [current] emperor of you Chinese does not rule fairly', because apart from allowing 'the eunuchs to take property' he persecuted 'those with property who are upright and honest'. The conclusion was obvious: '[Heaven] has given me the emperor's lands . . . Heaven favours me.' His son Dorgon used similar rhetoric when he arrived in Beijing in 1644. His first proclamation contained the declaration: 'The empire is not an individual's private empire. Whosoever possesses virtue holds it. The army and people are not an individual's private army and people. Whosoever possesses virtue commands them. We now hold it.'[54] Nurhaci and Dorgon thus sought to justify their assault on the Ming with the concept of the 'Mandate of Heaven', found in both the *Classic of History* and the *Classic of Songs* – texts by then 2,000 years old, with a status in East Asia equivalent to the Bible among Christians.[55]

In Christian states, too, historical precedents served to justify popular rebellions. During the Irish rebellion of 1641, a priest in County Tyrone read from 'Hanmer's "Chronicles", out of which [he] animated the rebels with the story of the Danes [in the eleventh century] who were discomfited by the Irish, though for the most part unarmed, and they paralleled that history with these times'; while in Donegal, some of 'the Rebells nowe expected the fulfilling of Columkill's Prophecie: which (as they did construe it to be) was that the Irish should conquer Ireland againe'.[56] Meanwhile Charles I's Scottish opponents drew strength both from documents such as the Declaration of Arbroath of 1320 that empowered the nobles of Scotland to protect their 'fundamental laws' against wayward kings, as well as from the Gaelic tradition of deposing unsatisfactory leaders, running back through Mary Stuart (Charles's grandmother) to Fergus, Scotland's legendary first king. Charles's English opponents also sometimes cited the tumultuous history of their northern neighbour. Three days before his execution in January 1649, the High Court of Justice tactlessly reminded Charles of 'several instances of kings being deposed and imprisoned by their subjects, especially in his own native kingdom of Scotland, where of 109 kings, most were deposed, imprisoned, or proceeded against for misgovernment; and his own grandmother removed'.[57] Other opponents harped on the fact that England possessed its own distinctive laws and customs. Some went back to 1066, when foreign invaders imposed a 'Norman Yoke', and urged 'true Englishmen' to regain their 'Ancient Constitution'. Others still demanded the abolition of any law or custom 'contrary to the Great Charter of England' (the Magna Carta of 1215); and when the gentlemen of Kent discussed the legality of Ship Money in 1637, they took comfort from the fact that 'the whole discourse of Fortescue' (written in the 1460s) clearly showed that in England 'the king had not an absolute power'.[58]

In Spain, Catalan scholars found and published privileges by Carolingian emperors in the ninth century that granted Barcelona and its hinterland the right to self-government under loose Frankish protection, guaranteed the use of its own Visigothic Laws and promised exemption from all future taxes. They therefore demanded that Philip IV do the same. In 1634, during its revolt against the salt monopoly, Guipúzcoa demanded that the central government respect 'the measures and arrangements that were in force when the region was incorporated into the kingdom of Castile' (in 1200).[59] Likewise, in France, the rebels of Périgord in the 1630s demanded a return to 'the same state we enjoyed during the reign of Louis XII' (d. 1515), while those of Normandy demanded respect for the charter granted to the duchy in 1315. In Italy in 1647–8 the rebels of Palermo insisted on a return to the 'days of King Peter of Aragon' (d. 1285); those of Naples wanted a restoration of the laws of Joan I (d. 1382), Joan II (d. 1435) and Charles V (d. 1558); most rebellious cities sought to recover their medieval status as independent communes. In Switzerland, finally, the rebels of 1653 drew strength from the legendary resistance of William Tell three hundred years before.[60]

Apologists for rebellion also regularly equated their leaders with biblical heroes and their opponents with biblical villains. Among Catholic rebels, Portuguese preachers compared Philip IV with Saul or Herod and equated John IV with David or Christ; they also likened John IV's acclamation as king with that of King David and compared the 60 years of rule from Madrid with the 'Babylonish captivity' of the Jews. In Naples, sermons by preachers sympathetic to the revolt hailed the insurgent leaders as Daniel, David and Moses while comparing Viceroy Arcos with Nebuchadnezzar, Goliath and Pharaoh; while royalists saw Viceroy Oñate (who restored order) as Gideon. Catalan pamphlets drew similarly invidious comparisons between Philip IV and those destroyed by God in the Old Testament.[61] On the Protestant side, some in England compared John Felton (the discontented veteran who murdered the duke of Buckingham) with Phineas and Ehud; as Felton went to his execution, a bystander cried 'God bless thee, little David'; and one of the score of poems composed to celebrate the duke's murder ended:

> Stout Machabee . . . thy most mightie arme,
> With zeale and justice arm'd, hath in truth wonne
> The prize of patriott to a British sonne.

A generation later some compared the earl of Essex, commander of the parliamentary army, with John the Baptist, and many saw Oliver Cromwell as Gideon. Dutch Calvinists regularly likened the kings of Spain to Pharaoh and equated the princes of Orange with Moses, Gideon, David and the Maccabees.[62]

Some Protestant apologists went further. In the Netherlands, Joost van den Vondel's epic poem of 1612, *Passcha* (Passover), included a specific 'Comparison between the deliverance of the children of Israel from Egypt and the liberation of the United Provinces of the Netherlands from Spain'; while a poem in praise of his native land written by a Dutch pastor declared simply:

> But most of all I give thanks to Him
> For making Holland Jerusalem.

In Scotland, the whole concept of a 'National Covenant' as the foundation of resistance came directly from the Old Testament. As Archibald Johnston of Wariston watched his compatriots 'subscribing' the parchment copy of the document in 1638, he discerned 'a very near parallel betwixt Israel and this church, the only two sworn nations to the Lord'. Many other Scots saw themselves as God's Chosen People fighting Pharaoh.[63]

All over Europe, dissidents embraced not only the texts but also the tone of Old Testament prophets to justify their resistance. At regular intervals the English Parliament heard sermons that claimed scriptural warrant for extreme measures against the king and his supporters, on texts such as 'Thou shalt smite them, and utterly destroy them; thou shalt make no covenant with them, nor show mercy unto them' (Deuteronomy 7: 2); 'I will ease me of mine adversaries, and avenge me of mine enemies' (Isaiah 1: 24); and 'Slay utterly old and young' (Ezekiel 9: 6). During the trial of the earl of Strafford in 1641, a preacher reminded Parliament (which served as the earl's judge and jury) about the fate of Achan and Achitophel, those 'troublers of Israel' who had rightly been punished by death for giving their ruler false council. In other parts of the Protestant world, preachers threatened (like

Jeremiah) eternal damnation for rulers who deviated from God's commandments; and insisted (like Haggai) that since the end of the world was imminent, if rulers refused to impose the necessary reforms then their subjects must take over.[64]

Catholic propagandists also used Scripture to justify extreme violence. The name 'Fronde', used by the opponents of Cardinal Mazarin, meant 'slingshot' and so possessed biblical overtones: both pamphlets and pictures compared the cardinal with Goliath and his enemies with David. Others compared France under Mazarin with the lot of the Israelites under Pharaoh.[65] After rebellion broke out in Ireland, a Franciscan exhorted his compatriots to 'fight to the end for our altars and hearths. We have no choice but to conquer or be conquered and either drive our enemies out of this land or be driven out ourselves. The country is too small for the English and the Irish.' A few years later, a Catholic commander informed his troops that 'You are the flower of Ulster ... Maccabbeans fighting against their enemy'; while, writing from the safety of Portugal, Conor O'Mahony, S.J., justified violent action against all non-Catholics in Ireland largely on the basis of Exodus 32: 27, wherein Moses ordered the destruction of thousands of idolaters.[66]

Finally, in looking to the past for subversive precedents, European dissidents scoured Roman and Greek texts as well as Scripture. Scholars in Naples published Classical texts with commentaries that unfavourably contrasted Spanish government by a viceroy with the parity between the nobles and the 'people' that had prevailed in the city's 'republican' past; while in England, according to Thomas Hobbes, 'As to rebellion, in particular against monarchy, one of the most frequent causes of it, is the reading of the books of policy, and histories, of the ancient Greeks and Romans'. He continued: 'From the reading, I say, of such books men have undertaken to kill their kings, because the Greek and Latin writers, in their books and discourses of policy, make it lawful and laudable for any man so to do – provided, before he do it, he call him a tyrant.' 'I cannot imagine how anything can be more prejudicial to a Monarchy,' he concluded, 'than the allowing of such books to be publicly read.'[67]

Justifying Disobedience II: Looking to the Future

Many rebels looked to the future as well as to the past, using prophecy, divination and portent to convince themselves and others of a favourable outcome to their resistance. In China, members of a popular religious sect known as the White Lotus Society had long predicted that a man named Li would one day be emperor, and as he strove to make this prediction come true, Li Zicheng consulted a medium. When the prophet unwisely stated that 'Zicheng is not a true Son of Heaven' and foretold the imminent demise of his power, Li executed him. Notwithstanding this disappointment, as he prepared to assault Beijing, Li turned to another seer to ascertain how best to achieve his goal. Perhaps learning from the fate of his predecessor, this prophet advised Li to place children in the vanguard of his forces (which he did, entering the capital virtually without a blow). Like most other Chinese, Li also placed great importance on portents. When a dust storm and yellow fog engulfed his temporary capital just after he proclaimed himself 'prince of Shun', Li panicked until his sycophantic seers assured him that it was an auspicious sign because, when a new Chinese dynasty arose, the sun and moon temporarily lacked light.[68]

In Europe, too, rebels turned readily for both illumination and support to those who claimed a hotline to heaven. Catholics had always recognized the spiritual authority of 'lowly personages', as Alexandra Walsham put it, 'set apart from his or her peers by virtue of a sacred commission'. Thus early in 1641, as the army of Philip IV suppressed the revolt of the Catalans, Sor Eufràsia Berenguer, a noble-woman who had taken the veil almost 30 years before, experienced visions of Christ, the Virgin Mary and Saint Eulàlia, the patron saint of Barcelona, all protecting the city. Her visions helped to embolden the city's defenders: the last one 'occurred on the 22nd [of January 1641] and on the 26th came the victory on the hill of Montjuich'.[69] Non-Catholics also sometimes consulted prophets. In 1638 many of Charles I's Scottish opponents drew comfort from 'the admirable speeches, exhorta-tions prayers [and] praises out of the mouth of a poor demoiselle, Margaret Mitchelson, who was transported in heavenly raptures and spoke strange things for the happy success of God's cause and Christ's crown in this kingdom, which was already enacted in heaven'. Margaret's ecstatic prophecies excited 'the astonishment of many thousand'; and some people who had previously harboured doubts 'were strongly confirmed and encouraged to add hand to this great work of God'.[70]

Some of the revolutionary prophets distributed their forecasts in print. William Lilly's *Prophecy of the White King* of 1644, which predicted the defeat and downfall of Charles I, sold 1,800 copies in the first three days. Lilly repeated his prediction in another pamphlet published on the very day of the king's defeat at the battle of Naseby in June 1645, which both cemented his reputation for accuracy and earned him an annual pension of £100 from the victors. 'His writings have kept up the spirits of the soldiers, the honest people of this realm, and many of us parliament men,' an MP later claimed.[71] In 1650 George Foster, a former officer of the New Model Army, published his visions that God had chosen Sir Thomas Fairfax as his 'instrument' to destroy Parliament and cut down 'all men and women, that he met with, that were higher than the middle sort, and raised up those that were lower than the middle sort and made them all equal'. Later, George changed his name to 'Jacob Israel Foster', and printed a prophecy that God would destroy the Pope in five years' time and the Ottoman sultan the year after that, which would usher in an age of abundance for all.[72]

Several Muslim, Jewish and Christian writers in the mid-seventeenth century prophesied the imminent end of the world, and some rebel leaders exploited the prevailing millenarian climate to claim Messianic powers for themselves. In Iran, in 1629, many Shi'ite Muslims hailed a rebellious provincial governor of Gilan as the Redeemer; while in the Sunni Ottoman empire, both Abaza Hasan (also a rebellious provincial governor) in 1658 and the son of a Kurdish Sufi in 1667 claimed to be the Mahdi (see chapter 7 above). In the 1670s the charismatic Muslim sheikh, Nasir al-Din, 'claimed that he was sent by God' and 'preached penitence' and 'spoke only of the law of God and of welfare and freedom' in Senegal (see chapter 15 above).

In Europe, Martin Laimbauer, a Protestant farmer who led a peasant revolt in Austria in 1635, sustained his cause for almost a year with his twin claims that the Apocalypse was imminent and that he was the Messiah. Many Englishmen claimed to be the Messiah during the 1640s and 1650s: James Nayler, who wore his hair and beard suggestively long, gained such a following that at Bristol, England's second city, on Palm Sunday 1656 – a year in which many prophets predicted the world would end – he imitated Christ and made a triumphal entry on a donkey while the people strewed palms before him. Most spectacular of all, in 1665 many Jews hailed Shabbatai Zvi as both king of the world and Messiah.[73]

Spanish America also produced Messianic rebel leaders. In 1647 in Santiago de Chile, an African slave proclaimed himself 'king of Guinea' and called for vengeance on the settlers; while a few years later Pedro Bohorques claimed to be descended from the Inca emperors and therefore the true ruler of Peru. In 1650 Don Guillén Lombardo (see page 462 above) escaped from the cells of the Mexican Inquisition and distributed 'infamous libels against the Inquisitors and the archbishop', including one (of which he had prepared many copies by hand) entitled *Proclamation of the just judgments of God*. Don Guillén composed Messianic poetry in between his interrogations by the Inquisitors until in 1659 they decided he was too dangerous to live and burnt him at the stake. Posthumously, his remarkable exploits apparently engendered the legend of Zorro.[74]

Justifying Disobedience III: Forging New Resistance Theories

When convenient precedents from Scripture, history and the Classics eluded them, and Messianic claims failed to win converts, those in Europe 'who hope only for a change' deployed three alternative strategies to justify resistance: creating bogus documents, borrowing arguments used by others elsewhere, and inventing brand-new reasons to resist. Several rebels forged documents that seemed to justify their actions. In 1641, in Ulster, Sir Phelim O'Neill brandished 'a parchment or paper with a great seal affixed which he affirmed to be a warrant from the King's Majestie for what he did'. The 'depositions' of many of the Protestant survivors testi-fied to its effectiveness in fooling them and others.[75] In 1647 the duke of Guise used an identical ruse to convince the leaders of the 'Most Serene Republic of Naples' that he possessed a letter from Louis XIV promising French support; while both Bohdan Khmelnytsky in Ukraine and Stenka Razin in Russia boasted to their Cossack followers that they possessed royal letters authorizing them to mobilize against their oppressors. Although in each case these documents received wide credence, they were all almost certainly forgeries.[76]

The second alternative strategy was to appropriate justifications for resistance invented by dissidents elsewhere. Thanks to their verbal diarrhoea, the leading Scottish Covenanters provided the most detailed accounts of this process. Thus in 1638, as the conflict with King Charles intensified, Archibald Johnston of Wariston read the history of the successful Dutch Revolt against the king of Spain written by Emanuel van Meteren and then 'studied all that week on *Althusii Politica*' – a

1,000-page treatise written by Johannes Althusius, which claimed that a contract or Covenant formed the basis of every association of human beings (from families, through professional groups, towns and provinces up to states), and that the representatives of the lower associations could in certain circumstances resist a tyrannical superior. The following year, Wariston 'began to fall to the hypothesis of resistance in Scotland' and to clear his mind he 'epitomized Brutus his reasons' – a reference to the French Calvinist treatise, *Vindiciae contra tyrannos*, published 60 years before to justify armed resistance.[77] Meanwhile Wariston's university preceptor, Robert Baillie, found justification for resistance in the writings of Martin Luther and other Protestants because they gave 'leave to subjects, in some cases, to defend themselves where the prince is absolute from any man, but not absolute from ties to the laws of church and state whereto he is sworn, which is the case of all Christian kings now'. Two weeks later, Baillie, Wariston and some radical Scottish clerics debated 'the lawfulness and necessity of *defending ourselves in this case by arms*'.[78] Alexander Henderson, too, turned to modern Dutch writers when he considered what circumstances might justify opposing the king's commands 'and taking arms therefore'. From Hugo Grotius's *On war and peace*, first published in 1625, he borrowed the argument that 'the great force of necessity' might 'justify actions otherwise unwarrantable'. 'In this extremity,' he continued, 'to sit still . . . waiting for our own destruction' would be 'not only against religion, but [against] nature'. There could be, Henderson concluded, 'no greater necessity' than the preservation of a country's religion and liberty because 'Necessity is a sovereignty, a law above all laws'.[79]

Charles I's English opponents also read and plundered Althusius, Grotius and other apologists of the Dutch revolt against Spain. In 1641 Calybut Downing, a Puritan minister who enjoyed the protection of the king's leading opponents, published a pamphlet that compared the current state of England with that of the Netherlands on the eve of their revolt in the 1560s. In particular, Downing drew a parallel between the duke of Alba, the 'tyrannical viceroy' sent by Philip II at the head of a Spanish army to crush his Dutch critics, and the earl of Strafford, widely suspected of planning to bring an army from Ireland to crush Charles's English critics, and concluded that eliminating the 'tyrannical' Strafford was the only way to prevent a 'civil war' in England similar to the one provoked by Alba in the Netherlands.[80]

In 1643 the gentleman scholar William Prynne revealed his preferred resistance theory in the title of his best-known book: *Soveraigne Power of Parliaments and Kingdomes, wherein the Parliament's present necessary defensive armes against their sovereignes, and their armies in some cases, is copiously manifested to be just.* It contained 200 closely printed pages of venomous attacks on King Charles, interspersed with quotations from the Bible, the Classics and modern writers (Catholic as well as Protestant), followed by an appendix of foreign examples of resistance, deposition and regicide from ancient Israel to modern France; the full text of the Act of Abjuration by which the Dutch had renounced their allegiance to Philip II in 1581; and extracts in English from the *Vindiciae contra tyrannos* (which would soon appear in an English translation with the combative title, *A defence of liberty against tyrants*).[81] For Prynne, England's problem lay not in tyrannical ministers but in its wayward monarch. Therefore, its only chance of salvation lay in creating a Republic.

Prynne could choose from two distinct republican visions: a state run by 'virtuous men' qualified to rule by their record of proven administrative competence, public service and legal expertise, such as the Dutch Republic; or an oligarchic state in which a few powerful families monopolized all power, as in Venice. Literature extolling both forms of government circulated widely in mid-seventeenth Europe. Above all, the Dutch Elzevier Press used their advanced printing technology, which allowed 'miniaturization', to publish a series of cheap volumes in small format that described various republics, ancient and modern: Athens and Sparta; the Hebrews and Rome; Venice and Genoa; the Swiss, the Hanseatic League and the Dutch. Written in a clear Latin, they enjoyed an extraordinary success: all major seventeenth-century libraries seem to have possessed a set, and their size made them easily portable by individuals. Many went through several editions.[82]

The impact of these and other republican works explains why, when Naples declared itself independent from Spain in 1647, it assumed the form 'Most Serene Republic', just like Venice, while the duke of Guise swore to defend 'the liberties of the Most Serene Republic of Naples just as the prince of Orange does in Holland'.[83] Likewise Irish Catholic exiles in the 1620s called for an invasion of their homeland 'in the name of the liberty of the fatherland', and the establishment of 'a Republic, which should be so called on its flags and in its commissions; and all other public ordinances should be in the name of the Republic and Kingdom of Ireland'. Some of the 1641 insurgents claimed 'that it was the Irish intencons to have a free state of themselves as they had in Holland, and not to bee tyde unto any kinge or prince whatsoever'.[84]

Such rhetoric alarmed kings and their ministers. In 1646 Cardinal Mazarin drew the attention of a new envoy setting forth for London to 'the example of the United Provinces of the Low Countries' which 'drain their own blood and spend more in one year to sustain war than they would have been willing to spend in fifty, if they had remained under the rule of the king of Spain, whatever war he had wished to wage'. Therefore, Mazarin predicted, a Republic in England would be far stronger than the Monarchy had been, 'especially if Scotland, a country where warlike and poor people abound, should become a part of this new Republic'.[85] Events soon proved the cardinal correct. In 1647 some officers and men of the victorious New Model Army voiced bold egalitarian principles such as 'The poorest he [male] that is in England has a life to live, [just] as the greatest he', so that 'every man that is to live under a government ought first by his own counsel to put himself under that government', while no one was bound to obey a 'government that he has not had a voice to put himself under' (see chapter 12 above). The following year some of those officers, assisted by like-minded politicians, set up a court to try 'Charles Stuart' (as they now called him), which condemned him to death and executed him – something never seen before (and rarely since). In the 1650s groups with even more radical programmes proliferated in both kingdoms, from the Levellers and the Diggers, who argued for an equitable division of property, to the Quakers, who claimed that women as well as men should all be equal.

These radical political and social ideas remained confined to Britain in the mid-seventeenth century; and even there, radicalism had its limits. The same army officers who had put the king on trial later crushed the Levellers; while some of the same Members of Parliament who had voted to execute the king also voted to execute the self-styled Messiah James Nayler for blasphemy.[86] Moreover, after the Restoration of the Monarchy in 1660, most of England's radical notions disappeared from public view for over a century. Nevertheless, the diffusion of resistance theories in so many parts of the world during the 1640s and 1650s was truly remarkable: never before had political news and ideas spread so far or so fast. Whereas previous opposition movements had involved hundreds, and at most thousands, many of those in the mid-seventeenth century involved a million or more. This transformation in scale rested upon two vital preconditions: both East Asia and Europe boasted not only a large number of eager readers, but also a large volume of printed material for them to read. Whether they appealed to Scripture or the Classics, to Ancient History or the Ancient Constitution, to Covenants or Contracts – the 'people who hope only for change' attracted many more followers in the mid-seventeenth century than any of their predecessors because they possessed the means to convey their arguments to audiences of unprecedented size.

'People of heterodox beliefs . . . who will join up with anyone who calls them': Disseminating Revolution[1]

IN *THE TIPPING POINT: HOW LITTLE THINGS MAKE A BIG DIFFERENCE* MALCOLM Gladwell evaluated the impact of Paul Revere's ride through Massachusetts on the night of 18/19 April 1775 to spread the word that the following day British troops in Boston would try to arrest the leading American Patriots in Lexington and capture the weapons of the local militia in Concord. The ensuing hostilities on 19 April began the American Revolutionary War. A critical element in Revere's success, according to Gladwell, was his status as a 'connector'. His work as a silversmith and his frequent business travel had allowed Revere to create a wide network of casual acquaintances, from many different social groups, whose trust he had earned. As opposition to the British grew, Revere frequently carried messages between the Patriot leaders. On the night of 18/19 April, therefore, he knew where to find the boats and horses essential to his journey as well as where to find each Patriot leader – and how to avoid the British patrols – along the way. Revere's role as a 'connector' enabled him to spread his news like a 'virus', and Gladwell hailed his ride as 'perhaps the most famous historical example of a word-of-mouth epidemic'.[2]

Several European observers in the mid-seventeenth century used similar medical metaphors to describe the remarkable speed with which revolts spread. The Spanish writer Francisco de Quevedo claimed in 1641 that revolts 'are the smallpox of kings: everyone gets them, and those who survive retain at least the marks of having had them'. A decade later, in his survey of the 'political uprisings of our times', the Italian historian Giovanni Battista Birago Avogadro declared: 'Popular uprisings are like contagious diseases, in which the deadly poison travels from one individual to another; and neither distance nor delay nor diversity of climate nor difference of life-styles can halt the effect of these dangerous contagions.' In 1676 the Governor of Barbados colony marvelled how the 'daily devastations of the Indians' had 'spread like a contagion over all the continent from New England ... to Maryland'. Nevertheless, as Hugh Trevor-Roper pointed out in his elegant 1957 essay that popularized the term 'General Crisis', although 'the universality of revolution owed something to mere contagion' nevertheless 'contagion implies receptivity: a healthy or inoculated body does not catch even a prevailing disease'.[3]

'Contagious diseases' and Composite States

It is noteworthy that both Quevedo and Birago Avogadro drew their examples of 'contagion' from a type of polity that showed unusual 'receptivity': the composite state. More than half the rebellions that broke out in seventeenth-century Europe occurred in such entities, largely because their governments tried to impose similar policies on communities with different political, fiscal and cultural institutions and traditions. In 1618 Ferdinand II attempted to apply the same religious uniformity he had already imposed in his hereditary lands upon the Bohemian lands he had just gained by election. Eleven years later, he initiated a similar process in the empire via the Edict of Restitution (see chapter 8 above). Shortly after his accession in 1625, Charles I declared that he wanted 'one uniform course of government in, and through, our whole monarchy', and he instructed his ministers to 'unite his three kingdoms in a strict union and obligation each to [the] other for their mutual defence when any of them shall be assailed, every one with such a proportion of horse, foot or shipping as may be rateably thought fit'. Charles modelled his scheme expressly on the 'Union of Arms' imposed on the Spanish Monarchy by Philip IV and Olivares.[4]

None of these ambitious plans prospered, yet they provoked spirited resistance – in part because of the inflexibility of their proponents. When some German *Catholics* expressed their fears about the risks of imposing the Edict of Restitution on all areas of Germany, Ferdinand II informed them that he was prepared to 'lose not only Austria but all his kingdoms and provinces and whatever he has in this world, provided he save his soul, which he cannot do without the implementation of his Edict'. A decade later, Charles I likewise protested that 'So long as this Covenant is in force, I have no more power in Scotland than as a Duke of Venice, which I will rather die than suffer'; while Olivares exclaimed that 'If the constitutions [of Catalonia] do not allow this, then the devil take the constitutions!'[5]

Not only did the proponents of uniformity usually fail to achieve their goals, they also seemed incapable of learning from their failure. In 1646 Don Juan de Palafox, who had served in both Aragon and Mexico (two 'peripheral' states of the Spanish Monarchy), observed to a colleague:

> Permit me, my lord, to tell you that Portugal was not lost in Portugal, or Catalonia in Catalonia, but rather in the heart of Madrid. And that is where [Spanish America] will be lost, just like [Portuguese Asia], because wherever public scandals receive rewards and honours, that is where the storms gather that later pour down on kingdoms which, through sins, wilful errors [*violencias*] and tyrannical rule, fragment and separate from the crown.

The same was true in other composite states. Thus despite numerous warnings that imposing on Scotland a Prayer Book modelled on English forms of worship would provoke opposition, Archbishop Laud made plans to impose it on Ireland too; while the failure to subdue the Scottish rebels by force in 1639 did not stop the earl of Strafford and Charles I from trying again in 1640 and, despite being roundly defeated, from contemplating a third attempt in 1641.[6]

Such obstinacy was dangerous because rebellions not only often *began* on the periphery of each composite state but also often *spread* around the periphery. Thus the revolt of Bohemia in 1618 was just the first domino to fall: almost all the other lands ruled by Ferdinand II – Hungary, Silesia, Moravia, Upper and Lower Austria – followed suit (see chapter 8 above). Two decades later in France, a judge commented that 'The news of the disorders that occurred in Lower Normandy' – the *Nu-Pieds* revolt – 'redoubled the courage of the populace in Rouen', the duchy's capital, so that 'these disorders became the staple of popular conversation among the common people, who publicized them as heroic actions'. Five days after crowds killed a tax collector in Rouen, the same thing happened in Caen, the second city of the duchy, 80 miles away. In 1640 a French diplomat sent to liaise with the Catalan rebels opined that Portugal 'would never have dared revolt without the example of Catalonia, fearing that it would be rapidly overwhelmed if it joined in so dangerous a dance alone'. Seven years later, on hearing that rioting had broken out in many towns of Andalucía, and that 'Sicily was on the brink of being lost', a phlegmatic Spanish minister remarked that 'In a Monarchy that comprises many kingdoms, widely separated, the first one that rebels takes a great risk because the rest can easily suppress it; but the second takes much less risk and from then onwards any others can try it without fear.'[7]

The 'connectors'

It is often difficult to reconstruct these 'dangerous dances' because those who sought to coordinate insurrections did their best to cover their tracks. The case of Portugal forms an exception. No sooner had Duke John of Bragança been acclaimed king in December 1640 than he sent messengers to foment rebellion elsewhere against his former sovereign. He sent two Jesuits to Barcelona to invite the Catalans to sign an alliance with him against Philip IV, and he sent a *fidalgo* to ask all parts of Portugal's overseas empire for their allegiance. Such coordination took time: to avoid interception, the *fidalgo* charged to convey the news to East Asia went first to London and thence took a neutral English ship to Java, where he waited until a Dutch ship took him to Taiwan. From there, the weary 'connector' finally reached Macao on 30 May 1642. Thereafter, of the entire Portuguese empire, only the city of Ceuta in North Africa remained loyal to Madrid (as it still does).[8]

'Connectors' also spread sedition in other composite states. In Sicily, news of the revolt that began in Palermo on 20 May 1647 triggered not only urban uprisings elsewhere in the island – Trapani on the 25th, Cefalù and Marsala on the 27th, Castronuovo and Sanfilippo on the 29th, and so on – but a veteran of the Palermo revolt who happened to be in Naples on 7 July 1647 led the uprising in the Piazza del Mercato; and after his death other Sicilians helped to radicalize the angry crowds. Their achievements inspired popular revolts throughout the kingdom of Naples (see Fig. 41). On 15 August, in Palermo, a recently returned eyewitness of Masaniello's revolution started a new revolt explicitly to secure the same concessions.[9] In Russia, the petitioners from provincial towns who had been in the capital in June 1648 likewise served as highly effective connectors in spreading revolution: as soon as they returned home with news of the Muscovites' defiance of the tsar, local uprisings followed. A generation later, supporters of Stenka Razin conducted an epistolary offensive that won him supporters in areas far from his Cossack base (see chapter 6 above). The peasants of Entlebuch who began the 'Swiss revolution' in 1653 sent envoys to mobilize support elsewhere in Canton Luzern and in adjacent cantons (see chapter 8 above). Finally, when James Howell sought to know 'upon whom to lay the blame' for the outbreak of the English Civil War, he argued (with his usual audacious mixture of metaphors), that the fire

> Was first kindled in Scotland. The Puritans there were the womb of it; though I must tell you withall, the loins that begot this centaur were the Puritans here in England. If the flint and steel had not struck fire in England, the tinder had never took fire in Scotland, nor had the flame ever gone over into Ireland.[10]

Nevertheless, discontented subjects did not always require human 'connectors' to 'kindle' their grievances: they could do it themselves. Thus Philip IV's Italian subjects carefully monitored the progress of the Catalan revolt through letters, pamphlets and books. In Naples, in 1646 (the year before Masaniello's uprising), Alexandre de Ros published his history of the Catalan revolt: although *Catalonia deceived* condemned the rebels, it provided a useful blueprint of how rebellions gathered momentum. Meanwhile, in Palermo, Vincenzo Auria (lawyer, poet and historian) reconstructed from the history books in his own library a full account of the earlier career of the unfortunate viceroy of Sicily, the marquis of Los Vélez, as viceroy of Navarre and Catalonia and ambassador in Rome, searching for a pattern of behaviour.[11] In the Stuart Monarchy, an Anglican bishop in Ireland complained in 1638 about the 'desperate example the contumacious Nonconformists [the Scottish Covenanters] have given both to England and to Ireland', and lamented that 'this contagion' had already begun to spread to Ulster. The following year, in the words of a professional 'letter-writer' (forerunner of newspaper reporters), 'The theatre for these kingdoms has now for a good while been chiefly placed at Edinburgh', so that others elsewhere would take 'what should be acted there' to 'frame the scene of their own interests accordingly'.[12]

No one watched Scottish events with greater attention than the Irish Catholics, who saw how 'the Scots, by pretending grievances and taking up arms to get them redressed, had not only gained divers privileges and immunities, but got £300,000 for their visit'. One Irish insurgent wanted to 'imitat Scotland, who gott a privilege by that course', in order to end 'the tyrannicall governement that was over them'; another boasted that 'The Scotts had theire willes by the force of armes and so would they heere in this kingdome'; while a third opined that 'if the Castle of Dublin hadd beene taken by the Lord Maguire, noe blowd had beene spilt, for they would only have held it till they hadd obteined their owne endes from his Majesty – which they thought was as reasonable to obteine as for the Scotts in England to obteine their desires'. Even more revealing was the response of a leading Irish confederate when his Protestant prisoner asked him: 'What? [Have you] made a Covenant amongst yow as the Scots did?' ' "Yea", said hee, *"The Scotts have taught us our A.B.C."* '[13]

The spread of the 'contagion' of revolution was not limited to composite states. In 1654 Birago Avogadro noted how an uprising against one ruler sometimes encouraged uprisings against another, because 'the example provided by the first suffices to provoke others in other states because the power of example in the mind of men is truly remarkable. We see that people are not only urged but expected and goaded into doing what they see others doing.'[14] The various rebellions against Charles I thus attracted much attention in continental Europe. In 1648 one-third of the 'extraordinary issues' of the French *Gazette* focused exclusively on British affairs, and almost half of all the documents and pronouncements it published came from the rebels. Germany, too, seemed fascinated by events across the Channel: between 1640 and 1660 some 50 German newspapers contained over 2,000 pages about events in Britain and Ireland, while German authors published more than 600 works on the subject. Likewise, in the Dutch Republic, one-third of all pamphlets published between 1640 and 1648 concerned English affairs; while the Catalan insurgents published not only pamphlets with news of the parallel revolts against Charles I, but also Irish Catholic manifestos in Catalan translation.[15]

The initial success of the 'revolution of Naples' against Philip IV similarly inspired sedition against other rulers. According to an ambassador, most Parisians believed 'that the Neapolitans have acted intelligently, and that in order to shake off oppression, their example should be followed'; and the crowds protesting against tax increases shouted 'Naples! Naples!' – a pointed reminder of the consequences of imposing unpopular taxes on a metropolis. In the Papal States, when insurrection broke out in Fermo in 1648, the first anniversary of Masaniello's revolt, many assumed that those who 'sacked and burned' the mansions of the wealthy merely imitated the 'example of the uprising of Naples'; and indeed several groups of revolutionaries crossed the border, encouraging insurgents in at least six other communities. They found their task eased by the disastrous harvest. A papal official reported that 'in all the places I visited, I found the spirits of vassals greatly agitated on account of the famine', so that if 'all the country people join together and form a union, a major conflagration may arise' (Fig 50).[16]

All over Europe, letters, newspapers, pamphlets, books and even plays provided details and drew conclusions about the events in Naples. One play printed in London in 1649, and entitled *The rebellion of Naples or the tragedy of Massenello*, concluded with a minatory *Epilogue* spoken by 'Masaniello' himself that began:

> Let kings beware how they provoke
> Their subjects with too hard a yoke,
> For when all's done, it will not do:
> You see, they break the yoke in two.

Two years later, in the Dutch Republic, rioters in Dordrecht hailed Masaniello as their hero.[17] Masaniello and his followers, in turn, drew inspiration from the Dutch. The 'Manifesto of the Most Faithful People of Naples', which declared that Philip IV was no longer their sovereign, resembled the document of 1581 by which the States-General of the Netherlands declared Philip II deposed; the duke of Guise took an

50. Revolts in the Papal States in 1648.
Although the revolt of Fermo against papal authority received most attention, both from contemporaries and from historians, at least six other towns – Viterbo, Todi, Perugia, Ascoli, Pontecorvo and Terracina – also rebelled. In each case, the arrival of insurgents from Naples triggered the outbreak.

oath as Protector 'with the same powers as those with which the Most Serene Prince of Orange defends the Republic and free states of Holland'; and a pamphlet reminded readers that the Spaniards had 'allowed themselves to be expelled from the seven provinces of Flanders by Dutch fishermen ... What, then, can they do ... against you?'[18]

The Neapolitans were not alone in drawing this conclusion. Earlier in the century, in his influential treatise on politics, Johannes Althusius claimed that the Dutch Republic's success in resisting Spain 'is so abundant that it overflows into neighbouring countries' and offered, 'for the imitation of others, those virtues' that had 'defended your commonwealth from tyranny and disaster'. A French writer made the same point: the Dutch had given 'warning to all rulers what duties they owe their peoples, and provide all peoples with a memorable example of what they can do against their rulers'. In Spain itself, Quevedo attributed the revolt of the Catalans to 'the example of Holland'; while in England, many blamed the rebellions against Charles I on the example set by the Dutch of how subjects who 'have revolted from their master' could 'yet prosper and flourish beyond all in Europe'. In 1641 an ambassador in London detected 'a secret intention to approach the Dutch form of government, for which the people here show far too much inclination'; and ten years later, Thomas Hobbes asserted that 'the late troubles in England [came] out of an imitation of the Low Countries'.[19]

The spate of rebellions in Europe also inspired malcontents in overseas colonies. The 'Declaration of Independence' prepared in Mexico by Don Guillén Lompart in 1642 cited the examples of others who 'have rebelled with good cause, having deliberated that it is better to die once for their restitution and liberty, than to live oppressed, tyrannized and violently subjected, as has been seen in the kingdoms of Portugal, Catalonia, Navarre and Biscay' – adding that 'in such remote and usurped kingdoms' as New Spain, abuses were 'far more widespread and grievous than over there' in Europe. The Native Americans oppressed by Philip IV, he reasoned, 'not only can, but should rise up' against him.[20] A decade later, when a group of frustrated Portuguese colonists in Goa deposed the viceroy, they 'gave as justification that Portugal had done the same, and so had the people of England – while, near at hand', they added, 'Ceylon had done it'. Meanwhile, in Anglo-America, in 1643 the colonists in New England noted how the Native Americans took comfort from 'those sad distractions in England, which they have heard of, and by which they know we are hindered' from receiving protection; while in 1676 the government in London learned with alarm that Nathaniel Bacon, leader of the rebellious planters of Virginia, 'had applied to the New England governments for assistance'.[21]

Exporting Revolution

Many rebel leaders besides Nathaniel Bacon appealed for outside aid. Thus in 1619–20 Frederick, the 'winter king' of Bohemia, vainly requested military assistance from his fellow Protestants in Scandinavia, Britain and the Dutch Republic, as well as from the Ottoman sultan and his vassal the prince of Transylvania (only the last obliged); while in 1626 the rebels of Upper Austria asked Christian IV of Denmark, who had just invaded Germany, to send assistance (it never materialized).[22] A decade later, the Scottish opponents of Charles I mounted a successful diplomatic offensive to secure munitions from Denmark, the Dutch Republic and above all Sweden (although their appeals to both the Catholic Louis XIII and the Protestant Swiss failed). The Portuguese also received favourable responses to their requests for aid: France, the Dutch Republic and eventually Britain all recognized the new regime and sent the money, troops and warships that prevented Spain from using its superior resources to reconquer its western neighbour.[23] The Irish Catholic Confederation likewise gained diplomatic recognition (as well as munitions and funds) from Spain, France and the Papacy until, for the first and last time before the twentieth century, Ireland boasted a *corps diplomatique*, headed by a papal nuncio. This was indeed a remarkable achievement because, as the representative of the Confederate government in the Dutch Republic reminded the States-General, previously 'we were naked men, destitute of arms, ammunition and experienced commanders', but 'with God's assistance we have provided ourselves of arms and ammunition and called home our experienced commanders and martial [men] from foreign services, and furnished ourselves with a considerable number of frigates and ships of war'. So now, friends and enemies alike 'look upon us as a considerable party, and parley with us, and give us leave to talk to them upon equal terms'.[24]

Some states offered assistance even before rebels elsewhere requested it. In 1637 Louis XIII made a secret offer to Duke John of Bragança to send 10,000 infantry and 1,000 cavalry if he decided to claim the Portuguese throne; and three years later, albeit with grave initial misgivings, he sent troops, treasure and advisers to the Catalans. Philip IV, for his part, signed a treaty of alliance with both the prince of Condé and the rebellious city of Bordeaux in 1651–2. These, however, were merely opportunistic and reactive efforts to sustain rebellions that had already started. The Dutch Republic sought to foment and support rebellions elsewhere more systematically.

According to Lieuwe van Aitzema, the official historian of the Dutch Republic, since 'the preservation of this state depended on the jealousy of its neighbours', its leaders always made haste to declare a common interest [gemeyn interesse] with any group around the world that shared its 'powerful enmity towards Spain'. They therefore signed alliances 'with all the princes and potentates who opposed the tyranny and pretended Universal Monarchy of the Spanish Monarchy': Catholic France and Venice, Protestant Denmark and Sweden, Orthodox Russia, Muslim Algiers and Tunis, and the Buddhist rulers of Sri Lanka. In 1638 Dutch Calvinist ministers attended the General Assembly of the Church of Scotland that abolished bishops, and Leiden University expressed support for the Scots' defence of their liberties. The Dutch authorities also allowed the Covenanters to come over and print pamphlets and purchase large quantities of arms and munitions; and they released numerous veterans from their army to serve against Charles I. A few months after the outbreak of civil war in England, a Dutch author argued that 'us Netherlanders' must not 'contribute to the suppressing of the Parliament' because 'if those that are on the king's side, together with him, get the upper hand' in England and Scotland, 'then shall they enter their action against us'.[25] Likewise, as soon as news of the 'revolution in Catalonia' in 1640 arrived in the Dutch Republic, the States-General established a special committee to coordinate support for their fellow rebels against Philip IV, and they asked Cardinal Richelieu to facilitate contact between The Hague and Barcelona. The following year they also accepted the credentials presented by an ambassador sent by John IV of Portugal – thus recognizing the legitimacy of the 'Restoration' – and sent a fleet of 12 warships to protect Lisbon against the threat of a Spanish seaborne attack.[26]

Charles I's opponents also sought to foment and support rebellions elsewhere. In 1642 the London preacher John Goodwin assured his compatriots that successful opposition to the king would be 'cheering and refreshing' to 'your brethren in their several plantations in far countries [America]'; while its 'heat and warmth' would 'pierce through many kingdoms great and large, as France, Germany, Bohemia, Hungary, Poland, Denmark, Sweden and many others'. Three years later, the Scots Parliament invited 'all Protestant potentates and republics to enter or join in the same or suchlike Solemn Covenant with the kingdoms of Great Britain, and so go on unanimously against the[ir] common enemy'. Most outspoken of all, in

1648 Hugh Peter delivered a sermon that claimed 'This army [the New Model] must root out monarchy, not only here but in France and other kingdoms round about.'[27] For a time, such views attracted some foreign support. Dutch printers published over 300 pamphlets on English affairs between 1640 and 1648, many of them directly commissioned by the English protagonists. In France, some speculated that 'the example of the neighbouring kingdom [England] would incite' Cardinal Mazarin's opponents to impose similar terms on the regency government, because 'Paris thinks itself no less than London', while others asserted that 'They speak openly in Paris of nothing but republics and liberties, and they say that the Monarchy is too old, and it was high time for it to end'.[28]

The execution of Charles I in January 1649 changed everything. Admittedly, the prolific French autodidact François Davant praised the regicides for reminding kings of the dangers of 'abusing their subjects', musing that 'troubled Monarchies may give birth to republics' as he considered Old Testament examples of kings whom God deposed, and he predicted that France would be next; while another radical pamphlet, *The divine nature of the disease of state*, also proclaimed that France was not alone in its struggle for liberty, since Naples and Catalonia as well as England had spearheaded a great movement of liberation from tyranny. But few other Europeans agreed. Instead, in France, a spate of pamphlets denounced 'the most horrible and detestable parricide ever committed by Christians'; Pierre Corneille wrote a sympathetic play; and four different French translations appeared almost immediately of the late monarch's apology, *Eikon Basilike* ('The king's image': see Plate 3).[29] Even those who had previously sided overwhelmingly with Parliament roundly condemned the regicide. The Dutch clergy excoriated it in their sermons, while as soon as news of the regicide arrived in Sweden, Marshal Jakob de la Gardie lamented that, because 'such a giddy spirit [*spiritus vertiginis*] has arisen' in Europe, no established government could feel safe (another minister hastened to publish a tract that denounced the execution).[30] In Germany, governments condemned all their critics as contaminated by England's 'Puritan principles', and dramatists (as in France) composed sympathetic plays. In the Polish capital, the nobleman Albrycht Stanisław Radziwiłł included a detailed account of Charles's last hours in his memoirs, adding fervently 'let there be no similar examples' in Poland. Most extreme of all, as soon as he received news of the regicide, Tsar Alexei expelled all English merchants from Russia.[31] The hostility continued. In 1651 Jakob de la Gardie warned the Swedish Council of State that some of his compatriots 'want to arrange things as they were in England some time past, making us all into pig's trotters'; while Queen Christina complained that 'neither king nor Parliament have their proper power, but the common man, the *canaille*, rules according to his fancy'. Three years later, on hearing that Cromwell had become Lord Protector, Christina also asserted that Axel Oxenstierna had wanted to do the same during her minority.[32]

To stem this unfavourable foreign tide, the English Republic appointed John Milton its 'Secretary for Foreign Tongues', and charged him with justifying the new regime abroad. He began with a translation of his vitriolic counterblast to 'The king's image', provocatively entitled *Eikonoklastes*, and prepared numerous pamphlets and official publications specifically for foreign distribution. Meanwhile the Republic produced a weekly newspaper in French, *Nouvelles ordinaires de Londres*, and maintained a 'Resident for the Parliaments of England and Scotland at Paris' who monitored and disseminated news of foreign rebellions from Naples to Ukraine. In 1654 Milton's *Second defence of the English people* defiantly imagined that

> From the pillars of Hercules [Cádiz in Spain] all the way to the farthest boundaries of [India], I seem to be leading home again everywhere in the world, after a vast space of time, Liberty herself, so long expelled and exiled ... I seem to introduce to the nations of the earth a product from my own country: ... the renewed cultivation of freedom and civic life that I disseminate throughout cities, kingdoms and nations.[33]

The success of these efforts can be measured by the German proclamations that prohibited the translation of any more 'books by the rebels', and owning or selling any work by John Milton; and Cardinal Mazarin's ban on all works by Milton, whom he accused of being 'the most impudent and most wily apologist of the blackest of all parricides, by which the English nation has just been sullied'.[34]

In 1652 English agents went to France with instructions to survey the defensive state of its ports and ascertain whether any of them might prove receptive to the republican form of government. Led by Edward Sexby, a prominent protagonist in the New Model Army's debates at Putney, the agents converged on the southwestern port of Bordeaux, mainly because it was already in revolt against the central government (the *Ormée*: see chapter 10). Sexby prepared two printed tracts that set out a blueprint for a republican form of government in the province of Guyenne (one of them clearly modelled on *An agreement of the people*, which he had drafted: see page 372 above), and the revolutionary government of Bordeaux sent delegates to London to secure English aid. Cromwell offered 40 warships and 5,000 men in return for control of Bordeaux itself, but although the city's leaders accepted the offer, Louis XIV forced their surrender before English aid could arrive.[35] One French pamphleteer now complained that the English leaders saw themselves as 'so many Moses and Josuahs' who 'boasted that they would offer the peoples of Europe forces sufficient to recover their liberty' and aspired to an 'empire of the universe'.[36]

A 'Public Sphere' in the West?

The ability to spread the 'contagion' of rebellion by words as well as deeds reflected both the production of an unprecedented multitude of texts and the existence of an immense audience capable of receiving and understanding them. In 1605 Johan Carolus of Strasbourg (in southwest Germany), who had previously made his living by compiling and circulating weekly handwritten newsletters, acquired a printing press and created the first printed newspaper in the world. Henceforth, instead of distributing 15–20 manuscript copies of his weekly bulletin for individual wealthy clients, he produced up to 500 copies for sale at a fraction of the cost. The Defenestration of Prague in 1618 – which almost everyone recognized as the harbinger of war (see chapter 8 above) – triggered a rapid expansion of the new medium: at least 15 cities published a German-language newspaper by 1620, rising to 30 by 1640. By then, Hamburg published two newspapers, each with a run of 2,500–3,000 copies; and in 1650 the first daily German newspaper began production.[37] Other printed media also expanded rapidly. In Germany, perhaps 10,000 political pamphlets and 2,000 broadsheets appeared during the course of the Thirty Years War, with peaks during the war for Bohemia and during Gustavus Adolphus's invasion (see Fig. 23). A century would pass before Germany produced as many printed works again.[38]

'Let the news be good or bad, it is always welcome to me because it tells me of the world,' wrote the Dutch intellectual Pieter Corneliszoon Hooft in 1640 – but others felt less enthusiastic. One French intellectual complained that newspapers 'make people know too much about their own affairs as well as about those of their neighbours. . . . It does not seem wise to me that ordinary people should know so much news: what is the point of informing them in such detail about the revolt of Naples, the insurgency in Turkey, and the regicide in England?' A generation later, an Italian political commentator went further. 'Ordinary people,' he observed, read the news *'as it is written, but interpret it as they wish, and they more often turn good news into bad than bad news into good'*. Previously, he continued,

> People had no reason to exercise their minds in the delusions and fantasies that they read in the newspapers, but were idle, everyone thinking about his own affairs instead of those of their rulers; but deluding and fantasizing has turned the people into princes, the ignorant into experts, the simpletons into sages, and the obedient into disobedient.

According to a colleague, the arrival of news about military developments proved particularly disruptive, because they 'caused wars about wars, and [the audience] did more skirmishing with lashing tongues than the soldiers had done with sharpened swords'.[39]

The audience for military (and other) news comprised not only readers but also illiterate listeners. For example, late in 1659 General George Monck issued a pamphlet explaining his motives for leading an army from Scotland to restore parliamentary government in England and calling for universal support. One copy reached a captain in the garrison of Leith, the port of Edinburgh, who read it himself, discussed it with another officer and then, since the pamphlet contained fewer than 1,000 words, he 'had it read to the soldiers' under his command. The same message thus reached hundreds of people, illiterate as well as literate, and if we imagine similar scenes throughout the army, the absence of effective resistance to Monck's march on London becomes more understandable (see chapter 12 above). The word had indeed become mightier than the sword.[40]

Taken together, the combination of multiple media with a large audience created a 'popular public sphere': a series of arenas, at least partially free from government interference, where for the first time in the world 'claims and counter-claims could be asserted and negotiated, and where the range of princely and imperial power could be questioned and contested.'[41] The destabilizing tendencies of this public sphere perplexed and frightened some contemporaries. 'It is strange to note how we have insensibly slid into this beginning of a civil war,' a Member of the English Parliament lamented in 1642, through 'paper combats, by declarations, remonstrances, protestations, votes, messages, answers and replies'; while a generation later a royalist argued that nothing had 'hurt the late king [Charles I more] than the paper bullets of the press'. In 1646 a Catalan cleric loyal to Philip IV made exactly the same point: 'In this day and age, we fight more with books than with armies,' he claimed, and intended the book he had just published to 'win back Catalonia in the same manner that it was lost'.[42] Rebels throughout Europe seemed able to find a printing press with ease: the Ormée of Bordeaux issued tracts; the *Nu-Pieds* of Normandy issued manifestos; and even Giuseppe Piantanida, whose proposed rebellion in Milan was discovered before it began, managed to print a proclamation. Naples produced so many *bandi* (ordinances) after the outbreak of rebellion in 1647 that, five months later, 'considering the importance of works in print, and the way they are believed throughout the world', its leaders ordered the printers of the city to submit all future texts for their imprimatur or face a heavy fine and the confiscation of their presses.[43]

Looking back just after the Restoration of Charles II in 1660, John Locke roundly condemned 'the scribbling of this age' and

> Accused the pens of Englishmen of as much guilt as their swords, judging that the issue of blood from whence such an inundation hath flowed had scarce been opened, or at least not so long unstopped had men been more unsparing of their ink; and that these furies, wars, cruelty, rapine, confusion, etc., which have so wearied and wasted this poor nation have been conjured up in private studies and from thence sent abroad to disturb the quiet we enjoyed.[44]

Some of Locke's contemporaries blamed education for the emergence of Europe's first 'public sphere'. In Spain, a government committee called on Philip IV to 'close down some grammar schools newly founded in villages and small towns, because with the opportunity of having them so near, the peasants divert their sons from the jobs and occupations in which they were born and raised, and put them to study'. In France, Cardinal Richelieu wanted to close three-quarters of the *collèges de plein exercice* (schools that provided a general education in Classical studies) because he, like Philip IV, reasoned that, if everyone received an education, 'the sons of the poor would desert the productive occupations of their parents for the comforts of office'. The French scholar Gabriel Naudé agreed, predicting in 1639 that 'the great number of colleges, seminaries and schools' would increase the frequency of 'revolutions of state'. Twenty years later, the marquis of Newcastle, sometime preceptor to Charles II, warned his illustrious charge that 'there are too many grammar schools' in England. The country, he asserted, needed only enough schools 'to serve the church, and moderately the Law, for else they run out to idle and unnecessary people that become a factious burden to the Commonwealth'. In America, Sir William Berkeley, the royalist Governor of Virginia, agreed. 'Learning', he complained in 1676, 'has brought disobedience, and heresy, and sects into the world; and printing has divulged them and libels against the best government. God keep us from both!'[45]

These critics made a valid point. A heightened appreciation of Classical learning (the Renaissance), followed by the religious fervour that called forth a more literate clergy and laity (the Reformation), had produced an 'educational revolution' in sixteenth-century Europe. Almost everywhere, schools sprang up to teach local children to read, write and undertake simple arithmetical calculations, until by the 1640s half the parishes in some parts of England and Wales, three-quarters of the parishes of Lowland Scotland and four-fifths of the parishes in and around Paris boasted their own school. Some preceptors explicitly set out 'to traine up young gentlemen, and all others whom we would have become wise men and good-commonwealths men', by fostering 'a free and bold speech', modelled on Classical precedents, that might inspire 'the hearts of princes and people' and thus 'turne and manage with their tongues, as with the helme in steerage, the floting vessels of states and empires'. Therein lay the danger: 'The immoderat libertie of speech given to orators who direct and guide the peoples' hearts and minds,' warned a French politician, could easily cause 'seditions and rebellions' because 'there is nothing that hath more force over the minds of men, than hath eloquence'. 'A powerful eloquence', echoed Thomas Hobbes in 1641, on the eve of the English Civil War, is 'the true feature of those who agitate and incite the people to revolution'.[46]

Many schoolteachers nevertheless failed to impart 'eloquence' to their pupils because education cost money. A survey of schools in Madrid in 1642 revealed that one-third of the pupils paid two *reales* a month just to learn to read, whereas those learning to read and write paid four, while those also learning arithmetic paid six. With up to 140 pupils per school, Richard Kagan has written, 'one can imagine the poorest students, the "readers" paying only two reales apiece, clustered in the back of the classroom and the sons of the more prosperous families who were each paying six reales seated in front'.[47] Nevertheless, since Spanish (like all European languages) uses an alphabet of around 26 characters, those with the necessary determination did not have to rely exclusively on schools in order to learn to read and to express themselves. Several seventeenth-century men and women from humble backgrounds described the progress of their self-instruction. When Oliver Sansom, born in Berkshire (England) in 1636, 'was about six years of age, I was put to school to a woman, to learn to read, who finding me not unapt to learn, forwarded me so well, that in about four months' time I could read a chapter of the Bible pretty readily'. At 'about five years old' Thomas Tryon, born two years earlier in Gloucestershire, started 'school, but being addicted to play, after the example of my young school-fellows, I scarcely learned to distinguish my letters before I was taken away to work for my living' since his father, a village craftsman 'having many children, was forced to bring them all to work betimes'. Thomas carded and spun wool and then became a shepherd, so that 'All this while, though now about thirteen years old, I could not read; then, thinking of the vast usefulness of reading, I bought me a primer' and persuaded other shepherds 'to teach me to spell, and so learned to read imperfectly,

my teachers not being ready readers; but in a little time' he 'learned to read competently well'. The shepherds could not teach him to write, because none of them knew
how; but Tryon persuaded 'a lame young man who taught some poor people's
children to read and write' to 'teach me to make the letters, and join them together'.
He eventually published some 20 books – a remarkable achievement for someone
whose formal schooling ended when he was six.[48] Some seventeenth-century
women also became literate without going to school. Elizabeth Angier, a clergyman's daughter from Lancashire, 'could read the hardest chapter in the Bible when
she was but four years of age' and 'at six years of age [could] write down passages of
the sermon in the chapel'. The Quaker Mary Fell, also from Lancashire, not only had
learned the Bible by heart but quoted extensive passages from memory in a book
she wrote in prison (albeit her 'virtual Bible' omitted those passages that enjoined
female subservience to men).[49]

Lutheran Sweden provides the most striking example of the extent of reading
ability in seventeenth-century Europe. Because most parishes contained huge areas,
the Church (backed by the government) devolved the task of teaching young children to memorize their catechism to all heads of households. Then, either at the
parish school or (more often) at the house of the pastor or a church elder, the children learned to read and comprehend what they already knew by heart. Next, the
minister examined both abilities annually and awarded one of six grades, ranging
from 'cannot read' to 'reads acceptably'. Finally, the local dean scrutinized and verified the examination registers. By the 1680s, these registers revealed 'acceptable'
reading rates of up to 90 per cent for both males and females. Eventually it was
possible to deny a licence to marry to those who could not read a passage of
Scripture satisfactorily.[50]

Because only Sweden systematically measured the ability to read, historians have
estimated literacy elsewhere via proxies: by counting the frequency of signatures (as
opposed to marks, or an admission of illiteracy) in documents such as marriage
registers or notarial deeds. Although the number in rural areas and among women
rarely rose above 10 per cent, in thriving cities like Amsterdam by the 1680s over
two-thirds of all males and over one-third of all females could sign their own name.
Since pupils all over Europe learned to write only after they could read, male functional literacy in Amsterdam (and perhaps in other major towns) probably
approached Swedish levels. Although an English tract of 1649 witheringly asked,
'who looks at school-books after he has left going to school?', distinct literary genres
developed in the seventeenth century expressly to inform the functionally literate.[51]

The most common medium for the semi-literate was the 'broadsheet', a
single sheet of printed paper not unlike the front page of a modern newspaper: a
striking 'headline' above an image with an explanatory text beneath (often
in rhyming verse, which made it easier for both readers and listeners to follow).
To attract purchasers, the headlines always stressed either novelty or alarm,
while the images showed both ingenuity and ambiguity. From 1606, the
printer Nicholas Oudot of Troyes (a French provincial town) used these same
techniques to produce booklets of 8 or 16 pages, sold by peddlers for a few pennies.

Most of these 'chapbooks' were devotional works (especially saints' lives), news of recent events (especially crimes and punishments), predictions ('almanacs'), stories (mostly romantic or escapist) and jokes (mostly obscene). Other chapbooks offered practical advice: how to play games, how to write a letter, how to succeed in love and in life, how to stay healthy. Oudot and his heirs printed most items in large type, with a striking image on the title page (similar to a broadsheet), short chapters and numerous illustrations. Some items achieved print runs of 100,000 copies. Although until the Fronde, censorship restrained Oudot (like other French printers) from publishing political news, in the words of a chronicler: 'The little books that circulate widely among the common people attract them like Manna'. Chapbooks thus played a crucial role in creating the broad reading public for the political polemics produced in the mid-seventeenth century. So, paradoxically, did official propaganda.[52]

France had no newspaper until 1631, when an official weekly *Gazette* began to appear. Although the government vetted its contents carefully (see chapter 10 above), like the chapbooks, the *Gazette*'s 'good-news' diet whetted the appetite of readers for political news and, when censorship collapsed in 1649, on some days no fewer than 12 new pamphlets appeared for sale in the streets of Paris (see Figs 32 and 33). So many publications targeted Cardinal Mazarin (hence their title: *Mazarinades*) that one critic jovially assured him that 'more attacks have been composed against you than against all the tyrants of Rome'. The 5,000 surviving *Mazarinades* fill over 50,000 printed pages.[53]

This initial attempt to mobilize French public opinion ended with the collapse of the Fronde in 1653, but another began almost at once when the Pope condemned five 'propositions' allegedly found in the writings of Cornelius Jansen (see chapter 10 above), whose emphasis on asceticism and devotion had won many followers. Four years later, one of Jansen's supporters began to publish a series of *Provincial Letters*, supposedly from a Parisian to a friend in the countryside, which made fun of the Jansenists' enemies. The author of these wickedly ironic epistles, Blaise Pascal, deliberately aimed at a general audience, and in 1656 he could claim that 'everybody has seen them, everybody understands them, and everybody believes them. They are not only in high repute among theologians: they have proved agreeable to men of the world and intelligible even to ladies.' The impact of the *Letters* can be gauged from the fact that Louis XIV ordered all of them to be shredded and burned.[54]

The first printed Spanish newspaper, the official weekly *La Gaçeta Nueva*, began to appear only in 1661, but just as in France, the failure to mention anything negative created a 'credibility gap', which a host of specialist writers filled by compiling manuscript *avisos* that conveyed news about 'the other Spain': assassinations and armed robberies; sodomy, rape and sexual promiscuity; political discontent, military defeats and, finally, rebellions. Discretion remained advisable, because several of those who criticized official policies in streets or taverns were never seen again; but anonymous manuscript newsletters avoided censorship and also appeared almost instantly. Some were the work of unemployed graduates, who reproduced a few pages on demand, almost like a modern photocopier, while others came from the pen of specialists who could reconstruct even a complex text (such as a play with five acts and multiple scenes) from memory in a single night – a remarkable feat that few today could match.[55]

As the situation of the Spanish Monarchy worsened, historiographer royal José de Pellicer y Tovar created a clandestine information network: he employed a team of scribes to write *avisos* to fellow scholars around the peninsula. Each one received a common core of news, together with additional items of local interest, and Pellicer expected full reports back to assuage what he called his 'sed de saber' (thirst for knowledge) – and to pass on to other correspondents in his next bulletin. These *avisos* left no doubt about the perils facing the Spanish Monarchy. On 12 June 1640 Pellicer transmitted the first news of the revolt in Barcelona (one week before) under the heading: 'Almost all the news reports today will be tragic and, more than tragic, extraordinary: things that neither the Spanish Monarchy nor many states in the past have seen before.'[56]

As in France, major changes occurred when rebellion put an end to censorship. Catalan pamphlet production, which averaged three items per year in 1620–34, and 13 per year in 1635–9, soared to 70 in 1641, reflecting the decision of the rebel regime to spend 5 per cent of its total war budget on printing and distributing propaganda 'to inform all Catalans, men and women, old and young, of the true state of affairs, so that they can distinguish truth from lies'. Catalan printers published more in the 1640s than ever before – and more than in any later decade before the mid-nineteenth century.[57] Much the same happened in Portugal, where publications leaped from two in 1640 to 133 in 1641, and the 800 Portuguese works published during the war with Spain (1640–68) exceeded the total of those produced during the rest of the century. In addition, the Portuguese printed a Gazette of their own modelled on the French precursor – the first newspaper to appear in that language – and, like other rebel regimes, kept those living abroad abreast of their aspirations and achievements through print. Many Catalan and Portuguese pamphlets were also published in France and the Dutch Republic, sometimes in translation; a dozen or more printed justifications of the two rebellions circulated in Germany, sometimes translated into German.[58]

The abolition of censorship in England had an even more dramatic impact on the ability to spread the 'contagion of revolution' through print. The year 1641 saw the publication of over 2,000 works there, more than ever before, and in 1642 the number doubled – an annual total unequalled until the eighteenth century (see Fig. 37). Interested readers living in the English provinces had long been able to pay correspondents in London (rather like Pellicer in Madrid) to send them weekly manuscript reports on political developments – so much so that Charles II's tutor, the marquis of Newcastle, believed that these professional news-writers had done immense damage to the king's cause 'for in a letter [one] might be bolder'. Whereas in the 1630s those who desired news from London had to pay £20 a year in return for perhaps one manuscript letter a week, a decade later a penny could buy thousands of words of printed news; and whereas only one newsbook appeared in England in 1639, and only three in 1641, over 60 periodicals and newspapers came out in 1642 and 70 in 1648 (the highest number for any year of the seventeenth century: see Fig. 36). A recent calculation showed that 23 newsbooks printed in the first six months of 1654 contained almost 900,000 words – and between 1642 and 1660 English presses turned out over 7,000 newsbooks. Each issue carried foreign and domestic news stories, including accounts of sermons and speeches taken down in shorthand by the first paid 'reporters' in history; and each newspaper had a 'party allegiance' (to king or Parliament) that gave its reporting a distinctive spin. The marquis of Newcastle advised Charles II to ban these, too, because they 'overheat your people extremely, and do Your Majesty much harm. . . . Every man is now become a statesman, and it is merely with the weekly corantos both at home and abroad'. A Scottish visitor to England in 1657 agreed: 'There have been of late,' he wrote, *'more good and more bad bookes printed and published in the English tongue than in all the vulgar languages of Europe'.*[59]

A 'public sphere' in China?

Just as no other seventeenth-century state became as politicized as England, so no other seventeenth-century state saw as many people participate in political upheavals as China. An unprecedented number of imperial subjects, from a wide range of backgrounds, reported and disseminated news throughout the empire in both speech and writing. According to Timothy Brook, 'More books were available, and more people read and owned more books, in the late Ming than at any earlier time in history, anywhere in the world'; and, based on a rigorous survey of extant sources, Lynn Struve has argued that 'the vocality in writing of the Chinese populace during the entire imperial era may never have been so great as it was in the early and middle seventeenth century'. This 'vocality' reflected the same combination of factors that occurred in Europe at the same time: a reading public of unprecedented size, reading material of unprecedented quantity, and unprecedented arenas in which to discuss them.[60]

As in Europe, China's enlarged public sphere reflected an 'educational revolution' in the sixteenth and early seventeenth centuries – but involving a very different infrastructure. Because Chinese is not an alphabetic language in which all words are composed from a relatively small number of characters, even functional literacy requires familiarity with several thousand characters, each one composed by several strokes in a specific order from upper left to lower right. We find no Chinese equivalent of Thomas Tryon, who learned to read without any formal instruction, or of Oliver Sansom, who could read a chapter of a complex work 'pretty readily' after only four months of school, let alone of Elizabeth Angier, who 'at six years of age [could] write down passages of the sermon in the chapel'.[61] Nevertheless, schools abounded in late Ming China. At the beginning of the seventeenth century, a survey of 500 Chinese counties revealed almost 4,000 schools: one-quarter in the towns and the rest in the countryside. In some areas, schools became so numerous that, according to a Gazetteer from Zhejiang province, 'nowadays even the very poor would be ashamed if they did not instruct their sons in the classics. From tradesmen to local-government runners, there are very few who cannot read or punctuate'. A Jesuit who travelled around rural Fujian in the 1620s concurred:

> Schools are extremely numerous in China. Scarcely a hamlet of twenty or forty houses lacks its school and in towns scarcely a street does not have several. We came upon one of them at almost every step, and could hear the children reciting the lesson by heart. Lots of schools are needed in view of the multitude of young boys and the fact that each teacher is only responsible, in his class, for between 12 and 15 pupils at a time.[62]

China's educational revolution seems to have reflected two distinct stimuli. Some of the Confucian scholars who stressed the need for introspection and intuition (page 121 above) believed that 'anyone could become a sage' and that moral principle might be found in the lives of 'ignorant men and women'. They therefore favoured education for all. Other scholars favoured the schooling system where boys learned to memorize and reproduce accurately the canon of Classical texts on ethics and history necessary to climb the ladder of examination success, with all the social and economic advantages that success brought (see chapters 5 and 18 above). This process normally required several years of classes that ran from dawn to dusk, with a short break for lunch, all year round (except for two weeks at New Year and a few holidays), because the canon required to pass even the *shengyuan* exam included 400,000 different characters of text, some of them archaic or arcane. Although some prodigies managed this feat by age 15 and most completed it before 20, many other students dropped out. Nevertheless, since even those who dropped out acquired *some* reading skills, the functionally literate public of mid-seventeenth-century China far exceeded a million and may have exceeded five million. Put another way, perhaps 20 per cent of the adult male population of late Ming China boasted respectable educational attainments.[63]

The existence of this huge potential readership fuelled a rapid expansion in printing. In the 1630s, 38 firms in Nanjing produced or sold books, with 37 more in Suzhou and 25 in Hangzhou (all in Jiangnan), and 13 more in Beijing. Although some enterprises specialized in producing a few high-quality items in which calligraphy mattered almost as much as content, others shifted to a simpler 'artisan style' of cutting characters that reduced costs. The cumulative impact was remarkable: of 830 commercial works known to have been printed in Nanjing during the Ming era (1368–1644), over 750 appeared after 1573. The output of other centres seems to have increased at a similar rate: by the early seventeenth century, the printers of Suzhou employed 650 woodblock carvers.[64]

Chinese printers enjoyed three advantages over their European colleagues. First, whereas over 50 written languages were current in early modern Europe, all subjects of the Chinese emperor used the same script (even though they spoke many different tongues), so that a book published anywhere in China could be bought and read by millions of people – a market far larger than that enjoyed by any European printer. Second, the development of cheap paper suitable for printing made from bamboo, rather than cloth fibres, brought down printing costs significantly. Finally, the use of carved woodblocks (xylography) meant that Chinese booksellers could produce illustrated works without either a printing press or a stock of type – two items of heavy capital expenditure essential for European printers who used movable type. Moreover, they could print only as many copies as the market required at any one time, storing the blocks for future use; and once the initial print run had sold out, it was easy to print more from the existing blocks without the need to re-compose the text (as with movable type).[65]

These various factors gave rise to a distinctive 'shengyuan culture' in Late Ming China, composed of satire and poetry, dictionaries and collections of famous texts, 'how-to' books (how to write letters, how to cure illnesses) and collections of successful examination essays. For the first time in Chinese history, men below the official class participated in book culture and so created an unprecedented 'public sphere': authors included merchants (who published poetry as well as commercial manuals) and commoners (who published fiction). Some of these works became best-sellers (notably primers for the examination system), and a European long resident in China marvelled at 'the exceedingly large numbers of books in circulation here and the ridiculously low prices at which they are sold'. Some bibliophiles in Jiangnan boasted collections of up to 10,000 volumes, some of them illustrated in black-and-white or in colour – because, as one editor complained in 1625, some books 'simply do not sell without pictures. So I, too, ape the fashion and furnish these illustrations for your pleasure. As they say, "Can't go against the tide" '.[66]

The last Ming emperors also resorted to print on an unprecedented scale. They not only issued innumerable posters for public display but also printed a daily broadsheet known as dibao (later the Peking Gazette) to inform all officials of imperial edicts and decrees, to announce promotions and demotions, and to provide news of domestic and foreign affairs. But still manuscript copies abounded because regional officials hired scribes – many of them no doubt failed examination candidates – in the capital to make and distribute copies of entries in the Gazette relevant to them. Some maintained a permanent news bureau where scribes copied unofficial as well as official news. Merchants produced commercial versions of these dibao, often adding local news and gossip to the official pronouncements, while news entrepreneurs also compiled excerpts from the Gazette and other sources and offered them for sale. The efficiency of this network is reflected in the memoirs of the minor official Yao Tinglin, living in a small town of Jiangnan. One day in 1644 he and 'other men of his family were drinking together when a friend rushed in in a panic, holding a "small gazetteer" ' – that is, an unofficial news-sheet – 'that said that the troops of the rebel Li Zicheng had captured Peking ten days earlier and that the Chongzhen emperor had committed suicide'. Confirmation from the official Peking Gazette arrived one day later.[67]

Yu Shenxing, a senior minister in Beijing, once complained about the false information spread by 'news bureau entrepreneurs who are out for the most miniscule profits and give no thought to matters of national emergency'. He asked, like so many later politicians frustrated by journalists, 'Why aren't they strenuously prohibited?'[68] But even had Yu prevailed, closing down the news bureaux would not have prevented the diffusion of information, whether true or false, because it also spread rapidly by word of mouth, via Ming China's excellent communications system. Travellers on the extensive network of highways would find courier relay stations (in theory) no more than 25 miles apart, connecting all provincial and prefectural capitals, and postal stations (in theory) every 4 miles along the main roads of each county. The Ming legal code decreed draconian penalties for delay in delivering messages: 20 lashes for a courier who was a day late, or for a postal worker who arrived three-quarters of an hour late (the greater severity of the penalties reflecting the fact that postal workers covered much shorter distances than couriers).

The network's impressive infrastructure promoted social intercourse at many levels. It enabled tens of thousands of students to travel to take examinations in prefectural, provincial and (for the successful) metropolitan capitals. It also facilitated the journeys of thousands of government officials required to travel to distant postings, and of hundreds more sent on tours of inspection around the empire, to say nothing of itinerant merchants (some of whom might also spend prolonged periods on the road), of peddlers carrying their wares between the different market towns in their area, or of refugees hoping to find better conditions elsewhere. In the words of Louis Le Comte, a French Jesuit who travelled thousands of miles around the Qing empire in the 1680s: 'All of China is on the move: on the roads, on the highways, on the rivers, and along the coasts of the maritime provinces you see hordes of travellers'. All these people wanted to hear news from home, and whatever their condition and wherever they went, travellers disseminated news of the 'outside world' to entertain those with whom they stayed and those they met on the road, while their servants also exchanged news in their humble overnight lodgings.[69]

In the 1620s Wei Zhongxian's persecution of Donglin alumni, and his subsequent fall from power (see chapter 5 above), offers an early snapshot of this developing 'public sphere'. Many intellectuals wrote private letters reporting each development that, together with the public edicts distributed by the courier and postal systems, excited public interest throughout China. Enterprising printers brought out compilations of personal accounts and official documents to satisfy public interest about what had happened and why; while the Suzhou rioters, punished so harshly for their support of the 'Donglin martyrs' (see chapter 18 above), became heroes of stage plays and popular literature, including four historical novels. The author of one novel assured readers that he had been at work for three years and 'based my book on what I read and heard', including scrutiny of a pile of copies of the *Peking Gazette* that stood 'more than three meters high', as well as 'several dozens of official documents and unofficial accounts'.[70]

According to historian John Dardess, 'probably no earlier event in China's long history has available for modern retelling anything like the archive available for the Donglin affair'; but, just one generation later, those who survived the violent transition from Ming to Qing rule produced even more memoirs, almost 200 of which still survive. Among these, Grace Fong has noted, Jiangnan (the lower Yangzi valley) produced 'a proportionately larger corpus of historical source materials' than any other area, reflecting the higher density of literate men and women living in the 'cultural and economic nexus of the Ming empire' who wanted to leave a written record of what they had seen and suffered before they died (many of them by their own hand). Lynn Struve estimates that the volume of documents concerning the political turmoil of the mid-seventeenth century 'was not surpassed as a distinct outpouring in Chinese cultural history until the latter part of the twentieth century'.[71]

This combination of the unprecedented diffusion of information about the common problems facing China with the unequalled number of readers allowed men and women in all regions to set their own experiences of adversity in a broader perspective and to develop comprehensive solutions. Huang Zongxi, a scholar whose father had been a Donglin martyr, probably exaggerated when he claimed in 1676 that in some areas of China, 'we find agricultural tenants, firewood gatherers, potters, brick burners, stone masons, and men from other humble walks of life attending public lectures and chanting classics'; but nevertheless several million imperial subjects took an active role in the Ming-Qing transition. The oldest state in the world had never seen anything like it – which is one reason why the transition claimed so many lives and lasted so long.[72]

A 'public sphere' Elsewhere?

Although Islam is a 'religion of the book', and although Arabic is an alphabetic language, few parts of the vast Muslim world saw the emergence of anything resembling a 'public sphere' in the seventeenth century. 'The Blacks' of West Africa, according to a French missionary, 'do not write: except for the *marabouts* [Sufi sheikhs] and some great lords, no one knows how to read or write'. Moreover, according to a French merchant who lived in Senegal in the 1670s, 'scarcely anyone, except those who want to be marabouts, study' – and even then, he added superciliously, 'they learn nothing except reading and writing. They devote themselves to no learned subject'.[73] It seems likely that many other parts of the Islamic world resembled Senegal: literacy remained confined to the clergy and involved only religious learning.

India, by contrast, boasted both a large literate population and a rich literary culture. In the Mughal empire, an army of scribes 'copied and produced manuscripts in the hundreds of thousands' both in Persian and in the various languages of the subcontinent, some of them dealing with statecraft and politics; but their readership – and therefore their impact on the political life of the richest state on earth – thus far remains unknown. In south India, however, 'everyday records were not penned on paper, but rather pressed into palm leaves, creating manuscripts that to survive had to be recopied each century'. Therefore most surviving Tamil documents from the period are poems, since only poems were deemed worthy of permanent preservation. In the Hindu states, finally, intellectuals deemed mere 'events' insignificant and so few written accounts recorded them.[74]

The intellectual life of the Ottoman empire was very different. The learned official Kâtib Çelebi (1609–57) read works both in Arabic and (thanks to the help of a French convert to Islam) in some Western languages, and eventually made a list of 'the many thousands of volumes in the libraries I had personally examined, and the books which for twenty years the book-sellers had been bringing me in a steady stream'. His bibliography contained almost 15,000 titles. Although the sultans allowed no work in Arabic to be printed, over 20 manuscript copies of Kâtib Çelebi's bibliography survive today, which suggests a widespread interest in learning.[75] Assessing the actual impact of this literature is far harder. For example, Kâtib Çelebi made no effort to circulate a penetrating analysis of the problems facing the Ottoman state, which he composed in 1653. 'Since I knew that my conclusions would be difficult to apply,' he wrote, 'I took no further trouble about it'. He merely hoped that 'a sultan of some future time will become aware of it' (see chapter 7 above).

The Ottoman sultans allowed only two groups of their subjects to use printing presses: Orthodox Christians and Jews. In 1627 Patriarch Cyril Lukaris of Constantinople (born a Venetian subject in Crete and educated at Padua University) imported a Greek-language printing press from England on which, with the aid of two Protestants, he produced editions of Patristic texts. But the jealous Catholics resident in the Ottoman capital persuaded the sultan that this was a seditious venture, and he shut down the printing press within a few months (and later deposed and executed Lukaris).[76] This development left only the presses of Jewish printers in Istanbul and Thessaloniki, who turned out Hebrew works in fascicles (rather than in completed books), which allowed authors to receive comments that could be addressed in later segments. These printed works were distributed at synagogues on Shabbat, deposited in libraries (some of them public) and sent to notable scholars (some of whom made copies for use by their students), ensuring that news and ideas circulated far and fast. In the 1650s the Jewish community of the Anatolian port-city of Izmir, of which Shabbatai Zvi had been a member, began to print works not only in Hebrew but also in Spanish, including a new edition of Manasseh ben Israel's influential *Hope of Israel*.[77]

Just as in China, travellers played a major role in spreading news and ideas within the Ottoman empire. The central government tried to ensure that its senior officials rotated posts, so that they did not 'put down roots' in any area, and although the system did not always succeed, thousands of senior administrators, judges and soldiers travelled from one location to another at regular intervals. The career of Evliyā Çelebi (1611–?80) offers an interesting example. Trained in Istanbul for a career in government service, he kept a detailed record of his assignments in Africa, Asia and Europe on military campaigns and on business, fiscal and diplomatic missions – during which he met and conversed with thousands of people. His account eventually filled ten volumes.[78] Many other Muslims travelled around the empire to study with noted teachers. For example, Sheikh Niyāzī-i Mişri (1618–94), born in a small Anatolian town, went to a neighbouring city with many medreses to study the Qur'an before migrating to Cairo (whose popular name at that time, 'Mişr', he adopted). For three years Niyāzī-i Mişri lived in the city, attending classes in the 'university' attached to the al-Azhar mosque, and residing in a Sufi lodge: both there and in the numerous marketplaces and coffee houses of Cairo, he met and conversed with scholars from all over the Muslim world. Then he wandered through western Anatolia and the Balkans, eventually attracting followers of his own who came to study with him. In the 1640s he went into exile, first on the island of Rhodes and then on Lesbos, for suggesting that Sultan Ibrahim, all his sons and his leading ministers were 'Jewish' – a taint that (if true) rendered them unfit to rule over Muslims – and proposing the replacement of the 'corrupted' house of Osman with the Crimean khans. Yet despite his exile, Mīṣri boasted many followers who read copies of his writings and formed a small Sufi order after his death.[79] Although Niyāzī-i Mīṣri never went to Mecca, many others did, for Islam expects every male Muslim to make a pilgrimage (hajj) there at least once. Along the way, as well as at their destination, pilgrims met people from other places with different experiences, skills and information, and thus expanded their mental horizons.

The history of two other religious movements – the Kadizadeli and the Shabbateans – demonstrates how far and how fast news and ideas could travel in the mid-seventeenth-century Muslim world. Disciples spread the teachings of Kadizade Mehmet all over the Ottoman empire. When Evliyā Çelebi visited a remote town in eastern Anatolia in the 1650s, he witnessed a government soldier who claimed to be a Kadizadeli destroy a beautifully illustrated Persian manuscript because, he said, it contained pictures of humans and so was contrary to the teachings of the Prophet. The numerous Ottoman soldiers stationed in Egypt also included disciples of Kadizade. As late as 1711, long after the movement had faded in the capital, a group of soldiers from Anatolia who had recently read the treatise that formed the cornerstone of Kadizadeli teaching ran amok in Cairo, defacing the tombs of local religious zealots and assailing the city's religious elite.[80]

The speed with which news of Shabbatai Zvi's meteoric career spread within the Ottoman empire and beyond is more surprising, both because Judaism was not the official faith of any state and because most rabbis and many Ottoman officials regarded him as a fraud (see chapter 7 above). Nevertheless, six months after Nathan of Gaza declared Shabbatai to be the Messiah in May 1665, the news had spread throughout the Jewish communities of North Africa from Cairo to Salé, on Morocco's Atlantic coast. It also reached Istanbul, and from there spread to Jewish communities in the Balkans, Hungary, Moldavia and the Crimea; while Jewish printers in the Ottoman capital published two volumes of devotions composed by Nathan, one for nocturnal use and the other 'arranged to be said daily, brought from the Land of Zvi [Palestine]'.[81] As soon as Shabbatai announced in December 1665 that he intended to travel to Istanbul to confront the sultan, thousands of Jews 'from Poland, the Crimea, Persia and Jerusalem, as well as from Turkey and the Frankish lands' converged on the Ottoman capital, and they were there to greet him when he arrived two months later.[82] Shabbatai's fame even reached the Americas: Jewish communities in the Caribbean islands expressed interest, while in Boston, Massachusetts, Increase Mather preached several sermons that drew attention to the 'constant reports' received 'that the Israelites were upon their journey towards Jerusalem, from sundry foreign parts in great multitudes'.[83]

This rapid diffusion of Shabbatai's message on four continents reflected not only its appeal at a time of millenarian excitement within both Judaism and Christianity, but also the impressive network of 'connectors' who linked the Jewish communities of the eastern Mediterranean with the rest of the world. Shabbatai himself had lived in many cities of the Ottoman empire before 1665, while his father had worked for the English merchants in Izmir, and his Polish-born wife had lived in Amsterdam, Venice and Livorno as well as in Egypt. Nathan of Gaza and the others rabbis who joined Shabbatai's entourage each boasted an extensive network of personal contacts whom they deluged with letters and (later) personal visits authenticating the Messiah's claims. In addition, western merchants and diplomats resident in the Ottoman empire wrote detailed reports to their principals, spreading the news along Europe's Atlantic coast as far as Hamburg, where the rabbis inserted a blessing for Shabbatai in their prayers. In just 18 months, Shabbatai and his network of 'connectors' had turned the claim made by an obscure Jewish scholar in Hebron into a world-wide movement. Only news of his apostasy in September 1666 put an end to it.[84]

The Rule of the Few

Despite the existence of extensive networks, new and old, for 'spreading the word' about important events, most of those events originated with a very small group of people who played a disproportionate role in 'turning the world upside down' (to use a popular phrase in Revolutionary England). Thus in 1640, a contemporary who watched the *segadors* rampage through the streets of Barcelona guessed that the hard core numbered no more than 500. The following year, Lord Maguire planned to take Dublin with fewer than 200 men (an enterprise that fewer than 40 English officers accomplished in 1659); and about the same number enabled Sir Phelim O'Neill to capture almost all the strongholds of Ulster. In 1647 Masaniello began with no more than 30 'ragazzi', many of them teenagers, when he turned a dispute over fruit excise in Naples into revolution; while Giuseppe d'Alesi had 12 co-conspirators when he seized control of Palermo. Both consolidated their authority with fewer than 500 'men and boys'.[85] The following year Bohdan Khmelnytsky began his Cossack revolt with no more than 250 followers; the men 'with blackened faces so they would not be known' who destroyed government records in the Andalusian town of Lucena also numbered 500; and Guru Hargobind, the Sikh leader, likewise led no more than '500 youths'. Even successful revolutions might involve surprisingly few actors. In 1640 the *coup d'état* in Lisbon, a city of 175,000 people, that permanently restored Portuguese independence, involved at most 40 noblemen with about 100 followers; while 20 years later, George Monck entered London, a city of perhaps 250,000 inhabitants, with fewer than 6,000 soldiers, exhausted after a 350-mile march in winter from the Scottish border. They nevertheless sufficed to end Britain's Republican experiment for ever.

The explanation for such asymmetry – for how 'little things make a big difference' – lies in contingency, and especially in timing. In the words of a frustrated but perceptive French diplomat in London during the Civil War, 'affairs here change so fast that one no longer reckons time by months and weeks, but by hours and even by minutes.'[86] The same was true elsewhere. In Ireland, the Catholic rebellion gained unstoppable momentum when the O'Neills and their allies persuaded the castellans of half a dozen Ulster forts to admit them on the night of 22–23 October 1641 – only a few hours before a warning arrived from Dublin. Six years later, the duke of Arcos lost control of events in Naples in the few minutes it took for Masaniello and his 'boys' to win over the holiday crowds in the Piazza del Mercato. In each case, the government disposed of far superior resources right up until the 'tipping point', but the failure to deploy them in timely fashion proved fatal because the new information networks rapidly spread the 'contagion' of revolutionary ideas – just as, a century later, the failure of British patrols to detain Paul Revere on his ride allowed him to spread the 'virus' that would begin the American Revolution.

PART V

BEYOND THE CRISIS[1]

THE POLITICAL, SOCIAL AND ECONOMIC UPHEAVALS KNOWN AS THE GENERAL Crisis largely ceased in the 1680s, yet global cooling continued for another generation. Average temperatures in 1687–1700 were 1.5°C lower than in the preceding decade; and in the Paris region, the *average* monthly temperature fell below freezing eight times between 1691 and 1697 – a phenomenon never seen again. The 1690s saw by far the coldest period in several long runs of European temperature records, leading climatologists to christen the decade the 'climax of the Little Ice Age'.[2] Although these oscillations may seem small, they were in fact enormous – especially in such a short period – since each change of 0.1°C advances or retards the ripening of crops by one day. The global cooling of the 1690s delayed harvests by an average of two weeks in temperate zones, and by far more in subboreal regions. Sea temperatures around the Orkney Islands and Scandinavia in the 1690s were 5°C lower than today. In June 1695, after perhaps the worst winter in the past 500 years, it snowed as far south as Lviv in the Ukraine; and a series of cool summers caused widespread crop failures.

Then, after a spell of warmer weather, in 1708–9 Europe suffered what survivors would call the 'Great Winter'. On the night of 5–6 January 1709, the temperature in Paris fell from 9°C to –9°C, and stayed well below freezing for almost three weeks; Saintes on France's Atlantic coast received 24 inches of snow; on France's Mediterranean coast temperatures plunged to –11°C; at Venice, the rich went skating on the lagoon. January 1709 was the coldest month recorded in the past 500 years. Although temperatures rose in February, they fell again just as the winter cereal crops began to sprout, killing them all. The price of grain reached its highest level of the entire *ancien regime* (Fig. 51).[3]

The underlying causes of this global cooling remained the same as before. Astronomers still saw virtually no sunspots. El Niño episodes increased in frequency (1687–8, 1692, 1694–5 and 1697). Volcanic activity peaked in 1693–4 (with major eruptions at Serua in Indonesia, Hekla in Iceland and Komagatake in Japan, all VEI 4; and at Vesuvius and Etna in Italy, both VEI 3) and again in 1707–8 (with at least ten major eruptions, including Vesuvius and Santorini, both VEI 3, and Mount Fuji, VEI 5, which released perhaps 30,000 cubic feet of volcanic ash, some of which fell on Edo, some 62 miles away). Temperatures fell throughout the northern hemisphere.[4]

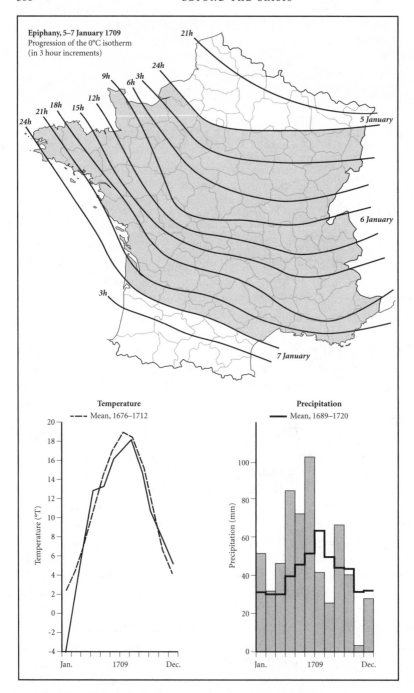

Epiphany, 5–7 January 1709
Progression of the 0°C isotherm
(in 3 hour increments)

51. The 'Great Winter' of 1708/9.
Dozens of people across France recorded the moment when rain turned to snow, and water turned to ice, at Epiphany 1709. Their attention reflected not only the rapid progress of Siberian air from Flanders to the Mediterranean – one of the last recorded 'extreme weather events' of the Little Ice Age – but also an increased awareness of climate change, and of the dangers that it posed. The year 1709 saw not only the coldest months recorded in the past five hundred years but also an abnormally wet summer.

As usual, extreme natural phenomena caused widespread human distress. In autumn 1690 Ottoman troops in the Balkans endured from 'snow, rain and frost. The snow, being as high as the horses' chests, barred the roads, and the infantry could no longer move on; many animals dying, the officers were left to go on foot.' Everyone experienced great 'shortage of provisions' and 'the hardships and sufferings they endured had never been seen before'. In China, an extensive drought produced widespread famine in 1691–2; while in New Spain, in those same years, hailstorms, a plague of locusts and torrential rains followed by drought and early frosts destroyed two maize harvests in a row and initiated a prolonged drought that lasted until 1697. Across the Atlantic, in Finland, some 500,000 people perished during the famine years of 1694, 1695 and 1696, and it took six decades for the country's population to recover.[5] In France, winter ice and summer rains in 1693–4 caused misery 'unknown in the memory of man' and 'without parallel in past centuries'; and between 1691 and 1701 climate change killed over a million people – a mortality, as Emmanuel Le Roy Ladurie has observed, equal to France's losses during the Great War, but culled from a population that numbered only 20 (not 40) million. A further 600,000 French men and women died during the Great Winter. In addition, those who survived these famines remained stunted for life, reaching an average height of only 5 feet – among the shortest Frenchmen ever recorded.[6]

As in the mid-seventeenth century, these episodes of climatic adversity occurred in wartime. Hostilities between Louis XIV of France and his enemies convulsed western Europe between 1689 and 1697, and again between 1702 and 1713; the Great Northern War between Charles XII of Sweden and his enemies affected much of eastern Europe between 1700 and 1721; the Qing emperor Kangxi led huge armies in the conquest of Inner Asia in the 1690s; while the Mughal emperor Aurangzeb campaigned ceaselessly against the Marathas and their allies in central India. All of these wars involved heavy taxation and caused widespread devastation.

It is therefore astonishing that although the persistence of war and global cooling caused misery and suffering on a scale that resembled the 1640s and 1650s, it was not accompanied by similar social and political upheavals – that is: the climax of the Little Ice Age did not coincide with the climax of the General Crisis. Admittedly, popular 'tumults' broke out in several cities of New Spain, including the viceregal capital, and in some regional capitals of the Ottoman empire; while in France, the famine of 1709 that followed the 'Great Winter' provoked almost 300 anti-tax revolts and far more bread riots. Even in Paris, crowds pillaged the bakeries and stoned the city guard. But none of these upheavals attracted the participation of 'people who hope only for a change' – the alienated aristocrats, intellectuals and clerics who had challenged and sometimes overthrown governments a generation before. Moreover the unrest of 1709 remained unequalled until 1789. There were no more Frondes. The 'fatal synergy' had ended.[7]

In his pioneering essay on 'The General Crisis Debate' in 1959, Hugh Trevor-Roper used a flamboyant metaphor to describe the impact of the revolutions of the mid-seventeenth century. Afterwards, he wrote, 'Intellectually, politically, morally, we are in a new age, a new climate. It is as if a series of rainstorms has ended in one final thunderstorm which has cleared the air and changed, permanently, the temperature of Europe' (page xvii above). The chapters in Part II offered support for these claims regarding France, Spain, Britain, Germany and its neighbours; and made parallel assertions for the 'temperature' in some areas beyond Europe (China, Russia, Poland and the Ottoman empire). The chapters in Part III argued that Tokugawa Japan, Spanish Italy, Mughal India and its neighbours, as well as some parts of Africa and the Americas, managed to avoid a 'final thunderstorm', but still experienced an unpleasant 'series of rainstorms'.

Trevor-Roper's metaphor does not do full justice to the magnitude of the change. Above all, massive mortality often accompanied the 'series of rainstorms', so that fewer – in many regions, far fewer – humans were alive in the 1680s than in the 1640s. In China, the Ottoman empire, Russia and much of Europe, prolonged wars as well as famine and disease caused the death of millions of men, women and children; while hundreds of thousands died in the Gujarat famine in India in 1630–2 and in the Kan'ei famine in Japan in 1641–3. Perhaps the most important characteristic of the 'new age' discerned by Trevor-Roper after the mid-century was thus one that he overlooked: *far fewer humans faced the risk of famine in the 1690s than in the 1640s and 1650s*. The demand for food no longer exceeded local supplies so egregiously.

Yet depopulation alone cannot explain the lack of political upheavals during the 'climax of the Little Ice Age'. Disasters, as Christof Mauch reminds us, often have a *phoenix effect*: those who survive a crisis often emerge better prepared to cope with any sequel. Catastrophes 'have improved emergency preparedness and spurred technological developments; they have also reduced the vulnerability of humans both in the emergent phase of natural catastrophes and during post-disaster recovery' – a phenomenon sometimes termed 'Creative destruction'.[8] Those who survived the mid-seventeenth century developed a wide variety of 'coping strategies'. Some involved escapism (indulging in pursuits that dulled the senses amid encircling horror: chapter 20). Others were innovative (limiting the spread of plague through quarantine, and of smallpox through inoculation; planting new crops with greater resistance to climate change; rebuilding towns in brick and stone to reduce the risk of catastrophic fires, and creating fire-insurance companies: chapter 21). Others still involved the resort to new forms of 'practical' or 'scientific' knowledge, in the hope not only of repairing the damage done by past catastrophes but also of reducing the impact of future ones – a legacy of the Global Crisis that helped to lay the foundations of the Great Divergence between the West and the Rest of the World (chapter 22).

Escaping the Crisis

Getting Away From It All

MANY OF THOSE WHO LIVED IN THE SEVENTEENTH CENTURY REACTED TO adversity and anxiety which they could neither explain nor avoid in much the same way as their descendants today: some killed themselves; others went to consult a therapist or a cleric; while others found solace in an absorbing pastime. All three categories are difficult to document, because they left few traces in the surviving sources. Some of those who committed suicide subsequently appeared in court records (such as the findings of the juries convened by the coroners of England) or in chronicles (like the *Mingmo zhonglie jishi*, 'True record of Late Ming extreme loyalty', which honoured over 1,000 Chinese men and women who killed themselves rather than obey the Qing conquerors). A few left a note of explanation, like the desperate Chinese elite women who wrote *tibishi*, 'poems inscribed on walls', before killing themselves; or like the Scottish Soldier of Fortune, Patrick Gordon, who became 'careles of myself' when he returned to his camp, wounded after trying to rescue his captain in battle, only to receive a reproach for breaking ranks. This 'did so vexe me' that, with 'a desperate resolution', he 'rode into the field betwixt' the two armies 'to seeke death . . . swinging my pistol about my head [to] provoke any of them out to exchange bullets'. He was lucky to survive this suicide mission with only flesh wounds.[1]

Most of those who in adversity sought the advice of doctors, therapists and clerics left even fewer documentary traces – often in the cryptic records kept by those they consulted. Thus the doctors of the first permanent Military Hospital in the world, at Mechelen in the Spanish Netherlands, began to encounter a new ailment among soldiers in the 1640s. They labelled it *el mal de corazón* – literally, 'heart-trouble' but apparently a sort of post-traumatic stress disorder that made men unfit for service. Another diagnosis that probably referred to the same condition was *estar roto* ('to be broken'); and, like those with *el mal de corazón*, sufferers were deemed useless for service and sent home.[2] Across the Channel, about forty people each month consulted William Lilly, the most famous astrologer in England, about their future. Most of them were women, who wanted to know 'Was she with child?' 'Should she go on a journey or not?'; 'If the man she loves be in France or England?'; 'How long her husband would live and which of them would die first'; 'Whether she has any enemies'; and, most simple of all, 'What sort of life she would have?' Lilly cast each patient's horoscope, on which he based his answer, before recording the details in his case books.[3] Lilly's contemporary Richard Napier, an English country parson who gained national fame as a 'therapist' (to use today's nomenclature), filled 15,000 folios with his notes on consultations with some 40,000 patients. He deemed over 2,000 to be 'troubled', and over 150 'suicidal'. Twice as many women as men sought his help with psychological distress, and roughly half of them reported anxieties about courtship, marriage and bearing children. A quarter of them had recently been bereaved. Most of the 'troubled patients' also reported economic stress, chiefly through debt (not surprising given the hard times in which they lived). One-third of his 'troubled' patients were in their twenties while one-twelfth were over 60 (these two age cohorts comprised, respectively one-quarter and one-fifth of the population at large); and servants formed by far the largest occupational category.[4]

Richard Napier determined that many of his troubled patients suffered from 'melancholy', or 'clinical depression', and the same diagnosis occurs in the case-books of Theodore Turquet de Mayerne, the most famous (and best paid) European physician of his day. His clients included Oliver Cromwell, the future Lord Protector, whom Turquet diagnosed in 1628 as '*valde melancholicus*' (exceedingly depressed); and Princess Elizabeth, Charles I's youngest daughter, of whom Turquet wrote in 1650 that 'after the death of her father, she fell into a great sorrow, whereby all the other ailments from which she suffered were increased'. She died shortly afterwards.[5]

Turquet and Cromwell had both read *The Anatomy of Melancholy*, a book by the Oxford academic Robert Burton that became a best-seller despite its enormous length (over 350,000 words in the first edition, rising to over 500,000 in later ones), which argued that 'melancholy' was 'a disease so grievous, so common' that 'in our miserable times' few 'feele not the smart of it'. He anatomized at great length the '*Melancholy* which goes and comes upon every smal occasion of sorrow, need, sicknesse, trouble, feare, griefe, passion, or perturbation of the minde, any manner of care, discontent, or thought, which causeth anguish, heavinesse and vexation of the spirits', concluding that 'from these melancholy dispositions, no man living is free'. Burton was no exception. He confessed to his readers that 'I write of melancholy, by being busie to avoid melancholy'; and like several of Napier's patients, the condition killed him – in 1640 he hanged himself in his college rooms.[6]

Patients with untreated 'melancholy' could endanger others as well as themselves. John Felton, an army officer, was described by his brother as having 'a melancholy disposition', while his former neighbour remembered him as 'a melancholy man much given to reading of books'. Among Felton's reading matter in 1628 was a 'Remonstrance' denouncing the duke of Buckingham, Charles I's Favourite. After brooding for several weeks over the accusations it contained, Felton decided to 'make himself a martyr for his country'. To this end he purchased a kitchen knife made of best Sheffield steel, sidled up behind the duke after breakfast one morning, and killed him with a single stab. Felton had no thought of escape: he had placed two statements justifying the deed inside his hat, in case he died in his attempt, and when instead he had the chance to escape amid the confusion, he announced 'I am the one' (thereby ensuring, as he must have anticipated, his arrest, torture and public execution).[7]

Robert Burton included the medieval Muslim physician and philosopher Avicenna among his numbing barrage of learned citations, because Avicenna's *Canon of medicine* contained a section on the 'melancholy' caused by fear, misfortune and thwarted affections. Burton's Muslim and Jewish contemporaries were, of course, also familiar with Avicenna and with the concept of melancholy (*ḥuzn* in Arabic) as a response to extreme stress, which emerges from a rare surviving report on someone who sought professional advice from a cleric. Although most individual conversations remain forever secret, when Jewish rabbis encountered thorny moral issues they sometimes sought written guidance from their learned colleagues, thus creating a paper trail. A case from the Little Ice Age that involved melancholy arose when a devout Sephardic Jew arrived in Egypt as the fiscal officer of a new provincial governor, leaving his wife behind him in Istanbul. 'From the day he arrived,' the local rabbis noted, 'he was afflicted with various terrible illnesses so that he was falling apart'. First the man consulted Jewish physicians and then, after they gave up on him, a Christian doctor who immediately diagnosed the problem: 'The illness had turned into *melancholia*' because the man's 'semen had built up and created an abscess in his body, and the vapors were rising to his head and reaching the heart'. The doctor predicted that if the official 'kept up in this way without discharging, the illness would overcome him'. Jewish doctrine ruled out masturbation, and the official's marriage contract explicitly prohibited bigamy. So he asked the local rabbis for advice. They responded by interviewing both the Jewish and Christian doctors themselves, and then 'conducted our own very thorough search in the books of the physicians to see whether an illness like this really exists in the world'. They eventually found that Avicenna's *Canon* contained a description that supported the diagnosis: sexual intercourse. Reasoning that even if they summoned the man's wife from Istanbul, the build-up of semen might kill him before she arrived, the rabbis allowed him to break his marriage oath and marry a second wife so he could ejaculate his way out of melancholy without committing the sin of Onan.[8]

Samuel Pepys would have had no problem here, for he committed that sin on many occasions and in many places, including the Chapel Royal during a Christmas Eve service – a feat that he recorded in the diary he kept for nine years. He also recorded his sexual encounters with over fifty women – several of them in 1665, when the departure of his wife and servants from London to avoid the Great Plague afforded him unusual freedom to sin. As disease ravaged the semi-deserted capital, according to the coded shorthand entries in his diary, he kissed and fondled waitresses in taverns, harassed maids in churches and bribed a waterman's daughter to masturbate him as her father rowed him down the Thames. He also committed adultery repeatedly, while 'next door on every side is the plague', with his mistress (and occasionally with his mistress's daughter). Sex even penetrated his dreams. As the death toll around him rose, he had 'the best [dream] that ever was dreamed – which was that I had my Lady Castlemaine [the king's mistress] in my arms and was admitted to use all the dalliance I desired with her'.[9] In September 1665 he wrote that 'in this sad time of plague everything else hath conspired to my happiness and pleasure, more for these last three months than in all my life before in so little time. God long preserve it'. The Creator evidently hearkened to His promiscuous servant, because at the end of the year Pepys wrote that 'I have never lived so merrily (besides that I never got so much [money]) as I have done this plague-time'.[10]

Seventeenth-century people elsewhere also sinned in order to avoid thinking about the disasters that surrounded them. In Germany, Elector Maximilian of Bavaria denounced in 1636 what he called the 'frivolous lifestyle' (leichtfertige Leben) that had developed among his subjects during 'the recent years of war'. He lamented that 'Illegitimate pregnancies, especially in the countryside, among unmarried peasants and other common people' and 'the abominable vice of adultery' had become 'just as common as cursing and blasphemy among old as well as young people of both sexes'. Magistrates and ministers in neighbouring Protestant states agreed: 'All vices, and particularly swearing, have grown rampant because of the war,' one lamented; 'Instead of making people more pious, the war made people nine times worse,' echoed another. In Japan, four years after watching thousands die in Edo's catastrophic Meireki fire of 1657, Asai Ryōi published his Tales of the floating world, which called upon his readers to 'live only for the moment' and to keep melancholy at bay by 'singing songs, drinking wine, diverting ourselves in just floating, floating; caring not a whit for the pauperism staring us in the face, refusing to be disheartened'.[11]

In China, many Ming intellectuals and scholar-officials escaped misery in a less flamboyant way by becoming 'monks on a scale unprecedented in any previous dynastic transition'. Some developed a religious vocation in response to 'the alienation from government affairs and feelings of despair, failure, worthlessness, and self-blame' felt by many Ming ministers; others did so after the Qing issued their edicts on tonsure and apparel, because Buddhist monks shaved their entire skull and wore traditional robes. They could therefore not be forced to grow a queue and wear Manchu dress, and could thus avoid overt rejection of the new dynasty (a choice that normally ended in death: see chapter 5 above).[12] Some of these refugees entered a monastery and spent the rest of their lives there; while others, especially those whom the Qing wanted to arrest, kept moving from one retreat to another. The latter group included Ye Shaoyuan, who wrote a three-part autobiography describing the misery he saw in and around Shanghai during the Ming-Qing transition. In August 1645, as 'the enemy descended south in great numbers' and 'the orders for cutting hair rained down fast', he and his four surviving sons began 'our journey to conceal ourselves as monks' in the mountains along the Jiangsu–Zhejiang border. Over the next three years Ye noted in his journal the people he met and the things he heard, revealing that the hills around his refuge teemed with former subjects of the Ming disguised as hermits and monks. They paid each other visits and exchanged news, poems and gifts; on one occasion Ye found almost 150 other 'monks' at a clandestine ceremony.[13]

Other discontented or disoriented members of the Han Chinese elite followed the example of their predecessors and cultivated elaborate gardens where they sought seclusion and composed poems, plays and prose. Others succumbed to fatalism. Thus Yao Tinglin, a minor Chinese official living near Shanghai, sensed that with a new dynasty, a new dress code and a new social hierarchy, by 1645 he had entered 'another world, with no restoring of the old order', and that he had been 'reborn in a new world' – a classic 'post-traumatic stress' response. After failing first as a trader and then as a farmer, in 1657 Yao became a minor government official – but he failed at this, too, running up considerable debts. As he entered his fourth decade in 1667, he wrote in his journal: 'I have the feeling that most of these forty years have been spent for nothing – that I have been through incredible hardship and yet have accomplished nothing so far'. The next year, he therefore resigned his official post, went back to the family village and opened a school. He worked as a teacher for the remaining three decades of his life.[14]

Some discontented and disoriented Europeans followed similar escapist strategies. In France, the chaos caused by the Fronde led the prominent critic of Mazarin, Robert Arnauld d'Andilly, who also looked after the gardens at the convent of Port Royal des Champs, near Paris, to publish a learned treatise on 'How to grow fruit trees', which offered an escape from insoluble political problems via raising, training and pruning trees to maximize their yields – an obvious metaphor for the peaceful pursuits that would restore prosperity. Throughout Europe, the seventeenth century saw the rise of the 'geometrical garden', which not only offered a secluded place of escape but allowed those wearied or intimidated by the malign force of nature to tame it at the microcosmic level through obsessively trimmed gardens.[15] In England, Charles I sought distraction during his final captivity by annotating his copy of Shakespeare's plays, to 'improve' the Bard's language, and wrote down 'my most impartial thoughts, touching the chief passages, which have been most remarkable or disputed, in my late troubles', interspersed with prayers, published posthumously as *Eikon Basilike*. Soon afterwards one of his disheartened supporters, Izaak Walton, wrote an overt invitation to escapism: *The Compleat Angler, or the contemplative man's recreation*, a conversation between a hunter, a falconer and a fisherman about pastimes that allowed the depressed to escape from the fractured world around them. First published in 1653, it has seen over 400 editions.[16]

Others escaped by fleeing abroad to avoid violence or vengeance. Thomas Hobbes left England for Paris in 1641, just before the Civil War, and did not return until it became clear that Parliament had won (and he had provided, in his *Leviathan*, a rationale for its rule that secured him a state pension); three years later, the marquis of Newcastle joined him, following the annihilation of his army at Marston Moor; and many other English royalists followed. Most of them remained in Europe until the Restoration in 1660 – when several of the leading British Republicans took their place. 'Bloodthirsty Mars' forced far more men and women to flee from central

Europe. Some were intellectuals at the height of their powers (like the musician Heinrich Schütz, the poet Martin Opitz, the mathematician and astronomer Johannes Kepler); others were country folk who could not protect their families, like the village shoemaker Hans Heberle, who had to flee with his family to Ulm 30 times during the Thirty Years War. Some went into exile alone, like Hugo Grotius after the execution of Oldenbarnevelt; others moved as a group, like the thousands of 'Masanielli', the unsuccessful Neapolitan rebels against Philip IV, who in 1648 took refuge in Rome, and the *malvizzi* from Messina 30 years later, hundreds of whom left for France on the fleet that evacuated the city's garrison.[17]

Escape was even more common in eastern Europe, where peasants could flee misery at home by joining the Cossacks or the Tartars to the south, or (in the case of Russian peasants) by crossing the Urals into Siberia. In addition, several Polish, Transylvanian and Austrian nobles took out 'dual citizenship' as a safeguard against potential catastrophe. Even Vasile Lupu (Basil the Wolf), prince of Moldavia, gained 'Polish citizenship' when his daughter married the son of Bohdan Khmelnytsky, explicitly with the intention of creating a safe haven in case his subjects should expel him.[18] In China, many vanquished supporters of the Ming also fled to escape situations that disheartened them: thousands of intellectuals who refused to serve the Qing, yet stopped short of open defiance, either took refuge in remote areas or moved from the household of one sympathetic colleague to another; some 60,000 Ming loyalists in 1661 followed their leader Coxinga to Taiwan, where they held out against the Qing for over two decades.

The violence of the mid-century also disheartened some of the victors. Sir Thomas Fairfax, for example, received £19,000 in salary as well as a cash gratuity of £10,000 and lands worth £4,000 per annum for his five years of service as Lord General of the New Model Army, and his name had appeared on the title page of some 700 pamphlets when in 1650, aged 38, he resigned his commission rather than lead his troops in a pre-emptive strike against Scotland. Instead he retired to his estate in Yorkshire where he composed melancholy verse (*The recreation of my solitude*) and filled 204 folio pages with his holograph translation of a Christianized Indian epic entitled *Barlaam and Josaphat*, whose highlight comes just after Josaphat, a general, 'renounced all his temporal grandure and glory'. At this point his ruler taunts him: 'Thou wast the first of my kingdom, and commander of all my forces' – Fairfax's translation deviated from the original so that it matched his own position – 'but hath mad thy selfe soe vile and contemptable as the very children mock att thee'. Fairfax remained in secluded retirement until his death in 1671.[19]

Similar sentiments afflicted Manchu Bannerman Dzengšeo, when he witnessed a 'friendly fire' incident on his way home after a tough but ultimately victorious campaign against the Three Feudatories (see chapter 5 above), mostly fought in mountains and jungle, often in torrential rain. The death of comrades profoundly upset him, and that night he recorded in his diary: 'In my heart I was frightened and, to keep myself safe, I pondered: "I have served on a military campaign for ten years, and have not lost my life in battle." ' One month later, after a victory parade before the emperor, Dzengšeo at last rejoined his family in Beijing – but still he felt unhappy, confiding to his journal: 'When I met my children and younger brothers I could not recognize them. Looking at them, the houses and the heated beds of the capital appeared even more odd, and suddenly it was like a confused, hazy dream. The more I thought about it, the more I marvelled at what seemed like being born again' (once again, a classic 'post-traumatic stress' response). Dzengšeo was a senior officer, perhaps equivalent to a lieutenant colonel, normally attended by seven or eight servants, whose family had acquired a prestigious mansion in the Chinese capital – yet neither wealth nor victory brought him mental peace after the horrors he had seen.[20]

Only the last part of Dzengšeo's campaign diary has survived, so perhaps the lost portions noted moments of intense satisfaction amid the general gloom, like those experienced by Peter Hagendorf, a Catholic foot soldier during the Thirty Years War. He, too, filled most of his diary with complaints about endless marches (he marched over 12,000 miles in under thirty years); family deaths (he buried one wife and eight children); and moments of danger (he concluded his account of Nördlingen with a series of curses: *'idiot, ass, fool, bitch* etc') – but he also noted times when he and his comrades 'lay in quarters, guzzling and boozing. It was great'. Best of all (for him), twice after the successful storm of a town, 'I got a pretty girl as my booty'. He only released them when his regiment moved on. One of Hagendorf's opponents, the Calvinist Scot Robert Monro, recalled with equal fondness the autumn of 1631, when he led his regiment through Germany:

> This march being profitable as it was pleasant to the eye. [So] we see that soldiers have not always so hard a life, as the common opinion is; for sometimes as they have abundance, so they have variety of pleasure in marching softly, without fear or danger, through fertile soils and pleasant countries, their marches being more like to a kingly progress than to wars, being in a fat land, as this was, abounding in all things except peace.

But later Monro's fortunes changed. He watched many of his comrades die; his regiment was disbanded; and in 1646, when commanding the Scottish Army in Ulster, his Catholic opponents routed him – leading him to conclude that 'the Lord of Hosts had a controversie with us to rub shame on our faces'. Two years later, like many other Scots he agreed to fight for the imprisoned Charles I against Parliament but was ignominiously captured in 'bed with his ladye' and imprisoned in the Tower of London for five years. Upon his release, like Sir Thomas Fairfax, Monro retired to his estates and remained there in seclusion until he died.[21]

Keeping Score

Such extreme swings of fortune led many seventeenth-century people to keep an intimate record of their actions. The radical Protestant Hugh Peter, a noted preacher in both England and New England, instructed his congregations that every day they should keep a journal and 'write down your sins on one side, and on the other side

God's little mercies'. Nehemiah Wallington, a London craftsman who heard (and recorded) this exhortation, rejoiced that 'by God's mercy I practice it already', and between 1637 and 1654 he filled eight volumes with his nightly 'introspections' on the public and private events that, he believed, reflected 'God's little mercies' towards him and those who shared his faith. In 1660 Samuel Pepys began his celebrated *Diary* as a spiritual journal and balance sheet, while at Whitsunday 1662, Isaac Newton (then a 19-year-old student at Cambridge) compiled a list of the 49 sins he could remember committing to that date – most of them involved disrespecting the Sabbath in some way, and beating people. (Interestingly, both Pepys and Newton compiled their record in shorthand, no doubt 'to conceal thoughts that he wished to set down for his own edification alone'.)[22] A generation later, the Reverend Gervase Disney saw no need for concealment, noting in his diary in longhand the 'mercies' and misfortunes of each day. For example, he 'took notice of the mercy shew'd my Wife, in delivering her from most acute Pains in the Tooth-Ache', and at the close of one day he proudly wrote, 'No actual Sin that I know of'. He urged his wife to follow his example. She must 'Spend thy week-days well, in the discharge of duties publick and private; keep an exact Diary of any sinful miscarriages, and be humbled every evening for them', and 'take notice of God's Mercies every day' and 'pen down God's Dealings with thee'.[23]

Devout Catholic contemporaries of Wallington, Pepys, Newton and Disney adopted similar strategies. In France, encouraged by Jansenist 'spiritual directors', some kept a record of their good and bad deeds remarkably like those enjoined by Puritan preachers across the Channel; while in Spain, a spirit of 'catastrofismo' (impending doom) led many to compose personal manuals for survival. Thus Dr Gaspar Caldera de Heredía, a gentleman of Seville, kept a journal entitled *Political tariff* (subtitled 'A guide to life in our time'), full of reflections on where his own life had gone wrong because of 'the general corruption of morals that normally characterize a great empire'.[24] Another common reaction to the crisis among seventeenth-century Catholics was to seek the intercession of saints – and the more, the better. The various communities of the kingdom of Naples 'elected' new patron saints, led by the capital city, which had seven patron saints in 1600 but over 200 a century later. There were already so many by 1624 that a special guide appeared, *Napoli sacra*, listing each shrine and its relics, together with its reputed powers. During the revolution of Naples in 1647–8 thousands of troubled men and women, conscious that those who made the wrong choice faced arrest and execution, flocked to their preferred chapel to beg for inspiration and protection. Anxious Catholics also founded, re-founded or expanded pilgrimage centres dedicated to the Virgin Mary, until in 1655 their number prompted the publication of a comprehensive guide, the *Atlas Marianus*, with an expanded edition in 1672 describing the location and 'powers' of 1,200 Marian pilgrimage centres (300 of them in Germany, almost all founded in the seventeenth century).[25]

In late Ming China, too, many worried individuals turned to introspection and self-criticism in the hope of averting disaster. Pre-printed *Ledgers of merit and demerit* (*Gongguoge: gong*, meaning 'merits'; *guo* meaning 'faults') provided a

calendar where its owner could record good and bad deeds, suggesting the appropriate 'points' for each action. It also left a space to enter a running tally.
Thus someone who gave money to the poor, and gained (say) five merits, but also
spread a slander about someone, receiving 30 demerits, would have to enter a net
score of 'minus 25'. In this way, as Cynthia Brokaw has noted, each person's 'monthly
balance helps him measure his moral progress, and at year's end his
total score indicates whether he can expect good or bad fortune from the gods in
the years ahead'.[26] Other educated Chinese kept a spiritual autobiography (in prose
for men, often in verse for women), or introspective 'travel records' (*youji*), wherein
the authors recorded and reviewed their daily deeds and thoughts. In the words
of one prominent intellectual: 'Everyday know your errors, everyday correct
your faults.' As one would expect, all three genres of 'self-writing' – ledgers,
autobiographies and travelogues – proliferated in precisely those areas of China
that experienced the greatest economic and social upheaval in the seventeenth
century: Jiangnan, Fujian and Guangdong.[27]

The Psychoactive Revolution

David Courtwright has argued that the prevailing 'melancholy' of the seventeenth
century caused the rapid spread of six substances that either stimulated or numbed
the human senses, a phenomenon he called 'the psychoactive revolution'.
Consumption of two (alcohol and opium) was already widespread, but the rest
(coffee, tea, chocolate and tobacco) were new – and several seem to have been more
potent then than they are now. Courtwright argued that consumption of these
commodities rose rapidly because they helped contemporaries to 'cope with lives
lived on the verge of the unliveable' – people, in short, 'who could use a smoke and
a drink'.[28]

And drink they did. In 1632 an English envoy to King Christian IV, then aged
55, primly remarked: 'Such is the life of that king: to drink all day and to lie with a
whore every night.' Some years earlier, one of Christian's councillors recorded the
court's drinking in his diary, grading the level of intoxication with one, two or three
crosses. On one memorable night, the diary has four crosses, followed by the prayer
'Libera nos domine' ('God spare us'). Christian and his court seem to have spent the
equivalent of one month of each year dead drunk.[29] Across the North Sea, the
English consumed over six million barrels of beer every year – more than a pint a day
for every man, woman and child – as well as two gallons of wine per person per year.
Samuel Pepys recorded in his *Diary* visits to well over 100 taverns in London in the
1660s where he drank both local ale and, thanks to the invention by English glassmakers of stronger bottle glass, more potent beers brewed in different parts of
England. Pepys and his contemporaries also relaxed in 'strong water houses' (another
seventeenth-century invention) to consume Dutch gin, French brandy, Scots and
Irish whisky and English rum. Some continental Catholics also often drank heavily
in the seventeenth century. In the aphorism of Dr Caldera's *Political tariff*, 'wine has
shipwrecked more boats than water'.[30]

The Mughal court in India also contained hard drinkers. Alcohol abuse claimed one of Emperor Jahangir's uncles, both of his brothers and a nephew; and the future emperor was himself imprisoned at one point by his father in an effort to dry him out. Jahangir nevertheless celebrated the first New Year after his accession by decreeing that 'everyone could drink whatever intoxicants or exhilarants he wanted without prohibition or impediment', and his memoirs refer to regular Thursday night parties at which he and his courtiers drank prodigiously in order to enjoy 'here on earth the future joys of paradise'. A court poet composed a witty couplet in honour of his bibulous master: 'I have two pairs of lips, one devoted to wine and the other apologizing for drunkenness.'[31] Jahangir also indulged in drugs – indeed, he employed one steward for his wine and another for his opium. According to a revealing entry in the emperor's *Autobiography*, while in hot pursuit of a rebellious son, 'When it was noon and the heat was at its hottest, I stopped for a moment in the shade of a tree and said to [an attendant] "Inasmuch as I, my composure notwithstanding, have not yet had the regular dose of opium I should have had at the beginning of the day, and no one has reminded me of it, imagine what state that wretch [my son] must be in."' As Lisa Balabanlilar has noted, 'Unapologetic drug use, and only slightly embarrassed alcoholism, received regular references in Jahangir's writings'; and even at the end of his life, when he was too ill to take opium 'of which he had been fond for forty years', he still enjoyed a few sips of wine.[32]

Visitors to other Muslim states likewise commented on the prodigious consumption of both opium and alcohol in the seventeenth century. Paul Rycaut, long time resident in the Ottoman empire, reported that it was normal for the sultan's subjects 'to be drunk, or intoxicate themselves with Aqua Vitae, opium, or any stupefying drugs'; while in Iran, although Shah Abbas II twice banned alcohol consumption and closed all taverns, at other times he and his courtiers indulged in prolonged and heavy drinking. In 1666, the year of the shah's death, his court consumed 145,000 litres of Shiraz wine. In addition, according to an English traveller, 'Opium (the juice of the poppy) is of great use' in Iran. It was, he opined, 'Good, if taken moderately; bad, nay mortal, if beyond measure; by practice they make that familiar which would kill us, so that their medicine is our poison. They chew it much, for it helps catarrhs, cowardice, and the epilepsy, strengthens (as they say) Venus.' He noted its 'use' by soldiers about to fight, messengers required to travel long distances at speed, and ordinary people trying to stave off fatigue, boredom and stress. Some ingested it as pills, others as a cordial, and a few adventurous addicts inserted it as a suppository. One French visitor claimed that only one Persian in ten did not use opium, and that, thanks to the prevailing drug culture, it was not uncommon 'to come across individuals hallucinating in the streets – speaking with or laughing at angels'. It would be easy to write off such extreme descriptions as Western bias, but in the 1660s the Iranian mullah Qummi claimed that the Sufis 'eat hashish so as to quicken' the process of attaining God, and they dispensed it freely to their disciples. Qummi also argued that the drugs associated with the Sufi lifestyle attracted many who lacked a true vocation, so that 'when one asks them what sainthood means, they say it means being a bachelor and homeless' (apparently an early formulation of Dr Timothy Leary's call to 'turn on, tune in and drop out').[33]

The consumption of coffee, tea, chocolate and tobacco also increased dramatically during the seventeenth century. In the Muslim world, coffee had long served two purposes: a stimulus to sustain religious zealots, such as Sufis and dervishes, as they sang, danced and chanted; and a social lubricant consumed in coffee houses where men gathered to talk. For precisely those reasons, the Ottoman, Mughal and Safavid governments periodically persecuted and even executed consumers – although evidently without stemming demand (see chapters 6 and 13 above). Coffee houses spread to Christian Europe somewhat later – Venice from 1645; Oxford and London from 1652; Paris from 1672 – but then proliferated rapidly. London had over 80 by 1665, and in one of them Samuel Pepys drank tea for the first time – 'I did send for a cupp of tee (a China drink) of which I never had drank before' – but found that it cost twenty times more by the pound than coffee. Consumption of both beverages remained modest in northwest Europe until the custom of taking them with sugar gained ground after the 1680s, prompting a cohort of Jesuit poets to extol their qualities in dithyrambic verses. Coffee drinkers, according to Guillaume Massieu, should consider themselves 'blessed' because 'thanks to this wonderful drink, you leap from your beds and hurry to do your duties, wishing the sun might rise earlier'. In particular, Massieu opined, preachers 'need to drink coffee because the liquid fortifies the weakened body, spreads a new vigour, a new life, in all actions, and gives the voice more strength'.[34]

Chocolate was believed to have similar properties. Samuel Pepys occasionally enjoyed a 'morning draft' in London in the 1660s; and in 1689, in Naples, Tommaso Strozzi (another Jesuit) filled three volumes with Latin verses in its honour: *On the mind's beverage; or, the manufacture of chocolate*, described the origins of cacao in the Americas, the proper way to prepare a draught, and its therapeutic powers, which (he claimed) range from curing diarrhoea (or constipation, depending on the dose), through reducing fevers, to stimulating the sexual appetite. At one point, Strozzi brought these attributes together in a notable anecdote about the recently canonized Santa Rosa of Lima, to whom an angel appeared one day bearing a drink of chocolate to cure her fever. She 'hungrily immerses her mouth and whole soul with the wounds of her crucified betrothed and, drawing deep, sucks in the delights and vital spirit from the Divinity'.[35] Drinking chocolate spread from Spain to France in the 1640s, and to England a decade later. One of London's many 'chocolate houses', where men gathered to discuss the issues of the day over a hot beverage, survives today: White's Chocolate House, opened in 1693 by an Italian immigrant, Francesco Bianco, is today White's, a Gentlemen's Club. It remains open to men only but it serves no chocolate beverages.

An English pamphlet about intoxicants reflected the rapid spread of the most popular and powerful stimulant: tobacco. The first edition, published in 1629, bore the title *Wine, beere and ale, together by the eares*; but a second edition the following year was retitled *Wine, beere, ale and tobacco, contending for superiority*. The reputation of tobacco as a prophylactic against plague led Pepys 'to buy some roll-tobacco to smell and chew' during the London plague: but his most remarkable encounter with smoking came two years later, when one of the horses pulling his coach became convulsed by shaking and seemed about to 'drop down dead' – until the coachman 'blew some tobacco [smoke] in his nose; upon which the horse sneezed, and by and by grows well and draws us the rest of our way'. When Pepys expressed surprise, the coachman observed phlegmatically: 'It's usual.' Seventeenth-century tobacco evidently contained far more powerful analgesic and psychotropic properties than any blend available today, because it not only resurrected half-dead horses but also eased pain, induced trances, suppressed hunger and staved off cold among humans. It also induced intoxication. In China in the 1620s the writer Yao Lü described how 'it can make one tipsy', and, three decades later, the German poet Jakob Balde entitled his satire on the abuse of tobacco: 'Dry drunkenness' (*Die truckene Trunckenheit*) (Plate 22).[36]

These qualities made tobacco a perfect refuge for the clinically depressed, which is no doubt why consumption soared despite the fact that in many countries consumers faced official discouragement and, sometimes, draconian punishments. In England, neither a minatory ode entitled *A counterblaste to tobacco*, composed by King James I, nor heavy taxes on those who persisted, reduced consumption: instead, annual imports of tobacco from England's American colonies rose from about 30 tons in the early 1620s to almost 1,000 tons in the late 1630s, and to over 5,000 tons by the end of the century. In China, the Chongzhen emperor tried different strategies. In 1639 he forbade tobacco cultivation, perhaps hoping to make his subjects economize, and decreed that anyone caught selling it in Beijing would be executed. He confirmed the death sentence for the first offender the following year; but, shortly afterwards, he revoked his decision in response to claims by military commanders that tobacco enabled their soldiers to withstand cold, damp and hunger. An essayist living in Shandong noted how rapidly tobacco smoking spread during the chaos of the 1640s and, as Timothy Brook has noted, 'Hundreds of poems on the subject of tobacco survive from the seventeenth and eighteenth centuries'. The elite of Qing China felt no shame about becoming 'tobacco's bond-servant' because (as one writer put it) it allowed the smoker to escape reality; indeed, claimed another, a true gentleman 'cannot do without it, however briefly, and to the end of their lives never tire of it'.[37]

In the Ottoman empire religious purists tried to eliminate tobacco precisely because it was a stimulant, and therefore prohibited by the Qu'ran. Nevertheless it grew in popularity, as did the mixture of tobacco and opium known as *barsh*, widely smoked in coffee houses and marketplaces. Periodic smoking bans had little effect until in 1633 Sultan Murad IV not only outlawed the production, sale and consumption of tobacco, but also had offenders summarily executed (see chapter 7 above). Nevertheless, as in China, soldiers broke the taboo: according to Katib Çelebi, who served as a clerk on Murad's campaigns in Iraq, hungry and tired soldiers smoked in the latrines to avoid detection until the ban lapsed. In 1691, despite continuing clerical opposition, the sultan started to tax the habit that he could not break.[38] In Russia, finally, seventeenth-century smokers ran grave personal risks. Russia could neither produce the crop domestically (like India, Iran and China) nor import it cheaply from a colony (like Britain): every pound had to be purchased abroad. This practice not only worried the government, because of the outflow of wealth, but also incurred the wrath of the Orthodox Church which condemned everything 'Western'. As in the Ottoman empire, buying and selling tobacco became a capital offence in 1633 (the following year the traveller Adam Olearius saw eight men and a woman flogged for selling tobacco); while the law code of 1649 (the *Ulozhenie*) contained 11 articles against tobacco, including one that reaffirmed the death penalty for possession and trading. Nevertheless, in Russia as elsewhere irrepressible demand led to rising consumption as the century advanced.[39]

Peace Breaks Out

Each of these *individual* 'coping strategies' to overcome the 'melancholy' induced by the crisis of the mid-seventeenth century emerged independently of – and often in spite of – the state. The same was true of several *collective* 'coping strategies'. All of them depended on the restoration of peace and a climate of security, sometimes after decades of war; and, as the nobility of Russia reminded their tsar in 1653, when he invited their views on attacking the Polish-Lithuanian Commonwealth: 'It is indeed easy to pull the sword from the scabbard, but not so easy to put it back when you want.' Their plea failed. A few months later, the tsar began a war that would last for 13 years.[40]

Except in Europe, seventeenth-century wars normally ended when one protagonist prevailed over its rivals by force of arms. Thus Japan's 'Warring States Era' ended when the armies of the Tokugawa Ieyasu defeated the forces of his remaining enemies in a series of battles around Osaka Castle, which they burnt down, and forced all the opposing leaders to commit suicide. Ieyasu then ordered the emperor to declare a new imperial era, *Genna*, and proclaimed his victory to be 'the Genna armistice' (*Genna enbu*). Likewise the 'Great Enterprise' of the Qing ended only when they had executed the last Ming Pretender and compelled the last Ming loyalists to submit and shave their foreheads; while the civil war among the four sons of the Mughal emperor Shah Jahan ended only when Aurangzeb had defeated and executed virtually all his male relatives.[41] In the Americas, both wars between the Europeans and the native inhabitants, and wars between different groups of native inhabitants, normally ended with the death of almost all the vanquished males and the enslavement of their families.

In Europe, by contrast, between 1648 and 1661 several wars that had ravaged the continent for a generation came to an end thanks to a series of delicate negotiated compromises born of exhaustion and popular anti-war sentiment. Western literature has always contained a strong anti-war component. In the 1620s a French writer observed that 'for every two soldiers enriched by war you will find fifty who received only injuries or incurable diseases'; and a decade later, a Danish nobleman quoted Pindar, a Greek poet of the fifth century BC, when he instructed his younger brother, about to go to war:

Consider carefully what you are seeking when you call yourself a soldier. Take
care that a vain and worldly desire to carry this name does not rule you, and
that being among those who shout *dulce bellum, dulce bellum* [sweet war, sweet
war], does not cause you to shout it along with them. Let it not be a joy for you to
see blood.[42]

Such sentiments multiplied as the wars dragged on, ruining people and property.
At the head of each double-page spread of his 'Historical notes and meditations' that
dealt with the campaigns of Charles I, the London craftsman Nehemiah Wallington
wrote '*Of the bitternesse of warre and the miseries that war brings*'. One English
pamphlet of 1642 warned that 'None knowes the misery of warre but those that see
it'; while another reminded readers of the 'manifold miseries' that civil war would
bring, to judge 'by the examples of Germany, France, Ireland and other places'.[43]
Four years later, some Welsh royalists noted that those who, back in 1642, had
'violently bed [bayed] for war', now 'prefer by far/An unjust peace before the justest
war'. As he travelled through southern England that year, the young Robert Boyle
was appalled by the general insecurity: 'Good God!', he wrote to his sister: 'That
reasonable creatures, that call themselves Christians too, should delight in such an
unnatural thing as war, where cruelty at least becomes necessity'. The following year,
in Germany, a desperate entry in a peasant family's diary reads: 'We live like animals,
eating bark and grass. No one could imagine that anything like this could happen to
us. Many people say there is no God.'[44]

Anti-war sentiments also multiplied in art and literature, especially after 1630.
Many painters and engravers emphasized the arbitrary and catastrophic nature of
war, seeking not only to document but also to deter. The stark engravings of Jacques
Callot's 'Grandes Misères de la Guerre' ('Miseries of War'), each one with a caption
condemning the barbarity of the soldiers, do not stand alone. In Germany, Hans
Ulrich Franck produced a series of 24 engravings known as 'The theatre of war' with
a title page on which curtains reveal a stage where an officer brandishes his weapon
while trying to keep his balance upon Fortune's globe. The motto reads: 'O hark!
Attend to the present; observe the future; and do not forget the end.' Even the enormous glass beakers known as *Humpen*, made to commemorate the end of the Thirty
Years War, showed 'God the Father leaning down out of heaven' to bless the emperor,
the king of France and the queen of Sweden, with an extremely long didactic legend
that began: 'Thy peace, thy peace, thy divine peace: never take it from us again. Let
the same be handed down to our children; Let it remain on the earth for our
descendants; Let the destroyed churches and schools be rebuilt; Let . . .'[45] Musicians,
too, hated war. As early as 1623, one composer lamented that the war had placed a
spear in the hand of princes with which to kill musicians, just as the Devil had
given Saul a spear to kill the harpist David: 'Saul's spear is . . . in the hands of court
finance ministers who lock their doors when they hear musicians approach'. Heinrich
Schütz, court musician of Electoral Saxony and the finest composer of his day,
was compelled to arrange short choral pieces of religious music for only 'one, two,
three or four voices with two violins, 'cello and organ', because the war left him

neither choirs nor orchestras for anything grander. 'The times neither demand nor
allow music on a big scale,' he complained. 'It is now impossible to perform music on
a large scale or with many choirs'. In the preface to his *Small spiritual concerti* of 1636,
he claimed that he published not so that his works could be performed, because few
places boasted sufficient musicians, but so that he would not forget how to compose.[46]
Of Schütz's 70 surviving works, 30 were lamentations.

Writers of both verse and prose cried out for peace with mounting stridency
as the wars continued. In 1642, at the first performance of his play *Friedens Sieg*
('The Victory of Peace'), written by Justus Georg Schottel, tutor to the duke of
Brunswick's children, his charges acted the leading parts while their parents and the
Elector of Brandenburg watched.[47] One of the moving hymns written by Lutheran
Pastor Paul Gerhardt began: 'Oh come on! Wake up, wake up you hard world: open
your eyes before terror comes upon you in swift sudden surprise'; while in Book II
of *Paradise Lost*, probably written in 1660, John Milton offered a powerful
denunciation of the long-term as well as the short-term evils caused by war:

> Say they who counsel warr, we are decreed,
> Reserv'd and destin'd to Eternal woe;
> Whatever doing, what can we suffer more,
> What can we suffer worse?
>
> ... And what peace can we return,
> But to our power hostility and hate,
> Untam'd reluctance, and revenge though slow,
> Yet ever plotting how the Conqueror least
> May reap his conquest, and may least rejoyce
> In doing what we most in suffering feel?[48]

In 1668, in Germany, Hans Jakob Christoffel von Grimmelshausen published *The
adventures of a German simpleton* expressly to remind 'posterity about the terrible
crimes that were committed in our German war'. It begins when the author, a farm
boy aged ten (and thus a 'simpleton' about the wider world), watches a group of
'iron men' (whom he later learns are cavalry troopers) torture the men and rape the
women on his farm, and then take away all they can carry and burn the rest.
Simplicissimus only survives to narrate later outrages because he feigns death
when one of the 'iron men' shoots at him before riding away. The book proved an
immediate best-seller.[49]

As Theodore K. Rabb observed in his landmark study, *The Struggle for Stability in
Early Modern Europe*: 'The shock of unbridled chaos, of a myriad of competing
claims battling each other to extinction, made thoughtful men realize that these
reckless assertions of private will were the surest route to disaster.' Since Classical
history formed an integral part of the educational curriculum in most parts of
Europe, many members of the elite no doubt drew parallels with the political
resignation that prevailed among the ruling elite after civil wars destroyed the
Roman Republic. Freedom 'was indeed lost, but most of the old nobility who best

understood it and prized it most highly perished in the wars and proscriptions; their few survivors were ready to pay the price for security'.[50] Similar conformist arguments gained ground in Europe in the mid-seventeenth century.

In 1647 a Welsh royalist confided to his journal that 'All innovation and change in government is very bad and dangerous. That form is always best which is in being, [because] the difficulties of alteration are so many and dangerous'. Four years later, Thomas Hobbes's *Leviathan* enjoined obedience to the new English Republic, regardless of its dubious legitimacy, because 'If a monarch subdued by war render himself subject to the victor' (Hobbes hardly needed to remind his readers that Charles I had just done this), then 'his subjects are delivered from their former obligation, and become obliged to the victor'. Many other English publications at the time, some sponsored by the Republican regime, advanced the same argument (albeit in a less comprehensive and memorable way).[51] In Catalonia, a French agent reported in 1644 that the local clergy 'say that since the obedience promised to France has no other foundation than the protection it promised, they are freed from their oath by the lack of such protection'; while five years later a Paris pamphleteer reminded his fellow subjects that monarchs 'owe us their protection just as we owe them our obedience'.[52]

A decade later John Locke welcomed the Restoration of King Charles II, not least because 'I no sooner perceived myself in the world but I found myself in a storm, which hath lasted almost hitherto'. Now, he felt obliged 'to endeavour [the] continuance' of the new regime 'by disposing men's minds to obedience to that government which brought with it quiet and settlement which our own giddy folly had put beyond the reach, not only of our contrivance, but hopes'. The 'storm' in England also appalled some foreign visitors. Peder Schumacher, from Denmark, spent three years studying at Queen's College, Oxford, where he may have read the political works of Thomas Hobbes. He certainly witnessed the decline and fall of the English Republic in 1658–60 before he went to Paris and observed Louis XIV's measures to consolidate his personal power. On his return to Denmark, Schumacher applied these experiences to draft the 'Royal Law' (*Kongelov*): the constitution of 1665 that conferred 'supreme power and authority' on the king.[53]

No More Wars

Other survivors of Europe's wars proposed mechanisms to avoid future wars entirely. Some wrote treatises advocating 'universal peace'. In 1623 the French monk Emeric Crucé proposed the creation of a permanent international assembly of ambassadors, to whom sovereigns would present their differences for adjudication, solemnly swearing to accept the majority decision (although, if they failed, states should enforce a settlement through economic and even military sanctions). It was to be a truly international body, and although Crucé proposed Venice as its ideal location, he felt confident that 'navigation can overcome [the] difficulty' that delegates from Persia, China and the Americas would face in getting there. Two years later, the Dutch polymath Hugo Grotius published a book entitled *The law of War and Peace*, proposing conventions to avoid needless wars, and also needless brutality in the wars that nevertheless occurred. In 1693 the Quaker colonizer William Penn published *An essay towards the present and future peace of Europe, by the establishment of an European Diet*, which suggested an international tribunal, very similar to Crucé's, to resolve international disputes peacefully, albeit only in Europe, and if any nation refuse to accept arbitration (or took up arms unilaterally) 'all other sovereignties, united as one strength, shall compel [its] submission'.[54]

These and other seventeenth-century writers who proposed universal solutions to what they perceived as a universal problem all wrote in wartime. Those who wrote just after a war, by contrast, tended to adopt a more limited and more pragmatic approach. In 1648 and again in 1652 the Estates of Hessen-Kassel submitted a formal petition asking the Supreme Court of the Holy Roman Empire to protect them with constitutional guarantees to safeguard them from 'being deprived of their liberties and from being led into one bloody massacre after another like innocent lambs'. When Hans Heberle, the long-suffering village shoemaker near Ulm, heard in 1667 that France had declared war on Spain again, he confided to his diary 'we beg God Almighty from the bottom of our hearts that he protect and shield our Germany and the whole Holy Roman Empire' from another incursion of 'foreign troops *because we experienced and suffered enough in the Thirty Years War*'.[55] Perhaps the most striking expression of such 'never again' sentiments came in 1661, when Sweden's regency government discussed whether or not to continue the wars inherited from the late King Charles X. Gustav Bonde, the treasurer, reminded his colleagues that

> War makes the most serious inroads upon the resources of the crown, and entails impoverishment and ruin of the subject; and we have learned by experience that no war in past times has brought renown, profit or advantage to king and country, without also exacting large annual expenditure of our resources, and burdening the subject with taxes and conscription ... It seems therefore necessary that we make up our minds to a period of peace, and lay aside all thought of war as long as peace is to be had.

Bonde conceded that recent wars had produced benefits for Sweden, but he still concluded that his colleagues should not

> Direct our thoughts to further wars, and make plans upon the supposition that God will always arrange for a similar outcome to all our actions. We should remember rather that the issue of war is always uncertain, and is frequently most disastrous for those who believe themselves to have the justest cause.[56]

Bonde's views prevailed – Sweden remained at peace for another decade – and although most states, including England and Russia as well as Sweden, would fight wars again, they did so with far less frequency than in the preceding half century. In England, for example, as soon as news arrived that Prince William of Orange had landed in southwest England with a powerful army in 1688, King James II and his ministers sent envoys to ask the prince to state his purpose, 'because they dread the thoughts of a war, for the bloudshed and all other evills that attend it alwaies'. This 'dread' helps to explain why the 'Glorious Revolution' involved no 'bloudshed' in England.[57]

One of the 'evills' that attended the wars of the mid-seventeenth century was their duration. In Europe, even the negotiations about ending hostilities could last for years – largely because neither side trusted the other. Thus in the summer of 1643 the French and Spanish governments sent 'Instructions' to their plenipotentiaries at the Congress of Westphalia that virtually precluded a settlement: 'Experience has shown that [the other side] does not honour the treaties it makes' – indeed, the two sides used identical words. Such incompatible views help to explain why it proved impossible to reconcile outstanding differences between these two protagonists at Westphalia (achieved only at the peace of the Pyrenees in 1659).[58] Negotiations between the other protagonists dragged on for five years not only through lack of political trust but also through incompatible religious demands. The Protestant and Catholic German delegates agreed on a common formula only in March 1648, and only by agreeing to differ:

> In matters of Religion, and in all other Affairs, wherein the States of the Empire cannot be considered as a single Body, and when the Catholic States and the Lutheran States are divided into two Parties; the Difference shall be decided *exclusively by amicable composition, without either side being coerced by a plurality of voices.*

Many wept when the measure passed, because it cleared the path to a final settlement (signed six months later) hailed by later generations as 'the foremost bulwark of freedom and equality, built with so much blood'. For over a century, armed conflicts between Catholics and Protestants had provided an excuse for foreign states to intervene, and so civil wars often engendered foreign wars. Henceforth, no German ruler could exploit religious divisions to provoke or prolong a war – and neither could foreign rulers.[59]

This marked a major step towards restoring stability because, as Thomas Hobbes forcefully stated in 1641: 'I am sure that experience teaches, thus much, that the dispute for [precedence] betwene the spirituall and civill power has of late more than any other thing in the world bene the cause of civill warres in all places of Christendome.' Two decades later, John Locke 'observed that almost all those tragical revolutions which have exercised Christendom these many years have turned upon this hinge'. Indeed, he continued, 'there hath been no design so wicked which hath not worn the visor of religion, nor rebellion which hath not' proclaimed 'a design either to supply the defects or correct the errors of religion'.

> Hence have the cunning and malice of men taken occasion to pervert the doctrine of peace and charity into a perpetual foundation of war and contention, all those flames that have made such havoc and desolation in Europe, and have not been quenched but with the blood of so many millions, have been at first kindled with coals from the altar, and too much blown with the breath of those that

attend the altar, who, forgetting their calling, which is to promote peace and meekness, have proved [to be] the trumpeters of strife and sounded a charge with a '*Curse ye Meros*'.[60]

Locke's citation of a text frequently used by radical preachers during the Civil War to incite political action did not stand alone. Samuel Butler's mock-epic poem *Hudibras*, 'written in the time of the late wars' and first published in 1662, recalled the time

When civil fury first grew high,
And men fell out, they knew not why;
When hard words, jealousies, and fears,
Set folks together by the ears,
And made them fight, like mad or drunk,
For Dame Religion . . .

He poured ridicule on those who

. . . do build their faith upon
The holy text of pike and gun;
Decide all controversies by
Infallible artillery;
And prove their doctrine orthodox
By apostolic blows and knocks;
Call fire and sword and desolation,
A godly thorough reformation.

According to Samuel Pepys, the book enjoyed immediate success – 'all the world cries up [the poem] to be the example of wit' – and it went through numerous editions.[61]

Although religious differences continued to affect European politics – some rulers expelled religious minorities, as the Catholic Louis XIV did the French Huguenots, while supporters hailed Protestant William III as Gideon and David when he went to war against Louis XIV – the views advanced by Locke and Butler steadily gained ground. Indeed, in 1689 Locke restated his condemnation of faith-based politics more forcefully in his *Letter concerning toleration*:

Nobody, therefore, in fine, neither single persons nor churches, nay, nor even commonwealths, have any just title to invade the civil rights and worldly goods of each other upon pretence of Religion. . . . No peace and security . . . can ever be established or preserved amongst men, so long as this opinion prevails: *that dominion is founded upon grace, and that religion is to be propagated by force of arms.*

According to Heinz Schilling, an eminent historian of religion, 'The end of confessional Europe, properly speaking, came around 1650' through 'the internal dissolution of orthodoxy and through the state's deconfessionalization of politics and society'; while, as his distinguished colleague Philip Benedict noted, 'religious conflicts spaced themselves out over time with diminishing frequency'.[62]

Signing a peace treaty after a prolonged war nevertheless marked just the beginning of efforts to heal the scars, end the fears and create a climate of trust. Many authorities prohibited any discussion of the recent contentious past. In 1648 the peace of Westphalia forbade 'any person to impugn in any place, in publick or in private, by preaching, teaching, disputing, writing or consulting, the Transaction of Passau [of 1552], the Peace of Religion [of 1555], and, above all, the present declaration or transaction; or to render them doubtful'. Already in London, the group of scholars who would later become the first Fellows of the Royal Society had resolved upon a similar accommodation: from its 'first ground and foundation' in 1645, at their weekly meetings, members 'barred all discourses of divinity, state-affairs, and of news ... confining ourselves to philosophical inquiries'.[63] Fifteen years later, on his return to England, Charles II followed their wise example and signed legislation that forbade the law courts to hear any suit arising from things 'counselled, commanded, acted or done' during 'the late distractions'. He also issued a temporary prohibition on even speaking about the recent past: 'If any person or persons, *within the space of three years next ensuing*, shall presume maliciously to call, or allege of, or object against any other person or persons any name or names, or other words of reproach, any way leading to revive the memory of the late differences, or the occasion thereof', the offender must pay a fine 'unto the party grieved'. He held those who served him to a higher standard. A naval lieutenant who in 1665 taunted his captain and another officer 'with their having been rebels and served under Cromwell's commission' was brought before a court martial chaired by Charles's brother, the future James II, in person:

> For which offences [the lieutenant] was adjudged to be cashiered from his employment in the fleet. His Royal Highness [James] very graciously was pleased to express the King's Majesty's and his own displeasure against recounting of former differences and parties. Said that all of the commanders were equally esteemed good subjects and officers, and he doubted not but they would so approve themselves in all occasions, and he would severely reprehend any expressions of past divisions.

The impact of this policy of forced reconciliation may be seen in the careful phrasing of the petitions by royalist veterans seeking compensation for losses and injuries during the war (they studiously avoided terms like 'rebel' and 'rebellion'), as in the requests of scientists like Samuel Hartlib for government funding (see chapter 22 below), who when explaining the delay in completing a project always referred to 'the troubles'.[64] Thus did England heal herself after almost two decades of war.

Her success was remarkable because, as Sir John Plumb pointed out, 'by 1688 conspiracy and rebellion, treason and plot, were a part of the history and experience of at least three generations of Englishmen'; and yet, 'by comparison, the political structure of eighteenth-century England possesses adamantine strength and profound inertia'. Plumb stressed that political stability (which he defined as 'the acceptance by society of its political institutions, and of those classes of men or officials who control them') did not become a common political phenomenon until relatively recently. Moreover, stability 'often happens to a society quite quickly'; and 'when achieved, it has seldom lasted'.[65] Plumb attributed the growth of political stability in England to three structural changes in the wake of the crisis of the mid-seventeenth century: a transition from population loss to population growth; the resumption and diversification of economic activity; and the decision of governments to invest both their attention and their resources in welfare instead of (or as well as) warfare. His model works not only for England but also for other states in the northern hemisphere where, taken together, the same three changes ended the fatal synergy that had first produced and then prolonged the crisis.

From Warfare State to Welfare State

The Phoenix Effect

H ANS JAKOB CHRISTOFFEL VON GRIMMELSHAUSEN CHOSE A STRIKING IMAGE for the frontispiece of his 1668 novel, *The adventures of a German simpleton*: a phoenix, pointing to an open book that contains images of war (Plate 23). The verse below the engraving began:

> Like a Phoenix I was born in the fire;

and continued with the question:

> What often grieved me, and seldom brought joy?
> What was it? I've written it down in this book.

Grimmelshausen's studied use of the past tense, and his image of a bird that rises from its own ashes, exuded confidence that the 'fire' was over; likewise the way his 'German simpleton' interspersed events from 'our German war' with those from Classical authors and the Bible implied that the age of wanton destruction of people and property had passed.

To test Grimmelshausen's perception, historians can consult quantitative data such as tolls and tax returns, harvest and tithe yields and baptismal registers; but since almost all of them relate to individual communities, they may not be 'typical'. By contrast the accounts of foreign travellers, though impressionistic, provide eyewitness observations that cover far larger areas. In 1663 Philip Skippon, the son of the eponymous English Civil War general and his German wife, undertook a 'Grand Tour' through Germany, Austria and Italy with his Cambridge tutor, Dr John Ray. He was immediately struck by the rapid post-war repopulation and reconstruction of Germany. 'Since the instrument of peace,' wrote Skippon (meaning the Peace of Westphalia in 1648), 'the people of this country have recruited themselves very much'. An anonymous Italian visitor the previous year confirmed this impression: 'although you see few people of fighting age,' he observed, 'there are an infinite number of children'. Skippon and Ray included numerous examples of renewal in their travelogues. For instance, although 'the wars destroyed all the old town' of Mannheim (ten miles from Heidelberg), now 'the streets are designed to be uniform' with 'all the buildings alike in broad and straight streets'. They found Heidelberg, too, 'populous, which is much considering the devastations made by the late wars in this country. The houses are most of timber, yet handsom and in good repair, which argues the inhabitants to be industrious and in a thriving condition'. Vienna likewise impressed both men: Skippon found it 'very populous' and its 'streets (except those at London) the most frequented we yet saw', while Ray considered it 'the most frequented and full of people that we have yet seen beyond the seas'.[1]

Such urban regeneration was not universal. The anonymous Italian visitor to Germany in 1662 remarked that 'few towns have managed to recover from the damage sustained during the war, and many of the largest ones remain virtually depopulated'; while the following year Dr Ray considered Augsburg 'for the bigness, not very populous and [it] is, I believe, somewhat decayed, and short of what it hath been, both as to riches and multitude of inhabitants; which may be attributed to the losses and injuries it susteined in the late wars'. In 1671 the Paris physician Charles Patin still found at Höchst, just outside Frankfurt, many signs of 'the deplorable consequences of the war. This beautiful city' was now 'no more than a village,' he wrote. Further east, between Jena and Leipzig, scene of several battles, Patin noted that the bodies of the 'nine or ten thousand men buried there still seems to provide manure for the fields' and predicted that 'all the surrounding towns will bear for a long time the sad traces of the war'. He concluded sagely and sadly: 'War spares nothing.'[2]

The rapid recovery of Germany's rural economy also impressed foreign visitors. Thus as he approached Munich in 1658, the itinerant Scots divinity student James Fraser admired the 'groves, gardins, parks, fertil cornfields and pretty brookes, fish ponds stored with carp and tinch and trout' all along his route – even though troops had repeatedly ravaged Bavaria during the second half of the Thirty Years War. Similarly, as he approached Regensburg (the scene of a protracted siege), Fraser found a 'croud of pedlers and pannier-bearers that passe here, selling baken bread, boiled eggs, fruits, stockings, shoes, caps or anything that yow need to the least needle . . . They are very curteous and discreet, and it's a wonder how cheap they sell those things.' In 1671, as Edward Brown (an English physician) passed through Hessen, ravaged by war for almost two decades, he found 'the whole country planted with wallnut trees, vines, corn and in some places with tobacco'. Further east, when Patrick Gordon (another itinerant Scot) and his regiment marched through 'the villages and little townes' of Poland, he found that they 'had abundance of all things – whereat I admired, considering how the countrey had been so often ruined by the enemyes, and no much better used by our owne soldiery'; but he later reflected that 'albeit many of their houses looke very waist lyke, as being destitute of hangings, standing beds, stooles or pictures . . . yet there is superfluity of good, well-dressed [prepared] victualls and liquor'. After serving as a battleground for a generation, the Polish population had evidently learned that it made sense to minimize possessions that could be taken as booty and maximize the portable necessities of life.[3]

In China, the nature of the surviving evidence complicates efforts to assess the devastation caused by the Ming-Qing transition. On the one hand, 'official records of harvests, grain prices, rainfall, granary stocks, and the like were carefully kept, but no one counted or recorded the number of deaths from disasters'; so there are no estimates of human losses. On the other hand, virtually no Han Chinese artists included military themes in their repertory, while Manchu artists (who did) naturally eschewed scenes of the destruction wrought by their troops. By contrast, as Grace Fong has observed, 'Chinese poetry from its very beginning has given full expression to the tragedies of war'; or, in the words of the poet Gui Zhuang, who lost one sister-in-law to soldiers and another to bandits: 'My grief has no outlet. I weep for her with poetry'.[4] The mid-seventeenth century crisis generated an outpouring of grief from men and women remarkable for both its intensity and variety. One particularly moving poem came from the pen of the Shanghai poet and Qing minister Li Wen. He became prominent in the *Fu she* ('Reformation Society') and remained in Beijing throughout 1644. When the soldiers of the Dashing Prince murdered his father, Li Wen offered his services to the Qing, and for the next two years he served as Dorgon's secretary, drafting most of the regent's Chinese procla-mations and public documents. In 1646 Li requested and received permission to visit his Jiangnan home, and the desolation that he encountered on his journey south left him appalled. He wrote a poem entitled 'On the road out: gazing in astonishment and seeing places which the bandits have destroyed':

> . . . Stark are the thousand miles over which the bandits came,
> Seared are the many hills beneath the sun.
> Travellers gladly leave these hearths behind;
> Residents rely [only] on low walls.
> If half the Central Plain is like this,
> How can one escape wind and frost?

Chen Bangyan, commander of Ming forces further south in Guangdong, wrote a short poem after Qing forces entered the city he was defending (they later tortured him to death):

> No fists, no braves left. No rations, no soldiers.
> Bonded with mountains and sea, I swore to help restore [the Ming.]
> Fate gave us no help. We were entangled in misfortune.
> One thousand autumns hence, let this solitary inscription give witness.[5]

Perhaps, however, some Chinese writers overlooked signs of post-war recovery. Although poets continued for over a century to use the metaphor 'the Weed-covered city' whenever they referred to Yangzhou, whose sack in 1645 was the most brutal episode of the entire Ming-Qing transition (see chapter 5 above), the city's school reopened within a year, and two years after that a dozen home-grown scholars took and passed the metropolitan examination – an unequivocal sign that some of the elite had survived the atrocities and accepted Qing rule. Within a decade Yangzhou boasted a new foundling home and several restored temples; and by 1664, according to one contemporary, more than one hundred gardens adorned the waterways just outside the city walls, where pleasure boats could be rented. After another decade, the local Gazetteer depicted Yangzhou as once again a suitable venue for scholars to meet and write, drink wine and tour the sites; and when the Kangxi emperor visited these sites, local merchants, officials, poets and artists entertained him with opera, banquets and lantern shows. The 'Weed-covered city' had come a long way.[6]

As in Europe, travel journals also illuminate the extent of postwar recovery. In 1658 Johannes Nieuhof, secretary of a Dutch diplomatic mission, kept a detailed illustrated journal of what he saw as he travelled the 1,500 miles that separate Canton from Beijing. Although he included no images of a ruined city (perhaps because the Qing official on his barge forbade him), Nieuhof noted that one town after another had been 'totally ruin'd and sack'd' by the Qing, starting with Canton, which was 'turn'd to a map of misery' when Tartars took it by storm in 1650, with 'more than 80,000 people slain, not including those who perished with hunger'. At Nanchang, a provincial capital, all but one of the 'rare buildings which had been formerly in this city were totally destroy'd by the Tartars'; while Hutron (Jiangxi province), 'a very pleasant city full of industry *before the distruction of China*', was now desolate.[7]

Nevertheless, like the poets who harped upon the 'Weed-covered city', Nieuhof exaggerated. First, as in Germany, some of the urban centres 'totally ruin'd' by troops made a rapid recovery. Thus only six years after the sack, Nieuhof found Canton once more a thriving commercial centre. 'Although this city was lamentably laid waste,' he wrote, 'it was in a few years after restor'd to its former lustre.' Second, Nieuhof conceded that while 'It is a maxim among the Tartars, that such cities as revolt against them, and are subdu'd by force of arms, should be serv'd after this manner' – that is, sacked – '*such as yield without any opposition, have no hurt done unto them*'. Since almost every town along the Grand Canal had opened its gates to the Qing 'without any opposition', north of Yangzhou Nieuhof found bustling economic activity and 'great store of rice' almost everywhere, and a countryside 'so full of buildings as if it were all but one continu'd village'.[8]

If only such optimistic parts of Nieuhof's travelogue had survived – or if Ray's *Observations* were the only source on post-war Germany – historians might with justification ask 'Crisis? What crisis?' Travellers, however, tend to follow the fastest and safest route between one notable tourist site and the next, and Nieuhof travelled up the Grand Canal in style aboard a special barge, while Ray did the same as he and his students travelled up the Rhine. The Scottish student James Fraser also took the highways, not the byways, and therefore tended to pass through precisely those areas likely to have recovered fastest – which would explain the presence of that 'curteous and discreet' 'croud of pedlers and pannier-bearers'. Nevertheless, the ashes of war, like a run of natural disasters, did not always produce a phoenix: sometimes they stifled rather than stimulated the survivors. To reprise just three rural examples: in the Scottish borders, farmers *never* returned to cultivate the Pentland Hills after global cooling and marauding troops ended the viability of their farms; in India, the cotton and cotton weavers of Gujarat *never* returned after famine and floods destroyed the market for their goods; and in China, sericulture *vanished* from the province of Shaanxi after the trauma of the Ming-Qing transition, despite a tradition that went back 2,000 years. The same was true of towns. For every Nanjing there was a Nanchang, for every Vienna there was a Höchst: places whose population would remain below – often far below – pre-war levels for the rest of the century and even beyond. Demographic recovery after the Global Crisis depended on a *benign synergy* of human and natural factors.

'Be Fruitful and Multiply'

Much of pre-industrial Europe saw a 'baby boom' whenever wars ceased because (in the words of a French man of letters) some areas were 'so fertile that what war destroys in one year regenerates in two'; while others (in the words of another scholar) 'resemble a fine fat bird: the more you pluck it, the more its feathers grow'. The later seventeenth century was no exception.[9] Abandoned farms on prime land normally recovered first and fastest, their natural fertility temporarily enhanced by enforced fallowing; and as soon as it was safe to do so, unmarried or widowed survivors took advantage of the vacant lands and houses left by each catastrophe (whether human or natural in origin) to marry, move in and start a family. In Italy's Aosta valley, war and plague killed 600 inhabitants of one village in 1630–1, leaving about 600 survivors; yet whereas the 1620s saw only 5 marriages a year, 14 took place in 1630 and 38 in 1631. Moreover, whereas the annual average number of baptisms in the 1620s had been 24, the year 1630 saw 42, and each year of the next decade saw 25 – meaning that a population half the size had managed to produce more babies.[10]

The return of security stimulated not only increases in the native population of war-ravaged villages on fertile land but also a flood of immigrants. Thus although the Thirty Years War reduced by 80 per cent the population of the lands ruled by the Benedictine monastery of Ottobeuren in south Germany (a fief consisting of a market town, 18 villages and scores of scattered hamlets), as soon as peace returned 'literally thousands of travellers' arrived 'from all over Germany and indeed from all over Europe'. Some were inhabitants returning after taking refuge elsewhere, while the rest included 'travelling players, demobilized soldiers, widows, orphans, and vagrants', such as 'Monsieur Robert de Villa, French nobleman', 'Nicholas Harp from London in England with four children' and the 'noble Irish lord' Raymond O'Dea 'plundered and driven into exile by the English heretics'. Many of these homeless refugees settled in the half-empty villages of the Ottobeuren lands: almost half of all the marriages in the estate in the 1650s involved at least one immigrant.[11]

Urban populations could also rebound swiftly after a catastrophe. In Italy, marriages in the port-city of Genoa during each of the three years after the plague of 1656–7 were twice as numerous as in the three years before – for much the same reasons as in the Aosta valley: the catastrophe had left a glut of vacant houses and jobs, and so people could afford to marry younger. Elsewhere, in-migration proved critical. In the Ottoman empire, the population of the port-city of Izmir (Smyrna) in Anatolia rose from perhaps 3,000 in 1603 to 40,000 in 1648 and over 100,000 in 1700, largely through migration – some from neighbouring villages, others from the Balkans (including the parents of Shabbatai Zvi), and others still from beyond, such as refugees from the massacres in the Polish-Lithuanian Commonwealth (including

Sarah, the wife of Shabbatai). In Spain, the population of the port-city of Cádiz tripled from 7,000 in 1600 to 22,000 in 1650, and almost doubled again to 41,000 in 1700, thanks to three factors: strong in-migration from the surrounding villages; a strict quarantine that excluded the plague epidemic that devastated its economic rival Seville in 1649–50; and the city's growing trade with the Americas (largely at the expense of Seville).[12]

Accommodating migrants sometimes required compromises. Thus the city of Venice lost almost 50,000 of its citizens during the plague of 1630–1, over half of them 'merchants and artisans' belonging to the city's guilds. Previously, all guilds had admitted only native sons, but for three years after the plague they welcomed qualified immigrants in order to restore their numerical strength. In Brandenburg, the 'Great Elector' Frederick William issued a decree 'by virtue of princely power and sovereign authority' that 'all persons prepared to rebuild a devastated and abandoned peasant farm must without exception be granted six years free of taxes, rents, and military quartering' – a measure that provoked widespread protests from landowners who resented the unilateral declaration of a rent 'holiday' and feared that foreign colonists would simply come, 'exhaust the soil' and then 'disappear into the dust'. Naturally the Great Elector ignored the protests. Most remarkable of all, the city-state of Lucca sought to replace its plague dead after 1631 by granting safe conduct and asylum to all outlaws from other states (provided they had not committed treason, heresy, counterfeiting or murder on the highway). The certificates of asylum issued expressly to restore the population to its pre-plague level fill two fat registers in the city archives.[13]

Many post-war migrants were veterans. Thus almost 5,000 infantry and 3,000 cavalry returned to Finland in 1650 after the end of the 'continental war', their pockets filled with the money provided by German taxpayers to pay their wage arrears. Even more veterans went home to Sweden, and since most of them were in their late teens and twenties, their return with money in their pockets added a substantial cohort of 'eligible bachelors' to communities where, for many years, women had far outnumbered men (see chapter 8 above).[14] In France, Spain, the Low Countries and Switzerland, too, the return of the veterans no doubt injected wealth into countless communities; while in England, between 1660 and 1662, the king's treasury paid out nearly £800,000 in wage arrears to the thousands of soldiers and sailors of the Republic who laid down their arms at the Restoration – and thus returned to civilian life far richer than they had left it.[15]

Nevertheless, despite a baby boom and an influx of migrants, the same factors that normally limited population growth in the early modern world still prevailed. Steady and significant demographic increase required not only the return of peace but also a respite from epidemic diseases, and the return of prosperity for merchants and manufacturers. Although this constellation prevailed in Japan and Mughal India after the 1650s, the population of most west European states began to recover only after the famine of 1660–2, while in China the 'Kangxi depression' (caused by the continuing war against Ming loyalists and the embargo on coastal trade) lasted until the 1680s. Moreover, even with optimal economic conditions, the 'depleted cohorts' created by major catastrophes earlier in the century – 1618–21, 1630–1, 1647–53, 1661–2 – continued to restrict growth. Not only did these cohorts lack the numbers to restore the previous population level, by a sad coincidence new episodes of famine or disease further reduced their numbers just as they reached marriageable age: 1672–5, 1694–6 and so on (see chapter 4 above). Finally, the 'urban graveyard effect' continued to take its toll. Thus in northern Italy, famine, plague and war ravaged the duchy of Mantua in 1630–1, affecting city and countryside alike; and yet, three decades later, some English tourists found Mantua 'a great city but not answerably populous, having not yet recovered it self of the losses it sustained when it was miserably sackt by the Emperor Ferdinand II's Army in the year 1630'. By contrast, they noted 'the country' round about' 'is very rich'. The tourists were correct: a census in 1676 revealed that the rural areas of the duchy had regained over 90 per cent of their pre-war population whereas the capital languished below 70 per cent.[16] Such imbalances, which occurred elsewhere in Europe, altered the balance of power between town and country. Thus in 1600 the magistrates of the town of Memmingen in Germany contemptuously dismissed the neighbouring peasants as bumpkins 'with neither enough cattle, grain nor other victuals or goods to justify the establishment of a single annual market'. A century later, by contrast, their descendants had to concede that the town and the surrounding villages 'are bound together, such that one always has need of the other, and in such a manner that each party must always uphold and maintain the motto "the one hand washes the other"'.[17]

Apparently the only European cities to escape post-war stagnation were the capitals, where the growth of central government and the conspicuous consumption of the court stimulated growth and attracted immigrants, and the North Atlantic ports, where burgeoning trade with America created both wealth and jobs. Most other cities would not regain either their pre-crisis populations or their economic dominance until the Industrial Revolution in the nineteenth century.

The lack of parish registers makes it more difficult to establish whether the end of the mid-seventeenth-century crisis also produced a 'baby boom' outside Europe, but in at least two areas this outcome seems unlikely. First, in those parts of West Africa where between one-third and one-half of all slaves captured and deported were female (notably west central Africa and the lands around the Bight of Biafra), it is hard to see how communities could have maintained a stable population, let alone increased. Second, in those parts of Asia where teenage female marriage was almost universal, and female infanticide was the principal means of easing population pressure, the demographic regime possessed no 'unused capacity' of fertility after the crisis to assist recovery. Births would therefore have remained low for at least one generation. Any increase in the Chinese population during the Ming-Qing transition therefore probably reflects some decrease in mortality and, even more, migration from poor to rich lands.

The new dynasty certainly did its best to promote resettlement. They briefly granted 'drifters' (liumin) who had settled on abandoned lands a permanent title to them, regardless of the claims of others. They also lent seed corn to poor cultivators;

created village pawnshops (for a while, the Kangxi emperor personally determined the amounts and terms of each loan); and offered incentives (such as travel costs, start-up loans, freehold land and farming stock and equipment) to any farmer prepared to migrate to the ravaged lands in the north and west. The number who took advantage of these schemes 'during the late seventeenth century and eighteenth centuries alone easily surpassed 10,000,000'. Thanks to these measures, the total cultivated land in the empire, which had fallen to 67 million acres in 1645, climbed back to 90 million acres in 1661 and to 100 million acres in 1685 – although since over 191 million acres of Chinese soil had been under cultivation in 1600, the heavy footprint of the Global Crisis remained perceptible well into the eighteenth century.[18]

A Second Agricultural Revolution

A baby boom normally stimulates the agricultural sector, since every new mouth needs to be fed, encouraging farmers to invest in irrigation and drainage works, to improve the yield of traditional crops and to introduce new ones. In Mughal India the versatile peasants of the Ganges valley, who already cultivated almost 50 different crops in the early seventeenth century, added maize (as well as tobacco, the other New World 'miracle crop') to their repertory; while the farmers of west central Africa began to plant not only maize but also manioc (originally a Brazilian crop) as a safeguard against the failure of the millet and sorghum harvests during drought. Manioc proved particularly valuable in wartime, since raiders might neglect the tubers below the ground. In the western Netherlands, and in eastern England, the disastrous harvests of the mid-seventeenth century encouraged the systematic rotation of cereal with root vegetables (such as carrots and turnips), and the sowing of clover and other crops rich in nitrogen. In 1650 Samuel Hartlib, a refugee from the Thirty Years War who settled in England, published *A discours of husbandrie used in Brabant and Flaunders*, later expanded to include information from New England and Ireland, showing how new methods of tillage and rotation made otherwise unproductive soils profitable; how to identify and to sow the strains best suited to each locality; and how to use chemical fertilizers to optimal effect. Hartlib also carried out experiments concerning the relative yields of different methods of farming. Some English historians have hailed these practical and theoretical efforts, which gathered momentum in the 1640s and 1650s, as an 'agricultural revolution'.[19]

Chinese farmers also innovated at this time, notably by cultivating maize, peanuts and sweet potatoes: three crops recently imported from the Americas, which thrived in marginal soils, resisted both droughts and locusts, did not require transplanting like rice, and produced twice as much as other dry-land crops with far less labour input. According to a Gazetteer from Jiangxi province, 'in general, maize is grown on the sunny side of the hills, sweet potatoes on the shady side' while maize 'provides half a year's food for the mountain dwellers'. Sucheta Mazumdar has hailed these improvements during the later seventeenth century as China's 'second agricultural revolution', one 'predicated on the maximum utilization of all crops and the development of complementary patterns of crop selection'. It allowed the average intake of adult males to rise above the vital threshold of 2,500 calories per day, and supplied more protein and vitamins – thereby both improving health and reducing hunger (see chapter 1 above).[20]

The Consumer Revolution

Domestic demand normally drove pre-industrial economies. Although the sight of stately East Indiamen returning to Europe's Atlantic ports filled with exotic goods from Asia captured the imagination of contemporaries, their cargoes amounted to (at most) 2 per cent of Europe's Gross Domestic Product. Put another way, all the goods transported by sea from Asia to Europe in an entire year would today fit inside a single container ship. The trade goods exchanged with Europe were even less significant as a percentage of Asia's Gross Domestic Product: as Jack Goldstone put it, 'The total volume of European trade was never more than just over 1 per cent of China's economy'.[21] Even the intercontinental trade between Europe and the Americas reached significant volume and value only in the 1690s. By contrast, the need to feed, clothe and house the 'baby boomers' and their families after the crisis of the mid-seventeenth century stimulated every sector of the economy.

In a bold study that focused on the production and consumption of households in northwest Europe and North America, economic historian Jan de Vries perceived a Western version of Japan's 'Industrious Revolution', starting around 1650. According to de Vries:

> A growing number of households acted to re-allocate their productive resources (which are chiefly the time of their members) in ways that increased *both* the supply of market-oriented, money-earning activities *and* the demand for goods offered in the marketplace. Increased production specialization in the household gives access to augmented consumption choices in the marketplace.

In short, the value as well as the volume of goods produced and consumed in the later seventeenth century increased because so many baby boomers wanted more than the bare necessities of life. To take the example of housing, all over northwest Europe, after 1650 'brick construction replaced wood and lime; functional spaces became better defined, as drawing rooms and dining rooms appeared in middle class homes and distinct bed chambers came to be defined ... and these interior spaces came to be filled with more, and more specialized, furniture'. Similar diversification characterized the consumption, and therefore the production, of apparel, food and beverages. Moreover, since technology could not provide the water, illumination, heat and hygiene sought by wealthier consumers, the heightened demand for many of these necessities also heightened the demand for domestic servants to provide them.[22]

A burgeoning demand for 'comfort items' also characterized late Ming China, but the trauma of the Ming-Qing transition brought it to an abrupt end in most areas. Suzhou, for example, with a population of 500,000, was in the early seventeenth century 'the most populous, and most prosperous, non-capital city on the face of the earth'; but famines, plagues and riots under the late Ming undermined its prosperity, and its defiance of the Qing led to a sack that left only 'broken tiles and walls' within the city, while 'outside the city, four or five out of every ten houses had been destroyed. What met the eye wounded the heart'.[23] Nevertheless, by 1676 four merchant guilds (including the printers and the drug merchants) as well as groups of 'foreign' merchants had founded or reconstructed lodges in the city, and 11 more followed suit over the next two decades: each lodge represented a major investment, and their multiplication reflected the construction both of merchant ships in the city (a new development) and of the quality goods to fill them. As he passed through Nanking in 1656, Johan Nieuhof noted that 'the shops of the chief citizens and merchants are fill'd with all manner of rich Chinese wares, as cottons, silk stuffs, China dishes [porcelain], pearls, diamonds'; while on the Yangzi 'the number of all manner of vessels is so great, that it seems as if all the shipping of the world were harbor'd there'.[24]

In Shanghai, the official-turned-schoolteacher Yao Tinglin noted in his journal in the 1680s how many things had altered since the fall of the Ming, focusing on the dramatic changes in apparel and foods available to ordinary people, thanks in part to the mass production of items that had been unknown or reserved for the rich under the Ming. Neighbouring Suzhou grew rich by catering to this market. An attempt by Qing officials to prevent the city's women from going to temples to burn incense (seen as an extravagance) had to be abandoned because it threw so many boatmen and sedan-chair carriers out of work; and when the Kangxi emperor visited in the 1680s, he noted disdainfully that the city's inhabitants 'set great store by the false and extravagant and are satisfied with comfort and pleasure; those who pursue commerce and crafts are many, those who till the fields are few'. Shortly afterwards, the emperor's trusted bondservant, Cao Yin, saw the situation rather differently. 'Suzhou,' he wrote, 'is heaven'.[25]

Again as in Japan, the 'industrious revolution' in China and Europe ran parallel to improvements to the damaged infrastructure. Dongting Lake, in Hunan province, became the largest lake in Ming China each autumn when the flood waters of the Yangzi flowed in, bringing nutrients and fish. At an early date, the central government constructed dikes to control the process, which allowed farming to develop on the fertile soil. This in turn encouraged private drainage projects, stimulated the production and export of crop surpluses and attracted both immigrant labour and grain merchants. Then, in the early seventeenth century, the state ceased to maintain its dikes, which compromised the private ventures and led to abandoned fields, emigration and the loss of the tax revenues required for repair. Local sources lamented the poverty of the area until the 1680s, but in the following decade the Qing provided subsidies to rebuild 16 of the major dikes, which once again stimulated private reclamation projects and the recovery of the area.[26] The same chronology characterized the recovery of another key element of infrastructure: transportation. Louis Le Comte, a French Jesuit who claimed to have 'travelled 2,000 leagues, covering almost every province' of China in the 1680s, was deeply impressed by

The care taken to make public highways accessible. They are about eighty feet wide, made of soil that is light and soon dries after rain. In some provinces you find (as with our [French] bridges) causeways for travellers on foot on the right and left hand, protected on both sides by an endless row of great trees, often enclosed by a wall eight or ten foot high on each side to keep passengers out of the fields.

Le Comte also noted with approval the post-stations and guard houses built at regular intervals along every road, and the numerous arches which, with few exceptions, displayed

A board on which characters that one can read a hundred paces away state the distance from the town one has just left and to the town to which the road leads. So guides are not necessary, and you always know where you are going, where you have been, how far you have travelled and how far you still have to go.[27]

Some of those highways remained in use in the twentieth century.

Water transport also improved. Above all, the Qing mobilized the full-time forced labour of 47,000 men to carry out repairs to the Grand Canal, the longest artificial waterway in the world, which allowed the relatively rapid transport of goods and passengers between Beijing and Jiangnan, a distance of 1,000 miles. Although Johannes Nieuhof came from a country studded with busy waterways, he believed that 'there is nothing more pleasant to be seen in all the world' than the Grand Canal, with its 'smooth large banks' and its 'extraordinary traffick'. Nieuhof's sketch of the canal at Tianjin, not far from Beijing, shows China's main thoroughfare in all its splendour in 1658, just 14 years after the Manchu invasion (Plate 24).[28]

Communications infrastructure in Europe also improved dramatically after the troubles of the mid-century subsided. When James Fraser arrived in London in 1657 he was amazed to find a postal network operated by 'a postmaster general and about 200 sub-postmasters', who conveyed letters at '120 miles in 24 houres'; and also 'hakeney [hackney] and stage coaches, wherin yow have yowr seat for a shilling the six miles, bravely sheltered from fowle ways and fowle wether'. The following year, a coach managed to travel up the Great North Road between London and York (apparently the first wheeled transport to do so), covering 200 miles in four days; and five years later, an Act of Parliament gave magistrates along the Great North Road powers to erect tollgates and apply the proceeds to highway improvement. Similar improvements evidently took place elsewhere, because a courier who left Dartmouth in Devon at 5 a.m. on 5 November 1688, bearing the alarming news that William of Orange and a fleet of 500 ships had just appeared off the English coast, reached Whitehall at 3 p.m. the following day: he had ridden 'above eight-score [160] miles in fewer than 24 hours'.[29] The English road network improved more rapidly after 1696 in response to a series of 'Turnpike Acts', which allowed magistrates to set up barriers (known as turnpikes) where they could collect tolls from travellers, and also to borrow money and appoint surveyors to improve highways. Almost 40 turnpike trusts existed in England by 1720.

Transporting bulky items could only be done efficiently by water, and here too the later seventeenth century saw important innovations throughout western Europe. Although building canals represented the greatest civil-engineering venture of the age, by 1665 the Dutch Republic boasted over 400 miles of inter-city transport canals at a cost of almost £500,000. Each canal possessed a towpath that permitted horse-pulled barges to convey passengers and freight quickly and cheaply between the principal cities of the coastal provinces, according to a regular schedule. Before long, fastidious Amsterdammers even sent their dirty washing by barge to the cheaper and cleaner laundries of Haarlem, 15 miles away. In France, in 1667 a group of investors directed the efforts of up to 12,000 labourers on the 150 miles of the 'Royal Canal of Languedoc', linking the Mediterranean and the Atlantic, which involved creating an artificial lake near the summit, several aqueducts and Europe's first tunnel constructed expressly for a canal. The first barges and almost 4,000 passengers paid to use the canal in 1682, its first year of operation, and traffic continued to use it until the drought of 1989 made it impassable.

Although the great age of English canal-building began somewhat later, from the 1650s local entrepreneurs started to invest their money in improving river navigation so that barges could convey goods to and from distant markets. The account books of Colonel Robert Walpole, an MP from Norfolk, reveal that when he went to London in the 1690s he bought both ale from Nottingham and Thomas Bass's beer from Burton (both locations that, thanks to the distinctive geology of the Trent valley, still produce outstanding brews) because they could be transported to the taverns of the capital entirely by water. He also bought Scotch whisky at three shillings a bottle, as well as countless other luxuries. The economy of connected 'shallow ponds' characteristic of the seventeenth century (see Fig. 9 above) had given way to an economy of mutually dependent regions (Fig. 52).[30]

Some condemned such purchases as sinful extravagance, and many states passed legislation (known as 'Sumptuary Laws') expressly designed to restrain consumption. In 1662 Sir William Petty, a distinguished economic theorist, argued that

> There are two sorts of riches, one actual and the other potential. A man is actually and truly rich according to what he eateth, drinketh, weareth, or any other way really and actually enjoyeth; others are but potentially or imaginatively rich, who, though they have power over much, make little use of it; these being rather stewards and exchangers for the other sort, than owners for themselves.

Petty therefore favoured imposing excise duties because they encourage 'thrift, the onely way to enrich a nation'. Such ideas soon went out of fashion. Thirty years later, Sir Dudley North, a merchant who had travelled the world and made a fortune through trade, observed succinctly that 'countries which have sumptuary laws are generally poor', because 'the main spur to trade, or rather to industry and ingenuity, is the exorbitant appetites of men, which they will take pains to gratifie, and so be disposed to work, when nothing else will incline them to it, for did men content themselves with bare necessaries, we should have a poor world'.[31]

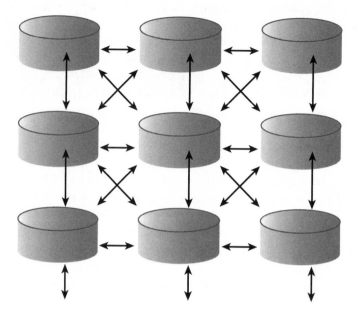

52. An economy of integrated regions.
Although each regional economy remains open, the domestic market has become integrated. The stronger regional economies include foreign trade, but even there multi-directional trade with other regional economies is more important. Compare with Figure 9 above.

Surviving household inventories in England, New England, the Dutch Republic and northern France suggest that the 'exorbitant appetites' of consumers like Colonel Walpole formed part of a consumer revolution. Early in the eighteenth century, Daniel Defoe included in his *Compleat English Tradesman* a chapter entitled 'Of the luxury and extravagancies of the age becoming virtues in commerce, and how they propagate the trade and manufactures of the whole nation', which argued (like Sir Dudley North) that the re-introduction of 'what we call sumptuary laws' would 'ruin thousands of families' because 'the luxury of the people is become a vertue in trade':

> If a due calculation were made of all the several trades besides labouring, manufac-
> turing, and handicraft business, which are supported in this nation merely by the
> sins of the people ... [namely by] the numberless gayeties of dress; as also by
> the gluttony, the drunkenness, and other exorbitances of life, it might remain a
> question, whether the necessary or the unnecessary were the greatest blessing to
> trade; and whether reforming our vices would not ruin the nation.

Although Defoe noted cautiously that 'heaven could, with but one dry or wet summer, bring us to the necessity of drastically reducing consumption', he considered the Britain in which he lived as 'the most flourishing and opulent country in the world'.[32]

A similar debate on the 'confusions of pleasure' took place in seventeenth-century China. The Confucian sage Mencius had pointed out the need for 'an intercommunication of the production of labour, and an interchange of men's services, so that one from his overplus may supply the deficiency of another'. A writer in Shanghai quoted this passage with approval, noting that although the frugality of a family 'can, perhaps, save it from becoming poor', the same was not true of larger communities because 'if a place is accustomed to extravagance, then the people there will find it easy to make a living, and if a place is accustomed to frugality, then the people there will find it difficult to make a living'. More specifically, when the rich 'are extravagant in meat and rice, farmers and cooks will share the profit; when they are extravagant in silk textiles, weavers and dealers will share the profit'. After the austerity of the Ming-Qing transition, China rediscovered the wisdom of Mencius: 'Spendthrifts may spend a million taels a day on foolish extravagances,' wrote a government official around 1680, 'but the expended treasure circulates among the people through the hands of those who obtain it', whereas 'a miser who saves up a sizable amount of money will impoverish numerous families around him'.[33]

'Seeing like a State'

In his paean of praise to conspicuous consumption, Daniel Defoe argued that 'exorbitances' of attire, food and drink had become 'so necessary to the support of the very government, as well as of commerce, that without the revenue now raised by them [through the excise], we can hardly see how the publick affairs could be supported'.[34] This was an extraordinary statement, considering that just one generation earlier, those same excise taxes ('gabelles' or 'gabelas' on the continent) had precipitated major revolts in the Spanish Monarchy, France and the Dutch Republic (see chapters 9, 10, 14 and 17 above); and that enraged crowds had burned down excise offices and attacked excise collectors (see chapters 12 and 14 above). The tax originated in England in 1643 as a temporary wartime measure but, as Scott Wheeler has noted, it 'brought "the state" to the English people in a way they had never experienced before'. Henceforth 'all Englishmen paid some taxes, regardless of their economic status' – indeed, excise became the crown's second largest source of revenue in peacetime and the third largest in wartime.[35]

Nevertheless the yield of the British excise, and also of customs duties and 'the Assessment' (later known as the 'Land Tax'), the three principal sources of public revenue, went almost entirely to defray the country's defence budget. The economic growth praised by Defoe reflected private rather than public finance. Even the costliest investments, such as improvements to roads and rivers, were effected by groups of private individuals known as 'undertakers'. The state nevertheless played a crucial role: it provided security and stability. Thus, every undertaker required government permission to start work and to collect tolls, but until 1688 England had two competing systems for obtaining and enforcing improvement rights: one through a patent granted by the crown, the other through Act of Parliament. Throughout the seventeenth century, each regime change threatened to ruin 'undertakers' who held a grant from the previous regime (for example, the Restoration settlement of 1660 included an Act that declared all 'orders and ordinances' made during the Interregnum 'to be null and void'). The Glorious Revolution ended this dual system: henceforth, crown and Parliament combined to provide a stable and predictable regulatory authority that made investment worthwhile and, thanks to the new climate of business confidence, individuals invested as much money in improving roads and rivers in the 15-year period 1695–1709 as in the 85-year period 1604–88. Moreover, their investment substantially reduced transport costs, which benefited investors and producers alike, and thus stimulated further investment.[36]

Increasing consumption made it possible for many governments to shift their fiscal base from direct to indirect taxes. In England, total revenues in 1650–9 exceeded £18 million, of which over one-third came from the 'Assessment' on landed property, whereas total revenues in 1680–9 fell below £15 million, of which only £530,000 came from the Assessment. In France, although the total revenues of Louis XIV rose from 84 million *livres* in 1661 to 114 million in 1688, the yield of the principal land tax (the *taille*) fell from 42 to 32 million. The statistics for other European states collected in the 'European State Finance Database' show similar trends.[37] These shifts – stable or rising state income, derived from taxes on consumption rather than on production – benefited both richer taxpayers, who spent proportionally less of their income on consumer goods, and the state, which gained a greater disposable income.

As Sheilagh Ogilvie has observed, the efforts of Europe's rulers to fund their wars in the first half of the seventeenth century 'affected more than taxation and warfare. The administrative instruments developed for *these* purposes could also regulate activities previously inaccessible to government'; and in his study, *Seeing like a state: how certain schemes to improve the human condition have failed*, James C. Scott examined the process by which modern governments impose order (something he called 'legibility') upon those activities that they want to regulate. He suggested that the process came at a cost, because 'certain forms of knowledge and control *require a narrowing of vision*':

> The great advantage of such tunnel vision is that it brings into sharp focus certain limited aspects of an otherwise far more complex and unwieldy reality. This very simplification, in turn, makes the phenomenon at the center of the field of vision more legible and hence more susceptible to careful measurement and calculation. Combined with similar observations, an overall, aggregate, synoptic view of a selective reality is achieved, making possible a high degree of schematic knowledge, control and manipulation.[38]

Scott traced both the growth of 'legibility' and the 'narrowing of vision' back to the mid-seventeenth century.

This chronology is not surprising. The trauma of the Global Crisis naturally made states want to 'know, control, and manipulate' both nature and society more effectively, in case they faced any repetition. Japan led the way: the cadastral surveys carried out by the Tokugawa shoguns (see chapter 16 above), which made both agriculture and demography 'legible', proved crucial in enabling them to mitigate the effects of the Little Ice Age. In China, the Kangxi emperor, mindful of the role played by harvest failure in the fall of the previous dynasty, considered the systematic collection and collation of accurate information about the weather crucial in promoting political stability. Although provincial officials of the Ming had normally included a 'rain report' in their regular accounts of local conditions, the central government paid little attention; the Kangxi emperor, by contrast, not only read the official weather reports but also requested reports from his Bannermen and bondservants on droughts, floods and harvest projections (especially for Jiangnan, which provided most of the capital's grain supply).[39]

Kangxi's example inspired at least one minister in Europe. Sébastien le Prestre, marquis of Vauban (1633–1707), acknowledged that his ambitious plan to replace the complex tax structure of Louis XIV's France with a poll tax was 'more or less what they do in China', citing the printed descriptions of the eyewitnesses Martino Martini (of which he owned a copy) and Louis Le Comte (Vauban attended the meeting of the Académie des Sciences at which Le Comte's observations were discussed).[40] In fact, the search for 'legibility' in France had already begun. In 1656 Jean-Baptiste Colbert informed Cardinal Mazarin (whom he served) that some Paris judges were 'searching in their registers for examples and arguments' that might help them to oppose the fiscal demands of his master, and suggested that 'perhaps it would not displease Your Eminence if I carried out a search of everything that has been said and done in this matter' to prepare an effective refutation. Mazarin welcomed the idea, adding 'It seems odd that no one has taken the trouble to keep such a register.' Colbert lost no time in filling this gap, systematically accumulating data about France's taxes, population size, land titles and economic output; and after Mazarin died in 1661, Colbert did the same for the king. Above all, each year he prepared a summary of the detailed accounts of public income and expenditure that he had laboriously prepared, and presented it to the king, specially written in a small book by a noted calligrapher and handsomely bound in red leather, so that Louis could carry it around with him at all times.[41]

Vauban bombarded the king with more ambitious statistics, but unlike Colbert, who almost always stayed at court and acquired most of his information indirectly, Vauban moved around almost ceaselessly to see things for himself, and he often presented his findings to Louis XIV in visual form. Thus after overseeing in person the construction or reconstruction of France's frontier fortresses, Vauban created a scale model of each one so that the king could visualize the defences of his kingdom without leaving his palace – an early form of 'Google Earth'. By 1700 almost 150 models existed, mostly on the same large scale of 1/600, with miniature walls, churches, houses and trees recreated in wood, silk, paper and sand. During a siege, the daily updates received from his field commanders could be reproduced on the model, allowing the king to micromanage operations via a stream of detailed instructions. It would be hard to find a better example of both the advantages and the perils of 'seeing like a state'.

Vauban also bombarded his master with other data acquired through a combination of personal observation, on-the-ground surveys and extensive reading; and where Colbert had concentrated on economics, Vauban focused on population. In the words of a document composed in 1686 (capitalized for emphasis), 'ONE MEASURES THE GRANDEUR OF KINGS BY THE NUMBER OF THEIR SUBJECTS', he called for an annual census to be undertaken. 'Would it not give the king great satisfaction,' Vauban asked rhetorically,

> To know at a fixed date every year the exact number of his subjects, in total and in detail, together with all the assets, wealth and poverty of each place? The number of his nobles, clergy, [and] officials ... by category, together with the place where they live? Would it not be a pleasure, but a useful and necessary pleasure, if he and his ministers could ascertain in just one hour's time the present and past state of the great kingdom that he rules?

Anticipating an affirmative answer, Vauban called on Louis to commission a series of 'general and regional maps' to which he could link the appropriate totals of population and assets, updated each year, so he would know 'precisely and easily the gains and losses, the growth or decline of his kingdom' and, if necessary, 'take appropriate measures'.[42] Vauban's archive abounds with meticulous censuses of communities, each one arranged according to parish and street, showing the gender, age and occupation of each resident, linked to a detailed map.

Vauban also undertook speculative exercises which he called 'supputations', based on his reading, his travels and the reports of others, on such topics as how to improve the yield of crops (to feed the king's armies better), how to make trees grow taller and straighter (to provide better masts for the king's warships), and even on how to get peasants to breed hogs so that in ten generations they would number over three million (to reduce the dependence of both peasants and soldiers on bread).[43] He also devoted much attention to France's overseas colonies, and especially to Canada, presenting the king with a memorandum in 1699 that suggested that the dispatch of more settlers every year would have a dramatic impact, because 'instead of the 13 to 14,000 souls that currently live in Canada, thirty years from now – that is, in about 1730 – there could be 100,000'. Moreover, if these men and women married and had four children each, Vauban predicted that the colony's population would double every generation so that 'around the year 2000 there might be 51 million people'.[44]

Such 'supputations' were of course totally unrealistic – the product of that 'narrowing of vision' identified by James Scott. The idea that peasant farmers would leave their hogs alive to breed while they themselves starved betrays remarkable ignorance of French rural life; while Vauban's addiction to geometry and calculations, although understandable given his background as a military engineer, led him to overlook other critical factors. Above all, although he cited 'the mortality of the year 1693 and the scarcity of food' as one reason for the decline in the number of Louis XIV's subjects, he 'considered climatic conditions as secondary', far less important than war and taxation. He even assured the king that 'dearth exists in the mind, not in reality'.[45]

The statistical approach of Colbert and Vauban nevertheless found many admirers abroad. In a provocative article on the spread of 'political arithmetic' in seventeenth-century Europe, Jacob Soll has observed that 'European states shared not only complex economic, military, political, social and spiritual crises but also comparable responses to them' – and examples are not hard to find, from the 'Cameralism' of many German states, to later Stuart England, where Sir John Plumb underlined the envy of many of Charles II's ministers for what they perceived as the 'systematic efficiency' of their French counterparts. Many royal officials became Fellows of the Royal Society, because they 'believed that the practical problems of life were best approached through knowledge'; and although their tunnel-vision often led them (like Vauban) 'into absurdities', by 1700 'Britain probably enjoyed the most efficient government machine in Europe'. There was more to political arithmetic in the seventeenth century than counting the reproductive potential of hogs.[46]

The Containment of Disease

James Scott drew attention to another consequence of 'seeing like a state'. Starting in the 1650s, he observed, European statesmen seemed

> Devoted to rationalizing and standardizing what was a social hieroglyph into a legible and administratively more convenient format. The social simplifications thus introduced not only permitted a more finely tuned system of taxation and conscription but also greatly enhanced state capacity. They made possible quite discriminating interventions of every kind, such as public-health measures, political surveillance, and relief of the poor.[47]

The 'discriminating interventions' in the field of public health were perhaps the most striking, since they included the containment of both of the two most lethal infections of the age: plague and smallpox.

We now know that bubonic plague is a bacillus spread by infected fleas that move first from rats (their normal 'hosts') to humans, and then among humans; but no one at the time (or, indeed, until the 1890s) knew this. Therefore, marginal groups often became a scapegoat for epidemics. When plague swept Milan in 1630, the city magistrates tried and executed several strangers whom, they claimed, had spread infection with 'pestiferous powders'. This judgment unleashed a 'great fear' far and wide: in Madrid, 1,000 miles away, rumours spread 'that some men had arrived sent by the devil to spread diabolical powders to kill people, as in Milan', and the city magistrates gave orders to stop 'any stranger who aroused suspicion' and to detain for three weeks anyone coming from a place suspected of plague infection. They even forbade monasteries to receive visiting clerics for fear that fugitives 'might make use of religious habits and garb' to pursue their evil plans. The magistrates of Seville, even further from Milan, held religious processions to plead for divine protection against the threat of 'pestiferous powders' – but also closed all the city gates.[48]

Although the diagnosis was wrong, the treatment was right – to prevent the movement of people and property in times of plague – and in every major city of Italy, a permanent Health Board staffed by both doctors and magistrates enforced draconian controls. In 1630 the Florence Health Board sanitized so many letters and packages that the city's mail revenues fell by 97 per cent – but, thanks to such strictness, although the plague ravaged all Italy north of Florence, killing up to one-quarter of the population, it never moved south of the Tuscan frontier. Such successes impressed governments outside Italy, and they began to follow suit. In France, a treatise of 1628 claimed irreverently that should God himself be 'suspect of contagion, it would be my duty to keep Him confined'; while in Spain, a cordon sanitaire stopped the plague epidemic of 1631 at the Pyrenees, and another in 1647–51 prevented it from entering Castile.[49] The lethality of the disease had not diminished – the epidemic that struck England in 1665 killed 100,000 Londoners, about one-quarter of the total population of the capital, rising to one-third in the poorer parishes, plus 100,000 more elsewhere in the kingdom – and few expected the Great Plague to be the last. Around 1690, the statistician Sir William Petty noted that plague epidemics struck England, on average, once every 20 years, and he predicted that the next visitation, which could not be far off, would kill 120,000 people in London alone. The city's magistrates were equally pessimistic, continuing to print the 'Bills of Mortality' with a special column for plague burials until 1703 (Plate 25). They were wrong. In France, although plague killed perhaps two million people in the course of the seventeenth century, each epidemic affected fewer places (Fig. 53). Even more remarkably, one area of Europe after another became entirely plague-free: Sicily after 1625, northern Italy (except for Genoa) after 1631, Scotland after 1649, Catalonia after 1651, England after 1665.[50]

Other governments managed to contain smallpox. Paradoxically, just as new and more virulent strains of the disease spread from Africa to the Americas, and perhaps to Europe, many people in Asia acquired immunity. The change began in north China. Smallpox decimated the Manchus after they invaded the Ming empire, killing even the emperor in 1661, and his son and successor the Kangxi emperor, a smallpox survivor, took a keen interest in the disease. He discovered that some Chinese doctors had developed a treatment called 'variolation': the deliberate administration of a mild form of the virus that most people survived, thereby gaining life-long immunity because smallpox only strikes each victim once.[51] According to his own account, Kangxi began to test the procedure 'on one or two people' (read: slaves) in the 1670s, and since it seemed to work, he insisted on inoculating his apprehensive family; then all the Banner troops on whom the safety of the Qing state depended; and finally over half the population of Beijing. 'This is an extremely important thing, of which I am very proud,' the emperor wrote in a testament for his children, because variolation 'has saved the health of millions of men'. His Majesty could have noted that variolation also brought great benefits to women, since contracting smallpox during pregnancy often proved fatal to both mother and child; and so, largely as a result of variolation, child mortality in

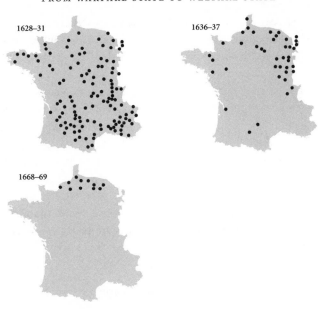

53. The conquest of plague in seventeenth-century Europe.
A steady reduction occurred in the number of places in France affected by plague during the epidemics of 1628–31, 1636–7 and 1668–9, largely thanks to the effective enforcement of quarantine restrictions.

China fell from 40 per cent to 10 per cent in the course of the eighteenth century.[52] From China, the technique spread slowly westwards to both the Ottoman and Mughal empires; and from there favourable reports reached western Europe. Although variolation arrived too late to save Queen Mary II of Great Britain (d. 1694), the heir of Louis XIV (d. 1711), or Emperor Peter II of Russia (d. 1730), deaths from smallpox plummeted wherever variolation was introduced. By any standard, this was a remarkable (and remarkably successful) public-health project.[53]

More 'discriminating interventions' in the field of public health could have occurred in the seventeenth century had the perverse prevailing medical orthodoxy not insisted that physical illnesses arose from general and not specific causes. Physicians therefore strove to balance the four 'humours' in each human body (often by blood-letting, sweating, vomiting or enemas), and deprecated any drug that did not produce some sort of excretion. This ruled out the bark of the cinchona tree (*Cinchona officinalis*), which contained quinine and so provided some protection against malaria. Jesuit missionaries in South America observed the therapeutic properties of 'Peruvian bark' and in the 1640s began to send regular shipments to Rome where, after extensive tests, doctors used it to stabilize feverish malaria patients. By the end of the century, over 30 books on the medicinal properties of the wonder drug had appeared in print – but some were hostile. In the mid-1650s some physicians claimed that although the drug produced short-term successes, it exacerbated the condition in the long term, leading many victims of the disease to refuse 'Jesuits' powder'. One of them was Oliver Cromwell, Britain's Lord Protector, whose death of malarial fever in 1658 doomed Britain's Republican experiment.[54]

Eventually, the new treatment prevailed. Robert Tabor carried out trials among malaria suffers in the Cambridge area until 1672, when he published his *Rational account of the cause and cure of agues*. His remedy cured Charles II, the heir to the French throne, and the queen of Spain. It also made him rich – according to an envious physician (who claimed that Tabor had plagiarized his knowledge of cinchona bark), although 'I never gott £10 by it, he hath gott £5,000' – and a knighthood.[55] Such rewards encouraged seventeenth-century medical practitioners, both licensed and amateur, to examine and test new remedies. In doing so they not only developed a sound methodology for experimental pharmacology, but also began to shift medical attention from applying remedies to individual patients according to their perceived 'humours', towards finding an efficient remedy for individual diseases.

Nourishing the People

After the 1650s, many governments also intervened to prevent their subjects from starvation in times of dearth. The Qing, for example, drew on 'more than two millennia of theoretical principles and institutional precedents' when they resuscitated the network of state-run granaries 'with a consistency, intensity, and degree of centralization unknown in previous eras'.[56] Each of China's counties boasted a public grain reserve known as the 'ever normal granary' (*changpingcang*), supplemented by community granaries (*shecang*) and charity granaries (*yicang*). Traditionally, each of them bought grain after harvest, when it was cheap, and sold it below the market price during late winter and spring to stabilize prices in good years and to prevent famine when necessary; but since the wars fought by the Late Ming left virtually nothing for welfare, by the 1640s almost all granaries lay in disrepair.

In 1654 the Shunzhi emperor ordered officials to re-establish both county and community granaries, with sufficient stocks to cope with any future famine relief; but it proved a slow process. In 1680 his son the Kangxi emperor began to issue a stream of legislation for efficient grain storage and, after some bad harvests, he also opened granaries and reduced or cancelled taxes even before reports arrived of actual famine. He accelerated these efforts after the drought-induced famine of 1691–2, with dramatic results: whereas the target reserve for each province under the late Ming was 1,500 tons, by the early eighteenth century at least 12 of China's provinces held a reserve of more than 50,000 tons each, while the state granaries in Yunnan, in the remote southwest, held 200,000 tons, and those of Gansu in the equally remote northwest held 272,000 tons (one million bushels). Above all, according to Louis Le Comte even though more than enough rice from Jiangnan arrived every year via the Grand Canal to feed the imperial household, 'they are so concerned about running short, that the granaries of Beijing always stock enough rice for three or four years ahead. It remains edible for a long time because they take care to dry and heat it first.'[57]

The Ottoman empire, too, maintained large granaries, above all in Istanbul and in Egypt, whose grain surplus maintained not only the capital but also the Holy Cities of Arabia. When in 1694 drought in the African interior meant that the Nile scarcely rose and receded quickly, leading to famine in Egypt, the sultan not only reduced or deferred taxes from affected areas (citing 'poor irrigation and drought') but also 'created a rationing system in which vouchers were distributed to peasants allowing them to claim an amount of food for themselves and their families. The vouchers could be bought and sold as currency.' Conditions worsened in 1695, with both continued drought and plague, leading to the migration of peasants to Cairo, where starving rioters looted 'the granaries and the wheat and barley storehouses in Rumayla Square at the foot of the citadel', the headquarters of Ottoman power. The sultan therefore dismissed the provincial governor, and his successor 'gathered the poor and starving', divided them into groups and assigned each group to 'a notable who was to provide the destitute individuals with bread and food'.[58]

In Europe, only the cities of the south managed to create permanent public granaries – none of them as large as those of the Qing and Ottoman empires. The Madrid granary (the *pósito* or *alhóndiga*) normally handled 20,000 tonnes of wheat each year, but during the famine of 1630–1 it distributed over 40,000 tonnes. The grain silos (*fosse del grano*) of Naples could hold up to 13,000 tonnes, and although a visitor to Naples in 1663 heard that 'here is always store enough to provide the city seven years', he suspected 'there might be enough to supply for two or three years', but not more. The *fosse* certainly did not suffice during the revolution of 1647–8, a famine year, when troops loyal to Philip IV cut the city off from its normal sources of supply and forced the authorities to decree that bread would only be issued '*per cartella*' (that is in exchange for a ration card), and that civilians would only be fed after soldiers.[59] The states of northern Europe fell far short of even this standard. Proposals by James I in 1619 to build public granaries in England perished through the greed of grain producers who wanted to obtain the highest price possible for their crops and opposed any measure that might affect their profits. Six years later, similarly selfish motives defeated the efforts of his son Charles I to persuade the Scottish Parliament to

> Mak, choise and designe suche placeis as thay sall think most fitte to be publict granaries whairin thair may be storehouses for preserving of all sortis of victuall and suche store of provisioun in the saidis storehouses as may prevent the extremitie of famine when bad yeiris sall happin, of the necessitie whairof we haif latelie had the experience.

In the 1620s the Swedish government also called in vain on each parish to establish a granary, repeating the call more insistently in 1642 (after a run of disastrous harvests), and again in the 1690s (after more famine years); but on each occasion it failed.[60] In France, although Nicholas La Reynie, Lieutenant General of Police in Paris, also failed to overcome resistance to creating a municipal granary, he found another way to nourish the inhabitants of the French capital. Every winter he required the Parisian clergy to report the exact number of people in their parish who needed relief, and he then arranged the distribution of a wide variety of items by his troops. According to the meticulous surviving 'Accounts of expenditure made during the winter from December 1, 1685, to April 30, 1686':

> Bread, soups, firewood, clothes, pants, wooden shoes, and shirts have been distrib-
> uted to the sick men and women, and remedies and food necessary for women who
> are sick and pregnant, the recently born receiving packages of swaddling clothes
> and small linens necessary for them, and milk and flour daily for the older babies
> who are still nursing; mattresses, sheets, covers and bed-frames for those who are
> sleeping on the floor, especially the poor weavers, ribbon makers, button-makers,
> embroiderers and others working inside whose work has ceased during this year.

La Reynie did not intend to see bread riots in the capital on his watch.[61.]

Since up to 90 per cent of all seventeenth-century people lived in villages, main-taining an effective rural safety net during famines was extremely important. In New Spain, the confraternities of many villages created a reserve of maize and beans, and a stock of cattle, in the course of the seventeenth century. Produced by communal labour, in normal years these assets were sold to support local religious rituals, but in times of dearth they formed a vital food reserve.[62] In Russia, the tsars ordered all monasteries along the Volga to maintain granaries; while in southern Europe, many villages and small towns created a 'loan bank' that kept a reserve of grain (perhaps grown in the town's own fields) which it lent to poor families in hard times – although usually it required both a pledge (usually a piece of clothing or a utensil) and a guarantor (a relative, a neighbour or an employer) and charged a small fee, payable after the next good harvest. Magistrates might also borrow money in times of dearth to purchase grain which they either gave away free or at a subsidized price.[63]

Governments also intervened to provide other forms of welfare during the unusu-ally harsh conditions of the seventeenth century. In Sweden, in 1633 the govern-ment established an orphanage in Stockholm, largely to accommodate the children of soldiers and sailors conscripted to fight in the 'continental war', because their mothers could not feed them; and in 1646 it created at Vadstena the earliest known home to care for injured and aged veterans. In Iceland, in 1651 the Danish crown established a hospital in each of the 'four quarters' of the island, donated crown land for their construction, and introduced a special tax to support them, to be paid by everyone. The legal obligation was critical because, in the words of an English pamphlet of 1601, 'In this obdurate age of ours, neither godly perswasions of the pastors, or pitifull exclamations of the poore, can moove any to mercie unless there were a lawe made to compell them: whereby it appeareth, that most give to the poore rather by compulsion then of compassion.'[64]

The date of the pamphlet's publication is significant, because in that year the English Parliament passed the most comprehensive legislation of the century, following a decade of global cooling. The Poor Law Act of 1601 required each parish in the kingdom to provide 'entitlements' (as we would call them today) in certain well-defined times of need – old age, widowhood, illness and disability, unemployment – but only to those normally resident within the parish. Funding for the system came from a tax on income from local property (primarily land and buildings), administered by 'overseers' chosen from among local property owners, who had to present their accounts annually for audit by the local magistrates. This devolution of public welfare to parish level proved a stroke of genius for two reasons. First, the involvement of magistrates (backed up, if necessary, by the royal courts) ensured that all the rich contributed. Second, the limitation of benefits to local residents meant that, in a crisis, the poor would stay in their parishes where their 'entitlements' were guaranteed, instead of seeking relief in the nearest town and overloading its resources (as happened elsewhere). The system was by no means perfect, and even the great dearths of 1629–31 and 1647–9 failed to persuade magistrates to tax the rich to support the poor; but this changed during the famine of the 1690s, when government pressure ensured that 'virtually every parish in the country was part of a nationally co-ordinated relief system' that brought benefits not only to the 10 per cent or so who needed charity to survive at any given time, but also to the much larger group who might require relief in some future crisis. The series of climate-induced crises that afflicted England between the 1590s and the 1690s thus gave rise to the world's first 'welfare state', and in doing so provided an essential precondition for the first Industrial Revolution.[65]

Creative Destruction

The numerous urban fires in the seventeenth century also stimulated some 'discriminating interventions'. In Germany some medieval guilds existed specifically to share fire risks, yet they could not cope with the proliferation of fires during the Thirty Years War; but in 1664, in Hamburg, regular guilds began to issue fire-insurance contracts known as 'Prudence in everything [*Alles mit Bedacht*]', which promised each member 1,000 thalers towards rebuilding costs if his house burned down, in return for a 10-thalers premium; and as in other towns, the Hamburg magistrates issued orders to promote fire prevention and punish arson.[66] It seems surprising that England did not immediately follow suit – after all, almost one hundred fires caused £1,000 or more of damage in the second half of the seventeenth century, a combined total of almost £1 million. Yet the only remedy for most of those afflicted was to secure a 'charity brief' from a sympathetic magistrate, authorizing them to collect money at the door of their local church. Even the Great Fire of London in 1666 failed to effect major changes. Admittedly, the following year, the London Rebuilding Act required the city corporation to straighten and widen some streets and all lanes, with compensation paid from a coal tax, and required future houses to be built of brick and stone; while Sir Christopher Wren oversaw the rebuilding of St Paul's Cathedral, 50 other churches and numerous public buildings in a uniform style. Yet so much more could have been done. The government received several imaginative plans for rebuilding the affected areas west of the Tower to create an imperial capital to rival Rome, but rejected all of them; while only seven provincial towns ravaged by fire in the seventeenth century followed London's example and secured a 'Rebuilding Act' that conferred special powers to realign streets and mandate construction in brick and stone.[67]

The 'peccatogenic' outlook of most Britons was partly responsible. Many initially blamed the Great Fire either on foreign residents, especially the French and the Dutch (crowds murdered several of them), or on Catholics. The 'Monument' erected after the Great Fire originally bore an inscription commemorating 'the most dreadful burning of this City; *begun and carried on by the treachery and malice of the Popish faction*' (a passage only removed in 1831). Nevertheless, 14 years after the Great Fire, Dr Nicholas Barbon (a physician turned property speculator) set up 'The Insurance Office for Houses' with a capital fund of £30,000. In its first three years of operation the office insured 4,000 London houses, receiving £18,000 in premiums (charging twice as much for timber as for brick houses), and paying out some £7,000 in claims. Barbon was aware of the risk – according to his prospectus, 'the insuring of houses being a new design, it is impossible to make a certain guess' of future profitability – but he considered it 'very improbable (unless the whole city be destroyed at once) that any loss at one time should exceed the fund'. His 'guess' proved correct, and the profits of Barbon's venture led to the creation of numerous Fire Insurance Societies, with the members of each one affixing a 'fire-insurance mark' to their property, so that the company's private fire brigade could find them.[68]

Some states reacted to the increased frequency of fires in the mid-seventeenth century by creating a permanent public fire brigade. Thus after the Meireki fire in Edo (1657), the shogun created an all-samurai fire service with four brigades at the centre, and special detachments assigned to bridges, granaries and other important structures; while London divided the city into four zones, each with 800 leather buckets, 50 ladders and 24 pickaxes. The basic technique of firefighters in both cities remained demolition, either tearing down or blowing up buildings to create a fire-break; but elsewhere the constant fire hazard prompted more sophisticated measures. Suzhou, the capital of Chinese silk production, created fire engines with forced water pumps mounted on wheeled vehicles, a technique also developed independently in Amsterdam, where the painter and entrepreneur Jan van der Heyden invented a suction-hose pump which he incorporated into fire engines equipped with hoses, each made of flexible leather with brass attachment fittings and 50 feet long (which remains the standard length of fire hoses in Europe). He set up a factory and sold 70 of his engines to the city – one for each of its wards. The benefits were immediate and dramatic: between 1669 and 1673, 11 fires in Amsterdam caused between them more than £100,000 of damage, but between 1682 and 1687 the 40 fires extinguished by the new engines caused, in all, less than £2,000 of damage. Van der Heyden's invention soon spread – to Britain, to Germany and even to Japan (although when it failed to cope with a blaze in Edo in 1658, 'the fire engine had been thrown into a pond nearby'), and to Russia (after Tsar Peter the Great saw one during his visit to the Dutch Republic in 1698) (Plate 26).[69]

Other public initiatives began to improve urban life. When James Fraser arrived in London in 1658, he marvelled that he could 'walke as safe in the darkest night' as by day, 'for in the twilight every house hangs out a glasse lanthern and lighted candle over the door, so that the streets ar as a lamp of light'. He noted that 'it was to prevent picking of pockets in the dark that those lights were appointed', and now 'if any offer to wrong yow', he 'could not escap, not through the narrowest lane or alley, unseen'.[70] A decade later, the Amsterdam town council went one better. Jan van der Heyden had invented a lamp capable of burning the whole night (thanks to wicks of Cyprus cotton made in his lamp factory), and in 1669 the city accepted van der Heyden's bid to erect 1,800 lamps placed between 125 and 150 feet apart (which, the inventor calculated, combined maximum lighting efficiency with minimum cost). Within six months the system was in operation, serviced by 100 municipal lamp-lighters. Visitors immediately noted how disorder and crime fell, thanks to both the lamps and a new 'neighbourhood watch' system maintained by most Dutch cities. By the 1660s Amsterdam paid 150 lightly armed citizens to patrol the streets each night, with as many again in reserve, and they summarily arrested anyone observed committing anti-social behaviour: beating their wives or servants; engaged in rape, theft or blatant street prostitution; acting in a drunk or disorderly manner.[71] Many cities in Germany and elsewhere in the Dutch Republic emulated the Amsterdam system and, by the end of the seventeenth century, humans had for the first time in world history tamed the night.

Non-Creative Destruction

In his influential analysis of 'Creative Destruction', Joseph Schumpeter recognized that, in certain circumstances, exceptions existed to the process of 'incessantly destroying' old economic structures and then 'incessantly creating a new one', which he saw as central to economic growth. He wrote:

> Let us assume that there is a certain number of retailers in a neighborhood who try to improve their relative position by service and 'atmosphere' but avoid price competition and stick as to methods to the local tradition – a picture of stagnating routine. As others drift into the trade that quasi-equilibrium is indeed upset, but in a manner that does not benefit their customers. The economic space around each of the shops having been narrowed, their owners will no longer be able to make a living and they will try to mend the case by raising prices in tacit agreement. This will further reduce their sales and so, by successive pyramiding, a situation will evolve in which increasing potential supply will be attended by increasing instead of decreasing prices and by decreasing instead of increasing sales.

'Such cases do occur,' Schumpeter noted, 'and it is right and proper to work them out. But as the practical instances usually given show, they are fringe-end cases to be found mainly in the sectors furthest removed from all that is most characteristic of capitalist activity. Moreover, they are transient by nature.'[72]

Schumpeter's assertion might have been true during the first half of the twentieth century – the period of which he had direct knowledge and about which he wrote – but it was entirely incorrect for the second half of the seventeenth century, when the 'stagnating routine' he described characterized almost every economic sector (not just 'fringe-end' cases). Moreover, instead of being 'transient', these exceptions persisted: in most parts of the world, survivors of the crisis reacted by trying to 'narrow the economic space' expressly to preserve the existing equilibrium and to prevent anything likely to upset their 'stagnating routine'. Indeed, the decision of most communities to enforce a 'low-pressure' economic regime, as opposed to the 'high-pressure' regime favoured in England and its neighbours, contributed to the 'Great Divergence' discerned by many historians between western Europe and the rest of the world.

The attitude of some European farmers towards 'alternative crops' is instructive here. Thus although maize usually survives adverse weather that will ruin cereals, and although it produces far better yields per acre, many farmers refused to cultivate it until virtually forced to do so by a crisis. In Spain, only after the famine of 1630–1 did maize cultivation spread – and, even then only in some of the worst-affected areas. A comparison of demographic and crop records for Galicia reveals that those communities that grew maize increased far more, and far more rapidly, than those that remained dependent on cereals alone. This partial embrace of maize enabled Galicia to experience sustained demographic growth during the seventeenth century – yet elsewhere in Spain, tradition trumped expediency: farmers used maize (if they used it at all) mainly for fodder. Attitudes towards rice were much the same. Although the farmers in the Tuscan village of Altopascio suffered from extreme climatic events in the mid-seventeenth century (unprecedented floods in 1654–6; drought in 1659), and saw deaths outnumber births one year in three, they still refused to diversify. Although they experimented with rice after one famine, they reverted to cereal cultivation as soon as possible because potential profits were higher, and they introduced maize only after the catastrophic harvest of 1710.[73]

A similar conservatism characterized many areas of Germany. For instance, whilst immediately after the Thirty Years War ended in 1648 the authorities of Ottobeuren welcomed immigrants who wanted to settle (page 616 above), as early as 1661 they denied permission for a penniless man from Tyrol to come and marry his local fiancée and settle, 'because there are still several native sons' who could take over vacant farms. This rejection ended the engagement and eventually the former fiancée left the monastery lands. Fewer than 20 per cent of all marriages in the 1660s involved an immigrant, and fewer than 10 per cent after the 1680s. The population of Ottobeuren therefore stood at only 72 per cent of the pre-war total in 1675 and still at only 92 per cent in 1707.[74]

The rural textile industry in the Black Forest region of Württemberg, centred on Calw, provides another striking example of 'stagnating routine'. On the eve of the Thirty Years War, villages in the area produced thousands of light woollen cloths (Zeuge or worsted), exporting them to Italy, Switzerland and Poland as well as other parts of the Holy Roman Empire. Spinning, weaving and dyeing cloth employed up to half the families in some villages; but hostile troops occupied Württemberg for much of the war, burning Calw to the ground in 1634, cutting trade routes, increasing risks and destroying several of its export markets. Once the war ended, the merchant-dyers formed an association and (supported by the local overlord) compelled the weavers' guilds to sign a permanent agreement with them which, they claimed, would guarantee a reasonable living for all. The contract contained three important restrictions. First, whereas previously each weaver had produced up to 200 cloths annually, henceforth the maximum would be 50 (carefully punctuated: no more than one cloth per week). Second, each year the merchant-dyers' association unilaterally fixed a price and agreed not to purchase above or sell below that price. Third, the weavers had to swear not to sell to anyone outside the merchant-dyers' association, or to compete with one another for apprentices, spinners, or raw materials. Although these restrictions harmed 'outsiders' (consumers, employees, women, migrants, Jews), they protected the interests of native merchant-dyers, the master-weavers and the male householders – at least until they eventually undermined the competitiveness of Württemberg textiles.

For similar reasons, guilds proliferated elsewhere in the wake of the crisis. Not far from Calw, on the Ottobeuren estates, before the war only potters and butchers had organized their own guilds, but between 1648 and 1700 rural guilds came to control virtually every sector of the economy: the activities of carters, blacksmiths, locksmiths, tailors, shoemakers, tanners, coopers, brewers, painters, gunsmiths, cutlers, rope-makers, bakers, millers, carpenters, cabinet-makers, glassmakers, masons, barbers and even bathhouse-keepers were regulated by guilds. In every case, the restrictive practices of the guilds guaranteed a living to all producers equally, and so facilitated a slow but sure recovery from the mid-century crisis; but in doing so they discouraged innovation and growth.[75]

The development of book printing in a cluster of villages in Sibao, a mountainous area in Fujian province in southeast China, offers a final example of a 'low-pressure' strategy for economic recovery. Devastation during the Ming-Qing transition left much abandoned land in the area until, with Qing encouragement, migrants 'who can farm mountain land come with their families and support themselves through their labour'. The sources often referred to the newcomers as *pengmin* ('shed people', because they lived in flimsy shacks), which conveys their initial poverty, but some of them turned a profit by cultivating bamboo that others used to make paper. Starting in 1663, other Sibao families took advantage of this cheap local paper to print cheap books from woodblocks. 'They targeted primarily the largest textbook market: the students at the base of the educational pyramid', who were preparing to sit the civil-service examinations. By 1700 Sibao boasted over a dozen publishing houses, each distributing their products through pedlars who travelled from market to market selling their wares.[76] The publishers of Sibao thus managed to create something from nothing, but creativity soon gave way to conservatism. They now strove, like the worsted producers of Calw, to eliminate competition, claiming thereby to maintain a fair share of profits for all. To begin with, although all male heirs got an equal share of their father's goods upon his death, a practice that led to the division of woodblocks and other printing stock along with other assets, the sons and their families might choose to remain under the same roof and run the print shop as a cooperative family business. Within this labour pool, which might include 70 relatives, the household head divided responsibilities and scrutinized accounts to eliminate competition and conflict; and even if fragmentation took place, with some sons taking a share of the blocks and setting up on their own, the families still minimized competition. At the end of each year the manager of each enterprise 'printed a sample cover page of each new work it planned to print in the coming year and posted these on the gate to its [premises]'. Should two enterprises propose the same title, the village elders would intervene to broker an agreement or, if that proved impossible, to impose a settlement. In the words of Cynthia Brokaw, who uncovered the methods of the Sibao printers, 'these measures aimed to ensure some profit for even the smallest [print] shops' and to inhibit 'large concerns from monopolizing these inexhaustibly popular educational texts'. In this goal they succeeded: the households that founded the prosperous printing industry of rural Sibao after 1663 were still producing the same texts almost three centuries later.[77]

The 'low-pressure' economic strategies observed in Calw, Ottobeuren and Sibao probably formed the norm before 1700, because few regions dared to adopt what might be called a 'high-pressure' strategy that allowed anyone – migrants, labourers, women, Jews – to participate in rural industries. Such a system was flexible, adapt-able and dynamic, but it also risked alienating vested interests and creating popular disorder. Even though opening up an enterprise to competition normally increased the size of the economic pie, the competitive melee usually left many with smaller slices. At least in the short term, it made good political and social sense to limit each enterprise to a closed corps of licensed experts, whose activities were micro-managed through their own professional associations, reinforced by state regula-tion, because vested interests remained content, minimizing the risk of disorder. Probably only regions with a sophisticated welfare system, such as England and the Dutch Republic, could take such risks.

Economic conservatism also involved risks, however. In 2011 an international team of economic historians headed by Robert C. Allen published data from around the eighteenth-century world concerning the number of 'baskets of basic goods' that unskilled labourers could purchase with their daily wages – something that might be called the 'welfare ratio'. Their study showed that important disparities existed in the 1730s, the first point at which comparative data become available, and that those disparities increased over time. In London the minimum daily wage could buy four 'baskets of basic goods', and in both Amsterdam and Oxford it could buy three, but in Beijing, Canton, Suzhou, Shanghai, Edo, Kyoto and Istanbul it could buy barely one. In addition, workers in the cities of central and southern Europe included in the survey had a welfare ratio no better than their comrades in Beijing; while no Asian city came close to achieving the welfare ratios already evident in parts of northwest Europe. Put another way, the available data suggest that by the 1730s (and probably earlier) a London labourer could support a family of four, while an Amsterdam or Oxford labourer could support a family of three, but a comrade in Asia or in south and east Europe could scarcely support himself. Moreover, in both England and Holland, wage labourers formed perhaps one-half of the working population in some towns by the early eighteenth century, whereas in Jiangnan (and in many parts of continental Europe) they formed less than one-fifth of urban and less than one-tenth of rural populations. This disparity magnified the differences in purchasing power.[78]

Although each 'basket of basic goods' contained enough food to provide 1,940 calories per day, mainly from the cheapest available carbohydrate, London workers did not of course eat four times as many carbohydrates as before. Instead they ate more expensive foods, drank more expensive beverages and bought a wide range of non-food items, thus fuelling the consumer revolution that so impressed Daniel Defoe. At least in Britain, it seems that the 'fatal synergy' that produced the mid-seventeenth century crisis had by 1700 given way to a 'benign synergy' in which demand for food no longer exceeded supply, while warfare did not stifle welfare, enabling a return of political stability, demographic recovery and economic growth, so that Grimmelshausen's phoenix could arise from the ashes. So why did it not arise everywhere, particularly in China?

The Great Divergence

THE 'GENERAL CRISIS', ACCORDING TO THE EMINENT SINOLOGIST SAMUEL Adshead in 1970, 'marks the decisive point of divergence between the modern histories of Europe and China'. In one of the few attempts to compare the experience of two distinct regions in the mid-seventeenth century, Adshead examined economic, social and political data, and concluded that 'European society emerged from this crisis reconstructed, more powerful and better integrated than before, while Chinese society remained relatively unchanged.' Thirty years later another eminent Sinologist, Kenneth Pomeranz, published a powerful comparative study, entitled *The Great Divergence* (a term that has subsequently gained widespread currency), that disagreed. On the basis of a comparison not only of leading economic indicators but also of learning and technology in the two regions, Pomeranz concluded that as late as 1750, little distinguished the economically advanced areas of China, such as Jiangnan, from the economically advanced areas of Europe, such as England.[1] Although the subsequent debate over the 'Great Divergence' has focused on economic contrasts, a comparison of the intellectual innovations in the wake of the Global Crisis at both 'ends' of Eurasia reveals some surprising similarities.

Educate and Punish

In 1654, just after the French government regained control of its capital, 'A Parish Priest of Paris' with 18 years of teaching experience published a 335-page book entitled *The parish school: or, how best to teach children in small schools.* The first section, which extolled 'the virtues of teachers', compared running a school with running an army. The key to successful instruction, claimed the anonymous author, was hierarchy and subordination: effective classroom teachers needed four 'observers' and 'admonishers', who noted the names of delinquents to be punished; eight 'visitors', who followed students home to see how they and their families behaved after school hours, and then denounced any faults to the teacher; and 12 'repeaters', who recited the lesson and showed the alphabet to the youngest pupils. The second section of *The parish school* discussed how to teach children piety; and then came two sections filled with 'best practices' on how to teach reading, writing, arithmetic and the rudiments of Latin. The author, later identified as abbé Jacques de Batencour, devoted many pages to the importance of discipline: segregating boys from girls; preventing children from talking to each other (therefore only one child at a time should leave the classroom to urinate); making sure the classroom had large windows ('to get rid of the evil smell of children'); and administering punishments that aimed to humiliate rather than to hurt, because their effects lasted longer. Batencour's 18 years in the classroom had also taught him the special difficulty of educating boys who were 'only children': having been spoiled at home, they required more humiliation and punishment at school than the rest.[2]

Such valuable pedagogical insights attracted a wide audience, and the book went through many editions. In addition, Louis XIV sent copies to his colony in Canada (Canadian libraries contain both extant copies of the first edition), while several French bishops praised its precepts and also commanded the schools of their diocese to follow them. Above all, Batencour's book set the agenda for the host of French charity schools founded during the later seventeenth century expressly 'to remedy the ignorance that prevails among the poor whose children, lacking money and unable to attend the parish schools, roam for the most part as vagabonds in the streets, without discipline and in total ignorance of the principles of religion'. To end this threat to public order, the government argued that 'There is no better cure than to establish charity schools in the principal parishes of the city, where the poor can be taught their catechism and at the same time learn to read and write'. Subsequent legislation to create primary schools included the same rationale, often word for word, and claimed that Louis XIV's initiative had not only educated the poor but also 'reformed the libertines whose excesses would have been a public scandal'.[3]

The 'Sun King' was not the only European ruler to see basic education as an effective antidote to the disorders fomented by the General Crisis. In 1651 Duke Augustus of Brunswick-Wolfenbüttel issued a comprehensive School Ordinance that mandated universal primary education explicitly to avoid the next generation turning into savages ('die Verwilderung der Jugend'). 'Unfortunately,' the duke thundered,

> Experience clearly shows that the accursed recent war has destroyed (among other things) the education of the young, and unless it is remedied in time we can expect no end to misfortune and misery. Instead of learning honour, virtue and well-being, young people have grown up with the example and experience of barbarism, so that we can expect in future, indeed in just a few years, nothing except wicked and indisciplined subjects of the state, who will shun neither evil nor injustice, but will instead continue the destruction of the ruins that remain of the State that God has graciously saved from the searing flames of war.

To avert these dangers, the duke continued (anticipating Batencour), 'Young people must be carefully educated, *with much wisdom and some severity*, in order to turn them away from evil and attract them to the good'. Therefore, he decreed, 'all parents must send their children' to school, 'to study for as many years as it takes them to learn to understand the Catechism and to read printed texts'.[4]

Similar concerns led other Protestant rulers to enjoin universal schooling – including those of Sachsen-Gotha in 1642, Hanover in 1646 and Württemberg in 1649 in Germany, and, on a much grander scale, Scotland in 1646. 'Considering how prejudicial the want of schools in many congregations has been, and how beneficial the founding thereof in every congregation will be to this kirk and kingdom', the Scots Parliament ordained 'that there be a school founded and a schoolmaster appointed in every parish' and that 'every congregation' in the kingdom must provide 'a commodious house for the school' together with 'a stipend to the schoolmaster'. By 1695, no fewer than 160 out of 179 Lowland parishes boasted a school and a schoolmaster.[5]

At the other 'end' of Eurasia, the Qing government also concluded that a thorough overhaul of China's educational system would accelerate recovery from the crisis. In 1652 an imperial edict called for the creation of a school in every village (whether by the community, a clan, a temple or a charity) and the process soon became so common that popular encyclopaedias included a specimen contract for hiring a teacher, leaving blanks for the variables:

> ─────── persons establishing a school: Now so that our sons and nephews [will] expound books, we cordially invite ─────── in ─────── year to take the teacher's seat on a lucky day, to guide the students, taking care that they seek the good, leading them throughout to achievement and to be grateful for beneficence, to respect virtue without limit. Respectfully, with our names and the salary stated below.

In 1658 another imperial edict imposed the 'national school curriculum' on regions not inhabited by Han Chinese: henceforth local chieftains in all areas of the empire must complete a standard education before they could govern.[6]

Other mid-seventeenth-century rulers also saw basic education as essential. The insistence of the Tokugawa rulers of Japan on conducting all the essential business of government in writing (see chapter 16 above) encouraged towns and fiefs to establish schools capable of creating cadres with the necessary reading, writing and arithmetical skills. A study of daimyō fiefs reveals that although only two boasted schools in the 1620s, and only eight by 1650, there were at least 20 by 1703.[7] Nevertheless, the post-crisis 'educational revolution' had its limits. In the Muslim world, religious schools (*medreses*) continued to function as before, primarily to impart religious instruction (see chapter 19 above); while even in Japan, China and Europe, where governments accepted the risks associated with promoting functional literacy and thus creating 'a public sphere', they showed little or no enthusiasm for higher education.

'The crisis of the universities'

In Europe, the first quarter of the seventeenth century saw the foundation or chartering of 20 new universities and over 40 other academies, bringing the total number of institutions of higher education close to 200; but the second quarter saw only eight new foundations, and 'after 1650', Jonathan Israel has observed, 'a combination of social and especially cultural factors plunged Europe's universities into the deepest and most prolonged crisis in their history', because 'most universities not only ceased growing but steadily contracted'. Total student numbers 'fell uninterruptedly from the 1680s throughout the eighteenth century'. New foundations virtually ceased.[8]

The reasons for this crisis were no secret. When in 1680 the Rector and Senate of Heidelberg University examined why 'student numbers are constantly in decline', they compiled a list of damning reasons (some of which still sound familiar): 'there are not enough professors', especially in the newer disciplines such as botany, anatomy and chemistry; in the older disciplines the instructors 'are careless in their lectures and public disputations'; 'discipline is either too strict or too soft'; 'fees and accommodation for students cost too much, and there are no scholarships'. These problems were not confined to Heidelberg, or to Germany. At the university of Pisa, mathematics teachers earned between one-sixth and one-eighth of the salary of philosophy professors; while at Leiden, mathematics professor Rudolf Snellius earned so little that he had to teach Hebrew in order to augment his salary, even though (on his own admission) 'he himself did not understand the rudiments of Hebrew'.[9] Confessionalization and bureaucratization ceased to stimulate university expansion, as they had formerly done throughout Europe. After the 1650s, church-building largely ceased and theology began to lose its dominant place in intellectual life; and although states still sought highly educated officials and diplomats, most universities failed to provide 'useful' courses in established subjects like history, geography, philosophy and modern languages, and no courses at all in new subjects like physics, chemistry and biology.

Only a substantial injection of public funds could have reversed this trend, creating new teaching posts, academic facilities and scholarships; but rulers remained reluctant, mindful of the prominence of highly educated scholars in recent rebellions (see chapter 18 above). In Naples, although Viceroy Oñate repaired the university faculty (the *palazzo degli studi*), damaged in the revolution of 1647–8, and although he assigned fixed salaries to instructors, in return he exacted a promise that they would not teach certain controversial courses, and he insisted that all students must take an oath of loyalty. In France, part of Louis XIV's efforts to harass and then expel his Huguenot subjects involved shutting down their Academies, which trained hundreds of young men in theology, philosophy and languages because, in the words of a Catholic bishop, 'the students here are serving their apprenticeship in rebellion and disobedience'. A Huguenot education, he asserted, was 'the source of all seditions'.[10] In England, in 1659 Lord Protector Richard Cromwell bowed to pressure from Oxford and Cambridge and refused to confirm the charter of Durham College, founded by his father, despite its rich store of 'books and mathematical instruments and all other instruments . . . relating to the practice of any of the liberal sciences', and a distinguished staff. That same year the marquis of Newcastle, Charles II's former tutor, wondered 'what all the learning of the universities did, or doe, against the red coats? [the nickname for Cromwell's soldiers] What did all the sages of the law doe against the red coats?'[11]

Such anti-intellectualism was not confined to Newcastle (a university 'drop out': in Cambridge he had 'tutors to instruct him, yet they could not persuade him to read or study much, he taking more delight in sports, than in learning'). Similar hostility to higher education appeared in a verse of the popular English song 'Heigh then up go we', first heard in 1640:

> We'll down with universities where learning is professed,
> Because they practise and maintain the language of the beast.
> We'll drive the doctors out of doors and arts what ere they be;
> We'll cry all arts and learning down, and *Heigh then up go we*.[12]

A decade later, English radicals likewise looked forward to the day when 'the Lord will raise up his word in the midst of [the universities], to destroy them, for the more the word of the Lord shall blow upon the university, the more shall this grass wither'; and argued that in an ideal world 'children shall *not* be trained up only to book learning, and no other employment', because 'through idleness and exercised wit therein they spend their time to find out policies to advance themselves to be lords and masters above their labouring brethren' – which 'occasions all the trouble in the world.' The Quakers, for their part, wanted to shut down all universities because they prepared ministers for the Established Church which they despised.[13]

Even had European universities received generous government support and general acclaim after 1650, it seems unlikely that they would have reformed their curricula to include new disciplines and methods, or even bought new books to create a 'universal library' that balanced authority with innovation. At Leiden University, violent disputes broke out between those who believed that mathematics offered the key to the universe (and therefore favoured an experimental approach in subjects such as astronomy, anatomy and botany), and those who saw no need to go beyond the published wisdom of the Greek philosopher Aristotle (who defined 'science' as the contemplation and organization of eternal truths already discovered). In 1648 a group of students invaded the class of a prominent Aristotelian philosopher, the émigré Scot Adam Steuart, and beat up his hearers, while others prevented Steuart from lecturing by stamping and banging, and disrupted doctoral exams on Aristotelian subjects. The university's Curators (equivalent to the Board of Trustees at a modern North American university) interrogated the professors (whom they held responsible for their students' behaviour) and, although they revoked Steuart's licence to teach metaphysics, they also insisted that only Aristotelian philosophy should be taught at Leiden. In addition, to reduce the risk of intellectual innovation, the Curators ruled that students could enter the university library on only two days per week, and forbade the library from purchasing any book that was not in Latin and on a traditional subject. The States of Holland, which had ultimate authority over public education, made clear its support for this conservative stance. It remained unchanged until 1689.[14]

In China, too, after 1650 the government frowned on higher education. The Qing believed that the intellectual elite had played a critical role in fomenting the 'troubles' faced by their predecessors, and they therefore closed down all Academies and

Learned Societies. Moreover, although they reintroduced the national system of civil-service examinations, holding special *jinshi* examinations in 1646, 1647 and 1649 before reverting to the traditional triennial pattern, they made some important changes. First, Manchu subjects received encouragement to compete in the examinations, and permission to submit answers in either Manchu or Chinese. Second, because there were never enough successful Manchu candidates, the Qing regularly filled senior positions with men who lacked a *jinshi* degree but boasted 'other qualifications' to govern. Finally, the new dynasty tolerated no irregularities in the examination process. In 1657 the Shunzhi emperor reacted savagely when evidence of cheating in the triennial *juren* examination came to light: he beheaded dozens of officials and examiners who had accepted bribes, as well as the intermediaries who had tampered with the scripts, and he deported hundreds of their family members to serve as slaves in Manchuria. Even successful candidates had to take the exam again.[15]

The New Learning

Nevertheless, government hostility to institutions of higher education failed to stifle intellectual speculation and innovation. On the contrary, to quote Jonathan Israel again:

> Down to around 1650, Western civilization was based on a largely shared core of faith, tradition and authority. By contrast, after 1650, everything, no matter how fundamental or deeply rooted, was questioned in the light of philosophical reason and frequently challenged or replaced by startlingly different concepts generated by the New Philosophy and what may still usefully be termed the Scientific Revolution.

The timeline of the 'New Philosophy' in England proposed by John Aubrey, author of the first books in English entirely devoted to archaeology, place names and folklore, vindicated Israel's claim. 'Till about the year 1649,' Aubrey wrote,

> 'Twas held a strange presumption for a man to attempt an innovation in learning, and not to be good manners to be more knowing than his neighbours and forefathers. Even to attempt an improvement in husbandry, though it succeeded with profit, was look't upon with an ill eie . . . 'Twas held a sinne to make a scrutinie into the waies of nature . . . In those times, to have had an invention and enquiring witt was accounted affectation, which censure the famous Dr. William Harvey could not escape for his admirable discovery of the circulation of the blood. He told me himself that upon his publishing that booke, he fell in his practice extremely.[16]

Aubrey condemned scholarship in the sixteenth century as 'Paedantry', because 'criticall learning, mathematics and experimental philosophy was not known'; and he considered even the first half of the seventeenth century 'a darke time' because '*Things* were not then studied. My lord Bacon first led that dance.'[17]

Aubrey exaggerated – as even his own examples revealed. Before he published his findings in 1628, William Harvey refined his theory concerning the circulation of the blood for over a decade by the repeated dissection and observation of numerous animals and by lectures and debates at London's College of Physicians; while as early as 1592 'my lord Bacon' – Francis Bacon, Lord St Albans – declared his intention 'to bring in industrious observations, grounded conclusions, and profitable inventions and discoveries', and to demonstrate how natural philosophy enhanced political power. He did this by preparing a six-part project for mapping all human knowledge, which he called *The Great Instauration*. Bacon published the first part in 1605, *The advancement of learning*, which boldly proposed that all knowledge could be organized according to the three intellectual faculties possessed by humans: memory (history), imagination (poetry) and reason (philosophy – including the sciences). This approach, he argued, both classified existing information and cleared the way for new discoveries. Bacon published the second part in 1620, entitled *Novum Organum* (a play on Aristotle's 'Organon' or 'logical works'), which proposed a method of scientific inquiry very different to that of Aristotle. Let 'the business be done as if by machinery', he argued, collecting and reviewing relevant cases in order to find 'certain and demonstrable knowledge'.[18] Bacon sent a copy of *Novum Organum* to King James I, together with a letter announcing that he was 'with hope'

> That after these beginnings, and the wheel once set on going, men shall suck more truth out of Christian pens, than hitherto out of heathen. I say 'with hope', because I hear my former book of *The advancement of learning* is well tasted in the universities here and the English colleges abroad: and this is the same argument sunk deeper.[19]

Poor Bacon! Someone with good links at court spitefully reported that the king 'cannot forbeare sometimes, in reading [Bacon's] last booke, to say that "*Yt is like the peace of God, that passeth all understanding*"'.[20] Likewise, neither Oxford nor Cambridge showed the slightest interest in the 'New Philosophy', and so their alumni left with little or no scientific knowledge. John Wallis, later an eminent mathematician, complained that when he was a student at Cambridge in the 1630s, the discipline was 'scarce looked upon as *accademical studies*, but rather *mechanical, as the business of traders*'. Therefore, 'amongst more than two hundred students' in his college, 'I do not know of any two (perhaps not any) who had more of mathematicks than I, (if so much), which was then but little; and but very few, in that whole university.' Wallis nevertheless managed to imbibe 'the principles of what they now call the *New Philosophy*' because:

> I made no scruple of diverting (from the common road of studies then in fashion) to any part of *useful learning*, presuming that knowledge is no burthen; and if, of any part thereof, I should afterwards have no occasion to make use, it would at least do me no hurt; and, what of it I might or might not have occasion for, I could not then foresee.[21]

When 'by our Civil Wars, Academical Studies were much interrupted in both our universities' (namely Oxford and Cambridge), Wallis moved to London, where in 1645 he joined the weekly meetings of 'divers worthy Persons, inquisitive into Natural Philosophy, and other parts of Humane Learning; and particularly of what hath been called the *New Philosophy or Experimental Philosophy*.' One of those 'worthy persons' was Robert Boyle, son of the richest man in Britain and the leading light of 'the invisible, or (as they term themselves) the philosophical college'. Boyle, like Wallis, applied himself to '*useful learning*' – or, in his own words, to 'natural philosophy, the mechanics, and husbandry according to the principles of our new philosophical college, that values no knowledge, *but as it hath a tendency to use*'. To this end, Boyle would consult 'the meanest' person, provided 'he can but plead reason for his opinion'.[22]

The 'Philosophical College' suffered from two handicaps. First, it numbered scarcely ten members; and, second, few scholars outside Great Britain read English. Francis Bacon eventually decided to have his *Advancement of Science* translated into Latin so it 'will live, and be a citizen of the world, as English books are not'.[23] He also sent complimentary copies to foreign scholars, including Galileo Galilei, who in 1609 had created a telescope powerful enough to carry out systematic observations of the moon (which he found to be irregular, not smooth) and Jupiter (where he detected four moons, which clearly rotated around the planet). The following year, Galileo published his findings in a short treatise in Latin (*Sidereus Nuncius*, 'The starry messenger'), and also sent copies of both his book and his telescope to foreign courts so that others could verify his claim – just as Bacon had suggested in his *Advancement*. Harvey went one step further than Bacon: he did not even publish in England. His now famous book describing how blood circulates first appeared in Latin in Frankfurt, Germany, with the revolutionary overthrow of Aristotle's explanation tucked away at the end. But if he hoped that these stratagems would deflect criticism, he miscalculated: both his book and its argument were either ignored or condemned by his compatriots (and also by most other Europeans) for two decades.[24]

René Descartes, a French philosopher living in Holland as a private scholar, proved an exception. In 1637 his influential *Discourse on method for the correct use of one's reason and for seeking truth in knowledge*, praised Harvey's theory (although even he did not name Harvey, citing merely 'an English doctor'); and, in an earlier work, Descartes approved Bacon's approach ('*la méthode de Verulamius*') because, although he had read all the Classical authors, he had reached his conclusions by rigorous experiments that anyone could replicate. Descartes also praised Galileo's 'application of mathematical reasoning to physics' (again without naming the author) and argued that, since 'all the things which come within the scope of human knowledge are interconnected', if someone began with simple notions and proceeded step by step, 'it does not take great skill and capacity to find them' (Plate 27). Descartes thus exalted experiment over theory.[25]

Just as Bacon's 'project' gained fame outside England, so Descartes's 'method' gained fame outside Europe. In Mughal India, the French traveller François Bernier, physician to Emperor Shah Jahan and his eldest son Dara Shikoh, translated some of

Descartes's work into Persian in the 1650s. Prince Dara had recently translated from Sanskrit into Persian over 50 of the Upanishads, ancient Hindu philosophical texts, which he called *Sirr-i Akbar* ('The Great Mystery') and composed a philosophical work entitled *Majma-ul-Bahrain* ('The Mingling of Two Oceans'), in which he stated that he 'became desirous of bringing in view all the heavenly books'. He there-fore examined the Hebrew Bible and the Christian Gospels, as well as the Upanishads and the Qu'ran, concluding that 'he did not find any difference, except verbal, in the way they all sought and comprehended Truth'. The prince also collected an impressive library and attracted to the holy city of Benares (Varanasi) a group of Sanskrit scholars who pursued *Navya Nayaya*, or 'new reason' (with the sense of 'evidence-based critical enquiry'). Bernier remained at Benares for four years, where he translated works by Descartes and other French 'natural philosophers' into Persian, while one of Dara's protégé's composed two treatises that confronted the 'new reason' and Cartesian philosophy.[26]

In China, in 1608 (the year before Galileo turned his new telescope on the moon), the scholar-official Xie Zhaozhe published a 1,414-page treatise entitled *Wa za zu* (*Fivefold Miscellany*). Had he read the book, Descartes would no doubt have approved of Xie's desire to correct Classical writers (albeit followers of Confucius rather than of Aristotle) through systematic observation. For example, Xie dismissed the 'popular saying' that snowflakes at the winter solstice had five points because 'Every year, as the winter moves into spring, *I have gathered snow-flakes and looked at them. All are six-pointed.*' Where Xie could not provide proof, he used his common sense: 'Since the conjunctions and the eclipses of the sun and the moon depend on their regular orbit, and they can be foreseen in numerical detail several tens of years in advance, it is not possible to escape them.' So 'is it not erroneous to point to them as portents of heaven?'[27] Xie's experimental approach did not stand alone. The 'foundation charter' of the *Fu She* ('Restoration Society') in 1629 expressed the hope that it would revitalize 'the ancient learning *and thus be of some use*'; while in 1637 (as Descartes oversaw the publication of his *Discourse*), Chen Zilong, another scholar-official, published *The Complete Book of Agricultural Science*, the posthumous work of a colleague who had converted to Christianity, which included material from many Western sources (including the translation of a treatise on hydraulic theory by a Jesuit). Chen justified the inclusion of foreign sources by twisting the traditional Confucian saying, 'If you have lost the proper way of doing things at court, *search for it in the countryside*': in China's present emer-gency, he asserted, 'If you have lost the proper way of doing things at court, *search for it among the foreigners.*'[28] Two years later, Chen and two colleagues published *Select Writings on Statecraft from the Ming Period*, a compendium of memoranda and advice submitted by over 400 officials from the fourteenth century to their own day, in the hope that they might suggest solutions to current Ming problems.[29]

Although Chen committed suicide rather than accept the Qing, some of his surviving colleagues promoted *kaozheng* ('evidentiary research': knowledge that could be verified empirically) and *Shixue* ('practical knowledge'). Gu Yanwu, from a gentry family in Jiangnan, epitomized the new approach. He memorized all the texts required to achieve *shengyuan* status in 1626, and later joined the 'Reformation Society', but repeatedly failed his further examinations. He and his friends managed to ignore both the Manchu and the bandit problems while they engaged in the traditional literary and social activities of educated young men, until another failure to pass the exams combined with regional disaster (the Little Ice Age struck Jiangnan with especial ferocity), led to a dramatic change of heart:

> Rejected in the autumn triennial examination in 1639, I retired and read books. Realizing the many grievous problems with which the state was faced, I was ashamed of the meager resources which students of the Classics possessed to deal with these problems. Therefore, I read through the twenty-one dynastic histories as well as gazetteers from the whole empire. I read the collected literary works of the famous men of each period as well as memorials and documents. I noted down what I gained from my reading.

Initially, Gu used his practical knowledge to support the Southern Ming state, preparing memorials that showed how, four centuries before, the Southern Song had kept northern invaders at bay in similar circumstances; but after the Qing conquered Jiangnan he shaved his head and feigned obedience in order to travel all over the empire. He visited the Shanhai Pass, through which the conquerors had entered China, to try and understand the strategic geography of the area, and he interviewed veteran soldiers for their recollections of what had happened – and 'if what they told him was not in conformity with what was commonly accepted, he retired indoors to correlate their information with that contained in his books'. Everywhere Gu acquired and read rare books, and copied down (or made rubbings of) inscriptions, using them to verify and if necessary correct Classical texts (which may have become corrupted) and historical chronicles (which may have been falsified). He also visited a host of friends and scholars – some lukewarm Qing subjects, others clandestine Ming loyalists – with whom he shared information. In their houses, Gu wrote books on history, archaeology and phonetics that exemplified the new 'scientific' outlook.[30]

Gu survived because the conquerors encouraged such pragmatism. In 1652 an imperial decree ordered that henceforth only 'studies of principle, works on governance, and other books that contribute positively to learned affairs' should be printed; while the Kangxi emperor later claimed that 'since my childhood I have always tried to find out things for myself', adding 'If you want to really know something, you have to observe or experience it in person; if you claim to know something on the basis of hearsay, or on happening to see it in a book, you'll be a laughingstock to those who really know.' He advised his subjects to 'Keep an open mind and you'll learn things', and stressed the need to 'Ask questions about everything and investigate everything.' Such views help to explain why the emperor studied mathematics, surveying, music, mechanics and astronomy with the Jesuit missionaries resident at his court; why he promoted a Jesuit to be director of the Imperial Bureau of Astronomy (which regulated the entire imperial calendar); and why he allowed the Western priests to teach his sons.[31]

Nothing Kangxi wrote or said could impress the scholars of Tokugawa Japan, who despised the Manchus as the barbarian descendants of Mongols who had tried to conquer the archipelago four centuries before – but they showed considerable interest in the epistemology of two other groups of foreigners. The professional translators (the *tolken*: eventually about twenty families), who worked with the Dutch physicians and surgeons based on Dejima island at Nagasaki (see chapter 16 above), alerted the central government to the potential importance of Western knowledge, and in 1667 the shogun asked the Dutch East India Company to send a physician with botanical and chemical experience. From a shortlist of five, the Company selected Dr Willem ten Rhijne, a pupil of the Dutch scholar who had published Descartes's work. He arrived in Edo in 1675 and returned the following year, but secured only one audience with the shogun, because in the words of the neo-Confucian scholar and physician, Genshō Mukai, co-editor of *Western Cosmography with critical commentaries*, Westerners 'are ingenious only in techniques that deal with appearance and utility' (a verdict that Descartes would no doubt have relished).[32] The Tokugawa showed far more interest in a second group of refugees in Nagasaki: the Ming scholars who followed the path of 'evidentiary research', called in Japanese *Jitsugaku*, or 'practical learning' (from the word *jitsu*, 'practical').

In Japan, as in China, 'practical learning' involved four assumptions: first, a belief that the present was different from the past; second, prioritizing experience over theory; third, seeing knowledge as a process of continuous experience and re-evaluation; and, finally, seeking knowledge of immediate utility. Also as in China, Japanese practitioners reacted to the seventeenth-century crisis by investigating how the world around them functioned, hoping to find some mechanism to escape from – or, at least, to mitigate – the catastrophe. Kaibara Ekken, the son of a samurai, trained as a doctor in Nagasaki before becoming preceptor to a daimyō family. He wrote over one hundred treatises on topics that ranged from botany and medicine, through astronomy and topography, to ethics and education, many of them in the form of self-help manuals directed at non-expert readers, male and female. One of his works stressed that 'One should not blindly regard all one has heard as true and reject what others say merely because they disagree, nor be stubborn and refuse to admit mistakes'; and, just like his contemporary Robert Boyle, Kaibara Ekken assured his readers that 'I followed up on what the townspeople spoke of, salvaged what I could prove out of even the most insane utterances, and made enquiries of people of the most lowly station. I was always willing to inquire into the most mundane and everyday matters and give consideration to all opinions.'[33]

Several scholars who endorsed 'practical learning' became counsellors to the leading daimyō of Japan, and through written and oral advice helped to introduce practical measures designed to assist economic recovery, and to prepare better for any recurrence of crisis. Yamazaki Ansai, the son of a samurai who worked for Hoshina Masayuki (grandson of Tokugawa Ieyasu and a senior regent after the death of Shogun Iemitsu), studied and wrote on mathematics and science; and at the Kimon School which he founded, he trained many others to consult and learn from a wide variety of sources. Kumazawa Banzan, another scholar from a samurai family, served the Ikeda daimyō at Bizen and played an important role in developing relief strategies and reconstruction in the wake of catastrophic floods in the 1650s. The Chinese refugee scholar Zhu Shunsui also became prominent in daimyō service. Like other members of his family, Zhu studied for the civil service examinations and read widely, and although he never became a minister of the Ming, and did not fight for them, he nevertheless refused to obey the head-shaving edict. He made several trips to both Japan and Annam to secure aid against the Manchus but, having failed, he settled in Nagasaki until in 1661, at the request of one of his Japanese disciples, he wrote a short tract explaining the fall of the Ming that reserved special blame for the 'empty' learning of the scholar-officials, who succeeded only because their meaningless examination essays were judged according to form rather than content; and he argued that even the most martial samurai needed a literary education. In 1665 his reputation secured an invitation from another grandson of Tokugawa Ieyasu to serve as his adviser and teacher, both in Edo and on his domain. In this role, Zhu stressed the need to 'nourish the people' and to provide them with a proper education through schools and public lectures, and he compiled an illustrated treatise of advice on how one must learn to 'cope with concrete situations'.[34]

In many seventeenth-century states, educated men bombarded rulers with suggested remedies for the crisis – 'projectors' in Stuart England; 'arbitristas' in Habsburg Spain; statecraft scholars in Ming China; memorialists in the Ottoman empire – but few received a hearing and even fewer achieved results. By contrast, men like Kaibara, Yamazaki, Kumazawa and Zhu managed to get many of their ideas implemented. Nevertheless, although Zhu always enjoyed universal respect and was buried close to his sponsor, suspicions about Kumazawa's ideas forced him to leave Ikeda service in 1657 for Kyoto, where he opened a school, but after a few years the magistrates closed it down and forced him to flee. He defiantly circulated the prospectus of a book to be called *Questions on the Great Learning*, which proposed reforms for the government of Japan. He spent the rest of his life in prison.[35]

The Thought Police

'If minds could be as easily controlled as tongues,' Benedict Spinoza observed in his *Theological-Political Treatise* of 1670, 'every government would be secure in its rule, and need not resort to force; for every man would conduct himself as his rulers wished, and his views as to what is true or false, good or bad, fair or unfair, would be governed by their decision alone'. Spinoza went on to predict that 'utter failure will attend any attempt in a commonwealth to force men to speak only as prescribed by the sovereign' – but most seventeenth-century rulers aimed to achieve precisely that goal.[36] Spinoza, like Kumazawa, knew all about censorship. His father had fled from his native Portugal, where he had professed to be a Catholic to escape the Inquisition (or 'Holy Office'), which sought to control the practice, expression and circulation of heterodox ideas. The Spanish Monarchy (of which Portugal then formed a part) boasted 24 tribunals, the last one founded in Madrid itself in 1638, and they stretched from Peru and Mexico in America, through the Canary Islands and Sicily, to Goa in India. The Inquisitors acquitted few of those who came before them (mostly as the result of an anonymous denunciation), and condemned some to death. (The Inquisitors of Coimbra, Portugal, who had jurisdiction over the village where Spinoza's father was born, tried almost 4,000 people between 1567 and 1631, and condemned over 250 of them to death.)

Many states in Italy also boasted Inquisitions, of which the 'Congregation of the Holy Office' in Rome handled 'public intellectuals' who held views of which the Church disapproved. One of the most celebrated trials involved Galileo Galilei of Florence, whose observations with telescopes suggested that the earth revolved around the sun, whereas certain passages of Scripture asserted the contrary. When some Jesuit astronomers corroborated Galileo's findings, the Inquisition agreed to tolerate *suggestions* that the solar system might be heliocentric, but threatened to punish anyone who claimed it as a fact (unless they could prove it). As one of his disciples once observed, Galileo resembled 'an insect whose bite is not felt by the victim at the time it is received, but plagues him for a long time afterwards'; and, although he respected the Inquisition's compromise while he searched for proof, he publicly ridiculed those (especially priests) who continued to claim that the sun circled the earth. Galileo therefore had many enemies ready to denounce him when, in 1632, he published a new book that discussed the rotation of sunspots as proof of the heliocentric theory. The Holy Office summoned Galileo to Rome, interrogated him, declared him guilty of heresy, banned his book and condemned him to life imprisonment. Although the Pope grudgingly commuted the sentence to house arrest, he also outlawed the publication of any of Galileo's books, past, present and future. In the phrase of a sympathizer, if Galileo requested a licence to print the Lord's Prayer, the Pope would refuse.[37]

Galileo's fate immediately stifled intellectual debate in much of Europe. His professed disciples suffered most. 'We are navigating with reefed sails, and we speak according to the narrow-mindedness of the present state of affairs', wrote Giovanni Ciampoli, a priest who had publicly defended Galileo and whom the Pope exiled to a remote Italian town. 'I have been burnt, I am terrified, and the perfidy of those who persecute has taught me to fear even the benevolence of patrons.' When Ciampoli died, the Inquisition confiscated his papers.[38] Even René Descartes, though living in the Dutch Republic, far beyond the reach of the Inquisition, was 'so astonished' by Galileo's fate 'that I have almost taken the decision to burn all my papers, or at least to let no-one see them'. He now abandoned the ambitious book he had just completed, called *The World*, because it asserted that the earth moved round the sun, and 'although I think [the assertion] is founded on very sure and very clear proofs, I would nevertheless not want to sustain them against the authority of the Church'. Descartes continued: 'I desire to live in peace and to continue the life I have begun under the motto *to live well you must live unseen*'. His book would not appear until a decade after its author's death.[39]

Descartes had been wise to seek anonymity. In 1637 he published his *Discourse on Method*, in which 'I try to prove the existence of God; and that the soul is distinct from the body' (Aristotle had argued that the soul was part of the body, and so of its 'essence'), and almost at once debates between supporters and critics of his views provoked shouting matches at Dutch universities, and denunciations by Calvinist ministers for dismissing the traditional proofs of God's existence. Some accused Descartes of seeking to corrupt 'ordinary people' because he had published in French instead of Latin. Deeply demoralized by the attacks, in 1649 he boarded a ship for Sweden (where he died the following year). Catholic theologians immediated denounced his opinions and the inquisitors soon placed all his philosophical works on the 'Index of Prohibited Books'.[40]

Spinoza also suffered for his beliefs. In 1656, when he was 24, the Jewish community of his native Amsterdam issued a *cherem* ('ban'), which forbade anyone to communicate with him, assist him, or read his work, because of his 'evil opinions'; and four years later, they denounced him to the city magistrates as a menace to 'all piety and morals' and called for his expulsion from Amsterdam. Ejected by his own community, Spinoza Latinized his name (from Baruch to Benedictus), had the Latin word '*caute*' ('Take care') engraved on his signet ring, and left Amsterdam to live secluded in villages and small towns while he worked on his *Theological-Political Treatise*. The almost universally hostile reaction that greeted his book discouraged Spinoza from publishing anything more. Even the colleagues who published his last work posthumously identified its author by initials alone.[41]

Although persecuted by the Republic's religious leaders, the Dutch government left both Descartes and Spinoza in peace. In France, in contrast, after the remarkable outpouring of pamphlets in both Paris and the provinces during the Fronde (see Figs 32 and 33), Louis XIV issued edicts that suppressed individual works while his police raided bookshops and searched travellers at the frontiers for forbidden publications: those found guilty of importing or selling contraband books were imprisoned or sent to the galleys. When the French historiographer royal brought out an *Abridged Chronology of the History of France*, which condemned the power exercised by Favourites and mentioned over-taxation and financial corruption as a cause of the Fronde, he lost his pension; and when he refused to change his text for a second edition, he lost his job. Such treatment soon led to self-censorship. The *Pensées* by Blaise Pascal, for example, were heavily abridged by their publisher: of his 50 *Pensées* on politics, only 17 appeared in print.[42] In England, a Licensing Act in 1662 prohibited the printing of any work without government permission, temporarily ending the publication of newspapers and reducing the spate of pamphlets to a trickle (see Figs 36 and 37). Fifteen years later, the crown tried to extend censorship to manuscripts, 'because it is notorious that not one in forty libels ever comes to the press, though by the help of manuscripts they are well-nigh as public'.[43]

Meanwhile, in India, the spread of the 'new reason' and Cartesian philosophy virtually ceased after 1658, when in the Mughal succession war Aurangzeb defeated the forces of his brother Dara Shikoh, captured him, had him declared an apostate from Islam, and finally had him murdered. In China, although the Shunzhi emperor did his best to win the support of the Han Chinese literary elite, even authorizing the compilation of an 'official history' of the previous dynasty, after his death in

1661 the Manchu regents for his young son, the Kangxi emperor, immediately reversed this policy.

Singletons and Multiples

In the wake of the mid-seventeenth century crisis, therefore, and largely as a result of it, the major states of both Europe and Asia witnessed an expansion of schooling combined with a limitation of higher education, and an efflorescence of 'new learning' combined with draconian censorship. And yet by 1700 the intellectual life of western Europe already diverged from that of other areas. A key difference was well expressed by the Dutch inventor Jan van der Heyden (see chapter 21 above), who began his dedication to the second edition of his *Description of Fire Engines* in 1690 by reminding his audience, the Amsterdam city council, that

> It is almost impossible to foresee and think through all that is necessary for the success [of any invention]. Small accidents often can spoil the whole result and demolish everything one believed unshakeable. Even the best-planned works are subject to endless chance and conflict, the more so when they are to be introduced for general use. So it happens, as has been accurately observed, that *of a hundred inventions of which trials had been made* (supposedly with good results and to which patents even had been granted) *hardly one succeeds*.

Van der Heyden knew whereof he spoke: he had been working on improving fire hoses and fire engines for almost forty years, and yet some of his prototypes 'caused more damage at fires than benefits'. He was probably unaware that the fire engine presented to the shogun of Japan had malfunctioned and been thrown into a pond, but he certainly knew that successful science requires 'trials', for which copious funds and the free exchange of knowledge were both imperative.[44]

In his study of India's 'new reason', Jonardon Ganeri astutely noted the absence of these preconditions. Although practitioners found patrons, even after the execution of Prince Dara in 1658, 'There were few institutions which brought together people of different intellectual persuasions, and certainly nothing like the Royal Society'. This meant that 'philosophers on the fringe and unusual sponsors define the emergence of early modernity in India'.[45] Likewise Qing China lacked learned societies, universities, museums and other institutions where scholars could meet together and freely present, discuss, re-evaluate and record their ideas. Although 'intermittent collaborations and occasional communications' took place between scholars, usually by letter, Mark Elvin has argued that 'the Chinese, in science, seem to have been loners in comparison with the Europeans'. This also reflected the lack of patrons. No doubt some members of the Chinese elite 'placed a high value on objective natural knowledge', just like their European counterparts; but, as Harold J. Cook observed, most of them 'had almost nothing to do with government. The kind of knowledge they valued most highly could therefore hardly become dominant.'[46] Finally, in Tokugawa Japan, Mary Elizabeth Berry has underlined that even the most original writers 'did not convert social knowledge into social science by analyzing the effects of the data and systems they described. And they did not convert information into news by reporting on events and opinions.' In short, they 'never shifted register from observation to commentary'.[47]

Of course, scholars throughout Asia still made important scientific advances, but those advances tended to be, in the phrase of the distinguished sociologist Robert K. Merton, 'singleton techniques', often discovered by chance; and while 'singletons' can sometimes have a significant impact, further refinements and adaptations tend to be limited and soon run into diminishing returns. By contrast, Merton argued, 'once science has been institutionalized, and significant numbers of men are at work on scientific investigations, the same discoveries will be made more than once'. Merton called these 'multiples', and he noted that almost 40 multiple discoveries occurred in the seventeenth century.[48]

Merton saw 'multiples' as a critical and unique component of European thought, and he traced them back to the research agenda established by Francis Bacon, whose *Novum Organum* had declared in 1620 that 'The path of science is not, like that of philosophy, such that only one man can tread it at a time'. Six years later, Bacon's *New Atlantis* described a 'college' (called 'Solomon's House'), with a staff divided into observers, experimenters, compilers, interpreters and 'merchants of light' (those who travelled afar in order to bring back knowledge), who would collaborate to extend natural knowledge and apply its practical benefits.[49] By then, in several European cities, men interested in knowledge already met together in 'academies', and a few admitted women (thus the Accademia dei Ricovrati of Padua elected 25 women in the course of the seventeenth century – albeit all but four of them were non-Italians, unlikely to attend any meetings).[50] The early academicians normally kept their activities secret. Even the noble members of the most famous Italian academy, the 'Lincei' ('Lynx-eyed') of Rome, at first used code names and wrote to each other in cypher; while in London, Wallis and his group of 'worthy persons, inquisitive into Natural Philosophy' significantly adopted the name 'the Invisible College'.

Gradually, the academies became less secretive. In 1649 some members of the 'Invisible College' moved from London to Oxford, where they reinforced another group, the 'Experimental Philosophical Club', whose members came from diverse social, religious and political backgrounds (which they agreed never to discuss). At first they met 'in an apothecaries house, because of the convenience of inspecting drugs, and the like, as there was occasion', and according to Wallis they made it their 'business to examine things to the bottom; and reduce effects to their first principles and original causes; thereby the better to understand the true ground of what hath been delivered to us from the Antients, and to make further improvements of it'.[51] They found a useful 'conduit pipe' for their discoveries in Samuel Hartlib, born in Poland of a German father and an English mother, who left home in 1628 to escape the continental wars and settled in London. Although Parliament rejected his proposal to establish an 'Office of Publike Addresse' to 'put in practice the Lord Verulam's designations *De augmentis scientiarum* [Bacon's *The Advancement of Science*] amongst the learned', they gave him some cash grants and an annual pension. Hartlib used these to employ a team of translators and scribes who copied and distributed details about rare books, inventions, scientific developments and technological innovations to members of the 'Hartlib Circle' – men who shared his belief that 'useful' knowledge could transform the world. Hartlib also received pamphlets and treatises from his correspondents, sent them to other members of his 'circle' for comment, revised them and finally then had them printed (often without the author's prior permission).[52]

The chaos that followed the resignation of Richard Cromwell as Lord Protector in 1659 (see chapter 12 above) destroyed the 'Hartlib Circle' and almost extinguished the 'Philosophical College', whose members were 'scattered by the miserable distractions of that fatal year', while 'the place of their meeting was made a quarter for soldiers'. Soon after the Restoration in 1660, Wallis, Wilkins, Boyle and nine other 'natural philosophers' reconvened to form 'a Colledge for the promoting of Physico-Mathematicall Experimentall Learning', which met every Wednesday. By the end of that year the college had grown to 30 Fellows, and nearly 100 by the time Charles II issued a charter that created the 'The Royal Society for promoting natural knowledge', authorized to dissect corpses, to conduct other experiments, to select a printer for books and to 'hold a correspondence on philosophical, mathematical or mechanical subjects with all sorts of foreigners'.[53] According to Thomas Sprat, the Society's first historian, from the outset the Fellows:

> Made the distribution, and deputed whom it [the Fellowship] thought fit for the prosecution of such, or such Experiments. And this they did, either by allotting the same Work to several men, separated one from another; or else by joyning them into Committees (if we may use that word in a Philosophical sence, and so in some measure purge it from the ill sound, which it formerly had). By this union of eyes and hands there do these advantages arise. Thereby there will be a full comprehension of the object in all its appearances; and so there will be a mutual communication of the light of one Science to another: whereas single labours can be but as a prospect taken upon one side.

Sprat considered the weekly meetings crucial because, 'in Assemblies, the Wits of most men are sharper, their Apprehensions readier, their thoughts fuller, than in their Closets'.[54]

Foreign observers agreed. Samuel Sorbière, a French gentleman interested in natural philosophy who attended several meetings of the Royal Society in 1662–3, waxed lyrical about Charles's foresight in creating such a forum 'for settling the peace, tranquility and imbellishment of his country upon a solid foundation' by 'perfecting the arts and useful sciences they have begun to cultivate'.[55] He urged his master, Louis XIV, to emulate the English example – which he did; but whereas the Royal Society met on its own premises, the Académie des Sciences normally met in the royal palace and received periodic instructions on what to do. Thus at its first formal session, the academicians were told to restrict their activities to 'five principal things: mathematics, astronomy, botany or the knowledge of plants, anatomy and chemistry'. Two years later, they were told to create a complete set of accurate maps of France, and although the king provided ample funds for the necessary equipment, it took them 17 years.[56]

Not all productive exchanges of scientific information took place in 'assemblies'. Henry Oldenburg, like Hartlib a refugee from Germany who settled in England, stayed in touch with his friends abroad and added new ones whenever he travelled to Europe, creating (in effect) an enormous 'list-serve' (Fig. 54).[57] After 1665, as founding Secretary of the Royal Society, Oldenburg also solicited papers from his correspondents, which he sent to other scholars for what we would now call 'peer review' before publishing them in the journal he edited: *Philosophical Transactions, giving some accompt of the present undertakings, studies and labours of the ingenious in many considerable parts of the world* – the world's oldest continuous scientific journal. Each issue had a print run of 500 copies, with (for a while) additional volumes in Latin translation as well as a partial French edition for the convenience of Louis XIV's academicians.[58]

By 1700, similar scientific journals existed all across Europe: the *Journal des Sçavans* (Paris, from 1665, in French), the *Acta eruditorum* (Leipzig, from 1682, in Latin), the *Nouvelles de la République des Lettres* (Amsterdam, from 1684, in French), the *Monatsgespräche* (Leipzig, from 1688, in German), the *Boekzaal van Europe* (Rotterdam, from 1692, in Dutch), and many more.[59] All of them reviewed and discussed books and ideas, and as such played a crucial role in disseminating

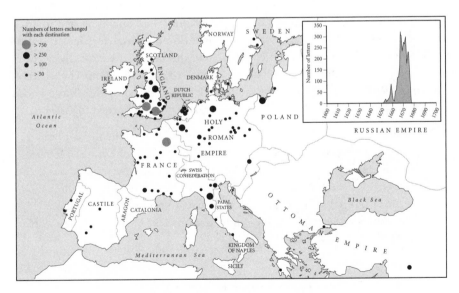

54. Henry Oldenburg's correspondents, 1641–77.
  Over 3,000 of Oldenburg's letters are known for the years 1641–77, revealing that he had contacts all over western Europe as well as in Scandinavia, Poland and the Ottoman empire. As founding secretary of the Royal Society of Great Britain, Oldenburg corresponded with far more scholars, and with scholars in far more countries, than any previous 'scientist'.

scholarship, despite the obstacles posed by distance. As the 1685 issue of the *Journal des Sçavans* put it: whereas in the past it had proved difficult to secure copies of recent works published abroad, 'today, by means of the learned journals', French scientists are 'informed of everything that happens; and we learn each month what we only used to find out after some years'.[60]

Personal contacts also advanced scientific knowledge. While Samuel Sorbière attended meetings of the Royal Society, two future Fellows, Philip Skippon and his Cambridge tutor John Ray were made welcome by scholars on the continent. At Heidelberg, they found that the Elector 'intends to erect a new college, which will be called "Collegium Illustre, or Lipsianum", because Lipsius was excellent in all sorts of learning; this college being designed for experiments, etc. as the Royal Society is at London'. In Naples, they attended some of the weekly meeting of the 'Academici Investigantes', joining about sixty others to hear a paper that 'defended the Lord Verulam's [Bacon's] opinion' and to watch an 'experiment'. Everyone, they found, was 'well acquainted with writings of all the learned and ingenious men' of Europe, whether dead (such as Bacon, Harvey, Galileo and Descartes) or alive (they named Robert Boyle, Thomas Hobbes and Robert Hooke).[61]

The 'Republic of Letters' also included practitioners who lived east of the Elbe and south of the Pyrenees. The Danzig brewer and astronomer Johannes Hevelius, who in 1647 published the lavishly illustrated *Selenographia*, the first lunar atlas (see Plate 1), had studied at Leiden and met scholars in England and France; became a Fellow of the Royal Society; and welcomed Edmond Halley and other prominent scientists to his impressive observatory in Danzig. In Spain, Miguel Marcelino Boix y Moliner asserted in a book entitled *Hippocrates illuminated* (1716) that 'the foreign doctors and philosophers of the last century' had only managed to 'make great advances' thanks to plagiarizing their Spanish precursors. He singled out the work of 'Gideon' Harvey on the circulation of the blood, 'Renato' Descartes on philosophy, and Richard Morton on cinchona bark, all of whom (he claimed) had simply replicated the earlier research by Spanish scholars – three little-known examples of 'contested multiples'. Jonathan Israel was surely correct to assert that

> No major cultural transformation in Europe, since the fall of the Roman Empire, displayed anything comparable to the impressive cohesion of European intellectual culture in the late seventeenth and early eighteenth century. For it was then that western and central Europe first became, in the sphere of ideas, broadly a single arena integrated by mostly newly invented channels of communication, ranging from newspapers, magazines, and the salon to the coffee-shop and a whole array of fresh cultural devices.[62]

The Limits of the Scientific Revolution

Europe's scientists had less success when they tried to understand and explain the Little Ice Age. Galileo had impressed on his illustrious pupil Grand Duke Ferdinand of Tuscany that instrumental observations and experiments could reveal the secrets of Nature, and members of Florence's Accademia del Cimento (Experimental Academy) invented an accurate rain-gauge (to measure precipitation), evaporimeter (to measure humidity), barometer (to measure air pressure), and thermometer (to measure atmospheric temperatures). In 1654 the Grand Duke established an international network of 11 stations, each one equipped with identical instruments and protocols, to perform synchronized measurements several times a day of temperatures (and, in one station, atmospheric pressure). Each station recorded its daily readings on a standard sheet, and dispatched copies to the Grand Duke. The network had assembled over 30,000 readings by 1667, when operations ceased under pressure from the Vatican, which feared that the results would reinforce Galileo's dangerous notion that instrumental ideas were superior to the Bible in interpretating Nature. Grand Duke Ferdinand's death three years later ended any hope of processing the data.[63]

Meanwhile, in England, Robert Hooke ('Curator of Experiments' of the Royal Society) proposed in 1663 a 'Method for making a history of the weather'. This would involve the measurement in numerous stations of eight variables: half by standardized instruments (wind direction, temperature, humidity and air pressure) and the rest by observation (cloud cover, thunderstorms, 'any thing extraordinary in the tides', 'aches and distempers in the bodies of men', and 'what conveniences or inconveniences may happen in the year, in any kind, as by flouds, droughts, violent showers etc'). Hooke designed a chart divided into columns, in which a month's daily observations could be recorded at each station; and he hoped to find 'in several parts of the world, but especially in distant parts of this kingdom, [people] that would undertake this work' of record-keeping. But therein lay the fatal flaw: making and distributing the delicate calibrated instruments, and paying the 'observers' in each station, required money – and the Society had none, since its budget consisted only of the annual dues from each Fellow (many of whom failed to pay). The scheme therefore remained unrealized (Plate 28).[64]

Several Englishmen nevertheless kept a 'weather diary', including the London schoolmaster John Goad, who made detailed observations between 1652 and 1685, when he published much of his data, juxtaposed with planetary movements, and a tentative analysis of the results. Goad also exchanged information with the antiquarian and astrologer Elias Ashmole, who like him made a daily record of observed precipitation, wind direction and so on. These men knew what they were about. 'Casualty is inconsistent with science,' Goad stated: since climate was not a matter of chance, scientific observation would reveal patterns, and so permit prediction. John Locke, who kept a 'Register of the weather' throughout the year 1692, agreed:

> If such a register as this, or one that was better contriv'd with the help of some instruments that for exactness might be added, were kept in every county in England and so constantly published, many things related to the air, winds, health, fruitfulness, etc., might by a sagacious man be collected from them and several rules and observations concerning the extent of winds and rains etc be in time established, to the great advantage of mankind.

Robert Plot, director of experiments for the Oxford Philosophical Society, likewise hoped that the close study of the weather would empower scientists to

> Learn to be forewarned certainly of divers emergencies (such as heats, colds, dearths, plagues, and other epidemical distempers) which are now unaccountable to us; and by their causes be instructed for prevention or remedies. Thence too we may hope to be informed how far the positions of the planets, in relation to one another and to the fixt stars, are concerned in the alterations of the weather, and in bringing and preventing diseases, or other calamities.[65]

Robert Plot's rationale reveals two important limitations of the 'scientific revolution'. First, the aim was admirable but unobtainable. Even in the twenty-first century, the wealth of meteorological data harvested via terrestrial and satellite observations does not suffice to forewarn us 'certainly of divers emergencies (such as heats [and] colds)', so that we can 'be instructed for prevention'. Even in August 2003 no one predicted – and, with the available technology, no one *could* have predicted – that the heat wave that struck many parts of Europe would last 11 days without remission and involve the highest temperatures ever recorded; yet in some areas that brief 'calamity' more than doubled the normal death rate for August and killed almost 70,000 people prematurely.[66]

Robert Plot's hope that systematic observation would show 'how far the positions of the planets' were 'concerned in the alterations of the weather, and in bringing and preventing diseases, or other calamities', revealed the second limitation of 'experimental philosophy': he still believed that occult forces shaped his environment. He was not alone. The last (and most popular) work written by Francis Bacon, *Sylva sylvarum*, contained a chapter on telepathy, wart-charming and witchcraft; William Harvey carried out 'experiments' to see whether or not those who claimed to be witches had supernumerary nipples or 'familiars' who performed supernatural tricks; while Robert Boyle sponsored a treatise to prove the existence of witchcraft (like Bacon, the last book he wrote examined the supernatural). Even Isaac Newton, knighted by the queen of England for his services to science, bought many books on magic, conducted alchemical experiments, and calculated from the Book of Daniel that the world 'will end A.C. [AD] 2060. It may end later, but I see no reason for its ending sooner.'[67] The appearance of two comets in 1664–5 spawned well over 100 publications, most of them filled with dire predictions of war, plague, famine, drought, gales, floods, the death of princes, the downfall of governments, and perhaps the end of the world. In Russia, locked in war with Poland, the tsar ordered prayer and fasting to beg God 'to send the peace we desire and to keep away from us all the evils that so many comets presage.'[68] Two other brilliant comets in 1680 and 1682 had a similar impact. Almost 100 works discussing their significance appeared in Germany and German-speaking Switzerland, over 30 in Spain, 19 in France and the Netherlands, 17 in England and its American colonies, and 6 in Italy. In Rome, ex-Queen Christina of Sweden offered a prize to anyone who could compute the comet's path (almost certainly to facilitate more accurate astrological predictions). In India, Dr John Fryer, a Cambridge graduate and physician, observed with amazement 'the rise and fall of the most prodigious comet I was ever witness to', and since 'it is certainly ominous', he prayed that 'it may not affect our Europe'. In England, John Evelyn, a founding Fellow of the Royal Society, wrote a detailed description of the fireball in his diary, adding: 'What this may portend (for it was very extraordinary) God only knows.' Like Fryer, he prayed that 'God avert his judgements: we have had of late several comets, which though I believe appear from natural causes, and of themselves operate not, yet I cannot despise them. They may be warnings from God.'[69]

These reactions differed little from those of educated observers elsewhere in the world. In Sri Lanka, in 1665, a chronicler associated the outbreak of rebellion against the king of Kandy with the 'fearful blazing star ... right over our heads'; while in India, 'during the whole duration of the comet' even Aurangzeb, a devout Muslim, 'drank only a little water and ate a small quantity of millet bread', and also 'slept on the ground with only a tiger skin over him'. In 1680, in China, the Manchu Bannerman Dzengšeo and his comrades fighting in Yunnan watched the progress of the comet with misgivings and argued 'that if it advanced towards the imperial palace it would be a bad omen'; and the official history of the Kangxi reign included a precise record of both that and the 1682 fireball.[70] Meanwhile, in Massachusetts, Increase Mather (preacher at the North Church in Boston and president of Harvard College) delivered a sermon about the 1680 comet entitled 'Heaven's alarm to the world', which warned 'that fearful sights and signs in heaven are the presages of great calamities at hand'. The fireball of 1682 inspired Mather to compose his comprehensive *Kometographia, or a discourse concerning comets*, which reminded his readers that the Thirty Years War and the destruction of the native population of New England had followed the comets of 1618, while the plague and fire that devastated London had followed that of 1664. It was only because 'we that live in America know but little of the great motions of Europe, much less in Africa and Asia, until a long time afterwards' that news of yet more catastrophic consequences had not reached Boston.[71]

Exactly half a century before, Descartes had expressed the hope that someone would publish in a single book all 'the observations of comets, with a table of the paths of each one'. He predicted that 'such a work would be of greater public utility than it might seem at first sight', but (he continued with a sigh) 'I have no hope that anyone will do it' because 'I think it is a skill beyond the reach of the human mind'. Isaac Newton took up this challenge in the 1680s, carefully copying into his notebooks the descriptions of comets that he found in Aristotle, medieval chronicles and more modern accounts, as well as the observations made by his contemporaries – not only Edmond Halley (who travelled to several European observatories to check their records) and John Flamsteed (the astronomer royal) but also the Jesuit Valentin Stansel from Brazil, the Harvard astronomer Thomas Brattle and his former schoolmate Arthur Storer, now a planter slave-owner in Calvert County, Maryland, who transmitted outstanding observations of the 1682 comet. Newton incorporated these and other findings gleaned from informants all around the world in his remarkable *Mathematical Principles* of 1687, of which the third book (entitled

'The System of the World') contained a long section about comets (Fig. 55).[72]
Newton also used his newly invented mathematical technique, later known as
calculus, to plot the course of the 1680 comet and concluded that it had come from
outer space on a parabolic curve around the sun and would never return.

Here Newton was wrong – and so were all but one of the scientists who calculated that comets followed an *elliptical* orbit and so periodically returned. The
French astronomer royal, Pierre Petit, argued (incorrectly) that the 1664 comet was
the same as that of 1618, and would reappear in 1710; his successor Giandomenico
Cassini deduced (also incorrectly) that the 1680 comet had previously appeared in
1577 and would therefore reappear in 1784. None of them won the prize set up by
ex-Queen Christina. Edmond Halley would also have reached the wrong conclusion
if he had decided to study the 1680 comet, but instead he focused on the fireball that
appeared two years later – which happened to be the only short-period comet that
is clear to the naked eye (others may be as bright, or brighter, but they appear only
once in a millennium or less).

Like Newton, Halley combined observation with historical study and his close
reading of the accounts of all previous apparitions convinced him that the comets
that appeared in 1531, in 1607 and in 1682 were one and the same, and that it must

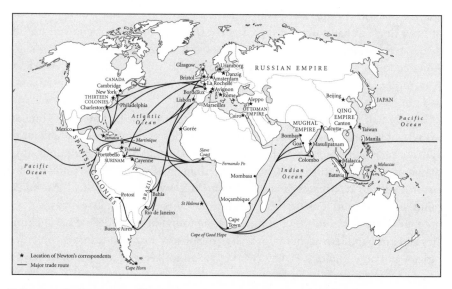

55. Sources of information used by Newton in *Principia Mathematica* (1687).
    Newton never left England (indeed, while working on the *Mathematical Principles*, he does not
    appear to have left Cambridge), but he received abundant data gathered by friends, and friends of
    friends, both Protestant and Catholic, from all the continents, which he used to form and support
    his hypotheses. The configuration of the principal trade routes of the 1680s explains the location
    of most of his data-gathering points.

therefore circle the sun in a 75- or 76-year cycle. He then calculated its exact orbit, using Newton's physics to account for the effect of the gravitational pull of the planets that it passed. In 1705 Halley published a short pamphlet in Latin and English that first set out his rationale about the orbit of comets in general, and the exact periodicity of the 1682 comet in particular, and then 'dare[d] venture to fore-tell' that the same comet 'will return again in the year 1758'. Although Halley did not live to see it, when a comet duly appeared in 1758, identical to the one described in 1682, contemporaries named it 'Halley's Comet' in his honour. Halley's short treatise included another prediction: although no previous comet 'has threaten'd the Earth', he noted that the orbits of some fireballs come close enough to raise the possibility that one day a collision might occur, and he ended his pamphlet with the ominous words: 'What might be the consequences' of 'the shock of celestial bodies (which is by no means impossible to come to pass), I leave to be discuss'd by the studious of physical matters'.[73]

Halley's 1705 pamphlet epitomized the dazzling achievements (and self-confidence) of the Scientific Revolution. It provided irrefutable proof that comets, like planets, orbited the sun; it offered an impressive test of Newtonian physics; and it also made two accurate predictions: the first vindicated when the comet returned after exactly 76 years, the second when part of a comet struck Jupiter with dramatic results almost three centuries later. Yet no one in 1705 – or even in 1750 – knew how dazzling Halley's achievement really was: even his first prediction could not be verified for 76 years. One might therefore object that, in the scientific sphere as in the field of education, the 'Great Divergence' between Europe and the rest of the world had not yet occurred; but this overlooks an important difference.

In his 'Introduction' to the 2009 special issue of the *Journal of Interdisciplinary History*, dedicated to the General Crisis in Europe, Theodore Rabb noted 'the transformation of attitudes toward science', which 'in the decades after 1640 went from concerns about its bewildering, contested and controversial quest for knowledge to the acceptance of scientific method as the magisterial form of intellectual endeavour. To move from the condemnation of Galileo to the knighthood of Isaac Newton is to traverse a fundamental divide in European thought.' In another article, Rabb stressed that this 'divide' lay not only in the advances made by scientists, but also in the political and social context in which their 'intellectual endeavour' took place. In the first half of the seventeenth century, it

> Corresponded closely with a growing malaise, as religious war, economic boom and bust, the spread of ever more virulent military conflicts, and the encroach-ment of centralizing governments on local autonomies caused widespread disrup-tion and distress. In this context the unprovable demands that the scientists were putting forward for jettisoning old ideas seemed both a symptom of, and a stimulus to, the fires of doubt.

After 1650, by contrast, 'looking to restore a sense of confidence, Europe's elite found reassurance and a tangible certainty in the increasingly united claims for new truths about the physical world'. Rabb argued that, on their own, 'the discoveries would not necessarily have gained wide acceptance. It was their role in restoring confidence in human capacity that gave them their magisterial status.' 'Useful' knowledge had ceased to be threatening.[74]

Even by the end of the seventeenth century, however, this new 'confidence' was neither complete nor universal in Europe. On their visit to Naples in 1663, Skippon and Ray heard complaints from the *Academici Investigantes* 'of the Inquisition, and their clergymen's opposition to the new philosophy; and of the difficulty they met with in getting books out of England, Holland etc'. Four years later, in Tuscany, papal pressure ended the Grand Duke's efforts to gather and study serial data on the climate. In England, Edmond Halley's doubts about the veracity of the Bible (for example, questioning the existence of a single act of Creation) cost him the chair of astronomy at Oxford University in 1691: the astronomer royal (one of his referees) warned that, if appointed, Halley would 'corrupt the youth of the university with his lewd discourse'. Newton and others duly prevented the election of such a subversive.[75] In Scotland, the High Court tried and executed a student at Edinburgh University for blasphemy in 1697.

It is here that Robert Merton's 'multiples' come into play: in Europe, censorship in one country no longer affected scientific innovation elsewhere. Thus, despite the papal ban on holding heliocentric opinions, in London, John Milton's *Paradise Lost*, first published in 1667, contains an admirable summary of Galileo's *Dialogue of the Two Systems* as well as numerous references to telescopic observation, rotating sunspots and irregularities on the moon's surface; while the 'Tuscan Artist' (Galileo) is the only contemporary mentioned in the entire work. Likewise, although in 1663 the Roman Inquisition placed the works of Descartes on the 'Index of Prohibited Books', a few years later Louis XIV chose Jacques Rohault, France's leading Cartesian, as mathematics and philosophy tutor to his heir; and in the 1670s the young man attended open discussions of the heliocentric theory at the Academy of Sciences, and followed the rotation of the comets, stars and planets during his visits to the Observatory created by his father.[76] The Scientific Revolution had been nationalized.

The situation in China was very different. In 1661 the Qing government set up a literary inquisition to review an unof–ficial *Ming History* published by a group of Han scholars in Jiangnan. Deeming it seditious, they executed some 70 men involved in the venture, including historians, printers and even purchasers of the work; exiled their male relatives and condemned their female relatives to serve as slaves in Manchu households; confiscated all their property; and burned all copies and all blocks of the book. As in Europe, harsh penalties led to widespread self-censorship among survivors.[77] Just over a century later, the central government initiated a massive bibliographic project known as 'The Complete Library of the Four Treasuries', which aimed to secure a copy of all known books for the imperial library – but 'If the books contain language that is anti-dynastic,' the emperor commanded, 'then the woodblocks and printed sheets must both be put to the flames. Heterodox opinions must be quashed, [so] that later generations may not be influenced.' The literary inquisition, which lasted for 15 years, destroyed 70,000 printing blocks and incinerated almost 4,000 works, while authors and printers purged many other works themselves, re-carving some individual blocks and removing censored names and statements from others.[78]

The Qing thus continued to see intellectual innovation and much 'useful knowledge' as a potential threat, not a potential asset. For them, 'new truths about the physical world' continued to seem 'both a symptom of, and a stimulus to, the fires of doubt'. Unlike rulers in northwest Europe, China's new masters refused to allow their leading scholars either freedom of expression or freedom to exchange ideas. Taken together with the different 'welfare ratio' that prevailed in the different locations by the early eighteenth century (see chapter 21 above), despite numerous similarities, the origins of the 'Great Divergence' lay in the Global Crisis.

Conclusion: The Crisis Anatomized

Winners and Losers

Crane Brinton's classic study *Anatomy of Revolution*, first published in 1938, sought 'uniformities' between the political upheavals in seventeenth-century England, eighteenth-century North America and France, and twentieth-century Russia. In the last chapter, Brinton asked 'What did these revolutions really change?', and he answered:

> Some institutions, some laws, even some human habits, they clearly changed in very important ways; other institutions, laws and habits they changed in the long run but slightly if at all. It may be that what they changed is more – or less – significant than what they did not change. But we cannot begin to decide the last matter until we have got the actual changes straight.

The preceding pages have attempted to 'get straight' what changed and what stayed the same in the seventeenth-century world; it now remains to assess their relative significance and to ascertain the 'uniformities' among the 50 or so revolutions and rebellions that occurred around the world between 1618 and 1688.[1]

At the individual level, the most 'significant' change for most contemporaries was a sharp deterioration in the overall quality of life. During the Indian famine of 1631, English merchants living in Gujarat considered that 'The times here are so miserable that never in the memory of man [has] the like famine and mortality happened.' Ten years later, in China, according to the diary kept by a young scholar, 'Jiangnan has never experienced this kind of disaster'. In 1647 a Welsh historian opined: ''Tis tru we have had many such black days in England in former ages, but those parallel'd to the present are to the shadow of a mountain compar'd to the eclipse of the moon'; while during the famine of 1649, a Scottish colleague wrote that 'The pryces of victuall and cornes of all sortes wer heigher than ever heirtofore aney[one] living could remember', so that 'the lyke had never beine seine in this kingdome heretofor, since it was a natione'.[2]

All ages produce pessimists who claim that the hardships they face are the 'worst in living memory', and the mid-seventeenth century produced unprecedented numbers of pessimists, and claims of unequalled misery – but the surviving evidence suggests that they were right. Because of the decrease in solar energy and the increase in volcanic and El Niño activity, the environmental deterioration has few parallels; while the frequency of wars and state breakdown created unprecedented political, social and economic instability.

Some groups suffered disproportionately. Slaves led the way. In China, in parts of Europe (notably Britain and Ireland), and above all in Africa, millions of men and women lost their liberty and often their lives because they became slaves; while millions more in Russia and eastern Europe also lost their liberty because they became serfs. Whether free or unfree, women also suffered disproportionately in most parts of the world. Women killed themselves because they had been raped and otherwise humiliated and could not 'live with the shame'; because they were destitute and could not face a life of hunger and deprivation; or because they did not wish to survive the death or disappearance of their loved ones. Many of the survivors faced a 'bitter living' (in the memorable words of 'a poor woman with only a small field or so to her name' in Germany): she and her sisters had to work harder and longer just to stay alive. Their desperate situation helps to explain why so many women around the seventeenth-century world aborted, killed or abandoned their infant children.[3]

Admittedly, some European women could use the 'weapons of the weak' to retaliate against their oppressors. Female workers and servants abused by their employers could seek revenge not only through foot-dragging, pilfering and slander but also (in extreme cases) through arson and murder. Wives could not only plead with their abusive husbands in private: they could complain to their neighbours and to the courts; they could seek (or threaten) divorce; and they could threaten (or *in extremis* inflict) grievous bodily harm. In London, Elizabeth Pepys used all of these strategies in 1668 after she discovered her philandering husband Samuel making love to their 16-year-old servant. After tears, reproaches and 'ranting', she threatened to tell their neighbours, to leave him, and even to join the Catholic Church. She also struck Samuel, attacked him with a pair of red-hot tongs and threatened to slit the servant's nose (a popular punishment for adultery). But Elizabeth's most effective weapon lay 'in matters of pleasure': she refused to sleep with him. Three weeks after his disgrace, Pepys confided to his diary that he was 'troubled to see how my wife is by this means likely for ever to have her hand over me, that I shall be for ever a slave to her'.[4] Only English and Dutch women seem to have enjoyed this limited power to 'retaliate', however. Their sisters in other areas of Europe might well ask, like Queen Christina of Sweden in the 1680s, 'What crime has the female sex committed to be condemned to the harsh necessity of being shut up all their days either as prisoners or slaves? I call nuns "prisoners" and wives "slaves"'.[5]

Queen Christina would no doubt have felt the same about her female contemporaries in much of Asia, where 'respectable' women lived in seclusion from puberty to menopause (a seclusion reinforced in China by the practice of foot-binding: see chapter 4 above). The only exceptions in the Muslim world were the mothers, wives and concubines of Mughal, Ottoman and Safavid rulers, especially during succession disputes. Thus Shah Jahan, who was absent from the Mughal court when his father Jahangir died in 1627, gained the throne only because his female relatives at court took control and outmanoeuvred those who supported other claimants. In the Ottoman empire Kösem, mother of Sultans Osman, Murad and Ibrahim, overthrew several Grand Viziers and even connived in the regicide of 1648, becoming the most powerful person in the state. Such power rarely lasted long: in 1651 Kösem was murdered at the behest of the mother of the new sultan, just as a generation earlier, in Iran, Shah Safi murdered scores of his female relatives because he feared they might try to overthrow him.[6]

Wars and revolutions killed, maimed and ruined large numbers of people, both directly through brutality and indirectly through forced migration and destruction of property. Deaths among young men rose with especial rapidity in western and central Europe during the Thirty Years War, in eastern Europe and Russia during the Thirteen Years War, and in China during the Ming-Qing transition. For many soldiers, as well as for thousands of civilians – Protestants and Catholics in Ireland, Jews and Poles in Ukraine, and Ming Clansmen in China – the World Crisis proved a terminal event. Taken together, these tragedies claimed the lives of so many millions, including so many members of the elite, that one might speak of a 'lost generation'.[7]

In some areas, a whole way of life disappeared. The violence of the Ming-Qing transition permanently destroyed sericulture in the province of Shaanxi, and the Gujarat famine and floods of 1628–31 did the same to one of India's premier cotton- and indigo-producing areas (see chapters 5 and 13 above). The plague epidemic that spread through southern Europe in the decade after 1649, killing one half of the inhabitants of Seville, Barcelona, Naples and other similar cities (see Fig. 11), set the seal on the decline of the Mediterranean as the heart of the European economy for ever. In many other areas, if the observations of Alex de Waal and Scott Cane concerning the effect of a prolonged 'hungry time' on farmers of marginal lands and on hunter-gatherers (see chapters 1 and 15 above) also prevailed in the seventeenth century, then many communities and countless families must have crossed 'a threshold of awfulness' and perished, leaving no trace.

Admittedly, the turmoil produced winners as well as losers. In East Asia, both Nurhaci and Tokugawa Ieyasu were revered as gods soon after their deaths and bequeathed to their numerous descendants a luxurious lifestyle that would endure for more than two centuries. Indeed, the numerous Tōshōgū shrines in Japan still honour the divinity of the first shogun, making him by far the most successful denizen of the seventeenth-century world. The descendants of Michael Romanov also prospered from the political, economic and social balance created by the crisis of 1648–9, cementing their control over an empire that expanded at the rate of 55 square miles a day – more than 20,000 square miles a year – for almost three centuries.[8] Many followers of these rulers also profited from the upheaval. In East Asia, tens of thousands of Manchu Bannermen and their families exchanged a precarious existence on the steppe for a life of plenty in one of the Tartar towns of China. Likewise, most of the military and civilian officials who swiftly transferred their allegiance from Ming to Qing prospered: of 125 senior officials who received the ambiguous title Er chen ('ministers who served both dynasties'), 49 became the president or vice-president of a department of state after the conquest.[9] In Japan, the Tokugawa clansmen and most of their daimyō allies enjoyed more than two centuries of peace and plenty following the proclamation of the 'Genna armistice' in 1615. In Russia, the boyars and their descendants who in 1649 won control over their serfs through the *Ulozhenie*, maintained their advantage for over two centuries. In India, the leaders who supported Aurangzeb when he challenged his father and brothers during the Mughal Civil War of 1657–9 shared some of the wealth of the richest state on earth.

In Europe, among civilians, government office allowed Samuel Pepys to increase his personal fortune from £25, when he began to serve in 1660, to £10,000 ten years later; while Jean-Baptiste Colbert, who at school 'was so dull that he was always bottom of the class', thanks to the favour first of Cardinal Mazarin and then of Louis XIV, died a millionaire and bequeathed a hereditary peerage to his son. Among soldiers, Sweden's commanders in Germany who survived the Thirty Years War returned home with immense wealth: the castle of Skökloster near Stockholm testifies even today to the booty brought home by General Karl Gustav Wrangel, while his colleague Hans Christoff Königsmarck, who began as a common soldier, died a nobleman with assets worth two million thalers. In England luck and good judgement during the Civil War allowed George Monck, the younger son of a squire (and fortunate as a young man to escape hanging for murdering a deputy sheriff), to become duke of Albemarle and commander-in-chief of England's armed forces in 1660, and to die with assets worth £60,000. Monck's followers also prospered. In return for facilitating the Restoration, the general insisted on full payment of the wage arrears of his men, and over the next two years the king's treasurers-at-war paid them £800,000.[10]

Often, soldiers gained at the expense of civilians. A Brandenburg lawyer and tax official, Johann Georg Maul, kept a diary between 1631 and 1645 in which he obsessively catalogued the descent of his family from prosperity to virtual destitution at the hands of soldiers who either robbed them, lodged with them, or demanded contributions from them. Maul's first experience of war cost him 280 thalers: a cavalry sergeant, three troopers and their lackey 'ate their way through' 55 thalers in food over 11 weeks; 'there was also 115 thalers . . . for 22 barrels of beer, which the aforementioned boozed away with his guests every night'. Maul also had to provide wine for some visiting officers, hay and straw for their guests, oats for the troopers' horses and, to add insult to injury, 'ten thaler for a horse which the major took as a mount for his Fool, who was called Pointynose'. Most subsequent years brought similar billeting demands, sometimes several times, which Maul grimly itemized along with robberies by troops living in his house, as well as endless demands for contributions to sustain troops billeted elsewhere. By 1640 Maul had enriched so many soldiers (and their camp-followers, like Pointynose) that he had virtually nothing left: when he defaulted on his contributions, the three troopers sent to extract payment 'saw for themselves that I had no money', so after drinking beer worth three thalers 'they agreed to leave, taking a handkerchief each which my wife gave them, worth a thaler, and some bread'.[11]

The upheavals of the age brought some women fame. Queen Christina said and did things after her abdication in 1654 that would have led other women to the gallows – making fun of religion; dressing, speaking and behaving as a man; ostentatiously kissing and sleeping with other women – but, as a prestigious convert to Catholicism as well as a former queen, she enjoyed unique freedoms.[12] Between 1649 and 1653, Madeleine de Scudéry published *The Great Cyrus*, the longest French novel ever written (2 million words; 13,000 pages; 10 volumes), which achieved enormous success because its protagonists were thinly disguised caricatures of Paris socialites and Frondeurs (Cyrus himself was obviously the prince of Condé, and so on). Yet Mlle de Scudéry was also a resolute feminist. Her novels implicitly attacked the prevailing idea of love as something rational, calculated and possessive: instead, her characters insist that love springs from the heart, not the head; and that love is only real when a man is overcome by a force stronger than himself and becomes totally submissive to a woman. Despite their enormous length, her books also appeared in English translation and reached a wide public. Elizabeth Pepys, who was not normally an avid reader, enjoyed Scudéry's books so much that one night she angered Samuel, as they travelled 'in the coach, in her long stories out of *Grand Cyrus*, which she would tell, though nothing to the purpose nor in any good manner'. (Did Samuel perhaps recognize the threat to his philandering ways posed by the book's feminist views?)[13]

Mlle de Scudéry also presided over a literary salon every Saturday, attended by the leading French intellectuals. One of its numerous female members was Marie-Madeleine, countess of La Fayette (1634–93), whose *Princess of Cleves* (1678) has been hailed as the first modern novel in French, since it offers both historical verisimilitude (it takes place at the French court a century earlier) and psychological analysis. It also reveals a noblewoman wrestling with the temptation to commit adultery with another courtier – a subject scarcely conceivable for a pre-Crisis novel, especially one written by a woman. *The Princess* is currently available in numerous printed editions, as a film, a 'Kindle' book, and a book-on-tape (duration: 5 hours 46 minutes); it forms part of France's National School Curriculum; and in 2008 Nicholas Sarkozy, then President of France, complained how much he had 'suffered' from being forced to read it at school. Fame indeed.[14]

Both Scudéry and La Fayette appear to have passed unscathed through the human and natural disasters of the mid-seventeenth century. Few women enjoyed such luck. Although there was no 'typical' experience of the global crisis, the lives of two other remarkable female survivors, and of their families, may be more representative. Wang Duangshu (c. 1621–1701) was the daughter of a scholar official in China's once wealthy Jiangnan region. Too old to fight the Qing, when their soldiers arrived in his town in 1645 her father posted on his door a sign that read 'NO SURRENDER' and refused to shave his head in the prescribed Manchu fashion. Instead, he fled to the mountains where he starved himself to death. Meanwhile his learned daughter, who had married an official who also refused to bow to the new regime, supported him as long as she could, through her teaching, writing and painting; but 'when the chill and hunger became unbearable' they left home together, taking turns at 'pushing a cart. Desolate while on the road, they sold her calligraphy, painting and writing for a living'.[15] That same year, 1645, Margaret Lucas, a lady-in-waiting to Queen Henrietta Maria of England who had followed her mistress into continental exile, married William Cavendish, marquis of Newcastle, the defeated royalist general at Marston Moor, 30 years her senior. The couple remained in exile until the Restoration of 1660, renting the exquisite town house that Peter Paul Rubens had used as his studio, where Margaret entertained literary luminaries and wrote books. In 1656 she presented the Antwerp City Library with a five-volume set of her own works; 11 years later she was the first woman to be allowed to visit the Royal Society (where she watched an 'experiment' performed by Robert Boyle); and by the time of her death in 1676 she had published over 20 books on subjects as diverse as natural philosophy, poetry, love (in verse and prose), and science fiction. She also composed an autobiography that, although expressing satisfaction with her social and literary successes, devoted far more attention to the loss of almost £1 million because Parliament had sequestered all her lands and revenues, and to the pain she felt at the death of her older brother Thomas from a head wound sustained while fighting for the king in Ireland, and the execution of her younger brother Charles by firing squad after the surrender of the royalist garrison of Colchester. Both died in 1648, and the following year her sister died of 'consumption' (no doubt tubercu-losis), followed by her mother. Margaret wrote that her mother's death was, 'I believe, hastned through grief' at having 'lived to see the ruin of her children'. She concluded sadly: 'I shall lament the loss so long as I live.' Despite her literary eminence, in her own eyes the balance sheet of her life, which ended before she was 50, was decidedly negative.[16]

The balance sheet of many states likewise showed both losses and gains. Thus although Qing China and Romanov Russia topped the list of successful dynasties, millions of their subjects lost either their lives or their freedom. In Ukraine, although Ruthenian culture flourished (and even spread to Russia), while serfdom disappeared, the name *Ruina* given by its historians testifies to the costs of the struggle to shake off Polish rule. Portugal exploited Spain's weakness to gain independence – the only entirely successful rebellion of the seventeenth century – but once again this success reflected immense material and personal sacrifices, including the permanent loss of most of the Lusitanian empire in Asia (and the temporary loss of its colonies in Africa and Brazil). The Dutch Republic gained formal recognition as an independent state, and carved out a lucrative trading empire in south and Southeast Asia at the expense of Portugal and inde-pendent rulers like the sultan of Mataram; but it lost its colonies in North and South America. Britain's brief Republican experiment secured the Caribbean island of Jamaica, and commercial dominance in the North Atlantic, but the Civil Wars caused the premature death of perhaps 500,000 people in Britain and Ireland, while Scotland and Ireland (the first states to rebel) temporarily lost their independence. The weakness of the Ottoman empire allowed the Austrian Habsburgs to conquer most of Hungary; while the weakness of the Spanish Habsburgs allowed Louis XIV to advance the frontiers of France – albeit, in both cases, at the cost of hundreds of thousands of lives.

Other states suffered grave political losses in the mid-seventeenth century and gained little or nothing. The kingdom of Kongo in Africa, and the Indian nations of New England, all perished; while the Polish-Lithuanian Commonwealth lost half its population, temporarily ceased to exist as an independent state, and lost for ever its status as a Great Power. The Spanish Monarchy, too, never recovered its political pre-eminence after the secession of Portugal and its overseas empire; and although Philip IV eventually overcame his rebels elsewhere, he did so only after making major concessions (in Catalonia, for example, he left the 'Constitutions' intact and pardoned virtually all those who had defied him). In East Asia, the short-lived Shun dynasty founded by Li Zicheng in China disappeared without trace; while the fall of the Ming forced a reconstruction of Korean identity, because it 'shattered the premise concerning the world order of which the Koreans felt they were a part' (just as it required Han Chinese intellectuals to refashion themselves). Around the Great Lakes of North America, the Hurons and their allies escaped famine, disease and the Iroquois by moving west where, as Daniel Richter noted, they 'recombined and reinvented themselves' to create a 'Middle Ground' between New England and New Mexico that lasted until the late eighteenth century – but they nevertheless lost all their ancestral lands.[17]

Above all, with the exception of Japan, New England and New France, the demographic balance of the seventeenth century was negative. Apart from the cases of drastic population loss already cited – Qing China; Romanov Russia and Ukraine; the Polish-Lithuanian Commonwealth; most of Germany – Philip IV ruled far fewer subjects at his death in 1665 than at his accession four decades before. Apart from the loss of his former vassals in Portugal and its empire, and along the French frontier, war devastated Catalonia, the areas of Castile along the Portuguese frontier, the Netherlands and Lombardy; while plague, recruiting and taxation depopulated large parts of the Spanish Mediterranean. Finally, in France, famines, epidemics and the civil war unleashed by the Fronde, 'the climax of the Little Ice Age' and the losses caused by his repeated wars meant that Louis XIV probably ruled over fewer subjects at his death in 1715 than when he began his personal rule in 1661.

In Search of Common Denominators

According to political scientist Mark Hagopian's book, *The Phenomenon of Revolution*, even

> When we have enumerated adequate sets of antecedent conditions with their respective empirical generalizations, [t]he resulting explanation or prognosis is bound to be highly complex, but *those seeking simplicity should study something else than the causes of revolution. In addition, there is good reason to doubt the 'completeness' that any explanation of revolution could possibly attain.*

Thus inspired, let us begin with the 11 'antecedent conditions' (or, as a historian might call them, 'causes') offered by Francis Bacon in his celebrated essay 'Of seditions and troubles', first published in 1612:

> The causes and motives of seditions are: innovation in religion; taxes; alteration of lawes and customs; breaking of priviledges; general oppression; advancement of unworthy persons; strangers; dearths; disbanded soldiers; factions growne desperate; and whatsoever, in offending people, joyneth and knitteth them in a common cause.[18]

Most of these categories can be broken down into components. Thus, in his lectures to the Statistical Society of London in 1878 on 'The famines of the world: past and present', Cornelius Walford proposed 13 distinct causes for just one of Bacon's categories: 'dearths'. Walford discerned six natural precipitants of harvest failure, including excessive rain, frosts, droughts, 'plagues of insects and vermin' and sunspot cycles, and seven more 'artificial' (read: human) precipitants, including war, 'defective agriculture', insufficient transport, legislative interference, currency manipulation, hoarding, and diverting grain from making bread to other purposes (such as brewing or distilling).[19]

Nevertheless although Walford relied mostly on nineteenth-century data from England and British India, the same combination of 'natural' and 'artificial causes' he identified also prevailed in the seventeenth century. Famines caused by unfavourable weather were often exacerbated by 'defective agriculture' (farmers who refused to cultivate maize and other crops more resistant to a harsher climate); by a shortage of vessels and carts to transport food from areas with a surplus to those in deficit; by grain merchants who withheld or diverted supplies in order to increase their profits while people around them starved; and by governments that promoted economic chaos by tampering with the currency, squandered resources that might have fed the starving, and refused to make peace in order to reduce demands for troops and taxes. The seventeenth century also witnessed an 'enigma', noted by Walford, that 'the very remedies which have been adopted to prevent, or to mitigate the severity of, these periodical visitations [of famine], have by some reflex action, apparently, either aided in producing them, or at least added very much to the severity of the results flowing from them' – results that often included rebellion and sometimes revolution. Nevertheless, Walford remained convinced that extreme climatic events normally played a greater role than human action in creating catastrophe.[20]

Does the seventeenth-century evidence support this analysis? Certainly, the major revolts almost all broke out in a period of unparalleled climatic adversity, notably when a 'blocked climate' produced either prolonged precipitation and cool weather or prolonged drought (1618–23, 1629–32, 1639–43, 1647–50, 1657–8 and 1694–6). Some areas suffered for longer: both Scotland (1637–49) and Java (1643–71) suffered the longest droughts in their recorded history. The century also saw a run of 'landmark winters', including some of the coldest months on record, and two 'years without a summer' (1628 and 1675); and an unequalled series of extreme climatic events – the freezing over of both the Bosporus (1620) and the

Baltic (1658); the drying up of China's Grand Canal (1641); the maximum advance of the Alpine glaciers in 1642–4. In 1641 the river Nile at Cairo fell to the lowest level ever recorded, while Scandinavia experienced its coldest winter ever recorded. These various climatic aberrations accompanied a major episode of global cooling that lasted at least two generations: something without parallel in the past 12,000 years. The famines caused by this change in the global climate caused what would today be called a 'humanitarian crisis' in which millions of people starved to death.

These same years of dearth also saw rebellions and revolutions, with two distinct 'peaks': Normandy, Catalonia, Portugal and its overseas empire, Mexico, Andalusia, Ireland and England in 1639–42; and Naples and Sicily, France, England (again) and Scotland, Russia, the Ottoman empire and Ukraine in 1647–8. Sometimes a link between rebellion and climate change is manifest. Thus, in Scotland, the summer of 1637 (in which Charles I sought to impose his new liturgy) was the driest in two decades, while 1638 (when he refused to make concessions to his Scottish opponents) was the driest in a century. Government innovation and inflexibility at a time of unprecedented climatic adversity led many Scots to join the Covenanting revolt. The earl of Lothian, a prominent landowner, spoke for many when (having described how, in October 1637, 'the earth has been iron in this land', ruining the harvest) he wrote 'I think I shall be forced this term to run away and let the creditors of the estate catch that catch may, for I cannot do impossibilities'. In the event, his lordship did not 'run away'. He had already signed the formal protest against the new Prayer Book; six months later he signed the National Covenant. In 1640 Lothian led a regiment in the invasion of England, declaring that 'necessitie made us come from home' and 'in our laufull defence WE DARE DIE'.[21] In Ireland, too, the failed harvests of 1638–41 caused widespread hardship among the Catholic population, disposing many to support the rebellion that began in October 1641, when ice and snow covered many parts of the island; and then followed 'a more bitter winter than was of some years before or since seen in Ireland', which turned the brutal mistreatment of Protestant settlers by their Catholic neighbours into a massacre that would in turn provoke massive retaliation.[22] Likewise, in East Asia, the repeated harvest failures caused by adverse weather in the early 1640s had two dramatic political effects. First, the famines and popular rebellions in Jiangnan fatally weakened the Ming as they struggled against the inroads of 'roving bandits' from the northwest. Second, drought and cold in Manchuria so reduced harvest yields that the Qing leaders concluded that invading China offered the only way to avoid starvation.[23]

Climate-induced dearth also contributed to many other rebellions. Perhaps, as Leon Trotsky wrote of the Russian Revolution of 1917, 'the mere existence of privations is not enough to cause an insurrection; if it were, the masses would always be in revolt' – but the privations inflicted by climate change in the mid-seventeenth century were an exception. The revolts in Évora in 1637, Palermo in 1647, Fermo in 1648, and the 'Green Banner' revolts of Andalusia in 1652, began in just the same way as the greatest rebellion of the twentieth century in Petrograd in 1917: when adverse weather ruined a harvest and thereby created a food shortage that brought hungry people onto the streets shouting 'bread'.[24]

In such a tense situation, even a small increase in government pressure could produce an apparently disproportionate popular reaction. The revolt of the towns of Sicily in 1647 began when the government decreed an end to the subsidy that had kept down the price of bread; while the Naples revolution a month later began when the viceroy reimposed an unpopular excise on fruit. In both cases, Philip IV overrode the misgivings of his ministers because he needed funds to pay for his wars – despite the fact that domestic rebellion opened a 'second front'. The same perverse logic prevailed in the French Monarchy, where Louis XIII repeatedly raised taxes in times of high food prices, so that his subjects had no money left to buy bread. 'Long live the king; death to taxes!' became the cry of rebellious subjects throughout Europe.

Governments could also stimulate or spread insurrections by other means. Charles I's insistence on imposing a new liturgy on Scotland in 1637 inflamed and united his opponents as nothing else could have done. The desecration by royal troops of the churches in villages that defied them had the same effect in Catalonia in 1640; as did the decision of the Qing regent Dorgon to enforce the head-shaving edict on all males in China in 1645. The revolt of the Catalans would last for 18 years; the resistance of Ming loyalists would last for 38 years. Ineptitude by rulers could also encourage resistance. In Naples the inability of the *eletto del popolo* to settle a squabble over who should pay the 'fruit excise' on the morning of 7 July 1647 allowed Masaniello and his 'boys' to galvanize irate bystanders into action. During the summer of 1648, revolts broke out in Moscow when the tsar refused to receive a 'Supplication' from his subjects that condemned corruption among his ministers, and in Paris when the regent botched an attempt to arrest her leading opponents as they left a service in Notre Dame cathedral. The ineffective use of force by governments in the initial stages of a rebellion could also prove disastrous. In Barcelona in 1640, in Naples at 1647 and in Messina in 1674, rebellions began just after the galley squadrons based in each port city departed to fight elsewhere.[25]

The most violent opposition to governments in the mid-seventeenth century often began in a capital city – a circumstance that reflected the greater vulnerability of all urban areas to both climatic change and to government abuse. The major revolts against Charles I and Philip IV all began in a political capital (in Edinburgh, Dublin and London against the former; in Barcelona, Lisbon, Palermo and Naples against the latter), as did other insurrections that rocked and sometimes toppled seventeenth-century regimes: Prague in 1618; Istanbul in 1622, 1648 and 1651; Manila in 1639; Paris in 1648; Moscow in 1648 and 1662; Edo in 1651.

Popular protests alone rarely brought down governments, however, and all the major rebellions of the mid-seventeenth century included members of the secular and, in most Christian and Muslim societies, also the clerical elite. Churchmen headed four rebel governments, at least for a time (Henderson in Scotland, Claris in Catalonia, Rinuccini in Ireland and Genoino in Naples); while throughout the French, Stuart and Spanish Monarchies, clerics preached sermons and published propaganda in support of the rebel cause. In the Polish Commonwealth, the Ukrainian clergy threw its weight behind Khmelnytsky; while in the Ottoman empire the Chief Mufti (the Şeyhülislam) played a pivotal role in legitimizing the deposition (and subsequent murder) of the sultan in 1622 and again in 1648.[26]

Noblemen, too, took the lead in several European revolts – Condé and Longueville in France; Argyle and Hamilton in Scotland; Antrim and Maguire in Ireland; Essex and Manchester in England – and, in all four countries, virtually the entire nobility participated in the resulting civil war. In Portugal, Duke John of Bragança founded a new royal dynasty in 1640; in Castile, the duke of Medina Sidonia sought to become the head of an independent Andalusia in 1641; while seven years later the duke of Guise established the short-lived 'Royal Republic of Naples'.[27] In the Mughal, Ottoman and Chinese empires, in contrast, the hereditary nobility played virtually no part because their fortunes were too closely linked to the state.

Most of the remaining leaders of the major mid-seventeenth rebellions belonged to the intellectual elite. At least 80 per cent of the members of the English House of Commons between 1640 and 1642, and many English peers, had either studied law at the Inns of Court, or gone to university, or both.[28] The Fronde in France began with the revolt of its senior judges. Those who had mastered China's national curriculum and started to climb its administrative 'ladder of success' by passing the state examinations took the lead both in paralyzing the Ming with factionalism and in opposing the Qing with suicidal energy.

Most insurgents in Europe claimed that they desired only the restoration of an earlier state of affairs which they considered preferable. Thus the rebels in Palermo and Naples demanded a return to the Charters granted by Charles V a century before; the Catalans called for respect for their ancient 'constitutions'; the Portuguese wanted a return to the relationship with the king created at the union of crowns in 1580 (and when they could not get it, a restoration of the constitutional situation that had prevailed *before* 1580). Initially, Charles I's enemies also called merely for a return to the past. In England, they demanded government by the crown-in-Parliament, as created by his predecessors; in Ireland the Catholics sought implementation of the 'Graces', which would end the recent trend in Protestant expansion at Catholic expense; in Scotland, the Covenanters insisted on retaining their traditional liturgy. In France, the judges wanted a return to the constitutional 'balance of power' that they believed had prevailed in the Middle Ages; while the nobles saw the 'liberties' and 'franchises' won by the blood of their ancestors in the service of the crown as their birthright, and to defend it they felt a 'duty to rebel'. In Russia, the crowd wanted the tsar to accept their petitions as he and his predecessors had done before.

Rebels in other parts of the world also drew strength from past precedents. In China, Li Zicheng, Zhang Xianzhong and the Qing, all of whom strove to replace the Ming dynasty, cited earlier examples (some of them two millennia earlier) of dynasties that had lost 'the Mandate of Heaven'; and Wu Sangui would do the same in 1673 when he initiated the Revolt of the Three Feudatories against the Qing. In the Ottoman empire, Kadizade Mehmet and his followers called for a return to the political and religious conventions that had prevailed at the time of the Prophet Mohammed a millennium before. Many others, such as the Swiss in Entlebuch and the Norman *Nu-Pieds*, demanded a return to a Golden Age when 'justice' had prevailed. To quote Crane Brinton once more: 'Revolutions cannot do without the word "justice" and the sentiments it arouses'.[29]

Attempts to gain 'justice' drew strength, at least in Europe, when supported by legal institutions of unquestioned legitimacy, such as the law courts or Parliament. To this end the rebel leaders in Scotland, Catalonia and Portugal immediately summoned the 'Estates of the Realm' to legitimize their challenge to established authority, as well as to enact appropriate policies and vote funds – thus creating an 'alternative government' capable of winning widespread support both at home and abroad.[30] In Ireland, since the Protestant-dominated Dublin government condemned the rebellion of 1641, the Catholic leaders created their own General Assembly and Supreme Council at Kilkenny, which served for a decade as the government of an independent Ireland (it even boasted its own corps of resident foreign diplomats: an achievement not repeated until the twentieth century). In England, Parliament was already in lawful session when the king declared its members rebels, but both Houses continued to sit until in January 1649 the surviving members of the House of Commons (the 'Rump') tried and executed him, and then proclaimed England a Republic with themselves as its sole sovereign body. Meanwhile, in the Dutch Republic, the States-General exploited the death in 1650 of William II of Orange to gain control over the executive functions that he had exercised. In Ukraine, finally, Hetman Bohdan Khmelnytsky from the first sought the approval of the assembly of Cossack freemen for his various actions, including a declaration of independence from the Polish Commonwealth and, later, a treaty of union with Russia that preserved most of the gains won by the initial revolt.[31]

The unifying appeal of these aims helps to explain why so many seventeenth-century insurgencies lasted so long. The revolt of Bohemia against Habsburg authority in 1618 initiated a war that lasted 30 years. The revolt of Portugal against Habsburg authority in 1640 began a conflict that lasted 28 years; while the Catalan Diputació's repudiation of Philip IV the following year turned the principality into a battleground for 19 years. In Ukraine, the Cossacks' rejection of the authority of the Polish crown in 1648 also led to 19 years of war. The execution of Charles I by his English subjects in 1649, and the proclamation of a Republic, inevitably led to hostilities against the Scots, the Irish and several American colonies (which proclaimed Charles II as their sovereign), and the former Stuart Monarchy remained on a war footing, with a large army and navy even in peacetime, right up to the Restoration in 1660.

Longevity, however, changed the character of most rebellions. As John Wallis later observed about England: 'As is usual in such cases, the power of the sword frequently [passed] from hand to hand', because of 'those who begin a war, not being able to foresee where it wil end'. None of the 'Five Members' whom Charles I tried to arrest early in 1642 possessed military experience, and few had held executive office, so they gave way to those like Oliver Cromwell whose actions demonstrated their ability to lead. Likewise, in Naples, the constitutional lawyers Genoino and Arpaja replaced the illiterate demagogue Masaniello, only to lose their places to Gennaro Annese and the duke of Guise, who possessed military experience.[32] The rise of a 'second generation' of more militant leaders, like Cromwell and Annese, helps to explain why revolutions became more violent the longer they lasted. The experience of resistance habituates leaders to actions that would earlier have seemed intolerable. Moreover, any government, whether established or insurgent, needs to take drastic measures when faced with climatic extremes, famine and war (and in the mid-seventeenth century such challenges occurred with unusual frequency), but regimes that lacked legitimacy (and experience) might resort to more extreme measures to enforce their policies.

Rebellious regimes might also appeal for foreign aid, and in so doing fragment their domestic support. In Ireland, the Catholic Confederacy turned to their co-religionists in Europe, and although the Papacy, France and Spain all provided valuable material assistance, each foreign power had its own agenda and did not scruple to create and exploit damaging domestic divisions in order to achieve them. In the Iberian Peninsula, the Catalan opponents of Philip IV appealed for French assistance; and although French troops and military advisers helped to save Barcelona, Louis XIII demanded that the Catalan leaders abandon their resolve to become an independent republic and instead recognize him as their sovereign. Most spectacular of all, in China, the Ming commander Wu Sangui appealed to his northern neighbours for military assistance against the 'roving bandits', and allowed the Manchu Grand Army to pass through the Great Wall to destroy Li's forces; but once this mission had been accomplished, the Manchus claimed that their victory conferred the Mandate of Heaven to rule all China, which they did until 1911.

Within the composite states of Europe, opponents of the same ruler in one area often took active steps to encourage others to rebel. Thus immediately after his 'acclamation', King John IV of Portugal sent envoys to Barcelona to make common cause with the Catalan rebels; and somewhat later his principal adviser, the Jesuit António Vieira, went to Rome to invite the Pope to invest John's son as king of Naples (a papal fief). In 1648 in Castile, Don Carlos de Padilla, lynchpin of the 'conspiracy of the duke of Híjar', looked to John IV of Portugal for support; and government agents found the name of Don Miguel de Iturbide, who had recently spearheaded successful opposition to royal policies in Navarre, among his papers (see chapter 9). Most striking of all, as soon as news arrived that riots in Palermo against excise duties in 1647 had secured their abolition, the citizens of Naples began to put up 'pungent and bitter invectives' calling for 'a revolution like Palermo'; and as soon as the revolution began, 'some people from Palermo' urged the Neapolitans 'to demand everything, in the same way that had happened in Palermo'. One of these 'Palermitanos' was Giuseppe d'Alesi, who returned to lead the movement in his native city that secured the same concessions as those granted the previous month to the rebels of Naples. In addition, in both kingdoms, revolt in the capital provoked copycat uprisings in numerous other towns (see chapter 14).

The opponents of Charles I in different parts of his Monarchy likewise created links across borders that aimed to improve their chances of success. Thus some Scottish ministers in northern Ireland found the hostility of the earl of Strafford's religious policies so intolerable that in 1639 they chartered a vessel to take them to Massachusetts (John Winthrop had visited Ulster the previous year), but storms drove them back to their native land. They saw this as a divine sign that they should 'find an America in Scotland' and, once arrived there, joined the Covenanters' opposition to Charles I. In Russia, too, disorders spread throughout the empire largely because in June 1648 the capital was full of petitioners from provincial towns, and local uprisings followed as soon as the petitioners returned home with news of the Muscovites' apparently successful defiance of the tsar (see chapter 6). Finally, the peasants of Entlebuch who began the 'Swiss revolution' in 1653 sent envoys to mobilize support elsewhere in Canton Luzern and its neighbours (see chapter 8).

If

Despite the unparalleled frequency of revolts in the mid-seventeenth century, it is possible to imagine a more peaceful world – even with the litany of 'antecedent conditions' listed above. As Charles I reminded the Long Parliament in November 1640, while explaining how the Scots had managed to defeat his forces so swiftly: 'Men are so slow to believe that so great a sedition should be raised on so little ground'.[33] 'Accidents' – totally unpredictable developments – could crucially affect the outbreak or outcome of a rebellion: the election by lot of two talented yet intransigent Catalan patriots, Pau Claris and Francesc de Tamarit, as the senior Diputats of Catalonia, in 1638 (see chapter 9); the interregnum in the Polish-Lithuanian Commonwealth created by the death of King Władysław IV just after the Cossack rebels routed its field army in 1648 (see chapter 6); the death from smallpox of William II of Orange without an adult heir just after he had defeated his domestic opponents in 1650 (see chapter 8).

Some 'accidents' were more predictable – especially those caused by distance, which was (in Fernand Braudel's adage) 'Public Enemy Number One'. Philip IV's advisers hesitated to react immediately to the revolt of Naples 'because the state of affairs over there changes from one moment to the next, and what seems appropriate today might not be so tomorrow'; while his envoy to the Irish Catholic Confederation complained that distance constituted 'the greatest problem of my job' because it meant that 'I can neither send successive accounts of what is happening nor receive in good time the royal orders of Your Majesty'.[34] Even within the Iberian Peninsula, as Sir John Elliott noted,

> The distance between Madrid and Barcelona meant that [the viceroy's] letters and those from Madrid never kept in step. While circumstances were changing from day to day in the Principality, Madrid was at least three days behind the news, and still legislating as if the situation was exactly the same as when the viceroy had written his last set of dispatches.[35]

Likewise, the central government in Madrid received the first reports of the Portuguese revolution that occurred in Lisbon on 1 December 1640 just one week later, but refused to believe them. 'It is possible that a popular tumult might have produced a good deal of what we have heard,' the Council of State informed Philip IV, 'but to proclaim a king the same day is not credible.' The king did not sign letters warning ministers in Europe about 'the accident of Portugal' until 15 December; he did not instruct colonial administrators to take defensive measures until 27 December; he did not warn the treasure fleets coming from America to avoid Portuguese harbours until 5 January 1641; and he did not order the closing of all frontiers, both in the peninsula and in America, to commerce with the rebels until 10 January.[36]

Conversely, 'accidents' could also unexpectedly derail rebellions. Thus Lord Maguire's plot to seize Dublin Castle in 1641 failed only because one of the conspirators decided to betray his colleagues – but even then the magistrates 'gave at first very little credit to so improbable and broken a [story], delivered by an unknown, mean man, well advanced in his drink', and so sent him away. He only managed to sabotage the plot because he made a second attempt – this time successful – to betray his colleagues (albeit now too late to send a warning of the plot to Ulster, where it succeeded: see chapter 11). Likewise, ten years later, the samurai plot to seize Edo and destroy the Tokugawa regime came to light only because one of the conspirators became delirious and unwittingly shouted out the details.[37] In each of these cases (and no doubt in many others) a minor 'rewrite' of the historical record would thus produce a dramatically different outcome; and the same is true of natural disasters, such as earthquakes and volcanic eruptions, which occur with little or no warning: *if only* the 1640s had not seen, at much the same time, the virtual disappearance of sunspots, much more volcanic activity, and double the number of El Niño episodes . . .

Nevertheless, although contingency (like catastrophe) cannot be written out of history, when constructing 'What if?' scenarios, historians must always consider second-order (or reversionary) counterfactuals: the possibility that rewriting the *short-term* historical record, as in the examples above, might still not alter the *long-term* outcome. Reversionary counterfactuals take two forms: one positive (an 'accident' could delay but not permanently derail a particular development) and the other negative (a development that was, so to say, 'an accident waiting to happen'). Positive examples are relatively easy to find. From the 'human archive', 22 years after the death of William II and the 'Dutch Revolution' that followed, his posthumous son William III recovered almost all of the traditional powers and influence of the princes of Orange; just as Charles II regained virtually all of his father's powers in all his dominions 11 years after the regicide in 1649. Turning to the 'natural archive', since some parts of the planet could only feed their inhabitants in 'good years', then even had fewer volcanic eruptions and El Niño episodes occurred in the 1640s, sooner or later 'bad years' would come, and they would still cause heavy mortality.

M. de Bellièvre, the French resident in London, provided a good example of a negative 'reversionary counterfactual' as he contemplated the situation in Ireland in 1648. He informed Cardinal Mazarin that

What surprises most of those who consider the affairs of that country [Ireland] is to see the people of the same country and the same religion, who know that the decision to exterminate them totally has been taken, so strongly divided by their private hatreds, so that zeal for their religion, the preservation of their country, and their own self-interest *does not suffice to make them abandon – at least for a while – the passions that incite them against each other.*[38]

The English conquest began the following year, and within three years Confederate Ireland was no more – but, in Bellièvre's view, even if the London government had delayed its campaign of repression, internal dissention still doomed the Catholic cause to ultimate defeat. Historian Julian Goodare has proposed a similar negative 'reversionary counterfactual' for Scotland: given the character of both Charles I and the leading Covenanters, 'the Scottish crisis of 1637–8, with its momentous consequences for Britain, *had been waiting to happen for some time; if the Prayer Book had not ignited it, something else soon would have done.*'[39]

Many of Charles's fellow rulers – Qing Regent Dorgon, Tsar Alexei Romanov, Gustavus Adolphus of Sweden and Christian IV of Denmark – displayed a similar inflexibility; and so did their principal ministers. None of them seemed prepared to contemplate alternatives to the policies they had adopted. Thus in 1632 Thomas Wentworth, later earl of Strafford, informed a colleague: 'Let the tempest be never so great, I will much rather put forth to sea, work forth the storm, or at least be found dead with the rudder in my hand' – an uncanny echo of the claim seven years earlier by the count-duke of Olivares that 'As the minister with paramount obligations, it is for me to die unprotesting, chained to my oar, until not a fragment is left in my hands.'[40] Although Philip IV's ministers never gave their political programme a boastful name like 'Thorough', they blindly pursued policies that were equally ambitious and equally unrealistic. However desperate the political situation seemed, introducing innovations and imposing additional burdens during the adverse economic and social situation caused by the Little Ice Age was sooner or later likely to provoke resistance and rebellion.

The Two Worlds of Robinson Crusoe

Robinson Crusoe, one of the most famous fictional inhabitants of seventeenth-century Britain, grew up during the Civil War and left home in 1651, just after the execution of Charles I; and after being marooned on a remote island he returned to his native land in 1687, just in time to witness the flight of James II and the Glorious Revolution. Yet Crusoe's 'Strange and surprizing adventures', first published in 1719, included not a word on these political changes. By contrast, Daniel Defoe, Crusoe's creator, repeatedly emphasized how the mental world in which his character grew up differed from the mental world of his readers. For example, Young Robinson kept a diary that initially resembled the spiritual journal and balance sheet maintained by many Puritans in the mid-seventeenth century (see chapter 20 above); but before long he filled it with balance sheets of profit and loss, reflecting the commercial outlook that had made England prosperous.[41] Moreover, whereas England in the mid-seventeenth century had been riven by confessional strife, Crusoe despised religious intolerance. He 'allow'd liberty of conscience throughout my dominions' to Catholics, Protestants and pagans alike; and he considered 'all the disputes, wranglings, strife and contention, which has happen'd in the world about religion, whether niceties in doctrines or schemes of church government, they were all perfectly useless to us, as for ought I can yet see, they have been to all the rest of the world'. Crusoe's enthusiasm for religious toleration did not stem from a desire to attract religious refugees (as under Cromwell) but because it was essential for profitable international trade (which Crusoe pursued with great success).[42] Finally, Crusoe successfully practised the 'new philosophy' (see chapter 22 above). He salvaged from his wrecked ship 'infinitely more than I knew what to do with', leading to the 'reflection, that all the good things of this world *are no farther good to us than they are for our use*'; and that, on the contrary, '*All I could make use of, was all that was valuable*'. Crusoe also became a successful planter, and soon found that his two most valuable assets were tools ('the carpenter's chest' he salvaged was 'much more valuable than a ship loading of gold would have been') and labour: Crusoe saved 'my man Friday', a Native American, from cannibals and immediately set him to work on his 'colony' (Crusoe's term), where the first English word he had to learn was 'Master'. So although Crusoe 'had never handled a tool in all my life' yet 'I improv'd myself in this time in all the mechanick exercises, which my necessities put me upon applying myself to'.[43] A clearer example of the impact of the new 'experimental philosophy' would be hard to find.

The world of 1719 differed from the world of 1651 in one other important respect: the frequency and violence both of volcanic eruptions and El Niño events diminished, the current 11-year sunspot cycle resumed, and the long episode of global cooling came to an end. The benign climate, coinciding with a more systematic exploitation of the environment, allowed the supply of goods to increase faster than demand for them, and so permitted rapid population growth in more fertile areas. In China, the Kangxi emperor noted in 1716 that the population grew 'day after day', unlike the available arable land, and complained – just like his predecessors a century before – about the increase in the number of 'unproductive consumers', singling out intellectuals, merchants and clerics. A few years later, a senior official in Fujian estimated that 'the population had doubled' during the previous six decades. He also complained that 'while the population increases daily, the amount of land under cultivation does not'. The following year, the central government launched a drive to bring more land under cultivation because 'population has increased of late, so how can [the people] obtain their livelihood? Land reclamation is the only solution.'[44] Thanks to such measures, by the mid-eighteenth century both East Asia and western Europe boasted a far denser population than ever before – but this time without a decline in life expectancies or standard of living. Equally important, the new equilibrium of population and resources made the demands of the fiscal-military state more bearable. The return of a warmer climate had broken the 'fatal synergy'.

Nevertheless, the same dynamic of subsistence prevailed, and continues to prevail. Societies in which the demand for food exceeds the supply must either increase supply (by adopting technological changes that improve crop yields per acre, by mobilizing a new source of energy, or by securing food elsewhere by trade or by force); or else they must reduce demand (by eating less, or by reducing the number of mouths to be fed through fewer births, increased migration, or more deaths). All these strategies played their part in coping with the problems caused by the fatal synergy of human and natural factors in the seventeenth century. Many starved and many more went hungry; while more abortions and infanticides, more delayed or forgone marriages, and more migration (both forced and voluntary) reduced the number of mouths to feed. Yet, since all these adaptive measures took effect only slowly, in most societies around the world food supply and demand only came back into equilibrium after 'enough' people had died.

Although blind, and confined to his house, John Milton understood this dynamic as clearly as any contemporary. He began to compose *Paradise Lost* in London during the landmark winter of 1658, and continued through the years of dearth that accompanied the Restoration of Charles II, so it is hardly surprising that unpredictable and unforgiving changes in the climate are central to his story. Milton's fictional world, like the real one in which he lived, was (as he termed it) a 'universe of death' at the mercy of extremes of heat and cold.

> At certain revolutions all the damned
> Are brought: and feel by turns the bitter change
> Of fierce extremes, extremes by change more fierce,
> From beds of raging fire to starve in ice
> Their soft ethereal warmth, and there to pine
> Immovable, infixed, and frozen round
> Periods of time; thence hurried back to fire.[45]

Epilogue: 'It's the climate, stupid'[1]

ONCE UPON A TIME, THE HISTORY OF CLIMATE WAS A 'HOT TOPIC'. In 1979 the World Meteorological Organization, the United Nations Environment Programme, the National Science Foundation, the Ford Foundation and the Rockefeller Foundation paid for 250 historians, geographers, archaeologists and climatologists from 30 countries to attend the first international 'Conference on Climate and History', hosted by the Climatic Research Unit at the University of East Anglia (England) – a unit sponsored by (among others) British Petroleum and Royal Dutch Shell. Cambridge University Press later published a volume containing the most innovative of the conference papers. That same year, the World Meteorological Organization created the 'World Climate Program' with a mandate to 'insert climatic considerations into the formulation of rational policy alternatives'. No one doubted then either that global climate had undergone dramatic changes in the past or that, sooner or later, it would undergo equally dramatic changes in the future.[2]

These initiatives took place in the shadow of a world food crisis: the price of wheat tripled and that of rice quintupled between 1972 and 1974, a reflection of harvest failures in South Asia, North America, the Sahel and the USSR, themselves a reflection of the strong El Niño episode of 1971–2 which suggested that a system of teleconnections might explain how the global climate 'worked'. The United Nations therefore convened a 'World Food Conference' in 1974, which made the solemn 'Declaration' that: 'As it is the common responsibility of the entire international community to ensure the availability at all times of adequate world supplies of basic food-stuffs by way of appropriate reserves, all countries should co-operate in the establishment of an effective world system of food security'. The Conference's equally solemn 'Resolutions' included:

- 'Achievement of a desirable balance between population and food supply'.
- 'Reduction of military expenditure for the purpose of increasing food production'; and
- '[Creating] a global information and early warning system on food and agriculture'.

Before governments had time to enact these resolutions, however, the 'shadow of a world food crisis' disappeared thanks to the 'Green Revolution': new high-yielding varieties of wheat, maize and rice, combined with the increased use of irrigation, fertilizers, pesticides and herbicides, dramatically increased food production. Famines virtually disappeared from the headlines and climate change virtually disappeared from the research agenda of historians.[3]

Then in 1990 the 'Intergovernmental Panel on Climate Change' (IPCC), another United Nations initiative, issued its first *Assessment Report*, summarizing the research of 'several hundred working scientists from 25 countries'. The document claimed that 'emissions resulting from human activities are substantially increasing the atmospheric concentrations of greenhouse gases', and that without immediate action to reduce greenhouse gas emissions, 'additional warming of the Earth's surface' was inevitable. To clarify the scale of the problem, the *Report* called on colleagues to 'further investigate changes which took place in the past'. The response of the scholarly community, including many historians, has been magnificent: since 1990 they have compiled thousands of data-sets and published hundreds of articles about past climate change, revealing a series of significant shifts that culminated in an unprecedented trend of global warming.[4]

Unlike the research presented in the 1970s, these new findings have been ignored, rejected and belittled; while suggestions that states should 'insert climatic considerations into the formulation of rational policy alternatives' also provoke passionate opposition. Just after he became Chairman of the Environment and Public Works Committee of the United States Senate in 2003, Senator James Inhofe declared global warming to be the 'greatest hoax ever perpetrated on the American people'.[5] In 2011 Senator Inhofe co-sponsored legislation (the Upton-Inhofe bill) that would prevent the federal government from 'promulgating any regulation concerning, taking action relating to, or taking into consideration the emission of a greenhouse gas to address climate change'; while later that year the United States House of Representatives defeated by 240 votes to 184 a motion known as the 'Waxman Amendment' stating that 'climate change is occurring, is caused largely by human activities, and poses significant risks for public health and welfare'.[6]

The Waxman Amendment conflated two distinct issues: determining whether 'human activities' (notably, the emission of greenhouse gases and deforestation) can produce climate change is not the same as proving that 'climate change' occurs. There may perhaps be residual doubts about the first proposition, just as some still deny that smoking tobacco increases the risk of lung cancer, but the historical record leaves no doubt that climatic change occurs, and that it can have catastrophic consequences for 'public health and welfare'. Although humans appear to have played no part in precipitating the climate changes of the seventeenth century, they suffered and died from its consequences all the same.

The surviving human and natural archives reveal episodes of major climate change in the fourteenth century and in 1816, as well as in the seventeenth century. A series of articles by economic historian Bruce Campbell demonstrates that the 1310s and 1340s saw both 'extreme instability' in the climate and lethal disease (rinderpest in 1316–25 and bubonic plague 1346–53), at a time when both the bovine and human populations had reached unprecedented densities. England's excellent surviving records suggest these natural disasters 'more than halved' the population.[7] The climate-induced catastrophe in 1816, another 'year without a summer', occurred when sunspots were few (the 'Dalton Minimum', 1795–1828), and just after the most powerful volcanic eruption recorded in the past 10,000 years, at Tambora in Indonesia: a combination that appears to have reduced average temperatures on earth by between 1° and 2°C – exactly the same variation as in the mid-seventeenth century. This sufficed to produce not only global cooling but also extreme climatic events. In North America, throughout the summer, fronts of Arctic air dumped snow north of a line stretching from British Columbia to Georgia, producing temperature oscillations from 35°C to freezing in a single day; and in September 1816, New Hampshire experienced 'the four greatest frosts known . . . at this season by any man living'. Across the Atlantic, intense cold prevailed for most of the summer from Finland to Morocco; rain fell on Ireland for 142 out of 153 days between May and September; England experienced the third coldest summer since continuous records began in 1659; and grapes in all French and Swiss vineyards ripened later than in any other year since continuous records began in 1437. In Asia, the monsoon failed in India, while snow fell in Jiangnan and Taiwan. In 1817 at Barnstead, New Hampshire, St Valentine's Day was 'the coldest day [that] has been for forty years'; while at Salem, Massachusetts, the Reverend William Bentley spent 'the first [day] in my life in which I kept house upon account of the cold'. The extreme weather also generated both disease and famine: a severe epidemic of typhus broke out in Europe while cholera ravaged India; scarcity of bread provoked widespread food riots in Europe; while 'through[out] New England scarcely a tenth part of the usual crop of sound corn will be gathered'. The price of wheat in New York City in 1816 would not be surpassed until 1973.[8]

The 'Yankee Chills' (as survivors in North America called their miserable summer) produced massive emigration from New England to the Midwest. 'The lands to the westward are luxuriant, and the climate mild and salubrious,' crooned a land promoter, and thousands of families believed him and abandoned their farms for the 'golden Ohio country': between 1817 and 1820 the population of the state of Ohio rose by 50 per cent, taking it above 500,000 for the first time. Most of the newcomers were New Englanders fleeing the sudden climate change.[9]

Two centuries later, flight to Ohio would offer little relief if 'Yankee Chills' (or any other natural disaster) should strike New England. In the words of the 2011 version of the state of Ohio's *Strategic Plan*: 'Getting food from farms to dinner tables involves a complex chain of events that could be interrupted at many different stages. Because food and agriculture are such vital industries to our state, Ohio must vigilantly protect animal, plant, and food supply chains' – but with over 11 million Ohioans, it is hard to see how the state could also feed 50 per cent more in an emergency.[10] Admittedly, if the 'chills' killed *only* corn, or *only* affected New England, the transport and distribution infrastructure that has developed in Ohio since 1816 could probably import sufficient emergency food rations from unaffected (or less affected) areas; but this might prove impossible in the wake of a natural disaster nearer home. In 2005 it took almost a week to get vital supplies of food and water into New Orleans after Hurricane Katrina struck, because the storm that flooded the city also severed road and rail links and disabled both landline and cellular telephones; while the evacuation of over one million people from areas of the Gulf Coast affected by the hurricane created a 'hollowed economy', with an infrastructure no longer capable of satisfying its basic food, water and health needs.[11]

Although Katrina was the costliest natural disaster in the history of the United States, it was only one among 432 reported natural disasters of 2005 around the world, causing between them $176 billion of economic damage. That figure remained the record until 2011 when, although the total of reported natural disasters fell to 302, the economic damage they caused exceeded $350 billion. This total included $2 billion caused by a tornado that struck Tuscaloosa, Alabama; $11 billion caused by the earthquake that struck Christchurch, New Zealand; $25 billion caused by another tornado that hit Joplin, Missouri; and $210 billion caused by the Tōhoku earthquake and tsunami in Japan. Between them, those four natural disasters killed well over 20,000 men, women and children. In addition, in 2011, over 106 million people around the world were affected by floods; almost 60 million more by drought; and a further 40 million by storms.[12]

No human intervention could have prevented these natural catastrophes – although a better early-warning system, better popular education about evasive strategies, and faster and more effective emergency responses would surely have mitigated the consequences. Likewise, no human intervention can prevent volcanic eruptions, halt an El Niño episode, or delay the onset of another sunspot minimum – despite the certainty that each will affect the climate, reduce harvest yields, and cause starvation, economic dislocation, political instability and death.[13] So what can be done to mitigate the consequences? The disastrous hurricane seasons of 2004 and 2005 (which included not only Katrina but 'seven of the nine costliest systems ever to strike the United States') led the National Hurricane Center, a division of the National Weather Service located at Miami, Florida, to pose just this question. The Center concluded sadly that another 'disastrous loss of life is inevitable in the future', mainly because the majority of those living in areas at risk have 'never experienced a direct hit by a major hurricane' and seem incapable of envisaging what one is like, while even the rest 'only remember the worst effects of a hurricane for about seven years'. For the National Hurricane Center, the problem lay less in the frequency of hurricanes than in the failure of human beings to learn from them: 'The areas along the United States Gulf and Atlantic coasts, where most of this country's hurricane-related fatalities have occurred are also experiencing the country's most significant growth in population' – striking testimony to the strong 'culture of denial' that prevails.[14]

Nevertheless, as the social psychologist Paul Slovik pointed out, 'The ability to sense and avoid harmful environmental conditions is necessary for the survival of all living organisms', while 'survival is also aided by an ability to codify and learn from past experience'. Moreover, Slovnik continued, '*Humans have an additional capability that allows them to alter their environment as well as respond to it*'.[15] This ability to 'alter' our environment presupposes two distinct skills: *learning processes* (the observation, measurement and classification of natural phenomena) and *learning steps* (the development of techniques, practices and instructions designed to reduce vulnerability in future hazards). History offers numerous examples of both in action. Repeated floods in the lands around the North Sea in the Middle Ages led to the evolution not only of preventive measures and coping strategies but also of permanent cadres of 'experts' and an unusually resilient entrepreneurial culture: all underpinned the rise of the Dutch Republic as a world power. Likewise, the crescendo of urban fires in the mid-seventeenth century gave rise in one city after another to both better fire-fighting measures and (at least in Europe) to the development of a system of specialized insurance companies that now form some of the most powerful business enterprises in the modern world.[16]

Nevertheless, in order to activate our 'additional capability to alter [our] environment', it seems that humans need to experience natural disasters '*not only in magnitude but in frequency as well. Without repeated experiences, the process whereby managers evolve measures of coping with [disasters] does not take place*.'[17] Effective measures to prevent and to mitigate floods and fires therefore only seem to evolve after *repeated* disasters of *unprecedented* severity strike a community. Perhaps this defect in human cognition explains why, despite the fact that 2010 saw the warmest global surface temperatures ever recorded, and was the 34th consecutive year with global temperatures above the twentieth-century average, the *Washington Post* proclaimed in 2011 that global warming had become 'a second-tier issue'.[18]

This strange disconnect prompted a team of researchers to ask over 67,000 people in 47 different countries to answer the question: 'How serious do you consider global warming?' The findings, published in the *Journal of Peace Research* in 2012, supported the assertion of the *Washington Post*: 'Global warming is not considered as an especially important environmental problem by the public.' The data also suggested five broad explanations:

- Concern about climate change correlates with education level, but not with age: those younger than 30 and those older than 60 both seem less concerned than those who are middle-aged.
- 'As countries become affluent, their citizens shift their concern from issues related to economic conditions and personal security' to 'issues related to political and individual freedom and environmental protection'.[19]
- 'A statistically significant negative correlation' exists between Biblical Fundamentalism and 'concern for the environment', particularly among Christians in the United States, for many of whom natural disasters are divine punishments for sins and so must be accepted.[20]
- Respondents in rich countries, and in countries with high carbon dioxide emission levels, showed less concern about global warming than those in poor countries, or in countries with low greenhouse gas emissions (perhaps because it is harder to accept global warming as a problem when it requires recognition that it is partly your fault: a relationship that has been labelled 'uncomfortable truth').

- Finally, the level of concern about global warming is negatively correlated with concern for climate-related natural disasters: that is, people living in countries highly exposed to natural disasters (such as droughts or earthquakes) are less concerned about global warming, either because they perceive the other environmental problems they face as more acute, or because prolonged exposure to natural adversity has taught them to live with it – or, in the words of a study entitled *The Culture of Disaster*: 'For the greater part of humanity, hazard and disaster are simply just accepted aspects of daily life.'[21]

Until recently, the fact that almost all people killed and most people affected by natural disasters lived outside North America and Europe fostered two assumptions in the West: that such things only happened 'somewhere else' (an assumption encouraged by terms such as 'Typhoon Alley', 'The ring of fire' or 'El Niño-prone'); and that certain groups are particularly 'vulnerable' not just because of *where* they live but also *how* they live (such as people who live in overpopulated cities or on marginal lands). Such views are not unfounded: for example, the Philippine archipelago really does experience more disasters than any other comparable area of the world, with 220 volcanoes (at least 12 of them active), 5 earthquakes a day, and up to 30 typhoons a year; while the Haitian earthquake of 2010 reminded the world that urban overcrowding and poverty magnify the impact of disasters.[22] But now, natural disasters are also striking North America and Europe, where each one becomes an 'insurance event'.

According to a White Paper prepared for the European Commission, almost two-thirds of all 'loss events' between 1980 and 2007 were 'directly attributable to weather and climate events (storms, floods and heat-waves)' while a further quarter 'are attributable to wild fires, cold spells, landslides and avalanches, which may also be linked to weather and climate'. Therefore, '95% of the overall losses of catastrophic events result from these weather and climate related events'. According to the same White Paper, 'overall losses caused by weather and climate related events have increased during the period 1980–2007 from a decadal average of less than €7.2 billion (1980–1989) to about €13.7 billion (1998–2007)'. The central European floods of 2002, alone, 'resulted in overall losses of €16.8 billion and insured losses of about €3.4 billion'.[23]

These striking data have not escaped the attention of the world's insurance companies – indeed, their own estimate in 2009 was that 'losses from weather events are growing at an annual 6 per cent, thus doubling every 12 years' – and, in response, they have made some dramatic changes in coverage and premiums. Thus in the Netherlands, where over one-third of the country would be under water without artificial barriers, flood insurance is now unavailable; while in Great Britain it is currently available only for properties built before 2009, and for them only until a government re-insurance system expires at the end of 2012.[24] In Florida, where in 1992 Hurricane Andrew caused more than $15 billion in insurance losses and bankrupted 12 insurance companies, the State government created a public alternative to the private market. Then came the hurricanes of 2004 and 2005, which forced private insurers to pay out a further $39 billion to 'rebuild Florida' – but when those insurers asked the State's permission to raise premiums to cover the increased risk, the State refused. Several private companies therefore refused to insure property in Florida, creating an 'insurance crisis' that has yet to be resolved. In the Bahamas, finally, where government declined to introduce a publicly guaranteed alternative to private insurance, after three major hurricanes between 1999 and 2004 'flood insurance (and consequently mortgage lending) became withdrawn [by private companies] for some low-lying areas and, without any State-backed alternative, houses have become abandoned as their value collapsed.'[25]

These developments led the International Association for the Study of Insurance Economics, also known as 'the Geneva Association', to conclude that 'Insurers need to emphasize that climate change brings societal problems to which insurance can only provide solutions in partnership with government and business'. This is easier said than done. Not everyone believes insurances companies, even when their message takes the form of dramatically higher premiums (if they did, no one would smoke tobacco because smokers pay so much more for life and health insurance.) Moreover, as the European Commission White Paper points out,

> In a number of regions, less populated and economically less performing, often located in areas that are particularly sensitive to climate change risks (coastal, mountainous), the costs to cover adaptation needs will be so huge that they exceed the capacity of public funding. In these areas, losses can take such massive dimensions also for the private sector that they rise eventually beyond the financial capacity of individual companies and businesses.[26]

The impact of the 2004 and 2005 hurricane seasons on the Florida property market demonstrates why neither insurers nor 'market forces' nor local government are likely to cope with all the consequences of climate change. In 2009 the Florida Chamber of Commerce composed a report entitled *Into the Storm*, warning that the state's entry into the insurance business had created a $2 trillion exposure in property risks, so that taxpayers face ruin when the next major hurricane strikes. The report recommended two obvious steps: offering incentives to owners who improved their properties to minimize storm damage (and thus reduce the cost of compensation and repair); and allowing the state insurance scheme to 'let risk determine rates' (that is, in the pungent phrase of former Representative Dennis Ross, 'The risk of living in high-risk areas should be borne by the people who choose to live in those areas'). The authors of *Into the Storm* envisaged only two other proposals: either to attract private insurers back by allowing them to raise premiums to levels that 'reflect the risks that property owners actually take'; or else to 'Push the Feds', because without private insurers 'We need to have a federal backstop for a Florida catastrophe'. The Chamber of Commerce recognized that neither proposal had much chance of success: allowing the 'free market' to determine property insurance premiums would result in rates that few owners could afford; while 'any national legislation that might serve as a back-up to Florida's potential catastrophic losses due to natural disasters still faces a very steep uphill battle from states that argue Florida's extreme exposure to natural disasters would pose an unfair burden to U.S. taxpayers'. As Dennis Ross might have put it: 'If you knew that devastating hurricanes strike Florida every year, why did you build a house here?'[27]

Pessimism regarding support from Washington does not lack scriptural warrant. In the twenty-first century, federal agencies have slightly increased funding to states and cities for disaster response planning; and they have spent rather more on 'mitigation' – that is, on moving things out of harm's way (such as relocating houses out of flood plains) and improving physical defences against natural hazards (such as restoring levees, canals and coastal wetlands in areas threatened by hurricanes and floods). The majority of federal disaster spending, however, has taken the form of aid to help state and local governments *to cope with disasters that have already happened.* These funds have normally gone to support short-term activities in the days and weeks after the event: search and rescue; law enforcement; putting out fires; providing temporary shelter; organizing the emergency distribution of food, water and medicine. Relatively little federal funding has gone into helping vulnerable localities prepare for *long-term* recovery in the wake of a future disaster: how to ensure that local government continues to operate; how to re-house displaced people; how to prepare for the inevitable health problems, mental as well as physical.

The pattern of federal emergency spending reflects a deep-seated fear of 'Big Government' in the United States. The principal rationale offered by the sponsors of the Upton-Inhofe bill (apart from the belief that global warming is 'a hoax') is that any attempt by a federal agency to mitigate or avert damaging climate change represents a 'power grab' by Washington that must at all costs be resisted. The same deep-seated fear also prevailed in seventeenth-century England. Plague epidemics in 1603, 1625 and 1636 had killed tens of thousands of Londoners, and so it was easy to anticipate the probable impact should a new epidemic spread from Holland in 1665. Nevertheless, neither the City nor the national government took appropriate action. Instead, when plague struck, the king and his court, many magistrates and almost all the rich fled the capital. When Charles II convened Parliament to debate appropriate intervention, no legislation passed because the peers demanded an exemption from restrictive measures such as quarantine and insisted that no plague hospitals be erected near their homes. One may wonder why the central government did not act unilaterally to save its capital; but, as a contemporary pamphlet pointed out, 'their power was *limited* and they must proceed legally' – the rule of Oliver Cromwell and his army officers a decade before had left a bitter taste, and as King Charles put it, he was 'too old to go again on my travels' and would not risk alienating his subjects with unpopular actions. The consequences of government inaction were therefore measured in the corpses of plague victims dumped daily in mass graves. In all, the Great Plague killed 100,000 Londoners, one-quarter of the total population of the capital, plus 100,000 more people elsewhere in England.[28]

In the twenty-first century, as in the seventeenth, coping with catastrophes on this scale requires resources that only central governments command. The construction of the Thames Barrier in southeast England offers an instructive example. The river Thames has frequently burst its banks and flooded parts of London. In 1663 Samuel Pepys reported 'the greatest tide that ever was remembered in England to have been in this river: all White Hall having been drowned'; and proposals to erect a barrier to prevent similar catastrophes began a century later – but the opposition of the London merchants, whose trade would suffer if ships could not sail up the Thames, and disagreements among competing jurisdictions over the cost, thwarted them all. Then in 1953 a tidal surge in the North Sea flooded some 150,000 acres of eastern England and drowned more than 300 people. A government minister assured the British House of Commons that 'We have had a sharp lesson, and we shall have only ourselves to blame if we fail to profit from it', and he set up a committee to propose remedies, which recommended the immediate construction in the Thames estuary of a 'suitable structure, capable of being closed'. The government eventually considered two types of barrier but, once again pressure from shipping interests and cash-strapped local authorities prevented action.[29]

Then in 1966 a new government asked its Chief Scientific Adviser, Professor Hermann Bondi, to examine the matter afresh. A mathematician by training, Bondi devoted much attention to assessing risks; but he also consulted historical sources and found that the height of storm tides recorded at London Bridge had increased by more than three feet between 1791 (when records began) and 1953, and he predicted that this trend would continue. Bondi compared the risk of another storm tide with other risks, such as a meteorite falling on central London – which would also cause immense damage – but, he noted, the probability was very low and there was no way to take evasive action. By contrast, 'a major surge flood in London would be a disaster of the singular and immense kind'; given the rising level of the North Sea, it was inevitable; and 'It would be indeed a knock-out blow to the nerve centre of the country.' Bondi therefore unequivocally recommended the construction of a Thames barrier, and although shipping interests and fragmented local government once again caused delay, in 1972 Parliament passed the Thames Barrier and Flood Protection Act, which authorized the project and promised to fund it. By 1982, when the barrier was complete, it had cost a stunning £534 million – but the value of the property it protects now exceeds £200 billion, including 40,000 commercial and industrial properties and 500,000 homes with 1¼ million residents. All would be inundated if another flood 'drowned' Whitehall, the heart of government now as in the time of Samuel Pepys, containing both Houses of Parliament and the offices where 87,000 members of the central administration work. It would also 'drown' the new Docklands economic development, and disable 16 hospitals, 8 power stations and many of the fire stations, police stations, shops and suppliers needed to repair and replace items damaged in the flood, as well as 200 miles of roads, 100 miles of railway, 51 rail stations and 35 Underground stations. Londoners would therefore lose not only their homes and jobs but also the essential means of response and recovery. In short, without the Thames Barrier, London would be like

New Orleans in 2005: vulnerable to a natural disaster that, like Katrina, is sooner or later inevitable.[30]

Completion of the Thames barrier came just in time – it had to be activated 39 times between 1983 and 2000, and 75 times between 2001 and 2010 – and its success, combined with the increased frequency of extreme weather, has encouraged a more proactive attitude towards climate change on the part of the British government. The 2004 Report by its Chief Scientific Officer, summarizing the research of nearly 90 experts on the risks of flooding, expressed the choice with engaging simplicity: '*We must either invest more in sustainable approaches to flood and coastal management or learn to live with increased flooding*.'[31] A similar choice exists for other climate-related risks (such as hurricanes), and indeed for other types of risks (such as the spread of diseases, perhaps accentuated by bio-terror or, for that matter, by 'bio-error'): societies can either 'pay to prepare', and commit substantial resources now to avoid far greater costs later, or else 'learn to live with increased' risks.

Despite the many differences between the seventeenth and the twenty-first centuries, governments during the Little Ice Age faced the same dilemma – although some needed more reminders than others of the need to choose. In Japan, at one extreme, the famine, rural revolts and urban riots of the Kan'ei era sufficed to convince Tokugawa Iemitsu and his advisers of the need to create more granaries, to upgrade the communications infrastructure, to issue detailed economic legislation, and to avoid foreign wars in order to accumulate sufficient reserves to cope with the possible return of extreme weather. England took somewhat longer. Despite the subsistence crises of the 1590s, 1629–31 and 1647–9, only in the 1690s did property owners accept the central government's argument that, in the long run, it was economically cheaper and more efficient (as well as more humane) to support those who became old, widowed, ill, disabled or unemployed, thus creating the first 'welfare state' in the world. Other societies endured even more disasters before they reached the same conclusion that welfare formed an essential and necessary part of collective risk management; but by the nineteenth century the 'welfare state' had become a hallmark of all economically advanced states.

Climatic adversity is a great leveller, because the human population in advanced societies shares many of the needs of the human population elsewhere. 'The hungry time', the term used by the aboriginal people of western Australian for the season between the end of one annual cycle and the beginning of the next (see chapter 15), sounds relatively simple for groups of hunters in another hemisphere, but climate change can create a 'hungry time' for those living in even the most advanced societies. Of course, the total human population in the seventeenth century was far less than the three billion in 1950, let alone the seven billion today; but the geographical distribution of the present population is changing in ways that increase the resemblance between the world today and that of the seventeenth century. Thus in 1950 Europe had three times the population of Africa, but in 2012 the population of Africa is at least 50 per cent larger than that of Europe – a disparity that widens every year as the former grows and the latter declines. This shift increases the percentage of the total population that spends a high proportion of its disposable income on basic needs such as food, energy and housing, often in areas where even central governments lack the effective means of dealing with big disasters, making them more vulnerable to the effects of climate change. Thus Hurricane Katrina in 2005 caused damage equivalent to 1 per cent of the Gross Domestic Product of the United States, but drought in 1999 caused damage equivalent to 16 per cent of the Gross Domestic Product of Kenya.

It is impossible to measure the human suffering caused by natural disasters. We cannot compare the misery of the women who went to the New Orleans Convention Center in 2005, expecting to find food, water, medical care and shelter in the aftermath of Katrina, but were instead raped, robbed and left to die, with the Australian women who starved as they watched their children die of hunger during an unusually long 'hungry time'; or with the poor women of Shanghai who found in 1642 that 'the only currency that could buy rice was children', and that the price of enough rice to feed one person for a week 'was two children'. Nor can we measure the true human cost of any of these catastrophes via some sort of 'body count'. Although some contemporaries speculated that 'a third of the world' died in the mid-seventeenth century, and although the surviving data confirm that some communities lost up to half of their populations, while others disappeared altogether, it is impossible to calculate a world-wide total. Certainly, the Global Crisis ended prematurely the lives of *millions* of people, just as a natural catastrophe of similar proportions today would end prematurely the lives of *billions* of people.

Historians who prophesy rarely receive much attention from their colleagues (or anyone else), and those who prophesy doom (whether or not they are historians) are normally dismissed as 'whiners' – *Hoggidiani*, to use the dismissive phrase in Secondo Lancellotti's book *Nowadays*. Yet the *Hoggidiani* are not always wrong. Some natural disasters occur so suddenly that, without advanced preparation, no escape is possible. George Gordon, Lord Byron, discovered this in 1816. He fled England to escape accusations of incest, adultery, wife-beating and sodomy, planning to spend a pleasant summer in a villa near Lake Geneva with a former mistress, his personal physician (and, perhaps, catamite) John Polidori, and a select group of close friends. Instead, the party spent a 'wet, ungenial summer' (Switzerland was one of the areas worst affected by global cooling), which forced Byron and his companions to spend almost all their time indoors. Among other recreations, they competed to see who could compose the most frightening story. Mary Wollstonecraft Shelley began work on *Frankenstein*, one of the first horror novels to become a best-seller, while Polidori wrote *The Vampyre*, the progenitor of the 'Dracula' genre of fiction. Byron himself composed a poem which he called 'Darkness'. All three works reflect the disorientation and desperation that even a few weeks of abrupt climate change can cause. Since the question today is not *whether* climate change will strike some part of our planet again, but *when*, we might re-read Byron's poem as we choose whether it is better to invest more resources in preparation today or live with the consequences of inaction tormorrow. After all, unlike our ancestors in 1816, and in the seventeenth century, we possess both the resources and the technology to make that choice.

Darkness by Lord Byron

I had a dream, which was not all a dream.
The bright sun was extinguish'd, and the stars
Did wander darkling in the eternal space,
Rayless, and pathless; and the icy earth
Swung blind and blackening in the moonless air.
Morn came and went – and came, and brought no day,
And men forgot their passions in the dread
Of this their desolation; and all hearts
Were chill'd into a selfish prayer for light:
And they did live by watchfires – and the thrones,
The palaces of crowned kings – the huts,
The habitations of all things which dwell,
Were burnt for beacons; cities were consum'd,
And men were gather'd round their blazing homes. . .

And War, which for a moment was no more,
Did glut himself again: a meal was bought
With blood, and each sat sullenly apart
Gorging himself in gloom: no love was left.
All earth was but one thought – and that was death
Immediate and inglorious; and the pang
Of famine fed upon all entrails. . .

Chronology of the leading events of the Global Crisis, 1618–88

Year	Europe	Americas	Asia & Africa	X = El Niño VEI = Major volcanic eruptions ** = Extreme climatic events	Year
1618	Bohemian Revolt; purges in Dutch Republic; deposition of Ottoman Sultan Mustafa		Manchu leader Nurhaci declares war on Ming and invades Liaodong	X Three comets; Sunspot minimum	1618
1619				X	1619
1620	Ottoman-Polish war → 1621 War spreads to Germany → 1648			** X	1620
1621	Spanish–Dutch war resumes (→ 1648); 'Kipper- und Wipper' period (→ 1623)			X	1621
1622	Ottoman regicide		Revolt of Shah Jahan against Jahangir; revolt of Abaza Mehmet Pasha → 1628	V4	1622
1623	Deposition of Ottoman Sultan Mustafa (again)				1623
1624	Danes invade Germany → 1629	Revolt against Viceroy in Mexico; Dutch seize Salvador → 1625	Donglin crisis in China; Ottoman war with Iran → 1639		1624

Year	Europe / Ottoman / other	Americas	Asia	Climate markers
1625	Act of Revocation (Scotland); Cossack revolt; French Huguenot revolt → 1629			V5; Sunspot maximum
1626	Revolt in Upper Austria		Manchus raid Korea	
1627				
1628	War of Mantua begins → 1631		Gujarat famine → 1631	** Year without a summer
1629	Edict of Restitution (Germany)		Manchus raid North China	
1630	Plague in Italy; Cossack revolt; Swedes invade Germany → 1648/1654	Dutch capture Pernambuco → 1654		X; **; V5, V4
1631	Rioting in Istanbul; Kadizadeli movement gathers strength			V5
1632	Russo-Polish war → 1634			
1633				
1634			Bandit armies invade Jiangnan	
1635	France declares war on Spain → 1659			X; **
1636	Croquants revolt (France) Revolt in Lower Austria		Hong Taiji proclaims Qing dynasty, raids North China and invades Korea	
1637	Cossack revolt → 1638; Scottish Revolution → 1651 Évora & S. Portugal revolt → 1638	Pequot war (New England)	Revolt at Shimabara, Japan → 1638	
1638				V4; X

Year	Europe	Americas	Asia & Africa	X = El Niño VEI = Major volcanic eruptions ** = Extreme climatic events	Year
1639	*Nu-Pieds* revolt (Normandy)		Chinese (Sangleys) revolt in Manila	X	1639
1640	Catalan revolt → 1659 Portugal declares independence: war with Spain →1668	'Beaver Wars' around Great Lakes		** two V4 & one V5	1640
1641	Irish rebellion → 1653 Conspiracy of Medina Sidonia (Andalusia)	'Panic in the Indies'	revolt of Portuguese Asia → 1668; Dutch capture Angola	X ** one V4 & one V5	1641
1642	English Civil War → 1646		Qing raid North China; Li Zicheng destroys Kaifeng	X	1642
1643	Sweden invades Denmark → 1645		Li Zicheng declares Shun era		1643
1644			Li Zicheng takes and loses Beijing; Qing invade China, capture Beijing and occupy Central Plain	Weakest monsoon recorded in East Asia	1644
1645	Turco-Venetian war → 1669	Portuguese colonists in Brazil rebel → 1654	Qing invade South China; 'Southern Ming' resistance → 1662	Prolonged sunspot minimum (Maunder Minimum) begins → 1715	1645
1646			Macao revolt	V4 X	1646

Year			
1647	**		Naples revolt → 1648 Sicily revolt → 1648 'Putney debates' (England)
1648	** X	Portuguese retake Angola	Fronde → 1653 Ukraine revolt → 1668 Hijar conspiracy (Madrid) Ottoman regicide and revolt Russian revolts → 1649 Second Civil War in England and Scotland Succession crisis in Denmark
1649			English regicide; the 'Rump' English army begins conquest of Ireland
1650	V4, V5 X		Dutch regime change → 1672 Swedish crisis England invades and occupies Scotland → 1660
1651	X	Yui conspiracy in Edo	Bordeaux Ormée → 1653 Istanbul riots; murder of Valide Sultan
1652	X	Colombo revolt	'Green Banner' revolts in Andalusia
1653		Goa revolt	Swiss Revolution Fall of 'Rump' in England
1654			Russo-Polish war → 1667 Last Swedish troops leave central Germany
1655	V4		Sweden invades Poland → 1661
1656			Istanbul riots

Year	Europe	Americas	Asia & Africa	X = El Niño VEI = Major volcanic eruptions ** = Extreme climatic events	Year
1657			Revolt of Abaza Hasan Pasha → 1659		1657
1658	Sweden invades Denmark		Mughal Civil War → 1662	***	1658
1659	English Republic restored; Spain and France make peace		Cape Colony at war → 1660	X	1659
1660	The 'Danish Revolution'; 'Restoration' in Scotland, Ireland and England			V6 & three V4 X	1660
1661			Qing order evacuation of all maritime areas → 1683	X	1661
1662	Moscow rebellion		Execution of last Ming claimant to Chinese throne		1662
1663	Ottoman-Habsburg war → 1664			V5	1663
1664				Comet	1664
1665			Portuguese and allies destroy Kongo; Shabbatai Zvi declared Messiah	Comet X	1665
1666		Revolt of Laicacota (Peru)			1666
1667	Russia and Poland make peace; French war against Spain → 1668			V5	1667

Year				Year
1668	Spain recognizes independence of Portugal and its empire			1668
1669	Venice and the Turks make peace	Dutch and allies defeat Makassar	X	1669
1670	Revolt of Stenka Razin → 1671			1670
1671		Portuguese and allies destroy Ndongo		1671
1672	Ottoman attacks on Poland → 1676; French attack Dutch Republic, leading to regime change and war →1678			1672
1673		'Revolt of the Three Feudatories' in China → 1681	V5	1673
1674				1674
1675	'Red bonnet' revolt in Brittany		** Year without a Summer	1675
1676,	King Philip's War (New England); Bacon's rebellion (Virginia)			1676
1677	Ottoman-Russian war → 1681			1677
1678				1678
1679				1679

Year	Europe	Americas	Asia & Africa	X = El Niño VEI = Major volcanic eruptions ** = Extreme climatic events	Year
1680				V5 comet	1680
1681			'Revolt of the Three Feudatories' ends		1681
1682	Moscow rebellion →1684			Last major comet of the century	1682
1683	Ottomans war against Habsburgs and Poland (and Venice from 1684) → 1699		Qing troops take Taiwan and permit maritime trade again	**	1683
1684			First visit by a Qing ruler to southern China	X	1684
1685					1685
1686			Drought in India & Indonesia → 1688		1686
1687				X	1687
1688	'Glorious Revolution' in England; Louis XIV starts war with Britain, Dutch, Spain and Empire (to 1697)				1688

Sources

- Sunspot chronology from Usoshin, 'Reconstruction' modified by Vaquero, 'Revisited sunspot data'.
- El Niño chronology from Gergis and Fowler, 'A history of ENSO events'
- Volcanic chronology from the Smithsonian Institution's site http://www.volcano.si.edu/world/largeeruptions.cfm

I have omitted two other major eruptions in the Smithsonian series because of imprecise dating: one V6 between 1640 and 1680 and another V4 between 1580 and 1680.

Acknowledgements

In February 1998, I suddenly decided I wanted to write this book, and I immediately sent an e-mail to Robert Baldock, then editing my *Grand Strategy of Philip II* at Yale University Press, with the news:

> I always thought that the idea of my next book would come to me quite unexpectedly. Last night I awoke at 4 AM and realized that I wanted to write a book about the General Crisis of the seventeenth century – not a collection of essays (been there, done that) but an integrated narrative and analytical account of the first global crisis for which we possess adequate documentation for Asia, Africa, the Americas, and Europe. My account would adopt a Braudelian structure, examining long-term factors (climate above all), medium-run changes (economic fluctuations and so on) and 'events' (from the English Civil War and the crisis in the French and Spanish Monarchies, through the murder of two Ottoman sultans, the civil wars in India and sub-Saharan Africa to the collapse of Ming China and the wars around the Great Lakes of North America). Besides examining each of the upheavals of the mid-century, the book would offer explanations of why such synchronic developments occur with so little warning and why they end. Although not the first 'general crisis' known to historians, it is the first one for which adequate data exists worldwide. Since it addresses issues of concern today – the impact of global climatic change and sharp economic recession on government and society – it should not lack interested readers.[1]

Although I had thus anticipated much of the structure of this book at the outset, I had no idea then how much travel it would take to research and how much time it would take to write. I should have known better. In the introduction to *Science and Civilization in China*, Joseph Needham warned: 'There is no substitute for actually seeing for oneself in the great museums of the world, and the great archaeological sites; there is no substitute for personal intercourse with the practising technicians themselves.' Needham followed this advice meticulously: he filled his magnificent multi-volume work with personal observations and testimony gathered during more than forty years of travel in China and around the world. He also selflessly furthered the work of students, and built on their achievements.[2] In researching my far more modest enterprise I have tried to follow Needham's precept and example. I have travelled extensively both to see for myself the places affected by the mid-seventeenth-century cataclysm and to consult 'the practising technicians' there who share my interest in them. Above all, I have tried to further the research of students and now I build on their achievements: I am particularly indebted to Lee Smith, with whom I edited a collection of essays on the subject (*The General Crisis of the Seventeenth Century*, London 1978; revised edition 1996); and to Tonio Andrade, Derek Croxton, Matthew Keith, Pamela McVay, Andrew Mitchell, Sheilagh Ogilvie, William M. Reger IV and Nancy van Deusen, all of whom graciously shared with me the fruits of their research on the seventeenth century.

Unfortunately, I lack Joseph Needham's dedication to languages (he started to teach himself Chinese at age 38) and, in any case, as John Richards (another pioneer of 'big history') observed, 'In the best of all worlds, the author would be proficient in a half-dozen more languages'.[3] I have therefore relied extensively on the skills of other colleagues and mentors. It is a particular pleasure to recall the assistance of Hayami Akira, who introduced me both to the wealth of surviving material on early modern Japanese history and to his extensive circle of erudite colleagues. I have learned more than I can say from him, and from Mary Elizabeth Berry, Phil Brown, Karen Gerhard, Iwao Seiichi, Ann Jannetta, Derek Massarella, Richard Smethurst and Ronald P. Toby, on the history of Japan. I am grateful for enlightenment to many other experts on seventeenth-century history: on China, to William S. Atwell, Cynthia Brokaw, Chen Ning Ning, Roger Des Forges, Nicola Di Cosmo, Kishimoto Mio, Joseph Needham, Evelyn S. and Thomas G. Rawski, Shiba Yoshinobu, Jonathan Spence, Lynn A. Struve, Joanna Waley-Cohen and Wang Jiafan; on Africa, to James de Vere Allen, John Lonsdale and Joseph C. Miller; and on South and Southeast Asia to Stephen Dale, Ashin das Gupta, Michael Pearson, Anthony R. Reid, Niels Steensgaard, Sanjay Subrahmanyam and George Winius. Dauril Alden, Nicanor Domínguez, Shari Geistberg, Ross Hassig, Karen Kupperman, Carla Pestana and Stuart Schwartz guided my steps towards relevant sources on the Americas; while Paul Bushkovitch, Chester Dunning, Robert Frost, Josef Polišenský, Matthew Romaniello and Kira Stevens did the same for Russia and Eastern Europe; as did Nicholas Canny, David Cressy, Jane Ohlmeyer and Glyn Redworth for Britain and Ireland; and Günhan Börekçi, Jane Hathaway and Mircea Platon for the territories formerly in the Ottoman empire. Yet more of my debts are acknowledged with gratitude in individual chapters. On the 'big picture', I owe much to the advice and inspiration of Jonathan Clark, Karen Colvard, Robert Cowley, Jack A. Goldstone, Richard Grove, Joe Miller, Paul Monod, Ellen Mosley-Thompson, Kenneth Pomeranz, Nicholas Rodger, Lonnie Thompson and Joel Wallman.

For vital assistance in acquiring and interpreting foreign-language sources I thank Alison Anderson (German); Bethany Aram (Spanish); Maurizio Arfaioli (Italian); Günhan Börekçi (Turkish); Przemysław Gawron and Dariusz Kołodziejczyk (Polish); Ardis Grosjean-Dreisbach (Swedish); Mary Noll and Matthew Romaniello (Russian); Mircea Platon (Romanian); Taguchi Koijiro and Matthew Keith (Chinese and Japanese); and Věra Votrubová (Czech and German). I also thank Peter Davidson for graciously making available to me his transcript of Aberdeen University Library, Ms 2538, the 'Triennial travels' of James Fraser, an Aberdeen University student.

A six-week stay at the International House of Japan in spring 2002 provided a wonderful opportunity to familiarize myself with materials concerning the crisis in East Asia, by speaking with other scholars in residence and then following up their suggestions in the western language materials available in its library. I started writing this book in a room overlooking its magnificent 'samurai' gardens, and completed the last phase of my research there on another visit in July 2010. I thank the community of I-House for their welcome, support and suggestions.

The cost of 'actually seeing for oneself', in East Asia and elsewhere, has increased prodigiously since Joseph Needham began his work, and my research would have been impossible without generous and prolonged financial support. I thank the Japan Society for the Promotion of Science, the Japanese Academy, the Carnegie Trust for the Scottish Universities and the British Academy for grants; and the Harry Frank Guggenheim and the John Simon Guggenheim Foundations for fellowships. I also thank the eight universities where I have taught over the past four decades for their support of my research on this and earlier related projects: namely Cambridge, St Andrews, Keio, British Columbia, Illinois, Oxford, Yale and, above all, Ohio State, where almost all the final planning and writing of this book took place. The sustained support of OSU's History Department and Mershon Center proved crucial in three areas: funding a course of lectures on the World Crisis, a succession of graduate research assistants, and prolonged periods of research abroad. The lectures given at the Mershon Center in 2001 by William Atwell, Paul Bushkovitch, Jack Goldstone, Richard Grove, Karen Kupperman, Anthony Reid, Stuart Schwartz and Joanna Waley-Cohen, and the discussions with them and my graduate seminar that followed, inspired and informed me as I started writing. Later on, their willingness to answer queries and to pass on references expanded my horizons and saved me from many mistakes.

The OSU graduate research assistants funded by the Mershon Center and the History Department helped me both to manage the material generated by this project and to maintain my enthusiasm. I thank Katherine Becker and Matthew Keith (both of whom also helped to organize the World Crisis lecture series), Günhan Börekçi, Andrew Mitchell and Leif Torkelsen. I also thank two other graduate students for their research assistance: Megan Wheeler in Oxford, and Taguchi Koijiro in Tokyo. Thanks to their help I completed the first draft of this book in July 2007 and sent it to three expert readers: Paul Monod, Kenneth Pomeranz and Nicholas Rodger. They, as well as four other anonymous Press 'readers', provided me with magnificent advice, almost all of which I eventually followed.

Other commitments prevented me from implementing this advice until 2010, when Rayne Allinson, Sandy Bolzenius, Kate Epstein and Mircea Platon (all at The Ohio State University) suggested numerous further improvements that inspired me to get back to work on the project. I am immensely grateful to all four of them for their friendship, guidance and encouragement as I strove to implement their suggestions – but especially to Kate, who started to send me comments, encouragement, and references in May 2006 and continued until the book went to press. I have also been very lucky in my editorial team at Yale University Press – Robert Baldock, my friend and publisher for 35 years; and Candida Brazil, Tami Halliday, Steve Kent, Rachael Lonsdale and Richard Mason, all of whom made wonderful suggestions and saved me from numerous errors. I am grateful to all of them for their expertise and their patience. Finally, I thank my four wonderful children – Susie and Ed, Richard and Jamie – and Alice Conklin for the love they have brought, and continue to bring, into my life.

Columbus–Oxford–Tokyo–Paris, 1998–2012

Conventions

1. All dates given are New Style, even for European countries like Britain, Sweden and Russia that did not adopt the Gregorian calendar until later – although, since histories of these countries normally use Old Style, I provide key dates in both forms. I have also converted all dates from Chinese, Islamic, Japanese and Jewish systems of reckoning time to the Gregorian calendar.

2. Where a recognized English version of a foreign place-name exists, I have used it (thus Brussels, Vienna, Moscow, Tokyo); otherwise I have preferred the style used today in the place itself (thus Bratislava and not Pressburg or Pozsony; Lviv and not Lwów or Lemberg). Likewise, with personal names, where an established English usage exists I have adopted it (Gustavus Adolphus, Philip IV). In all other cases, I have used the style and title employed by the person concerned.

3. I have used Pinyin rather than Wade-Giles Romanization for Chinese (except when quoting from a work that uses Wade-Giles); and I have given the family name first for all Japanese, Chinese and Turkish persons, past and present (thus Tokugawa Iemitsu, Hayami Akira and Kadizade Mehmet).

4. All italics, unless otherwise stated, are my emphasis.

Sources and Bibliography

Attempts by historians to understand and explain the wave of political, social and economic upheavals that swept the northern hemisphere in mid-seventeenth century began immediately. More than 30 accounts of individual rebellions appeared in print between 1643 and 1663; while, between them, *The history of the civil wars of these recent times* by Maiolino Bisaccione (1652), and *Memorable histories, containing the political uprisings of our times* by Giovanni Battista Birago Avogadro (1653), described the 'troubles' in Brazil, Britain, Catalonia, France, Moscow, Naples, the Papal States, Poland, Portugal, Sicily, Switzerland and the Ottoman empire. A century later, Voltaire linked the political upheavals of Europe with those in Asia and Africa, postulating for the first time that a *global* crisis had occurred.[1]

Comparative studies of the phenomena largely ceased until 1937, when Roger B. Merriman delivered a lecture entitled 'Six contemporaneous revolutions'. Merriman claimed that his subject 'has fascinated me for more than thirty years', and although he adopted a far narrower focus than Voltaire (looking only at western Europe, and even then only at six 'anti-monarchical rebellions' during the 1640s), he considered their common 'parallels and philosophies', stressed the 'cross currents' that linked them, and compared them with the European revolutions of 1848. Then the historiographical trail went cold again until the 1950s, when the English historians Eric Hobsbawm and Hugh Trevor-Roper launched a debate on what they called 'The General Crisis of the seventeenth century' with long articles published in the journal *Past & Present: A Journal of Scientific History*. In 1965 the journal's editor, Trevor Aston, republished them, together with five essays on England and case studies on France, Spain, Sweden and Ireland, in *Crisis in Europe, 1560–1660*. Five years later, Robert Forster and Jack Greene published the proceedings of a symposium on the subject, *Preconditions of Revolution in Early Modern Europe*, with case studies of rebellions in the 1640s in France, England and the Spanish Monarchy. Much later, 'as a survivor' of 'those dramatic days in the 1950s and 1960s' John Elliott published a magisterial overview of both the debate and the protagonists: 'The General Crisis in retrospect'.[2]

In 1968 Elliott gave an influential lecture entitled 'Revolution and continuity in early modern Europe,' which sought common denominators for the events of the 1640s, and also compared them with other 'waves' of resistance in early modern Europe. A decade later, this and other articles on the subject published since Aston's

Crisis in Europe appeared in Parker and Smith, *The General Crisis of the seventeenth century*; while a special issue of the journal *Revue d'histoire diplomatique* published studies of nine 'contemporaneous' revolts in western European (Portugal, Spain, England, Ireland, Spanish Italy, the Spanish Netherlands, Sweden, the Swiss cantons, and Lübeck). In 1976, Miroslav Hroch and Josef Petráň synthesized East European historical data and literature; while six years later, the journal *Renaissance and Modern Studies* published a special issue on '"Crisis" in Early Modern Europe' with eight more case studies from Europe, and Perez Zagorin, *Rebels and rulers, 1500–1800*, included case studies of over a dozen more.[3] The 1975 essay by Theodore Rabb, *The struggle for stability in early modern Europe*, looked not only at the crisis but also at its aftermath; and in 1999 Francesco Benigno, *Specchi della rivoluzione*, discussed the literature on the European upheavals of the mid-seventeenth century, and reviewed the vast historiography on the Fronde and on the revolt of Naples in detail.

The debate resumed a global perspective with a panel on 'The General Crisis in East Asia', held at the 1989 Annual Meeting of the American Association for Asian Studies, and published the following year in *Modern Asian Studies* (with essays by John Richards, William Atwell, Anthony Reid and Niels Steensgaard).[4] In 1991, Jack A. Goldstone's *Revolution and rebellion in the early modern world* systematically compared the contemporaneous state breakdowns in Stuart England, the Ottoman empire and Ming China. The following year, Ruggiero Romano's *Conjonctures opposées* presented data that linked the economic difficulties in both Europe and the Americas; while Sheilagh Ogilvie's essay 'Germany and the seventeenth-century crisis' provided the most satisfactory explanation to date of the crisis in western Europe. Finally, in 2008–9, two of the leading United States historical journals devoted special issues to the subject. It is hard to disagree with Theodore K. Rabb, who wrote in his Introduction to one collection: 'Like it or not, the Crisis seems here to stay.'[5]

With few exceptions, all works on the crisis relied almost exclusively upon political and economic sources. This is understandable, since the quantity of surviving manuscript and printed seventeenth-century material is almost overwhelming. For example, a census of accounts of the Naples revolution of 1647–8 held just in the libraries and archives of the city of Naples revealed almost 300 manuscripts, most of them written by contemporaries. In addition, over 20 printed contemporary accounts exist, as well as vivid paintings by a local artist, Micco Spadaro, that depict several leading episodes. So many descriptions of the contemporaneous rebellion of Fermo in central Italy have survived that one can follow its progress almost hour by hour. In England, the almost 400 extant accounts of the battle of Naseby in 1645 enable historians to reconstruct the action almost minute by minute. Despite this profusion, several important sources only came to light relatively recently: in the 1930s the papers of Samuel Hartlib and his circle were discovered in a London solicitor's office; in the 1970s the Chinese government opened the archives of the victorious Qing to researchers; and so on. Furthermore, many sources previously available in a single archive can now be consulted online. Perhaps the most spectacular example are the 20,000 pages of 'Depositions' dictated by over 3,000 Protestant survivors of the Irish rebellion in 1641, which have now been scanned, transcribed and indexed so that it is possible to 'search' for common denominators as well as for individuals. Other important examples include the entire 'State Papers' series in the Public Record Office in London, and the Hartlib papers at Sheffield University, both now available online.[6]

Nevertheless, the surviving written sources are often incomplete because of the destruction of documents that once existed – sometimes accidentally, sometimes deliberately. The sources concerning the numerous urban revolts that rocked Romanov Russia in 1648 offer a telling example of accidental loss. Only the revolt of the small Siberian town of Tomsk has left a considerable documentary trace, because officials stationed east of the Urals reported to the Siberian Ministry, whose archives remain largely intact. By contrast, their colleagues west of the Urals reported to other ministries in Moscow, most of whose archives were later either destroyed by fire or discarded. Historians can therefore reconstruct the minor troubles in Tomsk in considerable detail, whereas most of what we know about the major uprising in Moscow, which resulted in the murder of several ministers of the tsar and the burning of half his capital, comes from a couple of reports smuggled out of the country by foreigners (see chapter 6 above). Gaps that are not accidental but deliberate also abound. In Britain, in the 1630s, the growing tension between Charles I and his subjects led many protagonists to avoid entrusting their thoughts to paper. Some ceased to write at all (in 1639 an Irish nobleman wanted to visit a colleague because, he claimed, 'I have much to say to your lordship which I cannot trust to paper'), while others burnt sensitive correspondence ('The more I think of the business of this letter [of yours and my reply],' wrote a Caroline courtier, the more he favoured 'burning them so soon as their business is answered and ended'). In China, the victorious Qing announced in 1664 that 'should officials or commoners have in their homes books that record historical events of the late Ming, they should be sent in' to the nearest magistrate, who would destroy them.[7] It is particularly difficult for historians to fill silences like these, which have been deliberately created.

Two other 'silences' in the sources used by historians to explain the seventeenth-century crisis arose because data for systematic study became available only after the 1950s: records concerning climatic and population change. In 1955 the meteorologist Marcel Garnier published a study suggesting that the annual date on which French communities began to harvest their grapes reflected the prevailing temperature during the growing season. Looking back in 2011, Emanuel Le Roy Ladurie recalled that he decided to become a historian of climate upon reading Garnier's work, and he published his path-breaking *History of the climate since the year 1000* in 1967. Since then, climatologists have collected and published climatic observations from various locations around the world; while historians of climate – notably Hubert Lamb in the United Kingdom, Christian Pfister in Switzerland, Rudolf Brázdil in the Czech Republic, Mikami Takehiko in Japan, as well as Le Roy Ladurie in France, and their disciples – have studied the correlations and coincidences between these data and political and social upheavals.[8]

Just after Garnier published his article on how to measure climate before the era of scientific instruments, a team drawn from the French Institute of Demographic Studies and the French archives showed how to use the registers of births, marriages and deaths kept in each parish to reconstruct family size and demographic trends before the era of national censuses. First in France and then in other European countries, enthusiasts began to transcribe entries in surviving parish registers to create 'family dossiers', while scholars calculated rates of mortality and nuptuality. In the 1960s, after a visit to Europe, economic historian Hayami Akira realized that the annual registers of believers kept by every Buddhist temple in Japan offered, in some ways, a superior source to parish registers because they were already organized by families. In China, other demographers studied the detailed life records kept by the Qing dynasty of all its members. Here, too, teams of historians painstakingly transcribed records and calculated demographic trends.[9] By 2012, almost all the climatic and demographic data available around the world pointed to a series of major crises for much of the seventeenth century.

Since 2000, several path-breaking works have sought to link these serial data with specific historical events: Timothy Brook, *The troubled empire* (about China) and *Vermeer's hat* (a set of connected histories from the seventeenth century); John Richards, *The unending frontier* (an environmental history of the early modern world); Bruce Campbell, 'Nature as historical protagonist' (about the calamitous fourteenth century); and Sam White, *The climate of rebellion* (about the seventeenth-century Ottoman empire). All four authors placed environmental factors at the centre of their explanations, and I have learned much from their pioneering work. In particular, I gave careful consideration to the thesis advanced by John Richards that the early modern world progressed smoothly towards growing productivity, as ecological exchanges diversified food sources, while more intensive methods and expanding areas increased agricultural yields. Nevertheless, the mid-seventeenth century seemed to me a 'hiccup', a period of adjustment, in which adverse climatic, economic and political conditions retarded (and in some areas halted) the benefits of the broader environmental changes which Richards described. I deeply regret that I cannot sit down with him again to reconcile our slightly different perspectives.

Bruce Campbell's publications (listed below), use data from both the human and the natural archive to demonstrate that the northern hemisphere experienced a crisis in the fourteenth century similar in many respects to that of the seventeenth, with climatic adversity and microbial mutation leading to increasingly violent competition for resources, a wave of violent unrest, and massive mortality. Interested readers can therefore compare and contrast the two calamities, and draw conclusions about their relative severity – but it is already evident that our recent past includes major and prolonged environmental disasters that affect continents if not hemispheres. 'Like it or not', the role of climate change in inducing crises in human history is also 'here to stay'.

Abbreviations Used in the
Bibliography and Notes

ACA	Archivo de la Corona de Aragón, Barcelona
CA	*Consejo de Aragón* (Papers of the Council of Aragon)
AGI	Archivo General de Indias, Seville
IG	*Indiferente General* (*consultas* of the Council of the Indies)
México	(correspondence of the Council of the Indies with New Spain)
Perú	(correspondence of the Council of the Indies with Peru)
AGNM	Archivo General de la Nación, Mexico
CRD	*Cédulas Reales Duplicadas* (copies of orders received from Madrid)
AGRB	Archives Générales du Royaume/Algemeen Rijksarchief, Brussels
Audience	*Papiers d'État et d'Audience* (papers and correspondence of the Brussels government in French)
CC	*Chambre des Comptes* (treasury accounts of the Brussels government)
SEG	*Secrétairerie d'État et de Guerre* (papers and correspondence of the Brussels government in Spanish)
AGS	Archivo General de Simancas
CJH	*Consejos y Juntas de Hacienda* (papers of the Spanish Council of Finance)
CMC	*Contaduría Mayor de Cuentas* (with *época* and *legajo*: Spanish treasury papers)
CS	*Contaduría del Sueldo* (with *época* and *legajo*: Spanish treasury papers)
Estado	*Negociación de Estado* (papers of the Spanish Council of State)
GA	*Guerra Antigua* (papers of the Spanish Council of War)
SP	*Secretarías Provinciales* (papers of the Council of Italy)
AHEB	Arquivo Histórico do Estado de Bahia, Bahia, Brazil, *Seçâo Colonial* (correspondence of the viceroy of Brazil)
AHN	Archivo Histórico Nacional, Madrid
Consejos	*Consejos suprimidos* (papers of the Spanish Council of Castile)
Estado	*Consejo de Estado* (papers of the Spanish Council of State and of the Council of Portugal)
AHR	*American Historical Review*
AM	Archivo Municipal
AMAE (M)	Archivo del Ministerio de Asuntos Exteriores, Madrid, *Manuscritos*

AMAE (P)	Archives du Ministère des Affaires Étrangères, Paris
CPA	*Correspondance Politique: Angleterre* (correspondence of the French government with diplomats in Britain)
CPE	*Correspondance Politique: Espagne* (correspondence of the French government with diplomats in Catalonia)
ANF	Archives Nationales de France, Paris
AP	*Archives Privés* 260 and 261 (155 Mi 1–168 and 161 Mi 1–47) (Archive of Marshal Vauban)
APW	Repgen, K., ed., *Acta Pacis Westphalicae*: series I, Instructions; series II, Correspondence; series III, Diaries – each series with multiple sub-series (II Abteilung B, die französischen Korrespondenzen; Abteiling C, die schwedische Korrespondenzen; and so on); each Abteilung contains multiple volumes
AUB	Aberdeen University Library
Ms	*Ms* 2538, 'Triennial travels' of James Fraser, a Divinity student at Aberdeen University, in Europe 1657–8 (3 vols)
BL	British Library, London, Department of Western Manuscripts
Addl.	*Additional Manuscripts*
Cott.	*Cotton Manuscripts*
Eg.	*Egerton Manuscripts*
Harl.	*Harleian Manuscripts*
Lans.	*Lansdowne Manuscripts*
BNE	Biblioteca Nacional de España, Madrid, *Colección de manuscritos*
BNF	Bibliothèque Nationale de France, Paris, *Cabinet des Manuscrits*
Ff.	*Fonds français*
Ms. Esp.	*Manuscrit espagnol*
BNL	Biblioteca Nacional, Lisbon, Manuscripts
Bod.	Bodleian Library, Oxford, Department of Western Manuscripts
BR	Biblioteca Real, Madrid, *Colección de manuscritos*
BRAH	*Boletín de la Real Academia de Historia*
BRB	Bibliothèque Royale Albert 1er, Brussels, *Collection des manuscrits*
CC	*Climatic Change*
CHC	*Cambridge History of China*, ed. D. Twitchett et al., 15 vols, some in two parts (Cambridge, 1978–2009)
CHJ	*Cambridge History of Japan*, ed. J. W. Hall et al., 6 vols (Cambridge, 1988–99)
Co. Do. In.	*Colección de documentos inéditos para la historia de España*
CSPC	*Calendar of State Papers, Colonial Series, America and West Indies*, ed. W. N. Sainsbury et al., 45 vols (London, 1860–1994)
CSPD	*Calendar of State Papers, Domestic Series. Edward VI, Mary, Elizabeth I and James I*, ed. S. C. Lomax and M. A. Everett Green, 12 vols (London, 1856–72)
CSPD	*Calendar of State Papers, Domestic Series. Charles I*, ed. J. Bruce and W. D. Hamilton, 23 vols (London, 1858–97)

CSPI	*Calendar of State Papers relating to Ireland. James I*, ed. C. W. Russell and J. P. Prendergast, 5 vols (London, 1872–80)
CSPI	*Calendar of State Papers relating to Ireland of the Reign of Charles I*, ed. R. P. Mahaffy, 4 vols (London, 1900–4)
CSPV	*Calendar of State Papers and Manuscripts relating to English affairs, existing in the archives and collections of Venice, and in other libraries of Northern Italy, 1202–1674*, ed. H. F. Brown et al., 28 vols (London 1864–1947)
CSSH	*Comparative Studies in Society and History*
DMB	*Dictionary of Ming Biography*, ed. Carrington Goodrich and Fang Chaoying, 2 vols (New York, 1976)
ECCP	*Eminent Chinese of the Ch'ing Period*, ed. A. Hummel, 2 vols (Washington, DC, 1943)
EcHR	*Economic History Review*
EHR	*English Historical Review*
EI	*Encyclopedia of Islam*, 2nd edn, ed. P. J. Bearman et al., 12 vols (Leiden, 1960–2003, also accessible on the web)
HAG	Historical Archive, Goa, *Manuscripts* (correspondence of the viceroy of the Portuguese Estado da India and his Conselho da Fazenda)
HJ	*Historical Journal*
HMC	Historical Manuscripts Commission
IJC	*International Journal of Climatology*
IJMES	*International Journal of Middle Eastern Studies*
IVdeDJ	Instituto de Valencia de Don Juan, Madrid, Manuscript Collection (with 'envío' and folio number)
JAS	*Journal of Asian Studies*
JEEH	*Journal of European Economic History*
JESHO	*Journal of the Economic and Social History of the Orient*
JIH	*Journal of Interdisciplinary History*
JJS	*Journal of Japanese Studies*
JMH	*Journal of Modern History*
JWH	*Journal of World History*
MHE	Memorial Histórico Español
PLP	*Proceedings in the Opening Session of the Long Parliament*, ed. M. Jansson, 7 vols (Rochester, NY, 2002–7)
P&P	*Past & Present*
PRO	Public Records Office (now The National Archives), London
SP	*State Papers* (correspondence of the English secretaries of state)
RAS	Riksarkivet, Stockholm
	Diplomatica Muscovitica (correspondence from Swedish diplomats in Russia)
	Manuskriptsamlingen (manuscript collections)

RPCS	*Register of the Privy Council of Scotland*, 2nd series, ed. David Masson and P. Hume Brown, 6 vols (Edinburgh, 1899–1908)
SCC	*Science and Civilization in China*, ed. Joseph Needham and associates, 7 vols, vols 4–7 have multiple parts (Cambridge, 1954–2008)
SCJ	*Sixteenth Century Journal*
TCD	Trinity College Dublin
Ms	*Manuscripts:* the 33 volumes of 'Depositions', now available in digitized form at <1641.tcd.ie>
TRHistS	*Transactions of the Royal Historical Society*
WMQ	*William and Mary Quarterly*

Notes

Preface to the Paperback Edition

1 Works cited in the Bibliography are given in abbreviated form; other items are cited in full in the notes that follow. I thank Mary Elizabeth Berry, Fabian Drixler, Sir John Elliott, Kate Epstein, Patrick Lenaghan, Norm MacLeod, Theodore K. Rabb, Julia Adeney Thomas, and the contributors to the 'debates' in *Historically Speaking* XIV/5 (2013), and at the 2014 American Historical Association annual meeting, for wonderful feedback.
2 *Herald Scotland*, 24 Mar. 2013, review by Hugh Macdonald, chief sports writer.
3 Jack A. Goldstone, 'Climate lessons from history', in *Historically speaking*, XIV/5 (2013), 37.
4 Roger Lonsdale, ed., *Samuel Johnson: The Lives of the most eminent English poets with critical observations on their works*, 4 vols (Oxford, Clarendon Press, 2006), I, 290, written c. 1780, just over a century after Milton's death.
5 'Global Crisis: a Forum', with Kenneth Pomeranz, J. R. McNeill, and Jack Goldstone, in *Historically speaking*, XIV/5 (Nov. 2013), 29–39; 2014 American Historical Association annual meeting, session 115, on *Global Crisis*. The papers by Lauren Benton, Daniel Headrick, and Joseph C. Miller, together with a summary of the debate by Carla Gardina Pestana, the panel organizer, will appear in late 2014 in *Journal of World History*.
6 Jan de Vries, 'The Crisis of the Seventeenth Century: The Little Ice Age and the Mystery of the "Great Divergence"', in *The Journal of Interdisciplinary History*, XLIV (2013), 369–77, a review of *Global Crisis*. Quotation from p. 374. Goldstone, 'Climate lessons', 37, made the same complaint: 'One counterexample not dealt with is the Netherlands . . .'
7 Even the term 'golden age' [*gouden eeuw*] does not appear in Dutch dictionaries until the late nineteenth century, and its first appearance in a book title occurred in 1841 (I thank Rudolf Dekker for these details).
8 Pomeranz, 'Weather, war, and welfare: persistence and change in Geoffrey Parker's *Global Crisis*', in *Historically Speaking* XIV/5 (2013), 31, citing *Global Crisis*, 488.
9 Hayami, *The historical demography*; idem, *Population, family and society*; and idem, *Population and family in early-modern central Japan*; Saitō, 'The frequency of famines'. Farris, *Japan's Medieval Population*, 165–71, provides an excellent summary of the different views.
10 I am very grateful to Mary Elizabeth Berry for help in formulating the argument of this paragraph.
11 See, for example, recent articles about Karl Anders Pommerenning and Enomoto Yazaemon, whose writings formed a core source for (respectively) chapters 6 and 16: M. P. Romaniello, 'Moscow's Lost Petition to the Tsar, 2 June 1648', in *Russian History*, XLI (2014), 119–25; and L. Roberts, 'Name and Honor. A Merchant's Seventeenth-Century Memoir', in S. Frühstück and A. Walthall, eds, *Recreating Japanese Men* (Berkeley, 2011), 48–67.
12 *Diaries kept by the heads of the Dutch factory*, VI (1641–2), 208–9, letter of van Diemen to 'royal council of Japan, Batavia, 28 June 1642; *Deshima Dagregisters*, XI (1641–50), 263, account by the Dutch Factor of an Audience in Edo, 6 Jan. 1647; and 398, entry for 5 Aug. 1650. I thank Fabian Drixler for asking me about this.
13 *The Journal of Interdisciplinary History*, XL/1 (2009), 145–303, Rabb quotation from p. 150; Julia Adeney Thomas, 'Comment: Not yet far enough', in *American Historical Review*, CXVII (2012), 794–803.
14 *The Journal of Interdisciplinary History* XLIV/3 (2014), 299–377; Kelly and Ó Gráda, 'The waning of the Little Ice Age: climate change in early modern Europe', 301–25; White, 'The Real Little Ice Age', 327–52; Büntgen and Hellmann, 'The Little Ice Age in Scientific Perspective: Cold Spells and Caveats', 353–68. The 'new books' include S. K. Raphael, *Climate and political climate: environmental disasters in the medieval Levant* (Leiden, 2013); R. Ellenblum, *The collapse of the eastern Mediterranean: Climate change and the decline of the East, 950–1072* (Cambridge, 2014); and J. L. Brooke, *Climate Change and the Course of Global History: A Rough Journey* (Cambridge, 2014).

Prologue

1. Weiss, 'The genesis and collapse', noted the simultaneous collapse around 2200 BC of Akkad, the world's first empire, and of the Indus and other civilizations in western Asia amid evidence of general drought and

desiccation. Yancheva, 'Influence', noted the simultaneous collapse of the Maya and Tang and postulated a change in the monsoon pattern to explain it.

2. Campbell, 'Nature', 284; Brook, *The troubled empire*, 72.

3. Le Roy Ladurie, *Times of feast, times of famine*, 119, 289; de Vries, 'Measuring the impact of climate', 23. Mauelshagen, *Klimageschichte*, 16–35, charts the development of historical climatology down to 2009. In 2010 and 2011, Timothy Brook, Bruce Campbell and Sam White all published path-breaking studies (on China, western Europe and the Ottoman empire, respectively) that integrate climate into historical explanations.

4. Fortey, 'Blind to the end', *New York Times*, 26 Dec. 2005, http://www.nytimes.com/2005/12/26/opinion/26ihtedfortey.html. See also idem, *The earth: an intimate history*. On the long reign of the 'disaster deniers' see Bankoff, *Cultures of disaster*; Mauch and Pfister, *Natural disasters*; Juneja and Mauelshagen, 'Disasters'; and Benton, *When life nearly died*, ch. 3.

5. *2011 disasters in numbers* prepared by the International Disaster Database at the Université Catholique, Louvain, Belgium: www.emdat.be, accessed 12 Mar. 2012.

6. http://www.ncdc.noaa.gov/paleo/icecore.html contains ice-core data from throughout the world, including polar and low-level mountain ice caps and glaciers.

7. http://www.ncdc.noaa.gov/paleo/pollen.html contains pollen data series archived before 2005. Data contributed since then are available for download at http://www.neotomadb.org/.

8. http://www.ncdc.noaa.gov/paleo/treering.html, the International Tree-Ring Data Bank, contained in 2010 annual measurements of ring width or wood density from over 2,000 sites on six continents. Brázdil, 'European climate' and idem, 'Use', provide more detail on each category and also list recent publications based on them.

9. http://www.ncdc.noaa.gov/paleo/speleothem.html lists available data sets by continent, with links to each site.

10. For example, Barriendos, 'Climatic variations' and 'Climate and culture', used rogation ceremonies to measure drought in early modern Spain; while Neuberger, 'Climate', extracted meteorological information from some 12,000 paintings dated between 1400 and 1967 in 41 US and European art museums. Further examples in Brázdil, 'European climate', 10–13.

11. Mauelshagen, *Klimageschichte*, 36–59, and Garnier, *Les dérangements*, 24–48, provide excellent overviews of the sources, and a chronology of their exploitation.

12. Trevor-Roper, 'The general crisis', 50. A generation earlier, Sir George Clark had noted 'a change of atmosphere between the earlier part of the [seventeenth] century and the later, a change accompanied by storms' (Clark, *The seventeenth century*, ix).

13. Camuffo, 'The earliest temperature observations', a study based on almost 40,000 readings taken between 1654 and 1667 with identical thermometers at an international network of climate observation stations established by Tuscany.

14. F. E. Matthes, an expert on glaciers, coined the term 'Little Ice Age' in 1939: 'We are living in an epoch of renewed but moderate glaciation – a "little ice age".' The term now refers to the period 1350–1750, with its maximum intensity in the seventeenth century.

15. Le Roy Ladurie, *Times of feast*, 2. Presciently, Le Roy predicted that computers might change this: ibid., 303.

16. In 2012 the 'Euro-Climhist' database at Bern, Switzerland, included 1.2 million records, just for Europe.

17. BL *Harl* 390/211, Mede to Sir Martin Stuteville, 24 Feb. 1627. Mede's 'star pupil' at Christ's was John Milton.

18. Appleby, 'Epidemics and famine', 663.

Introduction

1. Burton, *The anatomy*, 3–4 ('Democritus to the Reader'); *Calendar of the Court Minutes*, i, Directors of the East India Company to their agents in Surat, Nov. 1644; Whitaker, *Ejrenopojos [The Peacemaker]*, 1–2, 9, on Haggai 2:7, 'And I will shake all nations'.

2. Elliott and La Peña, *Memoriales y cartas*, II, 276.

3. Porschnev, 'Les Rapports', 160, quoting Johan Adler Salvius; Mentet de Salmonet, *Histoire des troubles de la Grande Bretagne*, ii; Parival, *Abrégé*, 'Au lecteur' and 477.

4. Ansaldo, *Peste*, 16 (Fra Francesco); BL *Addl. Ms* 21,935/48 (Wallington); Mortimer, *Eyewitness accounts*, 185 (Thiele and Minck).

5. Howell, *Epistolae Ho-Elianae*, Book III, 26, to his nephew, 10 Dec. 1647, and Letter I, to Lord Dorset, '20 Jan. 1646' (but almost certainly 1649).

6. Hobbes, *Leviathan*, 89.

7. Bisaccione, *Historia* (1652), 2; Rushworth, *Historical collections*, I (1659), preface. Howell, *Epistolae*, also began his collection of letters on historical matters with the outbreak of 'the wars of Germany' in 1618.

8. Piterberg, *Ottoman tragedy*, 1, quoting Kâtib Çelebi; Peterson, *Bitter gourd*, 35, quoting Wu Yingji (1594–1645), *Liudu wenjian lu*.

9. Hobbes, *Behemoth*, 1.

10. Kessler, *K'ang-hsi*, 131, quoting the personal report of Xizhu to the emperor in 1684.

11. Mather, *Heaven's alarm to the world* (1681) and *Kometographia, or a discourse concerning comets* (1683).
12. Luterbacher, 'Monthly mean pressure reconstructions', 1,050. Subtelny, *Domination*, ch. 4, argued that the General Crisis did not grip many areas in eastern Europe until the 1690s: chapter 20 above argues against this interpretation.
13. Hugon, *Naples*, 16.
14. 'Thoughts on the late transactions respecting Falkland's islands' (1771), in Johnson, *Works*, X, 365–6, italics added. (I thank Jeremy Black for bringing this reference to my attention.)
15. Gladwell, *The tipping point* (a term first used in 1972, as opposed to 'turning point', which dates from 1836); Gaddis, *Landscape*, 98–9. See also the insights of Waldrop, *Complexity*, 12, 111.
16. Hill, *The world*, 13
17. Scott, *Weapons of the weak*, xvi–xvii.
18. TCD *Ms* 833/228v, Richard Plunkett's claim to Rev. George Creighton of Lurgan, Co. Cavan, in Creighton's deposition of 15 Apr. 1643.

Part I. The Placenta of the Crisis

1. Voltaire, *Essai*, II, 756–7. The marquise had read Bossuet's *Discourse on universal history* (1681) and proclaimed it both boring and Eurocentric. Voltaire set out to do better.
2. Ibid., II, 756–7, 794, 806 and 941–7 (*Remarques pour servir de supplément à l'essai sur les moeurs*, 1763).
3. In his analysis of the attempted military coup d'état in Spain on 23 Feb. 1981, Javier Cercas argued that the simultaneous hostility to the government of various distinct groups – politicians, journalists, bankers, businessmen, foreign governments, perhaps even the king – together formed '*the placenta of the coup, not the coup itself*. The nuance is key in understanding the coup' (Cercas, *The anatomy*, 28). A parallel nuance is the key to understanding the global crisis of the seventeenth century.

Chapter 1   The Little Ice Age

1. Special thanks for help in framing this chapter to William S. Atwell, Rudolf Brázdil, Günhan Börekçi, John Brooke, Richard Grove, Karen Kupperman, Mikami Takehiko, Christian Pfister and José M. Vaquero.
2. Cysat, *Collectanea*, IV.2, 898. See also Pfister and Brádzil, 'Climatic variability', 44–5.
3. Glaser, *Klimarekonstruktion*, 111, on the extremely cold winter in central Europe in 1620–1; other details from Thorndycraft, 'The catastrophic floods'; Barriendos and Rodrigo, 'Study', and Vanderlinden, 'Chronologie', 147.
4. See Pfister, 'Weeping in the snow', 33 and 50, and Garnier, 'Grapevine', 711, on 1626–8; Le Roy Ladurie, *Histoire humaine*, 337–48, on France's 'biennat super-aquatique' (1629–30); and ch. 13 above on India's 'perfect drought'.
5. García Acosta, *Desastres*, I, 177–8 (the clergy took the Virgin on procession six more times before 1668, an unequalled frequency); Dunn, *The Journal of John Winthrop*, 368, 384 and 387, Kupperman, 'The puzzle', 1,274, quoting Thomas Gorges. Ludlam, *Early American winters*, 15 and 18–22, charts New England's 'landmark winter' of 1641–2.
6. Arakawa, 'Dates', 222 (only 1699 and 1802 saw snow earlier); Aono, *Climatic reconstruction*, 92; Blair and Robertson, *The Philippine islands*, XXXV, 123 and 184, from reports on events in 1640–2 and 1643–4.
7. Teodoreanu, 'Preliminary observations', 190, quoting Achacy Taszychi; Yilmazer, *Topçular*, 1,145, 1,156, 1,164, 1,173; Odorico, *Conseils et mémoires de Synadinos*, 163, 169; www.ucm.es/info/reclido/es/basesdatos/rainfallindex.txt, accessed 31 Jan. 2010.
8. Naworth, *A new almanacke*, sig C2; BL *Harl. Ms* 5,999/29v, 'Discourse' by Henry Jones and others, Nov. 1643.
9. Buisman, *Duizend jaar weer*, IV, 469–70 (quoting a burgher of Liège); Peters, *Ein Söldnerleben*, 166, diary entry at Neustadt-an-der-Saale, 7 Aug. 1640 (I thank David Parrott for this reference).
10. Vicuña Mackenna, *El clima de Chile*, 43–4, Dean Tomás de Santiago to the Tribunal of Lima, 23 June 1640. Taulis, *De la distribution*, 17, shows a four-year drought in Chile 1636–9; Villalba, 'Climatic fluctuations', and Martínson, *Natural climate*, 27, both show cooler temperatures in Patagonia in the 1640s and 1660s.
11. Bamford, *A royalist's notebook*, 120–1; Laing, *Letters and Journals*, III, 62; Gilbert, *History of the Irish Confederation*, VI, 270–1.
12. Buisman, *Duizend jaar weer*, IV, 499–500.
13. Teodoreanu, 'Preliminary observations', 190, quoting Archdeacon Paul of Aleppo; Abbott, *Writings*, III, 225–8, Proclamation of 20/30 Mar. 1654; De Beer, *Diary of John Evelyn*, 388, 393.
14. Ådahl, *The sultan's procession*, 48, entry for 27 Feb. 1658; City Archives, Danzig, 694 f. 149 (I thank Robert Frost for this reference); Van Aitzema, *Saken*, IX, book 38, pp. 124–6. For the Swedish march, see ch. 8 above. Teodoreanu, 'Preliminary observations', 188, notes that Romanian sources recorded unusually severe winters in 1656–7, 1657–8 and 1659.
15. Garnier, *Les dérangements*, 85; Thirsk, 'Agricultural policy', 301; Hoskins, 'Harvest fluctuations', 18; Teodoreanu, 'Preliminary observations', 190, quoting Evliya Çelebi; Cernovodeanu and Binder, *Cavalerii Apocalipsului*, 90, quoting the *Journal* of Mihail Teleki, Chancellor of Transylvania, for 1661.

16. Gordon, *Diary*, II, 272; Goldie, *The entring book*, II, 450. Goad, *Astrometeorologia*, 77–8, printed data on ice in the Thames 'collected from the observations of leisure times of above thirty years'; Garnier, *Les dérangements*, figure 27, shows that winter 1683–4 was the coldest recorded in England (and almost in France, too)

17. Gordon, *Diary*, I, 132 (the Vistula froze so hard in Nov. 1656 that the Swedish army and its artillery marched across); Cyberski, 'History of the floods', 809–10; Teodoreanu, 'Preliminary observations', 191–2, quoting a Moldavian bishop in July 1670, and Philippe Le Masson du Pont in 1686.

18. Jones, *History and climate*, 12 (Russia) and 22–3 (Jan Antoni Chapowicki's diary); Ge, 'Winter half-year temperature reconstructions', 939, figure 3 (China); Evliya Çelebi, *Seyahatname*, X, 508 (Egypt: I thank Jane Hathaway for both reference and translation.)

19. Silvestre de Sancy, *Lettres*, III, 321 and 345, to Mme de Grignan, 28 June and 24 July 1675; Marks, *Tigers*, 195, quoting the *Da Qing sheng zu (Kangxi) shi lu* for 1717.

20. Smith, *Nakahara*, 107.

21. Smith, *The art of doing good*, 162, quoting Qi's diary; Wu, *Communication and imperial control*, 34–6, quoting Kangxi; poem in Scott, *Love and protest*, 140; Magisa, *Svcceso raro* – half of his six pages discussed possible 'implications'.

22. AM Cádiz 26/127, Cabildo of 21 Aug. 1648, with a copy of a letter from Don Diego de Riaño y Gamboa to all town councils, 1 Aug. 1648, ordering that it be transcribed in the council registers 'so that your successors will know about this letter'.

23. Haude, 'Religion', 541; and Firth and Rait, *Acts and Ordinances*, 26–7 and 1,070–2, 'Order for Stage-playes to cease' (12 Sep. 1642 NS) and 'An Ordinance for the utter suppression and abolishing of all Stage-Plays' (21 Feb. 1648 NS). England's theatres remained closed in law, if not always in fact, until the Restoration in 1660. Likewise, in Castile, Philip IV (although an avid theatregoer) ordered all theatres to close in 1644 after the death of his queen and again after the death of his son and heir in 1646; while his sister Anne, Queen Regent of France, also closed all the kingdom's theatres in 1648. I thank Rachael Ball for drawing this coincidence to my attention.

24. Balfour, *Historical works*, III, 436–7; Larner, *Source book*, sub annis 1649–50; Larner, *Enemies of God*, 61 and 74–5; Kuhn, *Soulstealers*, 229 (recognizing that his analysis applies to other cases of 'scape-goating' through the ages). I thank Kathryn Magee Labelle for the information on the Huron 'witch panic'. See further examples in Behringer, *Witches and witch-hunts*; Oster, 'Witchcraft'; and Roper, *Witch craze*.

25. Porschnev, 'Les rapports', 160, quoting Johann Adler Salvius; BNE *Ms* 2378/55, 'Reboluciones de Nápoles'; Bisaccione, *Historia*, 510.

26. BNE *Ms* 2371/634, *Prognosticon* (1640); Naworth, *A new almanacke* (1642), sig. C2; Graniti, *Diario*, I, 4 (Francesco Capecelatro); Bournoutian, *The Chronicle of Deacon Zak'aria of K'anak'er*, 156. The 1654 eclipse also caused widespread apprehension in Europe: see Labrousse, *L'entrée de Saturne*, and ch. 22 above.

27. Moosvi, 'Science and superstition'; Milton, *Paradise Lost*, book I, lines 596–9.

28. Anon., *A true and strange relation*, 7 (an account with two engravings of 'the burning island' created in July 1638); [Voetius], *Brittish lightning*, sig. A3.

29. Kâtib Çelebi, *Fezleke*, II, 326; Nicoară, *Sentimentul de insecuritate*, I, 77–8; Mallet and Mallet, *The earthquake catalogue*, plate IV, shows a peak in earthquake activity around 1650. Other sources testify to the prevalence of unusually destructive events: for example, earthquakes followed by tsunamis destroyed the Spanish colonial port cities of Santiago de Chile in 1657 (see Rosales, *Historia general*, 191–2), and Lima in 1684.

30. Bainbridge, *An astronomicall description*, 30–1; Pacheco de Britto, *Discurso*, fos A11–11v; Kepler, *Prognosticum astrologicum ... 1618*, 158, 163–4 and 171 (see also p. 176 for his glee at such accurate forecasting in his *Prognosticon* for the following year). See also Drake and O'Malley, *The controversy on the comets of 1618*; Urbánek, 'The comet of 1618'; and Thiebault, 'Jeremiah', 441, quoting the striking sermon of Elias Ehinger.

31. BR *Ms* II-551/120v–124v, Fray Diego de la Fuente to the count of Gondomar, London, 11 Apr. 1619.

32. Wakeman, *The great enterprise*, 57; Roth, 'The Manchu-Chinese relationship', 7–8; Biot, 'Catalogue', 56–7; Brook, *The confusions of pleasure*, 163–7; and Moosvi, 'Science and superstition', 115, quoting the *Iqbalnama-i Jahangiri*.

33. [Voetius], *Brittish lightning*, sig. A3; *The Moderate Intelligencer*, 202 (25 Jan.–1 Feb. 1649); Mather, *Kometographia* (1683), 108–11 – a book occasioned by concern over the comets of 1680 and 1682.

34. Xie Zhaozhe, *Wu za zu* (1608), quoted in Elvin, 'The man who saw dragons', 34; BNE *Ms* 2371/634, *Prognosticon* (1640); Burton, *Anatomy*, 1638 edn (Partition I, section I, subsection 1, 'Diseases in generall').

35. Birago Avogadro, *Turbolenze di Europa*, 369; Bainbridge, *An astronomicall description*, 30–1; Riccioli, *Almagestum novum*, 96. Hoyt and Schatten, *The role*, 106–7, review the opinions of Schyrler, Riccioli, Kirchner, Goad and Hooke (all of whom argued that sunspots affected climate).

36. Hoyt and Schatten, *The role*, 14–20, list observations of sunspots with telescopes between 1610 and 1650, corrected by Usoshin, 'Reconstruction', 302; and Vaquero, 'Revisited sunspot data', table 2. Spörer, 'Über die Periodicität der Sonnenflecken', and Maunder, 'The prolonged sunspot minimum', both noted that the few sunspots observed – in 1660, 1671, 1684, 1695, 1707 and 1718 – 'correspond, as nearly as we can expect, to the theoretical dates of maximum'. See also Moberg, 'Highly variable', and the attached database.

37. Auroras occur more often, and can be observed at more southerly latitudes, when sunspots are numerous.

38. Eddy, 'The "Maunder Minimum"', 268. Since Eddy's landmark paper of 1976, satellite images have confirmed that the sun's 'luminosity' matches the sunspot cycle, reaching its minimum during each sunspot minimum.

See also the graph showing how global surface temperatures track sunspot activity in Martinson, *Natural climate*, 98.

39. Amelang, *A journal of the plague year*, 100, from the chronicle of Andrés de la Vega; Atwell, 'Volcanism', 41; Yi, 'Meteor fallings', 205–6 and 217. The same Korean astronomers observed frequent meteor showers, with a peak in the 1640s, which could likewise create (or inspissate) dust veils.

40. Ovalle, *Histórica relación*, 302–3.

41. Magisa, *Svcceso raro de tres volcanes*. Delfin, 'Geological, 14C and historical evidence', identified the volcano as Mt Parker; Atwell, 'Volcanism', 33, proposed that this was a 'force six' eruption. Several European volcanoes also erupted at this time: notably Vesuvius in 1632, Etna in 1646 and Santorini in 1650. Each produced a dramatic local impact: the Santorini eruption covered the harvest with ash and caused a destructive tsunami: subsequent generations referred to this period as 'the time of evil' (see Friedrich, *Fire in the sea*).

42. Gergis and Fowler, 'A history of ENSO events', 370–1. Some of these dates differ slightly from those listed by Diaz and Markgraf, *El Niño*, 122–3, but this often reflects the fact that ENSO events often occur in winter and thus span two calendar years. McIntosh, *The way the wind blows*, 58 table (c), displays proxy data for Pacific Ocean temperatures around the Galápagos Islands that reveal the 1630s and 1640s as the greatest anomaly in the entire series 1600–2000. Jones, *Climatic variations*, 388–9, shows no coral formation at all in 1641 at Urvina Bay, in the Galápagos – the only year of zero growth ever recorded. For the weaker monsoons, and the suggestion that these reflect a reduction in solar energy received on earth, see Zhang, 'A test of climate'.

43. Liu, 'A 1000-year history', 458–9.

44. AGI *Filipinas* 28/100, Petition of Diego de Villatoro, 25 Aug. 1676, with further information in idem 28/90, Memorial from Villatoro. I thank Bethany Aram for locating these documents. García, 'Atmospheric circulation', 2,444 (especially the graph), 2,446–7 (ship losses) and 2,452 (return voyages), reveals the longer voyages around the time when Villatoro wrote his memorial, using a database of over 150 outward voyages from Acapulco to Manila and an unspecified number of returns between 1591 and 1802.

45. Rind and Overpeck, 'Hypothesized causes', 366–9, suggested that volcanic eruptions increased ENSO activity. Richard Grove and Lonnie Thompson suggested the converse possibility – that the shift of sea levels in the Pacific in El Niño years may increase volcanic activity – in a discussion at OSU's Mershon Center in April 2001.

46. Elvin, 'Blood and statistics', 149, quoting the prefectural *Gazetteer* of Jiaxing (Zhejiang). Pfister, 'Litte Ice Age-type impacts', 197–8, details how adverse temperature and precipitation affect grain, hay and vine production.

47. Song Yingxing, *Tiangong kaiwu*, translated as *Chinese technology in the seventeenth century*, 5.

48. Teodoreanu, 'Preliminary observations', 191, quoting a Moldavian bishop in July 1670. For another example (among many) of mice infestation, see Heberle, *Zeytregister*, 159.

49. Costin, *Letopisețul Țării Moldovei*, 196–7 (my thanks to Mircea Platon for finding and translating this item). Records from many other countries mention infestations of locusts (albeit not so vividly): see, for example, pages 125–6, 170 and 198 above.

50. Myllyntaus, 'Summer frost', 77–8 and 83. Significantly, the Finns have a special word for a summer frost: *kesähalla*.

51. Song Yingxing, *Tiangong kaiwu*, 4.

52. Kaplan, *The famine plot*, 62–3.

53. Ibid., 63; De Waal, *Famine that kills*, quoted in idem, 'A re-assessment', 470–1.

54. Cipolla, *Cristofano and the plague*, 149–50 (hospital in Prato); Fogel, 'The escape', 8–9 (the rest). In the seventeenth century, only English colonists in America attained current levels of nutrition: each male colonist in Virginia apparently consumed over 2,300 calories above his basic metabolic requirement (we lack figures for women and children).

55. Dyson, 'Famine in Berar', 99, quoting the *Hyderabad Residency Sanitary Report for 1897*.

56. Smith, *The art of doing good*, 54, quoting Yang, 'A record of distributing padded jackets (*Shi mianao ji*)' (1612); Sibbald, *Provision for the poor in time of dearth*, 1–2.

57. Hacquebord and Vroom, *Walvisvaart*, 133–4. When children are starving or seriously ill, their long bones cease to grow and instead form a small ridge visible on their skeletons known as 'Harris lines': many of the skeletons from Smeerenburg had 'Harris lines'. The measurement of surviving skeletons from northern Europe has revealed that average heights dropped by more than 2 inches between the 1450s and the 1750s: Steckel, 'New light on the "Dark Ages"'.

58. Komlos, 'An anthropometric history', 159; Hobbes, *Leviathan* (1651), quoted page xxiii above. Records for other early modern armies that measured soldiers at enlistment also show a marked reduction in height among those who grew up in periods of dearth. See, for example, Baten, 'Climate', 29 (on eighteenth-century Bavarian soldiers).

59. Semedo, *Historica relatione*, 6–7, 13. Semedo arrived in South China in 1613 and remained, with some breaks, until 1637. He wrote soon afterwards.

60. *Winthrop papers*, II, 111, 'General observations for the plantation of New England' (1629); Andrews, *The colonial period*, 612–13, quoting Gorges (1611), the Virginia Company (1624) and many others; Canny, *The origins of empire*, 20, quoting Thomas Bowdler's 'Common Place Book' for 1635–6.

61. *Qing shilu [Veritable records of the Ming]* VIII, ch. 86, p. 149, edict of the Yongzheng emperor 2 Nov. 1729 (translated by Ying Bao); Lenihan, 'War and population', 8, quoting Lawrence, *The interest of England*; Hull, *The*

economic writings, I, 149–51; Mortimer, *Eyewitness accounts*, 78, quoting Hans Conrad Lang; Antony and Christmann, *Johann Valentin Andreä*, 128; Arnauld, *Lettres*, II, 433, to the queen of Poland, 28 Jan. 1654 ('le tiers du monde étant mort').

62. Hayami and Tsubochi, *Economic and demographic developments*, 155 (Shi Zhihong); Lenihan, 'War and population', 20–1; Franz, *Der dreissigjährige Krieg*, 59; Jacquart, ' "La Fronde" ', and Garnier, 'Calamitosa tempora', 8–9 (see also Fig. 34 above).

Chapter 2   The 'General Crisis'

1. Doglio, *Lettere di Fulvio Testi*, III, 204: to Francesco Montecuccoli, Jan. 1641; Hobbes, *On the citizen*, 29 (a view reiterated ten years later in *Leviathan*, 88); Lind, 'Syndens', 342 (500 out of 4,500 items).

2. Brecke, 'Violent conflicts 1400 A D to the Present', Fig. 11, reproduced in Parker, 'Crisis and catastrophe', 1,057; Levy, *War*, 139–41; Aho, *Religious mythology*, 195.

3. Gough, *The history of Myddle*, 71–2 (Braddick, *God's Fury*, 389, provides an estimate of Myddle's population in 1640).

4. Carlton, *Going to the wars*, ch. 9; Gordon, *Diary*, I, 170, entry for 1656 but written about a decade later. Gordon served in the Swedish, Polish and Russian armies from 1655 until his death in Moscow in 1699.

5. Heberle, *Zeytregister*, 148, 225 ('Dan wir seyen gejagt worden wie das gewildt in wälden') and 158. The war forced Heberle and his family to abandon their home no less than 30 times.

6. Hobbes, *Leviathan*, 88–9; Scott, *England's troubles*, 410, quoting Charles II's communications to the two Houses of the Convention Parliament in June–July 1660; Gryphius, *Horribilicribrifax Teutsch*, Act I, scene 1; Rodén, 'The crisis', 100, quoting Christina's 'Ouvrage de loisir'. Monod, *The power*, 193–5, provides some similar quotations.

7. Struve, *Voices*, 2.

8. Chang and Chang, *Crisis and transformation*, 216, quoting *The miraculous reunion* by the Chinese scholar, writer and publisher Li Yu (1611–80); Struve, *Voices*, 48, from 'Ten days in Yangzhou' by Wang Xiuchu.

9. Struve, *Voices*, 48; Meyer-Fong, *Building culture*, 11–12 ('Weed-covered city'), 150–2 (later memories by survivors) and 261–2 (assessment of Wang's account).

10. Lahne, *Magdeburgs Zerstörung*, and Medick, 'Historisches Ereignis'. Hahn, *Zeitgeschehen*, 83, notes the later sermons. Further details in chs 4 and 8 above.

11. Struve, *Voices*, 47 (see also another rape described on p. 37). For suicide by Chinese women after they had been raped, see chs 4 and 5 above.

12. Helfferich, *The Thirty Years War*, 110, quoting Von Guericke, *Die Belagerung, Eroberung und Zerstörung der Stadt Magdeburg* (though he also noted that some 'honourable soldiers' showed respect for the women they captured and 'simply let them free or even married them').

13. Peters, *Ein Söldnerleben*, 144–5 (at Landshut 'habe ich als meine Beute ein hübscher Mädelein bekommen') and 147 (at Pforzheim 'habe ich auch ein junges Mädchen herausgeführt'). Ebermeier, *Landshut im Dreissigjährigen Krieg*, documents the scale of the city's destruction during and after the 1634 sack.

14. Parker, *Thirty Years War*, 187 (the ordeal of Frau Rörsch, from Linden near Rothenburg ob der Tauber, described by Christopher Friedrichs); TCD *Ms* 836/76, depositions of Christian Stanhawe and Owen Frankland, Armagh, 23 July 1642; Gordon, *Diary*, II, 10. Gordon reported many other rapes or attempted rapes by soldiers: see, e.g, I, 213–15 (a 'very beautifull virgin' whom Gordon saved from being gang-raped by Finnish soldiers).

15. Sreenivasan, *The peasants of Ottobeuren*, 286; TCD *Ms* 830/172, deposition of Christopher Cooe, Tuam, 21 Oct. 1645; Struve, *Voices*, 47.

16. Quoted by Zysberg, 'Galley and hard labor convicts', 96.

17. Boyle, *A treatise*, I, 15; Behr, *Der Verschantzte Turenne*, 'To the Reader'. Both authors published in 1677.

18. Elliott and La Peña, *Memoriales y cartas*, I, 244, 'Resumen que hizo el rey don Felipe IV' (1627), discussed in Parker, *Military revolution*, 193 n. 3; Lynn, *Giant of the Grand Siècle*, ch. 2, on French army size.

19. Botero, *Relatione*, fo. 19v; BNE *Ms* 2362/61–2, marquis of Aytona to Philip IV, 28 Dec. 1630, copy; Davenant, *Essay*, 26–7.

20. Estimates from Bonney, *The European dynastic states*, 383; Mantran, *Istanbul*, 253; and Hellie, 'Costs'.

21. Further details in ch. 5. The consequences were intensified because until the late nineteenth century the Chinese government never raised loans, and so had to fund its wars from current resources.

22. Wheeler, *The making of a world power*, 208–10; Ashley, *Financial and commercial policy*, 45, 104–7.

23. Stránský, *Respublica Bohemiae*, 495–6. On the revolts, see chs 6, 8 and 9 above.

24. Glete, *War and the state*, 215.

25. Krüger, 'Dänische und schwedische Kriegsfinanzierung', 291, based on Oxenstierna's 'alternative' computation of the cost of the coming campaign, 8 Mar. 1633.

26. Salm, *Armeefinanzierung*, 163 (quoting Hauptmann Holl in 1650).

27. Di Cosmo, *The diary*, 48, 55.

28. Kishimoto-Nakayama, 'The Kangxi depression', 229, quotation from Wei Jirui, secretary to the governor of Zhejiang, c. 1672; Mut, *El principe en la guerra*, 104 (part of a sustained, unfavourable comparison between Philip IV and Justinian); Seco Serrano, *Cartas*, I, 277–8, Sor María to Philip IV and reply, 1/12 June 1652.

29. Dardess, 'Monarchy in action', 20. I thank Professor Dardess for permission to cite his unpublished paper.

30. Haboush, 'Constructing the center', 81–2, quoting a memorial by Hŏ Mok, government inspector, in 1660.

31. Details from Roy, *Symbol of substance*, 191–7.

32. Foster, *The voyage of Thomas Best*, 176 (from the 'Journal' kept by Ralph Croft, who met the sultan in 1613); Reid, *Southeast Asia*, II, 257–8 (quoting Augustin de Beaulieu's account of his visit in 1619–22).

33. Fleischer, 'Royal authority', 49, cites this formulation of the 'Circle of Justice' from a sixteenth-century Ottoman writer, adapted via a Persian work from the Arab writer Ibn Khaldûn. See also Darling, ' "Do justice" '.

34. On the *Risâle* of Koçi Beg, see Fodor, 'State and society', 231–2; Murphey, 'The Verliyüddin Telhis'; and *EI*, II, 'Koçi Beg' (online); on how Murad acted on this advice, see ch. 7 above; on the *fatwās* (always very short, frequently just a 'yes' or 'no' rather like the similar opinions voiced by the confessors of the Spanish Habsburgs, noted below), see Imber, *Ebu's-su'ud*, 7, 29, 55; and *EI*, s.v. 'Fatwā'.

35. Brown, 'Tsar Aleksei', 140, quoting Gregorii Karpovich Kotoshikin, a clerk of the foreign affairs chancery who defected in 1664 and wrote a memoir about Russian government; other details from Rowland, 'Moscow', 603–9, and Baehr, *The paradise myth*, 25–33.

36. McIlwain, *The political works of James I*, 307–8, speech to Parliament, 31 Mar. 1609; Forster, *The temper*, 9: funeral sermon for George of Hessen-Darmstadt in 1661; Cardin Le Bret, *De la souveraineté du roy*, 1, and 193–5; Christina, *Apologies*, 320 (from 'Les sentiments').

37. Mormiche, *Devenir prince*, 232 (on the Rhineland) and 231 (on reading Commynes's *Mémoires* of the reign of Louis XI). Mormiche studied the education of some 40 members of the French royal family. See also Hoffman, *Raised to rule*, on the education of a dozen Spanish Habsburgs.

38. Mormiche, *Devenir prince*, 278, 290–1, and 472 (noting that Louis's grandson, the future Philip V of Spain, composed a booklet entitled *Don Quixote of La Mancha, volume V*).

39. Ibid., 213, quoting the preceptor of Louis XIV's heir, and 215 on scrofula. Only English monarchs also publicly 'touched' those afflicted by 'the King's Evil'.

40. Ibid., 427, quoting the duke of Montausier, best known for purging over 60 books of passages deemed inappropriate for the prince and then marked *Ad usum delphini* ('To be used by the Dauphin': a phrase still used pejoratively in France to indicate something unnecessarily censored); and 242 (the Dauphin's history of the 1672 campaign). See also pp. 241–2, on the educational programmes submitted to Louis by Bossuet in 1679 and by Fénelon in 1695.

41. Weiss, 'Die Vorgeschichte', 468: Frederick to Elizabeth, his wife, 19 Aug. 1619; Green, *The letters*, 70, Henrietta Maria to Charles, 11 May 1642 NS; Burnet, *Memoirs*, 203, Charles to Hamilton, Dec. 1642; Halliwell, *Letters*, II, 383–4, Charles I to Prince Rupert, Frederick and Elizabeth's son, 31 July 1645.

42. Examples from Polleross, *Das sakrale Identifikationsporträt*, II, #420–#502, and especially plates 25, 66, 103 and 158.

43. Brown, 'Tsar Aleksei', 140, quoting Kotoshikin. On confessors, see García García, 'El confesor fray Luis de Aliaga'; on the *Juntas de Teólogos*, see AGS *Estado* 8341/70–1 (the Spanish Match); Straub, *Pax et Imperium*, 212–13 n. 11 (French Protestants); Elliott, *Count-duke*, 340–1, 366, 416–18 (Mantua); Maffi, 'Confesionalismo', 479–90 (Valtelline); and Hugon, *Naples*, 238–9, Philip IV to Oñate, 6 Apr. 1648. Ch. 8 above provides examples of Ferdinand II and Maximilian of Bavaria consulting theologians on policy. Beik, *Louis XIV and absolutism*, 170–1, prints a remarkable letter of 1675 in which Bishop Bossuet warned the king that unless he ceased his sexual infidelity 'there is no hope of salvation'.

44. Elliott and de la Peña, *Memoriales y cartas*, I, 155, Memorial of 26 July 1626; Berwick y Alba, *Documentos escogidos*, 486, Philip IV to Haro, 21 Oct. 1652 (the day he heard of the surrender of Barcelona).

45. Bergh, *Svenska riksrådets protokoll*, XIII, 17, debate on 21 Feb. 1649 OS; Christina, *Apologies*, 345 ('Les sentiments', #266). In 1638 Gabriel Naudé, later Christina's adviser, had argued that religion served as a 'pretext' for political action (*Considérations politiques*, 148–51); so did the marquis of Hamilton: page 335 above.

46. Fernández Álvarez, *Corpus documental*, II, 104, Philip IV to don Gabriel Trejo Paniagua; Seco Serrano, *Cartas*, II, 42 and 48, Philip IV to Sor María, 11 Jan. and 19 Mar. 1656.

47. Jansson and Bidwell, *Proceedings in Parliament 1625*, 29, speech of Charles I to Parliament, 18 June 1625; Elliott, *Count-duke*, 378–9, Olivares's questions on 17 June 1629 and Philip's replies.

48. Mormiche, *Devenir prince*, 306, Louis to the Princess Palatine, 23 Aug. 1693; Rodger, *The command*, 66–7, quoting Sir William Coventry.

49. (Desmarets de Saint-Sorlin), *Europe*, 16–17. The play, apparently commissioned by Richelieu, received its first performance in Nov. 1642: see Lacour, *Richelieu dramaturge*, 141–65.

50. Pursell, *Winter king*, 226, Rusdorf to Frederick V, 13 Aug. 1624, reporting the views of Sir Edward Conway.

51. AHN *E libro* 714, unfol., *consulta* of the Council of State, 19 Oct. 1629; BRB *Ms.* 16147–48/139–40, marquis of Aytona to Olivares, 29 Dec. 1633; AGRB *SEG* 332/75, count of Oñate to the Cardinal-Infante, 8 Aug. 1634.

52. Both quoted in Odhner, *Die Politik Schwedens*, 5.

53. Peter Loofeldt, 'Initiarum Monarchia Ruthenicae' (on this occasion, common sense prevailed and the tsar did not 'pull the sword from the scabbard': see ch. 6 above); Scriba, 'The autobiography', 32; Morrice, *Entring book*, IV, 335.

54. Knowler, *Strafforde*, II, 243, Hopton to Wentworth, Madrid, 14/24 Nov. 1638; *APW*, 2nd series B, IV, pp. 579–81, Louis XIV [= Mazarin] to his 'plenipotentiaries' at Münster, 14 Oct. 1646.

55. Zaller, '"Interest of State"', 151, Digby to Aston, 15 Dec. 1620 OS. The ambassador wrote just after Spanish forces had occupied the Rhine Palatine, belonging to James I's nephew.
56. Séré, 'La paix', 255, Hugues de Lionne to Mazarin, 10 July 1656, quoting Haro.
57. *APW*, 2nd series, B V, p. 1,151, Louis XIV to plenipotentiaries, 26 Apr. 1647, drafted by Mazarin; *Co. Do. In*, LXXXIII, 312–14, Peñaranda to the marquis of Caracena, Governor of Lombardy, 27 June 1647; and 334, Peñaranda to the marquis of Castel Rodrigo, Governor-General of the Spanish Netherlands, 12 July 1647.
58. Fletcher, 'Turco-Mongolian monarchic tradition', 238–9.
59. The Safavids also adopted the 'cage' system in the seventeenth century, but without creating the same instability as the Ottomans: ch. 14 above. Many Muslim political writers supported the murder of all male relatives when a ruler succeeded: see Alvi, *Advice*, 22.
60. Romaniello, 'Ethnicity', and Goffman and Stroop, 'Empire as composite', argue that the Russian and Ottoman empires (respectively) were composite states. See also Elliott, 'A Europe of composite Monarchies'.
61. Álvarez, 'The role of inbreeding'.
62. Anon. (probably James Howell), *The times dissected*, sig. A2.
63. Bacon, *Essayes*, 46. The Chinese magistrate Huang Liuhong used exactly the same image to describe the danger of tolerating political disorder: 'When the accumulated hatred of the people towards their magistrate reaches the boiling point, a popular uprising may result and endanger the security of the state.' (Bailey, 'Reading between the lines', 56, quoting Huang, *A complete book concerning happiness*, based on his experience as a magistrate in Shangdong between 1674 and 1699). This paragraph owes much to discussions with Daniel Nexon and Leif Torkelsen.
64. Burnet, *The memoires*, 55–6, Charles to Hamilton, 11 June 1638; Elliott, *The revolt*, 374–5, Olivares to Santa Coloma, viceroy of Catalonia, 7 Oct. 1639.
65. Favourites had existed in earlier periods – Haman in the Book of Esther; Sejanus in the reign of Tiberius; Alvaro de Luna and Piers Gaveston in the Middle Ages – and many in the seventeenth century cited their misdeeds; but, except in the Ottoman empire, they were more numerous between the 1590s and the 1660s than ever before or since.
66. Bidwell and Jansson, *Proceedings in Parliament, 1626*, II, 220–4, Sir John Eliot's speech in the House of Commons on 10 May 1626. Charles immediately stormed to Parliament to protest the comparison, because if Buckingham was Sejanus '(he said) implicitly [Eliot] must intend himself for Tiberius', the emperor during whose reign Christ had been crucified (ibid., 235 n). For more on Buckingham, see chs 11 and 18 above.
67. *ODNB*, s.v, Francis Russell, 4th earl of Bedford (1587–1641), by Conrad Russell, quoting Bedford's *Commonplace book* (Bedford himself quoted the Spanish political theorist Juan de Mariana, S. J.).
68. Christina, *Apologies*, 142 (from her *Ouvrage de loisir* of the 1680s); Contamine, *Histoire militaire*, I, 391–2 (calculation by André Corvisier); Begley and Desai, *Shah Jahan Nama*, xvi n. 10; Wu, *Communication and imperial control*, 16; Spence, *Emperor of China*, 46.
69. Major, 'The crown', 639: quoting Father Joseph; Elliott, *Count-duke*, 42, exchange attributed to Olivares and Uceda, son and successor of the duke of Lerma, Philip III's 'Favourite' for 20 years.
70. Ogilvie, 'Germany and the seventeenth-century crisis', 68. Benigno, *Specchi della Rivoluzione*, 100–3, also suggests that it was style as much as substance that made 'Favourites' so loathed.
71. Cressy, 'Conflict', 134, 137, 138, 139. See page 357 above for the use of the metaphor (and the need) 'to wink' in a worried letter to Charles I from 1638.
72. Ras, *Hikajat Bandjar*, 329. The king wanted everyone to follow the dressing style (and other customs) of Java.
73. Rodger, *The command*, 67, quoting Sir William Coventry, secretary to James, duke of York, then Lord Admiral and the chief advocate of the war: see page 43 above.

Chapter 3   'Hunger is the greatest enemy'

1. Bacon, *Essayes*, 47 (first published in 1612).
2. Manuel de Melo, *Historia*, 25, 22; AMAE (M) Ms 42/15–16v, Chumacero to Philip IV, 22 Oct. 1647, and fos 45–8, *consulta*, 10 Sep. 1647; Bercé, 'Troubles frumentaires', 772, quoting 'rumore del popolo' in Fermo and neighbouring cities in 1648; Wildman, *Truths triumph*, 4–5; Sibbald, *Provision for the poor*, 1. Italics added throughout.
3. Details from Parry, 'Climatic change', and Dodgshon, 'The *Little Ice Age*' (quoting the marquis of Lorne, whose family owned Kintyre). Both articles contain striking maps and tables.
4. On yield ratios, see Aymard, 'Rendements', 483–7, and idem, 'Rese e profitti', 436; on Leonforte, see Davies, 'Changes', 393–7, and Ligresti, *Sicilia moderna*, 108.
5. *SCC*, IV.iii, 245, quoting Yan Sengfang, *Shang ting Chi*. See also the discussion of 'Internal frontiers and intensified land use in China' in Richards, *Unending frontier*, 112–47.
6. Ince, *Lot's little one*, 92–4; Jacquart, 'Paris', 108; Wrigley and Schofield, *Population history*, 79, 80, 168; Woods, *Death before birth*, 95–6, 194 and 196 (all data series peaked in the second half of the seventeenth century).
7. McIlwain, *Political works of James I*, 343–4, Speech to Star Chamber. The king claimed that, in this, England followed 'the fashion of Italy, especially of Naples'.

8. Jonson, *Epigrams*, CXXXIV, 'On the famous voyage' (1612); Howell, *Epistolae*, 25, to Captain Francis Bacon, Paris, 30 Mar. 1630; Dunstan, 'Late Ming epidemics', 7, quoting Xie Zhaozhe, *Wu-za-zu* (1608).

9. Keene, 'Growth', 20–1; Baer, 'Stuart London', 633–4, from the 'Settlement of tithes' of 1638.

10. Wakeman, *The great enterprise*, 455; Nef, *The rise*, 282–97 (quotation from the Venetian ambassador in London, 15 July 1644); Davenant, *The first days*, 54–5 and 84 (1656). Paris was no better: Newman, *Cultural capitals*, 12.

11. Quotations from Evelyn, *Fumifugium*, 5–16. See also Jenner, 'The politics of London air'.

12. Foster, *The voyage of Sir Henry Middleton*, 97–8 (Edmund Scott, 'Exact discourse of the subtilties . . . of the East Indians'). In East Asia, both religious and medical considerations encouraged the use of wood rather than stone in home building: see Pomeranz, *Great divergence*, 134–5.

13. Friedrichs, *The early modern city*, 276; Jones, Porter and Turner, *A gazetteer*, table 6; Hessayon, 'Gold tried in the fire', 4–5; Pepys, *Diary*, II, 128, entry for 30 June 1661. Seaver, *Wallington's world*, 54–6, notes how often Nehemiah Wallington reported major fires in mid-seventeenth century London (and, like a good Calvinist, he gloated when they consumed the property of sinful Sabbath-breakers).

14. Pepys, *Diary*, VII, 267–79, provided a memorable eyewitness account. Mauelshagen, *Klimageschichte*, 127–9, documents the climatic anomaly of the summer of 1666 and the prevalence of urban fires in Europe.

15. RAS, *Diplomatica Muscovitica* 39 unfol., Pommerenning to Christina, 16 July 1648 N. S (Ellersieck, 'Russia', 264, 343 and 353 discusses the frequency and causes of the numerous fires in mid-seventeenth century Moscow); Bernier, *Travels*, 246, described the Delhi fire; Mantran, *Istanbul*, 36, lists all seventeenth-century fires.

16. McClain, *Edo and Paris*, 106, quoting Asai Ryôi, *Musashi abumi*; Viallé and Blussé, *The Deshima Registers*, XII, 294, 2–9 March 1657 (diary entries of Zacharias Wagenaer), and 337 (12 Apr. 1658), final death toll.

17. Viallé and Blussé, *The Deshima Registers*, XII, 338, records the fire of Feb. 1658; idem, XIII, 7–10, that of 1661, and 247, that of 1668. Viallé and Blussé, *The Deshima Registers*, XII, 247, on the frequency of fires in Edo.

18. In July 2010 this 'core' from Hitotsubashi was on display in the Edo-Tokyo Museum, Tokyo, which also displayed three illustrations of the Meireki fire, including the one by Wagenaer.

19. Jones, Porter and Turner, *A gazetteer*, 13; Stoyle, ' "Whole streets converted to ashes" ', 141 (Exeter). Allemeyer, ' "Dass es wohl recht ein Feuer" ', lists fires in other early modern European cities.

20. Müller, *Der schwedische Staat*, 237–8 (Mainz); Ogilvie, *Germany*, 236, 241 (Nuremberg); Sparmann, *Dresden*, 15; Rizzo, 'Un economia in guerra', and idem, ' "Haver sempre l'occhio all'abbondanza" ' (Pavia); SIDES, *La popolazione*, 43–7, and Externbrink, 'Die Rezeption des "Sacco di Mantova" ' (Mantua); and Clark and Lepetit, *Capital cities*, 205–7 (Warsaw). See also the example of Magdeburg, ch.4 above.

21. Mote, *Imperial China*, 800 and 1,036 n. 52, quoting Wen Bing's chronicle of c. 1645 on Kaifeng.

22. Boyer, *La gran inundación*; Hoberman, 'Technological change'; and Gibson, *Aztecs*, 236–42 and 305–6 (on Mexico); Prieto, 'The Paraná river floods' (on Santa Fé); Le Roy Ladurie, *Histoire humaine*, 406–8 and 441–2, and Garnier, *Les dérangements*, 85 (on the Seine floods); Gottschalk, *Stormvloeden*, III, 166–8 (on 1651, with engraving) and 234–55 (with maps). See also Brázdil, *Hydrological Sciences Journal*, LI/5 (2006), 733–985, a special issue on 'Historical hydrology', with many articles on floods in early modern Europe.

23. Elvin, 'Market towns', 446–7, quoting the Gazetteer of Jiading county: for the effects see chs 1 above and 5 above. An official in Zhejiang province voiced similar fears in the 1660s: Nakayama, 'On the fluctuations', 77–8.

24. Mantran, *Istanbul*, 181; Inalcik and Quetaert, *An economic and social history*, 179–82; Murphey, 'Provisioning Istanbul'; Mikhail, *Nature and empire*, 103–13. On the Egyptian drought, see ch. 7 above.

25. AHN *Consejos libro* 1218/118 (extending the *pan de registro* area, 4 July 1630); and 1229/681 (allocation of bread among the households, 19 Oct. 1644). See also Bernardos Sanz, *Trigo castellano*.

26. AMAE (M) *Ms* 42/7, 11 and 15–16v, Chumacero to Philip IV, 6 Feb. and 20 May 1647.

27. AHN *Consejos* 7225/15, council of Castile to Philip IV, 25 May 1647 (no bread on sale in Madrid and emergency purchases in Zamora); *Consejos libro* 1232/20 (abolition of all exemptions, 23 Feb. 1647), 89 (enforcement of collection, 18 June 1647) and 765 (a petition for a reduction in the new bread quota dismissed with the lapidary phrase 'No a lugar' ['No way'], 30 Sep. 1647).

28. Despite criticisms of the economic model advanced by G. William Skinner (see his articles 'Marketing' and 'Cities', well summarized by Eastman, *Family*, 255 nn. 21–23), the 'macro-region' concept seems to me more plausible than the 'centre and periphery' model of Wallerstein, *The modern world-system*.

29. Warde, 'Subsistence', 300–1.

30. Perkins, *Agricultural development*, 333–44, presents statistics based on over 5,000 *dated* entries in the 'water control' sections of Chinese Gazetteers (out of a total of over 50,000 such entries); Yamamura, 'Returns on unification', 331–3, details Japanese projects.

31. Marks, *Tigers*, 112 (quotations, both from the Guangdong area in 1625–6).

32. Bray, *Technology and gender*, 228–9, quoting a Gazetteer of 1660 about the town of Luzhou; ch 13 above on Gujarat. On the fragile foundations of sugar production in south China, see Mazumdar, *Sugar and society*.

33. Mazumdar, *Sugar and society*, 188–9, and others have argued eloquently that workers in East Asia tended to increase production by adding labour rather than capital; but the production of silk, sugar, cotton and other commercial crops still required far more capital equipment than cultivating rice or wheat.

34. Kishimoto, *Shindai Chûgoku*, 29, writing of the early modern Chinese economy.

35. Van der Capellen, *Gedenkschriften*, I, 232 (noting also dearth, plague, floods and urban revolts). Data from Snapper, *Oorlogsinvloeden*, 71; Gutmann, *War*, 233; and Israel, *The Dutch Republic and the Hispanic world*, 150–2.
36. Lu, *Sources of Japanese history*, I, 216–18, prints some of the 'exclusion decrees'; Tashiro, 'Foreign relations', 292–3, gives details on who could trade and who could not. Tashiro Kazui, 'Tsushima', 97 n. 33, notes the order for an increase in silk imports via Korea and Tsushima.
37. HAG *Ms* 488/13v, viceroy to captain-general of Macao, 17 Apr. 1640 (on the loss of trade); Atwell, 'Some observations', 232–3.
38. *Diaries kept by the heads of the Dutch factory*, IV, 190–1, entry for 27 Apr. 1640 (on the flight and suicide of Osaka silk traders); HAG *Ms* 1163/206–7v, *asento* of the council of finance, Goa, 9 Feb. 1642, on what to do with '800,000 taeis de prata corrente pertenhentes aos japões'.
39. The Qing decision to depopulate the coastal regions of southeast China between 1661 and 1683 offers another example of a human-inflicted economic catastrophe that, in the words of a contemporary, caused 'the greatest conflagration and havoc the world has ever seen': Marks, *Tigers*, 152.
40. Subrahmanyam, *Money and the market*, 48, quoting a poem by Mulla Qudrati.
41. Von Glahn, *Fountain of fortune*, 176–81, 196–8, 205–6.
42. Kishimoto, 'Comments' at a conference in International House of Japan, Tokyo, 16 July 2010.
43. Nakayama, 'On the fluctuation of the price of rice', 76–7 (quoting a contemporary journal); Kishimoto, 'The Kangxi depression', 231, quoting Tang Zhen. Calculation and aphorism from Marks, *Tigers*, 154–60.
44. Cervantes Saavedra, *Segunda parte de el ingenioso hidalgo Quijote*, ch. 20: 'Dos linajes solos hay en el mundo, como decía una agüela mía, que son *el tener y el no tener.*'
45. Weisser, *The peasants of the Montes*, 38–42.
46. Hindle, 'Exhortation', 119; idem, *On the parish*, 22–5. The situation improved later: see ch. 21 above.
47. Gutmann, *War and rural life*, 165 (St Truiden), 199 (Emael) and 84–6 (tithe receipts from 14 parishes in the Lower Maas valley near Liège and Maastricht). See similar data from Germany in ch. 8 above.
48. Smith, 'Benevolent societies', 325–7; idem, *The art of doing good*, 97–9, quoting Chen Longzheng.
49. Spence, *Death of Woman Wang*, 4–4, and 42 quoting the 1673 county *Gazetteer*, and Huang Liuhong, *Fuhui quanshu [Complete book concerning happiness and benevolence]*.
50. Ono, *Enomoto Yazaemon*, 35; Mortimer, *Eyewitness accounts*, 77–8, quoting Hans Conrad Lang from near Ulm in 1635; Roupnel, *La ville*, 31–3 (quoting Girardot de Noseroy, *Histoire de dix ans de la Franche Comté de Bourgogne 1632–1642*); Mortimer, *Eyewitness accounts*, 185, quoting Pastor Minck, from near Darmstadt, circa 1650, and 22–3, quoting Sebastian Bürster, a monk living near Überlingen, in 1647.

Chapter 4 'A third of the world has died'

1. I thank Matthew Connelly, Eve Levin, Pamela McVay and Kenneth Pomeranz for help with drafting this chapter. I also thank Peter Laslett and Tony Wrigley for alerting me to the importance of demographic history during my first term of graduate studies in 1965. This chapter concentrates on demographic trends in areas that suffered the full force of the Little Ice Age and General Crisis – basically Europe and Asia. Ch. 15 examines the different demographic experience of Australia, Africa and the Americas.
2. Jacquart, 'La Fronde', 283, on France; Telford, 'Fertility', 70–3, and Beatty, *Land*, 47 and 133 on Jiangnan. See also page 76 above on Tancheng county; and quotations at page 24 above.
3. John Donne, *Devotions*, XVII. 'Any man's death diminishes me, because I am involved in mankind, and therefore never send to know for whom the bell tolls; it tolls for thee.' Kate Epstein reminds me that since Donne wrote these words in 1621–3, years of high mortality in London, he would have often heard bells tolling.
4. Flinn, *Scottish population history*, 130 (petition from the ministers of Orkney to the Privy Council, 1634); Questier, *Newsletters*, 85, John Southcot to Peter Biddulph, 11 May 1632, together with notes 251–2; Sym, *Life's preservative against self-killing*, Preface (by William Gouge, a famous Protestant preacher), and 124.
5. Figures from Macdonald and Murphy, *Sleepless souls*, 252–3 and 260–7. Nicholas Rodger, who listed the Eastern Circuit Assize Records from the reign of Charles II in the Public Record Office, noted that 'in the hard years of the mid-1660s both suicide and infanticide rose sharply'. I thank him for sharing this information
6. Houston, *Punishing the dead?*, tables 1, 2 and 4; Behringer, *Kulturellen Konsequenzen*, 259. I thank Rab Houston for pointing out that the increase in recorded suicides may reflect greater 'visibility' as well as greater numbers: in times of dearth, a coroner's jury might be more likely to declare a verdict of suicide for (say) a person found drowned in a mill-race.
7. Details from Meyer-Fong, *Building culture*, 17–18 (citing the lists of suicides in a 1675 gazetteer).
8. Fong, 'Writing from experience', 269–71. Idem, 'Signifying bodies', 116–21, narrates the equally harrowing story of Du Xiaoying, from Hunan, who committed suicide aged 16 after capture by Qing troops. She could have drowned herself at once, she wrote, but first wanted to write her epitaph: her 16 'poems on ending life' formed her last act.
9. Peterson, 'The life' 142. For more on this story, see ibid., 242–3.
10. Wakeman, *Great Enterprise*, 64–5 (Liaodong example); Struve, *Voices*, 31 (two letters from Shi Kefa).
11. Struve, *Voices*, 34 (Wang) and 30 (Struve's evaluation). Wang's wife tried to commit suicide twice.

12. Meyer-Fong, *Building culture*, 17–18 (quoting from the lists of suicides at Yangzhou in a 1675 gazetteer). More examples in Ho, 'Should we die?', 125–36, Mann, *Precious records*, 25, and Ko, *Teachers*, 130–5 and 185–7.

13. Ho, 'Should we die?', 136, quoting Qian Xing, *Jiashen zhuanxin lu*; Spence, *Death of Woman Wang*, 9 and 14, from the memoirs of Magistrate Huang Liuhong, published in 1694. Elvin, 'Female virtue', 128, discusses the 1688 edict. For more on those who committed suicide in the 1640s, and those who did not, see ch. 5 above.

14. Cherniavsky, 'The Old Believers', figure on p. 21. See also ch. 6 above.

15. Major, *Sati*, xxviii; Temple, ed., *The travels of Peter Mundy*, II, 34–6. Banerjee, *Burning women*, discusses the description of suttee by Mundy and 42 other Western travellers in India 1500–1712, and reproduces seven pictures.

16. Kolff and van Santen, *De geschriften van Francisco Pelsaert*, 328 ('d'welck in Agraa meest 2 a 3 maal des weecks geschiet': Pelsaert spent much of the 1620s in Agra). The British recorded almost 8,000 immolations in Bengal alone between 1815 and 1828 (the only period any government made a count): Major, *Sati*, 281–2.

17. Woods, *Death before birth*, 218, quoting Guillaume Mauqeste de la Motte, *Traité complète des accouchements naturels* (1722).

18. Nedham, *Medela medicinae*, 54. Miller, *The adoption of inoculation*, 30–1, and Razzell, 'Did smallpox reduce height?', 353–4, quote other contemporaries who thought that smallpox (and measles) became more virulent in the seventeenth century.

19. Bamford, *A royalist's notebook*, 23; Chang, 'Disease'.

20. Gatta, *Di una gravissima peste*, 6; Corsini and Delille, 'Eboli'.

21. Domínguez Ortiz, *La sociedad española*, 71.

22. Levin, 'Plague control in seventeenth-century Russia', citing statistics from a detailed report filed in Dec. 1654 by Treasury Official Kuzma Moshnin; Moote, *The Great Plague*, 178 and 258–61 (the 'Bill of Mortality' for the week listed 7,165 dead, but this excluded burials of those who died without identification or who did not belong to the Church of England).

23. See the tables in Slack, *The impact*, 58, and Livi-Bacci, 'Chronologie', 433. See similar frequency tables in Kostes, *Stom kairo*, 366–73 (Balkan Peninsula), and Dols, 'The second plague pandemic', 187 (Egypt, Palestine and Syria).

24. Dunstan, 'The late Ming epidemics'; Odorico, *Conseils et mémoires*, 163–81; Amelang, *Journal*. In Catalonia, the drought that destroyed the harvest in 1650, and therefore drastically reduced the seed corn available for the following harvest, facilitated the devastating plague of 1651.

25. Foster, *The English factories in India, 1630–1632*, 165–6, East India Company officials in Surat to their colleagues at Bantam, 8 Sep. 1631; and 178, same to London, 9 Dec. 1631.

26. Alfani, 'Plague', 18, 27 (the database consisted of 124 parish registers in 87 north Italian communities, of which only five escaped at least one plague epidemic in the seventeenth century); SIDES, *La popolazione*, 86, 110–11 and 253–6.

27. Ansaldo, *Peste*, 48 ('Plus a esté commis . . .' on 13 June 1630), and 199–202 (totals).

28. Amelang, *Journal*, 40, 50, 58, 61, 68, 62. Pérez Moreda, 'La peste', 14–23, presents evidence confirming that women died more frequently, as did almost all who carried the corpses (mostly the mentally retarded and slaves).

29. Amelang, *Journal*, 71; Garnier, *Les dérangements*, fig. 13, on the drought.

30. Hastrup, *Nature*, 234–5; Galloway, 'Annual variations', 498–500; Wrigley and Schofield, *Population history*, 398; Patz, 'The effects', 281–9; Cullen, *Famine in Scotland*, 143–5.

31. Schaufler, *Die Schlacht*, 7, quoting General Johann Werth. The Spanish film *Alatriste* (2006) ends with a moving portrayal of the last stand at Rocroi.

32. Rodger, *The command*, 73, quoting an officer who survived the Four Days Battle, which Rodger considers 'the greatest battle of the age of sail'; 214 (losses); and 101, Commissioner Taylor to Samuel Pepys, Harwich, 4 Apr. 1667 (10 shillings was half a pound sterling).

33. Hutchinson, *Memoirs*, 208; Carlton, *Going to the wars*, 173–9, offers these and other English examples. See also the disturbing case studies of seventeenth-century military violence in Meumann and Niefanger, *Ein Schauplatz herber Angst*.

34. *Quatre Dialogues de Paysans*, 67–8, from *L'entre-jeux de Paysans*, a short play printed in Liège circa 1635. I thank Myron Gutmann for drawing it to my attention. See some other examples in ch. 2 above.

35. Ayala, *De Iure*, 1.2 (Eng. edn, I, 10–11). See also Gentili, *De Iure Belli*, 3.7 (English edn, II, 320).

36. Pascal, *Pensées* 'Les hommes ne font jamais le mal si complètement et joyeusement que lorsqu'ils le font par conviction religieuse'. On Magdeburg, see Mortimer, *Eyewitness accounts*, 67–70 (stressing the *speed* of the destruction); Kaiser, ' "Excidium Magdeburgense" '; Droysen, 'Studien'; Cunningham and Grell, *Four horsemen*, 175–82.

37. Joshua 6: 21, 24. Hale, 'Incitement to violence', notes how frequently those who practised military atrocities justified them from the abundant precedents and injunctions which they found in the Old Testament.

38. Carlton, *Going to the wars*, 178–9, quoting contemporary accounts of the siege of Basing House. More atrocities, notably from China, Germany and New England, noted in chs 5, 8 and 15 above.

39. Abbott, *Writing and speeches*, II, 127, Cromwell to Speaker Lenthall, 17 Sep. 1649. (Cromwell chose not to explain why his troops had also killed many civilians not 'in arms', or why he allowed the slaughter to continue long after 'the heat of the action' had passed, especially knowing that most of the defenders were Protestants.)

40. Data from Lindegren, 'Men, money and means', 133, 140–1; idem, 'Soldatenleben', 142–3; Jespersen, *A revolution from above?*, 279–96; and Lappalainen, 'Finland's contribution', fig. 9.

41. *HMC Ormonde*, n.s. II, 130–1, Lords Justices to Irish Commissioners, 7 June 1642. See other examples of troops targeting women in ch. 2 above.

42. Ogilvie, *A bitter living*, 220–2; Roupnel, *La ville*, 91–2; Lindegren, 'Men, money and means', 156–7; Ailes, 'Wars, widows' (noting almost 250 petitions from war widows from five sample years).

43. Ogilvie, *A bitter living*, 1 (quoting Catharina Schill, 'ein arme Frau' who in 1654 'müesse sich seürlich nehren'); Rublack, *Crimes of women*, 144–5.

44. Hufton, *The prospect before her*, 81.

45. Moncada, *Restauración*, 135–8; Anes Álvarez, *Memoriales y discursos de Francisco Martínez de Mata*, 219–20; Wrigley, *People, cities and wealth*, 240.

46. Hindle, 'The problem of pauper marriage'; Wrightson, *Earthly necessities*, 222–3 (drawing on the reconstructions of the Cambridge Population Group).

47. Mauriceau, *The diseases of women with child*, 287; Goubert, *Beauvais*, 48–54.

48. Galloway, 'Secular changes in the short-term'.

49. Capp, *When gossips meet*, 37. Demographic data suggest that patricians of Geneva and Zurich began family planning in the seventeenth century (von Greyerz, 'Switzerland', 134), but they seem to have been unique.

50. Lee and Wang, *One quarter*, 10, 99. Note, however, that Lee and Wang derived most of their data from the Lower Yangzi, the southeast and southern Manchuria, where extended families controlled many resources and so had more carrots and sticks with which to influence individual couples than in other regions, where 'nuclear families' probably enjoyed greater autonomy. (I thank Kenneth Pomeranz for this point.)

51. Ko, *Teachers*, 261–3, describes the female market of Yangzhou and also quotes the poem. Elvin, 'Female virtue', 112–14, quotes a similarly revolting poem from Jiangnan about raising daughters explicitly to be prostitutes.

52. Bray, *Technology and gender*, 289; Lee, Wang and Campbell, 'Infant', 405, 408, 410–11; Lee and Wang, *One quarter*, 47–51, 98, 107–8.

53. Waltner, 'Infanticide and dowry', 201, quoting the 1625 gazetteer of Fuqing county; Elvin, 'Unseen lives', 145–6, poem by Wu Zhao of Jiangxi. Female infanticide was also common in Tokugawa Japan, see ch. 16 above.

54. Kaiser, 'Urban household composition', based mostly on urban household inventories; and Levin, 'Infanticide'.

55. Ransel, *Mothers of misery*, 25, 269–71.

56. Patin, *Lettres*, III, 226, to André Falconet, 22 June 1660 (a statistic occasioned by the death of a prominent courtier when she went to a 'sage femme' for an abortion). Schiebinger, *Plants and empire*, 122–4, prints the advice of some seventeenth-century writers on how to carry out abortions; Pollock, 'Embarking on a rough passage', 56–8, discusses examples.

57. Soman, *Sorcellerie*, I, 797 and IV, 22. Infanticide cases made up almost one-third of all homicide cases heard by the court and, according to Soman, the foremost expert on the subject, to suppose that the *Parlement* and other courts of early modern France executed 5,000 women for infanticide 'would be a conservative estimate'.

58. *Statutes of the realm*, 21 Jac. I c 27; Wrightson, 'Infanticide' (infanticide cases made up almost one-fifth of all homicides brought before the Essex courts 1624–64); Gowing, 'Secret births'.

59. William Shakespeare, *The tragical history of Hamlet, prince of Denmark* (c. 1600), Act 3, Scene 1: Hamlet, feigning madness, tells his beloved Ophelia: 'Get thee to a nunnery: why wouldst thou be a breeder of sinners?'

60. A census of all male religious in Italy and its adjacent islands (Corsica, Sardinia and Sicily) conducted in 1650 revealed almost 70,000 monks and friars (in over 6,000 convents): Boaga, *La soppressione*, 150. Since most towns recorded as many or more females as males in Holy Orders (albeit in fewer convents), the overall number of Italian nuns was probably about the same. I calculated the percentage of nuns in the total urban population by dividing the latter by two (approximately half the population was female).

61. 'Galarana Baratotti' [Elena Tarrabotti], *La simplicità ingannata* and *L'inferno monacale*. Quotation from the extracts translated in Dooley, *Italy in the Baroque*, 417.

62. The magistrates of Milan expressed alarm at the sharp increase in young women being sent to convents in 1627–32 – years of famine, plague and war. See Sperling, *Convents*, 26–8; Vigorelli, *Vita e processo*, 174–89; Zannetti, *La demografia*, 60; and Hunecke, 'Kindbett oder Kloster', 452–6.

63. For Madrid, Carbajo Isla, *La población*, 257–67, plus calculations from the number of baptized foundlings recorded in AHN *Consejos*, 41,391; for Seville, Álvarez Santaló, *Marginación social*, 44 and graph on p. 47; for London, Fildes, 'Maternal feelings', 143 (quotation) and 156 (graph of foundling totals and bread prices).

64. AHN *Consejos*, 41,391, n.p., 'Juez de comisión para la aberiguación de los fraudes que se an echo en el ospital de los niños expósitos' (I thank Fernando Bouza for bringing this volume to my attention). Álvarez Santaló, *Marginación social*, 213, provides another example of a first-person appeal (from Seville).

65. Viazzo et al., 'Five centuries', 78–87, based on the records of the Spedale degli Innocenti, the first dedicated foundling hospital in Europe.

66. For Scotland, see Canny, *Europeans on the move*, 80–5; Murdoch, *Scotland*, 14, 19–20; and Cullen, *Famine in Scotland*, ch. 6. Gordon, *Diary*, names almost 250 Scots whom he met in Poland and Russia between 1655 and 1667. For Portugal, I thank the demographers of the Gulbenkian Foundation at Oeiras for providing figures. Note that the Scottish migrants came disproportionately from the Highlands and the Portuguese overwhelmingly from the north.

67. Felix, *The Chinese in the Philippines*, I, 46; Blussé, *Strange company*, 74 and 83.
68. For details, and for the term 'co-colonization', see Andrade, *How Taiwan became Chinese*.
69. Ochoa, *Epistolaro español*, II, 64, Cristóbal Crespi, 16 May 1627.
70. Cervantes Saavedra, *La segunda parte de el ingenioso hidalgo*, ch. 24: 'A la guerra me lleva, mi necesidad/Si tuviera dineros, no fuera en verdad'; Corvisier, *L'Armée française*, 1, 317, quoting Marshal Villars.
71. Manuel de Melo, *Historia de los movimientos*, 38–40. On the urgent need for temporary labour in cultivating rice (and indeed cotton and silk), see Elvin, 'Blood and statistics', 149–51.
72. Manuel de Melo, *Historia de los movimientos*, 38–40; and ch. 9 above. Parets, *De los muchos sucesos* (Memorial Histórico Español, XX, 75–6) notes that the *segadors* almost rebelled during the famine of summer 1631 as well.
73. Stepto, *Lieutenant Nun*. For other examples of cross-dressing, which was more common than one might think, see Dekker and van de Pol, *The tradition of female transvestitism*.
74. Ko, *Teachers*, 171, quoting Hu. Nevertheless, surviving pairs of snow shoes, straw sandals and padded overshoes made for women with bound feet reproduced in Ko, *Every step*, 16, prove that they *could* travel; and in the 1660s bound feet did not prevent Woman Wang first from eloping and then from returning to her village after her lover abandoned her (Spence, *Woman Wang*, 117–24, 128, 136). Nor did foot-binding spare women from performing heavy labour (Mann, *Precious records*, 167–8). Sandy Bolzenius reminds me that since foot-binding no doubt increased the risk of rape, it would also have increased the likelihood of suicide by the victims.
75. Opitz, 'Trostgedichte', 194 (Opitz dared not publish his poem until 1633); Foster, *The English factories in India, 1630–2*, 146, the English factors at Surat to their colleagues in Java, 22 Apr. 1631 (see also ch. 13 above).
76. Chen Zilong, 'The little cart', from Waley, *Translations*, 325. William S. Atwell, who generously brought the poem to my attention, has shown that Chen must have written it while visiting North China in 1637.
77. MacKay, *The limits*, 137; Vassberg, *The village*, 113; Ruiz Ibáñez, *Dos caras*, 331 n. 1,873. The government sometimes marched its conscripts to 'hell' chained together, in order to avoid desertion: Ruiz Ibáñez, *Dos caras*, 334. For the same treatment of conscripts in Naples, see ch. 14 below.
78. Levi, 'Hindus beyond the Hindu Kush', 283–4, quoting the chronicle of François Pelsaert; *RPCS*, I, 385, Order of 22 Aug. 1626.
79. Kupperman, *The Jamestown project*, 292, quoting John Chamberlain in 1618 and Patrick Copland in 1622. Unfortunately, the Company did not send adequate provisions with these 'creatures', which explains why many starved: see ch. 15 above.
80. Baily, *A true & faithful warning*, 8–9 (Baily's experience turned him from Catholic to Quaker and he wrote 'A true & faithfull relation of some of his sufferings' from gaol); Donoghue, ' "Out of the land of bondage" ', 961.
81. Charbonneau, *Naissance*, 128 (about half of the 'Filles du Roy' came from the Paris orphanage: see Dumas, *Les filles du roi*, 48).
82. Hathaway, *Beshir Agha*, 18, quantifies the African slave trade to Ottoman Egypt.
83. Figures from Schwartz, 'Silver, sugar and slaves', 10–11, quoting Fernando de Silva Solís; and Donoghue, ' "Out of the land of bondage" ', 966. Further details in ch. 15 below.
84. T'ien, *Male anxiety*, 85 (poem); calculation in Lee and Wang, *One quarter*, 107–8; and Lee et al., 'Infant and child mortality', 404.
85. Goubert, *Beauvais*, 607–12, was the first to note the cyclical nature of these subsistence crises, each creating a 'classe creuse' (depleted cohort). In 1740–2 another famine struck the 'classe creuse' afflicted by the Great Winter.
86. Details in Peters, *Ein Söldnerleben*. Helfferich, *The Thirty Years War*, 276–302, includes details on these deaths in her partial English translation of Hagendorf's diary.
87. Sella, 'Peasant strategies', 468–9, quotes a visitor to an Alpine valley in 1625 who graphically described the impact of massive male migration on households now headed by women.
88. Goldstone, *Revolution and rebellion*, 138; table adapted from Adamson, 'England without Cromwell', 463 – both based on data assembled by the Cambridge Group for the History of Population and Social Structure.
89. Goldstone, *Revolution and rebellion*, 137–8. At p. 248 Goldstone notes that a similar increase in the size of the under-30 population also occurred in France in the decades before the revolution of 1789: a tantalizing parallel.
90. T'ien, *Male anxiety*, 31. Ng, 'Ideology', 68, links an apparent prevalence of sodomy in Fujian to the surplus of bachelors.
91. Sen, *Poverty and famines*, 1.
92. Kaplan, *The famine plot persuasion*, 2. Kaplan examines the 'plots' invoked to 'explain' six dearths in eighteenth-century France. He could also have found abundant evidence from the seventeenth century.
93. Bossuet, *Politics*, 65 (Book III, article iii).

Part II. Enduring the Crisis

1. Jia Yi, a Chinese political thinker of the second century BC, quoted in Elvin and Liu, *Sediments of time*, epigraph.
2. Elliott, 'Revolution and continuity', 110.
3. Clark, *The European crisis*, 3–5 (Clark) and 301 (Elliott); Kamen, *The iron century*, 335–6. Clark's volume included 16 studies of the various manifestations of crisis in Europe; but none noted that the same problems affected other continents or considered the episode of global cooling: see details in Parker, 'La crisis'.

4. See Des Forges, *Cultural centrality*, 40–1 and 76–7 on Yang Dongming and his *Album of the famished*.
5. These and other data quoted in Parker, 'La crisis'.
6. Steensgaard, 'The seventeenth-century crisis', 33, originally written in 1970.

Chapter 5   The 'Great Enterprise' in China, 1618–84

1. Special thanks for help with this chapter to Tonio Andrade, William S. Atwell, Cynthia Brokaw, Timothy Brook, Roger Des Forges, Nicola Di Cosmo, Ann Jannetta, Kenneth Pomeranz, Evelyn Rawski, Christopher Reed, Lynn Struve, Kenneth Swope, Joanna Waley-Cohen and Ying Zhang in the United States; to Wang Jiafan and Chen Ning Ning in China; and to Hayami Akira, Iwai Shigeki, Kishimoto Mio, Mikami Takekiho, Shiba Yoshinobu and Yanagisawa Akira in Japan. I thank Taguchi Kojiro for research assistance with material in East Asian languages. I have used Pinyin Romanization for all Chinese names, except when quoting from older works that used the Wade-Giles system.
2. Xia, *Xingcun lu* (1645) quoted in Struve, *Qing formation*, 334.
3. Brook, *The troubled empire*, 254–5.
4. Size based on Ho, *Population*, 102, but note that 1,161 million *mou* at 0.1647 acres per *mou* = 191.3 million acres and not 176 million acres as Ho stated.
5. Brook, *The troubled empire*, 243; CHC, IX, 40, quoting a Manchu document from 1615.
6. Iwai, 'The collapse', 6, quoting Mao Yuanyi; Nakayama, 'On the fluctuation', 74.
7. Details from Des Forges, *Cultural centrality*, 109, 166–8 and 178–80.
8. Fei, *Negotiating urban space*, ch. 1 (quotation from p. 43). The unusual name 'Single Whip' arose from the Chinese title *yitiao bianfa*, 'the conversion of tax assessments into a single item' – but because *bian* means not only 'convert' but also 'whip', 'single item' became 'single whip'.
9. Wakeman and Grant, *Conflict and control*, 7–10.
10. Data from Huang, *Taxation*, 145–7, 155, 173–4 and 261–5; idem, 'Military expenditures', 60; idem, 'Fiscal administration', 85 and 120–2; Des Forges, *Cultural centrality*, 18 and 32–4; and Chan, *Glory and fall*, 199–201 and 310–14. One minister proposed to cover the deficit with government promissory notes, but had no idea who would accept them.
11. Chan, *Glory and fall*, 189–97; Las Cortes, *Voyage en Chine*, 183–8; Semedo, *Historica relatione*, 126–7.
12. Las Cortes, *Voyage en Chine*, 183–8; Chang and Chang, *Crisis*, 269, quoting the *Mingshi*.
13. Dardess, *Blood and history*, 60, quoting Censor Zhou Zongjian. On the Donglin academy see, apart from Dardess, Busch, 'The Tunglin Academy'; and Dennerline, *The Chia-Ting Loyalists*, 158–71. Tonio Andrade reminds me that *jingshi jimin* appeared in such popular works of Ming China as *Romance of the three kingdoms*: see ch. 18 below.
14. On Wei's triumph, see Tong, *Disorder*, 112; ECCP, 846–7; Tsai, *The eunuch*, 4–6; and Wu, 'Corpses on display'. On the 'blacklists', see Zhang, 'Politics and morality', 166–71. Miller, *State versus gentry*, chs 4 and 5, argues convincingly that Wei was more efficient and Donglin more disruptive than often portrayed in Western sources.
15. Dardess, *Blood and history*, 163, quoting the 'Veritable records' of the Chongzhen reign.
16. Zhang, 'Politics and morality', 229–30.
17. Dardess, *Blood and history*, 166, quoting the *Mingshi*. Of course, since the official history of the Ming was compiled under the Qing, it sought to justify their 'Great Enterprise' rather than present an impartial account of events. (I thank Joanna Waley-Cohen for this point.)
18. Names from Parsons, *The peasant rebellions*, 8.
19. Tong, *Disorder*, 84, summarizes the penalties in the Ming Code for bandits; Song, *Zhongguo Gudai*, notes 'serious droughts' (*da han*) in Gazetteers from both Hebei and Shaanxi provinces. See also the annual climate maps in *Zhongguo Jin-wubai-nian*.
20. Details from Chan, *Glory and fall*, 336–8; Ch'ü, *Local government*, 154–5; and Wakeman, 'China and the seventeenth-century crisis', 13–14. Gu Yanwu, writing soon after 1644, blamed the fall of the Ming primarily on the decision to close the courier stations: Brook, *The confusions of pleasure*, 173–4.
21. Cheng and Lestz, *The search for Modern China*, 5, quoting Song Yingxing, a government official, in 1636. See Chan, *Glory and fall*, 233–4, and Parsons, *Peasant rebellions*, 24, for similar reports on the droughts and famines of these years; and Zhang, 'A test of climate', on the weak monsoons.
22. Chan, *Glory and fall*, 229–30, citing Wu Yingji, *Loushantang ji*, published in 1639. Wu (1594–1645) was a Donglin sympathizer, a member of the *Fu She*, a Ming loyalist and author of *Qizhen liangchao bofulu* ('Record of the calamities in the Tianqi and Chongzhen reigns', covering 1624–8).
23. Details from Song, *Zhongguo gudai*, gazetteer records from 1633–6 (categories 4–1 and 4–12); Perdue, *Exhausting the earth*, 208–9; Will, 'Un cycle hidraulique', 276; and *Zhongguo Jin-wubai-nian* (maps).
24. Wakeman, *Great Enterprise*, 168–90, describes the transfer of technology and the siege of Dalinghe. See also Elliott, *Manchu Way*, 75, and Rawski and Rawson, *China*, 156–7, on the Eight Banners.
25. Elliott, 'Whose empire'; Struve, *Ming-Qing conflict*, 167–8; and Crossley, *A translucent mirror*, part II.
26. Ko, 'The body as attire', 17, cites Hong Taiji's edicts.

27. Struve, *Ming-Qing conflict*, 173–4, notes the contrasting advice contained in a collection of Manchu state papers from 1638. See Perdue, *China marches west*, 119–20, on food shortages in Manchuria at this time.

28. *Ming shilu*, 'Treatise on the Five Elements' for the Chongzhen era (translation kindly provided by William S. Atwell).

29. Des Forges, *Cultural centrality*, 62, quoting the report of Wang Han, 'Sketches of a disaster', May 1640. The illustrations have apparently not survived (ibid., 350 n. 96) but probably resembled those of Yang Dongming during the famine of 1594: plates 5 and 17. See also Song, *Zhongguo gudai*, category 4–7 for 1640.

30. Dunstan, 'The late Ming epidemics', 9–10 and map 6 (1641); *Zhongguo Jin-wubai-nian* (climate maps); Brook, *The troubled empire*, 250–1 (Shanghai and Shandong). See also Song, *Zhongguo gudai*, categories 4–7 and 4–14 for 1641; and Sato, *Chukogu*, 243–4.

31. Janku, '"Heaven-sent disasters"', 233–4; Marks, *Tigers*, 134, 138–9, and especially the figures on 139 and 141.

32. Smith, *The art of doing good*, 162; Will and Wong, *Nourish the people*, 25–6 and 434; Needham and Bray, *SCC*, VI.ii, 64–70 (on Xu Guangqi's *Nong zheng chuan shu*) and 402–23 (on granaries). Further examples in ch. 1 above.

33. Chen Qide, *Zaihuang Zhishi* (Record of disastrous famine), quoted by Atwell, 'East Asia and the "World Crisis"', 6–7; Dunstan, 'The late Ming epidemics', 12; Nakayama, 'On the fluctuation', 74.

34. Brook, *Vermeer's hat*, 175; Smith, *The art of doing good*, 137 and 153, quoting the diary of Lu Shiyi, from Taicang in Nanzhili; and Will, 'Coming of age', 30, quoting Yao Tinglin, *Linian ji [Record of successive years]*. It is tempting to dismiss reports of cannibalism as mere rhetoric, but Li, *Fighting famine*, 34–7, 261, 273–4, 300, 304, 358–9 and 361, found the expression 'people ate each other' ('*ren xiang shi*') with some frequency in documents concerning seventeenth-century famines.

35. Semedo, *Historica relatione*, 7.

36. Ho, *Studies*, 261–2, quoting Xie Zhaozhe, *Wu za zu* (1608); and *Shenmiao liuzhong zoushu huiyao* 6.20b, a selection of memorials sent by ministers to the Wanli emperor, but tabled without action. Cynthia Brokaw informs me that this one, by Yao Yongji, referred to population pressure, especially in Jiangnan.

37. On the 'closing' of Japan, see ch. 3 above; total silver arrivals from Marks, *Tigers*, 142, and Atwell, 'Another look'; tax increases in von Glahn, *Fountain*, 177.

38. Robinson, *Bandits*, 5–6, on urban disorders; Marmé, 'Survival', 145; and idem, 'Locating linkages', 1,083, quoting Ye Shaoyuan.

39. Fong, 'Reclaiming subjectivity', 32 (quoting Ye on the looting of 1640). Will, 'Coming of age', 25–7, provides a graphic account of the sack of a Shanghai mansion.

40. Quotations from Tong, *Disorder*, 83–4; and Kessler, *K'ang-hsi*, 15, Memorial by Wei Yijie in 1660.

41. Agnew, 'Culture and power', 46, letter from the Kong dukes to a provincial official about the release of Li Mi, alias Wei Tongjiao, and 51, quoting the first Qing governor of Shandong in 1644.

42. Qin Huitian, *Wuli tongkao* (1761).

43. Data from Elman, *Cultural history* (especially pp. 128, 141, 177 and 424); Miyazaki, *China's examination hell*, 39–40; and Zhang, *Chinese gentry*, 33–42. The three levels of degree holder meant, literally, 'raw' or 'student' (*sheng*) member of a group (*yuan*); 'elevated' (*ju*) 'man' (*ren*); and 'advanced' (*jin*) 'scholar' (*shih*).

44. Naturally the system had serious flaws. Not only was it effectively limited to boys from families with sufficient resources to 'spare' a son to undertake prolonged intensive study, but it also excluded those from 'base professions' (such as actors, couriers and brothel-keepers). Moreover, although the exam itself was free, the cost of travel to the exam venue, lodging, thank-you gifts to the examiners and tips to the staff exceeded what many families could afford (Miyazaki, *China's examination hell*, 118).

45. Data from Elman, *Cultural history*, 143, 286, 290; Miyazaki, *China's examination hell*, 121–2; and *CHC*, VIII ii, 712–15.

46. Calculation from Ho, *Ladder*, 181. If there were 120 million Chinese around 1640, then perhaps 30 million were males aged 20 or above: 500,000 *shengyuan* thus meant one in 60 adult males. Brook, *The troubled empire*, 150, noted the number of students who failed, and also the 'body of students vying for spots in the Confucian schools'.

47. See Elman, *Cultural history*, 361–4, on the moral collapse of failed candidates. Ho, *Ladder*, 36, and Chow, *Publishing*, 50–1, describe scholars who 'ploughed with their ink stands'; Chow, 'Writing', and Elman, *op. cit*, 403–9, discuss the manuals on how to pass, written by those who had failed. See also ch. 19 below.

48. Miller, *State versus gentry*, 140, quoting the 'charter' of the *Fu she* composed by Zhang Pu, its founder. Statistics from Dennerline, *Chia-ting loyalists*, 30–9. Atwell, 'From education to politics', 344, notes that the *Fu she* was strongest in precisely those areas where Wei had hunted down Donglin supporters most brutally. See also ch. 19 below.

49. Chow, *Publishing*, 233–7, describes the *Guobiao* ('Models of the state') published by the *Fu she* in 1632.

50. Elman, *Cultural history*, 196–202 and 304–26, notes the various attempts to 'beat the system'. Other data from Ho, *Ladder*, 178; Des Forges, *Cultural centrality*, 127–8; and Peterson, *Bitter gourd*, 113–19.

51. Wakeman, *Great Enterprise*, 155, quoting a memorial by Zuo Maodi.

52. Details in Hucker, *Chinese government*, 69, and Dardess, 'Monarchy in action', 21.

53. Des Forges, *Cultural centrality*, 204–7, summarizes Li's early career. 'Zicheng' means 'complete by oneself'. Zhu Yuanzhang, founder of the Ming, offered the most recent example of a bandit leader who had founded an imperial dynasty – and some of Li's slogans were modelled on those of Zhu in his 'bandit phase'.

54. Des Forges, *Cultural centrality*, 275, quotes the ditty, which he dates to 1642. Li Yu's 1668 play *The miraculous reunion*, with Li Zicheng in the 'starring role' explaining his methods of fleecing civilians, shows how some civilians perceived the bandits: Chang and Chang, *Crisis and transformation*, 214–16.

55. See Des Forges, *Cultural centrality*, 276, 292–3 and 311 (on the administrative arrangements of the Shun regime), 235–6 and 268 (on the use of ancient precedents by Li and others); and 294–6 (on Shun civil service exams).

56. Wakeman, 'The Shun Interregnum', 45 (on first ditty) and 77 nn. 6–7, on the slogans; Des Forges, *Cultural centrality*, 275, for the second ditty.

57. Cheng and Lestz, *The search*, 7, for Li's proclamation to the citizens of Huangzhou; Des Forges, *Cultural centrality*, 211–12, on the punishment of Ming clansmen, and 275–6, on the egalitarian policies.

58. Zhang, 'Politics and morality', 1, quoting the *Ming Shi*.

59. Struve, *Voices*, 7, quoting the 'Short Record' of Liu Shangyou about his visit to Beijing in 1644.

60. Wakeman, *Great Enterprise*, 306, quotes the proclamation to the Han Chinese drafted by Fan Wencheng. Estimates of Qing strength at this point differ wildly. Fang, 'A technique', argues that 620 banner companies existed in spring 1644, each with around 300 fighting men, one-third of them liable for military service at any one time. This suggests a force of 186,000 warriors, of whom 62,000 would have been ready to invade. Elliott, *Manchu way*, 1, 117 and 363–4, estimates the number of free adult males in the Banners at between 300,000 and 500,000, with 120,000 ready to invade. Fang's lower estimate seems more plausible.

61. Cheng and Lestz, *The search*, 25–6, Wu's letter to Dorgon, preserved in the earliest draft of the *Veritable records of the Shunzhi emperor*. Hsi, 'Wu', points out that in this version, Wu used the term 'Northern State', as any loyal Ming subject would have done before the Qing entered Beijing (but not afterwards, when they would have written 'Great Qing State'). This supports its authenticity. Hay, 'The suspension of dynastic time', 171–97, notes how the Chinese system of giving all dates by reign forced people to choose between Ming and Qing.

62. Cheng and Lestz, *The search*, 26–7, Dorgon's reply to Wu (also drafted by Fan Wencheng). Both men pursued opportunistic policies: Wu approached Dorgon primarily for personal and family reasons while Dorgon wanted to acquire lands capable of feeding his people by whatever means possible.

63. Wakeman, *Great Enterprise*, 312 (the third line of the jest refers to the founder of the Han dynasty, who 'mounted the throne on horseback' and founded a legitimate dynasty – whereas Li did not).

64. Struve, *Voices*, 18–19, from a 'Memoir of residing in Beijing' (1644) by Liu Shangyou, a minor official from near Shanghai. The fate of the Ming crown prince remains a mystery: Li claimed to have captured him (and offered to surrender him to Dorgon), but he then disappeared – presumably murdered.

65. Wakeman, *Great Enterprise*, 316–17, Dorgon's edict of 5 June 1644; Zhang, 'Politics and morality', 324–5, notes Dorgon's astute strategy.

66. Wakeman, *Great Enterprise*, 318, quoting Xu Yingfen's *General record of experiencing the dynastic change*; and 418, quoting Song Quan (who in 1646 became a Grand Secretary).

67. Wakeman, *Great Enterprise*, 634–5 (letter from Antonio de Gouvea, S. J. to the General of the Order); Elvin, *Pattern*, 246 (quoting a county gazetteer). Lists of tenant revolts in Tong, *Disorder*, 185–6. For a graphic example of a slave uprising, see Cheng, *The search*, 39–44. For more on the chaos, see Will, 'Coming of age', 31–2; and, on the spate of popular revolts in Guangdong province, Mazumdar, *Sugar and society*, 202–4.

68. Fu, *Ming-Ch'ing*, 99–101, quoting the bondservant leader Song Qi, and the gazetteer of Baoshan county (I thank Christopher Reed for this reference).

69. Examples in Marks, *Tigers*, 143–7; Will, 'Un cycle hydraulique', 275–6.

70. Mote, *Imperial China*, 828, quoting Dorgon.

71. Wakeman, *Great Enterprise*, 456–7 and 458–61 (list of reforms proposed by former Ming officials).

72. See ibid., 425–7 and 439–40, on the preponderance of Shandong officials among the 'twice-serving ministers', and Agnew, 'Culture and power', 49–57, on the lamentable state of Shandong in 1643–4.

73. Elliott, *Manchu Way*, 98–116; Naquin, *Peking*, 289–97.

74. My analysis draws on Ko, 'The body as attire', 12–13 and 20; and Kuhn, *Soulstealers*, 58–9. Struve, *Voices*, 64, prints a first-hand account of scholarly resentment at shaving their heads.

75. Wakeman, *Great Enterprise*, 420–2, on Dorgon's reluctant revocation of the edict on 25 June 1644.

76. Struve, *Southern Ming*, 48, from the *Guoque* compiled by Tan Qian in the 1650s. On the embassy from Nanjing, see Wakeman, *Great Enterprise*, 405–11. The term 'Southern Ming' only became common in the twentieth century. No Ming loyalist at the time used it, because it would have recognized the legitimacy of the Manchus' seizure of the north; and no Qing writer used it, because it would have accorded legitimacy to the resisters. I use it here for convenience.

77. Wakeman, *Great Enterprise*, 556–63, and Meyer-Fong, *Building culture*, 14–20. For more on the sack of Yangzhou, see ch. 2 above. On the unique 1644 monsoon, see Yancheva, 'Influence', 76, fig. 3.

78. Wakeman, *Great Enterprise*, 584–8 (on the surrender of the officials) and 646–7 (order of Prince Dodo, 19 June 1645).

79. Kuhn, *Soulstealers*, 54, quoting Dorgon's outburst on 22 June and the decree of 8 July 1645. Cheng and Lestz, *The search*, 33–4, print the orders of the Board of Rites.

80. Martini, *Bellum*, 279. Nicola Di Cosmo reminds me that head-shaving epitomized a dilemma common to all foreign dynasties that conquered China: how far should they 'pander' to Chinese customs and how much should they allow their own followers to 'Sinicize'?

81. Wakeman, 'Localism and loyalism', offers a detailed reconstruction of these events, while Marmé, 'Survival', 156, records the sack of Suzhou after anti-tonsure riots. Brook, *The troubled empire*, 256–7, notes that resistance often began with a refusal to cut one's hair as the Qing demanded.

82. Will, 'Coming of age', 32–3, paraphrasing Yao's memoirs.

83. Naquin, *Peking*, 363–4, notes Qing vigilance concerning the capital's food supply, and a similar system for supplying salt. I have translated a *shi* of rice – 103.5 litres – as a 'bushel'.

84. Kessler, *K'ang-hsi*, 14, quoting a memorial by a governor-general in 1649 (presumably echoing the old saying 'You can conquer China on horseback, but you cannot rule it on horseback').

85. See Marks, *Tigers*, 139 and 195–202; Rawski, *The last emperors*, 222; Son, *Zhongguo gudai*, categories 3–17, 4–9, and 4–12 for the 1650s; Liu, 'A 1000-year history', 458–9, for the typhoons. See also the annual climate maps in *Zhongguo Jin-wubai-nian*.

86. Chang, 'Disease and its impact', notes that these strict measures increased Manchu paranoia about the disease.

87. Martini, *Bellum* 189–90. Other details from Bowra, 'The Manchu conquest of Canton'; Wakeman, *The Great Enterprise*, I, 558–65, 655–61 and II, 817–18; and Struve, *Southern Ming*, 139–43 (with useful campaign map).

88. On Coxinga's negotiations with the Qing in 1654, see Struve, *Voices*, 184–203 (quotations from 191, 194, 196). In 1646 a Southern Ming ruler bestowed on Zheng the imperial surname. Thereafter he was addressed as *guoxing ye* ('Gentleman of the imperial surname') which Westerners rendered as 'Coxinga'.

89. See Struve, *Southern Ming*, 154–66 and 178–93.

90. Nakayama, 'On the fluctuation', 76–8 (quoting several contemporary sources). For more on *shu huang* see ch. 2 above.

91. Will, 'Un cycle hydraulique', 276, details on Hanchuan county.

92. Struve, *Southern Ming*, 74 (for consistency, I have changed 'Ch'ing' to 'Qing' in this passage).

93. On these complex events, see again Struve, *Southern Ming*, 154–95.

94. Dennerline, 'Fiscal reform', 110; Wakeman, *Conflict and control*, 12, quoting one of those flogged and barred from taking exams. Wakeman, *op. cit.*, 10 n. 27, reports that at least one gentleman who protested against the tax demands called out under torture to the spirits of the Ming emperors, reinforcing belief that treason lay behind the protests.

95. Shi and Liu 'Estimation of the response of glaciers', 668–9.

96. *CHC*, IX, 144–5, contains a striking map of the suppression of the Three Feudatories. Di Cosmo, *Diary*, prints in English the campaign journal kept by a middle-rank Manchu officer in 1680 and 1681, with an impeccable introduction.

97. On the emperor's tours, see Chang, *A court on horseback*, 75–86 and 117; Spence, *Ts'ao-Yin*, 125–8; and Dott, *Identity reflections*, 177–8 (quoting the diary).

98. Marks, *Tigers*, 157–60 (Lingnan); Wakeman, *Great Enterprise*, 1,109 n. 77 (Sichuan).

99. Beattie, 'The alternative', 266, quoting a genealogy from Dongcheng county; Dardess, *A Ming society*, 42, report of Shi Junchang.

100. Peterson, 'The life', 149, quoting Gu's Memoirs. Lynn Struve estimated that the *Mingmo zhonglie jishi* ('True record of Late Ming extreme loyalty') submitted to the Kangxi emperor in 1702 included 'biographies and brief biographical notices of about 575 men and 360 women who died righteously in connection with the fall of the Ming': Struve, *Ming-Qing conflict*, 40–1 and 349–50.

101. Nieuhof, *An embassy*, 48. On the millions enslaved in 1644–5 by the Qing and their Han allies, see Elliott, *Manchu Way*, 227–9; on the vigorous defence of the fugitive slave laws by the Shunzhi emperor in 1655, see Kessler, *K'ang-hsi*, 16–17.

102. On slaves, see Mann, *Precious records*, 41 (on p. 242 n. 100, Mann notes that only after 1673 did the Qing Code forbid masters from having intercourse with their *married* slaves); on the rape clauses of the Qing Law Code issued in 1646, see Ng, 'Ideology and sexuality', who argues that these provisions reflected the new dynasty's concern to restrict the quantity of litigation: by increasing the burden of proof they hoped to deter legal suits.

103. Brook, *The troubled empire*, 258, prints this poem, together with another by widow Shang Jinglan. For more on Huang Yuanjie (c. 1620–c. 1669), who left over 1,000 poems at her death, see Ko, *Teachers*, 117–23. Widmer, 'The epistolary world', analyzes the increase in letters written and published by women during the Ming-Qing Transition.

104. Brook, *Confusions of pleasure*, 240–50. See also the similar lament of Xia Yungyi: page 115 above.

105. Waley-Cohen, *The culture of war*, 13; Will, 'Coming of age', 38–9, quoting from a final section of Yao's *Record*, which enumerated the changes he had witnessed, explicitly comparing his experience under Ming and Qing.

106. Brook, *The troubled empire*, 242, 249.

Chapter 6 'The great shaking'

1. Special thanks for help in preparing this chapter to Robert Frost, Przemysław Gawron, Dariusz Kołodziejczyk and James Lenaghan (on the Polish Commonwealth and Polish sources), and to Paul Bushkovitch, Irena Cherniakova, Chester Dunning, Mircea Platon, Matthew Romaniello, Mark Soderstrom and Kira Stevens (on Russia and Russian sources). I also thank Alison Anderson and Ardis Grosjean Dreisbach, respectively, for transcribing and translating German and Swedish documents, and Przemysław Gawron for translating Polish materials. Russia at this time used its own calendar, in which each year (counted from the Creation in 5508 BC) began on 1 September but in other respects followed the Julian Calendar, which Sweden also observed. In this chapter all dates have been converted to the Gregorian Calendar unless otherwise stated.

2. Data from Hellie, *Enserfment*, 112; Eaton, 'Decline', 220–3; and Dunning, *Russia's first civil war*, 466. At p. 481. Dunning notes the use of '*smuta*' by contemporaries.

3. Olearius, *Reisebeschreibung*, 143; LeDonne, *The Grand Strategy*, 29–35; Hittle, *The service city*, 23.

4. Baron, *Travels*, 120, quoting Olearius who had travelled through the grasslands himself in the 1630s. See also Davies, *State*, 30.

5. Although primarily a geographic term in the seventeenth century, in this chapter, 'Ukraine' refers to the three palatinates of Kiev, Bratslaw and Volhynia (incorporated into Poland in 1569), plus the palatinate of Chernihiv (annexed from Russia at the truce of Deulino in 1618 and added to the other three in 1635). All four shared a common legal code and official language (Ruthenian) and overwhelmingly adhered to Orthodox Christianity. In this chapter, the term 'Ruthenian' refers to the Orthodox population of Ukraine.

6. Romaniello, 'Ethnicity as social rank', notes that non-Russians often saw the agreements that made them part of the Muscovite state as 'alliances', not acts of submission, a classic characteristic of the 'composite state'.

7. Frost, *The northern wars*, 107, quoting Krzysztof Radziwill in 1622.

8. RAS, *Manuskriptsamlingen* 68, Peter Loofeldt, 'Initiarum Monarchiae Ruthenicae', p. 99, on 'zu Behauptunge ihren vermeinten kleinen Weldt'. The foreigners share the blame for their own ignorance: very few spoke Russian, and so, since virtually no Russians spoke any foreign language, most relied for information on professionals such as translators, doctors and military officers.

9. I thank Matthew Romaniello for this information.

10. Details in Kahan, 'Natural calamities', 371; Krenke, *Izmenchivost' klimata*, 87, 110, 113; Davies, *State*, 39; Stevens, *Soldiers on the steppe*, 42; and further data generously provided to me by Professor Stevens in Sep. 2004.

11. Cherniakova, *Karelia*, 101–5, data from Zaonezhskii Pogosts, near Lake Onega.

12. Hittle, *The service city*, 24; Hellie, 'The costs', 44; Stevens, *Russia's wars*, 132–8.

13. Details from Davies, *State*, 1–12, 70–2, 75, and 172; Shaw, 'Southern frontiers'; and Stevens, *Soldiers*, 34.

14. Vernadsky, *History*, V, 368.

15. Eaton, 'Early Russian censuses', 76–7; Hellie, *Enserfment*, 127–31. Moon, 'Peasant migration', 869, notes that migration involved a disproportionate number of healthy, young people who set up farmsteads and started families, but 'left behind the older, weaker people, who had passed their fertile years and were likely to die sooner'. He therefore plausibly suggests that population south of the Oka grew more rapidly, while population further north declined more rapidly than one might have expected.

16. Dunning, *Russia's first civil war*, 474, 464.

17. Romaniello, 'Through the filter', 919–20, describing the 'Stepennaia kniga', a manuscript chronograph of almost 800 folios in the Hilandar Research Library of the Ohio State University, Aronov Collection, 18. Dunning, *Russia's first civil war*, 475, dates the first use of 'Holy Russia'.

18. Kivelson, '"The Devil stole his mind"', 743.

19. Hellie, *Readings*, 192–6 (the 1645 petition); Loewenson, 'The Moscow rising', 147 (the Swedish envoy).

20. On the monopolies, see Hellie, *The economy*, 157 and 559 (salt) and 106–7 (tobacco). Torke, *Die staatsbedingte Gesellschaft*, 218–19, notes the unrest in autumn 1647.

21. Torke, *Die staatsbedingte Gesellschaft*, 219.

22. Baron, *Olearius*, 207. Torke, *Die staatsbedingte Gesellschaft*, 93–4, notes the significance of the presence in the capital in 1648 of the Moscow servitors who would normally have been deployed on the southern frontier.

23. Baron, *Olearius*, 142, 149–50; Gordon, *Diary*, II, 139.

24. Platonov, 'Novyi istochnik', 6–8: 'Kurtze vndt warhaftige Beschreibung desz gefährlichen Auffleutes des Gemeinen Pöbels Moscow'. Both this source (a manuscript from a private collection in Stockholm) and a dispatch from Ambassador Pommerenning mention a 'Supplication' on this day, yet no separate 'Supplication' has survived: only the one presented on 12 June 1648. However, the 'Beschreibung' states that the Supplication presented on both days was the same, which seems plausible.

25. RAS, *Diplomatica: Muscovitica* 39 contains the only surviving text of this document, a Swedish translation sent by Ambassador Karl Pommerenning to Queen Christina together with his letter of 16 July 1648 NS. Iakubov, 'Rossiia i Shvetsiia', printed a Russian translation of this Swedish text, and Hellie, *Readings*, 198–205, printed an English translation of Iakubov's Russian version. Since none of these texts seems reliable, I quote from a new translation of the Swedish original, and of Pommerenning's covering letter, prepared for me by

Ardis Grosjean-Dreisbach. The key terms are 'revolt' (*uppstånd*), 'great confusion' (*stoor oreeda*), and 'uprising and revolt' (*uppror och upstånd*).

26. Loewenson, 'Moscow rising', 153 (English translation of a Dutch eyewitness account); Platonov, 'Novyi istochnik', 9 ('Kurtze Beschreibung').

27. Baron, *Olearius*, 208 ('We must have you too'); RAS, *Diplomatica: Muscovitica* 39, Pommerenning to Christina, 16 July 1648 (the musketeers' answer); Loewenson, 'Moscow rising', 153 (their number and pay arrears); Platonov, 'Novyi istochnik', 10 (the soothing words). Note that the last source implies that 6,000 musketeers were involved, but this may mean 6,000 in the capital rather than 6,000 inside the Kremlin at the crucial moment. Kivelson, 'The Devil', 739, working from a Russian translation of this document, states that the crowd only entered the Kremlin *after* the musketeers declared in their favour, but the original states the reverse.

28. Loewenson, 'Moscow rising', 153. Platonov, 'Novyi istochnik', 13 ('they did not leave a nail in a wall').

29. Loewenson, 'Moscow rising', 154. See also Baron, *Olearius*, 208–9.

30. RAS, *Diplomatica: Muscovitica* 39, n.p., Pommerenning to Christina, 16 July 1648, mentioned 'houses on a list' (*annoterades huss*); Loewenson, 'Moscow rising', 155, noted 'some relation' of houses 'about 36 in number' to be burned. Kivelson, 'The Devil', 740 n. 21, and Platonov, 'Novyi istochnik', 14, quote sources that detail 70 or so houses burned.

31. RAS, *Diplomatica: Muscovitica* 39 n.p., Pommerenning to Christina, 16 July 1648.

32. Loewenson, 'Moscow rising', 155; RAS, *Manuskriptsamlingen* 68, Peter Loofeldt, *Initiarum Monarchiae Ruthenicae*, p. 91; RAS, *Diplomatica: Muscovitica* 39 n.p., Pommerenning to Christina, 16 July 1648.

33. Avrich, *Russian rebels*, 55; Platonov, 'Novyi istochnik', 19; Kivelson, 'The Devil', 747 (quoting a nobleman's servant).

34. Ellersieck, 'Russia', 89, citing Pommerenning to Christina, 6 July 1648, which Ellersieck decoded himself.

35. Torke, *Staatsbedingte Gesellschaft*, 223–4, notes 71 petitions submitted between 2 June and 31 July 1648 OS. Vernadsky, *Source book*, I, 246, prints the decree of 1 June 1649 OS expelling the English merchants.

36. Ladewig Petersen, *The crisis*, 34, showed that grain prices at Danzig – the largest mart for Baltic cereals – peaked in 1648. Stevens, *Soldiers*, 42, lists 1648 as a year of harvest failure; and PRO *PRO* 22/60, no 73, Charles I of Great Britain to Tsar Alexei, 1/11 June 1648, reported that his agents had been able to buy only 30,000 instead of 300,000 measures of grain because of the 'scarcity and conditions' in Muscovy.

37. See Pokrovskii, *Tomsk*, especially the tables on pp. 177 and 186.

38. Davies, *State*, 237, report of Governor Roman Boborykin. On the revolt of Kozlov, see ibid., 224–42.

39. Details from Anpilogov, 'Polozhenie gorodskogo'. Torke, *Staatsbedingte Gesellschaft*, 224–32, provides an admirable survey of the spread of unrest in 1648–9.

40. Hellie, *Enserfment*, 136, quoting later testimony from Patriarch Nikon.

41. Kivelson, 'The Devil', 752, quoting a memorandum later compiled by Prince Odoevskii, who headed the committee that drafted the code. Vernadsky, *Source book*, I, 222–3, prints the summons for Novgorod to choose delegates to the Zemskii Sobor, 26 July 1648, issued by the leading nobles and not by the tsar himself.

42. RAS, *Diplomatica: Muscovitica* 39 n.p., Pommerenning to Christina, 4 and 18 Oct. 1648 OS, with the translation of decoded passages as corrected by Ellersieck, 'Russia', 83–4. In his letter of 30 Dec. 1648, loc. cit., Pommerenning stated that each *strelets* had received 25 roubles in the course of the year.

43. Blum, *Lord and peasant*, 263 (a lord who murdered someone else's peasant *without* premeditation 'had to replace the slain peasant with the best of his own peasant families'). See also Kolchin, *Unfree labor*, 41–2; Hittle, *The service city*, 66–9; and the entire text at http://pages.uoregon.edu/kimball/1649-Ulj htm#ch11, accessed 9 Apr. 2012 (all but 4 of its 34 sections concerned fugitive serfs).

44. The fugitive-serf article was almost the last to be finalized, suggesting that it was the most contested: Hellie, *Enserfment*, 137–8.

45. RAS, *Diplomatica: Muscovitica* 39 n.p., Pommerenning to Christina, Moscow, 17 Nov. 1649.

46. Figures from Frost, *After the Deluge*, 7 n. 8 (Wiśniowiecki), and Sysyn, 'Ukrainian social tensions', 65 (landholders) and 57–8 (Jews). For distribution, see Stampfer, 'Maps of Jewish settlements'; for the Cossacks as a 'reservoir of malcontents', see Gordon, *Cossack rebellions*.

47. Plokhy, *The Cossacks*, 136, quoting a report by Stanislaw Koniecpolski to the Diet in 1631.

48. Sysyn, *Kysil*, 83, quoting Adam Kysil's second 'Discourse' on the Cossack problem in 1637. Beauplan, *Description*, described and drew Kodak fort just before the revolt.

49. Plokhy, *The Cossacks*, 143, chronicle of Lviv.

50. Hrushevsky, *History*, VIII, 222, report by Kysil, Feb. 1648.

51. Hannover, *Yaven Metzulah* (which literally means 'Deep mire', first published in 1653), 27–8. Beauplan, *Description*, 449, also commented on the extreme demands of the Polish landowners; Hrushevsky, *History*, VIII, 355–6, described the burden of billeting and the atrocities.

52. Hrushevsky, *History*, VIII, 350–5, and Plokhy, *The Cossacks*, 190–206, discuss evidence of Jewish exploitation. Raba, *Between remembrance and denial*, 14–18, discusses the spread of anti-Semitic propaganda.

53. Wrocław, Ossolineum, *Ms* 188/455v, 462, 463, 465v, 491, 499v, diary of Marcin Goliński of Kasimiersz (the Jewish quarter of Kraków); Beauplan, *Description*, 473–4 (on winters) and 471 (on locusts), reflecting 17 years living in Ukraine

54. Wrocław, Ossolineum, *Ms* 2389/1, A. Bielowski, 'Okolice i podania'; Wrocław, Ossolineum, *Ms* 188/516 (diary of Goliński); and Namaczyńska, *Kronika*, 27–9.

55. Hrushevsky, *History*, VIII, 370–1 and notes, and 396, discusses the royal response and letters, concluding that almost certainly Khmelnytsky lied.

56. Ibid., VIII, 397, quoting a Russian source. He also argues that the khan welcomed a rebellion against Władysław as a way to forestall his proposed attack.

57. Ibid., VIII, 411, Kysil to Primate Lubienski of Gniezno, 31 May 1648. Some Polish writers have asserted that Khmelnytsky issued a proclamation immediately after his victory at Korsun calling for a general revolt, but ibid., 412 n. 54 refutes them.

58. Ibid., VIII, 413 quotes both contemporary sources. I thank Mirosław Nagielski for pointing out the significance of the aristocratic arsenals.

59. Hrushevsky, *History*, VIII, 450–1, quoting the 'Victory March of the Khmelnytsky Uprising'. Yakovenko, 'The events of 1648–1649', provides other examples of the literature of hate generated by the revolt.

60. Hannover, *Abyss of despair*, 50–77; see also the testimony in Hrushevsky, *History*, VIII, 439–49, and the careful analysis of Stampfer, 'What actually happened?' All dates are given according to the Gregorian Calendar (New Style) used in Poland, and not according to the Old Style used in Ukraine and Russia.

61. Figures from Stampfer, 'What actually happened?'; Bacon, 'The House of Hannover', 179–80 and 191. Raba, *Between remembrance and denial*, ch. 1 reviews the numerous accounts of the massacre written by contemporaries. Many assumed that the massacre had been carefully planned but no evidence of preparation has materialized: sectarian hatred apparently sufficed. In 1650, Poland's Jewish leaders proclaimed a fast to commemorate the second anniversary of the day when the massacres began at Nemyriv, and commissioned a special elegy for what Jewish chronicles from the seventeenth century onwards called *Gezeirot ta'h ve-ta't*: 'The Decrees of 408–409' (that is, 5,408 and 5,409 in the Jewish calendar, or 1648–9 in the Christian one).

62. Wrocław, Ossolineum, *Ms* 189/56; *The moderate intelligencer*, CLXXVII (12–19 Oct. 1648 OS), quoting a report from Danzig dated 2 Oct. 1648.

63. See Plokhy, *The Cossacks*, 220–35; Hrushevsky, *History*, VIII, 517–19; and Sysyn, 'Ukrainian-Polish relations', 63, 67 and 69–71.

64. Hrushevsky, *History*, VIII, 535, Khmelnytsky speech to Kysil, Feb. 1649.

65. Plokhy, *The Cossacks*, 220; Hrushevsky, *History*, VIII, 520–1 and 541–2, Khmelnytsky's terms delivered to the commissioners, 24 Feb. 1649 OS.

66. Hrushevsky, *History*, VIII, 522, recording the commissioners' impressions in Dec. 1648 and Feb. 1649; Hrabjanka, *The great war*.

67. Hrushevsky, *History*, VIII, 589–90 (the Cossacks' demands) and 593–5 (the royal concessions) at Zboriv, both dated 18 Aug. 1649. Vernadsky, *History*, V, 447, reports negotiations between the Cossacks and Moscow.

68. RAS, *Manuskriptsamlingen* 68, Loofeldt, *Initiarum Monarchiae Ruthenicae*, pp. 93 and 97–9.

69. Ibid., pp. 98–9.

70. Davies, *Warfare*, 103–11, and Vernadsky, *History*, 463–81, provide a detailed account of the negotiations leading up to the 'Union' of January 1654 and the terms confirmed in Moscow the following March. What happened at Pereiaslav is bitterly contested by Ukrainian and Russian historians, the former claiming that the Union was intended only as a temporary measure, the latter asserting that it was meant from the first to be permanent. Whatever the Cossacks' intentions, it seems certain that from the first Alexei and his ministers saw the Union as permanent.

71. RAS, *Manuskriptsamlingen* 68, Loofeldt, *Initiarum Monarchiae Ruthenicae*, 99–100.

72. Roberts, *Sweden as a great power*, 163–9, minutes of the Swedish council of the realm, 8–12 Dec. 1654, reveals the reaction to Russia's invasion of Poland. The council approved mobilization, without deciding whether to attack Poland or, in return for certain concessions, to ally with Sweden against Russia. The council considered the risk that an invasion might lead Poland to collapse and then ally with Russia – precisely what happened – but deemed the risk of further Russian expansion far worse.

73. In 1886 Henryk Sienkiewicz entitled a historical novel about Poland in the mid–seventeenth century *Potop*, and the name has stuck. The current division of Ukraine between an eastern part that favours a closer union with Russia and a pro-Western part largely reflects the divisions created after 1656.

74. Brown, 'Tsar Alexei', 124, order of Alexei to Prince Trubetskoi, late May 1654.

75. Karpinski, *W walce z niedwidzialnym wrogiem*; Rykaczewski, *Lettres de Pierre des Noyers*, 393, letter from Poznań, 8 Apr. 1658; Namaczyńska, *Kronika*, 35.

76. Davies, *Warfare*, 132.

77. Gieysztorowa, *Wstep do demografii staropolskiej*, 188–90; Bogucka, 'Between capital, residential town and metropolis', 206–7; Reger, 'In the service of the tsar', 49; Stevens, *Russia's wars*, 160.

78. Jones, *History and climate*, 12.

79. Cherniakova, *Karelia*, 121 (families with sons in Megorsk Pogost according to the 1678 census), and 122 (details on the deaths of 1,092 males in the war).

80. Frost, *After the Deluge*, 72–3, quoting a report by Piotr Galiński, 30 Apr. 1656.

81. Hellie, 'The costs', 64–6.

82. Sargent and Velde, *Big problem*, 259–60, for the copper/silver exchange rate (with a striking graph). On the riots of 1662, see the eyewitness accounts of RAS, *Diplomatica Muscovitica* 602, n.p., Adolph Ebbers to King Charles XI, 10 and 18/24 June, 25/29 July and 21 Aug. 1662 (all dates Old Style); and Gordon, *Diary*, II, 159–62. See also Torke, *Die staatsbedingte Gesellschaft*, 244–52.

83. O'Brien, *Muscovy*, 120, quoting the French ambassador in Feb. 1667 and the English resident in Sep. 1667. Vernadsky, *A source book*, I, 304, prints parts of the truce of Andrusovo signed on 9 Feb. 1667 NS, including the clause that left Kiev under Russian control for two years. The truce stipulated that the parties should meet again in two years to reach a permanent settlement, failing which, they should meet again every two years until they agreed.

84. Crummey, 'The origins', 131, quoting Avraamii.

85. Michels, *At war*, 211–16, citing the investigation by church authorities after 1666 (quotation from p. 211).

86. Avrich, *Russian rebels*, 65, and Khodarkovsky, 'The Stepan Razin uprising', 8, both quote this 1667 document.

87. Avrich, *Russian rebels*, 76 and 78–9, quoting documents from 1670.

88. Details from ibid., 88–97, and Khodarkovsky, 'The Stepan Razin uprising', 14–18. No evidence exists that Razin possessed letters from Nikon: see Khmelnytsky's similar claim on page 170 above.

89. Avrich, *Russian rebels*, 115. Stenka Razin has inspired stories and folksongs: see idem, 121–2. In 1964, Yevgeny Yevtushenko composed the poem, 'The execution of Stenka Razin'.

90. Tsar and patriarch condemned all these religious dissidents as schismatics (*raskol'niki*) and, in order to identify them, used the new liturgy as a litmus test. This allowed later Old Believers to claim all dissidents as their precursors but Michels, *At war*, chs 4–6, shows that (until at least 1700) although all Old Believers were *raskol'niki*, not all *raskol'niki* were Old Believers.

91. Cherniavsky, 'The Old Believers', figure on p. 21. Cherniakova, *Karelia*, 231, provides a striking map of places in Karelia where peasants either rebelled against their ecclesiastical masters or burned themselves to death.

92. Sysyn, 'The Khmelnytsky rising', 167; Davies, *Warfare*, 188, followed by a detailed analysis of the later fate of each protagonist.

93. Details from Bushkovitch, *Religion and society*, chs 6–7, and Lewitter, 'Poland, the Ukraine and Russia'. Population figures from Davies, *Warfare*, 198–201. Subtelny, *Domination*, 130–7, notes the brief but unsuccessful bid for independence made by Hetman Mazeppa, 1706–9.

94. Hellie, *Enserfment*, 256 n. 59. Hellie, *The Muscovite Law Code*, provides a bilingual Russian and English edition. I thank Matthew Romaniello for sharing with me his insights on the *Ulozhenie*.

95. Gordon, *Diary*, II, 138–9, anno 1661 but probably written some years later.

96. Romaniello, 'Through the filter of tobacco', 914, citing a diplomat with the Carlisle mission in 1663.

Chapter 7   The 'Ottoman tragedy', 1618–83

1. Special thanks for help in preparing this chapter to Günhan Börekçi, John Curry, Kaan Durukan, Suraiya Faroqui, Matt Goldish, Jane Hathaway, Colin Imber and Oktay Özel. I thank Allen Clarke for translating Arabic material for me, and Günhan Börekçi not only for analyzing and translating Turkish sources but also for hosting me at the XI 'Congress of Social and Economic History of Turkey' in Ankara in 2008, at which I learned so much.

2. Firpo, *Relazioni*, XIII, 170, Relazione of Lorenzo Bernardo, 1592; Sandys, *A Relation of a Journey* (1615), 46. Distances from Pitcher, *An historical geography*, 134, and Çetin, *XVII. ve XVIII*, 17–22.

3. Baer, 'Death in the hippodrome', 64.

4. Details from Darling, *Revenue-raising*, 248–9, 281; *EI*, IV, 560–1, 'Kānūn'; and Fodor, 'Sultan, imperial council, Grand Vizier'. Although the council (*divan*) met in an open hall with a grill behind which, in theory, the sultan secretly listened, he rarely seems to have done so.

5. According to *EI*, s.v. 'Devshirme', recruiters might 'collect' one boy aged between 8 and 20 from every 40 Christian households in each village once every five years. They rarely recruited in towns, but promising boys captured in wars and raids often joined the 'sultan's slaves'.

6. Figures from Jennings, 'Firearms', 341, and Kunt, 'The Köprülü years', 31. The central government maintained strict segregation between sipahis and Janissaries in an attempt to prevent them making common cause.

7. See *EI*, s.v. 'Fatwā'. The *fatwā* was always very short, frequently just a 'yes' or 'no' (compare the similarly terse opinions voiced by the confessors of the Spanish Habsburgs: see ch. 9 above).

8. Tezcan, 'Searching for Osman', 105–9.

9. Zilfi, *Politics of piety*, 33, notes 'Slimey' Hüseyn. According to legend, the Janissaries' distinctive white headdress came from Hajji Bektash, whose disciples founded the Bektashi Order: Hathaway, *A tale*, 88, 100.

10. Öz, 'Population fall', Özel, 'Banditry' and Özel, 'Population changes', document the population losses in Anatolia; D'Arrigo, 'A 350-year (AD 1628–1980) reconstruction', provides climatic data.

11. Kiel, 'Ottoman sources' 99, 102, on Greece and Bulgaria; McGowan, *Economic life*, 106–7, on Manastir; Odorico, *Conseils et mémoires*, 163, 169 and 171 on Macedonia. Hütteroth, 'Ecology', 21–2, denies that the Little Ice Age affected the Ottoman empire, but cites only outdated research.

12. Grove and Conterio, 'The climate of Crete', 241–2, report the storm of January 1645 and note that it 'seems to have been more intense than those of the [twentieth] century'. Information on Safed gathered from local sources in 2002. On Egypt, see Mikhail, *Nature and empire*, 23 and 123; and Ibrahim, *Al-Azmat*, appendix 11.

13. Özel, 'Banditry', 69. His calculations of bandit size support those of Koçi Beg, *Risale*, in the 1630s. The size, structure and movement of the population of the Ottoman empire is the subject of great controversy: Özel, 'Population changes', offers an excellent overview. Details from ibid., 180-1, 186-7 and 190-2; Cook, *Population pressure*, 10-27; McGowan, *Economic life*, 139-40 and 145-6; Barkey, *Bandits*, 220-6; Faroqhi with Erder, 'Population rise'; Faroqhi, *Coping with the state*, 23-33, 40-3, and 86-97; and Inalcik, *An economic and social history*, 438-47 (also by Faroqhi).

14. On the title, applied by Katib Çelebi to the deposition and murder of Osman, see Piterberg, *Ottoman tragedy*, 1.

15. Börekçi, 'Factions and favorites', 82-3, quoting Francesco Contarini, the Venetian agent in Istanbul, 3 Jan. and 18 Sep. 1604.

16. Tezcan, *Searching for Osman*, 110, on the entitlements of the *mevali*, and 201, of Osman's revocation. Note that Osman also had his eldest brother murdered before leaving the capital, a fratricide that the Chief Mufti refused to sanction, giving the sultan another grievance against the clerical elite: Finkel, *Osman's dream*, 198.

17. White, *The climate*, 193, quoting Bostanzade Yahya; Anon., *The strangling and death*, 13. *Peçevi Tarihi*, II, 349-50, and *Topcular Katibi Abdulkadir (Kadri) Efendi Tarihi*, 687, both describe the freezing of the Bosporus early in 1621.

18. *Hasan Beyzade Tarihi*, 338-9 (my thanks to Günhan Börekçi for translating this reference); White, *The climate of rebellion*, 197-8, quoting Bostanzade Yahya. The sources are confused, but I follow the account of Tezcan, *Searching for Osman*, 229-30. Hathaway, 'The *Evlād-i 'Arab*', argues plausibly that tensions between the *devşirme* recruits raised in the Balkans and Anatolia, and those raised in the Caucasus and the Arab lands, contributed to the confrontations of 1622-3.

19. *Peçevi Tarihi*, II, 464; Roe, *A true and faithfull relation*, n.p., adding that if Osman's plan to create a military counterweight to the Janissaries and sipahis 'had taken effect, what events it might have produced by a civil war is not easy to judge'.

20. Pedani-Fabris, *Relazioni di ambasciatori veneti*, 557-8, Giorgio Giustinian (1627). Mustafa returned to the 'cage' and died there in 1639.

21. *Pecevi Tarihi*, 385; *Topcular Katibi Abdulkadir*, 944-6, 985; *Hasan Beyzade Tarihi*, 375. I thank Jane Hathaway for drawing to my attention the floods that partially destroyed the Kaaba in 1630.

22. Ibrahim, *Al-Azmat*, appendix 11; *Numarali Mühimme Defteri (H. 1040/1630-1631)*, entry 356. Grove and Conterio, 'The climate of Crete', 236, record a 'very severe' drought in winter and spring 1630.

23. *Numarali Mühimme Defteri (H 1040/1630-1631)*, analysis of contents by Günhan Börekci. By contrast, the register for 1617-18 (also published) records less than half the number of entries in all three categories.

24. Setton, *Venice*, 43 n. 14, quoting Sir Peter Wyche. See also Grehan, 'Smoking'. I thank Günhan Börekci for pointing out to me the coincidence between the Personal Rule of Murad (1632-40) and Charles I (1629-40).

25. Katib Çelebi, *The balance of truth*, 135-6 (from Katib Çelebi's autobiography, referring to a day in 1627-8). It is important to remember that, since the Kadizadeli movement failed to gain its objectives, most surviving sources on it come from its later critics (including Katib Çelebi).

26. Details in Zilfi, *Politics of piety*, 138-9, 146, 192 (quotation). Zilfi, 'The Kadizadelis', 253-5, lists the movement's 21-point programme. The underwear/spoon example comes from *Tarih-i Naima* VI, 226; the summary of practices condemned by the Kadizadelis from ibid., 219-20, and Çelebi, *Balance*, 97-100 and 110-23. I thank John Curry for these references.

27. Rycaut, *The present state*, part II, 128-31 on the Kadizadelis and 135-40 on the Sufis. For Rycaut's background, and its probable effect on his view of Ottoman affairs, see Darling, 'Ottoman politics through British eyes'; nevertheless Ottoman sources often corroborate Rycaut (see Terzioğlu, 'Sufi and dissident', 205, for an example).

28. Kâtib Çelebi, *Balance of Truth*, 43-4.

29. On the extreme weather of 1640-2, see *Topçular Katibi Abdülkadir*, 1,145, 1,156, 1,164, 1,173; D'Arrigo, Cullen and Touchan, 'Tree rings'; Odorico, *Conseils*, 163-81; White, *The climate*, 205-6; and pp. 4-5 above.

30. See Unat, 'Sadrazam Kemankeş', on the memorandum; and Uluçay, 'Sultan İbrahim', on the Sultan's administrative activity. Howard, 'Ottoman historiography', 64, notes that Koçi Beg composed one version of his *Risâle* (Treatise of Advice) for Murad and another for Ibrahim, and that he wrote the second in a notably simpler style, perhaps indicating real or perceived learning difficulties in the new sultan (I owe this point to Colin Imber).

31. See *EI*, s.v. 'Husayn Djindji Khodja'. Other data from Mantran, *L'histoire*, 237-9. Kunt, *The sultan's servants*, 70-5, showed that over half the provincial governors appointed between 1632 and 1641 remained in office for less than a year and only 10 per cent served for two years or more – a far faster turnover than before.

32. Setton, *Venice*, 121 n. 25, letter to Giovanni Soranzo, 1 Mar. 1645.

33. Dujčev, *Avvisi*, 111, Martino di Turra to the Pope, Ragusa, 12 Aug. 1647, forwarding information received from 'our friend in Constantinople' – probably Soranzo, the Venetian resident whom the sultan had placed under house arrest when war broke out.

34. Dujčev, *Avvisi*, 110-11, Turra to the Pope, Ragusa, 12 Aug 1647; Brennan, *The travel diary of Robert Bargrave*, 83.

35. Costin, *Letopisețul Țării Moldovei*, 196-7 (my thanks to Mircea Platon for finding and translating this item); Brennan, *The travel diary*, 135.

36. Kâtib Çelebi, *Fezleke*, II, 326; Dujčev, *Avvisi*, 120–1, Turra to the Pope, Ragusa, 9 July 1648, forwarding information sent from Istanbul on 12 June; Setton, *Venice*, 151 n 30, quoting Mormori, *Guerra di Candia*. Monconys, *Journal*, I, 49, letter from Istanbul, 24 Aug. 1648, also described the violence of the earthquake.

37. Monconys, *Journal*, I, 54, letter from Istanbul, 24 Aug. 1648, notes the Chief Mufti's legal consultation.

38. Emecan, 'İbrâhim', 280, narrates the deposition (see the fuller version, based on *Tarih-i Na'ima*, in Vatin and Veinstein, *Le sérail*, 243–7); Monconys, *Journal*, I, 54, letter from Istanbul, 24 Aug. 1648.

39. Monconys, *Journal*, I, 60, letter from Istanbul, 24 Aug. 1648.

40. Brennan, *The travel*, 87. Finkel, *Osman's dream*, 235–40, makes sense of impossibly confused events.

41. Behrnauer, 'Hâgî Chalfa's Dustûru'l-'amel', 125–32, a German translation of Kâtib Çelebi, 'The rule of action for the rectification of defects' (19 Mar 1653). See also the English summary in Lewis, *Islam in history*, 207–11. Erol Özvar has calculated Ottoman state income in 1648–9 at 89 tonnes of silver and expenditure at 154 tonnes, with corresponding figures in 1650 of 149 and 192 tonnes, and in 1652–3 of 145 and 215: Özvar, 'Fiscal crisis'.

42. Kunt, 'The Köprülü years', 20, citing *Tarih-i Na'ima*, and 31. On the other hand, in 1653 and 1656 the Ottomans rejected two Mughal requests for a declaration of war against Iran; see ch. 13 above.

43. Kâtib Çelebi, *Balance of truth*, 28–9.

44. Rolamb, 'Relation', 699. The Swedish envoy wrote of conditions 'at my arrival' in Istanbul, namely May 1657. Presumably the sultan's position six months before had been even more hazardous.

45. Zilfi, 'Kadizadelis', 252.

46. Kunt, 'The Köprülü years', 65.

47. Kunt, 'The Köprülü years', 76, quoting the history of Mehmed Halife, one of the pages chosen to recite the Qur'an. Kunt also notes that since both the emperor and his Vizier were named Mehmed, the exercise was particularly appropriate for rallying public support for their cause.

48. Kunt, 'The Köprülü years', 100–15 (messianic claims on p. 109); White, *The climate*, 214, on the extreme weather of 1657–9.

49. Kunt, 'The Köprülü years', 119–20, quoting from *Tarih-i Na'ima*.

50. On Romania, see Nicoară, *Sentimentul*, I, 37–8, quoting the chronicle of Radu Popescu and a sale contract by Gavril Niță, 1660 (and other similar ones); on Transylvania, see Cernovodeanu and Binder, *Cavalerii Apocalipsului*, 90, quoting the *Journal* of Mihail Teleki, Chancellor of Transylvania, for 1661 (my thanks to Mircea Platon for both the references, and the translations). See also the data in White, *The climate*, 214–15.

51. Details from Terzioğlu, 'Sufi and dissident', 205–6; and Baer, 'Death in the hippodrome', 80.

52. Anti-Semitic interpretations recorded by Baer, 'The Great Fire', 172–3, also noting the simultaneous elimination of other non-Muslims from the area. He notes that 'ethnic cleansing' in the capital began 'about a year after the fire', but does not connect that delay with the transfer of power from Köprülü Mehmed to his son.

53. Scholem, *Sabbatai Sevi*, 88, quoting the *Zohar*, a key text of the Kabbalah, and explaining how it was made to show '1648' as the year of the Apocalypse. Idel, 'Differing conceptions', provides a brilliant discussion of the 'unwillingness to adhere to the same answers that had been valid only a short time before' that led to the vision of Sabbatai and others. Menassah ben Israel, *Esperança de Israel* (Amsterdam, 1650; also published that same year in Hebrew, Portuguese, Latin and English).

54. Israel, 'Menasseh ben Israel', 390–2, expertly analyzes the first three disasters of 1645–8 but omits the fourth. On Philip IV's 1647 bankruptcy and anti-Jewish policies, see ch. 9.

55. Scholem, *Sabbatai*, 136, quoting a letter of Rabbi Solomon Laniado in 1669, relating his meeting with Shabbatai four years before. On Shabbatai as a 'fool', see ibid., 125–38, and Goldish, *The Sabbatean Prophets*, 1–2, 118–19 (as Goldish remarks, 'Shabbatai Zvi was a strange man in a strange age'). My thanks to Professor Goldish and to Benzion Chinn for helping me understand the 'Sabbatean phenomenon'. On Izmir's Jewish community – perhaps 2,000 out of a total population of 40,000 by 1648 – see Eldem, *The Ottoman city*, 98–102.

56. Goldish, *Sabbatean Prophets*, 2–3, notes that Shabbatai's preferred language was Spanish, and that the 1659 Izmir edition of *Esperança de Israel* appeared in that language.

57. Goldish, *Sabbatean Prophets*, 108, 119–20, quoting Leyb ben Oyzer, *Beschraybung fun Shabsai Zvi*, who based his account on interviews with those who 'ate and drank' with Shabbatai. On the networks that spread the word of Shabbatai, see ch. 18 above.

58. Goldish, *Sabbatean Prophets*, 102–5, quoting Thomas Coenen (a Dutch minister residing in Izmir at the time), *Ydele verwachtinge der Joden getoont in den persoon van Sabethai Zevi* (Amsterdam, 1669).

59. Pepys, *Diary*, VII, 47 (entry for 19 Feb. 1666 OS). Pepys added 'certainly this year of 1666 will be a year of great action, but what the consequence of it will be, God knows'.

60. Maier and Waugh, ' "The blowing of the Messiah's trumpet" ', document the tsar's interest and the importance of Christian as well as Jewish reports in spreading Shabbatai's claims. Benzion Chinn reminds me that Shabbatai's father was a purchasing agent for English merchants in Izmir.

61. Scholem, *Sabbatai*, 427–33, lists the 'kings' to whom Shabbatai gave a biblical name (King David, King Hezekiah, and so on). Hathaway, 'The Mawza' exile', links the Yemen rebellion of 1665–6 with Shabbatai.

62. Scholem, *Sabbatai*, 435, quoting a letter written by Fr. La Croix. The 'fall of the Crescent' was not an idle threat at this time: four sultans in living memory had been deposed – Mustafa in 1617 and again in 1623, and his nephews Osman in 1622 and Ibrahim in 1648.

63. The verdict of Scholem, *Sabbatai*, ix.
64. Finkel, *Osman's dream*, 276–7, offers two description of this gala. Kolodziejczyk, *Ottoman-Polish diplomatic relations*, prints the treaties of these years. Özvar, 'Fiscal crisis', calculated that the Ottoman treasury in 1670–1 received the equivalent of 147 tonnes of silver and spent 143 tonnes.
65. White, *The climate*, 215–22, provides an excellent summary of these harsh conditions after 1675.
66. Finkel, *Osman's dream*, 284, records the Grand Vizier's decision to reject the advice of the Chief Mufti and on p. 288 his similar rejection of a dream predicting disaster if he attacked the Habsburgs.
67. Xoplaki, 'Variability', 596–8, summarizes the extreme weather in the Balkans in the later seventeenth century.
68. Hathaway, *A tale*, 88–9, 181–2, 185–6, 190–1; and Hathaway, 'The *Evlād-i 'Arab*'.
69. Luterbacher and Xoplaki, '500-Year Winter Temperature', especially graph at p. 140; *Silahdar Tarihi*, II, 263–4 (I thank Jane Hathaway both for this reference and for the translation); and Faroqhi, 'A natural disaster'.

Chapter 8   The 'lamentations of Germany' and its Neighbours, 1618–88

1. I thank Katherine Becker and Leif Torkelsen for help with some German and Scandinavian sources; and Derek Croxton, Christopher Friedrichs and Paul Lockhart for valuable critiques of this chapter.
2. Von Krusenstjern and Medick, *Zwischen Alltag und Katastrophe*, 34 (order of catastrophes as listed); Koenigsberger, 'The European Civil War' (1971).
3. The geography of the Holy Roman Empire is extremely complex. Besides the territories named, northern Italy and (until 1648) the Swiss cantons and the Low Countries also owed nominal obedience to the emperor, but he rarely exercised direct power there (the war over Mantua, an imperial fief, in 1628–31, was an exception). Conversely, although after 1564 the emperors also ruled Hungary and Moravia, but they did not form part of the empire.
4. Dollinger, 'Kurfürst Maximilian', 298–9, Maximilian to his father (who had just abdicated), 21 June 1598.
5. MacHardy, 'The rise of absolutism', 436.
6. Polyxena Lobković quoted by Polišenský, *The Thirty Years' War*, 94; Landsteiner, 'Crisis of wine production', 326–7, shows unprecedented oscillation in yields during 1617–21.
7. Zillhardt, 'Zeytregister', 93.
8. Magen, *Reichsgräfliche Politik in Franken*, 190, statement of Hohenlohe's chancellor, June 1619.
9. Gindely, *Geschichte*, II, 164, Count Solms, Frederick's representative in Frankfurt, to his master, 28 Aug. 1619; Lee, *Dudley Carleton*, 270–1, letter of 18 Sep. 1619.
10. Weiss, 'Die Vorgeschichte', 468, Frederick to Elizabeth, his wife, 19 Aug. 1619.
11. Reade, *Sidelights*, I, 388, Sir Edward Conway to Secretary of State Naunton, Nov. 1620.
12. Wilson, *Thirty Years' War*, 353 (see 351–61 on the 'law of the conqueror').
13. Warde, 'Subsistence', 303, quoting J. Ginschopff, *Cronica* (1630); Helfferich, *The Thirty Years War*, 59, quoting *Münzbeschikung der Kipper und Wipper* (1621); Stránský, *Respublica Bohemiae* (1634), 495–6, quoted page 35 above. Langer, *Thirty Years' War*, 31–2 and 49, notes the rebellions. See also the broadsheets and commentary in Paas et al., *Kipper and Wipper*. 'Kippen' means 'to tilt' and 'Wippen' means both 'to wag' (like scales) and 'to torture', so *Kipper- und Wipperzeit* is rhyming slang (like 'hurley-burley' or 'pell-mell').
14. Supple, *Commercial crisis*, 75–6, 79 and 93, quoting Edward Misselden's pamphlet, *Free trade*, 1622.
15. Turbolo, *Copia*, 6.
16. Stouppe, *La religion des Hollandois*, 96–8 (the author was a Swiss Protestant officer garrisoned in Utrecht in 1673); Van der Woude and Mentink, 'La population'.
17. AGS *Estado*, 2327/168, *consulta* of the council of state, 12 June 1621.
18. Lockhart, *Denmark*, 55, quoting the earl of Leicester in 1632; other details from Ladewig Petersen, 'Conspicuous consumption', 64–5.
19. Mann, *Wallenstein*, 369, quoting the Bavarian council of war.
20. Jespersen, 'Slaget', 89, quoting Christian's holograph *Skrivekalender*: 'Sloges med Fjenden og mistede Slaget.'
21. Ernstberger, *Hans de Witte*, 166, Wallenstein to the imperial treasurer, 28 Jan. 1626. For more on military finance in the Thirty Years War, see ch. 2 above.
22. Zillhardt, 'Zeytregister', 117; further details in Pfister, *Klimageschichte der Schweiz*, 40–1, 118–22, 140; idem, 'Weeping in the snow', 33 and 50; and idem, *Wetternachhersage*, 194–8. Theibault, *German villages*, 184, notes that in Hessen-Kassel, 'Between 1626 and 1634. no year passed without some frost, drought, hail or blight to affect one of the crops'; while Garnier, 'Grapevine', 710, quotes a report from the French Jura region that 'the frost began at the end of November 1626 and continued until May [1627]'.
23. Behringer, 'Weather, hunger and fear', 11–12, on witch trials; and Bell, 'The Little Ice Age', 12–15, on 'der Wein Jud'; von Krusenstjern, '"Gott der allmechtig"', on the 'peccatological' explanations of Germans concerning bad weather at this time.
24. *Der Oberösterreichische Bauernkrieg*, 70–1, lists those executed, and at pp. 72–3 records the order extending the *Emigrationstermin* until Apr. 1628 on account of the appalling weather. Helfferich, *The Thirty Years War*, 83–4, prints two rebel broadsheets.
25. Robisheaux, *Rural society*, 210.
26. Bireley, *Religion and politics*, 54, Ferdinand's instructions to his representative at a meeting of the Electors at Mühlhausen, 4 Oct. 1627.

27. Urban, 'Druck'. Over one hundred copies of the edict survive in various forms: a remarkable number. Helfferich, *The Thirty Years War*, 91–8, prints the text in English.
28. Mann, *Wallenstein*, 700, Wallenstein to Oberst San Julian.
29. Bireley, *Religion and politics*, 125: eyewitness account of Kaspar Schoppe. Maximilian later argued that Lamormaini and other theologians had convinced him and other Catholic princes that God would grant their cause victory if they upheld the Edict but would punish them if they made concessions to the Protestants, as they proposed: see Albrecht, *Auswärtige Politik*, 379–81.
30. Symcox, *War, diplomacy and imperialism*, 102–13, prints an English version of Gustavus's *Declaration* of June 1630; Helfferich, *The Thirty Years War*, 99–103, prints his July manifesto.
31. O'Connell, 'A cause célèbre', 84, Louis to Brûlart, 22 Oct. 1630.
32. Suvanto, *Wallenstein*, 72, Questenberg to Wallenstein, 23 Apr. 1631 ('Jizt haists *Helff, helff*, und non est qui exaudiat').
33. Mortimer, *Eyewitness accounts*, 64–7 (Anna Wolff from Schwabach) and 21–3 (Pastor Johannes Schleyss of Gerstetten and Sebastian Bürster near Überlingen, which was besieged by the Swedes in 1632 and 1634. The city still holds an annual 'Sweden procession' to celebrate its deliverance).
34. Robisheaux, *Rural society*, 223.
35. Sreenavisan, *Peasants of Ottobeuren*, 282–6, quoting local parish registers; Mortimer, *Eyewitness accounts*, 78–9, quoting Raph, a town clerk near Stuttgart.
36. Vincent, *Lamentations*, 26, 33. My thanks to Jill Bepler for help in identifying the author of this work.
37. Theibault, *German villages*, 186 (frozen corn) and 184–5 (yield ratios); Peters, *Ein Söldnerleben*, 166; Theibault, 'The rhetoric', 283 (entry in the parish registers kept by Ludolf); Helfferich, *The Thirty Years War*, 205–12, Diary of Abbot Maurus Friesenegger of Andechs. Several writers in Bohemia also recorded heavy frosts in August and September 1641, in May and June 1642, and in May 1643: Brázdil, 'Meteorological records', 104–5.
38. Heberle, 'Zeytregister', 225; all other quotes from Mortimer, *Eyewitness accounts*, 172. Theibault, *German villages*, 125, makes the point that, before the war, homicide was rare, making the contrast once it began even more stark.
39. Mortimer, *Eyewitness accounts*, 178, quoting Thiele, writing in 1641.
40. Bireley, *Religion and politics*, 214–17 (quoting Ludwig Crasius, S. J. in 1635).
41. Bierther *Regensburger Reichstag*, 88 n. 69, Maximilian to his envoys, 27 Nov. 1640; Ruppert, *Kaiserliche Politik*, 243, on Ferdinand III and his 'Hoftheologen' in Feb. 1646.
42. Dickman, *Der Westfälische Frieden*, 115, quoting Johan Adler Salvius's open letter of April 1643. My account of peace-making has benefited from the generosity of Derek Croxton, who shared with me in advance of publication his work on *The last Christian peace*.
43. Odhner, *Die Politik Schwedens*, 163, Johan Adler Salvius to the Swedish regency council, 7 Sep. 1646. Salvius added the warning: 'People are beginning to see the power of Sweden as dangerous to the Balance of Power.'
44. *APW*, 2nd series, B II, p. 241, Mazarin to plenipotentiaries, 7 Apr. 1645; and B V, p. 1,151, Louis XIV to plenipotentiaries, 26 Apr. 1647, drafted by Mazarin.
45. *APW*, 1st series, I, pp. 440–52, Instruction of Ferdinand III to Trauttmansdorff, Linz, 16 Oct. 1645, holograph. Helfferich, *The Thirty Years War*, 233–40, provides an English translation of the whole document.
46. *APW*, 2nd series, B II, p. 369, Servien to Brienne, 27 May 1645.
47. Chéruel, *Correspondance de Mazarin*, II, 944, to Chanut, 30 Aug. 1647.
48. *Co. Do. In.*, LXXXIII 328 and 369, Peñaranda to Castel Rodrigo, 4 July and 2 Aug. 1647; Helfferich, *The Thirty Years War*, 250, quoting the diary of Clara Staiger; Buisman, *Duizend jaar weer*, IV, 487–500.
49. *Acta Pacis Westphalicae: Supplementa electronica*, provides the parallel texts of the 'instruments of peace' in the original and in several modern languages.
50. Johann Vogel of Nuremberg quoted in Glaser, *Wittelsbach und Bayern* II, 483 (in Matthew 19: 24, Christ said it was 'easier for a camel to go through the Needle's Eye than for a rich man to enter the kingdom of heaven'); Zillhardt, 'Zeytregister', 224, 226. Gantet, 'Peace celebrations', notes that the majority of almost 200 peace celebrations held in the empire between 1648 and 1660 were, like those in Ulm, both Protestant and urban: see map on p. 655.
51. Cooper, *The New Cambridge Modern History*, IV, 402, quoting Oxenstierna. See also Roberts, *Sweden as a great power*, 155–60, resolution of the Council of State on reasons for attacking Denmark, May 1643.
52. Quotation from Roberts, 'Queen Christina', 198. Leijonhufvud, 'Five centuries', 130–1, notes two 'completely cold decades' in the Baltic between 1614 and 1633, keeping ships ice-bound in Stockholm far longer than usual.
53. Roberts, *The Swedish imperial experience*, 25.
54. Data and quotations from Roberts, 'Queen Christina', 200, 201, 213 n. 62 and 217. Åström, 'The Swedish economy', 76–7, tabulates the creation of nobles; Roberts, *Sweden as a Great Power*, 41–3, prints excerpts from one of these Swedish *Mazarinades*.
55. Details from Nordmann, 'La crise', 221–2. On the surplus graduates, see ch. 18 below.
56. Data and quotations from Roberts, 'Queen Christina', 211, 203 n. 28, and 201.
57. Roberts, 'Queen Christina', 204, quoting Archbishop Lennaeus.
58. Roberts, *Sweden as a Great Power*, 101–5, prints the Supplication of 8 Oct. 1650 OS, and on pp. 105–8 the discussions of the noble Estate on 15 Oct. See also Roberts, 'Queen Christina', 205, 198–9.

59. Roberts, *Sweden as a Great Power*, 105–8, minutes of a meeting between 'representatives of all four estates' and the council, 15 Oct. 1650, quoting Oxenstierna, Count Per Brahe, and Archbishop Lennaeus.

60. Bergh, *Svenska riksrådets protokoll*, XV, 128, Jakob de la Gardie's speech to the council, 10 Oct. 1651. See also other examples of the Swedish council's concerns about foreign revolts in ch. 18 below.

61. Nordmann, 'La crise', 225–6.

62. Whitelocke, *A journal of the Swedish embassy*, I, 191–2 and 211–19; Roberts, 'Queen Christina', 202 n. 26, quoting Christer Bonde, councillor of state, in 1655, with a reference to a similar remark by the queen.

63. Bygdeå data from Lindegren, 'Frauenland und Soldatenleben', 149–51, and 'Men, money, and means', 155–6. See also ch. 3 above.

64. Data on Finland from Lappalainen, 'Finland's contribution', 182, and Villrand, 'Adaptation or protestation', 283 (conscription), 286–95 (desertion) and 308–9 (Jakob Göransson). See also Rodén, 'The crisis', 107–8.

65. Anon., *De na-ween vande Vrede*, sig. A2v.

66. Poelhekke, *Vrede van Munster*, 256, 258, quoting a resolution of the States of Holland, 28 Feb. 1646, and the pamphlet *Ongeveynsden Nederlandtschen Patriot* (1647).

67. Poelhekke, *Vrede van Munster*, 272, count of Castrillo to Philip IV, 3 June 1646; Prestage, *Correspondência diplomática*, II, 256, Sousa Coutinho to John IV, 17 Nov. 1647, quoting the French ambassador in The Hague. The marriage plan for Louis XIV fell through in October 1646 when the death of Prince Balthasar Carlos made María Theresa heiress to the Spanish throne. They nevertheless married in 1659 as part of the peace of the Pyrenees.

68. Poelhekke, *Vrede van Munster*, 387: Antoine Brun to the Dutch States-General, Münster, Feb. 1647.

69. Details from Buisman, *Duizend jaar weer*, IV, 494–508 (Reijer Anslo, 'Op het regenachtige weer in het jaar 1648' quoted pp. 494–5); and Gutmann, *War and rural life*, 233 (rye prices for Amsterdam, Liège and Maastricht; none reached such high levels again until the 1690s).

70. Israel, *The Dutch Republic and the Hispanic World*, 382–6, gives a good overview of the economic recession in the Netherlands. On the impact of garrison reductions, see idem, *The Dutch Republic: Its rise*, 612–15.

71. Anon., *De na-ween vande Vrede*, sig A3. Israel, *The Dutch Republic: Its rise*, 602, quotes other sermons that blamed the endless rain on the peace.

72. Israel, *The Dutch Republic and the Hispanic world*, 386 n. 31, quoting Antoine Brun to Philip IV, 25 Mar. 1650.

73. Van Aitzema, *Saken*, III, 440–3, letter of the Amsterdam magistrates to the States of Holland, 30 June 1650.

74. Buisman, *Duizend jaar*, IV, 646–55, details the unusual weather of 1672. Ten years later, Charles Le Brun painted the crossing of the Rhine as one of the episodes commemorated on the ceiling of the Hall of Mirrors at Versailles.

75. Israel, 'The Dutch role', 116 n. 33, quoting d'Avaux to Louis, Aug. 1688.

76. Grimmelshausen, *Der abenteurerliche Simplicissimus*, 376 (book V, ch. 1).

77. Von Greyerz, 'Switzerland', 133; Suter, *Der schweizerische Bauernkrieg*, 326–7 and 361 on grain prices.

78. Suter, *Der schweizerische Bauernkrieg*, 331, Supplication to the Basel authorities, 30 Nov. 1651, and 343–52 for the economic collapse after 1648. Compare the Dutch complaints in Anon., *De na-ween vande Vrede* (above).

79. Suter, *Der schweizerische Bauernkrieg*, 94–7, discusses how various Swiss pastors and peasants interpreted the comet, and at pp. 63–71, discusses the debasement.

80. On the 'troubles' in Bern and Zürich, see Wahlen and Jaggi, *Der schweizerische Bauernkrieg*, 10–106; on Salzburg, see Heinisch, *Salzburg*, ch. 15; on the frequent peasant revolts in Austria, see Bierbrauer, 'Bäuerliche Revolten', 66–7. For the banners see ch. 17 above.

81. Livet, 'La Guerre des Paysans', 131, De la Barde on 4, 21 and 26 Dec. 1652. He did not report the troubles in Entlebuch until 27 Feb. 1653 and did not see it as a 'civil war' for another two weeks.

82. Suter, *Der schweizerische Bauernkrieg*, 64, quotes the 'Neu Wilhelm Tellen Lied, im Entlebuch gemacht 1653'. The song was really about the currency devaluation, not about Tell.

83. Ibid., 150 and 330, 'Rede' of Pannermeister Hans Emmenegger, incorporated in the 'Bundesbrief' of the vassals (*Untertanen*) of Canton Luzern at Wolhusen, 26 Feb. 1653.

84. Ibid., 159–61 and 167, discusses the terms used in the correspondence between the cantonal authorities in spring 1653 to describe the troubles: 'Generalaufstand', 'Generalmachination' and (a neologism, no doubt from Italy) 'Revolution' that aimed at the 'Extermination unseres eydtgenössischen Standts' (161).

85. Suter, *Der schweizerische Bauernkrieg*, 429–37. See also Suter's detailed chronology ibid., 605–19.

86. Meadows, *A narrative*, 33–5. For more on the landmark winter of 1657–8 see ch. 1 above.

87. Ekman, 'The Danish Royal Law', 102–7, prints a translation of several clauses. Note that although Frederick signed the document, prepared by Schumacher, on 14/24 Nov. 1665, it remained unpublished until 1709.

88. Molesworth, *An account of Denmark*, 73, 74, 86.

89. Ogilvie, 'Communities and the second serfdom', 112 (slightly amended translation from the original in note 214).

90. Steinman, *Bauer und Ritter*, 87, quoting a letter from Baron Stein, after travelling through Mecklenburg in 1802. Hagen, 'Seventeenth-century crisis', provides a timely reminder that as long as areas remained depopulated, the 'serfs' could avoid the demands of their lords; the restrictive legislation was generally enforced only from the early eighteenth century.

91. Title from the evocative but misconceived pamphlet of Ergang, *The myth of the all-destructive fury of the Thirty Years War*.

92. Mortimer, *Eyewitness accounts*, 182 (Junius), 185 (Theile), 176–7 (Preis), and 185 (Minck); Theibault, 'The rhetoric', 271 (Ludolf). See also the summary data in Von Krusenstjern, *Selbstzeugnisse*.

93. Calculated from the list of occupations in Von Krusenstjern, *Selbstzeugnisse*, 259–60 (several authors had more than one occupation during their lives).

94. Von Krusenstjern, *Selbstzeugnisse*, rubric B 8, notes the 'Schreibmotiv' whenever an author gave one. See pp. 57 (Melchior Brauch of Nuremberg, a Lutheran baker, who stated explicitly that he wrote 'für mich'), 148 (Hans Conrad Lang, a Lutheran merchant, who wrote so that his 'Kindern mag zur Nachrichtung dienstlich sein') and 58 (Johannes Braun, a Lutheran pastor who fled into exile, where he wrote because 'die Schilderung unseres Unglücks und unserer Leiden ... kann unseren Nachkommen in vielen Dingen lehrreich sein').

95. Von Krusenstjern, *Selbstzeugnisse*, 194–5; Mortimer, *Eyewitness accounts*, 83, 88, chronological entries of Renner in his parish register. He paid a ransom of 400 thalers.

96. Mortimer, *Eyewitness accounts*, 170, quoting Schoolmaster Gerlach, near Würzburg.

97. Eckhert, *The structure of plagues*, 150; Outram, 'The socio-economic relations'; Lindegren, 'Men, money and means', 159.

98. In the words of Theibault, *German villages*, 165, referring to the Werra valley, 'The war undermined the ability of the village to reproduce itself'. See similar evidence in ch. 4 above and ch. 21 below.

99. Theibault, 'The demography', 12, 21.

100. Dipper, *Deutsche Geschichte*, 44, tabulating the estimates by Wolfgang Abel (1967), Karl Bosl and Eberhard Weis (1976), Eda Sagarra (1977), Hermann Kellenbenz (1977), Michael Mitterauer (1971) and Dipper himself. Wilson, *Thirty Years War*, 788, presents striking aggregate figures for the Habsburg hereditary lands.

101. Sreenivasan, *The peasants of Ottobeuren*, 289–91. The collapse of record-keeping, even parish registers, after 1634 makes it hard to attain greater precision on population losses.

102. Repgen, 'Über die Geschichtsschreibung', 10–12, on the use and meaning of 'Katastrophe' at this time.

103. Raynor, *A social history of music*, 115 and 203–4, quoting Burckhart Grossman and Heinrich Schütz. Nehlsen, 'Song publishing', provides a histogram of songs published in broadsheets and pamphlets 1618–49.

104. Tacke, 'Mars, the enemy of art', 245–8, quoting from Sandrart, *Teutsche Academie der Bau-, Bild- und Mahlerey-Künste* (1675); Robisheaux, *Rural society*, 202.

105. Wedgwood, *Thirty Years War*, 526.

106. Details from Gantet, 'Peace celebrations'. She highlights the choice of 8 August, rather than 24 October, for the annual celebration: on that day in 1629 the Edict of Restitution had abolished Protestant worship in Angsburg – so the annual ceremony also reminded subsequent generations about one cause of the war.

Chapter 9   The Agony of the Iberian Peninsula, 1618–89

1. For comments and references for this chapter I thank James Amelang, Bethany Aram, Sir John Elliott, Xavier Gil, Andrew Mitchell, Alberto Marcos Martín, Martha Peach and Lorraine White.

2. IVdeDJ 82/444, duke of Sessa to Zúñiga, 28 Sep. 1600, minute; AGRB *SEG* 183/170v–171, Zúñiga to Juan de Ciriza, 7 Apr. 1619, copy, evaluating whether or not to prolong the truce with the Dutch Republic.

3. Elliott, *Olivares*, 231, Olivares to the count of Gondomar, 2 June 1625.

4. Ibid., 293, about the 'Spanish Match' (1623); and 290–1, the Genoese ambassador (1629). See also Firpo, *Relazioni di ambasciatori Veneti*, X, 110, Contarini in 1641: Olivares 'ama le novità ed è facile ad abbraciale'.

5. Elliott, *Olivares*, 236, Olivares to Gondomar, 3 July 1625.

6. Elliott and La Peña, *Memoriales y cartas*, I, 183–93, on 'selling the Union' to Catalonia; Elliott, *Revolt of the Catalans*, 204 n. 2, Protonotorio Villanueva in Aug. 1626, on 'familiarizing the natives'.

7. Elliott, *Revolt*, 238, and Vilar, *La Catalogne*, I, 620 n. 1, record the false calculations; García Cárcel, 'La revolución catalana', 121, estimated the true figure at 'perhaps half a million people'.

8. Bronner, 'La Unión de Armas', 1,138 and 1,141 n. 31, Viceroy Chinchón (who had strong ties with Aragon) to a councillor of Castile, 14 Mar. 1628 and to Philip IV, 18 May 1629.

9. AHN *Estado libro* 857/180–1, 'Papel que escrivió Su Magestad al Consejo Real', Sep. 1629.

10. AHN *Estado libro* 714, n.p., *consulta* of the Council of State, 19 Oct. 1629, *voto* of the marques of Los Gelves; Elliott, *Olivares*, 365, records Olivares's prediction. Philip signed the peace of the Pyrenees in 1659.

11. AHN *Estado libro* 857/180–183v, 'Papel que escribió Su Magestad' [Sep. 1629]; AHN *Estado legajo* 727/59, 'Orden de Su Magestad sobre su yda a Italia y Flandes' [Oct. 1629].

12. AHN *Estado libro* 856, contains the proposals and the theologians' 32 recommendations, presented to the king on 23 Dec. 1629 (fos 159–60, recommendation of peace in Italy, and fo. 200, peace on all fronts, quoted here). The theologians also made a *separate* list of 15 fiscal recommendations for America on the same day: AGI *IG* 2690 and Bronner, 'La unión', 1,142–52 and 1,174–5.

13. BL *Addl. Ms* 14,007/229–230v, Olivares to Philip IV, 3 Jan. 1630, with royal rescript, both holograph.

14. Gelabert, *Castilla Convulsa*, 20, Miguel Santos de San Pedro, president of the council of Castile; Andrade e Silva, *Collecção chronológica*, 203–5, 'carta regia', 31 May 1631; Piqueras García, 'Cédula', 168.

15. BNL, *Codex Ms* 241/269–269v, Manuel de Faria e Sousa, 'Relação de Portugal'. I thank Lorraine White for this reference.

16. Anes Alvarez and Le Flem, 'Las crisis del siglo XVII', 17 and 34 (Hoyuelos); BNF *Ms. Esp.* 156/31–36v, *consulta* of the Council of State, 1631–2, copy. Marcos Martín, *Auge y declive*, was the first modern scholar to underline the scale of the crisis of 1628–31: see his graph at p. 231.

17. AGS *GA* 1037, n.f., royal decrees of 16 Feb. and 22 Mar. 1631; *GA* 1024, n.p., 'Papel' of the marquis of Castrofuerte, 10 Mar. 1631.

18. BNE *Ms* 6760/1–4, salt declarations from Madrid's Calle Fuencarral: Don Alonso de Aguilar declared that his household of 17 would need only 1 *fanega* of salt, while several other householders declared 'No salt wanted'. See ch. 11 below for Charles I's reliance on regalian rights in England, for much the same reasons, and with much the same adverse consequences.

19. Alba, *Documentos Escogidos*, 475, Olivares to the count of La Puebla, 28 May 1632.

20. See Gelabert, *Castilla Convulsa*, 71–2, quoting Philip IV.

21. Elliott, *Revolt*, 275–6, instructions to the Cardinal Infante as viceroy of Catalonia, 20 May 1632.

22. Ibid., 90, Viceroy to Philip IV, 31 Oct. 1626; Torres Sanz, *Nyerros i cadells*, appendixes 2 and 3.

23. Details from Simon i Tarrés, 'Els anys 1627–32'; Parets, *De los muchos sucesos*, I, 26–8, 29–30, 74–7, 92; Betrán, *La peste en Barcelona*, 96–8; Peña Díaz, 'Aproximación'; Vilar, *La Catalogne*, I, 589–93.

24. Quotations from Gelabert, *Castilla Convulsa*, 53; Guiard Larrauri, *Historia de la noble villa de Bilbao*, II, 90 and 102–3 (from an anonymous 'Relación de lo suçedido en los alborotos'); and Elliott, 'El programa de Olivares', 434, royal apostil to a *consulta* on 4 Nov. 1632.

25. Elliott, *Olivares*, 448, Olivares to the marquis of Aytona, 6 Oct. 1632; Subrahmanyam, *Explorations*, 129 and n. 78, Philip IV to Viceroy Linhares, 28 Feb. 1632.

26. Elliott, *Olivares*, 464, *consulta* of the Council of State, 17 Sep. 1633, vote of Olivares; and 482, Olivares to Pieter Roose, 29 Sep. 1634.

27. AGS *Guerra Antigua* 1,120, n.p., paper of Olivares written in Feb. 1635; Stradling, *Spain's struggle for Europe*, 116, Olivares *voto* of 16 Jan. 1635.

28. Gelabert, *Castilla Convulsa*, 148 (Quevedo) and 157 (*papel sellado*); BNE *Ms* 9402/2v (harvest failures 1635–8); Gascón de Torquemada, *Gaçeta*, 386–8 (half of Valladolid destroyed by floods, Feb. 1636).

29. AHN *Estado libro* 737/446–52, *consulta* of the Council of State, 16 Aug. 1624, *votos* of the royal confessor and the marquis of Montesclaros.

30. Schwartz, 'Silver, sugar and slaves', 1.

31. Manuel de Melo, *Epanáforas*, 566–79, prints three manifestos – one in verse – of Manuelinho.

32. Valladares, *Epistolario*, 138 and 154, Olivares to Basto, 26 Nov. and 18 Dec. 1638 ('no se pretendía el huevo, sino el fuero' – a phrase later made famous by Quevedo in a polemic: see Elliott, *Olivares*, 527).

33. Viñas Navarro, 'El motín de Évora', 47, Olivares to Fray Juan de Vasconcellos, his personal envoy to Portugal, [26 Nov. 1637]; AGS *SP libro* 1536/3v–4, royal reply to a *consulta* of the Junta Grande de Portugal, 6 Nov. 1637. Oliveira, 'Levantamientos', 47–54, describes the invasion plans, and at 66–74, the pardon.

34. Salvado and Münch Miranda, *Cartas*, II, 13–16, Instructions for Torre, 19–25 July 1638; and AHEB, *Seçâo Colonial* 256/121v–123, patent for La Torre, 25 July 1638.

35. Elliott, *Revolt*, 360, paper by Olivares, 12 Mar. 1639; and 363, Olivares to Santa Coloma, 18 June 1639.

36. Co. Do. In., LXXXIV, 538, 'Relaciones' of the count of Peñaranda to Philip IV, 8 Jan. 1651.

37. Elliott, *Revolt*, 130–7, describes the election process for the *Diputats*, concluding: 'Although it was luck alone that determined the outcome of the final lottery, a good deal more than luck was required to qualify for the draw.'

38. Ibid., 374–5, Olivares to Santa Coloma, 7 Oct. 1639; and ibid., 393, quoting Martí i Viladamor, *Noticia Universal*.

39. Manuel de Melo, *Historia*, 25, 22; Elliott, *Revolt*, 411, Dr Valonga to Villanueva, 24 Mar. 1640.

40. Parets, *De los muchos sucesos*, I, 147, and Pasqual de Panno, *Motines*, 60 and 126 (on the character of Monrodón); Simon i Tarrés, *Cròniques*, 253–4 (the Relation of Judge Rubí de Marimon); and Parets, *De los muchos sucesos*, I, 146–8 and 363–70 (on the death of Monrodón).

41. BNE *Ms* 2371/21, draft history of the year 1640 by Jerónimo de Mascarenhas. Simon i Tarrés, *Cròniques*, 264–5 (*Relación* of Rubí), recorded both predictions that 'something big' would happen on Corpus Christi Day and the departure of the galleys the day before.

42. BNE *Ms* 2371/21; Corteguera, *For the Common Good*, 163, quoting the diary of Miquel Parets, and 165 n. 34, quoting a servant of Santa Coloma. Vidal Pla, *Guerra dels segadors*, appendix I, lists the fate of the judges.

43. Corteguera, *For the common good*, 166, again quoting Parets; Simon i Tarrés, *Cròniques*, 268 (*Relación* of Rubí; cf. the account of random looting and burning in idem, 208–9: chronicle kept by the cathedral chapter).

44. Simon i Tarrés, *Cròniques*, 80 (*Dietari* of Bartolomeu Llorenci) and 269 (Rubí, who shaved his beard and got a tonsure in order to masquerade as a Jesuit), noted the murder of Castilians, with women playing a prominent role; PRO *SP* 94/41/336–7, 'Copy of a letter from Barcelona', 9 June 1640.

45. Elliott, *Revolt*, 452, royal rescript to a *consulta* of the Council of State, 12 June 1640; 489, Hopton to Cottington, 25 July 1640 NS; and 490, diary of Matías de Novoa.

46. Sanabre, *La acción de Francia*, 76, Granollers to the *Junta de Braços*.

47. Reula i Biescas, '1640–1647', notes the publication of Olivares's letters.

48. Quotations from AMAE (P) *CPE* 3/189 and 205, Duplessis-Besançon's long defence of his role: 'Première négotiation des françois en Cathalogne'.

49. Simón i Tarrés, *Els orígens ideològics*, 173–98; and Neumann, *Das Wort als Waffe*, ch. 2, discuss the *Proclamación Católica*; the *Justifació en conciència* by the 'Junta de teòlegs'; and Martí i Viladamor, *Noticia Universal* (written, ironically, in Castilian). Ettinghausen, *La Guerra*, published several shorter propaganda tracts.

50. Van Aitzema, *Saken van Staet*, II, 729. For the international impact of the most celebrated Catalan tract (also written in Castilian), Gaspar Sala i Berart's *Proclamación Católica*, see Grotius, *Briefwisseling*, XI, 640–4, letters to Camerarius and Oxenstierna, 1 Dec. 1640.

51. BNE *Ms* 2371/121–4, account of Mascarenhas; and Rubí, *Les Corts*, 262–8 (Los Vélez quoted on p. 266).

52. Révah, *Le Cardinal Richelieu*, 20–3, 47–8, Instruction to Jean de St Pé, 15 Aug. 1638.

53. PRO *SP* 94/41/1, Hopton to Coke, 14 Jan. 1639 NS.

54. Schaub, *Le Portugal*, 240, Vasconcelos to Soares, 30 Sep. 1640.

55. HAG *Ms* 28/514v–515, Viceroy of India to Philip IV, 2 Aug. 1641; and HAG *Ms* 488/24–24v, Viceroy to authorities in Manila, 26 Mar. 1641.

56. Valente, *Documentos históricos*, I, 442–5, resolution of 1 June 1640; Loureiro de Souza, *Documentos*, 10–16, Câmara to Philip IV, 13 Nov. 40, and to John IV, 16 Feb. and 30 Apr. 1641. They were right: Olivares's decision to denude Portugal of troops to suppress the Catalan revolt proved that he expected Brazil to fend for itself.

57. AGS *GA* 1331, n.p., *consulta* of the Junta de Ejecución, 7 Dec. 1640; PRO *SP* 94/42/73–4, Hopton to Windebank, 8 Dec. 1640. Valladares, 'Sobre reyes de invierno', 114–21, provides an excellent account of Bragança's personal road to rebellion.

58. AGS *GA* 1331, n.p., *consulta* of the Junta de Ejecución y Estado, 7 Dec. 1640; Elliott, *Olivares*, 600, *consulta* of 17 Dec. 1640, vote of Olivares.

59. Simon i Tarres, *Els orígens*, 199 n. 81, quoting Albert Tormé i Lliori.

60. AMAE (P) *CPE: Supplément* 3/228v, account of the battle by Duplessis-Besançon; Pérez Samper, *Catalunya*, 279, quoting Mascarenhas's *Relaçam* of his mission to Barcelona (written in July 1641).

61. Did royalist agents poison Claris? Although no direct evidence survives, Philip IV certainly ordered the assassination of two other opponents at this time: (a) Bragança's brother Don Duarte (BNE *MS* 10,984/28, Philip IV to Don Juan Chumacero, his special envoy to Rome, 15 Dec. 1640: 'encargo y mando que con gran secreto, y usando de los medios más eficazes, *procuraréis que se mate a Don Duarte*'); and (b) Bragança's ambassador to England (Elliott, *Olivares*, 606). Moreover, (c) in 1641 and again in 1647 Philip sponsored attempts to assassinate John IV (AHN *Estado libro* 699, s.v. 'Levantamiento' and 'Matar al tirano' – in itself a telling epigraph!). See also García Cárcel, *Pau Claris*, 120–3; and Sanabre, *La acción*, 139–40.

62. AGS *GA* 1376, n.p., Olivares at the Junta Grande, 19 June 1641 (my thanks to Lorraine White for drawing this document to my attention); AGI *México* 35/18, Marquis of Caldereyta to Philip IV, 6 Dec. 1641, noting the decision to hold back the treasure in July 1640: the arrival of 750,000 ducats might have turned the tide in the peninsular war.

63. Hespanha, 'La "Restauraçao"', details these general petitions and notes that most had also been voiced by the last Cortes, in 1619. In 1648 the Russian national assembly, the Zemskii Sobor, would also miss a golden opportunity to innovate: see ch. 6 above.

64. Parets, *De los muchos sucesos*, VI, 585–91; BNE *Ms* 2371/111–14, Nochera to Philip IV, 6 Nov. 1640, copy.

65. BNE *Ms* 18,723 no 58, 'Copia del papel que dió a Su Magestad el duque de Medina Sidonia', 21 Sep. 1641, quoting the duke of Nájera.

66. Valladares, *La rebelión*, 37–45 (details on the poison at p. 44); Marcos Alonso, 'El descubrimiento', based largely on BL *Egerton Ms*. 2081/138v, 'Memorial' of Francisco Sánchez Marqués.

67. BNE *Ms* 8177/141–5, 'Relación' of 16 May 1641; Borja Palomo, *Historia crítica*, 281–94; Archivo histórico de la Catedral de Burgos, *Sección de volúmenes*, VII, royal *cédula* of 6 Oct. 1642, printed; and *Libros de Actas Capitulares*, 83/597–600, acts of 16–17 Aug. 1642 (my thanks to Cristina Borreguero Beltrán for a transcript of these documents); AGI *IG* 429 leg. 38/193–4, one of 300 royal *cédulas* sent 6 Oct. 1642. For the record precipitation, see www.ucm.es/info/reclido/es/basesdatos/rainfallindex.txt, accessed 31 January 2010.

68. Elliott, *Olivares*, 611, Hopton to Vane, 3/13 April 1641; Pérez Samper, *La Catalunya*, 309–13; Marcos Martín, 'Tráfico de indulgencias'. For the link between the distribution of bulls and population size, see p. 259 above.

69. BL *Addl. Ms.* 12184/110–11, Sir Richard Browne to Secretary of State Nicholas, 12 Sep. 1642.

70. Elliott, *Olivares*, 280 and 646, Antonio Carnero to Pieter Roose, 16 Jan. 1643.

71. AHN *Estado libro* 969 n.p., Don Miguel de Salamanca to Olivares, Brussels, 14 July 1641.

72. AGS *Estado* 2667 n.p., and 8341/3, *consultas* of the Council of State, 30 Jan. and 3 Feb. 1643; *Co. Do. In.*, LIX, 304, Philip IV to Melo, 12 Feb. 1643, with a letter for Anne. (Queen Isabel also re-established direct contact with Anne: BNE *Ms* 9163/126.) Israel, *The Dutch Republic*, 351, notes Philip's peace initiative with the Dutch.

73. AGS *Estado* 2056 n.p., *consulta* of the Council of State 5 Dec. 1641, on Melo's letter of 11 Nov. (My thanks to Fernando González de León for this reference.)

74. AGS *Estado* 8341/3, *consulta* of the Council of State, 3 Feb. 1643, 'voto' of the count of Oñate (*'tendría el conde por conveniente dar un poco de tiempo al tiempo'*).
75. AGS *Estado* 2039 n.p., Melo to Philip IV, 23 May 1643.
76. Cueto, *Quimeras*, chs 5 and 6, reconstitute the prophets' summit. See also ch. 2 above.
77. AGS *Estado* 3848/154, *consulta* of the Junta of State, 23 Oct. 1643, *votos* of the counts of Monterrey and Oñate. On the consequences for Italy of this decision, see ch. 14 below.
78. Gelabert, 'Alteraciones', 364, Chumacero to Philip IV, June 1645; AMAE (M) *Ms.* 39/218, same to same, 22 July 1645 (a letter full of foreboding).
79. AGS *GA* 3255, n.p., Haro to Gerónimo de Torre, 13 Feb. 1646 (two letters), and to Philip IV, 14 Feb. 1646, all from Cadiz. On the 18th Haro declared that the storm was the worst anyone could remember 'in 30 or 40 years'.
80. BNE *VE* Ca 68–94, *Escrívense los sucessos de la Evropa desde Abril de 46 hasta junio de 47 inclusive*.
81. AMAE (M) *Ms* 42/15–16v, Chumacero to Philip IV, 22 Oct. 1647, and fos 45–8, *consulta*, 10 Sep. 1647.
82. Gelabert, 'Alteraciones', 367–72, narrates the revolt of Ardales.
83. Thompson, 'Alteraciones granadinos', 799; Morales Padrón, *Memorias de Sevilla*, 123–4; BNE *Ms* 11,017/106–19, 'Account of the troubles in Granada'.
84. AGS *Estado* 2668, n.p., *consulta* of the Council of State, 4 July 1648, incorporating the views of the Council of Castile; Seco Serrano, *Cartas*, I, 158–9, Philip IV to Sor María, 29 July 1648 (and yet, the king continued ominously, without 'abundant resources, we cannot defend ourselves').
85. Valladares, *Rebelión de Portugal*, 96, Haro to Philip IV, Dec. 1646.
86. Seco Serrano, *Cartas*, I, 170, Philip IV to Sor María, 8 Dec. 1648. Philip also executed the marquis of Ayamonte, still in prison for trying to lead Andalusia to independence seven years before (page 277 above), and imprisoned Don Miguel de Iturbide, a prominent member of the Navarre elite who 18 months before had come to court to explain the kingdom's opposition to new taxes and recruiting and whose name appeared in the papers of a friend of Híjar. Iturbide was never seen again: Gallastegui Ucín, 'Don Miguel', and Gelabert, *Castilla convulse*, 304–5 and 311–12.
87. *Co. Do. In.*, LXXXIV, 314–16 Peñaranda to Philip IV, 19 Aug. 1648.
88. AM Cádiz 26/161 and 168–74, resolutions of 26 Oct. and 24 Nov. 1648; Borja Paloma, *Historia crítica*, 297–9, quoting *Memorias Sevillanas*; Morales Padrón, *Memorias de Sevilla*, 115–17. Carbajo Isla, *Población*, 301–5, noted unparalleled peaks of 'párvulos' in 1651, 1654, 1657 and 1660.
89. Gelabert, *Castilla Convulsa*, 315, quoting an apocalyptic speech by the procurador of Valladolid in 1649; and idem, 'Alteraciones', 375, Tomás López to the marquess of Castel Rodrigo, Madrid, 2 Dec. 1651.
90. Gelabert, *Castilla convulsa*, 337, quoting a manuscript 'Tumultos de la Cyudad de Sevilla'; Domínguez Ortiz, *Alteraciones andaluzas*, 86, *real cédula*, 16 May 1652. Anes Álvarez, *Las crisis agrarias*, graph 9, shows dramatic drops in tithe yields for the archdiocese of Seville in 1647, 1650 and 1652.
91. These popular uprisings represent only a selection of the total: a host of minor revolts caused by taxes, billeting and recruiting at a time of chronic food shortage remain buried in obscure sources: see ch. 17 below.
92. Berwick y Alba, *Documentos escogidos*, 486, Philip IV to Haro, 21 Oct. 1652 (the day he heard of the surrender of Barcelona); Firpo *Relazioni*, X, 198, Relation of Pietro Bassadonna, 26 May 1653, beginning 'Correva l'anno 1647 ...'
93. Seco Serrano, *Cartas*, II, 42, Philip IV to Sor María, 11 Jan. 1656; Benito, 'Magnitude and frequency of flooding', 187–8.
94. AGS *Estado Francia* 1618/C.5, Junta of State, 7 Jan. 1659. Seco Serrano, *Cartas*, II, 131, letter to Sor María, July 1659. A few months later Mazarin agreed to the full reinstatement of Condé in return for the surrender of some more Spanish territory. See the brilliant reconstruction of these events by Séré, 'La paix'.
95. Valladares, *Rebelión*, 204, 'Junta sobre materias de Inglaterra', 17 June 1665. See other early modern examples of a reluctance to make peace through unwillingness 'to sacrifice all the treasure it has cost' in ch. 2 above.
96. Espino López, *Catalunya*, 74 and 78, *consultas* of the Council of State, 4 Nov. 1687 and 13 Apr. 1688; Kamen, 'The decline of Castile', 63, quoting Ambassador Carlo Russini in 1695. Other data taken from Kamen's article, and his monograph, *Spain* (see, for example, the map of the epidemics of 1676–85 at p. 45).
97. Parets, *De los muchos sucesos*, VI, 137–49, prints the royal confirmation of the privileges of Barcelona, 29 Nov. 1652. Other revolts against Philip IV that ended with concessions included Vizcaya in 1634, Portugal in 1637 and the Andalusian towns between 1647 and 1652 (see above), as well as Naples and Sicily (see ch. 14 below).
98. Pascual del Panno, *Motines de Cataluña*, 199–216: 'Lista de catalanes muertos y desterrados' (listing only 'cavalleros'); Vidal Pla, *Guerra dels segadors*, 187–215, names 470 war dead; Vilar, *Catalogne*, I, 634 (Barcelona), 193 (lost villages); Jordà i Fernández, *Església*, 134.
99. Kamen, *Spain*, 57; Solano Camón, *Poder monárquico*, 36; and Sanz Camañes, *Política, hacienda y milicia*, chs 5–7. Demographic and fiscal details from Kamen, *Spain*, 57–9; White, 'War and government', ch. 10 (especially pp. 330–6); and Nadal, 'La población española', 39–54.
100. Marquis of Villars (1681) quoted by Márquez Macías, 'Andaluces'. The marquis estimated that 6,000 people left for America each year.
101. Estimate by I. A. A. Thompson in Hoffman and Norberg, *Fiscal crises*, 176. Marcos Martín, '¿Fue la fiscalidad regia un factor de crisis?', 179 n. 7, evaluates the various estimates of modern historians of the total tax burden.

102. AM Cádiz, 26/132–8, *actos* of 16 Oct. 1648. Some groups exempt from paying regular taxes, such as the clergy and the nobility, contributed to the crown's expenses in other ways.
103. Marcos Martín, '¿Fue la fiscalidad regia un factor?', 197, makes this point eloquently; idem, 'Sobre la violencia', 215, *consulta* of the *consejo* de Hacienda, 30 Sep. 1634: 'les es más preciso su sustento que el vestido y calzado'.
104. Marcos Martín, '¿Fue la fiscalidad regia un factor?', 250–2, and table on p. 232.
105. BL *Egerton Ms.* 1820/340, Hopton to Secretary of State Coke, 6 Apr. 1634 NS. Brook quoted in ch. 5 above.
106. AGRB *SEG* 195/64, Philip IV to Infanta Isabella, his regent in the Netherlands, 9 Aug. 1626.
107. Seco Serrano, *Cartas*, I, 28, Philip IV to Sor María, 20 July 1645, holograph. When in 1665 Don Juan de Palafox analyzed the reasons for the 'ruina de nuestra monarchia' in his 'Juicio interior y secreto', written 'for my eyes alone', he singled out the failure to make peace in the Netherlands and the attack on Mantua. (Text printed by Jover Zamora, 'Sobre los conceptos'.)
108. Leman, *Richelieu et Olivarès*, charts the numerous peace offers by the two statesmen – each one abandoned as soon as they gained the upper hand.
109. Sessa in 1600 quoted page 254 above; Olivares in 1625 on page 255; Elliott and La Peña, *Memoriales y Cartas*, II, 279, Olivares to Antonio Carnero, 8 Aug. 1644; Monkhouse, *State Papers*, III, 16, Hyde to Nicholas, Madrid, 14 Apr. 1650 NS; Alcalá-Zamora, 'Razón de Estado', 341, quoting the marques of Los Vélez, viceroy of Naples, to Carlos II, 11 Nov. 1678.

Chapter 10   France in Crisis, 1618–88

1. I thank Robin Briggs, Laurence Brockliss, Oliver Herbert, David Parrott and Dale van Kley for their help in drafting this chapter.
2. Moote, *The Revolt*, 368.
3. Le Roy Ladurie, *Les fluctuations*, 72–3, documents the often overlooked cold conditions in France 1617–23.
4. Le Roy Ladurie, *Histoire humaine*, I, 337–9, and idem, *Les fluctuations*, 76–9, on the 'période hyper-pluvieuse' and on the worst mortality (after those of 1563 and 1694) to afflict France between 1560 and 1790.
5. Mousnier, 'Les mouvements populaires', 47, Marillac to Louis XIII, 15 July 1630; Grillon, *Les papiers*, V, 212, Richelieu paper of 13 Apr. 1630.
6. Porshnev, *Les soulèvements populaires*, 53, duke of Épernon to Chancellor Séguier, 26 June 1633. On the 'biennat super-aquatique' of 1629–30 and the famine of 1631, see Le Roy Ladurie, *Histoire humaine*, 337–47.
7. *APW*, 1st series I, 18–20, Louis XIII to Richelieu, 4 Aug. 1634 ('Not a living soul has seen this,' the king wrote on the outside of his ratiocinations). For proof that Spain planned to attack in 1635, see ch. 9 above.
8. Jansen, *Mars Gallicus*, first published in Aug 1635. Four editions, and a French and Spanish translation, had appeared by 1640.
9. See Bercé, *Histoire*, I, 365 (weather) and 368–93 (on the 'peasant assemblies'). Le Roy Ladurie, *Histoire*, 462–8, provides an excellent short overview of the Croquants.
10. Details from Bercé, *Histoire*, I, 402–6 (quotation from the *Histoire du duc d'Épernon*, the nobleman charged with suppressing the troubles, composed circa 1660).
11. Ibid., I, 412–14 lists the leaders; and at pp. 414–19 discusses the 14 surviving manifestos and the role of La Mothe.
12. Ibid., I, 443, quoting letters from royal ministers to Chancellor Séguier in June and July 1637. La Mothe survived in hiding until 1648 (445). On the vow, and the painting, see Monod, *The power of kings*, 120–1; for more on the 'etiquette' of rebellion, see ch. 17 above.
13. Both examples from Caillard, 'Recherches', 39–41.
14. Bonney, *Political change*, 252. Rural labourers earned 30 *livres* a year: Jacquart, *La crise rurale*, 613.
15. Foisil, *La révolte*, 62, Bullion to Richelieu, 11 Oct 1639 ('quasiment la quatriesme des impositions du royaume'). The *Nu-Pieds* revolt had begun in July. Bercé, *Histoire*, I, 78–96, examines both the exemptions and the government's efforts to end them.
16. Foisil, *La révolte*, 62, complaint of the États of Normandy, Feb. 1638.
17. Details in ibid., 93–101. The salt monopoly existed elsewhere in France but not in Normandy. Le Roy Ladurie, *Histoire*, 456–62, provides an excellent overview of the Nu-Pieds.
18. BNF *f. fr.* 3833/214, printed *Ordonnance* of 'General Jean Nud-Pieds'. BNF *f. fr.* 18937/227–40, 'Relation de la révolte de la Basse Normandie', identified all the leaders, and printed two verse manifestos.
19. Avenel, *Lettres*, VI, 500–1, Richelieu to Bouthillier, 29 Aug. 1639; Grotius, *Briefwisseling*, X, 611, to Nicolaes van Reigersberch, 17 Sep. 1639.
20. Foisil, *La révolte*, 285, quoting Séguier's journal. The chancellor sentenced scores of rebels to death, and hundreds to exile; imposed huge fines on towns implicated in the uprising (Caen had to pay over one million *livres*); and ordered reparations to those whose property had been damaged.
21. Avenel, *Lettres*, VI, 608 n., Bullion to Chavigny, 25 Oct. 1639; ibid., 881–2, Richelieu to Bouthillier, 10 Oct. 1641.
22. Ibid., VII, 302, Richelieu to Bouthillier, 28 Feb. 1642. See Bonney, 'Louis XIII', on Richelieu's reform plan of 1640.

23. AMAE (P) *CPE Supplément* 3/241, Bernard de Duplessis-Besançon's 'Première négotiation des françois en Cathalogne'; Grotius, *Briefwisseling*, XI, 496, Charles Marini to Grotius, 6 Sep. 1640.

24. Jacquart, *La crise*, 647, quoting the journal of Olivier d'Ormesson, 12 May 1644.

25. *APW*, 2nd series II B, IV, 283–4, Servien to Mazarin, 15 Apr. 1645 ('empire françois' and 'révolutions' in the original).

26. Ibid., 511–12, Brienne to the 'plenipotentiaries' at Münster, 4 Oct. 1646; and 241, Mazarin to d'Avaux, 20 July 1646.

27. Chéruel, *Histoire*, II, 497, quoting the *Journal manuscrit d'un bourgeois de Paris;* Chéruel, *Lettres*, II, 535, Mazarin to Longueville, 6 Dec. 1647; Decimon and Jouhaud, 'La Fronde en mouvement', 307, quote Richelieu's warning. Bercé, *Histoire*, I, 100, suggests 25,000 imprisoned 'tax delinquents' in 1646.

28. Motteville, *Mémoires*, II, 8 (the author accompanied the queen); Bluche, 'Un vent', 168, notes the tax burden on Paris; Jacquart, 'Paris', 116 n. 3, estimates the city's size.

29. Le Boindre, *Débats*, 44, Broussel on 5 Feb. 1648; Chéruel, *Histoire*, II, 501–2, quoting Talon's speech and the Venetian ambassador.

30. Retz, *Oeuvres*, II, 105–6. Compare the similar error of James VI and I a generation before: see p. 326 above.

31. Chéruel, *Lettres*, II, 917 and 948, Mazarin to Grimaldi, 4 July and 10 Sep. 1647; and 505, to Fontenay-Mareuil (French ambassador in Rome), 7 Oct. 1647.

32. Ranum, *Paris*, 283; Arnauld, *De la fréquente communion* (1643). Orcibal, *Jansénius*, 242, quotes Antoine Arnauld's claim that 'if [Jansen] had not been suspected of being the author of *Mars Gallicus* they would never have found heresy in his *Augustinus*'.

33. *Co. Do. In.*, LXXXIV, 230–1, 234–5, Peñaranda to Don Luis de Haro and to Philip IV, 18 May 1648.

34. Details from Charmeil, *Le Trésoriers de France*, 16, 73, 96–7, 146–7, 247 and 270. On 30 June 1648 a minister claimed that 'it is now six weeks since lending money ceased' – i.e. since mid-May: Bonney, *Political change*, 53.

35. Le Boindre, *Débats* 122, reports that on 17 June 1648, 'being unable to hold back their indignation', several judges interrupted the King's Advocate and 'broke the thread of his argument'. After three attempts to speak, he withdrew. Ranum, *Fronde*, 105, notes the forcible restraint of Molé.

36. Chéruel, *Lettres*, III, 159–60, Mazarin to Chanut, 31 July 1648, the day when *Parlement* registered the new edicts.

37. Ibid., III, 173–81, Mazarin to Servien, 14 Aug. 1648.

38. Mousnier, 'Some reasons', describes and analyzes these events on the basis of 14 eyewitness accounts.

39. See Bourgeon, 'L'Île de la Cité', 127–8, and Carrier, *Labyrinthe*, 429, on the 'Great Fear' ('appréhension') that gripped Paris.

40. Ranum, *Fronde*, 42, discusses the etymology of the term.

41. Chéruel, *Lettres*, III, 218–23, Mazarin to Servien, Paris, 23 Oct. 1648. The following day, 500 miles away in Münster, Servien signed the peace. Rohrschneider, *Der gescheiterte Frieden*, 407–16, provides a masterly account of the link between peace-making in Westphalia and the Fronde in Paris.

42. Motteville, *Mémoires*, II, 98, 214. (Mme de Motteville, whose Spanish mother had served as Anne's secretary, mentioned the Híjar conspiracy against Philip IV as well as the trial of Charles I in London.)

43. See the convincing argument by Bonney, 'The French Civil War', 76–7, drawing not only on pamphlets issued on behalf of the nobles but also on the 'cahiers de la noblesse' prepared in 1649 and 1651. Many aristocratic Frondeurs boasted an intellectual or family tradition of opposing the government: see Benigno, *Specchi*, 154–5.

44. Duccini, 'Regard', 322, quoting *L'adieu et le désespoir des auteurs et écrivains de la guerre civile.*

45. Carrier, *Fronde*, I, no. 3, Anon., *Epilogue, ou dernier appel du bon citoyen sur les misères publiques* (Mar 1649); *Advertissement aux rois* (1649), 6; and Carrier, *Fronde*, I, no. 8 [Louis Machon], *Les véritables maximes du gouvernement de la France* (Mar. 1652).

46. *La custode de la reyne, qui dit tout [The curtain around the queen's bed tells all]* (Paris, 1649), 8 pages, 26 verses; Merrick, 'The cardinal and the queen', 677 (quoting *Le ministre d'état flambé* also of 1649). Merrick, 'The cardinal and the queen', quotes many other *Mazarinades* that, in their sexual explicitness, have no parallel in early modern Europe; Beik, *Louis XIV*, 30–5, prints a scatological *Mazarinade* in English translation.

47. Jacquart, *Crise*, 652, 656, 765; Buisman, *Duizend Jaar*, IV, 499; Bourgeon, 'L'Île de la Cité', 119. Paris grain prices here and elsewhere from Baulant, 'Les prix', 539. Each *livre* contained 20 *sols* (or *sous*).

48. Motteville, *Mémoires*, II, 355.

49. Arnauld, *Lettres*, I, 416–17 (to Sister Geneviève, Apr. 1649) and 423–4 (to M. Macquet, 14 May 1649).

50. Carrier, *Labyrinthe*, 85, quoting two journals kept by Parisians. Other examples in Bonolas, 'Retz', 447–9.

51. Bonney, *Limits*, VII, 820–3, on Mazarin's submission, and 832 on Condé's wealth. Decimon and Jouhaud, 'La Fronde en mouvement', 317–18, evaluate Condé's strengths and weaknesses.

52. Chéruel, *Lettres*, IV, 619, Mazarin to Chanut, 28 Apr. 1650; Parival, *Abrégé de l'histoire*, 480.

53. Bercé, *Histoire*, I, 472–89; Pillorget, *Mouvements*, 647–70; and Carrier, *La Fronde*, II, no. 38, *Estat des pauvres de la frontière de Picardie* (Paris, 1650). On Provence, see Baehrel, *Une croissance*, 535.

54. Jouanna, *Devoir de révolte*, 262–73, discusses the Assembly of Nobles between 5 Feb. and 25 Mar. 1651, attended by 700–800 lords (of whom 463 signed the Act of Union on 18 Feb.), and other, smaller meetings in 1649 and 1652. The Assembly of the French clergy, meeting at the same time, made the same demands.

55. See Carrier, *La presse*, 432–5 (on purchasers) and 351–2 (on the 'wanted' poster).

56. Carrier, *La Fronde*, I, no. 11, Robert Arnauld, *La vérité toute nue*.

57. Descimon, 'Autopsie', provides an excellent account of the chaotic summer of 1652 in Paris.

58. Carrier, *Labyrinthe*, 148–9; Kötting, *Die Ormée*, passim; and ch. 12 above.

59. Bonney, *Limits*, IV.89, and VII.853, on Mazarin's bribes; and VIII.336–7, on revoking the edicts of *Parlement*.

60. Bonolas, 'Retz', and Carrier, *Labyrinthe*, 115–18, conclude that others wrote many of the radical pamphlets ascribed to Retz.

61. Golden, *The Godly rebellion*, 77 (attendance at the assemblies of the Paris curés, 1653–9), and 143–51 (evidence that perhaps two-thirds of the Paris priests were Jansenists).

62. Michel, *Jansénisme*, 327–66, on the religious polemics; Le Roy Ladurie, *Histoire humaine*, 441–3, on the 1658 floods; and ch. 8 above on Mazarin's praise of 'quitting when one is ahead'.

63. Carrier, *Labyrinthe*, 431, complaint by 'La Fleur', a famous 'empiric'; Arnauld, *Lettres*, II, 65, to prioress of Gif, Mar. 1652.

64. Arnauld, *Lettres*, II, 431–5, to the queen of Poland, 28 Jan. 1654; Garnier, 'Calamitosa tempora', 9 (Crétail); Jacquart, 'La Fronde', 283 (with several population graphs similar to Crétail).

65. Goubert, 'The French peasantry', 162–4, based on Goubert, *Beauvais et le Beauvaisis*, 510–11 and 607–12. Lebrun, *Les hommes*, 166, reported extreme dearth in Anjou in 1652–4.

66. Carrier, *Labyrinthe*, 150, Renaud de Sévigné to Christine de France, 19 July 1652; Arnauld, *Lettres*, II, 177, to the queen of Poland, 6 Sep. 1652; Jacquart, 'La Fronde', 279 quoting André d'Ormesson; *Mémoires de Mlle. de Montpensier*, II, 276, reporting the pessimism of Gaston, her father, at Easter 1655.

67. Robin Briggs: personal communication in May 2004. Dale van Kley reminds me that although revolution did not shake the integrity of France after 1789, it might well have done so after 1648.

68. Le Roy Ladurie, *Histoire humaine*, I, 452, estimates a loss of 500,000 due to famine amenorrhea, fewer marriages and what he is pleased to call 'les froideurs génitales'. See also Dupâquier, *Histoire de la population*, I, 204–5.

69. Louis XIV, *Mémoires*, 34.

70. Barnes, '"Playing the part"', 184, quoting René Le Voyer d'Argenson, *Annales de la Compagnie du Saint Sacrement* (manuscript completed in 1694). The fact that the Company preferred dissolution to accepting royal scrutiny no doubt convinced Mazarin that he was right.

71. Details from Dessert, 'Finances'. See also Dulong, 'Mazarin et ses banquiers'. Fouquet remained in prison until his death, 19 years later.

72. Beik, *Louis XIV*, 96–107, provides flow charts of Louis XIV's finances that would have made Colbert drool with envy.

73. Lough, *John Locke's travels*, 30–1, journal entry for 8 Feb. 1676. Blaufarb, 'The survival', reveals how this new balance between crown and estates worked to everyone's advantage.

74. Ranum, *Paris*, 145, quoting Nicholas Delamare, *Traité de la police*.

75. Louis XIV, *Mémoires*, 280, written in 1679. Beik, *Louis XIV*, 59–61, prints an interesting eyewitness account from 1673 of how Louis maintained control over his ministers.

76. *APW*, 3rd series, C II/1, Diarium Volmar, 214–17, entry for 17 Nov. 1644; *APW*, 2nd series, B I, 826, Servien to Brienne, 31 Dec. 1644; and idem, IV, 26, d'Avaux to Mazarin, 13 June 1646.

77. Mormiche, *Devenir prince*, 292, 281, 283, all quoting La Mothe Le Vayer, *De l'instruction de Monsieur le Dauphin* (1640), a work that attracted the favourable attention of Richelieu and led to La Mothe's appointment first as preceptor to Louis's younger brother and then to Louis himself. Note Louis XIII's ignorance regarding the likely cost of declaring war on Spain: see page 296 above.

78. Silvestre de Sancy, *Lettres*, III, 321 and 345, Mme de Sévigné to Mme de Grignan, 28 June and 24 July 1675; Le Roy Ladurie, *Histoire humaine*, 462–3 (Provence); Lough, *John Locke's travels*, 89, Journal entry for 1 May 1676. Climate data in Masson-Delmotte, 'Changes', and Garnier, 'Grapevine harvest dates'.

79. Komlos, 'An anthropometric history', 170–1; Corvisier, *L'Armée française*, 643.

Chapter 11   The Stuart Monarchy

1. Thanks for detailed comments and suggestions to Aidan Clarke, David Cressy, Richard Groening, Andrew Mackillop, Jane Ohlmeyer, Carla Pestana, Glyn Redworth and John Walter. Britain in the seventeenth century still used the Julian Calendar ('Old Style'), ten days earlier than the Gregorian Calendar common on the continent. Thus the Scottish Revolution began on 23 July 1637 in Edinburgh (and in this chapter), which in Paris, Rome and Madrid was 2 August.

2. Nalson, *An impartial collection*, I, iv–vi. Nalson even ridiculed Rushworth's dedication to Richard Cromwell, 'it being very improper to expect preferments and rewards, by telling the son that his father was a rebel and a murderer' *ODNB* s.v. Rushworth, quoting a letter to Anthony à Wood.

3. James I, *His maiesties speech to both houses of Parliament* (1607), sig D.

4. Ibid., sig. F2, a speech that James devoted to 'selling' the Union to Parliament.

5. Ibid., sig. H; Howell, *Cobbett's complete collection*, II, col. 114, the king's speech, 18 Apr. 1604; Davies, *A discovery*, 252; Silke, 'Primate Lombard', 131.

6. Calderwood, *History*, VII, 263.

7. Ibid., VII, 514; Appleby, *Epidemics and famine*, 126–7, 146–7; Thirsk, *Agrarian history*, IV, 582 (quoting letters by local magistrates to the Privy Council in 1623) and 631–2 (on the poor harvests of 1618–25 in England).

8. James I, *His maiesties speech* (1607), sig. Cv; Coke, *The third part of the Institutes*, 2, and Jansson and Bidwell, *Proceedings in Parliament, 1625*, 35, both referred to the 1624 Parliament as 'happy'; Cust, *Charles I*, 41.

9. Thirsk, *Agrarian history*, IV, 632–3; Bamford, *Royalist's notebook*, 27–8 and 54. See ch. 4 above on smallpox.

10. Kyle, 'Parliament and the palace of Westminster', and Kyle and Peacey, '"Under cover"', draw a fascinating picture of bustle and intimacy. The only forum that rivalled the Palace of Westminster in size and animated debate was the French Chambre Saint-Louis during the Fronde: see ch. 10.

11. Johnson et al., *Commons Debates 1628*, II, 58–60, Sir Benjamin Rudyerd's speech on 22 Mar. 1628.

12. Rushworth, *Historical Collections*, I, 631–8, Remonstrance presented on 17 June 1628.

13. Baker, 'Climate', 427 (from the diary of Richard Napier); Bamford, *Royalist's notebook*, 79; Wharton, *The history*, 47–9 and 51 (from Laud's *Diary*); PRO *SP* 16/282/134, a Latin poem on the 'most intense cold of January [1635] when the whole Thames froze over' (I thank David Cressy for this reference); *CSPV*, XXIV, 63, Anzolo Correr to Doge, 5 Sep. 1636.

14. Fincham, 'The judges' decision', 236, from Sir Roger Twysden's 'Remembrances'.

15. On the three men, see *ODNB* s v. John Bastwick, Henry Burton and William Prynne. In their journals, the Northampton attorney Robert Woodford, the Kent gentleman Sir Roger Twysden and the London craftsman Nehemiah Wallington all recorded the verdict with outrage: see New College, Oxford, *Ms* 9502, n.p., entries for 25 Aug. 1637 and 29 Nov. 1640; Fincham, 'The judges' decision', 237; and BL *Addl.* 21,935/40, 48, and 53–66v.

16. Clarendon, *History*, 92 (an encomium sustained in the three following pages), BL *Addl.* 21,935/48, Wallington's 'Historical notes'; Fincham, 'The judges' decision', 232–7, Sir Roger Twysden's summary of views expressed by his fellow gentry.

17. Firpo, *Relazioni*, I, 791–814, 'Relation' of Anzolo Correr, Richmond, 24 Oct. 1637, with large parts in cipher (summarized in *CSPV*, XXIV, 295–308). Correr's omission reflects the view at Charles's court: the first entry in Laud's diary that mentioned 'the Tumults in Scotland, about the Service-Book' was dated 29 Apr. 1638 (Wharton, *History*, 55). The 'Barons' Wars' took place in 1264–7.

18. PRO *SP* 16/527/103–7, draft proposal for the British Union of Arms (1627). Sir James Balfour, who had access to the relevant Scottish State Papers now lost, explicitly linked the Union of Arms scheme with the Revocation (Haig, *Historical Works*, II, 126). Quotations from ibid., 128, 134. Dickinson and Donaldson, *Sourcebook*, III, 67–77, publish various versions of the Revocation. Kishlansky, 'Charles I', 71, claims that the Revocation was promulgated by Parliament, not by Prerogative, but this is misleading: it did not receive Parliamentary approval until 1633.

19. Charles I, *A Large Declaration*, 16; Rushworth, *Historical Collections*, II, 321, prints Charles's proclamation ordering Archbishops Laud and Spottiswoode to prepare a liturgy for Scotland, 19 Apr. 1636.

20. Rushworth, *Historical Collections*, II, 470–1 (on Archie); Dickinson and Donaldson, *Sourcebook*, III, 88–9 (the Canons); Donaldson, *The making*, 100 (the Proclamation authorizing the Prayer Book); Charles I, *A large Declaration*, 18 (confirming that he had issued it by his own authority); *RPCS*, 2nd ser., VI, 448, Act of 13 June 1637 (placing non-compliers 'under pain of rebellion').

21. *RPCS*, 2nd ser., VI, 431–2, 438–9, 442–5, 454–6 (plague and scarcity of food) and 465 (coinage), 3, 8, 10 and 17 June 1637; Laing, *Correspondence*, I, 93–8, Lothian to his father, the earl of Ancram, 19 Oct. 1637 OS, a letter full of complaints about the economic disasters caused by bad weather. For confirmation from the 'natural archive', see Baker, 'Northwest Scotland stalagmite and climate reconstruction data'.

22. Rothes, *Relation*, 197 (use of proofs as wrapping paper); Braddick, *God's fury*, 3, quoting Montrose. Bennett, *The Civil Wars*, 3, named both the ministers and 'matrons' who met in April 1637.

23. Charles I, *A Large Declaration*, 23; Bennett, *The Civil Wars*, 3, quoting the earl of Wemyss and Bishop Guthrie.

24. *RPCS*, 2nd ser., VI, 509–13, entries for 4, 5 and 9 Aug. 1637; Rothes, *Relation*, 2–5.

25. Dickinson and Donaldson, *Sourcebook*, III, 95–104, print the Covenant, including the Oath and Subscription.

26. Paul, *Diary*, I, 327–31, Mar./Apr. 1638.

27. Ibid., I, 306–7 (22 Jan. 1638), 322 (27 Feb.) and 347 (4 May).

28. Russell, *Fall*, 56, Hamilton to Charles, June 1638; Burnet, *The memoires*, 55–6, Charles to Hamilton, 11 June 1638; Russell, *Fall*, 56–7, same to same, 26 June 1638.

29. Baker, 'Northwest Scotland stalagmite and climate reconstruction data'; *CSPV*, XXIV, *1636–1639*, 430, Francesco Zonca to Venice, London, 2 July 1638 NS (cyphered in the original).

30. Burnet, *The memoires*, 60–1, Charles to Hamilton, 25 June 1638; Hardwicke, *Miscellaneous State Papers*, II, 118, Hamilton to Charles I, Glasgow, 27 Nov. 1638.

31. Paul, *Diary*, I, 348 (19 May 1638: studying Althusius all week), 390 (20 Sep. 1638: discussion with Henderson and David Calderwood about armed resistance). See also ch. 18 below.

32. New College, Oxford, *Ms* 9502, Diary of Robert Woodford of Northampton, n.p., entry for 6 Apr. 1639 ('ten weeks' drought'); Wharton, *History*, 56–7, Laud's diary entries for 14 Jan. and 27 Dec. 1639; Aston, 'The Journal', (rain on 27 April, as the royal army travelled from York to Northallerton); Bruce, *Letters and papers*, 238, Sir Edmund Verney to Ralph Verney, Newcastle, 19 May 1639.

33. Bruce, *Letters*, 228, Sir Edmund Verney to his son Ralph, 1 May 1639; Aston, 'The Journal', 12, 14 (June 1639). Others considered the eclipse ominous: [Voetius], *Brittish lightning*, sig. A3.

34. Mormiche, *Devenir prince*, 281, quoting La Mothe le Vayer, *De l'instruction de Monsieur le Dauphin* (1640); Aston, 'The Journal', 28; Paul, *Diary*, 58–62.

35. Paul, *Diary*, 85 and 87–8 (entries for 15 and 17 June 1639); Adamson, 'England', 100.

36. Russell, *Fall*, 67 n. 135, Hamilton to Charles I, 8 July 1639.

37. Clarke, 'Ireland', 93.

38. Wharton, *History*, 57, Laud's diary entry for 5 Dec. 1639.

39. Adamson, *The noble revolt*, 23 and 17, quoting the king's speech on 5 May 1640. Adamson admits that the king might have decided on a 'surprise' dissolution simply to avoid a repeat of the chaotic end of the last Parliament, in 1629, when MPs held down the Speaker and continued to debate forbidden matters; but this time the parliamentary leaders had approved an immediate grant of £600,000 in return for the abolition of Ship Money. Why would Charles have walked away from that deal except through fear of something that threatened his whole policy, such as a motion calling for 'reconciliation'?

40. *HMC Third Report*, 3, rough minutes taken by Vane at the meeting of the 'committee of war' on 5 May 1640.

41. Bruce, *Notes*, viii, Northumberland to Lord Conway, 5 May 1640; Adamson, *The noble revolt*, 552 n. 211. Elliott, 'The year of the three ambassadors', 175–6, describes the complex negotiations between Strafford and Spain, December 1639 – September 1640.

42. Bruce, 'Notes', xiii, Windebank to Conway, 26 May 1640 ('the rendezvous is again put off till the 1st of August'); Adamson, *The noble revolt*, 551 n. 202, Northumberland to the earl of Leicester, 21 May 1640; Naworth, *A new Almanacke for … 1642*, sig. C2; *CSPD 1640*, 118 and 627, George Douglas to Roger Mowatt, Stepney, 5 May 1640, and Strafford to Cottington, Huntingdon, 24 Aug. 1640. *CSPD 1640–1*, 630, Vane to Windebank, York, 25 Aug. 1640, also lamented 'the great rains that fell on Saturday', hampering military operations; while *CSPV 1640–2*, 72, Giovanni Giustinian to Doge and Senate, 7 Sep. 1640, noted the havoc caused by 'the rain which has recently fallen most copiously'.

43. Haig, *Historical works*, II, 379, written in the 1650s.

44. Adamson, *The noble revolt*, 47, Lord Savile to Lord Loudun, 8 July 1640, together with an erudite demonstration of the authenticity of this (and of the letter signed by Savile and six other peers) at pp. 549–51.

45. Rushworth, *Historical Collections*, III, 1,214–15, Petition of the Yorkshire gentry, 28 July 1640.

46. *CSPD 1640–1*, 15, Vane to Windebank, York, 5 Sep. 1640. Hardwicke, *Miscellaneous State Papers*, II, 173, Vane to Windebank, York, 11 Sep. 1640, reported the king's 'great apprehension' concerning 'Newcastle and the coals' needed by London.

47. Hardwicke, *Miscellaneous State Papers*, II, 168–71, minutes of the council meeting, 2 Sep. 1640.

48. Gardiner, *Constitutional documents*, 134–5, Petition of 12 peers, 28 Aug. 1640, the same day as Newburn and the 'humble petition' of the Yorkshire gentry – although the peers, meeting in the earl of Bedford's house in London, of course knew of neither.

49. *CSPD 1640–1*, 15, Vane to Windebank, York, 5 Sep. 1640; and Hardwicke, *Miscellaneous State Papers*, II, 179, same to same, 14 Sep. 1640.

50. Hardwicke, *Miscellaneous State Papers*, II, 182, Vane to Windebank, York, 18 Sep. 1640; Rushworth, *Historical Collections*, III, 1,275, the king's speech on 24 Sep. 1640.

51. Hardwicke, *Miscellaneous State Papers*, II, 197, Vane to Windebank, York, 11 Oct. 1640.

52. Ibid., II, 193, Vane to Windebank, York, 1 Oct. 1640; Rushworth, *Historical Collections*, III, part 1, 11–12, the king's speech on 3 Nov. 1640; *PLP*, I, 63, 65 and 69.

53. Adamson, *The noble revolt*, 223.

54. Anon., *A declaration*, A4 (almost certainly by Oliver St John); page 340 above (on the minutes of 5 May 1640).

55. Knowler, *The earl of Strafforde's letters*, II, 416, Charles I to Strafford, 23 Apr. 1641.

56. *PLP*, IV, 164–5, the king's speech on 1 May 1641; Clarendon, *History*, 320–1, reporting his conversation with Essex on 26 Apr. 1641.

57. BL *Addl.* 21,935/138–9, Wallington's 'Historical notes and meditations' for 3 May 1641; Adamson, *The noble revolt*, 285–6, quoting Bishop Warner's diary (another source attributed these words to John Lilburne).

58. Adamson, *The noble revolt*, 288–91, quoting Pym and the earl of Stamford; Groen van Prinsterer, *Archives*, 2nd series, III, 459, Dutch ambassadors to the prince of Orange, 7 May 1641 OS ('bien plus générale et horrible que n'a esté celle de *la Fougade*'); and 465, Sommelsdyck to Orange, 9 May 1641 ('horible conspiration contre le parlement et la liberté *bien plus grande que celle de la Fougade*').

59. Cressy, 'The Protestation', 266–7, 271, 273 (quotations from John Turberville and Sir John Bramston; he also prints the text). Foreign ambassadors stressed the Scottish connection: the Protestation 'qu'ils appellent un *convenant*, comme en Écosse' (Groen van Prinsterer, *Archives*, 2nd series, III, 444, Rivet to prince of Orange, London, 4 May 1641 OS); 'a union exactly like the Covenant in Scotland' (*CSPV 1640–42*, 148, Giustinian to Doge and Senate, London, 6 May 1641 OS).

60. Sanderson, *Compleat history*, 418 (James Howell, in his preface, hailed Sanderson as 'an eye and ear witness'); Kilburn and Milton, 'The public context', 242, quoting Sir Philip Warwick. Hollar's remarkable engraving of the execution on 12 May 1641 is at http://upload.wikimedia.org/wikipedia/commons/1/16/Wenceslas_Hollar_-_Execution_of_Strafford_%28State_3%29.jpg

61. *CSPD 1641–3*, 17, Henry Vane to Sir Thomas Roe, Whitehall, 18 June 1641; Fletcher, *The outbreak*, 192–9 (details on the petitions); Adamson, *The noble revolt*, 121–2, citing *An order made to a select committee ... to receive petitions* (Dec. 1641) and the Commons Journals. One constituency agent claimed he had printed enough copies 'that every man of the House might have one' – if true, well over 500 copies: Kyle, 'Parliament', 94.

62. *Articles of the large treaty*, 48, treaty articles approved 7 Aug. 1641. *PLP*, VII, 231–2, lists the 53 senior appointees.

63. Marshall, *A peace-offering*, 45–6.

64. Perceval-Maxwell, 'Ulster 1641', 103, quoting the 'Desires concerning unity in religion' proposed by the Scottish commissioners; Gaunt, *The English Civil War*, 94 (from Russell's 1987 essay 'The British Problem and the English Civil War').

65. *HMC Fourth Report*, I, 164–7, sworn depositions of William Murray, Colonel Alexander Stewart and Colonel John Cochrane (quoting the bloody desire of the earl of Crawford) to a committee of the Scottish Parliament, 22–27 Oct. 1641. Colonel Stewart was absolutely clear about his willingness to murder the two noblemen, adding: '[This] is the custome of Germanie, where I have served, that if they sett uponn us eftir we have takin prisoners, with a greater partie, they use to kill the prisoners.'

66. Bray, *Diary*, IV, 78–9, Sir Edward Nicholas to Charles I, Westminster, 29 Sep. 1641, returned by Charles with marginal comments on 5 Oct. For the use of 'little Will: Murray' as a confidential courier, see ibid., 118, Queen Henrietta Maria to Nicholas, 10 Nov. 1641.

67. Adamson, *The noble revolt*, 394, Nicholas to Vane, 9 Oct. 1641 (Adamson notes the significance of the plural 'dominions', with the implication that the king intended to punish his enemies in England and Ireland too). Bray, *Diary*, IV, 86, Nicholas to Charles I, 11 Oct. 1641, stated that he had received 'Your Majestie's commaunds by apostile of the 5th present' on 'Satterday last', that is, 9 Oct.

68. Adamson, *The noble revolt*, 405, Endymion Porter to Nicholas, 19 Oct. 1641.

69. Bray, *Diary*, IV, 76 and 79, Nicholas to Charles I, 27 and 29 Sep. 1641.

70. TCD *Ms* 839/135, deposition of Mulrany Carroll, Co Donegal, 26 Apr. 1643.

71. Ohlmeyer, 'The "Antrim Plot" of 1641: a rejoinder', 434–7, printing Antrim's 'Information' in May 1650. The veracity of the earl's evidence, which deeply compromised Charles, has been hotly disputed ever since. See the summary of the debate in Lamont, 'Richard Baxter', 345–7, which confirms Professor Ohlmeyer's deduction that Antrim did not lie.

72. Gillespie, 'Destabilizing Ulster', 111, Edward Chichester to Ormond, May 1641; TCD *Ms* 838/30–1, deposition of Donnell Gorme McDonnell, gentleman, 11 Mar. 1653.

73. TCD *Ms* 809/14, Examination of Owen Connolly, 22 Oct. 1641. See similar quotes in ch. 19 above.

74. Gilbert, *History of the Irish Confederation*, I, 8–9 (who also records that the Justices received a warning even earlier but did not believe it); TCD 809/13v, examination of Connolly, 22 Oct. 1641. See also the sanitized account of the 'discovery' of the plot in *HMC Ormonde*, n.s. II, 1–3, Lords Justices to earl of Leicester, 25 Oct. 1641. Clarke, *Old English*, 161 n. 1, notes that Connolly's story is full of inconsistencies and contradictions, and speculates that they stemmed from his anxiety to conceal the extent of his own involvement. In 1659 a mere 30–40 conspirators captured Dublin Castle (ch. 12 below), which shows what a few men *could* achieve.

75. TCD *Ms* 816/133v, deposition of Roger Puttocke, 1 Mar. 1642; and *Ms* 834/92v deposition of Richard Grave, 25 Oct. 1641 (thus only two days after the events he described). Canny, *Making*, 469–70, gives an excellent account of the capture of the Ulster forts, and his maps at pp. 479 and 504 show the progress of the rising. Although the outbreak of rebellion may seem somewhat haphazard, the similar behaviour of plotters in different areas reveals considerable coordination: Perceval-Maxwell, *The outbreak*, 253.

76. BL *Harl Ms.* 5,999/29v, 'Discourse' by Henry Jones and others who compiled the depositions, Nov. 1643.

77. I have chosen depositions that give first-person testimony: TCD *Ms* 839/14v, John Kerdiff, Co. Tyrone, 28 Feb. 1642; *Ms* 833/28v, Dorcas Iremonger, Co. Cavan, 22 Mar. 1642; *Ms* 821/42v, Gilbert Johnstone, Tipperary, 20 Feb. 1643. See also *Ms* 817/35, deposition of Rev. Emanuell Beale, Queen's county, 11 Apr. 1642: the Catholics 'had no pittie upon poore Englishe people' and 'stript an infinite number of women and children, in the cold, which have died through the same'.

78. Clarke, 'The 1641 depositions', 113, estimated that one-fifth of all depositions mentioned settlers who died in 1641 through privation while another one-fifth mentioned those who died by violence. His subsequent research suggests that the weather killed more settlers than did the rebels (personal communication, July 2004). Corish, 'The rising of 1641', 291, argued that exposure to the weather killed twice as many Protestants as did the rebels.

79. TCD *Ms* 837/12–13, deposition of Thomas Richardson, Co. Down, 13 June 1642. (Hickson, *Ireland*, I, 312, prints this document with the wrong date, the wrong profession – she read 'taylor' instead of 'saylor' – and several errors of transcription.)

80. Castlehaven, *Memoirs*, 28–9; *HMC Ormonde*, n.s, II, 251–2, Lords Justices to Charles I, 16 Mar. 1643. Canny, *Making*, 488–91, 496–7, 520–4 and 527–8, and Perceval-Maxwell, *The outbreak*, 230–1, discuss the role of priests and friars in encouraging violence against the Protestants. ó Siochrú, 'Atrocity', details Protestant violence against Catholics.

81. TCD *Ms*, 830/41–2, deposition of Anthony Stephens, 25 June 1646.

82. Corish, 'The rising of 1641', 291–2; Ó Siochrú, 'Atrocity', 59–60. TCD *Ms*, 809/8v and 10v, deposition of Archdeacon Robert Maxwell, 22 Aug. 1642, twice mentioned the figure '154,000'; and the Lords Justices repeated it in March 1643 (Bradshaw, Hadfield and Maley, *Representing Ireland*, xx and 192–3). See also ch. 12 above.

83. Bray, *Diary*, IV, 97, Nicholas to Charles I, 25 Oct. 1641, with royal postscript dated 30th; TCD *Ms* 835/158, deposition of John Right, Co. Fermanagh, 5 Jan. 1642. Hickson, *Ireland*, I, 114–15, prints O'Neill's alleged royal commission, dated Edinburgh, 1 Oct. 1641, and the depositions she printed at pp. 169–73 and 188–9 reveal how well the forgery worked.

84. Kenyon, *Stuart Constitution*, 228–40, the Remonstrance presented to the king on 11 Dec. 1641. Adamson, *The noble revolt*, 387, records the first reference to 'King Pym' in early October 1641; and at p. 443 notes that the title *Grand* Remonstrance dates from the nineteenth century.

85. Nalson, *An impartial collection*, II, 668, speech by Sir Edward Dering, 22 Nov. 1641.

86. Details from letters calendared in *CSPD 1641–43*, 215–17. See also Pearl, *London*, ch. 4.

87. Catherine Macaulay, *History*, III, 150, printed the queen's high words but gave no source – however, since Henrietta Maria would later threaten to enter a convent unless her husband failed to do what she said (page 356 above), this outburst seems plausible. In a note, Macaulay added that the countess of Carlisle overheard the exchange and sent a warning to the House and again gave no source – but this time one of the 'Five Members', Sir Arthur Haselrig, himself confirmed the story and provided details of his narrow escape: Rutt, *Diary of Thomas Burton*, III, 93, Haselrig's speech on 7 Feb. 1659 (as quoted in the text).

88. Gardiner, *History*, X, ch. 103, produces a masterly account of these events in the course of which he wonders why Charles did not 'attempt to seize [the five members] in their beds, as the French parliamentary leaders were seized in 1851' – concluding that, first, Charles wanted 'to preserve the appearance of legality' and, second, that 'it was not in his character to expect a persistent refusal' (pp. 134–5).

89. *CSPD 1641–3*, 240–2, Thomas Wiseman and Robert Slingsby (one of the 'swordsmen' who entered the Commons) to Pennington, 6 Jan. 1642; Cressy, *England on edge*, 393, quoting John Dillingham. The Venetian ambassador commented on the 'constant bad weather': *CSPV 1640–2*, 269 and 276, letters of 3 and 17 Jan. 1642. Without Lady Carlisle's message, Charles would have found his 'birds' in the chamber and his armed entourage (which far outnumbered the MPs) would doubtless have tried to remove them by force. Since the MPs carried their swords in the chamber and since, given the rumours of a coup, some may also have come with concealed firearms, it is hard to see how the day could have ended without bloodshed in the Palace of Westminster.

90. BL *Addl.* 21,935/162, Wallington; Cressy, *England on edge*, 396, quoting Ellis Coleman; and Groen van Prinsterer, *Archives*, 2nd series, IV, 7, Heenvliet to Orange, London, 19 Jan. 1642 OS, relating an extremely indiscreet audience given by the queen the previous day.

91. Churchill, *The World Crisis*, 274 (on the escape of the *Goeben*, but adding that the same 'sinister fatality' would later 'dog' the Dardanelles campaign); Adamson, *The noble revolt*, 503, echoing and citing Russell, *Causes*, 10.

92. My argument contradicts Kishlansky, 'Charles I', who seems to me to select examples from England (and to a lesser extent, Scotland) that show the king in a favourable light. He entirely ignores Charles's Irish initiatives. No doubt Kishlansky will object that almost all my examples come from Scotland and Ireland, the countries that first rebelled. I plead guilty as charged.

93. Russell, *The Fall*, 524.

94. Sharpe, *Personal rule*, 183; Scott and Bliss, *The works*, V, pt 2, 317–70, prints Laud's accounts and royal apostils (quotations from pp. 319, 348 and 337); Donaldson, *The making*, 44–7.

95. The last sentence of James I, *His Maiesties speech* (1607), sig. Hv.

96. Clarendon, *History*, 567–8, Green, *The letters*, 65 (early May), 68–9 (11 May), and 80 (30 May 1642) – three rebukes written within a single month. Did any other early modern monarch endure such constant criticism?

97. Manchester's deputy, Oliver Cromwell, angrily retorted: 'My lord, if this be so, why did we take up arms at first? This is against fighting ever hereafter. If so, let us make peace, be it never so base.' Events would show that the earl was right. Woolrych, *Britain in Revolution*, 291, reconstructs the exchange from two later recollections.

98. Sharpe, *Personal rule*, 930; Braddick, *God's fury*, 42 and 95. On 'guilty as charged', see page 341 above.

99. Shagan, 'Constructing discord', is eloquent on this point. The Armada veteran in 1640 was Lord Mulgrave.

100. Burnet, *Memoirs*, 203, Charles to Hamilton, Dec. 1642.

101. Gardiner, *The Hamilton papers*, 6, Hamilton to Charles, Dalkeith, 7 June 1638. On the need for a 'willingness to wink' among seventeenth-century rulers, see ch. 2 above.

102. Wharton, *History*, 47, Laud's diary entry for 2 Dec. 1632: 'The small pox appeared upon his Majesty; but God be thanked, he had a very gentle disease of it.'

Chapter 12   Britain and Ireland from Civil War to Revolution, 1642–89

1. Rushworth, *Historical Collections the fourth and last part*, II, 1,397, the 'charge' read by John Cook; Hill quoted page xxvii above.

2. Balfour, *Historical works*, III, 409; Gilbert, *History of the Irish Confederation*, VI, 270–1; Anon., *A bloudy fight*, 8; Lenihan, 'War and population', 8, quoting Colonel Richard Lawrence in 1655, and 1, quoting Seán Ó Conaill, 'Tuireamh na hÉireann', a poem written between 1655 and 1659.

3. Bennett, *Civil Wars*, 363. Other data from Gentles, *The English Revolution*, 435–56; Aylmer, *Rebellion or revolution?*, 71; Porter, *Destruction*, 65–6; and Wheeler, *Making*, chs 6–8.

4. Morrill, *Cheshire*, 28–9, 108–9

5. Gentles, *The English Revolution*, 437; Plumb, *Growth*, 1.

6. Walter, *Understanding*, 201, the 'Humble petition' of Essex, 20 Jan. 1642 OS; Clifton, 'The popular fear', 29–31, lists the panics that occurred over the winter of 1641–2.

7. Aidan Clarke calculates that Jones's *Remonstrance* cited 78 of the 637 depositions then available. Orihel, '"A presse"', 129–37, lists pamphlets published in England between Nov. 1641 and Aug. 1642 that dealt with Ireland.

8. Baxter, *Holy commonwealth* (1659), 472–3 and 478–9 (explicitly citing 'the Examinations by the Irish Justices', and notably the exaggerated figure given by Archdeacon Robert Maxwell in his deposition: page 352 above); Lamont, 'Richard Baxter', 347–8, quoting Baxter's Memoirs.

9. Walter, *Understanding*, 319–20, on the Essex petition, and 325–6, on Stephen Marshall, *Meroz Cursed* (London 1642, on Judges 5:23), preached some 60 times as well as circulating widely in print. For a demonstration by women demanding measures to end unemployment two weeks before, and the use made of it by parliamentary leaders, see Pearl, *London*, 226–7.

10. Russell, *Fall*, 496, quoting Henry Wilmot.

11. Kenyon, *Stuart Constitution*, 244–7 and 21–3, prints the Nineteen Propositions (1 June 1642) and the king's response (18 June).

12. Walter, *Understanding popular violence*, 18, quoting Ephrain Udall, *The good of peace and the ill of warre*, and Smith, 'Catholic', 119, Lord Dorset to the countess of Middlesex, Aug. 1642. Jack Straw was another leader of the 1381 revolt; Robert Kett had led the Norfolk rebels in 1549.

13. Kenyon, *Stuart Constitution*, 194, marginal comment of the king on a letter in Nov. 1641; Russell, *Fall*, 437, quoting the reaction of some Kentishmen to the proclamation of 10 Dec.; Walter, *Understanding popular violence*, 129, instructions.

14. Walter, *Understanding popular violence*, 259, 'Humble Petition' of the Suffolk clothiers; 261, speech of Sir Simonds d'Ewes to the Commons; and 288, Sir Thomas Barrington's report to Parliament (with other similar statements).

15. *HMC Report on the Franciscan Manuscripts* (Dublin, 1906), 112, letter from London to Fr. Hugh Bourke, 29 Dec. 1641; ó Siochrú, 'Atrocity', 61–2, orders of the Lords Justices, Jan. and June 1642.

16. *CSPD 1641–43*, 508, Mr Harrison to John Bradley (in Paris), 28 Dec. 1643.

17. Abbott, *Writings and Speeches*, I, 314, Cromwell's speech in the House of Commons on 9 Dec. 1644.

18. [Parker,] *The king's cabinet* (published 14 July 1645), 1, Charles to the queen, 9 Jan. 1645, postscript.

19. Ibid.; Hirst, 'Reading', 213. Hirst also notes both the hostile reception, as recorded in the London newspapers, and the fact that Parliament put the original documents on display to demonstrate they were not forgeries. For the later career of Wallis, see ch. 22 above.

20. Symmons, *A vindication*, 241 (part of 'A true parallel between the sufferings of our Saviour and our Soveraigne'). Hirst, 'Reading', and Potter, *Secret rites*, 59–64, discuss both content and context of *The king's cabinet*.

21. Cressy, *England on edge*, 298, quoting Nehemiah Wallington's diary, 6 Feb. 1642 OS. See ch. 18 above for more on the 'educational revolution' in Tudor and Stuart England.

22. Ibid., 313–14, quoting Thomas Knyvett to his mother, May 1642; Eisenstadt and Schluter, 'Early modernities', 25.

23. [Parker,] *The king's cabinet*, preface, 43; Hirst, 'Reading', focuses on this important gender dimension.

24. [Parker,] *The king's cabinet*, 7–8, to Henrietta Maria, 5 Mar. 1645; 16, to Ormond, 27 Feb. 1645; 46–7 and 54–6 ('Annotations' arranged in six heads).

25. Woolrych, *Soldiers and statesmen*, 38; Firth, *The Clarke Papers*, I, 425–6, 'Colonel Wogan's narrative'. Although Wogan wrote much later, his reliability on these matters is upheld by Norris, 'Edward Sexby', 41–2.

26. Rushworth, *Historical Collections*, VI, 512, 'A solemn engagement of the army', 5 June 1647.

27. Ibid., VI, 564–70, 'A declaration, or representation from His Excellency Sir Thomas Fairfax and of the army under his command', 14 June 1647. Woolrych, *Britain*, 371, attributes its authorship 'essentially' to Ireton.

28. Gardiner, *Constitutional documents*, 316–26, 'The Heads of the Proposals ... to be tendered to the commissioners of Parliament residing with the army', debated by the General Council, 16–26 July 1647 OS; Firth, *Clarke Papers*, 1, 213, speech by William Allen. For the context, and for the senior officers' discussions with Charles, see Woolrych, *Soldiers and statesmen*, 153–79.

29. Macfarlane, *Diary of Ralph Josselin*, 87 (entry for 24 Feb. 1647); Bamford, *A royalist's notebook*, 112. Coates, *The impact*, 218, charts the impact of the 1646 harvest on London prices.

30. Adamson, 'The English nobility', 567–8, quotations from depositions of two eyewitnesses of the siege of Parliament on 26 July 1647. Clarendon later asserted that the decision of the Speakers, peers and MPs to take refuge with the Army 'appeared to every stander-by so stupendous a thing, that it is not to this day understood': *History*, IV, 244–5.

31. Gardiner, *Constitutional documents*, 333–5, *An Agreement of the People*. The author was either John Wildman (Morrill and Baker, 'The case', 121), or William Walwyn (Woolrych, *Soldiers and statesmen*, 215).

32. Firth, *Clarke Papers*, I, 301–2, 304 and 322–3: Rainborough, Ireton and Sexby in the debate on 29 Oct. 1647. Note that no one suggested extending the franchise to any 'she' – whether poor or propertied. Morrill and Baker, 'The case of the armie', argue that Sexby composed the pamphlet entitled *The case of the armie truly stated*, which triggered the debate at Putney and formed the basis for *The Agreement*. On his remarkable career, see *ODNB*, s.v. 'Sexby, Edward'.

33. [John Wildman, a Leveller spokesman at Putney], *A cal to all the souldiers of the Army*, 7 (second pagination: capitals in the original).

34. On the mutiny at Ware, and the *Remonstrance*, see Woolrych, *Soldiers and statesmen*, 279–86.

35. Hindle, 'Dearth', 65, quoting a verse written by the vicar of Hartpury, Gloucestershire, in his Parish Register.

36. Gardiner, *Constitutional documents*, 247–52, 'The Engagement between the king and the Scots', 26 Dec. 1647.

37. Thirsk, 'Agricultural policy', 301; Macfarlane, *Diary of Ralph Josselin*, 125, 129, entries for 9 May and 28 June 1648; Bamford, *A royalist's notebook*, 120–1.

38. Howell, *Epistolae*, III, 26, letter of 10 Dec. 1647 to his nephew (the output of the Mint fell by 90 per cent in 1648; see Coates, *Impact*, 229); Wildman, *Truths triumph*, 4–5 (published 1 Feb. 1648, describing his speech on 18 Jan.).

39. AMAE (P) *CPA* 50/24v–25, Mazarin to M. de Grignon, 10 Apr. 1648 NS, register copy. See a similar lament one month later in Chéruel, *Lettres*, III, 1,023.

40. Macfarlane, *Diary of Ralph Josselin*, 138, entry for 17 Sep. 1648; Abbott, *Writings and Speeches*, I, 636 and 641, Cromwell to Speaker Lenthall, Warrington, 20 Aug. 1648, and to the Derby House Committee, Wigan, 23 Aug. 1648.

41. Rushworth, *Historical Collections the fourth and last part*, II, 1,396–8 (the 'charge' read by John Cook, 'solicitor-general for the Commonwealth'); 1,406–14 (depositions); and 1,421 (sentence). *ODNB*, s.v. George Joyce, notes that astrologer William Lilly twice named Joyce as the executioner – once in testimony given at the Restoration and again in his autobiography – but casts doubt on his assertion. The changing composition of the High Court is chronicled in *ODNB* s.v. 'regicides'.

42. Firth and Rait, *Acts and Ordinances*, II, 2–4, 'An Act of thos present Parliament for constituting a counsell of state for the Comonwealth of England', 13 Feb. 1649; 18–20, 'An Act for abolishing the kingly office in England and Ireland, and the Dominions thereunto belonging', 17 Mar. 1649; 24, 'An Act for the abolishing the House of Peers', 19 Mar. 1649; and 122, 'An act declaring and constituting the people of England to be a Commonwealth and Free-State', 19 May 1649. None of these and other constitutional acts mentioned Scotland: only 'England and Ireland, and the Dominions thereunto belonging'.

43. Charles I, *Eikon Basilike* (2005 edition), 183–4.

44. Boulton, 'Food prices', 468 and 481–2; Firth, *Cromwell's army*, 184–5; Gaunt, *Natural and political observations*, 37. Macfarlane, *Diary of Ralph Josselin*, 152–85, entries for 7 Jan., 18 Feb., 15 Apr., 20 May, 7 Oct., 25 Nov. and 16 Dec. 1649 reported 'all things were wonderful dear'.

45. *A true representation* (24 May 1649). See similar heart-wrenching complaints from early 1649 in Thirsk and Cooper, *Seventeenth-century economic documents*, 51–2, and Hindle, 'Dearth', 84–6. Hindle notes with justified disapproval how 'historians have made so little attempt to take seriously the harvest crisis of the late 1640s': ibid., 65.

46. *Acts done*, 35–8, 'Proclamation of Charles the Second, king of Great Britain, France and Ireland', 5 Feb. 1649, and 'Act anent securing the Covenant, religion and peace of the kingdom', 7 Feb. 1649. Although the Rump abolished monarchy in England and Ireland, it said nothing about Scotland. It is ironic that it thus wished to disaggregate the composite state created in 1603, in which it saw no benefit – and that the Scots disagreed.

47. Bremer, 'In defence of regicide', 103, quoting John Hull's journal. Some committed themselves after news arrived of Cromwell's victory at Dunbar in September 1650, but commitment was neither official nor universal.

48. Anthony Ascham murdered in Spain; Isaac Dorislaus murdered in Holland. On the narrow escape of Bradshaw in Russia, see Gordon, *Diary*, I, 251–2.

49. Firth and Rait, *Acts and Ordinances*, II, 325–9, 'An Act for subscribing the Engagement', 2 Jan. 1650; Worden, 'The politics of Marvell's Horatian Ode', 526–7, quoting Sir Henry Vane, jr, former governor of Massachusetts.

50. MacDonald, *The poems of Andrew Marvell*, 118–21. Worden, 'The politics', 531, argues that the work 'was at least conceived in the week or so after Cromwell's return. The poem could have been completed then.'

51. Balfour, *Historical works*, III, 409 (prices), 432–3 (weather) and 436–7 (witches); Larner, *Source book*, sub annis 1649–50; Larner, *Enemies of God*, 61 and 74–5.

52. Hobbes, *Leviathan*, 491, 484, and 154 (for the dating of the work, probably begun early in 1649 and completed late in 1650, I follow Richard Tuck's introduction to the 1996 edition); Skinner, 'Conquest and consent', 97, quotes Hobbes's later boast (against criticisms by John Wallis); Knoppers, *Constructing Cromwell*, 56–7, reproduces and discusses the Dunbar medal; Bremer, 'In defense of the regicide', 118–24, prints and discusses John Cotton's sermon of thanksgiving for Dunbar; Bush, *The correspondence of John Cotton*, 458–64 and 468–70, prints Cotton's laudatory letter to Cromwell of 28 July 1651, and Cromwell's welcoming reply on 2 Oct.

53. Abbott, *Writings and Speeches*, II, 463 and 467, Cromwell to Lenthall, 4 and 8 Sep. 1651.

54. Ibid., 325, Cromwell to Lenthall, 4 Sep. 1650. Rommelse, 'The role of mercantilism', 597–8, stresses how the nature of the Rump facilitated state-building.

55. See ch. 15 below on the impact of the Republic on Anglo-America. The second fleet carried instructions that, if necessary, the fleet should 'rouse the planters' servants against their masters' – a truly revolutionary measure that, although never put into effect, would be bitterly recalled by the planters' descendants during the American Revolution a century later. My thanks to Thomas Ingersoll for this detail.

56. Scott, *Politics*, 201; Terry, *The Cromwellian Union*, xxi–xxiii, 'A declaration of the Parliament of England, concerning the settlement of Scotland', 28 Oct. 1651. The document proved hard for Scots Presbyterians to swallow, not only because it broke the Kirk's monopoly of legal worship but because it involved joining a Republic, which went against clause three of the Covenant (safeguarding monarchy).

57. Firth and Rait, *Acts and Ordinances*, II, 598–603, 'Act for the settlement of Ireland', 12 Aug. 1652. The 'Grand Remonstrance' of Dec. 1641 had already stated that the costs of suppressing the Irish rebellion would be reimbursed from estates forfeited by the rebels: Gardiner, *Constitutional documents*, 205. The Act of Settlement effectively sentenced around 100,000 Irish men and women to death – although relatively few were executed.

58. Woolrych, *Britain*, 528–36; Osborne, *Letters*, 76, to Sir William Temple, her future husband, 24 Apr. 1653.

59. Firth and Rait, *Acts and Ordinances*, II, 813–22, 'The government of the Commonwealth of England, Scotland and Ireland, and the Dominions thereunto belonging', 16 Dec. 1653. Although a few other states tolerated freedom of *private* worship, the Instrument of Government was the first to guarantee freedom of *public* worship.

60. Bush, *Cotton*, 461–2, on Cotton; Junge, *Flottenpolitik*, 246–7, on Gage. Cromwell had already sent forces to America in 1654, to seize both New Netherland and French forts in Acadia.

61. Firth, *Clarke Papers*, III, 207, 'Edward Montagu's notes on the debates in the Protector's council', 20 Apr. and 20 July 1654; Abbott, *Writings and Speeches*, III, 860, Cromwell to Admiral William Goodson.

62. Bethel, *The world's mistake in Oliver Cromwell*, 9; Abbott, *Writings and Speeches*, III, 857–8, Cromwell to General Fortescue, Oct. 1655; Worden, 'Oliver Cromwell and the Sin of Achan', 136–7, quoting 'A Declaration of his Highness, inviting the people of England and Wales to a day of solemn fasting and humiliation' (Mar. 1656). Gardiner, *Constitutional documents*, 447–59, prints *The humble petition and advice*. Worden, op. cit., 141–5, shows that the failure of the Western Design led Cromwell to decline the crown.

63. Gaunt, *Natural and political observations*, 37 ('sickly years'); De Beer, *Diary of John Evelyn*, 388, 393. Cromwell had intended to go to Westminster by boat to dissolve Parliament on 4 Feb. 1658, but because the river was partially ice-bound he had to travel by coach.

64. Macfarlane, *Diary of Ralph Josselin*, 435, entry for 28 Nov. 1658; Rutt, *Diary of Thomas Burton*, III, 256.

65. Gardiner, *Constitutional documents*, 465, the Declaration of Breda, issued by Charles on 4 Apr. 1660. Monck had followed just the same policy since February, leaving Parliament to make all the hard decisions. *ODNB*, s.v. 'Monck', by Ronald Hutton, probably comes as close as is possible to ascertaining Monck's motives.

66. Ohlmeyer, 'Seventeenth-century Ireland', 453–4, quoting 'A light to the blind', probably written by the Irish Catholic Nicholas Plunkett. No Union Parliament would meet again until 1802.

67. Stoyle, 'Remembering', 19–20; Gentles, 'The iconography', 101, and plate; TCD *Ms* 813/286, deposition of William Collis, Kildare, 4 May 1643 (the deposition originally gave the victim's name, but it was later deleted). See also *Ms* 831/176, the gang-rape described in the deposition of Andrew Adaire, Mayo, 9 Jan. 1643 ('severall of the rebells of Phelim o Dowles company ravished the wiffe of one Samuel Barber').

68. Thomas, *Religion*, 366 and 379 (see the originals in Bod. *Ashmole Ms*. 184, 'Figures set upon horary questions by Mr William Lilly' (for 1644–5) and *Ms*. 185 (for 1647–9)).

69. Cressy, *England on edge*, 85; Carlton, *Going to the wars*, 305–6. For similar expressions of grief by the wives and widows of men in naval service, see Rodger, *The command*, 127–8.

70. Bunyan, *The Pilgrim's Progress* (by 1688, the year of Bunyan's death, 11 editions of Part I and 2 of Part II, and translations into Dutch, French and (apparently) Welsh, had appeared); Fox, *A journal*, another classic of religious literature largely composed in the 1670s, was not published until 1694.

71. Kenyon, *Stuart Constitution*, 361, notes that only two statutes from 1641–2 were repealed: the Act excluding bishops from the House of Lords and the Triennial Act.

72. Wheeler, *Making*, 195. Admittedly, each monarch could only collect customs and excise legally after Parliament gave its consent at the start of each reign.

73. McKenny, 'Seventeenth-century land settlement', 198, Hyde to Mr Betius, 29 May 1654 OS.

74. Pestana, *English Atlantic*, 223, Instructions of Charles II to the governor of Virginia, 12 Sep. 1662.

75. Pepys, *Diary*, VIII, 262–9, entries for 12–13 June 1667; *CSPD 1667*, 185–90, letters dated 14 and 15 June 1667.

76. Grey, *Debates*, VIII, 264, speech of Sir Henry Capel, 7 Jan. 1681. Capel also noted how Richelieu and Mazarin had 'suppressed all the great men of France, and all to support absolute monarchy'.

77. Plumb, *The growth*, 60.

78. Kenyon, *Stuart Constitution*, 410–11, James II, 'Declaration of Indulgence', 27 Apr. 1688. On 4 May 1688 James ordered the public reading in churches to take place on 20 and 27 May in London and two weeks later elsewhere. Compare the orders issued by his father in 1637 to use 'Laud's Liturgy' in all the churches of Scotland.

79. Kenyon, *Stuart Constitution*, 441–2, the bishops' 'Petition', 19 May 1688 (the day before the first reading scheduled for the Declaration); and 443–5, Trial of the Seven Bishops, 29 June 1688, opinions of Justices Holloway and Powell. On 4 July, James deprived both these judges of their office (all dates Old Style).

80. Williams, *Eighteenth-century constitution*, 8–10, the 'invitation to William', 30 June 1688 OS.
81. Goldie, *The entring book*, IV, 340, Roger Morrice's entry for 17 Nov. 1688 OS. He added: 'And it's as well known the Parliament cannot sit here before six weekes be expired, and it will be longer before they can be supposed to dispatch any thing in a parliamentary way.'
82. Williams, *Eighteenth-century constitution*, 60 and 26, notes of discussions between William and the English peers in winter 1688–9; he also prints the Bill of Rights at pp. 26–33.
83. De Beer, *The correspondence of John Locke*, III, 545–6, Locke to Edward Clarke, 29 Jan 1689; and 538–9, Lady Mordaunt to Locke, 21 Jan. 1689.
84. *The weasel uncas'd*, a single printed sheet of verses, each one ending 'Which nobody can deny' (Lutaud, *Des révolutions*, 146–7, reviews other similar verse compositions); De Beer, *Diary of John Evelyn*, V, 288; Cullen, *Famine*, 2, 10, and 49; Sinclair, *The statistical account*, XVII, 483, report from Insch (Aberdeenshire), and II, 551, report from Kilmuir (Skye). See ch. 20 above for more on the 'climax of the Little Ice Age' in the 1690s.
85. Ingersoll, 'The lamp of experience', quoting Thomas Molyneux, MP; Anon., *An essay on government*, 95–6. (I thank Tom Ingersoll for bringing this remarkable reference to my attention.) On Masaniello, leader of the Naples revolution of 1647, see ch. 14 above.
86. Ingersoll, 'The lamp of experience'. For the numbing effect of the regicide in Europe at the time, see chs 12 and 19 above.
87. Burke, *Reflections*, 223–4; Kenyon, *Revolution principles*, 208, quoting Burke's *Appeal from the New to the Old Whigs* (1791). Lutaud, *Des révolutions*, describes how French Revolutionaries in 1789, 1830 and 1848 used precedents from the English revolutions of the seventeenth century.
88. Macaulay, *History*, II, 508–9. Plumb, quoted above, was the doctoral advisee of George Macaulay Trevelyan, Macaulay's great-nephew. It is again worth stressing that Plumb, like Macaulay, wrote only of England. The Revolution Settlement in both Scotland and Ireland involved great violence and prolonged material suffering.

Part III. Surviving the Crisis

1. Lancellotti, *L'hoggidi. Hoggidiani* literally means 'people nowadays'.
2. Lancellotti, *Oggidì, overo gl'ingegni non inferiori a' passati* (Venice, 1636).
3. Green, *Spain*, IV, 6, Quevedo to Don Francisco de Oviedo, 21 Aug. 1645; Hobbes quoted on page xxiii above; Sévigné and Arnauld on page 318 above; Gracián, *El Criticón*, 3 parts published 1651, 1653 and 1657. Gracián also used the word 'crisi' in other works, with the sense of 'judgement', criticizing the world in which he lived.

Chapter 13   The Mughals and their Neighbours

1. Special thanks for help in preparing this chapter to Lisa Balabanlilar, Stephen Dale, Scott Levi, Sanjay Subrahmanyam, Tristan Mostert and Stephan van Galen. Although members of the dynasty never used the term 'Mughal', an Arabized word for 'Mongol' picked up by Europeans in the sixteenth century (possibly as a term of opprobrium), it seems pedantic not to use it.
2. Details from Blake, *Shahjahanabad*. Although the Mongol Khan Batur Hongtaiji built a new capital at Zubak Zar in the 1640s and Coxinga built a Ming Memorial Capital on Amoy Island in the 1650s, these were towns not cities – and neither of them lasted long. Likewise the Dutch built new cities at Batavia (Java) after 1619 and at Recife (Brazil) after 1630, but these were colonial and not imperial centres. Finally, although the Maratha leader Shivaji created a new state, he chose an existing fortress, Raigad, as his capital.
3. Guha, *India in the seventeenth century*, I, 82 (from 'A voyage to Suratt in the year 1689' by John Ovington).
4. Dale, *The Muslim empires*, 107–8; Habib, *The agrarian system*, 4, 26–7.
5. Dale, *The Muslim empires*, 100.
6. Elliot and Dowson, *The history of India*, VII, 158.
7. Ibid., 156–9, print the description of Aurangzeb's exemplary piety in Bakhtawar Khan, *Mirat-i Alam* (1666).
8. Guha, *India*, I, 82 (Ovington in 1689); Sarkar, *Anecdotes of Aurangzeb*, 53, from Aurangzeb's advice to his son c. 1695. Beach and Koch, *King of the world*, 11, lists the major movements of Shah Jahan.
9. Guha, *India*, I, 82–3 (Ovington). He gave by way of example the Marathas' pillage of Surat in 1664.
10. Data from Richards, *Mughal Empire*, 138–40 (quoting Lahori's *Padshah Nama*). In 1689, Ovington gave much the same figure: see Guha, *India*, I, 82.
11. Begley and Desai, *Shah Jahan Nama*, 61–2 (a summary, composed in 1657–8, of the official chronicle compiled annually by the Imperial Historian: either Shah Jahan or his personal representative checked every word before it became the official record and could be copied). Habib, *The agrarian system*, 100–10, lists the famines.
12. Temple, *Travels of Peter Mundy*, II, 42–4, 47–9, 55–6: entries for Nov. – Dec. 1630; Foster, *The English factories in India, 1630–1633*, 122, 165, 178 and 218–19, letters from East India Company officials in Surat to London, 31 Dec. 1630, 8 Sep. and 9 Dec. 1631, and 8 May 1632 OS.
13. Temple, *Travels of Peter Mundy*, II, 265, 275–6, entries for April–May 1633; HAG Ms 1498/11–12, Viceroy Linhares to Philip IV, 10 Aug. 1631, copy. See also Disney, 'Famine', 260–1, based on the 78 entries in Linhares's diary between Mar. 1630 and Dec. 1631 concerning either the famine or problems arising from it. By 2010, although some 39 tree-ring series had been posted for India, only one included seventeenth-century data.

14. Foster, *The English factories 1634–1636*, 64–5, East India Company officials in Surat to London, 29 Dec. 1634 OS; Foster, *The English factories, 1630–1633*, 178–9, same to same, 9 Dec. 1631 OS.

15. Foster, *The English factories, 1630–1633*, 178–9, East India Company officials in Surat to London, 9 Dec. 1631 OS; Temple, *Travels of Peter Mundy*, II, 265, 275–6, entries for April–May 1633.

16. Elliot and Dowson, *The history of India*, VII, 24–5, quoting Lahori's *Padshah Nama*; Begley and Desai, *Shah Jahan Nama*, 62.

17. Raychaudhuri and Habib, *Cambridge economic history of India*, I, 184. See van Santen, 'De Vereenigde Oost-indische Compagnie', ch. 2, on the sudden Mughal decision to build great ships; Prakash, *The Dutch East India Company*, 34–41 and 234–40, on economic growth in Bengal under Shah Jahan; and Alam and Subrahmanyam, *The Mughal State*, 26–7, and Moosvi, 'Scarcities, prices and exploitation', 49, on the increasing revenues.

18. Subrahmanyam, 'A tale of three empires', 73. See Eaton, *The rise of Islam*, 156–7, on Mughal expansion into Bengal.

19. Foltz, 'The Mughal occupation', 51–2, quoting the *Shah Jahan-nama* and *Tazkira-i Muqim Kahni*. Balabanlilar, 'Lords of the auspicious conjunction', 72–8, notes that the Mughals called themselves *Guregeniyya* ('the dynasty of the son-in-law') in honour of Timur, who married a descendant of Chinggis Khan and adopted that title.

20. Foltz, 'The Mughal occupation', 57, quoting the *Tazkira-i Muqim Kahni*. Borgaonkar et al., 'Climate change', 32, 34, Himalayan tree-ring data, shows poor growing seasons in the 1640s.

21. Levi, 'Hindus beyond the Hindu Kush', 280, quotes the *Tazkira-i Muqim Kahni*, and notes that the sale of so many slaves in Central Asia in 1647 'was unique in the history of the region'.

22. Elliot and Dowson, *The history of India*, VII, 96–103, quoting Inayat Khan, *Shah Jahan Nama*.

23. Richards, *Mughal India*, 132–5, quoting the estimates in Muhammad Sadiq's *Shahjahan-Nama*.

24. McChesney, *Waqf*, 141, quoting a *Manshur* (confirmation) issued by the ruler of Balkh in 1668–9.

25. Faruqui, 'Princes and power', 299, quoting the *Waqiat-i Alamgiri*.

26. Elliot and Dowson, *The history of India*, VII, 178, quoting Muhammed Kazim, *Alamgir Nama*.

27. Moosvi, 'Scarcities', 55; Moinul Haq, *Khafi Khan's History*, 93–4. Although this entry in the *History* lacks a date, it comes immediately after events that occurred in Sep. 1659.

28. Foster, *The English factories, 1655–1660*, 263 and 256, letters from the English factors at Masulipatam, north of Madras, in Mar. and Oct. 1659; and 210 and 310, letters from the English factors in Surat, Sep. and Oct. 1659 and Apr. 1660; Foster, *The English factories in India, 1661–1664*, 32, letters from the English factors at Madras, 28 Jan. 1661 (all dates OS).

29. Moinul Haq, *Khafi Khan's History*, 130–1; Singh, *Region and empire*, 116, 'free kitchens' in Punjab 1658–60.

30. Foster, *The English factories, 1661–1664*, 200 and 321, letters from the English factors at Surat, 28 Jan. and 4 Apr. 1664; de Souza, *Medieval Goa*, 172 (graph of food prices in the city), van Santen, 'De Verenigde', 90–6.

31. Foster, *The English factories in India, 1661–1664*, 329, letter from the English factors at Surat, 26 Nov. 1664. Dutch sources document Indian famines in 1659, 1660, 1661, 1663, 1664 and 1666: Boomgaard, 'Fluctuations in mortality', 5. Rice and wheat prices increased sharply in Bengal in 1662–3: Moosvi, 'Scarcities', 47, and Prakash, *The Dutch East India Company*, 252–3. Kerala droughts in 1663, 1665 and 1666 recorded by Borgaonkar, 'Climate change', 51.

32. Bernier, *Travels*, 205, letter to Colbert written 'after an absence of twelve years' from France, which he left in 1656; Moosvi, 'Scarcities', 49–50 and 55; Moosvi, 'Indian economic experience', 332 (excluding Bengal, Orissa and Kashmir, because their revenues had already declined sharply between 1646 and 1656). See also the tax figures in Guha, *Health and population*, 33–4.

33. Moosvi, 'Scarcities', a pioneering effort to remedy the 'neglect of the short-term fluctuations in the cycle of production and consumption', such as famine and climate, in the economic history of Mughal India.

34. Love, *Indian records*, 558, Appendix VIII, 'Madras famines'.

35. Liu, *Asian population history*, 197–9 and 202–7. Peter Boomgaard, 'Fluctuations in mortality', documented poor harvests in Java in 1633–4, 1641–2, 1647, 1657 and 1659–62, and famine in 1618, 1625–7 and 1664–5; and poor harvests in the outer islands in 1633, 1638–9, 1644, 1646, 1648, 1651–3 and 1657, and famine in 1660 and 1664. See also ibid., 47–9; Reid, 'The crisis', 211–17; and Arakawa, *Climates*, 222.

36. Reid, *Southeast Asia*, I, 25, quoting Alcina, *History of the Visayan Islands* (1668); and, I, 18 and 19, quoting William Marsden, *History of Sumatra* (1783).

37. Boomgaard, 'Fluctuations in mortality', 5, noted the differing chronology of Indian and Indonesian droughts.

38. Reid, 'The crisis', 211 and 218–19. Dutch profits of course soared in proportion: Anthony Reid has calculated that 'the Dutch sold spices in Europe at about seventeen times, and in India at about fourteen times, the price for which they had bought them' in Indonesia.

39. Drewes, *Hakayat potjut Muhamat*, 167 (Prince Muhamat utters these words during an Achehnese civil war when he comes across abandoned fields); Reid, 'The crisis', 219, quoting the report of a Dutch factor in the southern Philippines, in 1699. See also the similar statement from a similar source in 1686: ibid., 218.

40. Skinner, *Sja'ir perang Mengkasar*, 215 (written 1669–70). On the Dutch struggle with Makassar, see Andaya, *The heritage of Arung Palakka*, 130–3; and Parker, 'The fortress', 213–15.

41. Boxer, *The Portuguese seaborne empire*, 106–7.

42. Foster, *The English factories, 1637–1641*, 228, William Fremlen to the East India Company, Dec. 1639 and 28 Jan. 1640. See also the similar verdict of Tavernier, *Travels in India*, 150–61.

43. Winius, *The fatal history*, 54–5, royal letter of Mar. 1641; Pissurlencar, *Assentos do Conselho do Estado*, II, 573–8, Viceroy Aveiras to John IV, 27 Sep. 1641.

44. Winius, *The fatal history*, 110, letter of 3 Apr. 1647, and 117, opinion of two councillors of war, Sep. 1649.

45. Boxer, *Fidalgos in the Far East*, 150, 153–4.

46. Bocarro, *O livro das plantas*, II, 155; Winius, *The fatal history*, 141, count of Óbidos, the deposed and imprisoned viceroy, to his brother. A replacement arrived from Lisbon two years later, arrested the conspirators and sent them back to Portugal in chains. See also de Souza, *Medieval Goa*, 115–17; and van Veen, 'Decay or defeat', 108–12.

47. Boxer, *Portuguese seaborne empire*, 128–9, quoting Manuel Godinho, *Relação do novo caminho que fez por terra e mar* (Lisbon, 1665). On Godinho, see Lobo and Correia-Afonso, *Intrepid itinerant*.

48. Boxer, *Portuguese India*, 7, viceroy to king, 26 June 1668.

49. Prestage and Laranjo Coelho, *Correspondência diplomática*, III, 354, Sousa Coutinho to Secretary of State Soares de Abreu, 4 May 1649; Boxer, *Portuguese India*, 23–4, viceroy to the king, Rio Licungo, 23 Oct. 1650.

50. Boxer, *Portuguese India*, 35, *consulta* of the Overseas Council to John IV, 9 Sep. 1649. Figures from Bruijn, *Dutch Asiatic shipping*, III, 75; and Subrahmanyam, *The Portuguese empire in Asia*, 163.

51. Boxer, *Portuguese India*, 7, letter of 14 Dec. 1658.

52. De Jonge, *Opkomst*, V, 248–9, van Diemen to the directors, 12 Dec 1641 (the Governor General himself added the italics).

53. Chardin, *Travels in Persia*, 128–9. On page 137, Chardin again stressed that 'Persia is, generally speaking, a barren country' but claimed that 'the *tenth* part of it is uncultivated'.

54. Newman, *Safavid Iran*, 74–5 and 202, describes the revolt and executions.

55. Dale, *The Muslim empires*, 218.

56. Floor, *The economy*, 61–2, quoting Chardin, *Voyages*. Climatic details from Newman, *Safavid Iran*, 94–5 and 131–2, and from Matthee, *Politics of trade*, 175–7. On devaluation, see also ch. 2 above.

57. Subrahmanyam cited at page 406 above. Berchet, *La Repubblica*, 50–2 and 215–19, documents an important but unsuccessful Polish-Venetian embassy to Iran in 1646–9 seeking a declaration of war against the Ottomans.

58. Chardin, *Travels in Persia*, 130.

59. Musallam, *Sex and society in Islam*, 10 (Hadith), 57–82 (pharmacy stocks and literature on abortion and contraception, including the 176 methods listed in one treatise), 89 (on *The Perfumed Garden*, which notes eight methods of birth control) and 118 (quotations from the treatises of Ibn Nujaim and Shawkani). Hindu as well as Muslim teaching permitted birth control and saw the ideal age of marriage for girls as 15.

60. Maussion de Favrières, *Les voyages*, 89 (La Boullaye-le-Gouz in 1644), and Babayan, *Mystics*, 441 (Chardin in 1676). The shah's predecessors had been less liberal: see ibid., pp. 442–3.

Chapter 14   Red Flag over Italy

1. I thank Brian Pullan, who first introduced me to Masaniello in his lecture course at Cambridge University in 1965, for commenting on this chapter, and Mario Rizzo, who has shaped my interpretation of 'Spanish Italy' ever since we first met in the Archivio di Stato in Naples in 1995. Early modern Italians used a twenty-four-hour clock, with each 'day' beginning half an hour after sunset: thus, regardless of the season, sunset occurred every day at 'ore 2330'. When Italians wrote that something happened 'ad un'ora di notte [at one o'clock at night]', they meant 'at 90 minutes after sunset'. In this chapter, I have converted the times given by contemporaries into their modern equivalents.

2. Grotius, *Briefwisseling*, XI, 609, to Nicolaes van Reigersberch, 10 Nov. 1640; Jacobs, *Epistolae*, I, 420–1, Howell letter from late 1640 (the date in the text – 3 Mar. 1638 – cannot be correct).

3. Gil Pujol, ' "Conservación" ', 88: 'Si busques bon govern/Napols, Messina y Palerm/bon exemple te an donat'.

4. Data from the pioneering articles of Maurice Aymard: 'La Sicilia' and 'In Sicilia' for population; 'Commerce et production' for silk exports; 'Rese' and 'Rendements' for crop yields; and from Davies, 'Changes', 387–8.

5. Ribot García, *La revuelta*, 57.

6. Di Marzo, *Biblioteca Storica*, III, 35–8 ('Diario' of Vincenzo Auria); AHN *Estado libro* 455, n.p., *consultas* of the Council of Italy 25 July 1645 and 14 Mar. 1646; Aymard, 'Bilancio', 990; and Ribot García, 'La época', 669.

7. Pocili, *Delle rivoluzioni*, 1; Collurafi, *Tumultazioni*, part I, 8. AGS *SP* leg. 1444, n.p., *consulta* of the Council of Italy, 3 Aug. 1647, on Los Vélez letters of 31 May and 5 June stating that Palermo spent 300 ducats a day on the bread subsidy. All Sicilian grain prices in this chapter come from the annual 'mete del frumento' (grain contract price) for Palermo, Trapani and other towns printed by Cancila, *Impresa*, 314–17.

8. Di Marzo, *Biblioteca storica*, III, 40–67 (Auria); ibid., IV, 64–6 and 70 (Rocco Pirri).

9. AGS *SP* leg. 1,444, n.p., Los Vélez to Philip IV, 23 May 1647. Los Vélez stated that he had reduced the loaves from 11.75 to 10 ounces 'para ajustar el gasto con el coste'.

10. Details from Pocili, *Delle rivoluzioni*, 4–5; Marzo, *Biblioteca storica*, III, 68–71 (Auria).

11. AGS *SP* leg. 1,444, n.p., Los Vélez to Philip IV, 23 May 1647.

12. Lionti, 'Cartelli sediziosi', 450–1, the petition of Caltabellotta, 23 June 1647.

13. Pocili, *Delle rivoluzioni*, 36–42, prints the new tax edict. On 11 July a *felucca* arrived in Palermo bearing news of the Naples uprising: AGS *SP* leg. 1,444, n.p., Los Vélez to Philip IV, 16 July 1647.

14. Capaccio, *Il forastiero*, 847. Opinions differ on the size of Naples. In 1634 Capaccio, *op. cit.*, 846, estimated 300,000; while Jean-Jacques Bouchard, who spent eight months there in 1632–3, thought the city and suburbs housed 'between seven and eight hundred thousand souls' (Kanceff, *Bouchard: Journal*, II, 254). In 1647 Viceroy Arcos opted for 600,000 (BNE *Ms* 2662/6, 'Relación del tumulto'); and a Jesuit guessed it was 800,000 (*Cartas de algunos padres*, VII (*MHE*, XIX), 94, 'Relación', 30 Aug. 1647). I follow De Rosa, 'Naples, a capital', 351, who suggested that 300,000 people lived in the city in 1630 and 365,000 on the eve of the plague of 1656.

15. Capaccio, *Il forastiero*, 703. Kanceff, *Bouchard: Journal*, II, 242, 265–70, and Capaccio, *Il forastiero*, 850, both mentioned the high-rise apartments. Benigno, *Specchi*, 276–82, discusses 'Who were the *Lazzari?*'

16. Details in Benigno, *L'ombra del re*, ch. 2, and Comparato, *Uffici*, 289–324.

17. Comparato, 'Toward the revolt', 291–2, quoting Francesco de Petri, *Responsa sive consilia* (Naples, 1634); Tutini, *Dell'origine e fundazione de' Seggi* (Naples, 1644). Tutini, a priest, claimed that the nobles never forgave him for his book and, after the revolt, insisted that he stay in permanent exile (which he did): Tutini and Verde, *Racconto*, xliii, letter of Tutini, 12 July 1649.

18. G. M. Novario, *De vassallorum gravaminibus tractatus* (3 vols, Naples 1634–42). In May 1647, even before news arrived of the revolt of Palermo, some 400 furious peasants attacked the noble administrator of a formerly royal domain near Cosenza: see Comparato, 'Toward the revolt', 306–7.

19. Villari, *Revolt*, 240 n. 89, *consulta* of the Sommaria, 3 Nov. 1643. Rovito, 'Rivoluzione', 374, quoting a *consulta* of the Council of Italy in August 1647, claims that 70,000 Neapolitans had invested in loans to be repaid from taxes.

20. Comparato, 'Toward the revolt', 280–1 and 315 (quotation from the 'Istoria' of Carlo Calà,); AGS *SP libro* 324/53, *consulta* of Council of Italy, 8 July 1647, noted that the tax on meat 'almost exceeds twice the sale price'.

21. Palermo, *Narrazioni*, 347, Medici to Grand Duke, 18 June and 25 June 1647.

22. Graniti, *Diario di Francesco Capecelatro*, I, 8–9 and 12–13, on the 'pessimo consiglio', 'gravissimo errore' and 'il secondo gravissimo errore che fece el duca d'Arcos'. Capecelatro was a colonel and so knew whereof he spoke. Santa Coloma had made exactly the same error in Barcelona in 1640 (ch. 9 above), which make Arcos's failure to learn from experience seem even more foolish.

23. Howell, *Exact historie*, 13; Capograssi, 'La rivoluzione', 178, Andrea Rosso to Doge, 9 July 1647. Tutini, *Racconto*, 19–21, claims the first leader of the revolt was 'un tale siciliano' who urged the crowd to demand the repeal of *all* gabelles, as in Palermo, until he was shot in a street brawl, opening the way for Masaniello to take over.

24. Graniti, *Diario di Francesco Capecelatro*, I, 15 and II, 67 ('Tenevano i popolari, come solevano, alberato lo stendardo rosso al torrione del Carmelo in segno di guerra'). On the goading by Sicilian refugees see BNE *Ms* 2662/4v–5, 'Relación del tumulto' prepared by or for Arcos ('Mezcláronse algunos Palermitanos . . .'); and *Cartas de algunos padres*, VII (*MHE*, XIX), 37–8, duchess of Arcos to her uncle, [15 July] 1647.

25. Palermo, *Narrazioni*, 385, Filomarino to Innocent X, 12 July 1647; Comparato, 'Toward the revolt', 306, quoting the diary of the notary Giovan Francesco Montanaro. Many sources dispute Masaniello's age and place of birth, but Graniti, *Diario di Francesco Capecelatro*, I, notes pp. 28–9, printed his entry in the baptismal register of Santa Caterina in Foro on 29 June 1620. He also married there in 1641. On the number of 'ragazzi', see ch. 19 below.

26. BNE *Ms* 2662/5–5v ('Relación del tumulto') and 41, Arcos to Philip IV, 15 July 1647, copy; Howell, *Exact history*, 26–30.

27. Howell, *Exact history*, 36–7, printed the list of 60 houses scheduled to be burned; Comparato, 'Toward the revolt', 308–10, categorized their owners; Musi, *La rivolta di Masaniello*, 103, showed the overlap between the list of those whose houses must be torched and Genoino's enemies.

28. Palermo, *Narrazioni*, 381, Filomarino to Innocent X, 8 July 1647 'alle 18 ore', or about 5 p.m.; Capograssi, 'La revoluzione', 181, Rosso to Doge, 9 July 1647, notes the unacceptable pardon.

29. Howell, *Exact history*, 85–95, gives the text of the 'Capitoli'; Musi, *La rivolta*, 338–40, analyzes their content; BNE *Ms* 2662/10, 'Relación', gives Arcos's view.

30. Capograssi, 'La revoluzione', 211, Rosso to Doge, 17 Sep. 1647. Tutini, *Racconto*, 137–8, recorded that 'molti preti di non buona vita' formed a militia company in Aug. 1647.

31. Tutini, *Racconto*, 24, and Correra, 'Inedita relazione', 362, on food at half price.

32. Capograssi, 'La revoluzione', 184, Rosso to Doge, and Palermo, *Narrazioni*, 387, Filomarino to Innocent X, both dated 16 July 1647. BNE *Ms* 2662/14v–15, 'Relación', describes in detail Arcos's arrangements for the murder, including his vow to donate a statue of the Virgin worth 2,000 ducats and provide dowries for 50 girls each year if the plot succeeded. Musi, *La rivolta*, 119–20, details rewards paid to the murderers.

33. Correra, 'Inedita relazione', 380; Capograssi, 'La revoluzione', 185, Rosso to Doge, 23 July 1647; Tontoli, *Il Mas'Aniello*, 154–5, BNE *Ms* 2662/16v–17; Musi, *La rivolta*, 123–31.

34. Hugon, *Naples*, 95 and 100, quoting the Tuscan and French envoys. Other data from ibid., 92–100.

35. Di Marzo, *Biblioteca storica*, III, 113–18 and 150–1.

36. La Lumia, *Storie siciliane*, IV, 127–33, prints the *49 Capitoli.*

37. Di Marzo, *Biblioteca storica*, IV, 174–5 (Pirri on the edict of 12 Oct., and on the arrival of the news from Naples).

38. AGS *SP* leg 1,444, n.p., *consulta* of 17 June (the same *legajo* contains Los Vélez's letter of 23 May, which had been deciphered and endorsed 'Received 16 June', so the council acted promptly); AGS *SP* 218/72, *consulta* of 27 Aug. 1647, reviewing many letters about the revolt of Naples.

39. ACA *CA* 679/4, *consulta* of 9 Mar. 1649, citing the archbishop's letter of 24 Sep. 1647; Seco Serrano, *Cartas*, I, 118, Philip IV to Sor María, 21 Aug. 1647, in reply to her letter of 1 Aug. (ibid., 117). On the 'troubles' in Valencia, see Casey, 'La Crisi General del segle XVII'.

40. Villari, *Per il re o per la patria*, 145–72, prints the key documents on Genoino's arrest and deportation. In the event, the viceroy of Sardinia sent Genoino to Spain to explain his actions but, aged 80, he died first.

41. Rovito, 'La rivoluzione', 414–17; Comparato, 'Toward the revolt', 312–15; and Musi, *La rivolta*, 138–43.

42. Graniti, *Diario di Francesco Capecelatro*, II, 46 (interestingly, red and black had been Masaniello's colours); Capograssi, 'La rivoluzione', 216–18, Rosso to Doge, 8 Oct. 1647; Conti, *Le leggi*, 52–3, proclamation of 25 Oct. 1647. The declaration was also published in Barcelona: Villari, *Elogi della dissimulazione*, 119.

43. Chéruel, *Lettres*, II, 466, Mazarin to Fontenay-Mareuil, 25 July 1647 (the day after he heard of Masaniello's revolt); xlvii–xlviii and 931, three letters to Cardinal Grimaldi, 26 July. See also Chéruel, *Histoire*, II, 381–2, on the council's decision on 30 July 1647.

44. Coryate's *crudities*, 92–3, 99: the author walked through the duchy in 1608. Manzoni's novel, *I promessi sposi*, provides a vivid and realistic portrait of the catastrophe. See also chs 8 and 9 above.

45. Vigo, *Nel cuore*, 37, quoting Count Onofrio Castelli; Raymond, *Itinerary*, 240; de Beer, *Diary of John Evelyn*, II, 501. D'Amico, 'Rebirth', 699, argues that the plague of 1630 halved the population of the city, but that it recovered from 75,000 in 1633 to 100,000 in 1648.

46. Buono, *Esercito*, 114–22, on Visconti's mission, quoting his Instructions of May 1640 and his report on an audience with Olivares on 4 July.

47. Ibid., 123–4, Council of Italy to Philip IV, 28 June 1641; Maffi, *Il baluardo*, 31, Philip IV to governor of Lombardy, 7 May 1641.

48. Maffi, *Il baluardo*, 40, Philip IV to governor of Lombardy, 30 Dec. 1643, 362 nn. 70–1, letters of Mar. 1648, and the tables at 340–4; Maffi, 'Milano in guerra', 403, Bartolomeo Arese to Philip IV, 29 July 1647.

49. Giannini, 'Un caso di stabilità', 153, quoting the Venetian resident in Milan on 7 Aug. 1647; and Signorotto, 'Stabilità', 734, Raimundo de la Torre to duke of Ferrara, 28 Aug. 1647 (an explicit link with events in Naples).

50. AGS *Estado* 3365/44–6, *consulta* of the Spanish Council of State, 14 Feb. 1648, enclosing a report of the arrest and a copy of Piantanida's manifesto. I thank Dr Davide Maffi for information on the plots: personal communication, October 2003.

51. Chéruel, *Histoire*, II, 433–4, Mazarin to Duplessis-Praslin, 29 Oct. 1647.

52. Giannini, 'Un caso di stabilità', 106–7, quoting Gualdo Priorato, *Relatione della città di Milano* (1666). Historical research has corroborated this controversial assertion, demonstrating the Lombard elite's unfaltering commitment to the Spanish Habsburg: see for instance Signorotto, *Milano spagnolo*, 32–4, 57, 131–45, 171–203; Maffi, *Il baluardo*, 176–91, 195–208; idem, *La cittadella*, 118–144; Rizzo, ' "Ottima gente da guerra" ', and idem, 'Influencia social'.

53. Mario Rizzo graciously drew my attention both to the emergence of a 'convivenza lombardo-asburgica' and to Spain's successful policy of creating Lombard 'stakeholders' in the regime: personal communications in Jan. and June 2007; his article ' "Rivoluzione dei consumi" ', 542; and his book *Alloggiamenti militari*, 146.

54. Venice and other states in the lower Po valley that suffered cruelly from the crisis of 1628–31 also remained politically quiescent in the 1640s and 1650s: see Sella, 'The survival', and Faccini, *La Lombardia*, 251–5.

55. In his 'Manifesto' of 4 Dec. 1647, Guise claimed that he reached an agreement with Annese on 24 Oct., two days before the declaration of the Republic: Conti, *Le legge*, 147–9. In his Memoirs, he claimed 'I was the first to suggest to them the title of "Republic" ': Petitot and Monmerque, *Mémoires du duc de Guise*, I, 89–90 (see pp. 85–90 for his earlier efforts). Chéruel, *Histoire*, II, 444–5, proves that Guise's alleged letter of support from Louis XIV was forged; Reinach, *Receuil*, X, 24, Mazarin to Duplessis-Besançon, 6 Apr. 1648, stressed his opposition to the idea of a Republic in Naples – ironically, the Republic collapsed that same day.

56. BL, C.55.i.3, *Documenti originali relativi alla rivoluzione di Tommaso Aniello*, is a collection of some 200 original *bandi*, many published in Conti, *Le legge*. Villari, *Elogio*, 60, notes the Italian translation of Alessandro de Ros's history of the Catalan revolt, published in Naples. Donzelli, *Partenope liberata, Parte 1a* (licensed by Annese and dedicated to Guise) took the story up to Guise's coup; Part II, which exists only in manuscript, narrated the rest of the story.

57. Conti, *Le legge*, 67–9 and 183–4, edicts of 4 Nov. and 17 Dec. 1647, exhorting the *regnicoli* to join the Republic.

58. Ibid., 150–2, edicts of 4–5 Dec. 1647.

59. Ibid., 198–9, 211–13, 245, edicts of 23–24 Dec. 1647 (Guise's proclamation of himself *Duce*), 30 Dec. 1647 (a Constitution for the 'most serene and royal republic), and 12 Jan. 1648; Graniti, *Diario di Francesco Capecelatro*, II, 376 (entry of 27 Dec. 1647).

60. *Co. Do. In*, LXXXIV, 129–30, Peñaranda to Pedro Coloma, 7 Feb. 1648; and 513–16, "Relaciones" by Peñaranda retracing the course of diplomatic negotiations, 1651. On the terms see chs 8 and 9 above. Philip signed the decree on 1 Oct. 1647.

61. Conti, *Le legge*, 382, edict on the banks, 31 Mar. 1648 – four days before the Spanish troops re-entered the city.

62. Benigno, *Specchi*, 282–3, on the arrival 16 Mar. 1648 of the news from Paris (see ch. 11).

63. AGS *SP libro* 443/31–32v, Philip IV to Oñate, 12 June 1648; *SP libro* 218/93 and 94, *consultas* of 17 and 20 May 1648 recommending the arrest and trial of Arcos. Hugon, *Naples*, 241–2, notes the rewards heaped upon d'Andrea.

64. Di Marzo, *Biblioteca storica*, III, 176–8 (Auria) records rain and 'scarsezza di fromento' throughout Sicily.

65. AHN *Estado libro* 455, n.p. royal rescript to a *consulta* of 18 July 1648; Di Marzo, *Biblioteca storica*, III, 332–3 (Auria); La Lumia, *Storie Siciliane*, IV, 117–19.

66. Ribot García, *La Monarquía*, 15.

67. Ribot García, *La revuelta*, 120, *consulta* of the Council of Italy, 9 Sep. 1669, and 124 n. 272, biography of Hoyo. France had sent its fleet to save Crete from the Turks, and the island's surrender (page 208 above) deprived it of a mission.

68. Ribot García, *La revuelta*, 166, viceroy to queen regent of Spain, 28 Sep. 1672. At pp. 141–2 Ribot lists and describes the numerous urban bread riots of 1671–2; and at 216–36 he lists the known members of the two factions.

69. Ribot García, *La Monarquía*, 34, Marquis of Astorga to queen regent, 27 July and 5 Aug. 1674.

70. Ibid., 45, Louis XIV to his ambassador in Rome (charged with coordinating French policy towards Messina), 7 Sep. 1674. On the similar assumptions of Richelieu and Mazarin, see chs 9 and 10 above, and 17 below.

71. Ibid., 119, quoting Louis's *Mémoires*.

72. Ibid., 638. Olivares quoted page 290 above.

73. Ribot García, *La Monarquía*, 524–618, expertly surveys these questions of loyalty during the rebellion and the war.

74. Lottin, *Vie et mentalité*, ch. 4, 'Français malgré lui'.

75. Di Marzo, *Biblioteca storica*, III, 332–3 (Auria); La Lumia, *Storie Siciliane*, IV, 117–19.

76. AGS *SP libro* 443/31–32v, Philip IV to Oñate, the new viceroy, 12 June 1648. See also *SP libro* 218/37 *consulta* of 5 May 1648, reluctantly agreeing to confirm Don Juan's concessions to the rebels; and Fusco, 'Il viceré di Napoli', 150, on the 'tax holiday' conceded to Naples after the plague of 1656.

Chapter 15   The 'dark continents'

1. I am very grateful to Dauril Alden, Rayne Allinson, John Brooke, William Russell Coil, Ross Hassig, Karen Ordahl Kupperman, John Lamphear, Kathryn Magee Labelle, Joseph C. Miller, Margaret Newell, Carla Pestana and Jason Warren for their valuable suggestions for improving this chapter; and to Andrew Ashbrook, Nicole Emke and Maria Widman for drawing to my attention sources on New England and New France.

2. Kessell, *Kiva*, 170; Richter, 'War and culture', 537. Both authors based their estimates on contemporary calculations.

3. Villalba, 'Climatic fluctuations', 355–6, shows that glaciers as well as the annual width and carbon-14 deposits in tree rings in Patagonia registered strikingly colder periods in the mid-seventeenth century. Further data from the 'natural archive' at www.ncdc.noaa.gov/paleo/ftp-treering.html show much the same pattern.

4. Ch. 1 above discusses the simultaneous increase in El Niño, volcanic and seismic activity in the mid-seventeenth century, and the possibility that they are connected.

5. McNeill, *Mosquito empires*, 91.

6. Franklin, 'Observations' (1751), paras 6–7. On the demographic history of New England, see Canny, *The origins*, 211–12; and Fischer, *Albion's seed*, 76–7.

7. *Winthrop papers*, III, 166, letter to Sir Nathaniel Rich, 22 May 1634 (only 2–3 adult deaths among the 4,000 colonists who arrived the previous year, and few child deaths); Wood, *New England* (1634), 4; Morton, *New English Canaan* (1637), 94; Anon., *New England's First Fruits* (1643), 246. Compare the description of the constant coughing and spitting of Londoners in ch. 3 above.

8. Percy, '*Trewe relacyon*' (written 1625, but describing 1609–10); Stahle, 'The lost colony', 567. Herrmann, 'The "tragicall historie"', suggests that the stories about the 'starveinge tyme' may have grown more horrific in retelling.

9. Kingsbury, *The records*, III, 485–90, Company to Governor of Virginia, London, 25 July 1621; and IV, 73–4, George Sandys to his brother Samuel, Jamestown, 30 Mar. 1623. Stahle, 'The lost colony', fig. 15, shows the drought of 1621–2 as recorded in the 'natural archive'.

10. Morton, *New English Canaan*, 94–5 and 121–2; on the landmark winter of 1641–2, see ch. 1 above; on that of 1657–8, see Collin, 'Observations' (citing the records of 'New Sweden').

11. See the quantitative data in Canny, *The origins*, 182–3 and 223–7, and Fischer, *Albion's seed*, 277. On El Niño, malaria and British Jamaica, see McNeill, *Mosquito empires*, 103.

12. Cushman, *The sin and danger*, 8; Morton, *New English Canaan*, 23; Salisbury, *Manitou and Providence*, 106.

13. Starna, 'The Pequots', 44.

14. *Winthrop papers*, III, 149 and 167, letters to John Endicott, 3 Jan. 1634, and to Sir Nathaniel Rich, 22 May 1634. Starna, 'The Pequots', 44–6, noted that native remedies like 'sweating' exacerbated rather than ameliorated some European diseases, and also suggested that some 'indigenous pathogens' such as tuberculosis and

syphilis, like smallpox and yellow fever, also 'appeared in increasingly virulent forms' in the seventeenth century.

15. *Winthrop papers*, III, 240, Williams to John Winthrop, Providence [3 July 1637]. Other details and quotations from Grandjean, 'New world tempests', 77–87.

16. Dunn, *Journal*, 75 (6 Nov. 1634). Figures from Starna. 'The Pequots', and Hauptman, 'The Pequot War'.

17. Gardiner, *History*, 10.

18. Underhill, *Newes*, 40, 81; Bradford, *History*, 339. Mason, *Brief History*, 10, put the death toll at 700, but neither he nor Underhill attempted a 'body count'. Hoffer, *Sensory worlds*, 277 n. 40, provides an ingenious calculation based on topography and ethnography that supports the lower figure of 400 proposed by Bradford and Underhill.

19. Salisbury, *Manitou and Providence*, 222; Mason, *A brief history*, 17; Karr, "'Why should you be so furious?"', 907 (quoting the treaty of Hartford, 21 Sep. 1638); Anon., *New England's First Fruits in respect of the progress of learning, in the Colledge at Cambridge in Massachusetts-Bay*, 246 (this marks Harvard's first serious effort at fund-raising in England).

20. Dunn, *Journal*, 181, 186, 256. See also the details in ch. 1 above.

21. Cressy, *Coming over*, 201, quoting *A brief relation of the state of New England* (London, 1689) by Increase Mather, who himself briefly returned to England. The regicide was Colonel Vincent Potter. Vane and Peter were executed after 1660 for their opposition to Charles I, even though they did not sign his death warrant. On their careers in England, and on the fate of Laud and Strafford, see chs 11 and 12 above.

22. Bradstreet, 'A dialogue', 189–90. (I deduce the date because, having spoken of the 1642 campaign, she wrote 'The seed time's come' which implies spring 1643.) Felons were hanged at Tyburn.

23. Pestana, *The English Atlantic*, 38, Freeholders of Barbados to the earl of Warwick, 1646. Pestana notes that the six colonies favouring the king all belonged to 'proprietors' whose powers stemmed from royal grants, whereas most of the settlements founded after 1629, often by the king's Puritan critics, declared for Parliament.

24. Anon., *New England's First Fruits*, 246.

25. Webb, *1676*, xv, uses the phrase 'concatenation of disasters' and mentions 'storm and plague' as well as 'Indian insurrection and civil war', but his book scarcely mentions natural disasters.

26. *CSPC 1675–1676*, 368, Governor Sir Jonathan Atkins to Secretary Williamson, Barbados, 3 Apr. 1676.

27. Gardiner, *History*, 26. Gardiner (architect of Fort Saybrook) was on Long Island with the Montauk when Miantonomo delivered his appeal in summer 1642. The sachem's injunction not to kill the cows offers eloquent testimony regarding the scarcity of other fauna.

28. 'Articles of Confederation of the United Colonies of New England', 19 May 1643, expanded 7 Sep. 1643: http://avalon.law.yale.edu/17th_century/art1613.asp, accessed 29 June 2011.

29. *CSPC 1675–1676*, 365, Berkeley to Secretary Williamson, 1 Apr. 1676.

30. Leach, *A Rhode Islander reports on King Philip's War*, 20–1. Briffa and Osborne's tree-ring records for Quebec and the Chesapeake both show the disastrous growing season of 1675. On livestock as a source of conflict in New England, see Anderson, *Creatures of Empire*.

31. *CSPC 1675–1676*, 366, Berkeley to Thomas Ludwell, his agent in London, 1 Apr. 1676.

32. Written evidence for the poor New England harvest of 1676 is hard to find, so I am grateful to Jason Warren for bringing to my attention Connecticut State Archives, *War: Colonial series I, 1675–1775*, Record Group 2, part 2, doc. 95, Secretary Allyn to the Assistants of New Haven and Fairfield Counties, Hartford, 27 June 1676, all about the need to remedy the shortage of wheat and 'Indian Corn'.

33. Quotations from Slotkin and Folsom, *So dreadfull a judgment*, 3–4; and Webb, *1676*, 411 and xvi. Other data from Mandell, *King Philip's War*, 134–7; and Warren, 'Connecticut unscathed', 18, 22–3.

34. *Massachusetts Historical Society Collections*, 4th ser., IX (1871), 184–7, 'Declaration of Nathaniel Bacon in the Name of the People of Virginia, July 30, 1676'; Webb, *1676*, 64–5.

35. Quotations from Webb, *1676*, 201–2 (for the quotations from Ireland echoed here, see chs 11 and 12 above). The royal fleet entered the Chesapeake in Jan. 1677 and accomplished its mission; but disease among the crews prevented it from proceeding to Boston as planned.

36. The Iroquois comprised five, later six, groups divided into two 'moieties': the Cayugas, Oneidas and, later, Tuscaroras, were the 'younger brothers' who deferred to the Mohawks, Onondagas and Senecas, the 'older brothers'. In the seventeenth century leaders of all the groups met regularly to discuss matters of mutual interest.

37. Ball and Porter, *Fighting Words*, 67, Tecumseh's plea to the Choctaw and Chickasaw in 1811. Interestingly, like seventeenth-century leaders, Tecumseh claimed that a comet and major earthquake that year vindicated his cause.

38. Henripin, *La population canadienne*, 3, 8, 13, 73, and graph on p. 128; Charbonneau, *Naissance*, 81 96–7, 128, 146–7. Totals in Dumas, *Les filles du roi*, 48 and 122. For Vauban's estimate, see ch. 21 below.

39. See Mann, *Iroquois women*, 241 (quotation) and 261–6 (on birth control).

40. Van der Donck, *A description* (1653), 184. See also Cook, *Born to die*, 192–8.

41. Van der Donck, *A description*, 210 (who appended to his account a special section 'Of the beaver'); Richards, *The unending frontier*, 467 (part of an excellent chapter on the American fur trade).

42. Brook, *Vermeer's Hat*, 31; Elliott, *Empires*, 63, quoting William Bradford. Like 'Mughals' (ch. 13 above, n. 1), the names of the Indian Nations used by the Europeans were rarely correct: the *Hurons* ('Boar's bristle' in

French) called themselves *Wendats*, 'Islanders'; *Mohawk* was an Algonquin insult meaning 'Cannibals'; while the *Iroquois* (the opprobrious Huron term for them, meaning 'Snakes') called themselves *Haudenosaunee*, 'Builders of the Longhouse'. *Algonquin* meant simply 'Allies'.

43. Thwaites, *Jesuit Relations*, XXIV, 295, Isaac Jogues, S. J., 'from the village of the Iroquois', 30 June 1643.

44. I thank Kathryn Magee Labelle for sharing with me the conclusions of her thesis 'Dispersed but not destroyed leadership, women and power in the Wendat diaspora, 1600–1701' (Ohio State University, 2011).

45. Perrot, *The Indian tribes*, 102 (the author lived in the region in 1665–84 as hunter, interpreter and official).

46. White, *The middle ground*, 41 and 48–9, quoting an account of La Salle's voyage down the Mississippi in 1682 These refugees included the ancestors of Tecumseh (page 455 above), who settled in what is now Alabama.

47. Richards, *The unending frontier*, 502–3.

48. Ibid., 504, 509.

49. Galloway, *Choctaw genesis*, 347–8.

50. Ibid., xiii; Cook et al., 'Drought reconstructions'; NOAA reconstructions for the Ozark highlands (by Stahl and Cleaveland: disastrous drought 1639–45); and Arizona, New Mexico and Utah (Cook: severe drought 1666–70). I thank Russell Barsch for alerting me to the oral tradition of the 'dogless period'.

51. DuVal, *The native ground*; White, *The middle ground*.

52. Smulders, *António Vieira's Sermon*, 164–6.

53. Van den Boogaart, *Johan Maurits*, 477, on yellow fever; Hemming, *Red gold*, 293, quoting two letters from São Luis: one by a Dutch official on 7 Apr. 1642, the other by the captain general of Maranhão on 14 Mar. 1645, who accused the Dutch of waging biological warfare because they 'brought with them Indians with smallpox, which is the plague of that land. They thus killed the majority of the best people in our Indian aldeias and almost all the settlers' slaves.'

54. Israel, *Diasporas*, 369, quoting Rabbi Isaac Aboab da Fonseca.

55. Ibid., 390–1, estimates the Jewish population of Dutch Brazil at 1,500 in 1645 and 650 by 1650, including Menassah ben Israel's brother. Some sailed directly to the Dutch and English colonies in North America, while others returned to the Dutch Republic.

56. Schwartz, 'Panic'; Álvarez de Toledo, 'Crisis', 272–4, quoting Don Juan de Palafox to Philip IV, 10 July 1641.

57. García Acosta, *Desastres agrícolas*, I, 176–9: data on 'carestía', 'hambre' and 'falta de lluvias', 1639–43.

58. Information and quotations from Crewe, 'Brave New Spain', based on the copious Inquisition records and a volume of Don Guillén's confiscated papers. His article includes a portrait of Don Guillén by Van Dijk (p. 61). See ch. 18 below on his later history.

59. AGI *Lima* 50/289–90, Viceroy Mancera to Philip IV, 8 June 1641, noted reports of the Portuguese revolt just received from Cartagena; AGI *Lima* 277, n.p., same to same, 22 July 1641, admitted that he had not believed the reports until confirmation came from Buenos Aires; AGI *Lima* 572 *libro* 52/234v, same to same, 23 July 1642, reported the Transandean expedition.

60. Schwartz, 'Panic', 220–1, quoting Mancera to Philip IV, 20 July 1642. It seems highly unlikely that the unfortunate Africans in the capital would 'love' the brutal slave drivers who had dragged them across the Andes.

61. Rosales, *Historia general*, 192–3, on earthquakes; Prieto, 'The Paraná river floods', on 'Ciudad Vieja'; García Acosta, *Desastres agrícolas*, I, 178, quoting the *Historia de Nuevo León*; Miguel Sánchez, *Imagen de la Virgen María* (Mexico, 1648); and Luis Laso de la Vega, *Huei tlamahuiçoltica* ('The Great Happening': Mexico, 1649). By 1730, the 'milagrosa imagen' had been taken on procession 24 times to intercede for rain, and one-third of these events occurred between 1641 and 1668.

62. Pérez de Ribas, *History*, 42; Treib, *Sanctuaries*, 268–95, with splendid photos of the surviving Salinas ruins.

63. Reff, 'Contact shock', 270. The revolt by the remaining Pueblo populations in 1680 destroyed (among other things) the archives that would have shed light on their earlier decline.

64. McNeill, *Mosquito empires*, 64. García Acosta, *Desastres agrícolas*, I, 181, quoting López Cogolludo, *Historia de Yucatán*. See also Cook, *Born to die*, 180 (part of an excellent overview of the epidemics that afflicted Latin America at pp. 167–82); and Kiple and Higgins, 'Yellow fever'.

65. Schiebinger, *Plants and empire*, 1, quoting the commentary to plate 45 of Merian's *Metamorphosis insectorum Surinamensium* – thus a book about caterpillars! Schiebinger presents more contemporary reports of slave abortion and infanticide at pp. 144–9.

66. Van Deusen, *Between the sacred and the worldly*, 11–12 (quote) and 176–7 (population). On European nuns, see ch. 4 above.

67. Lorandi, *Spanish king of the Incas*. See pp. 143–4 and 166 on his guns.

68. Guibovich and Domínguez, 'Para la biografía', describe the riots.

69. Glave, *Trajinantes*, 198–205, reviews the 'unease, disturbances and revolts' of the 1660s but finds no hard evidence of coordination (quotation at p. 199 n. 31, from a letter of 1671). AGI *Escribanía de Cámara* 561–565 contain testimony and evaluations concerning the 'revolt of Laicacota'.

70. McLeod, *Spanish Central America*, 217–23 and 307–9.

71. Van Deusen, *Between the sacred and the worldly*, 40, 241 n. 59 (quoting the history of the *Casa de Niñas Expósitas*); Mazet, 'Population et société', 61; and Mannarelli, *Pecados públicos*, 168–72, 251–2 (note, however, that Mannarelli's tables, from two parishes, represent only a quinquennial *sampling* of data. ibid., p. 169 n. 21).

72. Suárez, 'La "crisis"', 317.
73. Figures and details from Suárez, 'La "crisis"' and idem, *Desafíos transatlánticos*; and from Andrien, *Crisis and decline*, 34, 188–9 and 205.
74. Thom, *Journal*, I, 292–3 (10 Feb. 1655). See also Elphick, *Kraal and castle*, 110–16. 'Khoe' is the Nama word for 'person', and 'Khoekhoen' (Khoikhoi in some earlier sources) is the Nama word for 'people'.
75. Thom, *Journal*, III, 195–7 (5–6 Apr. 1660). Van Riebeeck concluded the meeting by telling the Khoekhoen leaders that, if they did not like his offer, they could try to 'drive us off. In such a case they would . . . become the owners of the fort and everything and would remain the owners for as long as they could retain it. If this alternative suited them, we would see what our course of action was to be' (ibid., 196).
76. Diaz and Markgraf, *El Niño*, 144; Mikhail, *Nature and empire*, 216–17; and Ibrahim, *Al-Azmat*, Appendix 11 on the Nile. See also ch. 7 above.
77. Webster, *Chronology*, 1. See a similar lament concerning West Africa in Harms, *River of wealth*, 8–9.
78. Webster, *Chronology*, chs 2 and 9, on Interlacustrine Africa; and Hathaway, *Beshir Agha*, 18–19, on the slave exodus from East Africa.
79. Based on the lucid analysis of Curtin, *Economic change*, 15–18.
80. Hair, *Barbot*, 76 and 83–4; Curtin, *Economic change, Supplementary evidence*, 3.
81. On the Niger Bend, see Curtin, *Economic change, Supplementary evidence*, 5; on Lake Chad, see Nicholson, 'Methodology'; and Martinson, *Natural climate variability*, 32–5 (by Nicholson).
82. Ritchie, 'Deux textes', 339, from Chambonneau's *Histoire de Tourbenan* (1678).
83. Ritchie, 'Deux textes', 352.
84. Details from Webb, *Desert frontier*, 24–35, and 68–87; and Alden and Miller, 'Unwanted cargoes', 47–8 and 78.
85. Hair, *Barbot*, 434; Thornton, *Warfare*, 15–16.
86. Harms, *River*, 33; Georg Oldendorp, quoted by Thornton, 'Warfare', 129 (see also Hair, 'The enslavement').
87. Hard copies of material from the database www.slavevoyages.org (which is regularly updated) are available in Eltis and Richardson, *Atlas*. Data in this paragraph from the maps on p. 14–15 and tables on pp. 23 and 89.
88. Climate data from Miller, 'The significance', 43–6; Thornton, 'Demography'; and Alden and Miller, 'Unwanted cargoes', 48, 78. In some years in the mid-seventeenth century, *all* slaves deported came from West Central Africa: http://www.slavevoyages.org/tast/assessment/estimates.faces
89. Boxer, 'Portuguese and Dutch colonial rivalry', 35 n. 78, Teixeira to John IV, Luanda, 10 Apr. 1653. Note that expeditionary forces from Brazil, not Europe, changed the allegiance of Angola in both 1641 and 1648.
90. Birmingham, *The Portuguese*, and Thornton, *Kingdom*, narrate these events; Miller, 'The significance', 25–8, links them to climate change.
91. Eltis and Richardson, *Atlas*, 192 and 194, 'Linguistic identifications of liberated Africans who embarked in Cameroon' and 'in the Sierra Leone region' in the early nineteenth century; and 163 ('Gender and age of slaves carried from African regions to the Caribbean, 1545–1700), and passim (quotations from ships' logs). The authors note one important exception: 'In West Central Africa other kinds of evidence suggest that slaves traveled much longer distances prior to embarkation.'
92. Grove, 'Revolutionary weather', 128. Heinrich, 'Interdecadal modulation', 63, noted the absence of suitable trees.
93. Martinson, *Natural climate variability*, 27; Mikami, *Proceedings*, 15; Cook, 'Warm season temperatures', 84, fig. 7A. Although on the previous page Cook and his co-authors declare that 'There is little indication for a "Little Ice Age" period of unusual cold', their graph shows a clear dip in 'warm-season temperature reconstruction' during the mid-seventeenth century. The same phenomenon appears in Pollack, 'Five centuries', 705, fig. 4A, while fig. 4B shows an even sharper dip in tree-rings from New Zealand.
94. Diaz and Markgraf, *El Niño*, 161–5.
95. Cane, 'Australian aboriginal subsistence', 395–6; Connor, *Australian frontier wars*, 2. Parenti, *Tropic of chaos*, correlates the rise in violence in Africa with times of climatic adversity.
96. Cane, 'Australian aboriginal subsistence', 391 and 431 (quotations). The previous paragraphs are closely based on Cane's research.
97. See the bark painting of Namarrkon, the 'Lightning spirit', from northern Australia in Sherratt, *A change in the weather*, 30.

Chapter 16   Getting it Right

1. I thank Hayami Akira for guiding my steps through Japanese demographic, economic and social history ever since my first visit to Japan in 1983; Mary Elizabeth Berry for a trenchant critique of earlier drafts of this chapter; William S. Atwell, Reinier Hesselink; Kishimoto Mio and Ronald P. Toby for valuable bibliographical advice; Matthew Keith and Taguchi Kojiro for assistance in researching, translating and interpreting Japanese materials; and the scholars who attended two seminars on this book organized by Professor Hayami at International House of Japan, Tokyo, in July 2010.
2. Elison, 'The cross and the sword', 55, quoting Ōta Gyūichi c. 1610 and Miura Jōshin in 1614; Reade, *Sidelights*, I, 183, Isaac Wake to Secretary of State Naunton, 15 June 1618; Lancellotti, page 397 above.

3. Figures from Smith, *The agrarian origins*, 3; Hayami, *Economic history*, 36–40; and idem, *Population and family*, 10–11 (suggesting a 1600 population total of 12m ± 2m). Note that rice production per village rose more slowly after 1700 (from an average of 2,340 bushels to only 2,400 bushels in 1830) – a further index of the remarkable strides made in the seventeenth century.

4. Figures and quotation from Hayami, *Economic history*, 43, 163 and 218.

5. Quotations from Totman, 'Tokugawa peasants', 465; statistics from Totman, *The green archipelago*, 53, 65, 68. See also the discussion of 'ecological strategies in Tokugawa Japan' in Richards, *Unending frontier*, 148–92.

6. Ono, *Enomoto Yazaemon*, 137–8; Nagakura, 'Kan'ei no kikin', 78–80, gives prices. The Kan'ei era began in 1624 and ended in 1643. Endō, *Kinsei seikatsushi nempyō*, 49–70, lists the natural disasters of this period while Yamamoto, *Kan'ei jidai*, 197–9, discusses many of them. Further data on the Kan'ei famine in Atwell, 'Some observations', 224–7; Atwell, 'A seventeenth-century "General Crisis"', 239–40; and ch. 1 above.

7. *Diaries kept by the heads of the Dutch factories*, VI, 87: entry for 15 July 1642, reporting news from the Japanese translators ('de tolcken') attached to the Dutch factory at Nagasaki.

8. Geerts, 'The Arima rebellion', 57–61 and 96–8, Koekebacker to van Diemen, Hirado, 18 Jan. and 25 Mar. 1638 (translated directly from the Dutch text, since Geerts's English translation is sometimes unreliable); contemporary Christian circulars quoted in Elison, *Deus destroyed*, 220–1. The 'messiah's original name was Masuda Shirō but, since he later took the name of the island of his birth, the sources call him Amakusa Shirō.

9. Bix, *Peasant protest*, xxii, on revolts; Fukuda, 'Political process', 55–8, on feuds.

10. Hayami, *Population and family*, 6–8; and idem, *Population, family and society*, 42–51 and 64–72. Hayami invented the now popular phrase 'Industrious Revolution' in a 1977 article.

11. Hayami, *Population and family*, 26–7. Hayami defined as 'rich' those who harvested 50 bushels or more of rice annually, and as 'poor' those who harvested only 5 bushels less.

12. Kazuki Gyûzan, *Fujin jusô*, discussed by Hanley and Nakamura, *Economic and demographic change*, 233–4. The Japanese, like the Chinese, seem to have considered infanticide as a sort of late-term abortion, and applied the term *mabiki* indiscriminately to both.

13. Cooper, *They came to Japan*, 58, quoting a letter from Cocks, English Factor in Hirado, 10 Dec. 1614. Cornell, 'Infanticide', argued that infanticide happened rarely – but ignored both contemporary testimony like that of Richard Cocks and demographic reconstructions like that of Smith, *Nakahara*. I thank Richard Smethurst for information on the 'abortion plaques' he observed in Zōjōji temple in Tokyo, founded in 1605. A typical message reads 'We'll meet in the next world and I'll apologize in person.'

14. Smith, *The agrarian origins*, 3, notes that surviving land registers compiled in early modern Japan 'reveal a remarkably uniform pattern of landholding'. The rest of this paragraph relies heavily on Smith's magisterial overview. Compare Fig. 10 above: the structure of a 'typical' European village.

15. Cooper, *This island of Japan*, 75–6 (by João Rodrigues, S. J.). Berry, *Japan*, 33 and 261, and Farris, *Japan's medieval population*, 191–208, argue that the last campaigns of the civil wars, although fewer, did extensive damage because of the increased size of the armies.

16. Cooper, *They came to Japan*, 57, Cocks to the earl of Salisbury, 10 Dec. 1614, about the innovations just introduced by Tokugawa Ieyasu.

17. Tsunoda et al., *The sources of Japanese tradition*, 328–31, prints Hideyoshi's 'Sword collection edict' (1588) and 'Restrictions on change of status and residence' (1591). Berry, *Hideyoshi*, 102–10, expertly discusses these edicts, noting that both were 'absolutely without precedent in Japan'.

18. Yamamura, 'From coins to rice', 359, from Hideyoshi's instructions to his surveyors, 1594. For more on the remarkable *Taikō kenchi*, see Berry, *Hideyoshi*, 111–18; Berry, *Japan*, 82–8; Brown, 'Practical constraints'; and idem, 'The mismeasurement'. Hideyoshi introduced the *kokudaka* system to his own estates c. 1580: Wakita, 'The *kokudaka* system'. Note the contrast between Hideyoshi's survey and the disastrous miscalculation of the resources of Catalonia and Castile by the count-duke of Olivares: ch. 9 above.

19. Yonemoto, *Mapping*, 9–16, and Berry, *Japan*, 40–3, 88–90 and 98, describe this map (which omitted Hokkaido), commissioned in 1605, completed around 1639 and revised in 1653. Harley and Woodward, *History of cartography*, II, book 2, plate 26, is a full-colour reproduction; Berry, *Japan*, reproduces one detail in black and white (p. 40) and one of the original provincial maps (p. 89).

20. Details from Vaporis, *Breaking barriers*, 19–20. Government messengers and officials, and nobles travelling to and from Edo on official business, used the system free and took precedence; merchants and other private individuals could pay to use the system.

21. 'The warning of Ōsaka and Edo', in Rekishi, *Senki Shiryô*, 377–8. I thank Matthew Keith for allowing me to use his translation of this striking document. Likewise, as soon as food rioters confronted the governor of Ōsaka in 1642 he 'sent a fast messenger to inform the central government of what had happened': *Diaries kept by the heads of the Dutch factories*, VI, 87: entry for 15 July 1642.

22. For English versions of the legislation, see Hall, *Feudal laws*, 276–83 (for the emperor and court nobles) and 288–92 (the *Buke Sho-hatto* for the *daimyō*). Both Ieyasu and Hidetada abdicated early in favour of their sons, but continued to exercise power: thus Iemitsu officially became shogun in 1623 but Hidetada exercised effective power until his death nine years later.

23. Keith, 'The logistics of power' provides an excellent translation and discussion of the 10-article edict, dated 18 May 1638. See also Vlastos, *Peasant protests*, 35–7, on Iemitsu's similar treatment of the fief of Shiraiwa, also in 1638, punishing not only the rebels but also the *daimyō* who had caused the rebellion.

24. *CHJ*, IV, 196 (from Bolitho's chapter 'The Han'). While massive land redistribution also occurred in other states – after the Bohemian revolt in the 1620s (ch. 8), and in Ireland in the 1650s (ch. 12) – it only occurred in exceptional (often unique) circumstances and never became established government practice.

25. In fact *sankin* could mean either 'reporting for audience' or 'reporting for service', depending on the character used for *kin*: the Tokugawa scribes normally used the former, but meant the latter. Hall, *Feudal laws*, 293–7, prints the full text of the 1635 *Buke Sho-hatto* which codified these measures.

26. The best guide to the *sankin kotai* system remains Tsukahira, *Feudal control*: on the different residence schedules (and the tardy daimyō of Morioka), see pp. 44–6; on exemptions and special arrangements, see pp. 52–6; on estimates of the cost to daimyō, see pp. 88–9 and 96–102. See also Vaporis, 'To Edo and back', on entourage size; and Yasaki, *Social change*, 193–7 and 209, on competitive spending among the daimyō.

27. Singer, *Edo*, 26 (quotation), together with illustrations from a 1998 exhibition; 'Regulations for villagers' in Lu, *Sources of Japanese history*, I, 209–10.

28. In 1634 Iemitsu persuaded a consortium of Nagasaki merchants to build the artificial island of Dejima (which means 'Jutting-out island') to house the Portuguese merchants. It covered 160,000 square feet and the Portuguese moved there two years later. After their expulsion, Iemitsu forced the Dutch to move there from their previous base at Hirado. A separate 'Chinatown' was completed in 1689, with housing for about 5,000 people (ibid., 77). For more on Iemitsu's regulation of foreign trade, see ch 3 above.

29. Cooper, *They came to Japan*, 402, Antonio Cardim's account of the ill-fated mission of 1640; Kuroita, *Shintei zōho kokushi taikei*, XL, 217, Iemitsu's order of 8 Feb. 1641 to the Kyushu daimyō (from the *Tokugawa jikki*). Lu, *Sources of Japanese history*, 216–18, prints some *sakoku* edicts. Some have claimed that the Tokugawa 'closed' Japan and prohibited all foreign contact, but this is manifestly false: see Toby, 'Reopening the question of *sakoku*'; and Innes, 'The door ajar'.

30. The proof provided by each household, carefully entered into 'Religious Investigation Registers' (*Shūmon Aratame-Chō*), and often annotated to show changes from the previous register, forms the best source on family structure generated anywhere in the early modern world: see Hayami, *Population, family and society*, 165–84.

31. Called Tōshōgū because they honour Tōshō Daigongen, as Tokugawa Ieyasu became known after his death. Nikkō formed the cornerstone of a series of ceremonial complexes in and around Edo, mostly built by the same team of architects and craftsmen: see Coaldrake, *Architecture and authority*, 164–92; and Gerhart, *The eyes of power*, chs 3–4. Today, the 'Tōshōgū League' links the 130 or so shrines dedicated to Ieyasu's divinity and issues a newsletter.

32. See Ooms, *Tokugawa ideology*, 129 (on Suzuki's Hobbesian views) and 131, quoting Suzuki, *Banmin tokuyō [Right action for all]* (1652).

33. Ono, *Enomoto Yazaemon*, 35–6 and 137–8; Nagakura, 'Kan'ei no kikin', 75–8 (Minami-Otari village in modern Nagano prefecture).

34. Kuroita, *Shintei zōho kokushi taikei*, XL, 258, 269–71, Iemitsu's orders of 1, 2, 8, 17, 22, 24 Feb., and 25 May 1642; Nagakura, 'Kan'ei no kikin', 75–8 (depopulation).

35. Ibid., XL, 279–81, 285 and 287–8, Iemitsu's orders of 28 June, 8 and 14 July 1642, and 20 and 21 Aug. (edict with 19 articles); *Diaries kept by the heads of the Dutch factories*, VI, 128–9, entry for 2 Sep. 1642 (reporting information received from Ōsaka); Nagakura, 'Kan'ei no kikin', 80–5 (legislation); Toyoda, *Aizu-Wakamatsu-shi*, II, 157–8 (the revolt of 1642).

36. White, 'State growth', 18–19 (restricting petitions); Fukuda, 'Political process', 55–8 (feuds); Bix, *Peasant protest*, xxii ('organized flight').

37. Shiveley, 'Sumptuary regulation', 129: legislation from 1648 and 1649. The concern for underwear stems from concern that it allowed forbidden materials to be worn with little risk of detection. The laws are known as 'Kei'an' because Iemitsu issued them in the 'Kei'an era' (1648–52).

38. Shiveley, 'Sumptuary regulation', 150–1 (laws for the *hatamoto*), and 152 (edict by Iemitsu).

39. Details from Sasaki, *Daimyō to hyakushō*, 243–53; and Hall, *Cambridge History of Japan*, IV, 203–4 (loans).

40. Kei'an Laws in Kodama and Ōishi, *Kinsei nōsei shiryōshû*, I, 35–40, summarized in Nakane and Ōishi, *Tokugawa Japan*, 41–2 (data collection noted in idem, 39–40); other measures from Yamamoto, *Kan'ei jidai*, 199–203; and Sasaki, *Daimyō to hyakushō*, 233–9. See also Shiveley, 'Sumptuary regulation', 153–5. That same year – 1649 – saw the issue in Russia of a far-reaching law code, immediately after a major crisis, that likewise regulated (among other things) agrarian society: the *Ulozhenie* (ch. 6 above).

41. Vlastos, *Peasant protests*, 38–9, Instruction of Hoshina Masayuki to his district magistrates; and 39–41 (from a chapter entitled 'The political economy of benevolence').

42. Hall, 'Ikeda', quotations from pp. 69–75. Ikeda's implicit assumption about a high rate of male literacy was not unreasonable: (see ch. 21 above).

43. Howell, *Capitalism*, 33; Sasaki and Toby, 'The changing rationale', 285, Instruction by Ikeda Mitsumasa, 1657.

44. *Diaries kept by the heads of the Dutch factory*, IX, 154 (10 Sept. 1646, the Nagasaki magistrates sent away Chinese crews 'na de maniere der Tartaaren geschooren' and told them 'niet wederom te coomen, tenwaare als Chineesen') and 167 (junks manned by men 'alle geschooren' also turned away on 16 Oct. 1646).

45. Toby, *State and diplomacy*, 113, 119–39, 148; Hesselink, *Prisoners from Nambu*, 81–2. Iemitsu only abandoned frugality when it came to building: he spent prodigiously in the 1620s and 1630s not only on the Tōshōgū shrine at Nikkō and the Ninomaru palace at Kyoto, which still stand, but also on the castles at Edo, Nagoya and Osaka, all subsequently destroyed. See the list of his projects in Gerhart, *The eyes of power*, 148–9.
46. See *Kodansha Encyclopedia of Japan*, IV, s. v. *junshi* ('following their lord in death'). Pflugfelder, *Cartographies of desire*, 37–8, notes the reason for the regents' suicide.
47. Berry, *Japan*, 32; see also Berry, 'Public life', 147–51.
48. Ono, *Enomoto Yazaemon* 189–92, recorded many details of the plot and its suppression in his *Memoranda*. Sansom, *History*, III, 53–8, gives a concise account (and of another abortive *rōnin* plot in 1652). Statler, *Japanese Inn*, 74–95, provides a delightful reconstruction, observed from one of the postal stations on the highway between Edo and Kyoto.
49. Viallé and Blussé, *The Deshima Registers*, XII, 16 (23 July 1651). The indiscreet interpreters also noted that 'the example' of Tokugawa Ieyasu 'is still fresh in their memories. He had likewise been appointed guardian of the rightful heir, but his desire for the crown had driven him to kill the heir', Toyotomi Hideyori.
50. Ibid., XII, 296 (3 Mar. 1657). Edo Castle, with a perimeter of perhaps 10 miles, covered a far larger area in the Tokugawa era than today. The five-storey donjon (*tenshudai*) destroyed in the Meireki fire stood 167 feet high and was thus the tallest building in Japan. See the ground plan at: http://en.wikipedia.org/wiki/File:Edo_Castle_plan_1849.svg
51. Hayami, *Economic history*, 169, tabulates the products listed in the 1637 *Kefukigusa*. See also Hayami, *Population, family and society*, 42–51.
52. White, *Ikki*, 281, noted that the central government often ordered local magistrates to punish protesters, but then itself punished the local magistrates who had allowed the 'incidents of contention' to occur. His conclusions rest on a study of almost 7,500 recorded 'incidents of contention' in Japan between 1590 and 1868.
53. Hayami, *Economic history*, 30–1. The rest of this paragraph rests on Hayami's insights except for the '1945 tax rate' analogy, for which I thank Mary Elizabeth Berry.
54. See the convincing evidence for tax evasion presented by Brown, 'Practical constraints'; and the examples of technological improvement in Nagahara and Yamamura, 'Shaping the process'.
55. Tokugawa, *The Edo inheritance*, 88; Viallé and Blussé, *The Deshima Registers*, XII, 345–6 (17–19 Mar. 1658).
56. Ooms, *Tokugawa ideology*, 297–8.
57. Hesselink, *Prisoners from Nambu*, 50–2, 62–4 and 101–2.
58. Ikegami, *Bonds of civility*, 307; Kornicki, *The book in Japan*, 63–5 (street vendors), and 324–52 (Chikamatsu's play, *Keisei Shimabara kaeru gassen*). For more on censorship, see ch. 22 above.
59. Berry, *Japan*, ch. 4, describes these rosters, known as *Mirrors*. On p. 122 she notes that, just as the timing of the rosters of nobles reflected Iemitsu's extension of the *sankin kōtai* system, so the appearance of the rosters of officials reflects Iemitsu's work in streamlining the Tokugawa administrative system.
60. Nakane and Ōishi, *Tokugawa Japan*, 60–2, stress the enormous volume of surviving village documents.
61. Ikegami, *Bonds of civility*, 300–2, quoting *Mukashi gome mangoku tsū* (1725). For examples of others who 'managed to learn to read from experience' in the seventeenth century, see ch. 18 above.
62. Data from Kornicki, *The book*, 20; Berry, *Japan*, 31; and Ikegami, *Bonds of civility*, 286. Compare, however, the 100 to 150 new titles printed each year in Japan, a country of 17 million, with the 2,000 new titles printed in England, a country of fewer than 5 million, in 1642: ch. 11 above.
63. Nakane and Ōishi, *Tokugawa Japan*, 119; Ikegami, *Bonds of civility*, 173, 181–2. Religious texts also predominated in seventeenth-century Europe.
64. Ikegami, *Bonds of civility*, 298; Pflugfelder, *Cartographies*, 23 note.
65. Lane, *Images from the floating world*, 11, quoting from Asai, *Ukiyo monegatori [Tales of the floating world]* (1661). *Uki-yo* was originally a Buddhist expression. *Yo* means 'world' and *uki* means 'sorrow', but with 'floating' as a homonym. The suffix *-e* means 'pictures'.
66. Ikegami, *Bonds of civility*, 142, from the *Kyōhabutei*. Berry, *Japan in print*, 1–12, offers a brilliant survey (with illustrations) of the guides and maps available to travellers (including, by 1700, some 200 maps of Tokyo).
67. Viallé and Blussé, *The Deshima Registers*, XIII, 8–9 (2 Apr. 1661), 371 (4 Apr. 1663) and 247 (1 Apr. 1668). See Asai's graphic account of the tragedy at page 63 above.
68. Totman, 'Tokugawa peasants', 464–5 and 467.

Part IV. Confronting the Crisis

1. Hobbes, *On the citizen*, 29; Anon., *The moderator*, 11; Vitrián, *Las memorias*, in Gil Pujol, 'L'engany de Flandes', 418; Pascal, *Les Pensées*, # 451.
2. Bacon, *Essayes*, 'Of seditions and troubles', 47; Carroll, 'The peace', 76; Ludden, *Peasant history*, 8; Smith, *Nakahara*, 112, 115. This paragraph owes much to the insights of Thurow, *Zero sum society*.
3. Beik, 'The violence', 77–8, 92; Sibbald, *Provision for the poor* (1699: quoted ch. 1 above).
4. Des Forges, *Cultural centrality*, 176–7, quoting a memorial of Lü Kun to the Wanli emperor. In Italy, Giovanni Botero made a similar analysis at almost the same time (1589): see Villari, *Baroque personae*, 101–2.

Chapter 17   'Those who have no means of support'

1. Special thanks to John Walter for help in framing the argument of this chapter, and to him, Cynthia Brokaw, David Cressy, Stephen Dale, Kaan Durukan, Suraiya Faroqhi, Jane Hathaway and Sanjay Subrahmanyam for references.

2. Bamford, *Royalist's notebook*, 60; Walter, *Crowds*, 69–70; Blickle, *Aufruhr*, 66–7 (Germany and Switzerland); Bercé, *Histoire des Croquants*, 682 (Aquitaine); Pillorget, *Les mouvements*, 988 (Provence).

3. Des Forges, *Cultural centrality*, 198, quoting Zheng Lian's *Outline history of the changes in Yu*. See the figures and graphs in Tong, *Disorder*, 47–9; and Parsons, *Peasant rebellions*, 86–7. *CHC*, VII/1, 624–5, provides excellent maps of Late Ming popular revolts. See chs 6 and 15 above on Russia and Japan.

4. Price, *Memoirs of the Emperor Jahangueir*, 225–6; Bercé, 'Troubles frumentaires', 789 and 777–8, Giuseppe Caetano and Alessandro Bini to Cardinal Panzirolo, 8 and 9 Aug. 1648.

5. BNE *Ms* 2375/5–10v, 'Relación del motín contra los Walones', in May 1643. See also otherwise unreported 'peasant furies' listed in Jago, 'The "Crisis of the Aristocracy"', 79 (against the dukes of Béjar), and in Lorenzo Cadarso, *Conflictos populares*, 72 (against the dukes of Nájera).

6. A. Domínguez Ortiz in *Manuscrits*, IX (1991), 263–4, in a 'Round Table' on the problems that faced the Spanish Monarchy in the 1640s; Calderón de la Barca, *El alcalde de Zalamea*, set in a village on the Portuguese front. Calderón himself served in the army that invaded Catalonia in 1640.

7. Walter, 'Public transcripts', 128–9.

8. Evans, *Seventeenth-century Norwich*, 113, from a petition to the Long Parliament by the mayor and council of Norwich; other details from Cressy, *England on edge*, 361–72 (which contain many other examples found in court records from 1640 to 1642).

9. Ebrey, *Chinese civilization*, 160, quoting 'Biography of Gentleman Wang' of 1591 (Wang Daokun, *Taihan ji*).

10. Bloch, *Les caractères originaux*, I, 175 (italics added); Scott, *Weapons of the weak*, xvi–xvii. See also Scott, *The moral economy*, and *Domination and the arts of resistance*.

11. See Barriendos, 'Climatic variations' and 'Climate and culture' and page 423 above for example of self-blame. Chs 1 and 8 above note the tendency to blame witches and Jews.

12. Nicolas, *La rébellion*, 223, offers a statistical analysis of grain riots on a national scale. In France between 1661 and 1789, over 1,500 riots, one-fifth of all those recorded, involved shortage of food. Of these, one-third involved pressure to establish a 'fair price' while almost half sought to prevent those trying to export local grain.

13. Gutiérrez Nieto, 'El campesinado', 70, quoting a manuscript treatise; Chéruel, *Lettres*, I, 413–14, Mazarin to the Intendant of Guyenne, 11 Oct. 1643. See similar letters of the same date to other officials in the south-west, loc. cit., pp. 414–16. On Catalonia and Ulster, see chs 9 and 11 above.

14. Lionti, 'Cartelli', 450–1, petition of Caltabellotta, 23 June 1647; Sella, *Crisis and continuity*, 54, quoting a farmer near Milan in 1631; Bercé, *Histoire des Croquants*, II, 657, Argenson to Séguier, 2 July 1644, visiting Poitou. In Ming China, too, abandoned land remained liable for tax arrears: see page 123 above.

15. Bailey, 'Reading between the lines', 71, quoting Huang Liuhong's 1699 manual for magistrates, *A complete book concerning happiness*; Bercé, *Histoire des Croquants*, II, 548 n. 44, count of Jonzac to Chancellor Séguier, 12 Dec. 1643; and ibid., II, 550–62, 570–1. The incident at Abjat left excellent records because the family of the late captain, a local nobleman, sued the village for damages.

16. Wood, 'Subordination', 66, and 'Fear', 810, stresses the extent of the humiliation required of poor petitioners, forced to plead in public on their knees and to use demeaning language. For the four factors, see Scott, *Weapons of the weak*, 242–8.

17. Wood, 'Subordination', 63; Walter, *Crowds*, 58 (staying within the law) and 187 ('no law now'); and ch. 5 above on the view that an interregnum meant the suspension of all laws in China too.

18. Bercé, *Histoire des Croquants*, II, 543. One-fifth of the riots studied by Bercé involved *only* women; as did one-quarter of rural and one-third of urban bread riots studied by Nicolas (*La rébellion*, 269). I thank John Mueller for reminding me that 'Chicks up front' became a battle-cry in United States protests during the 1960s, because, as in the seventeenth century, law-enforcement officials were slightly less likely to use physical violence against females.

19. Nicolas, *La rébellion*, 269–70. In the Dutch Republic (if not elsewhere), women also humiliated officials by raising their skirts and 'mooning'.

20. Dekker, 'Women in revolt', 343 (Haarlem); idem, *Holland in beroering*, 56–7 (Oudewater); Bennett, *Civil wars experienced*, 119 (Derby). See also Hugon, *Naples*, 82–4, on the role of women in the revolt of 1647–8.

21. Dekker, 'Women in revolt', 344 (quoting the same slogan in riots of 1621 and 1691); Walter, *Crowds*, 41, quoting William Lambarde's *Eirenarcha* (1619 edition) and a case from Star Chamber. Michael Dalton, *The Countrey Justice* (1622) said the same; and Capp, *Gossips*, 312–18, provides similar quotations. Interestingly, Englishwomen lost their immunity when they went to New England, where they received severe punishment for breaking the peace: Westerkamp, 'Puritan patriarchy', and idem, *Women and religion*, 35–52.

22. Tawney, *Land and labour in China*, 73, 77; Walter, *Crowds*, 44, quoting *A briefe declaration concerning the state of the manufacture of woolls* (1629); Nicolas, *La rébellion*, 281, quoting rioters in 1694, 1699 and 1709. See similar desperate views quoted in ch. 3 above, and two Spanish examples quoted on page 280 above.

23. *ODNB* s.v. 'Ann Carter' by John Walter (Ann was the only Englishwoman known to have been hanged for participation in a food riot; we do not know her age, but she married in 1620 and so by the time of the riots was probably in her late 20s); Dekker, 'Women in revolt', 351–2.

24. Bercé, *Histoire des Croquants*, II, 548: 'aux femmes les plus criardes'. On the prominent role of women in popular violence elsewhere in seventeenth-century Europe, see chs 9 (Bilbao, Barcelona and Lisbon), 10 (Paris) and 14 (Palermo and Naples) above; and Beik, *Louis XIV*, ch. 6.

25. Lindley, *Fenland riots*, 75, quoting a contractor's agent at Hatfield Level, 1626 (and 63 on the relative role of men and women); Simon i Tarrés, *Cròniques*, 269–70, account of Judge Ramon de Rubí; ch. 11 above on Scotland.

26. TCD *Ms* 837/5–5, deposition of Elizabeth Croker, Co. Down, 15 Mar. 1643 (on Lady Iveagh); *Ms* 836/73–74, deposition of Ann Smith and Margaret Clark, Co. Armagh, 16 Mar. 1643, and *Ms* 836/87–90, Joan Constable, Co. Armagh, 6 June 1643 (on Jane Hampton, 'formerly a Protestant, but a meere Irish woman and lately turned to Masse'). Ms. Croker signed herself only 'Eliza' while the other three women made their mark.

27. TCD *Ms* 834/111, deposition of Martha Culme, Co. Monaghan, 14 Feb. 1642; *Ms* 832/80, deposition of Marmaduke Batemannson, gent., Co. Cavan, 14 Apr. 1643 (about Rose ny Neill); *Ms* 812/202–8, deposition of Joseph Wheeler, gent., and others, Co. Kilkenny, 5 July 1643 (about Alice Butler). They also accused Florence Fitzpatrick of hanging six named Protestants 'and divers others'.

28. Khan, 'Muskets in the *mawas*', 93, quoting Manucci, *Storia do Mogor*.

29. In the nineteenth century, both the Taiping and Boxer rebels included female troops, but even then they played a subordinate role to male troops. Unlike their Chinese sisters, Indian women were prominent in the 'Great Rebellion' of 1857. I thank Cynthia Brokaw for help in formulating this paragraph.

30. Pillorget, *Mouvements*, 564 (catechism of Avignon, 1633, reprinted at Aix-en-Provence, 1647); Bercé, *Histoire des Croquants*, II, 553 (entry by the *curé* in the baptismal register of Rocamadour, 1653). Both authors noted clerical involvement in other popular revolts; so did Foisil (for the *Nu-Pieds* of Normandy); and Nicolas, *Rébellion*, 92–6. Clerics also provided political as well as spiritual leadership in several European revolts: see ch. 18 below.

31. Hugon, *Naples*, 153–6 (quotation from the chronicle of Tutino, one of the clerical fugitives). For more on Filomarino's ambiguous role, see chs 14 and 18 above.

32. Examples in Faroqhi, *Coping with the state*, 43–58; McGowan, 'Ottoman', 480–2; and Barkey, 'Rebellious alliances', 706 (who notes that Sufi convents rather than mosques normally served as the centre of social life). Cairo information kindly supplied by Jane Hathaway.

33. Wakeman, *Great Enterprise*, I, 627, describing events in Wujiang, near Lake Tai. Once again I thank Cynthia Brokaw for helping me to assess the Chinese data.

34. See Terzioglu, 'Sufi and dissident', 192, on Muslim 'holy fools' and ch. 7 above on Shabbatai Zvi.

35. On Avraamii, see Crummey, 'The origins'; on 'Manuelinho' the Fool, see Viñas Navarro, 'El motín', 339; on Archibald Armstrong, see page 333 above, Rushworth, *Historical Collections*, II, 470–1; and Rothes, *Relation*, 115, 208–9. Shannon, '"Uncouth language"', discusses the career of Archie, who outlived most other protagonists, dying in 1672.

36. For more examples of seditious posters, see Lorenzo Cadarso, *Los conflictos*, 75; and Lario, *El comte-duc d'Olivares*, 173. Walter, *Understanding popular violence*, 340–7, and 'Public transcripts', analyzes the various 'stages' of popular revolt in Stuart England before recourse to violence. Briggs, *Communities of belief*, 175–6, comments that revolts stood a better chance of success when they remained isolated and low-key: 'sufficient to drive away tax collectors without threatening any wider disruption'. See also the excellent analysis of 'norms and values' in early modern European revolts in Blickle, *Resistance*, 155–214.

37. Walter, *Understanding popular violence*, 36–9, quoting Bruno Rives, *Mercurius Rusticus*, Lady Rivers (the victim), and testimony from 1648 (see also a map of places attacked Aug.–Dec 1642 at pp. 34–5); Gentles, *The English Revolution*, 88, quoting a French envoy.

38. Simon i Tarrés, *Cròniques*, 269, account of Judge Ramon de Rubí, who only escaped by disguising himself as a Jesuit, shaving his beard and the crown of his head (ibid., 274).

39. TCD *Ms* 837/117, deposition of Captain Thomas Clarke, 12 May 1653; *Ms* 838/81, petition of Joan Todd, widow of John Hilhouse. Aidan Clarke estimates that more than half of Ulster depositions reported killings (personal communication, Sep. 2005).

40. Beik, 'The violence', 77 and 87.

41. Riches, *The anthropology of violence*, 25; Bercé, *Histoire des Croquants*, II, 582–3; Villari, *Revolt*, ch 2.

42. On Portugal, see Schaub, *Le Portugal*, 31–5, and Pérez Samper, *Catalunya*, 243; on Istanbul, see Brennan, *Bargrave*, 82; on Naples, see ch. 14 above, and Hugon, *Naples*, 303–8. For a similar etiquette at Évora in 1637, see ch. 9 above.

43. Wakeman and Grant, *Conflict and control*, 10 and 57, record ritual protests staged at temples. Other details from Parsons, *The peasant rebellions*, 4–5 and 187–8; Tsing Yuan, 'Urban riots'; Parsons, 'Attitudes', 179–80 and 185; Wakeman, *Great Enterprise*, 627; and Tong, *Disorder*, 162–3. Although the mass humiliation and slaughter of Ming clansmen in 1643–4 by Li Zicheng seems an exception, one might argue that (although numerous) they too formed a single category singled out for punishment.

44. Walter, '"Abolishing superstition"', 90–2; TCD *Ms.* 835/170, deposition of Edward Slacke, Co. Fermanagh, 4 Jan. 1642; Hickson, *Ireland*, I, 193–4, deposition of Rev. John Kerdiff, Co. Tyrone, 28 Feb. 1642; and TCD *Ms* 836/64, deposition of John Parrie, gentleman, Armagh, 31 May 1642.

45. Bercé, *Histoire des Croquants*, II, 647–8. In addition, 'in the epidemic of uprisings in 1637, 1643 and 1648' the villages along the Breton–Poitevin border were 'the first to rebel and the last to be pacified' (ibid., 648). Peasants from the same villages would also lead the Vendée uprising in 1793: Bercé, *Révoltes*, 161.

46. Bercé, *Histoire des Croquants*, II, 650–1: it belonged to the dukes of Bouillon. Once again, Bercé notes the survival of traditions: in the 1950s the anti-tax 'Poujade movement' scored its first successes in the areas that once belonged to the *vicomté* of Turenne (ibid., 652).

47. Hoffman, 'Zur Geschichte' (revolts in 1511–14, 1525, 1560, 1570 and 1595–7); Stoyle, '"Pagans" or "paragons"', 323 (the revolt of 1497 began in St Keverne's as did plans for another in 1537); Hill, *The world*, 110–13 (on Kingston). Clifton, *The last popular rebellion*, 48–56, notes a tradition of insurgency in Taunton and other parts of Somerset, culminating in their participation in Monmouth's rebellion in 1685.

48. Price, *Maroon societies*; Beckles, 'From land to sea'. I thank Carla Pestana for these references, and for discussing 'marronage' with me.

49. Wakeman, *Great Enterprise*, 430 n. 41 and 702, records bandit gangs in Liangshanbo in 1640–1 and 1647, until defeated by Qing troops. For more about *Water Margin*, see ch. 18 above.

50. Wilson, '"A thousand countries to go to"', 84. See a similar example in Wood, 'Subordination', 69.

51. Pillorget, *Les mouvements*, 406–10; Bercé, *Histoire des Croquants*, II, 564–5; Nicolas, *La rébellion*, 224–6; Di Marzo, *Diari*, III, 99, Diario of Auria, 20 June 1647.

52. See further details in ch. 14 above. English men and women commemorated several revolutionary anniversaries: 30 January (the regicide/martyrdom of Charles I), 3 September (Cromwell's victories at Dunbar and Worcester), 23 October (the Ulster Massacres), and 5 November (the Gunpowder Plot and later the landing of William of Orange) – but none triggered subsequent insurgency.

53. Failure to pay wages in full always ran the risk of provoking mutiny, as did failure to pay a bonus to the garrison of Istanbul upon the accession of a new sultan or (in provincial capitals) a new governor. On the events in Dublin and Paris, see chs 11 and 10 above.

54. Lebrun, *Les hommes*, 290, on the voracious wolves of Anjou; Nicolas, *La rébellion*, 412–13, on French arms.

55. Khan, 'Muskets in the *mawas*', 93, quoting Mundy, *Travels*, and Manucci, *Storia do Mogor*.

56. Morrill, *Revolt in the provinces*, 132–51, with afterthoughts at pp. 200–4; quotation from p. 144; Shy, *A people numerous and armed*, vii.

57. Bercé. *Histoire des Croquants*, I, 421–2, on the Croquants' military discipline. Their savagery of course reflected no more than the prevailing Laws of War. Bercé, *Révoltes*, ch. 3, discusses 'les meneurs', including veterans.

58. BNF *Fonds français* 18,937/233–40, 'Relation de la révolte de la Basse Normandie' provides details on the organization of the 'Nu-Pieds' and identifies their leaders. See also ch. 10 above.

59. Hugon, *Naples*, 196–204 (quoting Bissacioni, *Historia*). Further details in ch. 9 (Spain), 11–12 (Scotland and Ireland), 14 (Naples) and 15 (America) above.

60. See ch. 5 above. Parsons, *Peasant rebellions*, 228–37, notes that Zhang Xianzhong also began to attract former officers, which enabled him to conduct successful sieges in Sichuan.

61. Geerts, 'The Arima rebellion', 96–8, Koeckebacker to Anthonio van Diemen, 25 Mar. 1638 (I have made my own translation from the Dutch original); Blair and Robertson, *Philippine islands*, XXIX, 220, report of Juan López, S.J.; Dardess, *Blood and history*, 133, and Parsons, *Peasant rebellions*, 251, both note red flags among rebel bands. Elliott, *Empires*, 146, mentions the insignia in Mexico and Boston.

62. Graniti, *Diario*, II, 67; Anon., *The red-ribbon'd news*, 5; Kötting, *Die Ormée*, 111; pp. 322–3 above (on the 'bonnets rouges'). Rodger, *Safeguard of the sea*, 132, noted that from the thirteenth century 'among seamen everywhere' red flags 'signify war to the death'. Not all rebel flags were red: in Austria, the peasants led by Martin Laimbauer in 1636 deployed banners of white linen bearing slogans (Wilflingseder, 'Martin Laimbauer', 206–7); the Périgord 'Croquants' in 1637 marched under a blue and white banner, the colours of the Virgin Mary, whom their leader claimed had blessed the enterprise (Bercé, *Histoire des Croquants*, I, 423); the banner of the Republic of Naples, first unfurled in Oct. 1647, had the Virgin and San Gennaro on one side, and the fleur-de-lys of France on the other (Hugon, *Naples*, 152).

63. Maier and Waugh, '"The blowing of the Messiah's trumpet"', 146–7, on images of Shabbatai and Nathan. Knoppers, *Constructing Cromwell*, on Oliver; Hugon, *Naples*, 309–13, 328–57, discusses and reproduces many images of Masaniello. In addition, Palermo, *Narrazioni*, 353, Medici to Grand Duke 20 Aug. 1647, mentions two wax busts of Masaniello, done from life and made for Viceroy Arcos to send to Spain; Blok, *Nikolaus Heinsius*, 29–31, mentions the epigrams; Mastellone, 'Les révoltes', 167, mentions Spinoza's portrait as Masaniello; D'Alessio, *Contagi*, ch. 6, discusses early travel literature that mentioned Masaniello. Heilingsetzer, *Der oberösterreichische Bauernkrieg*, 36–7, records a contemporary likeness of Stephen Fadinger, leader of the Austrian revolt of 1626; and the Catalans circulated images of Pau Claris in 1640–1.

64. Hugon, *Naples*, 125–31, lists and discusses the 30 slogans recorded by two chroniclers and some revolutionary songs. Note also the *Knittelvers*, rhymed pairs of more or less regular iambic tetrameter lines, used for German broadsheets (ch. 8 above).

65. Cressy, *England on edge*, 337–8, prints the whole song (the verse on universities appears in ch. 18 below), and discusses others at pp. 330–46. Brome, *Rump*, was his third collection of Civil War songs.

66. See Heilingsetzer, *Der oberösterreichische Bauernkrieg*, 35–7; Wilflingseder, 'Martin Laimbauer', 206–7; Hrushevsky, *History*, VIII, 450–1; Suter, *Der schweizerische Bauernkrieg*, 64.

67. See Simon i Tarrés, *Orígens*, 212–13, on *Els Segadors*. Neumann, *Das Wort*, 214–18, and Lucas Val, 'Literatura i historia', discuss the songs, poems and plays of the Catalan revolt.

68. Valerius, *Neder-Landtsche Gedenck-Clanck*, 235–6. Nevertheless, songs never assumed the same importance in the 1640s as they did during the French Revolution: see Weber, *My France*, 92–102, 'Who sang the Marseillaise'.

69. Lorandi, *Spanish king of the Incas*, 23, quoting Bishop Juan de Vera of Cuzco in 1635; Valladares, *Epistolario*, 139, Olivares to Basto, 26 Nov. 163 (similar sentiments in his letter of 18 Dec. 1637: ibid., 157); Paul, *Diary*, 87–8, Johnston of Wariston's report of what he overheard Hamilton tell King Charles on 17 June 1639.

70. Bacon, *Essays* (1625), 'Of seditions and troubles'; Walter, *Understanding popular violence*, 259 (speech of John Pym on 25 or 26 Jan. 1642 OS). See also similar Spanish comments in chs 3 and 9 above.

71. Wood, 'Fear', 814; Hill, *World turned upside down*, 108, quoting *The mournfull cries* (and several other similar statements from 1648–9); Bercé, ''Troubles frumentaires', 772, report on the rioting at Fermo; Bercé, *Histoire des Croquants*, II, 546, account of the Bordeaux riots in Aug. 1648.

72. Huang, *Taxation*, 145–7; Cueto, *Quimeras y sueños*, 80–1, Philip IV's Instructions to his 'junta de conciencia'. Of course, the king's concern in 1641 might merely reflect fear that the revolts of Catalonia and Portugal could spread.

73. Spence, *Woman Wang*, 13; Darling, *Revenue-raising and legitimacy*, 248–67, provides a detailed analysis of a register of petitions to one treasury department, containing some 625 petitions received between 1634 and 1643: it rejected only two or three. See other examples in Faroqui, 'Political activity', especially pp. 31–2; and Barkey, 'Rebellious alliances', 706.

74. Mackay, *Limits*, ch. 4, provides some striking examples. For the role of petitions as a 'weapon of the weak' in early modern England, see Walter, 'Public transcripts', 137–43.

75. Lorenzo Cadarso, *Los conflictos*, 178–9. The nine included Aldeanueva de Ebro.

76. Ibid., 109, 179–80 and 192. Lope published *Fuenteovejuna* in 1619. Olivari, *Entre el trono*, 125–6, discusses its immediate popularity in Spain.

77. Bercé, *Histoire des Croquants*, II, 597–9 (Bayonne in June 1641). Two years later, the government revoked an unpopular property tax on the grounds that 'the costs and exactions arising from the collection of the said tax exceeded three- or fourfold the amount received by His Majesty' (loc. cit). For other 'strategic retreats' see ibid., 680 and Pillorget, *Mouvements*, 566 (both from France) and during Spain's 'Green Banner' revolts (ch. 9).

78. Robert von Friedeburg reminds me that resisting the power of the state is *always* a high-risk strategy: where early modern governments branded many of their opponents traitors, and reacted accordingly, their modern descendants brand many of their opponents 'terrorists', and react accordingly.

79. Blair and Robertson, *Philippines*, XXIX, 221–5, account of Juan López, S.J., on the brutal repression of the 1639 'sangley' revolt; and Spence, *Emperor of China*, 31–7 and ch. 3 above on the savagery of the Chinese Law Code.

80. RAS *Muscovitica* 602, n.p., Adolph Ebbers to Charles XI of Sweden, Moscow, 21 Aug. 1662; and Gordon, *Diary*, II, 159–62. In RAS *Livonica* II, vol. 176, n.p., Ebbers to Governor General Helmfelt, 26 Sep. 1662, noted that 'the boys whom I wrote about before, who were to have one ear cut off, have been pardoned; they will keep their ears but will receive a brand mark like the other [rioters]'. See also ch. 6 above on the brutal repression of the revolt led by Stenka Razin.

81. Price, *Memoirs of the Emperor Jahangueir*, 225–6.

82. Foisil, *La révolte*, 310–35; Bercé, 'L'émeute', 759–89.

83. Goldie, *The entring book of Roger Morrice*, III, 27–8 (Monmouth also 'said he could have had 20,000 or 30,000 men more, but he had no arms for them'); Clifton, *The last popular rebellion*, 231–41.

84. Hugon, *Naples*, 238–9, quoting Don Juan on 21 Feb. 1648, and Philip IV and Oñate after the surrender on 6 April; 243–56 and 263–6. Oñate nevertheless made some important concessions in order to preserve Spanish control: see ch. 14 above.

85. AHN *Estado libro* 961/56–59v, Olivares 'Relación' prepared for the duke of Bragança, Nov. 1637 (the same phrase appears in Viñas Navarro, 'El motín', 38, Philip IV to Duchess Margaret of Mantua, [undated]); AMAE (P) *CPE Supplément* 3/189–91, 'Première négociation des François en Cathalogne' by Bernard Duplessis-Besançon.

86. Chéruel, *Lettres*, III, 1,061, Mazarin to Ambassador Chanut in Stockholm, early Sep. 1648; Bercé, 'Troubles frumentaires', 789, Giuseppe Caetano, governor of Perugia, to Cardinal Panzirolo, 14 July 1648.

Chapter 18   'People who hope only for a change'

1. The title reprises the typology of rebellions proposed by Lü Kun of China: page 508 above.

2. Mandrou, 'Vingt ans après', 36, Fouquet to Chancellor Séguier, 1644; Argyll, *Instructions*, 8, written in 1661.

3. Briggs, 'Richelieu and reform', 72, Richelieu paper of 1624; Elliott and La Peña, *Memoriales y cartas*, I, 55, 62, the 'Gran Memorial' of 1624. See also the cardinal's view of the nobility in his *Testament politique*, 218–23.

Villari, *Baroque personae*, ch. 5, presents an excellent synopsis of the motives of seventeenth-century European rebels.

4. AGS *GA* 1331, n.p., *consulta* of the Junta de Ejecución, 7 Dec. 1640 (see Plate 12 above).

5. Such broad figures are misleading because of the striking inconsistencies within states. Thus in Spain, the average of 10 per cent conceals the fact that only 1 per cent in the province of Córdoba was noble, whereas *all* families in the northern provinces of Vizcaya and Guipúzcoa claimed nobility. In Poland, Mazovia boasted some villages composed entirely of nobles, whereas the region around Kraków had only 2 per cent. Moreover, as Hamish Scott reminds us: 'As more detailed research is undertaken on the demography of the nobility, employing fiscal and other records, previous estimates are having to be revised downwards': Scott, *The European nobilities*, I, 21.

6. See the luminous pages of Jouanna, *Devoir*, 268-70.

7. Jago, 'The influence of debt', 227-36, explains the system, the equivalent of 'Chapter XI bankruptcy protection'.

8. Lorenzo Cadarso, *Los conflictos*, 72-3. Other examples from ch. 9.

9. Duccini, *Faire voir*, 53; Carrier, *La presse de la Fronde*, I, 104-45 (on Condé).

10. Bercé, *Histoire des Croquants*, II, 557 (Bouillon). Idem, I, 413 and II, 570-1 and 574-5, cite other examples of noble participants in popular revolts. Corvisier, 'Clientèles et fidélités', describes some networks of clients.

11. Bercé, *Histoire des Croquants*, II, 737, anonymous relation of the Croquants of Angoumois and Saintonge, 1636 (noting the brutal murder of some officials from Paris). See ch. 9 above for the murder of anyone suspected of coming from Castile during the Catalan revolt of 1640.

12. Soares da Cunha, *A casa de Bragança*, 15-16 and 554-5, and ch. 9 above, on the duke's 'conservatism'.

13. Ohlmeyer, *Civil War*, 283, quoting Lord Clanricard in 1651 and Sir Lewis Dyve in 1650, with other similar examples on pp. 283-8.

14. I thank Cynthia Brokaw, Kenneth Pomeranz and Evelyn Rawski for help with the Chinese sources on this topic.

15. Ho, *The ladder*, 73, quoting Wang Daokun, *Taihan ji* (1591). See also p. 511 on Wang.

16. Details from Hucker, *Two studies*, 41-83; and Wakeman, *Great Enterprise*, 109-10.

17. Brook, *Confusions of pleasure*, 1-4, quoting the *Shexian zhi [She County Gazetteer]* of 1609 compiled by Zhang Tao.

18. Agnew, 'Culture and power', 47, complaint of Wang Shiying (himself a shengyuan) to the Kong dukes, who boasted enormous prestige and ruled vast lands thanks to their status as direct descendants of Confucius. Wang's experience helps to explain why landowners like the dukes of Kong welcomed the Qing.

19. AUB *Ms* 2538/21-2 and 37v, Fraser, 'Triennial travels'. The author spent almost three weeks in Oxford and four in Cambridge, visiting every college.

20. AUB *Ms* 2538/21-2, Fraser, 'Triennial travels'. Learning 'French to argue' seems an esoteric activity.

21. Kagan, *Students*, 85 and 182-5; Elliott, *Count-duke*, 15-18.

22. Curtis, 'Alienated intellectuals', 299, quoting Lord Chancellor Ellesmere; Quevedo, *La fortuna con seso y la hora de todos* (1632), I, 264; Roberts, 'Queen Christina', 217, quoting Magnus Gabriel de la Gardie in 1655; Zeman, 'Responses to Calvin', 45, quoting Ferdinand II. In his essay 'Of seditions and troubles', drafted c. 1610, Francis Bacon also predicted rebellion 'when more are bred schollers, then preferments can take off' *Essayes*, 47.

23. Amelang, 'Barristers and judges', 1,281-4 (suggesting that one might call the revolt of the Catalans 'the revolt of the lawyers'); Marques, *A parenética portuguesa e a Restauração*, I, 56. On Bohemia and Sweden, see ch. 8 above, on the Fronde, see ch. 10.

24. Hobbes, *Behemoth*, 40, 70-1, 144, 147-8.

25. Argyll, *Instructions*, 6, written in prison shortly before his execution for treason; Balfour, *Historical Works*, III, 426-7, final 'nota' to his 'Shorte memorialls and passages of this yeire 1649'.

26. Saltmarsh, *The smoke in the temple* (1646), 62; Anon., *Persecutio undecima* (published, perhaps significantly, on 5 Nov. 1648), 57.

27. Groenhuis, *Predikanten*, 31-2, from a sermon in Jan. 1626. Like many other self-righteous preachers, Smout sired an illegitimate child, which provoked much mirth among those he had criticized.

28. On the Dutch Republic, see ch. 8 above; on Scotland, Makey, *Church of the Covenant*, 102-3, Stevenson, 'Deposition of ministers', and Donaldson, 'The emergence of schism'; on England, see Green, 'The persecution'; idem, *The re-establishment*, ch. 8; and Holmes, *The Suffolk committees*.

29. Marques, *A parenética portuguesa e a Restauração*, I, 69, quoting Valenzuelo, *Portugal unido*; 54-6, statistics on 79 preachers; and II, table 1.2, sermons on 23 Dec. 1640 and Oct 1641, and table 2.1, analysis of five sermons from Dec. 1640. On the 'bonnets rouges', see pp. 322-3 above.

30. Neumann, *Das Wort als Waffe*, 206 (quoting *Triomphos del Amor*, 1642).

31. Monod, *Power of kings*, 181 (Torano and Nardò); Capograssi, 'La revoluzione', 211, Rosso to Doge, 17 Sep. 1647 (Naples).

32. Hugon, *Naples*, 153-6, and idem, 'Le violet et le rouge' (citing Capecelatro). The Primate of Naples occupied a unique position, because the kingdom was a papal fief, for which the king of Spain paid homage. Both before and after the revolution, Filomarino and the viceroys engaged in bitter disputes over jurisdiction. Hugon notes that the archives of the Spanish government at Simancas have an entire dossier entitled 'Filomarino', documenting disputes.

33. Perceval-Maxwell, *Outbreak*, 231, quoting a Jesuit chronicle of the rebellion, Dec. 1641; TCD *Ms* 817/37v, deposition of Rev. Thomas Fleetwood, Westmeath, 22 Mar. 1643; TCD *Ms* 816/8v, deposition of Charles Campbell, Monaghan, undated; *Ms* 831/191, deposition of Rev. Thomas Johnson, Mayo, 14 Jan. 1644, and *Ms* 821/154, deposition of Elizabeth Nelson, Tipperary, 16 Dec. 1642. All the deponents were Protestants, and so may have exaggerated the involvement of Catholic clerics, but it is unlikely that all their claims were false.

34. O'Mahony, *Disputatio apologetica*, discussed by ó hAnnracháin, '"Though hereticks and politicians"', 159–63.

35. Linz, 'Intellectual roles', 81–3, assumed 150,000 clerical positions to produce his 5 per cent estimate. Of his database of 116 elite intellectuals active in the seventeenth century, 33 per cent were in religious orders and a further 22 per cent were either secular clergy or in minor orders. Book production calculated from Antonio, *Biblioteca Hispana Nova*.

36. Santoro, *Le secentine napoletane*; Duccini, *Faire voir*; Reis Torgal, *Ideologia política*.

37. Marshall, *Meroz cursed*. See also the discussion of this text in Hill, *The English Bible*.

38. Cunningham, '"Zeal for God"', 116–18; Croix, *La Bretagne*, I,238. Villari, *Baroque personae*, 185–7, describes a theatrical sermon. Catholic priests also exerted influence as 'spiritual directors' to the rich and famous.

39. Cregan, 'The social and cultural background'; Walsh, *The Irish Continental College Movement*; Bergin, *The making of the French episcopate*, 187–8; Marques, *A parenética portuguesa e a Restauração*, I, 56.

40. ODNB, s.v. 'Henderson', quoting John Maxwell, deposed bishop of Ross, *The Burden of Issachar*, n.d.; analysis from Makey, *Church of the Covenant*, ch. 7.

41. See García Cárcel, *Pau Claris*, and ó hAnnracháin, *Catholic reformation*, and also chs 9 and 12 above, on the two protagonists. Although Giulio Genoino was a priest when he took control of the Naples revolution in 1647, he had achieved prominence as a lawyer.

42. Rycaut, *Present state*, II, 128 and 135 (italics added). Rycaut's hatred of English Puritans (who had forced him into exile) no doubt coloured his judgement: Darling, 'Ottoman politics through British eyes'.

43. Katib Çelebi, *Balance of truth*, 99. See ch. 7 above for more detail.

44. Clarendon, *Brief view*, 319–20 ('dirty people of no name'); Hill, *Puritanism*, 204–5 (the rest); ODNB, s.v. 'Pym'; Adamson, *The noble revolt*, 387, 582 and 681; Aston, *A collection*, sig. A2 (preface).

45. See ODNB, s.v. 'Sexby, Edward', and chs 12 and 19 above. Enemies of Cromwell belittled his origins by referring to him as 'King Copper-nose, Beelzebub's chief ale-brewer': Knoppers, *Constructing Cromwell*, 19–20.

46. Cressy, 'Protestation protested', 272, return from Middleton, Essex. Cressy adds: 'Female subscription occurred occasionally in more than half a dozen counties.' See also chapter 11 above.

47. Walsham, *Providence*, 213; Mack, *Visionary women*, 78–9 and 90–1. For more on Elizabeth Poole, see Firth, *Clarke Papers*, II, 150–4 and 163–70 (the minutes of the council meetings at which Poole appeared); Poole, *A vision* (her own account); Brod, 'Politics and prophecy'; Davies, *Unbridled spirits*, 137–41; and ODNB s.v. Poole and Cary. Many more women participated in the war by paying taxes, tending the sick and sustaining businesses and families.

48. BNE *Ms* 2371/21, draft history of the year 1640 by Jerónimo de Mascarenhas, on the 'Beata Paula'; see ch. 9 above on Philip IV and his prophets, some later imprisoned by the Inquisition on suspicion of heresy.

49. Hill, *World turned upside down*, 366; Smith, 'Almost revolutionaries'; Nicolas, *La rébellion*, 443. Not all insurgent leaders were young: Pierre Broussel was 73 when his arrest provoked the Day of the Barricades in Paris; Giulio Genoino was over 80 when he led the Neapolitan Republic in 1647.

50. See Terzioğlu, *Sufi and dissident*, 291–2 and 299, on Mişri's use of Alexander and Aristotle. See ch. 19 below for some of his other views.

51. Wakeman, *Great Enterprise*, I, 625–6, quoting a Jiangxi county Gazetteer.

52. Des Forges, 'Toward another Tang or Zhou?', 75.

53. Burkus-Chasson, 'Visual hermeneutics', 384 and 414 n. 37, records the paintings and playing cards; Ho, 'In defense of Sinicization', 142 n. 5, notes Nurhaci's knowledge of Chinese Classics. Crossley, *A translucent mirror*, 244–5, 287, notes Manchu editions of the *Romance* in 1647–50; Di Cosmo, *Diary*, 42, 82, 116, proves that Manchu soldiers read it. Brokaw, *Commerce and culture*, 570, notes that Mao Zedong, too, read and used *Water margin*.

54. Elliott, 'Whose empire?', 39, letters of Nurhaci to the Chinese inhabitants of Liaodong, late 1621 (see also ibid., 38, letter of Nurhaci to the Khalka Mongols, 1620, making a similar argument); Wakeman, *Great Enterprise*, 316–17, Dorgon's edict of 5 June 1644.

55. Des Forges, 'Toward another Tang or Zhou?', 82–9. Ch. 5 above notes the search of Li Zicheng and other protagonists in the Ming-Qing transition for historical precedents to justify their conduct. The commonest word for 'revolution' in China today remains *geming*: 'changing the Mandate'.

56. Hickson, *Ireland in the seventeenth century*, I, 194, deposition of Rev. John Kerdiff, Co. Tyrone, 28 Feb. 1642 citing Meredith Hanmer's *Chronicle of Ireland* (1571); TCD *Ms* 839/134v, deposition of Mulrany Carroll, Co. Donegal, 26 Apr. 1643.

57. Rutherford, *Lex, rex*, 449–53 (more examples in Cowan, 'The political ideas'); Rushworth, *Historical Collections the fourth and last part*, II, 1,420–1, President John Bradshaw to Charles I, 27 Jan. 1649.

58. Hill, 'The Norman Yoke'; Morrill, *Revolt in the provinces*, 143 (the Clubmen); Fincham, 'The judges' decision', 234 (with other examples of Fortescue's use by critics of the crown in the 1630s).

59. Neumann, *Das Wort als Waffe*, 107–11 (Catalonia); Truchuelo García, 'La incidencia', 89 (Guipúzcoa).

60. Bercé, *Histoire des Croquants*, II, 635–6 (Croquants); Foisil, *La révolte* (*Nu-Pieds*); Hugon, *Naples*, 108, 114, 146, 235 and 294; Bercé, 'Troubles frumentaires' (communal aspirations); and chs 14 and 8 above (on Palermo, Naples and Tell).

61. Marques, *A parenética portuguesa e a Restauração*, II, table 2.1, on Portugal; d'Alessio, *Contagi*, 88–93; Hugon, *Naples*, 85–6, and Benigno, *Specchi*, 242, on Naples; Simon i Tarrés, *Orígens*, 216, and Lucas Val, 'Literatura', 175, on Catalonia.

62. Fairholt, *Poems and songs*, xxviii and 70, and Braddick, *God's fury*, 43–5 and 53–4 (lionizing Felton); Adamson, 'Baronial context', 107 (Essex as John the Baptist); Hill, *The English Bible*, 453–5: an 'Index of Biblical persons and places' cited by seventeenth-century English authors.

63. Schama, *The embarrassment of riches*, 113 (Vondel's *Passcha* of 1612); Groenhuis, *De predikanten*, 81 (Lydius, *Belgium Gloriosum*, 1667); Paul, *Diary*, I, 344 (Feb. 1638).

64. Trevor-Roper, 'The Fast Sermons', 280–1, quoting Samuel Fairclough, *Troublers of Israel* (with other texts); German examples in Theibault, 'Jeremiah in the village', 444–53.

65. See, for example, Carrier, *La Fronde*, II, no. 36, *Lettre du père Michel* (1649), which made an explicit comparison. For France's 'Egyptian bondage' under Mazarin, see Benigno, *Specchi*, 133.

66. Lenihan, *Confederate Catholics*, 73, quoting Fr Anthony Geoghegan, Sep. 1642; Casway, 'Gaelic Maccabeanism', 178, speech by Owen Roe O'Neill (hailed by others as 'your present Maccabean and only champion'); O'Mahony, *Disputatio apologetica*.

67. Comparato, 'Barcelona y Nápoles'; Hobbes, *Leviathan*, 225–6, written just after the English regicide.

68. Parsons, *Peasant rebellions*, 189–99.

69. Mitchell, 'Religion, revolt', ch. 5, quoting the *Resumen de la vida de Sor Eufràsia Berenguer*.

70. Paul, *Diary*, I, 393, 395, 396 and 397 (Oct. and Nov. 1638). Wariston, who recorded these details, dutifully prayed that 'the Lord would continue Margaret's raptures and expressions till this great business were settled'. At the same time, in northern Ireland, a bishop complained that 'I have had Anabaptistical prophetesses come gadding up and down': *CSP Ireland, 1633–47*, 182, Bishop Bramhall of Derry to Laud, 23 Feb. 1638 OS. Further examples in Gillespie, *Devoted people*, 137–42, and Groenhuis, *De predikanten*, 98–102. See also page 550 above on Elizabeth Poole.

71. Hill, *The world turned upside down*, 87–106 ('A nation of prophets'), quotation from p. 90. Thomas, *Religion*, 371–2 and 441–4, lists prominent political figures (including Charles II) who consulted Lilly.

72. Foster, *The sounding of the last trumpet*, 17–18; Foster, *The pouring forth of the seventh and last viall*, 64–5. Foster's predictive powers should not be underestimated: Pope Innocent X *did* die in 1655 while Sultan Mehmet IV was *almost* overthrown in 1655–6. Hill, *The world turned upside down*, 223–4, and *ODNB* s.v. George Foster, both provide a short sketch of the man and his writings.

73. Wilflingseder, 'Martin Laimbauer'; *ODNB* s.v. 'James Nayler'. The Puritan minister Ralph Josselin noted in his Diary the common prediction that the world would end in 1655 or 1656 (Macfarlane, *Family life*, 23–4, 185, 189–91). Those who predicted this included François Davant (see Labrousse, 'François Davant'). In 1658 John Bunyan began to predict that 'the Day of Judgment is at hand'. On Shabbatai Zvi and the predictions that the world would end in 1666, see chs 7 and 19.

74. Price, *Marroon societies*, 37 (the king of Guinea); page 465 above on Bohorqués; Guijóo, *Diario*, I, 143–4 (26 Dec. 1650) and 220 (20 July 1653) on Lombardo. The fact that Guijóo, an ordinary priest, heard so much about Don Guillén shows how widely his fame spread. On Don Guillén's supposed metamorphosis into Zorro, see Troncarelli, *La spada e la croce*, 256–339.

75. TCD *Ms* 835/158, deposition of John Right, Co. Fermanagh, 5 Jan. 1642. Hickson, *Ireland*, I, 114–15, prints O'Neill's alleged royal commission, dated Edinburgh, 1 Oct. 1641, and at pp. 169–73 and 188–9, reveals how well the forgery worked. Gillespie, 'Political ideas', 113, quotes a Catholic bishop's admission that the document had been forged expressly to lead 'the common sort of people … into those forward actions and cruelties'.

76. On Guise's fraudulent letter, see ch. 14 above; on those of Khmelnytsky and Razin, see ch. 6 above. Not all anti-government letters published by rebels were false: those of Olivares published by the Catalans and those of Charles I published by his English opponents were both genuine: see chs 9 and 12 above.

77. Paul, *Diary*, I, 348 and 410–11 (19 May 1638 and 8–10 Feb. 1639). On the popularity in Scotland of Althusius's *Politica Methodice Digesta* (1603; expanded edn 1614), see Cowan, 'The making of the National Covenant'; and von Friedeburg, *Self-defence*, ch. 3. *ODNB*, s.v. 'Archibald Johnston', notes the other books in which Wariston 'set out to dig for corroborative arguments'.

78. Laing, *Letters and journals*, I, 116–17, Baillie to William Spang, 12 Feb. 1639; Paul, *Diary*, I, 411 (24 Feb. 1639).

79. Dunthorne, 'Resisting monarchy', 136–40, discusses Henderson's use of Grotius; Paul, *Diary*, I, 390 (Wariston's account of his discussion with Henderson and David Calderwood on foreign texts about resistance, 20 Sep. 1638).

80. Downing, *A discoursive coniecture*, 38 (which Adamson, *The noble revolt*, 207–9 and notes, dates to early 1641). Salmon, *French religious wars*, studies the reception of Althusius, Grotius and other writers in England.

81. Prynne, *Soveraigne Power*, Part IV, 153–99, is mostly a translation of the *Vindiciae* (the full English translation appeared in 1648).

82. On the series, in the compact 24° format published between 1626 and 1649, see Conti, *Consociatio civitatum*.

83. Hugon, *Naples*, 217–23; Mastellone, 'Holland as a political model'; idem, 'Les révoltes de 1647', 177–84; and Musi, *La rivolta*, 203–4, all provide a detailed discussion.

84. Casway, 'Gaelic Maccabeanism', 180–1, quoting a proposition sent to Philip IV of Spain in 1627; TCD *Ms* 829/311, deposition of William Fytton, Limerick, 8 July 1643.

85. Jusserand, *Recueil*, XXIV/1, 35–6, Instruction to M. de Bellièvre, 27 June 1646.

86. See ch. 12 above on the Levellers, and Peters, *Print culture*, ch. 8, on the 'Nayler Case'.

Chapter 19 'People of heterodox beliefs . . . who will join up with anyone who calls them'

1. This chapter owes much to lively discussions with Cynthia Brokaw and David Cressy. As with chs 17 and 18, the title incorporates the typology of rebellions suggested by Lü Kun of China: page 508 above.

2. Gladwell, *The tipping point*, 30–4 and 57–60. The 'most famous historical example of a word-of-mouth epidemic' in Europe occurred 14 years later: the 'Great Fear' of 1789 in France. See Lefebvre, *La Grande Peur*, especially Part III.

3. Quevedo, *La rebelión de Barcelona*, in *Obras*, I, 284; Birago Avogadro, *Turbolenze*, 369–70; *CSPC 1675–1676*, 368, Sir Jonathan Atkins to Secretary Williamson, 3 Apr. 1676; and Trevor-Roper, 'General Crisis', 61. Burke, 'Some seventeenth-century anatomists', 25–6, lists others who used similar metaphors.

4. Brigham, *British royal proclamations*, 53, 'A proclamation for settling the plantation of Virginia', 13 May 1625 OS; PRO *SP* 16/527/103–7, draft proposal for a British Union of Arms (1627). For the Spanish precedent, see ch. 9 above.

5. Lamormaini in 1630 quoted in ch. 8, Charles I in 1638 in ch. 11; and Olivares in 1639 in ch. 9 above.

6. Álvarez de Toledo, *Politics and reform*, 99, Palafox to the count of Castrillo, 1648 (translation slightly amended); Rothes, *Relation*, 10, reporting a conversation in which the archbishop of St Andrews mentioned the enthusiasm of an Irish bishop for 'Laud's liturgy'; and ch. 11 on the plans to invade Scotland.

7. Foisil, *Révolte*, 231, quoting the memoirs of Bigot de Monville; AMAE (P), *CPE Supplément* 3/240v–241, Duplessis-Besançon, 'Première négociation des françois en Cathalogne'; *Co. Do. In.*, LXXXIII, 313, count of Peñaranda, chief negotiator at Münster, to the marquis of Caracena, Governor of Milan, 27 June 1647.

8. Pérez Samper, *Catalunya*, 265 and 268–9, 271–2, 275, details the links with Portugal; Boxer, *Seventeenth-century Macau*, Part II, narrates the odyssey of Antonio Fialho Ferreira.

9. Hugon, *Naples*, 92–100, on the spread of revolution in Naples; Lionti, 'Cartelli sediziosi', charted the spread of revolt in Sicily from the dates of the 'seditious posters' in each place, some of which he printed. See also ch. 14 above.

10. [Howell], *A discourse*, 15. See also ch. 11 above, and Merriman, *Six contemporaneous revolutions*, 115–208.

11. Ros, *Cataluña desengañada*; Di Marzo, *Bibliote storica*, III, 206–11 (citing books by Assarino, Birago Avogadro and Collurafi). See also Villari, *Elogio*, 60–1.

12. *CSPI 1633–1647*, 182, Bishop Bramhall of Derry to Laud, 23 Feb. 1638 OS; Braddick, *God's fury*, 30, quoting John Castle to the earl of Bridgewater, 24 Oct. 1639.

13. Castlehaven, *Memoirs*, 13 (with corroborating statements at 14–16); TCD *Ms* 834/18, deposition of Gerrard Colley, Co. Louth, 2 May 1642; *Ms* 828/194v, deposition of Thomas Dight, Co. Kerry, 24 May 1642, quoting an Irish priest; *Ms* 836/64, deposition of John Parrie, gentleman, Armagh, 31 May 1642 (quoting 'George Sexton, Provost Marshall to the rebells of Ulster'); and *Ms* 833/228v, deposition of Rev. George Creighton, 15 Apr. 1643 (quoting Richard Plunkett). Italics added.

14. Birago Avogadro, *Le turbolenze*, 369–70.

15. Solomon, *Public welfare*, 160; Berghaus, *Aufnahme*, 24 and 109–402; Haan, 'The Treatment', 28–9; Mitchell, 'Religion, revolt'.

16. Te Brake, *Shaping history*, 109–10, quoting Ambassador Nani to the Doge and Senate of Venice, Sep. 1647; ch. 10 above (the French echo); Bercé, 'Troubles frumentaires', 770 (the magistrates of Fermo on the 'esempio forse de sollevati di Napoli'), and 772 (Cardinal Montalto, 7, 8, and 17 July 1648); 775 (map of rebellious areas of the Papal States in 1648) and 779 ('i Masanielli'); and idem, *La sommossa*, 53. Bisaccione, *Historie delle guerre civile* (1652), included a special section on the revolt of Fermo four years before.

17. 'T. B.', *The Rebellion of Naples*, 76–7 (discussed by D'Alessio, *Contagi*, 116–30, and Hugon, *Naples insurgée*, 328–35, together with other similar works). Burke, 'Masaniello: a response', 198, notes that rebels in Dordrecht in 1651 invoked the example of Masaniello. Polišenský, *War and society*, 186–95, and Villari, *Elogio*, 51–67, discuss other examples of the interest shown in the revolt by foreign governments.

18. Hugon, *Naples*, 219–21, citing the Manifesto and the Oath; Te Brake, *Shaping history*, 109, quoting *Discorso fatto al popolo napoletano per eccitarlo alla libertà* (1647).

19. Dunthorne, 'Resisting monarchy', 126, quoting Althusius and Guez de Balzac; Quevedo, *La rebelión de Barcelona* (1641) in *Obras*, I, 283; Parker, *The cordiall*, 30; *CSPV 1640–1642*, 220, Ambassador Giustinian to the Doge and Senate, 27 Sep. 1641 NS; Hobbes, *Leviathan*, 225. See Hill, *Intellectual origins*, 250–1, for other English praise for 'the example of Holland'.

20. Crewe, 'Brave New Spain', 77–8, quoting the paper that began 'Por quanto Dios Nuestro Señor compasivo de nuestros duelos inhumanos', confiscated at Lompart's arrest.

21. Winius, *Fatal history*, 141, Count of Óbidos, Goa, 1653; 'Articles of Confederation of the United Colonies of New England', 19 May 1643; Webb, *1676*, 237 n. 81 on Bacon's initiative.

22. Heiligsetzer, *Der oberösterreichische Bauernkrieg*, 17; ch. 8 above.

23. On Scotland's diplomatic successes, see ch. 11 above; on its failures, see Grotius, *Briefwisseling*, XI, 251, to Oxenstierna, 5 May 1640 (rejected appeal to Louis XIII); ibid., 329, from Charles Marini, Zurich, 4 June 1640; and *Theatrum Europeaum*, IV, 184–92, Andrew Ramsay to the Swiss Church, 1 April 1640 (also rejected).

24. Gilbert, *Irish Confederation*, VI, 233–4, Oliver French to the States-General, 5 May 1648.

25. Van Aitzema, *Saken*, I, 146 (alliance with Tunis and Algiers because they all 'een machtigh vyandt hadden aen Spangien'); 905 (jealousy); and 1,103 (Universal Monarchy); [Voetius], *Brittish lightning*, sig. B. Haan, 'The treatment', 39–48, discusses this pamphlet from 1643 (not 1642) – originally published in Dutch and French – and plausibly attributes it to Gisbertius Voetius. Sharpe, *Personal rule*, 833 n. 68 and ch. 11 above (support for the Scots).

26. See van de Haar, *De diplomatieke betrekkingen*, chs 2–3; and de Jong, 'Holland' (Dutch support for Portugal).

27. Goodwin, *Anti-Cavalierisme*, 5 and 50, published in October 1642 (see also *ODNB*, s.v. John Goodwin); Young, 'The Scottish Parliament', 92, quoting Instructions to Thomas Cunningham, Mar. 1645 (in Nov. 1643, the Scots Parliament also instructed its commissioners in England to seek allies abroad: ibid., 82–3); Markham, *Anarchia anglicana*, part ii, 49–50 (Hugh Peter's sermon).

28. Haan, 'The Treatment', 30–1; Carrier, *Labyrinthe*, 80, quoting Charles de Saumaise to Jacques Dupuy, 8 Sep 1648; 83, quoting Anon., *Epilogue, ou dernier appel du bon citoyen sur les misères publiques* (1649); and 108–19, on Republicanism in the *Mazarinades* and other publications of the day.

29. Carrier, *La Fronde*, I, no. 16, Davant, *Avis à la reine d'Angleterre et à la France* (1650), 3–6; Carrier, *Labyrinthe*, 111–12, citing *Le Ti θεĩου de la maladie de l'État* (Paris, 1649); Knachel, *England*, 66–70; Corneille, *Pertharite, Roy des Lombards*, first performed in 1651.

30. Van Aitzema, *Saken*, III (1645–57), 323 (news arrived in The Hague on 14 Feb. 1649); Bergh, *Svenska riksrådets protokoll*, XIII, 17, minutes of de la Gardie's speech at the Council of State on 21 Feb. 1649 OS – thus just three weeks after the regicide. The book was Caspar Salmasius, *Defensio Regia* (Stockholm, 1649).

31. Berghaus, *Aufnahme*, 56–8; Schilfert, 'Zur Geschichte', 129, Chancellor Schwarzkopf of Lower Saxony in 1651 (with similar fears voiced by the Elector of Brandenburg and others at ibid., pp. 129–30); Radziwiłł, *Memoriale*, IV, 116–18, written in Kraków on 18 Feb. 1649; Vernadsky, *Source book*, I, 246, decree of 1 June 1649 OS. Robin Briggs reminds me of a parallel process in 1793: the execution of Louis XVI discredited and paralyzed radicals in other countries.

32. Bergh, *Svenska riksrådets protokoll*, XIII, 128, minutes of de la Gardie's speech, 10 Oct. 1651; Christina quoted in Roberts, 'Queen Christina', 196–7; and Grosjean, *An unofficial alliance*, 247 n. 42.

33. BL *Addl. Ms* 4,200/14–70, letters from René Augier, 'Resident for the Parliaments of England and Scotland in Paris', to Giles Greene in London, 1646–8; Milton, *Complete prose works*, VIII, 555–6, *Pro populo anglicano defensio secundo*, May 1654.

34. Benigno, *Specchi*, 98; Berghaus, *Aufnahme*, 92.

35. Cosnac, *Souvenirs*, V, 256–77, 'Les principes, fondement et gouvernement d'une république' and 'Manifeste'; Carrier, *Labyrinthe*, 114. See also Knachel, *England*, 198–200, 212–13 and 267–9; Kötting, *Die Ormée*, 194–244 and passim; and Lutaud, *Des révolutions*.

36. Carrier, *La Fronde*, I no. 22, Anon., *Les cautelles de la paix* (May 1652), pp. 17–18 ('l'empire de l'univers'). No doubt the subsequent British attack on the Dutch Republic and the 'Western Design' to conquer part of Spain's empire in the Caribbean confirmed the author in his opinion. No group of rebels outside Europe seems to have 'exported revolution' in the mid-seventeenth century like the Dutch and the English.

37. Weber, 'The early German newspaper' (quotation from p. 74); Behringer, *Im Zeichen*, 303–80 and table on 414; and Berghaus, *Die Aufnahme*, I, 21–2. See also chs 10 and 12 above for some French and English statistics.

38. Schmidt, *Spanische Universalmonarchie*, 14 (pamphlet estimate); Paas, *The German Political Broadsheet*, II–VII, reproduced over 2,000 items published between 1618 and 1648, several of which survive in only a single copy. Many more items are known only by name, and no doubt others still have disappeared without trace.

39. Stolp, *De eerste couranten*, i, Hooft letter of 24 June 1640; Carrière, *Le labyrinth*, 156, quoting a pamphlet by Gabriel Naudé, Mazarin's librarian; Infelise, 'News networks', 66–7, quoting Gregorio Leti, *Dialoghi politici* (Rome 1666) and Francesco Fulvio Frugoni, *Del cane di Diogene* (Venice 1687). I have provided my own translation of the Italian texts.

40. Firth, *The Clarke papers*, IV, 231, Captain Newman of the Leith garrison to Monck, 31 Dec. 1659 OS (the pamphlet was *A letter of the officers of the Army of Scotland . . . to the officers of the Army of England*). Haan, 'The treatment', 2, notes how ordinary men and women in the Netherlands read political works on barges and ferries, and discussed them in taverns and squares.

41. Eisenstadt and Schluter, 'Early modernities', 25. Jürgen Habermas, who coined the phrase in 1962, has insisted that a 'popular public sphere emerged only in competition with the literary public sphere of the late eighteenth century', and so the term cannot be properly applied to an earlier period. Nevertheless, from the 1640s onwards western Europe witnessed both of the intersecting processes that Habermas considered essential ingredients of

the public sphere: first, 'the communicative generation of legitimate power'; and, second, 'the manipulative deployment of media power to procure mass loyalty, consumer demand and "compliance" with systemic imperatives'. Calhoun, *Habermas*, 452, 464–5 (from Habermas's response to his critics and his 'Concluding remarks'). See also the discussion in Dooley, 'News and doubts'; and Condren, 'Public, private'.

42. Whitelocke, *Memorials of the English affairs*, 176, speech on mobilizing an army, July 1642; Raymond, *The invention of the newspaper*, 186, quoting Dudley, Lord North, in 1671; Neumann, *Das Wort als Waffe*, 1, quoting Alexandre de Ros, *Cataluña desengañada* (Naples, 1646).

43. Conti, *Le leggei*, 92–3, *bando* of 15 Nov. 1647. Hugon, *Naples*, 128–37, discusses revolutionary writings.

44. Locke, *Political essays*, 5, from his 'First tract on government', written Sep.–Dec, 1660 but never published.

45. Kagan, *Students*, 45; Brockliss, 'Richelieu', 245–6; Naudé, *Considerations*, 127–8; Newcastle, *Advice*, 20; Bremner, *Children and youth*, 90, quoting 'The Report of Sir William Berkeley, Governor of Virginia, on the state of free schools, learning and the ministry of the colony, 1671'.

46. Brinsley, *Ludus literarius*, 176; Molinier, *A mirrour*, 356–7; Bodin, *The sixe bookes*, 543; Hobbes, *De Cive*, 139 (in a section entitled 'Causes dissolving a commonwealth').

47. Kagan, *Students*, 13–14.

48. Spufford, 'First steps', 410, 415–17, quoting the autobiographies of Sansom and Tryon (see also *ODNB* s.v. Thomas Tryon).

49. Ibid., 410–11, quoting Oliver Heywood's *Life of John Angier*, his father-in-law and Elizabeth's mother. Donawerth, 'Women's reading practices', reconstructed how Mary Fell, née Askew, wrote her *Women's speaking justified* while in prison in 1666, including quotations she had memorized from the Bible.

50. See Johansson, 'The History of Literacy in Sweden'. Since the state imposed no obligation to teach writing, scarcely a quarter of adult males and very few females in seventeenth-century Sweden could sign their names.

51. Hart, *Geschrift en Getal*, 131; Snel, *The right teaching of useful knowledge*, 314.

52. Cayet, *Chronologie novenaire* (1608), 22. Other details from Paas, *Kipper and Wipper*, and Bollême, *La Bibliothèque bleue*.

53. Carrier, *La presse*, 56 and 58 (quoting the complaints) and 71 (calculation of total printed *Mazarinades*; another 800 exist only in manuscript).

54. Pascal, *Lettres provinciales* (1657: trans. T. M'Crie), 'Reply of the provincial', 2 Feb. 1656.

55. Ezquerra Abadía, *La conspiración*, 12, lists those named in Pellicer's *Avisos* arrested for maligning the king and his policies. See Bouza, *Corre manuscrito*, 34–5, on the students; and 40–3 on copying plays and sermons.

56. Ettinghausen, 'Informació', 47, quoting Pellicer's *aviso* for 12 June 1640. Infelise, 'News networks', 55–62, describes the similar news network handled by Giovanni Quorli of Venice, 1652–68.

57. Neumann, *Das Wort als Waffe*, 193. On Catalan pamphlets, Ettinghausen, *Guerra dels Segadors*, 13–14, and Reula, '1640–1647'; on the Gazettes, see Ettinghausen, 'Informació', 54.

58. Schmidt, *Spanische Universalmonarchie*, 218–31 and 470–2 (list), and 371 (print).

59. Newcastle, *Advice*, 56 (see the 'young statesmen' reference on page 371 above); AUB Ms 2538/44, 'Triennial travels' of James Fraser. Figures from Raymond, *Invention*, 22–3, and Atherton, 'The press', 91. On 'spin', see Peacey, *Politicians and pamphleteers*. On the news-writers, see Atherton, *Ambition and failure*, 153–7; and Dooley and Baron, *The politics*, chs 2 and 9. The 1653–4 database may be consulted at http://www.ling.lancs.ac.uk/newsbooks.

60. Brook, *The troubled empire*, 199; Struve, *Ming-Qing conflict*, 8. Wong, *China transformed*, 112–13 and 125–6, has argued forcefully that 'Europe's public sphere' (which he defines as 'an arena in which politically engaged populations could express their claims against states') did not and could not exist in Qing China, mainly because of the lack of arenas 'in which reason could be heard and rationality could advance'. He does not consider the freedom of debate that took place in many 'arenas' during the Ming-Qing transition.

61. Note, however, the claim on page 502 above by a Japanese shopkeeper that he had 'managed to learn to read from experience' – even though Japanese contains a multitude of characters and more than one alphabet!

62. Rawski, *Education*, 92. The survey covered around one-third of the counties of Ming China; Ho, *Ladder*, 251, quoting a 1586 prefectural gazetteer; Las Cortes, *Le voyage*, 191–3.

63. See the ingenious calculations in Peterson in *CHC*, VIII ii, 714–15. Note, however, Cynthia Brokaw's reminder that the existence of so many different Chinese characters meant that someone able to read a text on one subject fluently might struggle to read works on something different (*Commerce*, 560–8).

64. Chia, 'Of Three Mountains Street', 128. Note, however, that China's output pales in comparison with Europe: although the 38 printers of Nanjing produced some 110 works between 1621 and 1644, the 30 printers of Naples brought out 94 works in a single year (1632: Santoro, *Le secentine*, 41).

65. Brokaw, *Commerce*, 13–17. In 1639 the imperial government began to print the 'Peking Gazette' from movable type, but only because the content changed every day.

66. Gallagher, *China*, 21, quoting Mateo Ricci (Brokaw, *Commerce*, 513–18, confirms the cheap price of books); Ko, *Teachers*, 50 (quoting an editor of *The peony pavilion*, a popular opera).

67. Will, 'Coming of Age', 31, quoting Yao's 'Record of successive years'. Yao also mentioned 'the publication in Jiangnan of a novel on the fall of Peking only two months after the event' (loc. cit.).

68. Brook, *Confusions*, 171–2, quoting Grand Secretary Yu Shenxing (1545–1608: note the similar protest of Lord Newcastle above). On *dibao*, see Struve, *Ming-Qing conflict*, 9–10, and Yin, *Zhongguo* (my thanks to Cynthia Brokaw for this reference).

69. Le Comte, *Nouveaux mémoires*, 498.

70. Wu, 'Corpses' 44, quoting Lu Yunlong, *Wei Zhongxian xiaosho chijianshu* ('Account to condemn the villainous Wei Zhongxian'). See Kishimoto, *Min shin kyōdai*, ch. 4, on the lionizing of the Suzhou rioters.

71. Dardess, *Blood and history*, 5; Fong, 'Writing from experience', 257–8; Struve, *The Ming-Qing conflict*, 7–9 and 33–4 (citing the histories of Ji Liuqi); and idem, *Ming formation*, 336.

72. Ho, *Ladder*, 199, paraphrasing the survey of Ming Confucian thought in Huang Zongxi, *Mingru xuean* (1676). The 1640s also saw the beginning of a 'Public Sphere' in Japan, discussed in ch. 16 above.

73. Labat, *Nouvelle relation*, II, 151 (adding that 'They use Arabic characters to write their own language'); Ritchie, 'Deux textes', 323–4, from Chambonneau's *Traité de l'origine des nègres* (1678).

74. Subrahmanyam, 'Hearing voices', 94–5; Ludden, *Peasant history*, 8.

75. Çelebi, *Balance*, 11, 143–4: the *Kashf al-zunā*. Professor Gottfried Hagen informs me that although not all copies date from the seventeenth century, this represents a substantial total for a work not prescribed for medrese study.

76. See Hering, *Ökumenisches Patriarchat*, and Trevor-Roper, 'The church of England'. Catholic missionaries also imported religious texts in Greek into the Ottoman empire, but the sultan would not allow them to be printed there.

77. See Hacker, 'The intellectual activities'. On Manasseh and his work, see ch. 7 above.

78. Evliyā Çelebi, *Seyahatname [Book of travels]*. (Since in Turkish Evliyā means 'Government Official' and Çelebi means 'Gentleman', this may have been a pseudonym.)

79. Terzioğlu, *Sufi and dissident*, 328–9, notes the 'Jewish' slur against Ibrahim; 346–53, on the Crimean option (Mişri met Crimean princes while exiled on the same island); and 464–90, on the Mişri Order and other legacies.

80. Ibid., 41, quoting Çelebi; Hathaway 'The Grand Vizier', 669 (the text was Birgeli Mehmet Efendi's *Risāle*, which had inspired Kadizade Mehmet)

81. Scholem, *Sabbatai*, 937–9, lists editions of the *Sefer Tiqqun ha-Laylah* and *Sefer Seder Tiqqun ha-Yom*, starting with the two Istanbul editions of 1666.

82. Scholem, *Sabbatai*, 604, quoting an Armenian living in Istanbul at the time. A single example: the father-in-law of Glückel of Hameln sold everything he owned to buy provisions for the journey from Hamburg to Israel: Lowenthal, *The Memoirs of Glückel of Hameln*, 46–7.

83. Scholem, *Sabbatai*, 549, quoting Mather.

84. This paragraph draws on the doctoral research of Benzion Chinn at the Ohio State University. I am most grateful to him for sharing it with me.

85. Different sources give different numbers for Masaniello's 'ragazzi': Graniti, *Diario*, 15, and Donzelli, *Partenope*, 7–8, both stated that he had eight companions, aged between 23 and 25; while Filomarino suggested that Masaniello commanded 25–30 boys aged 15 or less (Palermo, *Narrazioni*, 385, Filomarino to Innocent X, 12 July 1647). Giraffi later wrote that Masaniello trained at first 500 and eventually 2,000 boys specifically to mount a protest against the excise (Howell, *Exact history*, 11–12).

86. AMAE (P), CPA 54/101–7, M. de Bellièvre to Secretary of State Brienne, 31 Dec. 1646.

Part V. Beyond the Crisis

1. Special thanks to Derek Croxton, Kate Epstein, Jack Goldstone, Daniel Headrick, Paul Monod, Sheilagh Ogilvie and Kenneth Pomeranz for help in framing the final chapters of this book.

2. For two representative series that show the 1690s as the coldest on record see Brázdil et al., 'Use', fig. 2 (Germany since 1000); and Dobrovolný et al., 'Monthly', 93 (central Europe 1500–2007). See also Manley, 'Central England temperatures', 402 (data 1659–1973); and Xoplaki et al., 'Variability', 600–1.

3. Garnier, *Les dérangements*, 141–8, and figs 22–24, present the most recent round-up of west European data on 'the Great Winter'. For the experience of the Balkans, see Xoplaki et al., 'Variability', 598. Gabriele Bella's painting *The Frozen Lagoon in 1708* portrayed the Venetian skaters.

4. Shindel, 'Volcanic and solar forcing', 4,104, 'GCM simulation 1680 vs 1780 solar + volcano'; Luterbacher et al., 'European seasonal and annual temperature', 1,501–2; idem, 'Monthly mean pressure', 1,050, 1,062; Pfister, 'Weeping in the snow' 54, displays two weather maps reconstructing the unusual cold in 1695. http://www.volcano.si.edu/world/find_eruptions.cfm lists eruptions by year; http://en.wikipedia.org/wiki/File:Volcanic-ash-downfall_map_of_Mt.Fuji_Hoei-eruption01.jpg reconstructs the ash falls from Mount Fuji's 'Hōei eruption' in 1707–8.

5. Data from Teodoreanu, 'Preliminary observations', 189, quoting a Turkish chronicler; García Acosta, *Desastres agrícolas*, I, 203–14; Myllyntaus, 'Summer frost', 82. See also Xoplaki et al., 'Variability', 596–604.

6. Nicolas, *La rébellion*, 232–4, quoting the *intendants* of Limoges and Moulins; Lachiver, *Les années de misère*, ch. 8; and Le Roy Ladurie, *Les fluctuations*, 105–12, 114–15, 300–1. See also chs 4 and 10 above (on 'stunting') and ch. 12 (on Britain's weather).

7. See García Acosta, *Desastres agrícolas*, I, 211, on the 'tumultos' in New Spain; ch. 10 above on the French popular rebellions of the 1690s and 1709; Ze'evi, *An Ottoman century*, 5, 60, 83–4, on urban revolts in the Ottoman empire. Subtelny, *The domination*, chs 4–5, notes that small groups of discontented nobles in Livonia, Poland, Ukraine, Moldavia and Hungary all rebelled in the first decade of the eighteenth century; but none secured a broad base of support. Although Subtelny provided an excellent account of each of the five revolts, and noted some common denominators, none rivalled the upheavals of the 1640s and 1650s in scale or consequences.

8. Mauch and Pfister, *Natural disasters*, 6–7 (Mauch's introduction). The term 'Creative Destruction' is often misused. In 1848 Marx and Engels noted that most human societies face a 'crisis' whenever 'a famine [or] a widespread war of destruction cuts off every means of subsistence and destroys industry and trade'; and they argued that these setbacks stimulated both 'the conquest of new markets' and 'the more thorough exploitation of the old ones' (*Communist manifesto*, ch. 1). They did not use the term 'Creative Destruction', which first appeared a century later as the title of ch. 7 of Joseph Schumpeter's critique of Marxist theory, *Capitalism, socialism and democracy*. Schumpeter, however, expressly excluded 'wars, revolutions and so on' as the 'prime movers' of economic change. Instead, he meant by 'Creative Destruction' the *internal* process by which new economic markets, products and methods 'incessantly revolutioniz[e] the economic structure from within, incessantly destroying the old one, incessantly creating a new one' (*Capitalism*, 82–3). Like most historians, I perversely use Schumpeter's convenient term to describe Marx's useful insight.

Chapter 20   Escaping the Crisis

1. Gordon, *Diary*, I, 259–60 (perhaps an inspiration for Kevin Costner in the opening sequence of the film *Dances with Wolves*?). See ibid., 228, 260, and elsewhere for other examples of Gordon's fatalism. See ch. 5 above on the 'True record'. Mann, 'Women in East Asia', offers an excellent overview.

2. AGRB SEG 43 records at least six soldiers discharged from the Spanish Army in 1643–4 on account of *mal de corazón*; SEG 37/148 records a man of 42 discharged from the army who 'Por hallarse roto y con otros achaques está inhútil'.

3. Bodleian *Ms Ashmole* 185, 'Figures set upon horary questions by Mr William Lilly', vol. III, Aug. 1646–May 1647 – random entries from almost 300 questions asked by women during these nine months.

4. Macdonald, *Mystical Bedlam*, 36, 38, 40–1, 55, 73. Many 'troubled patients' of psychiatrists today have similar concerns, and the 6:4 male/female ratio is remarkably similar; but most are middle aged and virtually none are servants. For a similar distribution of suicide victims, see ch. 4 above. Napier had an enormous medical practice: his 'troubled' patients (1,286 female and 748 male) formed less than 5 per cent of the total he treated between 1597 and his death in 1634: see *ODNB* s.v. 'Napier'.

5. Trevor-Roper, *Europe's physician*, 8 (Cromwell) and 363–4 (Princess Elizabeth). Mayerne treated numerous patients for venereal disease, including the young Richelieu (ibid., 66). Macdonald, *Mystical Bedlam*, 150–64, discusses Napier's 'melancholy' and 'mopish' patients; Villari, *Baroque personae*, 29, also discusses 'manic depressives' of the day.

6. Burton, *Anatomy*, 5 and 76 ('Democritus to the Reader') and second pagination 11 (Partition I, section I, subsection V: 'Melancholy in disposition'); Aubrey, *Brief lives*, s.v. 'Burton', reports his suicide. Burton was just one of many English writers of his day on this subject, including John Donne (*Devotions upon emergent occasions*, 1624), John Milton ('Il pensoroso', 1645) and Sir Thomas Browne (*Hydriotaphia; Urn burial*, 1658). See Gowland, *The worlds of Renaissance melancholy*.

7. *ODNB*, s.v. 'Felton' by Alastair Bellany, quoting from trial papers; *CSPD 1628–1629*, 343, examination of Elizabeth Josselyn, 3 Oct. 1628. Although executed as a traitor, England celebrated Felton's action with toasts, poems and pamphlets: see ch. 18 above.

8. Goldish, *Jewish questions*, 131–3 (a 'responsum' first published in Venice in 1697). Avicenna (Ibn Sina) discussed melancholy in Part III of his treatise, dedicated to diseases of the brain.

9. Pepys, *Diary*, VIII, 588, entry for 24 Dec. 1667 (Pepys felt some remorse – 'God forgive me for it, it being in the chapel' – but consoled himself that he had profaned a Catholic and not an Anglican service); ibid., VI, 132, 145, 310 ('heavy petting'), 202 (the dexterous waterman's daughter); 162, 253, 294 (sex with his 'Valentine', whose first name he always omits, referring to her as 'Bagwell's wife'); 189, 201 (his Valentine's daughter); and 191 (dream).

10. Ibid., VI (1665), 240 (entry for 24 Sep. 1665) and 342 (verdict on the plague year).

11. Haude, 'Religion', 545–6, quoting Maximilian's directive (*Mandat*) of 20 Sep. 1636; the pastor of Hersbruck near Nuremberg; and Pastor Davis Wagentrotz of Brandenburg. Asai quoted ch. 16 above. Other crises loosened sexual restraints. Boccaccio's *Decameron*, although fiction, suggests that plague in the fourteenth century had much the same effect on the libidos of Florentines; while at a German railway station during an air-raid in 1944 Louis-Ferdinand Céline observed that 'Hunger and phosphorous make people rut and sperm and surrender without looking! . . . The whole waiting room and buffet exchanging lice, scabies, syphilis, and love!' (Céline, *Castle to castle*, 184. My thanks to Mircea Platon and Leif Torkelsen for these Pepysian items.)

12. Struve, 'Dreaming', 159–60, part of a study of Xue Cai (1598–1665, *jinshi* 1631), one of at least 160 prominent literati known to have entered a monastery. (A further 23 'entered the Dao'.) Peterson, *Bitter Gourd*, describes

how another prominent intellectual, Fang Yizhi, became a monk in 1650, after the collapse of the Southern Ming cause, and remained devoutly in his convent until his death 21 years later.

13. Fong, 'Reclaiming subjectivity', analyzes the copious autobiographical writings of Ye (b. 1589; *jinshi* 1625; retired 1630; d. 1648), and quotes Ye's *Jiaxing rizhu* ('Daily records') at p. 35. Brook, *Praying for power*, 114–16, notes that many Ming scholars used monasteries as 'retreats' where they prepared for their civil service exams or as public spaces for lectures and meetings – so they had already formed links with individual convents. At pp. 121–2 he notes that demoralized officials retired to monasteries in increasing numbers from the 1630s. The scale of monastic 'conversions' alarmed the Qing, who in 1653 tightened the rules on obtaining a licence to be a monk; but once the Ming cause foundered, this avenue of escape lost its appeal.

14. Will, 'Coming of age', 33.

15. Sieur Le Gendre [Robert Arnauld], *La manière de cultiver les arbres fruitiers* (1652). That same year Arnauld also published one of the most vicious *Mazarinades: La vérité toute nue*.

16. Walton, *The compleat angler* (the first edition in 1653 took the form of a dialogue between two characters, but he expanded this to three in the 1655 and subsequent versions). On *Eikon basilike*, see chs 2, 12 and 19 above.

17. Van Beneden and de Poorter, *Royalist refugees*, shows how Newcastle and his wife, Margaret Cavendish, survived in exile at what is today the Rubenshuis in Antwerp. On Hobbes, see ch. 12 above; on Heberle, Schütz, Opitz and Kepler, see ch. 8 above. On the Masanielli and *malvizzi*, see ch. 14; on the Polish and Russian peasants, see ch. 6 above.

18. Nicoară, *Sentimentul de insecuritate*, I, 189–92 (the ploy did not work: after his subjects overthrew him in 1653 he spent the rest of his life in a Turkish prison).

19. *ODNB*, s.v. 'Thomas Fairfax'; and Philip Major, 'Jumping Josaphat', *Times Literary Supplement*, 28 July 2006, p. 15. On other demoralized English victors (members of the Rump Parliament) see page 378 above.

20. Di Cosmo, *The diary*, 46, 83, 87 (from 1682).

21. Peters, *Ein Söldnerleben*, 42–3 (good living), 62 ('mit Vermeldung, oh lutrian, begfutu, Madtza, Hundtzfudt, etc'), 226 (the 'hübsches Mädelein'); Monro, *Expedition*, 218; Rushworth, *Historical Collections*, IV, part 1, 399; *ODNB* s.v. Monro.

22. Seaver, *Wallington's world*, 11; Pepys, *Diary* (see, for example, his annual entries on 26 March, the anniversary of a dangerous but successful operation to remove a kidney stone). On Newton, see Westfall, 'Short-writing', with the full text at http://www.newtonproject.sussex.ac.uk/view/texts/normalized/ALCH00069, accessed 12 Mar. 2012.

23. Disney, *Some remarkable passages*, 143 (entry for 14 Dec. 1685), 137 (12 Oct. 1685) and 125, 'Some few heads of advice' for his wife to observe after his death. See others examples quoted in Von Greyerz, *Versehungsglaube*, ch. 3. In Scotland, Calvinists like Johnston of Wariston also used their diaries for 'introspections': see the chapter on Wariston in Stevenson, *King or Covenant?*

24. Gallardo, *Ensayo*, II, cols 168–82, summarizes Caldera's *Arancel politico. Defensa del honor y práctica se la vida de nuestro siglo* (313 manuscript folios approved for publication but never printed); quotation from col. 174. Jover, *1635*, 430–3, documents the rise of 'catastrofismo' in Spain.

25. Sallmann, *Naples et ses Saints*, 345–6, calculated totals from the 'Visitor's Book' kept by the chapel that contained the bones of a local saint, Gaetano de Tiene; Guilielmo Gumppenberg, S.J., *Atlas Marianus sive de imaginibus Deiparae per orbem christianum miraculosis*, 2 vols (Ingolstadt, 1655), reprinted several times; expanded Latin and German editions in 1672.

26. Brokaw, *The ledgers*, 3–4.

27. Fong, 'Reclaiming', 28, quoting Yuan Huang *Liming wen [Essay on determining fate]* (1601), together with other 'egodocuments'. Kenneth Pomeranz reminds me of the difference between the 'introspections' of Wallington and other Christians, who envisaged a *single* Judgement Day, whereas their Chinese contemporaries saw the deeds that would earn a reward or a punishment as a *continuous* scorecard.

28. Courtwright, *Forces of habit*, 2, 59.

29. Lockhart, *Denmark*, 55, quoting the earl of Leicester in 1632; Ladewig Petersen, 'Conspicuous consumption', 64–5, quoting the diary of Esge Brock. (The entry is reproduced in Parker, *The Thirty Years War*, plate 24).

30. Pepys, *Diary*, X, 104–8 ('Drink'), and 416–18 ('Taverns'); Gallardo, *Ensayo*, II, col. 175. Clark, *The English alehouse*, 210–11, notes the impact of the black bottle on the consumption of beer.

31. Thackston, *Jahangirnama*, 320, quoting Taleb Amuli, the emperor's Persian-born poet laureate.

32. Ibid., 46 and 50; Balabanlilar, *Imperial identity*, 91.

33. Rycaut, *The present state*, 114; Matthee, *The pursuit of pleasure*, 107, quoting Thomas Herbert; Babayan, *Mystics*, 444–5, quoting Jean Chardin and Rafael du Mans, and 446–7, on Qummi. Seventeenth-century Europeans also used opium, but primarily for medication: see Maehle, *Drugs on trial*, ch. 3.

34. Pepys, *Diary*, I, 253, entry for 25 Sep. 1660; Massieu, *Caffaeum* (c. 1700). See also Thomas Fellon, SJ, *Faba Arabica, vulgo caffetum, carmen* (1696); and Pierre Petit, *Thia Sinensis* (1685), dedicated to a Jesuit. De Vries, *The industrious revolution*, 32–3 and 156–7, charts the slow spread of tea and coffee consumption.

35. Haskell, *Loyola's bees*, 94, quoting Strozzi, *De mentis potu, sive de cocolatis opificio libri tres* (Naples, 1689). Haskell devotes most of ch. 2 of her fascinating book to Strozzi.

36. Withington, 'Intoxicants', 631–8, discusses the anonymous pamphlet; Pepys, *Diary*, VI, 120 (7 June 1665), and VIII, 389–90 (18 Aug. 1667); Dikötter, '"Patient Zero"', 7, quoting Yao Lü. Grehan, 'Smoking', 1,373, notes that 'Middle Easterners still say today individuals "drink" their smoke.'

37. All quotations from Brook, *Vermeer's hat*, ch. 5, 'School for smoking' (quotation from p. 143, with examples at pp. 143–6).

38. Grehan, 'Smoking', 1,364–5 (quoting Katib Çelebi in 1653) and 1,355 (quoting 'Abd al-Ghani al-Nabulsi of Damascus in 1682). Ze'evi, *An Ottoman century*, 29, records widespread consumption of coffee, tobacco and hashish in seventeenth-century Jerusalem.

39. Romaniello, 'Through the filter of tobacco'. Mughal Emperor Jahangir banned smoking in 1617, but his son lifted the ban about a decade later. Shah Abbas of Iran took similar decisions at much the same time.

40. Account of a meeting of the Zemskii Sobor in 1653 by Peter Loofeldt, a Swedish diplomat: quoted page 174 above. A generation later, by contrast, similar fears *did* help to prevent bloodshed in England in 1688: page 608 above.

41. There was one exception. In 1689, after several decades of frontier warfare, China and Russia settled their differences by the treaty of Nerchinsk: the first of its kind in East Asia.

42. Crucé, *Nouveau Cynée*, 13; Lind, *Hæren*, 193 and 426 note, Jørgen Rosenkrantz to his brother Otto, 1636 (citing Pindar, 'Dulce bellum inexpertis': 'War is sweet to those who have never experienced it').

43. BL *Addl. Ms* 21,935/78v–79, 88–92 (Wallington); Anon., *The victorious proceedings*, 2; Parker, *The manifold miseries*, 1.

44. Bennett, *The Civil Wars*, 95 and 133, quoting Samuel Woods and Rowland Watkins; Birch, *The life*, I, 55, letter to Lady Ranelagh, 30 Mar. 1646; Kuczynski, *Geschichte*, 117, quoting a family Bible from Swabia in 1647.

45. One of these 1649 *Humpen* went on sale in 2012 for 40,000 euros. Full text reproduced at http://www. auctions-fischer.de/selling/highlights/glass-16th-19th-century.html?L=1&objekt=137&cHash=18f276ebbe, accessed 8 Feb. 2012. On Franck and other European military artists of the day, see the reproductions and discussions in van Maarseveen, *Beelden*, and Bussmann and Schilling, *1648*, vol. II: *Art and culture*.

46. Raynor, *A social history of music*, 115 and 203–4, quoting Burckhart Grossman and Heinrich Schütz.

47. Schottelius, *Neu erfundenes Freudens-Spiel genandt Friedens-Sieg* (Wolfenbüttel, 1648): digitized version available at http://diglib.hab.de/wdb.php?distype=img&dir=drucke%2Flo6992. Image 36 is an engraving of the first performance, showing the august players and audience.

48. Rabb, *The struggle*, 119, quoting Gerhardt; Milton, *Paradise Lost*, Book 2, lines 160–4, 335–40 (part of the Great Debate at Satan's court on whether or not another battle should 'be hazarded for the recovery of heaven'). Rabb, *The artist*, 101–18, dates the 'rise of a new, critical approach to war' among Western artists to the 1630s. Burke, 'The crisis', 251–5, provides a useful list of mid-seventeenth-century paintings and writings condemning war and revolution.

49. Grimmelshausen, *Der abentheurliche Simplicissimus teutsch*, first published 1668, soon reprinted, and the only German Baroque novel still widely read. The boy watches the sack of his family farm in Book I, ch. iv.

50. Rabb, *The struggle*, 119, citing English and German texts in support; Brunt, *Social conflicts*, 152–4 (I thank Nathan Rosenstein for drawing this reference to my attention).

51. Bod. *Ms. Eng. Hist.* c. 712 e.312 (The 'Commonplace Book' of Sir Roger Whitley for 1647–8), p. 47, 'Innovations and novelties'; Hobbes quoted page 379 above. Skinner, 'The ideological context', notes how many other English writers made the same point at this time.

52. AMAE (P) CPE 21/242–3v, Bishop Marca to Mazarin, Barcelona, 17 June 1644; Anon., *Avertissements aux rois*, 6. Also in 1644, in Beijing, Prince Dorgon proclaimed in June 1644 that the Mandate of Heaven had shifted to the Qing 'because we now hold it' (see ch. 18 above). In Japan, Suzuki Shōsan advanced much the same argument in his treatise *Banmin Tokuyō* (*Right action for all*) of 1652 (see ch. 16 above).

53. Locke, *Political essays*, 7, from his 'First tract on government', written Sep.–Dec., 1660 but never published. On the *Kongelov*, see ch. 8 above.

54. Crucé, *Nouveau Cynée*; Hugo Grotius, *De jure belli ac pacis, libri tres* (Paris, 1625); William Penn, *An essay towards the present and future peace of Europe, by the establishment of an European Dyet, Parliament or Estates*(London, 1693). Penn referred with approval to the 'Grand Design', proposed in the 1630s by Henry IV's former minister, the duke of Sully, for a European federation that would create a balance of power and thus promote peace. In 1671, in his *Traité des moyens de conserver la paix avec les hommes*, the French Jansenist Pierre Nicole argued that religious and moral restraint would reduce wars. Jacob, *Peace projects*, printed English versions of Grotius, Sully and Penn.

55. Von Friedeberg, 'The making', 916, deposition before the Imperial Chamber Council in 1652; Zillhardt, *Zeytregister*, 267 (note the early use of the term 'Thirty Years War' to describe the recent conflict).

56. Roberts, *Sweden as a great power*, 173–4, Gustav Bonde's Memorial to the Council of the Realm, 26 June 1661.

57. Morrice, *Entring book*, IV, 335.

58. Rohrschneider. *Der gescheiterte Frieden*, 81, 'La experiencia ha mostrado quan poco de puede fiar de las palabras y fee pública de Franceses en los tratados' (June 1643) and 'L'expérience nous fait cognoistre que les Espagnolz ne gardent leur traités' (Sep. 1643) – a stunning duplication of views, each composed in total secrecy.

59. *Instrumentum Pacis Osnabrugensis*, V, 52 ('*sola amicabilis compositio lites dirimat non attenta votorum pluralitate*'); Heckel, 'Itio in partes', quoting a constitutional tract of 1722. On the tears, see Dickmann, *Westfälische Frieden*, 460.

60. Tuck, *Philosophy*, 319, quoting Hobbes to the duke of Devonshire, July 1641; Locke, *Political essays*, 40–1, from his 'First tract on government', written Sep.–Dec. 1660. Sermons preached on the text 'Curse ye Meroz' (Judges 5: 23) are discussed in ch. 18 above.

61. Butler, *Hudibras,* Part I, canto 1, 1–6 and 195–202; Pepys, *Diary,* III, 294 (26 Dec. 1662), and IV, 35 (6 Feb. 1663). Pepys first bought a copy in Dec. 1662, found it 'silly', and therefore sold it at a loss later that same day. Two months later he bought another copy to find out what he had missed (but was still underwhelmed). Other readers enjoyed Butler's satirical reuse of phrases associated with former Puritans like Pepys.

62. Locke, *A letter,* 33; Schilling, 'Confessional Europe', 669; Benedict, 'Religion and politics', 133.

63. *Acta Pacis Westphalicae: supplementa electronica, IPO,* V:50; Wallis, *A defence of the Royal Society,* 7.

64. Kenyon, *Stuart Constitution,* 365–71, 'An Act of free and general pardon'; Anderson, *The journal,* 173, Court Martial, 7 Apr. 1665; Stoyle, ' "Memories of the maimed" '; Young, *Faith,* 54.

65. Plumb, *The growth,* xvi–xviii and 1. Scotland, Ireland and Anglo-America were, of course, a different story. I first heard Dr Plumb (as he then was) expound his thesis in Oxford in 1965, when I attended his Ford's Lectures. It was a thrill to discover, 45 years later, that it still rings true.

Chapter 21   From Warfare State to Welfare State

1. Meyer, 'Ein italienisches Urteil', 160–1; Ray, *Observations,* 81–2 (Mannheim and Heidelberg) and 140 (Vienna); Skippon, *An account,* 432 (Mannheim), 439–40 (Heidelberg), and 476 (Vienna). Both Englishmen became Fellows of the Royal Society through their prowess in observations. I thank Kenneth Pomeranz for many helpful comments on an earlier draft of this chapter.

2. Meyer, 'Ein italienisches Urteil', 160–1; Ray, *Observations,* 109; Patin, *Relations* (1671), 144, 199–200, 212.

3. AUB *Ms* 2538, 'Triennial travels', III/7v (Regensburg), 8 (Regensburg); Gordon, *Diary,* II, 8 and 36 (1659).

4. Li, *Fighting famine,* 9; Fong, 'Writing', 268–73. She observes 'The experience of loss and dislocation was so complex and traumatic that, for those who had the means and the skill, writing must have served as a therapeutic means of regaining some sense of control, order, and poetic dignity.' I thank Nicola Di Cosmo for pointing out the rarity of visual representations of military themes in Han Chinese art.

5. Li Wen, 'On the road', graciously translated for me by Lynn Struve (on Li's journey see Wakeman, *Great Enterprise,* 678–80); Wakeman, *Great Enterprise,* 761, printed Chen's poem (with another in note 127).

6. Meyer-Fong, *Building culture,* 134 (other data from ibid., 5, 12, 20, 77–8, 141–2 and 174–80).

7. Nieuhof, *An embassy,* 3 (preface), 85 (Yangzhou), and 64 (Nanchang). The English edition claims that only 8,000 were slain at Canton, but Nieuhof's original Dutch manuscript clearly states 80,000: see BNF, *Cartes et plans,* Ms In 8° 17, fo. 30. Likewise the English edition claims that Hukon enjoyed a lively trade when the Dutch visited in 1656, but Nieuhof's original text makes clear that this was 'voor de destructie van China': ibid., fo. 61.

8. Nieuhof, *An embassy,* 65 (Qing policy), 39 (Canton) and 84 (along the Grand Canal). Compare the similar expression of Semedo, just before the conquest: pages 23–4 above.

9. Brantôme, *Oeuvres,* VI, 326; La Noue, *Discours,* 160.

10. Ansaldo, *Peste,* 204–8. Del Pino Jiménez, 'Demografía rural Sevillana', 500–2, found the same surge immediately after the devastating plague of 1649 in the Andalusian towns he studied.

11. Sreenivasan, *Peasants,* 289–92 and 322–3 (all quotations). Theibault, *German villages,* 199, noted that, to repopulate his lands, the landgrave of Hessen-Kassel waived the normal 'residence tax' for any demobilized soldier who came and settled.

12. Felloni, 'Per la storia'; Eldem, *The Ottoman city,* 98–102 (by Daniel Goffman); Bustos Rodríguez, *Cádiz,* passim; and archival data communicated by Professor Bustos in Sep. 2006, for which I am most grateful.

13. *Venezia e la peste,* 98; Hagen, 'Seventeenth-century crisis', 325 (quoting the edict of 1661); Archivio di Stato, Lucca, *Anziani al tempo della libertà, buste* 707–8.

14. Jespersen, *A revolution,* 279–96; Lappalainen, 'Finland's contribution', fig. 9; Oschmann, *Der Nürnberger Exekutionstag* (on payments to veterans of the Swedish Army). The pleas of penniless war widows presented by Ailes, 'Wars, widows', show that for the families of many Swedish soldiers and sailors, the 'continental war' proved both a personal and a financial disaster.

15. Wheeler, *The making,* 212, notes the money paid to English veterans. Firth, *Cromwell's Army,* 197 and 206, noted that only those in service at the Restoration received their pay – the numerous officers purged in 1659 received nothing. Reece 'Military Presence', Appendix, suggests that 25,000 soldiers served in England in 1660.

16. Ray, *Observations,* 221, and Skippon, *An account,* 550–1 (both in 1663). On the destruction, see SIDES, *La popolazione,* 43–7; and Externbrink, 'Die Rezeption des "Sacco di Mantova" '.

17. Sreenivasan, *The peasants,* 348, quoting statements by the magistrates of Memmingen in 1600 and 1702.

18. Rawski, 'The Qing formation', 217–18, notes the pawnshops; demographic data from Pomeranz, 'Is there an East Asian development path?', 325–6; acreage from Ho, *Studies,* 102 (but note the caveat on page 730 n. 4 to ch. 5 above). Other information from Huang, *Peasant economy,* 85–6; Pomeranz, *The Great Divergence,* 84; and Will, 'Développement quantitatif'.

19. Hartlib, *Samuel Hartlib his legacie.* Kerridge, *The agricultural revolution,* first published in 1967, produced a barrage of examples of agrarian 'improvement' in England during the later seventeenth century. Mark Overton, *An agricultural revolution,* later dismissed this evidence and argued that little changed before 1750. The rival claims may be reconciled by noting that Kerridge drew most of his examples from East Anglia, where lighter soils facilitated innovation, whereas Overton concentrated on the Midlands, with heavier soils. For similar improvements in Japan, see ch. 16 above.

20. Ho, *Studies*, 146, quoting a Gazetteer of 1760; Mazumdar, 'The impact', 69; Wong, *China transformed*, 28 (calculations from lineages in Tongcheng county).
21. Goldstone, *Revolution*, 372.
22. Quotations from de Vries, *The Industrious Revolution*, 10 and 128, with more examples from his ch. 4, entitled 'Consumer demand', and his subsequent article, 'The limits'.
23. Clunas, *Superfluous things*, charted the Ming boom; on Suzhou, see Marmé, 'Survival', 145–55.
24. Marmé, 'Survival', 156–9 (guilds); Nieuhof, *An embassy*, 69 (shipping) and 75 (Nanjing). Compare the similar description of Semedo in the 1630s, page 24 above. In 2002 the number of vessels sailing up and down the Yangzi near Nanjing deeply impressed the present writer.
25. Marmé, 'Survival', 144, quoting Kangxi and Cao Yin, and 151 (*jinshi* score: 785 in the Qing period); Will, 'Coming of age', 38–9, quoting Yao's *Jishi shiyi* ('Remembrances not yet recorded').
26. Details from Perdue, 'Water control'. Dongting lake still expands from 2,000 to 12,000 square miles in the flood season (between July and September), but Poyang lake is now larger.
27. Le Comte, *Nouveaux mémoires*, I, 118–20.
28. Nieuhof, *An embassy*, 81 (Grand Canal) and 104 (Tianjin); Brook, *The confusions*, 48 (estimate by Gu Yanwu).
29. AUB *Ms* 2538, 'Triennial travels', I/29; Morrice, *Entring book*, IV, 331, entry for 6 Nov. 1688.
30. Once again, I thank Professor Kishimoto Mio for sharing her 'model' concept for China with me during a seminar at International House Tokyo in July 2010, and her speculation on that occasion that 'we can find some parallels on the other side of Eurasia as well'.
31. Hull, *The economic writings*, I, 91 and 94 (*A treatise of taxes*, ch. XV, 'Of excise'); North, *Discourses*, 14. De Vries, *The Industrious Revolution*, 58–64, makes the interesting suggestion that a positive attitude towards the 'new luxuries' originated with the Jansenists who saw 'self-love' as a useful and constructive passion.
32. Defoe, *The compleat English tradesman*, II, part 1, 99–102 and 107 (climate); the last hurrah appears in his *A tour*, I, 'the author's preface'.
33. Yang, 'Economic Justification for Spending', 51, quoting an essay by Lu Chi of Shanghai, c. 1540, quoting Mencius; Kishimoto-Nakayama, 'Kangxi depression', 241–2, quoting an essay by Wei Shixiao, c. 1680. Defoe made the same point: 'moderation', he wrote, would throw 'maid-servants' as well as farmers, craftsmen and tradesmen out of work: *The compleat English tradesman*, II, part 1, 99–102.
34. Defoe, *A tour*, I, 'The author's preface' (published in 1724, after 40 years of travels and observation); Defoe, *The compleat English tradesman*, II, part 1, 99–102.
35. Wheeler, *The making*, 148, 198. Its lineal successor, value added tax, remains the third largest source of British revenue: an extraordinary legacy of the Global Crisis.
36. Details from Bogart, 'Did the Glorious Revolution contribute?'
37. Wheeler, *The making*, 213; Mallet, *Comptes rendus*, 286–7 (when in the early eighteenth century Mallet reviewed the records of the French treasury, he found no meaningful figures for the quinquennium 1656–60, such was the fiscal chaos: ibid., 240); European State Finance Database, http://esfdb.websites.bta.com/Default.aspx, last accessed 4 Feb. 2012.
38. Ogilvie quoted page 52 above; Scott, *Seeing like a state*, 11.
39. Wu, *Communication*, 34–6 and 48–9; Janku, 'Heaven-sent disasters', 239–41.
40. Virol, 'Connaître', 851 and 855, demonstrates the Chinese influence on Vauban's plans for a 'Dîme royale'.
41. Colbert, *Lettres*, I, 251–2, Colbert to Mazarin, 30 Aug. 1656, and reply dated 9 Sep. Soll, 'Accounting', 234, describes the volume prepared each year for the royal pocket. Colbert, *Lettres*, II part 2, 771–83, published the contents of the volume for 1680 (which included a summary of state income and expenditure between 1662 and 1680). On the opposition of the judges to Mazarin, see chapter 10 above.
42. Vauban, *Méthode générale*, 14–15, published May 1686.
43. Virol, 'Connaître', and idem, *Vauban*, with additional data from Vauban's archive: ANF *AP* 155 Mi 1–68. The first detailed survey was carried out in the town of Douai, of which Vauban was governor, in 1682, and covers 91 folios: ANF *AP* 155 Mi 14/22; extract in Virol, 'Connaître', 873. Vauban thus amassed as much detail as the surveys of Japan by the Toyotomi and Tokugawa regimes, albeit not on a national scale (see ch. 16 above). See also Virol, *Vauban*, 192–4, for a 17-page 'Supputation' entitled 'Chronologie des cochons'.
44. 'Moyen de retablir nos colonies de l'Amérique et de les accroître en peu de temps' (1699), in Vauban, *Les oisivités*, 539–73, quotation from p. 571. The actual population of French Canada in 2000 was scarcely seven million (and that of all Canada not even 31 million).
45. Virol, *Vauban*, 204 ('Du nombre d'hommes'), 212 (noting that other practitioners of 'political arithmetic' made the same assumptions), and 213 (dearth is 'dans l'opinion et non dans la réalité': from a *Mémoire* of 1694).
46. Soll, 'Accounting', 237; Plumb, *The growth*, 11–13.
47. Scott, *Seeing like a state*, 3.
48. Pérez Moreda, *Las crisis*, 299; Morales Padrón, *Memorias de Sevilla*, 67.
49. Brockliss and Jones, *The medical world*, 350, quoting L'Érisse, *Méthode excellente et fort familière pour guérir la peste* (Vienne, 1628).
50. Lebrun, *Se soigner autrefois*, 162–3 (see the identical pattern in Switzerland described by Eckert, 'Boundary formation'); Moote, *The Great Plague*, 254.

51. Marks, *Tigers*, 147 n. 42, reports a successful variolation campaign in 1657 near Guangzhou. On the more virulent strains from Africa, see Alden and Miller, 'Unwanted cargoes', and ch. 4 above. Ch. 5 above noted the ravages of smallpox among the Manchus.

52. *SCC*, VI 6, 134–40 (Kangxi's personal testimony); Woods, *Death before birth*, 213–32 (smallpox, mothers and infants); Lee, Wang and Campbell, 'Infant and child mortality', 402–3 (spread of the technique in China). When describing variolation in Bengal in 1731, an English merchant claimed that the technique had been known there for 150 years: Guha, *Health and population*, 141.

53. Schiebinger, *Plants and empire*, 100–4, notes the spread of variolation to Europe. The parish returns printed in Sinclair, *The Statistical Account* (see, for example, vol. II, 12 and 551), record how variolation had often eliminated smallpox in Scotland even before Jenner pioneered vaccination.

54. No doubt Cromwell would have rejected *any* medicine monopolized by the Jesuits on ideological grounds, but his impeccably Catholic neighbour in the Spanish Netherlands, Archduke Leopold William, also refused to use cinchona in the 1650s: Maehle, *Drugs on trial*, 226–8.

55. *ODNB* s. v. Thomas Sydendam, letter to John Locke, 3 Aug. 1678.

56. Li, *Fighting famine*, 167.

57. Le Comte, *Nouveaux mémoires*, 125 (writing of his personal inspection in the 1680s). Other details from Li, *Fighting famine*; Will and Wong, *Nourish the people*; Shiue, 'Local granaries'; and Perdue, *China marches West*, 359–65. Early Tokugawa Japan, too, possessed a network of granaries: see ch. 16 above.

58. Mikhail, *Nature*, 216–17. Ibrahim, *Al-Azmat*, ch. 4, argued that the famine of 1694–5 was the worst of the seventeenth century.

59. Pullan, *Rich and poor*, 294–6, on Italian city granaries; Skippon, *An account*, 600; Hugon, *Naples*, 75, 139, 141, on Naples; and ch. 9 above on Madrid.

60. For England, see Thirsk, *The agrarian history*, IV, 619, for Scotland, see http://www.rps.ac.uk, article proposed by Charles I on 1 Nov. 1625; for Sweden see Myllyntaus, 'Summer frost', 92–4 (the situation changed only after 1726 and yet another series of catastrophic harvests: over 100 parishes boasted granaries by the end of the eighteenth century).

61. Ranum, *Paris*, 354–6. La Reynie, the first Lieutenant General (1667–97), belonged to the *dévôt* party that had long advocated spending on welfare, not warfare: see ch. 10.

62. Guthrie, 'A seventeenth-century "ever-normal granary"'; Farriss, *Maya society*, 269–70; and ch. 15 above.

63. Romaniello, 'Controlling the frontier', 435; See Bercé, 'Troubles frumentaires', 489–93, on the repertory of emergency relief measures taken in 1648 by the magistrates of Fermo.

64. Ailes, 'Wars, widows', 22, 25; Hastrup, *Nature*, 234–5; Anon., *An ease for overseers of the poore*, 22.

65. Hindle, *On the parish?*, 256; Solar, 'Poor relief', 4–6; Blaug, 'Poor Law Report', 229.

66. Allemeyer, '"Dass es wohl recht ein Feuer"', 218–20, noting orders from Braunschweig, 1647; Emden, 1666; Kirchward, 1673; Clausthal, 1687; Nürnberg, 1698. See also the Epilogue below about the importance of 'cumulative learning', because humans only evolve coping strategies for disasters that are frequent as well as severe.

67. Calculations from Thomas, *Religion*, 19–20; other data from Jones, *Gazetteer*, 52–3. See also ch. 3 above.

68. Barbon, *A letter*, 1–2.

69. McClain, *Edo and Paris*, 310–16; Needham and Wang, *SCC*, IV/ii, 218–22; van der Heyden, *A description*, 37, 81; Viallé and Blussé, *The Deshima Registers*, XII, 335–8.

70. AUB *Ms.* 2538, 'Triennial travels', I/29.

71. Israel, *Dutch Republic*, 680–2.

72. Schumpeter, *Capitalism*, 85. He concluded his argument: 'In the case of retail trade the competition that matters arises not from additional shops of the same type, but from the department store, the chain store, the mail-order house and the supermarket which are bound to destroy those pyramids sooner or later.' Note the caveat concerning the use of the term 'Creative Destruction' on page 780 n. 8 above.

73. Marcos Martín, *España*, 462–3, 479–82; McArdle, *Altopascio*, 52–4 and 91.

74. Quotations from Sreenivasan, *The peasants*, 289–92, 322–3 and 326.

75. Ogilvie, *State corporatism*, 106–9, 189 and 218–20; Sreenivasan, *The peasants*, 333–5, 345–8. See also Ogilvie, 'Guilds'.

76. Brokaw, *Commerce*, 226 and 405. For the size of the student market, see ch. 5 above.

77. Ibid., 179 (and all of her ch. 5 on 'Household division and competition').

78. Allen, 'Wages', passim. I thank Kenneth Pomeranz for discussing Allen's work with me.

Chapter 22   The Great Divergence

1. Adshead, 'The XVIIth century General Crisis' 265, 251; Pomeranz, *The Great Divergence*, passim. Although *The Great Divergence* contains relatively little on science and technology, Pomeranz compared the experience of early modern Europe and China in this regard in 'Without Coal? Colonies? Calculus?'. Once again, I thank Kenneth Pomeranz for sharing with me his erudition and his insights.

2. Batencour, *L'instruction méthodique*, 32–46, 'De la justice du maistre' (see p. 40 on the special wickedness of 'les garçons uniques'). I cite the 400-page 1669 re-edition of the 1654 original: *L'escole paroissiale ou la manière de bien instruire les enfans dans les petits escoles.*

3. Jolibert, *L'enfance*, 18, Plaidoyer before the Parlement of Paris, 25 Jan 1680; *Mélanges*, 7, Letter Patent of Louis XV, Sep. 1724, creating a charity school in Rouen.

4. Le Cam, 'Extirper la barbarie', 412–13, and idem, 'Die undeutlichen Grenzen', 50–1, quoting Duke Augustus of Brunswick-Wolfenbüttel's *Schulordnung* (1651) and *Allgemeine Landes-Ordnung* (1647), whose first two articles enjoined universal attendance at church and school – seen as the two pillars on which political stability rested.

5. Act of the Scottish Parliament registered 2 Feb. 1646 (http://www.rps.ac.uk/trans/1645/11/185, accessed 8 Feb. 2012).

6. Rawski, *Education*, 33–4 (on the 1652 schools edict) and 26 (citing an 'encyclopaedia' probably published in 1675–6); Herman, 'Empire' (on the 1658 edict on education for chieftains, the first of many). On China's 'national school curriculum', see chs 5 and 19 above.

7. Dore, *Education*, 20. Nevertheless, given the existence of 236 fiefs, in this respect Japan lagged far behind China and much of Europe.

8. Israel, *Radical enlightenment*, 128–9.

9. Hautz, *Geschichte der Universität Heidelberg*, II, 186–8, report of the Rector and debate by the Senate, 25 Feb. and 5 Mar. 1680; Tukker, 'The recruitment', 212 n. 4. See also the data on falling enrolments at Spanish universities in Kagan, *Students*.

10. Hugon, *Naples*, 266–7; Garrisson, 'Les préludes', 13, bishop of Montauban to Mazarin, 8 July 1659, a few days after students from the Protestant Academy had unwisely invaded the neighbouring Jesuit College and beaten up its students.

11. Rutt, *Diary of Thomas Burton*, II, 531–42, prints Oliver Cromwell's Letters Patent of 15 May 1657 founding 'a College at Durham', naming its instructors (mostly associates and protégés of Samuel Hartlib), and funding it from local church property; Newcastle, *Advice*, 20, written in 1659 (see Cavendish, *Life*, 186).

12. Cavendish, *Life*, 194; Cressy, *England on edge*, 337–8 (song).

13. Dell, *Several sermons*, 612–13 and 644–7, two sermons delivered in 1652–3 (Dell, once a chaplain of the New Model Army, was then Master of Gonville and Caius College, Cambridge); Winstanley, *The Law of freedom*, 68–9. For more on anti-university sentiment, see ch. 18 above.

14. On the vigorous life of students at Leiden, see Verbeek, *Descartes and the Dutch*, 34–70.

15. Ho, *Ladder*, 191–2. Mote, *Imperial China*, 863–4, gives much higher figures for those involved. Between 1677 and 1682, however, the emperor sold degrees to finance the repression of the Revolt of the Three Feudatories. For more on the civil service examination system, see chs 5 and 18 above.

16. Israel, *Radical enlightenment*, 3–4; Aubrey, *The natural history of Wiltshire*, 15 (the first paragraph of the Preface, written in the 1680s). The wonderful anecdote about Harvey *losing* patients as soon as he published a book reminds us that, besides being an acute observer of nature, Aubrey compiled scintillatingly wicked biographies of some 400 scientific luminaries, many of whom he had known personally, published posthumously in his *Brief Lives*. See also *ODNB* s.v. 'John Aubrey'.

17. Hunter, *John Aubrey*, 41–2, quoting from notes made by Aubrey for his projected biography of Bacon.

18. *ODNB*, s.v. 'Bacon'; Bacon's preface to the *Novum Organum*.

19. Bacon, *Works*, XIV, 120, Bacon to James I, 12 Oct. 1620.

20. McClure *Letters of John Chamberlain*, II, 339, to Sir Dudley Carleton, 3 Feb. 1623.

21. Scriba, 'The autobiography', 26–9 (italics added). See the similar contempt for mathematics as a matter for merchants and 'something inappropriate for a king' in France: ch. 10 above.

22. Scriba, 'The autobiography', 39–40; Birch, *Works*, I, 19–20, Boyle to Isaac Marcombes, 22 Oct. 1646, and to Francis Tallent (his Cambridge tutor), 20 Feb. 1647. Boyle's father was Richard, first earl of Cork. Villari, *Baroque personae*, 273–5, prints many similar statements by European scientists of their willingness to learn from anyone and anything.

23. Bacon, *Works*, XIV, 436, Bacon to Charles, prince of Wales, Oct. 1623, together with a Latin copy of *The advancement of learning*.

24. Weil, 'The echo'. Harvey thus anticipated the celebrated 1953 paper in *Nature* by James Watson and Francis Crick, describing the structure of DNA, which reserved its revolutionary implications for the terse penultimate paragraph that began 'It has not escaped our notice that . . .'.

25. Descartes, *Discours*, 51 and 22. Descartes praised Bacon ('Verulamius': the Latin version of St Albans, Bacon's title) to Mersenne, 23 Dec. 1630 and 10 May 1632: *Oeuvres*, I, 195–6 and 251.

26. Ganeri, *The lost age*, discusses the 'new reason' and its practitioners (quotations from Dara Shikoh at pp. 24–7). At pp. 16–17, Ganeri draws an explicit parallel between the approach of the 'new reason' philosophers and of Bacon.

27. Elvin, 'The man who saw dragons', provides a fascinating analysis of this work (quotations from pp. 12 and 34). Elvin also notes that, just as Galileo and Bacon had intellectual precursors, so did Xie (ibid., 3–7). See other common-sense quotations from *Wa za zu* in chs 1 and 5 above.

28. Miller, *State versus gentry*, 140, quoting Zhang Pu's declaration; Chen's 'Rules of Compilation' (*fanli*) to the *Nongzheng quanshu* by Xu Guangqi (1562–1633), one of the most prominent Chinese Christian converts of his day. Chen referred specifically to a treatise on hydraulics by Sabatino de Ursis, S.J., translated in Xu's work. My thanks to William S. Atwell for this reference.

29. Atwell, 'Ming statecraft', 68–9, on the *Huang Mingjingshi wenbian* of 1639, inspired by a similar compilation of political tracts from earlier periods published in 1635: Chang Pu, *Memorials by famous officials through the ages*. Chang and Chang, *Crisis*, 285–303, provide brief biographies of several Late Ming advocates of the new learning.

30. Details from Peterson, 'Ku Yen-wu' (quotations from p. 131, and 211, Gu's *Advantages and disadvantages of the provinces and prefectures of the empire*, completed in 1662). Gu's methods strikingly resemble those of English antiquaries of his day, such as John Aubrey. Pomeranz, 'Without coal?', 256–61, and Elman, *From philosophy*, ch. 2, offer excellent insights into Chinese 'evidentiary research'.

31. Struve, *Ming-Qing conflict*, 30, quotes the edict; Spence, *Emperor*, 65–8, quotes Kangxi's own writings. Waley-Cohen, *Sextants*, 105–21, provides a perceptive discussion of the benefits and limits of the Western knowledge that the Jesuits decided to release in China – cartography, artillery, art and architecture as well as 'science'.

32. Based on Cook, *Matters*, ch. 4, 'Translating what works', quotation from pp. 344–5 (Genshō, *Kenkon bensetsu*). Florentius Schuyle collated, translated and published Descartes's book as *De homine* in 1662.

33. Okada Takehiko, 'Practical learning', 270–1, quoting from the eight-volume complete works of Kaibara Ekken (1630–1714). This paragraph relies on the articles in de Bary and Bloom, *Principle and practicality*.

34. On Kumazawa (1619–91), and Zhu (1600–82), see McMullen, 'Kumazawa Banzan'; Ching, 'Chu Shun-Shui'; and idem, 'The practical learning'.

35. McMullen, 'Kumazawa Banzan'. Atwell, 'Ming observers', draws fascinating parallels between seventeenth-century *arbitristas* (from *arbitrio*, or 'remedy') in various countries.

36. Spinoza, *Tractatus theologico-politicus*, 291–2 (from the last chapter of the work, wherein 'It is shown that in a free commonwealth every man may think as he pleases and say what he thinks' – a quotation from Tacitus).

37. Drake and O'Malley, *The controversy*, xiii, Virginio Cesarini to Galileo, 1618 (the bite); other details from Drake, *Galileo at work*, and Redondo, *Galileo*.

38. Ciampoli, *Lettere*, 72–3, to Marcantonio Eugenii, 7 Dec. 1640. The Pope had asked Ciampoli to read Galileo's *Dialogues*, the book that contained the new passage on the heliocentric theory, and Ciampoli assured the Pope that it contained nothing against church doctrine, thus securing permission for its publication – and sealing his own fate.

39. Descartes, *Oeuvres*, I, 270–1 and 285–6, to Mersenne, Nov. 1633 and Apr. 1634 (in the original, the italicized words were *Bene vixit, bene qui latuit*, from Ovid, *Tristia*). *Le monde, ou traité de la lumière* only appeared in 1662.

40. Descartes made sure the first edition, published in Leiden, appeared anonymously; but the licence authorizing the French edition named him as its author. Descartes, *Oeuvres*, I, 338–41 to Mersenne, Mar. 1636, and 369, to someone involved in the licensing process, 27 Apr. 1637 (blaming Mersenne for naming him).

41. Spinoza, *Ethics*, 1–3 (from the introduction by Seymour Feldman).

42. Leffler, 'From humanist', 420, about François Eudes de Mézeray's *Abrégé chronologique de l'histoire de France*, 3 vols (Paris, 1668). For two prominent importers of contraband books (more than 1,700 of them) arrested in 1666 and condemned to the galleys, see Waquet, 'Guy et Charles Patin'.

43. Lord, *Poems*, I, xxxvii, quoting testimony of George L'Estrange, the chief censor, to the House of Lords in 1677 (the measure failed).

44. Van der Heyden, *A description of fire engines*, 3. See ch. 21 above on the ill-fated fire engine. In his *Essay of humane understanding* (1690), John Locke also stressed how often humans get things wrong: 'All Men are liable to Error': *Essay*, Book IV, ch. 19 (a section entitled 'Wrong assent or errour'), para 17.

45. Ganeri, *The lost age*, 248.

46. Elvin, 'The man who saw dragons', 22–3: Cook, *Matters*, 415. Elvin considers the examples of 'scholarly communication' presented in Elman, *From philosophy*, ch. 5, but rates them insignificant compared with Europe. He also notes that most of them occurred after 1700.

47. Berry, *Japan*, 51–2.

48. Merton, 'Singletons and multiples', 482–3. The argument between Newton and Leibniz, and between their disciples, over who first invented calculus is the best-known example of a seventeenth-century 'contested multiple'. For another, see Hall and Hall, 'The first human blood transfusion'.

49. Bacon, *Novum Organum*, aphorism CXIII; idem, *New Atlantis. A worke unfinished*.

50. One of the Italian fellows was Elena Lucrezia Cornaro Piscopia (1646–84), the first woman to obtain a doctorate (at Padua, 1678), who was fluent in Latin, Greek and Hebrew. She joined several academies, and ordered all her manuscripts to be destroyed at her death.

51. Scriba, 'The autobiography', 39–40.

52. Hartlib, *Considerations*, 46–8. Details on earlier attempts from Blome, 'Office of Intelligence', and *ODNB*, s v. 'Samuel Hartlib'.

53. Sprat, *History*, 57–8; charters to the Royal Society, 15 July 1662 and 22 Apr. 1663; *ODNB* s.v. 'Founder members of the Royal Society'.

54. Sprat, *History*, 84–5, 98. Wilkins oversaw the project and nominated Sprat, one of his own students, to write it p. 110.

55. Sorbière, *A voyage*, 49. See also the gushing account of the early meetings of the Royal Society by another French visitor: Balthasar de Monconys, *Journal*, II, 26–8, 37, 47–8 and 55–6.

56. Mormiche, *Devenir prince*, 329, 337.

57. Other scholars also served as 'clearing houses' for the exchange of scientific knowledge: 1,100 of Marin Mersenne's letters have survived for the years 1617–48, many of them accompanied by items sent by others which he forwarded as 'attachments'; Nicholas-Claude Fabri de Peiresc exchanged well over 10,000 letters with some 500 correspondents between 1598 and 1637; Ismael Boulliau left an estimated 10,000 letters at his death in 1694.

58. *Philosophical Transactions* did not become the official journal of the Royal Society of London until 1752: Oldenburg took personal responsibility (as well as the profits) for his work as editor (or 'author' as Oldenburg called himself). The *Journal des Sçavans*, which first appeared a few weeks earlier in 1665, at first included mostly book reviews.

59. Israel, *Radical enlightenment*, ch. 7, offers an excellent overview.

60. Bots, 'Le rôle des périodiques', 49, quoting Abbé Jean-Paul de la Roque, Director of the *Journal des Sçavans*.

61. Skippon, *An account*, 433 (Heidelberg) and 607 (Naples); Ray, *Observations*, 271–2 (Naples).

62. Boix y Moliner, *Hippocrates aclarado, prólogo*, n.f. (the author claimed that Harvey had learned about the circulation of the blood from a commentary on Ecclesiastes by Padre Juan de Pineda in 1620; while Descartes had plagiarized a book by Dr Gómez Pereyra, published in 1554); Israel, *Radical enlightenment*, vi.

63. Camuffo, 'The earliest temperature observations'. By a cruel irony, the records of this precocious experiment were severely damaged by an extreme climatic event: the Florence floods in 1966. When eventually processed in the twenty-first century, the data revealed winters more than 1°C cooler than in the twentieth century.

64. Sprat, *History*, I, 173–9, prints Hooke's proposal; Fleming, *Historical perspectives*, 34–7, provides an overview of this and other systematic attempts to collect weather data.

65. Goad, *Astro-meteorologica*; Baker, 'Climate', 428–32 (on Ashmole, Locke and Plot). Ashmole acquired the papers of other astrologers, including the 'weather diary' kept between 1598 and 1635 by Richard Napier (ch. 20 above). See also an interesting attempt in 1676 to compare the climates of Ireland and British North America in Vogel, 'The letter', especially p. 128.

66. In France, 56,000 people died in the first two weeks of August 2003, 15,000 more than usual, with particularly high mortality among women and those over age 45. One-third of that excess mortality occurred in Ile-de-France, with more than double the normal death rate in some areas: Hémon and Jougla, *Estimation*, 54–5.

67. Details from Gere, 'William Harvey's weak experiment' (Bacon and Harvey); Hunter, *Robert Boyle*, ch. 10 (entitled 'Magic, science and reputation' and mostly about Boyle's last book, *Strange reports*); Snobelen, 'A time' (Newton).

68. Lubienietski, *Theatrum Cometicum*, collected reports from all over Europe, accompanied by over 80 illustrations.

69. Robinson, *The great comet*, 120–6, and Álvarez de Miranda, 'Las controversías', list the works; Akerman, *Queen Christina*, 177; Fryer, *A new account*, III, 174–5, Fryer's letter from Surat, 25 Jan. 1681 OS; De Beer, ed., *The diary of John Evelyn*, IV, 235.

70. Lach and van Kley, *Asia*, III, 976; Tavernier, *Travels*, I, 309; Di Cosmo, *Diary of a Manchu soldier*, 57; *Kangxi Shilu*, XCII, pp. 14a and 20b (I thank Timothy Brook for this reference).

71. Mather, *Heaven's alarm*; idem, *Kometographia*, 118, 124 and 107.

72. Descartes, *Oeuvres*, I, 251–2, to Mersenne, 10 May 1632 (adding 'as Tycho [Brahe] did with the three or four that he observed: a reference to Brahe, *Liber de cometa*, 1603); Schaffer, *The information order*, 36–44. See the sources listed in Book III, lemma IV, of Newton's *Principia Mathematica*.

73. Halley, *A synopsis of the astronomy of comets* (London, 1705), 19, 21–22, 24. See Alvarez, *T-Rex*, 145–6 and colour plate facing p. 101, on the collision of a fragment of Comet P/Shoemaker-Levy 9 with Jupiter in 1994. It is possible that Halley knew that Cassini had seen something that *looked* like a comet hitting Jupiter in Dec. 1690, and had sketched it: Peiser, *Natural catastrophes*, 7. Halley was also lucky because the 1682 comet was the last one visible to the naked eye to appear for 60 years.

74. Rabb, 'Introduction', 149; Rabb, 'The Scientific Revolution', 509. I thank Mircea Platon for alerting me to the second item.

75. Skippon, *An account*, 607; Ronan, *Edmond Halley*, 124, Astronomer Royal John Flamsteed to Isaac Newton in 1691. Thirteen years later Halley became professor of geometry at Oxford, despite another critical letter from Flamsteed.

76. Milton, *Paradise Lost*, Book I: 287–91, and the beginning of Book VIII (I thank Kate Epstein for pointing out these references); Mormiche, *Devenir prince*, 338–9. The theologians of the Sorbonne protested at the discussion of Galileo's theory, until the Dauphin's religious preceptor Bossuet instructed them to desist. Compare Descartes's reaction when he read the sentence on Galileo: page 654 above.

77. See Kessler, 'Chinese scholars', 181–4, and Struve, *Ming-Qing conflict*, 30–2. The Chinese system of giving dates according to regnal titles and years identifed loyalty just as unequivocally as tonsures, and for the period after 1644 the authors of the *Ming History* used both Ming reign titles and the personal names (not the regnal titles) of the Qing rulers – which the regents took as clear signs of sedition.

78. Brook, 'Censorship', 177, quoting the Qianlong emperor's edict of 11 Dec. 1774. For an example of anti-Manchu literature that survived even this purge, see Chang and Chang, *Redefining history*, 136–41: some of the popular *Strange Stories from a Chinese Studio* (*Liaozhai Zhiyi*) written by Pu Songling in the 1670s.

Conclusion

1. Brinton, *Anatomy*, 237–8. I am particularly grateful to Rayne Allinson, Kate Epstein and Ken Pomeranz for their trenchant criticism of an earlier draft of this chapter.
2. Foster, *The English Factories in India, 1630–1633*, 218–19, letters from East India Company officials in Surat to London, 8 May 1632 OS; Smith, *The art of doing good*, 137, quoting Lu Shiyi's diary; Balfour, *Historical works*, III, 409; Howell, *Epistolae*, III, 26, letter of 10 Dec. 1647 to his nephew.
3. Ogilvie, *A bitter living*, 1, quoting Catharina Schill, 'ein arme Frau', in 1654. For the slaves see chs 5 (China), 12 (Britain) and 15 (Africa); for the serfs, see ch. 8. Examples of the enhanced impact of the crisis on women appear in chs 4–15 above.
4. Pepys, *Diary*, VIII, 337–414, narrates Elizabeth's revenge on him. See the brilliant summary in Capp, *Gossips*, 93–4, and his discussion of the arsenal of retaliation available to English wives and servants at pp. 84–126 and 166–81.
5. Cavaillé, 'Masculinité' para. 38, quoting Christina's 'Maxims'. Note the similarity between Christina's view of nuns and that of Elena Cassandra Tarrabotti: page 97–8 above.
6. Balabanlilar, *Imperial identity*, ch. 4, provides a brilliant analysis of the powerful 'begums and khanums' of the Mughal dynasty. See ch. 6 above for the power of the mothers of Ottoman sultans.
7. I thank Robert W. Cowley for suggesting the parallel between the quantitative and qualitative losses in the wars, revolutions and conquests of the seventeenth century and those of the twentieth.
8. Calculation by Nansen, *Through Siberia*, 283 (Nansen had just travelled around and across Siberia).
9. Wakeman, *Great enterprise*, 425–7 (notes on the careers of 23 senior Ming civil servants who surrendered first to the Shun and then to the Qing, and of 32 more who transferred their allegiance directly from Ming to Qing); and 1,129–33 (analysis of the origins and careers of the 125 men with an entry in the *Er chen zhuan*, 'Biographies of ministers who served both dynasties', and of members of the Han Chinese Banners).
10. D'Aubert, *Colbert*, 23 (quoting Lefèvre d'Ormesson); *ODNB*, s.v. 'Monck'; Wheeler, *The making*, 212. English soldiers who fought in Ireland in the 1640s and 1650s also did well from their military service: they received their wage arrears mostly in lands confiscated from the vanquished (see ch. 12 above). Parrott, *The business*, 241–9, offers a masterful survey of fortunes made and lost by military and naval commanders in seventeenth-century Europe.
11. Mortimer, *Eyewitness accounts*, 88–90.
12. Cavaillé, 'Masculinité', provides an excellent discussion of Christina's behaviour, and her critics.
13. Pepys, *Diary*, VII, 122, entry for 12 May 1666 (Samuel also mentioned his wife's delight in the book on 7 Dec. 1660 and 21 May 1667). *Artamène ou le Grand Cyrus* is available on line, with its own website http://www.artamene.org/
14. Admittedly, both Scudéry and La Fayette disguised their gender on the title page of their books, which claimed they were written by a man. *La Princesse* can be read on line http://www.inlibroveritas.net/lire/oeuvre2472. html. M. Sarkozy recorded his cultural 'suffering' at http://blogs.rue89.com/mon-oeil/2008/07/25/nicolas-sarkozy-kaercherise-encore-la-princesse-de-cleves, accessed 2 Mar. 2012.
15. Ko, *Teachers*, 129–36. Her husband was the son of one of the Donglin martyrs (ch. 5 above). Note the similarity with the poem 'The little cart' by Chen Zilong, quoted at page 103 above. Widmer, 'The epistolary world', presents a sensitive survey of Chinese women writers during the Ming-Qing transition.
16. Cavendish, *Nature's pictures*, 377–8 (from 'A true relation of my birth, breeding and life'). On Margaret and William in Antwerp, see the magnificent exhibition catalogue by van Beneden and de Poorter, *Royalist refugees*. Other details from Cavendish, *Life*; and *ODNB* s.v. Margaret Cavendish, Sir Thomas Lucas and Sir Charles Lucas.
17. Haboush, 'Constructing the center', 51; Richter, *Facing East*, 67–8; White, *The Middle Ground*, ch. 1.
18. Hagopian, *The phenomenon*, 123; Bacon, *Essayes*, 46. Bacon reprinted the essay, with certain changes, in the 1625 edition of his book, quoted here.
19. Walford, 'The famines', part II, 79. In Part I, 521–5, Walford discussed whether sunspots might influence harvests and hoped 'that the theory will receive the most critical investigation and elucidation'.
20. Ibid., part II, 217.
21. Laing, *Correspondence*, I, 93–8, and 105, Lothian to his father, the earl of Ancram, 19 Oct. 1637 and 8 Nov. 1640 (capitals in the original). The earl added: 'God's works have beane wrought by fewer then we are.'
22. BL *Harl. Ms.* 5,999/29v, 'Discourse by Henry Jones, Nov. 1643 (more details on climate and catastrophe in both Scotland and Ireland in ch. 11 above).
23. The threat of starvation may also have prompted Li Zicheng's daring 'long march' from Xi'an to Beijing early in 1644; but the destruction of his archives precludes certainty. See also ch. 5 above.
24. Trotsky, *History*, II, Introduction, and vol. I, ch. 7 ('Five Days'). For the origins of the other revolts, see chs 9 and 14 above.
25. See chs 9 (Barcelona), 14 (Naples and Messina), 6 (Moscow) and 10 (Paris) above. Brinton, *Anatomy*, 86–8, noted the same phenomenon in the American, French and Russian revolutions.
26. In addition, the enthusiasm of Kadizadeli and Sufi devotees helped to create the factions that wracked Istanbul (see chs 7 and 18 above). See Brinton, *Anatomy*, 99–100, on clerics and the American revolution.

27. Oliver Cromwell, although neither a nobleman nor a king, also founded a dynasty and, had he lived longer, the House of Cromwell rather than the House of Hanover might have replaced the Stuarts.

28. Brinton, *Anatomy*, 102, notes the prominence of university graduates among the American revolutionaries in the eighteenth century.

29. Ibid., 35.

30. Admittedly all three assemblies eventually lost their struggle: Portugal half a century later, when the inflow of revenue from Brazil enabled the crown to rule without a Parliament; Scotland and Catalonia when military force subjugated them a decade later.

31. Rebellions that did not gain control of the state's representative assembly normally collapsed relatively swiftly. In Naples, the 'Serenissima Reale Repubblica' planned to convene a *Parlamento* where represents of the 12 provinces of the kingdom could create a common cause, but the Spaniards regained control first; in Denmark and Sweden in 1650 the national Diet secured several concessions from the crown, but then fragmented and so lost them; in France in 1651 an Assembly of Nobles and an Assembly of Clergy forced the regent to summon the States-General of the kingdom but foolishly disbanded before it met (no assembly convened until 1789).

32. Scriba, 'The autobiography', 32. Once again Brinton makes this point eloquently for later revolutions: *Anatomy*, 122, 134–5, 137–8, 144.

33. Rushworth, *Historical Collections*, III part 1, 11–12, the king's speech, 3 Nov. 1640. See also ch. 11 above.

34. Braudel, *The Mediterranean*, I, part II, ch. 1, part 1; AGS *SP* 218/72, *consulta* of 27 Aug. 1647, reviewing many recent letters from Naples; AGS *Estado* 2566, n.p., Don Diego de la Torre to Philip IV, 18 Feb. 1648.

35. Elliott, *Revolt*, 407.

36. AGS *IG* 435 *legajo* 10/258v–259v, Fernando Ruiz de Contreras orders the Casa de Contratación in Seville to warn the fleet about 'el accidente de Portugal', 5 Jan. 1641, minute, and *IG* 429 *legajo* 38/177–182v, Philip IV to the viceroy of Peru and others, 7 Jan. 1641, minute. AGI *IG* 761, n.p., *consulta* of 27 Dec. 1640 – admittedly, someone endorsed this 'Luego, luego [At once, at once]', but noted that the council had delayed advising the king on the correct steps to take 'until there should be more specific and general information'. By contrast, Madrid sent news of the Catalan revolution to ministers in the New World almost immediately: AGI *IG* 589 leg. 13, n.p., Register of couriers dispatched to Seville, entry for 12 June 1640: a large packet of letters for American destinations left at '4 in the morning'.

37. One might object that *every* plot involving numerous participants runs a high risk that someone will betray it (some voluntarily, others involuntarily); yet no one betrayed the intentions of the 'matrons of the kirk' to disrupt the first reading of 'Laud's liturgy' in 1637, or the plan to restore Portuguese independence three years later.

38. AMAE (P) *CPA* 57/314–15, M. de Bellièvre to Secretary of State Brienne, London, 13 Nov. 1648.

39. Goodare, 'Debate: Charles I', 200–1; see also pages 354–8 above. For more on counterfactual protocols, see Tetlock, *Unmaking the West*, especially the Introduction.

40. Quotations from Elliott, 'The year of the three ambassadors', 181. For more on the character of Charles I, see ch. 11 above.

41. Starting with ch. 5, Crusoe narrated his experiences according to his 'Journal' (Defoe, *The life*).

42. Defoe, *The life*, 286, 262.

43. Ibid., 152, 58, 79, 170. My reading of the book owes much to Hill, 'Robinson Crusoe'.

44. Will, 'Développement quantitatif', 868, quoting the decrees of the Kiangxi emperor; Marks, *Tigers*, 291, quoting Han Liangfu in 1724 and the Yongzheng emperor in 1723. In a note, Will wonders how the emperors became convinced that China had become overpopulated, noting that memoranda from provincial governors on the question 'reflect imperial preoccupations rather than fuelling them'.

45. Milton, *Paradise Lost*, Book II, lines 597–603.

Epilogue

1. Apologies to James Carville, author of the mantra of the successful Clinton–Gore presidential campaign of 1992 'It's the economy, stupid'; and thanks to Oktay Özel who, at the panel on the 'Ottoman General Crisis' at the XI International Congress of Social and Economic History of Turkey, Ankara, 18 June 2008, suggested that our title should be 'It's the climate, stupid'. Thanks also to Derrin Culp, Kate Epstein, Daniel Headrick, James Lenaghan and Angela Nisbet, and to Greg Wagman and a group of gifted Honors Students at Notre Dame University for helpful references and suggestions.

2. I thank Christian Pfister and Martin Parry for sharing with me their recollections of the 1979 conference. Sanderson, *The history*, 285, notes BP and Shell sponsorship of the Climatic Research Unit, founded in 1971 as part of the University of East Anglia's School of Environmental Sciences. The Cambridge University Press volume was Wigley, *Climate and history*.

3. *Report of the World Food Conference, Rome, 5–16 November 1974* (New York, 1975), 6–8 (at FAORLC-41001WorldFoodConference doc, accessed 9 Mar. 2012. Note that in 1981, two years after the University of East Anglia conference, Amartya Sen published his influential *Poverty and famines*, arguing that famine reflected faulty distribution rather than defective production: see page 108 above.

4. Houghton, *Climate*, xi ('Executive summary') http://www.ipcc.ch/ipccreports/far/wg_I/ipcc_far_wg_ I_spm.pdf

5. http://inhofe.senate.gov/pressreleases/climateupdate.htm Speech by Senator Inhofe in the US Senate, 4 Jan. 2005 quoting with approval his speech on 28 July 2003. In another speech about 'the most media-hyped environmental issue of all time, global warming' on 25 Sep. 2006, the senator stated: 'The media often asks me about how much I have received in campaign contributions from the fossil fuel industry. My unapologetic answer is "Not Enough."' (http://epw.senate.gov/speechitem.cfm?party=rep&id=263759).

6. Text of the Upton-Inhofe Amendment at http://energycommerce.house.gov/media/file/PDFs/ETPA/ ETPA.pdf; defeat of the 'Waxman Amendment' (6 Apr. 2011) at http://clerk.house.gov/floorsummary/floor. aspx?day=20110406&today=20120310. The attached 'Roll 236' in this record named the 237 Republicans and 3 Democrats who voted 'no' and the 1 Republican and 183 Democrats who voted 'yes'.

7. Campbell, 'Panzootics', 178. See also his articles 'Physical shocks', and 'Nature'.

8. Mussey, 'Yankee Chills', 442, quoting an unnamed magazine in late 1816, quoting a Barnstead farmer and Bentley. More data in Heidorn, 'Eighteen hundred'; Post, *The last great subsistence crisis*, chs 2–3; Stommel, *Volcano weather*, 28–9 (map of the 'snow line' in New England in June 1816) and 83 (prices); and Harington, *The year without a summer?* (with spectacular fold-out map).

9. Mussey, 'Yankee Chills', 449 (Governor Wolcott of Connecticut) and 451 (statistics: Ohio's population rose from 380,000 to 580,000, and Indiana and Illinois also gained New England refugees). Many Europeans also migrated in 1816–17: to Russia, to South Africa and, above all, to North America Post; *The last great subsistence crisis*, 97–107.

10. *State of Ohio Homeland Security Strategic Plan* (2011), 6, at http://www.publicsafety.ohio.gov/links/Strategic_ Plan.pdf, accessed 10 Mar. 2012. The Plan says nothing about the need to 'vigilantly protect' the state's water supply.

11. Although they were entirely predictable, apparently no one foresaw the consequences of a Category 3 hurricane striking a port-city that stands only a few feet above sea level. Likewise, apparently no one foresaw the proba-bility that a Force 9 earthquake and a 46 feet tsunami would not only knock out all power at a nuclear site constructed right beside Japan's Pacific coast, at Fukushima, but also destroy the electrical cables that alone could supply the reserve power necessary to prevent a nuclear catastrophe.

12. Statistics from *2011 disasters in numbers* prepared by the International Disaster Database at the Université Catholique, Louvain, Belgium: www.emdat.be, accessed 12 Mar. 2012. These natural disasters caused many deaths – 36 at Tuscaloosa, almost 200 at Christchurch, over 550 at Joplin and at least 20,000 in northeast Japan – but other recent natural disasters have killed far more: the Sumatra-Andaman earthquake and tsunami of 2004 killed over 230,000 people; the Haitian earthquake of 2010 killed over 300,000; and so on.

13. Nordås and Gleditsch, 'Climate change and conflict,' criticize the failure of the IPCC to undertake systematic analysis of historical evidence to show how climate change acts as a 'threat multiplier for instability in some of the most volatile regions of the world' (p. 628, quoting a 2007 *National security and the threat of climate change Report from a panel of retired senior US military officers*). Their article introduces a special issue of the journal that contains five articles on the subject. I thank Sharmistha Bachi-Sen of the University of Buffalo for this reference. See also the special issue of *Journal of Peace Studies* in 2009 on the same subject.

14. Blake, *The deadliest, costliest, and most intense United States tropical cyclones*, 5, 6, 25.

15. Slovic, 'The perception of risk', 280, reprinted in his collected essays with the same title.

16. Israel, *The Dutch Republic: its rise, greatness and fall*, convincingly attributes the emergence and expansion of the Dutch Republic to the collective solidarity that evolved in the maritime provinces to cope with floods. On the emergence of fire insurance after 1650, see ch. 20 above.

17. Slovic, *The perception of risk*, 8, introduction by R. W. Kates.

18. http://www.noaanews.noaa.gov/stories2011/20110112_globalstats.html, accessed 11 Mar. 2012. The downgrade of global warming to a 'second-tier issue' appeared in the *Washington Post* for 9 June 2011: http://www. washingtonpost.com/politics/romney-draws-early-fire-from-conservatives-over-views-on-climate-change/2011/06/08/AGkUTaMH_story.html, accessed 11 Mar. 2012.

19. The authors found that many countries exposed to climate-related natural disasters also have less developed information systems, as well as populations with relatively low levels of education: both factors would further reduce concern about climate change.

20. In 2005 Televangelist John Hagee and others saw Hurricane Katrina as God's punishment on New Orleans for tolerating such 'abominations' as Gay Pride parades and clinics that offer abortions. For earlier 'peccatogenic' explanations, see ch. 1 above.

21. Bankoff, *Cultures*, 3; Kvaløy, 'The publics' concern', based on data collected from the 2005–9 'World Values Survey', quotations from pp. 11, 13–14, and 18. The authors asked respondents how serious they considered not only global warming but also 'loss of plant or animal species or biodiversity' and 'pollution of rivers, lakes and oceans'. Almost everywhere, concern for the last category came top, with global warming either second or last (p. 17). The findings strikingly parallel those of Diamond, *Collapse*, ch. 14, 'Why do some societies make disastrous decisions?'

22. Bankoff, *Cultures*, 10–13 and 32–3. Natural disasters in the Philippines also occurred in the seventeenth century (ch. 1 above) and led to the creation of the 'earthquake baroque' style: buildings specifically designed

to withstand seismic shock. For an example, the church at Paoay in northern Luzon, constructed 1694–1710, see http://heritageconservation.wordpress.com/2006/07/27/paoay-church/

23. *Adapting to climate change*, 97–8.

24. 'Revised statement of principles on the provision of flood Insurance', July 2008, http://archive.defra.gov.uk/environment/flooding/documents/interim2/sop-insurance-agreement-080709 pdf

25. Geneva Association, *The insurance industry*, 42 and 62–3 (Florida figures updated from Florida, *Into the storm*, 4). The Geneva Association is a non-profit organization comprising 80 chief executive officers from the world's leading insurance companies.

26. Geneva Association, *The insurance industry*, 70; *Adapting to climate change*, 24.

27. Florida, *Into the storm*, 2, 20, 23.

28. Cock, *Hygieine* sig. B1v (italics in the original). The author had tried to put his case to a sub-committee of the London council, but was 'silenc'd'; now he tried again 'in paper'. Further details from Moote, *The Great Plague*.

29. Pepys, *Diary*, IV, 323–4 (entry for 7 Dec. 1663); *Hansard House of Commons Debate*, 19 Feb. 1953, speech by Sir David Maxwell Fyfe; Horton, 'The Thames barrier project', 248; PRO *HLG* 145/151. Most of the Thames victims in 1953 died on Canvey Island, land reclaimed in the seventeenth century and provided with sea defences that were unequal to the higher waters three centuries later. It is notable that although the *reason* why the water level of the Thames had risen remained a mystery to those considering the Thames Barrier, they pressed on because of the *fact* that it had.

30. Data from *TE2100 Plan consultation document*, at ww.environment-agency.gov.uk/static/documents/Leisure/TE2100_Chapter01-04.pdf, accessed 12 Mar. 2012. Similar actions in the Netherlands following the 1953 floods resulted in the world's largest movable flood barrier at the mouth of the river Scheldt – once again, a preventive project so vast that only the central government could achieve it, and one that has thus far averted a repetition of another similar catastrophe.

31. Brázdil, 'Floods', 50; King, *Foresight, flood and coastal defence*.

Acknowledgements

1. E-mail to Robert Baldock, 21 Feb. 1998.

2. Needham, *SCC*, I, preface. Needham also quoted Raleigh, *History of the World* (1614): 'For all [history], without the knowledge of the places wherein it is performed, as it wants a great part of the pleasure, so it in no way enriches the knowledge and understanding of the reader.'

3. Richards, *The unending frontier*, 3.

Sources and Bibliography

1. Bisaccione, *Historia*; Birago Avogadro, *Delle historie memorabili*. Burke, 'Some seventeenth-century anatomists of revolution', surveys these and the other 'crisis' authors (two-thirds of them Italians, and one-quarter writing in 1647 and 1648). Voltaire, *Essay on the customs and character of nations* (see page 1 above).

2. Aston, *Europe in Crisis*; Elliott, 'The General Crisis'; and Merriman, *Six contemporaneous revolutions*. See also the historiographical discussions in Chaunu, 'Réflexions'; Parker, *Europe's seventeenth-century crisis*; Villari, 'Rivolte'; Wallerstein, 'Y-a-t-il une crise?' Te Brake, *Shaping history*, ch. 4; Dewald, 'Crisis'; Bitossi, 'Gli apparati statali'; Bilbao, 'La crisis'; Koenigsberger, 'The General Crisis'; and a special issue of the journal *Manuscrits*, IX (1991), 'Europa i Catalunya el 1640'.

3. *Revue d'histoire diplomatique*, XCII (1978), 5–232; Hroch and Petráñ, *Das 17 Jahrhundert – Krise der Feudalgesellschaft?* (first published in Czech in 1976); *Renaissance and Modern Studies*, XVI (1982), 1–107.

4. *Modern Asian Studies*, XXIV (1990), 625–97, mostly reprinted in the 1997 edition of Parker and Smith, *General Crisis*.

5. Goldstone, *Revolution and rebellion*; Romano, *Conjonctures opposés*; Ogilvie, 'Germany'; *AHR*, CXIII (2008), 1,029–99 ('The General Crisis of the seventeenth century revisited'); *JIH*, XL (2009), 145–303 ('The Crisis of the seventeenth century: interdisciplinary perspectives') – Rabb quoted from p. 150.

6. The depositions are available at <1641.tcd.ie>. See also the essays in Darcy, *The 1641 depositions*. 'State Papers Online' provides to institutional subscribers (only) the entire archives of the Tudor and Stuart governments.

7. Ohlmeyer, 'The Antrim Plot', 912, Lord Antrim to Hamilton, 13 July 1639; Scott and Bliss, *The works of William Laud*, VII, 211, Laud to Wentworth, 30 Nov. 1635; Struve, *Ming-Qing conflict*, 32.

8. Le Roy Ladurie, 'Naissance', pays tribute to Garnier's influence. In a conversation in February 2012, Le Roy Ladurie assured me that he had played down the climate-catastrophe connection in his 1967 book, 'because no one then would have believed me'.

9. Fleury and Henri, *Des registres paroissiaux*; Wrigley and Schofield, *The population history*; Hayami, *The historical demography*. See also Rosental, 'The novelty', and Séguy, 'L'enquête'.

Bibliography

A. Printed Primary Sources cited in the Notes

A true representation of the present sad and lamentable condition of the county of Lancaster (Wigan, 24 May 1649)

Abbott, W. C., ed., *Writings and Speeches of Oliver Cromwell*, 3 vols (Cambridge, MA, 1937–47)

Acta Pacis Westphalicae: Supplementa electronica, 1, 'Die Westfälischen Friedensverträge vom 24. Oktober 1648. Texte und Übersetzungen', http://www.pax-westphalica.de/ipmipo/

Acts done and past in the second session of the second Triennall Parliament of our soveraign lord Charles the I . . . and in the first Parliament of our soveraign lord Charles the II (Edinburgh, 1649)

Ådahl, K., ed., *The sultan's procession: The Swedish embassy to Sultan Mehmet IV in 1657–1658 and the Rålamb painting* (Istanbul, 2006)

Alba, *Documentos escogidos*, see Berwick y Alba

Alemán, Mateo, *Guzmán de Alfarache* (Madrid, 1599)

Allen, William, *A faithful memorial of that remarkable meeting of many officers of the army of England, at Windsor Castle, in the year 1648* (London, 1659)

Allom, Thomas, *China, in a series of views, displaying the scenery, architecture, and social habits of that ancient empire. Drawn, from original and authentic sources* (London, 1843)

Althusius, J., *see* Carney

Amelang, J., ed., *A Journal of the plague year: The diary of the Barcelona tanner, Miquel Parets, 1651* (Oxford, 1991)

Anderson, R. C., ed., *The journal of Edward Mountagu, first earl of Sandwich, admiral and general at sea, 1659–1665* (London, 1929: Navy Records Society, LXIV)

Andrade e Silva, J. de, *Collecção chronológica de legislação portugueza, 1627–33* (Lisbon, 1855)

Anes Álvarez, G., ed., *Memoriales y discursos de Francisco Martínez de Mata* (Madrid, 1971)

Anon., *An ease for overseers of the poore abstracted from the statutes, allowed by practise, and now reduced into forme, as a necessarie directorie for imploying, releeuing, and ordering of the poore* (Cambridge, 1601)

Anon., *The strangling and death of the Great Turke and his two sonnes* (London, 1622)

Anon., *A true and strange relation of fire, which by an eruption brake forth out of the bowels of the earth* (London, 1639)

Anon., *A Declaration shewing the necessity of the Earle of Straffords suffering* (London, 1641)

Anon., *The times dissected, or a learned discourse of several occurrences very worthy of observation to deter evill men and encourage good* (London, 1642)

Anon., *The victorious proceedings of the Protestants of Ireland* (London, 1642)

Anon., *Nicandro o antídoto contra las calumnias que la ignorancia y envidia ha esparcido por deslucir y manchar las heroicas y inmortales acciones del conde-duque de Olivares después de su retiro* (Madrid, 1643)

Anon., *The moderator, expecting sudden peace, or certaine ruine* (London, 1643)

Anon., *New England's First Fruits in respect of the progress of learning, in the Colledge at Cambridge in Massachusetts-Bay* (London, 1643), in *Collections of the Massachusetts Historical Society for the year 1792*, I (Cambridge and Boston, 1792), 242–50

Anon., *Escrívense los sucessos de la Evropa desde Abril de 46 hasta junio de 47 inclusive* (Madrid, 1647)

Anon., *The red-ribbon'd news from the army* (London, 1647)

Anon., *Persectio undecima. The churches eleventh persecution, or a briefe of the Puritan persecution of the Protestant clergy of the church of England* (London, 1648)

Anon., *Epilogue, ou dernier appel du bon citoyen sur les misères publiques* (Paris, 1649)

Anon., *La custode de la reyne, qui dit tout* (Paris, 1649)

Anon., *Le Ti θεῖον de la maladie de l'État* (Paris, 1649)

Anon., *Les cautelles de la paix* (Paris, 1652)

Anon., *Avertissements aux rois et aux princes pour la traité de la paix et le sujet de la mort du roi de la Grande Bretagne* (Paris, 1649)

Anon., *Avis à la reine d'Angleterre et à la France* (Paris, 1650)

Anon., *De na-ween vande Vrede. Ofte ontdeckinge vande kommerlijcke ghelegentheydt onses lieven Vaderlants: . . . met de remedien daer teghen* (Amsterdam, 1650)

Anon., *A bloudy fight in Ireland, between the Parliaments forces, commanded by Sir Charles Coot, and Col. Russels; and the King's forces* (London, 1652)

Anon., *A letter of the officers of the Army of Scotland, under the commander in chief there, to the officers of the Army of England* (London, 1659)

Anon., *The weasel uncas'd, or the in and outside of a priest drawn to the life* (undated, c. 1692)

Anon., *An Essay upon government adopted by the Americans. Wherein the lawfulness of revolutions are demonstrated in a chain of consequences from the Fundamental Principles of Society* (Philadelphia, 1775)

Antonio, Nicolás, *Biblioteca Hispana Nova*, 2 vols (Rome, 1696)

Antony, P. and H. Christmann, eds, *Johann Valentin Andreä: ein schwäbisher Pfarrer im dreissigjährigen Krieg* (Hildesheim, 1970)

Argyll, *Instructions, see* Slaughter

Arnauld, Angélique, *Lettres de la révérende mère Marie Angélique Arnauld*, 3 vols (Utrecht, 1741–2)

Arnauld, Antoine, *De la fréquente communion où Les sentimens des pères, des papes et des Conciles, touchant l'usage des sacremens de pénitence et d'Eucharistie, sont fidèlement exposez* (Paris, 1643)

Arnauld d'Andilly, Robert, *La vérité toute nue* (Paris, 1652)

[Arnauld d'Andilly, Robert] *La manière de cultiver les arbres fruitiers* (1652; reprinted 1671 and 1684)

Articles of the large treaty concerning the establishing of the peace betwixt the Kings Majesty, and his people of Scotland, and betwixt the two kingdomes: agreed upon by the Scottish, and English Commissioners in the city of Westminster the 7th day of August. 1641: allowed and published for the use of the Kingdome of Scotland (London, 1641)

Asselijn, Thomas, *Op- en ondergang van Masaniello* (Amsterdam, 1668)

Aston, John, 'The Journal of John Aston, 1639', in *Six North Country Diaries* (Edinburgh, 1910: Surtees Society, CXVIII), 1–34

Aston, Sir Thomas, *A collection of sundry petitions presented to the Kings most excellent majestie* (London, 1642)

Aubrey, John, *The natural history of Wiltshire*, ed. J. Britton (London, 1847)

Aubrey, John, *Brief lives chiefly of contemporaries set down by John Aubrey between the years 1669 and 1696*, ed. A. Clark (Oxford, 1898)

Avenel, D. L. M., ed., *Lettres, instructions diplomatiques et papiers d'état du cardinal de Richelieu*, 8 vols (Paris, 1853–77)

Ayala, Baltasar de, *De Iure et Officiis Bellicis et Disciplina Militari Libri III* (Douai, 1582; ed. J. Westlake, 2 vols (Washington DC, 1912))

Aykut, N., ed., *Hasan Beyzade Tarihi* (Istanbul, 1980)

Bacon, Francis, *The proficience and advancement of learning, divine and humane* (London, 1605)

Bacon, Francis, *Novum Organum Francisci de Verulamio Instauratio Magna* (London, 1620; English edn, *The new organon*, by L. Jardine and M. Silverthorne, Cambridge, 2000)

Bacon, Francis, *The essayes or counsels, civill and morall* (1625, ed. M. Kiernan, Oxford, 2000)

Bacon, Francis, *New Atlantis. A worke unfinished appended to: Sylva Sylvarum, or, a natural historie in ten centuries* (London, 1626)

Bacon, Francis, *The works of Francis Bacon, baron of Verulam, Viscount St. Alban, and Lord High Chancellor of England*, ed. J. Spedding, R. L. Ellis and D. D. Heath, 14 vols (London, 1861–79)

Baily [or Bayly], Charles, *A true & faithful warning unto the people and inhabitants of Bristol* (London, 1663)

Bainbridge, John, *An astronomicall description of the late comet from the 18. of November 1618. to the 16. of December following, with certain morall prognosticks or applications drawne from the comets motion* (London, 1619)

Balde, Jakob, *Satira contra abusum tabaci* (Nuremberg, 1657; trans. into German as *Die trückene Trünckenheit*, 1658)

Balfour, Sir James, *Historical works, see* Haig

Bamford, F. ed., *A royalist's notebook; The commonplace book of Sir John Oglander* (London, 1936)

Baranda, C., *María de Jesús de Ágreda. Correspondencia con Felipe IV: religión y Razón de Estado* (Madrid, 1991)

Baratotti, Galarana [Elena Tarrabotti], *La simplicità ingannata o La tirannia paterna* (Leiden, 1654; ed. F. Medioli, Turin, 1989)

Barbon, Nicholas, *A letter to a Gentleman in the Country, Giving an Account of the Two Insurance Offices; the Fire-Office and Friendly-Society* (London, 1685)

Barbot, Jean, *see* Hair et al.

Baron, S. H., *The travels of Olearius in seventeenth-century Russia* (Stanford, 1967)

[Barry, Henry?], *Remarks upon a discourse preached December 15th 1774* (New York, 1775)

[Batencour, Jacques de], *Instruction méthodique pour l'école paroissiale, dressée en faveur des petites écoles, dividée en quatre parties* (Paris, 1669)

Baxter, Richard, *A holy commonwealth, or Political aphorisms, opening the true principles of government: for the healing of the mistakes, and resolving the doubts, that most endanger and trouble England at this time: (if yet there may be hope)* (London, 1659)

Baykal, B. S., ed., *Peçevi Tarihi* (Ankara, 1982)

Bayle, Pierre, *Pensées diverses sur la comète* (1682); English. trans., *Various thoughts on the occasion of a comet*, ed. R. C. Bartlett (New York, 2000)

Beach, M. C. and E. Koch, *King of The world: The Padshahnama. An imperial Mughal manuscript from the Royal Library, Windsor Castle* (London, 1997)

Beauplan, *see* Le Vasseur

Begley, W. E. and Z. A. Desai, *The Shah Jahan Nama of 'Inayat Khan: An abridged history of the Mughal emperor Shah Jahan, compiled by his royal librarian* (Delhi, 1990)

Behr, Johann Heinrich, *Der Verschantzte Turenne oder grundliche Alt- und Neue Kriegsbaukunst* (Frankfurt, 1677)

Behrnauer, W. F. A., 'Hâgî Chalfa's Dustûru'l-'amel'. Ein Beitrag zur osmanischen Finanzgeschichte', *Zeitschrift der deutschen morganländischen Gesellschaft*, XI (1857), 111–32

Bekker, Balthasar, *Ondersoeck van de Betekeninge der Kometen* (Amsterdam, 1683)

Ben Israel, Manassah, *Esperança de Israel* (Amsterdam, 1650)

Bergh, S., ed., *Svenska riksrådets protokoll, 1621–1658*, 17 vols (Stockholm, 1878–1925)

Bernier, François, *Travels in the Mogul Empire, A. D. 1656–1668* (Westminster, 1891)

Berwick y Alba, Duchess of, *Documentos escogidos de la casa de Alba* (Madrid, 1891)

Bethel, Slingsby, *The world's mistake in Oliver Cromwell; or, A short political discourse shewing, that Cromwell's maladministration (during his four years, and nine moneths pretended protectorship) layed the foundation of our present condition, in the decay of trade* (London, 1668)

Bidwell, W. B. and M. Jansson, *Proceedings in Parliament, 1626*, 4 vols (New Haven, 1991–7)

Birago Avogadro, Giovanni Battista, *Delle historie memorabili che contiene le sollevationi di stato di nostri tempi* (Venice, 1653; reissued as *Turbolenze di Europa dall'anno 1640 sino al 1650*, Venice, 1654)

Birch, Thomas, *The life of the Honourable Robert Boyle* (London, 1741)

Bisaccione, M., *Historia delle guerre civili di questi ultimi tempi, cioê di Inghilterra, Catalogna, Portogallo, Palermo, Napoli, Fermo, Moldavia, Polonia, Svizzera, Francia, Turco* (1st edn, Venice, 1652; 4th edn, 'ricorretta et in molte parti accresciuta', Venice, 1655)

Blair, E. H. and J. A. Robertson, *The Philippine islands*, 55 vols (Cleveland, 1905–11)

Bocarro, Antonio, *O livro das plantas de todas as fortalezas, cidades e povoações do estado da India Oriental*, 3 vols (1635; ed. I. Cid, Lisbon, 1992)

Bodin, Jean, *The six bookes of a common-weale* (London 1606; English trans. by Richard Knolles from the French original)

Boix y Moliner, Miguel Marcelino, *Hippocrates aclarado y sistema de Galeno impugnado, por estar fundado sobre dos aphorismos de Hippocrates no bien entendidos, que son el tercero, y veinte y dos del primer libro* (Madrid, 1716)

Borja Palomo, Francisco, *Historia crítica de las Riadas o Grandes Avenidas del Guadalquivir en Sevilla desde su reconquista hasta nuestros días*, 2 vols (Seville, 1878)

Bossuet, Jean-Bénigne, *Politics drawn from the very words of Holy Scripture* (1679; Paris, 1709; English trans. Cambridge, 1990)

Bossuet, Jean-Bénigne, *Discours sur l'histoire universelle, à Monseigneur le Dauphin, pour expliquer la suite de la religion et les changemens des empires*, 2 vols (Paris, 1681)

Botero, Giovanni, *Relatione della Republica Venitiana* (Venice, 1605)

Bournoutian, G., *The Chronicle of Deacon Zak'aria of K'anak'er (Zak 'areay Sarkawagi Patmagrut'iwn)* (Costa Mesa, CA, 2004)

Boyle, Robert, *see* Birch

Boyle, Roger, earl of Orrery, *A treatise on the art of war*, 2 vols (London, 1677)

Bradford, William, *Bradford's History of Plymouth Plantation 1606–1646*, ed. W. T. Davis (New York, 1908)

Bradstreet, Anne, 'A dialogue between Old England and New', in *Tenth Muse lately sprung up in America* (London, 1650; facsimile edn, Gainesville, 1965)

Brantôme, Pierre de Bourdeille, seigneur de, *Oeuvres*, VI (Paris, 1787)

Bray, William, ed., *Diary and correspondence of John Evelyn, F. R. S., to which is subjoined the private correspondence between King Charles I. and Sir Edward Nicholas*, new edn, 4 vols (London, 1887)

Bremner, R. H., ed., *Children and youth in America: A documentary history*, I (Cambridge, MA, 1970)

Brennan, M. G., ed., *The travel diary of Robert Bargrave: Levant merchant (1647–1656)* (London, 1999: Hakluyt Society, 3rd series, III)

Brigham, C. S., ed., *British royal proclamations relating to America 1603–1783* (Worcester, MA, 1911)

Brinsley, John, *Ludus literarius: or, the grammar schoole, shewing how to proceede from the first entrance into learning, to the highest perfection required in the grammar schools* (London, 1612)

Brome, Alexander, *Rump: or an exact collection of the choycest poems and songs relating to the late times, by the most eminent wits, from anno 1639 to anno 1661* (London, 1662: an expanded edition of *Ratts rhimed to death*, 1660, and *The Rump*, 1660)

Brown, Edward, *An account of several travels through a great part of Germany, in four journeys* [1668] (London, 1677)

Bruce, John, ed., *Letters and papers of the Verney family down to the end of the year 1639* (London, 1853: Camden Society, LVI)

Bruce, John, ed., *Notes of the treaty carried on at Ripon between King Charles I and the Covenanters of Scotland, A. D. 1640* (London, 1869: Camden Society, C)

Bunyan, John, *The Pilgrim's Progress from this world to that which is to come, Part I* (London, 1678)

Burke, Edmund, *Reflections on the revolution in France* (1791; ed. J. C. D. Clark, Stanford, 2001)

Burnet, Gilbert, *The memoires of the lives and actions of James and William, dukes of Hamilton* (London, 1677)

Burton, Robert, *The Anatomy of Melancholy, What it is: With all the Kinds, Causes, Symptomes, Prognostickes, and Several Cures of it; in Three Partitions with their severall sections, members & Subsections. Philosophically, Medicinally, Historically, Opened & Cut Up* (1621; 4th edn, Oxford 1638)

Bush, S., ed., *The correspondence of John Cotton* (Chapel Hill, 2001)

Butler, Samuel, *Hudibras, Part I* (London, 1662)

Calderón de la Barca, Pedro, *El alcalde de Zalamea* (Alcalá de Henares, 1651)

Calderwood, David, *History of the Kirk of Scotland* (written in the 1640s), ed. T. Thomson, 7 vols (Edinburgh: Wodrow Society, 1842–5)

Calendar of the Court Minutes etc of the East India Company 1644–1649, ed. E. B. Sainsbury (Oxford, 1912)

Calendar of State Papers, Colonial Series, America and West Indies, 1675–1676, ed. W. N. Sainsbury (London, 1893)

Calendar of State Papers, Domestic Series. Edward VI, Mary, Elizabeth I and James I, ed. S. C. Lomax and M. A. Everett Green, 12 vols (London, 1856–72)

Calendar of State Papers, Domestic Series. Charles I, ed. J. Bruce and W. D. Hamilton, 23 vols (London, 1858–97)

Calendar of State Papers and manuscripts relating to English affairs, existing in the archives and collections of Venice, and in other libraries of Northern Italy, 1202–1674, ed. H. F. Brown et al., 28 vols (London, 1864–1947)

Calendar of State Papers relating to Ireland. James I, ed. C. W. Russell and J. P. Prendergast, 5 vols (London, 1872–80)

Calendar of State Papers relating to Ireland of the Reign of Charles I, ed. R. P. Mahaffy, 4 vols (London, 1900–4)

Callot, Jacques, *Les grandes misères de la Guerre* (Paris, 1633)

Campbell, Archibald, marquis of Argyll, *Instructions to a son, containing the rules of conduct in public and private life* (London, 1661)

Capaccio, Giovanni, *Il forastiero. Dialogi* (Naples, 1634)

Capecelatro, Francesco, *see* Graniti

Capograssi, A., 'La rivoluzione di Masaniello vista dal residente veneto a Napoli', *Archivio storico per le province napolitane*, NS, XXXIII (1952), 167–235

Cardin Le Bret, P., *De la souveraineté du roy* (Paris, 1632)

Carney, F. S., ed., *The politics of Johannes Althusius* (London, 1964)

Carrier, H., *La Fronde: contestation démocratique et misère paysanne. 52 Mazarinades*, 2 vols (Paris, 1982)

Cartas de algunos padres de la Compañía de Jesús sobre los sucesos de la monarquía entre 1634 y 1648, ed. Pascual de Gayangos, 7 vols (Madrid, 1861–5: *Memorial Histórico Español*, XIV–XIX)

Castlehaven, James Tuchet, earl of, *Memoirs of the Irish Wars* (1684; Delmar, NY, 1974)

Cavendish, Margaret, duchess of Newcastle, *Nature's pictures drawn by fancies pencil to the life* (London, 1656)

Cavendish, Margaret, duchess of Newcastle, *The life of William Cavendish, duke of Newcastle, to which is added 'The true relation of my birth, breeding and life'* (1667), ed. C. H. Firth (London, 1886)

Cayet, P. V., *Chronologie novenaire* (Paris, 1608; ed. Michaud and Poujoulat, Paris, 1838)

Cernovodeanu, Paul and Paul Binder, eds, *Cavalerii Apocalipsului. Calamitățile naturale din trecutul României (până la 1800)* (Bucharest, 1993)

Cervantes Saavedra, Miguel de, *Segunda parte de el ingenioso hidalgo, Don Quijote de la Mancha* (Madrid, 1615)

Chardin, Jean, *Sir John Chardin's travels in Persia* (Paris, 1676; London, 1724; New York, 2010)

Charles I, king of Great Britain, *A Large Declaration concerning the late tumults in Scotland* (London, 1639)

Charles I, king of Great Britain, *Eikon Basilike* (London, 1648/9; ed. J. Daems and H. F. Nelson, Peterborough, 2005)

Chen Zilong, 'The little cart', in A. Waley, *Translations from the Chinese* (New York, 1941)

Cheng Pei-kai and Michael Lestz, with J.D. Spence, *The search for modern China: A documentary collection* (New York, 1999)

Chéruel, Adolphe and Georges Avenel, eds, *Lettres du Cardinal Mazarin pendant son ministère*, 7 vols (Paris, 1872–93)

Christina, queen of Sweden, *Apologies*, ed. J.-F. de Raymond (Paris, 1994)

Churchill, A. and J., eds., *A collection of voyages and travels: some now first printed from original manuscripts, others now first published in English in six volumes* (London, 1732)

Ciampoli, Giovanni Battista, *Lettere* (Florence, 1650)

Clarendon, Edward Hyde, earl of, *The history of the rebellion and civil wars in England, begun in the year 1641*, ed. W. D. Macray, 6 vols (Oxford, 1888)

Clarendon, Edward Hyde, earl of, *Brief view and survey of the dangerous and pernicious errors to church and state in Mr. Hobbes's book entitled 'Leviathan'* (Oxford, 1676)

Clarendon State Papers, see Monkhouse

Cock, Thomas, *Hygieine, or, A plain and practical discourse upon the first of the six non-naturals, viz, air with cautionary rules and directions for the preservation of people in this time of sickness, very necessary for the gentry and citizens that are now in the country to peruse before they come into London* (London, 1665)

Coenen, Thomas, *Ydele verwachtinge der Joden getoont in den persoon van Sabethai Zevi* (Amsterdam, 1669)

Coke, Edward, *The third part of the Institutes of the Laws of England* (4th edn, London, 1669)

Colbert, Jean-Baptiste, *Lettres, instructions et mémoires de Colbert*, ed. Pierre Clément, 10 vols (Paris, 1861–73)

Collin, N., 'Observations made at an early period, on the climate of the country along the river Delaware, collected from the records of the Swedish colony', *Transactions of the American Philosophical Society*, NS, I (1818), 340–52

Collurafi, A., *Tumultazioni delle plebe di Palermo* (Palermo, 1661)

Conti, V., *Le leggi di una rivoluzione. I bandi della repubblica napoletana dall'ottubre 1647 all'Aprile 1648* (Naples, 1983)

Cooper, M., *The island of Japon: João Rodrigues' account of sixteenth-century Japan* (Tokyo, 1973)

Corneille, Pierre, *Pertharite, Roy des Lombards, Tragédie* (Paris, 1654)

Correra, L., 'Inedita relazione dei tumulti napoletani del 1647', *Archivio storico per le province napolitane*, XV (1890), 353–87

Coryate, Thomas, *Coryat's crudities, hastily gobled up in five months' travells ... newly digested, and now dispersed to the nourishment of the travelling members of this kingdom* (London, 1611)

Cosnac, Jules, Gabriel count of, *Souvenirs du règne de Louis XIV*, V (Paris, 1876)

Costin, Miron, *Letopisețul Țării Moldovei* (Bucharest, 1975)

Crucé, Émeric, *Nouveau Cynée ou Discours d'Estat représentant les occasions et moyens d'establir une paix générale et la liberté de commerce pour tout le monde* (Paris, 1623)

Cushman, Robert, *The sin and danger of self-love described, in a sermon preached at Plymouth, in New-England, 1621* (Boston, 1846)

Cysat, Renward, *Collectanea Chronica und denkwürdige Sachen pro Chronica Lucernensi et Helvetiae*, IV.2, ed. J. Schmid, (Luzern, 1969)

Dalton, Michael, *The Countrey Justice, containing the practice of the Justices of Peace out of their Sessions* (London, 1622)

Davant, François, *De la puissance qu'ont les roys sur les peuples, et du pouvoir des peuples sur les roys* (Paris, 1650)

Davenant, Charles, *An essay upon the ways and means of supplying the war* (London, 1695)

[Davenant, William], *The first days entertainment at Rutland-House* (London, 1656)

Davies, John, *A discovery of the true causes why Ireland was never entirely subdued* (1612; 3rd edn, London, 1666)

De Beer, E. S., ed., *The correspondence of John Locke*, 8 vols (Oxford, 1976–89)

De Beer, E. S., ed., *The diary of John Evelyn*, 6 vols (Oxford, 2000)

De Jonge, J. K. J., *De opkomst van Nederlandsch Gezag in Oost-Indië*, 16 vols (The Hague, 1862–1909)

Defoe, Daniel, *The life and strange surprizing adventures of Robinson Crusoe, of York, Mariner, who lived eight and twenty years all alone in an un-inhabited island on the coast of America, near the mouth of the great river of Oroonoque; Having been cast on Shore by Shipwreck, wherein all the Men perished but himself*, 4th edn (London, 1719)

Defoe, Daniel, *A journey thro' the whole island of Great Britain*, 4th edn, 4 vols (1724; London, 1748)

Defoe, Daniel, *The compleat English tradesman*, vol. II, in two parts (London, 1727)

Dell, William, *Several sermons and discourses* (London, 1652; reprinted 1709)

Descartes, René, *Discours de la méthode: pour bien conduire sa raison et chercher la vérité dans les sciences* (Leiden, 1637; bilingual English and French edn by G. Heffernan [Notre Dame, 1994])

Descartes, René, *Oeuvres de Descartes*, ed. C. Adam and P. Tannery, 12 vols (Paris, 1897–1913)

Desmarets de Saint-Sorlin, *Europe. Comédie héroïque* (Paris, 1643; reprinted, attributed to Cardinal Richelieu, Louvain, 2006)

Di Cosmo, N., ed., *The diary of a Manchu soldier in seventeenth-century China: 'My service in the army' by Dzengšeo* (New York, 2006)

Di Marzo, G., ed., *Biblioteca storica e letteraria di Sicilia. Diari dell città di Palermo dal secolo XVI al XIX*, III–IV (Palermo, 1869–71)

Diaries kept by the head of the Dutch factory in Japan, 1633–49, 11 vols (Tokyo, 1974–2012)

Dickinson, W. C. and G. Donaldson, eds, *A sourcebook of Scottish history*, III (Edinburgh, 1961)

Disney, Gervase, *Some remarkable passages in the holy life and death of Gervase Disney, Esq. to which are added several letters and poems* (London, 1692)

Documenti originali relativi alla rivoluzione di Tommaso Aniello (British Library: C.55.i.3)

Doglio, M. L., ed., *Lettere di Fulvio Testi*, 3 vols (Bari, 1967)

Donaldson, G., *The making of the Scottish Prayer Book of 1637* (Edinburgh, 1954)

Donne, John, *Devotions upon Emergent Occasions* (London, 1623)

Donzelli, Giuseppe, *Partenope liberata, o vero racconto dell'heroica risolutione fatta del popolo di Napoli per soltrarsi con tutto il regno dell'insopportabil giogo delli Spagnuoli* (Naples, 1648)

Dooley, B., ed., *Italy in the Baroque: Selected readings* (New York, 1995)

Downing, Calybute, *A discoursive coniecture upon the reasons that produce a desired event of the present troubles of Great Britaine, different from those of Lower Germanie* (London, 1641)

Drewes, G. W. J., ed., *Hakayat potjut Muhamat: An Achehnese epic* (The Hague, 1980)

Dujčev, I., *Avvisi di Ragusa. Documenti sull'Impero Turco nel secolo XVII e sulla guerra di Candia* (Rome, 1935: Orientalia Christiana Analecta, CI)

Dunn, R. S., J. Savage and L. Yeandle, eds, *The Journal of John Winthrop, 1630–1649* (Cambridge, MA, 1996)

Duplessis, Armand-Jean, Cardinal-duke of Richelieu, *Testament politique* (ed. L. André, Paris, 1947)

Elliot, H. M. and J. Dowson, *The history of India as told by its own historians: The Muhammadan Period*, 8 vols (London, 1867–77)

Elliott, J. H. and J. F. de la Peña, eds, *Memoriales y cartas del conde-duque de Olivares*, 2 vols (Madrid, 1978–81)

Evelyn, John, *Diary, see* De Beer

Evelyn, John, *Fumifugium: or the inconveniency of the aer and smoke of London dissipated* (London, 1661)

Evliyā Çelebi, *Seyahatname*, 15 vols (Istanbul, 1969–71)

Fairholt, F. W., *Poems and songs related to George Villiers, duke of Buckingham, and his assassination by John Felton* (London, 1850)

Fayol, Fray José de, *Epítome y relación general de varios sucesos de mar y tierra en las islas Filipinas* (Madrid, 1648; cited from the typescript copy in the Biblioteca Nacional de España: HA 37050)

Fellon, Thomas, S. J., *Faba Arabica, vulgo caffetum, carmen* (Rome, 1696)

Fernández Álvarez, M., *Corpus documental de Carlos V*, 5 vols (Salamanca, 1973–81)

Fincham, Kenneth, 'The judges' decision on Ship Money in February 1637: the reaction of Kent', *Bulletin of the Institute of Historical Research*, LVII (1984), 230–7

Firpo, Luigi, ed., *Relazioni di ambasciatori veneti al Senato, tratte dalle migliori edizioni disponibili e ordinate cronologicamente*, 14 vols (Turin, 1965–96)

Firth, C. H., ed., *The Clarke Papers: Selections from the papers of William Clarke*, 4 vols (London, 1891–1901: Camden Society, vols XLIX, LIV, LXI, LXII)

Firth, C. H. and R. S. Rait, *Acts and Ordinances of the Interregnum, 1642–1660*, 2 vols (London, 1911)

Fleming, David H., ed., *Diary of Sir Archibald Johnston of Wariston*, II (Edinburgh, 1919: Scottish History Society, XVIII); *see also* Paul

Fontenelle, Bernard le Bovier de, *La comète* (Paris, 1681)

Foster, George, *The pouring forth of the seventh and last viall upon all flesh and fleshlines, which will be a terror to the men that have great possessions or several visions which hath bin made out to me* (London, 1650)

Foster, George, *The sounding of the last trumpet or, severall visions, declaring the universall overturning and rooting up of all earthly powers in England, with many other things foretold, which shall come to passe in this year, 1650* (London, 1650)

Foster, William, ed., *The English factories in India, 1630–1633* (Oxford, 1910)

Foster, William, ed., *The English factories in India, 1634–1636* (Oxford, 1911)

Foster, William, ed., *The English factories in India, 1637–1641* (Oxford, 1912)

Foster, William, ed., *The English factories in India, 1655–1660* (Oxford, 1921)

Foster, William, ed., *The English factories in India, 1661–1664* (Oxford, 1923)

Foster, William, ed., *The voyage of Thomas Best to the East Indies, 1612–1614* (London, 1934: Hakluyt Society, 2nd series, LXXV)

Foster, William, ed., *The voyage of Sir Henry Middleton to the Moluccas, 1604–1606* (London, 1943: Hakluyt Society, 2nd series, LXXXVIII)

Fox, George, *A journal or historical account of the life, travels, sufferings, Christian experiences and labour of love in the work of the ministry, of that ancient, eminent and faithful servant of Jesus Christ, George Fox* (London, 1694)

Franklin, Benjamin, *Observations concerning the increase of mankind and the peopling of countries &c* (Philadelphia, 1751)

French, J. M., ed., *The life records of John Milton*, 4 vols (New Brunswick, 1949–58)

Fryer, John, *A new account of East India and Persia, being nine years' travels, 1672–1681*, ed. W. Crooke, 3 vols (London, 1915)

Galilei, Galileo and Christoph Scheiner, *On sunspots*, ed. E. Reeves and A. van Helden (Chicago, 2010)

Gallagher, L., ed., *China in the sixteenth century: The journals of Matthew Ricci, 1583–1610* (New York, 1951)

Gallardo, B. J., *Ensayo de una biblioteca española de libros raros y curiosos*, 2 vols (Madrid, 1863–89)

García Acosta, V., J. M. Pérez Zevallos and A. Molina del Villar, eds, *Desastres agrícolas en México. Catálogo histórico. I. Época prehispánica y colonial, 958–1822* (Mexico, 2003)

Gardiner, Lion, *A history of the Pequot War, or a relation of the war between the powerful nation of Pequot Indians, once inhabiting the coast of New-England, westerly from near Narraganset Bay, and the English inhabitants, in the year 1638* (1660; Cincinnati, 1860)

Gardiner, S. R., ed., *Debates in the House of Commons in 1625* (London 1873: Camden Society, NS, VI)

Gardiner, S. R., ed., *The Hamilton Papers* (London, 1880: Camden Society, NS, XXVII)

Gardiner, S. R., ed., *Constitutional documents of the Puritan Revolution* (London, 1906)

Gascón de Torquemada, G., *Gaçeta y nuevas de la Corte de España* (Madrid, 1991)

Gatta, G., *Di una gravissima peste che nella passata primavera e estate dell'anno 1656 depopulò la città di Napoli* (Naples, 1659)

Gaunt, John, *Natural and political observations, mentioned in a following index, and made upon the bills of mortality* (London, 1662)

Gilbert, J. T., ed., *A contemporary history of Affairs in Ireland from 1641 to 1652*, 6 vols (Dublin, 1879–80)

Gilbert, J. T., ed., *History of the Irish Confederation and the war in Ireland by Richard Bellings*, 7 vols (Dublin, 1882–91)

Ginschopff, J., *Cronica, oder eygendtlyche Beschreibung vieler denckwürdigen Geschichte* (Stuttgart, 1630)

Giraffi, Alessandro, *Le rivoluzioni di Napoli* (Venice, 1647; *see also*, Howell, James, *An exact historie*)

Girard, *Voyage en Chine, see* Las Cortes

Goad, J., *Astrometeorologia, or aphorisms and discourses of the bodies celestial, their nature and influence* (London, 1686)

Goldie, M., ed., *The entring book of Roger Morrice*, 7 vols (Woodbridge, 2007)

Gondi, Pierre de, cardinal de Retz, *Oeuvres*, II, ed. A. Feuillet (Paris, 1872)

Goodwin, John, *Anti-Cavalierisme, or, truth pleading as well the necessity as the lawfulness of this present war* (London, 1642)

Gordon of Auchleuchries, Patrick, *Diary of General Patrick Gordon of Auchleuchries 1635–99*, ed. D. Fedosov, 2 vols (Aberdeen, 2009)

Gough, R., *The history of Myddle* (written 1700–2), ed. D. Hey (Harmondsworth, 1981)

Gracián, Baltasar, S.J., *El Criticón*, 3 vols (Zaragoza, 1651, 1653, 1657)

Graniti, A., ed., *Diario di Francesco Capecelatro contenente la storia delle cose avvenute nel reame di Napoli negli anni 1647–50*, 3 vols (Naples, 1850–4)

Green, M. A. E., ed., *Letters of Queen Henrietta Maria including her private correspondence with Charles the First* (London, 1857)

Grey, Anchitell, *Debates of the House of Commons, from the year 1667 to the year 1694*, 10 vols (London, 1763)

Grillon, Pierre, *Les papiers de Richelieu: section politique interieure, correspondance et papiers d'État*, 6 vols (Paris, 1975–85)

Grimmelshausen, Hans Jacob Christoph von, *Der abentheuerliche Simplicissimus Teutsch* (1669; Tübingen, 1967)

Groen van Prinsterer, Guillaume, ed., *Archives ou correspondance de la maison d'Orange-Nassau*, 2nd series, 5 vols (Utrecht, 1857–61)

Grotius, Hugo, *Briefwisseling*, ed. P. C. Molhuysen, B. L. Meulenbroek and P. P. Witkam et al. online at http://grotius.huygens.knaw.nl/years

Gryphius, Andreas, *Horribilicribrifax Teutsch* (Breslau, 1663)

Guha, J. P., ed., *India in the seventeenth century*, 2 vols (New Delhi, 1984)

Guijóo, Gregorio Martín de, *Diario 1648–64*, ed. M. Romero de Terreros, 2 vols (México, 1952)

Guise, *Mémoires, see* Petitot

Gumppenberg, Guilielmo, S.J., *Atlas Marianus sive de imaginibus Deiparae per orbem christianum miraculosis*, 2 vols (Ingolstadt, 1655)

Haig, J., ed., *The historical works of Sir James Balfour of Denmylne and Kinnaird*, 3 vols (Edinburgh, 1825)

Hair, P. E. H., A. Jones and R. Law, eds, *Barbot on Guinea: The Writings of Jean Barbot on West Africa, 1678–1712*, 2 vols (London, 1992: Hakluyt Society, 2nd series CLXXV–CLXXVI)

Hall, J. C., ed., *Feudal laws of Japan* (Washington, DC, 1979)

Halley, Edmond, *A synopsis of the astronomy of comets* (Oxford, 1705)

Halliwell, J. O., ed., *Letters of the Kings of England*, 2 vols (London, 1846)

Hannover, Nathan, *Yaven Metzulah* (Venice, 1653: tr. A. J. Mesch as *Abyss of despair*, New York, 1950)

Hardwicke, Philip Yorke, earl of, ed., *Miscellaneous State Papers from 1501 to 1726* (London, 1778)

Hartlib, Samuel, *Considerations Tending to the Happy Accomplishment of England's Reformation in Church and State. Humbly presented to the piety and wisdome of the High and Honourable Court of Parliament* (London, 1647)

Hartlib, Samuel, *Samuel Hartlib his legacie; or, an enlargement of the discourse of husbandry used in Brabant and Flaunders* (London, 1650, incorporating the 'Discourse' compiled by Sir Richard Weston)

Harvey, William, *Exercitatio Anatomica de Motu Cordis et Sanguinis in Animalibus* (Frankfurt, 1628)

Harvey, William, *Exercitationes de generatione animalium* (Amsterdam, 1651)

Haust, J., ed., *Quatre dialogues de paysans (1631–1636)* (Liège, 1939)

Heberle, Hans, *see* Zillhardt

Hellie, R., *The Muscovite Law Code (Ulozhenie) of 1649* (Irvine, CA, 1988)

Hesse, Landgrave Herman IV of, *Historia meteorologica, das ist, vier und zwantzig jährige eigentliche und trewfleissige Observation und tägliche Verzeichnüss des Gewitters, erstlich demonstriret wird, ob und wie des tägliche Gewitter mit dem Gestirn uberein troffen, und warumb solches geschehen sey oder nicht?* (Cassel, 1651)

Hevelius, Johannes, *Selenographia sive Lunae descriptio* (Danzig, 1647)

Hickson, Mary, *Ireland in the seventeenth century, or the Irish massacres of 1641–2, their causes and results*, 2 vols (London, 1884)

Historical Manuscript Commission, *Third Report* (London, 1872)

Hobbes, Thomas, *On the citizen (De cive, 1641)*; English edn, ed. and tr. R. Tuck and M. Silverthorne (Cambridge, 1998)

Hobbes, Thomas, *Leviathan, or the matter, forme, and power of a common-wealth, ecclesiasticall and civill* (London, 1651; ed. R. Tuck, Cambridge, 1996)

Hobbes, Thomas, *Behemoth or The Long Parliament* (written 1668, first published 1679; 2nd edn, ed. F. Tönnies, London, 1969)

Holmes, C. A., ed., *The Suffolk committees for Scandalous Ministers, 1644–1646* (Ipswich, 1970: Suffolk Records Society, XIII)

Howell, James, *A discourse discovering some mysteries of our new state … shewing the rise and progress of England's unhappinesse, ab anno illo infortunato 1641* (Oxford, 1645)

Howell, James, *Epistolae Ho-elianae or familiar letters* (London, 1650; ed. J. Jacobs, London, 1890)

Howell, James, *An exact historie of the late revolutions in Naples and of their monstruous successes not to be parallel'd by any antient or modern history* (2nd edn, London, 1664: an English trans. of A. Giraffi, *Le revolutioni di Napoli*)

Howell, Thomas B., *Cobbett's complete collection of State Trials*, 33 vols (London, 1809–26)

Hrabjanka, H., *The great war of Bohdan Xmel'nyc'kyj* (1710: ed. Y. Lutsenko, Cambridge, MA, 1990)

Huang Liu-hung, *A complete book concerning happiness and benevolence: Fu-hui ch'üan-shu, A manual for local magistrates in seventeenth-century China* (1699), trans. and ed. Djang Chu (Tucson, 1984)

Hull, C. H., ed., *The economic writings of Sir William Petty*, 2 vols (Cambridge, 1899)

Hutchinson, Lucy, *Memoirs of the life of Colonel Hutchinson, Governor of Nottingham* (written c. 1665; 10th edn, London, 1863)

Hyde, Edward, *see* Clarendon

Iakubov, K., 'Rossiia i Shvetsiia v pervoi polovine XVII veku, VI. 1647–1650 gg. Doneseniia koroleve Khristine i pis'ma k korolevakeomu sekretariu shvedskogo rezidenta v Moskve Karla Pommereninga', *Chteniia v imperatorskom obshchestve istorii i drevnostei rossiskikh pri Moskovskom universitete*, I (1898), 407–74

Imperator, Francesco, *Discorso político intorno al regimento delle Piazze e della città di Napoli* (Naples, 1604)

Ince, William, *Lot's little one, or Meditations on Gen. 19 verse 20, being the substance of severall sermons sometimes delivered by William Ince* (Dublin, 1640)

İpşirli, M., ed., *Tarih-i Selâniki* (Istanbul, 1989)

Israel, Menassah ben, *Esperança de Israel* (Amsterdam, 1650)

Jacobs, J., ed., *Epistolae Ho-elianae, see* Howell

Jahangir, *Memoirs see* Price and Thackston

James I, king of Great Britain, *His Maiesties Speech to both the houses of Parliament, in his Highnesse great chamber at Whitehall* (London, 1607)

James I, *see* McIlwain

Jansen, Cornelius, *Augustinus, seu doctrina S. Augustini de humanae naturae sanitate, aegritudine, medicina, adversus Pelagianos et Massilienses*, 3 vols (Louvain, 1640; 2nd edn, Paris, 1641)

Jansen, Cornelius, *Mars Gallicus, seu de justitia armorum et feodorum regis Galliae* (Louvain, 1635)

Jansson, M., ed., *Proceedings of the opening session of the Long Parliament*, 7 vols (Rochester, NY, 2002–7)

Jansson, M. and W. B. Bidwell, eds, *Proceedings in Parliament, 1625* (New Haven, 1987)

Johnson, R. C., M. F. Keeler, M. Jansson and W. B. Bidwell, eds, *Commons Debates 1628*, 3 vols (New Haven and London, 1977)

Johnson, Samuel, *The works of Samuel Johnson. X. Political writings*, ed. D. J. Greene (New Haven and London, 1977)

Jonson, Ben, *Epigrams* (London, 1612)

Josselin, Ralph, *see* Macfarlane

[Junta de teòlegs], *Justifació en conciència de haver pres lo principat de Catalunya las armas per a resistir als soldats que de present la invadeixen y als altres que amenassan invadirla* (Barcelona, 1640)

Jusserand, J. J., ed., *Recueil des Instructions données aux ambassadeurs et ministres de France. XXIV. Angleterre* (Paris, 1929)

Kanceff, E., ed., *Oeuvres de Jean-Jacques Bouchard: Journal*, 2 vols (Turin, 1976–7)

Kâtib Çelebi, *Fezleke-i Tarih*, 2 vols (Istanbul, 1870)

Kâtib Çelebi, *The balance of truth* (1656: ed. and tr. G. L. Lewis, London, 1957)

Kenyon, J. P., ed., *The Stuart Constitution, 1603–1688: Documents and commentary* (Cambridge, 1966)

Kepler, Johannes, *Prognosticum astrologicum auff das Jahr ... 1618* (Linz, 1618), reprinted in V. Bialas and H. Grüssing, eds, *Johannes Kepler Gesammelte Werke*, XI part 2 (Munich, 1993)

Kingsbury, S. M., *The records of the Virginia Company of London*, 4 vols (Washington, DC, 1906–35)

Knowler, W., ed., *The earl of Strafforde's letters and dispatches*, 2 vols (London, 1739)

Kodama Kōta and Ōishi Shinzaburo, *Kinsei nōsei shiryōshû. I. Edo bakufu horei* (Tokyo, 1966)

Kolff, D. H. A., and H. W. van Santen, eds, *De geschriften van Francisco Pelsaert over Mughal Indië, 1627. Kroniek en Remonstrantie* (The Hague, 1979: Werken uitgegeven door de Linschoten Vereeniging, LXXXI)

Kuroita Katsumi, ed., *Shintei zôho kokushi taikei*, XL (Tokyo, 1964)La Lumia, M., *Storie siciliane*, 4 vols (reprint edn, Palermo, 1969)

La Noue, François, *Discours politique et militaire* (Basel, 1588)

Labat, Jean-Baptiste, *Nouvelle relation de l'Afrique occidentale: contenant une description exacte du Sénégal et des païs situés entre le Cap-Blanc et la rivière de Serrelionne*, 5 vols (Paris, 1728)

Laing, D., ed, *The letters and journals of Robert Baillie, 1637–62*, 3 vols (Edinburgh, 1841)

Laing, D., ed., *Correspondence of Sir Robert Kerr, first earl of Ancram, and his son William, third earl of Lothian*, 2 vols (Edinburgh, 1875: Roxburghe Club, C)

Lancellotti, Secondo, *L'hoggidì, overo il mondo non peggiore ne più calamitoso del passato* (Venice, 1623)

Lancellotti, Secondo, *Oggidì, overo gl'ingegni non inferiori a' passati* (Venice, 1636)

Lancellotti, Secondo, *Vita in prosa e in versi*, ed. M. Savini (Rome, 1971)

Larkin, J. F., and P. L. Hughes, eds, *Stuart royal proclamations*, 2 vols. (Oxford, 1973–83)

Larner, C. J., C. J. H. Lee and H. V. McLachlan, *A source book of Scottish witchcraft* (Glasgow, 1977)

Las Cortes, Alonso de, *Le voyage en Chine d'Adriano de las Cortes, S. J. (1625)*, ed. M. Girard (Paris, 2001)

Latham, R. C., and W. Matthews, eds, *The Diary of Samuel Pepys*, 11 vols (London, 2000)

[Laud, William,] *Arch-bishop Laud's annual accounts of his province, presented to the king in the beginning of every year; with the king's apostils or marginal notes* (London, 1695)

Laud, William, *see also* Heylyn, *Cyprianus*; Scott, *Works*; and Wharton, *History*

Lawrence, Richard, *The interest of England in the Irish transplantation stated* (London, 1655)

Le Boindre, J., *Débats du Parlement de Paris pendant la minorité de Louis XIV*, ed. R. Descimon and O. Ranum (Paris, 1997)

Le Comte, Louis, *Nouveaux mémoires sur l'état présent de la Chine*, 2 vols (Paris, 1691–7; English trans., London, 1698)

Le Gendre, Sieur, *see* Arnauld d'Andilly

Le Vasseur, Guillaume, sieur de Beauplan, *A description of Ukraine* (Rouen, 1651: English trans., New York, 1959)

Leach, D., ed., *A Rhode Islander reports on King Philip's War: The second William Harris letter* (Providence, RI, 1963)

Lee, M., ed., *Dudley Carleton to John Chamberlain, 1603–1624* (New Brunswick, 1972)

Leslie, John, earl of Rothes, *see* Rothes

Leyb ben Oyzer, *La beauté du diable. Portrait de Sabbatai Zevi. Présenté, annoté et traduit du yiddish amstellodamois du XVIIIe siècle par Nathan Weinstock* (Paris, 2011)

Lightfoote, John, *A few and new observations vpon the booke of Genesis, the most of them certaine the rest probable all harmelesse, strange, and rarely heard off before* (London, 1642)

Lionti, F., 'Cartelli sediziosi del 1647', *Archivio storico Siciliano*, NS, XIX (1894–5), 424–43

Locke, John, *A letter concerning toleration* (1689, ed. J. H. Tully, Indianapolis, 1983)

Locke, John, *An essay concerning humane understanding* (London, 1690)

Locke, John, *Political essays*, ed. M. Goldie (Cambridge, 1997)

Locke, *Travels*, *see* Lough

Loofeldt, Peter, 'Initiarum Monarchiae Ruthenicae', RAS, *Manuskriptsamlingen*, 68

Lord, George D., ed., *Poems on affairs of state: Augustan satirical verse 1660–1714*, vol. 1 (New Haven, 1963)

Loubère, S. de la, *A new historical relation of the kingdom of Siam* (Paris, 1693)

Lough, J., ed., *John Locke's travels in France, 1675–1679, as related in his journals, correspondence and other papers* (Cambridge, 1953)

Louis XIV, king of France, *A declaration of the Most Christian King Lovis the XIIIth [sic] King of France and Navarre* (London, 1649)

Louis XIV, king of France, *Mémoires de Louis XIV, suivi de Réflexions sur le métier du roi*, ed. J. Longnon (Paris, 1978)

Loureiro de Souza, A., ed., *Documentos históricos do Arquivo Municipal. Cartas do Senado 1638–1673* (Salvador, 1951)

Love, H. D., *Vestiges of Old Madras 1640–1800, traced from the East India Company's records preserved at Fort St. George and the India Office and from other sources*, 4 vols (London, 1913)

Lowenthal, M., ed., *The Memoirs of Glückel of Hameln* (New York, 1977)

Lu, J. D., *Sources of Japanese history*, I (New York, 1974)

Lubienietski, Stanislaus, *Theatrum Cometicum, duabus partibus constans, quarum altera frequenti Senatu Philosophico conspicua, Cometas anni 1664 & 1665* (Amsterdam, 1668)

Lydius, Jacobus, *Belgium Gloriosum* (Amsterdam, 1667)

McClure, N. E., ed., *The letters of John Chamberlain*, 2 vols (Philadelphia, 1939)

MacDonald, H., ed., *The poems of Andrew Marvell* (London, 1952)

Macfarlane, A., ed., *The diary of Ralph Josselin, 1616–1683* (London, 1976)

[Machon, Louis], *Les véritables maximes du gouvernement de la France* (Paris, 1652)

McIlwain, C. H., ed., *The political works of James I* (Cambridge, MA, 1918)

Mackiw, T., 'English press on Liberation War in Ukraine, 1648–50', *Ukrainian Quarterly*, XLIV (1986), 102–26 and 239–59

Magisa, Raymundo, *Svcceso raro de tres volcanes, dos de fuego y uno de agua, que reventaron a 4 de enero de este año de 1641 a un mismo tiempo en diferentes partes de islas Filipinas* (Manila, 1641)

Mallet, Jean-Roland, *Comptes rendus de l'administration des finances du royaume de France* (London, 1789)

Manucci, Niccolo, *Storia do Mogor, or Mogul India, 1653–1708*, ed. W. Irving, 4 vols (London, 1906)

Manuel de Melo, Francisco, *Historia de los movimientos, separación y guerra de Cataluña* (Lisbon, 1645; Madrid, 1912 edn)

Manuel de Melo, Francisco, *Epanáforas de vária história portuguesa* (Lisbon, 1660; ed. J. Serrão, Lisbon, 1976)

Markham, Clement ['Thodorus Verax'], *Anarchia anglicana, or the History of Independency, the second part* (London, 1649)

Marshall, Stephen, *A peace-offering to God a sermon preached to the honourable House of Commons assembled in Parliament at their publique thanksgiving, September 7, 1641: for the peace concluded between England and Scotland* (London, 1641)

Marshall, Stephen, *Meroz cursed or, A sermon preached to the honourable House of Commons, at their late solemn fast, Febr. 23, 1641* (London, 1642)

Martí i Viladamor, Francesc, *Noticia Universal de Cataluña* (Barcelona, 1640)

Martini, Martino, *Bellum Tartaricum, or the conquest of the great and most renowned empire of China* (London, 1654)

Mason, John. *A Brief History of the Pequot War: especially of the memorable taking of their Fort at Mistick in Connecticut in 1637* (Boston, 1736)

Massieu, Guillaume, *Caffaeum* (c. 1700, reprinted in Latin with French trans. in *Etrennes à tous les amateurs de café, pour tous les temps, ou Manuel de l'amateur de Café*, I (Paris, 1790), 81–109

Mather, Increase, *Heaven's alarm to the world, or, A sermon wherein is shewed that fearful sights and signs in heaven are the presages of great calamities at hand* (Boston, 1681)

Mather, Increase, *Kometographia, or a discourse concerning comets, wherein the nature of blazing stars is enquired into, with an historical account of all comets which have appeared since the beginning of the world* (Boston, 1683)

Mauriceau, François, *The diseases of women with child, and in childbed* (Paris, 1668; English trans., London, 1672)

Maussion de Favrières, J. de, ed., *Les voyages du sieur de La Boullaye-le-Gouz, gentilhomme angevin* (Paris, 1994)

Meadows, Philip, *A narrative of the principal actions occurring in the wars betwixt Sueden and Denmark before and after the Roschild treaty* (London, 1677)

Mélanges de notices diverses sur les frères des écoles chrétiennes (Paris, 1818)

Mentet de Salmonet, Robert, *Histoire des troubles de la Grande Bretagne* (Paris, 1649)

[Merana, Jean-Paul], *Letters writ by a Turkish Spy who lived five and forty years undiscover'd at Paris*, III (London, 1692)

Merian, Mattheas, *Theatrum Europeaum*, 21 vols (Frankfurt, 1633–1738)

Meyer, A. O., 'Ein italienisches Urteil über Deutschland und Frankreich um 1600', *Quellen und Forschungen aus italienischen Archiven und Bibliotheken*, IX (1906), 155–69

Milton, John, *A second defense of the people of England* (published in Latin in 1654); *Complete Prose works of John Milton*, VIII (New York, 1933)

Milton, John, *The ready and easy way to establish a free commonwealth* (1659); *Complete Prose works of John Milton*, VII (revised edn, New Haven, 1980)

Milton, John, *Paradise Lost* (2nd edn, revised and augmented, 1674; ed. B. K. Lewalski, Oxford, 2007)

Misselden, Edward, *Free trade, or, the meanes to make trade flourish, wherein the causes of the decay of trade in this kingdome* (London, 1622)

Moderate Intelligencer, The, weekly newspaper, ed. John Dillingham (London, 1645–49)

Moinul Haq, S., ed., *Khafi Khan's History of Alamgir* (Karachi, 1975)

Molé, Matthieu, *Mémoires*, ed. A. Champollion-Figeac, IV (Paris, 1857)

Molesworth, Robert, *An account of Denmark as it was in the year 1692* (London, 1694)

Molinier, Etienne, *A mirrour for Christian states: or, A table of politick vertues considerable amongst Christians* (London, 1635, trans. William Tyrwhit from French)

Moncada, Sancho de, *Restauración política de España* (Madrid, 1619; ed. Jean Vilar, Madrid, 1974)

Monconys, Balthasar de, *Iournal des voyages de Monsieur de Monconys, II: Angleterre, Pays-Bas, Allemagne et Italie* (Lyon, 1666)

Monconys, Balthasar de, *Journal des voyages de Monsieur de Monconys*, 3e partie (Lyon, 1666)

Monkhouse, Thomas, ed., *State Papers collected by Edward, earl of Clarendon*, 3 vols (Oxford, 1767–86)

Monro, Robert, *Monro his expedition with the worthy Scots regiment call'd Mackays* (London, 1637: ed. W. S. Brockington, Westport, 1999)

Montpensier, Mlle de, *Mémoires*, 2 vols (Paris, 1728)

Morales Padrón, F., *Memorias de Sevilla (1600–78)* (Córdoba, 1981)

Morrice, Roger, *see* Goldie

Morton, Thomas, *New English Canaan, or New Canaan containing an abstract of New England* (London, 1637)

Motteville, Mme de, *Mémoires*, 2 vols (Paris, 1904)

Mut, Vicente, *El príncipe en la guerra, y en la paz, copiado de la vida del emperador Iustiniano* (Madrid, 1640)

Naima, Mustafa, *Tarih-i Naima*, 4 vols (Istanbul, 1863–4)

Nalson, John, *An impartial collection of the great affairs of state from the beginning of the Scotch rebellion in the year MDCXXXIX to the murder of King Charles I*, 2 vols (London, 1682–3)

Naudé, Gabriel, *Considérations politiques sur les coups d'état* (Rome 1639; English edn: *Political considerations upon refin'd politicks and the master-strokes of state*, London, 1711)

Naworth, George [Sir George Wharton], *A new almanacke and prognostication for the yeere of our Lord and Saviour Iesus Christ, 1642* (London, 1642)

Nedham, Marchamont, *Medela medicinae. A plea for the free profession and a renovation of the art of physick … tending to the rescue of mankind from the tyranny of diseases* (London, 1665)

Newcastle, marquis of, *see* Slaughter

Newton, Isaac, *Philosophiae naturalis principia mathematica* (London, 1687)

Newton, Isaac, *The Chronology of Ancient Kingdoms Amended* (London, 1728)

Nieuhof (or Nieuhoff), Johannes, *Het gezantschap der Nederlandtsche Oost-Indische Compagnie aan de tartarischen cham* (1655–7; Amsterdam, 1665); English translation, *An embassy from the East-India Company of the United Provinces, to the Grand Tartar Cham, emperor of China* (London, 1673)

North, Sir Dudley, *Discourses upon trade, principally directed to the cases of the interest, coynage, clipping, increase of money* (London, 1691)

Novario, G. M., *De vassallorum gravaminibus tractatus*, 3 vols (Naples 1634–42)

Numarali Mühimme Defteri (H. 1040/1630–1631) (Ankara, 2001)

Nyren, E., *see* Pu Songling

O'Mahony, Conor, *Disputatio apologetica de iure regni Hiberniae pro Catholicis Hibernis adversus haereticos Anglos* (Lisbon, 1645; reprinted Dublin, c. 1828)

Ochoa, E. de, ed., *Epistolario español: cartas de personajes varios*, 2 vols (Madrid, 1870)

Odorico, P., ed., *Conseils et mémoires de Synadinos, prêtre de Serrès en Macédonie (17e siècle)* (Paris, 1996)

Olearius, Adam, *Vermehrte moscowitische und persianische Reisebeschreibung* (2nd edn, Schleswig, 1656) *see also* Baron

Ono Mizuo, ed., *Enomoto Yazaemon Oboegaki: kinsei shoki shōnin no kiroku* (Tokyo, 2001)

Opitz, Martin, *Gesammelte Werke. Kritische Ausgabe*, ed. G. Schulz-Behrend, 4 vols (Stuttgart, 1968–90)

Osborne, Dorothy, *Letters to Sir William Temple*, ed. K. Parker (Harmondsworth, 1987)

Ovalle, Alonso de, *Histórica relación del Reyno de Chile y de las missiones y ministerios que exercita en él la Compañía de Jesus* (Rome, 1646)

Paas, J. R., *The German political broadsheet 1600–1700*, 7 vols (Wiesbaden, 1985–2002)

Pacheco de Britto, Mendo, *Discurso em os dous phaenominos aereos do anno de 1618* (Lisbon, 1619)

Padrón, Morales, F., ed., *Memorias de Sevilla (1600–1678)* (Córdoba, 1981)

Palermo, F., *Narrazioni e documenti sulla storia del Regno di Napoli dall'anno 1522 al 1667* (Florence, 1846: *Archivio storico italiano*, IX)

Parets, M., *De los muchos sucesos dignos de memoria que han ocurrido en Barcelona y otros lugares de Cataluña: crónica escrita por Miguel Parets entre los años 1626 a 1660*, 6 vols (Madrid, 1851–1948: *Memorial Histórico Español*, XX–XXV)

Parival, J.-N. de, *Abrégé de l'histoire de ce siècle de fer, contenant les misères et calamitez des derniers temps, avec leurs causes et pretextes* (1653; 2nd edn, Brussels, 1655)

Parker, Henry, *The manifold miseries of civil warre and discord in a kingdome: by the examples of Germany, France, Ireland, and other places* (London, 1642)

[Parker, Henry], *The king's cabinet opened: or, certain packets of secret letters & papers written in the king's own hand and taken in his cabinet at Nasby-Field, June 14, 1645* (London, 1645)

Parker, Henry, *The cordiall of Mr. David Ienkins* (London, 1647)

Parliament of India, *The Commission of Sati (Prevention) Act, 1987* (No. 3 of 1988)

Pascal, Blaise, *Lettres provinciales* (Paris, 1657: trans. T. M'Crie)

Pascal, Blaise, *Les Pensées sur la religion et sur quelques autres sujets* (Paris, 1670; trans. W. F. Trotter)

Pasqual de Panno, Francisco, *Motines de Cataluña*, ed. I. Juncosa and J. Vidal (Barcelona, 1993)

Patin, Charles, *Relations historiques et curieuses de voyages, en Allemagne, Angleterre, Hollande, Bohême, Suisse, &c.*, 2nd edn (Lyon, 1676)

Patin, Guy, *Lettres*, ed. J. H. Reveillé-Parise, 3 vols (Paris, 1846)

Paul, G. M., ed. *The Diary of Archibald Johnston Lord Wariston 1639* (Edinburgh, 1896: Scottish Historical Society, XXVI)

Paul, G. M., ed., *Diary of Sir Archibald Johnston of Wariston. I: 1632–7* (Edinburgh, 1911: Scottish Historical Society, LXI), *see also* Fleming

Peçevi Tarihi, ed. B. S. Baykal, 2 vols (Ankara, 1982)

Pedani-Fabris, M. P., ed., *Relazioni di ambasciatori veneti, XIV: Costantinopoli. Relazioni inedite (1512–1789)* (Padua, 1996)

Pellicer de Tovar, José, *Avisos*, ed. J.-C. Chevalier and L. Clare, 2 vols (Paris, 2002–3)

Pelsaert, Francisco, *see* Kolff and van Santen

Pepys, Samuel, *see* Latham

Percy, George, 'A trewe relacyon of the procedeings and ocurrentes of momente which have hapned in Virginia', *Tyler's Quarterly Historical and Genealogical Magazine*, III (1922), 259–82

Pérez de Ribas, Antonio, *History of the triumphs of our Holy Faith among the most barbarous and fierce peoples of the new world* (1645: ed. D. T. Reff, Tucson, 1999)

Perrot, Nicholas, *The Indian tribes of the Upper Mississippi Valley and the region of the Great Lakes [Mémoire sur les mœurs, coustumes et religion des sauvages de l'Amérique septentrionale]*, ed. E. H. Blair (Cleveland, 1911)

Peters, J., *Ein Söldnerleben im Dreissigjährigen Krieg. Eine Quelle zur Sozialgeschichte* (Berlin, 1993)

Petit, Pierre, *Thia Sinensis* (Paris, 1685)

Petitot, A. and M. Monmerque, *Mémoires du duc de Guise*, 2 vols (Paris, 1826: *Collection des mémoires relatifs à l'histoire de France*, LV–LVI)

Petty, William, *see* Hull

Pissurlencar, P. S. S., *Assentos do Conselho do Estado, 1618–95*, 4 vols (Goa, 1953–6)

Pocili, A. [pseudonym for Placido Reina], *Delle rivoluzioni della città di Palermo avvenute l'anno 1648* [sic] (Verona, 1649)

Poole, E., *A vision wherein is manifested the disease and cure of the kingdom* (London, 1648)

Poole, E., *Another alarum for war* (London, 1649)

Prestage, E. and P. M. Laranjo Coelho, eds, *Correspondência diplomática de Francisco de Sousa Coutinho durante a sua embaixada em Holanda, 1643–50*, 3 vols (Lisbon, 1925–55)

Price, D., ed., *Memoirs of the Emperor Jahangueir written by himself* (London, 1829)

Prynne, William, *The Soveraigne Power of Parliaments and Kingdomes: divided into foure parts* (London, 1643)

Pu Songling, *The bonds of matrimony (Hsing shih yin yüan chuan)*, ed. E. Nyren (Lewiston, 1995)

Qing shilu, VIII (Beijing, 1985)

Questier, M. C., ed., *Newsletters from the Caroline Court, 1631–1638: Catholicism and the politics of the personal rule* (London, 2005: Camden Society, 5th series, XXVI)

Quevedo, Francisco de, *La fortuna con seso y la hora de todos, fantasia moral* (1632) in *Obras de Francisco de Quevedo Villegas*, 3 vols (Antwerp, 1699)

Quevedo, Francisco de, *La rebelión de Barcelona* (1641), in A. Fernández-Guerra y Orbe, ed., *Obras de Don Francisco de Quevedo y Villegas*, I (Madrid, 1876: Biblioteca de Autores Españoles, XXIII)

Radziwiłł, Albrycht Stanisław, *Memoriale rerum gestarum in Polonia, 1632–1656*, ed. A. Przyboś and R. Żelewski, 4 vols (Wrocław, 1968–74)

Ras, J. J., ed., *Hikajat Bandjar: A study in Malay historiography* (The Hague, 1968)

Ravenel, J. A. D., ed., *Lettres du cardinal Mazarin à la reine* (Paris, 1836)

Ray, John, *Observations topographical, moral, and physiological, made in a journey through part of the Low-countries, Germany, Italy, and France* (London, 1673)

Raymond, John, *An itinerary contayning a voyage made through Italy in the yeare 1646 and 1647* (London, 1648)

Register of the Privy Council of Scotland, 2nd series, ed. David Masson and P. Hume Brown, 6 vols (Edinburgh, 1899–1908)

Reinach, J., ed., *Recueil des instructions données aux ambassadeurs et ministres de France. X. Naples et Parme* (Paris, 1913)

Rekishi Toshosha, *Senki Shiryô: Amakusa Sôdô – Amakusa Shimabara Gunkishû* (Kyoto, 1980)

Repgen, K., ed., *Acta Pacis Westphalicae, Series I. Instrucktionen. Frankreich, Schweden, Kaiser*, I (Münster, 1962)

Repgen, K., ed., *Acta Pacis Westphalicae, Series II, Part B, Die französischen Korrespondenzen*, 7 vols to date (Münster, 1979–2011)

Riccioli, Giovanni Battista, *Almagestum novum, astronomiam veterem novamque* (Bologna, 1651)

Riccioli, Giovanni Battista, *Geographiae et cartographiae reformatae libri XII* (Bologna, 1661)

Richelieu, Armand-Jean Duplessis, Cardinal-Duke of, *Testament politique*, ed. L. André (Paris, 1947)

Richelieu, Armand-Jean Duplessis, Cardinal-Duke of, *see also* Desmaretz *and* Grillon

Ritchie, C. I. A., 'Deux textes sur le Sénégal (1673–1677)', *Bulletin de l'Institut fondamental de l'Afrique noire*, XXX, série B (1968), 289–353

Rives, Bruno, *Mercurius Rusticus, or the countries complaint of murthers, robberies, plundrings, and other outrages committed by the rebells on His Majesties faithfull subjects* (Oxford, 1643)

Roe, Sir Thomas, *A true and faithfull relation, presented to His Maiestie and the Prince, of what laterly happened in Constantinople* (London, 1622)

Rolamb, Nicholas, 'A relation of a journey to Constantinople', in Churchill, *A collection of voyages and travels*, V, 669–716

Ros, Alexandre, *Cataluña desengañada* (Naples, 1646)

Rosales, Diego de, *Historia general del reino de Chile, Flandes Indiano* (1652–3; 2nd edn, ed. M. Góngora, 2 vols, Santiago de Chile, 1986)

Rosenhane, Schering, *Observationes politicae super Galliae Motibus* (Stockholm, 1650)

Rothes, John Leslie, earl of, *A relation of proceedings concerning the affairs of the Kirk of Scotland, from August 1637 to July 1638*, ed. J. Nairne (Edinburgh, 1830: Bannatyne Club)

Rousse, Jean, *Décision de la question des temps* (London, 1649)

Rousseau, Jean-Jacques, 'Extrait du projet de paix perpétuelle de Monsieur l'Abbé de St Pierre' (1761), in *Oeuvres complètes de Jean-Jacques Rousseau*, III (Paris, 1964)

Rowen, H. H., *The Low Countries in early modern times* (New York, 1972)

Rubí, B. de, ed., *Les Corts Generals de Pau Claris. Dietari o procés de Corts de la Junta General de Braços del 10 de septembre de 1640 a mitjan març de 1641* (Barcelona, 1976)

Rushworth, John, *Historical Collections or private passages of state, weighty matters in law, remarkable proceedings in five parliaments, beginning the sixteenth year of King James, anno 1618*, 6 vols (London, 1659–1722)

Rutherford, Samuel, *Lex, rex: the law and the prince. A dispute for the just prerogative of king and people* (London, 1644)

Rutt, J. T., ed., *Diary of Thomas Burton, Esq., member in the Parliaments of Oliver and Richard Cromwell from 1656 to 1659*, 4 vols (London, 1828)

Rycaut, Paul, *The present state of the Ottoman empire* (London, 1668: facsimile edn, New York, 1971)

Rykaczewski, E., ed., *Lettres de Pierre des Noyers, secrétaire de la reine de Pologne Marie-Louise de Gonzague* (Berlin, 1859)

Sala i Berart, Gaspar, *Proclamación Católica a la Magestad piadosa de Felipe el Grande* (Barcelona, 1640)

Sala i Berart, Gaspar, *Secretos publicos, piedra de toque, de las intenciones del enemigo, y luz de la verdad … y añadidas a la fin las cartas que en esta van citadas* (Barcelona, 1641)

Saltmarsh, John, *The smoke in the temple wherein is a designe for peace and reconciliation of believers of the several opinions of these times about ordinances* (London, 1646)

Salvado, J.-P. and S. Münch Miranda, eds, *Cartas do primeiro conde da Torre*, 4 vols (Lisbon, 2002)

Sanderson, William, *A compleat history of the life and raigne of King Charles from his cradle to his grave* (London, 1658)

Sandys, George, *A relation of a Iourney begun An. Dom. 1610* (London, 1615)

Sarkar, J., ed., *Anecdotes of Aurangzeb* (English trans. of Ahkam-i Alamgiri, ascribed to Hamid-ud-din Khan Bahadur (3rd edn, Calcutta, 1949)

Sato Taketoshi, *Chukogu saigaishi nenpyo* (Tokyo, 1993)

Schottelius, Justus, *Neu erfundenes Freudens-Spiel genandt Friedens-Sieg* (Wolfenbüttel, 1648)

Schouten, Wouter, *Reys-togten naar en door Oost Indien* (Amsterdam, 1708)

Scott, W. and J. Bliss, eds, *The works of William Laud*, 7 vols (Oxford, 1847–60)

Scriba, C. J., 'The Autobiography of John Wallis, F.R.S.', *Notes and Records of the Royal Society of London*, XXV (1970), 17–46

Seco Serrano, C., ed., *Cartas de Sor María de Jesús de Ágreda*, 2 vols (Madrid, 1958)

Selden, John, *Table-talk, being the discourses of John Selden, Esq., or his sense of various matters of weight and high consequence, relating especially to religion and state* (2nd edn, London, 1696)

Semedo, Alvaro, S.J., *Historica relatione del gran regno della Cina* (Rome, 1653)

Sévigné, marquise de, *see* Silvestre de Sacy

Shakespeare, William, *A Midsummer Night's Dream* (c. 1595; London, 1623)

Shakespeare, William, *Hamlet*, (c. 1600; London, 1623)

Sibbald, Sir Robert, *Provision for the poor in time of dearth and scarcity* (Edinburgh, 1699)

Silahdar Findiklili Mehmed Ağa, *Silahdar Tarihi*, 2 vols (Istanbul, 1928)

Silvestre de Sacy, S. U., ed., *Lettres de Marie de Rabutin-Chantal, Marquise de Sévigné, à sa fille et à ses amis*, 11 vols (Paris, 1861)

Simon i Tarrés, A., ed., *Cròniques de la Guerra dels Segadors* (Barcelona, 2003)

Sinclair, John, *The Statistical Account of Scotland, drawn up from the communications of the different parishes*, 21 vols (Edinburgh 1791–99)

Skinner, C., ed., *Sja'ir perang Mengkasar (The rhymed chronicle of the Macassar War) by Entji' Amin* (The Hague, 1963)

Skippon, Philip, *An account of a journey through the Low Countries, Germany and France* (1663), in Churchill, *A collection of voyages and travels*, VI, 359–736

Slaughter, T. P., ed., *Ideology and politics on the eve of the Restoration: Newcastle's advice to Charles II* (Philadelphia, 1984)

Smulders, F., ed., *António Vieira's Sermon against the Dutch Arms (1640)* (Frankfurt, 1996)

Snel, George, *The right teaching of useful knowledg, to fit scholars for som honest profession* (London, 1649)

Song Yingxing, *Tiangong/Tienkung kaiwu* (1637)

Song Zhenghai, *Zhongguo Gudai Zhong de Ziran Zaihai he Yichang Nianbiao* (Guangzhou, 1992)

Sorbière, Samuel, *A voyage to England: containing many things relating to the state of learning and religion, and other curiosities of that kingdom* (1663; London, 1709)

Spinoza, Baruch, *Tractatus theologico-politicus* (1670; trans. S. Shirley, Leiden, 1991)

Spinoza, Baruch, *The Ethics: Treatise on the emendation of the intellect and selected letters* (1677; trans. S. Shirley, ed. S. Feldman (2nd edn, Indianapolis, 1992)).

Sprat, Thomas, *The history of the Royal-Society of London for the improving of natural knowledge* (London, 1667)

Stouppe, J.-B., *La religion des Hollandois, representée en plusieurs lettres écrites par un officier de l'armée du Roy, à un pasteur & professeur en théologie de Berne* (Paris, 1673)

Stránský, Pavel, *Respublica Bohemiae* (Leiden, 1634)

Struve, Lynn A., ed., *Voices from the Ming-Qing cataclysm: China in tigers' jaws* (New Haven, 1993)

Struve, Lynn A., *The Ming-Qing conflict, 1619–1683. A historiography and source guide* (Ann Arbor, 1998)

Summonte, Giovanni Antonio, *Historia della città e regno di Napoli*, 4 vols (Naples, 1601–43)

Sym, John, *Life's preservative against self-killing* (London, 1637)

Symmons, Edward, *A vindication of King Charles or, a loyal subject's duty manifested in vindicating his soveraigne from those aspersions cast upon him by certaine persons, in a scandalous libel, entitled, The Kings Cabinet Opened* (London, 1647)

'T. B.', *The Rebellion of Naples, or the Tragedy of Massenello Commonly so called: But Rightly Tomaso Aniello di Malfa Generall of the Neopolitans, Written by a Gentleman who was an eye-witness where this was really acted upon that bloudy Stage, the streets of Naples* (London, 1649)

Tadino, Alessandro, *Ragguaglio dell'origine e giornalieri della gran peste seguita in Milano nell'anno 1629 al 1632* (Milan, 1648)

Tang Xianzu, *The Peony pavilion: Mudan ting* (trans. C. Birch, 2nd edn., Bloomington, 2002)

Tarrabotti, Elena, *L'inferno monacale*, ed. F. Medioli (Turin, 1989); *see also* Baratotti

Tavernier, Jean-Baptiste, *Travels in India*, ed. V. Ball and W. Crooke, 2 vols (Oxford, 1925)

Taylor, John, *Religions enemies, with a brief and ingenious relation, as by Anabaptists, Brownists, Papists, Familists, Atheists* (London, 1641)

Temple, R. C., ed., *The travels of Peter Mundy in Europe and Asia, 1608–1667*, ed. R. C. Temple, 5 vols in 6 parts (London 1907–36: Hakluyt Society, 2nd series, XVII, XXXV, XLV, XLVI, LV, LXXVIII)

Terry, C. S., ed., *The Cromwellian Union: Papers relating to the negotiations for an incorporating Union between England and Scotland, 1651–52* (Edinburgh, 1902: Scottish Historical Society, XL)

Thackston, W. M., ed., *The Jahangirnama: Memoirs of Jahangir, emperor of India* (Oxford, 1999)

Thirsk, J. and J. P. Cooper, *Seventeenth-century economic documents* (Oxford, 1972)

Thom, H. B., ed., *Journal of Jan van Riebeeck*, 3 vols (Cape Town/Amsterdam, 1952–8)

Thurloe, John, *A collection of the State Papers of John Thurloe*, ed. W. Birch, 7 vols (London, 1742)

Thwaites, R. G., ed., *The Jesuit relations and allied documents: Travels and explorations of the Jesuit missionaries in New France 1610–1791*, 71 vols (Cleveland, 1898–1901)

Tontoli, Gabriele, *Il Mas'Aniello, overo discorsi narrativi la sollevatione di Napoli* (Naples, 1648)

Topçular Kâtibi 'Abdulkādir (Kadri) Efendi Tarihi, ed. Z. Yilmazer (Ankara, 2003)

Toyoda Takeshi, ed., *Aizu-Wakamatsu-shi, II: Kizukareta Aizu Han* (Aizu, 1965)

Turbolo, Giovanni Donato, *Copia di quattro discorsi* (Naples, 1629)

Tutini, Camillo, *Dell'origine e fundazione de' Seggi di Napoli* (Naples, 1642)

Tutini, Camillo and Mario Verde, *Racconto della sollevazione di Napoli acceduta nell'anno MDCXLVII* (1653; ed. P. Messina, Rome, 1997)

Underhill, John, *Nevves from America; or, A New and Experimentall Discoverie of New England: Containing, a True Relation of their War-like Proceedings these two yeares last past* (London, 1638)

Valente, O., ed., *Documentos históricos do Arquivo Municipal. Actos da Câmara*, I (Salvador, 1944)

Valenzuelo, Pedro, *Portugal unido y separado* (Madrid, 1659)

Valerius, Adriaan, *Neder-Landtsche Gedenck-Clanck, kortelick openbarende de voornaemste geschiedenissen van de 17 Neder-lantsche Provintien, 'tsedert den aenvang der inlandische beroerten ende troublen, tot den iaere 1625* (Haarlem, 1626)

Valladares, R., *Epistolario de Olivares y el conde de Basto (Portugal 1637–1638)* (Badajoz, 1998)

Van Aitzema, Lieuwe, *Notable revolutions, beeing a true relation of what hap'ned in the United Provinces of the Netherlands in the years MDCL and MDCLI somewhat before and after the death of the late Prince of Orange: according to the Dutch copie* (London, 1653)

Van Aitzema, Lieuwe, *Saken van Staet en Oorlogh, in ende omtrent de Vereenigde Nederlanden*, 6 vols (The Hague, 1669–72)

Van der Capellen, Adrian, *Gedenkschriften, 1621–54*, 2 vols (Utrecht, 1777)

Van der Donck, Adriaen, *A description of the New Netherlands* (1653: Madison, 2003: Wisconsin Historical Society Digital Library and Archives)

Van der Heyden, Jan, *A description of fire engines with water hoses and the method of fighting fires now used in Amsterdam* (1690; English edn by L. Multhauf, 1996)

Vanderlinden, E., *Chronique des évènements météorologiques en Belgique jusqu'en 1834* (Brussels, 1925: Mémoires publiés par la classe des sciences de l'Académie royale de Belgique, 2nd series VI)

Vauban, Sébastien le Prestre, marquis de, *Mémoire pour servir d'instruction dans la conduite des sièges et dans la défense des places* (written c. 1670: Leiden, 1740)

Vauban, Sébastien Le Prestre, marquis de, *Méthode géneralle et facile pour faire le dénombrement des peuples* (Paris, 1686)

Vauban, Sébastien Le Prestre, marquis de, *Les oisivités de Monsieur de Vauban*, ed. M. Virol (Paris, 2007)

Vernadsky, George, ed., *A source book for Russian history from early times to 1917* (New Haven, 1972)

Viallé, C. and L. Blussé, *The Deshima Registers. XI: 1641–1650* (Leiden, 2001: Intercontinenta, XXIII)

Viallé, C. and L. Blussé, *The Deshima Registers. XII: 1650–1660* (Leiden, 2005: Intercontinenta, XXV)

Viallé, C. and L. Blussé, *The Deshima Registers. XIII: 1660–1670* (Leiden, 2010: Intercontinenta, XXVII)

Vieira, António, *see* Smulders

Vigorelli, G., ed., *Vita e processo di Suor Virginia Maria de Leyva, monaca di Monza* (Milan, 1985)

Vincent, Philip, *The Lamentations of Germany wherein, as in a glasse, we may behold her miserable condition, and reade the woefull effects of sinne, composed by Dr. Vincent, Theol., an eye-witnesse thereof, and illustrated by pictures, the more to affect the reader* (London, 1638)

Vitrián y Ortuvia, Juan, *Las memorias de Felipe de Comines, señor de Argentón, de los hechos empresas de Luis Undécimo y Carlos Octavo, reyes de Francia, traducidas del francés con escolios propios*, 2 vols (Antwerp, 1643)

[Voetius, Gisbertius; 'G. L. V.'], *Brittish lightning, or, suddaine tumults in England, Scotland and Ireland to warne the United Provinces to understand the dangers and the causes thereof* (Amsterdam, 1643)

Voltaire, F. M. A. de, *Essai sur les mœurs et l'esprit des nations et sur les principaux faits de l'histoire depuis Charlemagne jusqu'à Louis XIII* (1741–2; first published 1756; Paris, 1963)

Voltaire, F. M. A. de, *Le siècle de Louis XIV* (Berlin, 1751)

Von Sandrart, Joachim, *Der Teutschen Academie, Zweyter und letzter Haupt-Teil, von der edlen Bau- Bild und Mahlerey-Künsten*, 3 vols (Nuremberg, 1679)

Voorbeijtel Cannenburg, W., ed., *De reis om de wereld van de Nassausche Vloot, 1623–1626* (The Hague, 1964: Werken uitgegeven van de Linschoten Vereeniging, LXV)

Wallington, Nehemiah, *see* Seaver *and* Webb

Wallis, John, *A defence of the Royal Society, and the Philosophical Transactions* (London, 1678)

Wallis, John, 'Autobiography', *see* Scriba

Walton, Izaak, *The Compleat Angler, or the contemplative man's recreation* (1653; 2nd edn, London, 1655)

Wariston, Archibald Johnston of, *see* Paul *and* Fleming

Webb, R., ed., *Historical notices of events occurring chiefly in the reign of Charles I by Nehemiah Wallington*, 2 vols (London, 1868–9)

Weise, Christian, *Von dem Neapolitanischen Haupt Rebellen Masaniello* (Zittau, 1682)

Wharton, Sir George, *see* Naworth

Wharton, Henry, ed., *The history of the troubles and tryal of the Most Reverend Father in God and blessed martyr, William Laud, Lord Arch-Bishop of Canterbury, wrote by himself during his imprisonment in the Tower; to which is prefixed the diary of his own life*, 2 vols (London, 1695–1700)

Whitelocke, Bulstrode, *Memorials of the English affairs* (1682: reprinted in 4 vols, Oxford, 1853)

Whitelocke, Bulstrode, *A journal of the Swedish embassy in the years 1653 and 1654*, 2 vols (London, 1772)

Whittaker, Jeremiah, *Ejrenopojos: Christ the settlement of unsettled times* (London, 1643)

Wildman, John, *A call to all the souldiers of the Army, by the free people of England* (London, 1647)

Wildman, John, *Truths triumph, or treachery anatomized* (London, 1648)

Wilkins, John, *Mathematical magick: or the wonders that may be performed by mechanicall geometry* (London, 1648)

Williams, E. Neville, *The eighteenth-century constitution, 1688–1815: Documents and commentary* (Cambridge, 1960)

Winstanley, Jerrard, *The Law of freedom in a platform, or true magistracy restored* (London, 1652)

Winthrop papers, 3 vols (Boston, 1929–43)

Winthrop, *see also* Dunn

Wood, William, *New England prospect. A true, lively and experimentall description of that part of America commonly called New England* (London, 1634)

Yang Dongming, *Jimin tushuo* (1594; first printed 1688)

Yilmazer, Z., ed., *Topçular Kâtibi 'Abdülkâdir (Kadrî) Efendi Tarihi* (Ankara, 2003)

Zhongguo Jin-wubai-nian Hanlao Fenbu Tu-ji (Beijing, 1981)

Zillhardt, G., ed., *Der dreissigjährige Krieg in zeitgenössischer Darstellung. Hans Heberles 'Zeytregister' (1618–1672)* (Ulm, 1975)

B. Secondary Works cited in the Notes

Adamson, J. S. A., 'The English nobility and the projected settlement of 1647', *HJ*, XXX (1987), 567–602

Adamson, J. S. A., 'The baronial context of the English Civil War', *TRHS*, 5th series, XL (1990), 93–120

Adamson, J. S. A., 'England without Cromwell: what if Charles I had avoided the Civil War?', in N. Ferguson, ed., *Virtual history: Alternatives and counterfactuals* (London, 1997), 91–123

Adamson, J. S. A., *The noble revolt: The overthrow of Charles I* (London, 2007)

Adapting to climate change: Towards a European framework for action (Commission of the European Communities: Commission staff working document SEC (2009))

Adshead, S. A. M., 'The XVIIth century General Crisis in China', *France-Asie/Asia*, XXIV/3–4 (1970), 251–65

Agnew, C. S., 'Culture and power in the making of the descendants of Confucius, 1300–1800' (University of Washington PhD thesis, 2006)

Aho, J. A., *Religious mythology and the art of war: Comparative religious symbolisms of military violence* (Westport, CT, 1981)

Ailes, M. E., 'Wars, widows, and state formation in 17th-century Sweden', *Scandinavian Journal of History*, XXXI/1 (2006), 17–34

Åkerman, S., *Queen Christina of Sweden and her circle: The transformation of a seventeenth-century philosophical libertine* (Leiden, 1991)

Alam, M. and S. Subrahmanyam, 'From an Ocean of Wonders: Mahmûd bin Amîr Walî Balkhî and his Indian travels, 1625–1631', in C. Salmon, ed., *Récits de voyage des Asiatiques. Genres, mentalités, conception de l'espace* (Paris, 1996), 161–89

Alam, M. and S. Subrahmanyam, eds, *The Mughal State, 1526–1750* (Delhi, 1998)

Albrecht, D., *Die auswärtige Politik Maximilians von Bayern 1618–1635* (Göttingen, 1962)

Alcalá-Zamora y Queipo de Llano, J., 'Razón de Estado y geoestrategia en la política italiana de Carlos II: Florencia y los presidios, 1677–81', *BRAH*, CLXXIII (1976), 297–358

Alden, D. and J. C. Miller, 'Unwanted cargoes: the origins and dissemination of smallpox via the slave trade, c. 1560–1830', in K. F. Kiple, ed., *The African exchange: Towards a biological history of Black People* (Durham, NC, 1987), 35–109

Alfani, G., 'Plague in seventeenth-century Europe and the decline of Italy: an epidemiological hypothesis' (IGIER Working Paper n. 377, accessed Feb. 2011)

Allemeyer, M. L., ' "Dass es wohl recht ein Feuer vom Herrn zu nennen gewesen . . .", Zur Wahrnehmung, Deutung und Verarbeitung von Stadtbränden in norddeutschen Schriften des 17. Jahrhunderts', in Jakubowski-Tiessen and Lehmann, *Um himmels Willen*, 201–34

Allen, R. C. et al., 'Wages, prices, and living standards in China, 1738–1925: in comparison with Europe, Japan, and India', *EcHR*, LXIV/S1 (2011), 8–38

Álvarez, G., F. C. Ceballos and C. Quinteiro, 'The role of inbreeding in the extinction of a European royal dynasty', PLoS ONE 4(4): e5174. doi:10.1371/journal.pone.0005174 (published 15 Apr. 2009)

Alvarez, W., *T-Rex and the crater of doom* (Princeton, 1997)

Álvarez de Miranda, P., 'Las controversias sobre los cometas de 1680 y 1682 en España', *Dieciocho; Hispanic Enlightenment*, XX, Extra; Anéjo 1 (1997), 21–52

Álvarez de Toledo, C., *Politics and reform in Spain and New Spain: The life and thought of Juan de Palafox (1600–49)* (Oxford, 2004)

Álvarez de Toledo, C., 'Crisis, reforma y rebelión en el mundo hispánico: el caso Escalona', in Parker, *La crisis de la Monarquía*, 255–86

Álvarez Santaló, L. C., *Marginación social y mentalidad en Andalucia occidental. Expósitos en Sevilla, 1613–1910* (Seville, 1980)

Alvi, S. S., ed., *Advice on the art of governance: Mau'izah-Jahângîri of Muhammad Bâqir Najm-Sânî* (New York, 1989)

Amelang, J. S., 'Barristers and judges in early modern Barcelona: the rise of a legal elite', *AHR*, LXXXIX (1984), 1, 264–84

Amelang, J. S., 'The bourgeois', in Villari, *Baroque personae*, 314–33

Amussen, S. D., *An ordered society: Gender and class in early modern England* (Oxford, 1988)

Andaya, L., *The heritage of Arung Palakka: A history of South Sulawesi (Celebes) in the seventeenth century* (The Hague, 1981)

Anderson, V. D., *Creatures of Empire: How domestic animals transformed early America* (Oxford, 2004)

Andrade, T., *How Taiwan became Chinese: Dutch, Spanish, and Han colonization in the seventeenth century* (New York, 2007)

Andrews, C. M., *The colonial period of American history. I. The settlements* (New Haven, 1934)

Andrien, K. J., *Crisis and decline: The viceroyalty of Peru in the seventeenth century* (Albuquerque, 1985)

Anes Álvarez, G., *Las crisis agrarias en la España moderna* (2nd edn, Madrid, 1974)

Anes Alvarez, G. and J. P. Le Flem, 'Las crisis del siglo XVII: producción agrícola, precios e ingresos en tierras de Segovia', *Moneda y Crédito*, XCIII (1965), 3–55

Anpilogov, G. N., 'Polozhenie gorodskogo i sel'skogo naseleniia Kurskogo uedza nakunune vosstaniia 1648 g.', *Vestnik Moskovskogo universiteta, seriia 9: Istoriia*, V (1972), 47–60

Ansaldo, M., *Peste, fame, guerra: cronache di vita Valdostana del secolo XVII* (Aosta, 1976)

Aono Ysuyuki, *Climatic reconstruction of spring-time temperatures using phenological data for flowering of cherry tree from old documents* (Osaka, 2006)

Appleby, A. B., 'Epidemics and famine in the Little Ice Age', *JIH*, X (1980), 643–63

Arakawa, H, 'Dates of first or earliest snow covering for Tokyo since 1632', *Quarterly Journal of the Royal Meteorological Society*, LXXXII (1956), 222–6

Arakawa, H., ed., *Climates of northern and eastern Asia* (Amsterdam, 1969: World Survey of Climatology, VIII)

Asch, R., ' "Wo der soldat hinkömpt, da ist alles sein": military violence and atrocities in the Thirty Years War reconsidered', *German History*, XVIII (2000), 291–309

Ashcraft, R., *Revolutionary politics and Locke's Two Treatises of Government* (Princeton, 1986)

Ashley, M., *Financial and commercial policy under the Cromwellian Protectorate* (2nd edn, London, 1962)

Aston, T. S., ed., *Crisis in Europe, 1560–1660* (London, 1965)

Aström, S.-E., 'The Swedish economy and Sweden's role as a Great Power, 1632–1697', in M. Roberts, ed., *Sweden's age of greatness 1632–1718* (London, 1973), 58–101

Atasoy, N. and J. Raby, *Iznik: The pottery of Ottoman Turkey* (London, 1989)

Atherton, I. J., *Ambition and failure in Stuart England: The career of John, first Viscount Scudamore* (London, 1999)

Atherton, I. J., 'The press and popular political opinion', in B. Coward, ed., *A companion to Stuart Britain* (Oxford, 2004), ch. 5

Atwell, W. S., 'From education to politics: the Fu She', in W. T. de Bary, ed., *The unfolding of Neo-Confucianism* (New York, 1975), 333–67

Atwell, W. S., 'Ming statecraft scholarship and some common themes in the political writings of Ch'en Tzu-lung (1608–47) and Ogyū Sorai (1666–1728)', in Yue-him Tam, ed., *Sino-Japanese cultural interchange: The economic and intellectual aspects. Papers of the International Symposium on Sino-Japanese cultural interchange*, III (Hong Kong, 1985), 61–85

Atwell, W. S., 'Some observations on the "17th-century crisis" in China and Japan', *JAS*, XLV/2 (1986), 223–44

Atwell, W. S., 'Ming observers of Ming decline: some Chinese views on the "17th-century crisis" in comparative perspective', *Journal of the Royal Asiatic Society of Great Britain and Ireland*, CXX (1988), 316–48

Atwell, W. S., 'A seventeenth-century "General Crisis" in East Asia?', in Parker and Smith, *The General Crisis*, 235–54

Atwell, W. S., 'East Asia and the "World Crisis" of the mid-seventeenth century' (lecture at the Mershon Center, Ohio State University, 2001)

Atwell, W. S., 'Volcanism and short-term climatic change in East Asian and world history, c. 1200–1699', *JWH*, XII (2001), 29–98

Atwell, W. S., 'Another look at silver imports into China, c. 1635–1644', *JWH*, XVI (2006), 467–89

Avrich, P., *Russian rebels 1600–1800* (London, 1972)

Aylmer, G. E., *Rebellion or revolution?* (London, 1985)

Aymard, M., 'Commerce et production de la soie sicilienne aux XVIe–XVIIe siècles', *Mélanges d'Archéologie et d'Histoire de l'École française de Rome*, LXXVII (1965), 609–40

Aymard, M., 'Rese e profitti agricoli in Sicilia, 1640–1760', *Quaderni storici*, XIV (1970), 416–38

Aymard, M., 'In Sicilia: sviluppo demografico e sue differenziazioni geografiche, 1500–1800', *Quaderni storici*, XVII (1971), 417–46

Aymard, M., 'Bilancio d'una larga crisi finanziaria', *Rivista storica italiana*, LXXXIV (1972), 988–1,021

Aymard, M., 'Rendements et productivité agricole dans l'Italie moderne', *Annales E. S. C.*, XXVIII (1973), 483–7

Aymard, M., 'La Sicilia: profili demografici', in *Storia di Sicilia*, VII (Palermo, 1978), 217–40

Babayan, K., *Mystics, monarchs and messiahs: Cultural landscapes of early modern Iran* (Cambridge, MA, 2002)

Bacon, G., ' "The House of Hannover": Gezeirot Tah in modern Jewish historical writing', *Jewish History*, XVII (2003), 179–206

Baehr, S. L., *The paradise myth in eighteenth-century Russia: Utopian patterns in early secular Russian literature and culture* (Stanford, 1991)

Baehrel, R., *Une croissance: la Basse-Provence rurale (fin XVIe siècle – 1789). Essai d'économie historique statistique* (Paris, 1961)

Baer, M. D., 'The Great Fire of 1660 and the Islamization of Christian and Jewish space in Istanbul', *IJMES*, XXXVI (2004), 159–81

Baer, M. D., 'Death in the hippodrome: sexual politics and legal culture in the reign of Mehmet IV', *P&P*, CCX (2011), 61–91

Baer, W. C., 'Stuart London's standard of living: re-examining the Settlement of Tithes of 1638 for rents, income, and poverty', *EcHR*, LXIII (2010), 612–37

Bailey, C. D. A., 'Reading between the lines: the representation and containment of disorder in Late Ming and Early Qing legal texts', *Ming Studies*, LIX (2009), 56–86

Baillie, M. G. L., 'Putting abrupt environmental change back into human history', in K. Flint and H. Morphy, eds, *Culture, landscape, and the environment: The Linacre lectures, 1997–8* (Oxford, 2000), 46–75

Baker, A., C. Proctor and B. Barnes, 'Northwest Scotland stalagmite and climate reconstruction data', NOAA Paleoclimatology Program and World Data Center for Paleoclimatology Data, Contribution Series #2000–011

Baker, J. N. L., 'The climate of England in the seventeenth century', *Quarterly Journal of the Royal Meteorological Society*, LVIII (1932), 421–39

Balabanlilar, L., 'Re-ordering societies and improving the world: the Grand Vizierate of Köprülük Mehmet Pasha, 1656–1661' (Ohio State University, MA thesis, 2003)

Balabanlilar, L., 'Lords of the auspicious conjunction: Turco-Mongol imperial identity on the subcontinent', *JWH*, XVIII (2007), 1–39

Balabanlilar, L., *Imperial identity in the Mughal Empire: Memory and dynastic politics in early modern south and central Asia* (London, 2012)

Baliński, M., *Dariusz Filipa Kazimierza Obuchowicza (1630 do 1654), Pamiętniki Obuchowiczów i Cedrowskiego. Pamiętniki historyczne XVII wieku* (Vilnius, 1859)

Ball, D. I. and J. Porter, *Fighting words: Competing voices from Native America* (Santa Barbara, 2009)

Banerjee, P., *Burning women: Widows, witches and early modern European travelers in India* (New York, 2003)

Bankoff, G., *Cultures of disaster: Society and natural hazard in the Philippines* (London, 2003)

Barkey, K., 'Rebellious alliances: the state and peasant unrest in early seventeenth-century France and the Ottoman empire', *American Sinological Review*, LVI (1991), 699–715

Barkey, K., *Bandits and bureaucrats: The Ottoman route to state centralization* (Ithaca, NY, 1994)

Barnes, A. E., ' "Playing the part of angels": the Company of the Holy Sacrament and the struggle for stability in early modern France', in Benedict and Gutmann, *Early modern Europe*, 168–96

Barrett, E. M., 'The geography of the Rio Grande Pueblos in the seventeenth century', *Ethnohistory*, XLIX (2002), 123–69

Barriendos, M., 'Climatic variations in the Iberian peninsula during the Late Maunder Minimum (AD 1675–1715): an analysis of data from rogation ceremonies', *The Holocene*, VII (1997), 105–11

Barriendos, M. and F. S. Rodrigo, 'Study of historical flood events on Spanish rivers using documentary data', *Hydrological Sciences Journal*, LI (2006), 765–83

Baten, J., 'Climate, grain production and nutritional status in southern Germany during the eighteenth century', *JEEH*, XXX/1 (2001), 9–47

Baulant, M., 'Le prix des grains à Paris de 1431 à 1788', *Annales E. S. C.*, XXIII (1968), 520–40

Beattie, H., 'The alternative to resistance: the case of T'ung-ch'eng', in Spence and Wills, *From Ming to Ch'ing*, 241–76

Beattie, H., *Land and lineage in China: A study of T'ung-ch'eng county, Anhwei, in the Ming and Ch'ing dynasties* (Cambridge, 1979)

Beckles, H., 'From land to sea: runaway Barbados slaves and servants, 1630–1700', *Slavery and Abolition*, VI (1985), 79–94

Behringer, W., 'Weather, hunger and fear: the origins of the European witch-hunts in climate, society and mentality', *German History*, XIII (1993), 1–27

Behringer, W., *Im Zeichen des Merkur: Reichspost und Kommunikationsrevolution in der frühen Neuzeit* (Göttingen, 2003)

Behringer, W., *Witches and witch-hunts: A global history* (Cambridge, 2004)

Behringer, W., H. Lehmann and C. Pfister, eds, *Kulturelle Konsequenzen der 'Kleinen Eiszeit'* (Göttingen, 2005)

Beik, W., *Louis XIV and absolutism: A brief study with documents* (Boston, 2000)

Beik, W., 'The violence of the French crowd from Charivari to Revolution', *P&P*, CXCVII (2007), 75–110

Bell, D. P., 'The Little Ice Age and the Jews: environmental history and the mercurial nature of Jewish-Christian relations in early modern Germany', *AJS Review*, XXXII/1 (2008), 1–27

Benedict, P., 'Religion and politics in the European struggle for stability, 1500–1700', in Benedict and Gutmann, eds, *Early modern Europe*, 120–38

Benedict, P. and M. P. Gutmann, eds, *Early modern Europe: From crisis to stability* (Newark, DE, 2005)

Benigno, F., *L'ombra del re. Ministri e lotta politica nella Spagna del Seicento* (Venice, 1992)

Benigno, F., *Specchi della Rivoluzione. Conflitto e identità politica nell'Europa moderna* (Rome, 1999)

Benito, G. et al., 'Magnitude and frequency of flooding in the Tagus Basin (central Spain) over the last millennium', *CC*, LVIII (2003), 171–92

Bennassar, B., *Recherches sur les grandes épidémies dans le Nord de l'Espagne à la fin du XVIe siècle* (2nd edn, Paris, 2001)

Bennett, M., *The Civil Wars experienced: Britain and Ireland 1638–1661* (London, 2000)

Benton, M. J., *When life nearly died: The greatest mass extinction of all time* (London, 2005)

Bercé, Y.-M., 'Troubles frumentaires et pouvoir contralisateur: l'émeute de Fermo dans les Marches (1648)', *Mélanges d'archéologie et d'histoire de l'École française de Rome*, LXXIII (1961), 471–505, and LXXIV (1962), 759–803

Bercé, Y.-M., *Histoire des Croquants. Étude des soulèvements populaires au XVIIe siècle dans le sud-ouest de la France*, 2 vols (Geneva, 1974)

Bercé, Y.-M., *Révoltes et révolutions dans l'Europe moderne, XVIe–XVIIIe siècles* (Paris, 1980)

Bercé, Y.-M., *La sommossa di Fermo del 1648, con le cronache di Maiolino Bisaccioni, Francesco Maria e Domenico Raccamadori e una memoria inedita di Giuseppe Fracassetti* (Fermo, 2007)

Berchet, G., *La Repubblica di Venezia e la Persia* (Turin, 1865)

Berghaus, G., *Die Aufnahme der englishen Revolution in Deutschland 1640–1669* (Wiesbaden, 1989)

Bergin, J., *The making of the French episcopate* (New Haven, 1996)

Bergin, J. and L. W. B. Brockliss, eds, *Richelieu and his age* (Oxford, 1992)

Bernardos Sanz, J. U., *Trigo castellano y abasto madrileño: Los arrieros y comerciantes segovianos en la Edad Moderna* (Salamanca, 2003)

Berry, M. E., *Hideyoshi* (Cambridge, MA, 1982)

Berry, M. E., 'Public life in authoritarian Japan', *Daedalus*, CXXVII/3 (1998), 133–65

Berry, M. E., *Japan in print: Information and nation in the early modern period* (Berkeley, 2006)

Betrán, J. L., *La peste en la Barcelona de los Austrias* (Lleida, 1996)

Bierbrauer, P., 'Bäuerliche Revolten im Alten Reich. Ein Forschungsbericht', in P. Blickle et al., eds, *Aufruhr und Empörung? Studien zum bäuerlichen Widerstand im Alten Reich* (Munich, 1980), 1–68

Bierther, K., *Der Regensburger Reichstag von 1640/1641* (Kallmünz, 1971)

Bilbao, L. M., 'La crisis del siglo XVII en su lectura económica. Un debate inconcluso', *Areas. Revista de ciencias sociales*, X (1989), 51–72

Biot, E., 'Catalogue des comètes observées en Chine depuis l'an 1230 jusqu'à l'an 1640 de notre ère', *Connaissance des Temps* (Paris, 1843), 44–59

Biraben, J. N., *Les hommes et la peste en France et dans les pays européens et méditerranéens*, 2 vols (Paris, 1975)

Biraben, J.-N. and D. Blanchet, 'Essai sur le mouvement de la population de Paris et de ses environs depuis le XVIe siècle', *Population*, LIII (1998), 215–48

Bireley, R., *Religion and politics in the age of the Counter-Reformation: Emperor Ferdinand II, William Lamormaini, S. J., and the formation of imperial policy* (Chapel Hill, NC, 1981)

Birmingham, D., *The Portuguese conquest of Angola* (London, 1965)

Bitossi, C., 'Gli apparati statali e la crisi del Seicento', in N. Tranfaglia and M. Firpi, eds, *La Storia. I grandi problemi dal Medioevo all'Età contemporanea. V. L'Età Moderna, iii: stati e società* (Turin, 1986), 169–98

Bix, H., *Peasant protest in Japan, 1590–1884* (New Haven, 1986)

Blake, E. S., E. N. Rappaport and C. W. Landsea, *The deadliest, costliest, and most intense United States tropical cyclones from 1851 to 2006 (and other frequently requested hurricane facts)* (Miami, 2007: NOAA Technical Memorandum NWS TPC-5)

Blake, S. P., *Shahjahanabad: The sovereign city in Mughal India* (Cambridge, 1991).

Blaufarb, R., 'The survival of the *Pays d'États*: the example of Provence', *P&P*, CCIX (2010), 83–113

Blaug, M., 'The Poor Law Report re-examined', *Journal of Economic History*, XXIV (1964), 229–45

Blickle, P. et al., *Aufruhr und Empörung. Studien zur bäuerliche Widerstand im Alten Reich* (Munich, 1980)

Blickle, P., ed., *Resistance, representation and community* (Oxford, 1997)

Bloch, M., *Les caractères originaux de l'histoire rurale française* (1931; 2nd edn, 2 vols, Paris, 1952–6)

Blok, F. F., *Nikolaus Heinsius in Napels (april–juli 1647)* (Amsterdam, 1984)

Blome, A., 'Offices of intelligence and expanding social spaces', in Dooley, ed., *The dissemination*, 207–22

Bluche, F., 'Un vente de Fronde' in Bluche and S. Rials, eds, *Les révolutions françaises. Les phénomènes révolutionnaires en France du Moyen Age à nos jours* (Paris, 1989), 167–79

Blum, J., *Lord and peasant in Russia: From the ninth to the nineteenth century* (Princeton, 1961)

Blussé, L., *Strange company: Chinese settlers, mestizo women and the Dutch in VOC Batavia* (Dordrecht, 1986)

Boaga, E., *La soppressione innocenziana dei piccoli conventi in Italia* (Rome, 1971)

Bogart, D., 'Did the Glorious Revolution contribute to the transport revolution? Evidence from investment in roads and rivers', *EcHR*, LXIV (2011), 1,073–1,112

Bogucka, M., 'Between capital, residential town and metropolis: the development of Warsaw in the sixteenth to eighteenth centuries', in Clark and Lepetit, *Capital cities*, 198–216

Bolitho, H., *Treasures among men: The Fudai daimyō in Tokugawa Japan* (New Haven, 1974)

Bollême, G., *La bibliothèque bleue: Littérature populaire en France du XVIIe au XIXe siècle* (Paris, 1971)

Bollême, G., *La bibliothèque bleue. Anthologie d'une littérature 'populaire'* (Paris 1976)

Bonney, R. J., 'The French Civil War, 1649–53', *European History Quarterly*, VIII (1978), 71–100

Bonney, R. J., *Political change in France under Richelieu and Mazarin, 1624–1661* (Oxford, 1978)

Bonney, R. J., *The European dynastic states, 1494–1660* (Oxford, 1991)

Bonney, R. J., 'Louis XIII, Richelieu, and the royal finances', in Bergin and Brockliss, eds, *Richelieu and his age*, 120–33

Bonney, R. J., *The limits to absolutism in ancien régime France* (Aldershot, 1995)

Bonney, R. J., ed., *The rise of the fiscal state in Europe, c. 1200–1815* (Oxford, 1999)

Bonolas, P., 'Retz, épigone de Cromwell?', *XVIIe siècle*, CLXIX (1990), 445–55

Boomgaard, P., et al., 'Fluctuations in mortality in seventeenth-century Indonesia', in *Conference on Asian Population History* (Beijing: Academia Sinica, 1996), 1–11

Börekçi, G., 'Factions and favorites at the Courts of Sultan Ahmed I (r. 1603–17) and his immediate predecessors' (Ohio State University, PhD. thesis, 2010)

Borgaonkar, H. P., A. B. Sikder, Somaru Ram and G. B. Pant, 'Climate change signature in tree-ring proxies from the Indian subcontinent' (Asia-2K Workshop, Nagoya, 2010)

Borja Palomo, F., *Historia crítica de las riadas o grandes avenidas del Guadalquivir en Sevilla* (Seville, 2001)

Bots, H., 'Le rôle des périodiques néerlandais pour la diffusion du livre (1684–1747)', in C. Berkvens-Stevelinck, et al., eds, *Le magasin de l'univers: The Dutch Republic as the centre of the European book trade* (Leiden, 1992), 49–70

Bottigheimer, K. S., *English money and Irish Land: The 'Adventurers' in the Cromwellian settlement of Ireland* (Oxford, 1971)

Boulton, J., 'Food prices and the standard of living in London in the "Century of Revolution", 1580–1700', *EcHR*, LIII (2000), 455–92

Bourgeon, J.-L., 'L'Île de la Cité pendant la Fronde. Structure sociale', *Paris et Île-de-France – Mémoires*, XIII (1962), 22–144

Bouza, F., *Corre manuscrito. Una historia cultural del Siglo de Oro* (Madrid, 2001)

Bowra, E. C., 'The Manchu conquest of Canton', *China Review*, I (1872–3), 228–37

Boxer, C. R., *Fidalgos in the Far East, 1550–1700: Fact and fancy in the history of Macao* (The Hague, 1948)

Boxer, C. R., 'Portuguese and Dutch colonial rivalry 1641–1661', *Studia*, II (1958), 7–42

Boxer, C. R., *The Portuguese seaborne empire, 1415–1825* (London, 1969)

Boxer, C. R., *Portuguese India in the mid-seventeenth century* (Delhi, 1980)

Boxer, C. R., *Seventeenth-century Macau in contemporary documents and illustrations* (Singapore, 1984)

Boyer, R. E., *La gran inundación. Vida y sociedad en Mexico 1629–1638* (Mexico, 1975)

Braddick, M. J., *God's fury, England's fire: A new history of the English Civil Wars* (London, 2008)

Braddick, M. J., and J. Walter, eds, *Negotiating power in Early Modern society: Order, hierarchy, and subordination in Britain and Ireland* (Cambridge, 2001)

Bradley, R. S., *Paleoclimatology: Reconstructing climates of the Quaternary* (2nd edn, London, 1999)

Bradley, R. S. and P. D. Jones, eds, *Climate since A.D. 1500* (London, 1992)

Bradshaw, B., A. Hadfield and W. Maley, eds, *Representing Ireland: Literature and the origins of conflict, 1534–1660* (Cambridge, 2010)

Bradshaw, B. and J. Morrill, eds, *The British problem, c. 1534–1707: State formation in the Atlantic archipelago* (New York, 1996)

Braudel, F., *The Mediterranean and the Mediterranean world in the age of Philip II*, 2 vols (London, 1972–3)

Bray, F., *Technology and gender: Fabrics of power in late imperial China* (Berkeley, 1997)

Brázdil, R., *Historické a současné porodně v České Republice* (Brno, 2005)

Brázdil, R., ed., *Hydrological Sciences Journal*, LI/5 (2006), 733–985 (a special issue dedicated to 'Historical hydrology')

Brázdil, R. et al., 'Historical climatology in Europe – the state of the art', *CC*, LXX (2005), 363–430

Brázdil, R. and O. Kotyza, 'Floods in the Czech Republic in the past millennium', *L'houille blanche*, V (2004), 50–5

Brázdil, R., P. Dobrovolný and J. Luterbacher, 'Use of documentary data in European climate reconstructions: state of the art and recent progress' (paper delivered at the 'Climate and History' conference at the Deutsches Historisches Institut, Paris, 3–4 Sep. 2011)

Brázdil, R., H. Valášek and O. Kotyza, 'Meteorological records of Michel Stüeler of Krupka and their contribution to the knowledge of the climate of the Czech Lands in 1629–1649', in D. Drbohlav, J. Kalvoda and V. Voženílek, eds, *Czech geography at the dawn of the millennium* (Olomouc, 2004), 95–112

Brázdil, R. et al., 'European climate of the past 500 years: new challenges for historical climatology', CC, CI (2010), 7–40

Brecke, P., 'Violent conflicts 1400 A.D. to the present in different regions of the world' (Paper prepared for the 1999 Meeting of the Peace Science Society International, Ann Arbor, Michigan)

Bremer, F. J., 'In defence of regicide: John Cotton on the execution of Charles I', WMQ, 3rd series, XXXVII (1980), 103–24

Brenner, R., *Merchants and revolution: Commercial change, political conflict, and London's overseas traders, 1550–1653* (Cambridge, 1993)

Briffa, K. R. and T. J. Osborn, 'Blowing Hot and Cold', *Science*, CCXCV (2002), 2,227–8

Briggs, R., 'Richelieu and reform: rhetoric and political reality', in Bergin and Brockliss, eds, *Richelieu and his age*, 71–97

Briggs, R., *Communities of belief: Cultural and social tension in early modern France* (Oxford, 1989)

Brinton, C., *Anatomy of Revolution* (1938; 2nd edn, New York, 1965)

Brockliss, L., 'Richelieu, education and the state', in Bergin and Brockliss, eds, *Richelieu and his age*, 237–72

Brockliss, L. and C. Jones, *The medical world of early modern France* (Oxford, 1997)

Brod, M., 'Politics and prophecy in seventeenth-century England: the case of Elizabeth Poole', *Albion*, XXXI (1995), 395–413

Brokaw, C. J., *The ledgers of merit and demerit: Social change and moral order in late Imperial China* (Princeton, 1991)

Brokaw, C. J., *Commerce in culture: The Sibao book trade 1663–1946* (Cambridge, MA, 2007)

Brokaw, C. J. and Kai-Wing Chow, eds, *Printing and book culture in late imperial China* (Berkeley, 2004)

Bronner, F., 'La Unión de Armas en el Perú. Aspectos político-legales', *Anuario de estudios americanos*, XXIV (1967), 1,133–71

Brook, T., 'Censorship in eighteenth-century China: a view from the book trade', *Canadian Journal of History*, XXII (1988), 177–96

Brook, T., *Praying for power: Buddhism and the formation of gentry society in late-Ming China* (Cambridge, MA, 1993)

Brook, T., *The confusions of pleasure: Commerce and culture in Ming China* (Berkeley, 1998)

Brook, T., *Vermeer's hat: The seventeenth century and the dawn of the global world* (New York, 2008)

Brook, T., *The troubled empire: China in the Yuan and Ming dynasties* (Cambridge, MA, 2010)

Brooks, G. E., *Landlords and strangers: Ecology, society and trade in Western Africa, 1000–1630* (Boulder, CO, 1993)

Brown, P. B., 'Tsar Aleksei Mikhailovich: Muscovite military command style and legacy to Russian military history', in Lohr and Poe, *The military and society in Russia*, 119–45

Brown, P. C., 'Practical constraints on early Tokugawa land taxation: annual versus fixed assessments in Kaga domain', *JJS*, XIV (1988), 369–401

Bruijn, J. R. et al., *Dutch Asiatic shipping in the 17th and 18th centuries*, 3 vols (The Hague, 1979–87)

Brunt, P.A., *Social conflicts in the Roman Republic* (London, 1971)

Buisman, J., *Duizend jaar weer, wind en water in de Lage Landen. IV. 1575–1675* (Franeker, 2000)

Bulman, W. J., 'The practice of politics in the English Civil War and the "resolutions" of Henrietta Maria and Charles I', P&P, CCVI (2010), 43–78

Buono, A., *Esercito, istituzioni, territorio. Alloggiamenti militari e 'case herme' nello Stato di Milano (secoli XVI e XVII)* (Florence, 2009)

Burke, P., 'The Virgin of the Carmine and the revolt of Masaniello,' P&P, XCIX (1983), 3–21

Burke, P., 'Masaniello: a response', P&P, CXIV (1987), 197–9

Burke, P., 'Some seventeenth-century anatomists of revolution', *Storia della storiografia*, XXII (1992), 23–35

Burke, P., 'The crisis in the arts of the seventeenth century: a crisis of representation?', JIH, XL (2009), 239–61

Burkus-Chasson, A., 'Visual hermeneutics and the act of turning the leaf: a genealogy of Liu Yuan's *Lingyan ge*', in Brokaw and Chow, eds, *Printing and book culture*, 371–416

Busch, H., 'The Tunglin Academy and its political and philosophical significance', *Monumenta serica*, XIV (1949–55), 1–163

Bushkovitch, P., *Religion and society in Russia in the sixteenth and seventeenth centuries* (Oxford, 1992)

Bussmann, K. and H. Schilling, eds, *1648: War and peace in Europe*, 3 vols (Münster, 1998)

Bustos Rodríguez, M., *Cádiz en el sistema atlántico. La ciudad, sus comerciantes y la actividad mercantil, 1650–1830* (Madrid, 2006)

Caillard, M., 'Recherches sur les soulèvements populaires en Basse Normandie (1620–1640)', in M. Caillard, *À travers la Normandie des XVIIe et XVIIIe siècles* (Caen, 1963)

Calhoun, C., ed., *Habermas and the public sphere* (Boston, 1992)

Cambridge History of China, see Twitchett

Campbell, B. M. S., 'Nature as historical protagonist: environment and society in pre-industrial England', *EcHR*, LXIII (2010), 281–314

Campbell, B. M. S., 'Physical shocks, biological hazards, and human impacts: the crisis of the fourteenth century revisited', in S. Cavaciocchi, ed., *Le interazioni fra economia e ambiente biologico nell'Europe preindustriale. Seccoli XIII–XVIII* (Prato, 2010), 13–32

Campbell, B. M. S., 'Panzootics, pandemics and climatic anomalies in the fourteenth century', in B. Herrmann, ed., *Beiträge zum Göttinger Umwelthistorischen Kolloquium 2010–2011* (Göttingen, 2011), 177–215

Camuffo, D. and C. Bertolin, 'The earliest temperature observations in the world: the Medici network (1654–1670)', *CC*, CXI (2012), 335–62

Cancila, O., *Impresa, redditi, mercato nella Sicilia moderna* (Palermo, 1993)

Cane, S., 'Australian aboriginal subsistence in the Western Desert', *Human Ecology*, XV (1987), 391–434

Canny, N., *Making Ireland British, 1580–1650* (Oxford, 2001)

Canny, N., ed., *Europeans on the move: Studies in European migration 1500–1800* (Oxford, 1994)

Canny, N., ed., *The origins of empire: British overseas enterprise to the close of the seventeenth century* (Oxford, 1998: The Oxford History of the British Empire, I)

Capp, B., *When gossips meet: Women, family and neighbourhood in early modern England* (Oxford, 2003)

Capp, B., 'Life, love and litigation in Sileby in the 1630s', *P&P*, CLXXXII (2004), 55–83

Carbajo Isla, M., *La población de la villa de Madrid, desde finales del siglo XVI hasta mediados del siglo XIX* (Madrid 1987)

Carlton, C., *Going to the wars: The experience of the British Civil Wars 1638–1651* (London, 1992)

Carrier, H., *La presse de la Fronde (1648–53): les Mazarinades* (Geneva, 1989)

Carrier, H., *Le labyrinthe de l'Etat. Essai sur le débat politique en France au temps de la Fronde (1648–1653)* (Paris, 2004)

Carroll, S., 'The peace in the feud in sixteenth- and seventeenth-century France', *P&P*, CLXXVII (2003), 74–115

Carroll, S., *Blood and violence in early modern France* (Oxford, 2006)

Casey, J., 'La Crisi General del segle XVII a València 1646–48', *Boletín de la Sociedad Castellonense de Cultura*, XL VI/2 (1970), 96–173

Casey, J., *The kingdom of Valencia in the seventeenth century* (Cambridge, 1979)

Castellanos, J. L., ed., *Homenaje a don Antonio Domínguez Ortiz*, 3 vols (Granada, 2008)

Casway, J., 'Gaelic Maccabeanism: the politics of reconciliation', in Ohlmeyer, *Political thought*, 176–88

Cavaillé, J.-P., 'Masculinité et libertinage dans la figure et les écrits de Christine de Suède', *Les Dossiers du Grihl* (online), 2010–01 | 2010, accessed 4 Mar. 2012. URL: http://dossiersgrihl.revues.org/3965; DOI: 10.4000/dossiersgrihl.3965

Céline, L.-F., *Castle to castle* (Urbana, IL, 1997)

Cercas, J., *The anatomy of a moment: Thirty-five minutes in history and imagination* (New York, 2011)

Çetin, Cemal, *XVII. ve XVIII. Yüzyıllarda Konya Menzilleri*, unpublished M.A. thesis (Selçuk University, Konya, 2004)

Ch'ü T'ung-Tsu, *Local government in China under the Ch'ing* (Cambridge, MA, 1962)

Chan, A., *The glory and fall of the Qing dynasty* (Norman, OK, 1982)

Chang Chia-Feng, 'Disease and its impact on politics, diplomacy and the military: the case of smallpox and the Manchus (1613–1795)', *Journal of the History of Medicine and Allied Sciences*, LVII/2 (2002), 177–97

Chang Chun-shu and S. Hsueh-lun Chang, *Crisis and transformation in seventeenth-century China: Society, culture, and modernity in Li Yü's world* (Ann Arbor, 1992)

Chang Chun-shu and S. Hsueh-lun Chang, *Redefining history: Ghosts, spirits, and human society in P'u Sung-ling's world, 1640–1715* (Ann Arbor, 1998)

Chang, M. G., *A court on horseback: Imperial touring and the constitution of Qing rule, 1680–1785* (Cambridge, MA, 2007)

Charbonneau, H., *Naissance d'une population. Les français établis au Canada au 17e siècle* (Montréal, 1987)

Charmeil, J. P., *Les Trésoriers de France à l'époque de la Fronde* (Paris, 1964)

Chaunu, P., 'Réflexions sur le tournant des années 1630–1650,' *Cahiers d'Histoire*, XII (1967), 249–68

Cherniakova, I. A., *Karelia na perelome epokh: ocherki sotsialnoi i agrarnoi istorii XVII veka* (Petrozavodsk, 1998)

Cherniavsky, M., 'The Old Believers and the new religion', *Slavic Review*, XXV (1966), 1–39

Chéruel, A., *Histoire de France pendant la minorité de Louis XIV*, 2 vols (Paris, 1879)

Chia, L., 'Of Three Mountains Street: the commercial publishers of Ming Nanjing', in Brokaw and Chow, eds, *Printing and book culture*, 128–51

Ching, J., 'Chu Shun-Shui, 1600–82: a Chinese Confucian scholar in Tokugawa Japan', *Monumenta Nipponica*, XXX/2 (1975), 177–191

Ching, J., 'The practical learning of Chu Shun-Shui (1600–82)', in de Bary and Bloom, eds, *Principle and practicality*, 189–229

Chow Kai-Wing, 'Writing for success: printing, examinations, and intellectual change in late Ming China', *Late Imperial China*, XVII/1 (1996), 120–57

Chow Kai-Wing, *Publishing, culture and power in early modern China* (Stanford, 2004)

Christianson, P., 'Arguments on billeting and martial law in the Parliament of 1628', *HJ*, XXVII (1994), 539–67

Church, W. F., *Richelieu and reason of state* (Princeton, 1972)

Churchill, W. S., *The world crisis, 1911–1918*, 6 vols (London, 1923–31)

Cipolla, C. M., *Cristofano and the plague: A study in the history of public health in the age of Galileo* (London, 1973)

Cipolla, C. M., *Public health and the medical profession in the Renaissance* (Cambridge, 1976)

Cipolla, C. M., *Before the Industrial Revolution: European society and the economy 1000–1700* (3rd edn, London, 1993)

Clark, G. N., *The seventeenth century* (2nd edn, Oxford, 1947)

Clark, P., *The English alehouse: A social history, 1200–1830* (London, 1983)

Clark, P., ed., *The European crisis of the 1590s: Essays in comparative history* (London, 1985)

Clark, P. and B. Lepetit, eds, *Capital cities and their hinterlands in early modern Europe* (Aldershot, 1996)

Clarke, A., 'Ireland and the General Crisis', *P&P*, XLVIII (1970), 79–99

Clarke, A., 'The 1641 depositions', in P. Fox, ed., *Treasures of the Library, Trinity College Dublin* (Dublin, 1986), 111–22

Clarke, A., *The Old English in Ireland, 1625–42* (2nd edn, Dublin, 2000)

Clifton, R., 'The popular fear of Catholics during the English Revolution', *P&P*, LII (1971), 23–55

Clifton, R., *The last popular rebellion: The Western Rising of 1685* (London, 1984)

Clunas, C., *Superfluous things: Material culture and social status in early modern China* (Cambridge, 1991)

Coaldrake, W. H., *Architecture and authority in Japan* (London, 1996)

Coates, B., *The impact of the English Civil War on the economy of London, 1642–1650* (Aldershot, 2004)

Comparato, V. I., *Uffici e società a Napoli (1600–1647). Aspetti dell'ideologia del magistrate nell'età moderna* (Florence, 1974)

Comparato, V. I., 'Toward the revolt of 1647', in A. Calabria and J. A. Marino, eds, *Good government in Spanish Naples* (New York, 1990), 275–316

Comparato, V. I., 'Barcelona y Nápoles en la búsqueda de un modelo político: analogías, diferencias, contactos', *Pedralbes: revista d'historia moderna*, XVIII (1998), 439–52

Condren, C., 'Public, private and the idea of the "Public Sphere" in early-modern England', *Intellectual History Review*, XIX (2009), 15–28

Connor, J., *The Australian frontier wars, 1788–1838* (Sydney, 2005)

Contamine, P., ed., *Histoire militaire de la France. I. Des origines à 1715* (Paris, 1992)

Contamine, P., ed., *War and competition between states* (Oxford, 2000)

Conti, V., *Consociatio civitatum. Le repubbliche nei testi elzeviriani (1625–1649)* (Florence, 1997)

Cook, E. R., 'Southwestern USA Drought Index Reconstruction'. International Tree-Ring Data Bank. IGBP PAGES/World Data Center for Paleoclimatology Data Contribution Series #2000–053

Cook, E. R., B. M. Buckley, R. D. D'Arrigo and M. J. Peterson, 'Warm-season temperatures since 1600 BC reconstructed from Tasmanian tree rings and their relationship to large-scale sea surface temperature anomalies', *Climatic Dynamics*, XVI (2000), 79–86

Cook, H. J., *Matters of exchange: Commerce, medicine and science in the Dutch Golden Age* (New Haven and London, 2007)

Cook, M. A., *Population pressure in rural Anatolia, 1450–1600* (London, 1972)

Cook, N. D., *Born to die: Disease and new world conquest, 1492–1650* (Cambridge, 1998)

Cooper, J. P., ed., *The New Cambridge Modern History*, IV (Cambridge, 1970)

Cooper, M., ed., *They came to Japan: An anthology of European reports on Japan, 1543–1640* (Berkeley, 1965)

Corish, P., 'The rising of 1641 and the Catholic confederacy, 1641–5', in Moody et al., eds, *A new history of Ireland*, III, 289–316

Cornell, L., 'Infanticide in early modern Japan? Demography, culture and population growth', *JAS*, LV (1996), 22–50

Corsini, C. A. and G. Delille, 'Eboli e la peste del 1656', in *I congreso hispano-luso-italiano de demografía histórica* (Barcelona, 1987), 244–50

Corteguera, L. R., *For the common good: Popular politics in Barcelona 1580–1640* (Ithaca, NY, 2002)

Corvisier, A., *L'Armée française de la fin du XVIIe siècle au ministère de Choiseul. Le Soldat*, 2 vols (Paris, 1964)

Corvisier, A., 'Clientèles et fidélités dans l'armée française aux XVIIe et XVIIIe siècles', in Y. Durand, ed., *Hommage à Roland Mousnier. Clientèles et fidélités en Europe à l'époque moderne* (Paris, 1981), 213–36

Courtwright, D. T., *Forces of habit: Drugs and the making of the modern world* (Cambridge, MA, 2001)

Cowan, E. J., 'The making of the National Covenant', in J. S. Morrill, ed., *The Scottish National Covenant in its British context* (Edinburgh, 1990), 68–90

Cowan, E. J., 'The political ideas of a covenanting leader: Archibald Campbell, marquis of Argyll 1607–1661', in R. A. Mason, ed., *Scots and Britons: Scottish political thought and the union of 1603* (Cambridge, 1994), 241–61

Cregan, D., 'The social and cultural background of a Counter-Reformation Episcopate, 1618–1660', in A. Cosgrove and D. MacCartney, eds, *Studies in Irish History presented to R. Dudley Edwards* (Dublin, 1979), 85–117

Cressy, D., *Coming over: Migration and communication between England and New England in the 17th century* (Cambridge, 1987)

Cressy, D., 'Conflict, consensus and the willingness to wink: the erosion of community in Charles I's England', *Huntington Library Quarterly*, LXI (1999–2000), 131–49

Cressy, D., 'The Protestation protested, 1641 and 1642', *HJ*, XLV (2002), 251–79

Cressy, D., *England on edge: Crisis and revolution 1640–1642* (Oxford, 2006)

Cressy, D., *Dangerous talk: Scandalous, seditious, and treasonable speech in pre-modern England* (Oxford, 2010)

Crewe, R. D., 'Brave New Spain: an Irishman's independence plot in seventeenth-century Mexico', *P&P*, CCVII (2010), 53–97

Croix, A., *La Bretagne aux 16e et 17e siècles: la vie, la mort, la foi* (Paris, 1981)

Crossley, P. K., *A translucent mirror: History and identity in Qing imperial ideology* (Princeton, 1999)

Croxton, D., *Peacemaking in early modern Europe: Cardinal Mazarin and the Congress of Westphalia* (Cranbury, NJ, 1999)

Croxton, D., *The last Christian peace: The Congress of Westphalia in context* (forthcoming)

Crummey, R. O., 'The origins of the Old Believers' cultural system: the works of Avraamii', *Forschungen zur osteuropäischen Geschichte*, L (1995), 121–38

Crummey, R. O., 'Muscovy and the "General Crisis of the seventeenth century"', *Journal of Early Modern History*, II (1998), 156–80

Cueto, R., *Quimeras y sueños. Los profetas y la monarquía católica de Felipe IV* (Valladolid, 1994)

Cullen, K. J., *Famine in Scotland: The 'Ill Years' of the 1690s* (Edinburgh, 2010)

Cunningham, A. and O. P. Grell, *The four horsemen of the Apocalypse: Religion, war, famine and death in Reformation Europe* (Cambridge, 2000)

Cunningham, B., ' "Zeal for God and for souls": Counter-Reformation preaching in early seventeenth-century Ireland', in A. Fletcher and R. Gillespie, eds, *Irish preaching 700–1700* (Dublin, 2001), 127–44

Curtin, P. D., *Economic change in Precolonial Africa: Senegambia in the era of the slave trade*, 2 vols (Madison, 1975)

Curtis, M. H., 'The alienated intellectuals of early Stuart England', *P&P*, XXIII (1962), 25–43 (reprinted in Aston, ed., *Crisis in Europe*, 295–316)

Cust, R., *Charles I: A political life* (Harlow, 2005)

Cyberski, J. et al., 'History of the floods on the river Vistula', *Hydrological Sciences Journal*, LI (2006), 799–817

D'Alessio, S., *Contagi. La rivolta napoletana del 1647–48: linguaggio e potere politico* (Florence, 2003)

D'Amico, S., 'Rebirth of a city: immigration and trade in Milan, 1630–1659', *SCJ*, XXXII (2001), 697–721

D'Arrigo, R. and H. M. Cullen, 'A 350-year (AD 1628–1980) reconstruction of Turkish precipitation', *Dendrochronologica*, XIX (2001), 169–77

D'Aubert, F., *Colbert. La vertue usurpée* (Paris, 2010)

Dale, S. F., *The Muslim empires of the Ottomans, Safavids and Mughals* (Cambridge, 2010)

Darcy, E., A. Margey and E. Murphy, *The 1641 depositions and the Irish rebellion* (London, 2012)

Dardess, J. W., *A Ming society: T'ai-ho county, Kiangsi, fourteenth to seventeenth century* (Berkeley, 1996)

Dardess, J. W., *Blood and history in China: The Donglin faction and its repression, 1620–1627* (Honolulu, 2002)

Dardess, J. W., 'Monarchy in action: Ming China' (unpublished paper)

Darling, L. T., 'Ottoman politics through British eyes: Paul Rycaut's *The present state of the Ottoman empire*', *JWH*, I (1994), 71–97

Darling, L. T., *Revenue-raising and legitimacy: Tax collection and finance administration in the Ottoman empire, 1560–1660* (Leiden, 1996)

Darling, L. T., ' "Do justice, do justice, for that is paradise": Middle Eastern advice for Indian Muslim rulers', *Comparative Studies of South Asia, Africa and the Middle East*, XXII/1–2 (2002), 3–19

Davies, B. L., *State, power and community in early modern Russia: The case of Kozlov, 1635–1649* (London, 2004)

Davies, B. L., *Warfare, state and society on the Black Sea steppe, 1500–1700* (London, 2007)

Davies, S., *Unbridled spirits: Women of the English Revolution, 1640–1660* (London, 1998)

Davies, T., 'Changes in the structure of the wheat trade in seventeenth-century Sicily and the building of new villages', *JEEH*, XII (1983), 371–405

De Bary, W. T. and I. Bloom, eds, *Principles and practicality: Essays in neo-Confucianism and practical learning* (New York, 1979)

De Jong, M., 'Holland en de Portuguese Restauratie van 1640', *Tijdschrift voor Geschiedenis*, LV (1940), 225–53

De Rosa, L., 'Crise financière, crise économique et crise sociale: le royaume de Naples et la dernière phase de la Guerre de Trente Ans (1630–44)', *Bulletin de l'Institut historique belge de Rome*, XLIV (1974), 175–99

De Rosa, L., 'Naples, a capital', *JEEH*, XXVI/2 (1997), 349–73

De Souza, T. R., *Medieval Goa: A socio-economic history* (New Delhi, 1979)

De Vries, J., 'Measuring the impact of climate on history: the search for appropriate methodologies', *JIH*, X (1980), 559–630, reprinted in R. I. Rotberg and T. K. Rabb, eds, *Climate and history: studies in interdisciplinary history* (Princeton, 1981), 19–50

De Vries, J., *The industrious revolution: Consumer behavior and the household economy, 1650 to the Present* (Cambridge, 2008)

De Vries, J., 'The limits of globalization in the early modern world', *EcHR*, LXIII (2010), 710–33

De Waal, A., 'A re-assessment of entitlement theory in the light of recent famines in Africa', *Development and Change*, XXI (1990), 469–90

Dekker, R., *Holland in beroering. Oproeren in de 17e en 18e eeuw* (Baarn, 1982)

Dekker, R., 'Women in revolt: popular revolt and its social bias in Holland in the seventeenth and eighteenth centuries', *Theory and Society*, XVI (1987), 337–62

Dekker, R. and L. van de Pol, *The tradition of female transvestitism in early modern Europe* (London, 1989)

Del Pino Jiménez, A., 'Demografía rural Sevillana en el antiguo regimen: Utrera, Los Palacios-Villafranca y Dos Hermanos, 1600/1800' (Seville University PhD thesis, 2000)

Delfin, F. G. et al., 'Geological, 14C and historical evidence for a 17th-century eruption of Parker volcano, Mindanao, Philippines', *Journal of the Geological Society of the Philippines*, LII (1997), 25–42

Dennerline, J., 'Fiscal reform and local control: the gentry-bureaucratic alliance survives the conquest', in Wakeman and Grant, eds, *Conflict and control*, 86–120

Dennerline, J., *The Chia-Ting loyalists: Confucian leadership and social change in seventeenth-century China* (New Haven and London, 1981)

Des Forges, R. V., *Cultural centrality and political change in Chinese history: Northeast Henan in the fall of the Ming* (Stanford, 2003)

Des Forges, R. V., 'Toward another Tang or Zhou? Views from the Central Plain in the Shunzhi reign', in L. Struve, ed., *Time, temporality and change of empire: East Asia from Ming to Qing* (Honolulu, 2005), 73–112

Descimon, R., 'Autopsie du massacre de l'Hôtel de Ville (4 juillet 1652). Paris et le "Fronde des Princes"', *Annales HSS*, LIV (1999), 319–51

Descimon, R. and C. Jouhaud, 'La Fronde en mouvement: le développement de la crise politique entre 1648 en 1652', *XVIIe siècle*, CXLV (1984), 305–22

Dessert, D., 'Finances et société au XVIIe siècle: à propos de la Chambre de Justice', *Annales E.S.C.*, XXIX (1974), 847–81

Dewald, J., 'Crisis, chronology, and the shape of European social history', *AHR*, CXIII (2008), 1,031–52

Diamond, J., *Collapse: How societies choose to fail or succeed* (London, 2005)

Diaz, H. F. and V. Markgraf, eds, *El Niño: Historical and paleoclimatic aspects of the Southern Oscillation* (Cambridge, 1993), 251–63

Dickmann, F., *Der Westfälische Frieden* (Münster, 1959)

Dikötter, F., ' "Patient Zero": China and the myth of the "Opium Plague" ' (Inaugural lecture, SOAS, London, 2003)

Dils, J. A., 'Epidemics, mortality and the civil war in Berkshire, 1642–6', in R. C. Richardson, ed., *The English Civil Wars: Local aspects* (Stroud, 1997), 144–55

Dipper, C., *Deutsche Geschichte, 1648–1789* (Frankfurt, 1991)

Disney, A., 'Famine and famine relief in Portuguese India in the sixteenth and early seventeeth centuries', *Studia*, XLIX (1989), 255–82

Dobrovolný, P., A. Moberg and R. Brázdil, 'Monthly, seasonal and annual temperature reconstructions for Central Europe derived from documentary evidence and instrumental records since AD 1500', *CC*, C (2010), 69–107

Dodgshon, R. A., 'The *Little Ice Age* in the Scottish Highlands and Islands: documenting its human impact', *Scottish Geographical Journal*, CXXI (2005), 321–37

Dollinger, H., 'Kurfürst Maximilian I. von Bayern und Justus Lipsius', *Archiv für Kulturgeschichte*, XLVI (1964), 227–308

Dols, M. W., 'The second plague pandemic and its recurrences in the Middle East, 1347–1894', *JESHO*, XXII (1979), 162–89

Domínguez Ortiz, A., *La sociedad española en el siglo XVII*, I (Madrid, 1963)

Domínguez Ortiz, A., 'La conspiración del duque de Medina Sidonia y el marqués de Ayamonte', in idem, *Crisis y decadencia de la España de los Austrias* (Barcelona, 1969), 113–53

Domínguez Ortiz, A., *Alteraciones andaluzas* (Madrid, 1973)

Donaldson, G., 'The emergence of schism in seventeenth-century Scotland', in D. Baker, ed., *Schism, heresy and religious protest* (Cambridge, 1972: Studies in Church History, IX), 277–94

Donawerth, J., 'Women's reading practices in seventeenth-century England: Margaret Fell's *Women's speaking justified*', *SCJ*, XXXVII (2006), 985–1,005

Donoghue, J., ' "Out of the land of bondage": the English revolution and the Atlantic origins of abolition', *AHR*, CXV (2010), 943–74

Dooley, B., *Italy in the Baroque: Selected readings* (New York, 1995)

Dooley, B., 'News and doubt in early modern culture: or, are we having a public sphere yet?', in Dooley and Baron, eds, *The politics*, 275–90

Dooley, B., ed., *The dissemination of news and the emergence of contemporaneity in early modern Europe* (Aldershot, 2010)

Dooley, B. and S. Baron, eds, *The politics of information in early modern Europe* (London, 2001)

Dore, R., *Education in early modern Japan* (Berkeley, 1965)

Dott, B., *Identity reflections: Pilgrimages to Mount Tai in late imperial China* (Cambridge, MA, 2004)

Drake, S., *Galileo at work: His scientific biography* (Mineola, NY, 1995)

Drake, S. and C. D. O'Malley, eds, *The controversy on the comets of 1618: Galileo Galilei, Horatio Grassi, Mario Guiducci, Johan Kepler* (Philadelphia, 1960)

Droysen, G., 'Studien über die Belagerung und Zerstörung Magdeburgs, 1631', *Forschungen zur deutsche Geschichte*, III (Göttingen, 1863), 433–606

Duccini, H., 'Regard sur la littérature pamphlétaire en France au XVIIe siècle', *Revue Historique*, CCLX (1978), 313–39

Duccini, H., *Faire voir, faire croire. L'opinion publique sous Louis XIII* (Seyssel, 2003)

Dulong, C., 'Mazarin et ses banquiers', in *Il cardinale Mazzarino in Francia* (Rome, 1977: Atti della Accademia Nazionale dei Lincei, XXXV), 17–40

Dumas, S., *Les filles du roi en Nouvelle-France: Étude historique avec répertoire biographique* (Québec, 1972)

Dunning, C. S. L., *Russia's first civil war: The Time of Troubles and the founding of the Romanov dynasty* (University Park, PA, 2001)

Dunstan, H., 'The late Ming epidemics: a preliminary survey', *Ch'ing-shih wen- t'i*, III.3 (Nov. 1975), 1–59

Dunthorne, H., 'Resisting monarchy: the Netherlands as Britain's school of revolution in the late sixteenth and seventeenth centuries', in R. Oresko, G. C. Gibbs and H. M. Scott, eds, *Royal and republican sovereignty in early modern Europe: Essays in memory of Ragnhild Hatton* (Cambridge, 1997), 125–48

Dupâquier, Jacques, ed., *Histoire de la population française. I. Des origines à la Renaissance* (Paris, 1988)

DuVal, K., *The native ground: Indians and colonists in the heart of the continent* (Philadelphia, 2006)

Dyson, T., 'Famine in Berar, 1896–7 and 1899–1900: echoes and chain reactions', in Dyson and Ó Gráda, *Famine demography*, 93–112

Dyson, T. and C. Ó Gráda, *Famine demography: Perspectives from the past and present* (Oxford, 2002)

Eastman, L. E., *Family, fields and ancestors: Constancy and change in China's social and economic history, 1550–1949* (Oxford, 1988)

Eaton, H. L., *Early Russian censuses and the population of Muscovy, 1550–1650* (University of Illinois PhD thesis, 1970)

Eaton, H. L., 'Decline and Recovery of the Russian Cities from 1500 to 1700', *Canadian-American Slavic studies*, XI (1977), 220–52

Eaton, R., *The rise of Islam and the Bengal frontier* (Berkeley, 1993)

Ebermeier, W., *Landshut im Dreissigjährigen Krieg* (Landshut, 2001)

Ebrey, P. B., ed., *Chinese civilization and society: A sourcebook* (New York, 1981)

Eckert, E. A., 'Boundary formation and diffusion of plague: Swiss epidemics from 1562 to 1669', *Annales de démographie historique* (1978), 49–80

Eckert, E. A., *The structure of plagues and pestilences in early modern Europe: Central Europe, 1560–1640* (Basel, 1996)

Eddy, J. A., 'The "Maunder Minimum": sunspots and climate in the reign of Louis XIV', in Parker and Smith, eds, *The General Crisis*, 264–97

Eddy, J. A., P. A. Gilman and D. E. Trotter, 'Anomalous solar rotation in the early 17th century', *Science*, CXCVIII (25 Nov. 1977), 824–9

Eisenstadt, S. N. and W. Schluter, eds, 'Introduction: paths to early modernities: a comparative view', *Daedalus*, CXXVII.3 (1998), 1–18

Ekman, E., 'The Danish Royal Law of 1665', *JMH*, XXVII (1959), 102–7

Eldem, E., D. Goffman and B. Masters, *The Ottoman city between east and west: Aleppo, Izmir and Istanbul* (Cambridge, 1999)

Elison, G., *Deus destroyed: The image of Christianity in early modern Japan* (Cambridge, MA, 1973)

Elison, G., 'The cross and the sword: patterns of Momoyama history', in G. Elison and B. Smith, eds, *Warlords, artists and commoners: Japan in the sixteenth century* (Honolulu, 1981), 55–85

Ellersieck, H. E., 'Russia under Aleksei Mikhailovich and Fedor Alekseevich, 1645–1682: the Scandinavian sources' (UCLA PhD thesis, 1955)

Elliott, J. H., *The revolt of the Catalans: A study in the decline of Spain* (Cambridge, 1963)

Elliott, J. H., 'The year of the three ambassadors', in H. Lloyd-Jones et al., eds, *History and imagination: Essays in honour of H.R. Trevor-Roper* (London, 1981), 165–81

Elliott, J. H., 'El programa de Olivares y los movimientos de 1640', in J. M. Jover Zamora, ed., *La España de Felipe IV* (Madrid, 1982: Historia de España Espasa-Calpe, XXV), 335–62

Elliott, J. H., *The count-duke of Olivares: The statesman in an age of decline* (New Haven and London, 1986)

Elliott, J. H., 'A Europe of composite Monarchies', *P&P*, CXXXVII (1992), 48–71

Elliott, J. H., 'Revolution and continuity in early modern Europe', in Parker and Smith, *The General Crisis*, 108–27

Elliott, J. H., 'The General Crisis in retrospect: a debate without end', in Benedict and Gutmann, *Early Modern Europe*, 31–51

Elliott, J. H., 'Yet another crisis?', in Clark, ed., *The European crisis of the 1590s*, 301–11

Elliott, J. H., *Empires of the Atlantic world: Britain and Spain in America 1492–1830* (New Haven and London, 2006)

Elliott, J. H. et al., *1640: La monarquía hispánica en crisis* (Barcelona, 1992)

Elliott, J. H. and A. García Sanz, eds, *La España del conde-duque de Olivares* (Valladolid, 1990)

Elliott, M. C., 'Whose empire shall it be? Manchu figurations of historical process in the early seventeenth century', in Struve, ed., *Time, temporality and imperial transition*, 31–72

Elliott, M. C., *The Manchu Way: The eight banners and ethnic identity in late imperial China* (Stanford, 2001)

Elman, B. A., *From philosophy to philology: Intellectual and social aspects of change in Late Imperial China* (Cambridge, MA, 1985)

Elman, B. A., *A cultural history of civil examinations in Late Imperial China* (Berkeley, 2000)

Elphick, R., *Kraal and castle: Khoikhoi and the founding of white South Africa* (New Haven and London, 1977)

Eltis, D. and D. Richardson, *Atlas of the transatlantic slave trade* (New Haven and London, 2010)

Elvin, M., *The pattern of the Chinese past* (Stanford, 1973)

Elvin, M., 'Market towns and waterways: the county of Shanghai from 1480 to 1910', in G. W. Skinner, ed., *The city in late imperial China* (Stanford, 1977), 441–73

Elvin, M., 'Female virtue and the state in China', *P&P*, CIV (1984), 111–52

Elvin, M., 'The man who saw dragons: science and styles of thinking in Xie Zhaozhe's Fivefold Miscellany', *Journal of the Oriental Society of Australia*, XXV–XXVI (1993–4), 1–41

Elvin, M., 'Unseen lives: the emotions of everyday existence mirrored in Chinese popular poetry of the mid-seventeenth to the mid-nineteenth century', in R. T. Ames, T. Kasulis and W. Dissanayake, eds, *Self as image in Asian theory and practice* (Albany, NY, 1998), 113–99

Elvin, M., 'Blood and statistics: reconstructing the population dynamics of late imperial China from the biographies of virtuous women in local gazetteers', in H. T. Zurndorfer, ed., *Chinese women in the imperial past: New perspectives* (Leiden, 1999), 135–222

Elvin, M. and Ts'ui-Jung Liu, eds, *Sediments of time: Environment and society in Chinese history* (Cambridge, 1998)

Emecan, F., 'İbrâhim', *Türkiye Diyanet Vakfı İslam Ansiklopedisi* (Istanbul, 1988)

Encyclopedia of Islam, ed. B. Lewis et al. (new edn, 4 vols, Leiden, 1961–71)

Endō Motoo, *Kinsei seikatsushi nempyō* (Tokyo, 1982)

Environment Agency, The, *Thames Estuary 2010 Plan for consultation* (London, 2010)

Ergang, R., *The myth of the all-destructive fury of the Thirty Years War* (Pocono Pines, PA, 1956)

Ernstberger, A., *Hans de Witte, Finanzmann Wallensteins* (Wiesbaden, 1954)

Espino López, A., *Catalunya durante el reinado de Carlos II. Política y guerra en la frontera catalana, 1679–1697* (Bellaterra, 1999)

Ettinghausen, H., *La Guerra dels Segadors a través la premsa de l'època*, 4 vols (Barcelona, 1993)

Ettinghausen, H., 'Informació, comunicació i poder a l'Espanya del segle XVII', *Manuscrits*, XXIII (2005), 45–58

Evans, J. T., *Seventeenth-century Norwich: Politics, religion and government, 1620–1680* (Oxford, 1979)

Externbrink, S., 'Die Rezeption des "Sacco di Mantova" im 17. Jahrhundert. Zur Wahrnehmung, Darstellung und Bewertung eines Kriegsereignisses', in Meumann and Niefanger, eds, *Ein Schauplatz herber Angst*, 205–21

Ezquerra Abadía, R., *La conspiración del duque de Híjar (1648)* (Madrid, 1934)

Faccini, L., *La Lombardia fra '600 e '700. Riconversione economica e mutamenti sociali* (Milan, 1988)

Fagan, B., *The long summer: How climate changed civilization* (New York, 2004)

Fang Chaoying, 'A technique for estimating the numerical strength of the early Manchu military forces', *Harvard Journal of Asiatic Studies*, XIII (1950), 192–215

Faroqhi, S., 'Political activity among Ottoman taxpayers and the problem of sultanic legitimation', *JESHO*, XXXV (1992), 1–39

Faroqhi, S., *Coping with the state: Political conflict and crime in the Ottoman empire, 1550–1720* (Istanbul, 1995)

Faroqhi, S., 'A natural disaster as an indicator of agricultural change: clouding in the Edirne area, 1100/1688–9', in E. Zachariadou, ed., *Natural disasters in the Ottoman empire* (Rehtymnon, 1999), 251–63

Faroqhi, S., ed., *The Cambridge History of Turkey, III: The later Ottoman empire, 1603–1839* (Cambridge, 2006)

Faroqhi, S. with L. Erder, 'Population rise and fall in Anatolia, 1550–1620', *Middle Eastern Studies*, XV (1979), 322–45

Farris, N., *Maya society under colonial rule: The collective enterprise of survival* (Princeton, 1984)

Farris, W. W., *Japan's medieval population: Famine, fertility and warfare in a transformative age* (Honolulu, 2006)

Faruqui, M. D., 'Princes and power in the Mughal empire, 1569–1657' (Duke University, PhD thesis, 2002)

Fei Si-yen, *Negotiating urban space: Urbanization and Late Ming Nanjing* (Cambridge, MA, 2009)

Felix, A., ed., *The Chinese in the Philippines*, 2 vols (Manila, 1966–9)

Felloni, G., 'Per la storia della populazione di Genova nei secoli XVI e XVII', *Archivio Storico Italiano*, CX (1952), 236–53

Ferrarino, L., *La guerra e la peste nella Milano dei 'Promessi sposi'. Documenti inediti tratti dagli archivi Spagnoli* (Madrid, 1975)

Fildes, V., 'Maternal feelings re-assessed: child abandonment and neglect in London and Westminster, 1550–1800', in Fildes, ed., *Women as mothers*, 139–78

Fildes, V., ed., *Women as mothers in pre-industrial England: Essays in memory of Dorothy McLaren* (London, 1990)

Finkel, C., *Osman's dream: The story of the Ottoman empire* (London, 2005)

Firth, C. H., *Cromwell's Army: A history of the English soldier during the Civil Wars, the Commonwealth and the Protectorate* (4th edn, London, 1962)

Fischer, D. H., *Albion's seed: Four British folkways in America* (Oxford, 1989)

Fleischer, C., 'Royal authority, dynastic cyclism and "Ibn Khaldûnism" in sixteenth-century Ottoman letters', *Journal of Asian and African Studies*, XVIII (1983), 183–220

Fleming, J. R., *Historical perspectives on climate change* (Oxford, 1998)

Fletcher, A., *The outbreak of the English Civil War* (London, 1981)

Fletcher, J., 'Turco-Mongolian monarchic tradition in the Ottoman empire', *Harvard Ukrainian Studies*, III–IV/1 (1979–80), 236–51

Fleury, M. and L. Henri, *Des registres paroissiaux à l'histoire de la population: manuel de dépouillement et d'exploitation de l'état civil ancien* (Paris, 1956)

Flinn, M., ed., *Scottish population history from the seventeenth century to the 1930s* (Cambridge, 1977)

Floor, W., *The economy of Safavid Persia* (Wiesbaden, 2000)

Flores, J. and S. Subrahmanyam, 'The shadow sultan: succession and imposture in the Mughal Empire, 1628–1640', *JESHO*, XLVII (2004), 80–121.

Florida Chamber of Commerce, *Into the storm: Framing Florida's looming property insurance crisis* (Talahassee, 2009)

Fodor, P., 'State and society, crisis and reform, in 15th–17th century Ottoman Mirror for Princes', *Acta Orientalia Academiae Scientiarum Hungaricae*, XL (1986), 217–40

Fodor, P., 'Sultan, imperial council, Grand Vizier: changes in the Ottoman ruling elite and the formation of the Grand Vizieral *Telhis*', *Acta Orientalia Academiae Scientiarum Hungaricae*, XLVII (1994), 67–85

Foisil, M., *La révolte des Nu-Pieds et les révoltes normandes de 1639* (Paris, 1970)

Foltz, R., 'The Mughal occupation of Balkh, 1646–1647', *Journal of Islamic Studies*, VII (1996), 49–61

Fong, G. S., 'Signifying bodies: the cultural significance of suicide writings by women in Ming-Qing China', *Nan nü: Men, women and gender in Early and Imperial China*, III.1 (2001), 105–42

Fong, G. S., 'Reclaiming subjectivity in a time of loss: Ye Shaoyuan (1589–1648) and autobiographical writing in the Ming-Qing transition', *Ming Studies*, LIX (2009), 21–41

Fong, G. S., 'Writing from experience: personal records of war and disorder in Jiangnan during the Ming-Qing transition', in N. Di Cosmo, ed., *Military culture in Imperial China* (Cambridge MA, 2009), 257–77

Forster, L. W., *The temper of 17th-century German literature* (London, 1952)

Forster, R. and J. P. Greene, eds, *Preconditions of revolution in early modern Europe* (Baltimore, 1970)

Fortey, R. A., *Earth: An intimate history* (New York, 2004).

Fortey, R. A., 'Blind to the end', *New York Times*, 26 Dec. 2005

Franz, G., *Der dreissigjährige Krieg und das deutsche Volk* (1940; 4th edn, Stuttgart, 1979)

Friedrich, W. L., *Fire in the sea: Volcanism and the natural history of Santorini* (Cambridge, 2000)

Friedrichs, C. R., *The early modern city, 1450–1750* (London, 1995)

Frost, R. I., *After the deluge: Poland-Lithuania and the second northern war, 1655–60* (Cambridge, 1993)

Frost, R. I., *The northern wars: War, state and society in northeastern Europe, 1558–1721* (London, 2000)

Fu I-ling, *Ming-Ch'ing Nung-Ts'un she-hui ching-chi* (Beijing, 1961)

Fukuda Chizuru, 'The political process in the first half of the seventeenth century', *Acta Asiatica*, LXXXVII (2004), 35–58

Fusco, I., 'Il viceré di Napoli, conte di Castrillo, e l'epidemia di peste del 1656', in Rizzo, et al., eds, *Le forze del príncipe*, 137–77

Gaddis, J. L., *The landscape of memory: How historians map the past* (Oxford, 2002)

Galasso, G., *Napoli spagnola dopo Masaniello; politica, cultura, società*, 2 vols (Florence, 1982)

Galasso, G., *En la periferia del imperio. La monarquía hispánica y el reino de Nápoles* (Barcelona, 2000)

Gallasteguí Ucín, J., 'Don Miguel de Iturbide y Navarra en la crisis de la monarquía hispánica (1635–48)', *Cuadernos de historia moderna*, XI (1991), 177–94

Galliker, J. F., 'Die Hoheitszeichen der Talschaft Entlebuch', *Entlebucher Brattig* (1991), 37–45

Galloway, P., 'Annual variations in deaths by age, deaths by cause, prices and weather in London, 1670 to 1830', *Population Studies*, XXXIX (1985), 487–505

Galloway, P., 'Secular changes in the short-term preventive, positive and temperature checks to population growth in Europe, 1460 to 1909', *CC*, XXVI (1994), 3–63

Galloway, P. K., *Choctaw genesis, 1500–1700* (Lincoln, NE, 1995)

Ganeri, J., *The lost age of reason: Philosophy in early modern India, 1450–1700* (Oxford, 2011)

Gantet, C., 'Peace celebrations commemorating the peace of Westphalia', in Bussmann and Schilling, eds, *1648*, II, 649–56

García Cárcel, R., *Pau Claris. La revolta catalana* (Barcelona, 1980)

García Cárcel, R., 'La revolución catalana: algunos problemas historiográficos', *Manuscrits*, IX (1991), 115–42

García García, B., 'El confesor fray Luis de Aliaga y la conciencia del rey', in F. Rurale, ed., *I religiosi a Corte. Teologia, politica e diplomazia in Antico Regime* (Rome, 1998), 159–94

Garcia, R. G. et al., 'Atmospheric circulation changes in the tropical Pacific inferred from the voyages of the Manila Galleons in the sixteenth–eighteenth centuries', *Bulletin of the American Meteorological Society*, LXXXII (2001), 2,435–55

Gardiner, S. R., *A history of England from the accession of James I to the outbreak of the Civil War*, 10 vols (London, 1883–91)

Garnier, E., *Les dérangements du temps. 500 ans de chaud et de froid en Europe* (Paris, 2010)

Garnier, E., 'Calamitosa tempora, pestis, fames. Climat et santé entre les XVIIe et XIXe siècles' (http://hal.archives-ouvertes.fr/docs/00/59/51/45/PDF/6-JSE-2009-Garnier-Manuscrit-2009-03-09.pdf, accessed 5 April 2012)

Garnier, E., V. Daux, P. Yiou, P. and I. García de Cortázar-Atauri, 'Grapevine harvest dates in Besançon (France) between 1525 and 1847: social outcomes or climatic evidence?', *CC*, CIV (2011), 703–27

Garrisson, C., 'Les préludes de la Révocation à Montauban (1659–1661)', *Société de l'histoire du Protestantisme français: Bulletin historique et littéraire*, XLII (1893), 7–22

Gaunt, P., ed., *The English Civil War: The essential readings* (Oxford, 2000)

Ge Quangsheng et al., 'Winter half-year temperature reconstructions for the middle and lower reaches of the Yellow River and Yangtze River, China, during the past 2000 years', *Holocene*, XIII (2003), 933–40

Geerts, A. J. M., 'The Arima rebellion and the conduct of Koekebacker', *Transactions of the Asiatic Society of Japan*, XI (1883), 51–116

Gelabert González, J. E., 'Alteraciones y Alteraciones (1643–1652)', in Castellanos, *Homenaje*, II, 355–78

Gelabert González, J. E., *Castilla Convulsa (1631–52)* (Madrid, 2001)

Geneva Association, *The insurance industry and climate change – contribution to the global debate* (Geneva, 2009: Geneva Reports, Risk and Insurance Research, II)

Gentili, A., *De Iure Belli* (1589; English edn, 2 vols, Oxford, 1933)

Gentles, I., 'The iconography of revolution: England 1642–1649', in Gentles, J. Morrill and B. Worden, eds, *Soldiers, writers and statesmen of the English Revolution* (Cambridge, 1998), 91–113

Gentles, I., *The English Revolution and the wars of the three kingdoms, 1638–1652* (London, 2007)

Gere, C., 'William Harvey's weak experiment: the archaeology of anecdote', *History Workshop Journal*, LI (2001), 19–36

Gergis, J. L. and A. M. Fowler, 'A history of ENSO events since A.D. 1525: implications for future climate change', *CC*, XCII (2009), 343–87

Gerhart, K. M., *The eyes of power: Art and early Tokugawa authority* (Honolulu, 1999)

Giannini, M. C., 'Un caso di stabilità politica nella monarchia asburgica: comunità locali, finanza pubblica e clero Stato di Milano durante le prima metà del 600', in F. J. Guillamón Álvarez and J. J. Ruiz Ibañez, eds, *Lo conflictivo y lo consensual en Castilla. Sociedad y poder político 1521–1785. Homenaje a Francisco Tomás y Valiente* (Murcia, 2001), 99–162

Gibson, C., *The Aztecs under Spanish rule* (Stanford, 1964)

Gieysztorowa, I., *Wstep do demografii staropolskiej* (Warsaw, 1976)

Gil Pujol, X., ' "Conservación" y "Defensa" como factores de estabilidad en tiempos de crisis: Aragón y Valencia en la década de 1640', in Elliott et al., *1640*, 44–101

Gil Pujol, X., 'L'engany de Flandes. Les anàlisis de l'aragonès Juan Vitrián sobre la monrquia espanyola i la seva proposta d'abandonar Flandes (1643)', in *Miscellània Ernest Lluch i Martín* (Vilassar de Mar, 2006), 411–29

Gillespie, R., 'Harvest crises in early seventeenth-century Ireland', *Irish Economic and Social History*, XI (1984), 5–18

Gillespie, R., 'The end of an era: Ulster and the outbreak of the 1641 rising', in C. Brady and R. Gillespie, *Natives and newcomers: Essays on the making of Irish colonial society* (Dublin, 1986), 191–213

Gillespie, R., 'Destabilizing Ulster', in MacCuarta, ed., *Ulster 1641*, 107–22

Gillespie, R., 'Political ideas and their social contexts in seventeenth-century Ireland', in Ohlmeyer, ed., *Political thought*, 107–27

Gillespie, R., *Devoted people: Belief and religion in early modern Ireland* (Manchester, 1997)

Gindely, A., *Geschichte des Dreissigjährigen Krieges*, 4 vols (Prague, 1869–80)

Gladwell, M., *The tipping point: How little things can make a big difference* (New York, 2000)

Glaser, H., ed., *Wittelsbach und Bayern II. Um Glauben und Reich: Kurfürst Maximilan I. 2. Katalog der Ausstellung* (Munich and Zürich, 1980)

Glaser, R., *Klimarekonstruktion für Mainfranken, Bauland und Odenwald* (Stuttgart, 1991)

Glaser, R., *Klimageschichte Mitteleuropas: 1000 Jahre Wetter, Klima, Katastrophen* (Darmstadt, 2001)

Glaser, R. et al., 'Spatio-temporal change of climate induced regional vulnerability and resilience in Central Europe since AD 1000' (paper delivered at the 'Climate and History' conference at the Deutsches Historisches Institut, Paris, 3–4 September 2011)

Glave, L. M., *Trajinantes. Caminos indígenas en la sociedad colonial, siglos XVI/XVII* (Lima, 1989)

Glete, J., *War and the state in early modern Europe: Spain, the Dutch Republic and Sweden as fiscal-military states, 1500–1660* (London, 2002)

Goffman, D. and C. Stroop, 'Empire as composite: the Ottoman polity and the typology of dominion', in B. Rajan and E. Sauer, eds, *Imperialisms: Historical and literary investigations, 1500–1900* (London, 2004), 129–45

Golden, R. M., *The Godly rebellion: Parisian curés and the religious Fronde 1652–62* (Chapel Hill, NC, 1981)

Goldish, M., *The Sabbatean prophets* (Cambridge, MA, 2004)

Goldish, M., *Jewish questions: Responsa on Sephardic life in the early modern period* (Princeton, 2008)

Goldstone, J. A., 'East and West in the 17th century: political crises in Stuart England, Ottoman Turkey and Ming China', *Comparative Studies in Society and History*, XXX (1988), 103–42

Goldstone, J. A., *Revolution and rebellion in the early modern world* (Berkeley and Los Angeles, 1991)

Gommans, J., *Mughal warfare* (London, 2002)

Goodare, J., 'Debate. Charles I: A case of mistaken identity', *P&P*, CCV (2009), 189–201

Gordon, L., *Cossack rebellions: Social turmoil in sixteenth-century Ukraine* (Albany, NY, 1983)

Gottschalk, M. K. E., *Stormvloeden en rivieroverstromingen in Nederland. III. 1600–1700* (Amsterdam, 1977)

Goubert, P., 'The French peasantry of the seventeenth century: a regional example', in Aston, ed., *Crisis*, 141–65

Goubert, P., *Beauvais et le Beauvaisis de 1600 à 1730. Contribution à l'histoire sociale de la France au XVIIe siècle* (Paris, 1960)

Gowing, L., 'Secret births and infanticide in seventeenth-century England', *P&P*, CLVI (1997), 87–115

Gowland, A., *The worlds of Renaissance melancholy: Robert Burton in context* (Cambridge, 2006)

Grandjean, K. A., 'New world tempests: environment, scarcity, and the coming of the Pequot war', *WMQ*, 3rd series, LXVIII (2011), 75–100

Green, O. H., *Spain and the western tradition: The Castilian mind in literature from* El Cid *to* Calderón, IV (Madison and London, 1966)

Green, I., *The re-establishment of the Church of England, 1660–1663* (Oxford, 1978)

Green, I., 'The persecution of "scandalous" and "malignant" parish clergy during the English Civil War', *EHR*, XCIV (1979), 507–31

Green, I., 'Career prospects and clerical conformity in the early Stuart church', *P&P*, XC (1981), 71–115

Greengrass, M. et al., eds, *Samuel Hartlib and universal reformation: Studies in intellectual communication* (Cambridge, 1994)

Grehan, J., 'Smoking and "early modern" sociability: the great tobacco debate in the Ottoman Middle East (seventeenth to eighteenth centuries)', *AHR*, CXI (2006), 1,352–77

Groenhuis, G., *De predikanten. De sociale positie van de gereformeerde predikanten in de Republiek der Verenigde Nederlanden voor c. 1700* (Groningen, 1977)

Grosjean, A., *An unofficial alliance: Scotland and Sweden 1569–1654* (Leiden, 2003)

Grove, A. T., 'The "Little Ice Age" and its geomorphological consequences in Mediterranean Europe', *CC*, XLVIII (2001), 121–36

Grove, A. T. and A. Conterio, 'The climate of Crete in the sixteenth and seventeenth centuries', *CC*, XXX (1995), 223–47

Grove, R., 'Revolutionary weather: the climatic and economic crisis of 1788–1795 and the discovery of El Niño', in T. Sharratt, T. Griffiths and L. Robin, eds, *A change in the weather: Climate and culture in Australia* (Sydney, 2005), 128–39

Guha, S., *Health and population in South Asia from earliest times to the present* (London, 2001)

Guiard Larrauri, T., *Historia de la noble villa de Bilbao*, II (Bilbao, 1906)

Guibovich Pérez, M. and N. Domínguez Faura, 'Para la biografía de Espinosa Medrano: dos cartas inéditas de 1666', *Boletín del Instituto Riva-Agüero*, XXVII (2000), 219–42

Guthrie, C. L., 'A seventeenth-century "ever-normal granary": the Alhóndiga of colonial Mexico City', *Agricultural History*, XV (1941), 37–43

Gutiérrez Nieto, J. I., 'El campesinado', in J. Alcalá-Zamora, ed., *La vida cotidiana en la España de Velázquez* (2nd edn, Madrid, 1999), 43–70

Gutmann, M. P., *War and rural life in the early modern Low Countries* (Princeton, 1980)

Haan, R. L., 'The treatment of England and English affairs in the Dutch pamphlet literature, 1640–1660' (University of Michigan PhD thesis, 1959)

Habib, I., *The agrarian system of Mughal India (1556–1707)* (Bombay, 1963)

Haboush, JaHyun Kim, 'Constructing the center: the ritual controversy and the search for a new identity in seventeenth-century Korea,' in JaHyun Kim Haboush and Martina Deuchler, eds, *Culture and the state in late Chosôn Korea* (Cambridge, MA, 1999), 46–90, 240–9

Hacker, J., 'The intellectual activities of the Jews of the Ottoman empire during the sixteenth and seventeenth centuries', in Twersky and Septimus, eds, *Jewish thought*, 95–135

Hacquebord, L. and W. Vroom, eds, *Walvisvaart in de Gouden Eeuw. Opgraving op Spitsbergen* (Amsterdam, 1988)

Hagen, W. W., 'Seventeenth-century crisis in Brandenburg: the Thirty Years' War, the destabilization of serfdom, and the rise of absolutism', *AHR*, XCIV (1989), 302–35

Hagopian, M. N., *The phenomenon of revolution* (New York, 1974)

Hahn, J., *Zeitgeschehen im Spiegel der lutherischen Predigt nach dem dreissigjährigen Krieg. Das Beispiel des kursächsischen Oberhofpredigers Martin Geier (1614–80)* (Leipzig, 2005)

Hair, P. E. H., 'The enslavement of Koelle's informants', *Journal of African History*, VI (1965), 193–203

Hale, J. R., 'Incitement to violence? English Divines on the theme of war, 1578–1631', in Hale, *Renaissance war studies* (London, 1984), 487–517

Hall, A. R. and M. B. Hall, 'The first human blood transfusion: priority disputes (Henry Oldenburg)', *Medical History*, XXIV (1980), 461–5

Hall, J. W., 'Ikeda Mitsumasa and the Bizen flood of 1654', in A. M. Craig and D. H. Shively, eds, *Personality in Japanese History* (Berkeley, 1970), 57–84

Hall, J. W., ed., *The Cambridge History of Japan*, IV (Cambridge, 1991)

Hall, J. W., K. Nagahara and Kozo Yamamura, eds, *Japan before Tokugawa: Political consolidation and economic growth, 1500–1650* (Princeton, 1981)

Hanley, S. B. and K. Nakamura, *Economic and demographic change in pre-industrial Japan, 1600–1868* (Princeton, 1977)

Harington, C. R., *The year without a summer? World climate in 1816* (Ottawa, 1992)

Harley, J. B. and D. Woodward, eds, *The history of cartography: Cartography in the traditional east and southeast Asian societies*, 2 vols (Chicago, 1994)

Harms, R. W., *River of wealth, river of sorrow: The central Zaire basin in the era of the slave and ivory trade, 1500–1891* (New Haven and London, 1981)

Harrell, S., ed., *Chinese historical micro-demography* (Berkeley, 1995)

Hart, S., *Geschrift en Getal. Een keuze uit de demografisch-, sociaal- en economisch-historische studiën, op grond van Zaanse en Amsterdamse archivalia, 1600–1800* (Dordrecht, 1976)

Haskell, Y. A., *Loyola's bees: Ideology and industry in Jesuit Latin didactic poetry* (Oxford, 2003)

Hastrup, K., *Nature and policy in Iceland 1400–1800: An anthropological analysis of history and mentality* (Oxford, 1990)

Hathaway, J., 'The Grand Vizier and the false Messiah: the Sabbatai Sevi controversy and the Ottoman reform in Egypt', *Journal of the American Oriental Society*, CXVII (1997), 665–71

Hathaway, J., *A tale of two factions: Myth, memory, and identity in Ottoman Egypt and Yemen* (Albany, NY, 2003)

Hathaway, J., *Beshir Agha, chief eunuch of the Ottoman imperial harem* (Oxford, 2005)

Hathaway, J., 'The *Evlâd-i 'Arab* ('Sons of the Arabs') in Ottoman Egypt: a re-reading', in C. Imber and K. Kiyotaki, eds, *Frontiers of Ottoman studies: State, province, and the West*, I (London, 2005), 203–16

Hathaway, J., 'The *Mawza*' exile at the juncture of Zaydi and Ottoman Messianism', *Association of Jewish Studies Review*, XXIX (2005), 111–28

Haude, S., 'Religion während des Dreissigjährigen Krieges (1618–1648)', in G. Litz, H. Munzert and R. Liebenberg, eds, *Frömmigkeit, Theologie, Frömmigkeitstheologie/Contributions to European church history. Festschrift für Berndt Hamm zum 60. Geburtstag* (Leiden, 2005), 537–53

Hauptman, L. M., 'The Pequot War and its legacies', in Hauptman and Wherry, eds, *The Pequots*, 69–80

Hauptman, L. M. and J. D. Wherry, eds, *The Pequots in southern New England: The fall and rise of an American Indian nation* (Norman, OK, 1990)

Hautz, J. F., *Geschichte der Universität Heidelberg*, 2 vols (Mannheim, 1862–4)

Hay, J., 'The suspension of dynastic time', in J. Hay, *Boundaries in China* (London, 1994), 171–97

Hayami, A., *The historical demography of pre-modern Japan* (Tokyo, 2001)

Hayami, A., *Population, family and society in pre-modern Japan* (Folkestone, 2009)

Hayami, A., *Population and family in early-modern central Japan* (Kyoto, 2010)

Hayami, A. and Y. Tsubochi, eds, *Economic and demographic developments in rice-producing societies: Some aspects of East Asian economic history, 1500–1900* (Louvain, 1990)

Hayami, A., O. Saitō and R. P. Toby, *The economic history of Japan, 1600–1990. I. Emergence of economic society in Japan, 1600–1859* (Oxford, 2004)

Heidorn, K. C. 'Eighteen hundred and froze to death: the year there was no summer', http://www.islandnet.com/~see/weather/history/1816.htm, accessed 13 Mar. 2012.

Heilingsetzer, G., *Der oberösterreichische Bauernkrieg 1626* (Vienna, 1976: Militärhistorische Schriftenreihe, XXXII)

Heinisch, R. R., *Salzburg im dreissigjährigen Krieg* (Vienna, 1968)

Heinrich, I. et al., 'Interdecadal modulation of the relationship between ENSO, IPO and precipitation: insights from tree-rings in Australia', *Climate Dynamics*, XXXIII (2009), 63–73

Helferrich, T., *The Thirty Years War: A documentary history* (Indianapolis, 2009)

Hellie, R., *Readings for 'Introduction to Russian civilization': Muscovite society* (Chicago, 1970)

Hellie, R., *Enserfment and military change in Muscovy* (Chicago, 1971)

Hellie, R., *The economy and material culture of Russia, 1600–1625* (Chicago, 1999)

Hellie, R., 'The costs of Muscovite military defence', in Lohr and Poe, eds, *The military and society*, 41–66

Hemming, J., *Red gold: The conquest of the Brazilian Indians* (London, 1978)

Hémon, D. and E. Jougla, *Estimation de la surmortalité et principale caracteristiques epidemiologiques: Rapport remis au Ministre de la Santé, de la Famille et des Personnes Handicapées le 25 septembre 2003* (Paris, 2003)

Henderson, F., " 'Posterity to Judge': John Rushworth and his "Historical Collections" ', *Bodleian Library Record*, XV (1996), 247–59

Henripin, J., *La population canadienne au debut du XVIIIe siècle* (Paris, 1954)

Hering, G., *Ökumenisches Patriarchat und europäische Politik, 1620–1638* (Wiesbaden, 1968)

Herman, J. E., 'Empire in the southwest: early Qing reforms to the native chieftain system', *JAS*, LVI (1997), 47–74

Herrmann, R. B., 'The "tragicall historie": cannibalism and abundance in colonial Jamestown', *WMQ*, LXVIII (2011), 47–74

Hespanha, A. M., 'La "Restauração" portuguesa en los capítulos de las cartas de Lisboa de 1641', in Elliott et al., *1640*, 123–68

Hessayon, A., *'Gold tried in the fire': The prophet TheaurauJohn Tany and the English Revolution* (Aldershot, 2007)

Hesselink, R., *Prisoners from Nambu: Reality and make-belief in seventeenth-century Japanese diplomacy* (Honolulu, 2002)

Hill, C., 'The Norman Yoke', in idem, *Puritanism and Revolution*, 46–111

Hill, C., 'Lord Clarendon and the Puritan Revolution' in idem, *Puritanism and Revolution*, 181–94

Hill, C., *Puritanism and Revolution. Studies in the interpretation of the English Revolution of the seventeenth century* (London, 1958)

Hill, C., *The world turned upside down: Radical ideas during the English Revolution* (2nd edn, London, 1972)

Hill, C., 'Robinson Crusoe', *History Workshop Journal*, X (1980), 7–24

Hill, C., *The English Bible and the seventeenth-century revolution* (London, 1993)

Hill, C., *Intellectual origins of the English revolution revisited* (new edn, Oxford, 1997)

Hille, M., 'Mensch und Klima in der frühen Neuzeit. Die Anfänge regelmässiger Wetterbeobachtung, "Kleine Eiszeit", und ihre Wahrnehmung bei Renward Cysat (1545–1613)', *Archiv für Kulturgeschichte*, LXXXIII (2001), 63–91

Hindle, S., 'Exhortation and enlightenment: negotiating inequality in English rural communities, 1550–1650', in Braddick and Walter, eds, *Negotiating power*, 102–22

Hindle, S., 'The problem of pauper marriage in seventeenth-century England', *TRHistS*, 6th series, VIII (1998), 71–89

Hindle, S., *On the parish? The micro-politics of poor relief in rural England, c. 1550–c. 1750* (Oxford, 2004)

Hindle, S., 'Dearth and the English Revolution: the harvest crisis of 1647–1650', *EcHR*, LXI Special Issue: 'Feeding the Masses' (2008), 64–98

Hirshman, A., *Exit, voice, loyalty: Responses to decline in firms, organizations and states* (Cambridge, MA, 1970)

Hirst, D., 'Reading the royal romance: or, intimacy in a king's cabinet', *Seventeenth Century*, XVIII (2003), 211–29

Hittle, J. M., *The service city: State and townsmen in Russia, 1600–1800* (Cambridge, MA, 1979)

Ho, K.-P., 'Should we die as martyrs to the Ming cause? Scholar-officials' views on martyrdom during the Ming-Qing transition', *Oriens Extremus*, XXXVII (1994), 123–57

Ho, P.-T., *Studies in the population history of China* (revised edn, Cambridge, MA, 1967)

Ho, P.-T., *The ladder of success in Imperial China: Aspects of social mobility, 1368–1911* (2nd edn, New York, 1980)

Ho, P.-T., 'In defense of Sinicization: a rebuttal of Evelyn Rawski's "Re-envisioning the Qing"', *JAS*, LVII (1998), 123–55

Hoberman, L. S., 'Technological change in a traditional society: the case of the *desagüe* in colonial Mexico', *Technology and Culture*, XXI (1980), 386–407

Hoffer, P. C., *Sensory worlds in early America* (Baltimore, 2003)

Hoffman, A., 'Zur Geschichte der Schaunbergischen Reichslehen', *Mitteilungen des Oberösterreichischen Landesarchivs*, III (1954), 381–436

Hoffman, M. K., *Raised to rule: Educating royalty at the court of the Spanish Habsburgs, 1601–1634* (Baton Rouge, 2011)

Hoffman, P. T. and K. Norberg, eds, *Fiscal crises, liberty, and representative government, 1450–1789* (Stanford, 1994)

Horner, R. W., 'The Thames Barrier Project', *Geographical Journal*, CXLV (1979), 242–53

Hoskins, W. G., 'Harvest fluctuations and English economic history, 1620–1759', *Agricultural History Review*, XVI (1968), 15–31

Houghton, J. T., G. J. Jenkins and J. J. Ephraums, eds, *Climate Change: The IPCC Scientific Assessment Report prepared for Intergovernmental Panel on Climate Change by Working Group I* (Cambridge, 1990)

Houston, R. A., *Punishing the dead? Suicide, lordship and community in Britain, 1500–1830* (Oxford, 2010)

Howard, D. A., 'Ottoman historiography and the literature of "decline" of the sixteenth and seventeenth centuries', *Journal of Asian History*, XXII (1988), 52–77

Howell, D. L., *Capitalism from within: Economy, society and the state in a Japanese fishery* (Berkeley, 1995)

Hoyt, D. V. and K. H. Schatten, *The role of the sun in climate change* (Oxford, 1997)

Hroch, M. and J. Petráň, *Das 17 Jahrhundert – Krise der Feudalgesellschaft?* (Hamburg, 1981)

Hrushevsky, M., *History of Ukraine-Rus'*, VIII (1913–22; English trans, Edmonton, 2002)

Hsi, A., 'Wu San-kuei in 1644: a reappraisal', *JAS*, XXXIV (1975), 443–53

Huang, P. C. C., *The peasant economy and social change in North China* (Stanford, 1985)

Huang, R., 'Military expenditures in sixteenth-century Ming China', *Oriens Extremus*, XVII (1970), 39–62

Huang, R., *Taxation and government finance in sixteenth-century China* (Cambridge, 1974)

Huang, R., 'Fiscal administration during the Ming dynasty', in Hucker, ed., *Chinese government*, 73–128

Hucker, C. O., *Chinese government in Ming times: Seven studies* (New York, 1969)

Hucker, C. O., ed., *Two studies on Ming History* (Ann Arbor, 1971: Michigan papers in Chinese Studies, XII)

Hufton, O., *The prospect before her: A history of women in western Europe 1500–1800* (New York, 1995)

Hugon, A., 'Le violet et le rouge. Le cardinal-archevêque Filamarino, acteur de la révolution napolitaine (1647–1648)', *Cahiers du CRHQ*, I (2008) [www.crhq.cnrs.fr/cahiers/1/c1a4_Hugon.pdf]

Hugon, A., 'Les violences au cours de la révolution napolitaine (1647–1648) et des révoltes andalouses (1647–1652)', in M. Biard, ed., *Combattre, tolérer ou justifier?: écrivains et journalistes face à la violence d'État (XVIe–XXe siècle)* (Rouen, 2009), 55–71

Hugon, A., 'Naples 1648: le retour à l'ordre après la révolte dite de Masaniello', in Pernot and Toureille, eds, *Lendemains de guerre*, 417–26

Hugon, A., *Naples insurgée 1647–1648. De l'événement à la mémoire* (Rennes, 2010)

Hunecke, V., *Die Findelkinder von Mailand. Kinderaussetzung und aussetzende Eltern vom 17. bis zum 19. Jahrhundert* (Stuttgart, 1987)

Hunecke, V., 'Kindbett oder Kloster. Lebenswege venezianischer Patrizierinnen im 17. und 18. Jahrhunderts', *Geschichte und Gesellschaft*, XVIII (1992), 446–76

Hunter, M., *John Aubrey and the realm of learning* (London, 1975)

Hunter, M., *Robert Boyle, 1627–1691: Scrupulosity and science* (Woodbridge, 2000)

Hütterroth, W.-D., 'Ecology of the Ottoman lands', in Faroqui, ed., *Cambridge History of Turkey*, 18–43

Ibrahim, Nasir Ahmad, *Al-Azmat al-ijtima 'iyya fi misr fi al-qarn al-sabi' 'ashar* (Cairo, 1998)

Idel, M., 'Differing conceptions of Kabbalah in the early seventeenth century', in Twersky and Septimus, eds, *Jewish thought*, 137–200

Ikegami, E., *Bonds of civility: Aesthetic networks and the political origins of Japanese culture* (Cambridge, 2005)

Iklé, F. C., *Every war must end* (New York, 1991)

Imber, C. H., *Ebu's-su 'ud: The Islamic legal tradition* (Stanford, 1997)

Inalcik, H. and D. Quetaert, eds, *An economic and social history of the Ottoman empire*, 2 vols (Cambridge, 1994)

Infelise, M., 'News networks between Italy and Europe', in Dooley, ed., *The dissemination*, 51–67

Ingersoll, T. N., 'The lamp of experience and the shadow of Oliver: history and politics in 1776' (unpublished manuscript)

Ingram, M. J., 'Child sexual abuse in early modern England', in Braddick and Walter, eds, *Negotiating power*, 63–84

Innes, R. L., 'The door ajar: Japan's foreign trade in the seventeenth century' (University of Michigan PhD thesis, 1980)

Israel, J. I., *The Dutch Republic and the Hispanic world, 1606–1661* (Oxford, 1982).

Israel, J. I., *Empires and entrepots: The Dutch, the Spanish Monarchy and the Jews, 1585–1713* (London, 1990)

Israel, J. I., *The Dutch Republic: Its rise, greatness and fall 1477–1806* (Oxford, 1995)

Israel, J. I., 'The Dutch role in the Glorious Revolution', in Israel, *The Anglo-Dutch moment*, 105–62

Israel, J. I., *Radical Enlightenment: Philosophy and the making of modernity, 1650–1750* (Oxford, 2001)

Israel, J. I., *Diasporas within a diaspora: Jews, crypto-Jews and the world maritime empires (1540–1740)* (Leiden, 2002)

Israel, J. I., ed., *The Anglo-Dutch moment: Essays on the Glorious Revolution and its world impact* (Cambridge, 1991)

Iwai Shigeki, 'The collapse of the Ming and the rise of the Qing in the seventeenth-century general crisis' (conference paper, Tokyo, July 2010)

Jacob, J. R. and M. C. Jacob, *Peace projects of the seventeenth century* (New York, 1972)

Jacob, M. C., *Scientific culture and the making of the industrial West* (Oxford, 1997)

Jacquart, J., 'La Fronde des Princes dans la région parisienne et ses consequences matérielles', *Revue d'histoire moderne et contemporaine*, VII (1960), 257–90

Jacquart, J., *La crise rurale en Ile-de-France, 1550–1670* (Paris, 1974)

Jacquart, J., 'Paris: first metropolis of the early modern period', in Clark and Lepetit, eds, *Capital cities*, 105–18

Jago, C. J., 'The influence of debt on the relations between crown and aristocracy in seventeenth-century Castile', *EcHR*, XXVI (1973), 218–36

Jago, C. J., 'The "Crisis of the Aristocracy" in seventeenth-century Castile', *P&P*, LXXXIV (1979), 60–90

Jakubowski-Tiessen, M. and Harmut Lehmann, eds, *Um himmels Willen. Religion in Katastrophezeiten* (Göttingen, 2003)

Janku, A., ' "Heaven-sent disasters" in late imperial China: the scope of the state and beyond', in Mauch and Pfister, eds, *Natural disasters*, 233–64

Janssens, P., 'L'échec des tentatives de soulèvement aux Pays-Bas sous Philippe IV (1621–65)', *Revue d'histoire diplomatique*, XCII (1978), 110–29

Janssens, P., 'La Fronde de l'aristocratie belge en 1632', in Thomas and de Groof, eds, *Rebelión y resistencia*, 23–40

Jenner, M., 'The politics of London air: John Evelyn's *Fumifugium* and the Restoration', *HJ*, XXXVIII (1995), 535–51

Jennings, R. C., 'Firearms, bandits and gun-control: some new evidence on Ottoman policy towards firearms in the possession of reaya, from judicial records of Kayseri, 1600–27', *Archivum Ottomanicum*, VI (1980), 339–58

Jespersen, K. J. V., 'Slaget ved Lutter am Barenberg, 1626', *Krigshistorisk tidsskrift*, IX (1973), 80–9

Jespersen, L., ed., *A revolution from above? The power state of sixteenth- and seventeenth-century Scandinavia* (Odense, 2000)

Johansson, E., 'The history of literacy in Sweden', in H. J. Graff, ed., *Literacy and social development in the West: A reader* (Cambridge, 1981), 151–82

Jolibert, B., *L'enfance au 17e siècle* (Paris, 1981)

Jones, E. L., S. Porter and M. Turner, *A gazetteer of English urban fire disasters 1500–1900* (Norwich, 1984: Historical Geography Research Series, XIII)

Jones, P. D., R. S. Bradley and J. Jouzel, eds, *Climatic variations and forcing mechanisms of the last 2000 years* (Berlin, 1996)

Jones, P. D. et al., eds, *History and climate: Memories of the future?* (New York, 2001)

Jordà i Fernández, A., *Església i poder a la Catalunya del segle XVII. La seu de Tarragona* (Monserrat, 1993)

Jorio, M., ed., *1648. Die Schweiz und Europa. Aussenpolitik zur Zeit des Westfälischen Friedens* (Zürich, 1999)

Jouanna, A., *Le devoir de révolte. La noblesse française et la gestation de l'État moderne (1559–1661)* (Paris, 1989)

Jouhaud, C., *Mazarinades. La Fronde des mots* (Paris, 1985)

Jover Zamora, J. M., *1635: historia de una polémica y semblanza de una generación* (Madrid, 1949)

Jover Zamora, J. M., 'Sobre los conceptos de monarquía y nación en el pensamiento político español del siglo XVII', *Cuadernos de historia de España*, XIII (1950), 138–50

Juneja, M. and F. Mauelshagen, 'Disasters and pre-industrial societies: historiographic trends and comparative perspectives', *Medieval History Journal*, X (2007), 1–31

Junge, H.-C., *Flottenpolitik und Revolution. Die Entstehung der englischen Seemacht während der Herrschaft Cromwells* (Stuttgart, 1980)

Kagan, R. L., *Students and society in early modern Spain* (Baltimore, 1974)

Kagan, R. L. and G. Parker, eds, *Spain, Europe and the Atlantic world: Essays in honour of J. H. Elliott* (Cambridge, 1995)

Kahan, A., 'Natural calamities and their effect upon the food supply in Russia', *Jahrbücher für Geschichte Osteuropas*, NS XVI (1968), 354–77

Kaiser, D. E., *Politics and war: European conflict from Philip II to Hitler* (2nd edn, Cambridge, MA, 2000)

Kaiser, D. H., 'Urban household composition in early modern Russia', *JIH*, XXIII (1992), 39–71

Kaiser, M., ' "Excidium Magdeburgense". Beobachtungen zur Wahrnehmung und Darstellung von Gewalt in Dreissigjährigenh Krieg', in Meumann and Niefanger, eds, *Ein Schauplatz herber Angst*, 43–63

Kamen, H., 'The decline of Castile: the last crisis', *EcHR*, 2nd series, XVII (1964–5), 63–76

Kamen, H., *The Iron Century: Social change in Europe 1550–1660* (London, 1971)

Kamen, H., *Spain in the later seventeenth century 1665–1700* (London, 1980)

Kaplan, S. L., *The famine plot persuasion in eighteenth-century France* (Philadelphia, 1982: *Transactions of the American Philosophical Society*, LXXII, part 3)

Karpinski, A., *W walce z niedwidzialnym wrogiem. Epidemie chorób zakaźnych w Rzeczpospolitej w XVI–XVII wieku* (Warsaw, 2000)

Karr, R. D., ' "Why should you be so furious?" The violence of the Pequot war', *Journal of American History*, LXXXV (1998), 876–909

Kates, R. W., 'The interaction of climate and society', in R. W. Kates, J. H. Ausubel and M. Berberian, eds, *Climate impact assessment: Studies of the interaction of climate and society* (Chichester, 1985), 7–14

Keene, D., 'Growth, modernization and control: the transformation of London's landscape, c. 1500–c. 1760', in Clark and Gillespie, eds, *Two capitals*, ch. 2

Keith, M. E., 'The logistics of power: Tokugawa response to the Shimabara rebellion and power projection in seventeenth-century century Japan' (Ohio State University PhD thesis, 2006)

Kenyon, J. P., *Revolution principles: The politics of party 1689–1720* (Cambridge, 1977)

Kenyon, J. P. and J. H. Ohlmeyer, eds, *The civil wars: A military history of England, Scotland and Ireland 1638–1660* (Oxford, 1998)

Kerridge, E., *The agricultural revolution* (London, 1967)

Kessell, J., *Kiva, cross and crown: The Pecos Indians and New Mexico, 1540 to 1840* (Washington, DC, 1979)

Kessler, L. D., 'Chinese scholars and the early Manchu State', *Harvard Journal of Asiatic Studies*, XXXI (1971), 179–200

Kessler, L. D., *K'ang-hsi and the consolidation of Ch'ing rule 1661–1684* (Chicago, 1976)

Khan, I. A., 'Muskets in the *mawas*: instruments of peasant resistance', in Panikkar et al., eds, *The making of history*, 81–103

Khodarkovsky, M., 'The Stepan Razin uprising: was it a "peasant war"?', *Jahrbücher für Geschichte Osteuropas*, XLII (1994), 1–19

Kiel, M., 'Ottoman sources for the demographic history and the process of Islamisation of Bosnia-Hercegovina and Bulgaria in the fifteenth-seventeenth centuries: old sources, new methodologies', *International Journal of Turkish Studies*, X (2004), 93–119

Kilburn, T. and A. Milton, 'The public context of the trial and execution of Strafford', in Merritt, ed., *The political world*, 230–51

King, D., *Foresight, flood and coastal defence project* (London, 2004) at http://www.publications.parliament.uk/pa/cm200304/cmselect/cmenvfru/558/4051202.htm, accessed 12 Mar. 2012.

Kiple, K. and B. T. Higgins, 'Yellow fever and the Africanization of the Caribbean', in Verano and Ubelaker, eds, *Disease and demography*, 237–48

Kishimoto Mio, 'The Kangxi depression and early Qing local markets', *Modern China*, X (1984), 227–56

Kishimoto Mio, *Shindai Chûgoku no buka to keizai hendô* (Tokyo, 1997)

Kishimoto Mio, *Min shin kyôdai to Kônan shakai* (Tokyo, 1999)

Kishlansky, M. A., 'Charles I: a case of mistaken identity', *P&P*, CLXXXIX (2005), 41–80 and CCV (2009), 175–237

Kivelson, V. A., ' "The Devil stole his mind": the Tsar and the 1648 Moscow Uprising', *AHR*, XCVIII (1993), 733–56

Knachel, P. A., *England and the Fronde: The impact of the English Civil War and revolution in France, 1649–58* (Ithaca, NY, 1967)

Knoppers, L. L., *Constructing Cromwell: Ceremony, portrait and print 1645–1661* (Cambridge, 2000)

Ko, D., *Teachers of the inner chambers: Women and culture in seventeenth-century China* (Stanford, 1994)

Ko, D., 'The body as attire: the shifting meanings of footbinding in seventeenth-century China', *Journal of Women's History*, VIII/4 (1997), 8–27

Ko, D., *Every step a lotus: Shoes for bound feet* (Berkeley, 2001)

Kodansha Encyclopedia of Japan, IV (Tokyo, 1983)

Koenigsberger, H. G., 'The European Civil War', in Koenigsberger, *The Hapsburgs and Europe, 1516–1660* (Ithaca, NY, and London, 1971), ch. 3.

Koenigsberger, H. G., 'The General Crisis: a farewell', in Koenigsberger, *Patrons and Virtuosi* (London, 1986), ch. 7

Kolchin, P., *Unfree Labor: American slavery and Russian serfdom* (Cambridge, MA, 1987)

Kolodziejczyk, D., *Ottoman-Polish diplomatic relations (fifteenth-eighteenth centuries)* (Leiden, 2000)

Komlos, J., 'An anthropometric history of early-modern France', *European Review of Economic History*, VII (2003), 159–89

Kornicki, P., *The book in Japan: A cultural history from the beginnings to the nineteenth century* (Honolulu, 2001)

Kostes, K. P., *Stom kairo tes panoles* (Herakleion, 1995)

Kötting, H., *Die Ormée (1651–3). Gestaltende Kräfte und Personenverbindungen der Bordelaiser Fronde* (Münster, 1983: Schriftenreihe der Vereinigung zur Erforschung der neueren Geschichte, XIV)

Krenke, A. N., ed., *Izmenchivost' klimata Evropy v istoricheskom proshlom* (Moscow, 1995)

Kroener, B., 'Conditions de vie et origine sociale du personnel militaire subalterne au cours de la Guerre de Trente Ans', *Francia*, XV (1987), 321–50

Krüger, K., 'Dänische und schwedische Kriegsfinanzierung im Dreissigjährigen Krieg bis 1635', in Repgen, ed., *Krieg und Politik*, 275–98

Kuczynski, J., *Geschichte des Alltags des deutschen Volkes. I: 1600–50* (Berlin, 1981)

Kuhn, P. A., *Soulstealers: The Chinese sorcery scare of 1768* (Cambridge, 1990)

Kunt, I. M., *The Köprülü years, 1656–1661* (Princeton, 1971)

Kunt, I. M., *The sultan's servants: The transformation of Ottoman provincial government, 1550–1650* (New York, 1983)

Kupperman, K. O., 'The puzzle of the American climate in the early colonial period', *AHR*, LXXXVIII (1982), 1,262–89

Kupperman, K. O., *The Jamestown project* (Cambridge, MA, 2007)

Kvaløy, B., H. Finseraas and O. Listhaug, 'The publics' concern for global warming: a cross-national study of 47 countries', *Journal of Peace Research*, XLIX (2012), 11–22

Kyle, C. R., 'Parliament and the palace of Westminster: an exploration of public space in the early seventeenth century', in C. Jones and S. Kelsey, eds, *Housing Parliament: Dublin, Edinburgh and Westminster* (Edinburgh, 2002), 85–98

Kyle, C. R. and J. Peacey, ' "Under cover of so much coming and going": public access to Parliament and the political process in early Modern England', in Kyle and Peacey, eds, *Parliament at work: Parliamentary committees, political power and public access in early modern England* (Woodbridge, 2002), 1–23

Labelle, K. M., 'Dispersed but not destroyed: leadership, women and power in the Wendat diaspora, 1600–1701' (Ohio State University PhD thesis, 2011)

Labrousse, E., *L'entrée de Saturne au lion: l'éclipse de soleil du 12 août 1654* (Leiden, 1974)

Labrousse, E., 'François Davant: l'autobiographie d'un autodidacte', *XVIIe siècle*, CXIII (1976), 78–93

Lach, D. F. and E. J. van Kley, *Asia in the making of Europe*, 3 vols (Chicago, 1965–93)

Lachiver, M., *Les années de misère: la famine au temps du Grand Roi 1680–1720* (Paris, 1991)

Lacour, L., *Richelieu dramaturge, et ses collaborateurs* (Paris, 1926)

Ladewig Petersen, E., *The crisis of the Danish nobility, 1580–1660* (Odense, 1967)

Ladewig Petersen, E., 'Conspicuous consumption: the Danish nobility of the seventeenth century', *Kwartalnik historij kultury materialnej*, I (1982), 57–65

Lahne, W., *Magdeburgs Zerstörung in der zeitgenössischen Publizistik* (Magdeburg, 1931)

Lamb, H. H., *Climate: Past, present and future*, 2 vols (London, 1977)

Lamont, W., 'Richard Baxter, "Popery" and the origins of the English Civil War', *History*, LXXXVII (2002), 336–52

Landsteiner, E., 'The crisis of wine production in late sixteenth-century Europe: climatic causes and economic consequences', *CC*, XLIII (1999), 323–34

Lane, R., *Images from the floating world: The Japanese print, including an illustrated dictionary of Ukiyo-e* (New York, 1982)

Langer, H., *The Thirty Years' War* (Poole, 1980)

Lappalainen, J. T., 'Finland's contribution to the war in Germany', in K.-R. Böhme and J. Hansson, eds, *1648 and European security proceedings* (Stockholm, 1999), 179–91

Lario, D. de, *El comte-duc d'Olivares i el regne de València* (Valencia, 1986)

Larner, C. J., *Enemies of God: The witch-hunt in Scotland* (London, 1981)

Lassen, A., 'The population of Denmark in 1660', *Scandinavian Economic History Review*, XIII (1965), 1–30

Le Cam, J.-L., 'Extirper la barbarie. La reconstruction de l'Allemagne protestante par l'École et l'Église au sortir de la Guerre de trente Ans', in Pernot and Toureille, eds, *Lendemains de Guerre*, 407–14

Le Cam, J.-L., 'Über die undeutlichen instutionellen Grenzen der Elementarbildung. Das Beispiel des Herzogtums Braunschweig-Wolfenbüttel im 17. Jahrhundert', in A. Hanschmidt and H.-U. Musolff, eds, *Elementarbildung und Berufsausbildungs, 1450–1750* (Cologne, 2005: Beiträge zur historischen Bildungsforschung, XXXI), 47–72

Le Roy Ladurie, E., *Times of feast, times of famine: A history of climate since the year 1000* (London, 1973: original French edn, Paris, 1967)

Le Roy Ladurie, E., *Historie humaine et comparée du climat*, 3 vols (Paris, 2004–9)

Le Roy Ladurie, E., 'Naissance de l'histoire du climat' (paper delivered at the 'Climate and History' conference at the Deutsches Historisches Institut, Paris, 3 Sep. 2011)

Le Roy Ladurie, E., D. Rousseau and A. Vasak, *Les fluctuations du climat: de l'an mil à aujourd'hui* (Paris, 2011)

Lebrun, F., *Les hommes et la mort en Anjou aux 17e et 18e siècles. Essai de démographie et de psychologie historiques* (Paris/The Hague, 1971)

Lebrun, F., *Se soigner autrefois. Médécins, saints et sorciers aux 17e et 18e siècles* (Paris, 1983)

LeDonne, J., *The Grand Strategy of the Russian empire, 1650–1831* (Oxford, 2004)

Lee, J. Z. and F. Wang, *One quarter of humanity: Malthusian mythology and Chinese realities, 1700–2000* (Cambridge, 1999)

Lee, J. Z., F. Wang and C. Campbell, 'Infant and child mortality among the Qing nobility: implications for two types of positive check', *Population Studies*, XLVIII (1994), 395–411

Lefebvre, G., *La Grande Peur de 1789* (Paris, 1932)

Leffler, P. K., 'From Humanist to Enlightenment historiography: a case study of François Eudes de Mézeray', *French Historical Studies*, X (1978), 416–38

Leijonhufvud, L., et al., 'Five centuries of Stockholm winter/spring temperatures reconstructed from documentary evidence and instrumental observations', *CC*, CI (2010), 109–41

Leman, A., *Richelieu et Olivarès: leurs négociations secrètes de 1636 à 1642* (Lille, 1932: Mémoires et travaux des facultés catholiques de Lille, XLIX)

Lenihan, P., 'War and population, 1649–1652', *Irish Economic and Social History*, XXIV (1999), 1–21

Lenihan, P., *Confederate Catholics at war, 1641–1649* (Dublin, 2001)

Lepore, J., *The name of war: King Philip's War and the origins of American identity* (New York, 1999)

Lětopis Samovidca o wojnach Bohdana Chmielnickoho (Moscow, 1846)

Leupp, G., *Male colors: The construction of homosexuality in Tokugawa Japan* (Berkeley, 1995)

Levi, S. C., 'Hindus beyond the Hindu Kush: Indians in the Central Asian slave trade,' *Journal of the Royal Asiatic Society*, 3rd series, XII (2002), 277–88

Levin, E., 'Infanticide in pre-Petrine Russia', *Jahrbücher für Geschichte Osteuropas*, XXXIV (1986), 215–24

Levin, E., 'Plague control in seventeenth-century Russia' (unpublished paper)

Levy, J. S., *War in the modern great power system, 1495–1975* (Lexington, MA, 1983)

Lewis, B., *Islam in history* (London, 1973)

Lewitter, L. R., 'Poland, the Ukraine and Russia in the seventeenth century', *Slavonic and East European Review*, XXVII (1948–9), 157–71 and 414–29

Li, L., *Fighting famine in North China: State, market, and environmental decline, 1690s–1990s* (Stanford, 2007)

Li Bozhong, *Agricultural development in Jiangnan, 1620–1850* (London, 1998)

Ligresti, D., *Sicilia moderna: le città e gli uomini* (Naples, 1984)

Lind, G., *Hæren og magten i Danmark 1614–1662* (Odense, 1994)

Lind, G., 'Syndens straf og mandens ære. Danske tolkninger af krigen 1611–1660', *Historisk Tidskrift [Dansk]*, CXXVIII (2008), 339–65

Lindegren, J., 'Frauenleben und Soldatenleben. Perspektiven auf Schweden und den dreissigjährigen Krieg', in von Krusenstjern and Medick, eds, *Zwischen Alltag und Katastrophe*, 135–58

Lindegren, J., 'Men, money and means', in Contamine, ed., *War and competition*, 129–62

Lindegren, J., 'Soldatenleben. Perspektiven auf Schweden und den Dreissigjährigen Krieg', in von Krusenstjern and Medick, eds, *Zwischen Alltag und Katastrophe*, 136–58

Lindley, K., *Fenland riots and the English Revolution* (London, 1982)

Linz, J. J., 'Intellectual roles in sixteenth and seventeenth-century Spain', *Daedalus*, CI/3 (1972), 59–108

Liu Kam-biu, Caiming Shen and Kin-sheun Louie, 'A 1000-year history of typhoon landfalls in Guangdong, southern China, reconstructed from Chinese historical documentary records', *Annals of the Assocation of American Geographers*, XCI (2001), 453–64

Liu, Ts'ui-Jung, J. Lee, D. S. Reher, O. Saito and W. Feng, eds, *Asian population history* (Oxford, 2000)

Livet, G., 'La Guerre des Paysans de 1653 en Suisse vue par l'Ambassadeur de France: témoinage et interprétation', *Revue d'histoire diplomatique*, XCII (1978), 130–65

Livi-Bacci, M., 'Chronologie, intensité et diffusion des crises de mortalité en Italie, 1600–1850', *Population*, XXXII (1977), 401–40

Lobo, V. and J. Correia-Afonso, *Intrepid itinerant: Manuel Godinho and his journey from India to Portugal in 1663* (Bombay, 1990)

Lockhart, P. D., *Denmark in the Thirty Years War 1618–1648* (Cranbury, NJ, 1996)

Loewenson, 'The Moscow rising of 1648', *Slavonic and East European Review*, XXVII (1948–9), 146–56.

Lohr, E. and M. Poe, *The military and society in Russia, 1450–1917* (Leiden, 2002)

Lorandi, A. M., *Spanish king of the Incas: The epic life of Pedro Bohorques* (Pittsburgh, 2005)

Lorenzo Cardoso, P. L., *Los conflictos sociales en Castilla (siglos XVI–XVII)* (Madrid, 1996)

Lottin, A., *Vie et mentalité d'un Lillois sous Louis XIV* (Lille, 1968)

Lucas Val, N. de, 'Literatura i historia. Identitats collectives i visions de "l'altre" al segle XVII', *Manuscrits*, XXIV (2006), 167–92

Ludden, D., *Peasant history in south India* (Princeton, 1985)

Ludlam, D. M., *Early American winters* (Boston, 1966)

Lutaud, O., *Des révolutions d'Angleterre à la Révolution française. Le tyrannicide et Killing no murder (Cromwell, Athalie, Bonaparte)* (Leiden, 1973)

Luterbacher, J., 'Monthly mean pressure reconstruction for the late Maunder Minimum period (AD 1675–1715)', *IJC*, XX (2000), 1,049–66

Luterbacher, J. et al., 'The late Maunder Minimum', *CC*, XLIX/4 (2001), 441–62

Luterbacher, J. and E. Xoplaki, '500-year winter temperature and precipitation variability over the Mediterranean area and its connection to the large-scale atmospheric circulation', in H.-J. Boehle, ed., *Mediterranean climate. Variability and trends* (Heidelberg, 2003), 133–53

Luterbacher, J., D. Dietrich, E. Xoplaki, M. Grosjean and H. Wanner, 'European seasonal and annual temperature variability, trends, and extremes since 1500', *Science*, CCCIII (5 Mar. 2004), 1,499–1,503

Lynn, J. A., *Giant of the Grand Siècle: The French army, 1610–1715* (Cambridge, 1997)

McArdle, F., *Altopascio: A study in Tuscan rural society, 1587–1784* (Cambridge, 1978)

Macaulay, C., *The history of England from the accession of James I. to that of the Brunswick line*, 8 vols (London, 1763–83)

Macaulay, T. B., *History of England since the accession of James the Second*, 5 vols (New York, 1848)

McCants, A. E. C., E. Bever and J. de Vries, 'Commentaries', *JIH*, XL (2009), 295–303

McCavitt, J., *Sir Arthur Chichester, Lord Deputy of Ireland 1605–1616* (Belfast, 1998)

McChesney, R. D., *Waqf in Central Asia: Four hundred years in the history of a Muslim shrine, 1480–1889* (Princeton, NJ, 1991)

McClain, J. L. et al., *Edo and Paris: Urban life and the state in the early modern era* (Ithaca, NY, 1994)

MacCuarta, B., ed., *Ulster 1641: Aspects of the rising* (Belfast, 2nd edn, 1997)

Macdonald, M., *Mystical Bedlam: madness, anxiety and healing in seventeenth-century England* (Cambridge, 1981)

Macdonald, M. and T. R. Murphy, *Sleepless souls: Suicide in early modern England* (Oxford, 1990)

McGowan, B., 'Ottoman political communications', in H. D. Laswell, D. Lerner and H. Speir, eds, *Propaganda in world history* (Honolulu, 1979), 444–92

McGowan, B., *Economic life in Ottoman Europe: Taxation, trade and the struggle for land, 1600–1800* (Cambridge, 1981)

MacHardy, K., 'The rise of absolutism and noble rebellion in early modern Habsburg Austria, 1570 to 1620', *CSSH*, XXXIV (1992), 407–38

McIntosh, R. J. et al., eds, *The way the wind blows: Climate, history and human action* (New York, 2000)

McKenny, K., 'The seventeenth-century land settlement in Ireland: towards a statistical interpretation', in Ohlmeyer, ed., *Ireland*, 181–200

McLeod, M. J., *Spanish Central America: A socio-economic history, 1520–1720* (Berkeley, 1973)

McMullen, I. J., 'Kumazawa Banzan and "Jitsugaku": toward pragmatic action', in de Bary and Bloom, eds, *Principle and practicality*, 337–73

McNeill, J. R., 'China's environmental history in world perspective', in Elvin and Liu, eds, *Sediments of time*, 31–49

McNeill, J. R., *Mosquito empires: Ecology and war in the greater Caribbean, 1620–1914* (Cambridge, 2010)

Mack, P., *Visionary women: Ecstatic prophecy in seventeenth-century England* (Berkeley, 1992)

Mackay, R., *The limits of royal authority. Resistance and obedience in seventeenth-century Castile* (Cambridge, 1999)

Maehle, A.-H., *Drugs on trial: Experimental pharmacology and therapeutic innovation in the eighteenth century* (Amsterdam and Atlanta, 1999)

Maffi, D., 'Confesionalismo y Razón de Estado en la Edad Moderna. El caso de la Valtelina (1637–39)', *Hispania sacra*, LVII (2005), 467–89

Maffi, D., 'Milano in guerra. La mobilitazione delle risorse in una provincia della Monarchia, 1640–1659', in Rizzo et al., eds, *Le forze del príncipe*, I, 345–408

Maffi, D., *Il baluardo della corona. Guerra, esercito, finanze e società nella Lombardis seicentesca (1630–1660)* (Florence, 2007)

Maffi, D., *La cittadella in armi. Esercito, società e finanza nella Lombardia di Carlo II, 1660–1700* (Milan, 2010)

Magen, F., *Reichsgräfliche Politik in Franken. Zur Reichspolitik der grafen von Hohenlohe zur Vorabend und Beginn des dreissigjährigen Krieges* (Schwäbische Hall, 1975)

Maier, I. and D. C. Waugh, ' "The blowing of the Messiah's trumpet" ': reports about Sabbatai Sevi and Jewish unrest in 1665–67', in Dooley, ed., *The dissemination of news*, 137–52

Major, A., ed., *Sati: A historical anthology* (Oxford, 2007)

Major, J. R., 'The crown and the aristocracy in Renaissance France', *AHR*, LXIX (1964), 631–45

Major, P., 'Jumping Josaphat', *Times Literary Supplement*, 28 July 2006, 15

Makey, W., *The Church of the Covenant, 1637–1651* (Edinburgh, 1979)

Mallet, R. and J. W. Mallet, *The earthquake catalogue of the British Association with the discussion, curves and maps etc* (London, 1858)

Mandell, D. R., *King Philip's War: Colonial expansion, native resistance, and the end of Indian sovereignty* (Baltimore, 2010)

Mandrou, R., 'Vingt ans après, ou une direction de recherches fécondes: Les révoltes populaires en France au XVIIe siècle', *Revue Historique*, CCXLII (1969), 29–40

Manley, G., 'Central England temperatures: monthly means 1659 to 1973', *Quarterly Journal of the Royal Meteorological Society*, C (1974), 389–405

Mann, B. A., *Iroquois women: The Gantowisas* (New York, 2000)

Mann, G., *Wallenstein* (Frankfurt, 1971)

Mann, S., *Precious records: Women in China's long eighteenth century* (Stanford, 1997)

Mann, S., 'Women in East Asia: China, Japan, and Korea', in B. G. Smith, ed., *Women's history in global perspective*, II (Urbana, IL, 2005), 47–94

Mannarelli, M. E., *Pecados públicos: la ilegitimidad en Lima, siglo XVII* (Lima, 1993)

Mantran, R., *Istanbul dans la seconde moitié du XVIIe siècle* (Paris, 1962)

Manzoni, A., *The betrothed* (1827; Harmondsworth, 1972)

Marcos Martín, A., *Auge y declive de un nucleo mercantil y financiero de Castilla la Vieja. Evolución demográfica de Medina del Campo durante los siglos XVI y XVII* (Valladolid, 1978)

Marcos Martín, A., *España en los siglos XVI, XVII y XVIII. Economía y sociedad* (Barcelona, 2000)

Marcos Martín, A., 'Tráfico de indulgencias, guerra contra infieles y finanzas regias. La Bula de Cruzada durante la primera mitad del siglo XVII' in M. Rodríguez Cancho, ed., *Historia y perspectivas de investigación. Estudios en memoria del profesor Angel Rodríguez Sánchez* (Mérida, 2002), 227–36

Marcos Martín, A., '¿Fue la fiscalidad regia un factor de crisis en la Castilla del siglo XVII?', in Parker, ed., *La crisis de la Monarquía*, 173–253

Marcos Martín, A., 'Sobre la violencia del impuesto en la Castilla del siglo XVII', in J. J. Lozano Navarro and J. L. Castellano, eds, *Violencia y conflictividad en el universo barroco* (Granada, 2010), 197–240

Marks, R. B., *Tigers, rice, silk and silt: Environment and economy in late imperial South China* (Cambridge, 1998)

Marmé, M., 'Survival through transformation: how China's Suzhou-centred world economy weathered the general crisis of the seventeenth century', *Social History*, XXII/2 (2007), 144–65

Marmé, M., Locating linkages or painting bull's-eyes around bullet holes? An East Asian perspective on the seventeenth-century crisis', *AHR*, CXIII (2008), 1080–9

Marques, J. F., *A parenética portuguesa e a dominação filipina* (Porto, 1986)

Marques, J. F., *A parenética portuguesa e a Restauração 1640–1668. A revolta e a mentalidade*, 2 vols (Porto, 1989)

Márquez Macías, R., 'Andaluces en América. Recuerdos y añoranzas', *Trocadero*, XXI–XXII (2009–10), 9–20

Marshall, C. R., ' "Causa di Stravaganze". Domenico Gargiulo's *Revolt of Masaniello*', *Art Bulletin*, LXXX (1998), 478–97

Martinson, D. G., ed., *Natural climate variability on decade-to-century time scales* (Washington, DC, 1995)

Masson-Delmotte, V. et al., 'Changes in European precipitation seasonality and in drought frequencies revealed by a four-century-long tree-ring isotopic record from Brittany, western France', *Climate Dynamics*, XXIV (2005), 57–69

Mastellone, S., 'Les révoltes de 1647 en Italie du Sud. Étaient-ils paysannes ou urbaines?', *Revue d'histoire diplomatique*, XCII (1978), 166–88

Mastellone, S., 'Holland as a political model in Italy in the seventeenth century', *Bijdragen en Mededelingen voor de Geschiedenis der Nederlanden*, XCVIII (1983), 568–82

Matthee, R. P., *The politics of trade in Safavid Iran: Silk for silver 1600–1730* (Cambridge, 1999)

Matthee, R. P., *The pursuit of pleasure: Drugs and stimulants in Iranian history, 1500–1900* (Princeton, NJ, 2005)

Mauch, C. and C. Pfister, eds, *Natural disasters, cultural responses: Case studies towards a global environmental history* (Lanham, MD, 2009)

Mauelshagen, F., *Klimageschichte der Neuzeit, 1500–1900* (Darmstadt, 2010)

Maunder, E. W., 'The prolonged sunspot minimum, 1645–1715', *Journal of the British Astronomical Association*, XXXII (1922), 140–5

Mazet, C., 'Population et société à Lima aux 16e et 17e siècles: la paroisse de San Sebastián', *Cahiers des Amériques Latines*, XIII–XIV (1976), 51–100

Mazumdar, S., *Sugar and society in China: Peasants, technology and the world market* (Cambridge, MA, 1998)

Mazumdar, S., 'The impact of New World food crops on the diet and economy of China and India, 1600–1900', in R. Grew, ed., *Food in global history* (Boulder, CO, 2000), 58–78

Medick, H., 'Historisches Ereignis und zeitgenössische Erfahrung: die Eroberung und Zerstörung Magdeburgs 1631', in von Krusenstjern and Medick, eds, *Zwischen Alltag und Katastrophe*, 377–407

Merrick, J., 'The cardinal and the queen: sexual and political disorders in the Mazarinades', *French Historical Studies*, XVIII (1994), 667–99

Merriman, R. B., *Six contemporaneous revolutions* (Oxford, 1938)

Merritt, J. F., 'Power and communication: Thomas Wentworth and government at a distance during the personal rule, 1629–35', in Merritt, ed., *The political world*, 109–32

Merritt, J. F., ed., *The political world of Thomas Wentworth, earl of Strafford, 1621–1641* (Cambridge, 1996)

Merton, Robert K., 'Singletons and multiples in scientific discovery', *Proceedings of the American Philosophical Society*, CV (1961), 470–86

Meumann, M. and D. Niefanger, eds, *Ein Schauplatz herber Angst: Wahrnehmung und Darstellung von Gewalt im 17. Jahrhundert* (Göttingen, 1997)

Meyer-Fong, T., *Building culture in early Qing Yangzhou* (Stanford, 2003)

Micco Spadaro: Napoli ai tempi di Masaniello (Naples, 2002)

Michałowski, J., *Księga pamiętnicza (1647–1655)*, ed. Z. A. Helcel (Kraków, 1864)

Michel, M.-J., *Jansénisme et Paris, 1640–1740* (Paris, 2000)

Michels, G. B., *At war with the church: Religious dissent in seventeenth-century Russia* (Stanford, 1999)

Mikami Takehiko, ed., *Proceedings of the International Symposium on the Little Ice Age Climate* (Tokyo, 1992)

Mikhail, A., *Nature and empire in Ottoman Egypt: An environmental history* (Cambridge, 2011)

Miller, G., *The adoption of inoculation for smallpox in England and France* (Philadelphia, 1957)

Miller, H., *State versus gentry in Late Ming Dynasty China, 1572–1644* (London, 2008)

Miller, J. C., 'The significance of drought, disease and famine in the agriculturally marginal zones of West-Central Africa', *JAH*, XXIII (1982), 17–61

Mitchell, A. J., 'Religion, revolt, and the creation of regional identity in Catalonia, 1640–1643' (Ohio State University PhD thesis, 2005)

Mitchell, H. J., 'Reclaiming the self: the Pascal-Rousseau connection', *Journal of the History of Ideas*, LIV (1993), 637–58

Miyazaki, I., *China's examination hell: The civil service examinations of Imperial China* (New Haven, 1976)

Moberg, A. et al., 'Highly variable northern hemisphere temperature reconstructed from low- and high-resolution proxy data', *Nature*, CCCXXXIII/7026 (2005), 613–17

Monod, P., *The power of kings: Monarchy and religion in Europe, 1589–1715* (London and New Haven, 1999)

Moody, T. W., F. X. Martin and F. J. Byrne, eds, *A new history of Ireland, III: 1534–1691* (Oxford, 1976)

Moon, D., 'Peasant migration and the settlement of Russia's frontiers, 1550–1897', *HJ*, XL (1997), 859–93

Moosvi, S., 'Scarcities, prices and exploitation: the agrarian crisis, 1658–70', *Studies in History*, I (1985), 45–55

Moosvi, S., 'Science and superstition under Akbar and Jahangir: the observation of astronomical phenomena,' in I. Habib, ed., *Akbar and his India* (Delhi, 1997), 109–20

Moosvi, S., 'The Indian economic experience 1600–1900: a quantitative study', in Panikkar, ed., *The making of history*, 328–57

Moote, A. L., *The revolt of the judges: The Parlement of Paris and the Fronde, 1642–1652* (Princeton, 1971)

Moote, A. L. and D. C. Moote, *The Great Plague: The story of London's most deadly year* (Baltimore, 2004)

Mormiche, P., *Devenir prince. L'école du pouvoir en France, XVIIe–XVIIIe siècles* (Paris, 2009)

Morrill, J. S., *Cheshire 1630–1660: County government and society during the 'English Rebellion'* (Oxford, 1974)

Morrill, J. S., *The revolt of the provinces: Conservatives and radicals in the English Civil War, 1630–1650* (London, 1976)

Morrill, J. S. *Revolt in the provinces: The people of England and the tragedies of war, 1630–1648* (2nd edn, London, 1999)

Morrill, J. S. and P. Baker, 'The case of the armie truly restated', in M. Mendle, ed., *The Putney Debates of 1647. The army, the Levellers and the English state* (Cambridge, 2007), 103–24

Mortimer, G., *Eyewitness accounts of the Thirty Years War 1618–1648* (London, 2002)

Mote, F. W. *Imperial China, 900–1800* (Cambridge, MA, 1999)

Mousnier, R., 'Les mouvements populaires en France avant les traités de Westphalie et leur incidence sur ces traités', in M. Braubach, ed., *Forschungen und Studien zur Geschichte des westfälischen Friedens* (Münster, 1965: Schriftenreihe der Vereinigung zur Erforschung der neueren Geschichte, I), 36–61

Mousnier, R., 'Some reasons for the Fronde: the revolutionary days in Paris in 1648', in P. J. Coveney, ed., *France in Crisis, 1620–1675* (London, 1977), 169–200

Müller, H. D., *Der schwedische Staat in Mainz, 1631–1636* (Mainz, 1979)

Murdoch, S., ed., *Scotland and the Thirty Years War 1618–1648* (Leiden, 2001)

Murphey, R., 'The Verliyüddin Telhis: notes on the sources and interrelations between Koçi Bey and contemporary writers of advice to kings', *Belleten*, XLIII (1979), 547–71

Murphey, R., 'Provisioning Istanbul: the state and subsistence in the early modern Middle East', *Food and Foodways*, II (1988), 217–63

Murphey, R., *Ottoman warfare, 1500–1700* (London, 1998)

Musallam, B. F., *Sex and society in Islam: Birth control before the nineteenth century* (Cambridge, 1983)

Musi, A., *La rivolta di Masaniello. Nella scena politica barocca* (2nd edn, Naples, 2002)

Mussey, B., 'Yankee chills, Ohio fever', *New England Quarterly*, XXII (1949), 435–451

Myllyntaus, T., 'Summer frost as a natural hazard with fatal consequences in Preindustrial Finland', in Mauch and Pfister, eds, *Natural disasters*, 77–102

Nadal, J., 'La población española durante los siglos XVI, XVII y XVIII. Un balance a escala regional', in V. Pérez Moreda and D. S. Reher, eds, *Demografía histórica de España* (Madrid, 1988), 39–54

Nagahara, K. and Kozo Yamamura, 'Shaping the process of unification: technological progress in sixteenth- and seventeenth-century Japan', *JJS*, XIV (1988), 77–109

Nagakura Tamotsu, 'Kan'ei no kikin to bakufu no taio', in Kodama Kota et al., eds, *Edo jidai no kikin* (Tokyo, 1982), 75–85

Nakane, C. and S. Ōishi, eds, *Tokugawa Japan: The social and economic antecedents of modern Japan* (Tokyo, 1990)

Nakayama, M., 'On the fluctuation of the price of rice in the Chiang-nan region during the first half of the Ch'ing period (1644–1795)', *Memoirs of the Research Department of the Toyo Bunko*, XXXVII (1979), 55–90

Namaczyńska, S., *Kronika klęsk elemntarnych w Polsce i w krajack sąsiednich w latach 1648–1696* (Lwów, 1937)

Nansen, F., *Through Siberia: The land of the future* (New York, 1914)

Naquin, S., *Peking: Temples and city life, 1400–1900* (Berkeley, 2000)

Needham, J. et al., *Science and civilization in China*, 7 vols in 27 parts to date (1954–)

Nef, J. U., *The rise of the British coal industry*, 2 vols (London, 1932)

Nehlsen, B., 'Song publishing during the Thirty Years War', in Bussmann and Schilling, eds, *1648*, II, 431–7

Neuberger, H., 'Climate in art', *Weather*, XXV (1970), 46–56

Neumann, K., *Das Wort als Waffe: politische Propaganda im Aufstand der Katalanen 1640–1652* (Herbolzheim, 2003)

Newman, A. J., *Safavid Iran: Rebirth of a Persian empire* (London, 2006)

Newman, K., *Cultural capitals: Early modern London and Paris* (Princeton, NJ, 2007)

Ng, V., 'Ideology and sexuality. Rape laws in Qing China', *JAS*, XLVI (1987), 57–70

Nicholson, S. E., 'The methodology of historical climate reconstruction and its application to Africa', *Journal of African History*, XX (1979), 31–49

Nicoară, Toader, ed., *Sentimentul de insecuritate în societatea românească la începuturile timpurilor moderne 1600–1830*, 2 vols (Cluj, 2002–5)

Nicolas, J., *La rébellion française. Mouvements populaires et conscience sociale 1661–1789* (Paris, 2002)

Nordås R. and N. P. Gleditsch, 'Climate change and conflict', *Political Geography*, XXVI (2007), 627–38

Nordmann, C., 'La crise de la Suède au temps de Christine et de Charles X Gustave (1644–1660)', *Revue d'histoire diplomatique*, XCII (1978), 210–32

Norris, M. A., 'Edward Sexby, John Reynolds and Edmund Chillenden: Agitators, "Sectarian Grandees" and the relations of the New Model Army with London in the spring of 1647', *Historical Research*, LXXVI (2003), 30–53

ó hAnnracháin, T., ' "Though hereticks and politicians should misinterpret their goode zeal": political ideology and Catholicism in early modern Ireland', in Ohlmeyer, ed., *Political thought*, 155–75

ó hAnnracháin, T., *Catholic reformation in Ireland: The mission of Rinuccini 1645–1649* (Oxford, 2002)

ó Siochrú, M., 'Atrocity, codes of conduct and the Irish in the British Civil Wars 1641–1653', *P&P*, CXCV (2007), 55–86

Der Oberösterreichische Bauernkrieg, 1626. Ausstellung des Landes Oberösterreich (Linz, 1976)

O'Brien, C. B., *Muscovy and the Ukraine from the Pereiaslavl Agreement to the Truce of Andrusovo, 1654–67* (Berkeley, 1963)

O'Connell, D. P., 'A cause célèbre in the history of treaty-making: the refusal to ratify the peace of Regensburg in 1630', *British Yearbook of International Law*, XLII (1967), 71–90

Odhner, C. T., *Die Politik Schwedens im Westfälischen Friedenscongress und die Gründung der schwedischen Herrschaft in Deutschland* (Gotha, 1877)

Ogilvie, S. C., ed., *Germany: A new economic and social history, II. 1630–1800* (London, 1996)

Ogilvie, S. C., *State corporatism and proto-industry: The Württemberg Black Forest, 1580–1797* (Cambridge, 1997)

Ogilvie, S. C., *A bitter living: Women, market and social capital in early modern Germany* (Oxford, 2003)

Ogilvie, S. C., 'Germany and the seventeenth-century crisis', in Parker and Smith, eds, *The General Crisis*, 57–86

Ogilvie, S. C., 'Guilds, efficiency and social capital: evidence from German proto-industry', *EcHR*, LVII (2004), 286–333

Ogilvie, S. C., 'How does social capital affect women? Guilds and communities in early modern Germany', *AHR*, CIX (2004), 325–59

Ogilvie, S. C., 'Communities and the second serfdom in early modern Bohemia', *P&P*, CLXXXVII (2005), 69–119

Ohlmeyer, J. H., 'The Antrim Plot of 1641 – a myth?', *HJ*, XXXV (1992), 905–19

Ohlmeyer, J. H., *Civil War and Restoration in the three Stuart kingdoms: The career of Randal MacDonnell, marquis of Antrim, 1609–1683* (Cambridge, 1993)

Ohlmeyer, J. H., 'The "Antrim Plot" of 1641: a rejoinder', *HJ*, XXXVII (1994), 434–7

Ohlmeyer, J. H., ed., *Ireland from Independence to Occupation, 1641–1660* (Cambridge, 1995)

Ohlmeyer, J. H., 'Seventeenth-century Ireland and the new British and Atlantic histories', *AHR*, CIV (1999), 446–62

Ohlmeyer, J. H., ed., *Political thought in seventeenth-century Ireland: Kingdom or colony* (Cambridge, 2000)

Okada Takehiko, 'Practical learning in the Chu Hsi school: Yamazaki Ansai and Kaibara Ekken', in de Bary and Bloom, eds, *Principles and practicality*, 231–305

Olivari, M., *Entre el trono y la opinión. La vida política castellana en los siglos XVI y XVII* (Valladolid, 2004)

Ooms, H., *Tokugawa ideology: Early constructs, 1570–1680* (Princeton, 1985)

Orcibal, J., *Jansénius d'Ypres (1585–1635)* (Paris, 1989)

Orihel, M. L., ' "A presse full of pamphlets" on Ireland: stereotypes, sensationalism and veracity in English reactions to the 1641 Irish rebellion, November 1641 – August 1642' (Queen's University, Kingston, Ontario, MA thesis, 2001)

Oschmann, A., *Der Nürnberger Exekutionstag 1649–1650: Das Ende des Dreissigjährigen Krieges in Deutschland* (Münster, 1991: Schriftenreihe der Vereinigung zur Erforschung der neueren Geschichte, XVII)

Oster, E., 'Witchcraft, weather and economic growth in Renaissance Europe', *Journal of Economic Perspectives*, XVIII (2004), 215–28

Outram, Q., 'The socio-economic relations of warfare and the military mortality crises of the Thirty Years' War', *Medical History*, XLV (2001), 151–84

Overton, M., *The agricultural revolution in England: The transformation of the agrarian economy 1500–1850* (Cambridge, 1996)

Öz, M., 'Population fall in seventeenth-century Anatolia (some findings for the districts of Canik and Bozok)', *Archivum Ottomanicum*, XXII (2005), 159–71

Özel, O., 'Population changes in Ottoman Anatolia during the 16th and 17th centuries: the "demographic crisis" reconsidered', *IJMES*, XXXVI (2004), 183–205

Özel, O., 'Banditry, state and economy: on the financial impact of the *Celali* movement in Ottoman Anatolia', *Proceedings of the IXth International Congress of Economic and Social History of Turkey* (Ankara, 2007), 65–74

Özvar, E., 'Fiscal crisis of the Ottoman empire in the seventeenth century?' (unpublished paper at the XI Congress of Social and Economic History of Turkey, Ankara, 2008)

Paas, J. R., M. W. Paas and G. C. Schoolfield, *Kipper and Wipper inflation 1619–1623: An economic history with contemporary German broadsheets* (New Haven and London, 2012)

Pamuk, S., 'The price revolution in the Ottoman empire reconsidered', *IJMES*, XXXIII (2001), 69–89

Panikkar, K. N., T. J. Byres, and U. Patnaik, eds, *The making of history: Essays presented to Irfan Habib* (London, 1985)

Parenti, C., *Tropic of Chaos: Climate change and the new geography of violence* (New York, 2011)

Parker, C. H., *The Reformation of the community: Social welfare and Calvinist charity in Holland, 1572–1640* (Cambridge, 1998)

Parker, D., *Europe's seventeenth-century crisis: A Marxist review* (London, 1973)

Parker, G. *Spain and the Netherlands, 1559–1659. Ten studies* (2nd edn, London, 1990)

Parker, G., *Europe in crisis* (2nd edn, Oxford, 2001)

Parker, G., 'The artillery fortress as an engine of European overseas expansion, 1480–1750', in Parker, *Success is never final: Empire, war and faith in early modern Europe* (New York, 2002), 192–218

Parker, G., 'Crisis and catastrophe: the global crisis of the 17th-century reconsidered', *AHR*, CXIII (2008), 1052–79

Parker, G., *The military revolution. Military innovation and the rise of the West, 1500–1800* (3rd edn, Cambridge, 2008)

Parker, G., 'States make war but wars also break states', *Journal of Military History*, LXXIV (2010), 11–34

Parker, G., 'La crisis de la década de 1590 reconsiderada: Felipe II, sus enemigos y el cambio climático', in A. Marcos Marín, ed., *Libro Homenaje para José Luis Rodríguez de Diego* (Valladolid, 2011), 643–70

Parker, G., ed., *The Thirty Years War* (2nd edn, London, 1996)

Parker, G., ed., *La crisis de la Monarquía de Felipe IV* (Barcelona, 2006)

Parker, G. and L. M. Smith, *The General Crisis of the seventeenth century* (2nd edn, London, 1997)

Parrott, D., *The business of war: Military enterprise and military revolution in early modern Europe* (Cambridge, 2012)

Parry, M. L., 'Climatic change and the agricultural frontier: a research strategy', in Wrigley et al., *Climate and history*, 319–36

Parsons, J. B., 'Attitudes towards Late Ming rebellions', *Oriens Extremus*, VI (1959), 177–91

Parsons, J. B., *The peasant rebellions of the late Ming dynasty* (Tucson, AZ, 1970)

Peacey, J., *Politicians and pamphleteers: Propaganda during the English Civil Wars and Interregnum* (Aldershot, 2004)

Pearl, V., *London and the outbreak of the Puritan revolution: City, government and national politics, 1625–43* (Oxford, 1961)

Peña Díaz, M., 'Aproximación a la climatología en la Catalunya del siglo XVII', in *Primer congrés d'història moderna de Catalunya*, I (Barcelona, 1984), 255–65

Perceval-Maxwell, M., 'Ulster 1641 in the context of political developments in the three kingdoms', in MacCuarta, ed., *Ulster*, 93–106

Perceval-Maxwell, M., *The outbreak of the Irish rebellion of 1641* (Quebec, 1994)

Peiser, B. J., *Natural catastrophes during Bronze Age civilizations* (Oxford, 1998)

Perdue, P. C., 'Water control in the Dongting lake region during the Ming and Qing periods', *JAS*, XLI (1982), 747–65

Perdue, P. C., *Exhausting the earth: State and peasant in Hunan, 1500–1800* (Cambridge, MA, 1987)

Perdue, P. C., *China marches west: The Qing conquest of Central Eurasia* (Cambridge, MA, 2005)

Pérez Moreda, V., *Las crisis de mortalidad en la España interior: siglos XVI–XIX* (Madrid, 1980)

Pérez Moreda, V., 'La peste de 1647–57 en el Mediterraneo occidental', *Boletín de la Asociación de Demografía Histórica*, V (1987), 14–23

Pérez Samper, M. A., *Catalunya i Portugal el 1640: Dos poles en una cruilla* (Barcelona, 1992)

Perkins, D. H., *Agricultural development in China, 1368–1968* (Chicago, 1969)

Pernot, F. and V. Toureille, eds, *Lendemains de Guerre. De l'Antiquité au monde contemporain, les hommes, l'espace et le récit l'économie et le politique* (Brussels, 2010)

Perrenoud, A., *La population de Genève du 16e au début du 19e siècle. Étude démographique* (Geneva, 1979: Mémoires et documents publiés par la société d'histoire et d'archéologie de Genève, XLVII)

Pestana, C. G., *The English Atlantic in an age of revolution, 1640–1661* (Cambridge, MA, 2004)

Peters, K., *Print culture and early Quakers* (Cambridge, 2005)

Peterson, W. J., 'The life of Ku Yen-wu (1613–1682)', *Harvard Journal of Asiatic Studies*, XXVIII (1968), 114–56, and XXIX (1969), 201–47

Peterson, W. J., *Bitter Gourd: Fang I-chih and the impetus for intellectual change* (New Haven and London, 1979)

Pfister, C., *Klimageschichte der Schweiz 1525–1860 und seiner Bedeutung in der Geschichte von Bevolkung und Landwirtschaft*, 2 vols (Bern, 1988)

Pfister, C., *Wetternachhersage. 500 Jahre Klimavariationen und Naturkatastrophen (1496–1995)* (Berlin, 1999)

Pfister, C., 'Documentary evidence', *PAGES-News*, X/3 (December 2002: special issue)

Pfister, C., 'Learning from nature-induced disasters: theoretical considerations and case studies from western Europe", in Mauch and Pfister, eds, *Natural disasters*, 17–40

Pfister, C., 'Little Ice Age-type impacts and the mitigation of social vulnerability to climate in the Swiss canton of Bern prior to 1800', in R. Costanza, L. M. Graumlich and W. Steffen, eds, *Sustainability or collapse? An integrated history and future of people on earth* (Berlin, 2005), 191–208

Pfister, C., 'The vulnerability of past societies to climatic variation: a new focus for historical climatology in the twenty-first century', *CC*, C (2010), 25–31

Pfister, C., 'Weeping in the snow: the second period of Little Ice Age-type impacts, 1570–1630', in Behringer et al., *Kulturelle Konsequenzen der 'Kleinen Eiszeit'*, 31–86

Pfister, C. and R. Brázdil, 'Climatic variability in sixteenth-century Europe and its social dimension: a synthesis', *CC*, XLIII (1999), 5–53

Pflugfelder, G., *Cartographies of desire: Male-male sexuality in Japanese discourse* (Berkeley, 1999)

Pillorget, R., *Les mouvements insurrectionnels de Provence entre 1596 et 1715* (Paris, 1975)

Piqueras García, M. B., 'Cédula de Felipe IV sobre el derecho de la media anata', *Trocadero*, XXI–XXII (2009–10), 165–90

Pitcher, D. E., *An historical geography of the Ottoman empire* (Leiden, 1972)

Piterberg, G., *An Ottoman tragedy: History and historiography at play* (Berkeley, 2003)

Platonov, S. F., 'Novyi istochnik istochnik dlia istorii Moskovskikh volnenii', *Chteniiia v imperatorskom obshchestve istorii i drevnostei Rossiiskikh Moskovskom universitete* (1893/1), 3–19

Plokhy, S., *The Cossacks and religion in early modern Ukraine* (Oxford, 2001)

Plumb, J. H., *The growth of political stability in England, 1675–1725* (London, 1967)

Poelhekke, J. J., *De Vrede van Munster* (The Hague, 1948)

Pokrovskii, N. N., *Tomsk 1648–1649 gg: voevodskaia vlast' i zemskie miry* (Novosibirsk, 1989)

Polišenský, J. V., *The Thirty Years' War* (London, 1971)

Polišenský, J. V., *War and society in Europe 1618–1648* (Cambridge, 1978)

Pollack, H. N., S. Huang and J. E. Smerdon, 'Five centuries of climate change in Australia: the view from underground', *Journal of Quaternary Science*, XXI (2006), 701–6

Polleross, F. B., *Das sakrale Indentifikationsporträt: ein höfischer Bildtypus vom 13. bis zum 20. Jahrhundert*, 2 vols (Vienna, 1988)

Pollock, L., 'Embarking on a rough passage: the experience of pregnancy in early-modern society', in Fildes, ed., *Women as mothers*, 39–67

Pomeranz, K. W., *The Great Divergence: China, Europe, and the making of the modern world economy* (Princeton, 2000)

Pomeranz, K. W., 'Is there an East Asian development path? Long-term comparisons, constraints, and continuities', *JESHO*, XLIV (2001), 322–62

Pomeranz, K. W., 'Without coal? Colonies? Calculus? Counterfactuals and industrialization in Europe and China', in Tetlock et al., eds, *Unmaking the West*, 241–76

Porschnev, B. F., 'Les rapports politiques de l'Europe occidentale et de l'Europe orientale à l'époque de la Guerre de Trente Ans', in *Rapports du XIe Congrès des Sciences Historiques* (Stockholm, 1960), IV, 136–63

Porschnev, B., *Les soulèvements populaires en France avant la Fronde* (Paris, 1963)

Porter, S., *Destruction in the English Civil War* (Gloucester, 1994)

Post, J. D., *The last great subsistence crisis in the Western World* (Baltimore, 1977)

Post, J. D., *Food shortage, climatic variability and epidemic disease in pre-industrial Europe: The mortality peak in the early 1740s* (Ithaca, NY, 1985)

Potter, L., *Secret rites and secret writing: Royalist literature, 1641–1660* (Cambridge, 2009)

Potts, R., *Humanity's descent. The consequences of ecological instability* (New York, 1996)

Prakash, O., *The Dutch East India Company and the economy of Bengal 1630–1720* (Princeton, 1985)

Price, R., ed., *Maroon societies: Rebel slave communities in the Americas* (2nd edn, Baltimore, 1996)

Prieto, M. del R., 'The Paraná river floods during the Spanish colonial period', in Mauch and Pfister, eds, *Natural disasters*, 285–303

Prown, P. C., 'The mismeasurement of land: land surveying in the Tokugawa period', *Monumenta Nipponica*, XLII (1987), 115–55

Przybylak, R. et al., 'Temperature changes in Poland from the sixteenth to the twentieth centuries', *IJC*, XXV (2005), 773–91

Pullan, B. S., *Rich and poor in Renaissance Venice: The social institutions of a Catholic state, to 1620* (Oxford, 1971)

Pullan, B. S., *Orphans and foundlings in early modern Europe* (Reading, 1989)

Pursell, B., *The Winter King: Frederick V of the Palatinate and the coming of the Thirty YearsWar* (Aldershot, 2002)

Raba, J., *Between remembrance and denial: The fate of the Jews in the wars of the Polish Commonwealth during the mid-seventeenth century as shown in contemporary writing and historical research* (Boulder, CO: East European Monographs, CDXXVIII, 1995)

Rabb, T. K., *The struggle for stability in early modern Europe* (Oxford, 1975)

Rabb, T. K., 'The Scientific Revolution and the problem of periodization', *European Review*, XV (2007), 503–12

Rabb, T. K., 'Introduction: the persistence of the "Crisis"', *JIH*, XL (2009), 145–50

Rabb, T. K., *The artist and the warrior: Military history through the eyes of the Masters* (New Haven and London, 2011)

Radkau, J., *Nature and power: A global history of the environment* (Cambridge, 2008)

Ransel, D., *Mothers of misery: Child abandonment in Russia* (Princeton, 1988)

Ranum, O., *Richelieu and the councillors of Louis XIII* (Oxford, 1963)

Ranum, O., *The Fronde: A French revolution, 1648–1652* (New York, 1993)

Ranum, O., *Paris in the Age of Absolutism: An essay* (2nd edn, University Park, PA, 2002)

Rawski, E. S., *Education and popular literacy in Ch'ing China* (Ann Arbor, 1979)

Rawski, E. S., *The last emperors: A social history of Qing imperial institutions* (Berkeley, 2001)

Rawski, E. S., 'The Qing formation and the early-modern period', in Struve, ed., *Qing formation*, 207–41

Rawski, E. S. and J. Rawson, eds, *China: The Three Emperors, 1662–1795* (London, 2005)

Raychaudhuri, T. and I. Habib, eds, *The Cambridge economic history of India*, I (Cambridge, 1982)

Raymond, J., *The invention of the newspaper: English newsbooks 1641–1649* (Oxford, 1996)

Raynor, H., *A social history of music* (London, 1972)

Razzell, P., 'Did smallpox reduce height?', *EcHR*, LI (1997), 351–9, and LIV (2001), 108–9

Reade, H. G. R., *Sidelights on the Thirty Years' War*, 3 vols (London, 1924)

Reay, B., *The Quakers and the English Revolution* (London, 1985)

Redondo, P., *Galileo: Heretic* (Princeton, 1987)

Reece, H. M., 'The military presence in England, 1649–1660' (Oxford University D. Phil. thesis, 1981)

Reff, D. T., 'Contact shock in northwestern New Spain, 1518–1764', in J. W. Verano and D. H. Uberlaker, eds, *Disease and demography in the Americas* (Washington, DC, 1992), 265–76

Reger, W., 'In the service of the Tsar: European mercenary officers and the reception of military reform in Russia, 1654–1667' (University of Illinois PhD thesis, 1997)

Reher, D. S., 'Castilla y la crisis del siglo XVII: contextos demográficos para un ajuste de larga duración', in E. Martínez Ruíz, ed., *Madrid, Felipe II y las ciudades de la Monarquía*, II (Madrid, 2000), 347–74

Reid, A. R., 'The crisis of the seventeenth century in southeast Asia', in Parker and Smith, eds, *The General Crisis*, 206–34

Reid, A. R., *Southeast Asia in the age of commerce, 1450–1680*, 2 vols (New Haven, 1988–93)

Reis Torgal, L., *Ideologia política e teoria do estado na Restauração*, 2 vols (Coimbra, 1981–2)

Repgen, K., 'Über die Geschichtsschreibung des Dreisigjährigen Krieges: Begriff und Konzeption', in Repgen, ed., *Krieg und Politik, 1618–1648*, 1–84

Repgen, K., ed., *Krieg und Politik, 1618–1648. Europäische Probleme und Perspektiven* (Munich, 1988)

Reula i Biescas, J., '1640–1647: una aproximació a la publicística de la guerra dels segadors', *Pedralbes: revista d'historia moderna*, XI (1991), 91–108

Révah, I. S., *Le Cardinal Richelieu et la Restauration du Portugal* (Lisbon, 1950)

Ribot García, L. A., *La revuelta antiespañola de Mesina. Causas y antecedentes (1591–1674)* (Valladolid 1982)

Ribot García, L. A., 'La época del conde-duque de Olivares y el reino de Sicilia', in Elliott and García Sanz, eds, *La España del Conde Duque*, 655–77

Ribot García, L. A., *La Monarquía de España y la guerra de Mesina (1674–1678)* (Madrid, 2002)

Richards, J., *The Mughal empire* (Cambridge, 1993)

Richards, J., *The unending frontier: An environmental history of the early modern world* (Berkeley, 2003)

Riches, D., *The anthropology of violence* (Oxford, 1986)

Richter, D. K., 'War and culture: the Iroquois experience', *WMQ*, 3rd series, XL (1983), 528–59

Richter, D. K., *The ordeal of the Longhouse: The peoples of the Iroquois League in the era of European colonization* (Chapel Hill, NC, 1992)

Richter, D. K., *Facing East from Indian Country: A native history of early America* (Cambridge, 2001)

Rind, D., and J. Overpeck, 'Hypothesized causes of decade-to-century scale climate variability: climate model results', *Quaternary Science Review*, XII (1993), 357–74

Ringrose, D. R., *Madrid and the Spanish economy, 1560–1850* (Berkeley, 1983)

Riquer i Permanyer, B. de, ed., *Encyclopèdia Catalana: Historia política, societat i cultura dels paisos Catalans* (Barcelona, 1997)

Rivero Rodríguez, M., 'Técnica de un golpe de estado: el inquisidor García de Trasmiera en la revuelta siciliana de 1647', in F. J. Aranda Pérez, ed., *La declinación de la Monarquía hispánica* (Madrid, 2004: VIIa Reunión de la Fundación Española de Historia Moderna), 129–53

Rizzo, M., 'University, administration, taxation and society in Italy in the sixteenth century: the case of fiscal exemptions for the University of Pavia', in *History of Universities*, VIII (1989), 75–116

Rizzo, M., 'Un economia in guerra: Pavia nel 1655', *Annali di storia pavese*, XXVII (1999), 339–60

Rizzo, M., '"Haver sempre l'occhio all'abbondanza dei viveri". Il governo dell'economia pavese durante l'assedio del 1655', in A. M. Bernal, L. de Rosa and F. D'Esposito, eds, *El gobierno de la economía en el imperio español* (Seville and Naples, 2000), 471–507

Rizzo, M., *Alloggiamenti militari e riforme fiscali nella Lombardia spagnola tra cinque e seicento* (Milan, 2001)

Rizzo, M., '"Ottima gente da guerra". Cremonesi al servizio della strategia imperiale', in G. Politi, ed., *Storia di Cremona. L'età degli Asburgo di Spagna (1535–1707)* (Cremona, 2006), 126–45

Rizzo, M., '"Rivoluzione dei consumi", "state-building" e "Rivoluzione militare". La domanda e l'offerta di servizi strategici nella Lombardia spagnola, 1535–1659', in I. Lopane and E. Ritrovato, eds, *Tra vecchi e nuovi equilibri economici. Domanda e offerta di servizi in Italia in età moderna e contemporanea* (Bari, 2007), 447–74

Rizzo, M., 'Influencia social, conveniencia económica, estabilidad política y eficiencia estratégica. Notables lombardos al servicio de los Habsburgo en la segunda mitad del siglo XVI', in J. F. Pardo Molero and M. Lomas Cortés, eds, *Oficiales reales. Los ministros de la Monarquía Catolica (siglos XVI–XVII)* (forthcoming)

Rizzo, M., J. J. Ruiz Ibáñez and G. Sabatini, eds, *Le forze del príncipe. Recursos, instrumentos y límites en la práctica del poder soberano en los territorios de la Monarquía Hispánica*, 2 vols (Murcia, 2003)

Roberts, M., 'Queen Christina and the General Crisis of the seventeenth century', in Aston, ed., *Crisis in Europe*, 195–221

Roberts, M., *Sweden as a Great Power 1611–1697: Government, society, foreign policy* (London, 1968)

Roberts, M., *The Swedish imperial experience, 1560–1718* (Cambridge, 1979)

Robinson, D. M., *Bandits, eunuchs and the Son of Heaven: Rebellion and the economy of violence in mid-Ming China* (Honolulu, 2001)

Robinson, J. H., *The great comet of 1680: A study in the history of rationalism* (Northfield, MN, 1916)

Robisheaux, T., *Rural society and the search for order in early modern Germany* (Cambridge, 1989)

Rodén, M. L., 'The crisis of the seventeenth century: the Nordic perspective', in Benedict and Gutmann, eds, *Early modern Europe*, 100–19

Rodger, N. A. M., *The safeguard of the sea: A naval history of Britain, 1660–1649* (London, 1997)

Rodger, N. A. M., *The command of the ocean: A naval history of Britain, 1649–1815* (London, 2004)

Rodrigo, F. S. et al., 'On the use of the Jesuit private correspondence records in climate reconstructions: a case study from Castile (Spain) for 1634–1648', *CC*, XL (1998), 625–45

Rohrschneider, M., *Der gescheiterte Frieden von Münster: Spaniens Ringen mit Frankreich auf dem Westfälischen Friedenskongress (1643–1649)* (Münster, 2007: Schriftenreihe der Vereinigung zur Erforschung der neueren Geschichte, XXX)

Romaniello, M. P., 'Controlling the frontier: monasteries and infrastructure in the Volga region, 1552–1682', *Central Asian Survey*, XIX (2000), 429–43

Romaniello, M. P., 'Ethnicity as social rank: governance, law and empire in Muscovite Russia', *Nationalities Papers*, XXXIV (2006), 447–69

Romaniello, M. P., 'Through the filter of tobacco: the limits of global trade in the early modern world', *CSSH*, XLIX (2007), 914–37

Romano, R., *Conjonctures opposées. La crise du 17e siècle en Europe et en Amérique latine* (Geneva, 1992)

Rommelse, G., 'The role of mercantilism in Anglo-Dutch political relations, 1650–1674', *EcHR*, LXIII (2010), 591–611

Ronan, C. A., *Edmond Halley: Genius in eclipse* (New York, 1969)

Roper, L., *Witch craze: Terror and fantasy in Baroque Germany* (New Haven, 2004)

Rosental, Paul-André, 'The novelty of an old genre: Louis Henry and the founding of historical demography', *Population (English)*, LVIII/1 (2003), 97–130

Rossi, P., 'The scientist', in Villari, ed., *Baroque personae*, 263–89

Roth, G., 'The Manchu-Chinese relationship, 1618–1636', in Spence and Wills, eds, *From Ming to Ch'ing*, 4–38

Roupnel, G., *La ville et la campagne au XVIIe siècle: étude sur les populations du pays dijonnais* (2nd edn, Paris, 1955)

Rovito, P. L., 'Le rivoluzione constitutionale di Napoli (1647–48)', *Rivista storica italiana*, XCVII (1986), 367–462

Rowen, H. H., *The Low Countries in early modern times* (New York, 1972)

Rowland, D. B., 'Moscow – the Third Rome or the New Israel', *Russian Review*, LV (1996), 591–614

Roy, V. N., D. Shulman and S. Subrahmanyam, *Symbol of substance: Court and state in Nâyaka-period Tamil Nadu* (Delhi, 1992)

Rublack, U., *The crimes of women in early modern Germany* (Oxford, 1999)

Ruíz Ibañez, J. J., *Las dos caras de Jano. Monarquía, ciudad e individuo. Murcia, 1588–1648* (Murcia, 1995)

Ruppert, K., *Die kaiserliche Politik auf dem Westfälischen Friedenskongress (1643–1648)* (Münster, 1979: Schriftenreihe der Vereinigung zur Erforschung der neueren Geschichte, X)

Russell, C., 'The British problem and the English Civil War', *History*, LXXII (1987), 395–415

Russell, C., *The fall of the British monarchies, 1637–1642* (Oxford, 1991)

Saitō Osamu, 'The frequency of famines as demographic correctives in the Japanese past', in Dyson and Ó Gráda, eds, *Famine demography*, 218–39

Salisbury, N., *Manitou and Providence: Indians, Europeans and the making of New England, 1500–1643* (Oxford, 1982)

Sallmann, J.-M., *Naples et ses Saints à l'âge baroque (1540–1750)* (Paris, 1994)

Salm, H., *Armeefinanzierung im Dreissigjährigen Krieg. Die Niederrheinisch-Westfälische Reichskreis, 1635–1650* (Münster, 1990: Schriftenreihe der Vereinigung zur Erforschung der neueren Geschichte, XVI)

Salmon, J. H. M., *The French religious wars in English political thought* (Oxford, 1959)

Sanabre, J., *La acción de Francia en Cataluña en la pugna por la hegemonía de Europa (1640–1659)* (Barcelona, 1956)

Sandberg, B., *Warrior pursuits: Noble culture and civil conflict in early modern France* (Baltimore, 2010)

Sanderson, M., *The history of the University of East Anglia 1918–2000* (London, 2002)

Sansom, G., *A history of Japan, 1615–1867* (Stanford, 1963)

Santoro, M., *Le secentine napoletane della Biblioteca Nazionale di Napoli* (Rome, 1986)

Sanz Camañes, P., *Política, hacienda y milicia en el Aragón de los últimos Austrias entre 1640 y 1680* (Zaragoza, 1997).

Sargent, T. J. and F. R. Velde, *The big problem of small change* (Princeton, 2002)

Sasaki Junnosuke, *Daimyô to hyakushô* (Tokyo, 1966)

Sasaki Junnosuke and R. Toby, 'The changing rationale of daimyo control in the emergence of the bakuhan state', in Hall et al., eds, *Japan before Tokugawa*, 271–94

Schaffer, S., *The information order of Isaac Newton's* Principia Mathematica (Uppsala, 2008)

Schama, S. M., *The embarrassment of riches: An interpretation of Dutch Culture in the Golden Age* (New York, 1987)

Schaub, J. F., *Le Portugal au temps du comte-duc d'Olivares (1621–1640). Le conflit de juridictions comme exercice de la politique* (Madrid, 2002)

Schaufler, H. H., *Die Schlacht bei Freiburg im Breisgau* (Freiburg, 1979)

Schiebinger, L., *Plants and empire: Colonial bioprospecting in the Atlantic world* (Cambridge, MA, 2004)

Schilfert, G., 'Zur Geschichte der Auswirkungen der englischen bürgerlichen Revolution auf Nordwestdeutschland', in F. Klein and J. Streisand, eds, *Beiträge zum neuer Geschichtsbild, zum 60. Geburtstag von Alfred Meusel* (Berlin, 1956), 247–57

Schilling, H., 'Confessional Europe', in T. A. Brady, H. A. Oberman and J. D. Tracy, eds, *Handbook of European History, 1400–1600*, 2 vols (Cambridge, 1995), II, 641–81

Schmidt, P., *Spanische Universalmonarchie oder "teutsche Libertet". Das spanische Imperium in der Propaganda des Dreissigjährigen Krieges* (Stuttgart, 2001: Studien zur modernen Geschichte, LIV)

Schoffeleers, J. M., *River of blood: The genesis of a martyr cult in Southern Malawi, circa A.D. 1600* (Madison, 1992)

Scholem, G., *Sabbatai Sevi: The mystical Messiah, 1626–1676* (Princeton, 1973)

Schüller, K., *Die Beziehungen zwischen Spanien und Irland im 16. und 17. Jahrhundert. Diplomatie, Handel und die soziale Integration katholischer Exulanten* (Münster, 1999)

Schumpeter, J. A., *Capitalism, socialism and democracy* (1942; ed. R. Swedberg, London, 2003)

Schwartz, S. B., 'Panic in the Indies: the Portuguese threat to the Spanish empire' in Thomas and de Groof, eds, *Rebelión y resistencia*, 205–17

Schwartz, S. B., 'Silver, sugar and slaves: how the empire restored Portugal' (EUI conference paper, 2003)

Scott, D., *Politics amd war in the three Stuart kingdoms, 1637–1649* (Basingstoke, 2004)

Scott, H. M., ed., *The European nobilities of the 17th and 18th centuries*, 2 vols (London, 1995)

Scott, J., *Love and protest: Chinese poems from the sixth century AD to the seventeenth century AD* (London, 1972)

Scott, J., *England's troubles: Seventeenth-century English political instability in European context* (Cambridge, 2000)

Scott, J. C., *The moral economy of the peasant: Rebellion and resistance in Southeast Asia* (New Haven, 1976)

Scott, J. C., *Weapons of the weak: Everyday forms of peasant resistance* (New Haven, 1985)

Scott, J. C., *Domination and the arts of resistance: Hidden transcripts* (New Haven, 1990)

Scott, J. C., *Seeing like a state: How certain schemes to improve the human condition have failed* (New Haven, 1998)

Seaver, P. S., *Wallington's world: A Puritan artisan in seventeenth-century London* (Stanford, 1985)

Seed, P., *To love, honor and obey in colonial Mexico: Conflicts over marriage choice, 1574–1821* (Stanford, 1988)

Séguy, J., 'L'enquête sur la population de la France de 1500 à 1700 (J.-N. Biraben): présentation, sources, bibliographie', *Population*, LIII (1998), 181–213

Sella, D., *Crisis and continuity: The economy of Spanish Lombardy in the seventeenth century* (Cambridge, MA, 1979)

Sella, D., 'The survival of the urban economies of central and northern Italy in the seventeenth century: recent studies and new perspectives', *Journal of Mediterranean Studies*, X (2000), 275–85

Sella, D., 'Peasant strategies for survival in northern Italy, XVI–XVII centuries', *JEEH*, XXXVII/2–3 (2008), 455–69

Sen, A. K., *Poverty and famines: An essay on entitlement and deprivation* (Oxford, 1981)

Séré, D., 'La paix des Pyrénées ou la paix du roi: le rôle méconnu de Philippe IV dans la restauration de la paix entre l'Espagne et la France', *Revue d'histoire diplomatique*, CXIX (2005), 243–61

Séré, D., *La Paix des Pyrénées. Vingt-quatre ans de négociations entre la France et l'Espagne, 1635–1659* (Paris, 2007)

Serra i Puig, E., *La revolució catalana de 1640* (Barcelona, 1991)

Setton, K. M., *Venice, Austria and the Turks in the seventeenth century* (Philadelphia, 1991)

Shagan, E., 'Constructing discord: ideology, propaganda and English responses to the Irish rebellion of 1641', *Journal of British Studies*, XXXVI (1997), 4–34

Shannon, A., '"Uncouth language to a princes ears": Archibald Armstrong, court jester, and early Stuart politics', *SCJ*, XLII (2011), 99–112

Sharpe, K., *The personal rule of Charles I* (New Haven, 1992)

Shaw, D. J. B., 'Southern frontiers of Muscovy, 1550–1700', in J. H. Bater and R. A. French, eds, *Studies in Russian Historical Geography*, I (London, 1983), 117–42

Shaw, S. J., *History of the Ottoman empire and modern Turkey*, 2 vols (Cambridge, 1976–7)

Shennan, J. H., *The Parlement of Paris* (London, 1968)

Sherratt, A., 'Climatic cycles and behavioural revolutions: the emergence of modern humans and the beginning of farming', *Antiquity*, LXXI (1997), 271–87

Shi Yafeng and Liu Shiyin, 'Estimation of the response of glaciers in China to the global warming in the twenty-first century', *Chinese Science Bulletin*, XLV (2000), 668–72

Shindell, D. T., 'Volcanic and solar forcing of climate change during the Preindustrial Era', *Journal of Climate Change*, XVI (2003), 4,094–4,107

Shiue, C. H., 'Local granaries and central government disaster relief: moral hazard and interregional finance in eighteenth- and nineteenth-century China', *Journal of Economic History*, LXIV (2004), 100–24

Shiveley, D. H., 'Sumptuary regulation and status in early Tokugawa Japan', *Harvard Journal of Asiatic Studies*, XXV (1964–5), 123–64

Shy, J., *A people numerous and armed: Reflections on the military struggle for American independence* (2nd edn, Oxford, 1990)

SIDES, *see* Società italiana di demografia storica

Signorotto, G., *Milano spagnola. Guerra, istituzioni, uomini di governo (1635–1660)* (Florence, 1996)

Signorotto, G., 'Stabilità politica e trame antispagnole nella Milano del Seicento', in Y. Bercé and E. Fasano Guarini, *Complots et conjurations dans l'Europe moderne* (Rome, 1996), 721–45

Silke, J. J., 'Primate Lombard and James I', *Irish Theological Quarterly*, XXII (1955), 143–55

Simas Bettencourt Amorim, M. N., *Guimarães de 1580 a 1819. Estudo demográfico* (Lisbon, 1987)

Simón i Tarrés, A., 'Catalunya en el siglo XVII. La revuelta campesina y popular de 1640', *Estudi general I. Col.legi Universitari de Girona*, I (1981), 137–47

Simón i Tarrés, A., 'Els anys 1627–32 i la crisi del segle XVII a Catalunya', *Estudis d'Història Agrària*, IX (1992), 157–80

Simón i Tarrés, A., *Els orígens ideològics de la revolució catalana de 1640* (Barcelona, 1999)

Singer, R. T., *Edo art in Japan 1615–1868* (Washington, DC, 1998)

Singh, C., *Region and empire: Panjab in the seventeenth century* (Delhi, 1991)

Skinner, G. W., 'Marketing and social structure in rural China', *JAS*, XXIV (1964), 3–43, XXV (1965), 195–228 and 363–99

Skinner, G. W., 'Cities and the hierarchy of local systems', in Skinner, ed., *The city in late imperial China* (Stanford, 1977), 275–352

Skinner, Q. R. D., 'Conquest and consent: Hobbes and the Engagement controversy' in Skinner, *Visions of politics*, III, 287–307

Skinner, Q. R. D., 'The ideological context of Hobbes's political thought', in Skinner, *Visions of politics*, III, 264–86

Skinner, Q. R. D., *Visions of politics*, 3 vols (Cambridge, 2002)

Slack, P., *The impact of the plague in Tudor and Stuart England* (London, 1985)

Slotkin, R. and J. K. Folsom, eds, *So dreadful a judgement: Puritan responses to King Philip's War, 1676–1677* (Middletown, CT, 1978)

Slovic, P., 'The perception of risk', *Science*, NS, CCXXXVI (1987), 280–5

Slovic, P., *The perception of risk* (London, 2000)

Smith, D. L., 'Catholic, Anglican or Puritan? Edward Sackville, fourth earl of Dorset and the ambiguities of religion in early Stuart England', *TRHistS*, 6th series, II (1992), 105–24

Smith, J. H., 'Benevolent societies: the reshaping of charity during the late Ming and early Ch'ing', *JAS*, XLVI (1987), 309–37

Smith, J. H., *The art of doing good: Charity in late Ming China* (Berkeley, 2009)

Smith, R. E. F., *Peasant farming in Muscovy* (Cambridge, 1977)

Smith, S. R., 'Almost Revolutionaries: the London apprentices during the Civil Wars', *Huntington Library Quarterly*, XLII (1978–9), 313–28

Smith, T. C., *The agrarian origins of modern Japan* (Stanford, 1959)

Smith, T. C., *Nakahara: Family farming and population in a Japanese village, 1717–1830* (Stanford, 1977)

Smuts, R. M., ed., *The Stuart court and Europe: Essays in politics and political culture* (Cambridge, 1996)

Snapper, F., *Oorlogsinvloeden op de overzeese handel van Holland 1551–1719* (Amsterdam, 1959)

Snobelen, S. D., ' "A time and times and the dividing of time": Isaac Newton, the Apocalypse, and 2060 A.D.', *Canadian Journal of History* (Dec. 2003)

Soares da Cunha, M., *A casa de Bragança, 1560–1640: práticas senhoriais e redes clientalares* (Lisbon, 2000)

Società italiana di demografia storica [SIDES], *La popolazione italiana nel '600* (Bologna, 1999)

Solano Camón, E., *Poder monárquico y estado pactista (1626–52): los aragoneses ante la Unión de Armas* (Zaragoza, 1987)

Solar, P. M., 'Poor relief and English economic development before the industrial revolution', *EcHR*, XLVIII (1995), 1–22

Soll, J., 'Accounting for Government: Holland and the rise of political economy in seventeenth-century Europe', *JIH*, XL (2009), 215–38

Soll, J., *The information master: Jean-Baptiste Colbert's Secret State Intelligence System* (Ann Arbor, 2009)

Solomon, H. M., *Public welfare, science and propaganda in seventeenth-century France: The innovations of Théophraste Renaudot* (Princeton, 1972)

Soman, A., *Sorcellerie et justice criminelle (16e–18e siècles)* (Guildford, 1992)

Sparmann, E., *Dresden während des 30-jährigen Krieges* (Leipzig, 1914)

Spence, J. D., *Ts'ao-Yin and the K'ang-hsi emperor: Bondservant and master* (New Haven and London, 1966)

Spence, J. D., *Emperor of China: Self-portrait of K'ang-hsi* (New York, 1974)

Spence, J. D., *The death of Woman Wang: Rural life in China in the seventeenth century* (London, 1978)

Spence, J. D. and J. E. Wills, eds, *From Ming to Ch'ing: Conquest, region, and continuity in seventeenth-century China* (New Haven, 1979)

Sperling, J., *Convents and the body politic in late Renaissance Venice* (Chicago, 1999)

Spooner, F., 'From hoards to safe havens: some transfers abroad in the seventeenth and eighteenth centuries', *JEEH* XXXIV (2005), 601–24

Spörer, G. F. W., *Üeber die Periodicitätder sonnenflecken seit dem Jahre 1618* (Halle, 1889)

Spufford, M., 'First steps in literacy: the reading and writing experiences of the humblest 17th-century Spiritual autobiographers', *Social History*, IV (1979), 405–35

Sreenivasan, G. P., *The peasants of Ottobeuren, 1487–1726: A rural society in early modern Europe* (Cambridge, 2004)

Stade, A., ed., *Carl X Gustaf och Danmark* (Stockholm, 1965)

Stahle, D. W. et al., 'The Lost Colony and Jamestown droughts', *Science*, CCLXXX (1998), 564–7

Stahle, D. W. et al., 'Tree-ring data document 16th-century megadrought over North America', *EOS*, 81/12 (March 21, 2000), 121–5

Stampfer, S., 'Maps of Jewish settlements in Ukraine in 1648', *Jewish History*, XVII/2 (2003), 107–14

Stampfer, S., 'What actually happened to the Jews of Ukraine in 1648?', *Jewish History*, XVII/2 (2003), 207–27

Starna, W. A., 'The Pequots in the early seventeenth century', in Hauptman and Wherry, eds, *The Pequots*, 33–47

Statler, O., *Japanese Inn* (New York, 1961)

Steckel, R. H., 'New light on the "Dark Ages": the remarkably tall stature of northern european men during the medieval era', *Social Science History*, XXVIII (2004), 211–30

Steensgaard, N., 'The seventeenth-century crisis', in Parker and Smith, *The General Crisis*, 32–56

Steinman, P., *Bauer und Ritter in Mecklenburg. Wandlungen der gutsherrlich-bäuerlichen Verhältnisse im Westen und Osten Mecklenburgs von 12/13 Jahrhundert bis zur Bodenreform 1945* (Schwerin, 1960)

Stepto, G., ed., *Lieutenant Nun: Memoir of a Basque transvestite in the New World. Catalina de Erauso* (Boston, 1996)

Stevens, C. B., *Soldiers on the steppe: Army reform and social change in early modern Russia* (Dekalb, IL, 1995)

Stevens, C. B., *Russia's wars of emergence, 1460–1730* (London, 2007)

Stevenson, D., 'Deposition of ministers in the church of Scotland under the Covenanters 1638–51', *Church History*, XLIV (1975), 321–35

Stevenson, D., *King or Covenant? Voices from the Civil War* (East Linton, 1996)

Stolp, A., *De eerste couranten in Holland. Bijdrage tot de geschiedenis der geschreven nieuwstijdingen* (Haarlem, 1938)

Stommel, H. and E., *Volcano weather: The story of 1816, the year without a summer* (Newport, RI 1983)

Stoyle, M. J., '"Whole streets converted to ashes": property destruction in Exeter during the English Civil War', *Southern History*, XVI (1994), 62–81

Stoyle, M. J., '"Pagans" or "paragons"? Images of the Cornish in the English Civil War', *EHR*, CXI (1996), 299–323

Stoyle, M. J., '"Memories of the maimed": the testimony of Charles I's former soldiers, 1660–1730', *History*, LXXXVIII (2003), 204–26

Stoyle, M. J., 'Remembering the English Civil War', in P. Gray and K. Oliver, eds, *The memory of catastrophe* (Manchester, 2004), 19–30

Stradling, R. A., *Spain's struggle for Europe, 1598–1668* (London, 1994)

Straub, E., *Pax et Imperium. Spaniens Kampf um seine Friedensordnung in Europa zwischen 1617 und 1635* (Paderborn, 1980)

Struve, L. A., *The Southern Ming, 1644–1662* (New Haven, 1984)

Struve, L. A., *Time, temporality, and Imperial transition: East Asia from Ming to Qing (Asian Interactions and Comparisons)* (Honolulu, 2002)

Struve, L. A., 'Dreaming and self-search during the Ming collapse: the Xue Xiemeng Biji, 1642–1646', *T'oung Pao*, XCIII (2007), 159–92

Struve, L. A., ed., *The Qing formation in world-historical time* (Cambridge, MA, 2004)

Sturdy, D., 'La révolte irlandaise (1641–1650)', *Revue d'histoire diplomatique*, XCII (1978), 51–70

Suárez, M., 'La "crisis del siglo XVII" en la región andina', in M. Burga, ed., *Historia de América Andina. Formación y apogeo del sistema colonial*, II (Quito, 2000), 289–317

Suárez, M., *Desafíos transatlánticos. Mercaderes, banqueros y estado en Perú virreinal 1600–1700* (Lima, 2001)

Subrahmanyam, S., *The Portuguese empire in Asia, 1500–1700: A political and economic history* (London, 1993)

Subrahmanyam, S., ed., *Money and the market in India, 1100–1700* (Delhi, 1994)

Subrahmanyam, S., 'Hearing voices: vignettes of early modernity in South Asia, 1400–1750', *Daedalus*, CXXVII.3 (1998), 75–104

Subrahmanyam, S., *Explorations in connected history: Mughals and Franks* (Oxford, 2005)

Subrahmanyam, S., 'A tale of three empires: Mughals, Ottomans and Habsburgs in a comparative context', *Common Knowledge*, XII.1 (2006), 66–92

Subtelny, O., *The domination of eastern Europe: Native nobilities and foreign absolutism, 1500–1715* (Montreal, 1986)

Supple, B. E., *Commercial crisis and change in England, 1600–1642* (Cambridge, 1959)

Suter, A., *Der schweizerische Bauernkrieg von 1653. Politische Sozialgeschichte – Sozialgeschichte eines politischen Ereignisses* (Tübingen, 1997)

Sutherland, W., *Taming the wild field: Colonization and empire on the Russian steppe* (Ithaca, NY, 2004)

Suvanto, P., *Wallenstein und seine Anhänger am Wiener Hof zur Zeit des zweiten Generalats, 1631–1634* (Helsinki, 1963)

Symcox, G., ed., *War, diplomacy and imperialism, 1618–1763* (London, 1974)

Sysyn, F. E., 'Ukrainian-Polish relations in the seventeenth century: the role of national consciousness and national conflict in the Khmelnytsky movement', in P. J. Potichnyj, ed., *Poland and Ukraine: Past and present* (Edmonton, 1980), 58–82

Sysyn, F. E., *Between Poland and the Ukraine: The dilemma of Adam Kysil, 1600–1653* (Cambridge, MA, 1985)

Sysyn, F. E., 'Ukrainian social tensions before the Khmel'nyts'kyi uprising', in S. H. Baron and N. S. Kollmann, eds, *Religion and culture in early modern Russia and Ukraine* (Dekalb, IL, 1997), 52–70

Sysyn, F. E., 'The Khmel'nyts'kyi Uprising: a characterization of the Ukrainian revolt', *Jewish History*, XVII (2003), 115–39

't Hart, M., *The making of a bourgeois state: War, politics and finance during the Dutch Revolt* (Manchester, 1993)

't Hart, M., 'The United Provinces, 1579–1806', in R. Bonney, ed., *The rise of the fiscal state in Europe, c. 1200–1815* (Oxford, 1999), ch. 9

T'ien Ju-K'ang, *Male anxiety and female chastity: A comparative study of Chinese ethical values in Ming-Ch'ing times* (Leiden, 1988)

Tacke, A., 'Mars, the enemy of art: Sandrart's *Teutsche Academie* and the impact of war on art and artists', in Bussmann and Schilling, eds, *1648*, II, 245–52

Talbot, M., 'Ore italiane: the reckoning of the time of day in pre-Napoleonic Italy', *Italian Studies*, XL (1985), 51–62

Tashiro Kazui, 'Tsushima Han's Korean trade, 1684–1710', *Acta Asiatica*, XXX (1976), 85–105

Tashiro Kazui, 'Foreign relations during the Edo period: *Sakoku* re-examined', *JJS*, VIII (1982), 283–306

Taulis M.E., *De la distribution des pluies au Chili. La périodicité des pluies depuis 400 ans* (Geneva, 1934: Matériaux pour l'étude des calamités publiés par les soins de la Société de Géographie de Genève, XXXIII/1), 3–20

Tawney, R. H., *Land and labor in China* (London, 1932)

Tazbir, J., 'La polonisation du catholicisme après le concile de Trente', *Memorie domenicane*, new series, IV (1973), 217–40

Te Brake, W., *Shaping history: Ordinary people in European politics 1500–1700* (Berkeley, 1998)

Telford, T. A., 'Fertility and population growth in the lineages of Tongcheng County, 1520–1661', in Harrell, ed., *Chinese historical micro-demography*, 48–93

Teodoreanu, E., 'Preliminary observations on the Little Ice Age in Romania', *Present Environment and Sustainable Development*, V (2011), 187–94

Terzioğlu, D., 'Sufi and dissident in the Ottoman empire: Niyāzī-i Mişri (1618–94)' (Harvard University PhD thesis, 1999)

Tetlock, P. E., R. N. Le Bow and G. Parker, eds, *Unmaking the West: 'What-If? Scenarios that rewrite world history* (Ann Arbor, 2006)

Tezcan, B., 'Searching for Osman: a reassessment of the deposition of the Ottoman Sultan Osman (1618–1622)' (Princeton University PhD thesis, 2001)

Theibault, J. C., 'The rhetoric of death and destruction in the Thirty Years War', *Journal of Social History*, XXVII/2 (1993), 271–90

Theibault, J. C., 'Jeremiah in the village: prophecy, preaching, pamphlets and penance in the Thirty Years' War', *Central European History*, XXVII (1994), 441–60

Theibault, J. C., *German villages in crisis: Rural life in Hesse-Kassel and the Thirty Years War, 1580–1720* (Atlantic Highlands, NJ, 1995)

Theibault, J. C., 'The demography of the Thirty Years War revisited: Günther Franz and his critics', *German History*, XV (1997), 1–21

Thirsk, J., 'Agricultural policy: public debate and legislation, 1640–1750', in Thirsk, *The agrarian history of England and Wales. V. 1640–1700*, 2 vols (Cambridge, 1985), II, 298–388

Thomas, K. V., *Religion and the decline of magic: Studies in popular belief in 16th- and 17th-century England* (London, 1971)

Thomas, W. and B. de Groof, eds, *Rebelión y resistencia de el mundo hispánico del siglo XVII* (Louvain, 1992)

Thompson, I. A. A., 'Alteraciones granadinos: el motín de 1648 a la luz de un nuevo testimonio presencial', in Castellanos, ed., *Homenaje*, II, 799–812

Thompson, I. A. A. and B. Yun Casalilla, eds, *The Castilian crisis of the seventeenth century* (Cambridge, 1994)

Thorndycraft, V. R., et al., 'The catastrophic floods of AD 1617 in Catalonia (northeast Spain) and their climatic context', *Hydrological Sciences Journal*, LI (2006), 899–912

Thornton, J. K., 'Demography and history in the kingdom of Kongo, 1550–1750', *Journal of African History*, XVIII (1977), 507–30

Thornton, J. K., *The kingdom of Kongo: Civil war and transition 1641–1718* (Madison, 1983)

Thornton, J. K., *Warfare in Atlantic Africa, 1500–1800* (London, 1999)

Thornton, J. K., 'Warfare, slave trading and European influence: Atlantic Africa 1450–1800', in J. M. Black, ed., *War in the early modern world, 1450–1815* (London, 1999), 129–46

Thurow, L. C., *The zero-sum society: Redistribution and the possibilities for economic change* (New York, 1981)

Toby, R. P., 'Reopening the question of *sakoku*: diplomacy in the legitimation of the Tokugawa bakufu', *JJS*, III (1977), 323–63

Toby R. P., *State and diplomacy in early modern Japan* (Princeton, 1984)

Tokugawa, Tsunenari, *The Edo Inheritance* (Tokyo, 2009)

Tong, J. W., *Disorder under heaven: Collective violence in the Ming dynasty* (Stanford, 1991)

Torke, H. J., *Die staatsbedingte Gesellschaft im Moskauer Reich. Zar und Zemlja in der altrussischen Herrschaftsverfassung, 1613–1689* (Leiden, 1974)

Torres Sanz, X., *Nyerros i cadells. Bàndols i bandolerisme a la catalunya moderna (1590–1640)* (Barcelona, 1993)

Totman, C., 'Tokugawa peasants: win, lose or draw?', *Monumenta Nipponica*, XLI (1986), 457–76

Totman, C., *The green archipelago: Forestry in pre-industrial Japan* (Berkeley, 1989)

Totman, C., *Early modern Japan* (Berkeley, 1993)

Treib, M., *Sanctuaries of Spanish New Mexico* (Berkeley, 1993)

Trevor-Roper, H. R., 'The general crisis of the seventeenth century', *P&P*, XVI (1959), 31–64

Trevor-Roper, H. R., 'The Fast Sermons of the Long Parliament', in idem, *Religion, the reformation and social change* (2nd edn, London, 1972), 273–316

Trevor-Roper, H. R., 'The church of England and the Greek church in the time of Charles I', in D. Baker, ed., *Studies in church history. XV: Religious motivation* (Oxford, 1978)

Trevor-Roper, H. R., *Europe's physician: The various life of Sir Theodore de Mayerne* (New Haven and London, 2006)

Troncarelli, F., *La spada e la croce. Guillén Lombardo e l'inquisizione in Messico* (Rome, 1999)

Trotsky, L., *The history of the Russian Revolution*, 3 vols (1930; English edn, 1932)

Truchuelo García, S., 'La incidencia de las relaciones entre Guipúzcoa y el poder real en la confirmación de los fueros durante los siglos XVI y XVII', *Manuscrits*, XXIV (2006), 73–93

Tsai, S-S. H., *The eunuch in the Ming dynasty* (New York, 1996)

Tsing Yuan, 'Urban riots and disturbances', in Spence and Wills, eds, *From Ming to Ch'ing*, 280–320

Tsukahira, T. G., *Feudal control in Tokugawa Japan: The Sankin Kôtai system* (Cambridge, MA, 1966: Harvard East Asian Monographs, XX)

Tsunoda, R., W. T. de Bary and D. Keene, *The sources of Japanese tradition*, 2 vols (New York, 1958)

Tuck, R., *Philosophy and government, 1572–1651* (Cambridge, 1993)

Tukker, C. A., 'The recruitment and training of Protestant ministers in the Netherlands in the sixteenth century', in D. Baker, ed., *Miscellanea Historiae Ecclesiasticae*, III (Louvain, 1970), 198–215

Turner, H. A., *Hitler's thirty days to power: January 1933* (New York, 1996)

Twersky, I. and B. Septimus, eds, *Jewish thought in the seventeenth century* (Cambridge, MA, 1987)

Twitchett, D. and F. W. Mote, eds, *The Cambridge History of China VIII, Part 2: The Ming* (Cambridge, 1998)

Uluçay, C., 'Sultan İbrahim Hakkinda Vesikalar', *Yeni Tarih Dergisi*, I/5 (1957)

Unat, R., 'Sadrazam Kemankeş Kara Mustafa Paşa Layihasi', *Tarih Vesikalari* I/6 (1942), 443–80

Urban, H., 'Druck und Drücke des Restitutionsedikt von 1629', *Archiv für Geschichte des Buchwesens*, XIV (1974), 609–54

Urbánek, V., 'The comet of 1618: eschatological expectations and political prognostications during the Bohemian revolt', in J. R. Christianson et al., eds, *Tycho Brahe and Prague: Crossroads of European science* (Prague, 2002)

Usoshin, I. G. et al., 'Reconstruction of monthly and yearly group sunspot numbers from sparse daily observations', *Solar Physics*, CCXVIII (2003), 295–305

Valladares, R., 'Sobre reyes de invierno. El diciembre portugués y los 40 fidalgos (o algunos menos, con otros más)', *Pedralbes: revista d'historia moderna*, XV (1995), 103–36

Valladares, R., *La rebelión de Portugal. Guerra, conflicto y poderes en la Monarquía Hispánica (1640–1680)* (Valladolid, 1998)

Van Beneden, B. and N. de Poorter, *Royalist refugees: William and Margaret Cavendish in the Rubens House, 1648–1660* (Antwerp, 2006)

Van de Haar, C., *De diplomatieke betrekkingen tussen de Republiek en Portugal, 1640–1661* (Groningen, 1961)

Van den Boogaart, E., ed., *Johan Maurits of Nassau-Siegen, 1604–79: A humanist prince in Europe and Brazil* (The Hague, 1979)

Van der Woude, A. and G. Mentink, 'La population de Rotterdam au XVIIe et XVIIIe siècle', *Population*, XXI (1966), 1,165–90

Van Deusen, N., *Between the sacred and the worldly: The institutional and cultural practice of recogimiento in Colonial Lima* (Stanford, 2001)

Van Maarseveen, M. P. et al., eds, *Beelden van een strijd. Oorlog en kunst vóór de Vrede van Munster, 1621–1648* (Delft, 1998)

Van Nouhuys, T., *The age of the two-faced Janus: The comets of 1577 and 1618 and the decline of the Aristotelian world view in the Netherlands* (Leiden, 1998)

Van Santen, H. W., 'De Verenigde Oost-indische Compagnie in Gujarat en Hindustan, 1620–1660' (Leiden University PhD thesis, 1982)

Van Veen, E., *Decay or defeat? An inquiry into the Portuguese decline in Asia, 1580–1645* (Leiden, 2000)

Vaporis, C. N., 'To Edo and back: alternative attendance and Japanese culture in the early modern period', *JJS*, XXIII (1997), 25–67

Vaporis, C. N., *Breaking barriers: Travel and the state in early modern Japan* (Cambridge, MA, 1994)

Vaquero, J. M. et al., 'Revisited sunspot data: a new scenario for the onset of the Maunder Minimum', *Astrophysical Journal, Letters*, DCCXXXI (2011) L 24

Vassberg, D. E., *The village and the outside world in Golden Age Castile: Mobility and migration in everyday rural life* (Cambridge, 1996)

Vatin, N. and G. Veinstein, *Le sérail ébranlé. Essai sur les morts, dépositions et avènements des sultans ottomans (XIVe–XIXe siècles)* (Paris, 2003)

Venezia e la peste, 1348–1797 (Venice, 1980)

Verano, J. W., and D. H. Uberlaker, eds, *Disease and demography in the Americas* (Washington, DC, 1992)

Verbeek, T., *Descartes and the Dutch: Early reactions to Cartesian philosophy, 1637–50* (Carbondale, IL, 1992)

Vernadsky, G., *History of Russia, V: The tsardom of Moscow, 1547–1682* (New Haven, 1969)

Viazzo, P. P., M. Bortolotto and A. Zanotto, 'Five centuries of foundling history in Florence', in C. Panter Brick and M. J. Smith, eds, *Abandoned children* (Cambridge, 2000), 70–91

Vicuña Mackenna, B., *El clima de Chile. Ensayo histórico* (Buenos Aires, 1970)

Vidal Pla, J., *Guerra dels segadors i crisi social. Els exiliats filipistes 1640–52* (Barcelona, 1984)

Vigo, G., *Nel cuore della crisi. Politica economica e metamorfosi industriale nella Lombardia del 600* (Pavia, 2000)

Vilar, P., *La Catalogne dans l'Espagne moderne*, I (Paris, 1962)

Villalba, R., 'Climatic fluctuations in northern Patagonia during the last 1000 years as inferred from tree-ring records', *Quaternary Research*, XXXIV (1990), 346–60

Villari, R., 'Rivolte e conscienza rivoluzionaria nel secolo XVII', *Studi storici*, XII (1971), 235–64

Villari, R., 'Masaniello: contemporary and recent interpretations,' *P&P*, CVIII (1985), 117–32

Villari, R., *Elogi della dissimulazione. La lotta politica nel '600* (Rome, 1987)

Villari, R., ed., *Baroque personae* (Chicago, 1991)

Villari, R., *Per il re o per la patria. La fedeltà nel Seicento* (Bari, 1991)

Villari, R., *The revolt of Naples* (Cambridge, 1993; original Italian edn, 1967)

Villstrand, N. E., 'Adaptation or protestation: local community facing the conscription of infantry for the Swedish armed forces 1620–79', in Jespersen, ed., *A revolution from above?*, 249–313

Viñas Navarro, A., 'El motín de Évora y su significación en la restauración portuguesa de 1640', *Boletín de la Biblioteca Menéndez y Pelayo*, VI (1924), 321–39, and V (1925), 29–49

Virol, M., 'Connaître et accroître les peuples du royaume: Vauban et la population', *Population*, LVI (2001), 845–75

Virol, M., *Vauban: de la gloire du roi au service de l'État* (Seyssel, 2003)

Vlastos, S., *Peasant protests and uprisings in Tokugawa Japan* (Berkeley, 1986)

Vogel, B., 'The letter from Dublin: Climate change, colonialism, and the Royal Society in the seventeenth century', *Osiris*, XXVI (2011), 111–27

Volpp, S., 'The literary circulation of actors in seventeenth-century China', *JAS*, LXI (2002), 949–84

Von Friedeburg, R., 'The making of patriots: love of Fatherland and negotiating monarchy in seventeenth-century Germany', *JMH*, LXXVII (2005), 881–916

Von Glahn, R., *Fountain of fortune: Money and monetary policy in China, 1000–1700* (Berkeley, 1996)

Von Greyerz, K., 'Switzerland during the Thirty Years War', in Bussmann and Schilling, eds, *1648*, I, 133–9

Von Greyerz, K., *Vorsehungsglaube und Kosmologie: Studien zu englischen Selbstzeugnissen des 17. Jahrhunderts* (Göttingen and London, 1990)

Von Kreusenstjern, B., *Selbstzeugnisse der Zeit des Dreissigjährigen Krieges: Beschreibenden Verzeichnis* (Berlin, 1997)

Von Kreusenstjern, B., '"Gott der allmechtig der das weter fiehren kan, wohin er will". Gottesbild und Gottesverständnis in frühenneuzeitlichen Chroniken', in Behringer et al., eds, *Kulturelle Konsequenzen*, 179–94

Von Krusenstjern, B. and H. Medick, eds, *Zwischen Alltag und Katastrophe. Der Dreissigjährige Krieg aus der Nähe* (Göttingen, 1999)

Wahlen, H. and E. Jaggi, *Der schweizerische Bauernkrieg, 1653, und die seitherige Entwicklung des Bauernstandes* (Bern, 1952)

Wakeman, F. C., 'The Shun Interregnum of 1644', in Spence and Wills, eds, *From Ming to Ch'ing*, 39–87

Wakeman, F. C., *The Great Enterprise: The Manchu reconstruction of imperial order in 17th century China* (Berkeley, 1985)

Wakeman, F. C., 'China and the seventeenth-century crisis', *Late Imperial China*, VII (1986), 1–26

Wakeman, F. C., 'Localism and loyalism during the Ch'ing conquest of Kiangnan', in Wakeman and Grant, eds, *Conflict and control*, 44–85

Wakeman, F. C. and C. Grant, eds, *Conflict and control in Late Imperial China* (Berkeley, 1975)

Wakita Osamu, 'The *kokudaka* system: a device for unification', *JJS*, I (1975), 297–320

Waldron, A., *The Great Wall of China, from history to myth* (Cambridge, 1990)

Waldrop, M. M., *Complexity: The emerging science on the edge of order and chaos* (New York, 1992)

Waley-Cohen, J., *The sextants of Beijing: Global currents in Chinese history* (New York, 1999)

Waley-Cohen, J., *The culture of war in China: Empire and the military under the Qing dynasty* (London, 2006)

Walford, C., 'The famines of the world: past and present', *Journal of the Statistical Society of London*, XLI (1878), 433–535, and XLII (1879), 79–275

Wallerstein, I., *The modern world-system: Capitalist agriculture and the origins of the European world-economy in the sixteenth century* (London, 1974)

Wallerstein, I., 'Y-a-t-il une crise du XVIIe siècle?', *Annales E. S. C.*, XXXIV (1979), 126–44

Walsh, T. J., *The Irish Continental College Movement: The colleges at Bordeaux, Toulouse, and Lille* (Dublin, 1973)

Walsham, A., *Providence in early modern England* (Oxford, 1999)

Walter, J., *Understanding popular violence in early modern England: The Colchester plunderers* (Cambridge, 1999)

Walter, J., ' "Abolishing superstition with sedition"? The politics of popular iconoclasm in England, 1640–2', *P&P*, CLXXXIII (2004), 79–123

Walter, J., 'Public transcripts, popular agency and the politics of subsistence in early modern England', in Braddick and Walter, eds, *Negotiating power*, 123–48

Walter, J., *Crowds and popular politics in early modern England* (Manchester, 2006)

Waltner, A., 'Infanticide and dowry in Ming and early Qing China', in A. B. Kinney, ed., *Chinese views of childhood* (Honolulu, 1995), 193–217

Wang Lingmao, 'Migration in two Minnan lineages in the Ming and Qing periods', in Harrell, ed., *Chinese historical micro-demography*, 183–213

Wang Shaowu, 'Climate of the Little Ice Age in China', in Mikami Takehito, ed., *Proceedings of the International Symposium on the Little Ice Age Climate* (Tokyo, 1992), 116–21

Waquet, F., 'Guy et Charles Patin, père et fils, et la contrebande du livre à Paris au XVIIe siècle', *Journal des savants* (1979/2), 125–48

Warde, P., 'Subsistence and sales: the peasant economy of Württemberg in the early seventeenth century', *EcHR*, LIX (2006), 289–319

Warren, J., 'Connecticut unscathed: victory in the Great Narragansett War (King Philip's War), 1675–1676' (Ohio State University PhD thesis, 2011)

Watson, E. and Luckman, B. H., 'Tree-ring based reconstructions of precipitation for the southern Canadian cordillera', *CC*, LXV (2004), 209–41

Webb, J., *Desert frontier: Ecological and economic change along the western Sahel, 1600–1850* (Madison, 1995)

Webb, S. S., *1676: The end of American independence* (New York, 1984)

Weber, E., *My France: Politics, culture, myth* (Cambridge, MA, 1991)

Weber, J., 'The early German newspaper – a medium of contemporaneity', in Dooley, ed., *The dissemination*, 69–79

Webster, J. B., ed., *Chronology, migration and droughts in interlacustrine Africa* (London, 1979)

Wedgwood, C. V., *The Thirty Years War* (London, 1938)

Wedgwood, C. V., 'The scientists and the English Civil War', in *The logic of personal knowledge: Essays presented to Michael Polanyi on his seventieth birthday* (London, 1961), 59–70

Weil, E., 'The echo of Harvey's De motu cordis (1628), 1628 to 1657', *Journal of the History of Medicine*, XII/4 (1957), 167–174

Weiss, H., 'The genesis and collapse of third millennium North Mesopotamian civilization', *Science*, CCLXI (1993), 995–1,004

Weiss, J. G., 'Die Vorgeschichte des böhmischen Abenteuers Friedrichs V. von der Pfalz', *Zeitschrift für die Geschichte des Oberrheins*, new series, LIII (1940), 383–492

Weisser, M. R., *The peasants of the Montes: The roots of rural rebellion in Spain* (Chicago, 1976)

Westerkamp, M. J., 'Puritan patriarchy and the problem of revelation', *JIH*, XXIII (1993), 571–95

Westerkamp, M. J., *Women and religion in early America, 1600–1850: The Puritan and evangelical tradition* (London, 1999)

Wheeler, J. S., *The making of a world power: War and the military revolution in seventeenth-century England* (Stroud, 1999)

White, J. W., 'State growth and popular protest in Tokugawa Japan', *JJS*, XIV (1988), 1–25

White, J. W., *Ikki: Social conflict and political unrest in early modern Japan* (Ithaca, NY, 1995)

White, L. G., 'War and government in a Castilian province: Extremadura 1640–1668' (University of East Anglia PhD thesis, 1985)

White, L. G., 'Strategic geography and the Spanish Monarchy's failure to recover Portugal, 1640–1668', *Journal of Military History*, LXXI (2007), 373–409

White, R., *The Middle Ground: Indians, empires and republics in the Great Lakes region 1650–1800* (Cambridge, 1991)

White, S., *The climate of rebellion in the early modern Ottoman empire* (Cambridge, 2011)

Widmer, E., 'The epistolary world of female talent in seventeenth-century China', *Late Imperial China*, X/2 (1989), 1–43

Wigley, T. M. L., M. Ingram and G. Farmer, eds, *Climate and history: Studies in past climate and their impact on Man* (Cambridge, 1981)

Wilflingseder, F., 'Martin Laimbauer und der Unruhen im Machlandviertel, 1632–6', *Mitteilungen des oberösterreich-ischen Landesarchivs*, VI (1959), 136–208

Will, P.-E., 'Un cycle hydraulique en Chine: la province de Hubei du 16e au 19e siècles', *Bulletin de l'école française d'Extrême Orient*, LXVI (1980), 261–88

Will, P.-E., 'Développement quantitatif et développement qualitatif en Chine à la fin de l'époque impériale', *Annales HSS*, XLIX (1994), 863–902

Will, P.-E., 'Coming of age in Shanghai during the Ming-Qing transition: Yao Tinglin's (1628-after 1697) *Record of the successive years*', *Gu jin lung heng*, XLIV (2000), 15–38

Will, P.-E. and R. Bin Wong, *Nourish the people: The state civilian granary system in China, 1650–1850* (Ann Arbor, 1991)

Wills, J. E., *1688: A global history* (New York, 2001)

Wilson, H. S., *The imperial experience in sub-Saharan Africa since 1870* (Minneapolis, 1977)

Wilson, J. E., '"A thousand countries to go to": peasants and rulers in late eighteenth-century Bengal', *P&P*, CLXXXIX (2005), 81–109

Wilson, P. H., *The Thirty Years War: Europe's tragedy* (Cambridge, MA, 2009)

Winius, G., *The fatal history of Portuguese Ceylon: Transition to Dutch rule* (Cambridge, MA, 1971)

Withington, D., 'Intoxicants and society in early modern England', *HJ*, LIV (2011), 631–57

Wong, R. Bin, *China transformed: Historical change and the limits of European experience* (Ithaca, NY, 1997)

Wood, A., 'Subordination, solidarity and the limits of popular agency in a Yorkshire valley, c. 1596–1615', *P&P*, CXCIII (2006), 41–72

Wood, A., 'Fear, hatred and the hidden injuries of class in early modern England', *Journal of Social History*, XXIX (2006), 803–26

Woods, R., *Death before birth: Fetal health and mortality in historical perspective* (Oxford, 2009)

Woolf, D. R., *The social circulation of the past: English historical culture 1500–1730* (Oxford, 2003)

Woolrych, A., *Soldiers and statesmen: The General Council of the Army and its debates, 1647–1648* (Oxford, 1987)

Woolrych, A., *Britain in Revolution, 1625–1660* (Oxford, 2002)

Worden, B., 'The politics of Marvell's Horatian Ode', *HJ*, XXVII (1984), 525–47

Worden, B., 'Oliver Cromwell and the Sin of Achan', in D. Beales and G. Best, eds, *History, society and the churches: Essays in honour of Owen Chadwick* (Cambridge, 1985), 125–45

Worden, B., 'Providence and politics in Cromwellian England', *P&P*, CIX (1985), 55–99

Wrightson, K. E., 'Infanticide in earlier seventeenth-century England', *Local Population Studies*, XV (1975), 10–22

Wrightson, K. E., *Earthly necessities: Economic lives in early modern Britain* (Cambridge, 2000)

Wrigley, E. A., *People, cities and wealth: The transformation of traditional society* (Oxford, 1987)

Wrigley, E. A., and R. S. Schofield, *The population history of England, 1541–1871: A reconstruction* (2nd edn, Cambridge, 1989)

Wu, H. L., 'Corpses on display: representations of torture and pain in the Wei Zhongxian novels', *Ming Studies*, LIX (2009), 42–55

Wu, S., *Communication and imperial control in China: Evolution of the palace memorial system, 1693–1735* (Cambridge, MA, 1970)

Xoplaki, E., M. Panagiotis and J. Luterbacher, 'Variability of climate in meridional Balkans during the periods 1675–1715 and 1780–1830 and its impact on human life', *CC*, XLVIII (2001), 581–615

Yakovenko, N., 'The events of 1648–1649: contemporary reports and the problem of verification', *Jewish History*, XVII (2003), 165–73

Yamamoto Hirofumi, *Kan'ei jidai* (Tokyo, 1989)

Yamamura, K., 'Returns on unification: economic growth in Japan, 1550–1650', in J. W. Hall, N. Keiji and K. Yamamura, eds, *Japan before Tokugawa* (Princeton, 1981), 327–72

Yamamura, K., 'From coins to rice: hypotheses on the *Kandaka* and *Kokudaka* systems', *JJS*, XIV (1988), 341–67

Yancheva, G. et al., 'Influence of the intertropical convergence zone on the East Asian monsoon', *Nature*, CCCXLV (4 January 2007), 74–7

Yang, Lien-Sheng, 'Economic justification for spending – an uncommon idea in traditional China', *Harvard Journal of Asiatic Studies*, XX/1 (1957), 36–52

Yasaki Takeo, *Social change and the city in Japan from earliest times through the Industrial Revolution* (Tokyo, 1968)

Yi Tae-jin, 'Meteor fallings and other natural phenomena between 1500–1750, as recorded in the Annals of the Chosön dynasty (Korea)', *Celestial mechanics and dynamical astronomy*, LXIX (1998), 199–220

Yin Yungong, *Zhongguo Mingdai xinwen chuanbo shi* (Chongqing, 1990)

Yonemoto, M., *Mapping early modern Japan: Space, place and culture in the Tokugawa period (1603–1868)* (Berkeley, 2003)

Young, J. R., *The Scottish Parliament 1639–1661: A political and constitutional analysis* (Edinburgh, 1996)

Young, J. T., *Faith, medical alchemy and natural philosophy: Johann Moriaen, reformed intelligencer, and the Hartlib Circle* (Aldershot, 1998)

Zagorin, P., *Rebels and rulers 1500–1660*, 2 vols (Cambridge, 1982)

Zaller, R., '"Interest of State": James I and the Palatinate', *Albion*, VI (1974), 144–75

Zannetti, D. E., *La demografia del patriziato Milanese nei secoli XVII, XVIII, XIX* (Rome, 1972)

Ze'evi, D., *An Ottoman century. The district of Jerusalem in the 1600s* (Albany, NY, 1996)

Zeman, J. K., 'Responses to Calvin and Calvinism among the Czech brethren (1540–1605)', *American Society for Reformation Research. Occasional Papers*, I (1977), 41–52

Zhang, D. D., H. F. Lee, P. Brecke, Y.-Q. He and J. Zhang, 'Global climate change, war, and population decline in recent human history', http://www.pnas.org/content/104/49/19214.full, accessed 20 April 2011

Zhang Pingzhong et al., 'A test of climate, sun, and culture relationships from an 1810-year Chinese cave record', *Science*, CCXXXII (2008), 940–2

Zhang Ying, 'Politics and morality during the Ming-Qing dynastic transition' (University of Michigan PhD thesis, 2010)

Zhang Zhongli [Chang Chung-li], *The Chinese gentry: Studies on their role in nineteenth-century Chinese society* (Seattle, 1955)

Zhang, Z., H. Tian, B. Cazelles, K. L. Kausrud, A. Bräuning, F. Guo and N. C. Stenseth, 'Periodic climate cooling enhanced natural disasters and wars in China during AD 10–1900', *Proceedings of the Royal Society*, B, LXXXIX (2010), 1–9

Zhihong, Shi, 'The development and underdevelopment of agriculture during the early Qing period (1644–1840)', in Hayami and Tsubouchi, eds, *Economic and demographic developments*, 69–88

Zilfi, M., 'The Kadizadelis: discordant revivalism in seventeenth-century Istanbul', *Journal of Near Eastern Studies*, XLV (1986), 251–69

Zilfi, M., *The politics of piety: The Ottoman Ulema in the post-classical age* (Minneapolis, 1988)

Zysberg, A., 'Galley and hard labor convicts in France (1550–1850)', in P. Spierenburg, ed., *The emergence of carceral institutions: Prisons, galleys and lunatic asylums 1550–1900* (Rotterdam, 1984), 78–124

Index